AN AMERICAN DILEMMA

ALSO BY GUNNAR MYRDAL

AN AMERICAN DILEMMA

*The Negro Problem
and Modern Democracy*

Volume I

by
GUNNAR MYRDAL

WITH THE ASSISTANCE OF
RICHARD STERNER
AND
ARNOLD ROSE

PANTHEON BOOKS
A Division of Random House, New York

Library of Congress Cataloging in Publication Data

Myrdal, Gunnar, 1898-
An American Dilemma.

Reprint of the 20th anniversary ed. published by
Harper and Row, New York.
Bibliography: pp. 1144–80.
    1. Negroes. I. Sterner, Richard Mauritz Edvard,
1901-   joint author. II. Rose, Arnold Marshall,
1918-1968, joint author. III. Title.
E185.6.M95 1975   301.45'19'6073   74-18494
ISBN 0-394-73042-9 (v. 1)

*This study was made possible by funds granted by Carnegie
Corporation of New York. That corporation is not, however,
the author, owner, publisher, or proprietor of this publication
and is not to be understood as approving by virtue of its grant
any of the statements made or views expressed therein.*

CONTENTS
Volume I

    1. The Negro Problem as a Moral Issue
    2. Valuations and Beliefs
    3. A White Man's Problem
    4. Not an Isolated Problem
    5. Some Further Notes on the Scope and Direction of This Study
    6. A Warning to the Reader

PART I. THE APPROACH

    1. Unity of Ideals and Diversity of Culture
    2. American Nationalism
    3. Some Historical Reflections
    4. The Roots of the American Creed in the Philosophy of Enlightenment
    5. The Roots in Christianity
    6. The Roots in English Law
    7. American Conservatism
    8. The American Conception of Law and Order
    9. Natural Law and American Puritanism
    10. The Faltering Judicial Order
    11. Intellectual Defeatism
    12. "Lip-Service"
    13. Value Premises in This Study

    1. On the Minds of the Whites
    2. To the Negroes Themselves
    3. Explaining the Problem Away
    4. Explorations in Escape
    5. The Etiquette of Discussion

Volume II

PART VI. JUSTICE

PART VII. SOCIAL INEQUALITY

PART X. THE NEGRO COMMUNITY

PART XI. AN AMERICAN DILEMMA

*The footnotes to Volume I which immediately follow page 520 of the text retain the original pagination of the one-volume edition, pages 1181 through 1335, as does the Index to both volumes, pages 1441 through 1483.

LIST OF TABLES

LIST OF FIGURES

AUTHOR'S PREFACE TO THE TWENTIETH
ANNIVERSARY EDITION

When two decades ago I labored with this book, I came increasingly to understand that I had happened to come to the study of the Negro problem in America at a time when big changes were pending and a new trend was at the point of asserting itself. As my study dragged me through all the serious imperfections of American life related to the Negro problem, I became ever more hopeful about the future. This sense of hopefulness, together with the complete identification I could feel with the moral force, which in this book I referred to as the American Creed, made it subjectively easier for me to carry out an assignment which, in fact, called upon me to become an expert —more so than any other European scholar of this generation—on almost everything that is wrong in America. For the Negro problem is intertwined with all other social, economic, political, and cultural problems, and its study affords a perspective on the American nation as a whole.

Since the national compromise worked out in the 1870's, the relative status of the Negro people had been rising but the pace of change had been exceedingly slow, and in some fields there had even been retreats. The most important conclusion of my study was, however, that an era of more than half a century during which there had been no fundamental change was approaching its close. "Ten years from now this (past) period in the history of inter-racial relations in America may come to look as a temporary interregnum. The compromise was not a stable power equilibrium." Or more positively: "Not since Reconstruction has there been more reason to anticipate fundamental changes in American race relations, changes which will involve a development towards American ideals." At that time I had little backing for this conclusion in the contemporary literature on the Negro problem in America, nor could I feel myself to have much support from the social scientists then working in the field of race relations, whose views in the main were more static, fatalistic, and, more particularly, lacking in an appreciation of the importance for social change of the moral, ideological, and political forces in the nation. A student who has often been wrong in his forecasts will be excused for pointing to a case when he was right.

Often have I been challenged during these twenty years to come back and to review my findings in the light of all that has happened since I left the scene of my study. I have felt tempted to do so. But I have found it impossible. The task would have involved much time-consuming work, and commitments to other responsibilities—practical and political, and, more recently for some years, purely scientific in another field—have kept me fully occupied. The present book will have to remain my first and my last contribution to the study of the Negro problem in America. As I did not want to express views on a subject on which I could no longer constantly follow the discussion, I have refrained from making further comments on the Negro issue* and even from answering criticisms of my own study.

In these circumstances I am particularly gratified that my friend and former collaborator, Arnold Rose, has contributed to the present volume a lucid though compressed review of changes in the status of the Negro in American society in the past twenty years. Among the scholars working in the field he is certainly the most competent and also the most appropriate one for that task. When he worked as one of my two assistants in preparing the book, he was a young graduate, though of unusually great brilliance and youthful learnedness. In the original preface I have accounted for his important contribution to the study. Since then he has maintained his interest in the field of race relations and is now a distinguished professor at a distinguished university. In an old and cherished tradition, he has also taken his part in popular education and practical action; he has thus, as a citizen, helped to shape the events he is describing. His effort in writing this epilogue to the present edition of the old book has deepened my feeling of personal obligation and gratitude to him.

Before concluding this preface I should like to stress again a point which, from the beginning, I have always felt to be important about this study: that, in a minor way, its very initiation by one of America's great national institutions for the advancement of learning and for the dissemination of knowledge was a new demonstration of the moral concern, the rationalism, the liberalism, and the optimism which, as is often pointed out in this book, are distinguishing traits of American culture. Only to a nation dedicated to democratic ideals and convinced of its own basic soundness and strength could it have occurred to invite a foreigner—particularly one from a country entirely spared of racial problems and, moreover, a social scientist who, if anything, was certainly not renowned for a willingness to pass

---

* I made one exception in 1948 when, at the winding up of the Julius Rosenwald Fund, I gave a paper "Social Trends in America and Strategic Approaches to the Negro Problem," published in *Phylon*, vol. IX, no. 3, 1948.

over or conceal uncomfortable facts—to review this most sensitive and serious national problem. As the study was continued after the outbreak of World War II and America's involvement in it, the problem it dealt with became, of course, an even more acute source of national worry. Nevertheless, the book was published during the most anxious months of the war. I know of no other country where such a thing could have happened. Americans as citizens have much greater reason to feel intensely proud of the initiation, pursuit, and publication of this study during a time of national emergency than have I for being chosen as an instrument of a nation's urge for objective self-scrutiny.

At this time, I want to refer somewhat more fully to the role of the late Dr. Frederick P. Keppel, at that time the president of the Carnegie Corporation, in the preparation of this study. He was truly a great American, an open, warmhearted, generous, truth-loving human being of highest culture and unflinching courage. I reckon it as one of the great good fortunes in my life that, for some years, I was closely associated with him. He always referred to Newton D. Baker, who had been one of the trustees of the Corporation, as the man who conceived the idea of this study; but from circumstantial evidence, it is clear to me that Keppel was the major force in planning and pushing this undertaking even before I was engaged to carry it out. He then followed the study with intense interest. I know that it meant much to him, and not only because—as he told me once in a letter after the work was finished—he had risked so much of his own reputation upon it.

On his advice I started the study, not by reading books but by traveling around the country, in particular in the South, to see things with my own eyes. I was shocked and scared to the bones by all the evils I saw, and by the serious political implications of the problem which I could not fail to appreciate from the beginning. When I returned to New York I told Mr. Keppel of my deep worries. I should confess that I even suggested a retreat to him: that we should give up the purely scientific approach and instead deal with the problem as one of political compromise and expediency—a different type of inquiry, but one with which I had also had some experience. As mentioned in the original preface, I proposed that I should work with a three-man committee, composed of a Southern white, a Northern white, and a Negro, and I even proposed names for its membership. In such a group we could have taken considerations of political feasibility into account and worked out a basis for practical understanding, to which each could have subscribed. But if I was afraid, Keppel was not. Without a moment's hesitation, he told me that I was not going to have a committee to lean upon. The facts were before me. My job was simply to apply my professional tools to discover the truth for myself, without any side glances toward what might be politically desirable or possible. And so this matter was settled.

Frederick Keppel read the whole manuscript as it was produced and still earlier familiarized himself with the plans and outlines. I knew he was deeply disturbed by what he learned and increasingly so as the study proceeded. Indeed, he went through an ordeal as the facts were assembled and the conclusions drawn. But never once did he retreat from the position he had taken: that I was in America to uncover the truth as I saw it and to present my findings in unabridged form to the American public. There was never an attempt on his part to censor me. I remember that towards the end of my work, I received a letter from the State Department asking whether it would be possible to have a copy of my manuscript. I referred the request to Mr. Keppel. We agreed that it did not necessarily imply an attempt at censorship. As the Negro problem was such a grave matter in the national situation, it was indeed natural that the government should seek to draw on my findings. But Keppel advised me politely to decline the request, and so I did. The freedom of a scholar's thought and expression, he said, was too precious a treasure to risk—even in war— the merest hint of any collusion with official authority.

I have recalled these personal memories of a true liberal and a great American because I feel a personal urge to do so. As long as America has men like Keppel placed in responsible positions, periods of reaction and of intimidation of free scholars will pass, as they have done before. The trend toward ever greater fulfillment of the liberal ideals cannot be reversed, and America will remain a bastion of intellectual freedom and social progress.

GUNNAR MYRDAL

Stockholm, March, 1962
The Institute of International Economic Relations
Stockholm University

POSTSCRIPT TWENTY YEARS LATER

SOCIAL CHANGE AND THE NEGRO PROBLEM

The changes of twenty years in the American Negro problem have been too extensive to record in a postscript. A comprehensive survey would be required to bring *An American Dilemma* truly up-to-date. But then, a book that analyzed the Negro problem on the eve of its greatest changes would have to be rewritten, and it would necessarily be a new book. Instead it is proposed merely to point out the dynamic forces of change and to illustrate some of the specific changes. We believe that the prognosis of twenty years ago has proved to be quite accurate: Changes have occurred at a considerably more rapid rate than was generally anticipated at that time; the changes have occurred without revolution, in harmony with the traditions of the American Creed; the sources of change have been numerous and not exerted through only one institution (some had considered the economic structure to be the only possible source of change). The changes have been cumulative in the sense that a change in one sphere has stimulated changes in other spheres; the changes have been most complete in the economic sphere, next in the legal and political spheres, and least in the sphere of social relationship. Twenty years is a long time for a social science prognosis to hold up, and while we still consider it valid we recognize that a new prognosis can include additional elements.

An analysis of the dynamic forces operating in the present situation inevitably involves the selection of what is most significant from the complexity of current reality. The need for brevity prevents a full exposition of assumptions and bases of selection. Suffice it to say that I shall follow the outlines of the book in giving greatest weight to forces involving social power, both economic and political; secondary weight to changes in public ideologies; and tertiary weight to factors usually singled out as "psychological" (although it seems to me that a better socio-psychological analysis would not separate the individual psychological factors from those involving social power and ideologies).

The major forces causing the rapid change in race relations since 1940 seem to have been continuous industrialization and technological advance, the high level of mobility among the American people, economic prosperity, the organization and political education of minority groups, an increased American awareness of world opinion, a consistent support for civil rights on the part of the Supreme Court and a lesser support from the other branches of the federal government and of the Northern state governments, and the propaganda and educational effort for more equal civil rights. Some of these forces are likely to continue to exert the same push as they have in the recent past; others are likely to change in their influence; and new forces are likely to have increasing influence.

THE EFFECTS OF INDUSTRIALIZATION

Industrialization has operated to create changes in race relations in several ways. First, it has eliminated cotton agriculture as the dominant source of Southern wealth. Racism grew up as an American ideology partly in response to the need to maintain a reliable and permanent work force in the difficult tasks of growing cotton. While American Negro slavery was older than extensive cotton agriculture, it took on major economic and political significance in connection with the rise of "King Cotton" after the 1790's, and the patterns of discrimination and prejudice that have carried on until the present day took their form originally in the cotton-growing areas. Cotton agriculture remained as a dominant element in the economy of the Southern states until the 1930's, but then the diversification of agriculture and the rise of manufacturing significantly replaced it. The continuation of racism after cotton was no longer "king" is an example of the sociological principle that ideologies continue after the condition that gave rise to them no longer exist. Nevertheless, the decline of cotton agriculture permitted other forces to weaken racism.

Industrialization moved people from rural areas into the cities, not only for factory jobs but for service occupations as well. Urbanization has always been associated with the weakening of traditional social structures. The caste system governing the relations between whites and Negroes in the South not only had its birth in the rural areas but also its integration into the social structure of a relatively static rural society. When Negroes moved into the cities—and even in the South the majority of them now live in cities—the elaborate requirements of the caste system could hardly be maintained. Relationships in the city are too casual and too instrumental to require the constant manifestations of subordination on the part of Negroes that characterized the rural caste system. Segregation became more physical than symbolic, and behind the walls of segregated isolation Negroes were better able to build a resistance to subordination.

Industrialization also brought migration away from the South. While the great migration of Negroes was to the Northern cities until about 1940, it became increasingly a westward migration after that time. The outward migration was, of course, partly due to the lag in Southern industrialization, but even with that lag now being overcome, the especially strong discrimination against Negroes in the South will keep them migrating out of the region. But the majority of Negroes no longer live in the Deep and Upper South (the old Border states have realigned themselves largely into Northern states), so that the outward migration must necessarily slow down. The main significance of the northward and westward migrations for the Negroes was that it separated them from the full-blown caste system of the South, even though they met other forms of discrimination and prejudice in the other regions of the country. In the North (which we shall refer to as including the West also), they could vote freely and have almost the full protection of the laws and the law-enforcement machinery. They, as well as the whites, get a better education in the North, and this has been a factor in improving their status. Thus Negroes have been much better able to improve their condition in the North, and they have used their improved condition (especially their vote) to help Negroes still living in the South.

TECHNOLOGICAL PROGRESS

While technological progress is by no means the sole factor which has contributed to the high level of prosperity since 1940, it has been an important element in it. The prosperity—and the almost full employment associated with it during the period 1940-1954—has been especially beneficial to Negroes. While measures vary, it has been estimated that the rise of average real income among Negroes since 1940 has been two to three times that among whites. Since average income among Negroes is still significantly below that among whites, their rapid improvement must be seen against the backdrop of great economic discrimination and poverty in the pre-1940 period. The prospects for further automation and the industrial use of nuclear energy will involve still higher productivity and a higher standard of living for employed workers in the future, and Negroes are no longer being excluded from this (especially in the North). The rise in average family income among Negroes since 1940 has not only meant a fuller participation in the material benefits of the modern economy but also a greater opportunity to get more education and other cultural benefits. Further, continuing prosperity among the whites has tended to reduce one major source of frustrations that sometimes contribute to scapegoating and race-baiting.

Technological change—especially in the form of automation—is having another effect on the position of Negroes in the United States, and this is partly a negative one. As a relatively unskilled element in the working population, the Negro is frequently the most rapidly displaced worker when changing technology requires an upgrading of skills. This influence is abetted by the fact that many Negroes are relative newcomers to the ranks of Northern industrial workers, and thus have the least unionization and lowest seniority. Hence, Negroes are the hardest hit by technological unemployment, and technological change and low seniority have for all practical purposes replaced discrimination as the main forces in excluding Negroes from factory jobs in the North and West. Negroes thus again constitute a disproportionately large number of the "permanently unemployed," and their rate of becoming unemployed was about double that of white workers during the several recessions that have occurred since 1955. Occupational training for Negroes is thus seen as crucial. If minority workers get the new job training, they will not only cease to be subject to special handicaps, but they will no longer be behind the already skilled workers of the majority group because the latter now also need retraining.

HEIGHTENED GROUP IDENTIFICATION

The development of an educated elite and of a lively sense of group identification among Negroes have been significant factors in changing American race relations in a more equalitarian direction since the turn of the century. They have exerted their influence mainly by the organization of a wide range of protest and pressure associations, sometimes with and sometimes without the collaboration of liberal whites. Although this movement was highly developed by 1940, it has taken on some significant additional elements since then. The nonviolent resistance technique, borrowed from Gandhi, was apparently first used in the United States as a means of achieving desegregation in 1942, with the organization of the Congress on Racial Equality (CORE) in Chicago. Working first in selected Northern cities, it gradually moved to the Border states and did not begin work in the South until about 1954. The technique caught nation-wide attention in 1957 with the spontaneous and independent development of the Montgomery (Alabama) bus strike, led by Rev. Martin Luther King. After the successful conclusion of this effort, King organized the Southern Christian Leadership Conference (SCLC), which then worked for desegregation in several other Southern cities. In 1958 the CORE technique of "sit-ins," operated for years on an interracial basis, was adopted spontaneously by groups of Southern Negro college students and used all over the South with considerable success. While these students formed the Student Nonviolent Coordinating Committee (SNCC), a sympathetic group of Northern students (both white and Negro) formed the Students for Integration (SFI) to provide moral and physical aid to the Southern SNCC and to CORE. The significance of the development of all of these organizations was not simply that the Gandhian technique of nonviolent resistance was successfully added to the repertoire of those seeking equal rights for Negroes, but also that large sections of the Negro masses were now directly participating in the efforts for the improvement of their status. The new organizations, rivals to some extent among themselves, placed themselves in partial opposition to the older NAACP and Urban League because the latters' techniques did not lend themselves to direct participation. The competition was healthy, however, for while the Negro youth joined the newer organizations, the growing Negro middle class (adult) was stimulated to give increasing support to the older organizations.

Violence as a technique for changing the pattern of race relations was also developed in the post-World War II period. Some of this was purely spontaneous in response to white violence and did not take an organized form, as in the case of the Florida Negroes who flogged a white employer for beating his Negro employee. But of greater significance was the acceptance of a philosophy of violence by a small number of fairly well-educated Negroes, such as the group led by James Lawson of the United African Nationalist Movement.

While cold conflict with white America had been found among the Negro lower class ever since the Garvey movement of the 1920's, it was never so well organized as in the Negro self-styled Muslim movement of the 1950's. This disciplined organization, probably reaching a membership of almost 100,000 by 1960, had as its stated goal a segregated territory within the United States, and it espoused— vaguely so as not to violate the law—future violence to attain this goal.

These were the new organized power currents that developed among Negroes in the post-World War II era. While not all of them sought integration, all did seek equality. They suggested a heightened group identification and impatience among Negroes and, since they occurred at a time when desegregation was becoming a reality, they suggested that Negroes themselves might delay integration in its final stages. That is, group identification may become so strong that Negroes, like many American Jews, may not want full integration.

Increasing Awareness of World Opinion

Just as the Negro population was becoming more politically alert to the possibilities of changing race relations, so was the white population becoming more aware of the need to change its traditional ways of associating with and thinking of Negroes. Perhaps the most important force here was the Second World War itself. It transformed the United States from an isolationist, isolated nation into a leading world power, with responsibilities in every part of the world. The American people had to take the point of view of other peoples toward themselves, and they found the major domestic criticism to be America's handling of its racial minorities. Newspapers all over the world reported on American discriminations and racial violence, and expressions of protest in various forms were voiced. What was particularly new was that a significant number of Americans became aware of this criticism, and it had its effect back on their consciences, particularly among the educated upper classes and intellectuals who were in close touch with world movements. The world reaction gained greater significance as those colored nations of Asia and Africa which had formerly been under colonial rule gained their independence. As the United States government partly realigned its foreign policy toward these new nations, so it was obliged to encourage a more equalitarian treatment of their racial co-members at home. The formation of new independent African nations after 1957 increased race pride among American Negroes and thus also strengthened their drive toward equality.

The Second World War and its aftermath brought unprecedented numbers of Americans in touch with other peoples. The armed services transported millions of Americans to Europe and Asia, and the tourist trade sent millions more to all parts of the world. Asians and Africans, especially students, began to visit the United States in significant numbers. Residents of New York City and Washington, D. C., were almost as likely to pass a foreign colored man on the street as a native one, and even Southerners could no longer be sure whether the Negroes they saw in their cities were Americans or Africans. Perhaps more pervasive was the change in the nation's mass media: Before 1940 newspapers, movies, and radio either ignored the Negro or stereotyped him unfavorably; after 1950 these media paid the Negro —foreign or native—a great deal of objective or favorable attention.

Some social science researches and certain novels made the Negro almost popular in certain white circles, mainly intellectual. With the rising living standards of the American Negro, and his efforts to integrate himself into American life, white Americans generally were also much more likely to have direct contact with middle-class Negroes.

CIVIL RIGHTS ON THE FEDERAL SCENE

As mentioned, the more educated white Americans and those in closest contact with foreign opinion were the ones most likely to lead the effort to eliminate discrimination and prejudice. This included the chief federal government officials. The United States Supreme Court led the way, perhaps because it was closer to the Constitution, which had been thoroughly equalitarian since 1868. The Supreme Court had generally sought to guarantee Negroes some legal protection, but it had equivocated, until 1944, about the vote and about equal use of public facilities. That year saw a unanimous Court declare unequivocally that the "white primary" was illegal, and that such subterfuges to prevent Negroes from voting in the South were unconstitutional. Since then, the Court has consistently decided, with undivided opinions, that no branch of any government in the United States could show any discrimination whatsoever on grounds of race, religion, or nationality.

Perhaps the most important of these decisions was the one handed down on May 17, 1954, which held that it was unconstitutional for the public schools to segregate the races. This decision withdrew the last legal support from the Southern states' effort to segregate public facilities—including parks, playgrounds, libraries, bathing beaches, as well as schools—by claiming that it was trying to provide "separate-but-equal" facilities. The decision also applied to privately owned facilities engaged in interstate commerce, including rail and bus terminal waiting rooms and restaurants. Only a small proportion of the local governments affected took immediate steps to desegregate, but through various pressures the elaborate caste system of the South began to be dismantled. The federal courts faced many cases after 1954 to implement the Supreme Court's historic decision wiping out "separate but equal" but it could go no further in principle, for it was now operating in full accord with the Constitutional provisions for full equality.

The executive branch of the federal government began to move to implement its responsibilities for enforcing equality during the 1930's, when the Roosevelt administration (1933-1945) practiced equality in the administration of some of its programs and hired Negroes in other than custodial or honorary capacities. The main program of the Roosevelt era, however, was one forced on the President by the combined pressure of all the Negro organizations during wartime: the Fair Employment Practices Commission (FEPC), which had as its task to prevent discrimination in employment on the part of industries holding contracts with the federal government. The Truman administration (1945-1953) went further in eliminating discrimination in federal employment and in the operation of federal programs, although it lost the FEPC in 1946 because of Congressional disapproval. Its main achievements along these lines were the virtual abolition of discrimination and segregation in the armed services and the support and publicity given to the President's Civil Rights Commission.

The Eisenhower administration (1953-1961) continued the existing nondiscriminatory policies and gave administrative support to the courts' rulings on school desegregation—even to the point of calling out federal troops to enforce school desegregation in Little Rock, Arkansas. The Kennedy administration (1961-   ) pumped life into the government committee to enforce nondiscrimination in employment by industries having contracts with the government (thereby reviving in fact the FEPC for major manufacturing companies), and extended administrative support to the courts' rulings on nondiscrimination by the states and by agencies of interstate transportation (most important was the 1961 ruling by the Interstate Commerce Commission that rail and bus terminals might not segregate). There remained considerable opportunities for executive branch action to enforce nondiscrimination and desegregation at the beginning of 1962.

The legislative branch has the greatest potential but the record of least achievement, largely because of the presence within it of congressmen from the South. The latter are a minority but hold the balance of power between the conservatives and liberals (which they use to trade off against the enactment of civil rights legislation), and they have a disproportionate share of the leadership positions because of their seniority. The Congress' main contribution to the equalization of the races has been a negative one: It has not sought to reverse the aforementioned actions of the judicial and executive branches (except for killing the FEPC in 1946). In 1957, Congress passed its first statute since the 1870's to enforce civil rights, a weak law giving federal authorities some power to restrain local polling officials from preventing Negroes' voting. In 1960 it passed a second statute slightly strengthening this law. It has been questioned whether these statutes helped the position of Negroes sufficiently to justify the damage the political bargaining to gain their passage did to other liberal legislation (for example, to the bill to provide federal aid for education). Negroes would benefit along with other groups by the passage of many bills which the Southern congressmen block in vote-trading with the conservatives; scarcely a bill comes before Congress these days (except occasionally in the fields of defense and foreign policy) which does not have a "race angle" attached to it. Either the legislation is perceived as having the potential in itself to enhance the equalization of the Negroes, or the Southern congressmen are willing to trade votes with the conservatives in such a way that the latter will vote against civil rights' bills if the Southern Democrats will support the conservative position on other measures. Unless a new factor comes along to change the present structure or to give a different perspective to it, it may thus not be strategic for proponents of civil rights to seek new legislation from Congress. Much of what they want from the federal government can be provided by the executive branch as well as by the legislative branch, and the votes of Negroes are more effective for the President than for the Congress. It is doubtful, however, whether civil rights groups will curtail their efforts to get federal legislation; the main effort in 1960-1961 was to modify certain procedural rules in the Congress so that substantive civil rights legislation would be easier to pass.

CIVIL RIGHTS AT THE STATE LEVEL

The Northern state governments and some of the local governments have been effective sources of change in American race relations. After the federal FEPC was killed, New York led the states in passing legislation setting up FEPC's within their jurisdictions. By the late 1950's most of the Northern and Western states and cities with any sizeable Negro population had such legislation, which effectively prevented discrimination in employment. A more difficult problem for the North was discrimination in housing, but in 1958, New York again led the way by making it illegal to discriminate against a person on grounds of race, religion, or nationality in the sale or rental of most categories of housing. By 1961 nine states had passed legislation of this sort. At the time of writing (January 1962), it is too early to ascertain the effectiveness of these statutes.

OPPOSITION OF THE SOUTHERN WHITES

Such have been the main forces promoting the equalization of Negroes in American society in the years since 1940. The main forces maintaining the subordination and segregation of Negroes have been

those in tradition and the status quo. In 1954, however, a new factor
entered, which has undoubtedly prevented change from being more
rapid than it might otherwise have been. This was the organization of
Southern white opposition, mainly into the Citizens' Councils. There
had been no effective organization to hold the Negro in a subordinate
position since the decline of the Ku Klux Klan in the late 1920's.
Minor and local organizations had sporadic effects, but the leading
reactionary movements of the era 1930-1954 avoided any attack on
the position of Negroes. It is significant that the reaction to the rapid
changes of the post-1940 period took until 1954 to gain organized expression. Racists did not resist changes in the caste system in any
effective manner until the very keystone of that system was in danger:
It was the Supreme Court decision to desegregate the public schools
that led to the concerted resistance. It is significant that economic,
political, and legal aspects of the caste system had already changed
materially, and the pattern of social segregation was under threat
before the proponents of the caste system organized themselves to protest it. The old racist ideology was vigorously reasserted once again
after 1954 (there had been periodic spokesmen for it, but they had
been given little public attention after 1930), even though the original
source of it and most of the material benefits to be gained from it had
disappeared. The ideology of racism was no longer a response to a
conflict between economic-political forces and the idealism of the
American Creed, but rather an expression merely of a traditional
psychology.

The Southern resistance movement drew strength from all social
classes, but there were also defectors in all classes. Many of the leaders
of the White Citizens' Councils were upper class, and they used their
economic power to hurt Negroes who sought a greater measure of
civic equality. But some of the economic leaders of the South took
the position that resistance to the Supreme Court decision was disturbing to the social order and bad for business, and that the South
should stop "fighting the War Between the States" and become forward-looking and efficient. Political and other organizational leaders
were similarly divided; while few whites claimed to be pro-Negro or
in favor of equality, many of the influential people of the South felt
that the effort to subordinate the Negro should be relegated to the
past. It is difficult to know how the less articulate whites of the South
divided, but they did divide. While many participated in violent
activities to prevent desegregation, a majority of the voters of Little
Rock, Arkansas, voted for a school board that announced its intention
of desegregating the public schools in accord with the federal court

order, and there were similar evidences in other parts of the South that significant numbers of whites were quietly resigned to desegregation. The articulate and organized group, however, was the one favoring the maintenance of the caste system, and it used boycotts, effective appeals to the Southern legislatures, violence, and other means to resist the changes. In general, this group is larger and more effective in the Deep South than in the Upper South, and it has practically ceased to exist in the Border states. With some exceptions, the only ones to benefit from the caste system today are those, mainly in the lower classes, who get psychological satisfaction out of a sense of racial superiority.

Some of the leaders of the resistance are those who believe that leaders should follow the wishes of the led. But there are also other types of leaders: A few have sought to make money by exploiting the fears of the white South; an example was Bryant Bowles, whose main purpose in organizing the National Association for the Advancement of White People in 1955 was to collect dues. Another minor type—represented by John Kasper—seems to have a psychological drive to lead violent movements. Still another rare type—exemplified by John Hamilton—hoped to build a full-scale fascist movement out of the Southern resistance to desegregation. But all of these minor types of leaders were frustrated in one way or another, and soon disappeared from the scene. Except for spontaneous leaders who stand out for a day or two of violence, all of the continuing leaders of the Southern resistance are persons with some traditional and legitimate authority. They apparently have a strong racist ideology, and strong personal desires to keep the Negro subordinate, but they also have a vested interest in keeping things on an even keel, and generally tend to hold their followers back from unplanned violence. Violence directed against Negroes can easily spread to white-owned property and other institutions, and so the traditional leaders try to keep excitement in check.

RESISTANCE IN THE NORTH

Resistance to change in race relations in the North is practically unorganized, although there are small property-owners associations which oppose the movement of Negroes into certain neighborhoods and oppose the passage of "fair housing" or "open occupancy" legislation. There are a great number of unorganized white Northerners who resist personal association with Negroes, particularly as neighbors and as social club members. Usually they no longer try to keep them out of co-employment or out of the large, impersonal voluntary associations, churches, or trade unions, but they still resist intimate association.

For a few years following the development of the Southern resistance, there was an unorganized but articulate movement among some Northern leaders to put brakes on the trend toward equalization, particularly as regards the South. These individuals took up the Southern theme of "leaving the South alone to work out its own problems," and argued that "both kinds of extremists are dangerous." But the majority of Northern leaders seem to have been persuaded that the South has always moved more rapidly toward better race relations when prodded by the North. The Northern proponents of "moderation" were articulate mainly in the period 1955-1958, but they probably would be heard from again if widespread violence were to occur in the South.

There is a continuing dilemma for some segments of Northern opinion which have strong ties with the South. They include not merely those who have family and personal connections with Southerners, but Northern businessmen and trade union leaders who have Southern branches. The national AFL-CIO, for example, has not moved as forthrightly on integration within its own ranks as it might because of pressures from Southern (and even some Northern) locals and because of its hopes of organizing more white Southern workers. In 1959, Negro labor leaders formed the Negro American Labor Council to pressure the AFL-CIO toward a position of complete integration. For a period, the leadership of the national labor movement refused to recognize the Negro group except in the critical terms of "dual unionism." By the end of 1961, however, president George Meany of the AFL-CIO verbally capitulated and set up some organizational machinery to eliminate discrimination and segregation in the member unions.

Improvement in Employment Opportunities

In the dynamic situation created by all these forces, any description of the position of Negroes at any one moment is bound to be dated before it can be printed. The picture as of the winter of 1962 will be painted in broad strokes so that it is also superficial and incomplete. Whereas in 1940, Negroes were excluded from most occupations outside of agriculture and service, by 1962 some Negroes were to be found in nearly every occupation. Considerable employment discrimination remained in the South and even in the Border states, but it was all but eliminated in the Northern and Western states. This did not mean that Negroes were approaching occupational equality, for there was the heritage of inadequate training, low skill orientations, poor general education, and low seniority. The training lag was most serious as union seniority and company seniority rules often made it impossible for Negroes to get training for better jobs even if they had a positive attitude toward getting it. Discrimination in government economic benefits—poor relief, unemployment compensation, old age assistance, public housing, and lesser forms—had been all but wiped out, except where there was local control in some Southern communities. A notable exception arose in Louisiana in 1960 where the "Aid to Dependent Children" program was curtailed for those mothers who had additional illegitimate children while receiving ADC aid for their older children (this was applied almost exclusively to Negroes).

GETTING THE VOTE

Negroes were voting without restriction in most areas of the Upper South, and in some cities of the Deep South. The only state where they were almost systematically excluded from the polls (as they had been throughout the South in 1940) was Mississipppi. Here, and in many rural areas of the other Deep Southern states, they were prevented illegally from voting by the arbitrary whim of local polling officials and by threats of violence. The poll tax still existed in five states, and several Southern states had literacy and "understanding" tests for voting, but their main discriminatory effect on Negroes was through their misapplication. Negroes occasionally ran for the lower local offices, and in Atlanta a Negro was elected to the school board with the aid of white voters. The main changes in Southern politics resulting from Negro voting were the election of liberal Democrats in several states and the breaking of the barriers which hitherto prevented conservatives from voting Republican. Hence, the two-party system began to develop in the South (especially in Texas and Florida). In the 1948 and 1960 presidential elections, Negro votes in several Southern as well as Northern states provided the margin of victory for the Democratic candidate. There were four Negro congressmen in 1960 and many local public officials, predominantly in Northern cities, and Negroes were thoroughly integrated into the local political parties of the Northern States. The great majority of Negroes were voting Democratic, although there was some evidence of their "flexibility" in switching party affiliation when a local Republican candidate seemed more pro-Negro than his Democratic counterpart.

LAW ENFORCEMENT

In 1940 the enforcement of law in the South could be characterized as absent when Negroes were the victims (whether whites or
other Negroes were the criminals), and overenforced when whites
were the victims and Negroes the violators. By the 1950's there were
many cases, even in the Deep South, where white persons committing
crimes against Negroes were prosecuted and punished, although this
was by no means general. Negro criminals whose victims were other
Negroes were much more likely to be handled according to the law
by law enforcement officials. Practically all Southern cities employed
Negro policemen after 1945 to maintain law and order in Negro
communities, and Southern judges were no longer likely to release
Negro criminals on the word of a white man. There was still considerable "overenforcement" of the law when Negroes were apprehended for crimes against whites, but civil suits between a white and
a Negro were handled much more equitably. Despite the mass violence
which attended many instances of desegregation, extralegal violence of
the everyday, person-to-person basis which was characteristic of the
pre-1940 period was now greatly reduced. Lynching was a rare event
after 1950, and even murders of Negro prisoners by white policemen
and jailers became infrequent. Thus, even while tension mounted between the races in the South, total violence declined. This seemed to
be due to the fact that potential white perpetrators of violence were
aware that they were in some danger of retribution from the law or
from retaliating Negroes. In the North police brutality remained
sporadic and individual, never was it a matter of policy, and there was
no evidence of discrimination by judges. While the war years saw
some major race riots in the North and West, the formation of interracial citizens' committees in practically all Northern cities practically
eliminated them from 1944 on. The major exception was in Chicago
and some of its suburbs, where there were numerous small riots all
through the 1940's and 1950's when Negroes moved into new
residential neighborhoods or attempted to swim at the "white" public
bathing beaches.

HOUSING

The aforementioned changes in the economic, political, and legal
spheres were occurring regularly and generally with little public attention or controversy. Changes in the area of social relations, however,
were occuring in some areas but not in others, and received a great
deal of notice. The movement of Negroes into the Northern and
Southern cities was attended by increasing housing segregation, and
with housing segregation came the inevitable segregation of neighbor-

hood facilities, overcrowding, high rents, run-down buildings, slums, and expansion into new neighborhoods attended by conflict with whites. This became the most serious aspect of the race problem, certainly in the North. The chief legal buttress for housing segregation was the restrictive covenant, a clause written into a deed for property preventing its use by members of specified groups, mainly Negroes.

In 1948 the U.S. Supreme Court decided that the restrictive covenant was unenforceable in the courts, thus wiping out the legal support for housing segregation and allowing it to rest on voluntary action. The decision eased the situation for Negroes somewhat, and it was followed by various organized efforts to develop integrated housing in the North. Publicly subsidized housing was no longer segregated, and some privately sponsored integrated housing projects were developed. But the great bulk of urban Negroes remained segregated, and there was some evidence that the segregation was increasing in the South. Negroes themselves fought the housing restrictions generally only when there was insufficient space to live; only a few of them sought to break the pattern of segregation itself. By the end of the 1950's some Northern states passed statutes making it illegal to refuse to rent or sell housing to Negroes, and generally in the North the space pressures on Negroes eased considerably.

In late 1961 it was rumored that the President was contemplating issuing an executive order which would prohibit the lending of money with government guarantees (covering around 90 per cent of the credit for housing construction and purchases) if the housing affected was not available for lease or purchase by minority groups. Political considerations delayed this executive order in 1962, but if it should ever be issued and enforced it would remove the strongest barrier to housing integration from the white side. Whether Negroes would move in large numbers to take advantage of it is more questionable. At the time of writing, housing segregation remains as the most serious and least soluble aspect of the race problem, at least in the Northern states.

SEGREGATION IN PUBLIC AND PRIVATELY OWNED FACILITIES

Segregation of other public and privately-owned-but-open-to-the-public facilities remained a function of housing segregation in the North. Forced segregation of schools, playgrounds, restaurants, hotels, and other public and commercial establishments became exceptional in the North as the climate of opinion changed and the old civil rights statutes of the Northern states once again became operative. In the South desegregation of these types of facilities began as a result of the court decisions and organized movements already examined. By 1961 school systems were formally desegregated in all the Border states, in many scattered areas of the Upper South and in a few cities of the Deep South. Violence had attended school desegregation in Dover, Delaware; Clinton and Nashville, Tennessee; Little Rock, Arkansas; and New Orleans, Louisiana. But it was accomplished peacefully and more thoroughly in the larger school systems of Washington, D.C.; St. Louis, Missouri; Dallas, Texas; and Atlanta, Georgia. By 1961 only Mississippi, Alabama, and South Carolina had none of their schools desegregated. But there was only spotty and token desegregation in all of the other Deep Southern states and some of the Upper South states.

Desegregation of the other public and the privately owned commercial establishments took roughly the same pattern, although a few years later. In the two years of 1959 and 1960 the sit-in movement opened some restaurants to Negroes in about 200 cities of the South. But the majority of restaurants in these cities remained segregated, and Negro patronage of the nonsegregated restaurants was rare. An issue arose over the exclusion of dark-skinned representatives of foreign nations from the highway restaurants of Maryland, a Border state, and the federal government intervened with partial success. Hotels, theaters, and recreational facilities were opened to Negroes on approximately the same basis as restaurants: in every state except Mississippi and Alabama there were at least some desegregated, but the majority in the Deep South and even some areas of the Upper South remained segregated, and Negro patronage of the desegregated facilities was rare. Interstate transportation was effectively desegregated, and—after the Montgomery, Alabama, bus strike of 1957—so was the transportation within many Southern cities.

One of the major gains in the North was the desegregation of most of the major voluntary associations. The major professional associations were desegregated in the South also. Except for weak, formal associations (such as the PTA's), most other Southern voluntary associations remained segregated. Social clubs and informal groups remained segregated throughout the country, with a few exceptions in the North. College fraternities and sororities remained mainly segregated in fact, although a campaign in the North to remove formal barriers was largely successful. Almost the same could be said of the churches, although in mixed neighborhoods churches sometimes served members of both races (especially the Roman Catholic churches).

INTER-RACIAL MARRIAGES

Inter-racial marriages were probably on the increase in the North, although they were still not frequent. In the South inter-racial marriage continued to be illegal. This was the one type of law discriminating among the races still on the statute books of the Southern states; not even the Negro organizations sought to challenge it, and hence the courts had no occasion to declare it unconstitutional. The probability is that the courts would declare it unconstitutional, for they had nullified a California statute barring marriage between whites and Orientals. But apparently the Negro leadership thought it unwise to challenge this last formal barrier of the caste system, at least until other forms of desegregation should be accomplished in greater degree.

The formerly elaborate "etiquette of race relations" was crumbling in the South, and it became common to hear Negroes addressed by whites by their formal titles of "Mr.," "Mrs.," and "Miss." The self-demeaning manner of Negroes in the presence of whites declined except in the rural areas. With the improvement in occupational opportunities, Negroes were much less likely to be domestic servants. The barriers to serious conversations between the races broke down in the North, but remained in the South. The results of these changes were that Northern whites could perceive Negroes as human beings for the first time, while relations between the races in the South grew cold as they became increasingly restricted to matters of common economic interest. The white Southerners were no longer sure they understood "their" Negroes, and Negroes could no longer be relied on to maintain their "place" in the presence of whites. A Gallup Poll taken in January, 1961, showed that 76 per cent of white Southerners expected that there would soon be complete integration of the races in public places.

SUMMARY

There could be no doubt that the races were moving rapidly toward equality and desegregation by 1962. In retrospect, the change of the preceding twenty years appeared as one of the most rapid in the history of human relations. Much of the old segregation and discrimination remained in the Deep South, and housing segregation with its concomitants was still found throughout the country, but the all-encompassing caste system had been broken everywhere. Prejudice as an attitude was still common, but racism as a comprehensive ideology was maintained by only a few. The change had been so rapid, and caste and racism so debilitated, that I venture to predict the end of all formal segregation and discrimination within a decade, and the decline of informal segregation and discrimination so that it would be a mere shadow in two decades. The attitude of prejudice might remain indefinitely, but it will be on the minor order of Catholic-Protestant prejudice within three decades. These changes would not mean that there would be equality between the races within this time, for the heritage of past discriminations would still operate to give Negroes lower "life chances." But the dynamic social forces creating inequality will, I predict, be practically eliminated in three decades. It would only be appropriate to guess that most sociologists would find these predictions "optimistic." But then, most sociologists found the predictions contained in *An American Dilemma* of twenty years ago optimistic, and most of these predictions have since come true.

While to the student of social change, who must have historical perspective and be aware of continuities and rigidities in the social structure, the changes in American race relations from 1940 to 1962 appear to be among the most rapid and dramatic in world history without violent revolution, to the participants themselves the changes did not appear to be so rapid. People generally live from day to day, and from month to month, without historical perspective, and hence tend not to perceive changes that occur over a period of years. The "social present" usually means much more to people than does social change. Young people who have come to awareness of the world around them during the latter part of the period under consideration see only the conditions of the last few years; for them the conditions of the pre-1940 period are "ancient history," and hence the changes of twenty years are not part of their image of the modern world. These things are true for all social change. But of particular significance for our analysis is the fact that Negroes *still* experience discrimination, insult, segregation, and the threat of violence, and in a sense have become more sensitive and less "adjusted" to these things. To them the current problems and current conflicts have much more significance than those of ten or twenty years ago. Schooled as they are by the American Creed, their standard of comparison for the present situation is not what existed in 1940 but what the Constitution and "the principles of democracy" say should be. Further, most American Negroes are aware of great changes going on in Africa, and in fact are inclined to exaggerate the "improvements" there resulting from the demise of old-fashioned colonialism. From these perspectives, the changes occurring in the United States seem much too slow. White Americans, who can also take the point of view of their own Constitution and of their country's role in a world whose population is two-thirds colored, might agree with them.

ARNOLD ROSE

University of Minnesota
Minneapolis, June 1962

order, and there were similar evidences in other parts of the South that significant numbers of whites were quietly resigned to desegregation. The articulate and organized group, however, was the one favoring the maintenance of the caste system, and it used boycotts, effective appeals to the Southern legislatures, violence, and other means to resist the changes. In general, this group is larger and more effective in the Deep South than in the Upper South, and it has practically ceased to exist in the Border states. With some exceptions, the only ones to benefit from the caste system today are those, mainly in the lower classes, who get psychological satisfaction out of a sense of racial superiority.

Some of the leaders of the resistance are those who believe that leaders should follow the wishes of the led. But there are also other types of leaders: A few have sought to make money by exploiting the fears of the white South; an example was Bryant Bowles, whose main purpose in organizing the National Association for the Advancement of White People in 1955 was to collect dues. Another minor type—represented by John Kasper—seems to have a psychological drive to lead violent movements. Still another rare type—exemplified by John Hamilton—hoped to build a full-scale fascist movement out of the Southern resistance to desegregation. But all of these minor types of leaders were frustrated in one way or another, and soon disappeared from the scene. Except for spontaneous leaders who stand out for a day or two of violence, all of the continuing leaders of the Southern resistance are persons with some traditional and legitimate authority. They apparently have a strong racist ideology, and strong personal desires to keep the Negro subordinate, but they also have a vested interest in keeping things on an even keel, and generally tend to hold their followers back from unplanned violence. Violence directed against Negroes can easily spread to white-owned property and other institutions, and so the traditional leaders try to keep excitement in check.

RESISTANCE IN THE NORTH

Resistance to change in race relations in the North is practically unorganized, although there are small property-owners associations which oppose the movement of Negroes into certain neighborhoods and oppose the passage of "fair housing" or "open occupancy" legislation. There are a great number of unorganized white Northerners who resist personal association with Negroes, particularly as neighbors and as social club members. Usually they no longer try to keep them out of co-employment or out of the large, impersonal voluntary associations, churches, or trade unions, but they still resist intimate association.

For a few years following the development of the Southern resistance, there was an unorganized but articulate movement among some Northern leaders to put brakes on the trend toward equalization, particularly as regards the South. These individuals took up the Southern theme of "leaving the South alone to work out its own problems," and argued that "both kinds of extremists are dangerous." But the majority of Northern leaders seem to have been persuaded that the South has always moved more rapidly toward better race relations when prodded by the North. The Northern proponents of "moderation" were articulate mainly in the period 1955-1958, but they probably would be heard from again if widespread violence were to occur in the South.

There is a continuing dilemma for some segments of Northern opinion which have strong ties with the South. They include not merely those who have family and personal connections with Southerners, but Northern businessmen and trade union leaders who have Southern branches. The national AFL-CIO, for example, has not moved as forthrightly on integration within its own ranks as it might because of pressures from Southern (and even some Northern) locals and because of its hopes of organizing more white Southern workers. In 1959, Negro labor leaders formed the Negro American Labor Council to pressure the AFL-CIO toward a position of complete integration. For a period, the leadership of the national labor movement refused to recognize the Negro group except in the critical terms of "dual unionism." By the end of 1961, however, president George Meany of the AFL-CIO verbally capitulated and set up some organizational machinery to eliminate discrimination and segregation in the member unions.

IMPROVEMENT IN EMPLOYMENT OPPORTUNITIES

In the dynamic situation created by all these forces, any description of the position of Negroes at any one moment is bound to be dated before it can be printed. The picture as of the winter of 1962 will be painted in broad strokes so that it is also superficial and incomplete. Whereas in 1940, Negroes were excluded from most occupations outside of agriculture and service, by 1962 some Negroes were to be found in nearly every occupation. Considerable employment discrimination remained in the South and even in the Border states, but it was all but eliminated in the Northern and Western states. This did

FOREWORD

I have been asked to write a prefatory note for this book, because of the part played by the Carnegie Corporation in inaugurating the comprehensive study of which it is the outcome. In the public mind, the American foundations are associated with gifts for endowment and buildings to universities, colleges and other cultural and scientific institutions, and to a lesser degree with the financial support of fundamental research. It is true that a great part of the funds for which their Trustees are responsible have been distributed for these purposes, but the foundations do other things not so generally recognized. There are, for example, problems which face the American people, and sometimes mankind in general, which call for studies upon a scale too broad for any single institution or association to undertake, and in recent years certain foundations have devoted a considerable part of their available resources to the financing of such comprehensive studies.

The primary purpose of studies of this character is the collection, analysis and interpretation of existing knowledge; it is true that considerable research may prove necessary to fill the gaps as they reveal themselves, but such research is a secondary rather than a primary part of the undertaking as a whole. Provided the foundation limits itself to its proper function, namely to make the facts available and let them speak for themselves, and does not undertake to instruct the public as to what to do about them, studies of this kind provide a wholly proper and, as experience has shown, sometimes a highly important use of their funds.

As examples, we may take the inquiry and report of the Committee on the Costs of Medical Care (1928-1933), made possible by a group of foundations. Lord Hailey's memorable study, *An African Survey*, in the thirties was financed by the Carnegie Corporation. The significance of such undertakings cannot be measured by their cost. The volumes on the Poor Whites of South Africa, published in 1932, represent a relatively modest enterprise, but they have largely changed the thinking of the South Africans upon a social question of great importance to them.

While the underlying purpose of these studies is to contribute to the general "advancement and diffusion of knowledge and understanding," to quote the Charter of the Carnegie Corporation, it sometimes happens that a secondary factor, namely the need of the foundation itself for fuller light in the formulation and development of its own program, has been influential in their inception. This is true in the present case. The wide sweep of Andrew Carnegie's interests included the Negro, he gave generously to Negro institutions, and was closely identified with both Hampton and Tuskegee Institutes. The Corporation which he created maintained that interest, and during the years between its organization in 1911 and the inauguration of the present study, it made grants of more than two and one-half million dollars in direct response thereto.

In 1931, the late Newton D. Baker joined the Corporation Board. He was the son of a Confederate officer, attended the Episcopal Academy in Virginia and the Law School of Washington and Lee University, and spent the greater part of his early years in the Border states of West Virginia and Maryland. His services first as City Solicitor and later as Mayor of Cleveland gave him direct experience with the growing Negro populations in Northern cities, and as Secretary of War he had faced the special problems which the presence of the Negro element in our population inevitably creates in time of national crisis.

Mr. Baker knew so much more than the rest of us on the Board about these questions, and his mind had been so deeply concerned with them, that we readily agreed when he told us that more knowledge and better organized and interrelated knowledge were essential before the Corporation could intelligently distribute its own funds. We agreed with him further in believing that the gathering and digestion of the material might well have a usefulness far beyond our own needs.

The direction of such a comprehensive study of the Negro in America, as the Board thereupon authorized, was a serious question. There was no lack of competent scholars in the United States who were deeply interested in the problem and had already devoted themselves to its study, but the whole question had been for nearly a hundred years so charged with emotion that it appeared wise to seek as the responsible head of the undertaking someone who could approach his task with a fresh mind, uninfluenced by traditional attitudes or by earlier conclusions, and it was therefore decided to "import" a general director—somewhat as the late Charles P. Howland was called across the Atlantic to supervise the repatriation of the Greeks in Asia Minor after the close of the first World War. And since the emotional factor affects the Negroes no less than the whites, the search was limited to countries of high intellectual and scholarly standards but with no background or traditions of imperialism which might lessen the confidence of the Negroes in the United States as to the complete impartiality of the study and the validity of its findings. Under these limitations, the obvious places to look were Switzerland and the Scandinavian countries, and the search ended in the selection of Dr. Gunnar Myrdal, a scholar who despite his youth had already achieved an international reputation as a social economist, a professor in the University of Stockholm, economic adviser to the Swedish Government, and a member of the Swedish Senate. Dr. Myrdal had a decade earlier spent a year in the United States as a Fellow of the Spelman Fund, and when the invitation was extended to him by the Corporation in 1937, was about to make a second visit at the invitation of Harvard University to deliver the Godkin Lectures.

It was understood that he should be free to appoint and organize a staff of his own selection in the United States and that he should draw upon the experience of other scholars and experts in less formal fashion, but that the report as finally drawn up and presented to the public should represent and portray his own decisions, alike in the selection of data and in the conclusions as to their relative importance. Upon him rested the responsibility, and to him should go the credit for what I for one believe to be a remarkable accomplishment.

The difficulties of Dr. Myrdal's task, which would have been great enough in any event, were much increased by the outbreak of the present war. At a critical point in the development of the enterprise, he returned to Sweden to confer with his colleagues in the Government and the University, and only after nine months was he enabled to return by a long and circuitous route. Meanwhile, defense and war needs here had taken more and more of the time and energies of his collaborators. Despite all these difficulties, delays and complications, his task has now been completed and is presented in these volumes. The Carnegie Corporation is under deep and lasting obligation to Dr. Myrdal. The full degree of this obligation will be appreciated only when the material he has gathered and interpreted becomes generally known.

Though he has achieved an extraordinary mastery of the English language, Dr. Myrdal is not writing in his mother tongue. As a result, there is a freshness and often a piquancy in his choice of words and phrases which is an element of strength. Here and there it may lead to the possibility of misunderstanding of some word or some phrase. This is a risk that has been deliberately taken. It would have been possible for some American to edit the very life out of Dr. Myrdal's manuscript in an effort to avoid all possibility of offending the susceptibilities of his readers, but the result would have been a less vital and a far less valuable document than it is in its present form.

Thanks are also due to the Director's many associates and advisers, and in particular to Professor Samuel A. Stouffer and Dr. Richard Sterner, who during Dr. Myrdal's absence carried the burden of direction and decision, and to Messrs. Shelby M. Harrison, William F. Ogburn and Donald R. Young for their generously given editorial services in connection with the publication of some of the research memoranda prepared by Dr. Myrdal's collaborators.

When the Trustees of the Carnegie Corporation asked for the preparation of this report in 1937, no one (except possibly Adolf Hitler) could have foreseen that it would be made public at a day when the place of the Negro in our American life would be the subject of greatly heightened interest in the United States, because of the social questions which the war has brought in its train both in our military and in our industrial life. It is a day, furthermore, when the eyes of men of all races the world over are turned upon us to see how the people of the most powerful of the United Nations are dealing *at home* with a major problem of race relations.

It would have been better in some ways if the book could have appeared somewhat earlier, for the process of digestion would then have taken place under more favorable conditions, but, be that as it may, it is fortunate that its appearance is no longer delayed.

I venture to close these introductory paragraphs with a personal word dealing with a matter upon which Dr. Myrdal himself has touched in his preface, but which I feel moved to state in my own words. It is inevitable that many a reader will find in these volumes statements and conclusions to which he strongly objects, be he white or colored, Northerner or Southerner. May I urge upon each such reader that he make every effort to react to these statements intellectually and not emotionally. This advice, I realize, is much more easy to give than to follow, but it is given with a serious purpose. The author is under no delusions of omniscience; as a scholar, he is inured to taking hard knocks as well as giving them, and he will be the first to welcome challenges as to the accuracy of any data he has presented, the soundness of any general conclusions he has reached, and the relative weight assigned by him to any factor or factors in the complicated picture he draws. Criticism and correction on these lines will add greatly to the value of the whole undertaking.

F. P. Keppel

December 15, 1942.

AUTHOR'S PREFACE TO THE FIRST EDITION

Late in the summer of 1937 Frederick P. Keppel, on behalf of the Trustees of the Carnegie Corporation of New York, of which he was then President, invited me to become the director of "a comprehensive study of the Negro in the United States, to be undertaken in a wholly objective and dispassionate way as a social phenomenon."

> Our idea, so far as we have developed it, would be to invite one man to be responsible for the study as a whole, but to place at his disposal the services of a group of associates, Americans, who would be competent to deal as experts with the anthropological, economic, educational and social aspects of the question, including public health and public administration.[a]

After some correspondence and, later, personal conferences in the spring of 1938, when I was in the United States for another purpose, the matter was settled. It was envisaged that the study would require a minimum of two years of intensive work, but that it might take a longer time before the final report could be submitted.

On September 10, 1938, I arrived in America to start the work. Richard Sterner of the Royal Social Board, Stockholm, had been asked to accompany me. On Mr. Keppel's advice, we started out in the beginning of October on a two months' exploratory journey through the Southern states. Jackson Davis, of the General Education Board, who has behind him the experiences of a whole life devoted to improving race relations in the South and is himself a Southerner, kindly agreed to be our guide, and has since then remained a friend and an advisor.

> We traveled by car from Richmond, Virginia, and passed through most of the Southern states. We established contact with a great number of white and Negro leaders in various activities; visited universities, colleges, schools, churches, and various state and community agencies as well as factories and plantations; talked to police officers, teachers, preachers, politicians, journalists, agriculturists, workers, sharecroppers, and in fact, all sorts of people, colored and white . . .
>
> During this trip the State Agents for Negro Education in the various states were our key contacts. They were all extremely generous with their time and interest, and were very helpful.
>
> The trip was an exploratory journey: we went around with our eyes wide open and gathered impressions, but did not feel ready, and in any case, had not the necessary time to collect in an original way data and material for the Study. The experience

[a] Letter from Mr. Frederick P. Keppel, August 12, 1937.

however, was necessary. Without it our later studies will have no concrete points at which to be fixed.[a]

After a period of library work a first memorandum on the planning of the research to be undertaken was submitted to Mr. Keppel on January 28, 1939. It was later mimeographed, and I had, at this stage of the study, the advantage of criticisms and suggestions, in oral discussions and by letter, from a number of scholars and experts, among whom were: W. W. Alexander, Ruth Benedict, Franz Boas, Midian O. Bousfield, Sterling Brown, W. O. Brown, Ralph J. Bunche, Eveline Burns, Horace Cayton, Allison Davis, Jackson Davis, John Dollard, W. E. B. Du Bois, Edwin Embree, Earl Engle, Clark Foreman, E. Franklin Frazier, Abram L. Harris, Melville J. Herskovits, Charles S. Johnson, Guion G. Johnson, Guy B. Johnson, Eugene Kinckle Jones, Thomas Jesse Jones, Otto Klineberg, Ralph Linton, Alain Locke, Frank Lorimer, George Lundberg, Frank Notestein, Howard W. Odum, Frederick Osborn, Robert E. Park, Hortense Powdermaker, Arthur Raper, Ira DeA. Reid, E. B. Reuter, Sterling Spero, Dorothy Swaine Thomas, W. I. Thomas, Charles H. Thompson, Edward L. Thorndike, Rupert B. Vance, Jacob Viner, Walter White, Doxey A. Wilkerson, Faith Williams, Louis Wirth, L. Hollingsworth Wood, Thomas J. Woofter, Jr., Donald R. Young.

During the further planning of the study in terms of specific research projects and collaborators, Donald R. Young of the Social Science Research Council, Charles S. Johnson of Fisk University, and Thomas J. Woofter, Jr., then of the Works Progress Administration, were relied upon heavily for advice. Mr. Young, in particular, during this entire stage of the study, was continuously consulted not only on all major questions but on many smaller concerns as they arose from day to day, and he placed at my disposal his great familiarity with the field of study as well as with available academic personnel. Upon the basis of the reactions I had received, I reworked my plans and gradually gave them a more definite form in terms of feasible approaches and the manner of actually handling the problems. A conference was held at Asbury Park, New Jersey, from April 23 to April 28 inclusive, at which were present: Ralph J. Bunche, Charles S. Johnson, Guy B. Johnson, Richard Sterner, Dorothy S. Thomas, Thomas J. Woofter, Jr., and Donald R. Young. As a result of the conference I submitted to Mr. Keppel, in a letter of April 28, 1939, a more definite plan for the next stage of the study. The general terms of reference were defined in the following way:

> The study, thus conceived, should aim at determining the social, political, educational, and economic status of the Negro in the United States as well as defining opinions held by different groups of Negroes and whites as to his "right" status. It must, further, be concerned with both recent changes and current trends with respect

[a] Memorandum to Mr. Keppel, January 28, 1939.

to the Negro's position in American society. Attention must also be given to the total American picture with particular emphasis on relations between the two races. Finally, it must consider what changes are being or can be induced by education, legislation, interracial efforts, concerted action by Negro groups, etc.

Mr. Keppel, who from the start had given me the benefit of his most personal interest and advice, and who had followed the gradual development of the approach, gave his approval to the practical plans. Needed were a working staff, consisting of experts who could devote their whole time to the project, and, in addition, the collaboration of other experts to prepare research memoranda on special subjects. I was most fortunate in securing the cooperation needed. The following staff members were engaged, besides Richard Sterner: Ralph J. Bunche, Guy B. Johnson, Paul H. Norgren, Dorothy S. Thomas, and Doxey A. Wilkerson. Norgren did not join the staff until November 1, 1939. Mrs. Thomas left the study on January 15, 1940, for another engagement. Outside the staff, the following persons undertook various research tasks, namely: M. F. Ashley-Montagu, Margaret Brenman, Sterling Brown, Barbara Burks, Allison Davis, J. G. St. Clair Drake, Harold F. Dorn, G. James Fleming, Lyonel C. Florant, E. Franklin Frazier, Herbert Goldhamer, Melville J. Herskovits, T. Arnold Hill, Eugene L. Horowitz, Eleanor C. Isbell, Charles S. Johnson, Guion G. Johnson, Dudley Kirk, Louise K. Kiser, Otto Klineberg, Ruth Landes, Gunnar Lange, T. C. McCormick, Benjamin Malzberg, Gladys Palmer, Arthur Raper, Ira DeA. Reid, Edward Shils, Bernhard J. Stern, Louis Wirth, T. J. Woofter, Jr. There were the following assistants to staff members and outside collaborators, who worked for various periods: Berta Asch, Lloyd H. Bailer, Louis Boone, Frieda Brim, Vincent Brown, William B. Bryant, Elwood C. Chisolm, Walter Chivers, Kenneth Clark, Belle Cooper, Lenore Epstein, Edmonia Grant, Louis O. Harper, James Healy, Mary C. Ingham, James E. Jackson, Jr., Wilhelmina Jackson, Anne De B. Johnson, Louis W. Jones, Alan D. Kandel, Simon Marcson, Felix E. Moore, Jr., Rose K. Nelson, Herbert R. Northrup, Edward N. Palmer, Lemuel A. Penn, Glaucia B. Roberts, Arnold M. Rose, George C. Stoney, Joseph Taylor, Benjamin Tepping, Harry J. Walker, Richard B. Whitten, Milton Woll, Rowena Wyant, and Walter Wynne. Mrs. Rowena Hadsell Saeger was the executive secretary of the study throughout this stage.

During the summer of 1939 I prepared a detailed plan for the study.[a] The work on the various research memoranda started gradually during the summer and fall of 1939, and I remained in close touch with all my collaborators. As I wanted to be able to corroborate, as far as possible,

[a] "Memorandum on the Disposition of the Study on the American Negro."

information in the literary sources and in the research memoranda being prepared for the study, by looking at interracial relations in various parts of the country with my own eyes, I continued to reserve as much of my time as possible for work in the field.

After the Germans had invaded Denmark and Norway in April, 1940, Mr. Keppel and I agreed that my duty was to go home to Sweden. Samuel A. Stouffer—who, meanwhile, had undertaken the responsibilities on the staff which Mrs. Thomas had left—agreed to take upon himself the burden of directing the project in my absence. Without reserve, he unselfishly devoted all his talents and all his energy to the task of bringing the research to completion by September 1, 1940, and he succeeded. I shall always remain in deep gratitude to Stouffer for what he did during those months and for the moral support he thereafter has unfailingly given me and the project.

Because of the delay in the completion of the work—and, indeed, the uncertainty as to whether I would ever be able to return to the task of writing a final report—the Corporation decided, in the fall of 1940, to facilitate the publication of some of the memoranda. A Committee to advise in the selection of those contributions most nearly ready for publication was appointed, consisting of Donald R. Young, Chairman, Shelby M. Harrison and William F. Ogburn. Samuel A. Stouffer served as Secretary to this committee. The following volumes have been published:

Melville J. Herskovits, *The Myth of the Negro Past*. New York: Harper & Brothers, 1941.

Charles S. Johnson, *Patterns of Negro Segregation*. New York: Harper & Brothers, 1943.

Richard Sterner, *The Negro's Share*. New York: Harper & Brothers, 1943.

A fourth volume is to be published later:

Otto Klineberg, editor, *Characteristics of the American Negro*. New York: Harper & Brothers.

This volume contains the following research memoranda, the manuscripts of which will be deposited in the Schomburg Collection of the New York Public Library.

Otto Klineberg, "Tests of Negro Intelligence," "Experimental Studies of Negro Personality."

Benjamin Malzberg, "Mental Disease among American Negroes: A Statistical Analysis."

Louis Wirth and Herbert Goldhamer, "The Hybrid and the Problem of Miscegenation."

Eugene L. Horowitz, " 'Race' Attitudes."

Guy Johnson, "The Stereotypes of the American Negro."

The following unpublished manuscripts, prepared for the study—after some provision has been made to preserve the authors' rights—are being deposited in the Schomburg Collection of the New York Public Library where they will be available for scientific reference:[a]

M. F. Ashley-Montagu, "Origin, Composition and Physical Characteristics of the American Negro Population."

Margaret Brenman, "Personality Traits of Urban Negro Girls."

Sterling Brown, "The Negro in American Culture" (fragment).

Ralph Bunche, "Conceptions and Ideologies of the Negro Problem," "The Programs, Ideologies, Tactics, and Achievements of Negro Betterment and Interracial Organizations," "A Brief and Tentative Analysis of Negro Leadership," "The Political Status of the Negro."

Barbara Burks, "The Present Status of the Nature-Nurture Problem as It Relates to Intelligence."

Allison Davis, "Negro Churches and Associations in the Lower South."

Harold F. Dorn, "The Health of the Negro."

J. G. St. Clair Drake, "Negro Churches and Associations in Chicago."

G. James Fleming, "The Negro Press."

Lyonel C. Florant, "Critique of the Census of the United States," "Negro Migration—1860-1940" (revised edition, 1942, of the Stouffer-Florant manuscript).

E. Franklin Frazier, "Recreation and Amusement among American Negroes," "Stories of Experiences with Whites."

T. Arnold Hill, "Digest and Analysis of Questionnaires Submitted by Urban League Secretaries for 'The Negro in America.' Churches and Lodges, Negro Business and Businessmen, Racial Attitudes, Recreation and Leisure Time."

E. C. Isbell, "The Negro Family in America," "Statistics of Population Growth and Composition."

Guion G. Johnson, "A History of Racial Ideologies in the United States with Reference to the Negro."

Guion G. Johnson and Guy B. Johnson, "The Church and the Race Problem in the United States."

Guy B. Johnson and Louise K. Kiser, "The Negro and Crime."

Dudley Kirk, "The Fertility of the Negro."

Ruth Landes, "The Ethos of the Negro in the New World."

Gunnar Lange, "Trends in Southern Agriculture," "The Agricultural Adjustment Program and the Negro" (fragment).

T. C. McCormick, "The Negro in Agriculture."

Benjamin Malzberg, "A Study of Delusions among Negroes with Mental Diseases."

Paul Norgren, "Negro Labor and Its Problems."

[a] In addition to the unpublished research memoranda listed, the following material is also deposited in the Schomburg Collection:

Memorandum to Mr. Keppel, January 28, 1939 (containing the first plan of the Study)

Memorandum to the Staff, "Disposition of the Study on the American Negro," September 10, 1939 (containing the definitive research program)

Memorandum to the Staff, "Main Viewpoints and Emphases of the Study," February 8, 1940

Memorandum to the Staff, "Preparation of Manuscripts," February 8, 1940

Memorandum to the Staff, "Bibliographies," October 31, 1939

E. Nelson Palmer, "A Note on the Development of Negro Lodges in the United States."

Arthur Raper, "Race and Class Pressures."

Ira DeA. Reid, "The Negro in the American Economic System."

Edward A. Shils, "The Bases of Social Stratification in Negro Society."

Bernhard J. Stern, "The Negro in Adult Education."

Samuel A. Stouffer and Lyonel C. Florant, "Negro Population and Negro Population Movements: 1860-1940, in Relation to Social and Economic Factors."

Doxey Wilkerson, "The Negro in American Education" (fragment).

T. J. Woofter, Jr., "The Negro and Agricultural Policy."

The Advisory Committee appointed by the Corporation has gone through all the published and unpublished memoranda listed above. Coming to the material from outside and viewing it with fresh eyes, the Committee felt justified in giving the following appraisal:

> The Committee found that every manuscript submitted offered significant contributions. In serving the purposes of the Study so well, the contributors necessarily subordinated their individual publication interests to the interests of the central project. This is evidence of unselfish team-play which deserves respect and commendation.[a]

To this high appreciation, which needs no amplification on my part, I want to add some words of personal gratitude to my colleagues in the first stage of the study. The collaboration in the study—which embraced, in friendship and concerted efforts, white and Negro men and women of different specialties, ages, and previous accomplishments—gave more than is contained in the 15,000 typewritten pages of manuscript. Even about the specific problems of race relations, which we were studying together, I learned much more from our informal conferences than I can ever duly account for in this book.

To Mrs. Rowena Hadsell Saeger I remain grateful for her great devotion and, specifically, for the efficient manner in which she relieved me of much office work in directing the study, thereby allowing me to use much of the year for continuing my field trips.

The National Association for the Advancement of Colored People, The Urban League, The Commission for Interracial Cooperation, private and public research institutions, several branches of the federal government, and state and municipal authorities in different parts of the country, and, in addition, a great number of individuals, have aided me and my collaborators to an extent which makes any detailed acknowledgment difficult.

The first stage of the study closed with the completion of the several research memoranda which are published or, in unpublished form, are made available for students of the Negro problem.

[a] Foreword by the Committee to: Melville J. Herskovits, *The Myth of the Negro Past* (1941), p. x.

The second stage of the study began when I returned to America on March 6, 1941. In writing the present book, which has been produced during this second stage, I have utilized the unpublished manuscripts, prepared for the study during its first stage, in the same manner as I have used the printed literature. I have, therefore, had frequent occasion to cite them. As a glance at the footnotes will reveal, the *unpublished* manuscripts on which I have relied most heavily are those by Bunche, Norgren, Raper, Stouffer and Florant, and, in the next place, those of Dorn, Drake, Kirk and Lange. I have, of course, depended upon the printed literature to an even greater extent than upon the specially prepared monographs. Much of the library work was done during the summer of 1941 in the excellent Baker Library of Dartmouth College, Hanover, New Hampshire. Use was also made of the Columbia University Library, the New York Public Library, the Princeton University Library and the Russell Sage Foundation's library. I have also drawn upon my personal observations of conditions and attitudes in various parts of the country and upon the observations of Sterner and Rose. Most of the book was written in Princeton, New Jersey.

In September, 1941, I was joined by Richard Sterner and Arnold Rose, whose names rightly appear on the title page as assistants. Richard Sterner has been my associate in this work from the first day. Together we explored the Negro problem in America, which was so new and foreign to us both, and together we discussed the task to be accomplished. Sterner assisted in an essential way in outlining the program for the first stage of the work. Besides the special investigation of the Negro's standard of living, which he later undertook as one of the staff members and which resulted in his now published book, *The Negro's Share: In Income, Consumption, Housing and Public Assistance*, he kept, upon my request, a general interest and a general responsibility for the wider economic problems of the Negro in America. For the present book he has prepared manuscripts in draft form for nine chapters in Part IV on economic problems. Appendix 6, "Pre-War Conditions of the Negro Wage Earner in Selected Industries and Occupations," is written by him. He has carefully gone through the several succeeding drafts of other parts of the book and has given me criticism which has not only referred to details but often to fundamental views and arrangement. For the final shape of Part V on the political problems, for instance, his criticism has been of greatest importance since it has led me to stress, much more than I had succeeded in doing in a first draft, the elements of actual and pending change in the political scene of the South. His critique of this and other parts has had a specific functional value for the writing of this book, as he, being a stranger like myself and having the same cultural background, was inside the points of view which have been applied throughout the work. I should also mention that when statements in this book are made in a conjectural form and based on personal observations, these observations are often made by Sterner or by both Sterner and myself.

Arnold Rose has prepared drafts for Chapters 5, 6, 7, and 8 on problems connected with race and population, Chapter 22 on the present political scene, Chapter 29 on the patterns of discrimination, Chapters 41 and 42 on church and education, and Appendices 4, 7 and 8. He has also prepared drafts for many sections of other chapters. For still other chapters he has assembled data and filled in gaps. For the final formulation of the main methodological analysis in Appendix 2 on facts and values in social science, his contribution has been of great importance. He has read the manuscripts of all parts and edited them. His editing work has included much more than polishing the English. It has, rather, been a most conscientious checking of basic data as well as of inferences, and a critical consideration of arrangement, viewpoints and conclusions. Both his criticisms and suggestions have, with few exceptions, led to changes in the final manuscript, and many of these changes are important. His wide knowledge of the social science literature and his sound judgment on methodological problems have, in this critical work, been significant. When I delivered the manuscript and departed from America, there was still a great deal of checking to be done and gaps to be filled in for which he was responsible, as well as for the proof reading. He also had to write Chapters 43 and 44, on the Negro community and culture, and Sections 1 and 4 of Appendix 10. For the present form of these two chapters and the appendix, Rose is himself responsible.

About the contributions of both Sterner and Rose I want to add the following. The size of the book, and still more the scope of the problems involved, will make it understandable even to the reader who is not himself familiar with many of the specific fields, that the work done has been immense. We have had to dig deep into primary sources in many fields of social science and a major part of this digging has been done by them. The collaboration, which stretched ruthlessly over evenings and weekends, has been a sheer pleasure to me, as I have felt more than I have ever experienced before the stimulation of an ideal cooperation where we not only added together the results of our labor but imagined that we in our concerted endeavors sometimes reached higher than an arithmetical sum. A similar outlook on the methodological problems of social science and a mutually shared scientific curiosity in seeing our structure of hypothesis, data, and conclusion rise, have given to our collaboration a spirit of intellectual exploration which I will not soon forget.

To Miss Ruth Moulik, who has been our secretary and who will continue to stay with the book until it has come through the press, we are grateful for her skill and great devotion. Besides the responsibility for the office and, particularly, for the typing and checking of the manuscript, she has helped us by statistical computations, by digging up sources in the library, by checking statistical data and quotations, and in many other ways.

In the last, hectic stage of the study, from September through December, 1942, Caroline Baer Rose was a member of the little group of three who had to carry on after Sterner and I departed for Sweden. She worked unselfishly through all hours, including evenings and weekends, and brought to the study her frank personality and broad background. She assisted Mr. Rose in checking data and filling in gaps and was especially helpful in doing these things on the economics part. She also wrote the first draft of Chapter 44, Section 4, on "Recreation."

Before making my final revision of the manuscript I have had the invaluable help of having it read critically and carefully by two friends who are at the same time outstanding social scientists with a great familiarity with the problems treated in the book: Professors E. Franklin Frazier of Howard University and Louis Wirth of the University of Chicago. They have not spared any effort, and as a result I have had their criticisms and suggestions often from page to page, referring to everything from the syntax and the arrangement of chapters and appendices to fundamental problems of approach and to conclusions. In my revision nearly every point raised by them has caused omissions, additions, rearrangements, clarifications or other alterations. Paul H. Norgren has read Appendix 6 and a first draft of Chapter 19. Gunnar Lange has read Chapters 10 to 12 and a first draft of Chapter 18. The final manuscript has benefited by their criticism. Alva Myrdal has read various chapters; her criticism of Appendix 1 and Chapter 41 on Negro education has been particularly valuable.

The relation of the study to the Carnegie Corporation of New York must be accounted for. The study has an unusual character as it was not initiated by any individual scholar or academic institution but sponsored by the Carnegie Corporation itself and, in a sense, carried out within the Corporation. The general plan that a number of American experts should be asked to collaborate by preparing research monographs while the director himself should write a final report, was also developed by the Corporation. All decisions on practical and financial matters have been taken on the responsibility of the Corporation. The Trustees of the Corporation have been most generous and prompt in appropriating necessary funds for the study.

Mr. Keppel has had to keep in closer touch with the progress of the work than is usual when a study is sponsored by an outside institution. No conventional words of appreciation can express what his unfailing personal interest in the project has meant in upholding the courage of the present author throughout his tribulations. Charles Dollard, the Assistant to the President of the Carnegie Corporation, has followed the work in all its practical details and has, with Keppel, contributed most in terms of moral support and advice. Both Keppel and Dollard have read the manuscript and given me their criticisms and suggestions, which have been very valuable.

For the content of the book, I am solely responsible.

The scope and main direction of this book will be explained in the "Introduction." There are, however, some few notes of a more personal character for which the proper place is at the close of this preface. To invite a foreigner—someone "in a nonimperialistic country with no background of domination of one race over another" who, presumably "would approach the situation with an entirely fresh mind"; I am here again quoting Keppel's first letter, August 12, 1937—to review the most serious race problem in the country, is an idea singularly American. In any other country such a proposal would have been defeated by afterthoughts of practical and political expediency. Many will deem it a foolish idea. But more fundamentally it is a new demonstration, in a minor matter, of American moralism, rationalism, and optimism—and a demonstration of America's unfailing conviction of its basic soundness and strength. Early in the course of this work, when I had found out the seriousness of the task before me, I proposed to Mr. Keppel that a committee be formed of a Southern white, a Northern white, and a Negro. In such a group we could have allowed for political considerations and worked out a basis for practical understanding, to which each one could have subscribed, since the representation of different viewpoints would have accounted for the intellectual compromises involved. This was, however, not at all what he wanted. He told me that everyone would generously help and advise me— and there he proved right—but that I would have to find out for myself, and upon my own responsibility, the truth in the matter without any side glances as to what was politically desirable and expedient.

This book is the result. Let it be added at once that the author does not have any pretension of having produced the definitive statement of the Negro problem in America. The problem is too big and too complicated, and also things are rapidly changing while one writes. Time has, as always, been a limitation. When I now leave the work, I know that many chapters could be improved. But apart from such shortcomings, there is a more basic relativism which the reader should keep in mind. *Things look different, depending upon "where you stand"* as the American expression runs. The author fully realizes, and hopes the reader will remember, that he has never been subject to the strains involved in living in a black-white society and never has had to become adjusted to such a situation—and that this condition was the very reason why he was asked to undertake the work. He was requested to see things as a stranger. Indeed, he was asked to be both the subject and the object of a cultural experiment in the field of social science.

As he, in this problem—to which he previously had given hardly a thought—was nearly stripped of all the familiar and conventional moorings of viewpoints and valuations, he had to construct for himself a system of coordinates. He found this in the American ideals of equality and liberty. Being a stranger to the problem, he has had perhaps a greater awareness of the extent to which human valuations everywhere enter into our scientific discussion of the Negro problem. In two appendices on valuations, beliefs, and facts he has attempted to clear the methodological ground for a scientific approach which keeps the valuations explicit and hinders them from going underground in the form of biases distorting the facts. And he has followed the rule all through the book of inserting the terms "the American Creed" and "value premise" and of specifying those value premises and printing them in italics. The reader will be less irritated by their repetition if he understands that these terms are placed as signs of warning to the reader and to the writer alike: the search for scientific knowledge and the drawing of practical conclusions are dependent upon valuations as well as upon facts.

When, in this way, the data on the American Negro problem are marshaled under the high ideals of the American Creed, the fact must be faced that the result is rather dark. Indeed, as will be pointed out in the first chapter, the Negro problem in America represents a moral lag in the development of the nation and a study of it must record nearly everything which is bad and wrong in America. The reading of this book must be somewhat of an ordeal to the good citizen. I do not know if it can be offered as a consolation that the writing of the book, for much the same reason, has been an ordeal to the author who loves and admires America next to his own country—and does it even more sincerely after having had to become an expert on American imperfections. To a scholar a work is always something of a fate. His personal controls are diminutive; he is in the hands of the facts, of his professional standards, and of the fundamental approach chosen.

If this book gives a more complete record than is up to now available of American shortcomings in this field, I hope, however, that it also accounts more completely for the mutability in relations, the hope for great improvement in the near future and, particularly, the dominant role of ideals in the social dynamics of America. When looking back over the long manuscript, one main conclusion—which should be stressed here since it cannot be reiterated through the whole book—is this: that *not since Reconstruction has there been more reason to anticipate fundamental changes in American race relations, changes which will involve a development toward the American ideals.*

To the friends, colleagues, experts, and administrators of both races who have been helpful to me in the course of this study, 1 want to say plainly that in a job of this kind the attempt to be completely honest involves the author in the risk of losing friends. If this does not happen in the present instance, I shall ascribe this to the singular American magnanimity which is demonstrated in the very initiative of calling for this study.

GUNNAR MYRDAL

Stockholm, October, 1942
University of Stockholm

Acknowledgments

Permission has been granted by the following publishers to quote from the copyright material listed below. The place and date of publication will be found in the Bibliography.

American Council on Education:
Children of Bondage by Allison Davis and John Dollard.
Color, Class, and Personality by Robert L. Sutherland.
Color and Human Nature by W. Lloyd Warner, Buford H. Junker and Walter A. Adams.
Growing up in the Black Belt by Charles S. Johnson.
Negro Youth at the Crossways by E. Franklin Frazier.

D. Appleton-Century Company:
Below the Potomac by Virginius Dabney.
Race Distinctions in American Law, by Gilbert T. Stephenson.

Albert and Charles Boni:
The New Negro edited by Alain Locke.

The Atlanta University Press:
Economic Cooperation Among Negro Americans edited by W. E. B. Du Bois.

Chapman & Grimes, Inc.:
The Negro's God by Benjamin E. Mays.

Chapman & Hall, Ltd. (London):
Through Afro-America by William Archer.

The University of Chicago Press:
The Biology of the Negro by Julian H. Lewis.
Deep South by Allison Davis, Burleigh B. Gardner and Mary R. Gardner.
The Etiquette of Race Relations in the South by Bertram Wilbur Doyle.
Introduction to the Science of Sociology by Robert E. Park and Ernest W. Burgess.
Negro Politicians by Harold F. Gosnell.
The Negro Press in the United States by Frederick G. Detweiler.
Shadow of the Plantation by Charles S. Johnson.

The Clarendon Press (Oxford):
The Relations of the Advanced and Backward Races of Mankind by James Bryce.

The Cleveland Foundation:
   Criminal Justice in the American City—A Summary by Roscoe Pound.
Columbia University Press:
   American Caste and the Negro College by Buell G. Gallagher.
   The Anthropometry of the American Negro by Melville J. Herskovits.
The John Day Company and David Lloyd, agent:
   American Unity and Asia, copyright 1942, by Pearl S. Buck.
R. S. Crofts & Co.:
   The Roots of American Civilization by Curtis P. Nettels.
Doubleday, Doran and Company:
   Booker T. Washington by Emmett J. Scott and Lyman Beecher Stowe.
   Following the Colour Line by Ray Stannard Baker.
   Penrod by Booth Tarkington.
   The Story of the Negro by Booker T. Washington.
   Studies in the American Race Problem by Alfred H. Stone.
   Up From Slavery by Booker T. Washington.
   What the Negro Thinks by Robert R. Moton.
Duke University Press:
   Race Relations and the Race Problem edited by Edgar T. Thompson.
Lee Furman, Inc.:
   A Long Way From Home by Claude McKay.
University of Georgia Press:
   What Negro Newspapers of Georgia Say About Some Social Problems
      by Rollin Chambliss.
Ginn and Company:
   The Basis of Racial Adjustment by Thomas J. Woofter, Jr.
   Folkways by William Sumner.
Harcourt, Brace and Company:
   Black Reconstruction by W. E. B. Du Bois.
   Darkwater by W. E. B. Du Bois.
   Dusk of Dawn by W. E. B. Du Bois.
   Main Currents of American Thought by Vernon L. Parrington.
Harper & Brothers:
   American Minority Peoples by Donald R. Young.
   Divine White Right by Trevor Bowen.
   The Negro's Church by Benjamin E. Mays and Joseph W. Nicholson.
   Negro Problems in Cities by Thomas J. Woofter, Jr. and Associates.
   Preface to Eugenics by Frederick Osborn.
   The Story of a Pioneer by Anna Howard Shaw.
   We Europeans by Julian S. Huxley and A. A. Haddon.
Harvard University—Peabody Museum:
   Study of Some Negro-White Families in the United States by Caroline
      Bond Day.

Harvard University Press:
Population: A Problem For Democracy by Gunnar Myrdal. Reprinted by permission of the President and Fellows of Harvard College.

Hastings House and Hampton Institute:
The Negro in Virginia prepared by the Federal Writers' Project.

D. C. Heath and Company:
Race Relations by Willis D. Weatherford and Charles S. Johnson.

Henry Holt and Company:
American Regionalism by Howard W. Odum and Harry E. Moore.
Black Yeomanry by Thomas J. Woofter, Jr.
The Frontier in American History by Frederick Jackson Turner.
The Negro in American Civilization by Charles S. Johnson.
Planning for America by George B. Galloway and Associates.

The Johns Hopkins Press:
The Industrial Revolution in the South by Broadus Mitchell and George S. Mitchell.

Alfred A. Knopf, Inc.:
The Autobiography of an Ex-Coloured Man by James Weldon Johnson.
Black Manhattan by James Weldon Johnson.
The Mind of the South by Wilbur J. Cash.
The Racial Basis of Civilization by Frank H. Hankins.

Little, Brown & Company:
The Road to Reunion by Paul H. Buck.

Little, Brown & Company and Atlantic Monthly Press:
The Epic of America by James Truslow Adams.

Longmans, Green and Co., Inc.:
The Basis of Ascendancy by Edgar Gardner Murphy.
Problems of the Present South by Edgar Gardner Murphy.

A. C. McClurg & Co.:
The Souls of Black Folk by W. E. B. Du Bois.

McGraw-Hill Book Company, Inc.:
Race Mixture by E. B. Reuter.

The Macmillan Company:
The American Commonwealth by James Bryce.
Democracy and Race Friction by John M. Mecklin.
The Mind of Primitive Man by Franz Boas.
Race Questions by Josiah Royce.
Studies in the Theory of Human Society by Franklin H. Giddings.

Julian Messner, Inc.:
Sinful Cities of the Western World by Hendrik De Leeuw.

Methuen and Company, Ltd. (London):
The Negro in the New World by Sir Harry Johnston.

The University of North Carolina Press:

The Collapse of Cotton Tenancy by Charles S. Johnson, Edwin R. Embree and W. W. Alexander.

The Legal Status of the Negro by Charles S. Mangum, Jr.

Liberalism in the South by Virginius Dabney.

Human Geography of the South by Rupert B. Vance.

The Negro College Graduate by Charles S. Johnson.

Preface to Peasantry by Arthur F. Raper.

Tar-Heel Editor by Josephus Daniels.

W. W. Norton & Company, Inc.:

American Faith by Ernest Sutherland Bates.

The Oxford University Press:

American Farmers in the World Crisis by Carl T. Schmidt.

Race, Class and Party by Paul Lewinson.

The University of Pennsylvania Press:

The Philadelphia Negro by W. E. B. Du Bois.

G. P. Putnam's Sons:

Darker Phases of the South by Frank Tannenbaum.

Freedom and Culture by John Dewey.

The Ronald Press Company:

The Course of American Democratic Thought by Ralph H. Gabriel.

Russell Sage Foundation:

"*Youth Programs*" by M. M. Chambers in the *Social Work Year Book, 1941* edited by Russell H. Kurtz.

Charles Scribner's Sons:

America's Tragedy by James Truslow Adams.

Heredity and Human Affairs by Edward M. East.

The Marginal Man by Everett V. Stonequist.

The Negro: The Southerner's Problem by Thomas Nelson Page.

The Negro Question by George W. Cable.

The Old South by Thomas J. Wertenbaker.

The Passing of the Great Race by Madison Grant.

The Rising Tide of Color Against White World Supremacy by Lothrop Stoddard.

The Twentieth Century Fund:

Facing the Tax Problem.

The Viking Press:

Along This Way, copyright 1933 by James Weldon Johnson.

After Freedom, copyright 1939 by Hortense Powdermaker.

Alien Americans by B. Schrieke, copyright 1936.

Brown America by Edwin R. Embree, copyright 1931.

Negro Americans, What Now?, copyright 1934 by James Weldon Johnson.

University of Virginia:
  Negro Crime in a Small Urban Community by Robert M. Lightfoot.
Yale University Press:
  Caste and Class in a Southern Town by John Dollard.
  Essays of William Graham Sumner edited by Albert G. Keller and
    Maurice R. Davie.
  New Haven Negroes by Robert Austin Warner.
  Social Life of a Modern Community by W. Lloyd Warner and Paul S.
    Lunt.
Xavier University:
  The Negro in Louisiana by Charles B. Roussève.

INTRODUCTION

1. The Negro Problem as a Moral Issue

There is a "Negro problem" in the United States and most Americans are aware of it, although it assumes varying forms and intensity in different regions of the country and among diverse groups of the American people. Americans have to react to it, politically as citizens and, where there are Negroes present in the community, privately as neighbors.

To the great majority of white Americans the Negro problem has distinctly negative connotations. It suggests something difficult to settle and equally difficult to leave alone. It is embarrassing. It makes for moral uneasiness. The very presence of the Negro in America[a]; his fate in this country through slavery, Civil War and Reconstruction; his recent career and his present status; his accommodation; his protest and his aspiration; in fact his entire biological, historical and social existence as a participant American represent to the ordinary white man in the North as well as in the South an anomaly in the very structure of American society. To many, this takes on the proportion of a menace—biological, economic, social, cultural, and, at times, political. This anxiety may be mingled with a feeling of individual and collective guilt. A few see the problem as a challenge to statesmanship. To all it is a trouble.

These and many other mutually inconsistent attitudes are blended into none too logical a scheme which, in turn, may be quite inconsistent with the wider personal, moral, religious, and civic sentiments and ideas of the Americans. Now and then, even the least sophisticated individual becomes aware of his own confusion and the contradiction in his attitudes. Occasionally he may recognize, even if only for a moment, the incongruence of his state of mind and find it so intolerable that the whole organization of his moral precepts is shaken. But most people, most of the time, suppress such threats to their moral integrity together with all of the confusion, the ambiguity, and inconsistency which lurks in the basement of man's soul. This, however, is rarely accomplished without mental strain. Out of the strain comes a sense of uneasiness and awkwardness which always seems attached to the Negro problem.

The strain is increased in democratic America by the freedom left open

---

[a] The word *America* will be used in this book as a synonym for continental United States.

—even in the South,^a to a considerable extent—for the advocates of the Negro, his rights and welfare. All "pro-Negro" forces in American society, whether organized or not, and irrespective of their wide differences in both strategy and tactics, sense that this is the situation. They all work on the national conscience. They all seek to fix everybody's attention on the suppressed moral conflict. No wonder that they are often regarded as public nuisances, or worse—even when they succeed in getting grudging concessions to Negro rights and welfare.

At this point it must be observed that America, relative to all the other branches of Western civilization, is moralistic and "moral-conscious." The ordinary American is the opposite of a cynic. He is on the average more of a believer and a defender of the faith in humanity than the rest of the Occidentals. It is a relatively important matter to him to be true to his own ideals and to carry them out in actual life. We recognize the American, wherever we meet him, as a practical idealist. Compared with members of other nations of Western civilization, the ordinary American is a rationalistic being, and there are close relations between his moralism and his rationalism. Even romanticism, transcendentalism, and mysticism tend to be, in the American culture, rational, pragmatic and optimistic. American civilization early acquired a flavor of enlightenment which has affected the ordinary American's whole personality and especially his conception of how ideas and ideals ought to "click" together. He has never developed that particular brand of tired mysticism and romanticism which finds delight in the inextricable confusion in the order of things and in ineffectuality of the human mind. He finds such leanings intellectually perverse.

These generalizations might seem venturesome and questionable to the reflective American himself, who, naturally enough, has his attention directed more on the dissimilarities than on the similarities within his culture. What is common is usually not obvious, and it never becomes striking. But to the stranger it is obvious and even striking. In the social sciences, for instance, the American has, more courageously than anywhere else on the globe, started to measure, not only human intelligence, aptitudes, and personality traits, but moral leanings and the "goodness" of communities. This man is a rationalist; he wants intellectual order in his moral set-up; he wants to pursue his own inclinations into their hidden haunts; and he is likely to expose himself and his kind in a most undiplomatic manner.

In hasty strokes we are now depicting the essentials of the American *ethos*. This moralism and rationalism are to many of us—among them the author of this book—the glory of the nation, its youthful strength, perhaps the salvation of mankind. The analysis of this "American Creed" and its

^a The more precise meaning of the words, *South, North,* and other terms for regions in America will be explained in Appendix 4.

implications have an important place in our inquiry. While on the one hand, to such a moralistic and rationalistic being as the ordinary American, the Negro problem and his own confused and contradictory attitudes toward it must be disturbing; on the other hand, the very mass of unsettled problems in his heterogeneous and changing culture, and the inherited liberalistic trust that things will ultimately take care of themselves and get settled in one way or another, enable the ordinary American to live on happily, with recognized contradictions around him and within him, in a kind of bright fatalism which is unmatched in the rest of the Western world. This fatalism also belongs to the national *ethos*.

The American Negro problem is a problem in the heart of the American. It is there that the interracial tension has its focus. It is there that the decisive struggle goes on. This is the central viewpoint of this treatise. Though our study includes economic, social, and political race relations, at bottom our problem is the moral dilemma of the American—the conflict between his moral valuations on various levels of consciousness and generality. The "American Dilemma," referred to in the title of this book, is the ever-raging conflict between, on the one hand, the valuations preserved on the general plane which we shall call the "American Creed," where the American thinks, talks, and acts under the influence of high national and Christian precepts, and, on the other hand, the valuations on specific planes of individual and group living, where personal and local interests; economic, social, and sexual jealousies; considerations of community prestige and conformity; group prejudice against particular persons or types of people; and all sorts of miscellaneous wants, impulses, and habits dominate his outlook.

The American philosopher, John Dewey, whose immense influence is to be explained by his rare gift for projecting faithfully the aspirations and possibilities of the culture he was born into, in the maturity of age and wisdom has written a book on *Freedom and Culture*, in which he says:

> Anything that obscures the fundamentally moral nature of the social problem is harmful, no matter whether it proceeds from the side of physical or of psychological theory. Any doctrine that eliminates or even obscures the function of choice of values and enlistment of desires and emotions in behalf of those chosen weakens personal responsibility for judgment and for action. It thus helps create the attitudes that welcome and support the totalitarian state.[1]

We shall attempt to follow through Dewey's conception of what a social problem really is.

2. VALUATIONS AND BELIEFS

The Negro problem in America would be of a different nature, and, indeed, would be simpler to handle scientifically, if the moral conflict raged only between valuations held by different persons and groups of persons. The essence of the moral situation is, however, that the conflicting valuations are also held by the same person. *The moral struggle goes on within people and not only between them. As people's valuations are conflicting, behavior normally becomes a moral compromise. There are no homogeneous "attitudes" behind human behavior but a mesh of struggling inclinations, interests, and ideals, some held conscious and some suppressed for long intervals but all active in bending behavior in their direction.*

The unity of a culture consists in the fact that all valuations are mutually shared in some degree. We shall find that even a poor and uneducated white person in some isolated and backward rural region in the Deep South, who is violently prejudiced against the Negro and intent upon depriving him of civic rights and human independence, has also a whole compartment in his valuation sphere housing the entire American Creed of liberty, equality, justice, and fair opportunity for everybody. He is actually also a good Christian and honestly devoted to the ideals of human brotherhood and the Golden Rule. And these more general valuations—more general in the sense that they refer to all human beings—are, to some extent, effective in shaping his behavior. Indeed, it would be impossible to understand why the Negro does not fare worse in some regions of America if it were not constantly kept in mind that behavior is the outcome of a compromise between valuations, among which the equalitarian ideal is one. At the other end, there are few liberals, even in New England, who have not a well-furnished compartment of race prejudice, even if it is usually suppressed from conscious attention. Even the American Negroes share in this community of valuations: they have eagerly imbibed the American Creed and the revolutionary Christian teaching of common brotherhood; under closer study, they usually reveal also that they hold something of the majority prejudice against their own kind and its characteristics.

The intensities and proportions in which these conflicting valuations are present vary considerably from one American to another, and within the same individual, from one situation to another. The cultural unity of the nation consists, however, in the fact that *most Americans have most valuations in common* though they are arranged differently in the sphere of valuations of different individuals and groups and bear different intensity coefficients. This cultural unity is the indispensable basis for discussion between persons and groups. It is the floor upon which the democratic process goes on.

In America as everywhere else people agree, as an abstract proposition, that *the more general valuations—those which refer to man as such and not to any particular group or temporary situation—are morally higher.* These valuations are also given the sanction of religion and national legislation. They are incorporated into the American Creed. The other valuations—which refer to various smaller groups of mankind or to particular occasions—are commonly referred to as "irrational" or "prejudiced," sometimes even by people who express and stress them. They are defended in terms of tradition, expediency or utility.

Trying to defend their behavior to others, and primarily to themselves, people will attempt to conceal the conflict between their different valuations of what is desirable and undesirable, right or wrong, by keeping away some valuations from awareness and by focusing attention on others. For the same opportune purpose, *people will twist and mutilate their beliefs of how social reality actually is.* In our study we encounter whole systems of firmly entrenched popular beliefs concerning the Negro and his relations to the larger society, which are bluntly false and which can only be understood when we remember the opportunistic *ad hoc* purposes they serve. These "popular theories," because of the rationalizing function they serve, are heavily loaded with emotions. But people also want to be rational. Scientific truth-seeking and education are slowly rectifying the beliefs and thereby also influencing the valuations. In a rationalistic civilization it is not only that the beliefs are shaped by the valuations, but also that the valuations depend upon the beliefs.[a]

Our task in this inquiry is to ascertain social reality as it is. We shall seek to depict the actual life conditions of the American Negro people and their manifold relations to the larger American society. We must describe, in as much detail as our observations and space here allow, who the American Negro is, and how he fares. Whenever possible, we shall present quantitative indices of his existence and of the material conditions for his existence. But this is not all and, from our point of view, not even the most important part of social reality. We must go further and attempt to discover and dissect the doctrines and ideologies, valuations and beliefs, embedded in the minds of white and Negro Americans. We want to follow through W. I. Thomas's theme, namely, that when people define situations as real, they *are* real.[2] We shall try to remember throughout our inquiry that material facts in large measure are the product of what people think, feel and believe. The actual conditions, as they are, indicate from this point of view the great disparities between the whites' and the Negroes' aspirations and realizations. The interrelations between the material facts and people's valuations of and beliefs about these facts are precisely what make the Negro a social problem.

It is sometimes assumed to be the mark of "sound" research to disregard the fact that people are moral beings and that they are struggling for their conscience. In our view, this is a bias and a blindness, dangerous to

[a] The theory of human behavior and its motivation, which is sketched in the text and is basic to our approach to the Negro problem, is explained in Appendix 1, "A Methodological Note on Valuations and Beliefs."

the possibility of enabling scientific study to arrive at true knowledge. Every social study must have its center in an investigation of people's conflicting valuations and their opportune beliefs. They are social facts and can be observed by direct and indirect manifestations. We are, of course, also interested in discovering how these inclinations and loyalties came about and what the factors are upon which they rest. We want to keep free, however, at least at the outset, from any preconceived doctrine or theory, whether of the type making biological characteristics, or economic interests, sexual complexes, power relations, or anything else, the "ultimate" or "basic" cause of these valuations. We hope to come out with a type of systematic understanding as eclectic as common sense itself when it is open-minded.

When we thus choose to view the Negro problem as primarily a moral issue, we are in line with popular thinking. It is as a moral issue that this problem presents itself in the daily life of ordinary people; it is as a moral issue that they brood over it in their thoughtful moments. It is in terms of conflicting moral valuations that it is discussed in church and school, in the family circle, in the workshop, on the street corner, as well as in the press, over the radio, in trade union meetings, in the state legislatures, the Congress and the Supreme Court. The social scientist, in his effort to lay bare concealed truths and to become maximally useful in guiding practical and political action, is prudent when, in the approach to a problem, he sticks as closely as possible to the common man's ideas and formulations, even though he knows that further investigation will carry him into tracts uncharted in the popular consciousness. There is a pragmatic common sense in people's ideas about themselves and their worries, which we cannot afford to miss when we start out to explore social reality. Otherwise we are often too easily distracted by our learned arbitrariness and our pet theories, concepts, and hypotheses, not to mention our barbarous terminology, which we generally are tempted to mistake for something more than mere words. *Throughout this study we will constantly take our starting point in the ordinary man's own ideas, doctrines, theories and mental constructs.*

In approaching the Negro problem as primarily a moral issue of conflicting valuations, it is not implied, of course, that ours is the prerogative of pronouncing on *a priori* grounds which values are "right" and which are "wrong." In fact, such judgments are out of the realm of social science, and will not be attempted in this inquiry. Our investigation will naturally be an analysis *of* morals and not *in* morals. In so far as we make our own judgments of value, they will be based on explicitly stated value premises, selected from among those valuations actually observed as existing in the minds of the white and Negro Americans and tested as to their social and political relevance and significance. Our value judgments are thus derived and have no greater validity than the value premises postulated.

3. A White Man's Problem

Although the Negro problem is a moral issue both to Negroes and to whites in America, we shall in this book have to give *primary* attention to what goes on in the minds of white Americans. To explain this direction of our interest a general conclusion from our studies needs to be stated at this point. When the present investigator started his inquiry, his preconception was that it had to be focused on the Negro people and their peculiarities. This is understandable since, from a superficial view, Negro Americans, not only in physical appearance, but also in thoughts, feelings, and in manner of life, seemed stranger to him than did white Americans. Furthermore, most of the literature on the Negro problem dealt with the Negroes: their racial and cultural characteristics, their living standards and occupational pursuits, their stratification in social classes, their migration, their family organization, their religion, their illiteracy, delinquency and disease, and so on. But as he proceeded in his studies into the Negro problem, it became increasingly evident that little, if anything, could be scientifically explained in terms of the peculiarities of the Negroes themselves.

As a matter of fact, in their basic human traits the Negroes are inherently not much different from other people. Neither are, incidentally, the white Americans. But Negroes and whites in the United States live in singular human relations with each other. All the circumstances of life—the "environmental" conditions in the broadest meaning of that term—diverge more from the "normal" for the Negroes than for the whites, if only because of the statistical fact that the Negroes are the smaller group. The average Negro must experience many times more of the "abnormal" interracial relations than the average white man in America.[a] The more important fact, however, is that practically all the economic, social, and political power is held by whites. The Negroes do not by far have anything approaching a tenth of the things worth having in America.

It is thus the white majority group that naturally determines the Negro's "place." All our attempts to reach scientific explanations of why the Negroes are what they are and why they live as they do have regularly led to determinants on the white side of the race line. In the practical and political struggles of effecting changes, the views and attitudes of the white Americans are likewise strategic. The Negro's entire life, and, consequently, also his opinions on the Negro problem, are, in the main, to be considered as secondary reactions to more primary pressures from the side of the dominant white majority.

[a] This is less true, of course, in communities where the ratio between the number of Negroes and the number of whites diverges sharply from the average ratio of one to ten for the whole nation.

The Negro was brought to America for the sake of the white man's profit. He was kept in slavery for generations in the same interest. A civil war was fought between two regional groups of white Americans. For two years no one wanted Negroes involved in the fighting. Later on some two hundred thousand Negro soldiers fought in the Northern army, in addition to all the Negro laborers, servants, spies, and helpers in both armies. But it was not the Negroes' war. As a result of the war, which took a toll of some half million killed and many more wounded, the four million Negro slaves were liberated. Since then the Negro's "place" in American society has been precarious, uncertain and changing; he was no longer so necessary and profitable to the white man as in slavery before the Civil War. In the main, however, the conflicting and vacillating valuations of the white majority have been decisive, whether the issue was segregation in the schools, discrimination with reference to public facilities, equal justice and protection under the laws, enjoyment of the franchise, or the freedom to enter a vocation and earn an honest living. The Negro, as a minority, and a poor and suppressed minority at that, in the final analysis, has had little other strategy open to him than to play on the conflicting values held in the white majority group. In so doing, he has been able to identify his cause with broader issues in American politics and social life and with moral principles held dear by the white Americans. This is the situation even today and will remain so in the foreseeable future. In that sense, "this is a white man's country."

This stress in the formulation of our problem, it must be repeated, is motivated by an ambition to be realistic about the actual power relations in American society. It should not be taken as a doctrinaire approach. In the degree that the Negro people succeed in acquiring and institutionalizing footholds of power in society with the help of interested white groups— for example, if they can freely use their votes, as they can in the North, or press themselves into the industrial labor market and the trade unions— they will increasingly be able to act and not only to react. Under all circumstances, in fact even in slavery, the attitudes and activities of the Negro people do, to a certain extent, influence the attitudes and policies of the white majority group in power, as account is taken by the whites of the Negro's reactions. Even if the prevailing power situation is reason enough to look for the primary responsibility for what happens in the valuations of the white people, these same valuations are themselves the product of a two-way interracial relationship.

4. NOT AN ISOLATED PROBLEM

Closely related to the thesis that the Negro problem is predominantly a white man's problem is another conclusion, which slowly dawned upon the author, though it undoubtedly is not news to many of his American readers: *The Negro problem is an integral part of, or a special phase of, the whole complex of problems in the larger American civilization. It cannot be treated in isolation.* There is no single side of the Negro problem—whether it be the Negro's political status, the education he gets, his place in the labor market, his cultural and personality traits, or anything else—which is not predominantly determined by its total American setting. We shall, therefore, constantly be studying the American civilization in its entirety, though viewed in its implications for the most disadvantaged population group.

There is a natural tendency on the part of white people in America to attempt to localize and demarcate the Negro problem into the segregated sector of American society where the Negroes live. This tendency is visible even in many scientific treatments of the Negro problem. The Negro spokesmen, on their side, are often equally tempted to stress the singularity of their grievances to the extent of not considering the broader setting. The fact of segregation also often makes them less familiar with the American society at large. The Negro social scientists have their special opportunity in knowing intimately the Negro community and will—with a few outstanding exceptions [3]—treat their problems in isolation.

The assumption underlying the approach in this book is, on the contrary, that the Negro problem exists and changes because of conditions and forces operating in the larger American society. Establishing this integration is thought to make the analysis more realistic. This will explain and, the author believes, justify the fact that in all parts of this inquiry attention is given to the characteristics of the American society at large in which the Negro becomes a problem.

The relationship between American society and the Negro problem is not one-sided. The entire structure of American society is itself greatly conditioned by the presence of the thirteen million Negro citizens. American politics, the labor market, education, religious life, civic ideals, art, and recreation are as they are partly because of the important conditioning factor working throughout the history of the nation. New impulses from the Negro people are constantly affecting the American way of life, bending in some degree all American institutions and bringing changes in every aspect of the American's complex world view. While primary attention will be focused on the Negro people and on the influences *from* the larger society working on them, their influence *back on* white society will not be ignored.

This plan of keeping the entire American culture within the focus of our study will, of course, increase the difficulties of our task. There are some ideas concerning the larger society, in which our special problem has its play, which are so general that they are hard to grasp and give definite form and, in any case, almost impossible to prove. Everyone has such ideas, and of necessity, they determine the scientific treatment of a specific social problem. In few instances is it possible to check them by present-day scientific tools. It is still less possible to check one's ideas about the larger society within the frame of a specialized investigation. In the main, they remain unchecked, as they are derived by common sense intuition and everyday reflection. They are generalized inductions from a vast mass of unassorted, scientifically uncontrolled personal experience. Few of them are obtained from books dealing with the larger society. But since they determine the study, they should be accounted for as far as possible. This is usually difficult, as these ideas—in the degree they conform to the cultural *milieu*—do not stand out clearly in the consciousness of an investigator. No doubt most social scientists honestly believe they have no such preconceptions. Their prevalence becomes obvious, however, when time has passed and the *milieu* has changed. Then we see how the scientists in the past period unconsciously worked under certain preconceptions, which we now find erroneous or not adequate for the present situation. These general ideas can also become explicit when one becomes acquainted with a different civilization and views one's own society through the prism of such an alien *milieu*.

The present writer has been looking not only at the Negro people but at all America from the outside. In fact, it has been his chief and sometimes overwhelming difficulty in this work that he had to start from the beginning and try to understand not only the Negro problem but the entire American culture in which it is encompassed. Comparatively little in American civilization is natural to him. He is constantly reminded of the preconceptions he utilizes to understand the larger American society. The difference is not that he has preconceptions and his American colleagues do not. The difference is that, being an outsider, he is compelled to be more conscious of them, and has had to try to reach them by deliberate intellectual efforts. In this situation he is tempted to turn a deficiency into a virtue. At any rate, he is under the pressure to state to himself what he thinks about this somewhat strange culture. He can then attempt an experiment in more rigorous social science methods in the interests of objectivity by laying open even this type of preconception. He is thereby attempting rationally to assist his critics. Not only in the next few chapters but everywhere in the book I express general views on the larger American society; many general statements about the Negro and race relations belong to the same type of judgment.

Some readers may disagree with many of my preconceptions of America. All will probably disagree with some. Just because in this experiment the preconceptions are not hidden but are openly set out, the reader is offered a guide to the specific mistakes which, in pursuing the study, might have been committed on account of false preconceptions about the larger American society and the Negro problem. If the reader is equally careful he will, however, also remember that, at least in the present stage of social research, it is next to impossible to judge rationally our most general assumptions concerning a civilization. The possibility always remains, therefore, that on some points he is wrong, and I am right. But a good result will in any case be reached, as we shall have determined the locus of fundamental disagreement, and thus we shall be better prepared to direct further research toward its scientific solution.

These assumptions are all, in a sense, subjective. I have, naturally, tried to acquire as objectively true an understanding of America and the American Negro as I am capable of reaching. And, equally naturally, it would be most fortunate to the investigation if these main assumptions approached objective truth and were relevant to the problems under study. But they are, of course, not proved; they are not part of scientifically verified truth. The only definite statement I can make is that the picture is subjectively "true"; that is, that it faithfully represents what the author, upon careful consideration, believes to be true.

5. Some Further Notes on the Scope and Direction of this Study

This book is an analysis, not a description. It presents facts only for the sake of their meaning in the interpretation. Since, however, an attempt at a comprehensive analysis was made, the scope of the facts, even when compressed into outline form, is extensive, though, we hope, selective. The author had available not only the vast existing published literature, but also some specially prepared research memoranda, a portion of which are being published, and all of which are made available to the inquiring reader.[a]

On the theoretical[b] side, the aim of this book is to formulate tentative generalizations on the basis of known facts. A corollary of this scientific task is to indicate gaps in knowledge. These gaps will be noted in passing, and in some respects positive suggestions for investigation will be offered. Undoubtedly, we shall sometimes be found to have overlooked existing sources. In view of the scope of the investigation this is inevitable but, nevertheless, regrettable.

As the known and verified facts are scarce, a courageous use will be made of the writer's own observations. Their conjectural character will always be made explicit. They are the author's best judgments, when published data

[a] A list of these will be found in the Preface. The unpublished memoranda can be consulted in the Schomburg Collection of the New York Public Library.

[b] The terms *theoretical* and *practical* (or *political*) are used in this book as in the discipline of philosophy. The former word implies thinking in terms of causes and effects; the latter words imply thinking in terms of means and ends. (See Appendix 2, Section 4.)

are insufficient, as to what is the truth, and they should be taken only for what they are. For the outlining of further research they may serve as the projection of plausible hypotheses.

On the practical side, the aim of this book is to throw light on the future, and to construct, in a preliminary way, bases for rational policy. This is one reason why the theoretical analysis will stress interrelations and trends. Even though reliable prognoses cannot be made in many respects, various possibilities can be presented and their probabilities estimated.

Explicit value premises will be introduced, usually in the beginning of each main part of the inquiry. As a source for the value premises, the relatively comprehensive and definite body of political ideals contained in the "American Creed" will be used; we shall sketch the historical origin of the American Creed in the first chapter. The use of explicit value premises serves three main purposes: (1) to purge as far as possible the scientific investigation of distorting biases which are usually the result of hidden biases; (2) to determine in a rational way the statement of problems and the definition of terms for the theoretical analysis; (3) to lay a logical basis for practical and political conclusions.[a]

Our aim is to organize the entire treatise around one single sequence of thoughts. We shall proceed from the American scene at large to the facts and problems of Negro life, to the trends, to the specific policies, to their final integration into the structure of national policies. This plan is, within limits, the basis of organization for each major part of the inquiry.

The main axes to be drawn through our subject and in accordance with which we shall organize the materials are pretty much determined by the object under study. Those of most general relevance are: color, region, urban-rural residence, social class, education, sex, and age. Comparisons between Negroes and whites—in such things, for example, as vital indices, criminality, family patterns—will not be made indiscriminately but, as far as possible, will be standardized by comparing Negroes with a duly defined control group of whites, or by comparing subgroups of Negroes and whites of equal social, economic, and educational status. This attempt is, however, all too often frustrated through insurmountable difficulties due to the scarcity of available data.

The book concentrates on present conditions but does not neglect the future. While it would add to our comprehension to examine the historical development behind the existing situation, this is beyond the scope of our inquiry. In a sense and to a degree present conditions and trends can be analyzed without consideration of their antecedents. This should not be

---

[a] The problem of bias, of theoretical and practical research, and of the utilization of the scientific technique of explicit value premises are treated in Appendix 2, "A Methodological Note on Facts and Valuations in Social Science." The author may be allowed to point out that a critical study of this inquiry assumes the reading of Appendix 2.

taken to mean that the author has not tried—within the time available—
to familiarize himself with the history of the Negro problem in America,
but merely that this book has a limited scope and does not intend to give
the history of the Negro problem. Where, in the course of the presentation,
it is deemed necessary to review some aspect of the past in order to understand present problems, historical outlines will be offered. We are, however, not concerned with the past for its own sake, but merely in so far as
important happenings in the past have influenced present situations and
trends. Even in this narrower sphere we do not have the historian's interest in the "uniquely historical datum" but the social scientist's interest in
broad and general relations and main trends.

Other problems of race relations in the United States and the Negro
problem in areas outside of the United States will be left entirely outside
the scope of the present inquiry. Good reasons could be given for stretching
the boundaries of the study considerably in both directions. Unquestionably
it could contribute vastly to a more complete understanding of the American Negro problem. Obvious restrictions of space and capacity, however,
stand in the way.

The book has grown to considerable length, and the author realizes that
some readers cannot afford the time or energy to read it all. The main parts
have, therefore, been arranged so that they can be read independently.
This has involved some repetitions of facts and main viewpoints. Even for
the reader who reads the whole book, the repetitions have been thought
to be less burdensome than the risk of obscurity. When he surveyed a wide
field of American culture, James Bryce said:

> Whenever it has been necessary to trace a phenomenon to its source or to explain
> the connection between several phenomena, I have not hesitated, knowing that one
> must not expect a reader to carry in his mind all that has been told already, to re-state
> a material fact, or re-enforce a view which gives to the facts what I conceive to be
> their true significance.[4]

Technical terms will be avoided except when they are necessary for
clarity. Words will be used in their common sense meaning unless the
danger of ambiguity forces us explicitly to restrict the meaning of the
term. Some of the main terms which are understood to be value loaded—
such as discrimination, disfranchisement, caste, and class—will be expressly
defined in relation to our set of value premises.[a]

If we have departed from the usual techniques of style in minor respects,
we have done so with the hope of helping the reader. One thing may be
mentioned here: We have classified footnotes into two groups. Those
marked by letters of the alphabet are placed at the bottom of the page;
we believe that they should be read with the text since they are integral

---

[a] See Appendix 2, Section 4.

parts of it, but would make the text clumsy if they were to be inserted in it. Those marked by numbers are placed at the end of the book; they are mainly for scholars who wish concrete evidence of sources, but we believe the general reader will wish to skim over them. Our classification is subjective and does not rigidly follow any rules.

6. A WARNING TO THE READER

Before embarking upon the study, the simple old reminder should be repeated that no person or culture can be judged solely by its imperfections. The subject of this book—American attitudes and actions with respect to the Negro and the disparity between American ideals and behavior in this field—forces us to dig in dark corners and to wash dirty linen in public. But we wish to warn the reader that we do not, and he should not, regard our analysis as a complete evaluation of America.

As interests in social studies are often concentrated on problem groups and areas, a delusion is easily created that the situation in America is worse than it actually is. "Moral statistics" consist traditionally of a recording of all the negative items in a culture: crime, illegitimacy, suicide and so on. This tradition has arisen because data for abnormalities are available. Figures on divorces have been calculated in all countries—and, of course, America ranks among the highest—but there has never been any comprehensive enumeration of the happy marriages. There are statistics on crime—and they are ugly for America—but none on civil decency. The method of measuring moral levels by statistics and descriptions of what is extremely bad and wrong in a society is thus heavily loaded against a nation with a particularly wide range of moral behavior. This is a fact not always taken into account even by the American specialists on the evils and the wrongs of society.

In setting out upon investigating a subject matter, which is bound to deal for the most part with various forms of social pathology in America, the author must stress that, in his opinion, large groups of the American population probably live a more "righteous" life, measured by whatever standard one chooses, than any large group of people anywhere else in the Western world. Even in the large cities with a shocking amount of political corruption, crime, and vice, by far the greater part of the population has no more contact with these phenomena than if they lived in another country. *The moral latitude is so very wide in America: if there is abnormally much that is very bad, there is also unusually much that is extremely good.*

Thus a study of America centered upon the Negro problem must not be expected to give a comprehensive and balanced cultural analysis of the nation any more than would a study centered on crime or political corruption. Under a broader perspective the Negro is only a corner—although a fairly big one—of American civilization. This corner is one of the least

clean in the national household: we shall see plenty of law-breaking, crime
and corruption, poverty and distress, heartlessness and ignorance. We shall
continuously be dealing with the frictions, worries and shortcomings of
America.

Studying the Negro problem gives a "frog-perspective" of the cultural
situation, not a bird's eye view. Although the frog-perspective does reveal
some of the real virtues of a society, as we shall find, it focuses more completely on its faults. For a general purpose, it is not a true perspective.[5]
I am eager to have the warning expressly stated in the introduction to this
book, that *anyone who uncritically utilizes the viewpoints and findings of
this inquiry on the American Negro problem for wider conclusions concerning the United States and its civilization than are warranted by its
direction of interest is misusing them.*

PART I

THE APPROACH

CHAPTER I

AMERICAN IDEALS
AND THE AMERICAN CONSCIENCE

1. UNITY OF IDEALS AND DIVERSITY OF CULTURE

It is a commonplace to point out the heterogeneity of the American nation and the swift succession of all sorts of changes in all its component parts and, as it often seems, in every conceivable direction. America is truly a shock to the stranger. The bewildering impression it gives of dissimilarity throughout and of chaotic unrest is indicated by the fact that few outside observers—and, indeed, few native Americans—have been able to avoid the intellectual escape of speaking about America as "paradoxical."

Still there is evidently a strong unity in this nation and a basic homogeneity and stability in its valuations. Americans of all national origins, classes, regions, creeds, and colors, have something in common: a social *ethos*, a political creed. It is difficult to avoid the judgment that this "American Creed" is the cement in the structure of this great and disparate nation.

When the American Creed is once detected, the cacophony becomes a melody. The further observation then becomes apparent: that America, compared to every other country in Western civilization, large or small, has the *most explicitly expressed* system of general ideals in reference to human interrelations. This body of ideals is more widely understood and appreciated than similar ideals are anywhere else. The American Creed is not merely—as in some other countries—the implicit background of the nation's political and judicial order as it functions. To be sure, the political creed of America is not very satisfactorily effectuated in actual social life. But as principles which *ought* to rule, the Creed has been made conscious to everyone in American society.

Sometimes one even gets the impression that there is a relation between the intense apprehension of high and uncompromising ideals and the spotty reality. One feels that it is, perhaps, the difficulty of giving reality to the *ethos* in this young and still somewhat unorganized nation—that it is the prevalence of "wrongs" in America, "wrongs" judged by the high standards of the national Creed—which helps make the ideals stand out so clearly. America is continously struggling for its soul. These principles of social ethics have been hammered into easily remembered formulas. All means of intellectual communication are utilized to stamp them into everybody's mind. The schools teach them, the churches preach them. The courts pronounce their judicial decisions in their terms. They permeate editorials with a pattern of idealism so ingrained that the writers could scarcely free themselves from it even if they tried. They have fixed a custom of indulging in high-sounding generalities in all written or spoken addresses to the American public, otherwise so splendidly gifted for the matter-of-fact approach to things and problems. Even the stranger, when he has to appear before an American audience, feels this, if he is sensitive at all, and finds himself espousing the national Creed, as this is the only means by which a speaker can obtain human response from the people to whom he talks.

The Negro people in America are no exception to the national pattern. "It was a revelation to me to hear Negroes sometimes indulge in a glorification of American democracy in the same uncritical way as unsophisticated whites often do," relates the Dutch observer, Bertram Schrieke.[1] A Negro political scientist, Ralph Bunche, observes:

> Every man in the street, white, black, red or yellow, knows that this is "the land of the free," the "land of opportunity," the "cradle of liberty," the "home of democracy," that the American flag symbolizes the "equality of all men" and guarantees to us all "the protection of life, liberty and property," freedom of speech, freedom of religion and racial tolerance.[2]

The present writer has made the same observation. The American Negroes know that they are a subordinated group experiencing, more than anybody else in the nation, the consequences of the fact that the Creed is not lived up to in America. Yet their faith in the Creed is not simply a means of pleading their unfulfilled rights. They, like the whites, are under the spell of the great national suggestion. With one part of themselves they actually believe, as do the whites, that the Creed is ruling America.

These ideals of the essential dignity of the individual human being, of the fundamental equality of all men, and of certain inalienable rights to freedom, justice, and a fair opportunity represent to the American people the essential meaning of the nation's early struggle for independence. In the clarity and intellectual boldness of the Enlightenment period these tenets were written into the Declaration of Independence, the Preamble of the Constitution, the Bill of Rights and into the constitutions of the several states. The ideals of the American Creed have thus become the highest law of the land. The Supreme Court pays its reverence to these general principles when it declares what is constitutional and what is not. They have been elaborated upon by all national leaders, thinkers and statesmen. America has had, throughout its history, a continuous discussion of the principles and implications of democracy, a discussion which, in every epoch, measured by any standard, remained high, not only quantitatively but also qualitatively. The flow of learned treatises and popular tracts on the subject has not ebbed, nor is it likely to do so. In all wars, including the present one, the American Creed has been the ideological foundation of national morale.

2. American Nationalism

The American Creed is identified with America's peculiar brand of nationalism, and it gives the common American his feeling of the historical mission of America in the world—a fact which just now becomes of global importance but which is also of highest significance for the particular problem studied in this book. The great national historian of the middle nineteenth century, George Bancroft, expressed this national feeling of pride and responsibility:

> In the fulness of time a republic rose in the wilderness of America. Thousands of years had passed away before this child of the ages could be born. From whatever there was of good in the systems of the former centuries she drew her nourishment; the wrecks of the past were her warnings . . . The fame of this only daughter of freedom went out into all the lands of the earth; from her the human race drew hope.[3]

And Frederick J. Turner, who injected the naturalistic explanation into history that American democracy was a native-born product of the Western frontier, early in this century wrote in a similar vein:

> Other nations have been rich and prosperous and powerful. But the United States has believed that it had an original contribution to make to the history of society by the production of a self-determining, self-restrained, intelligent democracy.[4]

Wilson's fourteen points and Roosevelt's four freedoms have more recently expressed to the world the boundless idealistic aspirations of this American Creed. For a century and more before the present epoch, when the oceans gave reality to the Monroe Doctrine, America at least applauded heartily every uprising of the people in any corner of the world. This was a tradition from America's own Revolution. The political revolutionaries of foreign countries were approved even by the conservatives in America. And America wanted generously to share its precious ideals and its happiness in enjoying a society ruled by its own people with all who would come here. James Truslow Adams tells us:

> The American dream that has lured tens of millions of all nations to our shores in the past century has not been a dream of merely material plenty, though that has doubtless counted heavily. It has been much more than that. It has been a dream of

being able to grow to fullest development as man and woman, unhampered by the barriers which had slowly been erected in older civilizations, unrepressed by social orders
which had developed for the benefit of classes rather than for the simple human being
of any and every class. And that dream has been realized more fully in actual life here
than anywhere else, though very imperfectly even among ourselves.[5]

This is what the Western frontier country could say to the "East." And
even the skeptic cannot help feeling that, perhaps, this youthful exuberant
America has the destiny to do for the whole Old World what the frontier
did to the old colonies. *American nationalism is permeated by the American
Creed,* and therefore becomes international in its essence.

3. SOME HISTORICAL REFLECTIONS

It is remarkable that a vast democracy with so many cultural disparities
has been able to reach this unanimity of ideals and to elevate them
supremely over the threshold of popular perception. Totalitarian fascism
and nazism have not in their own countries—at least not in the short range
of their present rule—succeeded in accomplishing a similar result, in spite
of the fact that those governments, after having subdued the principal
precepts most akin to the American Creed, have attempted to coerce the
minds of their people by means of a centrally controlled, ruthless, and
scientifically contrived apparatus of propaganda and violence.

There are more things to be wondered about. The disparity of national
origin, language, religion, and culture, during the long era of mass immigration into the United States, has been closely correlated with income
differences and social class distinctions. Successive vintages of "Old Americans" have owned the country and held the dominant political power; they
have often despised and exploited "the foreigners." To this extent conditions in America must be said to have been particularly favorable to the
stratification of a rigid class society.

But it has not come to be. On the question of why the trend took the
other course, the historians, from Turner on, point to the free land and
the boundless resources. The persistent drive from the Western frontier—
now and then swelling into great tides as in the Jeffersonian movement
around 1800, the Jacksonian movement a generation later, and the successive third-party movements and breaks in the traditional parties—could,
however, reach its historical potency only because of the fact that America,
from the Revolution onward, had an equalitarian creed as a going national
ethos. The economic determinants and the force of the ideals can be shown
to be interrelated. But the latter should not be relegated to merely a
dependent variable. Vernon L. Parrington, the great historian of the development of the American mind, writes thus:

> The humanitarian idealism of the Declaration [of Independence] has always
> echoed as a battle-cry in the hearts of those who dream of an America dedicated to

democratic ends. It cannot be long ignored or repudiated, for sooner or later it returns to plague the council of practical politics. It is constantly breaking out in fresh revolt. . . . Without its freshening influence our political history would have been much more sordid and materialistic.[6]

Indeed, the new republic began its career with a reaction. Charles Beard, in *An Economic Interpretation of the Constitution of the United States*,[7] and a group of modern historians, throwing aside the much cherished national mythology which had blurred the difference in spirit between the Declaration of Independence and the Constitution, have shown that the latter was conceived in considerable suspicion against democracy and fear of "the people." It was dominated by property consciousness and designed as a defense against the democratic spirit let loose during the Revolution.

But, admitting all this, the Constitution which actually emerged out of the compromises in the drafting convention provided for the most democratic state structure in existence anywhere in the world at that time. And many of the safeguards so skillfully thought out by the conservatives to protect "the rich, the wellborn, and the capable" against majority rule melted when the new order began to function. Other conservative safeguards have fastened themselves into the political pattern. And "in the ceaseless conflict between the man and the dollar, between democracy and property"—again to quote Parrington[8]—property has for long periods triumphed and blocked the will of the people. And there are today large geographical regions and fields of human life which, particularly when measured by the high goals of the American Creed, are conspicuously lagging. But taking the broad historical view, the American Creed has triumphed. It has given the main direction to change in this country. America has had gifted conservative statesmen and national leaders, and they have often determined the course of public affairs. But with few exceptions, only the liberals have gone down in history as national heroes.[9] America is, as we shall point out, conservative in fundamental principles, and in much more than that, though hopefully experimentalistic in regard to much of the practical arrangements in society. But *the principles conserved are liberal* and some, indeed, are radical.

America got this dynamic Creed much as a political convenience and a device of strategy during the long struggle with the English Crown, the London Parliament and the various British powerholders in the colonies. It served as the rallying center for the growing national unity that was needed. Later it was a necessary device for building up a national morale in order to enlist and sustain the people in the Revolutionary War. In this spirit the famous declarations were resolved, the glorious speeches made, the inciting pamphlets written and spread. "The appeal to arms would seem to have been brought about by a minority of the American people, directed by a small group of skillful leaders, who, like Indian scouts, covered their tracks so cleverly, that only the keenest trailers can now follow their course and understand their strategy."[10]

But the Creed, once set forth and disseminated among the American people, became so strongly entrenched in their hearts, and the circumstances have since then been so relatively favorable, that it has succeeded in keeping itself very much alive for more than a century and a half.

4. THE ROOTS OF THE AMERICAN CREED IN THE PHILOSOPHY OF ENLIGHTENMENT

The American Creed is a humanistic liberalism developing out of the epoch of Enlightenment when America received its national consciousness and its political structure. The Revolution did not stop short of anything less than the heroic desire for the "emancipation of human nature." The enticing flavor of the eighteenth century, so dear to every intellectual and rationalist, has not been lost on the long journey up to the present time. Let us quote a contemporary exegesis:

Democracy is a form of political association in which the general control and direction of the commonwealth is habitually determined by the bulk of the community in accordance with understandings and procedures providing for popular participation and consent. Its postulates are:

1. The essential dignity of man, the importance of protecting and cultivating his personality on a fraternal rather than upon a differential basis, of reconciling the needs of the personality within the frame-work of the common good in a formula of liberty, justice, welfare.
2. The perfectibility of man; confidence in the possibilities of the human personality, as over against the doctrines of caste, class, and slavery.
3. That the gains of commonwealths are essentially mass gains rather than the efforts of the few and should be diffused as promptly as possible throughout the community without too great delay or too wide a spread in differentials.
4. Confidence in the value of the consent of the governed expressed in institutions, understandings and practices as a basis of order, liberty, justice.
5. The value of decisions arrived at by common counsel rather than by violence and brutality.

These postulates rest upon (1) reason in regarding the essential nature of the political man, upon (2) observation, experience and inference, and (3) the fulfillment of the democratic ideal is strengthened by a faith in the final triumph of ideals of human behavior in general and of political behavior in particular.[11]

For practical purposes the main norms of the American Creed as usually pronounced are centered in the belief in equality and in the rights to liberty.[12] In the Declaration of Independence—as in the earlier Virginia Bill of Rights—equality was given the supreme rank and the rights to liberty are posited as derived from equality. This logic was even more clearly expressed in Jefferson's original formulation of the first of the "self-evident truths": "All men are created equal *and from that equal creation* they derive rights inherent and unalienable, among which are the preservation of life and liberty and the pursuit of happiness."[13]

Liberty, in a sense, was easiest to reach. It is a vague ideal: everything turns around *whose* liberty is preserved, to *what extent* and *in what direction*. In society liberty for one may mean the suppression of liberty for others. The result of competition will be determined by who got a head start and who is handicapped. In America as everywhere else—and sometimes, perhaps, on the average, a little more ruthlessly—liberty often provided an opportunity for the stronger to rob the weaker. Against this, the equalitarianism in the Creed has been persistently revolting. The struggle is far from ended. The reason why American liberty was not more dangerous to equality was, of course, the open frontier and the free land. When opportunity became bounded in the last generation, the inherent conflict between equality and liberty flared up. Equality is slowly winning. The New Deal during the 'thirties was a landslide.[a]

5. THE ROOTS IN CHRISTIANITY

If the European philosophy of Enlightenment was one of the ideological roots of the American Creed, another equally important one was Christianity, particularly as it took the form in the colonies of various lower class Protestant sects, split off from the Anglican Church.[b] "Democracy was envisaged in religious terms long before it assumed a political terminology."[14]

It is true that modern history has relegated to the category of the pious patriotic myths the popular belief that *all* the colonies had been founded to get religious liberty, which could not be had in the Old World. Some of the colonies were commercial adventures and the settlers came to them, and even to the religious colonies later, to improve their economic status. It is also true that the churches in the early colonial times did not always exactly represent the idea of democratic government in America but most often a harsher tyranny over people's souls and behavior than either King or Parliament ever cared to wield.

But the myth itself is a social reality with important effects. It was strong

---

[a] New Dealers, like most American liberals today, pronounce liberty before equality. But they do so in the eighteenth century Jeffersonian sense, not in the American businessman's sense. The "four freedoms" of Franklin D. Roosevelt are liberties, but they are liberties to get equality, not liberties of the stronger to infringe on the weaker. In this sense, equality is logically derivable from liberty, just as liberty is from equality: if there is real liberty for all there will be equal opportunity and equal justice for all, and there will even be social equality limited only by minor biological inequalities.

[b] While the Protestant sects emphasized the elements of the American Creed, it should not be forgotten that there was an older trait of humanitarianism and equalitarianism in the creed of the Medieval Church.

already in the period of the Revolution and continued to grow. A small proportion of new immigrants throughout the nineteenth century came for religious reasons, or partly so, and a great many more wanted to rationalize their uprooting and transplantation in such terms. So religion itself in America took on a spirit of fight for liberty. The Bible is full of support for such a spirit. It consists to a large extent of the tales of oppression and redemption from oppression: in the Old Testament of the Jewish people and in the New Testament of the early Christians. The rich and mighty are most often the wrongdoers, while the poor and lowly are the followers of God and Christ.

The basic teaching of Protestant Christianity is democratic. We are all poor sinners and have the same heavenly father. The concept of natural rights in the philosophy of Enlightenment corresponded rather closely with the idea of moral law in the Christian faith:

> The doctrine of the free individual, postulating the gradual escape of men from external political control, as they learned to obey the moral law, had its counterpart in the emphasis of evangelicism upon the freedom of the regenerated man from the terrors of the Old Testament code framed for the curbing of unruly and sinful generations. The philosophy of progress was similar to the Utopian hopes of the millennarians. The mission of American democracy to save the world from the oppression of autocrats was a secular version of the destiny of Christianity to save the world from the governance of Satan.[15]

But apart from the historical problem of the extent to which church and religion in America actually inspired the American Creed, they became a powerful container and preserver of the Creed when it was once in existence. This was true from the beginning. While in Europe after the Napoleonic Wars the increasing power of the churches everywhere spelled a period of reaction, the great revivals beginning around 1800 in America were a sort of religious continuation of the Revolution.

> In this way great numbers whom the more-or-less involved theory of natural rights had escaped came under the leveling influence of a religious doctrine which held that all men were equal in the sight of God. Throughout the Revival period the upper classes looked upon the movement as "a religious distemper" which spread like a contagious disease, and they pointed out that it made its greatest appeal to "those of weak intellect and unstable emotions, women, adolescents, and Negroes." But to the poor farmer who had helped to win the Revolution only to find himself oppressed as much by the American ruling classes as he had ever been by Crown officials, the movement was "the greatest stir of Religion since the day of Pentecost."[16]

Religion is still a potent force in American life. "They are a religious people," observed Lord Bryce about Americans a half a century ago, with great understanding for the importance of this fact for their national ideology.[17] American scientific observers are likely to get their attentions fixed upon the process of progressive secularization to the extent that they do not see this main fact, that America probably is still the most religious country in the Western world. Political leaders are continuously deducing the American Creed out of the Bible. Vice-President Henry Wallace, in his historic speech of May 8, 1942, to the Free World Association, where he declared the present war to be "a fight between a slave world and a free world" and declared himself for "a people's peace" to inaugurate "the century of the common man," spoke thus:

> The idea of freedom—the freedom that we in the United States know and love so well—is derived from the Bible with its extraordinary emphasis on the dignity of the individual. Democracy is the only true political expression of Christianity.
>
> The prophets of the Old Testament were the first to preach social justice. But that which was sensed by the prophets many centuries before Christ was not given complete and powerful political expression until our Nation was formed as a Federal Union a century and a half ago.[18]

Ministers have often been reactionaries in America. They have often tried to stifle free speech; they have organized persecution of unpopular dissenters and have even, in some regions, been active as the organizers of the Ku Klux Klan and similar "un-American" (in terms of the American Creed) movements. But, on the whole, church and religion in America are a force strengthening the American Creed. The fundamental tenets of Christianity press for expression even in the most bigoted setting. And, again on the whole, American religion is not particularly bigoted, but on the contrary, rather open-minded. The mere fact that there are many denominations, and that there is competition between them, forces American churches to a greater tolerance and ecumenical understanding and to a greater humanism and interest in social problems than the people in the churches would otherwise call for.

I also believe that American churches and their teachings have contributed something essential to the emotional temper of the Creed and, indeed, of the American people. Competent and sympathetic foreign observers have always noted the generosity and helpfulness of Americans.[19] This and the equally conspicuous formal democracy in human contacts have undoubtedly had much to do with the predominantly lower class origin of the American people, and even more perhaps, with the mobility and the opportunities—what de Tocqueville called the "equality of condition"—in the nation when it was in its formative stage. But I cannot help feeling that the Christian neighborliness of the common American reflects, also, an influence from the churches. Apart from its origin, this temper of the Americans is part and parcel of the American Creed. It shows up in the Americans' readiness to make financial sacrifices for charitable purposes. No country has so many cheerful givers as America. It was not only "rugged individualism," nor a relatively continuous prosperity, that made it possible for America to get along without a publicly organized welfare policy almost up to the Great Depression in the 'thirties but it was also the world's most generous private charity.

6. The Roots in English Law

The third main ideological influence behind the American Creed is English law. The indebtedness of American civilization to the culture of the mother country is nowhere else as great as in respect to the democratic concept of law and order, which it inherited almost without noticing it. It is the glory of England that, after many generations of hard struggle, it established the principles of justice, equity, and equality before the law even in an age when the rest of Europe (except for the cultural islands of Switzerland, Iceland, and Scandinavia) based personal security on the arbitrary police and on *lettres de cachet*.

This concept of a government "of laws and not of men" contained certain fundamentals of both equality and liberty. It will be a part of our task to study how these elemental demands are not nearly realized even in present-day America. But in the American Creed they have never been questioned. And it is no exaggeration to state that the philosophical ideas of human equality and the inalienable rights to life, liberty, and property, hastily sowed on American ground in a period of revolution when they were opportune—even allowing ever so much credit to the influences from the free life on the Western frontier—would not have struck root as they did if the soil had not already been cultivated by English law.

Law and order represent such a crucial element both in the American Creed and in the spotty American reality that, at a later stage of our argument in this chapter, we shall have to devote some further remarks to this particular set of ideological roots.

7. American Conservatism

These ideological forces—the Christian religion and the English law—also explain why America through all its adventures has so doggedly stuck to its high ideals: why it has been so conservative in keeping to liberalism as a national creed even if not as its actual way of life. This conservatism, in fundamental principles, has, to a great extent, been perverted into a nearly fetishistic cult of the Constitution. This is unfortunate since the 150-year-old Constitution is in many respects impractical and ill-suited for modern conditions and since, furthermore, the drafters of the document made it technically difficult to change even if there were no popular feeling against change.

The worship of the Constitution also is a most flagrant violation of the

American Creed which, as far as the technical arrangements for executing the power of the people are concerned, is strongly opposed to stiff formulas. Jefferson actually referred to the American form of government as an experiment. The young Walt Whitman, among many other liberals before and after him, expressed the spirit of the American Revolution more faithfully when he demanded "continual additions to our great experiment of how much liberty society will bear." Modern historical studies of how the Constitution came to be as it is reveal that the Constitutional Convention was nearly a plot against the common people. Until recently, the Constitution has been used to block the popular will: the Fourteenth Amendment inserted after the Civil War to protect the civil rights of the poor freedmen has, for instance, been used more to protect business corporations against public control.[a]

But when all this is said, it does not give more than one side of the cult of the Constitution. The common American is not informed on the technicalities and has never thought of any great difference in spirit between the Declaration of Independence and the Constitution. When he worships the Constitution, it is an act of American nationalism, and in this the American Creed is inextricably blended. The liberal Creed, even in its dynamic formulation by Jefferson, is adhered to by every American. The unanimity around, and the explicitness of, this Creed is the great wonder of America. The "Old Americans," all those who have thoroughly come to identify themselves with the nation—which are many more than the Sons and Daughters of the Revolution—adhere to the Creed as the faith of their ancestors. The others—the Negroes, the new immigrants, the Jews, and other disadvantaged and unpopular groups—could not possibly have invented a system of political ideals which better corresponded to their interests. So, by the logic of the unique American history, it has developed that the rich and secure, out of pride and conservatism, and the poor and insecure, out of dire need, have come to profess the identical social ideals. The reflecting observer comes to feel that this spiritual convergence, more than America's strategic position behind the oceans and its immense material resources, is what makes the nation great and what promises it a still greater future. Behind it all is the historical reality which makes it possible for the President to appeal to all in the nation in this way: "Let us not forget that we are all descendants from revolutionaries and immigrants."

8. THE AMERICAN CONCEPTION OF LAW AND ORDER

While the Creed is important and is enacted into law, it is not lived up to in practice. To understand this we shall have to examine American

[a] See Chapter 20, Section 5.

attitudes toward law. It is necessary to discuss the legal tradition of America at the outset, since it gives a unique twist to each of the specific problems that we shall take up in ensuing chapters.[a]

Americans are accustomed to inscribe their ideals in laws, ranging from their national Constitution to their local traffic rules. American laws thus often contain, in addition to the actually enforced rules (that is, "laws" in the ordinary technical meaning of the term), other rules which are not valid or operative but merely express the legislators' hopes, desires, advice or dreams. There is nothing in the legal form to distinguish the latter rules from the former ones. Much of the political discussion has to do with the question of strengthening the administration of laws or taking other measures so as to enforce them. Between the completely enforced rules and the unenforceable ones there are many intermediary types which are sometimes, under some conditions, or in some part, only conditionally and incompletely enforced.

To an extent this peculiar cultural trait of America is explainable by the fact that the nation is young and, even more, that it owes its state structure to a revolution—a revolution in the courageously rationalistic age of Enlightenment. Americans have kept to this custom of inscribing their ideals in laws.[b]

The "function," from the legislator's point of view, of legislating national ideals is, of course, a pedagogical one of giving them high publicity and prestige. Legislating ideals has also a "function" of dedicating the nation to the task of gradually approaching them. In a new nation made up of immigrants from all corners of the world and constantly growing by the arrival of other immigrants, carrying with them a greatly diversified cultural heritage, these goals must have stood out as important to statesmen and political thinkers.

Another cultural trait of Americans is a relatively low degree of respect for law and order. This trait, as well as the other one just mentioned, is of paramount importance for the Negro problem as we shall show in some detail in later chapters. There is a relation between these two traits, of high ideals in some laws and low respect for all laws, but this relation is by no means as simple as it appears.

[a] Our analysis is somewhat parallel to that of James Truslow Adams, "Our Lawless Heritage," *Atlantic Monthly* (December, 1928), pp. 732-740.

[b] Other countries, and I am thinking primarily of Great Britain, Holland, and Scandinavia, also sometimes commit their ideals to legislation, but they do so rarely and with great circumspection and extreme caution. On the whole, these countries have left even the essential liberties of citizens in a democracy unformulated as merely implied in all legislation and judicial procedure. Yet they have afforded a greater protection of the common citizens' liberties under the law than America (although they have not faced the same problems as America).

9. NATURAL LAW AND AMERICAN PURITANISM

On this point we must observe somewhat more closely the moralistic attitude toward law in America, expressed in the common belief that there is a "higher law" behind and above the specific laws contained in constitutions, statutes and other regulations.

The idea of a "natural law" has long been a part of our common line of legal tradition. When the elected "lawman" in pre-Christian times "spoke the law" to the assembled arm-bearing freemen, he was not assumed to make the law or invent it but to expound something which existed prior to and independent of himself and all others participating in the procedure. The idea of a "higher law," as well as the whole procedure of letting it become a social reality and, indeed, the entire legal system as it functioned and grew in the northern countries, had deep roots in primitive religion and magic, as is revealed by studies of the contemporary mythology and the peculiar formalistic mechanisms of the creation and operation of law. The distinguishing mark of the particular type of magical thinking in these countries was, however, that out of it developed what we now understand to be the characteristic respect for law of modern democracy.

When representative bodies, among them the English Parliament, emerged as political institutions, they also did not conceive of themselves as "legislatures" in the modern sense, but pretended only to state the law that already "existed." Even when these legislatures began to take on new functions and to make rules to meet new situations, they still kept up the fiction that they only "declared" or "explained" the law as it existed. The modern idea of creating laws by "legislation" is thus a late product in the historical development of Western democracy, and it was never totally freed from the connotation of its subordination to a "higher law" existing independent of all formally fixed rules.

In America the Revolution gave a tremendous spread to this primitive idea of "natural law" as it, in the meantime, had been developed in the philosophies of Enlightenment under the further influences of Greek speculation, Roman law, medieval scholasticism, and free naturalistic speculation since Francis Bacon, Thomas Hobbes and Hugo Grotius. American religion supported it strongly. The idea fixed itself upon the entire American state structure. "A peculiarity of American democracy had been from the beginning that it put its faith in a higher law rather than in the changing will of the people."[20] The role given to the Supreme Court and the tradition of this tribunal not to "legislate," which as a court it could hardly have the right to do, but to refer to the higher principles back of the Constitution strengthened still more the grip of this old idea on the mind of the Americans.

The adherence even in modern times to this idealistic conception of the origin and reality of the judicial order undoubtedly, in one way, raised its moral prestige among the American people as it had done earlier in the history of the Old World. No careful observer of the present American scene should miss seeing, in spite of everything we shall discuss presently, the common American's pride in and devotion to the nation's judicial system and its legal institutions. Government authorities constantly appeal to this idealistic pride and devotion of the citizens in order to enforce the law. In America, there is a continuous endeavor to keep the judicial system orderly, and there is a continuous educational campaign on behalf of this idealism. Undoubtedly *the idealistic concept of American law as an emanation of "natural law" is a force which strengthens the rule of law in America.*

But, in another way, it is at the same time most detrimental to automatic, unreflecting law observance on the part of the citizens. Laws become disputable on moral grounds. Each legislative statute is judged by the common citizen in terms of his conception of the higher "natural law." He decides whether it is "just" or "unjust" and has *the dangerous attitude that, if it is unjust, he may feel free to disobey it.*[21] The strong stress on individual rights and the almost complete silence on the citizen's duties in the American Creed make this reaction the more natural. The Jeffersonian distrust of government—"that government is best which governs least"—soon took the form, particularly on the Western frontier, of a distrust and disrespect for the enacted laws. The doctrine of a higher law fosters an "extra-legal" disposition towards the state and excuses illegal acts.

But the frontier was not, in this respect, fundamentally different from the old colonies. Without stepping outside the American tradition, Garrison could pronounce even the Constitution to be a "compact with Hell" on the slavery issue. This, by itself, would not have been dangerous to democracy, if he had meant to argue only for a change of the Constitution. But he and many more Northerners of conscientious inclinations found it a moral obligation not to obey the fugitive slave laws. Here the citizen does not stop to criticize the laws and the judicial system and demand a change in them, but he sets his own conception of the "higher law" above the existing laws in society and feels it his right to disobey them. It is against this background also that we shall have to study the amazing disrespect for law and order which even today characterizes the Southern states in America and constitutes such a large part of the Negro problem. This anarchistic tendency founded upon a primitive concept of natural law has never left American political speculation or American popular thought.[22]

This anarchistic tendency in America's legal culture becomes even more dangerous because of the presence of a quite different tendency: *a desire to regulate human behavior tyrannically by means of formal laws.* This last tendency is a heritage from early American puritanism which was sometimes fanatical and dogmatic and always had a strong inclination to mind other people's business. So we find that this American, who is so proud to announce that he will not obey laws other than those which are "good" and "just," as soon as the discussion turns to something which in his opinion is bad and unjust, will emphatically pronounce that "there ought to be a law against . . ." To demand and legislate all sorts of laws against this or that is just as much part of American freedom as to disobey the laws when they are enacted. America has become a country where exceedingly much is permitted in practice but at the same time exceedingly much is forbidden in law.

By instituting a national prohibition of the sale of liquor without taking adequate steps for its enforcement, America was nearly drenched in corruption and organized crime until the statute was repealed. The laws against gambling have, on a smaller scale, the same effect at the present time. And many more of those unrespected laws are damaging in so far as they, for example, prevent a rational organization of various public activities, or when they can be used by individuals for blackmailing purposes or by the state or municipal authorities to persecute unpopular individuals or groups. Such practices are conducive to a general disrespect for law in America. Actually today it is a necessity in everyday living for the common good American citizen to decide for himself which laws should be observed and which not.

10. THE FALTERING JUDICIAL ORDER

We shall meet this conflict as a central theme in all angles of the Negro problem. The conflict should not, however, be formulated only in terms of the national ideology. Or, rather, this ideology is not fully explainable in terms of the thoughts and feelings out of which the American Creed was composed.

A low degree of law observance already became habitual and nationally cherished in colonial times when the British Parliament and Crown, increasingly looked upon as a foreign ruler by the Americans, insisted upon passing laws which the Americans considered unwise, impractical or simply unjust. The free life on the frontier also strained legal bonds. There the conflict between puritanical intolerance and untamed desire for individual freedom clashed more severely than anywhere else. The mass immigration and the cultural heterogeneity were other factors hampering the fixation of a firm legal order in America. The presence of states within the nation with different sets of laws and the high mobility between states were contributing factors. The jurisdictional friction between states and the federal government, the technical and political difficulties in changing the federal Constitution, the consequent great complexity of the American legal system, and the mass of legal fiction and plain trickery also are among the important factors. For example, it cannot be conducive to the highest respect for the legal system that the federal government is forced to carry out important social legislation under the fiction that it is regulating "interstate commerce," or that federal prosecuting agencies punish dangerous gangsters for income tax evasion rather than for the felonies they have committed.

So this idealistic America also became the country of legalistic formalism. Contrary to America's basic ideology of natural law and its strong practical sense, "the letter of the law," as opposed to its "spirit," came to have an excessive importance. The weak bureaucracy[a] became tangled up in "red tape." The clever lawyer came to play a large and unsavory role in politics, in business, and in the everyday life of the citizens. The Americans thus got a judicial order which is in many respects contrary to all their inclinations.

Under the influence of all these and many other factors the common American citizen has acquired a comparatively low degree of personal identification with the state and the legal machinery. An American, when he accidentally comes by the scene of a crime or of an attempt by the police to seize an offender, is, on the average, more inclined to hurry on in order not to get involved in something unpleasant, and less inclined to stop and help the arm of the law, than a Britisher or a Scandinavian would be under similar circumstances. He is more likely to look on his country's and his community's politics and administration as something to be indulged and tolerated, as outside his own responsibility, and less likely to think and act as a would-be legislator, in a cooperative endeavor to organize a decent social life.[b] He is even inclined to dissociate himself from politics as something unworthy and to take measures to keep the worthy things "out of politics." This is part of what Lord Bryce called "the fatalism of the multitude" in America. This political fatalism and the lack of identification and participation work as a vicious circle, being both cause and effect of corruption and political machine rule.

The authorities, when not relying upon the idealistic appeal, will most often meet the citizen's individualistic inclinations by trying to educate him to obey the law less in terms of collective interest than in terms of self-interest. They try to tell the young that "crime does not pay," which, in some areas, is a statement of doubtful truth.

In the exploitation of the new continent business leaders were not particular about whether or not the means they used corresponded either with the natural law or with the specific laws of the nation or the states. This became of greater importance because of the central position of business in the formation of national aspirations and ideals. When Theodore

[a] See Chapter 20, Section 2.
[b] The low degree of participation will be discussed in Chapter 33.

Roosevelt exclaimed: "Damn the law! I want the canal built," he spoke the language of his contemporary business world and of the ordinary American.

We have to conceive of all the numerous breaches of law, which an American citizen commits or learns about in the course of ordinary living, as psychologically a series of shocks which condition him and the entire society to a low degree of law observance. The American nation has, further, experienced disappointments in its attempts to legislate social change, which, with few exceptions, have been badly prepared and inefficiently carried out. The almost traumatic effects of these historical disappointments have been enhanced by America's conspicuous success in so many fields other than legislation. One of the trauma was the Reconstruction legislation, which attempted to give Negroes civil rights in the South; another one was the anti-trust legislation pressed by the Western farmers and enacted to curb the growth of monopolistic finance capitalism; a third one was the prohibition amendment.

11. INTELLECTUAL DEFEATISM

Against this background, and remembering the puritan tendency in America to make all sorts of haphazard laws directed at symptoms and not at causes and without much consideration for social facts and possibilities,[23] it is understandable that the social scientists, particularly the sociologists, in America have developed a defeatist attitude towards the possibility of inducing social change by means of legislation.[a] The political "do-nothing" tendency is strong in present-day social science in America. It is, typically enough, developed as a *general* theory—actually as a scientific translation of the old natural law idea in its negative import. The social scientists simply reflect the general distrust of politics and legislation that is widespread among the educated classes of Americans.

Of particular importance to us is that this view is common even among Negro intellectuals when reflecting on various aspects of the Negro problem. The failure of Reconstruction had especially severe effects on them. Younger Negro intellectuals are disposed to express disbelief in the possibility that much can be won by politics, legislation, and law suits, and have become inclined to set their hopes on what they conceive of as more fundamental changes of the economic structure. Sometimes they think in terms of an economic revolution. But, whether their thoughts take such a radical direction or stay conservative, a common trait is fatalism in regard to politics and legislation. Fatalism in regard to *res publica* is, however,

---

[a] These points are developed at greater length in Appendix 2. We are here referring not to the specialists on law and law enforcement but to the general sociologist, economist, or political scientist when he meets legislation as an angle of his respective problems.

by no means a Negro characteristic. It is a common American disease of the democratic spirit which is on the way to becoming chronic.

We shall meet this tendency as it affects various aspects of the Negro problem as we go along. A few critical remarks on the general theory that "stateways cannot change folkways" need to be made at the start. In this abstract form and as applied to various specific problems, the theory cannot be true, since in other parts of the world similar changes are effectuated by means of legislation. The theory must, therefore, be qualified in the light of specific American conditions. But even in America new legislation, infringing upon old customs and upon individual and local interests, is often made fairly watertight nowadays.[24] The general explanation why some laws have been more successful than others in America is that *they have been better prepared and better administered*.

This means that, among the explanations for the general disrepute and deficiency of law and order in America, there are two other factors: *the habit of passing laws without careful investigation, and the relatively low standard of American administration of law*. To the latter point we shall return in a later chapter,[a] where we shall point also to the new but strong tendency in America toward the building up of an independent and legal administration. On the former point we shall restrict ourselves to quoting a high authority: "For nothing is done with so little of scientific or orderly method as the legislative making of laws."[25]

These two factors are strategic. When the foolish attempts to suppress symptoms of ills while leaving the causes untouched become censored, and when lawmaking increasingly becomes an important task of scientific social engineering, and when, further, administration becomes independent, legal, impartial, and efficient, better laws will be made, and they will be better enforced even in America. It is a problem to explain why lawmaking and administration have been so backward in a nation where private business and also private agencies for public good are often excellently organized.

The mere possibility of change in these two factors shows the fallacy of the general theory that law cannot change custom. In the face of the tendency in American society toward more careful lawmaking and improved administration the theory appears politically as well as theoretically biased; biased against induced change. In this book we shall meet other dynamic tendencies in American society favoring the same development, the chief among them being, perhaps, the growing cultural homogeneity and the increasing political and social participation of the masses. Many social scientists tend not only to ignore these changes, but to deny them and, in some cases, to oppose them.

If in the course of time Americans are brought to be a law-abiding people, and if they at the same time succeed in keeping alive not only their

[a] See Chapter 20.

conservatism in fundamental principles and their pride and devotion to their national political institutions, but also some of their puritan eagerness and courage in attempting to reform themselves and the world—redirected somewhat from the old Biblical inclination of thinking only in terms of prescriptions and purges—this great nation may become the master builder of a stable but progressive commonwealth.

12. "Lip-Service"

The conflict in the American concept of law and order is only one side of the "moral overstrain" of the nation. America believes in and aspires to something much higher than its plane of actual life. The subordinate position of Negroes is perhaps the most glaring conflict in the American conscience and the greatest unsolved task for American democracy. But it is by no means the only one. Donald Young complains:

> In our more introspective moments, nearly all of us Americans will admit that our government contains imperfections and anachronisms. We who have been born and brought up under the evils of gang rule, graft, political incompetence, inadequate representation, and some of the other weaknesses of democracy, American plan, have developed mental callouses and are no longer sensitive to them.[26]

The *popular* explanation of the disparity in America between ideals and actual behavior is that Americans do not have the slightest intention of living up to the ideals which they talk about and put into their Constitution and laws. Many Americans are accustomed to talk loosely and disparagingly about adherence to the American Creed as "lip-service" and even "hypocrisy." Foreigners are even more prone to make such a characterization.

This explanation is too superficial. To begin with, the true hypocrite sins in secret; he conceals his faults. The American, on the contrary, is strongly and sincerely "against sin," even, and not least, his own sins. He investigates his faults, puts them on record, and shouts them from the housetops, adding the most severe recriminations against himself, including the accusation of hypocrisy. If all the world is well informed about the political corruption, organized crime, and faltering system of justice in America, it is primarily not due to its malice but to American publicity about its own imperfections. America's handling of the Negro problem has been criticized most emphatically by white Americans since long before the Revolution, and the criticism has steadily gone on and will not stop until America has completely reformed itself.

Bryce observed: "They know, and are content that all the world should know, the worst as well as the best of themselves. They have a boundless faith in free inquiry and full discussion. They admit the possibility of any number of temporary errors and delusions."[27] The present author remembers, from his first visit to this country as an inexperienced social scientist at the end of the 'twenties, how confused he often felt when Americans in all walks of life were trustingly asking him to tell them what was "wrong with this country." It is true that this open-mindedness, particularly against the outside world, may have decreased considerably since then on account of the depression, and that the present War might work in the same direction, though this is not certain; and it is true also that the opposite tendency always had its strong representation in America. But, by and large, America has been and will remain, in all probability, a society which is eager to indulge in self-scrutiny and to welcome criticism.

This American eagerness to get on record one's sins and their causes is illustrated in the often quoted letter by Patrick Henry (1772), where he confessed that he had slaves because he was "drawn along by the general inconvenience of living here without them."

> I will not, I cannot, justify it. However culpable my conduct, I will so far pay my devoir to virtue as to own the excellence and rectitude of her precepts, and lament my want of conformity to them.[28]

American rationalism and moralism spoke through Patrick Henry. America as a nation is like its courageous and eloquent son of the Revolution. It is continuously paying its *devoir* to virtue; it is repeating its allegiance to the full American Creed by lamenting its want of conformity to it. The strength and security of the nation helped this puritan tradition to continue. No weak nation anxious for its future could ever have done it. Americans believe in their own ability and in progress. They are at bottom moral optimists.

In a great nation there is, of course, division of labor. Some Americans do most of the sinning, but most do some of it. Some specialize in muck-raking, preaching, and lamentation; but there is a little of the muckraker and preacher in all Americans. On the other hand, superficially viewed, Americans often appear cynical. Their social science has lately developed along a deterministic track of amoralistic nonconcernedness; but this is itself easily seen to be a moralistic reaction. As a matter of fact, this young nation is the least cynical of all nations. It is not hypocritical in the usual sense of the word, but labors persistently with its moral problems. It is taking its Creed very seriously indeed, and this is the reason why the ideals are not only continuously discussed but also represent a social force—why they receive more than "lip-service" in the collective life of the nation. The cultural unity of the nation is this common sharing in both the consciousness of sins and the devotion to high ideals.

Americans accuse themselves, and are accused by others, of being materialists. But they are equally extreme in the other direction. Sometimes an American feels moved to put the matter right, as Josiah Royce did when he explained:

When foreigners accuse us of extraordinary love for gain, and of practical materialism, they fail to see how largely we are a nation of idealists. Yet that we are such a nation is something constantly brought to the attention of those whose calling requires them to observe any of the tendencies prevalent in our recent intellectual life in America.[29]

The American problem to be studied in this book would, indeed, have an entirely different prognosis if this fact were forgotten.

13. VALUE PREMISES IN THIS STUDY

For the study of a national problem which cuts so sharply through the whole body politic as does the Negro problem, no other set of valuations could serve as adequately as the norm for an incisive formulation of our value premises as can the American Creed. No other norm could compete in authority over people's minds. "The American democratic faith is a pattern of ideals providing standards of value with which the accomplishments of realistic democracy may be judged," observes an author surveying the historical trends of American thinking.[30]

And there is no doubt that these ideals are active realities. The student of American history must be professionally near-sighted or blinded by a doctrinal belief in a materialistic determinism if he fails to see the significance of tracing how the Creed is gradually realizing itself. *The American Creed is itself one of the dominant "social trends."* "Call it a dream or call it vision," says John Dewey, "it has been interwoven in a tradition that has had an immense effect upon American life."[31] Or, to quote a distinguished Negro thinker, the late Kelly Miller:

> In this country political, social and economic conditions gravitate toward equality. We may continue to expect thunderstorms in the political firmament so long as there exists inequality of political temperature in the atmosphere of the two regions. Neither Massachusetts nor Mississippi will rest satisfied until there is an equality of political condition in both States. . . . Democratic institutions can no more tolerate a double political status than two standards of ethics or discrepant units of weight and measure.[32]

But apart from trends, the American Creed represents the national conscience. The Negro is a "problem" to the average American partly because of a palpable conflict between the status actually awarded him and those ideals.

The American Creed, just because it is a living reality in a developing democracy, is not a fixed and clear-cut dogma. It is still growing. During the Revolutionary epoch the interests of statesmen and philosophers and of the general public were focused on the more formal aspects of freedom, equality and justice. After a long period of material expansion but not rapid spiritual growth, the American Creed is in this generation again in a formative stage. It is now discovering its ideals in the social and economic sphere and in the realm of international organization.

While this is going on, there are great disparities in opinions even on fundamentals in these new fields of valuation—as there were during the Revolution concerning the ideals which then became crystallized. Some Americans see in trade unions a denial of the rights to human liberty; others see in the unions an expression of the common man's right to reach for greater equality and freedom. Some Americans want to tax property and nationalize public utilities in order to defend equality of opportunity for the masses of the people and to preserve their liberties; others see in such attempts an assault upon American principles of liberty. In the international field American ideals in recent decades and even today seem divided and rambling in the wide space of the triangle marked by the three points: absolute isolationism, an organized world democracy, and American world imperialism.

These great disparities of opinion would, in any other social problem, considerably increase the technical difficulties of utilizing the Creed as a set of specified and definite value premises for research. When in later chapters we face the task of defining our value premises specifically, we shall find that this is not the case in the Negro problem. The Creed is expressive and definite in practically all respects of importance for the Negro problem. Most of the value premises with which we shall be concerned have actually been incorporated for a long time in the national Constitution and in the constitutions and laws of the several states.

The deeper reason for the technical simplicity of the value aspect of the Negro problem is this: From the point of view of the American Creed the status accorded the Negro in America represents nothing more and nothing less than a century-long lag of public morals. In principle the Negro problem was settled long ago; in practice the solution is not effectuated. The Negro in America has not yet been given the elemental civil and political rights of formal democracy, including a fair opportunity to earn his living, upon which a general accord was already won when the American Creed was first taking form. And this anachronism constitutes the contemporary "problem" both to Negroes and to whites.

If those rights were respected, many other pressing social problems would, of course, still remain. Many Negroes would, together with many whites, belong to groups which would invoke the old ideals of equality and liberty in demanding more effective protection for their social and economic opportunities. But there would no longer be a *Negro* problem. This does not mean that the Negro problem is an easy problem to solve. It is a tremendous task for theoretical research to find out why the Negro's status is what it is. In its unsolved form it further intertwines with all other social problems. It is simple only in the technical sense that in America the value premises—if they are conceived to be the ideals of the American Creed—are extraordinarily specific and definite.

Finally, in order to avoid possible misunderstandings, it should be explained that we have called this Creed "American" in the sense that it is adhered to by the Americans. This is the only matter which interests us in this book, which is focused upon the Negro problem as part of American life and American politics. But this Creed is, of course, no American monopoly. With minor variations, some of which, however, are not without importance, the American Creed is the common democratic creed. "American ideals" are just humane ideals as they have matured in our common Western civilization upon the foundation of Christianity and pre-Christian legalism and under the influence of the economic, scientific, and political development over a number of centuries. The American Creed is older and wider than America itself.

CHAPTER 2

ENCOUNTERING THE NEGRO PROBLEM

1. On the Minds of the Whites

When we say that there is a Negro *problem* in America, what we mean is that the Americans are worried about it. It is on their minds and on their consciences.

To begin with, the Negro is a problem to himself. If a multitude of first-hand random observations, such as we have made over the whole country, are any evidence, the contented Negro, whose mind is at peace on the race issue, is a rare phenomenon. As a generalization he is definitely a myth. Whether the myth was ever wholly true in the past, I cannot say. It is evident, however, that for a long time the Negro protest has been rising. This trend became sharply accentuated during the First World War. The present War will, in all probability, increase their discontent with their status in America.

The Negro problem is working on the white man's mind too, even, and not least, when he wants to convince himself and others that it is settled for all time. The problem has varying degrees of importance in different regions, depending partly on their historical backgrounds and on the relative proportion of Negroes in their populations, as also in different social classes and under different religious, educational and ideological influences. Over large areas of America where there are few or no Negroes, the Negro problem is of minor importance to the people living there. To these ordinary white Americans, the only reason why the Negro problem has a higher salience than, say, the problem of British imperialism in India or, earlier, the Irish question, is his citizenship in the United States and, consequently, his feeling of national responsibility. The frequent reminders in the press and in public discussions of the practice of lynching and the agitation around the proposed anti-lynching legislation, the reports of Negro criminality, the continuous recollections of discrimination in education and in the labor market, and just now the public discomfort around the racial angle of both the larger world conflict and the war efforts at home—all constantly actualize to some degree this feeling of responsibility.

This national participation in the Negro problem should not be exaggerated. Neither should it be minimized. It is the writer's conclusion that even in those Northern states with few Negroes, the Negro problem is always present though relatively quiescent. Nearly everybody in America is prepared to discuss the issue, and almost nobody is entirely without opinions on it. The opinions vary. They may be vague and hesitating or even questioning, or they may be hardened and articulate. But few Americans are unaware of the Negro problem.

So it seems always to have been. Wandering around the stacks of a good American library, one is amazed at the huge amount of printed material on the Negro problem. A really complete bibliography would run up to several hundred thousand titles.[1] Nobody has ever mastered this material exhaustively, and probably nobody ever will. The intellectual energy spent on the Negro problem in America should, if concentrated in a single direction, have moved mountains.

This does not imply that the Negro problem approaches the status of a dominant issue. It is not now a main divider of opinions in national politics, although it was so in the decades before and after the Civil War. There were other periods in American history, however, when it was in the background, perhaps never so much as in the decades before the First World War. But as a secondary problem and as a peculiar influence on all the dominant national issues, it has always held a rank among the most conspicuous. Through the generations, it has disturbed the religious moralists, the political philosophers, the statesmen, the philanthropists, the social scientists, the politicians, the businessmen and the plain citizens.

A number of factors underlie the present trends—such as the danger of continued and, after the Second World War, intensified economic dislocation with its serious effects on Negro employment; the rising tension around democracy as a form of government and a way of life; and, finally, the rising educational level and intensified group consciousness and discontent of the Negro people themselves. All this makes it probable that the Negro problem in America is again going to mount high in relative importance among national issues.

2. TO THE NEGROES THEMSELVES

To the Negro himself, the problem is all-important. A Negro probably seldom talks to a white man, and still less to a white woman, without consciousness of this problem. Even in a mixed white and Negro group of closest friends in Northern intellectual circles, and probably even in an all-Negro group, the Negro problem constantly looms in the background of social intercourse. It steers the jokes and the allusions, if it is not one of the dominant topics of conversation. As an inescapable overtone in social relations, "race" is probably just as strong as sex—even in those most emancipated American environments where apparently sex is relatively released and "race" is suppressed.

The Negro leader, the Negro social scientist, the Negro man of art and letters is disposed to view all social, economic, political, indeed, even esthetic and philosophical issues from the Negro angle. What is more, he is expected to do so. He would seem entirely out of place if he spoke simply as a member of a community, a citizen of America or as a man of the world. In the existing American civilization he can grow to a degree of distinction, but always as a representative of "his people," not as an ordinary American or an individual in humanity. He might protest; if he does it for the proper audience and in the proper forms, he is allowed to protest: but he protests as a Negro. He can criticize, but only as a Negro defending Negro interests. That is the social role awarded him, and he cannot step out of it. He is defined as a "race man" regardless of the role he might wish to choose for himself. He cannot publicly argue about collective bargaining generally in America, the need of a national budgetary reform, monetary schemes for world organization, moral philosophies and esthetic principles.

Even if originally he should have had the interests and the aptitudes for wider knowledge and a broader career, the pressure of this expectancy on the part of society conditions his personality and forces him, willy-nilly, into the role of a Negro champion. This expectancy is entrenched in all institutions in American society, including universities, learned societies and foundations. It animates even the staunchest friends and protectors of the Negro minority, often, indeed, for the reason that the Negroes sorely need their leadership. The same expectancy of their leaders is shared by the Negro people. The Negro leader, sensing that his own people need him and conscious that his racial origin offers him an easy opportunity for a role in life, thus acquires his characteristic direction. Even women in modern times do not have their souls so pressed into one single narrow furrow of human interests by the tyrannic expectancy of society, although the women's lot in this, as in many other respects, offers the nearest analogy. The Negro genius is imprisoned in the Negro problem. There is throughout the entire history of the United States no single example of an exception to this rule important enough to be cited.[2]

The difference in this respect between the Negro and other "racial" minorities—the Jews, for example—is notable. The difference is not explainable simply in terms of differences in natural and cultural abilities between the two groups. A Jewish economist is not expected to be a specialist on Jewish labor. A Jewish sociologist is not assumed to confine himself always to studying the Ghetto. A Jewish singer is not doomed eternally to perform Jewish folk songs. A Jew is not out of place either as a governor of a state or as a planner of world reconstruction. The Jew is discriminated against in America, but there is a quantitative difference between this and the discrimination against the Negro which is so great that it becomes qualitative. On the intellectual level, which we are now discussing, the fettering of the Negro spirit within the Negro problem is not accomplished so much by simple discrimination as by the prejudice inherent even in the most friendly but restrictive expectancy, including the expectancy of the Negro people.

So far we have been commenting on the fate of those rare persons with extraordinary talents who, if any, should have both the intellectual strength and the opportunities to break out of the prison of the Negro problem. To the ordinary members of the Negro upper and middle class, even the window shutters of the prison are closed. It will be the theme of following chapters to show in some detail how Negro preachers, teachers, professionals, and businessmen have had to build their whole economic and social existence on the basis of the segregation of their people, in response to the dictates of the white society. To state the situation bluntly: these upper class Negroes are left free to earn their living and their reputation in the backwater of discrimination, but they are not free to go into the main current of the river itself. On the one hand, they are kept fully aware of the wider range of opportunities from which they are excluded by segregation and discrimination. On the other hand, they know equally well how they are sheltered by the monopoly left to them in their little world apart. In their whole outlook on life and society they are forced into an impossible and tragic dilemma.

The masses of the Negro people, however, unlike the more advantaged leaders, professionals, and businessmen, derive almost none of the compensatory gains from the caste system. They sense how they are hampered and enclosed behind the walls of segregation and discrimination more acutely than might be expected.

They do not usually spend too much of their mental energy on theorizing over the Negro problem. Their days are filled with toil and more personal troubles and pleasures. But, as we shall find, in most of these varied activities, the Negro problem enters as a loud overtone. It is heard in church, in school, on the work place, in the play yard and on the street. They, too, are imprisoned in the Negro problem.

The broad masses of Negroes are also enclosed in the prison as effectively by the restrictive expectancy of their friends as by the persecutions of their enemies.

> The patronizing attitude is really more damning than the competitive struggle. The stone wall of calm assumption of his inferiority is to the Negro a keener hurt and a greater obstacle than the battle which admits an adversary worth fighting against. It is hard to keep ambition alive and to maintain morale when those for whom you have fondness and respect keep thinking and saying that you are only children, that you can never grow up, that you are cast by God in an inferior mould.[4]

The late James Weldon Johnson sums up this situation of the Negro people in the following way:

> And this is the dwarfing, warping, distorting influence which operates upon each and every coloured man in the United States. He is forced to take his outlook on all things, not from the view-point of a citizen, or a man, or even a human being, but from the view-point of a *coloured* man. It is wonderful to me that the race has progressed so broadly as it has, since most of its thought and all of its activity must run through the narrow neck of this one funnel.[4]

3. EXPLAINING THE PROBLEM AWAY

To the white Americans the possibilities of keeping the Negro problem out of their minds are, naturally, greater and, in addition, they have certainly good selfish reasons for keeping it below the level of consciousness. To be sure, it was a not unusual experience of the writer to be told confidently sometimes by the learned, but most often by the laity, that there is "no Negro problem" in America and that, if there ever was one, it is solved and settled for all time and to the full satisfaction of both parties. Everything is quiet on the racial front. We think the Negroes are all right in their place; and they on their part do not want things changed. In fact, they are the happiest lot on earth. Just look at them: how they laugh and enjoy themselves; how they sing and praise the Lord.

This attitude was met most frequently and expressed most emphatically in the Deep South. It was often maliciously added that there was surely a Negro problem in the North, but only because the Yankees have not yet learned to know the Negro and how to keep him in his proper place. The situation, if true, would certainly deserve to be called paradoxical: The Negroes should be least of a problem to the whites in the regions where they are most numerous. They should show up among the human and national worries, though certainly not as a principal one, of a Minnesota farmer who never sees Negroes, but be no problem at all to the Southern planter who works them in scores and is always surrounded by them.

All this is not true, of course. A contrary statement, that the white South is virtually obsessed by the Negro problem, that the South has allowed the Negro problem to rule its politics and its business, fetter its intelligence and human liberties, and hamper its progress in all directions, would be nearer the truth.[5] A brilliant Northerner, Frank Tannenbaum,[6] has taken up this thought and, presumably fully in earnest, suggested, as the only hope of solving the Southern problem, that the Southerners get other worries to keep their minds off the Negro: they should get labor troubles, try to get immigrants and develop a complex at home against white "foreigners," and generally get some real issues into their petty politics. This might be carrying an idea to an extreme for educational purposes, but certainly there is a kernel of sense in it.

Apart from the few intellectuals of pronounced liberal leanings, however, statements to the effect that there really is no Negro problem have become part of the common stock of stereotyped opinions in the South, and they are not entirely absent from the North. But such statements cover a volcanic ground of doubt, disagreement, concern, and even anxiety—of moral tension and need for escape and defense. To furnish such a covering is, from a psychological point of view, their very "function." The prevalence of such opinions and the intensity with which they are expressed might serve as an index of the latent interracial tension felt in the white world.

The usefulness of this escape rationalization has a limit, however. The limit is reached when overt interracial struggles appear. The notion of "no Negro problem" is then suddenly transformed into an alarming awareness that the contrary is so. This contrary reaction can be invoked experimentally, simply by directing attention to the potentialities of conflict. Particularly when talking to people among the poorer classes of whites with less intellectual control over their thoughts and feelings, the writer has repeatedly observed the most flagrant contradictions on this point, sometimes appearing within the same sentence. A white Southerner can defend, for instance, the suppression of the Negroes by saying that they are satisfied with their status and lack a desire for change. Without any intermediate remarks, he can then proceed to explain that suppression is necessary, that Negroes must be kept down by all means, and that Negroes have an ineradicable craving to be like white people. Attempts on the part of the interlocutor to draw attention to the contradiction have seldom succeeded.

Some light might be thrown on this state of mind of many American whites by observing the different state of mind of the Negroes. The Negroes cannot, of course, feel an equivalent need for this special type of self-defense, that there is "no Negro problem," which in the white world is a defense against one's own thoughts and feelings and the opinions of other whites. Actually, it often happened that the writer was told by Negroes in the South that race relations in their part of the country offered no particular difficulties and were not much of a problem. White people present at such pronouncements took great pleasure in the corroboration of their own statements. It would seem that such statements from Negro leaders are part of the moral tribute expected from those leaders at all public interracial affairs, such as school festivals, programs of entertainment centered around Negro singers, interchurch meetings, and other occasions where white representatives are present. That the Negroes should be allowed to voice complaints, even though only in a cautious tone, constituted the radical departure in the innovation of interracial commissions after the First World War. Their meetings are between the "best people of the two races," and are typically not open to the general public.

Statements that interracial relations are good thus belong in the South to the etiquette of Negro college presidents, principals and teachers of Negro schools, and all other Negroes enjoying upper or middle class status under the sanction of the power of appointment and dismissal in the hands of white boards or officials. They are also widely accepted as a way of getting along by a considerable number of Negro preachers and by the handful of thriving and successful Negro businessmen. In return, these persons are allowed much leeway, particularly in the Upper South. These sentiments are sometimes also expressed by Negro professionals who are aware of the local requirements for successful leadership.

But, even in these cases, the statements that there is "no Negro problem" have an easily detected difference in tone when pronounced by Negroes. To begin with, they are usually restricted expressly to the local community, and often qualified by certain reservations as to this or that which might need improvement, while the corresponding white pronouncements are mostly broad and absolute in character. They are, further, as a defense mechanism, primarily directed against provoking the suspicions of the other group. They are, finally, not to be taken too seriously. The writer repeatedly made the observation, both in the Deep South and in the Upper South, as well as in the North, that a Negro seldom took this position when talking freely and when there was no point in hiding his real feelings.

The difference between the two groups, with respect to the recognition of the Negro problem, corresponds, of course, to the fundamental fact that the white group is above and the Negro group is below, that the one is intent upon preserving the *status quo*, while the other wants change and relief from the pressure of the dominant group. The one group is tempted to convince itself and others that there is "no problem." The other group has a contrary interest to see clearly and even make visible to others the existence of a real problem. This latter group may be hushed by fear or opportunistic calculations. These calculations can, of course, be of the most respectable character; indeed, they often are part of the cautious Negro patriot's wise policy of trying to safeguard his people from needless sufferings and to gain favors for them from the dominating white group. But, in any case, the explanation is not to be sought in such deep-seated internal tensions as with the white people. The Negro's rationalization, when it is articulated, is likely to be much more overt and, indeed, sometimes cynically so. It has not the same character of a self-deceiving defense construction against one's own moral feelings.

4. Explorations in Escape

In a big city in the Deep South I was once taken by a friend to an upper class club for a social luncheon party. The conversation turned around world affairs, the business trend, art, literature and some personal gossiping; the tone was most congenial and free, perhaps even carefree, and had the distinctive mark of skeptical openmindedness which accompanies social security and a lifelong experience of unhampered cultural opportunities. Near the intended end of the party, my friend announced the peculiar reason for my being in America at the present time and invited the company to tell me their frank opinions on the Negro problem.

For a moment a somewhat awkward silence descended upon our party, a queer feeling that our relation of human understanding was broken. An illusion was shattered. Here we had all been behaving on the understanding that we were men of the world, members of that select cosmopolitan fellowship which senses no strong local ties and whose minds meet in most broad topics of general and human interest; and then suddenly my friend had violated this understanding by addressing all the others as a local fraternity sharing a dark secret together, while I was marked off as the stranger peeping in on them and their secret, the Negro problem.

The situation most urgently had to be redefined. The responsibility was shouldered by an elderly, very distinguished doctor. He made a short speech (the discussion had suddenly turned very formal) to the effect that in the South there was "no Negro problem"; a static equilibrium had been reached, and was going to remain, and it fitted the situation as a glove fits the hand. More particularly, he went on, the relations between the two races in the South corresponded to their inherited abilities and aptitudes. A long time ago those relations had been stratified into "folkways and mores," known and respected by both races and taken for granted, or rather as self-evident, in view of the inferior endowments of the African race and the superior qualities of the Anglo-Saxon master race. The doctor ended up by pointing out that it was, in fact, inherent in this very notion of "mores," that they could never be questioned or disputed or even consciously analyzed. There could, indeed, by definition, never be a "problem" concerning the mores of society. The very question was nonsensical. The mores were the ground everybody walked upon, the axioms of social life, even more unquestioned than the religious truths and for more substantial psychological reasons.

The doctor finished. Everybody agreed, and there was really nothing in the issue to discuss. The few moments' stress was eased, and a measure of congeniality again restored. I then reflected that the South was, as I was finding out, now on the way to giving the Negroes a real chance in education. I referred to the continuous improvement of public schools even for Negroes and to the growing number of Negro youths who were permitted to acquire a higher education of a kind, even in the South. It had occurred to me, I continued, that this tread in education—leaving many other primary causes of change unmentioned—represented a dynamic factor of cumulative importance. If it was given time, and if the direct and indirect effects in all spheres of life were allowed to accumulate, the resultant social change might finally attain a momentum where it could seriously challenge, or at least move quite a bit, the "folkways and mores" our doctor had rooted so firmly, not only in tradition, but in the very nature of things and particularly in the biology of the races. Yes, it might make it difficult to keep the Negro in his place. It might, for instance, make it much less easy to hold him disfranchised; in all certainty it would soon render obsolete one of the principal arguments and constitutional instruments for denying him the ballot—namely, his illiteracy.

After this remark, I did not need to say anything more for the next hour or two but could lean back and listen to one of the most revealing and most ably performed, though sometimes heated, intellectual debates on the Negro problem in America I had, up till then, and even thereafter, heard. This was not a theater performance staged for my benefit; the arguments were too well considered and reasoned to be suspected of being improvised for the occasion; I was, indeed, happily forgotten most of the time. There was genuine concern, and there was serious disagreement. Professor Sumner's theory of folkways and mores had evaporated into the thinnest nothing; even the doctor never said a word more about the mystically unproblematic "mores." At the end I had the opportunity to restore good feeling between the debaters in a roar of understanding laughter when I closed my thanks for Southern hospitality with the observation that apparently they seemed to have a most disturbing Negro problem on their minds down in the Old South.

A situation in the Negro world parallel to this experience showing how the problem burns under the cover of a placid stereotype was given me in one of the very first weeks of my study of the Negro problem in America. When I and my Swedish associate (accompanied at this occasion by a white friend of the Negro people, a professor at a Southern university) visited a Negro leader prominent in banking and insurance in a city of the Upper South, he had kindly arranged for a gathering in his office of a group of about thirty Negro gentlemen of upper class status, representing business, church, university and professions. One of his subordinates had been given the function of relating statistics on the progress of Negro business in America. He fulfilled his task with much ability and eloquence. The figures sometimes rose to millions and hundreds of millions and, nevertheless, were presented to the last unit; they marched along solemnly and created an illusion of greatness and success. The lecture ended up in a cheerful and challenging mood. All had listened as to a sermon and felt duly elevated.

This spirit prevailed until I happened to touch off some of the unfortunate realities so guardedly concealed within the statistical house of cards that had just been erected. I referred to the facts, that one of the white companies alone had more Negro insurance business than all the Negro companies together, while the latter had practically no white business at all; that Negro banking had a rather serious record of bankruptcies; that Negroes were practically excluded from all production and wholesale trade; that they controlled only an inconsiderable fraction of retail trade even in the Negro consumers' market and practically none in the white market.

My remarks were formulated as questions, and I was hoping for some discussion. But I had never expected the tumultuous and agitated controversy which, much to the embarrassment of our dignified host, broke loose. The comforting unanimity a few minutes before was suddenly decomposed into the wide and glaring spectrum of American Negro ideologies, bearing not only on business but on all other aspects of life as well. All possible opinions were vented in a debate where seldom one spoke at a time, ranging from an old-fashioned revolutionism demanding violent resistance and aggression by force against the white suppressors, on the infra-red end, to a pious religious plea, voiced by an elderly preacher, for endurance, forbearance, and patience under the sufferings, on the ultra-violet end.

As these two occurrences exemplify, the artificially constructed escapist consensus is liable to crash if pushed from the outside. It is inherent in the situation, however, that such pushes do not originate from inside, or, if they do, that an attempt is made to canalize them safely. An unstable equilibrium is retained and actually believed to be stable.

I once visited an art exhibition in one of the cultural centers of the Old South where everything from the city plan to the interests and manners of the people carries the cherished memories of the romantic, glorious past. Among other exhibits was a man-sized sculpture in terra cotta called "Soldier in Rain," representing a Negro man lynched by hanging. The piece was forcefully done; and, as I thought, a real masterpiece. The hanging man was clothed only in a shirt and a pair of trousers tightly stretched around the body by the rain. On the chest there was a medal affixed to the shirt; a raindrop was suspended under the medal. I was absorbed in admiring the sculpture with two ladies who were supervising the exhibition. They were true experts in art appreciation and had kindly followed me around and told me many things which I could not otherwise have seen for myself.

Quite unintentionally I happened to refer to the sculpture as representing a lynching. My hostesses immediately reacted as to a shock and explained eagerly that I was totally mistaken. The sculpture represented a soldier being hanged, probably behind the front for some offense, a soldier *in abstracto*, "just any soldier." It had nothing to do with the Negro problem. They were bent on convincing me that I was wrong; they mentioned that none of all the thousands of visitors to the exhibition had ever hinted at the possibility that the sculpture represented a lynched Negro and eagerly showed me newspaper clippings with reviews where the sculpture was discussed in terms of "a soldier," "a simple soldier," "a soldier behind the line." I answered that soldiers were never anywhere executed by hanging either at or behind the line, and that in the whole world hanging was, in the popular conception, which is the important thing for an artist, usually associated with the English custom of hanging petty thieves and with American lynching parties. I was even brought to point out that the sculptor had endowed the hanged man with the long limbs and facial characteristics commonly ascribed to the Negro race. But no arguments had any weight. I am convinced that they sincerely believed they were right, and I preposterously wrong. The visit ended with some mutually felt embarrassment.

As my curiosity was awakened, I went to see the sculptor. He is an immigrant from one of the republics of Latin America and is of nearly pure Indian descent. I was told later that because of his slightly dark color, he sometimes had met some difficulties when he was not personally recognized. On one occasion, quite recently, he had been beaten by the police when he had appeared on the street one night with a white woman. I now told him about my experience at the exhibition and asked him to clear up the matter for me. His first answer was that there was nothing to clear up: his sculpture was an abstract piece of art and represented a soldier being hanged, "any soldier." We discussed the matter for a while on this line. But gradually, I must confess, I came to feel slightly exasperated, and I said, "If you, the artist, do not know what you have created, I know it as an art spectator. You have depicted a lynching, and, more particularly, a lynching of a Negro." The sculptor then suddenly changed personality, became intimate and open, and said: "I believe you are right. And I have intended it all the time." I asked, "Don't you think everybody must know it?" He said, "Yes, in a way, but they don't want to know it." I asked again, "Why have you spent your time in producing this piece? You understand as well as I that, even if it is admirable and is also being greatly admired by the whole public, nobody is actually going to buy it. Personally, I would not dare to have it in the cellar of my house, still less in a room where I lived." He answered, "I know. I suppose that I have made this for myself. I am going to keep it in a closet. This is the 'American Skeleton in the Closet.' That would be the right name of my sculpture. 'Soldier in Rain' is only a fake, a deception between me and the public down here."

The situation described is a beautiful crystallization of moral escape. A sculptor, with so much color in his skin and such life experiences because of his skin color that a degree of identification with the American Negro people has been established, is living out his aggression in a piece of art which, in reality, is meant as an accusation against society. In the layer of his mind where his artistic imagination works and directs his skilful hands, he is clear and bent on his purpose; and the result is forceful and exact. In the layer where he meets the community, there is twilight. He gave me two contradictory statements as to what the sculpture actually represented, and he was, as I believe, serious and honest both times. The art appreciative public in this refined old city shares in his twilight. They accept his fake with grace and gratitude. To some extent they also share in the deep meaning of the sculpture to its creator. They probably even "get a kick" out of an obvious association which, however, they suppress. Probably none of the visitors to the exhibition would ever take part in a lynching or have anything but regret for its occurrence. But they partake in a national and regional responsibility. Lynching, further, stands only as a symbol for a whole system of suppression measures, in which they daily are participants. Their valuations are in conflict. Art, particularly when presented in such a tactful way, has a function of releasing the tension of suppressed moral conflicts.

5. THE ETIQUETTE OF DISCUSSION

Generally the form of a matter becomes important when the matter itself is touchy. Explosives must be handled with care. Educators, reformers, and journalists with liberal leanings in the South have a standard text which they recite to please one another and the visitor. Everything can be said in the South if it is said "in the right way." Criticisms and even factual statements should be phrased in such a manner that they do not "offend" or create "embarrassment." I have listened again and again to the pronouncements of this theory of Southern indirectness from liberal white Southerners who have been most eager that I should understand, not only the esthetics, but also the pragmatic purpose of this escape machinery. I have been told countless examples, where, as my interlocutor confided to me, he was able to "get by" in saying so and so to such and such a person because he phrased it in this or that way, or how this or that change for the better in interracial relations was "put over" on the public by letting it appear in a euphemistic light. I have sensed the high subjective pleasure of this persistent balancing on the margins and the corresponding pleasures of the less liberal audience in being merely teased but never affronted by the sore points. I have come to understand how a whole system of moral escape has become polite form in the South. This form is applicable even to scientific writings and, definitely, to public discussion and teaching on all levels. It is sometimes developed into an exquisite and absorbing art.

It renders the spoken or written word less effective. It is contrary to the aims of raising issues and facing problems; it makes difficult an effective choice of words. It represents an extra encumbrance in intellectual intercourse. At the same time as it purposively opens a means of escape, it also fetters everything to the very complex suppressed by this means: the Negro problem on their minds.

This form has even crystallized into a peculiar theory of induced social change. It has become policy. There is nearly common agreement in the South that reforms in interracial relations should be introduced with as little discussion about them as possible. It is actually assumed that the race issue is a half dormant, but easily awakened, beast. It is a complex which is irrational and uncontrollable, laden with emotions, and to be touched as little as possible.

When talking about the Negro problem, everybody—not only the intellectual liberals—is thus anxious to locate race prejudice outside himself. The impersonal "public opinion" or "community feelings" are held responsible. The whites practically never discuss the issue in terms of "I" or "we" but always in terms of "they," "people in the South," "people in this community," or "folks down here will not stand for . . ." this or that. One can go around for weeks talking to white people in all walks of life and constantly hear about the wishes and beliefs of this collective being, yet seldom meeting a person who actually identifies himself with it. But he follows it.

In the more formal life of the community the Negro problem and, in fact, the Negro himself, is almost completely avoided. "In effect the Negro is segregated in public thought as well as in public carriers," complains Robert R. Moton.[7] The subject is only seldom referred to in the church. In the school it will be circumvented like sex; it does not fit naturally in any one of the regular courses given. Sometimes, but rarely, the topic will be taken up for ostentatious treatment as part of an effort toward interracial good-will. The press, with remarkable exceptions, ignores the Negroes, except for their crimes. There was earlier an unwritten rule in the South that a picture of a Negro should never appear in print, and even now it is rare. The public affairs of community and state are ordinarily discussed as if Negroes were not part of the population. The strange unreality of this situation becomes apparent when one comes to realize that for generations hardly any public issue of importance has been free from a heavy load of the race issue, and that the entire culture of the region— its religion, literature, art, music, dance, its politics and education, its language and cooking—are partly to be explained by positive or negative influences from the Negro.

If the Negro is a shunned topic in formal intercourse among whites in the South, he enters all informal life to a disproportionate extent. He creeps up as soon as the white Southerner is at ease and not restraining himself. He is the standard joke. It is interesting to notice the great pleasure white people in all classes take in these stereotyped jokes and in indulging in discussions about the Negro and what he does, says and thinks. It is apparently felt as a release. Ray Stannard Baker, surveying the South and the Negro problem a generation ago, told a story, which the present writer has encountered several times and which seems to define the situation properly.[8]

> A Negro minister I met told me a story of a boy who went as a sort of butler's assistant in the home of a prominent family in Atlanta. His people were naturally curious about what went on in the white man's house. One day they asked him: "What do they talk about when they are eating?"
>
> The boy thought a moment; then he said:
> "Mostly they discusses us cullud folks."

As Baker adds, the same consuming interest exists among Negroes. A large part of their conversation deals with the race question. One gets the feeling that the two groups are sitting behind their fences, publicly ignoring each other but privately giving free rein to a curiosity emotionalized to the highest degree.

The stories and the jokes give release to troubled people. It is no accident that Americans generally are a story-telling nation, and that jokes play a particularly important role in the lives of the Southerners, white and black, and specifically in race relations. It should not surprise us that sex relations are another field of human life with a great prolification of jokes. There is much of human brotherhood in humor—a sort of fundamental democracy in a plane deeper than the usual one. It usually conveys a notion that we are all sinners before the Lord. When people are up against great inconsistencies in their creed and behavior which they cannot, or do not want to, account for rationally, humor is a way out. It gives a symbolic excuse for inperfections, a point to what would otherwise be ambiguous. It gives also a compensation to the sufferer. The "understanding laugh" is an intuitive absolution between sinners and sometimes also between the sinner and his victim. The main "function" of the joke is thus to create a collective surreptitious approbation for something which cannot be approved explicitly because of moral inhibitions. To the whites the Negro jokes further serve the function of "proving" the inferiority of the Negro. To the

Negroes the function of anti-white jokes is partly to pose the whites in a ridiculous light, which to them is a compensation. Partly it is a mechanism of psychological adjustment; they "laugh off" their misfortunes, their faults, their inferiority.

In this situation the minds of people are, however, likely to show signs of deep-seated ambivalence. White Southerners like and love individual Negroes and sometimes Negroes in general; they apparently also hate them. I have often witnessed how the feeling tone can pass from the one emotional pole to the other abruptly as a result of a remark changing the imagined type of interrelation toward which the person reacts.

What applies to the emotional level may also be found on the intellectual level. Thus a Southerner, while extolling the virtues of the "good old Negroes" he used to know and deploring the vices of the young who go to school and are recalcitrant, may suddenly turn an intellectual somersault and bemoan the ignorance and backwardness of the older group and become enthusiastic about the intelligence and progressiveness of the young. I have come to know how fundamental and common this ambivalence of Southern white people is toward the relative value of the different Negro generations and how strategically important it is for policy, educational policy particularly.

Sometimes mental contradictions are elaborated into theories and find their way into learned treatises and documents of state policy. An example is the theory that Negroes have "lower costs of living," which defends— in the writers' minds— lower salaries for Negroes against the equalitarian principles of the Constitution. The all-embracing Jim Crow doctrine "equal but separate" belongs to the same category of systematized intellectual and moral inconsistency. A partial blinding of a person's knowledge of reality is sometimes necessary. There are plenty of people in the South who will tell you, honestly and sincerely, that Negroes have equal educational opportunities with whites. I think they believe it—for a moment, in a way, and with a part of their minds. Their conviction rests on two contradictory principles between which they shift.

This mental training of the Southerner, which makes him shift between principles according to momentary change or stimulus, spreads from the Negro problem to other issues. The Negro problem is unique only in intensity. But in most of the other issues, the Negro problem is, directly or indirectly, involved. One meets it in the attitude toward trade unionism, factory legislation, social security programs, educational policies, and virtually all other public issues.

I once went to see the director of the Department of Labor in a Southern capital. The discussion started by his asking me if trade unions were strong in Sweden, to which I answered, "Yes." Without any initiative from my side, he then told me how the trade union movement in this region had the great sympathy of the state and municipal authorities, and how it was favored in all ways. I said to him, "Look here, I am an economist. I know that this state is not rich. Your infant industry has to overcome a ruthless competition from the North where industry is long established. Trade unions mean higher production costs. Is it really a wise policy to lay this extra burden upon your young industry?" My interlocutor immediately changed mood. "Now you hit the point. And this is the reason why we try to keep the unions out of this state." Then he started to tell me the techniques used to keep out labor organizers from the state.

I changed the subject of conversation and told him I had been visiting some mills and felt that there was too little interest shown for security measures to protect the workers against accidents. The official started out to give me a vivid impression of factory legislation and factory inspection as being the very thing nearest to the legislators' hearts in this state. Again I invoked my profession as an economist, emphasized the cost factor and the competitive situation; and again I got the answer, "You hit the point" and the totally different story about the attitude of the state.

These inconsistencies and contradictions should not be taken as indicating simply personal insincerity. They are, rather, symptoms of much deeper, unsettled conflicts of valuations. The absorbing interest in the form of a matter; the indirectness of approach to a person, a subject, or a policy; the training to circumvent sore points and touchy complexes—which we consider as symptoms of escape—are developing into a pattern of thinking and behavior which molds the entire personality. People become trained generally to sacrifice truth, realism, and accuracy for the sake of keeping superficial harmony in every social situation. Discussion is subdued; criticism is enveloped in praise. Agreement is elevated as the true social value irrespective of what is to be agreed upon. Grace becomes the supreme virtue; to be "matter of fact" is crude. It is said about the Southern Negro that he is apt to tell you what he thinks you want him to say. This characteristic ascribed to the Negro fits, to a considerable extent, the whole civilization where he lives.

This escape mechanism works, however, only to a point. When that point is reached, it can suddenly be thrown out of gear. Then grace and chivalry, in fact, all decent form, is forgotten; criticism becomes bitter; opinions are asserted with a vehemence bordering on violence; and disagreement can turn into physical conflict. Then it is no longer a question of escape. The conflict is raging in the open.

6. THE CONVENIENCE OF IGNORANCE

In this connection the remarkable lack of correct information about the Negroes and their living conditions should at least be hinted at. One need not be a trained student of the race problem to learn a lot in a couple of days about the Negroes in a community which is not known by even its otherwise enlightened white residents. To an extent this ignorance is not simply "natural" but is part of the opportunistic escape reaction.

It thus happens that not only the man in the street, but also the professional man, shows ignorance in his own field of work. One meets physicians who hold absurd ideas about the anatomical characteristics of the Negro people or about the frequency of disease among the Negroes in their own community; educators who have succeeded in keeping wholly unaware of the results of modern intelligence research; lawyers who believe that practically all the lynchings are caused by rape; ministers of the gospel who know practically nothing about Negro churches in their own town. In the North, particularly in such groups where contacts with Negroes are lacking or scarce, the knowledge might not be greater, but the number of erroneous conceptions seems much smaller. The important thing and the reason for suspecting this ignorance to be part of the escape apparatus is that knowledge is constantly twisted in one direction—toward classifying the Negro low and the white high.

The ignorance about the Negro is the more striking as the Southerner is himself convinced that he "knows the Negro," while the Yankee is supposedly ignorant on the subject. The insistence on the part of the Southern whites that they have reliable and intimate knowledge about the Negro problem is one of the most pathetic stereotypes in the South. In fact, the average Southerner "knows" the Negro and the interracial problem as the patient "knows" the toothache—in the sense that he feels a concern—not as the diagnosing dentist knows his own or his patient's trouble. He further "knows" the Negro in the sense that he is brought up to use a social technique in dealing with Negroes by which he is able to get them into submissive patterns of behavior. This technique is simple; I have often observed that merely speaking the Southern dialect works the trick.

Segregation is now becoming so complete that the white Southerner practically never sees a Negro except as his servant and in other standardized and formalized caste situations. The situation may have been different in the old patriarchial times with their greater abundance of primary contacts. Today the average Southerner of middle or upper class status seems to be just as likely as the typical Northerner to judge all Negroes by his cook, and he is definitely more disposed than the Northerner to draw the widest conclusions from this restricted source of information. I have also found that the white participants in the work of the local interracial commissions—who are not typical Southerners because they are extraordinarily friendly to the Negro and are looked upon as local experts on the race problem—regularly stress the importance of those meetings in bringing together representatives of the two races so that they can "come to know each other." They often confess how vastly their own knowledge of the Negro has increased because they, in these meetings, had a chance to talk to Reverend So-and-so or Doctor So-and-so. These testimonies are the more telling when one has been present at a few of these interracial meetings and observed how strictly formal and ruled by mental inhibitions they are. It is also astounding to observe that at such meetings Negro members, by relating simple and obvious facts in the local situation, can reveal things unknown to the whites present. Even when true friendliness is the basis for the approach, the awkwardness and anxiety shown in these interracial contacts is often apparent.

The ignorance about the Negro is not, it must be stressed, just a random lack of interest and knowledge. It is a tense and highstrung restriction and distortion of knowledge, and it indicates much deeper dislocations within the minds of the Southern whites. The blind spots are clearly visible in stereotyped opinions. The "function" of those stereotypes is, in fact, to serve as intellectual blinds.[9] Thinking and talking in terms of stereotypes appear to be more common in the Negro problem than in other issues and more dominant in the regions of America where the race problem is prominent.

The stereotypes are ideological fragments which have been coined and sanctioned. They are abstract and unqualified, as popular thinking always tends to be. They express a belief that "all niggers" are thus and so. But, in addition, they are loaded with pretention to deep insight. It is because of this emotional charge that they can serve to block accurate observation in everyday living and detached thinking. They are treated as magical formulas. It is amazing to see the stern look of even educated people when they repeat these trite and worn banalities, inherited through the generations, as if they were pointing out something new and tremendously important, and also to watch their consternation and confusion when one tries to disturb their conventional thoughtways by "outlandish" questions.

7. NEGRO AND WHITE VOICES

What is at the bottom of this elaborated escape psychology? Has the old Negro fighter and scholar W. E. B. Du Bois struck a vein of truth when he remarks:

> Nor does the paradox and danger of this situation fail to interest and perplex the best conscience of the South. Deeply religious and intensely democratic as are the mass of the whites, they feel acutely the false position in which the Negro problems place them. Such an essentially honest-hearted and generous people cannot cite the caste levelling precepts of Christianity, or believe in equality of opportunity for all men, without coming to feel more and more with each generation that the present drawing of the color-line is a flat contradiction to their beliefs and professions.[10]

He certainly expresses the opinion of enlightened Negroes. Booker T. Washington said, in essence, the same thing when, in discussing white people's prejudice against and their fear of the Negro, he explained that they

. . . are moved by a bad conscience. If they really believe there is danger from the Negro it must be because they do not intend to give him justice. Injustice always breeds fear.[11]

James Weldon Johnson, a third Negro leader, pointed out that

. . . the main difficulty of the race question does not lie so much in the actual condition of the blacks as it does in the mental attitude of the whites.[12]

And again:

The race question involves the saving of black America's body and white America's soul.[13]

White people have seen the same thing. Ray Stannard Baker wrote:

It keeps coming to me that this is more a white man's problem than it is a Negro problem.[14]

A Southern academician, Thomas P. Bailey, whose book on the Negro problem has not been surpassed in scrupulous moral honesty, said:

The real problem is not the negro but the white man's attitude toward the negro.

and

Yes, we Southerners need a freedom from suspicion, fear, anxiety, doubt, unrest, hate, contempt, disgust, and all the rest of the race-feeling-begotten brood of viperous emotions.[15]

The Negroes base their fundamental strategy for improving their status on this insight. Moton tells us:

. . . the careful observer will discover another characteristic of Negro psychology— his quick perception of physical disadvantage and his equally quick adjustment to secure the moral advantage. In all the agitation concerning the Negro's status in America, the moral advantage has always been on his side, and with that as a lever he has steadily effected progress in spite of material disadvantages.[16]

James Weldon Johnson puts it this way:

Black America is called upon to stand as the protagonist of tolerance, of fair play, of justice, and of good will. Until white America heeds, we shall never let its conscience sleep. . . . White America cannot save itself if it prevents us from being saved.[17]

And the moral situation of white Southerners is such that Johnson can confidently explain:

Negroes in the South have a simple and direct manner of estimating the moral worth of a white man. He is good or bad according to his attitude toward colored people. This test is not only a practical and logical one for Negroes to use, but the absolute truth of its results averages pretty high. The results on the positive side are, I think, invariably correct; I myself have yet to know a Southern white man who is liberal in his attitude toward the Negro and on the race question and is not a man of moral worth.[18]

The white man is driven to apologies, not by the Negro, because the Negro is not so strong, but by his own moral principles. We shall have to study those apologies intensively in this inquiry. Only as a foretaste we quote James Truslow Adams, who pleads:

> The condition of the portion of that continent from which he came was one not only of savagery but of chronic warfare, quite irrespective of the activities of the slave traders. A negro in his native land was liable at any moment to be attacked, captured, enslaved by other blacks, torn from his family, or killed and in some cases eaten. Would the 12,000,000 of negroes in the United States today prefer that their ancestors had never been enslaved and that therefore they themselves, if alive, should at this moment be living as savages or barbarians in the African jungle? Would a DuBois prefer to be head man to an African chief instead of a Harvard graduate, scholar and writer? Would a Robeson prefer beating a tom tom to thrilling audiences throughout the world with his beautiful voice? Would the colored washerwoman I had in the North give up her comfortable house and her car, in which she motored her family to Virginia each summer, for the ancestral grass hut in the jungle? [19]

An editorial commenting upon certain demands raised by a committee of Negro citizens of the City of New York and presented under the auspices of a wartime organization for the propagation of democracy in America reads:

> . . . as a group, even in this great free city, they [the Negroes] haven't enjoyed equality of opportunity. They have been at a disadvantage in housing. . . . For no reason except color, they find many jobs closed to them . . . the Negro suffers from an undeserved historic misfortune. He does not enjoy, anywhere in the United States, opportunities equal to his individual capacity. . . . It is time that more of his white neighbors stopped being so patient about this situation. An injustice to any group, whether we realize the truth or not, hurts all of us.[20]

And so the conflict in the troubled white man's soul goes on.

8. THE NORTH AND THE SOUTH

In the North the observer finds a different mental situation in regard to the Negro problem. The South is divergent from the rest of the country not only in having the bulk of the Negro population within its region but also in a number of other traits and circumstances—all, as we shall find, directly or indirectly connected with the Negro problem.

There has been less social change in the South. Industrialization has lagged until recently. The South is more agricultural and rural. Parts of it are isolated. There has been relatively little immigration from foreign countries or from the North; practically all migration has been internal or outward. The South is poorer on the average: it is true both that there are more poor people in the South and that they are poorer than in the North.[a] Farm tenancy is common in the South but rarer in the North. The tradition of the "independent farmer" is largely a Northern tradition. On the other hand, the tradition of aristocracy is much stronger in the South; "the Southern gentlemen," "the Southern lady," and "Southern hospitality" are proverbial, even if stereotyped.

Because of this tradition and because of the relative lack of industrialization, a main way to get and remain rich in the South has been to exploit the Negroes and other weaker people, rather than to work diligently, make oneself indispensable and have brilliant ideas. The South has been relatively intolerant of reform movements of any sort. Circumstances connected not only with the Negro problem but also with such traditions as state's rights make change seem more hazardous than in the North. Education for all groups and on all levels has been inferior in the South. The trauma of the Civil War is still acute. The observer finds many Southerners still "fighting" the Civil War. In the North it is forgotten.

The mere existence of a more rapid tempo of life in the North, the constant changes, and the feeling of progress push the Negro problem into the background. And the human capacity for interesting oneself in social problems is crowded by many other worries. There have been more frequent clashes of political opinions in the North. The North has been made to feel labor problems. The Northern farmers have been more restless and articulate in their demands. The continuous mass immigration of foreigners has created local problems of exploitation and poverty, maladjustment and cultural assimilation. Placed beside these problems a local Negro problem, where it existed in the North, became robbed of its singularity and shrank in significance.

The Negro problem has nowhere in the North the importance it has in the South. "Too often we find," complained a Southern student of the Negro problem long ago, "that when our Northern journalism discusses wrongs at the North or at the West, it criticizes the *wrongs,* but when it discusses wrongs at the South, it criticizes the *South.*"[21] This is a correct observation. But the explanation and, we must add, the justification of this fact is, first, that the Negro problem actually is a main determinant of all local, regional, and national issues, whether political, economic, or broadly cultural, in the South, while this is not true in the North; and, second, that there is a "Solid South" backing the "wrongs" in the one region, while opinions are much more diversified in the North.

[a] Contrary to the general impression, however, the well-to-do whites in the South are in about the same proportion in the population as are the well-to-do whites in the North. (We except here the very few tremendous fortunes in the North which are more numerous than in the South.) Also, the Southern whites *as a whole* have about the same income as do Northern whites: a large proportion of the poor in the South are Negroes. (See Chapter 16.)

There are few Negroes living in most of the North. This is especially true of the rural regions. Where Negroes live in small cities, particularly in the New England states, they are a small element of the population who have never been much of a problem. In the big cities where the greater part of the total Northern Negro population lives, the whites are protected from getting the Negro problem too much on their minds by the anonymity of life and the spatial segregation of racial, ethnic, and economic groups typical of the metropolitan organization of social relations.

The Northern whites have also been able to console themselves by comparing the favorable treatment of Negroes in the North with that of the South. Negroes have votes in the North and are, on the whole, guaranteed equality before the law. No cumbersome racial etiquette in personal relations is insisted upon. The whole caste system has big holes in the North, even if prejudice in personal relations is pronounced, and the Negroes are generally kept out of the better jobs. Reports of how Negroes fare in the South tend to make the Northerners satisfied with themselves, if not smug, without, in most cases, making them want to start again to reform the South. We fought a Civil War over the Negroes once, they will say; it didn't do any good and we are not going to do it again.

The mass migration of Southern Negroes to the North since the beginning of the First World War leads naturally—especially in periods of economic depression—to the reflection on the part of the Northerners that improvement of conditions for Negroes in their own communities is dangerous as it will encourage more Southern Negroes to come North. Most white Northerners seem to hold that the Negroes ought to stay on Southern land, and that, in any case, they cannot be asked to accept any responsibility for recent Negro migrants. Few Northerners have any idea that the Negroes are being pushed off the land in the South by the development of *world* competition against Southern agricultural products in combination with a *national* agricultural policy discriminating severely against the Negroes. This argument that Negroes should not be encouraged to come North—which is in the minds of many Northern city authorities—is a chief factor in hampering a sound welfare policy for Negroes.

This "passing the buck" is, of course, not only a device of Northerners to quiet their conscience. It is prominently displayed also by Southerners. The latter get satisfaction out of every indication that Negroes are not treated well in the North and, indeed, that groups other than Negroes are living in distress in the North. Such things help to assuage their own conscience. They need a rationalization against their sympathy for the underdog and against their dislike of the caste pressure inflicted upon the Negro. This situation has prevailed since before the Civil War. The horrors of Northern free-labor slavery and Northern city slums have never left the Southerner's mind. The object of this maltreatment, namely, the poor

Negro in both South and North, is the loser. Meanwhile each of the two guilty regions points to the other's sins—the South assuaging its conscience by the fact that "the Negro problem is finally becoming national in scope" and the North that "Negroes are much worse off in the South."

The Civil War, even if it does not figure so highly in Northern consciousness as the corresponding memories in the South, is a definite source of historical pride in the North. Many families, particularly in the higher social classes which contain "Old Americans," have ancestors who fought in the War, the recollection of which carries emotional identification with the Northern cause. The teaching in the schools of the North spreads an identification and a vicarious pride even to the Northerners whose ancestors were Europeans at the time of the Civil War. The liberation of the slaves plays an important part in this idealization. But, paradoxically enough, it turns against the Negro in his present situation: "We gave him full citizenship," the Northerner will say. "Now it is his own funeral if he hasn't got the guts to take care of himself. It would be an injustice in the opposite direction to do more for him than for people in general just because of his race. The Negro shouldn't be the ward of the nation. Look at all other poor, hardworking people in America. My grandfather had to sweat and work before he got through the mill."

This rationalized political valuation, which can be heard anywhere in the North, goes back to the Northern ideological retreat and the national compromise of the 1870's. It still, in disguised forms, creeps into even the scientific writings of Yankee authors. Donald Young, for example, writes:

> With the Civil War came emancipation, enfranchisement, and guaranties of equal rights for black and white. If anything, Northern politicians did their best to give the Negro a favored status which in effect would have made him almost a ward of the government. . . . Although a reaction to slavery was naturally to be expected, it would have been a mistake to give the freedman any more protection from private or public persecution than is afforded a citizen of any other color. Fortunately, the United States Supreme Court and the post-Civil War decline in emotionalism and increase in political sanity prevented the consummation of such attempts at special Negro legislation protection as the Fourteenth and Fifteenth Amendments and Sumner's Civil Rights Bill originally intended.[22]

The logic of this argument is weak. From the basic equalitarian assumption, it could not, of course, be deemed to be an unjust favoring of the Negro people on account of their race, if they were protected from the specific discriminations which are inflicted upon them just because of their race. Guaranteeing them civil liberties as citizens could not be said to be making them the wards of the nation in this particular sense. But even if this Northern rationalization is, in fact, an escape notion like many others we have found in the South, it is not charged with much emotion. The

Northerner does not have his social conscience and all his political thinking permeated with the Negro problem as the Southerner does.

Rather, he succeeds in forgetting about it most of the time. The Northern newspapers help him by minimizing all Negro news, except crime news. The Northerners want to hear as little as possible about the Negroes, both in the South and in the North, and they have, of course, good reasons for that. The result is an astonishing ignorance about the Negro on the part of the white public in the North. White Southerners, too, are ignorant of many phases of the Negro's life, but their ignorance has not such a simple and unemotional character as that in the North. There are many educated Northerners who are well informed about foreign problems but almost absolutely ignorant about Negro conditions both in their own city and in the nation as a whole.

This has great practical importance for the Negro people. A great many Northerners, perhaps the majority, get shocked and shaken in their conscience when they learn the facts. The average Northerner does not understand the reality and the effects of such discriminations as those in which he himself is taking part in his routine of life. *To get publicity is of the highest strategic importance to the Negro people.* The Negro protection and betterment organizations and many white liberals see this clearly and work hard to articulate the sufferings of the Negroes.

There is no doubt, in the writer's opinion, that a great majority of white people in America would be prepared to give the Negro a substantially better deal if they knew the facts. But to understand the difficulty the Negroes have to overcome in order to get publicity, we must never forget the opportunistic desire of the whites for ignorance. It is so much more comfortable to know as little as possible about Negroes, except that there are a lot of them in Harlem, the Black Belt, or whatever name is given to the segregated slum quarters where they live, and that there are still more of them in the South; that they are criminal and of disgustingly, but somewhat enticingly, loose sexual morals; that they are religious and have a gift for dancing and singing; and that they are the happy-go-lucky children of nature who get a kick out of life which white people are too civilized to get.

Just one note more should be added: the Southerners are not entirely different on this last point from the Northerners. I have become convinced also that a majority even of Southerners would be prepared for much more justice to the Negro if they were really brought to know the situation. The younger generations of Southern whites are less indoctrinated against the Negro than their parents were. But they are also farther away from him, know less about him and, sometimes, get more irritated by what little they see. We do not share the skepticism against education as a means of mitigating racial intolerance which recently has spread among American sociologists as a reaction against an important doctrine in the American Creed. *The simple fact is that an educational offensive against racial intolerance, going deeper than the reiteration of the "glittering generalities" in the nation's political creed, has never seriously been attempted in America.*

CHAPTER 3

FACETS OF THE NEGRO PROBLEM

1. AMERICAN MINORITY PROBLEMS

For some decades there has been a tendency to incorporate the American Negro problem into the broader American minority problem.[1] In the United States, the term "minority people" has a connotation different from that in other parts of the world and especially in Central and Eastern Europe, where minority problems have existed. This difference in problem is due to a difference in situation. The minority peoples of the United States are fighting for status in the larger society; the minorities of Europe are mainly fighting for independence from it. In the United States the so-called minority groups as they exist today—except the Indians and the Negroes—are mostly the result of a relatively recent immigration, which it was for a long time the established policy to welcome as a nationally advantageous means of populating and cultivating the country. The newcomers themselves were bent upon giving up their language and other cultural heritages and acquiring the ways and attitudes of the new nation. There have been degrees of friction and delay in this assimilation process, and even a partial conscious resistance by certain immigrant groups. But these elements of friction and resistance are really only of a character and magnitude to bring into relief the fundamental difference between the typical American minority problems and those in, say, the old Austrian Empire. Of greatest importance, finally, is the fact that the official political creed of America denounced, in general but vigorous terms, all forms of suppression and discrimination, and affirmed human equality.

In addition to a cultural difference between the native-born and the foreign-born in the United States, there was always a class difference. At every point of time many of those who were already established in the new country had acquired wealth and power, and were thus in a position to lay down the rules to late-comers. The immigrants, who left their native lands mainly because they had little wealth, had to fit themselves as best they could into the new situation. Their lack of familiarity with the English language and ways of life also made them an easy prey of economic exploitation. But as long as the West was open to expansion, immigrant groups could avoid becoming a subordinate class by going to a place where they were the only class. Gradually the frontier filled up, and free land no longer offered the immigrants cultural independence and economic self-protection. Increasingly they tended to come from lands where the cultures were ever more distant from the established American standards. They became distinguished more markedly as half-digested isolates, set down in the slums of American cities, and the level of discrimination rose.

The first stage of their assimilation often took them through the worst slums of the nation. Group after group of immigrants from every part of the world had their first course in Americanization in the squalid and congested quarters of New York's East Side and similar surroundings. They found themselves placed in the midst of utter poverty, crime, prostitution, lawlessness, and other undesirable social conditions. The assimilation process brought the immigrants through totally uncontrolled labor conditions and often through personal misery and social pressures of all kinds. The American social scientist might direct his curiosity to the occasional failures of the assimilation process and the tension created in the entire structure of larger society during its course. To the outside observer, on the other hand, the relative success will forever remain the first and greatest riddle to solve, when he sees that the children and grandchildren of these unassimilated foreigners are well-adjusted Americans. He will have to account for the basic human power of resistance and the flexibility of people's minds and cultures. He will have to appreciate the tremendous force in the American educational system. But it will not suffice as an explanation. He will be tempted to infer the influence upon the immigrant of a great national *ethos*, in which optimism and carelessness, generosity and callousness, were so blended as to provide him with hope and endurance.

From the viewpoint of the struggling immigrant himself, the harsh class structure, which thrust him to the bottom of the social heap, did not seem to be a rigid social determinant. In two or three generations, if not in one, the immigrant and his descendants moved into, and identified themselves with, the dominant American group, and—with luck and ability—took their position in the higher strata. Only because of this continuous movement of former immigrants and their descendants up and into the established group could the so-called "Americans" remain the majority during a century which saw more than a score of millions of immigrants added to its population. The causal mechanism of this social process has been aptly described as a continuous "push upwards" by a steady stream of new masses of toiling immigrants filling the ranks of the lower social strata. The class structure remained, therefore, fairly stable, while millions of individuals were continuously climbing the social ladder which it constituted. The unceasing process of social mobility and the prospect of its continuation, and also the established Creed of America promising and sanctioning social mobility, together with many other factors of importance, kept the minority groups contented and bent on assimilation.

Religious differences, differences in fundamental attitudes, and "racial" differences entered early as elements of friction in the process of assimilation and as reasons for discrimination while the process was going on. With the growing importance of the new immigration from Southern and Eastern Europe in the decades before the War, these factors acquired increased importance. They are, in a considerable degree, responsible for the fact that even recent community surveys, undertaken decades after the end of the mass immigration, give a picture of American class stratification which closely corresponds to the differentiation in national groups. This type of differentiation is one of the most distinguishing characteristics of the American social order.

The split of the nation into a dominant "American" group and a large number of minority groups means that American civilization is permeated by animosities and prejudices attached to ethnic origin or what is popularly recognized as the "race" of a person.[a] These animosities or prejudices are commonly advanced in defense of various discriminations which tend to keep the minority groups in a disadvantaged economic and social status. They are contrary to the American Creed, which is emphatic in denouncing differences made on account of "race, creed or color." In regard to the Negro, as well as more generally to all the other minorities, this conflict is what constitutes the problem, and it also contains the main factors in the dynamic development. Taking a cross-sectional view at any point of time, there is thus revealed an inconsistency in practically every American's social orientation. The inconsistency is not dissolved, at least not in the short run. Race prejudice and discrimination persist. But neither will the American Creed be thrown out. It is a hasty conclusion from the actual

[a] The popular term "race prejudice," as it is commonly used, embraces the whole complex of valuations and beliefs which are behind discriminatory behavior on the part of the majority group (or, sometimes, also on the part of the minority group) and which are contrary to the equalitarian ideals in the American Creed. In this very inclusive sense the term will be used in this inquiry. It should be noted that little is explained when we say that "discrimination is due to prejudice." The concept "race prejudice" unfortunately carries connotations that the intergroup situation is fairly stable and that the complex of attitudes behind discrimination is homogeneous and solid. (This is, incidentally, the danger with the concept of "attitude" as it is often used; see Appendix 1.) For a discussion of the empirical study of race prejudice, see Appendix 10, Section 4.

We do not need to enter into a discussion of whether "anti-minority feelings" in general are different from the "race prejudices" as they are displayed against Negroes. On the one hand, people in general also refer the former attitude to what they usually perceive of as "race." As Donald Young points out, there is also something of a common pattern in all discriminations (see footnote 1 to this chapter). On the other hand, there is this significant difference which we shall stress, that in regard to the colored minorities, amalgamation is violently denied them, while in regard to all the other minorities, it is welcomed as a long-run process.

facts of discrimination that the Creed will be without influence in the long run, even if it is suppressed for the moment, or even that it is uninfluential in the short run.

In trying to reconcile conflicting valuations the ordinary American apparently is inclined to believe that, as generations pass on, the remaining minority groups—with certain distinct exceptions which will presently be discussed—will be assimilated into a homogeneous nation.[2] The American Creed is at least partially responsible for this, as well as for the American's inclination to deem this assimilation desirable. Of course, this view is also based on the memories of previous absorption of minority groups into the dominant "American" population. Even the American Indians are now considered as ultimately assimilable. "The American Indian, once constituting an inferior caste in the social hierarchy, now constitutes little more than a social class, since today his inferior status may be sloughed off by the process of cultural assimilation."[3] This, incidentally, speaks against the doctrine that race prejudice under all circumstances is an unchangeable pattern of attitudes.

This long-range view of ultimate assimilation can be found to coexist with any degree of race prejudice in the actual present-day situation. In many parts of the country Mexicans are kept in a status similar to the Negro's or only a step above. Likewise, in most places anti-Semitism is strong and has apparently been growing for the last ten years.[4] Italians, Poles, Finns, are distrusted in some communities; Germans, Scandinavians, and the Irish are disliked in others, or sometimes the same communities. There are sections of the majority group which draw the circle exclusively and who hate all "foreigners." There are others who keep a somewhat distinct line only around the more exotic peoples. The individual, regional, and class differentials in anti-minority feeling are great.[5]

In spite of all race prejudice, few Americans seem to doubt that it is the ultimate fate of this nation to incorporate without distinction not only all the Northern European stocks, but also the people from Eastern and Southern Europe, the Near East and Mexico. They see obstacles; they emphasize the religious and "racial" differences; they believe it will take a long time. But they assume that it is going to happen, and do not have, on the whole, strong objections to it—provided it is located in a distant future.

2. The Anti-Amalgamation Doctrine

The Negroes, on the other hand, are commonly assumed to be unassimilable and this is the reason why the characterization of the Negro problem as a minority problem does not exhaust its true import.[a] The Negroes are set apart, together with other colored peoples, principally the Chinese and

[a] See Chapter 4.

the Japanese. America fears the segregation into distinctive isolated groups of all other elements of its population and looks upon the preservation of their separate national attributes and group loyalties as a hazard to American institutions. Considerable efforts are directed toward "Americanizing" all groups of alien origin. But in regard to the colored peoples, the American policy is the reverse. They are excluded from assimilation. Even by their best friends in the dominant white group and by the promoters of racial peace and good-will, they are usually advised to keep to themselves and develop a race pride of their own.

Among the groups commonly considered unassimilable, the Negro people is by far the largest. The Negroes do not, like the Japanese and the Chinese, have a politically organized nation and an accepted culture of their own outside of America to fall back upon. Unlike the Oriental, there attaches to the Negro an historical memory of slavery and inferiority. It is more difficult for them to answer prejudice with prejudice and, as the Orientals may do, to consider themselves and their history superior to the white Americans and their recent cultural achievements. The Negroes do not have these fortifications for self-respect. They are more helplessly imprisoned as a subordinate caste in America, a caste [a] of people deemed to be lacking a cultural past and assumed to be incapable of a cultural future.

To the ordinary white American the caste line between whites and Negroes is based upon, and defended by, the anti-amalgamation doctrine. This doctrine, more than anything else, gives the Negro problem its uniqueness among other problems of lower status groups, not only in terms of intensity of feelings but more fundamentally in the character of the problem. We follow a general methodological principle, presented previously, when we now start out from the ordinary white man's notion of what constitutes the heart of the Negro problem.

When the Negro people, unlike the white minority groups, is commonly characterized as unassimilable, it is not, of course, implied that amalgamation is not biologically possible. But crossbreeding is considered undesirable. Sometimes the view is expressed that the offspring of crossbreeding is inferior to both parental stocks. Usually it is only asserted that it is inferior to the "pure" white stock. The assumption evidently held is that the Negro stock is "inferior" to the white stock. On the inherited

[a] In this inquiry we shall use the term "caste" to denote the social status difference between Negroes and whites in America. The concept and its implications will be discussed in some detail in Part VIII. It should be emphasized that, although the *dividing line* between Negroes and whites is held fixed and rigid so that no Negro legitimately can pass over from his caste to the higher white caste, the *relations* between members of the two castes are different in different regions and social classes and changing in time. It is true that the term "caste" commonly connotes a static situation even in the latter respect. However, for a social phenomenon we prefer to use a social concept with too static connotations rather than the biological concept "race" which, of course, carries not only static but many much more erroneous connotations.

inferiority of the Negro people there exists among white Americans a whole folklore, which is remarkably similar throughout the country. To this we shall refer in the next chapter.

Whether this concept of the inferiority of the Negro stock is psychologically basic to the doctrine that amalgamation should be prohibited, or is only a rationalization of this doctrine, may for the moment be left open. The two notions, at any rate, appear together. The fact that one is used as argument for the other does not necessarily prove such a causal psychic relation between them. In many cases one meets an unargued and not further dissolvable *primary* valuation, which is assumed to be self-evident even without support of the inferiority premise. Miscegenation [a] is said to be a threat to "racial purity." It is alleged to be contrary to "human instincts." It is "contrary to nature" and "detestable." Not only in the South but often also in the North the stereotyped and hypothetical question is regularly raised without any intermediary reasoning as to its applicability or relevance to the social problem discussed: "Would you like to have your sister or daughter marry a Negro?" This is an unargued appeal to "racial solidarity" as a primary valuation. It is corollary to this attitude that in America the offspring of miscegenation is relegated to the Negro race.

A remarkable and hardly expected peculiarity of this American doctrine, expounded so directly in biological and racial terms, is that it is applied with a vast discretion depending upon the purely social and legal circumstances under which miscegenation takes place. As far as lawful marriage is concerned, the racial doctrine is laden with emotion. Even in the Northern states where, for the most part, intermarriage is not barred by the force of law, the social sanctions blocking its way are serious. Mixed couples are punished by nearly complete social ostracism. On the other hand, in many regions, especially in the South where the prohibition against intermarriage and the general reprehension against miscegenation have the strongest moorings, illicit relations have been widespread and occasionally allowed to acquire a nearly institutional character. Even if, as we shall find later when we come to analyze the matter more in detail,[b] such relations are perhaps now on the decline, they are still not entirely stamped out.

Considering the biological emphasis of the anti-amalgamation doctrine and the strong social sanctions against intermarriage tied to that doctrine, the astonishing fact is the great indifference of most white Americans

---

[a] Miscegenation is mainly an American term and is in America almost always used to denote only relations between Negroes and whites. Although it literally implies only mixture of genes between members of different races, it has acquired a definite emotional connotation. We use it in its literal sense—without implying necessarily that it is undesirable—as a convenient synonym of amalgamation.

[b] See Chapter 5.

toward real but illicit miscegenation. In spite of the doctrine, in some regions with a large Negro population, cohabitation with a Negro woman is, apparently, considered a less serious breach of sexual morals than illicit intercourse with a white woman. The illicit relations freely allowed or only frowned upon are, however, restricted to those between white men and Negro women. A white woman's relation with a Negro man is met by the full fury of anti-amalgamation sanctions.

If we now turn to the American Negro people, we can hardly avoid the strong impression that what there is of reluctance in principle toward amalgamation is merely in the nature of a reaction or response to the white doctrine, which thus stands as primary in the causal sense and strategic in a practical sense. It is true that white people, when facing the Negro group, make an ideological application of the general Jim Crow principle—"equal but separate" treatment and accommodations for the two racial groups—and proceed from the assertion that both races are good to the explanation that there is a value in keeping them unmixed. They appeal also to the Negroes' "race pride" and their interest in keeping their own blood "pure." But this is a white, not a Negro, argument.

The Negro will be found to doubt the sincerity of the white folks' interest in the purity of the Negro race. It will sound to him too much like a rationalization, in strained equalitarian terms, of the white supremacy doctrine of race purity. "But the outstanding joke is to hear a white man talk about race integrity, though at this the Negro is in doubt whether to laugh or swear." [6] Even the Negro in the uneducated classes is sensitive to the nuances of sincerity, trained as he is both in slavery and afterwards to be a good dissembler himself. The Negro will, furthermore, encounter considerable intellectual difficulties inherent in the idea of keeping his blood pure, owing to the fact that the large majority of American Negroes actually are of mixed descent. They already have white and Indian ancestry as well as African Negro blood. And in general they are aware of this fact.

In spite of this, race pride, with this particular connotation of the undesirability of miscegenation, has been growing in the Negro group. This is, however, probably to be interpreted as a defense reaction, a derived *secondary* attitude as are so many other attitudes of the Negro people.[a] After weighing all available evidence carefully, it seems frankly incredible that the Negro people in America should feel inclined to develop any particular race pride at all or have any dislike for amalgamation, were it not for the common white opinion of the racial inferiority of the Negro people and the whites' intense dislike for miscegenation. The fact that a large amount of exploitative sexual intercourse between white men and Negro women has always been, and still is, part of interracial relations, coupled with the further fact that the Negroes sense the disgrace of their women who are

[a] See Appendix 10, Section 4.

not accepted into matrimony, and the inferior status of their mixed off-spring, is a strong practical reason for the Negro's preaching "race pride" in his own group. But it is almost certainly not based on any fundamental feeling condemning miscegenation on racial or biological grounds.

On this central point, as on so many others, the whites' attitudes are primary and decisive; the Negroes' are in the nature of accommodation or protest.

3. THE WHITE MAN'S THEORY OF COLOR CASTE

We have attempted to present in compressed and abstract formulation the white supremacy doctrine as applied to amalgamation, sex relations and marriage. The difficulty inherent in this task is great. As no scientifically controlled nation-wide investigations have been made, the author has here, as in other sections, had to rely on his own observations.[7]

Every widening of the writer's experience of white Americans has only driven home to him more strongly that the opinion that the Negro is unassimilable, or, rather, that his amalgamation into the American nation is undesirable, is held more commonly, absolutely, and intensely than would be assumed from a general knowledge of American thoughtways. Except for a handful of rational intellectual liberals—who also, in many cases, add to their acceptance in principle of amalgamation an admission that they personally feel an irrational emotional inhibition against it—it is a rare case to meet a white American who will confess that, if it were not for public opinion and social sanctions not removable by private choice, he would have no strong objection to intermarriage.

The intensity of the attitude seems to be markedly stronger in the South than in the North. Its strength seems generally to be inversely related to the economic and social status of the informant and his educational level. It is usually strong even in most of the non-colored minority groups, if they are above the lowest plane of indifference. To the poor and socially insecure, but struggling, white individual, a fixed opinion on this point seems an important matter of prestige and distinction.

But even a liberal-minded Northerner of cosmopolitan culture and with a minimum of conventional blinds will, in nine cases out of ten, express a definite feeling against amalgamation. He will not be willing usually to hinder intermarriage by law. Individual liberty is to him a higher principle and, what is more important, he actually invokes it. But he will regret the exceptional cases that occur. He may sometimes hold a philosophical view that in centuries to come amalgamation is bound to happen and might become the solution. But he will be inclined to look on it as an inevitable deterioration.[a]

[a] The response is likely to be anything but pleasant if one jestingly argues that possibly a small fraction of Negro blood in the American people, if it were blended well with all

This attitude of refusing to consider amalgamation—felt and expressed in the entire country—constitutes the center in the complex of attitudes which can be described as the "common denominator" in the problem. It defines the Negro group in contradistinction to all the non-colored minority groups in America and all other lower class groups. The boundary between Negro and white is not simply a class line which can be successfully crossed by education, integration into the national culture, and individual economic advancement. The boundary is fixed. It is not a temporary expediency during an apprenticeship in the national culture. It is a bar erected with the intention of permanency. It is directed against the whole group. Actually, however, "passing" as a white person is possible when a Negro is white enough to conceal his Negro heritage. But the difference between "passing" and ordinary social climbing reveals the distinction between a class line, in the ordinary sense, and a caste line.

This brings us to the point where we shall attempt to sketch, only in an abstract and preliminary form, the social mechanism by which the anti-amalgamation maxim determines race relations. This mechanism is perceived by nearly everybody in America, but most clearly in the South. Almost unanimously white Americans have communicated to the author the following logic of the caste situation which we shall call the *"white man's theory of color caste."*

(1) The concern for "race purity" is basic in the whole issue; the primary and essential command is to prevent amalgamation; the whites are determined to utilize every means to this end.

(2) Rejection of "social equality" is to be understood as a precaution to hinder miscegenation and particularly intermarriage.

(3) The danger of miscegenation is so tremendous that the segregation and discrimination inherent in the refusal of "social equality" must be extended to nearly all spheres of life. There must be segregation and discrimination in recreation, in religious service, in education, before the law, in politics, in housing, in stores and in breadwinning.

This popular theory of the American caste mechanism is, of course, open to criticism. It can be criticized from a valuational point of view by main-

---

the other good stock brought over to the new continent, might create a race of unsurpassed excellence: a people with just a little sunburn without extra trouble and even through the winter; with some curl in the hair without the cost of a permanent wave; with, perhaps, a little more emotional warmth in their souls; and a little more religion, music, laughter, and carefreeness in their lives. Amalgamation is, to the ordinary American, not a proper subject for jokes at all, unless it can be pulled down to the level of dirty stories, where, however, it enjoys a favored place. Referred to society as a whole and viewed as a principle, the anti-amalgamation maxim is held holy; it is a consecrated taboo. The maxim might, indeed, be a remnant of something really in the "mores." It is kept unproblematic, which is certainly not the case with all the rest of etiquette and segregation and discrimination patterns, for which this quality is sometimes erroneously claimed.

taining that hindering miscegenation is not a worthwhile end, or that as an end it is not sufficiently worthwhile to counterbalance the sufferings inflicted upon the suppressed caste and the general depression of productive efficiency, standards of living and human culture in the American society at large—costs appreciated by all parties concerned. This criticism does not, however, endanger the theory which assumes that white people actually are following another valuation of means and ends and are prepared to pay the costs for attaining the ends. A second criticism would point out that, assuming the desirability of the end, this end could be reached without the complicated and, in all respects, socially expensive caste apparatus now employed. This criticism, however adequate though it be on the practical or political plane of discussion, does not disprove that people believe other-wise, and that the popular theory is a true representation of their beliefs and actions.

To undermine the popular theory of the caste mechanism, as based on the anti-amalgamation maxim, it would, of course, be necessary to prove that people really are influenced by other motives than the ones pronounced. Much material has, as we shall find, been brought together indicating that, among other things, competitive economic interests, which do not figure at all in the popular rationalization referred to, play a decisive role. The announced concern about racial purity is, when this economic motive it taken into account, no longer awarded the exclusive role as the *basic* cause in the psychology of the race problem.

Though the popular theory of color caste turns out to be a rationalization, this does not destroy it. For among the forces in the minds of the white people are certainly not only economic interests (if these were the only ones, the popular theory would be utterly demolished), but also sexual urges, inhibitions, and jealousies, and social fears and cravings for prestige and security. When they come under the scrutiny of scientific research, both the sexual and the social complexes take on unexpected designs. We shall then also get a clue to understanding the remarkable tendency of this presumably biological doctrine, that it refers only to legal marriage and to relations between Negro men and white women, but not to extra-marital sex relations between white men and Negro women.

However these sexual and social complexes might turn out when analyzed, they will reveal the psychological nature of the anti-amalgamation doctrine and show its "meaning." They will also explain the compressed emotion attached to the Negro problem. It is inherent in our type of modern Western civilization that sex and social status are for most individuals the danger points, the directions whence he fears the sinister onslaughts on his personal security. These two factors are more likely than anything else to push a life problem deep down into the subconscious and load it with emotions. There is some probability that in America both complexes are particularly laden with emotions. The American puritan tradition gives everything connected with sex a higher emotional charge. The roads for social climbing have been kept more open in America than perhaps anywhere else in the world, but in this upward struggle the competition for social status has also become more absorbing. In a manner and to a degree most uncomfortable for the Negro people in America, both the sexual and the social complexes have become related to the Negro problem.

These complexes are most of the time kept concealed. In occasional groups of persons and situations they break into the open. Even when not consciously perceived or expressed, they ordinarily determine interracial behavior on the white side.

4. The "Rank Order of Discriminations"

The anti-amalgamation doctrine represents a strategic constellation of forces in race relations. Their charting will allow us a first general overview of the discrimination patterns and will have the advantage that white Americans themselves will recognize their own paths on the map we draw. When white Southerners are asked to rank, in order of importance, various types of discrimination,[a] they consistently present a list in which these types of discrimination are ranked according to the degree of closeness of their relation to the anti-amalgamation doctrine. This rank order—which will be referred to as *"the white man's rank order of discriminations"*—will serve as an organizing principle in this book. It appears, actually, only as an elaboration of the popular theory of color caste sketched above. Like that theory, it is most clearly and distinctly perceived in the South; in the North ideas are more vague but, on the whole, not greatly divergent. Neither the popular theory of caste nor the rank order of discriminations has been noted much in scientific literature on the Negro problem.

The rank order held nearly unanimously is the following:

Rank 1. Highest in this order stands the bar against intermarriage and sexual intercourse involving white women.

Rank 2. Next come the several etiquettes and discriminations, which specifically concern behavior in personal relations. (These are the barriers against dancing, bathing, eating, drinking together, and social intercourse generally; peculiar rules as to handshaking, hat lifting, use of titles, house entrance to be used, social forms when meeting on streets and in work, and so forth. These patterns are sometimes referred to as the denial of "social equality" in the narrow meaning of the term.)

[a] In this introductory sketch the distinction between "segregation" and "discrimination" is entirely disregarded. This distinction, signified by the popular theory and legal construct "separate but equal," is mainly to be regarded as an equalitarian rationalization on the part of the white Americans, indicating the fundamental conflict of valuations involved in the matter. "Segregation" means only separation and does not, in principle, imply "discrimination." In practice it almost always does. (See Chapter 28.)

Rank 3. Thereafter follow the segregations and discriminations in use of public facilities such as schools, churches and means of conveyance.

Rank 4. Next comes political disfranchisement.

Rank 5. Thereafter come discriminations in law courts, by the police, and by other public servants.

Rank 6. Finally come the discriminations in securing land, credit, jobs, or other means of earning a living, and discriminations in public relief and other social welfare activities.

It is unfortunate that this cornerstone in our edifice of basic hypotheses, like many of our other generalizations, has to be constructed upon the author's observations.[8] It is desirable that scientifically controlled, quantitative knowledge be substituted for impressionistic judgments as soon as possible.[9] It should be noted that the rank order is very apparently determined by the factors of sex and social status, so that the closer the association of a type of interracial behavior is to sexual and social intercourse on an equalitarian basis, the higher it ranks among the forbidden things.

Next in importance to the fact of the white man's rank order of discriminations is the fact that *the Negro's own rank order is just about parallel, but inverse, to that of the white man.* The Negro resists least the discrimination on the ranks placed highest in the white man's evaluation and resents most any discrimination on the lowest level. This is in accord with the Negro's immediate interests. Negroes are in desperate need of jobs and bread, even more so than of justice in the courts, and of the vote. These latter needs are, in their turn, more urgent even than better schools and playgrounds, or, rather, they are primary means of reaching equality in the use of community facilities. Such facilities are, in turn, more important than civil courtesies. The marriage matter, finally, is of rather distant and doubtful interest.

Such reflections are obvious; and most Negroes have them in their minds. It is another matter, however, whether the white man is prepared to stick honestly to the rank order which he is so explicit and emphatic in announcing. The question is whether he is really prepared to give the Negro a good job, or even the vote, rather than to allow him entrance to his front door or to ride beside him in the street car.

Upon the assumption that this question is given an affirmative answer, that the white man is actually prepared to carry out in practice the implications of his theories, this inverse relationship between the Negro's and the white man's rank orders becomes of strategical importance in the practical and political sphere of the Negro problem. Although not formulated in this way, such a relationship, or such a minimum moral demand on the ordinary white man, has always been the basis of all attempts to compromise and come to a better understanding between leaders of the two groups. It has been the basis for all interracial policy and also for most of the practical work actually carried out by Negro betterment organizations. Followed to its logical end, it should fundamentally change the race situation in America.

It has thus always been a primary requirement upon every Negro leader —who aspires to get any hearing at all from the white majority group, and who does not want to appear dangerously radical to the Negro group and at the same time hurt the "race pride" it has built up as a defense—that he shall explicitly condone the anti-amalgamation maxim, which is the keystone in the white man's structure of race prejudice, and forbear to express any desire on the part of the Negro people to aspire to inter-marriage with the whites. The request for intermarriage is easy for the Negro leader to give up. Intermarriage cannot possibly be a practical object of Negro public policy. Independent of the Negroes' wishes, the opportunity for intermarriage is not favorable as long as the great majority of the white population dislikes the very idea. As a defense reaction a strong attitude against intermarriage has developed in the Negro people itself.[10] And the Negro people have no interest in defending the exploitative illicit relations between white men and Negro women. This race mingling is, on the contrary, commonly felt among Negroes to be disgraceful. And it often arouses the jealousy of Negro men.

The required soothing gesture toward the anti-amalgamation doctrine is, therefore, readily delivered. It is iterated at every convenient opportunity and belongs to the established routine of Negro leadership. For example, Robert R. Moton writes:

> As for amalgamation, very few expect it; still fewer want it; no one advocates it; and only a constantly diminishing minority practise it, and that surreptitiously. It is generally accepted on both sides of the colour line that it is best for the two races to remain ethnologically distinct.[11]

There seems thus to be unanimity among Negro leaders on the point deemed crucial by white Americans. If we attend carefully, we shall, however, detect some important differences in formulation. The Negro spokesman will never, to begin with, accept the common white premise of racial inferiority of the Negro stock. To quote Moton again:

> . . . even in the matter of the mingling of racial strains, however undesirable it might seem to be from a social point of view, he [the Negro] would never admit that his blood carries any taint of physiological, mental, or spiritual inferiority.[12]

A doctrine of equal natural endowments—a doctrine contrary to the white man's assumption of Negro inferiority, which is at the basis of the anti-amalgamation theory—has been consistently upheld. If a Negro leader publicly even hinted at the possibility of inherent racial inferiority, he would immediately lose his following. The entire Negro press watches the Negro leaders on this point.

Even Booker T. Washington, the supreme diplomat of the Negro people through a generation filled with severe trials, who was able by studied unobtrusiveness to wring so many favors from the white majority, never dared to allude to such a possibility, though he sometimes criticized most severely his own people for lack of thrift, skill, perseverance and general culture. In fact, there is no reason to think that he did not firmly believe in the fundamental equality of inherent capacities. Privately, local Negro leaders might find it advisable to admit Negro inferiority and, particularly earlier, many individual Negroes might have shared the white man's view. But it will not be expressed by national leaders and, in fact, never when they are under public scrutiny.[13] An emphatic assertion of equal endowments is article number one in the growing Negro "race pride."

Another deviation of the Negro faith in the anti-amalgamation doctrine is the stress that they, for natural reasons, lay on condemning exploitative illicit amalgamation. They turn the tables and accuse white men of debasing Negro womanhood, and the entire white culture for not rising up against this practice as their expressed antagonism against miscegenation should demand. Here they have a strong point, and they know how to press it.[14]

A third qualification in the Negro's acceptance of the anti-amalgamation doctrine, expressed not only by the more "radical" and outspoken Negro leaders, is the assertion that intermarriage should not be barred by law. The respect for individual liberty is invoked as an argument. But, in addition, it is pointed out that this barrier, by releasing the white man from the consequences of intimacy with a Negro woman, actually has the effect of inducing such intimacy and thus tends to increase miscegenation. Moton makes this point:

> The Negro woman suffers not only from the handicap of economic and social discriminations imposed upon the race as a whole, but is in addition the victim of unfavourable legislation incorporated in the marriage laws of twenty-nine states, which forbid the intermarriage of black and white. The disadvantage of these statutes lies, not as is generally represented, in the legal obstacle they present to social equality, but rather in the fact that such laws specifically deny to the Negro woman and her offspring that safeguard from abuse and exploitation with which the women of the white race are abundantly surrounded. On the other side, the effect of such legislation leaves the white man, who is so inclined, free of any responsibility attending his amatory excursions across the colour line and leaves the coloured woman without redress for any of the consequences of her defencelessness; whereas white women have every protection, from fine and imprisonment under the law to enforced marriage and lynching outside the law.[15]

But even with all these qualifications, the anti-amalgamation doctrine, the necessity of assenting to which is understood by nearly everybody, obviously encounters some difficulties in the minds of intellectual Negroes. They can hardly be expected to accept it as a just rule of conduct. They tend to accept it merely as a temporary expedient necessitated by human weakness. Kelly Miller thus wrote:

> . . . you would hardly expect the Negro, in derogation of his common human qualities, to proclaim that he is so diverse from God's other human creatures as to make the blending of the races contrary to the law of nature. The Negro refuses to become excited or share in your frenzy on this subject. The amalgamation of the races is an ultimate possibility, though not an immediate probability. But what have you and I to do with ultimate questions, anyway?[16]

And a few years later, he said:

> It must be taken for granted in the final outcome of things that the color line will be wholly obliterated. While blood may be thicker than water, it does not possess the spissitude or inherency of everlasting principle. The brotherhood of man is more fundamental than the fellowship of race. A physical and spiritual identity of all peoples occupying common territory is a logical necessity of thought. The clear seeing mind refuses to yield or give its assent to any other ultimate conclusion. This consummation, however, is far too removed from the sphere of present probability to have decisive influence upon practical procedure.[17]

This problem is, of course, tied up with the freedom of the individual. "Theoretically Negroes would all subscribe to the right of freedom of choice in marriage even between the two races,"[18] wrote Moton. And Du Bois formulates it in stronger terms:

> . . . a woman may say, I do not want to marry this black man, or this red man, or this white man. . . . But the impudent and vicious demand that all colored folk shall write themselves down as brutes by a general assertion of their unfitness to marry other decent folk is a nightmare.[19]

Negroes have always pointed out that the white man must not be very certain of his woman's lack of interest when he rises to such frenzy on behalf of the danger to her and feels compelled to build up such formidable fences to prevent her from marrying a Negro.

With these reservations both Negro leadership and the Negro masses acquiesce in the white anti-amalgamation doctrine. This attitude is noted with satisfaction in the white camp. The writer has observed, however, that the average white man, particularly in the South, does not feel quite convinced of the Negro's acquiescence. In several conversations, the same white person, in the same breath, has assured me, on the one hand, that the Negroes are perfectly satisfied in their position and would not like to be treated as equals, and on the other hand, that the only thing these Negroes long for is to be like white people and to marry their daughters.

Whereas the Negro spokesman finds it possible to assent to the first rank of discrimination, namely, that involving miscegenation, it is more difficult for him to give his approval to the second rank of discrimination, namely, that involving "etiquette" and consisting in the white man's refusal to extend the ordinary courtesies to Negroes in daily life and his expectation of receiving certain symbolic signs of submissiveness from the Negro. The Negro leader could not do so without serious risk of censorship by his own people and rebuke by the Negro press. In all articulate groups of Negroes there is a demand to have white men call them by their titles of Mr., Mrs., and Miss; to have white men take off their hats on entering a Negro's house; to be able to enter a white man's house through the front door rather than the back door, and so on. But on the whole, and in spite of the rule that they stand up for "social equality" in this sense, most Negroes in the South obey the white man's rules.

Booker T. Washington went a long way, it is true, in his Atlanta speech in 1895 where he explained that: "In all things that are purely social we [the two races] can be as separate as the fingers, yet one as the hand in all things essential to mutual progress."[20] He there seemed to condone not only these rules of "etiquette" but also the denial of "social equality" in a broader sense, including some of the further categories in the white man's rank order of discrimination. He himself was always most eager to observe the rules. But Washington was bitterly rebuked for this capitulation, particularly by Negroes in the North. And a long time has passed since then; the whole spirit in the Negro world has changed considerably in three decades.

The modern Negro leader will try to solve this dilemma by iterating that no Negroes want to intrude upon white people's private lives. But this is not what Southern white opinion asks for. It is not satisfied with the natural rules of polite conduct that no individual, of whatever race, shall push his presence on a society where he is not wanted. It asks for a general order according to which *all* Negroes are placed under *all* white people and excluded from not only the white man's society but also from the ordinary symbols of respect. No Negro shall ever aspire to them, and no white shall be allowed to offer them.

Thus, on this second rank of discrimination there is a wide gap between the ideologies of the two groups. As we then continue downward in our rank order and arrive at the ordinary Jim Crow practices, the segregation in schools, the disfranchisement, and the discrimination in employment, we find, on the one hand, that increasingly larger groups of white people are prepared to take a stand against these discriminations. Many a liberal white professor in the South who, for his own welfare, would not dare to entertain a Negro in his home and perhaps not even speak to him in a friendly manner on the street, will be found prepared publicly to condemn disfranchisement, lynching, and the forcing of the Negro out of employment. Also, on the other hand, Negro spokesmen are becoming increasingly firm in their opposition to discrimination on these lower levels. It is principally on these lower levels of the white man's rank order of discriminations that the race struggle goes on. The struggle will widen to embrace all the thousand problems of education, politics, economic standards, and so forth, and the frontier will shift from day to day according to varying events.

Even a superficial view of discrimination in America will reveal to the observer: first, that there are great differences, not only between larger regions, but between neighboring communities; and, second, that even in the same community, changes occur from one time to another. There is also, contrary to the rule that all Negroes are to be treated alike, a certain amount of discretion depending upon the class and social status of the Negro in question. A white person, especially if he has high status in the community, is, furthermore, supposed to be free, within limits, to overstep the rules. The rules are primarily to govern the Negro's behavior.

Some of these differences and changes can be explained. But the need for their interpretation is perhaps less than has sometimes been assumed. The variations in discrimination between local communities or from one time to another are often not of primary consequence. All of these thousand and one precepts, etiquettes, taboos, and disabilities inflicted upon the Negro have a common purpose: to express the subordinate status of the Negro people and the exalted position of the whites. They have their meaning and chief function as symbols. As symbols they are, however, interchangeable to an extent: one can serve in place of another without causing material difference in the essential social relations in the community.

The differences in patterns of discrimination between the larger regions of the country and the temporal changes of patterns within one region, which reveal a definite trend, have, on the contrary, more material import. These differences and changes imply, in fact, a considerable margin of variation within the very notion of American caste, which is not true of all the other minor differences between the changes in localities within a single region—hence the reason for a clear distinction. For exemplification it may suffice here to refer only to the differentials in space. As one moves from the Deep South through the Upper South and the Border states to the North, the manifestations of discrimination decrease in extent and intensity; at the same time the rules become more uncertain and capricious. The "color line" becomes a broad ribbon of arbitrariness. The old New England states stand, on the whole, as the antipode to the Deep South. This generalization requires important qualifications, and the relations are in process of change.

The decreasing discrimination as we go from South to North in the United States is apparently related to a weaker basic prejudice. In the North the Negroes have fair justice and are not disfranchised; they are not Jim-Crowed in public means of conveyance; educational institutions are less segregated. The interesting thing is that the decrease of discrimination does *not* regularly follow the white man's rank order. Thus intermarriage, placed on the top of the rank order, is legally permitted in all but one of the Northern states east of the Mississippi. The racial etiquette, being the most conspicuous element in the second rank, is, practically speaking, absent from the North. On the other hand, employment discriminations, placed at the bottom of the rank order, at times are equally severe, or more so, in some Northern communities than in the South, even if it is true that Negroes have been able to press themselves into many more new avenues of employment during the last generation in the North than in the South.

There is plenty of discrimination in the North. But it is—or rather its rationalization is—kept hidden. We can, in the North, witness the legislators' obedience to the American Creed when they solemnly pass laws and regulations to condemn and punish such acts of discrimination which, as a matter of routine, are committed daily by the great majority of the white citizens and by the legislators themselves. In the North, as indeed often in the South, public speakers frequently pronounce principles of human and civic equality. We see here revealed in relief the Negro problem as an American Dilemma.

5. RELATIONSHIPS BETWEEN LOWER CLASS GROUPS

It was important to compare the Negro problem with American minority problems in general because both the similarities and the dissimilarities are instructive. Comparisons give leads, and they furnish perspective.

This same reason permits us to point out that the consideration of the Negro problem as one minority problem among others is far too narrow. The Negro has usually the same disadvantages and some extra ones in addition. To these other disadvantaged groups in America belong not only the groups recognized as minorities, but all economically weak classes in the nation, the bulk of the Southern people, women,[a] and others. This country is a "white man's country," but, in addition, it is a country belonging primarily to the elderly, male, upper class, Protestant Northerner. Viewed in this setting the Negro problem in America is but one local and temporary facet of that eternal problem of world dimension—how to regulate the conflicting interests of groups in the best interest of justice and fairness. The latter ideals are vague and conflicting, and their meaning is changing in the course of the struggle.

There seems to be a general structure of social relations between groups on different levels of power and advantage. From a consideration of our

[a] The parallel between the status of Negroes and of women, who are neither a minority group nor a low social class, is particularly instructive; see Appendix 5, "A Parallel to the Negro Problem."

exaggeratedly "typical" case—the Negro—we may hope to reach some suggestions toward a more satisfactory general theory about this social power structure in general. Our hypothesis is that in a society where there are broad social classes and, in addition, more minute distinctions and splits in the lower strata, *the lower class groups will, to a great extent, take care of keeping each other subdued,* thus relieving, to that extent, the higher classes of this otherwise painful task necessary to the monopolization of the power and the advantages.

It will be observed that this hypothesis is contrary to the Marxian theory of class society, which in the period between the two World Wars has been so powerful, directly and indirectly, consciously and unconsciously, in American social science thinking generally. The Marxian scheme assumes that there is an actual solidarity between the several lower class groups against the higher classes, or, in any case, a potential solidarity which as a matter of natural development is bound to emerge. The inevitable result is a "class struggle" where all poor and disadvantaged groups are united behind the barricades.

Such a construction has had a considerable vogue in all discussions on the American Negro problem since the First World War. We are not here taking issue with the political desirability of a common front between the poorer classes of whites and the Negro people who, for the most part, belong to the proletariat. In fact, we can well see that such a practical judgment is motivated as a conclusion from certain value premises in line with the American Creed. But the thesis has also been given a theoretical content as describing actual trends in reality and not only political *desiderata.* A solidarity between poor whites and Negroes has been said to be "natural" and the conflicts to be due to "illusions." This thesis, which will be discussed in some detail in Chapter 38, has been a leading one in the field and much has been made of even the faintest demonstration of such solidarity.

In partial anticipation of what is to follow later in this volume, we might be permitted to make a few general, and perhaps rather dogmatic, remarks in criticism of this theory. Everything we know about human frustration and aggression, and the displacement of aggression, speaks against it. For an individual to feel interest solidarity with a group assumes his psychological identification with the group. This identification must be of considerable strength, as the very meaning of solidarity is that he is prepared to set aside and even sacrifice his own short-range private interests for the long-range interests of his group. Every vertical split within the lower class aggregate will stand as an obstacle to the feeling of solidarity. Even within the white working class itself, as within the entire American nation, the feeling of solidarity and loyalty is relatively low.[a] Despite the

* See Chapter 33.

considerable mobility, especially in the North, the Negroes are held apart from the whites by caste, which furnishes a formidable bar to mutual identification and solidarity.

It has often occurred to me, when reflecting upon the responses I get from white laboring people on this strategic question, that my friends among the younger Negro intellectuals, whose judgment I otherwise have learned to admire greatly, have perhaps, and for natural reasons, not had enough occasion to find out for themselves what a bitter, spiteful, and relentless feeling often prevails against the Negroes among lower class white people in America. Again relying upon my own observations, I have become convinced that the laboring Negroes do not resent whites in any degree comparable with the resentment shown in the opposite direction by the laboring whites. The competitive situation is, and is likely to remain, highly unstable.

It must be admitted that, in the midst of harsh caste resentment, signs of newborn working class solidarity are not entirely lacking; we shall have to discuss these recent tendencies in some detail in order to evaluate the resultant trend and the prospects for the future.[a] On this point there seems, however, to be a danger of wishful thinking present in most writings on the subject. The Marxian solidarity between the toilers of all the earth will, indeed, have a long way to go as far as concerns solidarity of the poor white Americans with the toiling Negro. This is particularly true of the South but true also of the communities in the North where the Negroes are numerous and competing with the whites for employment.

Our hypothesis is similar to the view taken by an older group of Negro writers and by most white writers who have touched this crucial question: that the Negro's friend—or the one who is least unfriendly—is still rather the upper class of white people, the people with economic and social security who are truly a "noncompeting group." There are many things in the economic, political, and social history of the Negro which are simply inexplicable by the Marxian theory of class solidarity but which fit into our hypothesis of the predominance of internal lower class struggle. Du Bois, in *Black Reconstruction*, argues that it would have been desirable if after the Civil War the landless Negroes and the poor whites had joined hands to retain political power and carry out a land reform and a progressive government in the Southern states; one sometimes feels that he thinks it would have been a possibility.[21] From our point of view such a possibility did not exist at all, and the negative outcome was neither an accident nor a result of simple deception or delusion. These two groups, illiterate and insecure in an impoverished South, placed in an intensified competition with each other, lacking every trace of primary solidarity, and marked off from each other by color and tradition, could not possibly be expected to

[a] See Chapter 18.

clasp hands. There is a Swedish proverb: "When the feed-box is empty, the horses will bite each other."

That part of the country where, even today, the Negro is dealt with most severely, the South, is also a disadvantaged and, in most respects, backward region in the nation. The Negro lives there in the midst of other relatively subordinated groups. Like the Negro, the entire South is a problem. We do not want to minimize other obvious explanations of the harsher treatment of the Negro in the South: his concentration there in large numbers, the tradition of subordination retained from slavery, and the traumatic effect of the Civil War and Reconstruction; but we do want to stress the fact that the masses of white Southerners are poor and to keep in mind the tendency of lower class groups to struggle against each other.[a]

[a] The great similarity in cultural situation—on a different level—between the Negro people in all America and the white South should not be overlooked. Many of the general things which can be said about the Negroes hold true, in large measure, of the white Southerners, or something quite similar can be asserted. Thus, just as the Negro sees himself economically excluded and exploited, so the Southern white man has been trained to think of his economy as a colony for Yankee exploitation. As the Negro has been compelled to develop race pride and a "protective" community, so the white South has also a strong group feeling. The white South is also something of a nation within a nation. It is certainly no accident that a "regional approach" in social science has been stressed in the South. The Southerner, like the Negro, is apt to be sensitive and to take any personal remark or observation as a rebuke, and a rebuke not only against himself but against the whole South. In analyzing himself, he finds the same general traits of extreme individualism and romanticism which are ascribed to the Negro. His educators and intellectual leaders find it necessary to complain of the same shortcomings in him as he finds in the Negro: violence, laziness, lack of thrift, lack of rational efficiency and respect for law and social order, lack of punctuality and respect for deadlines. The rickety rocking-chair on the porch has a symbolic meaning in the South not entirely different from that of the Negro's watermelon, although there is more an association of gloom and dreariness around the former stereotype, and happy-go-lucky carefreeness around the latter. The expression "C.P.T."—colored people's time—is often referred to in the South, but nearly as frequently it is jestingly suggested that it fits the folkways also of the white Southerners. The casual carrying of weapons, which is so associated in the Northerners' minds with the Negro, is commonplace among white Southerners. Both groups are on the average more religious than the rest of America, and the preacher is, or has been, more powerful in society. In both groups there is also a tendency toward fundamentalism and emotionalism, the former characteristic more important for the whites, the latter for the Negroes. The general educational level in the South has, for lack of school facilities, been lower than the national norm, and as a result an obvious double standard in favor of Southerners is actually being applied by higher educational institutions and by such organizations as foundations awarding fellowships and encouraging research projects. The Yankee prejudice against the South often takes the form of a paternalistic favoring of a weaker group. The white writers of the South, like the Negro writers, are accustomed to work mainly for a "foreign" public of readers. And they have, for the benefit of the out-group, exploited the in-group's romance and oddness. During the 'twenties both groups had a literary renaissance, commonly described in both cases as an emancipation from outside determinants and as a new earthbound realism. This list could be continued to a considerable length, but it has already been made understandable both why the Negro in a way feels so much at home in the South and why his lot there sometimes becomes so sad and even tragic.

A few remarks are now relevant on the internal social stratification of the Negro group itself. The stratification of the Negro caste into classes is well developed and the significance attached to class distinctions is great. This is not surprising in view of the fact that caste barriers, which prevent individuals of the lower group from rising out of it, force all social climbing to occur within the caste and encourage an increase in internal social competition for the symbols of prestige and power. Caste consigns the overwhelming majority of Negroes to the lower class. But at the same time as it makes higher class status rarer, it accentuates the desire for prestige and social distance within the Negro caste. It fact it sometimes causes a more minute class division than the ordinary one, and always invests it with more subjective importance.[a] The social distinctions within a disadvantaged group for this reason become a fairly adequate index of the group's social isolation from the larger society.

Caste produces, on the one hand, a strong feeling of mutuality of fate, of in-group fellowship—much stronger than a general low class position can develop. The Negro community is a protective community, and we shall, in the following chapters, see this trait reflected in practically all aspects of the Negro problem. But, on the other hand, the interclass strivings, often heightened to vigorous mutual repulsion and resentment, are equally conspicuous.

Negro writers, especially newspapermen, particularly when directing themselves to a Negro audience, have always pointed out, as the great fault of the race, its lack of solidarity. The same note is struck in practically every public address and often in sermons when the preacher for a moment leaves his other-worldliness. It is the campaign cry of the organizations for Negro business. Everywhere one meets the same endless complaints: that the Negroes won't stick together, that they don't trust each other but rather the white man, that they can't plan and act in common, that they don't back their leaders, that the leaders can't agree, or that they deceive the people and sell out their interests to the whites.

In order not to be dogmatic in a direction opposite to the one criticized, we should point out that the principle of internal struggle in the lower classes is only one social force among many. Other forces are making for solidarity in the lower classes. In both of the two problems raised—the solidarity *between* lower class whites and Negroes and the internal solidarity *within* the Negro group—there can be any degree of solidarity, ranging between utter mistrust and complete trustfulness. The scientific problem is to find out and measure the degree of solidarity and the social forces determining it, not just to assume that solidarity will come about "naturally" and "inevitably." The factors making for solidarity are both irrational and rational. Among the irrational factors are tradition, fear, charisma, brute

[a] See Chapter 32.

force, propaganda. The main rational factors are economic and social security and a planned program of civic education.

While visiting in Southern Negro communities, the writer was forced to the observation that often the most effective Negro leaders—those with a rational balance of courage and restraint, a realistic understanding of the power situation, and an unfailing loyalty to the Negro cause—were federal employees (for example, postal clerks), petty railway officials, or other persons with their economic basis outside the local white or Negro community and who had consequently a measure of economic security and some leisure time for thinking and studying. They were, unfortunately, few. Generally speaking, whenever the masses, in any part of the world, have permanently improved their social, economic, and political status through orderly organizations founded upon solidarity, these masses have not been a semi-illiterate proletariat, but have already achieved a measure of economic security and education. The vanguards of such mass reform movements have always belonged to the upper fringe of the lower classes concerned.

If this hypothesis is correct and if the lower classes have interests in common, the steady trend in this country toward improved educational facilities and toward widened social security for the masses of the people will work for increased solidarity between the lower class groups. But changes in this direction will probably be slow, both because of some general factors impeding broad democratic mass movements in America[a] and—in our special problems, solidarity between whites and Negroes— because of the existence of caste.

In this connection we must not forget the influence of ideological forces. And we must guard against the common mistake of reducing them solely to secondary expressions of economic interests. Independent (that is, independent of the economic interests involved in the Negro problem) ideological forces of a liberal character are particularly strong in America because of the central and influential position of the American Creed in people's valuations.

It may be suggested as an hypothesis, already fairly well substantiated by research and by common observation, that those liberal ideological forces tend to create a tie between the problems of all disadvantaged groups in society, and that they work for solidarity between these groups. A study of opinions in the Negro problem will reveal, we believe, that persons who are inclined to favor measures to help the underdog generally, are also, and as a part of this attitude, usually inclined to give the Negro a lift. There is a correlation between political opinions in different issues,[b] which probably rests upon a basis of temperamental personality traits and has its

[a] See Chapter 33.
[b] For a discussion of the correlation of opinions in different issues, see Appendix 2, Section 1.

deeper roots in all the cultural influences working upon a personality. If this correlation is represented by a composite scale running from radicalism, through liberalism and conservatism, to reactionism, it is suggested that it will be found that all subordinate groups—Negroes, women, minorities in general, poor people, prisoners, and so forth—will find their interests more favored in political opinion as we move toward the left of the scale. This hypothesis of a system of opinion correlation will, however, have to be taken with a grain of salt, since this correlation is obviously far from complete.

In general, poor people are not radical and not even liberal, though to have such political opinions would often be in their interest. Liberalism is not characteristic of Negroes either, except, of course, that they take a radical position in the Negro problem. We must guard against a superficial bias (probably of Marxian origin) which makes us believe that the lower classes are naturally prepared to take a broad point of view and a friendly attitude toward all disadvantaged groups. A liberal outlook is much more likely to emerge among people in a somewhat secure social and economic situation and with a background of education. The problem for political liberalism—if, for example, we might be allowed to pose the problem in the practical, instead of the theoretical mode—appears to be first to lift the masses to security and education and then to work to make them liberal.

The South, compared to the other regions of America, has the least economic security, the lowest educational level, and is most conservative. The South's conservatism is manifested not only with respect to the Negro problem but also with respect to all the other important problems of the last decades—woman suffrage, trade unionism, labor legislation, social security reforms, penal reforms, civil liberties—and with respect to broad philosophical matters, such as the character of religious beliefs and practices. Even at present the South does not have a full spectrum of political opinions represented within its public discussion. There are relatively few liberals in the South and practically no radicals.[a]

The recent economic stagnation (which for the rural South has lasted much more than ten years), the flood of social reforms thrust upon the South by the federal government, and the fact that the rate of industrialization in the South is higher than in the rest of the nation, may well come to cause an upheaval in the South's entire opinion structure. The importance of this for the Negro problem may be considerable.[b]

6. THE MANIFOLDNESS AND THE UNITY OF THE NEGRO PROBLEM

The Negro problem has the manifoldness of human life. Like the women's problem, it touches every other social issue, or rather, it represents an angle of them all. A glance at the table of contents of this volume

[a] See Chapter 21, Section 5.
[b] See Chapter 21, Section 4.

shows that in our attempt to analyze the Negro problem we have not been able to avoid anything: race, culture, population, breadwinning, economic and social policy, law, crime, class, family, recreation, school, church, press, organizations, politics, attitudes.

The perplexities and manifoldness of the Negro problem have even increased considerably during the last generation. One reason is migration and industrialization. The Negro has left his seclusion. A much smaller portion of the Negro people of today lives in the static, rather inarticulate folk society of the old plantation economy. The Negro people have increasingly stepped into the midst of America's high-geared metropolitan life, and they have by their coming added to the complication of these already tremendously complicated communities. This mass movement of Negroes from farms to cities and from the South to the North has, contrary to expectation, kept up in bad times as in good, and is likely to continue.

Another and equally important reason why the Negro problem shows an increasing involvement with all sorts of other special problems is the fact that America, especially during the last ten years, has started to use the state as an instrument for induced social change. The New Deal has actually changed the whole configuration of the Negro problem. Particularly when looked upon from the practical and political viewpoints, the contrast between the present situation and the one prior to the New Deal is striking.

Until then the practical Negro problem involved civil rights, education, charity, and little more. Now it has widened, in pace with public policy in the new "welfare state," and involves housing, nutrition, medicine, education, relief and social security, wages and hours, working conditions, child and woman labor, and, lately, the armed forces and the war industries. The Negro's share may be meager in all this new state activity, but he has been given a share. He has been given a broader and more variegated front to defend and from which to push forward. This is the great import of the New Deal to the Negro. For almost the first time in the history of the nation the state has done something substantial in a social way without excluding the Negro.

In this situation it has sometimes appeared as if there were no longer a Negro problem distinct from all the other social problems in the United States. In popular periodicals, articles on the general Negro problem gave way to much more specific subjects during the 'thirties. Even on the theoretical level it has occurred to many that it was time to stop studying the Negro problem in itself. The younger generation of Negro intellectuals have become tired of all the talk about the Negro problem on which they were brought up, and which sometimes seemed to them so barren of real deliveries. They started to criticize the older generation of Negroes for their obsession with the Negro problem. In many ways this was a movement which could be considered as the continuation, during the 'thirties, of the "New Negro Movement" of the 'twenties.

We hear it said nowadays that there is no "race problem," but only a "class problem." The Negro sharecropper is alleged to be destitute not because of his color but because of his class position—and it is pointed out that there are white people who are equally poor. From a practical angle there is a point in this reasoning. But from a theoretical angle it contains escapism in new form.[a] It also draws too heavily on the idealistic Marxian doctrine of the "class struggle." And it tends to conceal the whole system of special deprivations visited upon the Negro only because he is not white. We find also that as soon as the Negro scholar, ideologist, or reformer leaves these general ideas about how the Negro should think, he finds himself discussing nothing but Negro rights, the Negro's share, injustices against Negroes, discrimination against Negroes, Negro interests—nothing, indeed, but the old familiar Negro problem, though in some new political relations. He is back again in the "race issue." And there is substantial reason for it.

The reason, of course, is that there is really a common tie and, therefore, a unity in all the special angles of the Negro problem. All these specific problems are only outcroppings of one fundamental complex of human valuations—that of American caste. This fundamental complex derives its emotional charge from the equally common race prejudice, from its manifestations in a general tendency toward discrimination, and from its political potentialities through its very inconsistency with the American Creed.

7. THE THEORY OF THE VICIOUS CIRCLE

A deeper reason for the unity of the Negro problem will be apparent when we now try to formulate our hypothesis concerning its dynamic causation. The mechanism that operates here is the "principle of cumulation," also commonly called the "vicious circle."[b] This principle has a much wider application in social relations. It is, or should be developed into, a main theoretical tool in studying social change.

Throughout this inquiry, we shall assume a general interdependence between all the factors in the Negro problem. White prejudice and discrimination keep the Negro low in standards of living, health, education, manners and morals. This, in its turn, gives support to white prejudice. White prejudice and Negro standards thus mutually "cause" each other. If things remain about as they are and have been, this means that the two

[a] See Chapter 38, Sections 5 to 7.
[b] See Appendix 3, "A Methodological Note on the Principle of Cumulation." We call the principle the "principle of cumulation" rather than "vicious circle" because it can work in an "upward" desirable direction as well as in a "downward" undesirable direction.

forces happen to balance each other. Such a static "accommodation" is, however, entirely accidental. If either of the factors changes, this will cause a change in the other factor, too, and start a process of interaction where the change in one factor will continuously be supported by the reaction of the other factor. The whole system will be moving in the direction of the primary change, but much further. This is what we mean by cumulative causation.

If, for example, we assume that for some reason white prejudice could be decreased and discrimination mitigated, this is likely to cause a rise in Negro standards, which may decrease white prejudice still a little more, which would again allow Negro standards to rise, and so on through mutual interaction. If, instead, discrimination should become intensified, we should see the vicious circle spiraling downward. The original change can as easily be a change of *Negro standards* upward or downward. The effects would, in a similar manner, run back and forth in the interlocking system of interdependent causation. In any case, the initial change would be supported by consecutive waves of back-effects from the reactions of the other factor.

The same principle holds true if we split one of our two variables into component factors. A rise in Negro employment, for instance, will raise family incomes, standards of nutrition, housing, and health, the possibilities of giving the Negro youth more education, and so forth, and all these effects of the initial change, will, in their turn, improve the Negroes' possibilities of getting employment and earning a living. The original push could have been on some other factor than employment, say, for example, an improvement of health or educational facilities for Negroes. Through action and interaction the whole system of the Negro's "status" would have been set in motion in the direction indicated by the first push. Much the same thing holds true of the development of white prejudice. Even assuming no changes in Negro standards, white prejudice can change, for example, as a result of an increased general knowledge about biology, eradicating some of the false beliefs among whites concerning Negro racial inferiority. If this is accomplished, it will in some degree censor the hostile and derogatory valuations which fortify the false beliefs, and education will then be able to fight racial beliefs with more success.

By this we have only wanted to give a hint of an explanatory scheme of dynamic causation which we are going to utilize throughout this inquiry. As pointed out in Appendix 3, and as we shall find in later chapters, the interrelations are in reality much more complicated than in our abstract illustrations, and there are all sorts of irregularities in the reaction of various factors. But the complications should not force us to give up our main hypothesis that a cumulative principle is working in social change. It is actually this hypothesis which gives a theoretical meaning to the Negro problem as a special phase of all other social problems in America. Behind the barrier of common discrimination, there is unity and close interrelation between the Negro's political power; his civil rights; his employment opportunities; his standards of housing, nutrition and clothing; his health, manners, and law observance; his ideals and ideologies. The unity is largely the result of cumulative causation binding them all together in a system and tying them to white discrimination. It is useful, therefore, to interpret all the separate factors from a central vantage point—the point of view of the Negro problem.

Another corollary from our hypothesis is practical. In the field of Negro politics any push upward directed on any one of those factors—if our main hypothesis is correct—moves all other factors in the same direction and has, through them, a cumulative effect upon general Negro status. An upward trend of Negro status in general can be effected by any number of measures, rather independent of where the initial push is localized. By the process of cumulation it will be transferred through the whole system.

But, as in the field of economic anti-depression policy, it matters a lot how the measures are proportioned and applied. The directing and proportioning of the measures is the task of social engineering. This engineering should be based on a knowledge of how all the factors are actually interrelated: what effect a primary change upon each factor will have on all other factors. It can be generally stated, however, that it is likely that *a rational policy will never work by changing only one factor*, least of all if attempted suddenly and with great force. In most cases that would either throw the system entirely out of gear or else prove to be a wasteful expenditure of effort which could reach much further by being spread strategically over various factors in the system and over a period of time.

This—and the impracticability of getting political support for a great and sudden change of just one factor—is the rational refutation of so-called panaceas. Panaceas are now generally repudiated in the literature on the Negro problem, though usually without much rational motivation. There still exists, however, another theoretical idea which is similar to the idea of panacea: the idea that there is *one* predominant factor, a "basic factor." Usually the so-called "economic factor" is assumed to be this basic factor. A vague conception of economic determinism has, in fact, come to color most of the modern writings on the Negro problem far outside the Marxist school. Such a view has unwarrantedly acquired the prestige of being a particularly "hard-boiled" scientific approach.

As we look upon the problem of dynamic social causation, this approach is unrealistic and narrow. We do not, of course, deny that the conditions under which Negroes are allowed to earn a living are tremendously important for their welfare. But these conditions are closely interrelated to all other conditions of Negro life. When studying the variegated causes of discrimination in the labor market, it is, indeed, difficult to perceive what precisely is meant by "the economic factor." The Negro's legal and political status and all the causes behind this, considerations by whites of social prestige, and everything else in the Negro problem belong to the causation of discrimination in the labor market, in exactly the same way as the Negro's low economic status is influential in keeping down his health, his educational level, his political power, and his status in other respects. Neither from a theoretical point of view—in seeking to explain the Negro's caste status in American society—nor from a practical point of view—in attempting to assign the strategic points which can most effectively be attacked in order to raise his status—is there any reason, or, indeed, any possibility of singling out "the economic factor" as basic. In an interdependent system of dynamic causation there is no "primary cause" but everything is cause *to* everything else.

If this theoretical approach is bound to do away in the practical sphere with all panaceas, it is, on the other hand, equally bound to encourage the reformer. The principle of cumulation—in so far as it holds true—promises final effects of greater magnitude than the efforts and costs of the reforms themselves. The low status of the Negro is tremendously wasteful all around—the low educational standard causes low earnings and health deficiencies, for example. The cumulatively magnified effect of a push upward on any one of the relevant factors is, in one sense, a demonstration and a measure of the earlier existing waste. In the end, the cost of raising the status of the Negro may not involve any "real costs" at all for society, but instead may result in great "social gains" and actual savings for society. A movement downward will, for the same reason, increase "social waste" out of proportion to the original saving involved in the push downward of one factor or another.

These dynamic concepts of "social waste," "social gain," and "real costs" are mental tools originated in the practical man's workshop. To give them a clearer meaning—which implies expressing also the underlying social value premises—and to measure them in quantitative terms represents from a practical viewpoint a main task of social science. Fulfilling that task in a truly comprehensive way is a stage of dynamic social theory still to be reached but definitely within vision.

8. A Theory of Democracy

The factors working on the white side in our system of dynamic causation were brought together under the heading "race prejudice." For our present purpose, it is defined as discrimination by whites against Negroes. One viewpoint on race prejudice needs to be presented at this point, chiefly because of its close relation to our hypothesis of cumulative causation.

The chemists talk about "irreversible processes," meaning a trait of a chemical process to go in one direction with ease but, for all practical purposes, to be unchangeable back to its original state (as when a house burns down). When we observe race prejudice as it appears in American daily life, it is difficult to avoid the reflection that it seems so much easier to increase than to decrease race prejudice. One is reminded of the old saying that nineteen fresh apples do not make a single rotten apple fresh, but that one rotten apple rapidly turns the fresh ones rotten. When we come to consider the various causative factors underlying race prejudice—economic competition; urges and fears for social status; and sexual drives, fears, jealousies, and inhibitions—this view will come to be understandable. It is a common observation that the white Northerner who settles in the South will rapidly take on the stronger race prejudice of the new surroundings; while the Southerner going North is likely to keep his race prejudice rather unchanged and perhaps even to communicate it to those he meets. The Northerner in the South will find the whole community intent upon his conforming to local patterns. The Southerner in the North will not meet such concerted action, but will feel, rather, that others are adjusting toward him wherever he goes. If the local hotel in a New England town has accommodated a few Negro guests without much worry one way or the other, the appearance one evening of a single white guest who makes an angry protest against it might permanently change the policy of the hotel.

If we assume that a decrease in race prejudice is desirable—on grounds of the value premise of the American Creed and of the mechanism of cumulative wastage just discussed—such a general tendency, inherent in the psychology of race prejudice, would be likely to force us to a pessimistic outlook. One would expect a constant tendency toward increased race prejudice, and the interlocking causation with the several factors on the Negro side would be expected to reinforce the movement. Aside from all valuations, the question must be raised: Why is race prejudice, in spite of this tendency to continued intensification which we have observed, nevertheless, on the whole not increasing but decreasing?

This question is, in fact, only a special variant of the enigma of philosophers for several thousands of years: the problem of Good and Evil in the world. One is reminded of that cynical but wise old man, Thomas Hobbes, who proved rather conclusively that, while any person's actual possibilities to improve the lot of his fellow creatures amounted to almost nothing, everyone's opportunity to do damage was always immense. The wisest and most virtuous man will hardly leave a print in the sand behind him, meant Hobbes, but an imbecile crank can set fire to a whole town. Why is the world, then, not steadily and rapidly deteriorating, but rather, at least over long periods, progressing? Hobbes raised this question. His answer was, as we know: the State, *Leviathan*. Our own tentative answer to the more specific but still overwhelmingly general question we have raised above will have something in common with that of the post-Elizabethan materialist and hedonist, but it will have its stress placed differently, as we shall subsequently see.

Two principal points will be made by way of a preliminary and hypothetical answer, as they influence greatly our general approach to the Negro problem. The first point is the American Creed, the relation of which to the Negro problem will become apparent as our inquiry proceeds. The Creed of progress, liberty, equality, and humanitarianism is not so uninfluential on everyday life as might sometimes appear.

The second point is the existence in society of huge institutional structures like the church, the school, the university, the foundation, the trade union, the association generally, and, of course, the state. It is true, as we shall find, that these institutional structures in their operation show an accommodation to local and temporary interests and prejudices—they could not be expected to do otherwise as they are made up of individuals with all their local and temporary characteristics. As institutions they are, however, devoted to certain broad ideals. It is in these institutions that the American Creed has its instruments: it plays upon them as on mighty organs. In adhering to these ideals, the institutions show a pertinacity, matched only by their great flexibility in local and temporary accommodation.

The school, in every community, is likely to be a degree more broadminded than local opinion. So is the sermon in church. The national labor assembly is prone to decide slightly above the prejudice of the median member. Legislation will, on the whole, be more equitable than the legislators are themselves as private individuals. When the man in the street acts through his orderly collective bodies, he acts more as an American, as a Christian, and as a humanitarian than if he were acting independently. He thus shapes social controls which are going to condition even himself.

Through these huge institutional structures, a constant pressure is brought to bear on race prejudice, counteracting the natural tendency for it to spread and become more intense. The same people are acting in the institutions as when manifesting personal prejudice. But they obey different moral valuations on different planes of life. In their institutions they have invested more than their everyday ideas which parallel their actual behavior. They have placed in them their ideals of how the world rightly ought to be. The ideals thereby gain fortifications of power and influence in society. This is a theory of social self-healing that applies to the type of society we call democracy.

Part II

RACE

CHAPTER 4

RACIAL BELIEFS

1. BIOLOGY AND MORAL EQUALITARIANISM

Few problems are more heavily loaded with political valuations and, consequently, wishful thinking than the controversy concerning the relative importance of nature and nurture. Opinions on this question signify more than anything else where each of us stands on the scale between extreme conservatism and radicalism. The liberal is inclined to believe that it is the occasion that makes the thief, while the conservative is likely to hold that the thief is likely to create the occasion. The individual and society can, therefore, according to the liberal, be purposively improved through education and social reform. The conservative, on the other hand, thinks that it is "human nature" and not its environment which, on the whole, makes individuals and society what they are. He sees therein a reason and a justification for his skepticism in regard to reforms.[a]

The liberalism of the Enlightenment which later developed such strong roots in this country tended to minimize the differences between individuals and peoples as to inborn capacities and aptitudes. To Locke, the newborn child was a *tabula rasa* upon which the "sensations"—that is, in modern language, the entirety of life experiences—made their imprint. Environment was thus made supreme. As to the inborn capacities and inclinations, men were, on the whole, supposed to be similar; apparent differences were of cultural origin, and men could be changed through education. This was the basis for the philosophical radicalism and the rationalistic optimism which French, and also some English, writers developed during the eighteenth century. Individual differences in mental traits were sometimes recognized. But so far as groups of people were concerned—social classes, nations, and what was beginning to be called "races"—equality of natural endowments was the general assumption.

It should be remembered that these philosophers were primarily reacting

[a] The generalization expressed in this paragraph has its exceptions. Though it is hardly possible to be a true biological determinist and yet a political liberal, it is possible to be an environmentalist and yet a conservative. The easiest rationalization in the latter case is to perceive of the environment as very tough against politically induced changes. William Sumner and his theory of mores is the classical American example of such a marriage between a radical environmentalism and an extreme political conservatism. (See Appendix 2.)

against that particular extension of feudalism into modern times which was represented in their home countries by the theories of mercantilism and the social order of estates and privileges. Dissimilar minority races were not much in the foreground of their political thinking, but social classes were. The upper classes in England and France, as everywhere else, developed a vague popular theory that the lower classes, urban proletariat, and rural peasantry were less well endowed by nature.ª It was against this convenient belief that the radical philosophers of the Enlightenment reacted. Their main interest was, however, not naturalistic but moralistic. Equality in "natural rights of man," rather than equality in natural endowments, was central in their thought.

The former equality was, of course, not necessarily made dependent upon the latter. Even if some people were weaker, the moral philosophers did not think that this was a sound reason for giving them less protection in their natural rights. But the radical and optimistic belief in the possibility of social improvement, which they also held, did require the environmentalistic assumption. Thus a strong tendency toward a belief in natural equality became associated with the doctrine of moral equality in the philosophy of the Enlightenment.

When transferred to America the equality doctrine became even more bent toward the moral sphere. There are several reasons for this. Originally the doctrine had a function in the political disputes with the mother country, England. These disputes concerned rights and not natural endowments. The strong impact of religion in America following the Revolution is another reason. A third reason was the actual presence within America of a different "race."

There is thus no doubt that the declaration that all men were "created equal" and, therefore, endowed with natural rights has to be understood in the moral sense that they were born equal as to human rights. Nevertheless, the moral equality doctrine carried with it, even in America, a tendency toward a belief in biological equalitarianism. Among the educated classes, race prejudice was low in the generation around the Revolution. This is easily seen even by a superficial survey of the American political literature of the age.

2. The Ideological Clash in America

When the Negro was first enslaved, his subjugation was not justified in terms of his biological inferiority. Prior to the influences of the Enlightenment, human servitude was taken as a much more unquestioned element in the existing order of economic classes and social estates, since this way

ª It should be noted that just as a biological rationalization was then and is now invoked to justify class, so arguments concerning the "social order" have always been employed to justify Negro slavery and, later, color caste. (See Chapter 28, Section 5.)

of thinking was taken over from feudal and post-feudal Europe. The historical literature on this early period also records that the imported Negroes—and the captured Indians—originally were kept in much the same status as the white indentured servants.[1] When later the Negroes gradually were pushed down into chattel slavery while the white servants were allowed to work off their bond, the need was felt, in this Christian country, for some kind of justification above mere economic expediency and the might of the strong. The arguments called forth by this need were, however, for a time not biological in character, although they later easily merged into the dogma of natural inequality. The arguments were broadly these: that the Negro was a heathen and a barbarian, an outcast among the peoples of the earth, a descendant of Noah's son Ham, cursed by God himself and doomed to be a servant forever on account of an ancient sin.[2]

The ideas of the American Revolution added their influence to those of some early Christian thinkers and preachers, particularly among the Quakers, in deprecating these arguments. And they gave an entirely new vision of society as it is and as it ought to be. This vision was dominated by a radically equalitarian political morality and could not possibly include slavery as a social institution. The philosophical ideas of man's natural rights merged with the Golden Rule of Christianity, "Do unto others as you would have them do unto you."

How it actually looked in the minds of the enlightened slaveholders who played a prominent role in the Revolution is well known, since they were under the urge to intellectual clarity of their age, and in pamphlets, speeches, and letters frequently discussed the troubles of their conscience. Most of them saw clearly the inconsistency between American democracy and Negro slavery. To these men slavery was an "abominable crime," a "wicked cause," a "supreme misfortune," an "inherited evil," a "cancer in the body politic." Jefferson himself made several attacks on the institution of slavery, and some of them were politically nearly successful. Later in his life (1821) he wrote in his autobiography:

> . . . it was found that the public mind would not bear the proposition [of gradual emancipation], nor will it bear it even at this day. Yet the day is not far distant when it must bear it, or worse will follow. Nothing is more certainly written in the book of fate than that these people are to be free.[3]

It was among Washington's first wishes ". . . to see a plan adopted for the abolition of it [slavery]; but there is only one proper and effectual mode by which it can be accomplished and that is by legislative authority. . . ."[4] In this period the main American religious denominations also went on record to denounce slavery.

Even in terms of economic usefulness slavery seemed for a time to be a decaying institution. Slave prices were falling. Public opinion also was definitely in motion. In the North where it was most unprofitable, slavery was abolished in state after state during this revolutionary era. Also Southern states took certain legislative steps against slave trade and relaxed their slave codes and their laws on manumission. It is probable that the majority of Americans considered Negro slavery to be doomed. But in the South the slaves represented an enormous investment to the slave owners, and the agricultural economy was largely founded on slave labor. When the Constitution was written, slavery had to be taken as an economic and political fact. It is, however, indicative of the moral situation in America at that time that the words "slave" and "slavery" were avoided. "Somehow," reflects Kelly Miller, "the fathers and fashioners of this basic document of liberty hoped that the reprobated institution would in time pass away when there should be no verbal survival as a memorial of its previous existence."[5]

In the first two decades of the nineteenth century, the Abolitionist movement was as strong in the South as in the North, if not stronger. A most fateful economic factor had, however, entered into the historical development, and it profoundly changed the complexion of the issue. Several inventions in the process of cotton manufacture, and principally Eli Whitney's invention of the cotton gin in 1794, transformed Southern agriculture. Increased cotton production and its profitability gave impetus to a southward and westward migration from the old liberal Upper South, and raised the prices of slaves which had previously been declining.[6]

In explaining the ensuing ideological reaction in the South we must not forget, however, that the revolutionary movement, typified by the Declaration of Independence, represented a considerable over-exertion of American liberalism generally, and that by the time of the writing of the Constitution a reaction was on its way. In Europe after the Napoleonic Wars a reaction set in, visible in all countries and in all fields of culture. The North released itself rather completely from the influences of the European reaction. The South, on the contrary, imbibed it and continued on an accentuated political and cultural reaction even when the European movement had turned again toward liberalism. Around the 1830's, the pro-slavery sentiment in the South began to stiffen. During the three decades leading up to the Civil War, an elaborate ideology developed in defense of slavery. This Southern ideology was contrary to the democratic creed of the Old Virginia statesmen of the American Revolution.

The pro-slavery theory of the *ante-bellum* South is basic to certain ideas, attitudes, and policies prevalent in all fields of human relations even at the present time.[a] The central theme in the Southern theory is the moral and political dictum that slavery did not violate the "higher law," that it was

---

[a] See Chapters 10, 20, 24 and 28.

condoned by the Bible and by the "laws of nature," and that "free society," in contrast, was a violation of those laws.

More and more boldly as the conflict drew nearer, churchmen, writers, and statesmen of the South came out against the principle of equality as formulated in the Declaration of Independence. This principle came to be ridiculed as a set of empty generalities and meaningless abstractions. Common experience and everyday observation showed that it was wrong. Indeed, it was "exuberantly false, and arborescently fallacious":

> Is it not palpably nearer the truth to say that no man was ever born free and no two men were ever born equal, than to say that all men are born free and equal? . . . Man is born to subjection. . . . The proclivity of the natural man is to domineer or to be subservient.[7]

Here we should recall that Jefferson and his contemporaries, when they said that men were equal, had meant it primarily in the moral sense that they should have equal rights, the weaker not less than the stronger.[8] This was fundamentally what the South denied. So far as the Negroes were concerned, the South departed radically from the American Creed. Lincoln later made the matter plain when he observed that one section of the country thought slavery was *right* while the other held it to be *wrong*.

The militant Northern Abolitionists strongly pressed the view that human slavery was an offense against the fundamental moral law. Their spiritual ground was puritan Christianity and the revolutionary philosophy of human rights. They campaigned widely, but most Northerners—sensing the dynamite in the issue and not liking too well the few Negroes they had with them in the North—kept aloof. In the South the break from the unmodified American Creed continued and widened. Free discussion was effectively cut off at least after 1840. Around this central moral conflict a whole complex of economic and political conflicts between the North and the South grew up.[a] The most bloody contest in history before the First World War became inevitable. De Tocqueville's forecast that the abolition of slavery would not mean the end of the Negro problem came true. It is with the American nation today, and it is not likely to be settled tomorrow.

It should be observed that in the pro-slavery thinking of the *ante-bellum* South, the Southerners stuck to the American Creed *as far as whites were concerned*; in fact, they argued that slavery was necessary in order to establish equality and liberty for the whites. In the precarious ideological situation—where the South wanted to defend a political and civic institution of inequality which showed increasingly great prospects for new land exploitation and commercial profit, but where they also wanted to retain the democratic creed of the nation—*the race doctrine of biological inequality*

---

[a] The role of the Negro and slavery as causative factors for the War will be commented upon in Chapter 20.

between whites and Negroes offered the most convenient solution.[9] The logic forcing the static and conservative ideology of the South to base itself partly on a belief in natural inequality is parallel but opposite to the tendency of the original philosophy of Enlightenment in Europe and the American Revolution to evolve a doctrine of natural equality in order to make room for progress and liberalism.[10]

3. THE IDEOLOGICAL COMPROMISE

After the War and Emancipation, the race dogma was retained in the South as necessary to justify the caste system which succeeded slavery as the social organization of Negro-white relations. In fact, it is probable that racial prejudice increased in the South at least up to the end of Reconstruction and probably until the beginning of the twentieth century.[11]

The North never had cleansed its own record in its dealing with the Negro even if it freed him and gave him permanent civil rights and the vote. In the North, however, race prejudice was never so deep and so widespread as in the South. During and after the Civil War it is probable that the North relaxed its prejudices even further. But Reconstruction was followed by the national compromise of the 1870's when the North allowed the South to have its own way with the Negroes in obvious contradiction to what a decade earlier had been declared to be the ideals of the victorious North and the polity of the nation. The North now also needed the race dogma to justify its course. As the North itself did not retreat from most of the Reconstruction legislation, and as the whole matter did not concern the average Northerner so much, the pressure on him was not hard, and the belief in racial inequality never became intense. But this period was, in this field, one of reaction in the North, too.

The fact that the same rationalizations are used to defend slavery and caste is one of the connecting links between the two social institutions. In the South the connection is psychologically direct. Even today the average white Southerner really uses the race dogma to defend not only the present caste situation but also *ante-bellum* slavery and, consequently, the righteousness of the Southern cause in the Civil War. This psychological unity of defense is one strong reason, among others, why the generally advanced assertion is correct that the slavery tradition is a tremendous impediment in the way of improvement of the Negro's lot. The caste system has inherited the defense ideology of slavery.

The partial exclusion of the Negro from American democracy, however, has in no way dethroned the American Creed. This faith actually became strengthened by the victorious War which saved the Union and stopped the Southerners from publicly denouncing the cherished national principles that all men are born equal and have inalienable civil rights. The question can be asked: What do the millions of white people in the South and in the North actually think when, year after year, on the national holidays dedicated to the service of the democratic ideals, they read, recite, and listen to the Declaration of Independence and the Constitution? Do they or do they not include Negroes among "all men"? The same question is raised when we observe how, in newspaper editorials and public speeches, unqualified general statements are made asserting the principles and the fact of American democracy. Our tentative answer is this: In solemn moments, Americans try to forget about the Negroes as about other worries. If this is not possible they think in vague and irrational terms; in these terms the idea of the Negroes' biological inferiority is a nearly necessary rationalization.

The dogma of racial inequality may, in a sense, be regarded as a strange fruit of the Enlightenment. The fateful word *race* itself is actually not yet two hundred years old. The biological ideology had to be utilized as an intellectual explanation of, and a moral apology for, slavery in a society which went out emphatically to invoke as its highest principles the ideals of the inalienable rights of all men to freedom and equality of opportunity. It was born out of the conflict between an old harshly nonequalitarian institution—which was not, or perhaps in a short time could not be, erased—and the new shining faith in human liberty and democracy. Another accomplishment of early rationalistic Enlightenment had laid the theoretical basis for the racial defense of slavery; the recognition of *Homo sapiens* as only a species of the animal world and the emerging study of the human body and mind as biological phenomena. Until this philosophical basis was laid, racialism was not an intellectual possibility.

The influences from the American Creed thus had, and still have, a double-direction. On the one hand, the equalitarian Creed operates directly to suppress the dogma of the Negro's racial inferiority and to make people's thoughts more and more "independent of race, creed or color," as the American slogan runs. On the other hand, it indirectly calls forth the same dogma to justify a blatant exception to the Creed. The race dogma is nearly the only way out for a people so moralistically equalitarian, if it is not prepared to live up to its faith. A nation less fervently committed to democracy could, probably, live happily in a caste system with a somewhat less intensive belief in the biological inferiority of the subordinate group. *The need for race prejudice is, from this point of view, a need for defense on the part of the Americans against their own national Creed, against their own most cherished ideals.* And race prejudice is, in this sense, a function of equalitarianism. The former is a perversion of the latter.[12]

4. REFLECTIONS IN SCIENCE

This split in the American soul has been, and still is, reflected in scientific thought and in the literature on the Negro race and its characteristics.

Thomas Jefferson, the author of the Declaration of Independence and the supreme exponent of early American liberalism, in his famous *Notes on Virginia* (1781-1782) deals with the Negro problem in a chapter on "The Administration of Justice and the Description of the Laws." He posits his ideas about race as an argument for emancipating the slaves, educating them, and assisting them to settle in Africa:

> Deep-rooted prejudices entertained by the whites; ten thousand recollections, by the blacks, of the injuries they have sustained; new provocations; the real distinctions which nature has made; and many other circumstances, will divide us into parties, and produce convulsions, which will probably never end but in the extermination of the one or the other race.[13]

He goes on to enumerate the "real distinctions" between Negroes and whites and gives a fairly complete list of them as they were seen by liberal people of his time: color, hair form, secretion, less physiological need of sleep but sleepiness in work, lack of reasoning power, lack of depth in emotion, poverty of imagination and so on. In all these respects he is inclined to believe that "it is not their condition, then, but nature, which has produced the distinction." But he is cautious in tone, has his attention upon the fact that popular opinions are prejudiced, and points to the possibility that further scientific studies may, or may not, verify his conjectures.[14]

This guarded treatment of the subject marks a high point in the early history of the literature on Negro racial characteristics. In critical sense and in the reservation for the results of further research, it was not surpassed by white writers until recent decades. As the Civil War drew nearer, intellectuals were increasingly mobilized to serve the Southern cause and to satisfy the Southern needs for rationalization. After Reconstruction their theories were taken over by the whole nation. Biology and ethnology were increasingly supplanting theology and history in providing justification for slavery and, later, caste. Even the friends of the Negroes assumed great racial differences, even if, out of charity, they avoided elaborating on them. The numerous enemies of the Negro left a whole crop of pseudo-scientific writings in the libraries, emphasizing racial differences. Robert W. Shufeldt's book, *America's Greatest Problem: the Negro*[15] which had considerable influence for a time—illustrating the inferiority argument by a picture of a Negro lad between two monkeys and filled with an imposing mass of presumed evidences for Negro inferiority—is a late example of this literature at its worst.[16]

Without much change this situation continued into the twentieth century. At this time the heavily prejudiced position of science on the race problem was, however, beginning to be undermined. Professor Franz Boas and a whole school of anthropologists had already come out against these arguments for racial differences based on the primitive people's lack of culture.[17] The outlines of a radically environmentalistic sociology were being drawn by W. G. Sumner, W. I. Thomas and C. H. Cooley. The early research on intelligence pronounced that there were considerable racial differences but it had already encountered some doubts as to validity.[a] Improved techniques in the fields of anatomy and anthropometry had begun to disprove earlier statements on Negro physical traits.[b]

The last two or three decades have seen a veritable revolution in scientific thought on the racial characteristics of the Negro. This revolution has actually a much wider scope: it embraces not only the whole race issue even outside the Negro problem, but the fundamental assumptions on the nature-nurture question. The social sciences in America, and particularly sociology, anthropology, and psychology,[18] have gone through a conspicuous development, increasingly giving the preponderance to environment instead of to heredity.

In order to retain a proper perspective on this scientific revolution, we have to recall that American social science is not many decades old. The biological sciences and medicine, firmly entrenched much earlier in American universities, had not, and have not yet, the same close ideological ties to the American Creed. They have been associated in America, as in the rest of the world, with conservative and even reactionary ideologies.[19] Under their long hegemony, there has been a tendency to assume biological causation without question, and to accept social explanations only under the duress of a siege of irresistible evidence. In political questions, this tendency favored a do-nothing policy. This tendency also, in the main, for a century and more, determined people's attitudes toward the racial traits of the Negro. In the years around the First World War, it exploded in a cascade of scientific and popular writings [20] with a strong racialistic bias, rationalizing

[a] Cooley challenged Galton's hereditary explanation of racial genius in 1897. (Charles H. Cooley, "Genius, Fame and the Comparison of Races," *Annals of the American Academy of Political and Social Science* [May, 1897], pp. 317-358); see Chapter 6, Section 3.

[b] Several scientists, for example, had criticized much of the early research on brain and skull differences. One of the most notorious of the exposés was that of Robert B. Bean by Franklin P. Mall. Bean was a Southern student of Mall's in the latter's laboratory at Johns Hopkins. In an elaborate study of Negro skulls and brains, he attempted to show that the skulls were smaller than the skulls of white men, and that the brains were less convoluted and otherwise deficient. After Bean published his findings (Robert B. Bean, "Some Racial Peculiarities of the Negro Brain," *American Journal of Anatomy* [September, 1906], pp. 27-432), Mall repeated the measurements on many of the same specimens and found that Bean had completely distorted his measurements and conclusions. (Franklin P. Mall, "On Several Anatomical Characters of the Human Brain, Said to Vary According to Race and Sex, With Especial Reference to the Weight of the Frontal Lobe," *American Journal of Anatomy* [February, 1909], pp. 1-32). Bean's sample, too, was grossly inadequate; it consisted of 103 Negroes and 49 whites in the Baltimore morgue who had been unclaimed at death.

the growing feeling in America against the "new" immigrants pouring into a country whose last frontier was now occupied and congregating in the big cities where they competed with American labor. In addition to the social friction they created, the idea that these newcomers represented an inferior stock provided much of the popular theory for the restrictive immigration legislation.[21]

The wave of racialism for a time swayed not only public opinion but also some psychologists who were measuring psychic traits, especially intelligence, and perhaps also some few representatives of related social sciences.[22] But the social sciences had now developed strength and were well on the way toward freeing themselves entirely from the old biologistic tendency. The social sciences received an impetus to their modern development by reacting against this biologistic onslaught. They fought for the theory of environmental causation. Their primary object of suspicion became more and more the old static entity, "human nature," and the belief that fundamental differences between economic, social, or racial groups were due to "nature."

From the vantage point of their present research front, the situation looks somewhat like this: a handful of social and biological scientists over the last fifty years have gradually forced informed people to give up some of the more blatant of our biological errors. But there must be still other countless errors of the same sort that no living man can yet detect, because of the fog within which our type of Western culture envelops us. Cultural influences have set up the assumptions about the mind, the body, and the universe with which we begin; pose the questions we ask; influence the facts we seek; determine the interpretation we give these facts; and direct our reaction to these interpretations and conclusions.

Social research has thus become militantly critical. It goes from discovery to discovery by challenging this basic assumption in various areas of life. It is constantly disproving inherent differences and explaining apparent ones in cultural and social terms. By inventing and applying ingenious specialized research methods, the popular race dogma is being victoriously pursued into every corner and effectively exposed as fallacious or at least unsubstantiated. So this research becomes truly revolutionary in the spirit of the cherished American tradition. A contrast is apparent not only in comparison with earlier stands of American social science but also with contemporary scientific trends in other countries. The democratic ones have, on the whole, followed a similar course, but America has been leading. It is interesting to observe how on this point the radical tendency in American social research of today dominates even the work and writings of scientists who feel and pronounce their own political inclination to be conservative.

What has happened is in line with the great traditions of the American

Creed, the principles of which are themselves, actually, piecemeal becoming substantiated by research and elaborated into scientific theory. American social scientists might—in a natural effort to defend their objectivity—dislike this characterization, but to the outsider it is a simple and obvious fact that the social sciences in America at present have definitely a spirit in many respects reminiscent of eighteenth century Enlightenment. The ordinary man's ideas have not, however, kept up to those of the scientist. Hardly anywhere else or in any other issue is there—in spite of intensive and laudable efforts to popularize the new results of research—such a wide gap between scientific thought and popular belief. At least potentially these ideas have, however, a much greater importance in America than could be assumed upon casual observation and for the reason that the ordinary American has a most honored place in his heart for equalitarianism.

This trend in social sciences to discount earlier notions of great differences in "nature" between the advantaged and the disadvantaged groups (rich-poor, men-women, whites-Negroes) runs parallel to another equally conspicuous trend in American political ideology since the First World War: an increased interest and belief in social reforms. The latter trend broke through in the course of the Great Depression following the crisis of 1929; and it materialized in the New Deal, whose principles, even if not methods, are now widely accepted. We have already stressed the strategic importance for political liberalism and radicalism of the modern social science point of view on the basic problem of nurture *versus* nature. The scientific trend in non-democratic countries during the same period—and specifically the sway of racialism over German universities and research centers under the Nazi regime—provides a contrast which vividly illustrates our thesis.

As always, we can, of course, assume that basically both the scientific trend and the political development in a civilization are functions of a larger synchronized development of social ideology. A suspicion is, then, natural that fundamentally the scientific trend in America is a rationalization of changed political valuations. This trend has, however, had its course during a remarkable improvement of observation and measurement techniques and has been determined by real efforts to criticize research methods and the manner in which scientific inferences are made from research data. It has, to a large extent, been running against expectation and, we may assume, wishes. This is the general reason why, in spite of the natural suspicion, we can feel confident that the scientific trend is, on the whole, a definite approach toward objective truth.

5. THE POSITION OF THE NEGRO WRITERS

As creators of original scientific theories and as independent research workers in the field of social science, as in other fields, the Negroes came late and are even now rather exceptional. This is a consequence of the

American caste system. But for a much longer time they have had gifted essayists well in touch with the trends in social sciences. From the beginning, Negro writers took the stand that the American dogma of racial inequality was a scientific fake.[23] The late Kelly Miller, particularly, knew how to present the Negro's case effectively. He had well digested the anthropological criticism against the argument that the Negroes had never produced a culture of their own in Africa and knew how to turn it around:

> Because any particular race or class has not yet been caught up by the current of the world movement is no adequate reason to conclude that it must forever fall without the reach of its onward flow. If history teaches any clear lesson, it is that civilization is communicable to the tougher and hardier breeds of men, whose physical stamina can endure the awful stress of transmission. To damn a people to everlasting inferiority because of deficiency in historical distinction shows the same faultiness of logic as the assumption that what never has been never can be. The application of this test a thousand years ago would have placed under the ban of reproach all of the vigorous and virile nations of modern times.[24]

and:

> ... history plays havoc with the vainglorious boasting of national and racial conceit. Where are the Babylonians, the Assyrians and the Egyptians, who once lorded it over the earth? In the historical recessional of races they are "one with Nineveh and Tyre." Expeditions must be sent from some distant continent to unearth the glorious monuments of their ancestors from beneath the very feet of their degenerate descendants. The lordly Greeks who ruled the world through the achievements of the mind, who gave the world Homer and Socrates and Phidias in the heyday of their glory, have so sunken in the scale of excellence that, to use the language of Macaulay, "their people have degenerated into timid slaves and their language into a barbarous jargon." On the other hand, the barbarians who, Aristotle tells us, could not count beyond ten fingers in his day subsequently produced Kant and Shakespeare and Newton.[25]

Miller reminds his white countrymen:

> Our own country has not escaped the odium of intellectual inferiority. The generation has scarcely passed away in whose ears used to ring the standing sneer, "Who reads an American book?" It was in the day of Thomas Jefferson that a learned European declared: "America has not produced one good poet, one able mathematician, one man of genius in a single art or science." In response to this charge Jefferson enters an eloquent special plea. He says: "When we shall have existed as a people as long as the Greeks did before they produced a Homer, the Romans, a Virgil, the French, a Racine, the English, a Shakespeare and Milton, should this reproach be still true, we will inquire from what unfriendly cause it has proceeded." How analogous to this is the reproach which you [Thomas Dixon, Jr.] and Mr. Watson, treading the track of Thomas Nelson Page, and those of his school of thought, now hurl against the Negro race? The response of Jefferson defending the American colonies from the reproach of innate inferiority will apply with

augmented emphasis to ward off similar charges against the despised and rejected Negro.[26]

To the Southerners particularly he gave the following rejoinder:

The white people of the South claim, or rather boast of, a race prepotency and inheritance as great as that of any breed of men in the world. But they clearly fail to show like attainment.[27]

and added maliciously:

Has it ever occurred to you that the people of New England blood, who have done and are doing most to make the white race great and glorious in this land, are the most reticent about extravagant claims to everlasting superiority? You protest too much. Your loud pretensions, backed up by such exclamatory outburst of passion, make upon the reflecting mind the impression that you entertain a sneaking suspicion of their validity.[28]

This is heated polemics but not without its point. On the central issue his best formulated argument is probably contained in the following sentences:

The Negro has never, during the whole course of history, been surrounded by those influences which tend to strengthen and develop the mind. To expect the Negroes of Georgia to produce a great general like Napoleon when they are not even allowed to carry arms, or to deride them for not producing scholars like those of the Renaissance when a few years ago they were forbidden the use of letters, verges closely upon the outer rim of absurdity. Do you look for great Negro statesmen in States where black men are not allowed to vote?[29]

Concerning the physical disabilities of the Negro, he was full of scorn:

Do you recall the school of pro-slavery scientists who demonstrated beyond doubt that the Negro's skull was too thick to comprehend the substance of Aryan knowledge? Have you not read in the now discredited scientific books of that period with what triumphant acclaim it was shown that the shape and size of the Negro's skull, facial angle, and cephalic configuration rendered him forever impervious to the white man's civilization? But all enlightened minds are now as ashamed of that doctrine as they are of the one-time dogma that the Negro had no soul.[30]

If at the time when he was writing, he could have seen the modern development of intelligence research, on which we shall comment in a later chapter, he would have had still more arrows for his bow.

Miller has been quoted at some length here because his attitude is typical of the thinking of the intellectual Negroes on this issue for several decades,[31] in fact, from the first time the Negro people had a group of individuals trained to independent scholarly thinking. These early Negro intellectuals were in all certainty just as much driven by their rationalization interests as their white colleagues. Only their interest went in the opposite direction. In the development of intelligence research it is apparent that Negroes and members of other minority groups always had a tendency to find environmental explanations for differences in intelligence performance, while the "American" scientists and, particularly, Southerners and other Americans who for one reason or other felt tender toward the Southern cause, for a long time labored under the bias of expecting to find innate differences.

From one point of view it is, of course, merely an historical accident that modern research has tended to confirm the Negroes' view and not the whites'. The Negro writers constantly have proceeded upon the assumption, later formulated by Du Bois in *Black Reconstruction*: ". . . that the Negro in America and in general is an average and ordinary human being, who under given environment develops like other human beings. . . ."[32] This assumption is now, but was not a couple of decades ago, also the assumption of white writers.[33] Negro writings from around the turn of the century, therefore, sound so much more modern than white writings. It is mainly this historical accident which explains why, for example, Du Bois' study of the Philadelphia Negro community,[34] published in the 'nineties, stands out even today as a most valuable contribution, while white authors like H. W. Odum and C. C. Brigham have been compelled—and have had the scientific integrity and personal courage—to retreat from writings of earlier decades even though they were published after Du Bois' study.[35] The white authors have changed while the Negro authors can stand by their guns. It is also apparent, when going through the literature on the Negro, that the whole tone, the "degree of friendliness" in viewpoints and conclusions, has been modified immensely in favor of the Negro since the beginning of the 'twenties.[36] This trend is, of course, intimately related to the general trend in social sciences, referred to above, and to the still broader political and social development in the American nation.

The Negro intellectuals' resistance to the white race dogma has been widely popularized among the Negro people through the Negro press, the Negro school and the Negro pulpit. As it corresponds closely to Negro interests, it will now be found to emerge as a popular belief in all Negro communities in America, except the backward ones. It may be assumed that formerly the Negroes more often took over white beliefs as a matter of accommodation.

The spread of the same conclusions from modern research has been much slower among whites, which is also natural, as they do not coincide with their interest in defending the caste order, and in any case, do not have the same relevance to their own personal problems of adjustment. One most important result is, however, that *it is now becoming difficult for even popular writers to express other views than the ones of racial equalitarianism and still retain intellectual respect*. This inhibition works also on the journalists, even in the South and even outside of the important circle of Southern white liberals. The final result of this change might, in time, be considerable. Research and education are bolstering the American Creed in its influence toward greater equalitarianism.

6. THE RACIAL BELIEFS OF THE UNSOPHISTICATED

Our characterization of the race dogma as a reaction against the equalitarian Creed of revolutionary America is a schematization too simple to be exact unless reservations are added. Undoubtedly the low regard for the Negro people before the eighteenth century contained intellectual elements which later could have been recognized as a racial theory in disguise. The division of mankind into whites, blacks, and yellows stretches back to ancient civilization. A loose idea that barbarism is something inherent in certain peoples is equally old. On the other hand, the masses of white Americans even today do not always, when they refer to the inferiority of the Negro race, think clearly in straight biological terms.

The race dogma developed gradually. The older Biblical and sociopolitical arguments in defense of slavery retained in the South much of their force long beyond the Civil War. Under the duress of the ideological need of justification for Negro slavery, they were even for a time becoming increasingly elaborated. Their decline during recent decades is probably a result of the secularization and urbanization of the American people, which in these respects, as in so many others, represents a continuation of the main trend begun by the revolutionary ideological impulses of the eighteenth century. In this development, the biological inferiority dogma threatens to become the lone surviving ideological support of color caste in America.

In trying to understand how ordinary white people came to believe in the Negro's biological inferiority, we must observe that there was a shift from theological to biological thinking after the eighteenth century. As soon as the idea was spread that man belongs to the biological universe, the conclusion that the Negro was *biologically* inferior was natural to the unsophisticated white man. It is obvious to the ordinary unsophisticated white man, from his everyday experience, that the Negro is inferior. *And inferior the Negro really is;* so he shows up even under scientific study. He is, on the average, poorer; his body is more often deformed; his health is more precarious and his mortality rate higher; his intelligence performance, manners, and morals are lower. The *correct* observation that the Negro is inferior was tied up to the *correct* belief that man belongs to the biological universe, and, by twisting logic, the *incorrect* deduction was made that the inferiority is biological in nature.

Race is a comparatively simple idea which easily becomes applied to certain outward signs of "social visibility," such as physiognomy. Explanations in terms of environment, on the contrary, tax knowledge and imagination heavily. It is difficult for the ordinary man to envisage clearly how such factors as malnutrition, bad housing, and lack of schooling actually deform the body and the soul of people. The ordinary white man cannot be expected to be aware of such subtle influences as the denial of certain outlets for ambitions, social disparagement, cultural isolation, and the early conditioning of the Negro child's mind by the caste situation, as factors molding the Negro's personality and behavior. The white man is, therefore, speaking in good faith when he says that he sincerely believes that the Negro is racially inferior, not merely because he has an interest in this belief, but simply because he has seen it. He "knows" it.

Tradition strengthens this honest faith. The factors of environment were, to the ordinary white man, still less of a concrete reality one hundred years ago when the racial dogma began to crystallize. Originally the imported Negro slaves had hardly a trace of Western culture. The tremendous cultural difference between whites and Negroes was maintained [a] and, perhaps, relatively increased by the Negroes being kept, first, in slavery and, later, in a subordinate caste, while American white culture changed apace. By both institutions the Negroes' acculturation was hampered and steered in certain directions. The Negroes, moreover, showed obvious differences in physical appearance.

From the beginning these two concomitant differences—the physical and the cultural—must have been associated in the minds of white people. "When color differences coincide with differences in cultural levels, then color becomes symbolic and each individual is automatically classified by the racial uniform he wears."[37] Darker color, woolly hair, and other conspicuous physical Negro characteristics became steadily associated with servile status, backward culture, low intelligence performance and lack of morals. All unfavorable reactions to Negroes—which for social if not for biological reasons, are relatively much more numerous than favorable reactions—became thus easily attributed to *every* Negro as a Negro, that is, to the *race* and to the individual only secondarily as a member of the race. Whites categorize Negroes. As has been observed also in other racial contacts, visible characteristics have a power to overshadow all other characteristics and to create an illusion of a greater similarity between the individuals of the out-race and a greater difference from the in-race than is actually warranted.[38]

This last factor is the more important as the unsophisticated mind is much more "theoretical"—in the popular meaning of being bent upon simple, abstract, clear-cut generalizations—than the scientifically trained mind.[39] This works in favor of the race dogma. To conceive that apparent differences in capacities and aptitudes could be cultural in origin means a deferment of judgment that is foreign to popular thinking. It requires

[a] When we say that cultural differences were maintained, we do not refer one way or the other to the retention of African culture.

difficult and complicated thinking about a multitude of mutually dependent variables, thinking which does not easily break into the lazy formalism of unintellectual people.

We should not be understood, however, to assume that the simpler concept of race is clear in the popular mind. From the beginning, as is apparent from the literature through the decades, environmental factors to some extent, have been taken into account. But they are discounted, and they are applied in a loose way—partly under the influence of vulgarized pre-Darwinian and Darwinian evolutionism—to the race rather than to the individual. The Negro race is said to be several hundreds or thousands of years behind the white man in "development." Culture is then assumed to be an accumulated mass of memories *in the race*, transmitted through the genes. A definite biological ceiling is usually provided: the mind of the Negro race cannot be improved beyond a given level. This odd theory is repeated through more than a century of literature: it is phrased as an excuse by the Negro's friends and as an accusation by his enemies. The present writer has met it everywhere in contemporary white America.

Closely related to this popular theory is the historical and cultural demonstration of Negro inferiority already referred to. It is constantly pointed out as a proof of his racial backwardness that in Africa the Negro was never able to achieve a culture of his own. Descriptions of hideous conditions in Africa have belonged to this popular theory from the beginning. Civilization is alleged to be the accomplishment of the white race; the Negro, particularly, is without a share in it. As typical not only of long literature but, what is here important, of the actual beliefs among ordinary white people in America, two quotations from a fairly recent exponent of the theory may be given:

> To begin with, the black peoples have no historic pasts. Never having evolved civilizations of their own, they are practically devoid of that accumulated mass of beliefs, thoughts, and experiences which render Asiatics so impenetrable and so hostile to white influences. . . . Left to himself, he [the Negro] remained a savage, and in the past his only quickening has been where brown men have imposed their ideas and altered his blood. The originating powers of the European and the Asiatic are not in him.[40]
>
> The black race has never shown real constructive power. It has never built up a native civilization. Such progress as certain negro groups have made has been due to external pressure and has never long outlived that pressure's removal, for the negro, when left to himself, as in Haiti and Liberia, rapidly reverts to his ancestral ways. The negro is a facile, even eager, imitator; but there he stops. He adopts, but he does not adapt, assimilate, and give forth creatively again. . . .
>
> Unless, then, every lesson of history is to be disregarded, we must conclude that black Africa is unable to stand alone. The black man's numbers may increase prodigiously and acquire alien veneers, but the black man's nature will not change.[41]

Without any doubt there is also in the white man's concept of the Negro "race" an irrational element which cannot be grasped in terms of either biological or cultural differences. It is like the concept "unclean" in primitive religion. It is invoked by the metaphor "blood" when describing ancestry. The ordinary man means something particular but beyond secular and rational understanding when he refers to "blood." The one who has got the smallest drop of "Negro blood" is as one who is smitten by a hideous disease. It does not help if he is good and honest, educated and intelligent, a good worker, an excellent citizen and an agreeable fellow. Inside him are hidden some unknown and dangerous potentialities, something which will sooner or later crop up. This totally irrational, actually magical, belief is implied in the system of specific taboos to be analyzed in Part VII. White intellectuals, particularly in the South, have often, in attempting to clarify to the writer their own attitude toward taboos, referred to this irrational element and described it in the terms utilized above. They sometimes talked of it as an "instinct," but were well aware that they could not grasp it by this too sober physio-psychological analogy.

In this magical sphere of the white man's mind, the Negro is inferior, totally independent of rational proofs or disproofs. And he is inferior in a deep and mystical sense. *The "reality" of his inferiority is the white man's own indubitable sensing of it, and that feeling applies to every single Negro.* This is a manifestation of the most primitive form of religion. There is fear of the unknown in this feeling, which is "superstition" in the literal sense of this old word. Fear is only increased by the difficulties in expressing it in rational language and explaining it in such a way that it makes sense. So the Negro becomes a "contrast conception." He is "the opposite race"— an inner enemy, "antithesis of character and properties of the white man."[42] His name is the antonym of white. As the color white is associated with everything good, with Christ and the angels, with heaven, fairness, cleanliness, virtue, intelligence, courage, and progress, so black has, through the ages, carried associations with all that is bad and low: black stands for dirt, sin, and the devil.[43] It becomes understandable and "natural" on a deeper magical plane of reasoning that the Negro is believed to be stupid, immoral, diseased, lazy, incompetent, and *dangerous*—dangerous to the white man's virtue and social order.

The Negro is segregated, and one deep idea behind segregation is that of quarantining what is evil, shameful, and feared in society.[a] When one speaks about "Americans" or "Southerners," the Negro is not counted in. When the "public" is invited, he is not expected. Like the devil and all his synonyms and satellites, he is enticing at the same time that he is

---

[a] To illustrate this point and to exemplify how racial beliefs develop in an individual, we have included as footnote 44 to this chapter one of the clearest analyses of his own former prejudices by a Southerner to be found in the literature.

disgusting. Like them he is also humorous in a way, and it is possible to pity him. As the devil with his goat's foot is earth-bound in a sinister sense, so the Negro is also more part of "nature" than the white man. The old theologians of the South meant something specific when they equipped the Negro with a disproportionate amount of original sin just as Christian theologians generally characterize the devil as a fallen angel. Behind all these associations is the heritage of magic and primitive religion which we carry from prehistoric time and which is always with us in metaphorical meanings attached to the words we use.

The stereotyped opinions of the Negro express themselves in institutionalized behavior, in jokes and stories, and in fiction. Fiction as a sounding board for, and as a magnifier of, popular prejudices is an object for research which deserves much more attention. The printed word has an easily detected magical import and authority for the unintellectual mind.[a] It is generalized. People want to see their favorite opinions set forth and elaborated in print.[45] One of the sources for studying the stereotyped opinions on the Negro is, therefore, fiction.[46]

7. BELIEFS WITH A PURPOSE

The low plane of living, the cultural isolation, and all the resulting bodily, intellectual, and moral disabilities and distortions of the average Negro make it natural for the ordinary white man not only to see that the Negro is inferior but also to believe honestly that the Negro's inferiority is inborn. This belief means, of course, that all attempts to improve the Negro by education, health reforms, or merely by giving him his rights as a worker and a citizen must seem to be less promising of success than they otherwise would be. The Negro is judged to be fundamentally incorrigible and he is, therefore, kept in a slum existence which, in its turn, leaves the imprint upon his body and soul which makes it natural for the white man to believe in his inferiority.[b] This is a vicious circle; it is, indeed, one of the chief examples of cumulative causation.[c] From a practical point of view, it signifies that one of the ways, in the long run, to raise the white man's estimate of the Negro is to improve the Negro's status and, thereby, his qualities. It means also, however, that one of the chief hindrances to improving the Negro is the white man's firm belief in his inferiority. ". . . what the greater part of white America merely *thinks* about us is an influ-

[a] Every lawyer knows from experience that by presenting a printed blank of a drafted contract, he can much more easily get anyone to sign it than if it was written for the occasion.

[b] ". . . the haughty American Nation . . . makes the negro clean its boots and then proves the moral and physical inferiority of the negro by the fact that he is a shoeblack." (George Bernard Shaw, *Man and Superman* [1916; first edition, 1903], p. xviii.)

[c] See Chapter 3, Section 7.

ential factor in making our *actual condition* what it is," complains James Weldon Johnson.[47]

The Negro's situation being what it is and the unsophisticated white man's mind working as it does, the white man can honestly think and say that his beliefs are founded upon close personal experience and hard facts. He is not deliberately deceiving himself; but the beliefs are opportunistic. The typical white individual does not fabricate his theory for a purpose. The ordinary white American is an upright and honest fellow who tries to think straight and wants to be just to everybody. He does not consciously concoct his prejudices for a purpose.

But unscrupulous demagogues do it all the time with great profit. Many other white individuals will occasionally find it to their private interests to stretch their biased beliefs a little more in a direction unfavorable to the Negro. Much of this might happen just on the margin of what is consciously acknowledged. Practically no white people are sufficiently incited by self-interest to scrutinize their beliefs critically. And so *through the generations, strengthened by tradition and community consensus, a public opinion among whites is formulated which is plainly opportunistic in the interest of the majority group.* The individual in the group can remain confident in his moral and intellectual integrity. He "sees" the facts for himself. Tradition and consensus seem to him to be additional intellectual evidence and moral sanction for what he already believes. They relieve him of any duty he otherwise might have felt to criticize seriously his observations and inferences. The recognition that the racial beliefs thus have a social purpose opens up a perspective on the causal mechanism behind their formation and gives us a clue for the further study of their structure, to which we now proceed.

If white Americans can believe that Negro Americans belong to a lower biological species than they themselves, this provides a motivation for their doctrine that the white race should be kept pure and that amalgamation should, by all means, be prevented. The theory of the inborn inferiority of the Negro people is, accordingly, used as an argument for the anti-amalgamation doctrine. This doctrine, in its turn, has, as we have seen, a central position in the American system of color caste.[a] The belief in biological inferiority is thus another basic support, in addition to the no-social-equality, anti-amalgamation doctrine, of the system of segregation and discrimination. Whereas the anti-amalgamation doctrine has its main importance in the "social" field, the belief in the Negro's biological inferiority is basic to discrimination in all fields. White Americans have an interest in deprecating the Negro race in so far as they identify themselves with the prevailing system of color caste. They have such an interest, though in a lower degree, even if their only attachment to the caste order

[a] See Chapter 3, Section 2.

is that they do not stand up energetically as individuals and citizens to eradicate it.

We are not under any obligation, of course, to extend civil courtesies, equal justice, suffrage, and fair competition to animals, however much we love them. Kind treatment of animals is not a "right" of theirs but is rather construed as an obligation to our own humane feelings and to those of our equals. In so far as the Negro can be placed lower in the biological order than the white man and nearer to the animals, he is also, to an extent, kept outside the white man's social and moral order. The white man's entire system of discrimination is then in no need of moral defense. The Negro becomes deprived of the "natural rights of man," and will, instead, have his protection in the civil kindness toward inferior and dependent beings, which behooves a Christian society. He will be asked not to insist on "rights" but to pray for favors.

> . . . the thought of the older South—the sincere and passionate belief that somewhere between men and cattle, God created a *tertium quid*, and called it a Negro— a clownish, simple creature, at times even lovable within its limitations, but straitly foreordained to walk within the Veil. To be sure, behind the thought lurks the afterthought—some of them with favoring chance might become men, but in sheer self-defense we dare not let them, and we build about them walls so high, and hang between them and the light a veil so thick, that they shall not even think of breaking through.[48]

Another analogy may be found in the status of women and children.[*] They, too, were—in a considerable measure—wards of the adult males, particularly in the period when the race dogma was being built up. They did not enjoy "equal rights" but had to rely for their protection upon kindly considerations from their superiors. Their status was also partly explained and justified by biological inferiority or lack of maturity. The Negro can be classified as nearer the animal but still a man, although not a mature man. Unlike children, he can be assumed never to grow to full maturity. Not only the individual Negro but the Negro race as a whole can be said to be "undeveloped" and "childish."

The dominant interest in rationalizing and defending the caste system can be specified in the demand that the following statements shall be held true:

(1) The Negro people belongs to a separate race of mankind.
(2) The Negro race has an entirely different ancestry.
(3) The Negro race is inferior in as many capacities as possible.
(4) The Negro race has a place in the biological hierarchy somewhere between the white man and the anthropoids.
(5) The Negro race is so different both in ancestry and in characteristics

[*] See Appendix 5.

that all white peoples in America, in contradistinction to the Negroes, can be considered a homogeneous race.

(6) The individuals in the Negro race are comparatively similar to one another and, in any case, all of them are definitely more akin to one another than to any white man.

Our assumption is that the abstract scheme of opportunistic ideas, stated in the six points above, represents the ordinary white American's *ad hoc* theory on the Negro race. The assumption is based on the fact that the scheme closely corresponds to obvious needs for rationalization inherent in the American caste situation. Not only can the scheme be deduced from the rationalization needs, but it has been induced from our observations of opinions actually held among unsophisticated whites over the whole country. Such beliefs seem to have particular strength in the South and in other regions and groups where the Negro problem has a high salience. Their strength seems everywhere to stand in a close inverse relation to the individual white's level of education. Its relation to social class—*if standardized for education*—seems more doubtful. The white upper class person might feel a greater biological distance from the average Negro, but he has not the same need to emphasize the race dogma, since the social distance is so great and so secure. He will often be found both more willing to recognize individual Negroes as exceptions to the race dogma and more likely to classify poor whites as of an inferior stock, and, sometimes, "just as bad as" the average Negro. The lower classes of whites seem to be much more careful to keep the race dogma straight in both these respects.

In adhering to this biological rationalization, specified in the six points stated above, the white man meets certain difficulties. A factual difficulty to begin with is that individual Negroes and even larger groups of Negroes often, in spite of the handicaps they encounter, show themselves to be better than they ought to be according to the popular theory. A whole defense system serves to minimize this disturbance of the racial dogma, which insists that *all* Negroes are inferior. From one point of view, segregation of the Negro people fulfills a function in this defense system. It is, of course, not consciously devised for this purpose, and it serves other purposes as well, but this does not make its defense function less important. Segregation isolates in particular the middle and upper class Negroes,[a] and thus permits the ordinary white man in America to avoid meeting an educated Negro. The systematic tendency to leave the Negro out when discussing public affairs and to avoid mentioning anything about Negroes in the press except their crimes also serves this purpose.[b] The aggressive and derogatory attitude toward "uppity" Negroes and, in particular, the

[a] See Chapter 30, Section 2, and Chapter 32.
[b] See Chapter 2, and Chapter 30, Section 3.

tendency to relegate all educated Negroes to this group also belongs to the defense system.[a]

Since he has a psychological need to believe the popular theory of Negro racial inferiority, it is understandable why the ordinary white man is disinclined to hear about good qualities or achievements of Negroes. "The merits of Negro soldiers should not be too warmly praised, especially in the presence of Americans," reads one of the advices which the French Military Mission, stationed with the American Expeditionary Army during the First World War, circulated but later withdrew.[49] It should be added that white people who work to help the Negro people and to improve race relations see the strategic importance of this factor and direct their work toward spreading information about Negroes of quality among the whites.

Another difficulty has always been the mulatto.[b] White Americans want to keep biological distance from the out-race and will, therefore, be tempted to discount the proportion of mulattoes and believe that a greater part of the Negro people is pure bred than is warranted by the facts. A sort of collective guilt on the part of white people for the large-scale miscegenation, which has so apparently changed the racial character of the Negro people, enforces this interest.

The literature on the Negro problem strengthens this hypothesis. Only some exceptional authors, usually Negroes, gave more adequate estimates of the proportion of mixed breeds,[50] and it was left to Hrdlička and Herskovits in the late 'twenties to set this whole problem on a more scientific basis.[c] The under-enumeration of mulattoes by the census takers decade after decade and also, until recently, the rather uncritical utilization of this material, indicate a tendency toward bias. The observations of the present author have, practically without exception, indicated that the non-expert white population shows a systematic tendency grossly to underestimate the number of mulattoes in the Negro population.

It may, of course, be said against this assumption of a hidden purpose that one should not assume the ability of uninformed and untrained persons to distinguish a mulatto from a pure bred Negro. But the facts of historical and actual miscegenation are fairly well known, at least in the South, and are discussed with interest everywhere. And if a wrong estimate systematically goes in the same direction, there is reason to ask for a cause. It has also

[a] See Chapter 31. The term "uppity" is a Southern white man's term for all Negroes who try to rise, or have risen, out of the lower classes. Negroes use the term also, but are more inclined to substitute "biggity" for it.

[b] The term "mulatto" is, according to American custom, understood to include all Negroes of mixed ancestry, regardless of the degree of intermixture and the remoteness of its occurrence. The term includes in addition to "true" mulattoes also quadroons and octoroons and all other types of cross-breeds. In America they are all grouped with the Negro race. (See Chapter 5, Section 1.)

[c] See Chapter 5, Section 6.

been observed that the ordinary white American gets disturbed when encountering the new scientific estimates that the great majority of American Negroes are not of pure African descent. Similarly, the ordinary white American is disturbed when he hears that Negroes sometimes pass for white. He wants, and he must want, to keep biological distance.

But the mulatto is a disturbance to the popular race theory not only because of his numbers. The question is also raised: Is the mulatto a deteriorated or an improved Negro? In fact, there seems never to have been popular agreement among white Americans whether the mulatto is worse than the pure bred Negro, or whether he is better because of his partially white ancestry. The former belief should *per se* strengthen the anti-amalgamation doctrine, in fact, make adherence to it to the interest of the entire society. The second belief can serve a purpose of explaining away Negro accomplishments which are, with few exceptions, made by mulattoes and which then could be ascribed to the white blood.[51] Actually, I have often heard the same man use both arguments.

8. SPECIFIC RATIONALIZATION NEEDS

When analyzing the actual beliefs, we must take account of much more specific needs for rationalization. Specific beliefs seem to have specific rationalization purposes besides the general one of justifying the caste order as a whole. Practically every type of white-Negro relation, every type of discrimination behavior, every type of interracial policy, raises its own peculiar demands for justification. And practically every special Negro characteristic, actual or only presumed, opens the possibility of meeting one or more of these special demands.

The specific demands are embraced in the general one, in the same way as the caste order consists after all of the aggregate of a great number of specific discriminations and disabilities. Some of the beliefs are directly connected with a purpose of rationalizing a particular phase of the caste order. Others are only indirectly connected with such a specific purpose. The connection is sometimes obvious, as when a certain belief is regularly brought forward as a reason for a certain item of the caste order. Sometimes the connection is less apparent to the observer; we shall even have to expect that at times it will be hidden from both the consciousness of the believer and the superficial observation of the investigator. The following exemplifications in most cases indicate only those direct connections between beliefs and specific purposes which are more apparent. All the beliefs to be mentioned have been scientifically disproved, as we shall find in the next two chapters.

The beliefs that Negroes get sleepy when working with machines and that they, on the whole, lack mechanical aptitudes, serve a need for justification of their being kept out of industry. The beliefs of their general unreliability, their inborn lack of aptitude for sustained mental activity, and, particularly, their lower intelligence, help to justify this vocational segregation and to excuse the barriers against promotion of Negroes to skilled and supervisory positions. The beliefs that the Negro race is "childish," immature, undeveloped, servile, lacking in initiative, are used to justify the denial of full civic rights and suffrage to Negroes.

The Negro's presumed lower intelligence and the belief that the mind of the Negro cannot be improved beyond a given level have always been main arguments for discrimination in education, and, specifically, for directing Negro education toward developing his hands and not his brains. The beliefs that Negroes have a much smaller cranial capacity and lower brain weight, a less complicated brain structure, thicker skull bones, an earlier closing of the cranial sutures, have a function to explain and fortify the beliefs in the lesser development of the Negro's higher brain centers and, consequently, his lower intelligence and reasoning power.

The beliefs in the Negro's inborn laziness and thriftlessness, his happy-go-lucky nature, his lack of morals, his criminal tendencies, and so on, serve the purpose of easing the conscience of the good, upright white citizen when he thinks of the physical and moral slum conditions which are allowed in the Negro sections of all communities in America. They also rationalize the demand for housing segregation, and tend, on the whole, to picture the Negro as a menace to orderly society unless "kept in his place" by the caste system. The exaggerated beliefs in the Negro's higher susceptibility to various diseases have, in particular, the function to explain, in a way less compromising for the larger community, the high mortality rates and the bad health conditions among the Negro population. Until recently, these beliefs have discouraged all programs of health improvement among Negroes.

The belief in a peculiar "hircine odor" of Negroes, like similar beliefs concerning other races, touches a personal sphere and is useful to justify the denial of social intercourse and the use of public conveniences which would imply close contact, such as restaurants, theaters and public conveyances. It is remarkable that it does not hinder the utilization of Negroes in even the most intimate household work and personal services.

There are many popular beliefs deprecating the mulatto: that they are more criminally disposed even than Negroes in general; that they tend to be sterile; that they—having parents of two distinct races—are not harmoniously proportioned, but have a trait of one parent side by side with a trait of the other parent, paired in such a way that the two cannot function together properly; that they are more susceptible to tuberculosis; that, because Negroes have relatively long, narrow heads, Negro women, with narrow pelvises, and their mulatto offspring are endangered when they bear children of white men whose heads are rounder, and so on.

These beliefs are all of a nature to discourage miscegenation and to keep up biological distance even in regard to cross-breeds. The assertion, particularly common among Southerners, that there are infallible signs to detect everyone with the slightest amount of Negro blood, which is so easy for the observer to disprove by experiment, is a reassuring belief with a similar function.

The belief that practically all Negro women lack virtue and sexual morals bolsters up a collective bad conscience for the many generations of miscegenation. At the same time, it is, occasionally, a wishful expression of sexual appetite on the part of white men. The belief in the strong sexual urge and the superior sexual skill and capacity of Negro women (the "tigress" myth) has more obviously this latter function. The belief that Negro males have extraordinarily large genitalia is to be taken as an expression of a similar sexual envy and, at the same time, as part of the social control devices to aid in preventing intercourse between Negro males and white females.

There are also popular beliefs which are friendly and actually ascribe some sort of superiority to the Negro: for example, that he is more gifted in music, the arts, dancing, and acting than white people; that he is better in handling animals or, sometimes, children; that he is loyal and reliable as a servant (often the opposite is, however, asserted); that he is, on the whole, a more happy and mentally balanced human being; that he has more emotional warmth; that he can take sorrows and disappointments more easily; that he is more religious in his nature. All such favorable beliefs seem to have this in common, that they do not raise any question concerning the advisability or righteousness of keeping the Negro in his place in the caste order. They do not react against the major need for justification. They rather make it natural that he shall remain subordinate.

The list of beliefs with specific purposes could be made much longer. The underlying hypothesis is this, that in analyzing the popular beliefs, we have to work as a detective reconstructing the solution of a crime from scattered evidence. For both the student of popular beliefs on the Negro and the detective, the guide to the explanation is given in the question: To whose good? Beliefs are opportune; they are in the service of interests. It is these general and specific rationalization needs which give the beliefs their pertinacity. They give to the stereotypes their emotional load, and their "value" to the people who hold to them.[52]

9. Rectifying Beliefs

The rationalization needs do not work in an intellectual vacuum. They must have raw material to shape into the desired form. This material consists of white people's experiences of Negroes, how they behave and what they are, from his point of view. We have already observed that the ordinary white man's actual observations of average Negroes in their present inferior status make most of his beliefs natural and reasonable to him. The dependent Negro's attempts to accommodate to the wishes and expectations of the dominant white group facilitate this tendency. This all refers to the South. In the North, white people may have few personal experiences of Negroes, but they take over the myths, legends, and stereotypes that are existent in their culture.

Assuming as our *value premise* that we want to reduce the bias in white people's racial beliefs concerning Negroes,[a] our first practical conclusion is that we can effect this result to a degree by actually improving Negro status, Negro behavior, Negro characteristics. The impediment in the way of this strategy is, of course, that white beliefs, directly and indirectly, are active forces in keeping the Negroes low. We have already referred to this vicious circle.

A second line of strategy must be to rectify the ordinary white man's observations of Negro characteristics and inform him of the specific mistakes he is making in ascribing them wholesale to inborn racial traits. We may assume that, until the Negro people were studied scientifically—which in a strict sense of the term means not until recent decades—the raw material for beliefs which the average white man had at his disposal in the form of transmitted knowledge and personal observations placed only the most flexible limits to his opportunistic imagination. When, however, scientific knowledge is being spread among people and becomes absorbed by them through popular literature, press, radio, school, and church, this means that the beliefs are gradually placed under firmer control of reality. *People want to be rational, to be honest and well informed.* This want, if it is properly nourished, acts as a competing force among the opportunistic interests. To a degree the desire to be rational slowly overcomes the resistance of the desire to build false rationalizations. The resistance is, however, keen. Professor Young tells us:

> More than five hundred students of the author continued to rank the "American" as the superior "race" *after* completing a course on race relations! The "will to believe" . . . is strong![53]

The paramount practical importance of scientific research on the Negro is apparent for improvement of interracial relations. It is no accident that popular beliefs are biased heavily in a direction unfavorable to the Negro people—because they are steered by white people's needs for justification of the caste order. And it is, consequently, no accident either that scientific research, as it is progressing, is unmasking and rejecting these beliefs and giving rational reasons for beliefs more favorable to the Negroes. It is

[a] The desire to be rational, to know the truth, and to think straight is—as need not be elaborated upon—central in the American Creed, and is accepted by everybody in principle.

principally through encouraging research and through exposing the masses of people to its results that society can correct the false popular beliefs— by objectivizing the material out of which beliefs are fabricated. Seen in long-range perspective, a cautious optimism as to the results of gathering and spreading true information among the American people in racial matters seems warranted. The impression of the author is that the younger, and better educated, generation has, on the whole, somewhat fewer superstitious beliefs, and that, during the last decade at least, the racial beliefs have begun to be slowly rectified in the whole nation.

A third line of strategy is, naturally, to attack the valuations for the rationalization of which false beliefs are employed. This must mean strengthening the American Creed in its primary function of bending people's minds toward equalitarianism. Everything done to modify the caste order must diminish the moral conflict in the hearts of the Americans and thus decrease the defense needs which give emotional energy to the false racial beliefs. Indirectly, the valuations conflicting with the Creed also are becoming deflated as beliefs are becoming rectified. Valuations depend, to an extent, on the availability of functional beliefs in which they can be "lived out" and expressed.[a]

In this way the moral and the intellectual tasks of education are closely related. The interrelation extends even to our first line of strategy. Every improvement of the actual level of Negro character will increase the effectiveness of both the intellectual and moral education of white people in racial matters and *vice versa*. It is this mechanism of mutual and cumulative dynamic causation which explains the actual situation in theory and, at the same time, affords the basis for constructive practical policy.

10. THE STUDY OF BELIEFS

It should by this time be clear that *it is the popular beliefs, and they only, which enter directly into the causal mechanism of interracial relations.* The scientific *facts* of race and racial characteristics of the Negro people are only of secondary and indirect importance for the social problem under study in this volume. In themselves they are only virtual but not actual social facts. ". . . to understand race conflict we need fundamentally to understand *conflict* and not *race*." [54] We have concluded, further, from the actual power situation in America *that the beliefs held by white people rather than those held by Negroes are of primary importance.*[b]

The popular beliefs concerning the Negro race pose two different tasks for scientific research. One task is to criticize and refute the beliefs when they are wrong. American anthropology and psychology have, in recent decades, worked in this direction. It was, in fact, a necessary work to be

[a] See Appendix 1.
[b] See Introduction, Section 3

performed in order to free science itself from the load of inherited racial bias. Another task which, in the end, might turn out to be of equal practical importance and which has a more central theoretical relevance is *to study the racial beliefs themselves as social facts:* to record them carefully; to analyze their causation and explain their role in people's emotions, thoughts, and actions; their "function" in the caste order of American society.

Practically nothing has been done in a comprehensive and systematic compass to study the popular racial beliefs as social facts.[55] The racial beliefs have not even been recorded in a scientifically controlled manner. It is true that the beliefs can be perceived by an observer in America. They can also be recorded from the press and the popular literature. Selected fragments of evidence on various sectors of racial beliefs have, for a long time, been recorded in the scientific literature on the Negro problem.[56] Until a few decades ago, however, even this literature had more the character of folklore itself than of a study of folklore. Impressionistic information of this type permits discussion of the problem in a hypothetical manner. It allows the outlining of a problem for study but not its solution. The foregoing pages are written in this vein. In order to lay the factual basis for a truly scientific analysis, which is more than suggestive and conjectural in character, *beliefs must be observed and recorded in a systematic way under controlled research conditions.*[57]

In such studies the assumption should be that *people's beliefs are not necessarily consistent.* The utmost care should be taken not to press upon the informants a greater systematic order than there actually exists in their beliefs. For our assumption is, further, that *the very inconsistencies are illuminating* and of highest importance, particularly for the analytical approach to the deeper problem of the causation of the beliefs. Our hypothesis is that *the beliefs are opportunistic* and have the "function" to defend interests. The ordinary American's interests in the Negro problem should not be assumed to be simple and harmonious. They are, instead, complicated and conflicting. The conflicts are largely suppressed and only vaguely conscious.

The analysis of the racial beliefs will, therefore, reach down to the deeper-seated *conflicts of valuations.* As people's thought, speech, and behavior regularly are in the nature of moral compromises, this deeper analysis cannot be accomplished simply by recording and systematizing the actual beliefs themselves, but must endeavor—by comparing various beliefs and particularly their inconsistencies—to understand them by inferences as to their "function" in the individual's opportunistic world view.

In this deeper analysis—and only in this stage of the belief study—the scientific facts of race and racial traits become of importance. They have no direct importance *per se;* indirectly they are of importance in that they always, to an extent determined by exposure to education, form part of the raw material out of which actual beliefs are shaped. But in the analysis of beliefs they contribute *the objective norms in relation to which the degree of incompleteness and the degree and direction of falsification of the actual beliefs can be scientifically ascertained and measured.* As the distortion of truth in the beliefs is assumed to signify the opportunism of the latter, its measurement opens the door to *a scientific study of the fundamental conflicts in valuations.*[a]

The main conclusion from this conjectural discussion of racial beliefs is, therefore, that a set of most fascinating research problems of great theoretical and practical importance is waiting for investigation. Such studies will demonstrate to what extent the hypotheses developed above will hold true when tested against properly recorded research data.

[a] See Appendix 1, Section 3.

CHAPTER 5

RACE AND ANCESTRY

1. THE AMERICAN DEFINITION OF "NEGRO"

The "Negro race" is defined in America by the white people. It is defined in terms of parentage. Everybody having a *known* trace of Negro blood in his veins—no matter how far back it was acquired—is classified as a Negro. No amount of white ancestry, except one hundred per cent, will permit entrance to the white race. As miscegenation has largely been an affair between white men and Negro women, it is a fair approximation to characterize the Negro race in America as the descendants of Negro women and Negro or white men through the generations—minus the persons having "passed" from the Negro into the white group and their offspring.[a]

This definition of the Negro race in the United States is at variance with that held in the rest of the American continent. "In Latin America whoever is not black is white: in teutonic America whoever is not white is black."[1] This definition differs also from that of the British colonies and dominions, primarily South Africa, where the hybrids (half-castes) are considered as a group distinct from both whites and Negroes. Even in the United States many persons with a mixture of Indian and white blood are regarded as whites (for example, ex-Vice President Curtis and Will Rogers).

Legislation in this respect tends to conform to social usage, although often it is not so exclusive.[2] In some states one Negro grandparent defines a person as a Negro for legal purposes, in other states any Negro ancestor —no matter how far removed—is sufficient. In the Southern states definitions of who is a Negro are often conflicting. Since Reconstruction, there has been a tendency to broaden the definition. The Northeastern states generally have no definition of a Negro in law. These legal definitions and their changes and differences should not be taken too seriously, however. The more absolutistic "social" definition is, in most life situations, the decisive one.[3]

[a] This approximative summary neglects, of course, the Indian element in the ancestry of some Negroes, and the passing of part-Negro persons into the American Indian population. as well as the relatively few part-Negro offspring of white mothers.

This social definition of the Negro race, even if it does not change any-thing in the biological situation, increases the number of individuals actually included in the Negro race. It relegates a large number of individuals who look like white people, or almost so, to the Negro race and causes the Negro race to show a greater variability generally than it would show if the race were defined more narrowly in accordance with quantitative ethnological or biological criteria. "The farcical side of the color question in the States"—says Sir Harry H. Johnston—"is that at least a considerable proportion of the 'colored people' are almost white-skinned, and belong in the preponderance of their descent and in their mental associations to the white race." [4] In the American white population the so-called Nordic type, which is popularly assumed to be the opposite extreme from the black Negro, is a rare phenomenon. This statement is especially true after the "new" immigration from Southern and Eastern Europe and from the Near East. But even the "Old American stock" was preponderantly "non-Nordic." [a] There are, however, also American Negroes with the clearest of white skin, the bluest of blue eyes, and the long and narrow head which happens to be both a Negro and a "Nordic" trait.

The popular belief rationalizing the exclusive social definition of the Negro race is well expressed by the high priest of racialism in America, Madison Grant, in the following words:

> It must be borne in mind that the specializations which characterize the higher races are of relatively recent development, are highly unstable and when mixed with generalized or primitive characters tend to disappear. Whether we like to admit it or not, the result of the mixture of two races, in the long run, gives us a race revert-ing to the more ancient, generalized and lower type. The cross between a white man and an Indian is an Indian; the cross between a white man and a Negro is a Negro; the cross between a white man and a Hindu is a Hindu; and the cross between any of three European races and a Jew is a Jew. [5]

The fact that this belief is contrary to scientifically established truth does not diminish its force as a belief. An additional fortification in the sphere of beliefs is the "black baby myth," the popular theory that the slightest amount of Negro ancestry in an individual, who does not show even a trace of Negro characteristics, can cause a "throw-back" and that he—in a mating with a white individual—can become the parent of a black baby. [b]

There has been much speculation about how this very exclusive racial

[a] In making his famous study of the physical traits of "Old Americans" (practically all of English, Scotch, Irish, Dutch, French, or German ancestry), Hrdlička encountered great difficulty in finding persons of pure "Nordic" ancestry. (See Aleš Hrdlička, The Old Americans [1925], especially p. 5.)

Even in the population of Sweden, supposed to be the purest "Nordic" stock in existence, only some 15 per cent can be classified as "Nordics" on strict anthropometric grounds.

[b] Here two additional popular beliefs are added to our list in Chapter 4, Section 7, of beliefs with a special purpose. Concerning the black baby myth, see Section 7 of this chapter.

definition came to fasten itself on America. These speculations run all the way from an often asserted, particularly strong "racial instinct" in the "Anglo-Saxon race" to Embree's remark that "this custom grew up during slavery in order to increase the number of slaves, who constituted valuable property."[6] When attempting to account for the historical origin of the social definition of the Negro, the fact should be taken into account that mixed offspring were almost always the result of illegitimate sex relations in which, according to common law, the ordinary paternal lineage becomes broken. This question of how the very inclusive definition of the Negro race arose in American cultural history is not solved.

The definition of the "Negro race" is thus a social and conventional, not a biological concept. The social definition and not the biological facts actually determines the status of an individual and his place in interracial relations.[a] This also relieves us of the otherwise cumbersome duty of explaining exhaustively what we, in a scientific sense, could understand by "race" as an ethnological and biological entity.[7] In modern biological or ethnological research "race" as a scientific concept has lost sharpness of meaning, and the term is disappearing in sober writings. In something even remotely approaching its strict sense, it applies only to exceptionally isolated population groups, usually with a backward culture, which thus seems to be the concomitant of "racial purity."

Thus the scientific concept of race is *totally inapplicable at the very spots where we recognize "race problems."* It is being replaced by quantitative notions of the relative frequency of common ancestry and differentiating traits. "Racial purity" is thus relativized, and the hybridity of all peoples on earth is no longer minimized. Only the ignorant talk about the "Swedish" or "Scandinavian race," not to speak of the "Anglo-Saxon" or "German race." The "white American race" is gradually beginning to be merely a joke even among the populace, except in the South. The great variability of traits among individuals in every population group is becoming stressed, and the considerable amount of overlapping between all existing groups increasingly recognized. Besides the recognized differences among individuals in any one group, the differences among averages of groups tend to pale into insignificance.

The fundamental unity and similarity of mankind—above minor individual and group differentials—is becoming scientifically established. While formerly attention was fixed on the few obvious distinguishing characteristics, and while the assumption was always that there existed

---

[a] In recognition of this, we regularly substitute in this book the terms the "Negro people," the "Negro group" or the "Negro population" for the term, the "Negro race." When we sometimes, for the sake of convenience, talk about "race," "racial" characteristics, or "racial" relations, we should be understood to refer to the popular conception of the word, not the scientific one.

other differences in regard to less observable facts, scientists now stress the unity of mankind and are skeptical of differences until they are demonstrated. The old custom of describing population groups in terms of "types" —the so-called "Nordic" type, for instance—which were not true types in the statistical sense but idealized, or caricatured, types, is being discredited. Even the use of average or modal figures for measuring traits is beginning to be considered scientifically unsatisfactory. It is recognized that the representation of the traits of a group should be made in the form of curves of frequency distribution or scatter diagrams. An absolutistic metaphysical system of opportunistic beliefs is, in this way, gradually being demolished, and humble, relativistic scientific knowledge raised on its ruins. Qualitative conceptions are translated into quantitative ones. This is a common trend of modern scientific development.

The common belief that the races could be ordered as higher or lower in an evolutionary series, so that Negroids could be deemed more ape-like than Caucasoids, is entirely discredited. It is now commonly assumed by expert opinion that man—the species *Homo sapiens*—evolved only once, and that such average differences as now exist between men are due to living under different geographic conditions after having separated from the common place of origin. Independent of this hypothesis, which, of course, can hardly be checked, it is a fact that the Negro is no more akin to the apes than the white man is. Of the four most noticeable characteristics generally ascribed to the average or typical Negro—dark skin, broad nose, woolly hair, thick lips—only the first two make him slightly more similar to the apes. The white man's thin lips and straight hair are, on the other hand, much nearer to the traits of the apes.

When all this is said, when anticipating some later conclusions, it is recognized that the great majority of American Negroes have Caucasoid ancestry as well as Negroid, and when it is also recognized that modern psychological research has discounted the previously held opinions that there are great innate mental differentials between racially defined population groups, it still does not follow that the race concept is unimportant in the Negro problem, and that continued and intensified ethnological, biological, and psychological research on the American Negro people is unnecessary. In spite of all heterogeneity, the average white man's unmistakable observation is that *most Negroes in America have dark skin and woolly hair*, and he is, of course, right.

He is also right in ascribing the occurrence of these characteristics to African ancestry. His delineation of the Negro race might be ever so arbitrary and scientifically inaccurate; his ideas about concomitant mental and moral traits might be fantastic and untenable; but the fact is that "race" in *his* definition is the basis of the social caste system as it exists in America. Because of social visibility and of community knowledge of the parentage of individuals, "race" has tremendous cultural consequences. Under the exposure of science and education the white people in America might, in times to come, gradually rectify their opportunistic beliefs and even change their valuations to agree more with the national Creed of justice and equality of opportunity, so that these cultural consequences will be mitigated or obliterated. But for the time being, this is not so.

From one viewpoint the entire Negro problem in America hinges upon this social definition of "race." Should America wake up one morning with all knowledge about the African ancestry of part of its population and all memories of color caste absolutely forgotten and find all the outward physical characteristics of the Negro people eradicated, but no change in their mental or moral characteristics, nothing we know about this group and other population groups in America would lead us to believe that the American Negro would not rapidly come to fit in as a well-adjusted ordinary American. His poverty and general backwardness would mean a low starting point and cause a larger portion of this population group to remain in the lower social strata. But, having been relieved of the specific caste deprivations and hindrances, his relative preponderance in the disadvantaged classes would, from the beginning, decrease.

His earlier relative isolation in America through slavery and subordinate caste position and, perhaps, also a few faint traditions and customs kept from Africa, would, for a time, endow him with remnants of some peculiar cultural and personality traits. But they would be negligible even in the beginning—if, as we assume, they are unrelated through social visibility to his caste status—compared with the much more glaring and "non-American" peculiarities of various groups of recent immigrants.

But this is only a dream. The Negro has to be defined according to social usage, and his African ancestry and physical characteristics are fixed to his person much more ineffaceably than the yellow star is fixed to the Jew during the Nazi regime in Germany. With the social definition comes the whole stock of valuations, beliefs, and expectations in the two groups, causing and constituting the order of color caste in America.

This defines our problem in this and the next chapters. Our task is to describe the ancestry and the characteristics of this clearly delineated social group in America which is known under the somewhat incorrect term of the Negro "race."

2. AFRICAN ANCESTRY

Part of the ancestry of the American Negro people is African, and it is proper to start out from this line of parentage as it is the one from which their name and status are derived. Too, the fact must not be ignored that the major proportion of their ancestors, back to the time of the first contact between Negroes and whites, is African Negro.[8]

No official registration records were kept of the number of slaves imported, but compilations have been made on the basis of ship captains' reports and port records. The compilation which has been most extensively quoted has been that of Henry C. Carey, as modified by the United States Bureau of the Census. Carey estimated that a total of about 333,000 Negroes had been imported into the United States up to 1808, when federal law prohibited the slave trade.[9] Of this figure the Census Bureau said, "It is claimed, however, that this total is too small, and that a closer estimate would bring the number to 370,000 or even 400,000."[a] These slaves were brought from Africa and from the West Indies.[b]

TABLE 1

CAREY'S ESTIMATES OF THE NUMBER OF SLAVES IMPORTED
INTO THE UNITED STATES AT VARIOUS TIME PERIODS

Time Period	Number of Slaves Imported	Avrage Import Pe Year
Prior to 1715	30,000	—
1715–1750	90,000	2,500
1751–1760	35,000	3,500
1761–1770	74,500	7,400
1771–1790	34,000	1,700
1791–1808	70,000	3,900
Total	333,500	

Source: Henry C. Carey, The Slave Trade (1853), p. 18.

Some 50,000 more slaves were brought within the boundaries of the United States between 1790 and 1860 by annexations of territory—principally of Louisiana, Florida and Texas.[10] There are not even private records to guide us in estimating how many slaves were smuggled into the country between 1808 and 1860. Herskovits mentions the fantastically high figure of two and a half millions.[11] Dublin, after examining the data on smuggling and on births and deaths, concluded: "The unlawful trade in Negroes can at most account for the increase of less than one-half of 1 per

[a] U. S. Bureau of the Census, A Century of Population Growth in the United States: 1790-1900 (1909), p. 36. A figure of slightly below 400,000 slaves imported before 1808 seems reasonable in the light of the fact that the total Negro population was only 757,000 in 1790 and that this estimate allows for an import of 330,000 up to 1790.

[b] It is impossible to estimate how many came from Africa and how many from the West Indies, not only because no adequate records were kept, but also because there was the custom of bringing slaves intended for the United States first to the West Indies for a few years where they were made accustomed to their new life by the older West Indian slaves. It seems to be the consensus of opinion, however, that the proportion of West Indian slaves brought to the United States did not become significant until the nineteenth century.

cent a year. The rest of the increase, namely, about 2 per cent . . . represented the excess of births over deaths."[12] Dublin's proportion of smuggled Negroes is equivalent to an absolute figure of about 563,000,[a] but even this must be taken, as he says, to be a maximum figure. All estimates of the number of slaves smuggled in between 1808 and 1860 must be regarded in the light of the fact that apparently only 330,000 to 400,000 Negroes were imported during the entire period before 1808, when the slave trade was federally legal. Although it is possible that there were more slaves smuggled into the United States between 1808 and 1860 than there were legally imported in the two centuries before 1808, it is probable that the former figure was, at best, not much larger. A good many of the Negro slaves who were liberated after the Civil War were African-born. Whatever historical research ultimately determines these two figures to be, it is extremely likely that the total number of slaves imported into the United States before 1860, by whatever means, was less than a million.

The Negroid element in the ancestry of the present-day American Negro people, whether brought here directly or via the West Indies, had its original home in Africa and in the islands close to that continent.[13] The population of Africa was not homogeneous during the period of the slave trade.[14] In the region of the Sahara Desert and surrounding districts, there had been intermixtures between Negroids and Caucasoids for an unknown number of centuries. In the Southern portion of the Continent were the Bushmen and the Hottentots. In the section known as the "West Coast"—which is really only the central part of the African coast facing the Atlantic Ocean—lived the "true Negro."[b] The remainder of Central and Southern Africa was inhabited by various groups of Negroes who are often lumped together for convenience and called the "Bantu-speaking stocks."

These problems—from what regions and from what Negroid peoples in Africa the Negro ancestors of the present-day American Negroes came, and in what proportions during various periods of the slave trade the direct and indirect import to America was furnished—are still far from settled in a conclusive way. Since anthropometric evidence is difficult or impossible to bring to bear on these problems—due, among other things, to the later miscegenation of the various Negro groups in America—anthropologists have had to rely on the relatively meager historical evidence that can be discovered, scanty oral traditions in Africa, and cultural remnants in the

---

[a] The census reports an increase of 3,064,022 Negroes between 1810 and 1860. The application of Dublin's ratio (4 to 1) to this gives 612,804 Negroes who had to be accounted for by factors other than natural increase. Some 50,000 of these came into the country when new territory was annexed. This leaves 562,804 as a maximum figure for the number smuggled.

[b] This is a technical anthropological term, according to Herskovits, and should not be taken to imply a value judgment that the West Coast Negroes are "truer" Negroes than any others.

New World.[15] This evidence seems to indicate that the great majority of slaves brought directly to the United States came from the West Coast and hence belonged predominantly to that racial group known as the "true Negroes." A small proportion of the slaves came from other points in Central and South Africa and from Madagascar, some few also from East Africa and North Africa.[16] It would seem probable, however, that the proportion of slaves from parts of Africa other than the West Coast increased toward the end of the slave trade era, as it became increasingly difficult to get enough West Coast Negroes. But the proportion from other parts of Africa never became predominant. During the later period also, slaves were brought from the West Indies, and the Negro ancestors of these people came from all over Africa.[17]

Since Emancipation there has been an addition to the American Negro population through immigration. This has never been large, however. In 1940 there were only about 84,000 foreign-born Negroes in the entire United States. Three-fourths of these were from the West Indies and so may be presumed to have a significant proportion of white and Indian ancestry.[18] Only about 1,000 came from Africa, but this does not necessarily mean that they were of unmixed Negroid stock.[a] In common with most foreign-born groups, these foreign-born Negroes have a high birth rate,[19] and so tend to have an effect on the genetic composition of the American Negro people in slightly larger proportion than their small numbers would indicate. This effect is largely offset, however, by the facts that they are genetically much more like the native American Negro and that they are concentrated in Northern cities where the birth rate rapidly becomes depressed. Consequently, they will tend not to have such an important effect on the genetic composition of the American Negro population.

3. CHANGES IN PHYSICAL APPEARANCE

Even if we ignore the fact that there has been an admixture of white and Indian blood[b] into the American Negro population, there have been some changes in this population stock which make it different from those African tribes from which it has descended. Those who became slaves in America were only a selection of Africans, not a representative sample of them. They were probably made even less representative by the rigors of the displacement from Africa to America, which killed off a certain number of them. After the Negroes came to America, their biological composition was probably changed by differential reproductivity and possibly by mutations. There may also have been environmentally caused changes in

[a] While the total figures are from the 1940 Census, the proportions from the West Indies and from Africa are from the 1930 Census. The latter figures for 1940 are not yet available. It is probable that these proportions have not changed significantly from 1930 to 1940.

[b] Race mixture will be discussed in the following sections.

physical appearance which have no relation to genetic changes. About the effects of most of these causes of change, our knowledge is conjectural.

The slave trade itself could be assumed to follow a selective pattern. It has been part of the system of popular beliefs of white people in America to assume that the captured slaves were predominantly of low class origin, of a docile nature and with less intelligence and courage than the average in their homeland. Modern research tends to rectify the idea of the extreme submissiveness shown by the American Negro in slavery—a belief which became of particularly great importance as part of the Southern ideological armor before and immediately after the Civil War—and also to render probable that the slaves were a cross-section of the population from which they were drawn.[20] Several instances of African royalty and nobility are recorded among the slaves. The means by which Africans were made slaves cannot be used to argue for any unfavorable selection. Persons who had been captured in war, who had committed crimes, or who had failed to pay their debts, were sold to traders. Other slaves were those who were simply kidnapped by the white traders or by their black assistants. Warfare and kidnapping were nonselective. Punishment for crimes or debt was certainly socially selective, but there is no evidence that it was biologically selective. In any case, this source of slaves was of rather small importance.

Another source of selectivity—this one in the positive direction—might have been the rigors of the voyage from Africa to America. Available evidence is contradictory as to the extent of mortality during the period from the seizure of slaves in Africa to their ultimate sale in America. The old standard evidence pointed to a death rate as high as five-sixths of all Negroes captured. Some recent sources of information, however, mention a mortality as low as 13 per cent.[21] Even if the evidence were not contradictory as to the extent of mortality, the biologically selective nature of this mortality would not be definitely known—although it seems reasonable to suppose that the weakest died first. More definitely selective than the death rate was the unwillingness of the slavers to ship sick, disabled or weak persons. They were looking for the able-bodied to be sent as slaves.

Slavery as an institution must, in various ways, have had selective effects upon the genetic composition of the American Negro population. Plantation owners, particularly in the slave-breeding states in the Upper South during the first half of the nineteenth century, took measures of positive eugenics in controlling mating.[22] The slave breeders can generally be assumed to have favored the reproduction of docile and physically strong specimens of the slave population. The historical sources give frequent references to such practices. Other practices—such as the killing of slaves who attempted to escape and the selling of "bad niggers" down the river to the Deep South where life expectancy was shorter—may also have had some genetic effect.

It is also possible to speculate about the eugenic effects of such selective factors of reproduction as the bad health conditions and the high mortality rates in the freed Negro population up to the present time and of the looser sex mores in the Negro population. But in these respects, as in regard to all the other sources of selectiveness mentioned above, the prudent conclusion must be that our factual knowledge of each source is next to nothing, and that there is no possibility of weighing them together into a conclusion concerning their resultant effect upon the genetic composition of the Negro people. It is probable that we shall *never* come to know, in a scientific way, what these various selective factors have meant for the genetic composition of the American Negro people.

Mutations, as well as selection, may have made the American Negro different in some respects and in some degree from the corresponding population groups of the African continent. There is no knowledge as to the number or character of the genetic mutations that have occurred in the Negro population since coming to the Western Hemisphere, but there have undoubtedly been some. Since the cessation of the slave trade, the Africans, too, must have had mutations that did not get transmitted to the American Negro people because of isolation. About this we know nothing.

Such mutations must be distinguished from changes which appear to be "biological" but yet are not, or may not be, inherited by transmission of genes. In recent decades there have been many studies, usually not with specific reference to the Negro, indicating how such things as glandular activity, diet, and physical handling of infants may affect physical traits. Since Negroes experienced changes in climate, diet, and customary practices in care of infants, and perhaps even in glandular activity, when they made the drastic transition from Africa to America, their physical traits may be expected to have changed. The studies of physical changes of immigrants inaugurated by Boas [23] open the possibility that changes may occur even in such standard traits as head form. Since no anthropometric studies were made of Negroes before they were shipped to America, knowledge is lacking as to the specific character of the changes in physical form. But that there were some of this type, there is good reason to expect.[24] Changes in cultural conditions since the period of slave importation, and the more recent migration from the rural South to the urban North, may also have modified the Negro's physical appearance since he landed on American shores.[a]

The influences affecting the Negro's physical appearance are sometimes of an intentional type which do not need gross changes in environment to exert their effects. The Negro woman can, and does, lighten her face

---

[a] In this paragraph we are considering only the physical changes due to direct environmental influences. The psychic changes—which are probably more important—will be treated in Chapter 6.

with powder and bleaches. The Negro can—but does not, usually, because of the high cost—remodel the shape of his nose and lips. The changes which can be effected by this conscious type of modification of physical appearance are not numerous, but they may increase with advances in medical and surgical knowledge.

4. EARLY MISCEGENATION

The slaves imported from Africa by no means represented "pure Negro races." Of the original tribal stocks many had an admixture of Caucasoid genes from crosses with Mediterranean peoples. During the slave trade more white genes were added. The Portuguese who settled on the Guinea Coast had relations with the natives. The slave traders themselves were known frequently to have had promiscuous intercourse with their female merchandise. Even more important as a source of infiltration of white blood into the Negro slave population before arriving in what is now the United States was slavery in the West Indies. While some of the slaves in these islands came directly from Africa, others were brought indirectly by way of Spain and Portugal. The importation of Negro slaves into those European countries was in practice by the beginning of the sixteenth century, and by 1539 there is some evidence that it reached the figure of 10,000 to 12,000 a year.[25] It seems that there was extensive miscegenation in these two European nations. Part of the offspring remained and became engulfed in the population of the Iberian Peninsula. Those brought over to the West Indies formed a large proportion of their slave population. This continuously received further additions of non-Negro blood from the white and Indian inhabitants of these islands. No one knows exactly what proportion of the slave population of the United States was brought by way of the West Indies, but the proportion would be significant. As the slave import from the West Indies formed an increasing proportion of all slave importation during the later periods of slavery in America, and as Negro immigration after Emancipation has been largely from the West Indies, the elements in the American Negro people with the shortest line of ancestry in this country are, therefore, not of purer breed but rather the contrary.[26]

Upon their arrival in the New World, one type of mixture which is important, although not often referred to in this relation, did not *per se* involve Indian and white stock. We refer to the wholesale mingling of the various African stocks with each other. Historical sources from the period often ascribe to the slaveholders a conscious purpose to break up tribal coherence and allegiance between the slave masses in order to decrease their resistance against slavery. It was part of their being "broken in." [27] But even apart from such a purpose, a compulsory labor system managed by persons who, in any case, had no feeling for upholding tribal differentiation, even when they did not consciously follow the opposite policy, must have had this result. This intermingling between the African tribes also had its beginnings in Africa, where commerce and wars, slaveholding and slave trade, for thousands of years, had this effect.[28] The extensive slave trading by Europeans after the discovery of the New World, and the stirring up of population movements in Africa caused thereby, only intensified a process already taking place. Its final consummation occurred in America.[a]

In the United States miscegenation with Indians and whites occurred from the very beginning. Indians were held as slaves in some of the American colonies while Negro slaves were being imported. Equality of social status between Indians and Negroes favored intermingling. The whites had little interest in hindering it.[29] As the number of Negro slaves increased, the Indian slaves gradually disappeared into the larger Negro population. Whole tribes of Indians became untraceably lost in the Negro population of the South.[b] Some Indian tribes held Negro slaves with whom they mingled, and some were active in the internal Negro slave trade. Runaway Negro slaves and free Negroes often took refuge in the Indian camps, where they then were kept as slaves or were adopted. They took part in the wars and insurrections and became completely amalgamated in the Indian tribes with which they lived. In a few cases the intermixture produced a group that was recognized neither as Indian nor as Negro. A few isolated groups of this type remain to the present day.[30]

During the nineteenth century, the Indians declined as a significant element in the population of the South, and those who remained began to take on the attitudes of the white man toward the Negro. From this time on, Indian-Negro mixture was probably no more important than Indian-white mixture in the South. But the early interbreeding between Negroes and Indians has been of greater importance for the genetic composition of the American Negro population than has until recently been realized.[31] Twenty-seven and three-tenths per cent of the Negro sample of 1,551 individuals examined by Herskovits claimed some Indian ancestry.[32]

The relations between Negro and white indentured servants during the seventeenth century had much the same social basis as the Negro-Indian intermixture. As already pointed out, some time lapsed before the imported Negroes were pushed down to the lower status of chattel slavery, and racial prejudice developed only gradually. All through the colonial period, the white population showed a marked excess of males and a scarcity of females—as did also the Negro population—which *per se* is a factor tending

---

[a] This intermingling, both in Africa and in America, will be considered again when we discuss the possible consequence of a new "brown race" in America. (See Section 9 of this chapter.)

[b] Many other Indian tribes, of course, moved West, so that the relative absence of Indians in the South is by no means due solely to amalgamation with the more numerous Negroes.

to promote interracial sex relations.[33] It seems from the historical records that the two dependent groups—Negro and white servants—were often bound together by considerable sympathy during most of the seventeenth century; the extreme contempt and hatred between Negroes and poor whites which has prevailed into the present time seems, in any case, to be a later development.[34]

Sexual relations occurred under these conditions rather freely and a half-breed stock appeared early. Some of those early relations involved, as the sporadic historical sources reveal, white women; some of the relations in both directions had the character of legal marriage. But from the beginning the much larger portion of the intermixture occurred between white men and Negro women and most of it was extra-marital. When a mulatto generation came into existence, it served as a new stimulus to relations between the Negro and white groups, as mulatto women were preferred to pure-blooded Negroes as sexual objects. Even if in these early relations it seems that most of the time the white male partner belonged to the lower classes, the higher classes, who owned and could dispose of their slave women, already had given a share to the paternity of the growing Negro population of America.

Parallel to the stratification of the lower slave status for Negroes, the various states started to pass laws against intermarriage and other types of interracial sex relations.[35] It is apparent from a casual inspection of these laws that they were largely guided by the property holders' interest in keeping parents and offspring in slavery.[a] Their chief effect upon interracial sex relations was probably to drive them even more toward the illicit type. It probably did not diminish their actual occurrence to any appreciable degree, since there was practically no attempt to enforce the law prohibiting interracial intercourse outside of marriage.

5. ANTE-BELLUM MISCEGENATION

As the slavery and plantation system became more firmly established in the early eighteenth century, a second stage was reached in Negro-white sex relations. White servitude was already on the decline while the number of Negro slaves was increasing. Some authors hold the opinion that, as a result, miscegenation decreased considerably, but their arguments are not convincing.[36]

A final answer to this question will probably never be reached, the less so as the matter of interracial sex relations had become an important issue between the white Southerners and the Northern Abolitionists in the decades preceding the Civil War. The accusation that there was sexual

[a] Before these laws were passed, there was some question as to whether the offspring of a free person and a slave was free or not. There was also some question as to the legal status of both parents in such a case.

exploitation of Negro women was one of the most effective means of consolidating public opinion against slavery in the puritan North. Thus Southern writers of the period avoided mentioning the point, especially as it involved white men of the master class and their female slaves. What the present writer has been able to read in historical sources and, in addition, to learn from the rumors in the South leads him to believe that Wirth gives a balanced statement on the "amount of miscegenation during the period of slavery" when he says:

> The contemporary observers, on the whole, tend to leave an impression that no likely looking Negro, or more especially mulatto, girl was apt to be left unmolested by the white males; that very few of the young white men grew up "virtuously," and that their loss of virtue was scarcely to be attributed to cohabitation with white women. While such impressionistic statements lead to the inference that interracial sexual relations were normal experiences for at least the white men of well-to-do families, they reveal nothing concerning the proportion of Negro women and, of lesser importance, of Negro men, who entered into interracial unions. It is quite conceivable that the very great emphasis on the sexual activities of the white male has tended to obscure the extent to which large numbers of Negro women may have been free from any sexual experiences with men of the white race.[37]

It should not be assumed that interracial sex relations were a pattern only of the Southern rural plantations. There is general agreement, among the authors who have studied the question of interracial sexual relations of this period, that such relations—measured in proportion to Negro women involved—were even more frequent in the Southern cities and in the North. The Negro population in these urban communities contained a larger proportion of mulattoes, partly as a result of race mixture there and partly because slaveholding fathers of mulatto children sometimes freed their offspring and moved them to the cities or to the free territory in the North. The North contained more light-colored Negroes also because there were many states without laws prohibiting intermarriage. Mulatto women have always been preferred to full-blooded Negroes as sex mates. A large proportion of city Negroes were free; in the North all Negroes were free. City life—both in the South and in the North—was more anonymous, even for the slaves. In cities a larger proportion of Negroes were engaged in household work. They were fewer and were more scattered through the white population. All these factors tended to make interracial sex relations relatively more numerous in the Southern and Northern cities than in the Southern rural areas. The only factor, apparently, working in the opposite direction—to decrease sex contacts between the races in the North—was the North's lack of interest in breeding mulattoes for the slave market. These interracial sex relations in the North and in Southern cities had only a minor influence on the genetic composition of the total Negro population, however, since the bulk of the Negro population during the slavery period was rural Southern.

6. MISCEGENATION IN RECENT TIMES

The third stage of Negro-white sex contact came with the Civil War and its aftermath. The Northern army left an unknown amount of Yankee genes in the Southern Negro people.[38] The prolonged disturbances following the War were probably even more important. Reuter summarizes the situation in these words:

> The emancipation of the slaves and the breakdown of the master-slave relationship was followed by a prolonged period of profound disorganization. Restraints were removed and the manumitted slaves wandered in celebration. The period was one of more or less unrestrained promiscuity.[39]

This period was not a short one. When the Negro population gradually settled down in the caste status which had been substituted for slavery, sexual mores can be assumed to have been continued much along *ante-bellum* lines. The only new element in the situation, apparently, was the lack of interest in breeding mulatto children for the slave market, because the latter no longer existed. What evidence there is on interracial sexual relations during the later decades of the nineteenth century does not indicate that such relations were considerably less frequent than during slavery; they might even have been somewhat more frequent.

It is more difficult to form even a conjectural judgment as to the amount of interracial sexual relations during the twentieth century and as to the present trend than it is to ascertain broadly the facts for earlier periods. Interracial sexual relations are more closely guarded than ever, and life is more anonymous and less fixed in groups about whose behavior simple and valid generalizations might be made. The slight increase in scientific research on the subject has not compensated for these trends. Among factors which might have tended to increase interracial sexual contact must be reckoned: increased Negro migration to cities and the North; slow but gradual urbanization even of rural districts in the South; and the secularization of sexual morals, particularly among the white population. Among factors tending to have an opposite effect are: in the white population, the gradual breakdown of the sexual double standard (making for easier accessibility of white women for extra-marital purposes), the balancing of the sex ratio, and the publicity about the high rate of venereal disease among Negroes; in the Negro population, the gradually increasing race pride, the relatively lessened value of concubinage with a white man, the slowly spreading middle class morality in sex matters. Public opinion in the South also has become firmer in condemning white men's sex relations with Negro women, and the segregation of the Negro people has become more complete.

There have been no scientific studies which even suggest tentatively the actual quantitative trend of interracial sexual relations. Most of the informants the writer has questioned on local trends—but by no means all—have agreed in the belief that sex relations between members of the two groups are decreasing. The same opinion is expressed in the literature.[40] It should, however, be considered with the greatest reservation, as such an opinon is opportune in both the white and the Negro groups. The matter is of great social importance because of the way in which the Negro problem has been defined in America, and it is, therefore, urgent that science should bring light upon this phase of social life—in spite of the natural reluctance and perhaps even resistance from the side of the public.

But even if interracial sexual relations were not decreasing, the offspring from intermixture may be decreasing. The scanty evidence available seems to point in this direction.[41] In considering trends in the injection of white genes into the American Negro population, the amount of sex relations between members of the two races is not the only factor which must be taken into consideration.

An increased utilization of effective contraception, decreasing the relative and absolute amount of mixed offspring, has the same genetic effect as decreased interracial sexual relations. Writers who have considered recent trends in miscegenation generally tend to ignore trends in use of contraceptive devices.[42] It is possible that, as means of effective birth control have become spread among the American population, they have been utilized with particular eagerness and efficiency in mixed sexual relations.[43] The writer has, from the information he has been able to gather from doctors, social workers, Negroes with wide community knowledge, and, occasionally, from average Negroes themselves, got the impression that, at least in cities, even Negroes in lower strata have kept pace with knowledge about contraceptives.[44]

Even more important is a change in the character of interracial sexual relations. The more stable type of sex unions—marriage and concubinage—have probably been decreasing,[45] and these are the types of relations most productive of offspring.[a] On the other hand, prostitution is mostly sterile, while other casual types of relations may have increasingly involved the use of contraceptives.[46]

The probable decline in offspring with one white parent and one Negro parent should, therefore, not be taken to mean that interracial sex contacts have necessarily decreased: a rise in prostitution and other casual sex contacts may have counterbalanced the decline in marriage and concubinage. From a genetic standpoint, the only sex relations which matter are those

[a] The cultural, social, and personal side of miscegenation, the different types of sexual unions, the legislation against intermarriage and the research on intermarriage will be dealt with in later chapters on discrimination and caste. (See Chapters 29 and 31.)

leading to mixed offspring. The scanty quantitative evidence and general opinion seem to indicate that there has been a decline in the rate at which white genes are being added to the Negro population.

7. "PASSING"

Because of the American caste rule of classifying all hybrids as Negroes, it might be thought that no Negro blood would ever get into the white population. However, some extremely light Negroes—usually having more white ancestry than Negro—leave the Negro caste and become "white." "Passing" is the backwash of miscegenation, and one of its surest results. Passing must have been going on in America ever since the time when mulattoes first appeared. Passing may occur only for segmented areas of life—such as the occupational or recreational—or it may be complete; it may be temporary or permanent; it may be voluntary or involuntary; it may be with knowledge on the part of the passer or without his knowledge; it may be individual or collective.[47] Usually the only kind that is important for the genetic composition of both the white and the Negro population is that kind which is complete and permanent.[a]

Usually only the lighter colored Negroes pass in the United States. However, some of the darker do also by pretending to be Filipinos, Spaniards, Italians or Mexicans. Day's study further reveals how capable of passing are persons with one-fourth, three-eighths, and even one-half, Negro blood, not to speak of persons with even smaller admixtures.[48] Because those who pass usually have more white ancestors than Negro, it is genetically less important that these people go over into the white world than if they were to remain in the Negro. Passing, therefore, involves far greater change in social definition of the individual than it does in his biological classification.

It is difficult to determine the extent of passing. Those who have passed conceal it, and some who have passed permanently are not even aware of it themselves because their parents or grandparents hid the knowledge from them. Census data and vital statistics are not accurate enough to permit of estimates within reasonable limits. The possible methods for estimating the extent of passing are: (1) getting at genealogies by direct questioning or other means; (2) noting discrepancies between the observed numbers of Negroes in the census and those which may be expected on the basis of the previous census and birth and death figures for the intercensal years; (3) noting deviations from normal in the sex ratio of Negroes. All these methods have been employed, but—for one reason or another— have not permitted us to state the extent of passing.[49]

[a] The cultural, social, and personal problems raised by the phenomenon of passing will be discussed in Chapter 31.

Passing has genetic significance for both whites and Negroes.[a] The whites get a certain admixture of Negro genes. This may modify certain characteristics of their physical structure to an extent which must be slight, on account of both the great size of the white population and the predominance of Caucasoid genes in the passers. It cannot make the white population much darker even if continued for a long time.[50] The main genetic consequence of passing for the Negro people is that some of the near-Caucasoid elements are being constantly removed from the possibility of reducing the proportion of Negroid genes in the remaining American Negro population. This is, of course, a relative matter, since far from all light Negroes attempt to pass, and since many who cannot pass have a large admixture of white blood. Passing is apparently more common to men than to women, judging by opinion and the sex ratio.[b] This does not reduce the genetic significance of passing, however, since the contribution of genes by a father is just as great as that by a mother. Of some consequence for genetic composition is the fact that young adults are those who pass most frequently. These are the persons who bear most children, who are, consequently, usually lost to the Negro group.

8. Social and Biological Selection

There are no data to permit the conclusion that, in the rural South where most of the miscegenation has taken place, one social class of the white population was more responsible for the existence of the mixed-blood population than corresponds to its relative proportion in the population. Neither does the available evidence allow the contrary conclusion. But even if one social class of white people in the South should have been more predominantly involved in miscegenation, this would not necessarily have great genetic importance, since it is not scientifically established that social classes of whites in the South differed significantly in genetic composition, in spite of the popular opinion that poor whites are degenerate.[51] It is also not possible to state that within the various social classes of whites, miscegenation has followed any pattern of *individual* selection.

Turning to the Negro partners in miscegenation it would, however, on *a priori* grounds, seem probable that a factor of positive selection in mating could have been at work, at least until recent times when Negro pride became important. The Negro girl whose physical appearance and cultural manners approximated the prevalent standards in the higher caste would

[a] In the following discussion and throughout the book, we discuss certain implications of the inheritance of skin color as an example of all physical traits which have significance for social status, such as breadth of nose, thickness of lips and hair form.

[b] This probably occurs because passing usually involves economic advantages to Negro males who must compete in a white man's world, but economic disadvantages to a Negro female who could get a white husband only from the lower classes, but possibly a Negro husband from the upper classes.

certainly be preferred as a sexual partner. Such girls tended, at least after the first generation in America, to be mulattoes rather than pure-blooded Negroes. The fact that a similar preference probably occurred in the choice of Negro girls for household work, where they became more exposed to sexual advances, would strengthen its importance. Within the Negro marriage market the mulattoes' lighter skin has had, and continues to have, a strong competitive value. This can again be assumed to work as a factor of positive selection favoring the mulatto group: Dark males who have distinguished themselves in any way tend to take light mulatto women as wives.

> As a result of this marriage selection, whatever talent there is among the mulattoes remains among the mulattoes; whatever talent there is among the black group marries into the mulatto caste. In either event the talent of the Negro race finds its way into the mulatto groups. The descendants of these talented men are mulattoes, and whatever of the father's superior mentality and energy they may show or carry becomes an asset to the mulatto group, and the full-blood group is correspondingly impoverished. The mulatto caste loses none of its native worth and is constantly reinforced by the addition to it of the best of the variant types which appear among the numerically larger group.[52]

We cannot accept this line of reasoning, however, without qualifications, since it is not certain that whites have predominantly selected innately superior Negro girls to have sex relations with, or that socially successful dark Negroes who marry light girls are also biologically superior, or that the inferiority of the white parents of mulattoes has not balanced the superiority of their Negro parents. The proof that mulattoes are biologically superior to full-blooded Negroes must go beyond the finding that mulattoes have made greater achievements than pure-blooded Negroes, since the latter have had more social handicaps than the former.[53]

Differences in fertility and mortality between groups with a varying degree of white ancestry must, through the generations, have affected the results of miscegenation upon the genetic composition of the present-day American Negro people. While opportunistic opinions have been expressed both to the effect that mulattoes were sterile, or more sterile, than full-blooded Negroes, on the one hand, and that they were unusually prolific, on the other hand, there is not the slightest shred of scientific evidence for either of these opposing popular beliefs.[54]

It is certain, however, that mulattoes are concentrated in cities in the higher economic brackets, where—because of greater use of effective birth control—they have a lower fertility than the Negro population as a whole. Nor does the probable lower death rate of mulattoes entirely counterbalance their lower birth rate. This differential reproductivity has been tending to reduce the proportion of white genes in the total Negro population. While other effects on genetic composition by differential reproductivity have been claimed (such as the presumed selective migration of superior Negroes to the cities, where the birth rate is low),[55] these have thus far no basis in demonstrated facts.

Length of residence of different elements of the Negro population in the United States must have had an influence on the genetic composition of the American Negro people. Because the Negro net reproduction rate has, until recently, been far above unity—so that a given group of American Negroes has always more than reproduced itself in the next generation—the earlier a certain element has entered the American Negro population, the greater the proportion of the total Negro population does this element form,[a] in relation to its original size. This factor operates on the genetic distribution of the descendants of the various African races in favor of the "true Negroes" from the West Coast, since Africans outside this latter group were probably not brought to America in significant numbers until the nineteenth century. The factor also makes less important the relative numbers of Negroes coming *via* the West Indies, who also did not come in significant numbers until relatively recently. It also enhances the genetic significance of the earlier interracial sex contacts with the Indians and the indentured white servants brought from Europe in the seventeenth century. Finally, it makes more important the interracial sex contacts with the North and West Europeans that occurred in the earlier days than those with South and East Europeans that have tended to become relatively more numerous since the Civil War.

9. Present and Future Genetic Composition Trends

Everything said so far about the racial character of the slaves originally imported, about miscegenation and passing in this country, and about the various general factors which have influenced the American Negro stock, has been highly conjectural and speculative. Summing up this unsatisfactory knowledge can hardly lead to anything more than an expectation that the American Negro people should show up as a considerably mixed population group. It is the merit of Professor Melville J. Herskovits[56] that he has finally approached this problem directly and, taking his departure in anthropometric research of the present Negro group in America and its genealogy, has tried to ascertain the actual composition of the group.

Herskovits' most significant finding was that 71.7 per cent of his presumably representative sample of 1,551 Negroes had knowledge of some white ancestry, and that 27.2 per cent knew of some Indian ancestry.[57] Herskovits claims that his sample is representative because the groups of Negroes from various sections of the country were found to be similar in several

---

[a] The element need not have remained intact in certain family lines, of course. The statement in the text refers to the proportion of genes in the Negro population, therefore, and not to the proportion of persons.

physical traits. This does not constitute proof of representativeness, however, because it is likely that each group of Negroes (from each section of the country) is an upper class group, and Herskovits does not define the degree of closeness of trait which constitutes similarity. Too, the list of traits which were compared does not include color or other important differentiating traits. It is likely that Herskovits' sample contains too many upper class Negroes who are known to have a disproportionate amount of white ancestry.[a] The fact that many Negroes may not know of white ancestry of several generations back[58] may, however, counterbalance the selective factor in Herskovits' sample and leave his figure of 71.7 per cent with white ancestry not too inaccurate. Thus, while we cannot say that existing research permits a definitive answer to the question as to how many Negroes have some white blood, the best available evidence and expert opinion point to a figure around 70 per cent. This figure must tend to increase with time, if for no other reason than that full-blooded Negroes intermarry with mixed bloods and their offspring become mixed bloods. Herskovits' other important conclusion—that in many physical traits the present American Negro population shows less variability than its parent African Negro, American white, and American Indian populations, and so are rapidly forming a genetically homogeneous group—cannot be accepted as demonstrated.[59]

A forecast of the future trend of genetic changes must, in its very nature, be highly conjectural, and, if stretched beyond the next few decades, it cannot possibly be more than an amateurish guess. Even for the immediate future it can amount to little more than an enumeration of the relevant factors and a consideration of their interrelations. Any statement concerning the resultant effect of the forces at play has no greater validity than the specific premises stated concerning the primary factors at work.

Miscegenation between American Negroes and whites is commonly believed to be on the decrease. Even if it is not certain that sex relations between members of the two groups are decreasing, there is more reason to feel confident that children of white-Negro unions are becoming rarer, in both absolute numbers and relative proportions. Information on, and accessibility to, contraceptive devices is increasing; and their further technical perfection is generally expected among population experts. A decreasing rate of birth of offspring with parents representing the two races will not, of course, decrease the proportion of white genes in the Negro people but will slow down their further increase and postpone the distant possibility of full amalgamation.

Passing is becoming easier in the more mobile and anonymous society of today and tomorrow. The more recent immigration of darker peoples

---

[a] It also seems that Herskovits' sample contains too many Negroes from the Atlantic seaboard states. who are known to have a disproportionate amount of white ancestry.

from Eastern Europe and from around the Mediterranean Sea and also from Latin America, especially from Mexico, and the rising social respectability of the American Indian, have made passing easier for the Negro. Warmer relations with the republics of South America will perhaps be an influence in the same direction. The increasing segregation, on the other hand, which tends to create economic and social monopolies for the Negro upper class (to which most of the light-colored mulattoes belong) will tend to decrease the desire to pass. So also will the rising race pride.[a] America is unique among all countries having a mixed population—not excluding countries like Brazil where discrimination is so much milder—in having a significant number of white or almost white Negroes, who could easily pass but prefer not to do so.

As the individuals who pass must be near-white, the extent of passing is a function of the number of such individuals. Continued miscegenation between whites and Negroes will tend to increase that number; miscegenation between mulattoes and darker Negroes—as well as low reproduction rates for mulattoes—will tend to decrease it. What the trend of passing is, and will be, resulting from the interplay of these various factors, is impossible to ascertain on the basis of present evidence.

The effect of passing, whatever its extent, is to neutralize the effect of miscegenation on the genetic composition of the Negro people.[b] It is even possible to conceive of a temporary condition in which the rate of passing would exceed the rate of addition of new white blood into the Negro group so that there would be a tendency for the American Negro group to become more negroidized.

Differential reproductivity is a factor which can be expected to have a continuing importance within the next decades.[60] Our knowledge of social and economic conditions among the Negro people and of the development of differential reproductivity in other countries which are more advanced in birth control rather favors the forecast that present fertility differences between the various Negro groups are not going to decrease much for a long time.[c] Infant mortality and, generally, mortality in the lower age groups may be expected, on the other hand, to become gradually more equalized.[d] There are, further, no sure signs that light-colored people will not remain in the upper class. Since, with increasing segregation, the Negro

[a] See Chapter 30, Section 2.

[b] The effect of passing on the American *white* population can never become important because those who pass usually have more Caucasoid genes than Negroid, and because the numbers who pass are insignificant compared to the huge American white population.

[c] Fertility differentials may decrease, however, if Southern states extend the policy, which a few of them now have, of setting up birth control clinics in rural areas. (See Chapter 7, Section 7.)

[d] See Chapter 7, Section 2.

upper class is relatively growing, it can come to include a relatively greater number of black Negroes without losing many of its mulattoes.

Reproduction differences have, in the main, the same effect on the Negro group as passing, except that the effect is not so exclusively concentrated on the extremely light-colored Negroes.[a] This factor, therefore, enters into the balance between miscegenation and passing and makes it more probable that the effects of miscegenation can be fully, or more than fully, counterweighted.

Internal miscegenation within the Negro group between individuals with a varying degree of white ancestry is, and will in the future be, going on. The result is a tendency toward a slow but continuous equalization of Negro and white genes in the Negro people, decreasing the relative numbers at both the black and white extremes and concentrating the individuals ever closer to the average. The changes in position of the average itself will depend upon the balance, referred to above, between white-Negro miscegenation, on the one hand, and passing and reproductivity differentials, on the other hand.

Immigration of Negroes (and mixed bloods) from the West Indies and from South America—the latter of which might become more important in the future—will, in so far as the immigrants enter the country as Negroes, somewhat change the genetic composition of the Negro people in a direction dependent upon the genetic constitution of the newcomers. As the stocks are not very different,[b] this factor, even if the immigration should increase, will not effect great changes in the American Negro people.

The three main problems to be stressed in a theoretical analysis starting out from such considerations as those stated above—assuming immigration inconsequential, and disregarding the effects on the white population—are:

(1) The interdependence between the various factors. Passing is, for example, a function of Negro-white and Negro-mulatto miscegenation and of differential reproductivity.

(2) The position of the average in the various traits which differentiate whites from Negroes. This position is a function of miscegenation, passing and differential reproductivity.

(3) The homogeneity of the Negro population. The degree of dispersion around the average is generally a function of internal miscegenation and, particularly in regard to the form of the frequency curve at the white end, a function of external miscegenation, passing and differential reproductivity.

[a] It has, of course, in contradistinction to passing, no effects at all on the white population.

[b] They contain, however, relatively more genes of other original African stocks than the "true Negro," which predominated in the import to the United States, and of different groups of Indians than those that were to be found in the United States. They also bring their own mutations and other physical changes of the last four hundred years.

The above generalizations may be integrated into a system of simple mathematical equations. In view of the paucity of data on the extent and trends of miscegenation, passing, and differential reproductivity, such a mathematical formulation could not be used to predict the probable future genetic composition and physical appearance of American Negroes. However, it might have the value of allowing the student to realize more easily the logical possibilities in the future. It may also have the value of checking the looser type of judgments made even by respectable authors. The construction of such a theoretical model, however, is a major task in itself and is beyond the scope of this book.

This chapter has mainly been a review of a great number of questions upon which science does not as yet provide precise and definite answers. We can, however, state confidently that there are no reasons to believe that a more complete amalgamation between whites and Negroes will occur within the surveyable future. It is even possible, though not certain, that the proportion of very light mulattoes who now, so to speak, form a bridge between the two population groups will decrease by passing and by marriage with darker Negroes. That the Negro group is not disappearing will be a theme of Chapter 7. Finally, we remind the reader again that the concept of the American Negro is a social concept and not a biological one. Even considerable changes in the genetic composition of the Negro people may leave the social problems, around which this inquiry is centered, unchanged.

CHAPTER 6

RACIAL CHARACTERISTICS

1. PHYSICAL TRAITS

In our discussion of "racial" characteristics, which is only a brief summary, we are separating those traits which are physical from those which are psychic, thus following the traditional division between anthropology and psychology. In presenting the facts, particularly on the physical traits, but also on the psychic traits, we have to build upon studies mainly concerned with those traits in which Negroes differ from whites, which, by itself, represents a biased statement of the problem tending to exaggerate differences and minimize similarities. We are, furthermore, limited almost to what we have ourselves criticized—namely, presenting differences between the means of the two groups—because these are practically all the facts available. The dispersion around the means is usually measured only by standard deviation and other abstract indices which do not allow an intensive study of the concrete distribution and of overlapping. Still worse, the available data are so weak that even the differences between means cannot be said to be satisfactorily established.

Ascertaining the differences between Negroes and whites in respect to physical traits involves not only measurements of Negroes but also the establishment of a "standard" set of measurements of whites. No anthropometric measurements of the American population have ever been undertaken on such a large scale and with such methodological precautions that valid comparisons between one sub-group and the rest of the population are made possible. Nearest the ideal in regard to large number of cases was the Army study,[1] but the technique of measurement had several weaknesses.[2]

There are, however, a large number of studies on small samples of American Negroes and various groups of whites. For the Negroes, Herskovits' study is by far the best available. During his investigations, Herskovits tried to determine the representativeness of his sample; we have in the preceding chapter accounted for the general reasons why we cannot accept his claims. The investigators of white samples have not even made efforts to get representativeness.

Apart from this question of representativeness, which is particularly important because of the heterogeneous origin of the American population, the samples are often too small to allow even for reliability in a formal statistical sense, especially after differences in age and sex have been taken into account. There are also differences in criteria and in techniques of measurement utilized in the various studies which make comparisons extremely hazardous. Some of these differences can be accounted for, but some are hidden in the results and, consequently, unknown. Only when the two groups have been studied by one investigator in one integrated study is there full security on this point, but few such studies have been made; and they have no claims to representativeness and reliability.[3]

The white population most often used for furnishing a standard set of measurements of whites has been Hrdlička's *Old Americans*.[4] Hrdlička's sample—which includes 900 complete and 1,000 incomplete cases of individuals measured over a period of 15 years—is not, and was never meant to be, representative of the white American population. It is instead a sample of those white Americans whose ancestors had been longest in this country—predominantly British, Germans and Scandinavians. To get his sample, Hrdlička took only Americans whose ancestors on both sides had been in the United States for at least two generations. The exclusiveness as to ancestral stock implied in this selection is coupled with a definite bias toward including a disproportionate number of persons of high socio-economic status. Only those "Old Americans" who did not marry the poorer immigrants from Southern and Eastern Europe were accepted as proper ancestors to the individuals in the sample. An even stronger source of bias in the same direction was Hrdlička's device of selecting persons from patriotic societies, especially the Daughters of the American Revolution, and from large Eastern universities.[5] Also he made an intentional selection of persons who were healthy and "normal." The socio-economic bias generally, and particularly the demand for healthiness and "normality," must be considered to be the more important as several physical traits are known, and some others are suspected, not to be true hereditary traits but to be determined also by nutrition and other environmental factors.

Thus, to sum up, when Negroes are compared with whites, in the United States, and Hrdlička's sample is used, they are compared with a vaguely defined group of "normal," healthy, white persons of Western European ancestry in which the upper classes were heavily over-represented. Hrdlička's study has many outstanding qualities, but it offers a poor substitute for the standard set of measurements of a representative sample of the American white population needed for comparison when Negro physical traits are to be determined.

It is no exaggeration to say that no physical difference between the average American Negro and the average American white, not even difference in color, has yet been measured quantitatively by research methods which conform to the rigid standards of statistics. The present undeveloped state of this field of physical anthropology should not lead us to accept low scientific standards and to make conclusions which are not warranted. At the maximum we are justified in drawing from available studies only rather qualitative statements concerning average differences, the actual quantities of which—as well as the actual spreads around the means—are not known or known only approximately, so that words and not figures are their more appropriate expressions.

Compared to the average white man, the average Negro of the present day seems to exhibit the following physical traits:[6] head slightly longer and narrower; cranial capacity slightly less; interpupillary distance greater; nose broader; lips thicker; external ear shorter; nasal depth greater; nose and head shorter; torso shorter; arms and legs longer; pelvis narrower and smaller; stature shorter; skin with greater amount of black pigment; hair wavy, curly, frizzly or woolly; distribution of hair less thick; more sweat glands. Prognathism is greater, not because the brain case stops growing in early childhood, but because the upper jawbone continues to grow after the age at which that of the white man stops. A larger proportion of Negroes have brown eyes, black hair, and sacral pigment spots than do Old Americans.[7] This summary contains all those physical traits, reported by more than one anthropologist, that distinguish the American Negro from the Old American. The traits vary greatly among different groups of Negroes and in the total population of Negroes at different times, since—as we have seen—Negroes are not genetically homogeneous and stable. Stature, cranial capacity, and perhaps other traits are also modifiable by environmental changes over time, and the differences do not, therefore, necessarily, or wholly, represent hereditary traits.

In many of these traits Negroes differ only slightly from white men; in nearly all of them there is some overlapping between Negroes and whites. The average person is, for these reasons, not aware of some of these differences. Some of the traits are outstanding and easily visible in the average Negro—although nearly or entirely lacking in many individual members of the Negro group—such as dark skin, woolly hair, broad nose, thick lips and prognathism. They are the basic traits that account for the Negro's "social visibility."

The white man might be aware of other differences but grossly exaggerates them in his imagination, not because he has observed the differences, but because he has certain opportunistic beliefs which he fortifies by hearsay testimony and by such occasional experiences of his own as happen to confirm his beliefs. He also usually attaches an incorrect interpretation to them. An example is the slightly smaller cranial capacity of the average Negro which the white man associates with alleged lower reasoning power of the Negro despite the fact that no connection has been proved between cranial capacity and mental capacity.

Certain traits are found only in popular beliefs and have no foundation at all in fact. Such are the beliefs that the time of suture closure in the brain case of the Negro is earlier than that of the Caucasoid, that the Negro's hands and feet are larger, and that his forehead slopes more. It would be instructive to trace the psychological significance of these and other false beliefs to those who hold them.[a] To the same category belongs the belief that the Negro has different vocal cords. This is associated with the rather unique pronunciation and speech habits of a large proportion of the Negro population.[b]

Certain common beliefs have as yet not been checked by scientific research. This is, for instance, true of the beliefs that male Negroes have extraordinarily large genitalia and all Negroes a peculiar odor.[8] These beliefs have a strategic function in the justification of the American caste system.[c] Occasionally even social scientists express the stereotypes with no evidence behind them. These beliefs are certainly not "the cause" of race prejudice, but they enter into its fixation.

Since measurements of the American Negro are intended to be those of the average individual, and since the majority of American Negroes are mulattoes, the traits measured are predominantly those of mulattoes. Little is known of the actual mechanism of inheritance of the various traits when races cross, except that it is far from being simple Mendelian inheritance. Anthropologists who have studied the biological effects of miscegenation have been forced to use the indirect technique of observing what differences are found on the average between persons of varying degrees of white blood. They find the changes in traits from those of the pure Negro type to be roughly proportional,[9] on the whole, to the amount of admixture of white blood.[10]

Little is known about the functional correlates of the physical traits of Negroes, although it might be expected that there are some. There has been some speculation, for example, as to what anatomical traits of Negroes cause their supposed superiority in athletics, but no one has yet succeeded in proving any hypothesis, and, therefore, it is not known whether the superiority, if it exists, has a genetic basis or not.[11]

2. Biological Susceptibility to Disease

There is one type of physical trait which has not usually been discussed by anthropologists but which has occupied medical students for generations

[a] See Chapter 4, Section 7.
[b] Such cultural differences will be discussed in Chapter 44.
[c] See Chapter 4, Section 7, and Chapter 28, Section 5.

and which, if substantiated, would have great practical importance. We refer to the possibility of a differential susceptibility to various diseases.

The discussion concerning whether the Negro is innately susceptible to certain diseases has had a history similar to the discussion concerning whether the Negro is mentally inferior to the white man.[12] The first inference was that the difference in specific disease rates was due to differences in biological constitution. An elaborate explanation was built up in terms of the Negro's biological inability to adapt to a cold climate, the dark color of the Negro's viscera, the maldistribution of the Negro's nerve cells, and so on. The great decline in the Negro death rate since the turn of the century, almost paralleling, at a higher level, the decline in the white death rate,[a] forced investigators to recognize environmental factors.

The mode of investigation then became one of holding constant a few environmental factors—such as rural-urban residence and economic status—and attributing the remaining discrepancies to differences in innate susceptibility. In some studies the explicit assumption is made, without evidence, that there are no other relevant differences in the average living conditions of Negroes and whites. In other studies the same assumption is made implicitly. Few, if any, investigators have realized fully that the whole mode of existence of Negroes—with their segregation, over-crowding, and ignorance—helps to create a higher disease rate as compared to whites; and that these factors cannot be held constant completely because there is no group exactly comparable in the white world.

The implication is that only an experimental procedure, in which all environmental factors were controllable, would answer the question as to what degree the present difference in disease and death rates is due to an inferior biological constitution on the part of the Negroes. This experiment would have to take into consideration the fact that resistance to disease is a function not only of heredity and environment at a certain time, but also of environmental conditions throughout the life history of the individuals under observation—for resistance to disease is built up in an individual during his childhood and even before his birth.[13]

We may briefly consider the facts concerning differences in disease and death rates between Negroes and whites.[14] First, we must observe that the reporting of deaths and the designation of a cause of death are very inadequate. This has significance in studying differences between Negroes and whites, for Negroes are concentrated in those population groups for which reporting is least complete. Second, the fact that certain beliefs are prevalent about Negro susceptibilities, and that there is often a question as to what shall be reported as the "cause of death," make the official statistics an imperfect source for determining ethnic differences in disease. This is especially important in the case of those diseases to which Negroes

[a] See Chapter 7, Section 2.

are traditionally supposed to be relatively immune, such as scarlet fever and diabetes. Diseases which are not frequently a cause of death are reported so badly or are reported for such inadequate samples that it is almost inevitable that Negroes would appear to be immune to them even if they were not really so. Such diseases include hookworm, gout, goiter and skin diseases.

Most of the discussion, however, has been relative to the diseases to which Negroes may be especially susceptible, because their rates in these diseases are higher than those for whites. A large number of such diseases have been recorded by different investigators,[15] but we shall consider only those which are important as causes of death and those for which the differences between Negroes and whites are large enough to indicate that they are due to real differences and not to errors in sampling[16] or observation. This narrows our problem down to pellagra, syphilis, nephritis, tuberculosis, and pneumonia-influenza as important diseases which are definitely more prevalent among Negroes than among whites. No one seems to have advanced the claim that the Negro's higher death rates due to pellagra, syphilis, or nephritis result from his biological constitution. The question of innate racial differences seems to have cropped up mainly with reference to tuberculosis and pneumonia-influenza. Enough facts are available to indicate that the main reasons for the discrepancy between Negroes and whites in the incidence of tuberculosis are environmental and not hereditary:

1. A study made before the Civil War shows that the incidence of tuberculosis at that time was considerably higher for whites than for Negroes.[17] A survey made by Dr. Frederick L. Hoffman indicated: "The opinion of southern physicians who practised among Negroes before the Civil War was almost unanimous that consumption was less frequent among the colored population than among the whites."[18] It was only after Emancipation that the Negro rate jumped high above that of the whites.

2. Negro deaths from tuberculosis have decreased considerably in recent years as public health facilities have been improved and made more available to Negroes. Between 1920 and 1933, the rate per 100,000 population declined from 344 to 232 in the North, and from 229 to 130 in the South.[19]

3. While, since the Civil War, the Negro tuberculosis rate has always been higher than the white tuberculosis rate, the Negro rate today is lower than the white rate was a few decades ago.[20]

4. In a few unusual communities in Tennessee, where the Negroes have a higher occupational status than whites, the tuberculosis rates are higher for whites than for Negroes.[21]

There is not so much direct evidence that the higher pneumonia-influenza rate for Negroes is due to environmental causes. However, other etiological studies of these allied diseases have not succeeded in finding a strong hereditary susceptibility. Also a report by Love and Davenport,[22] on the incidence of these diseases among World War troops, indicates that Negroes are no more susceptible to both these diseases together but are more likely to get the more dangerous pneumonia and less likely to get the less dangerous influenza. This suggests that when influenza strikes, it takes a more serious form among Negroes because their constitution is not so strong—which, of course, does not indicate a hereditary trait—but that Negroes are no more susceptible in the first instance to pneumonia-influenza.

In trying to determine whether Negroes have any special susceptibility to *mental* disease, there are even more difficulties than in the case of physical disease.[a] The only information comes from hospitals, which vary greatly in their policy respecting admittance. Some of the mental diseases have a known physical basis; for others no physical basis has been discovered. When Pollock, for example, tried to show that Negroes were more susceptible to dementia praecox, by pointing out that in Illinois, Negroes had a rate of 57.1 as compared to 15.6 for whites, it was easy to disprove his conclusion.[23] In New York, the discrepancy between the races was not so great.[24] In both Illinois and New York, Negroes were concentrated in cities, which generally have a rate twice as high as the rural areas. Negroes were also concentrated in those age and income groups with the highest rates of dementia praecox. Further, the Negro population of New York and Chicago contained a much larger proportion of recent migrants, and instability seems to have a connection with dementia praecox.

Another type of difficulty in the way of determining whether there is any hereditary difference in susceptibility is illustrated by the data on general paresis. The rate for Negroes in New York State (1929-1931) was 25.0 as compared to 7.0 for whites. The ratio of the Negro rate to the white rate remained high when considered for New York City alone (3.9 to 1) and when standardized for age (4.1 to 1). The explanation seems to be simply that New York Negroes have much more syphilis than whites, and syphilis is the major cause of paresis. Thus, Negroes have a greater incidence of paresis because they have more syphilis, but no racial susceptibility to syphilis has been demonstrated. In view of all these complications, recent students of mental disease have tended to avoid completely the question as to whether Negroes have any special susceptibilities to mental disease.

In general, we must conclude that no innate susceptibilities or immunities to specific diseases on the part of the Negro have yet been conclusively demonstrated. Disease is the result of a complicated interplay of hereditary and environmental factors, and no one has yet succeeded in holding constant

[a] At this point we shall consider only the question as to whether there are hereditary racial differences in mental disease. For other aspects of mental disease, see Chapter 44, Section 3.

the environmental factors to determine that the heredity of the Negro is such as to make him more or less susceptible to certain diseases than the white man. Even disease susceptibilities and immunities that are passed on from parent to child may not be genetic, since infection may occur before or after birth, and some environmental influences on the mother are visited upon her unborn children.

That there may be hereditary differences in mental or physical diseases we cannot deny.[a] But what we do know about the changes in the disease rate and the differentials in incidence under different environmental conditions leads us to the conclusion that any hereditary differentials in susceptibility (which may ultimately be detected) are likely to be small in comparison to the changes which can be brought about by varying the mode of living and the quality of medical care. Too, susceptibility does not mean disease: for proper preventive efforts can reduce the ill-effects of any degree of susceptibility. Our practical conclusion is, therefore, that there is no reason for feeling complacent about the higher disease and death rates of Negroes on the ground that they have a greater innate susceptibility.

3. Psychic Traits

Most of the physical differences between Negroes and whites may be directly translated into terms of esthetic valuation, capacity for physical labor, and bodily healthiness. Except in the first respect, which, of course, is subjective, they do not, even if exaggerated, warrant any great depreciation of the Negro as a fellow human being. The differences, assumed or factual, as to size and structure of the brain have, in addition, been utilized for supporting beliefs in innate characteristics which are vastly more important—namely, the Negro's mental abilities and general psychic inclinations, and, consequently, his capacity for culture and morals. The

[a] The fact that the Negro is somewhat different physically from the white man makes it likely that there are small racial differences in susceptibility. But nothing is definitely known about this, and the physical differences may have a complicated effect, as the following example will show. The black pigment in the Negro's skin is a protection against sunlight, and some investigators—but not all—think this involves a lessening of the amount of ultra-violet light absorbed by Negroes. Since ultra-violet light is a preventive of rickets, and since Negroes seem to have more than their fair share of rickets, some have claimed that the Negro's black skin has given him a greater biological susceptibility to rickets. But the skin of Negroes secretes more sebum, which makes ultra-violet light more potent. Too, diet deficiencies are a demonstrated cause of rickets, and Southern Negroes have notorious diet deficiencies. (See Julian Herman Lewis, *The Biology of the Negro* [1942], pp. 94-96.)

Similarly, the Negro's supposed emotional traits have been advanced to explain certain of the diseases for which he has a high rate. For example, his excitability is supposed to cause hypertension of the heart, but his lack of excitability has been advanced by some to explain his high rate of angina pectoris—another heart disease. Neither the emotional traits nor their connection with the diseases in Negroes have been demonstrated. (*Ibid.*, pp. 291-299.)

belief in the innate inferiority of the Negro in mental capacities and moral traits has naturally been central in the race dogma from the beginning. It is strategic in the justification of color caste. Obvious culture inferiorities, existing in the Negro population, made an inference back to innate cultural capacities not only opportune but also easy and, in fact, to be expected.

When direct attempts were made to study scientifically these psychic differences and to measure their magnitude, virtually no one—or at least very few [25]—had any doubts that they really existed as biological traits, and that they were large. The history of the measurement of the psychic traits of the American Negro began with attempts to quantify what was already "known" about him. And usually the scientists found what they were seeking.

Ferguson,[26] for example, proceeding on his "demonstration" that the superiority of whites was "indubitable," even after various environmental influences were held "constant," correlated performance with skin color and found a perfect upward progression from pure Negro, through three-fourths pure Negro, mulattoes, and quadroons.[27] Ferguson even went so far as to attempt a quantitative statement of intelligence differences among the different color groups. "It is probably correct to say that pure Negroes, Negroes three-fourths pure, mulattoes and quadroons, have, roughly, 60, 70, 80, and 90 per cent, respectively, of white intellectual efficiency." He dismissed the possibility that social differences may have caused the differences in performance: "Among Negroes in general there are no considerable social distinctions based on color. A colored person is a Colored person, whether he be mulatto or Negro, and all mingle together as one race." Another example may be taken from the report of one of the earliest and most publicized studies of Negro-white personality differences.[28] The author, who concludes that Negroes are much less able to inhibit their impulses, significantly begins his paper with the statement: "It is with the issue here raised that the present study primarily concerns itself. Namely: what is the psychological explanation of the impulsiveness, improvidence and immorality which the Negro everywhere manifests?"

For a time it seemed as if finally a firm basis was being laid for a science of psychic racial differences, extending our knowledge, not only by quantifying the apparent differences in innate cultural capacities, but by specifying the particular respects in which the Negro was inherently inferior to the white man. When we now look back on this stage of psychological research, we must remember that there was this common belief of Negro inferiority and, in addition, that many of the earlier studies had a direct or indirect connection with practical questions, such as segregation in schools, which tended to enforce the opportunistic bias.

Independent of any special bias, or of the general bias inherent in the total cultural situation of American caste society, the scientist of that day had to say to himself, as most authors are saying today, that psychic differences simply are to be expected. We know that individuals are different, and that heredity is an appreciable component in individual differences. We know also that there are average physical differences between Negroes and whites, although we have not succeeded in measuring them. Hence why should there not be innate *psychic* differences as well? Why should not the differences in ancestry and in the natural and cultural factors which have influenced biological history somewhat differently for the average American Negro also show up in differences as to average character, temperament, sensory powers and intelligence? Professor Boas, who certainly did not share in any bias in favor of racial differences, said:

> It does not seem probable that the minds of races which show variations in their anatomical structure should act in exactly the same way. Differences of structure must be accompanied by differences of function, physiological as well as psychological; and, as we found clear evidence of difference in structure between the races, we must anticipate that differences in mental characteristics will be found.[29]

With particular reference to Negro-white differences, Boas said:

> . . . it would be erroneous to assume that there are no differences in the mental make-up of the Negro race and of other races, and that their activities should mix in the same lines. On the contrary, if there is any meaning in correlation of anatomical structure and physiological function, we must expect that differences exist.[30]

Such statements are made by almost everyone who touches the problem.

In view of these presumptions and biases, whether valid or invalid, the startling thing is that psychological research has failed to prove what it set out to prove. Huxley and Haddon—who, like most of the others, emphasize that "It is clear that there must exist innate genetic differences between human groups in regard to intelligence, temperament, and other psychological traits . . ."[31]—make the important remark that it is "not without significance that such an enormous mass of investigation has failed to demonstrate what so many are eager to prove."[32] This fact is of some importance as it should increase our right to feel confident in the results of the scientific trend, on the part of scientists, toward finding no psychic difference between Negroes and whites. The desire to attain methodologically valid results is tending to overcome—in the long run—presumptions and biases.

Research on psychic differences has, almost from the beginning, been dominated by methodological criticism and a gradual refinement of research methods. The story has been told several times in technical and popular works and will not be retold here.[33] A few generalizations may suffice.

As in the case of the similar problems in regard to the differences between social classes and between the two sexes, the great differences between individuals within each of the two groups tended from the beginning to make judgments more relativistic concerning the differences between the averages of the groups. The large amount of overlapping brought out the fact that both Negroes and whites belonged to the same human species and had many more similarities than differences. The averages themselves tended to come nearer each other when the measurements were refined to exclude more and more the influences of differences in environment, such as education, cultural background and experience, socio-economic class; and the social factors in the test situation itself, such as motivation and rapport with the tester.

The intensive studies of these last influences proved, in addition, that no psychological tests yet invented come even close to measuring innate psychic traits, absolutely undistorted by these influences. They rather rendered it probable that average differences would practically disappear if all environmental factors could be controlled. Psychologists are coming to realize that they are not, and probably never will be, measuring innate traits directly but are, rather, measuring performance in a limited number of selected tasks, and that performance is determined—in a most complex fashion—by many influences besides innate capacity.

Most of this work has concerned intelligence, as measured by the Intelligence Quotient. The inferences to be drawn are, on the whole, negative as far as hereditary differences are concerned: it has not been possible to prove beyond doubt the existence of any differences at all in innate intelligence between American Negroes and whites; neither has it been possible to prove, on the other hand, that no differences exist. In regard to environmental factors the inferences are, however, positive: it has been proved that environmental differences account for large differences in the measured intelligence performances. Present evidence seems, therefore, to make it highly improbable that innate differences exist which are as large as is popularly assumed and as was assumed even by scholars a few decades ago.

What is here said about the general level of intelligence applies also to more specific mental traits. Nothing is definitely proved in the nature of qualitative differences; even the suggestion that Negro children have superior memory is not proved.[34] Neither is it made credible that there are fewer Negroes in the highest ranges of intelligence.[35] The earlier assumed difference that the intelligence of Negro youth ceases to develop at an earlier age does not stand criticism.[36] Nothing is proved concerning differences between Negroes and whites in sensory powers. Other personality traits have been studied, but such studies have yielded no conclusions with regard to innate differences which could be considered valid.[37] Finally it should be mentioned that studies of different groups of American Negroes with a different amount of white blood have not given more positive results.[38]

These negative conclusions from many decades of the most painstaking scientific labor stand in glaring contrast to the ordinary white American's firm conviction that there are fundamental psychic differences between Negroes and whites. The reason for this contrast is not so much that the ordinary white American has made an error in observation, for most studies of intelligence show that the average Negro in the sample, if judged by performance on the test, is inferior to the average white person in the sample,[a] and some studies show that the average Negro has certain specific personality differences from the white man,[b] but that he has made an error in inferring that observed differences were innate and a part of "nature." He has not been able to discern the influence of gross environmental differences, much less the influence of more subtle life experiences. The fact should not be ignored, however, that he has also made many observational errors, because his observations have been limited and biased.

Even as long ago as 1930—and that is long ago in this field of study, which is comparatively recent and has developed rapidly—a questionnaire circulated among "competent scholars in the field of racial differences" revealed that only 4 per cent of the respondents believed in race superiority and inferiority.[c] It is doubtful whether the proportion would be as large

[a] Summaries of studies using intelligence tests make it quite clear that Negroes rank below whites. See: (1) T. R. Garth, Race Psychology (1931); (2) Paul A. Witty and H. C. Lehman, "Racial Differences: The Dogma of Superiority," Journal of Social Psychology (August, 1930), pp. 394-418; (3) Rudolph Pintner, Intelligence Testing (1931), pp. 432-433; (4) Otto Klineberg (editor), Characteristics of the American Negro, prepared for this study; to be published, manuscript pages 1-119. Not all groups of Negroes have been found inferior to all groups of whites, however. In the Army intelligence tests during the First World War, for example, the Negroes of the Northern states of Ohio, Illinois, New York, and Pennsylvania topped the whites of the Southern states of Mississippi, Arkansas, Kentucky and Georgia. See Otto Klineberg, Negro Intelligence and Selective Migration (1935), p. 2.

[b] It is not so much in the simple personality traits—measurable by existing psychological tests—that Negroes differ from whites, but in the complex traits connected with the cultural differences. Klineberg's recent summary shows that few, if any, psychological studies indicate Negro-white personality differences. ("Experimental Studies of Negro Personality," in Klineberg (editor), Characteristics of the American Negro, manuscript pages 1-65.) For a discussion of Negro personality and culture, see Chapters 36, 43 and 44.

[c] Charles H. Thompson, "The Conclusions of Scientists Relative to Racial Differences," The Journal of Negro Education (July, 1934), pp. 494-512. Although this study was not published until 1934, the questionnaire on which it was based was circulated in 1929-1930.

This trend toward the repudiation of all positive findings with respect to racial differences may be exemplified further by a statement made by Professor C. C. Brigham, whose A Study of American Intelligence (1923) was one of the references most frequently cited by those who held to Negro-white differences in intelligence. After reviewing studies made by others in the late 'twenties, Brigham concludes:

"This review has summarized some of the more recent test findings which show that comparative studies of various national and racial groups may not be made with existing tests, and which show, in particular, that one of the most pretentious of these comparative racial studies—the writer's own—was without foundation." ("Intelligence Tests of Immigrant Groups," Psychological Review (March, 1930), p. 165).

today. The attitude of the psychologists reflects the state of the scientific findings in their field.

But while they seem to be negative, these conclusions of psychological research have probably been more revolutionary and practically important, with respect to the Negro problem, than the conclusions from any other sphere of science. It is true that science's last word has not been said even on the Negro's innate intelligence and still less on his other psychic traits. But the undermining of the basis of certitude for popular beliefs has been accomplished. Also the research literature on the subject indicates that even if future research should be able to establish and measure certain innate psychic differences between American Negroes and whites, on the average, *it is highly improbable that such differences would be so large, that—particularly when the overlapping is considered—they could justify a differential treatment in matters of public policy, such as in education, suffrage and entrance to various sections of the labor market.* This is a practical conclusion of immense importance.

For the theoretical study of the Negro problem in all its other branches —from breadwinning and crime to institutions and cultural accomplishments—the negative results in regard to heredity and the positive findings in regard to *milieu* are also of paramount importance. It means that when *we approach those problems on the hypothesis that differences in behavior are to be explained largely in terms of social and cultural factors, we are on scientifically safe ground. If we should, however, approach them on the hypothesis that they are to be explained primarily in terms of heredity, we do not have any scientific basis for our assumption.*

4. FRONTIERS OF CONSTRUCTIVE RESEARCH

The main need in physical anthropology is an application of some of the general precepts of statistics. No accurate description can be made of the physical traits of a group of people unless one measures a representative sample of that group. It may be stated bluntly that no anthropologist has yet measured a representative sample of Americans, or any specific sub-group of Americans.[a] In making measurements, differences in age, sex, economic status, and ethnic background need to be taken into consideration. These demands on representativeness and specification will imply demands for larger samples than individual investigators can be expected to handle on their own resources and, consequently, planned cooperative work is necessary.[39] In the selection of traits to be measured, a more unbiased and comprehensive approach should be adhered to, so that interest is awarded equally to traits where groups can be expected to be similar on the average and to traits where the expectation is the contrary. Instead of reporting results only in terms of abstract averages, standard deviations, and coeffi-

[a] See footnotes 3, 4, and 5 of this chapter.

cients of correlation, they should be presented in terms of the concrete frequency distributions as well, so that dispersion, exceptions, overlapping, and number of cases may be easily determined.[40]

The importance of environmental factors for physical traits needs more stress. Indeed a new direction in problems for research may be had by turning from *existing* averages and limits to *changes* in traits which accompany certain unplanned or induced changes in environment and biological functions. Boas' research[41] on the changes in the physical traits of immigrants opened up problems for further research which are still far from solved after an interval of over thirty years. For the anthropology of the Negro, it may be observed that the possible physical correlates of the northward migration, of the improvements in diet, of the decline in many specific disease rates, of the increased wearing of shoes, and of many other changes, have never been studied. Controlled biological experiments on the Negro are not out of the question: Concentrated vitamin B_1 has been administered to white persons and the effects of greater energy and optimism and lesser susceptibility to fatigue noted.[42] Is it not a reasonable and verifiable hypothesis that the administration of concentrated doses of vitamins would have even greater effects on Negroes, whose diets are, on the average, even more deficient than those of whites?

The possibilities of redirecting psychological investigation are perhaps even greater. Even if the intelligence and personality measurement devices cannot be used to measure innate differences between Negroes and whites, they may be invaluable in detecting cultural differences and thereby in suggesting spots where education could improve Negroes. Recently, students of the Negro—following the lead of social anthropologists[43]—have been putting mental testing devices to this use.[44] In general, psychological measuring devices can be used as instruments for detecting social differences, for predicting individual behavior in certain types of situations, and for suggesting techniques of control and improvement.

The idea of using the intelligence tests as devices for measuring the psychological effects of unplanned or induced changes is not new to the psychologists. A large number of studies have been made of the effects of foster homes on the Intelligence Quotient of children.[45] In 1935, Klineberg reported a study in which he showed that there was a correlation between the I.Q. of Negro school children who had immigrated to New York from the South and the length of their residence in New York.[46] Canady has reported that a group of Negro students showed an average I.Q. six points higher when tested by a Negro psychologist than when tested by a white psychologist, and that a group of white students showed an average I.Q. six points lower when tested by a Negro psychologist than when tested by a white psychologist.[47]

While many other examples could be cited of the use of intelligence tests to measure the influences of various environmental changes on the I.Q., this field has, however, as yet scarcely been tapped. With reference to the Negro, the writer knows of no studies which have been made to determine the effect on test performance of such influences as: the shock of the Negro child when he first learns that he is a Negro and realizes the social import of this fact; foster-placement in white homes; isolated development in white neighborhoods while still in the parental Negro home; shock of news about lynching as compared to other types of shock unconnected with race relations; group testing of Negroes isolated among white children as over against group testing of these same Negroes among other Negro children; various locations for the administration of tests to the same group of Southern Negroes, such as Negro schools, white schools, and courthouses; new schools and educational equipment in the same or different locales; special training in language usage, vocabulary, and logic; special rewards of different types (having some significance in the Negro world and in race relations) for high performance; and other significant influences.[48] To determine the effect on test performance of such influences the experiment must be set up very carefully. The effect of the influences should be noted, not only on intelligence test performance, but also on performance on the various types of personality trait measurement devices.

The type of research suggested here would involve a radical change in point of view in psychological research. It would be freed from the traditional discussion of *racial* traits and no longer look upon the environmental factors and their psychic effects as simple modifiers which hinder the attempt to determine psychic traits conceived of as static biological entities, a measurement of which would be eternally valid. It would rather look on environmental factors and their effects as the main objects for study. The psychic traits would be comprehended as continually changing ways of acting, and as the product of an individual's original endowment and all his life experiences as actively integrated by him into a unity.

Environmental stimuli would be studied as experiences from the point of view of the individual, and effects on intelligence and personality would be correlated with these experiences and not simply with external economic status, education, housing and so on. The effect of a new experience is not simply one of addition or subtraction, since an individual defines this experience in terms of all his previous experiences. No environmental stimulus has the same effect upon different individuals since it affects different individuals after they have had different experiences in different succession.

The question as to what extent and in what ways biological constitution determines individual differences in performance on intelligence and personality tests can no longer be answered by conceiving of certain inherited traits as constituting independent variables which can be thought of as isolated. Two of the specific questions which should be asked—from the point of view discussed here—to determine the role of heredity in intelligence and personality have been stated in a report sponsored by the Social Science Research Council:

> In studying this problem two questions should be considered. First, to what extent do individuals differ in degree of flexibility to environmental influences—i.e., are the congenital attributes of some persons less subject to modification by environmental forces than are those of other persons? Secondly, to what extent does the congenital equipment of the person determine his subsequent environment—i.e., to what extent do his congenital traits predispose him to select or modify various aspects of his environment? [49]

Little of the existing research on the role of heredity in the determination of psychic traits and capacities has been undertaken with either of these two questions in mind. As we have seen, the presumption has been—and still is, among most students—that, because there are certain physical differences between Negroes and whites, there may also be expected to be certain psychological differences. This does not necessarily follow, however, and the use of the presumption as a working hypothesis is a source of bias, for the following reason: Everything we know—from the work of the child psychologists, the psychiatrists, and the social psychologists—about development in the individual indicates that specific psychic traits, especially personality traits, but also the components of intelligence,[50] are *not* present at birth and do not "maturate" but *actually develop through experience*. Specific psychological traits, therefore, cannot be compared with specific physical traits in respect to their hereditary determination.

Whether underlying capacities and the most general personality traits—speed of reaction, for example—differ in average between the two races is not known, but it should not be forgotten that *they are never subject to direct observation in the same sense that physical traits are*. Thus, even if there were some hereditary differences in psychic traits and capacities, it would still not be necessary for empirically observable traits and capacities to differ at all between the two races. It is possible that we shall never know if there are hereditary differences in psychic traits between the average Negro and the average white man. The fact of being a Negro is so interwoven with all other aspects of a Negro's life that to hold constant these other aspects (e.g., economic and social status, education, and so on) would be equivalent to holding the racial factor constant also.

From the standpoint of the attainment of pure scientific knowledge, it is, of course, unfortunate that the early measurement of psychic traits of different social groups was guided by biased assumptions. When viewed in an historical context, however, it becomes apparent that biased popular opinion gave psychologists the stimulus to go out and try to measure the things which were previously only the subjects of impression. After the biased conclusions were made, they came to be criticized on grounds of methodological inadequacy. Thus began a trend toward improvement of techniques and qualification of conclusions that led to much of the present knowledge about the actual forces determining the intelligence and personality of disadvantaged groups. Such knowledge has been used and is being used to great advantage in the correction of popular beliefs.

Now that this phase of scientific effort is coming to a climax, psychologists can begin to direct their efforts in a more positive direction. While the pioneer outposts of this new research have given us several stimulating hints of the direction of this research, the field is still open for challenging hypotheses as yet not thought of.

Part III

POPULATION AND MIGRATION

CHAPTER 7

POPULATION

....

1. The Growth of the Negro Population

There were about 17 times as many Negroes in the United States in 1940 as there were in 1790, when the first census was taken, but in the same period the white population increased 37 times (Figure 1). Negroes were 19.3 per cent of the American population in 1790, but only 9.8 per cent in 1940. Except for the first decade in the nineteenth century and the 1930's, this proportion has been steadily declining. The trend in the propor-tion has been governed by the natural increase of the two population stocks, by expansion of the territorial limits of the United States and by immigration. Since all figures on these things are uncertain, it is not possible to make an accurate imputation of the changes in the relative importance of these factors. Since descendants of immigrants after the second genera-tion are included in the category of "native born," it is still less possible to calculate what the proportion of Negroes would have been had there been no immigration of either race to the United States after 1790.

In a previous chapter we have discussed the considerable slave import, legal up to 1808 and illegal from then until the Civil War. After the War immigration of Negroes became inconsequential.[a] The immigration of whites from Europe was much heavier, even in relation to the larger white stock, during practically the whole period.[b] There is no doubt that this factor accounts for the great decline in the proportion of Negroes until recently. Additions of territory to continental United States have brought in a more than proportional share of whites.[c]

There has been a radical change in these factors, a change which promises to stop the downward trend of the proportion of Negroes and probably send it slightly upward. There have been no acquisitions of continental territory for a long while, and it is not likely that there will be any more. Immigration from Europe was largely halted by the First World War,

[a] See Chapter 5, Section 2.

[b] The immigration of foreign-born whites has meant much not only for its direct addi-tions to the white American population, but also because the foreign-born have had a high birth rate.

[c] Only the acquisition of Louisiana in 1803 and of Florida in 1819 brought in significant numbers of Negroes.

FIGURE I. NEGRO POPULATION OF THE UNITED STATES: 1790 TO 1940

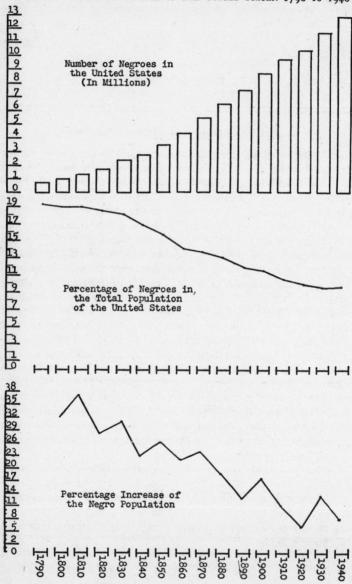

Source: United States Census.

Note: Population of 1870 taken as midpoint between population of 1860 and 1880.

and the restrictive legislation of the 1920's [a]—not likely to be repealed—has continued to hold that immigration low. Economic stagnation during the 1930's operated to reduce the immigration below the legal quota, even when the latter was temporarily further reduced by Executive Order.[1] Only the refugees coming after 1933 made the immigration from Europe at all significant. It is not likely that immigration from Europe will rise after the present War. We can assume that from now on, as during the 1930's, the immigration from Europe will not greatly exceed the emigration to Europe.

Both white and Negro population groups are, therefore, now changing and will continue to change—if our assumption is correct—almost entirely in accord with their respective birth and death rates. One important exception to this is the continuing immigration of Mexicans and Canadians.[b] These groups will continue to provide a small but steady addition to the white population. Like immigration, passing may be ignored as relatively negligible in the estimation of probable changes in the relative numbers of Negroes and whites.[c]

While there are more statistics on population than in most other fields, they are less adequate for many of the problems we are interested in. There is continuous registration of births and deaths, compiled annually, but the failure to register large numbers of births and deaths makes it extremely hazardous to use these statistics.[2] Much more complete is the decennial census, but for our purposes this also is inadequate since young children are frequently overlooked (in different degree for the different regions and races), and since the census asked no direct question on internal migration until 1940.[3]

The inadequacies of both vital registration and census enumeration are greater for the South than for the North, greater for rural areas than for urban, and even in the same areas, greater for Negroes than for whites. We are handicapped also by the fact that, at the time of writing (summer, 1942) the compilation of the 1940 Census is far from complete, and the 1930 Census is too old to be of much use in showing the present situation. For all these reasons it will be somewhat hazardous to present the facts about population beyond the crude trends we have already noted. We shall present only those facts about which we feel fairly certain, but it should be understood that the figures cited are approximations.

[a] See Chapter 4, footnote 21.

[b] Although there is no provision in law setting quotas on immigrants from other American countries, actually there are serious restrictions which keep down this immigration. Every prospective immigrant must pass a strict examination before the American consul to whom he applies for his permit: he must meet certain standards of physical and mental health, literacy, and show the ability to support himself. There is no appeal from the decision of the consul.

[c] See Chapter 5, Section 7.

For our first observation of Negro and white natural increase—that is, the balance of births and deaths—we may turn to the *net reproduction rate*. This rate is a combined measure of the birth and death rates adjusted to a stable age distribution of the population. It is the number of girls which 1,000 newborn girls may be expected to bear during their lifetime, assuming existing rates of fertility and mortality. Estimates of the Bureau of the Census, based on a 5 per cent cross-section of the 1940 Census returns, indicate a net reproduction of 107 for nonwhites and 94 for whites including Mexicans (Table 1).[4] For 1930 the comparable rates—calculated from all census returns—were 110 and 111, respectively.[5] Despite errors in the data, it is possible to derive the following tentative conclusions: (1) that Negroes,

TABLE 1

NET REPRODUCTION RATES BY COLOR AND URBAN-RURAL RESIDENCE,
FOR THE UNITED STATES, BY REGIONS: 1930 AND 1940

(1940 data are estimates based on a preliminary tabulation of a
5 per cent cross-section of the 1940 Census returns.)

Region and Color	1940				1930			
	Total	Urban	Rural-nonfarm	Rural-farm	Total	Urban	Rural-nonfarm	Rural-farm
All Classes								
United States	96	74	114	144	111	88	132	159
North	87	74	109	133	103	90	128	150
South	111	75	118	150	127	86	138	165
West	95	75	120	138	101	80	129	155
White								
United States	94	74	114	140	111	90	133	159
North	87	74	109	133	104	91	128	150
South	110	76	120	145	132	92	145	169
West	94	76	119	134	99	79	128	151
Nonwhite								
United States	107	74	114	160	110	75	119	156
North	83	79	(a)	(a)	87	82	(a)	(a)
South	113	71	112	160	115	71	116	153
West	119	(a)	(a)	(a)	157	(a)	(a)	(a)

Source: Sixteenth Census of the United States: 1940. Population. Preliminary Release; Series P-5, No. 13

(a) Rates not shown for those population groups which, in 1940, had fewer than 20,000 females under 5 years old.

like whites, are not reproducing themselves so rapidly as they used to, (2) that probably their rate is now higher than that of the whites, and (3) that this differential is a new phenomenon, at least in so far as it is significant. If such a differential continues into the future and if it is not fully compensated for by immigration of whites, the proportion of Negroes in the American population may be expected to rise, though slowly.[6]

While in the country as a whole, around 1930, the net reproduction rate for Negroes and for whites was about the same, the Negro rate was significantly below the white rate in each region of the country and in rural and urban areas taken separately. This situation occurred, of course, because Negroes were concentrated in the South and in rural areas, which have high rates for both whites and Negroes compared to other areas. In other words, it was only because of their unusual geographic distribution that Negroes were reproducing themselves as rapidly as whites. During the 1930's, however, it would seem that a fundamental change took place: the white rates had dropped until they were no longer above the Negro rates in each region and in rural and urban areas taken separately.[a] If the 1940 rates for the whole country are "standardized" to show what the rates would be if both color groups were distributed by residence areas in the same proportion as the total population, the whites rise from 94 to 97 and the nonwhites drop from 107 to 102.[7] That is, even if differences in regional and rural-urban residence are "held constant," Negroes now have a higher net reproduction rate than whites. Since the errors in the census are greater for Negroes than for whites and, therefore, the discrepancy is greater—if anything—than shown by the figures we have presented, we feel justified in presenting the following as a fourth conclusion from the net reproduction figures: (4) Even within regions and rural-urban areas taken separately, Negroes are no longer reproducing themselves at a lower rate than whites. In fact, the figures suggest that they are reproducing themselves more—thus reversing the position they held in 1930 and earlier.

2. Births and Deaths

To determine the causes of these differentials and trends, we shall first have to go to the birth and death rates which compose the net reproduction rates. Unfortunately these rates are even more unreliable than the composite net reproduction rate.[8] Certain general conclusions are justified, however, even if we cannot rely on the exact magnitudes.

The Negro birth rate, like the white birth rate, has been falling at least since 1880 and perhaps longer.[9] And since 1850 it has been consistently higher than the white birth rate. These important generalizations about the birth rate have held true in recent years: in 1928-1932 the corrected gross reproduction rate[b] was 136 for Negroes—as compared to 122 for whites (1930)—and by 1933-1937 the Negro rate had fallen to 130.[10]

[a] These rates apply in the North only to the urban areas.
[b] The gross reproduction rate is a refined birth rate adjusted to a stable age distribution. It is the number of girl babies born to the average woman throughout her reproductive period. It is computed by applying crude birth rates to a life table population of 1,000 women and summing the age specific fertility rates thus obtained. The rates for Negroes were calculated and corrected for under-registration by Kirk, and the rates for whites were calculated by Lotka from the Metropolitan Life Insurance Company's files. (See

While there are proportionately more Negro than white infants born, significantly fewer of the Negro infants live. During 1940, 73 out of every 1,000 live Negro infants were recorded to have died before reaching their first birthday, as compared to 43 white babies out of every 1,000 born.[11] If the official statistics were more accurate, they would undoubtedly reveal a much greater differential in infant mortality rates. While a good many more Negro infants die than white infants, in proportion to their total numbers, the difference in death rates for children and mature adults is apparently even greater.[12] Only at ages above 50 does the Negro death rate apparently begin to fall to the level of the white death rate. If a Negro child is born alive,[13] it has (in 1930), on the average, a life expectancy of roughly 48.5 years, while the average white newborn child can expect to reach the age of 60.9 years.[14] For a stationary population with a stable age distribution, these expectancy figures would correspond to a death rate for Negroes of 20.6 per thousand population and for whites of 16.4. The actually registered death rates were, in 1930, 16.5 per thousand for Negroes and 10.8 for whites.[15] The lower actual rates are due not only to under-registration, but also to the abnormal age structure: both Negroes and whites have a disproportionate number of young adults.

As we said, the birth rate has been falling for both Negroes and whites. The fall in fertility is the major factor behind the secular decline in net reproduction for both population groups; the decrease in mortality has not been able to effect more than a rather slight checking of this decline. It is probable that since 1930 the birth rate for whites has fallen more rapidly than the birth rate for Negroes.[16]

The existing data regarding trends in the death rate are so faulty and self-contradictory that it is hardly worth while to quote them. The available data do not permit us to compare trends in the Negro and white death rates.[17] If the death rates have been falling for both groups, it would seem that they were falling more rapidly for whites than for Negroes until 1930. In 1930 the mortality rate for the Negro population was higher than the rate for the white population thirty years previously, in 1900.[18] It is likely that since 1930 the death rate has fallen more rapidly for Negroes than for whites.[19]

The decline in the birth rate for both whites and Negroes has been changing the *age structure* of the populations and this, in turn, is having certain effects on both birth and death rates. Even if the age specific birth rates (that is, the birth rate for each age group of women) should remain constant, the crude birth rate (that is, the birth rate for the entire population) will ultimately drop as the population grows older. The crude birth rate is now

Dudley Kirk, "The Fertility of the Negroes," unpublished manuscript prepared for this study [1940], p. 14.) Not only are there errors due to under-registration in these calculations, but there are also errors due to misreporting of age by women.

abnormally high, since there is an abnormally large number of persons in the child-bearing age groups (this is so because they were born in a period with higher fertility). This is slightly more true of Negroes than of whites, since most of the foreign-born are white, and they are now mostly in the older age groups. In 1940, 41.1 per cent of the nonwhite females, as compared to 39.2 per cent of the white females, were between the ages of 20 and 45.[20] The effect on the white birth rate will come sooner, both because Negroes have had a somewhat higher birth rate and because they, as a result of higher mortality and fewer foreign-born, have, and probably will continue to have, a relatively smaller proportion of persons in ages above the fertile age groups. Likewise, even though the death rate declines some-what for each age group of both white and Negro populations, the crude death rate will tend to increase as the proportion of persons in high age groups increases. And for the same reasons, the rise in the death rate will come sooner for whites than for Negroes.

Considering the differences in age structure alone, which are causing the decline in the crude birth rate and the rise in the crude rate to come sooner for whites than for Negroes, we have another reason why—for a while at least—the proportion of Negroes in the total population will increase. It must be remembered, however, that future changes in fertility and mortality will change the entire pattern. Of particular interest for our present problem would be the effects of a large-scale disease prevention campaign. Since Negro death rates are now considerably higher than white death rates, it is more possible to bring them down. Any impartial efforts to reduce sickness and death in the nation will have much more effect on Negroes than on whites simply because Negroes have much more pre-ventable and curable disease to begin with.[a] We have observed that a more rapid fall of Negro mortality has probably already occurred during the 'thirties.

Migration will continue to be a great importance for future trends in Negro birth and death rates. Migration from rural to urban areas universally reduces the birth rate.[21] It has been related to the main set of causal factors behind the reduction of both white and Negro fertility over the last 70 years. In recent decades the effects have probably been more pronounced for the Negroes than for the whites, since a larger proportion of Negroes have left the farms for the cities, and since the rural South and the urban North represent more the extremes of country and city than the places whites predominantly come from and go to.[22] Even within the South the places to which Negroes have been migrating—the larger cities and the rural areas of the Mississippi Valley[23]—are those of lowest birth rate. While whites also are moving to cities and to rural areas in the western part of the South, their birth rates are apparently not lowered so

[a] See Section 5 of this chapter.

much as those of Negroes.[24] In the migration to cities the Negro birth rate is affected by two special factors: (1) When they migrate to cities, Negro women seek jobs more than white women do, and all urban occupations, especially domestic service, in which Negroes are concentrated, make child-bearing disadvantageous.[25] (2) When Negroes have migrated to cities, the men have gone more to some cities and the women more to other cities than in the case of the whites. This is because Negro women seek jobs in cities more than do white women, and they have gone mainly to commercial cities where there is a greater demand for domestic servants. Negro men, on the other hand, find more opportunities in industrial cities than the Negro women do. The result is that migration involves a greater unbalancing of the *sex ratio* for Negroes than for whites, and consequently the birth rate is reduced more.

Also, migration has probably meant a somewhat reduced death rate for the Negroes,[26] but the decline in death rate has not balanced the decline in birth rate. In 1940, the nonwhite net reproduction rate for rural-farm areas was 154, as compared to 76 for urban areas; for whites the comparable figures were 132 and 76, respectively.[27]

The future of Negro migration is, of course, uncertain. In following chapters we shall find that there are reasons to anticipate that Negroes, more than whites, will be pushed from the Southern land and also that they, more than whites, will attempt to come North. If we consider migration alone, therefore, the effects of urbanization on fertility seem likely to continue to be somewhat greater for Negroes than for whites. This is uncertain, however, as the fertility of urban whites now has dropped sharply and may continue to fall more rapidly than Negro fertility. The sex ratio for Negroes has been tending to even out and will continue to do so. Negroes are becoming more accustomed to the strains of city life and its effects on their health may not be so great as has been the case in the last two decades. The death rate of Negroes in Northern cities might also decrease considerably if better health facilities are made available to them and taken advantage of by them. For all these reasons, the net reproduction rate might reach a lower limit which would be higher than the white rate.

Other differentials between various classes and groups of Negroes are important in estimating trends in Negro population. First, there is the *income differential*. Among Negroes, as among whites, the larger the income, the lower the birth rate, the lower the death rate, and the lower the net reproduction rate.[28] These relations are characteristic only during the period before the practice of birth control is taken up by the lower socio-economic groups. But for America as a whole, and particularly for the Negro people, this phase is likely to last for many more decades. What significance these differentials will have for the future of the Negro population it is difficult to say. As we do not foresee any great rise of economic status for the masses of Negroes in the immediate future, and not even a great increase in the small upper and middle strata,[a] it is not likely that the factor of a rising standard of living will *per se* be of great importance for either fertility or mortality.

The future development of *welfare policy* might become much more important, but its effect would be different from a direct rise in income. If the social security system is extended and if allowances are going to be given to children, and if other welfare policies—in regard to public housing, nutrition, and health—are developed and directed more upon the welfare of children, this might stop the decline in fertility, decrease mortality and raise net reproduction. These effects would be greater for poor people than for the well-to-do people, and therefore would be greater for Negroes than for whites—since Negroes are more concentrated in the lower income strata. If there is an increased spread of information on *birth control*, there will be a decrease in fertility, mortality and net reproduction.

Another possible influence on the future of Negro population in the United States is *immigration*. In the 1940 Census, there were enumerated only 84,000 foreign-born Negroes in the entire country.[29] In 1900, there were 41,000 foreign-born Negroes in the country. The total Negro population in that year was 8,833,994.[30] The bulk of the foreign-born Negroes came from the West Indies. Lack of opportunities for Negroes in the United States makes it improbable that the rate of Negro immigration will become significant, but there is always a possibility. Despite the fact that the majority of these immigrant Negroes live in New York City, and most of the remainder live in other cities, they seem to have a high fertility.[31]

3. SUMMARY

Popular theories on the growth of the Negro population in America have been diverse. At times it has been claimed that Negroes "breed like rabbits," and that they will ultimately crowd out the whites if they are not deported or their procreation restricted. At other times it has been pronounced that they are a "dying race," bound to lose out in the "struggle for survival." Statistics—both of the comprehensive kind in the United States Census and the limited kind gathered in sample surveys—have been used to bolster both arguments.[32]

With the very insufficient and inadequate measures of the factors of change affecting the reproduction of the Negro population in America, it is difficult to piece together a satisfactory prediction of the future course of the total number and the proportion of Negroes in the United States. It can be stated confidently, though, that both these extremes of popular

[a] See Part IV.

ideas are wrong. *In their reproduction American Negroes are like American whites and show the same sort of differentials by regions and groups.*

From 1790 to 1930 the proportion of Negroes in America decreased to about a half of what it had been in the beginning of this period (Figure 1). But this was due, not to any peculiarities in reproduction, but to the overweight of white immigration. The situation began to change during the First World War and the 'twenties: the immigration of whites from Europe fell until it was no longer significant. If there is no substantial change in foreign immigration again, and if conditions affecting births and deaths of both whites and Negroes remain about the same as they are now, or change so that the effect on whites is similar to the effect on Negroes, it is probable that the proportion of Negroes in the total population will rise slowly. There was a rise of one-tenth of 1 per cent of the proportion of Negroes in the total population during the 'thirties. This increase may continue and even become somewhat more marked, but not much. The main reason for this is that Negroes are concentrated in the rural South where the birth rate is generally very high.

If Negroes continue to migrate to Southern and Northern cities, the rate of Negro reproduction will be lowered in relation to the white rate—although possibly not so much as in the past. If there were an economic improvement among Negroes, which does not seem immediately likely, it would seem probable that this would also tend to decrease fertility more than mortality. The development of a social welfare policy, which seems much more probable, would in all likelihood brake the fall in fertility as well as decrease mortality. A mitigation of discrimination in the granting of medical and other health advantages to Negroes, particularly if concomitant with a general improvement of these advantages for all poor people, would have profound effects in reducing the large Negro death rate and in raising Negro reproduction. The spread of birth control among Negroes will decrease the rate of reproduction. Immigration of foreign-born Negroes—which does not promise to become important—would increase the Negro population, not only because it adds directly to their numbers, but also because these immigrants seem to have a high fertility.

Of course, changes affecting the Negro population will not go on *in vacuo*, and there will be similar changes in the white population—all of which will affect the future proportion of Negroes in the total population of the United States. A dominating factor will be the decline in fertility in both population groups. Comparisons with other countries, as well as between different groups in America, make it seem highly probable that this decline will continue. But for several reasons which we have noted, it is likely that, for a short time at least, the decline in the white birth rate will be more rapid than the decline in the Negro birth rate.

4. ENDS AND MEANS OF POPULATION POLICY[a]

As is apparent from what we have said, several of the factors of change are dependent upon policy, and we shall now turn to programs instead of prognoses. Our discussion of population policy will have to be most abstract and, in part, conjectural. For not only are the basic data poor, but there has been less thinking in America devoted to the broad problem of a rational population policy than to other spheres of social engineering.

One reason for the inarticulateness and inadequacy of American discussion of population policy is the heterogeneity of America's population, and the fact that some of its component groups are commonly considered to be inferior. This complicates tremendously the formulation of a rational and unified population policy. It creates conflicts of valuations which make it uncomfortable to discuss the problem. The strength of church and religion in America presents another inhibition. Specifically, the fundamentalistic Protestant religion in some of the regions where fertility is highest in the South and the Catholic Church in the big Northern cities are against discussions of population policy.[33]

We shall avoid the unsettled problem of an American population policy at large and restrict our treatment to the Negro angle of it. In stating our *value premises* a distinction must be made between ends and means.[34] We shall find that for the white people the desired quantitative goal conflicts sharply with their valuation of the means of attaining that goal. For Negroes no such conflict is present.

If we forget about the means, for the moment, and consider only the quantitative goal for Negro population policy, there is no doubt that *the overwhelming majority of white Americans desire that there be as few Negroes as possible in America*. If the Negroes could be eliminated from America or greatly decreased in numbers, this would meet the whites' approval—*provided that it could be accomplished by means which are also approved*. Correspondingly, an increase of the proportion of Negroes in the American population is commonly looked upon as undesirable. These opinions are seldom expressed publicly. As the opinions, for reasons which we shall develop, are not practicable either, they are not much in the foreground of public attention. But as general valuations they are nearly always present. Commonly it is considered a great misfortune for America that Negro slaves were ever imported. The presence of Negroes in America today is usually considered as a "plight" of the nation, and particularly of the South. It should be noted that the general valuation of the desirability

---

[a] This section will be concerned with policy only as it deals with the total number of Negroes in the United States. Population policy as it deals with the distribution of Negroes within the United States will be discussed in the next chapter. Population policy as it deals with the migration of the Negro people will be discussed in Chapter 17, Section 3.

of a decrease of the Negro population is not necessarily hostile to the Negro people. It is shared even by enlightened white Americans who do not hold the common belief that Negroes are inferior as a race. Usually it is pointed out that Negroes fare better and meet less prejudice when they are few in number.

There is an important qualification to be made to these statements. As we have found at many points in this study, people are not always consistent in their valuations. Many white Southerners live by exploiting Negroes, and many fortunes have been built up by cheating Negroes; many white Southerners realize their economic dependence on the Negro and would not like to lose him. Many white Southerners have opposed all "back-to-Africa" or "forty-ninth State" movements, which would eliminate Negroes from their midst. When Negroes began to migrate northward in great numbers during the First World War, many white Southerners made strenuous efforts to stop them: propaganda was distributed; threats were made; Negro leaders were bribed; favors were bestowed; Northern labor agents were prohibited, fined or beaten up. The dominant upper and middle classes of whites in the South realize, for the most part, that they would stand to lose economically if the Negro were to disappear. With the decline of the cotton economy, which we shall analyze in Chapters 11 and 12, the valuation is not so strong now as in 1917-1918. Too, the valuation is not held by most Northerners or by Southern poor whites. And this valuation in the economic sphere is not necessarily tied to the Negro. If poor whites could be exploited with the same facility, the dominant white Southerners would be glad to be rid of the Negro. The valuation in the socio-political sphere, however, *is* tied to the Negro: the Negro is a problem and practically all Southerners (as practically all Northerners) would like to get rid of him. More important from a practical and political standpoint is that the valuation in the economic sphere is only a short-time attitude. Southerners who gain economically from the presence of the Negro are concerned only that the Negro should not disappear during their lifetime or, at most, their children's lifetime. When they think in terms of a long span of future generations, the valuation that the Negro should be eliminated is almost completely dominant. And as we shall presently see, all white Americans agree that, if the Negro is to be eliminated, he must be eliminated slowly so as not to hurt any living individual Negroes. Therefore, the dominant American valuation is that the Negro should be eliminated from the American scene, but *slowly*.

The Negroes cannot be expected to have the same view on the quantitative goal of Negro population. Of course Negroes are familiar with the general fact that prejudice against them is in part a function of their number. But I have never met a Negro who drew the conclusion from this that a decrease of the American Negro population would be advantageous.

Rather it is sometimes contended that the Negro's power would increase with his numbers, and that the most virile people is the one that survives in the universal struggle. With the increase in "race pride" and "race consciousness," which is a consequence of the rising tide of the Negro protest,[a] *almost every Negro, who is brought to think about the problem, wants the Negro population to be as large as possible.* This is sometimes even expressed in writing. W. Montague Cobb, for instance, opens his summary "prescription" for the Negro with the following precepts:

1. He should maintain his high birth rate, observing the conditions of life necessary to this end. This alone has made him able to increase, in spite of decimating mortality and hardships. If the tide should turn against him later, strength will be better than weakness in numbers.
2. He should make a fetish of health. Progressive eradication of tuberculosis, venereal disease, pneumonia, and maternal and infant mortality, will give him sounder and more abundant parental stock and offspring.
3. He should cultivate excellence in sports. This spreads healthful habits.[35]

While whites and Negroes have widely divergent valuations in regard to the desirable quantity of the American Negro population, they agree on the qualitative goal. It is implicit in the American Creed, with its stress on the value and dignity of the individual human being, that *both white and Negro Americans in principle find it desirable to raise the quality of the Negro people* Du Bois, for example, criticized those Negroes who

. . . are quite led away by the fallacy of numbers. They want the black race to survive. They are cheered by a census return of increasing numbers and a high rate of increase. They must learn that among human races and groups, as among vegetables, quality and not mere quantity really counts.[36]

Since the biological principles of eugenics cannot be applied until environmental conditions are more equalized,[37] and since the American Creed places inhibitions in the way of applying eugenics, to improve the quality of the Negro people means primarily to improve their environmental conditions. It is true that the average white American does not want to sacrifice much himself in order to improve the living conditions of Negroes. This is the explanation of discrimination in public service generally. But on this point the American Creed is quite clear and explicit, and we can proceed safely on the value premise that *the medical and health facilities and, indeed, all public measures in the field of education, sanitation, housing, nutrition, hospitalization and so forth, to improve the quality of the population and to advance individuals and groups physically, mentally, or morally, should be made just as available for Negroes as for whites in similar circumstances and with similar needs.* This value premise has, in fact, sanction in the Constitution of the United States.

[a] See Chapter 35.

In our further discussion of the means in Negro population policy we might start out from the desire of the politically dominant white population to get rid of the Negroes. This is a goal difficult to reach by approved means, and the desire has never been translated into action directly, and probably never will be. All the most obvious means go strongly against the American Creed. The Negroes cannot be killed off. Compulsory deportation would infringe upon personal liberty in such a radical fashion that it is excluded. Voluntary exportation of Negroes could not be carried on extensively because of unwillingness on the part of recipient nations as well as on the part of the American Negroes themselves, who usually do not want to leave the country but prefer to stay and fight it out here.[a] Neither is it possible to effectuate the goal by keeping up the Negro death rate. A high death rate is an unhumanitarian and undemocratic way to restrict the Negro population and, in addition, expensive to society and dangerous to the white population. The only possible way of decreasing Negro population is by means of controlling fertility. But as we shall find, even birth control—for Negroes as well as for whites—will, in practice, have to be considered primarily as a means to other ends than that of decreasing the Negro population.

In the final analysis *all these theoretically possible policies to effectuate the white desire to decrease the Negro population are blocked by the American Creed* (except birth control which, however, is largely attached to other ends). This is why the desire is never publicly expressed. The influence of the American Creed goes even further. Should America in the future, when the net reproduction of the nation has decreased still further, embark upon a policy to stimulate the bearing and rearing of children, the democratic Creed of this country will come to prescribe that aids to families be *equally available to Negroes and other unpopular groups, "independent of creed, color or race."*

In sum, if America does not turn fascist, the numerically and politically dominant white population will be driven by its national *ethos* to abstain from taking any practical measures to realize its desire to decrease the Negro population. Instead, it will be compelled to extend to the Negroes the population measures taken primarily to build up the white population. *This is, of course, exactly what the Negroes want, and a unity of purpose becomes established on the basis of the American Creed.*

Meanwhile, the basic conflict of valuations on the part of the dominant whites is, as we pointed out, one of the explanations why there is so little discussion of broad population policy in America. It helps, further, to explain much of the discrimination and indifference about Negro welfare and the great difficulty in stamping it out. On the other hand, it should, at least, give an extra impetus to make effective birth control available

[a] See, however, Chapter 38, Section 12.

to Negroes. We can see signs of this already in several of the Southern states.

5. CONTROLLING THE DEATH RATE

Since there is no evidence at present that certain diseases are genetically more characteristic or less characteristic of Negroes than of whites— although it is possible that slight differences in one direction or the other may some day be revealed—it is not necessary to single out Negroes for special attention in any efforts to cure or prevent disease.[a] The application of the equalitarian principles of "need" in the cure of disease and ill health and of "equality of opportunity" in their prevention—which are our value premises in this section—will suffice to eliminate any special Negro disabilities.

If disease prevention work is to be effective, it must be planned on a national basis without regard to the color of the inhabitants. In the South as well as in the North there is an increasing popular recognition among whites that "diseases cannot be segregated," and that high rates of death, sickness, and poor health among Negroes carry tremendous social costs, directly and indirectly, even if they cannot be calculated accurately in dollars and cents.

There are special social costs connected with infant mortality. There are costs to society as well as to the parents of bearing and raising a child if it dies before it contributes to the world by its labor and other personal qualities. From practically any point of view, it would be better not to have certain children born at all rather than to have them die before completing a normal lifetime. And if healthy children are born, it is in the interest of everyone to see that they are given the opportunity to remain healthy.

These considerations apply to both Negroes and whites. But they apply with greater forcefulness to Negroes since differential death rates reveal that equalization of health conditions, even without advance in medical knowledge or practice, would pull the Negro death rate down sharply. To give Negroes adequate medical facilities fits in both with the equalitarian Creed and with the interests of whites. The observer finds in the South that the propaganda by experts and humanitarians regularly and bluntly makes this appeal to "enlightened self-interest."

Medical knowledge has advanced beyond medical practice, and medical practice has advanced far beyond most people's opportunity to take advantage of it. A reduction in these lags would have tremendous consequences for the well-being and happiness of every person in the nation. Of special significance to the Negroes is the lag of opportunity for some people to obtain the advantages of medical practices available to other people. Area for area, class for class, Negroes cannot get the same advantages in the

[a] See Chapter 6, Section 2.

way of prevention and cure of disease that the whites can. There is discrimination against the Negro in the availability to him of medical facilities.

It is hard to separate the effects of discrimination from those of concentration of Negroes in areas where medical facilities are not easily available and in those income brackets which do not permit the purchase of medical facilities in the competitive market. Discrimination increases Negro sickness and death both directly and indirectly and manifests itself both consciously and unconsciously. Discrimination is involved when hospitals will not take in Negro patients; or when—if they do permit Negro patients —they restrict their numbers, give them the poorest quarters, and refuse to hire Negro doctors and nurses to attend them.[a] The number of hospital beds recently available to Negroes in the South is not known except in Mississippi (1938)[38] where there were 0.7 beds per 1,000 Negroes as compared to 2.4 per 1,000 whites, and in the Carolinas (1938)[39] where there were 1.2 beds per 1,000 Negroes as compared to 2.1 per 1,000 whites. In 1928 there was available in the United States one hospital bed for each 139 of the white population, but only one hospital bed for each 1,941 of the colored population. This means that at that time each white inhabitant of the United States had 14 times as good a chance for proper hospital care as had the colored citizen.[40] The facilities for Negroes are generally of a much poorer quality than for whites. In 1937 only about 35 per cent of Southern Negro babies were delivered by a physician, as compared to 90 per cent of Southern white babies and 98 per cent of Northern white and Negro babies.[41] In the whole United States in 1930 there were only about 3,805 Negro doctors, 5,728 Negro nurses, and 1,773 Negro dentists, and a disproportionate number of these were employed in the North.[42] It is true, of course, that Negroes cannot afford doctors and hospitals to the same extent as whites, but that does not eliminate the fact of discrimination.

Discrimination manifesting itself against the Negro's health is indirect as well as direct, and fits into the pattern of the vicious circle. Inadequate education for Negroes, partly due to economic inability to keep young people in schools and partly due to inferior schools for Negroes in the South, not only prevents the training of Negro medical experts, but also keeps knowledge about sanitation and health in the general population at an extremely low level. Magical and superstitious practices continue in an unenlightened Negro population,[43] and customary patterns of behavior dangerous to health are brought from the South to the North. Ill health reduces the chances of economic advancement, which in turn operates to

---

[a] For a summary of the facts on health facilities and medical care for Negroes, see Harold F. Dorn, "The Health of the Negro," unpublished manuscript prepared for this study (1940), pp. 94a-114b and 131-208. Efforts by the government and private organizations to improve health conditions among Negroes will be taken up in Chapter 15, Section 4.

FIGURE 2. RATIO OF NONWHITE TO WHITE MORTALITY RATES FOR SELECTED CAUSES OF DEATH, UNITED STATES: 1929-1931

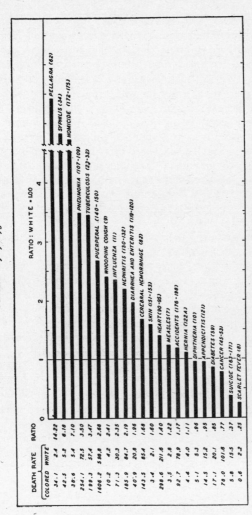

DEATH RATE		RATIO
COLORED	WHITE	
34.1	2.4	14.22	PELLAGRA (62)
42.5	5.2	8.18	SYPHILIS (34)
38.6	5.4	7.10	HOMICIDE (172-173)
254.1	72.5	3.50	PNEUMONIA (107-109)
199.3	57.4	3.47	TUBERCULOSIS (23-32)
1606.2	596.8	2.68	PUERPERAL (140-150)
10.2	4.2	2.41	WHOOPING COUGH (9)
71.3	30.3	2.35	INFLUENZA (11)
185.9	84.7	2.19	NEPHRITIS (130-132)
40.9	20.8	1.96	DIARRHEA AND ENTERITIS (119-120)
143.5	85.4	1.68	CEREBRAL HEMORRHAGE (82)
3.4	2.1	1.60	SKIN (151-153)
298.6	211.6	1.40	HEART(90-95)
3.5	2.8	1.22	MEASLES(7)
92.7	78.9	1.17	ACCIDENTS (176-198)
4.4	4.0	1.11	HERNIA (122A)
5.1	5.3	.96	DIPHTHERIA (10)
14.5	15.2	.95	APPENDICITIS(121)
17.1	20.1	.85	DIABETES (59)
78.0	101.8	.77	CANCER (45-53)
5.8	15.5	.37	SUICIDE (163-171)
0.6	2.2	.25	SCARLET FEVER (8)

RATIO: WHITE = 1.00

Source: Harold F. Dorn, "The Health of the Negro," unpublished manuscript prepared for this study (1940), figure 7.

Note: The figure "1" indicates that the two races have the same death rate, the figure "2" indicates that the nonwhite rate is twice the white rate, and so on. Texas is not included in the computations, since data were not available for it. Nonwhite rates were standardized on the total white population of death registration states of 1930. The rate for puerperal causes is per 100,000 births, including stillbirths.

reduce the chances of getting adequate medical facilities or the knowledge necessary for personal health care.

Any intelligent efforts to reduce Negro morbidity and mortality will result in striking success. This we may deduce from a knowledge of the vicious circle mechanism and from a knowledge of existing Negro-white differentials. Perhaps the greatest need of the Negroes, in the way of reducing sickness and death, is for a dissemination of knowledge on how to take care of the body in both its normal and its pathological state. Other needs are indicated by the diseases for which the Negro rate is strikingly higher than the white rate (Figure 2).[a] These include pellagra (a result of dietary deficiency), syphilis (a function of inadequate information, on the one hand, and social disorganization, on the other), homicide (partly a result of cultural isolation of a subordinated people and lack of police protection in Negro communities),[b] pneumonia and influenza (a function of inadequate care), and tuberculosis (a result, largely, of inadequate sanitation and poor diet).[c] These diseases not only kill, but also reduce the efficiency of Negroes to a much greater extent than that of whites. Pellagra, syphilis, and tuberculosis, at least, can easily be recognized as public problems—the eradication of which is necessary to the health and efficiency of the entire nation.

The infant mortality rate as registered is 69 per cent higher among Negroes than among whites (1940); the actual difference is probably even greater.[44] The discrepancy in maternal mortality rates between the two races is much higher—official figures indicate that the rate for Negro mothers is two and one-half times as high as the rate for white mothers (1940).[45] Both infant mortality and maternal mortality among the Negroes have been declining in the last decade. But the fact that they are still much higher for Negroes indicates that much can yet be done to reduce these types of death among Negroes.

Ill health reduces the birth rate in ways other than killing off mothers in their child-bearing period. In the first place, it increases sterility among men and women. That there is more sterility among Negroes than among whites is shown by the fact that there are more childless women, both married and unmarried, among Negroes and that the higher Negro birth rate is due to a higher average number of children per mother.[46] This sterility is not innate, as Pearl[47] has demonstrated, but is caused by general

[a] We use the data on causes of death to get an index of Negro-white differentials in disease. Only the causes of death which have a marked differential effect on Negroes and whites are mentioned here. Practically all causes have some differential effects in favor of the whites. The only possible exceptions—which seem to affect whites more than Negroes—are scarlet fever, cancer, diabetes, and perhaps a few of the minor rich man's diseases such as gout.

[b] See Parts V and IX.

[c] See Chapter 6, Section 2.

diseases, venereal diseases, induced abortion and organic deficiencies. All these things may be reduced by means available to modern science or by more general diffusion of a few simple items of information. The same causes keep the Negro stillbirth rate high, and so lower the birth rate. In 1940, the reported Negro stillbirth rate was 58.1 per 1,000 live births as compared to 27.6 for whites.[48] If the unreported stillbirths and spontaneous abortions were added to this, the discrepancy would, no doubt, be much greater.

All these types of death rates have apparently been falling recently, for Negroes as well as for whites. It is useless to cite statistics because the reporting of deaths has progressively improved and, therefore, no adequate comparison can be made between two periods.[a] But the direct and indirect evidence available shows a decline in the death rates.[49] The greatest progress seems to be in reducing deaths among Negroes due to tuberculosis, syphilis, diphtheria, whooping cough, diarrhea, and enteritis. But the Negro rates are still much higher than the white rates, and there is much that can be done for both Negroes and whites.

In Chapter 15, Section 4, we shall comment somewhat more in detail both upon what is being done in the way of public policy to prevent and cure disease and upon the actual discrimination against the Negroes which up to now has rendered the public measures less effective for them. We can conclude from known facts and the stated value premises that what is needed in the way of special attention to Negroes is constant vigilance against popular and official prejudice in the application of a general medical and health program. In view of the racial attitudes prevalent in the South, and in view of the generally greater needs and smaller resources of the South, it is almost necessary that national organizations, and specifically the federal government, take a firm lead in this work. A national policy, working toward an improvement of health and a decline in disease, will increase the happiness and efficiency, not only of those directly served, but also of the general population. It will also, if carried out with intelligence and fairness, be a major example of the democratic process.

6. The Case for Controlling the Negro Birth Rate

Aside from any desire on the part of white people to check the growth of the Negro population, there are in the South a great number of Negroes —as of whites—who are so destitute that from a general social point of view it would be highly desirable that they did not procreate. The same is true, though to a much lesser degree, about the North. Many of these people are

---

[a] It is not reasonable to compare Negro death rates even in those Northern states that have had adequate registration for a long while, since in these states the Negro population has changed drastically due to migration from the South. For the available data, however, see Section 2 of this chapter.

so ignorant and so poor that they are not desirable parents and cannot offer their children a reasonably good home. The chances of their children dying at any early age are much greater than those of other children. No social policy, however radically framed, would be able to lift the standards of these people immediately. The most direct way of meeting the problem, not taking account of the value premises in the American Creed, would be to sterilize them. The fact that most whites would want to decrease the Negro population—particularly the lower class Negroes—would strengthen the argument for sterilization of destitute Negroes.

We find, however, that such proposals, if they are made at all, are almost as repugnant to the average white American in the South and the North as to the Negro. In general he is not inclined to consider sterilization as a means of birth control except to prevent the reproduction of the feeble-minded, the insane, and the severely malformed when a hereditary causation can be shown.[50] Outside of those rare cases he is against sterilization even if entirely voluntary.

For this he gives not only the reason that in many regions of the South the political and judicial system is such that, for Negroes and perhaps other poor people, a system of "voluntary" sterilization might in practice turn out to be compulsory. His resistance goes deeper. He reacts against the idea that any individual, for reasons which have no biological but only social causes, should undergo an unnatural restriction of his procreative possibilities. Outside the narrow field of negative eugenics, sterilization is, therefore, excluded as a means of controlling fertility. Except for individual cases in which life or health is threatened by child-bearing, the average American takes a similar attitude toward induced abortion. In his opinion, life should not be extinguished. Abortion, further, is not entirely free from health risks.[a]

The type of birth control which we shall have to discuss as a means of population policy is thus for all practical purposes restricted to contraception. As we have already seen, the whites' desire to decrease the Negro population becomes, even in regard to birth control, entirely overshadowed by quite other valuations centered on the health and happiness of the individual parents and children, which are all backed by the American Creed and shared by the Negroes. The full possibilities of these latter valuations in permitting a birth control policy in America have not yet been realized. Under their sanction birth control facilities could be extended relatively more to Negroes than to whites, since Negroes are more concentrated in the lower income and education classes and since they now know less about modern techniques of birth control. On this score there would probably be no conflict of policy between Negroes and whites.

[a] The prevalence of this political attitude does not prevent individuals from resorting to abortion when they want to interrupt undesired pregnancies.

Without going into the general reasons for spreading birth control in any population,[51] a few remarks on the special reasons for Negroes are in point. One of the most obvious misfortunes which a reduced birth rate could relieve is the poverty of the Negro masses. This is especially true as new legislation, urbanization, and technological advance operate to diminish child labor. It is particularly strong as long as the state shares only slightly in paying for the investment in a new generation and leaves the rising costs of bearing and rearing children almost entirely to the individual families. Since Negro women are employed to a greater extent than white women, the periods of pregnancy, delivery, and dependency are a relatively greater economic burden to Negro families. If pregnancies occur too frequently, the mother's health is endangered. To poor Negro mothers in communities which do not provide proper natal and pre-natal care for Negroes, any pregnancy is a health risk.

Besides poverty, there are other conditions among Negroes which motivate birth control. One is the high disease rate. In so far as diseases of parents are transmitted to their children, killing or permanently maiming them, such parents ought to be encouraged not to have children. The special reference here, of course, is to the venereal diseases which afflict Negroes to a much greater extent than whites.[52] Poindexter[53] estimates that of the conceptions of untreated syphilitic women, about 30 per cent die *in utero*, 40 per cent die within the first two years of life, and the remaining 30 per cent, while they live past the age of two, usually have some permanent defect. There can be no excuse for having children under such circumstances, and the provision of contraceptive information and devices would be to everyone's advantage. There are in the United States over 2,500 clinics[54] the function of which is to cure cases of venereal disease. Since a good proportion of the cost of these clinics is borne by the federal government,[55] they are roughly distributed in accordance with need. Thus the South, with only 31 per cent of the total population but 79 per cent of the Negro population, had 61 per cent of these clinics in 1940.[56] In connection with the work of these clinics there is much publicity on the prevention and cure of venereal disease. It would be a simple matter, and one much in accord with the purpose of this work, for the clinics to provide, and give information about, contraceptives to those who have the diseases which they are combating. The funds for these activities need to be increased, and clinics set up where none are now available. A case could also be made for extending the scope of the circumstances under which physicians may legally perform therapeutic abortions.[57]

A third special problem in connection with the formation of a policy toward Negro fertility is suggested by the extremely high illegitimacy rate among Negroes.[a] Reported illegitimate births constituted 16.2 per cent of

---

[a] The causes of this high birth rate to unmarried mothers will be considered in Chapter 43, Section 2.

all reported births among nonwhites in 1936, and 2.0 per cent among whites. The illegitimate child is under many handicaps and seldom has the opportunity to develop into a desirable citizen.[58] Even if he has a good mother, she cannot give him the proper care since she must usually earn her own living and cannot afford to place him under proper supervision. The absence of a father is detrimental to the development of a child's personality, as is the mockery from the outside world which the illegitimate child is sometimes forced to experience.[a] Too, the unwed mother tends —although there are many exceptions—to have looser morals and lower standards, and in this respect does not provide the proper *milieu* for her child. It would be better both for society in general and for the mother if she had no child.

In all these respects the extra strength of the reasons for birth control among Negroes is due only to the fact that, as a group, they are more touched by poverty, disease, and family disorganization than is common among the whites in America. If caste with all its consequences were to disappear, there would, from these viewpoints, be no more need for birth control among Negroes than among whites. But the general reasons for family limitation would remain, and they would have a strength depending upon the extent to which society was reformed to become a more favorable environment for families with children.[59] Until these reforms are carried out, and as long as the burden of caste is laid upon American Negroes, even an extreme birth control program is warranted by reasons of individual and social welfare.

7. Birth Control Facilities for Negroes

The birth control movement in America was one which had the support of liberals but met the fiercest opposition of the Catholic Church and other organized groups with conservative leanings. It also had to deal with the inertia and puritanical morality of the masses.[60] Only in the last fifteen years has it become possible to discuss the subject publicly without being criticized or condemned as immoral. Only in the last five years has the legal prohibition against dissemination of information about birth control let up significantly, and there are still all sorts of legal obstacles to the movement.[61]

In the last decade some significant changes have occurred. Public opinion, as measured by polls, is increasingly in favor of birth control. National magazines have had frank articles on it. The number of contraceptive clinics rose from 34 in 1930 to 803 in 1942.[62] In three states—North Carolina, South Carolina, and Alabama—*public* health authorities have taken the lead in bringing birth control clinics to rural areas, where they are most

[a] There is much less social derogation of the illegitimate child among Negroes than among whites. See Chapter 43, Section 2.

needed. Several other Southern states are on the verge of following the example of these three. In 1937 the conservative American Medical Association accepted birth control as an "integral part of medical practice and education." These rapid changes are partly the result of the general trend toward social amelioration and secularization. They are also the result of the excellent propaganda and organizational work under the movement now known as the Planned Parenthood Federation of America. The leading spirit in the movement, since 1916, has been Mrs. Margaret Sanger.

While the birth control movement is generally considered to be a liberal movement, and the South is generally the least hospitable section of the country to liberal movements, the South now leads other sections of the country in accepting birth control.[63] The relative absence of Roman Catholics in the South, the great attention recently of the birth control organizations to the South, and the greater need of the South are important reasons for this. But it is reasonable to assume that the large number of undesired Negroes in the rural districts also has something to do with the lack of opposition on the part of the white South.[a]

There is some variation in the technical organization of the programs in the three Southern states which now have public birth control clinics, but there is enough in common to describe a general pattern.[64] These clinics were started by the action of the chief health officer in each state; he sent letters to each of the local health officers to ask them if they would accept birth control clinics as a part of their regular health clinics. Those who accepted[b]—and this now includes most of the local health officers in North Carolina and a significant proportion in South Carolina and Alabama —received advice, instruction and special supplies. The regular local health offices—some of which, therefore, now have birth control clinics—are paid for by the state governments and by the Children's Bureau of the federal government on a grant-in-aid basis, but they are under the control of locally appointed health officers. The cost of birth control supplies is often borne by the private birth control organization of the state. When the public clinics began in North Carolina, a nurse whose salary and expenses were paid by the Planned Parenthood Federation of America gave instruction and supplies to the local doctors and nurses. The clinics in the other states had a similar start. Thus at the beginning the expenses of the program were borne by private groups, but there is a strong tendency

---

[a] As we observed in the previous sections of this chapter, Southerners will never publicly admit that they would like to see the Negro population decrease, but they do point to the poverty that could be avoided if there were fewer Negroes. Another indication that the presence of the Negroes is a main reason for the lack of opposition to birth control in the South is that, despite lack of opposition to it, birth control is taboo as a subject for public or polite conversation even more in the South than in the North.

[b] In many cases the local health officer had to get the approval of the county medical society.

toward state support with federal aid. Sometimes the patients pay a nominal fee.

Most of the 452 privately supported birth control clinics in the United States in 1942 were under the sponsorship of the Planned Parenthood Federation of America or its local affiliates. Most of these are in cities. The Harlem section of New York got a clinic in 1930. The Federation—with funds made available by a white philanthropist—is conducting two demonstration projects important to Negroes: one in urban Nashville, Tennessee, and the other in rural Berkeley County, South Carolina. Both projects are for Negroes only. The Federation has a Division of Negro Service whose primary function is educational. Aided by a national Negro Advisory Council of 34 eminent Negro leaders, it works through the Urban Leagues, Negro doctors and nurses, the National Hospital Association, the Negro press and Negro clubwomen.[65] Some 200 of the Negro Jeanes teachers have requested information of the Federation's Division of Negro Service, as have hundreds of Southern white health officers and doctors.[66]

The activity of the birth control movement's workers, the Southern whites, and the Negro leaders—all with the same aim of spreading birth control among Negroes—promises a great development of the movement in the future. Since few Negroes are Catholics, and since they do not live in areas where Catholics predominate, the chief remaining weakness, as far as Negroes are concerned, is the lack of funds for educational work. It would seem that, more and more, the Southern states are on the way to making public funds available for birth control work. Too, it is likely that philanthropy will be more willing to come into this field since it has become legal and popularly acceptable in the last five years.

A more serious difficulty is that of educating Southern Negroes to the advantages of birth control. Negroes, on the whole, have all the prejudices against it that other poor, ignorant, superstitious people have.[67] More serious is the fact that even when they do accept it, they are not very efficient in obeying instructions and sometimes they come to feel that it is a fake.[68] An intensive educational campaign is needed, giving special recognition to the prejudices and ignorance of the people whom the campaign is to benefit. The use of Negro doctors and nurses is essential.

With the growing popular and legal acceptance of birth control, it would seem that a shift in emphasis is needed.[69] None of the present activities should be cut out, but the time has come for more direct and more widespread educational work. The birth control organizations, having been stung so many times, are chary of direct propaganda that might antagonize doctors and others among the "best people." It is true that they seek to reach the masses of Negroes through the Urban Leagues, Negro newspapers, Jeanes teachers, and Negro clubwomen. But they only tell people to see a doctor and so do not get over the fact that there are more easily accessible devices for birth control and venereal prophylaxis than the ones usually prescribed by physicians.[70]

Of course special cases do require medical attention, and all persons should be told to see a doctor if possible.[71] Medical advice will always be an asset in getting over improved techniques of birth control, in adjusting individual problems and in securing general health improvement. But there is no need for all people to refrain from birth control or prophylaxis until they have seen a doctor. So far contraception has been most successful on a mass basis among city people who learn about simple methods from their friends, not from doctors. What city Negroes now know—as evidenced by their low birth rate—merely needs to be told to country Negroes. The birth control organizations can do this more effectively, more speedily, and more scientifically, than can rumors and jokes.

The main reason for advocating this shift in emphasis is that mass instruction and propaganda reach more people in less time and at lower cost than the clinics run by doctors and nurses.[72] The need for birth control is common, and is only slightly touched by present activities, despite their high cost. If birth control is to achieve mass utilization, there must be a shift in emphasis from time-consuming and expensive instruction of individuals to a speedy and inexpensive education of groups. And there should not only be groups of women, but also groups of men. Birth control is fundamentally a simple matter, and it calls for adult education before clinical consultation.

CHAPTER 8

MIGRATION

1. OVERVIEW

There are no comprehensive statistics on internal migration in America. Census data on population increase of the several regions from one decade to another, and on the state of birth of individuals, will have to be relied upon for giving what indirect information on migration they can. What we get from these sources is merely *a very approximate measure of the trend of long-range net migration, between regions, of Negroes as compared with whites.*[1] Our interest in this chapter will be focused on migration defined in this way.

Ever since they were brought to this country as slaves, Negroes have been concentrated in the South. There had been little use for slaves in the North, and the Northern state governments early abolished what slavery there was. The South, on the other hand, after an initial period of experimentation, came to regard slavery as an essential part of its economy, and brought Negroes in as long as it was legally possible to do so, and after that bred and smuggled them to increase the number of slaves. Part of the frontier was then in the Southeast and the Negroes were brought along as slaves in the great southward and westward movement of the plantation economy. The restriction of slavery to the South, among many other factors, limited this forced migration to this new region. The stream of free Negroes and fugitive slaves to the North, though highly important politically, was not quantitatively significant.[2] If the southward and westward movement within the slave territory be ignored, the distribution of Negroes in the main regions of the country was substantially the same in 1860 as it was in 1790. In 1860 there was only a scattering of Negroes in the North and practically none in the West.[a]

The Civil War removed the legal restrictions on Negro mobility. It also removed the slave owners' interest in moving the Negroes to places where they could be most profitably used. There was apparently much

---

[a] In 1860, 94.9 per cent of the Negroes in the United States lived in the South (including Missouri). Only one-tenth of 1 per cent lived in non-Southern states west of the Mississippi River, and the remaining 5 per cent lived in Northern states east of the Mississippi River. (*Eighth Census of the United States: 1860.* Vol. I, p. xiii.)

wandering locally. Perhaps, Negroes moved locally more than did whites in the South since Emancipation gave them a psychological release, and since they did not own much land to tie them down. Even today Negroes are less "attached to the soil" than whites, and the turnover of Negro share tenants is high.[a] But there was, for a long time, little long-distance migration out of the South. And even within the South the Negroes seem, on the whole, to have become rather more tied to the districts where they lived before Emancipation than they had been earlier when they were productive capital owned by the employers, and when the plantation economy was in its expanding stage. Outside the local migration, the only numerically significant migration of Negroes between the Civil War and the World War was from rural areas to cities within the South (including Washington, D.C.).

The proportion of Negroes in the North and West[b] rose from 5.1 per cent in 1860 to 10.4 per cent in 1910. In 1910 Negroes made up only 1.6 per cent of the total Northern and Western population (it was 1.2 per cent in 1860). In 1910, 79.3 per cent of all Northern Negroes lived in cities (it was 64.3 per cent in 1860). The urban Negro population in the South increased during the same period from 6.7 to 22.0 per cent of the total Negro population in the region. In 1860 Negroes constituted 19.3 per cent of the Southern urban population and 24.5 per cent in 1910.

The Great Migration, starting in 1915 and continuing in waves from then on, has brought changes in the distribution of Negroes in the United States. The proportion of all Negroes living in the North and West rose to 23.8 per cent in 1940, which signifies a total net migration between 1910 and 1940 of about 1,750,000 from the South.[3] Negroes constituted, in 1940, 3.7 per cent of the total Northern population. Practically all of the migrants had gone to the cities and almost all to the big cities. In 1940, 90.1 per cent of all Negroes in Northern and Western states outside of Missouri lived in urban areas. New York City alone claimed 16.9 per cent of all Negroes living in the North and West. If the Negroes of Chicago, Philadelphia, Detroit, Cleveland, and Pittsburgh are added to those of New York, the proportion rises to 47.2 per cent. The rural North and West still remain practically void of Negroes. The total Negro rural-farm population outside the South was only 269,760 in 1940[c] as against 190,572 in 1910. In most smaller cities in the North Negroes are also absent, or

---

[a] See Chapter 11, Section 8.

[b] In this chapter we include Missouri in the South together with the 16 states and the District of Columbia, defined by the census as the South. The West, as we define it here, includes all states west of the Mississippi River except Louisiana, Arkansas, Missouri, Texas and Oklahoma.

[c] Of these 269,760 Negroes, 218,963 were rural-nonfarm Negroes and only 50,797 were rural farm Negroes. A comparable breakdown in the figures for 1910 is not available.

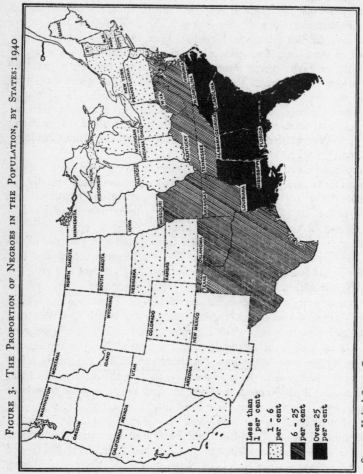

FIGURE 3. THE PROPORTION OF NEGROES IN THE POPULATION, BY STATES: 1940

Less than
1 per cent

1 - 6
per cent

6 - 25
per cent

Over 25
per cent

Source: United States Census.

the small stock of old Negro inhabitants has not been materially increased.

In the South the proportion of the Negro population that lived in cities increased from 22.0 per cent to 37.3 per cent between 1910 and 1940. Negroes now make up 22.3 per cent of the total urban population of the South, while a generation ago the corresponding figure was 24.5 per cent. The Southern rural Negro population has shrunk from 78.0 per cent of the total number of Southern Negroes in 1910 to 62.7 per cent in 1940. The rural Negroes are still distributed in various parts of the South in much the same way as in 1910 and, indeed, as in 1860 on the eve of the Civil War.

In spite of the considerable mobility in the last thirty years, the great majority of Negroes in the United States still live in the South (Figure 3).

2. A CLOSER VIEW

Why has the Negro not moved around more in America? And why have his moves—even in the last generation—been so restricted to a few main streams? A satisfactory answer cannot be given because of fragmentary knowledge. Our attempted answer will have to be abstract, as practically all phases of the Negro problem are involved.[a]

After Emancipation the great masses of American Negroes were concentrated in the rural South, actually some four-fifths of the total Negro population. Theoretically, there were four possible types of places where they could move. First, they could leave the United States. Second, they could take part in the settlement of the frontier West. Third, they could move to the growing cities of the South or to other rural areas in the South. Finally, they could go North. A consideration of why the Negro did, or did not, make each of these types of movements, and of his motives for so doing, will at least formulate some of the main problems involved.[b]

Colonization abroad had been attempted in the *ante-bellum* South as a method of getting rid of the free Negroes. The back-to-Africa movement is interesting from an ideological point of view.[c] Its quantitative effects upon the Negro population in America were, however, almost nothing. Not many white people were ever deeply interested; fewer still were prepared to make the necessary financial sacrifices for the passage and settlement of Negroes abroad. Most Negroes were not willing to leave

[a] For a more intensive treatment of several factors only hinted at in this chapter, we refer the reader to later parts of this book, particularly Part IV on the economic status of the Negro.

[b] Most of the factual material for this discussion has been taken from Samuel A. Stouffer and Lyonel C. Florant, "Negro Population and Negro Population Movements:—1860-1940, in Relation to Social and Economic Factors," unpublished manuscript prepared for this study (1940, revised by Lyonel Florant under title, "Negro Migration:—1860-1940" [1942]).

[c] See Chapter 38, Section 12. Also see Stouffer and Florant, *op. cit.*, pp. 35-38.

America. Nevertheless, the idea of mass emigration to Africa or some other place outside the United States is still not completely out of American thinking,[a] although in practice it has not amounted to much so far.

Some ten thousand Negroes went to Liberia and some thousands to Haiti before the Civil War, but after the War this emigration practically ceased.[4] Particularly after the Civil War, Negroes in small numbers traveled back and forth between the United States and the West Indies, but there has been little opportunity for any large-scale emigration to these heavily populated, small islands. South America—especially Brazil, where there is already a large proportion of Negroes—would seem to offer many possibilities to Negroes who wish to leave the United States. Although it is conceivable that the closer cultural relations now opening between the United States and South America will lead to a significant intermigration between these two areas, few have yet taken advantage of those opportunities.

Negroes did not participate in the settlement of the West. In fact, there are not many Negroes in the West even today. In 1940 only 2.2 per cent of all American Negroes lived west of the Mississippi River (outside of Texas, Oklahoma, Louisiana, Arkansas, Missouri, which states may be considered as part of the South rather than the West). Most of the Negro migration to the West has occurred in the last decade: the Western population of Negroes increased 21.1 per cent between 1930 and 1940. But there was little migration when the West was a frontier, and land was cheap. In 1890 there were only 100,986 Negroes in the West, in 1910 still only 135,872.

The reasons for this are not clear, and some historian can do a service by investigating the problem. We know that the settlement of Negro freedmen in the West was a frequently discussed possibility immediately after the Civil War. A few movements to get away from the South developed rather soon. By far the biggest one was to Kansas, and may have brought as many as 40,000 Negroes to that state.[5] There are reasons to believe that the lack of capital and experience on the part of Southern Negroes is only a small part of the explanation as to why westward migration generally became abortive. There were Negroes who had the little capital necessary to get started on their own in the West; others could have begun as laborers, who were needed not only on the farms but in the huge construction work going on. The primary explanation seems to be that in rural areas of the West, white settlers decided that there were not to be any Negroes.[b] The same seems to have been true in most rural areas of the Northeast and in

---

[a] See Chapter 38, Section 12.

[b] This is all the more incomprehensible because Chinese were imported to do the construction work in the West, and there was much greater prejudice against them than against Negroes.

most small towns of the entire North. The closer neighborhood controls in smaller communities seem to have blocked the Negro from moving in when he was no longer protected as a slave. Even apart from actual pressure there must have been imagined pressure: individuals in a lower caste, like the Negroes, are always on the lookout for discrimination and intimidation and probably felt that it was not safe to venture into the loneliness of a small community. At any rate, it soon became a popular belief among Southern Negroes that the only outlet from the Southern Black Belt was to the cities and preferably to the big cities, where Negro neighborhoods were already established. Negro migration thus early tended to become migration between fairly large-sized Negro communities or to be stopped altogether.

But there were cities in the West, and a few of these grew rapidly. In them small Negro communities developed, and the Negro inhabitants found that there was less prejudice in these new cities than even in the Northeastern cities. James Weldon Johnson described San Francisco, for example, in 1905:

> I was delighted with San Francisco. Here was a civilized center, metropolitan and urbane. With respect to the Negro race, I found it a freer city than New York. I encountered no bar against me in hotels, restaurants, theaters, or other places of public accommodation and entertainment. We hired a furnished apartment in the business area, and took our meals wherever it was most convenient. I moved about with a sense of confidence and security, and entirely from under that cloud of doubt and apprehension that constantly hangs over an intelligent Negro in every Southern city and in a great many cities of the North. . . . The black population was relatively small, but the colored people that I met and visited lived in good homes and appeared to be prosperous. I talked with some of them about race conditions; the consensus of their comment was that San Francisco was the best city in the United States for a Negro. This may, of course, have been in some degree a reflex of prevalent Pacific Coast boosting.[6]

It is surprising that cities like San Francisco, Los Angeles, and Seattle did not attract a greater Negro population. Perhaps the long and expensive journey to the Western cities has been a deterrent. The competition from Orientals and Mexicans as domestics and laborers also has played a role. But we are not satisfied with this explanation, although we have nothing better to offer.

The South also had its western frontier. In 1860, there was relatively little population in the large area which is now Oklahoma and Western Texas. After 1860, whites began to flow in from more eastern places in the South. Later, as the boll weevil, erosion, and mechanization shifted cotton westward; and as new occupations developed in agriculture, in livestock production, in mining, and in manufacturing in these areas, whites moved in at an increasing rate. But Negroes did not come in any significant numbers. By 1940, Negroes constituted only 12.5 per cent of the population of Texas and Oklahoma, and they were not often employed in the new occupations. Oil and gas wells in these two states gave employment to 90,000 in 1930, of whom only 800 were Negroes. In the cities, Negroes had little opportunity outside of domestic and personal service: in 1930 they constituted only 8 per cent of the gainfully occupied in nonagricultural pursuits aside from domestic and personal service. Negroes did not even get much of a share in the new cotton production of these states.[a] Southern prejudice against the Negro seems to be the most potent factor in keeping the Negro out of the new opportunities in Texas and Oklahoma. In some towns Negroes are not permitted to remain over 24 hours; everywhere the Negro is "kept in his place." Another factor has been the competition from the Mexicans, who went into the lowest occupations and filled the traditional "Negro jobs."

Negroes did go to the Southern cities but not nearly to the same extent as did the whites. In 1940, Negroes constituted only 22.4 per cent of the population of Southern cities over 100,000, and 22.5 per cent of the cities of that size having 20 per cent of their employed workers in manufacturing and construction industries. The growth of the city represents the greatest economic change in the South that has occurred since the Civil War. The Industrial Revolution, with all its connotation of modern progress and new opportunity, came to the South later than it did to the North, but it did come. Negroes, however, were not allowed to share in many of its fruits. The tradition persisted that Negroes could not operate machines, or at least this was the rationalization used to keep them from the new occupations. Negroes lost out in many of the skilled occupations they had formerly had. In the Southern city, the Negro is now mainly an unskilled laborer or a servant.[b]

While the Negroes have probably moved around locally in the South a great deal since 1860, the net result of this movement has been surprisingly insignificant. Negroes have not been permitted to take advantage of new opportunities in rural areas any more than they have been in urban areas. By a reclassification of the South into 140 districts which are much more homogeneous in regard to Negroes than the political units formerly used by the Census Bureau,[7] Stouffer and Wyant have shown three striking facts:

1. Those Southern districts which tended to have relatively few Negroes in 1860 grew faster both absolutely and relatively between 1860 and 1930 than those with many Negroes. The former included most of the districts which were destined to be most heavily urban in 1930.

[a] See Chapter 11, Section 4, and Chapter 12, Section 6.
[b] For a more detailed description of the Negro in Southern industry, see Chapter 13.

2. Those Southern districts which tended to have relatively few Negroes in 1860 also had relatively few in 1930.[8]

3. In 1930, as in 1860, the regions of dense Negro population were concentrated in the crescent, sometimes narrow, sometimes broad, between the Potomac and Texas and between the mountains and the sea (see Figure 2). This old plantation belt is "black" today, as it was at the time of Emancipation, although the proportion of Negroes in the population has declined. The two great mountain regions—the Appalachians and the Ozarks—were still almost entirely devoid of Negroes, and areas in the Border states outside the mountains tended to show decreases rather than increases in the percentage Negro.

Not only did the Negro not share in the expanding opportunities in the South, but also the areas in which the Negroes lived declined from an economic standpoint. Most important was the deterioration of cotton production in the Black Belt of the Southeast. In the states east of Mississippi, Negro-operated farms produced 643,000 fewer bales of cotton in 1929 than in 1909, while white-operated farms increased production by 90,000 bales.[9]

Thus we have seen that the Negro did not share much in the growth of the West and of the South. For a long while—until the World War, in fact—it did not seem that he would share in the even greater growth of the North. During and immediately after the First World War came the Great Migration, and ever since then Negroes have not stopped coming to the urban North.[10] Negroes probably came in greater relative numbers than the Southern whites who had more opportunities within the old South and in the new South of Texas and Oklahoma, but they did not come as rapidly after 1915 as did the white immigrants from Europe before the First World War. By 1940 there were 2,439,201 Negroes living in the North, east of the Mississippi River, or 19.0 per cent of the total Negro population in the country and 3.9 per cent of the total Northern population. Population distribution within the South was, of course, somewhat affected by the northward migration after 1914. Many Negroes went North from the Border states, and their number was not quite replenished by Negroes coming from farther South. Those portions of Virginia, the Carolinas, and Georgia which lie east of the mountains lost Negro population most heavily, but have made it up—except for the Piedmont area—by natural increase.[11]

The inadequate explanation that we gave in discussing lack of migration to the West is all we have to account for the extreme concentration in a few Northern cities. There is enough industrial activity, and there could be opportunity for anonymity, as well as a low level of race prejudice, in many of the smaller cities of the North to permit a significant immigration of Negroes. That Negroes have not migrated to these places is as much of a mystery as the relative absence of migration to the West.

Another mystery—which is not entirely outside our problem, as the conditions and behavior of Negroes are constantly compared with those of their white neighbors—is why poor white Southerners during the entire period after the Civil War did not move in greater numbers to the North than they did. The Industrial Revolution came to the Northern cities long before the Civil War. But the period since 1860 has witnessed the greatest mechanization and expansion of industry. Over-population and poverty have loomed over the South all the time. It is true that the whites could move to the Southwest which was mostly closed to the Negroes. The whites also reserved for themselves most of the jobs in the developing industry in the South. But industrial wages were low and many whites were pressed down to share tenancy in the rural districts.[a] As compared to the European immigrants, who formed the bulk of the labor supply for the factories in the North, they should have had the advantage of knowing the language and of being more familiar with American ways and manners.

In 1930 the percentage of all Southern-born Negroes who lived in the Northern states east of the Mississippi River was double the percentage of Southern-born whites living in these Northern states. Most of the Southern whites living in the North were from the Border states. If we leave the Border states out of consideration, the proportion of Negroes born in the Lower South and living in the North outnumbered, by a ratio of five to one, the proportion of whites born in the Lower South and living in the North. Despite the fact that most Southern-born whites living in the North came from the Border states, Negroes born in the Border states and living in the North outnumbered, by a ratio of two to one, the proportion of whites born in the Border states and living in the North.[12] This lack of migration of whites from the South is especially striking when it is realized that there were almost as many Northern-born whites in the South as there were Southern-born whites in the North. In 1930 there were 1,931,799 Southern-born whites living in the Northern states outside of the Mountain and Pacific Divisions; but there were 1,821,678 whites born in these Northern states living in the South.[13] Even if we subtract Northern-born whites living in Washington, D.C., from the latter figure, we have 1,732,120 Northern-born whites living in the South.[14]

The corresponding figures for Negroes were: 1,355,789 Southern-born Negroes living in the Northern states outside of the Mountain and Pacific Divisions and 52,338 Negroes born in these Northern states living in the South. Of the latter, 4,621 were living in Washington, D.C., which left only 47,717 Northern-born Negroes living in the rest of the South.[15] The difference between numbers of Southern whites and Southern Negroes

[a] See Chapter 11.

living in the North is even more striking when it is remembered that there were more than two and a half times as many whites born in the South as there were Negroes. Thus, when discussing the causes as to why the stream of Negro migrants to the North before 1915 was so small, it should be remembered that the Southern whites followed the same pattern. And the Great Migration of Negroes after 1915 is the more significant when it is realized that it was much bigger—relative to the size of the respective populations—than the corresponding migration of Southern whites.

3. THE GREAT MIGRATION TO THE URBAN NORTH[16]

For the average Negro, living conditions in the North have always been more favorable than in the South. The North has—in spite of considerable discrimination—offered him more economic opportunities (in relief if not in employment), more security as a citizen, and a greater freedom as a human being. The concrete import of this general statement will become clearer as we proceed in our inquiry. Nevertheless, this great difference did not, by itself, cause more than a tiny stream of northward migration for almost two generations.

On the whole, the difference was probably widening after 1870. Jim Crow legislation and disfranchisement were being perfected in the South in the decades around the turn of the century. Lynching and legal insecurity did not start to decrease until the 1890's, and the drop was not great until the 1920's. Schools for Negroes were generally improved but not so fast as for the whites and not nearly so fast as in the North. The slow trend toward Negro landownership was broken just after the turn of the century. The natural increase of the Southern population was large, and the corresponding expansion of employment opportunities retarded. Negroes were not allowed to share much in the opportunities that did develop. Whites began to monopolize the new cotton growing in the Southwest and also to infringe on the traditional "Negro jobs." Except for a small proportion of Negro professionals and businessmen who served their own people, few Negroes in the South had opportunity to improve their economic position. At least in a subjective sense—which is the important thing in discussing human motivation—the difference in desirability between South and North widened as Southern Negroes became more educated and came to know the outside world better.

In the North, industrial expansion was tremendous after the Civil War, creating new employment opportunities for millions of immigrants. The few Negroes in the North were largely kept out of industrial employment but found a ready demand as domestics and in other service jobs. In many places it was a fashion among the wealthy to hire Negroes as servants in preference to European immigrants. Many middle class whites also came to prefer Negroes—largely because they did not object to the hardest work and did not expect much in wages. A second important demand factor came from the big industries when white workers went out on strike. A third element in the migration before the First World War was the escape

FIGURE 4.   THE NORTHWARD MIGRATION

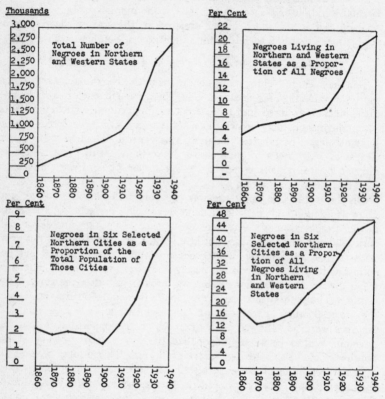

Source: United States Census.

Notes: In each diagram, the calculation for 1870 is based on the assumption that the figures are mid-way between those of 1860 and 1880. Missouri is considered as part of the South.

The six selected Northern cities are: New York, Chicago, Philadelphia, Detroit, Cleveland and Pittsburgh. These cities are those Northern ones, outside of cities in Missouri, which contained the largest Negro populations in 1930. Brooklyn is included in New York City even before the date on which it was legally incorporated with it.

of upper class Negroes who desired to improve themselves. These were few in number, and many managed to get placed in commerce and industry on an almost equal basis with the whites.[17]

But—except for occasional sudden influxes of Negroes as a result of the demands for strikebreakers—the stream of Negroes moving to the North never swelled much (Figure 4). In the normal case the industrial employers found their demand for unskilled labor well filled by European immigrants. The workers themselves often resented Negro competition. This is not a full explanation of why the North did not attract more Negroes, however, since the labor market was immense in comparison to the supply of Negro labor, and since the service occupations would, even at that time, have been preferable to Southern Negroes, particularly when we remember all the other advantages for a Negro in the North. The slow but accelerating increase in northward Negro net migration (Figure 4) confirms our general hypothesis of a widening gap in the subjective desirability between the two regions as places to live. But, as we said, the rate of migration did not become large until the World War. Much in the Great Migration after 1915 is left unexplained if we do not assume that there was before 1915 *an existing and widening difference in living conditions between South and North which did not express itself in a mass migration simply because the latter did not get a start and become a pattern.*

In this situation of accumulated migration potentialities several factors of change coincided and created a shock effect after 1915. In the South "white infiltration" into the types of work formerly monopolized by Negroes, the relative shift westward of cotton growing, and the ravages of the boll weevil made the Negro cotton farmer still worse off. Drought, too, made farming difficult in 1916 and 1917. The First World War stirred up people's minds and prepared them for change. The draft actually moved a great number of Negro men from their home communities. The draft of white workers, the stopping of immigration, and the general war prosperity forced Northern industry to turn actively to Negroes for new workers. There was a "push" in the South and there was a "pull" in the North, widening tremendously the already existing differences in opportunities for a Negro in the two regions. When factors of inertia were once overcome and the northward mass migration was started, the movement quickly took on momentum. A new pattern of behavior was set; a new hope in the possibilities in the North was created. Lines of communication between North and South were established.

If the migration is thus explained in terms of "conditions" and "factors" and a "difference in opportunities," it should, of course, not be assumed that an accurate picture has thereby been given of the actual motivation of the individuals moving. The motivation was probably different for each Negro who migrated, and it involved a conscious consideration of all the personal elements in the situation that the individual happened to think of and judged as relevant—not only, and sometimes not even primarily, the economic opportunities.[18] It also involved a number of poorly-thought-out elements, unconscious influences and "chance" factors. The precipitating "cause" of migration of an individual might be such an event as the spurning of a young man by his sweetheart, or the death of a grandmother who was too old to be moved.[19]

What actually happened to a great number of Negroes at the start of the Great Migration must have been that they were unsettled, like everyone else, by the War and by all the changes occurring in the industrial system and the labor market. They found their chances in the South particularly bad. In addition, they heard about new openings in the North. Negroes already in the North wrote letters to relatives or friends in the South. Such letters were often passed around the community or their contents were passed on by word of mouth among the illiterates. To these means of communication were added those of the Negro press and the labor agents. Negro newspapers stimulated migration not only by printing advertisements of specific jobs, but also by editorials and news comments on the better conditions for Negroes in the North. These affected individual Negroes and also set the topic of friendly social discussion in many Negro communities.

It is impossible to estimate the influence of agents, both white and Negro, sent out by Northern industries. At first they were ignored by the Southern whites, but during the boom days of 1917 and thereafter, their activities were hampered in many ways, both legally and illegally. Not only were there agents with specific promises of jobs and money to pay the railroad fare of Negroes who desired to take these jobs, but there were rumors of agents who did not exist except in the distorted perceptions or imaginations of rumor-spreaders. Negroes who were influenced by such rumors did not have much difficulty in getting jobs during the War, but they had to pay their own railroad fare when they had not expected to.

A desire to improve oneself economically by going North was, of course, a chief motive for migration. Many had heard about specific job opportunities, and many had friends who had become well-to-do in the North, but just as important was the general myth of Northern prosperity. Generally, the Negro was sought as an unskilled laborer and in such an occupation, for the most part, he had to stay. The North, as well as the South, has been hesitant to mix the machine and the Negro;[a] and yet, whether measured in terms of proportions in "desirable" occupations, average income, availability of unemployment relief, or of other types of social security benefits, the Negro is considerably better off in the North than in the South.[b]

Allied with the desire for economic improvement was a desire for social improvement. Like many other oppressed people, Negroes placed a high premium on education. In the North, Negroes not only had access to more

[a] For evidence, see Chapter 13.
[b] For statistical documentation of these statements, see Chapters 13, 14, 15 and 16.

and better schools, but they could more easily earn the money to go to them. Many Negroes also felt they could no longer tolerate their subordinate and restricted position. Both the fact and the myth of Northern equality played a role in stimulating some Negroes to go North. Such Negroes were usually those who had some taste of a society in which their position was not so low—such as those who read books or corresponded with Northern friends, or those who had served in the United States Army during the World War. The general freedom, excitement, and anonymity of city life also attracted many rural Southern Negroes. A small number of Negroes went North because they found themselves *persona non grata* with Southern whites for one reason or another.

There were a number of things which retarded migration. Even the Great Migration during and after the World War brought only a small proportion of Southern Negroes to the North. Perhaps a majority of them were not even considering migrating. Except during the war boom, Negroes realized that there were only a limited number of jobs in the North. Owners of Northern industry were not very willing to hire Negro workers except when orders were pilling up, and European immigrant laborers could not be had because of the War or legal restrictions on immigration. Northern industrialists often believed in the stereotype of the lazy and inefficient Negro, and often their limited observations strengthened their belief. Some had the legitimate doubt whether Negroes, used to forced labor on farms, could be adapted to free labor in factories. Too, they did not wish to offend their white workers, who were in the majority. Most white unions, faced with Negroes coming into their industries, fought the Negroes; and white workers generally opposed black competition. On the other hand, some Negroes were, or felt they were, fairly well established economically in the South. In some cases the economic tie was actually a chain. In the turpentine industry, for example, Negroes worked and lived in isolated camps, and were forced to buy in company stores. The owners, in order to maintain a steady and cheap labor supply, saw to it that the Negro laborers ran into debt, and connived with the law-enforcement agencies to prevent Negroes from escaping that debt.

There were not only economic ties, but also all sorts of social ties. Few persons like to leave permanently their families and friends and places familiar to them to go to a strange place. This fear of the unknown was enhanced by the stories that grew up about the North as a lawless and licentious place. It was—being North—a cold place, where Negroes—being used to warm climates—died in droves. A few migrants disliked the North so much that they returned South, and discouraged their friends.[20] Then, too, many Negroes did not know how to go about getting a train ticket and others did not have enough money to buy one.

Negro leaders were divided as to the desirability of a northward migra tion. Some saw the North as a place where members of their race could get a new start in life, economically, socially and politically. Others felt that migration was a disrupting force, and that the Negro problem could not be solved by running away from it. Some professionals and businessmen in the South were afraid of losing their clientele, and some community leaders were afraid of losing their communities. A number of them joined in the caravan, but the ones left behind were not particularly happy about it all. The upper class Negroes in the North had mixed feelings with respect to the new migration. On the one hand, they saw their own social status decreasing: prejudice mounted against Negroes in the North as a reaction to the sudden influx of rough Southern Negroes.[a] On the other hand, the economic basis of their businesses or professions broadened as the Negro community grew.

4. Continued Northward Migration

After the First World War many of the same influences continued, and Negroes kept up their migration northward. After a few years of depression, unprecedented prosperity brought a new demand for industrial goods. Immigration laws effectively kept out competitors to American labor, except for Mexicans and a few French-Canadians. Cotton production in the South Atlantic and East South Central states was still in the doldrums, though not so badly as during the War. Also important was the fact that a pattern of migration had been well started; fear and local ties were no longer so potent in deterring migration as they had been before the War. Jobs, however, were not so plentiful in the North, and a housing shortage for Negroes, who were kept in segregated quarters of the cities, caused rents to eat up a large part of the Negro's wage.

With the depression beginning in 1929, a new set of circumstances arose to determine the extent of the Negro's migration northward. There were no longer new jobs for Negroes in the North; in fact, Negroes there were laid off by the thousands. In November, 1937, 39 per cent of the male nonwhite labor force in Northern states outside of the Rocky Mountain and Pacific Coast Divisions were unemployed.[21]

[a] An elderly upper class Negro woman who had lived all her life in the North told an interviewer in 1927:

"The Negro invasion began about 1915. Until that time we had been accepted as equals but as soon as the Southern Negroes began coming in we were relegated to their class. Our white friends shunned us and we were really without social life until our own group was better organized. . . . We really do not mingle with the Southern Negro and they do not come near us as they know that we are Northerners."

This woman was president of a local society composed of Negroes who had lived in the North for at least 35 years, or their descendants. (Unpublished document in possession of the Social Science Research Committee of the University of Chicago, "History of Douglas," document No. 15).

But a new form of livelihood arose to take the place of jobs. This was public assistance in its many forms. It was much harder for Negroes who needed it to get relief in the South than in the North. In 1935 around half of all Negro families in the North were on relief.[a] Hence Negroes were again attracted northward—though not to the same extent as during the period of the World War and the 1920's. Many Northern states set up residence requirements—ranging up to five years—to keep out migrants seeking relief. These requirements were not rigorously enforced in the early days of the depression, but even when they were, Negroes felt it better to trust to luck for odd jobs or to their friends until the residence requirements had been met, rather than to meet almost sure starvation in the South.[b] Relief and the residence requirements for relief also had the effect of cutting down on the remigration to the South.[c]

Economic conditions had become relatively worse for Negroes in the South during the depression. Whites who had lost their small farms or their better jobs in the cities began to encroach on the Negroes in the heavy unskilled occupations and even in the service occupations—the traditional jobs of the Southern Negro. Southern agriculture became worse, and the poorest owners and tenants—which included a disproportionate share of Negroes—were forced out. The Agricultural Adjustment Administration of the federal government—in an effort to aid Southern agriculture—forced out the poorest among both white and Negro agriculturists even more.[d] Most of these—including practically all the whites—went on relief, but many of the Negroes could not get relief and so moved North where no color distinction was made in the administration of public assistance.[e]

Most experts believed, during the 'thirties, that the northward Negro migration had diminished considerably. Now that the preliminary results of the 1940 Census are available, we know that it has kept up. It was not so high during the 'thirties as it had been from 1915 to 1930, but the remarkable thing is that it has kept up at all in the absence of employment opportunities in the North.[22]

5. THE FUTURE OF NEGRO MIGRATION

Taking the long historical view, the main observations to be made about Negro migration are that the Negro people have tended to stay where

[a] See Chapter 15.

[b] See Chapter 16.

[c] Also, persons who are able to support themselves after a fashion but know that they may be in need of relief sometime in the future, often consider local relief differentials when deciding on whether or not they want to migrate. Such potential relief clients are particularly numerous, of course, in the Negro group.

[d] See Chapter 12.

[e] For the statistical facts on unemployment, public assistance, and agriculture in the South, see Part IV of this book.

they were. Their movements between the regions of the country have been decidedly more restricted in amount and direction than those of the whites. This trend is as significant as the slower growth of the Negro population when compared with the white population, which we analyzed in the preceding chapter.

The restriction of long-range mobility of Negroes is—to an extent and in a certain direction—a thing of the past. We found that the long immobility of the Negroes was not unrelated to the white immigration, which filled, the demand for unskilled labor in the fast-growing industrial structure of the North. The white Southerners had a natural increase large enough to fill most of those jobs in the lagging industry of the South. The stopping of immigration during the First World War was one of the factors suddenly giving the Negro a chance in Northern industry. But the influence of immigration as a cause of immobility and the stoppage of immigration as a cause, later, of greater mobility were interwoven in a complicated fashion with many other factors. Northern industry went into a period of mechanization, decreasing tremendously its demand for unskilled labor. During the 'thirties a great industrial stagnation hampered the growth of employment opportunities. But once unleashed, the northward Negro migration continued through good and bad times.

To forecast the future of Negro migration is, of course, difficult. It will be determined by social trends and by public policy. Certain of the main conditioning factors stand out rather clearly.

The liberty of the individual to move freely in the country is a firmly entrenched principle of the American Creed. The future development will probably be to reinforce still more in practice the individual's freedom to migrate.[23] It is true that Northern cities are usually not desirous of having Negroes move in. There are a number of measures which can be taken in order to keep out Negro migrants. But none are effective, at least not in the big cities where Negroes have already gained a strong foothold. Smaller cities have often kept out Negroes by social pressure or resort to intimidation. In the South peonage or semi-peonage has prevented some Negroes from moving away. This practice has largely been stamped out during the 'thirties by legal action or is losing its motivation because of the oversupply of Negro labor.[a]

There would, on the contrary, be *a possibility of establishing a positive migration policy of helping the Negroes get to the places where their opportunities on the labor market are best.* Such a policy would be consistent with the American Creed.[b] It seems not improbable that such a labor information service will develop as part of the public control of the labor

---

[a] See Chapter 12 and Chapter 26, Section 2.

[b] See Chapter 9. The details of our suggestion will be presented in Chapter 27, Section 3.

market which is beginning to take shape during the present War and which will become still more of a necessity in the post-war economic crisis.

Leaving this prospect aside, there seem to be good reasons to expect a continuation of the northward migration, in spite of depressions and booms. The pattern is now set and the lines of communication established. The War and the post-war crisis are again stirring up the Negro people, and the psychological effects will probably be cumulative as in the First World War. The general level of education and knowledge of the outside world is rising among Southern Negroes. In the South the continued crisis in cotton growing, which we foresee, and the concentration of its effects on the Negro farmers will continue to act as a tremendous push.[a] The low Negro reproduction rate in Southern cities will, by itself, give space for a continual influx from the surrounding rural areas. Industrialization in the South also is perhaps going to continue at a more rapid rate than in the North.[b] One would expect that this would draw whites away from the poorer, unskilled, and service jobs in the cities and so make more room for Negroes at the bottom of the Southern urban occupational structure. But over-population is so serious in the region and the pattern of giving all new industrial jobs to whites only is so firmly established that it does not seem likely that the industrial development will, directly or indirectly, give Negroes anything like the number of jobs required.

In the North, there are fair prospects of a somewhat decreased economic discrimination against Negro workers. If, in a later stage of the present War, Negroes are brought into industry to a greater extent,[c] this might condition white workers in the North to be better prepared to accept Negroes as co-workers. And there are other factors working in the same direction.[d] The great size of the Northern labor market compared with the Negro population there also keeps employment opportunities better. The fact that Northern Negroes are not reproducing their numbers from generation to generation, while there is a positive natural increase among Southern Negroes, tends also to promote a steady shift of Negroes from the South to the North. The existing differentials in public assistance treatment accorded Negroes between the South and the North will probably continue.[e] The importance of this factor for keeping up migration in depressions has been seen during the 'thirties.

With the West opened up, it would seem that it would be no different from the North in attracting Negroes. It is the writer's impression that, on

[a] See Chapter 12.
[b] The faster rate of industrialization in the South than in the North is a development of the last two decades.
[c] See Chapter 19.
[d] See Chapter 45.
[e] See Chapter 16.

the whole, Negroes meet relatively less discrimination in the West than in parts of the Middle West and the East. This, of course, does not apply to much of the Southwest where Southern whites have gone and have brought their attitudes toward the Negro with them. The small number of Negroes already in the West, the relatively small amount of race prejudice there, and the heavy demand for servants in California will perhaps make the West Coast cities more popular as places for Negro immigration than Northern cities in the Eastern half of the country. The relatively great extent of Negro migration to California in the last decade is perhaps indicative of a future trend.[24] Since Negroes get practically their only new economic opportunities in growing cities, we may expect that most of the westward migration will be to the cities of the West Coast and not to inland cities and rural districts.[25]

A great deal will depend upon the future development of employment opportunities in the war boom, the post-war crisis, and the solution found for this crisis. The development through these future emergencies will be shaped, not only by the free play of economic forces in a market, but increasingly by governmental policies called forth by these emergencies. We shall come back to these problems in Chapter 19.

As a concluding note, it should be stressed that there is no doubt that migration to the North and West is a tremendous force in the general amelioration of the Negro's position. It is even more: northward migration is a necessity if the economic status of Southern Negroes is not to deteriorate as cotton growing disappears as a means of getting a living for the masses of rural Negroes. Migration out of the South, further, means not only *economic* improvement to the Negro. It also gives him a social status approaching equality.[a] It increases the Negro vote, which might become of rising importance for national policy.[b] The experience of the migration of 1917-1919 also suggests that emigration of a significant number of Negroes is one of the surest ways of stimulating the Southern whites to give more consideration to the Negroes that remain in the South. At any rate it seems certain that a concentration of unemployed Negroes on relief in the South will only deteriorate race relations in that region.

Many writers have felt that the partial exodus of the Negro population from the South to the North would "solve" the Negro problem. In doing this, some Northern writers have been thinking of the effects on the Southern white people.[26] Some others, mainly among Southern writers, have thought about the effect on Northern whites: They believe that race prejudice will rise with the proportion of Negroes present in Northern communities; and they feel that when Northern attitudes become more like the Southern attitudes, they will lay the basis for a more unified

[a] See Part VII.
[b] See Part V.

national opinion about how to treat Negroes.[27] Still others, and to this group belong most Negro writers, have their attention fixed on the rise in education, general culture, and political power of the Negro people, and believe that the northward migration will improve the Negro's position in both North and South.[28]

We shall not take part in this dispute, except to emphasize three things: first, that there is probably some truth in the first two statements; second, that, independent of this, migration to the North means a tremendous amelioration of the Negro's status in America; but, third, that the "solution" of the Negro problem—even taken in a relativistic sense of developing a gradual but steady improvement of race relations—is much too complicated to be solved by migration. Governmental intervention is rising, and this trend means that the change of race relations is no longer determined by such "natural" developments as migration but by a complex of intentional policies affecting not only migration but all other spheres of the problem.

Part IV

ECONOMICS

CHAPTER 9

ECONOMIC INEQUALITY

1. NEGRO POVERTY

The economic situation of the Negroes in America is pathological. Except for a small minority enjoying upper or middle class status, the masses of American Negroes, in the rural South and in the segregated slum quarters in Southern and Northern cities, are destitute. They own little property; even their household goods are mostly inadequate and dilapidated. Their incomes are not only low but irregular. They thus live from day to day and have scant security for the future. Their entire culture and their individual interests and strivings are narrow.

These generalizations will be substantiated and qualified in the following chapters. For this purpose the available information is immense, and we shall, in the main, be restricted to brief summaries. Our interest in this part of our inquiry will be to try to unravel the causal relations underlying the abnormal economic status of the American Negro. We want to understand how it has developed and fastened itself upon the economic fabric of modern American society. It is hoped that out of a study of trends and situations will emerge an insight into social and economic dynamics which will allow inferences as to what the future holds for the economic well-being of the American Negro people. This future development will depend in part upon public policy, and we shall discuss the various alternatives for induced change. Certain value premises will be made explicit both in order to guide our theoretical approach and to form the basis for the practical analysis.

Before we proceed to select our specific value premises, let us ask this question: Why is such an extraordinarily large proportion of the Negro people so poor? The most reasonable way to start answering this question is to note the distribution of the Negro people in various regions and occupations. We then find that the Negroes are concentrated in the South, which is generally a poor and economically retarded region. A disproportionate number of them work in agriculture, which is a depressed industry. Most rural Negroes are in Southern cotton agriculture, which is particularly over-populated; backward in production methods; and hard hit by soil exhaustion, by the boll weevil, and by a long-time fall in international demand for American cotton. In addition, few Negro farmers own the land they work on, and the little land they do own is much poorer and less well-equipped than average Southern farms. Most Negro farmers are concentrated in the lowest occupations in agriculture as sharecroppers or wage laborers. In the North, there are practically no Negroes in agriculture.

Nonagricultural Negro workers are, for the most part, either in low-paid service occupations or have menial tasks in industry. Few are skilled workers. Most of the handicrafts and industries in the South where they have a traditional foothold are declining. The majority of manufacturing industries do not give jobs to Negroes. Neither in the South nor in the North are Negroes in professional, business, or clerical positions except in rare instances and except when serving exclusively the Negro public—and even in this they are far from having a monopoly.

The unemployment risk of Negroes is extraordinarily high. During the depression, government relief became one of the major Negro "occupations." Indeed, the institution of large-scale public relief by the New Deal is almost the only bright spot in the recent economic history of the Negro people.

Such a survey, however, even when carried out in greater detail, does not, by itself, explain why Negroes are so poor. The question is only carried one step backward and at the same time broken into parts: Why are Negroes in the poorest sections of the country, the regressive industries, the lowest paid jobs? Why are they not skilled workers? Why do they not hold a fair proportion of well-paid middle class positions? Why is their employment situation so precarious?

We can follow another approach and look to the several factors of economic change. In most cases changes in the economic process seem to involve a tendency which works against the Negroes. When modern techniques transform old handicrafts into machine production, Negroes lose jobs in the former but usually do not get into the new factories, at least not at the machines. Mechanization seems generally to displace Negro labor. When mechanized commercial laundries replace home laundries, Negro workers lose jobs. The same process occurs in tobacco manufacture, in the lumber industry and in the turpentine industry. When tractors and motor trucks are introduced, new "white men's jobs" are created out of old "Negro jobs" on the farm and in transportation. Progress itself seems to work against the Negroes. When work becomes less heavy, less dirty, or less risky, Negroes are displaced. Old-fashioned, low-paying, inefficient enterprises, continually being driven out of competition, are often the only ones that employ much Negro labor.

Although there are no good data on employment trends by race, it seems that the business cycles show something of the same tendency to work against Negroes as do technical changes. It is true that Negroes, more

than whites, are concentrated in service industries and in certain maintenance occupations (janitors, floor-sweepers, and so forth) which are
relatively well-protected from depressions. On the other hand, the Negro
agricultural laborer is more likely to be forced out by depressions than is
the white farmer and farm worker. In fact, in almost every given occupation Negroes tend to be "first fired" when depression comes. Even in the
service and maintenance occupations, Negroes are fired to give jobs to
white workers. When prosperity returns, the lost ground is never quite
made up. As cycle succeeds cycle, there is a tendency toward cumulative
displacement of Negroes. The general level of unemployment, depression
or no depression, is always higher for Negroes than for whites, and the
discrepancy is increasing.

Likewise the organization of the labor market by trade unions has,
most of the time, increased the difficulties for Negroes to get and to hold
jobs. Even social legislation instituted in order to protect the lowest paid
and most insecure workers—among whom the Negroes ordinarily belong—
is not an undivided blessing to Negro workers. When the employer finds
that he has to take measures to protect his workers' health and security and
to pay them higher wages, he often substitutes, voluntarily or under pressure, white workers for Negroes. Sometimes sweatshop industries, existing
only because of low-paid Negro labor, are actually driven out of business
by legislation or union pressure, and the Negro is again the victim instead
of the beneficiary of economic and social progress.

Of course, Negroes are pressing hard in all directions to get jobs and
earn a living. The number of job-seeking Negroes is constantly increased,
as the shrinkage of the international cotton market, the national agricultural policy under the A.A.A. program, and the displacement of Negroes
from traditional jobs, all create a growing unemployment. Negroes are
willing—if it were allowed them—to decrease their demand for remuneration, and they are prepared to take the jobs at the bottom of the
occupational hierarchy. But still their unemployment is growing relative
to that of the whites.

Again we are brought to ask: Why are the Negroes always the unlucky
ones? What is this force which, like gravitation, holds them down in the
struggle for survival and economic advance? To these questions—as to the
closely related questions stated above—we shall find the detailed answers
as diverse as the structure of modern economic life itself. But there will be
a common pattern in the answers.

2. OUR MAIN HYPOTHESIS: THE VICIOUS CIRCLE

This common pattern is the vicious circle of cumulative causation out-
lined in Chapter 3 and Appendix 3.

There is a cultural and institutional tradition that white people exploit

Negroes. In the beginning the Negroes were owned as property. When slavery disappeared, caste remained. Within this framework of adverse tradition the average Negro in every generation has had a most disadvantageous start. Discrimination against Negroes is thus rooted in this tradition of economic exploitation. It is justified by the false racial beliefs we studied in Chapter 4. This depreciation of the Negro's potentialities is given a semblance of proof by the low standards of efficiency, reliability, ambition, and morals actually displayed by the average Negro. This is what the white man "sees," and he opportunistically exaggerates what he sees. He "knows" that the Negro is not "capable" of handling a machine, running a business or learning a profession. As we know that these deficiencies are not inborn in him—or, in any case, in no significant degree—we must conclude that they are caused, directly or indirectly, by the very poverty we are trying to explain, and by other discriminations in legal protection, public health, housing, education and in every other sphere of life.

This scheme of causal interrelation is as important in explaining why Negroes are so poor and in evaluating the wider social effects of Negro poverty, as it is in attempting practical planning to raise the economic level of the Negro people. The dynamics of the problem is this: A primary change, induced or unplanned, affecting any one of three bundles of interdependent causative factors—(1) the economic level; (2) standards of intelligence, ambition, health, education, decency, manners, and morals; and (3) discrimination by whites—will bring changes in the other two and, through mutual interaction, move the whole system along in one direction or the other. No single factor, therefore, is the "final cause" in a theoretical sense. From a practical point of view we may, however, call certain factors "strategic" in the sense that they can be controlled.

The statistics of the system can be illustrated by the following comments on the Negro sharecropper in the rural South:

> Shiftlessness and laziness are reported as reasons for the dependent state, whereas, in fact, in so far as they exist, they are not necessarily inherent, but are caused by the very conditions of the share-cropping system. . . . It is a notorious and shameful fact that the stock arguments employed against any serious efforts to improve the lot of the cotton tenant are based upon the very social and cultural conditions which tenancy itself creates. The mobility of the tenant, his dependence, his lack of ambition, shiftlessness, his ignorance and poverty, the lethargy of his pellagra-ridden body, provide a ready excuse for keeping him under a stern paternalistic control. There is not a single trait alleged which, where true, does not owe its source and continuance to the imposed status itself.[1]

The same type of vicious circle controls the situation for the poverty-stricken Negroes outside of cotton agriculture. Poverty itself breeds the conditions which perpetuate poverty.

The vicious circle operates, of course, also in the case of whites. Few people have enough imagination to visualize clearly what a poor white tenant or common laborer in the South would look like if he had had more opportunities at the start. Upper class people in all countries are accustomed to look down upon people of the laboring class as inherently inferior. But in the case of Negroes the deprecation is fortified by the elaborate system of racial beliefs, and the discriminations are organized in the social institution of rigid caste and not only of flexible social class.

3. THE VALUE PREMISES

The system of social ideals which we have called the American Creed, and which serves as the source of the instrumental value premises in this study, is less specified and articulate in the economic field than, for instance, in regard to civic rights. There is, in regard to economic issues, considerable confusion and contradiction even *within* this higher plane of sanctified national ideals and not only—as elsewhere— *between* those ideals and the more opportunistic valuations on lower planes. In public discussion opposing economic precepts are often inferred from the American Creed. A major part of the ideological battle and of political divisions in the American nation, particularly in the decade of the Great Depression, has concerned this very conflict of ideals in the economic sphere. "Equality of opportunity" has been battling "liberty to run one's business as one pleases."

Meanwhile the battle-front itself has been moving—on the whole definitely in favor of equality of opportunity. American economic liberalism was formerly characterized by "rugged individualism"; it is now gradually assimilating ideals of a more social type. There was always the vague popular ideal of "an American standard of living," but now a more definite and realistic conception is growing out of it. A new kind of "inalienable rights"—economic and social—is gradually taking shape within the great political canon of America and is acquiring the respectability of common adherence even if not of immediate realization. As an exemplification of the new way of thinking, without assuming that it has advanced to the level of a national ideal, we may quote the following statement by the National Resources Planning Board, which is an elaboration of President Roosevelt's pronouncement of "freedom from want" as one of the human liberties:

> We look forward to securing, through planning and cooperative action, a greater freedom for the American people. . . . In spite of all . . . changes, that great manifesto, the Bill of Rights, has stood unshaken 150 years and now to the old freedoms we must add new freedoms and restate our objectives in modern terms. . . . Any new declaration of personal rights, any translation of freedom into modern

terms applicable to the people of the United States, here and now must include:

1. The right to work, usefully and creatively through the productive years.
2. The right to fair pay, adequate to command the necessities and amenities of life in exchange for work, ideas, thrift, and other socially valuable service.
3. The right to adequate food, clothing, shelter, and medical care.
4. The right to security, with freedom from fear of old age, want, dependency, sickness, unemployment, and accident.
5. The right to live in a system of free enterprise, free from compulsory labor, irresponsible private power, arbitrary public authority, and unregulated monopolies.

. . . .

9. The right to rest, recreation, and adventure; the opportunity to enjoy life and take part in an advancing civilization.[2]

The most convenient way of determining our value premises for the economic part of our inquiry is, perhaps, to start from the viewpoint of what the American does *not* want. The ordinary American does not, and probably will not within the surveyable future, raise the demand for full *economic equality* in the meaning of a "classless society" where individual incomes and standards of living would become radically leveled off. Such an ideal would be contrary to the basic individualism of American thinking. It could hardly be realized while upholding the cherished independence of the individual. It would nullify the primary responsibility of the individual for the economic fate of himself and his family. It would rob the individual of his chance to rise to wealth and power. It would thus bury the American Dream. It runs contrary to the common belief that it is the individual's hope for economic advancement which spurs him to do his utmost and at the same time acts as the main driving force behind progress in society. The strength of these individualistic ideals is extraordinary in America even today, in spite of the important changes of basic conditions which we shall presently consider.

Although there is a great deal of inequality of income and wealth in America, the American Creed has always been definitely adverse to class divisions and class inequalities. Americans are, indeed, hostile to the very concept of class.[a] But the observer soon finds that this hostility is generally directed only against a rigid system of privileges and social estates in which the individual inherits his status, and not against differences in wealth as such. The American demand is for *fair opportunity and free scope for individual effort.*

In a new nation with rapid social mobility—which is practically always in an upward direction as new immigrants always fill the lower ranks—this way of reconciling liberty with equality is understandable. Social mobility permitted a relative uniformity of social forms and modes of thinking to

_____
[a] See Chapter 31, Sections 1 and 2.

exist side by side with a great diversity of economic levels of living. Cultural heterogeneity within the nation and huge geographical space also permitted a measure of anonymity and ignorance of distress. On account of the rapid tempo of economic progress and the rapidly growing market, economic adversities never did appear so final and hopeless.[a] Land was abundant and practically free, and there was at least an avowed national ideal of free education for all individuals.

The principle of noninterference on the part of the State in economic life, therefore, did not seem incompatible with the prinicple of equality of opportunity. This ideal has had, of course, more influence in America than in any comparable European country. There have always been qualifications, however, even in this country. In recent times the qualifications have been increasing in relative importance, slowly remolding the entire configuration of this part of the American Creed. Probably most Americans are today prepared to accept a considerable amount of *public control* for the purpose of preserving natural resources. Land and other natural assets are today almost entirely occupied and are no longer free. In the whole nation, a vivid realization has grown up of the waste and damage done to these national assets in reckless exploitation and speculation.

In regard to the personal resources of the nation, Americans are not as willing to have public control. But in the one field of education, they have been the pioneering radical interventionists of the world bent upon improving the human material by means of proper schooling. The spirit of interventionism by education is continually gaining in momentum. It early became a self-evident qualification of American economic liberalism. Within the last decades this spirit has spread to other fields. Social legislation has been instituted to regulate children's and women's work, safety measures, and other working conditions in industry, and—later—wages, hours and labor organizations. A system of social insurance has gradually been taking form.

The mass unemployment during the depression of the 'thirties—mounting higher than ever before and higher over a long period than in any other country—and the realization that whole regions and occupational groups can be brought to destitution through no fault of their own caused the development to full consciousness of a sense of public responsibility for these things. For the first time America saw itself compelled to organize a large-scale system of public relief. For the first time also, America made substantial exertions in the field of public housing. The school lunch program, the food stamp plan, and the direct distribution of surplus commodities represent other activities in the same direction, as do also the attempts to

[a] Another factor which prevented economic adversity from appearing to be so hopeless was the belief in the power of private philanthropy to remedy economic distress and the obligation on everybody to practice philanthropy.

induce Southern farmers and sharecroppers to have year-round gardens. Public health programs were expanded, and the nation is even gradually facing the task of organizing the care of the sick in a more socially protective way than hitherto.

Behind this great movement there is an unmistakable trend in social outlook and political vaulations. As articulate opinion is gradually taking form that there is *a minimum standard of living* below which no group of people in the country should be permitted to fall. This idea, of course, is not new in America; it is a development of the spirit of Christian neighborliness which has been present in the American Creed from its beginning.[a] But the emphasis is new. Now it is not only a question of humanitarianism; it is a question of national social and economic welfare. Neither the political conflicts raging around the proper means of providing help by public measures nor the widespread uncertainty and disagreement concerning the actual height of the minimum standard to be protected by those measures should conceal the important fact that *the American Creed is changing to include a decent living standard and a measure of economic security among the liberties and rights which are given this highest moral sanction.*

As usual in America, the ideals are running far ahead of the accomplishments. The new belief that the health, happiness, and efficiency of the people can be raised greatly by improved living conditions is already just as much in the forefront of public attention in America as in most progressive countries in Europe and the British Dominions. Nowhere are so many housing investigations carried out to demonstrate the correlation between bad housing conditions and juvenile delinquency, tuberculosis, and syphilis as in America.

Contrary to *laissez-faire* principles, various industries have long been given government protection in the United States—most often by means of the tariff. The recent development has shifted the motivation from "assistance-to-business" terms to "social welfare" terms. This change in motivation is not always carried out in the measures actually taken. The agricultural policy may be pointed to as an example. If we except the work of the Farm Security Administration, there are only weak attempts to administer the public assistance given the farmers in accordance with their individual needs; those farmers who have the highest incomes most often also get the highest relief benefits from the A.A.A. If the trend does not change its course, however, all economic policy is bound to come under the orbit of social welfare policy.

At the same time, social welfare policy proper—by an increasing stress upon the preventive instead of the merely curative aspects—is becoming integrated with economic policy. *Social welfare policy is bound to become looked upon in terms of the economic criterion of national investment.*[3]

[a] See Chapter 1, Section 5.

Another change is that of an increasing interest in the distribution of income and wealth as such. The rise of taxation to pay for social policy—and now also for the War—is forcing public attention to this problem. The old idea in public finance that taxation should leave the distribution of incomes and wealth between individuals and classes "unchanged" has become impractical. There is a strong tendency to expect some leveling off of the differences through taxation. It is rationalized by giving a new meaning to the old normative formula that taxes should be imposed according to "ability to pay." Similarly, there is a trend away from the attempt to construct social welfare policies in such a manner that they would not have any influence on the labor market.

All these trends are gradually decreasing the sanctity of individual enterprise, which is slowly coming under public control, although not necessarily public ownership. The American public has been critical of the huge "monopoly" and the "holding company" for over fifty years. The general trend for big business and corporate finance to grow at the expense of small business—which will be accentuated by the present War—has made Americans more and more willing to have government restrictions on private business. Even if big business still utilizes the old individualistic formulas for its purposes, the observer feels that its success in this is declining.[4] Private property in business itself seems less holy to the average American when it is no longer connected to individually-run enterprise and when large-scale interferences are necessitated by international crises and when taxation is mounting and its burden must be placed somewhere. In agriculture, the increase in tenancy and migratory labor and the decline of the independent farmer are having a similar effect.

In all these respects the American Creed is still in flux. The change has, however, only strengthened the basic demand for equality of opportunity. But it is becoming apparent to most Americans that conditions have so changed that this demand will require more concerted action and even state intervention to become realized. It is commonly observed that the closing of the frontier and the constriction of immigration tend to stratify the social order into a more rigid class structure. Occupational mobility and social climbing are tending to become possible mainly by means of education, and a significant shift now takes two generations instead of one. The self-made man is a vanishing social phenomenon.

The perfection of the national educational system, while increasingly opening up fairer chances for individuals starting out even from the lowest social stratum, is at the same time restricting opportunities to move and to rise for individuals who have passed youth without having had the benefit of education and special training. If they are in the laboring or farming classes they will, in all probability, have to stay there. As this situation is becoming realized among the masses, and as cultural heterogeneity is

decreasing, a new impetus is given toward mass organizations.ª Throughout America collective interest groups are gradually getting the sanction
of public approval.[5] The growth of labor unions is on the verge of becoming
looked upon as a realization of the American belief in the independence and
integrity of the individual.

When all these trends have reached their maturity, the meaning of
economic individualism in the American Creed will have changed considerably. For the time being, however, the American Creed is somewhat disorganized in respect to economic life. For our present purpose of selecting,
out of the main stream of national thinking, the relevant value premises for
studying the economic aspects of the American Negro problem, a satisfactory minimum of clear-cut economic ideals seems to be available in spite
of this state of flux.

We shall, in our inquiry, assume that the following norms are generally
and explicitly held on the higher or national plane of the valuation sphere
in the hearts of ordinary Americans:

1. *There is nothing wrong with economic inequality by itself.* The mere
fact that the Negro people are poorer than other population groups does
not *per se* constitute a social problem. It does not challenge the American
Creed. This first value premise will not be conspicuous in our inquiry. Its
main significance is the negative one of keeping our study within the conservative reformist limits of average American economic discussion.

2. Somewhat less precise is our second value premise: *that no American
population group shall be allowed to fall under a certain minimum level of
living.* This premise also assumes Negro poverty and all other poverty as
a matter of fact. It insists only that poverty shall not go too far without
being given public attention and amelioration. It offers a means of evaluating the social effects of poverty and affords a motivation for social welfare
policy. Even if the general principle of a minimum level of living must now
be considered as established in national thinking, it is still undecided how
high or low this minimum level should be.

3. Our third value premise is bound to be the most significant one for
our inquiry as it brings out the principal chasm between American ideals
and practices: *that Negroes shall be awarded equal opportunities.* In so far
as Negro poverty is caused by discrimination, the American Creed is
challenged in one of its most specific and longest established precepts.
Equality of opportunity, fair play, free competition—"independent of race,
creed or color"—is deeply imprinted in the nationally sanctioned social
morals of America. This value premise must direct every realistic study
of the Negroes' economic status in America.

Discrimination is, for this reason, the key term in such a study. This term
is *defined in relation to the norm of equality of opportunity* in the American
Creed. In this sense it is, naturally, a "value-loaded" term, and rightly so.

ª For some further comments upon this development, see Chapter 33.

But it lacks nothing in scientific preciseness and definiteness. An inquiry into the Negro problem in America which shrinks from this valuation is devoid of social perspective and, indeed, interest. Discrimination will be our central concept for our analysis of both the utilization of Negro productivity and the distribution of goods and services for Negro consumption.

4. THE CONFLICT OF VALUATIONS

By formulating these value premises, and particularly the third one, demanding fair play, we again confront the split in American personality and the ambivalence in American social morals. Our central problem is neither the exploitation of the Negro people nor the various effects of this exploitation on American society, but rather the moral conflict in the heart of white Americans.

In passing we might glance at some of the standard rationalizations by which the American white man tries to build a bridge of reason between his equalitarian Creed and his nonequalitarian treatment of the Negroes. It should be understood that the popular theories are based upon what the ordinary white man conceives to be his own observations and upon what he believes to be common knowledge. We shall first refer to the folklore in the South.

Sometimes a mere reference to custom is advanced as a reason for economic discrimination against Negroes. A report on teachers' salaries prepared by a university in one of the Border states reads:

> An additional argument in favor of the salary differential is the general tradition of the South that negroes and whites are not to be paid equivalent salaries for equivalent work. The attitude may be considered wrong from whatever angle it is viewed, but the fact remains that the custom is one that is almost universal and one that the practical school administrator must not ignore.[6]

For not a few, this moral logic that "what was and is, shall be and ought to be" seems sufficient.

Interestingly enough, only rarely will a white man in the South defend economic discrimination in terms of white people's interest to have cheap labor available.[a] Nearest to such a motivation come oblique statements like: "This is a white man's country"; or more expressively: "We don't have money enough to pay our white workers decent wages"; or, in regard to discrimination in the school system: "The appropriations do not suffice even to give the white children good schools."

Such statements are common in the whole South. They are made even by intellectuals. Often there is a further rationalization behind such pronouncements to the effect that "Negroes are the wards of the white people" —an American version of the doctrine of English imperialism about "the

---

[a] In this, economic discrimination is different from social discrimination. See Chapter 28.

white man's burden." "Negroes couldn't live at all without the aid and guidance of the white people," it is said. "What little they have, they have got from the whites." Their own sacrifices apparently do not count. Their poverty itself becomes, in fact, the basis of the rationalization. "The whites give them all the jobs." "Actually, they live on us white people." "They couldn't sustain themselves a day if we gave them up." "The whites pay all the taxes, or don't they?"

Then, too, economic inequality "has to" be maintained, for it is the barrier against "social equality":[a] "you wouldn't let your sister or daughter marry a nigger." The sister or the daughter comes inevitably even into the economic discussion.

This is the ordinary Southerner explaining the matter in plain words to the inquisitive stranger. He is serious and, in a sense, honest. We must remember that the whole white Southern culture, generation after generation, is laboring to convince itself that there is no conflict between the equalitarianism in the American Creed and the economic discrimination against Negroes. And they can never get enough good reasons for their behavior. They pile arguments one on top of the other.[7]

The most important intellectual bridge between the American Creed and actual practices in the economic sphere is, of course, the complex of racial beliefs discussed above in Chapter 4. Their import in the economic sphere is that the Negro is looked upon as inherently inferior as a worker and as a consumer. God himself has made the Negro to be only a servant or a laborer employed for menial, dirty, heavy and disagreeable work. And, since practically all such work is badly paid, it is God's will that the Negro should have a low income. Also, any attempt to raise Negro incomes goes against "the laws of supply and demand" which are part of the order of nature. The Negro is bad as a consumer too. "If you give him more pay, he will stop working"; he will "drink it up and start a row." "Higher wages will make the nigger lazy and morally degraded." This last belief particularly, but also many of the others, bears a striking similarity to ideas about the laboring class as a whole developed in a systematic form by European mercantilist writers in the seventeenth and eighteenth centuries.[b]

---

[a] See Part VII.

[b] See Eli F. Heckscher, *Mercantilism* (translated by Mendel Shapiro, 1935; first published, 1931).

The whole ideology displays a static, precapitalistic tendency. When white Southerners object to a conspicuous rise in Negro levels of living, they act much like the upper classes in most European countries centuries ago when they frowned upon lower class people's rise to higher levels of consumption, and even instituted legal regulations forbidding the humbler estates to have servants, to own certain types of dress, and so on. An American Negro in a luxurious car draws unfavorable comment, and so—in previous times—did a Swedish maid who "dressed like a lady." In the static pre-competitive society, tradition was in itself a value.

On the other hand, it is said that the Negro is accustomed to live on little. "It is a marvel how these niggers can get along on almost nothing." This would actually imply that the Negro is a careful consumer—but the conclusion is never expressed that way.

This touches upon the second main logical bridge between equalitarianism and economic discrimination: the cost-of-living and the standard-of-living arguments. The first of these two popular theories is—again quoting the already mentioned university publication—presented in the following way:

> ... observation alone would suggest to the unbiased observer that the negro teacher will be able to purchase within her society a relatively higher standard of living than the white teacher will be able to secure with the same amount of money.[8]

Statistical investigations are referred to which seem to indicate the remarkable fact that Negro teachers with smaller salaries spend less money for various items of the cost-of-living budget than better paid white teachers.

Scientifically, this is nonsense, of course. A cost-of-living comparison has no meaning except when comparing costs for equivalent budget items and total budgets. That poor people get along on less has nothing to do with cost of living. They *must* get along on less, even when cost of living, in the proper sense, is higher for them. We have quoted this statement only to illustrate a popular theory which, though it now seldom gets into respectable print, is widespread in the South and constitutes a most important rationalization among even educated people.[a]

Sometimes an attempt is made to give the theory greater logical consistency by inserting the idea that "Negroes don't have the same demands on life as white people." "They are satisfied with less." It should be remembered that equal pay for equal work to women has been objected to by a similar popular theory in all countries. The underlying assumption of a racial differential in psychic wants is, of course, entirely unfounded.

Others are heard expressing the theory of lower demands on life in the following way: "Their cost of living is obviously lower since they have a lower standard of living." Lower wages and lower relief grants are generally motivated in this way. A great number of more or less confused notions are held together in such expressions. Having "a low standard of living," for one thing, means to many to be a "no-account" person, a worthless individual. It also means that, being able to live as they are

---

[a] In relief work the popular theory of the Negroes' "lower cost of living" as a motivation for discrimination is often given in terms more directly and more honestly related to actual customs and social policy. Some social workers in the Deep South explained to Richard Sterner that the appropriation did not suffice for the full "budgetary deficiency" of the clients, for they had to give each one just the barest minimum they could get along with. Rents usually were lower for Negro clients, since they lived in the Negro sections. It was readily admitted that this was so because housing was poorer in Negro neighborhoods. But even so, money had to be saved on the small appropriations wherever possible.

living, Negroes have a peculiar ability to manage a household. Oblique statements to this effect are often made when discussing this type of popular theory; one social worker in a responsible position came out straight with the argument. It probably also means that people accustomed to suffer from want do not feel poverty so much as if they had seen better days. This, of course, is a much more common popular theory: all over the world the "people who have seen better days" are believed to be worse off than other paupers. In the case of the Negro there is the additional belief that he has a particularly great capacity to be happy in his poverty. He is a child of nature. And he has his religion. He can sing and dance.

The rationalizations amount to this: since Negroes are poor and always have been poor, they are inferior and should be kept inferior. Then they are no trouble but rather a convenience. It is seldom expressed so bluntly. Expressions like "standard of living" and "cost of living" are employed because they have a flavor of scientific objectivity. They avoid hard thinking. They enable one to stand for the *status quo* in economic discrimination without flagrantly exposing oneself even to oneself. For their purpose they represent nearly perfect popular theories of the rationalization type.

These are only a few examples to illustrate the way of thinking utilized in the South of today to justify economic discrimination. In the North there exists practically nothing of these piled-up, criss-crossing, elaborated theories. In matters of discrimination the ordinary Northerner is unsophisticated. Most Northerners, even in those parts of the country where there are Negroes, know only vaguely about the economic discriminations Negroes are meeting in their communities. They are often uninformed of the real import of those discriminations in which they themselves participate.

It is generally held in the North that such discrimination is wrong. When the matter occasionally comes up for public discussion in newspapers and legislatures, it is assumed that discrimination shall be condemned. Some states have, as we shall see, made laws in order to curb discrimination in the labor market. The present writer is inclined to believe that, as far as such discriminations are concerned, a large majority of Northerners would come out for full equality if they had to vote on the issue and did not think of their own occupations. Northern states and municipalities, on the whole, hold to the principle of nondiscrimination in relief, and this is probably not only due to considerations of the Negro vote but also in obedience to the American Creed.

As we shall find, however, there is plenty of economic discrimination in the North. In situations where it is acute and where it becomes conscious, the average Northerner will occasionally refer to the interest of himself and his group in keeping away Negro competition—a thing which seldom or never happens in the South. On this point he might be cruder. His rationalizations will seldom go much further than presenting the beliefs in the Negroes' racial inferiority and the observation that he "just does not want to have Negroes around" or that he "dislikes Negroes." Southern-born white people in the North usually keep more of the complete defense system and also spread it in their new surroundings. Even in the North it happens occasionally, when economic discrimination is discussed, that the "social equality" issue and the marriage matter are brought up, though with much less emotion.

A main difference between the types of rationalization in the two regions seems to be that the Southerners still think of Negroes as their former slaves, while the association with slavery is notably absent from the minds of Northerners. To Northerners, the Negro is, more abstractly, just an alien, felt to be particularly difficult to assimilate into the life of the community. But in the South, the master-model of economic discrimination—slavery—is still a living force as a memory and a tradition.

CHAPTER 10

THE TRADITION OF SLAVERY[a]

1. Economic Exploitation

To the *ante-bellum* South slavery was, of course, a tremendous moral burden. Human slavery, in spite of all rationalization, was irreconcilably contrary to the American Creed. The South had to stand before all the world as the land which, in modern times, had developed and perfected that ignominious old institution.

But, in a sense, exploitation of Negro labor was, perhaps, a less embarrassing moral conflict to the *ante-bellum* planter than to his peer today. Slavery then was a lawful institution, a part of the legal order, and the exploitation of black labor was sanctioned and regulated. Today the exploitation is, to a considerable degree, dependent upon the availability of extralegal devices of various kinds.

Moreover, slavery was justified in a political theory which had intellectual respectability,[b] which was expounded in speeches, articles, and learned treatises by the region's famous statesmen, churchmen and scholars. The popular theories defending caste exploitation today, which have been exemplified in the previous chapter, bear, on the contrary, the mark of intellectual poverty. Even a reactionary Southern congressman will abstain from developing the detailed structure of those theories in the national capital. Hardly a conservative newspaper in the South will expound them clearly. The liberal newspapers actually condemn them, at least in general terms. The change in the moral situation, brought about in less than three generations, is tremendous.

If we look to actual practices, however, we find that the tradition of human exploitation—and now not only of Negroes—has remained from slavery as a chief determinant of the entire structure of the South's economic life. The observer is told that a great number of fortunes are achieved by petty exploitation of the poor, a practice sometimes belonging to the type referred to in the region as "mattressing the niggers." As contrasted with the North, there is less investment, less market expansion, less inventiveness and less risk-taking. Sweatshop labor

[a] This chapter is the first of a set of three on Southern agriculture.
[b] See Chapter 20, Section 4.

conditions are more common. Even the middle strata of the Southern white population depend on exploitation of labor.

The white workers, in their turn, often seek to defend themselves against the potential or actual competition from Negro labor by extra-economic devices. They themselves are often held in paternalistic economic and moral dependence by their employers. As is often pointed out, the South as a region is competing against the North by its recourse to low-paid docile white and Negro labor. It has actually advertised this as an opportunity for outside capitalists. ". . . the South remains largely a colonial economy,"[1] complains Vance, one of the region's outstanding social scientists, and explains: "The advance of industry into this region then partakes of the nature, let us say it in all kindliness, of exploiting the natural resources and labor supply . . ."[2]

This pattern of common exploitation—where everyone is the oppressor of the one under him, where the Negroes are at the bottom and where big landlords, merchants, and Northern capital are at the top—is obviously the extension into the present of a modified slavery system. As Vance points out,[3] the "geography and biology" of the region are not to be blamed for its economic position, but it is history that has molded the type of organization.

The South tries to blame its economic backwardness on the differential in freight rates, the national tariff system, and other economic irregularities, but these are, in the final analysis, rather minor matters; they are hardly more than symptoms of poverty and political dependence. The destruction of material and human values during the Civil War and its aftermath was large, but, by itself, it does not explain the present situation. About three generations have lapsed since then, and we know from other parts of the world how rapidly such wounds can be healed. The same is true about the head start in industrialization which the North had: it could have been overcome. To complain about the lack of capital in the region is rather to beg the question. In modern dynamic economics we do not look upon capital so much as a prerequisite for production but rather as a result of production. The investment in the South of Northern capital has not been detrimental but is, on the contrary, a reason why the South is not more backward economically than it is.

The explanation for the economic backwardness of the South must be carried down to the rigid institutional structure of the economic life of the region which, historically, is derived from slavery and, psychologically, is rooted in the minds of the people.

2. SLAVERY AND CASTE

In some respects, the remnants of the outmoded slavery system of the Old South—which we call caste—have been even more important impediments to progress and economic adjustment than slavery itself could ever have been. It is often argued—and in the main rightly—that the static, noncompetitive slavery institution and the quasi-feudal plantation system did not fit into modern American capitalism. The economic interpretation of the Civil War makes much of this thought. To quote a typical remark: "Slavery stands against our technical trends which demand a mobile, replaceable labor supply and which generate useful energy in individuals by offering them hope of advancement."[4]

But in certain respects the surviving caste system shows even more resistance to change than did slavery. The main economic significance of slavery was that the employer really owned his labor. Because of that he also had a vested interest in its most profitable utilization. This fundamental unity of interest between capital and labor—as labor *was* capital—constituted a main point in the pro-slavery theory.[a]

It is true that the slaves were robbed of their freedom to move on their own initiative. But as factors of production, they were moved by the economic interest of their owners to their "most advantageous uses." Before Emancipation the Negroes took part in the westward movement of production and people. From this point of view the fight of the South to widen the realm of slavery in the United States prior to the Civil War was also a fight to bring Negro labor to those places where it could be put to most advantageous use. After Emancipation the freedmen could move individually in the regions where they were already settled. But they were, as a group, practically blocked from entering new rural territory in the Southwest. Only the cities in the South and the North left them an outlet for migration.[b]

Before Emancipation it was in the interest of the slave owners to use Negro slaves wherever it was profitable in handicraft and manufacture.[c] After Emancipation no such proprietary interest protected Negro laborers from the desire of white workers to squeeze them out of skilled employment. They were gradually driven out and pushed down into the "Negro jobs," a category which has been more and more narrowly defined.

There is no doubt that, compared with the contemporary caste system, slavery showed a superior capacity to effectuate economic adjustment, even if the slave owners and not the slaves reaped the profits. Even to many Negroes themselves slavery, again in certain limited respects, was a more advantageous economic arrangement than the precarious caste status into which they were thrown by Emancipation. To the owners, slaves represented valuable property. The prices of slaves tended to rise until the Civil War.[5] The slave owner had the same rational economic interest in caring for the

[a] See Chapter 20, Section 4.
[b] See Chapter 8.
[c] See Chapter 13.

material welfare of the slaves, their health and productive standards, as any good proprietor engaged in animal husbandry. As the slaves were his own Negroes in a literal sense, he could develop the same pride, attachment, and even affection, which the devoted proprietor-manager is likely to feel toward his own livestock.

The apologetic literature of the South gave much stress to examples of such paternalistic idyls. Stories of the kindly relations between masters and slaves are always particularly touching, both because they stand out against the background of the intrinsic cruelty and arbitrariness implied in a system under which some human beings were owned by others and because they represent this unreserved feeling of kindness which we can hardly feel toward other objects than those which are absolutely under our dominance as are our domestic animals. It is commonly asserted that the slaves fared particularly well in the slave-breeding and slave-exporting states of the Upper South, and that they there also showed themselves to be "happy" in spite of the regularly recurring necessity of leaving near relatives when they were sold into the Deep South.[6]

The rise in sickness and death rates which seems to have occurred following the Civil War[a] bears out the general opinion that the first economic effect of freedom was a decreased level of living for the Negro people. The implication would be that, since the plantation owners lost their property interest in upholding a level of living which preserved the capital value of the Negro, this level dropped below the subsistence standard.

Important for the development of the new labor structure into which the freed Negro slaves were pressed and which has determined their economic fate and, to a considerable extent, the economic history of the South until this day was the fact that Emancipation was not related to any change of mind on the part of white people. The reform was thrust upon the South and never got its sanction. It became rather a matter of sectional pride to resist the change to the utmost. When it became apparent that the North could not, or would not, press its demands with force, the white South found a revenge for the defeat in the War by undoing as far as possible the national legislation to protect the freedman. This negative direction of Southern political will is still, three generations after the Civil War, apparent to the observer. The South did not want—and to a great extent still does not want—the Negro to be successful as a freedman. White Southerners are prepared to abstain from many liberties and to sacrifice many advantages for the purpose of withholding them from the Negroes.[b]

To the whites the temporary Negro vagrancy that followed the Civil War[7] must have appeared as a confirmation of their dominant conviction, that most Negroes are inherently incapable of persistent work, unless kept

[a] See Chapter 6, Section 2.
[b] See Chapter 20.

under severe discipline. To blame it on the inherent racial character of the Negro was the most convenient way out. It did not involve any new and strenuous thinking. It offered an escape from the difficult task of having to introduce a basically new pattern of dealing with labor. A well-entrenched system of slavery has probably nowhere been completely abolished by one stroke. The plantation South was ruined through the War, and the Emancipation forced upon it—ruined, it was felt, because of the Negro. Under such circumstances it was likely that the South would try to build up a labor organization as similar as possible to slavery.

As the years passed, the old plantation system reestablished itself. Negro labor was on hand in spite of much short-distance wandering. A considerable portion of the old plantation owners were killed in the War, went bankrupt or left the land for other reasons. Much land became forfeit to creditors and tax authorities. But, as cotton prices soared, it was profitable for anybody who could lay hands on cash to buy land and hire Negro labor. After some attempts with a wage system, sharecropping became the labor pattern into which the Negroes and, later on, poor whites were pressed.[8]

3. The Land Problem

An economic reconstruction of the South which would have succeeded in opening the road to economic independence for the ex-slaves would have had to include, besides emancipation, suffrage and full civil liberties: rapid education of the freedmen, abandonment of discrimination, land reform. Some measures in all these directions were actually taken.

Concerning land reform, there were spurious attempts to break up the plantation system and to distribute the land to the cultivators. There were some few statesmen who grasped the importance of such a basic economic reform for the Reconstruction program. Thaddeus Stevens and Charles Sumner saw it.[9] But their strivings came to practically nothing. A small amount of abandoned and confiscated land was turned over to Negroes by the Union Army, by Union administrators of various kinds and, later, by the Freedmen's Bureau. But the latter institution had to use most of its small appropriations—totaling less than $18,000,000—for general relief or for educational purposes. Besides, it was allowed to operate for only seven years (1865-1872).[10]

To have given each one of the million Negro families a forty-acre freehold would have made a basis of real democracy in the United States that might easily have transformed the modern world,[11] reflects Du Bois. This may be true enough, but it should be kept clear that the historical setting would hardly have allowed it. From an historical point of view it is even more Utopian to think through anew the Reconstruction problem in terms of modern social engineering. It is not entirely useless, however, as such an intellectual experiment defines our norms and gives perspective to what actually took place.

After the Civil War, the overwhelming majority of Negroes were concentrated in Southern agriculture. Consequently, the greatest problem was what to do with these great masses of Southern Negroes, most of whom were former slaves. Even the Negroes not in Southern agriculture were influenced by the patterns set, since the Northern Negro laborer was recruited, in later decades, from the rural South.

A rational economic reform of Southern plantation economy, which would preserve individual property rights to the maximum (always of greatest importance for a smooth readjustment) but also utilize the revolutionary situation for carrying into effect the aims of Reconstruction, could have included the following points besides freeing the slaves:

1. Remunerating fully the slave owners out of federal funds.
2. Expropriating the slave plantations or a larger part of them and remunerating fully their owners out of federal funds.
3. Distributing this land in small parcels to those cultivators who wished it, against mortgaged claims on their new property, and requiring them to pay for the land in yearly installments over a long period.
4. Creating for a transition period a rather close public supervision over the freedmen and also certain safeguards against their disposition of their property; also instituting an effective vocational education of Negro farmers, somewhat along the lines of the F.S.A. of the 1930's.
5. Instituting a scheme of taxation to pay off the former slave- and land-owners and, perhaps, to allow repayments for the land by the new owners to be kept down under the actual expropriation costs.
6. As a partial alternative, in order to relieve the Negro population pressure in the South and in order to help keep down the scope of the reconstruction program: helping Negroes take part in the westward rural migration.

The cheapness of land in America would have been a factor making a land reform easier to execute than in most other countries where it has been successfully carried out when abolishing serfdom. Even if the burden on the public finances were reckoned as economic costs—which, of course, is a totally wrong way of calculating costs in a national economy, as they are meant to be profitable investments in economic progress—those costs would have been trifling compared with what Reconstruction and Restoration, not to speak of the Civil War, actually cost the nation. What happened, however, was that the slaves were freed without any remuneration being paid their former owners; and that, with few exceptions, the freedmen were not given access to land.

The explanation of why there was no land reform in America to complement the emancipation of the slaves, during the short period when the South did not have much of a say and had not yet deeply fortified its own mental resistance, is usually given in terms of the reluctance of the North to intrude upon the rights and interests of property ownership. But the North obviously did not hesitate to expropriate the slave property[a] and let it loose on the region without any provision for its economic maintenance. The owners must have felt this to be a grave injustice inflicted upon them, and even Northerners must have reflected that this property was acquired under the law and in a system of rights where it was exchangeable for other property. The dominating North defended its action by asserting that slave property was unjust, which is a pretty revolutionary doctrine from the property point of view. Undoubtedly property in land stood in another category to the Northerners. But the Union authorities occasionally dealt rather harshly also with land property in the South during Reconstruction, even if they did not often give it away to the Negroes.

A more important reason why there was no land reform was, in all probability, consideration of a narrow financial sort. The Civil War had left the Union with a great national debt. The North—which refused to let the federal government assume the war debts of the Confederate states and to pay for the expropriated slave property—did not feel inclined to carry the fiscal costs for a land reform on the national budget.

Under these circumstances, the road to the national compromise of the 1870's was actually well paved from the beginning. Except for a Republican party interest in the Negro vote and the general craving for revenge against the Southern rebels, there seems not to have been much interest among most Northerners in helping the Negroes.[b] This was particularly so since the North now acquired a frame of mind where the puritan social idealism of *ante-bellum* days, of which abolitionism had only been one of the expressions, succumbed for decades to the acceptance of industrialization, expansion, mechanical progress and considerable political corruption.

The white South was, as has been said, for the most part violently against any constructive program framed to raise the Negro freedmen to economic independence.[12] A liberal Southerner of the older generation with great political experience, Josephus Daniels, tells this story:

> When I was eighteen I recall asking an old Confederate, "What was so bad about the promise to give every Negro head of a family forty acres and a mule? Wouldn't that have been better help than to turn the ignorant ex-slave without a dollar over to the mercy of Republican politicians, white and black, who made political slaves

[a] Only the slave owners of the District of Columbia were compensated for the price of their slaves. See William H. Williams, "The Negro in the District of Columbia During Reconstruction." *The Howard Review* (June, 1924), p. 102.

[b] There were many exceptions, however, and the compromise was a gradual development. Not only was there a small remnant of the Abolition movement, but even a man like James G. Blaine made a vigorous plea in 1879 that the Negro be given full rights and opportunities. (Symposium: "Ought the Negro to be Disfranchised," *North American Review* [March, 1879].)

of them? And if each Negro had been given a piece of land, for which Uncle Sam would pay the Southern owner, wouldn't it have been better for the white man and the Negro?"

The old man looked at me as if I were a curious individual to be raising such an unheard-of question. "No," he said emphatically, "for it would have made the Negro 'uppity,' and, besides, they don't know enough to farm without direction, and smart white men and Negroes would have gotten the land away from them, and they'd have been worse off than ever. . . . The real reason," pursued the old man, "why it wouldn't do, is that we are having a hard time now keeping the nigger in his place, and if he were a landowner he'd think he was a bigger man than old Grant, and there would be no living with him in the Black District. . . . Who'd work the land if the niggers had farms of their own . . . ?"[13]

In spite of the lack of a land reform and against heavy odds in practically all respects, there was a slow rise of Negro small-scale landownership in the South until the beginning of this century. But the proportion of Negroes owning their own land has never been large, and it has been declining for the last 30 or 40 years.[a]

4. THE TENANCY PROBLEM

But even if a rational land reform was not carried out, some of the goals could have been reached by a legal regulation of the tenancy system, aimed not only at protecting the tenants as well as the landlords, but also at preserving the soil and raising the economic efficiency of Southern agriculture. There were individuals who saw clearly what was at stake. The Freedmen's Bureau was futilely active in regulating labor and tenant contracts. But it had neither the political backing nor the clear purpose necessary to accomplish much of lasting importance. And it was not given the time or the resources. Hence, a most inequitable type of tenancy fixed itself upon the South.

A survey of the legal organization of landlord-tenant relations in Southern states today reveals a system which has no real parallel in other advanced parts of the Western world. There are a great number of state laws—some of the most extravagant character—to defend the planters' interests. There are few laws which defend the tenants' interests. The tenant does not have any right to permanency of tenure on the land he cultivates. He seldom has any right to reimbursement for permanent improvements which he makes on the land.[14] The tenant is not secured in his contractual rights. Woofter, writing in the 'twenties, makes the rather obvious point that "passage of laws to the effect that no tenant contract is enforceable unless it is written would . . . help," but no such laws have been passed.[15]

On the other hand, there is, as we said, elaborate legislation to protect

[a] See Chapter 11, Section 6.

the planters' interests against the tenants. Reference should here be made to the Black Codes, instituted by eight Southern states immediately after the Civil War (1865-1867) before Congressional Reconstruction. Mangum characterizes these laws as follows:

> These Black Codes gave the Negro population very little freedom. The colored man was free in name only in many cases. The apprentice, vagrancy, and other provisions of these statutes forced the Negro into situations where he would be under the uncontrolled supervision of his former master or other white men who were ready and willing to exploit his labor.[16]

The historical background for these laws was the need for some kind of regulations of the freedmen's labor conditions, the Southerners' disbelief in free labor, and their intention of restoring as far as possible the *antebellum* relation between the two races.[17] The Black Codes were among the factors which stimulated Congress to carry out Reconstruction along more drastic lines. These laws were abolished, but after Reconstruction they made their reappearance in various forms.

One type is the various kinds of lien laws.[18] They are sometimes strengthened by laws making a tenant a criminal when he is deemed negligent in his duties.[19] During the 'thirties, federal agencies have been more active in stamping out debt peonage[a] by bringing up test cases in the federal courts. Several laws of this or other kinds have been held unconstitutional by state and federal courts.[20] Nevertheless, debt peonage still exists.[b]

Another present-day vestige of the Black Codes is the vagrancy laws.[c] They make it possible for employers to let the police act as labor agents. Apprehended vagrants are made to choose between accepting the employment offered them and being sentenced by the court to forced labor in chain-gangs. The literature is filled with descriptions of how the police and the courts were utilized to recruit forced labor. Convicts were hired out, sometimes in chain-gangs, to planters, mine owners, road contractors and turpentine farmers. There were plantations and other enterprises that depended almost entirely on convict labor. In recent years this practice has been practically stamped out.[d]

More difficult to stamp out has been the practice of white employers getting Negro tenants or laborers by paying their fines at court. It is parallel

[a] The term "peonage" means a condition of compulsory service based on the indebtedness of the laborer to his employer; see Mangum, *op. cit.*, pp. 164 ff.

[b] See Chapter 11, Section 8; Appendix 6, Section 4; and Chapter 26, Section 2; also, Mangum, *op. cit.*, p. 172.

[c] The very concept "vagrancy" is a dangerous one as it has not the same definiteness as other crimes. In all countries there have at times been attempts to press poor people into peonage by such laws.

[d] See Chapter 26, Section 2.

to the transaction whereby an employer pays a Negro's debt to a former employer or to a merchant and, by taking over the debt, also takes over the worker. The police and the courts have often been active in "creating" the debts by exacting fines for petty offenses or upon flimsy accusations. Sometimes a number of Negroes are "rounded up" and given out for the price of the fines to interested employers who are short of labor. More often the police and the courts only act to enforce an existing situation of debt peonage.[21]

The background of the difficulty of stamping out peonage is the fact that the South has a weak legal tradition. As we shall show in Part VI, the police and the courts have traditionally been active as agents for white employers. Traditionally the planters and other whites have little scruple against taking the law into their own hands. Threats, whippings, and even more serious forms of violence have been customary caste sanctions utilized to maintain a strict discipline over Negro labor which are seldom employed against white labor. The few laws in favor of the Negro tenant have not often been enforced against the white planter.

The legal order of the South is, however, gradually becoming strengthened. But, even if we assume full enforcement—which is far from being reached as yet, particularly in the Black Belt where most of the plantations and the rural Negroes are concentrated—the entire system of laws regulating the relations between employers and employees in Southern agriculture is heavily stacked against the latter.

CHAPTER II

THE SOUTHERN PLANTATION ECONOMY AND THE
NEGRO FARMER

1. Southern Agriculture as a Problem

The main facts of rural Southern poverty and the distress of the rural
Negro people in the South have been well-known for a long time. The
plantation-tenant system is one of America's "public scandals."[a] Even
before the Civil War there were many Southern patriots who saw some of
the detrimental factors working to undermine the welfare of the region.
When Hinton Helper, on the eve of the Civil War, came out with his
blunt exposure of the *ante-bellum* myth of how efficient and perfectly
balanced the Southern economic system was, he could quote passages in
support of his position like the following by C. C. Clay:

> I can show you, with sorrow, in the olden portions of Alabama, and in my native
> county of Madison, the sad memorials of the artless and exhausting culture of cotton.
> Our small planters, after taking the cream off their lands, unable to restore them
> by rest, manures, or otherwise, are going further West and South, in search of other
> virgin land, which they may and will despoil and impoverish in like manner. Our
> wealthier planters, with greater means and no more skill, are buying out their poorer
> neighbors. . . . In traversing that county [Madison County], one will discover
> numerous farm houses, once the abode of industrious and intelligent freemen, now
> occupied by slaves, or tenantless. . . . Indeed, a county in its infancy, where fifty
> years ago scarce a forest tree had been felled by the axe of the pioneer, is already
> exhibiting the painful signs of senility and decay, apparent in Virginia and the
> Carolinas.[1]

At least from the 'eighties, when Henry Grady coined the promising
phrase "the New South," the propagation of an agricultural reform program has belonged to the established Southern traditions. Like the dedica-
tion "the New South," this program has in fundamentally unchanged form
been taken over by generation after generation of public-spirited Southern
liberals and is today one of their dearest aims. In fact, the same remedies
of encouraging independent land ownership, crop diversification, and soil
conservation have been recommended through the decades by unanimous

[a] See Appendix 2, Section 1.

230

expert opinion. In a sense, this is one of the most discouraging things about Southern agriculture, that the faults have been recognized and the remedial plans worked out for such a long time without much being accomplished—at least up to the Great Depression and the New Deal.

The revolutionary changes within the last decade—and particularly the effects of the A.A.A. on rural Negroes—are less well-known. We shall leave those latest developments to be analyzed in the next chapter. In this chapter we want, mainly by way of presenting some illustrative quantitative relations, to give a short survey of the familiar topics: the plight of the rural South and of the Negro farmer.

2. OVER-POPULATION AND SOIL EROSION

Rural farm areas in the United States in 1940 had a population of about 30,000,000. More than half of this population, or over 16,000,000, was in the South; and over one-fourth of the Southern farm population (around 4,500,000) was Negro. But the South had only 35 per cent of all land in farms in the country, and the value of this farm land, as well as of the buildings on the land, the farm implements and machinery, constituted but 28 per cent of the national figure. Only 8 per cent of the Southern farm land was operated by Negro owners, tenants, and croppers, and their share in the value of Southern farms, buildings, implements, and machinery was equally small.[2] For the rest, Negroes participated in the Southern agricultural economy only as wage laborers, at low wages and usually without the assurance of year-round employment.

The import of these broad facts is as simple as it is significant. They are behind all the rural poverty of the South. The agricultural South is over-populated,[a] and this over-population affects Negroes much more than whites. This applies particularly to the Old South, including the Delta district, which contains the main concentration of Negroes. In this Black Belt the over-population has—on the whole—been steadily increasing. "Since 1860 the amount of land in southeastern farms has remained stationary, new lands being cleared about as rapidly as old land was exhausted,"[3] while the number of male agricultural workers in the same area rose from around 1,132,000 in 1860 to 2,102,000 in 1930.[4]

A cultural heritage from times of pioneering, colonization, and slavery makes the conditions even worse than can be visualized by the ratio of population to land alone. The early colonists and the later land speculators did not have to economize in their use of the land. To the *ante-bellum*

---

[a] It is true that countries like Denmark have a much higher population density in their agricultural areas but, nevertheless, preserve a much higher living level. But both objective market conditions and the rural culture are incomparably more favorable than they can be, in the surveyable future, in Southern agriculture. Our term "over-population" has the pragmatic meaning indicated by this observation.

plantation owners, it was the slaves that represented the main capital—not the land. This set a pattern also for other Southern farmers. To become rich from the land was to become a plantation owner and a slave owner—not to care for the soil. This tradition has continued until the present time. In the fall of 1938 the writer traveled for two days through a beautiful forest in Tennessee. The woods were burning everywhere. The smoke often made driving difficult. Local newspapers told about small organized forces which were out to fight the fires. From the highways they were nowhere to be seen. There were plenty of people around in several places, but few, if any, seemed to care much about the fires.

Experiences like this make it possible, for even the stranger, to understand the psychology of soil erosion, soil mining, and "selling the soil in annual installments."[5] A sample study made in 1933 suggested that one-third of the Southern land was eroded and that at least half of all eroded land in the country was in the South.[6]

It is generally assumed that the soil in the South originally had a relatively high fertility.[7] "The South was potentially a section of varied and rich agriculture," writes Woofter. "It could have become fully as diversified as France. The reasons why it did not are historical and economic rather than physical."[8] The soil is usually light, and there is heavy rainfall in most parts of the region. The traditional concentration upon cash crops such as cotton and other plants, which fail to bind the top soil and rapidly deplete fertility—without a rational scheme of crop rotation or other preventive measures—is a chief causal factor behind soil erosion. The high rate of tenancy, leaving the immediate care of the land to people who are not only utterly dependent and ignorant but also lack an individual economic interest in maintaining the productivity of the land, is another cause. In the final analysis soil erosion is more a consequence than merely an aspect of protracted rural over-population.

Lange summarizes:

> We may therefore conclude as changes in land in farms have been rather insignificant, that the agricultural population and among this population the Negroes in the old South at present have less land resources to support themselves on than they had a generation ago. The trend is continuing in the same direction, indicating that if strong action is not taken to prevent further erosion the farm population will have in the future even less land resources at its disposal than at present.[9]

3. Tenancy, Credit and Cotton

The literature, today as earlier, contains excellent descriptions of how the plantation system, tenancy, and the one-sided cultivation of cotton and corn—and, in some areas, tobacco, rice, or sugar—have contributed to soil erosion; how the credit system, by favoring cash crops, has made it difficult to break away from the vicious circle; how this credit-cotton-tenancy-erosion circle has become loaded downward through some of its own major effects: poverty for most, economic insecurity for all, widespread ignorance, low health standards, relative lack of an enterprising spirit, high birth rates and large families.

The extent to which Southern cash-crop production is based on tenancy is indicated by the following figures. Almost three-fourths of all Southern cotton farms and more than half of the crop-specialty farms (tobacco, potatoes, peanuts, and so on)[a] were, in 1929, operated by tenants. About two-thirds of all tenants in the South, and almost three-fourths of the croppers, worked on cotton farms. Of the full owners, on the other hand, less than one-third had farms where cotton accounted for 40 per cent or more of the gross income. Most of the other two-thirds owned farms which were characterized as crop-specialty, general or self-sufficing.[10]

Negro farmers have always been dependent on the cotton economy to a much greater extent than have been the white farmers in the South. By 1929 three out of four Negro farm operators, as against two out of five white farmers, received at least 40 per cent of their gross income from cotton. Although not more than about one-tenth of the Southern farm land was cultivated by Negro owners, tenants and croppers, almost one-third of the total output in cotton was produced on this Negro-operated land.[11] In addition, an unknown, but probably considerable, quantity of cotton was produced by Negro wage labor on holdings operated by white farmers. The importance of cotton growing for the Negro farmer can thus hardly be over-estimated.

In the main, cotton is cultivated by means of a primitive and labor-consuming agricultural technique which has not changed much since slavery. Cotton is largely responsible for the fact that the Southeast alone had to pay more than half of the national bill for commercial fertilizers.[12] One-third of the national total for all kinds of fertilizer was expended on cotton farms.[13] Cotton growing, as any one-sided agriculture—if it is not lifted up by high techniques to a level where intelligence is constantly used and prosperity secured—has also psychological effects: it "limits interests . . . limits spiritual growth, makes people narrow, single-grooved, helpless."[14] It invites child labor and causes retardation in schools. It favors large families.

The wide fluctuations of the price of cotton[15]—which seem to have

[a] The type of farm classification in the 1930 Census of Agriculture is based on gross income. Farms for which 40 per cent or more of the gross income was derived from cotton were characterized as cotton farms. By the same token, farms for which 40 per cent or more of the income came from one or several of certain specified crops (tobacco, peanuts, potatoes, soybeans, cowpeas, and so on) were classified as crop-specialty farms. When no product accounted for as much as 40 per cent of the gross income, the farm was "general." Self-sufficing farms were defined as those for which 50 per cent or more of the value production was consumed by the farm family.

become more frequent after 1914, due to wars, inflation, deflation, as well as intensified competition from other countries—make cotton a most hazardous crop, and the farmers who specialize in cotton run extraordinarily heavy risks which are outside their intelligent control.[16] The gambling tradition has been hard to overcome, although almost everybody seems to know that no solid material culture can ever be built on the poor man's speculation. But more fundamentally, the continued cultivation of cotton is called forth—as highly labor-consuming, simple in technique, and easily supervised—by the plantation and tenancy system; or, from another point of view, by over-population and tenancy, and—as a cash crop—by the dependence of Southern agriculture on short-term credit.

The peculiar credit system of the rural South has often been analyzed.[17] It has its historical roots in the slavery economy and, later, in the emergence of the plantation system in the impoverished South after the Civil War. Since then the rural South has been greatly dependent on outside credit both because of the low standards of income and saving in the region and because of the comparatively high requirements on operating capital for cotton growing. The wide fluctuation of cotton prices and farm incomes have added their influence to make lending abnormally risky and, consequently, to make loans expensive. Also, from the point of view of business administration, the organization of banking and credit was most inadequate, and it remained so because of the low plane of political life in the South[a] and the lack of active desire and ability to create large-scale cooperative organizations.

As part of the federal agricultural policy, great improvements have lately been made by the organization of new credit agencies.[b] But still credit is expensive and difficult to get in the rural South, and this is undoubtedly part of the explanation for the insufficient investment in land and buildings and for the slowness of mechanization. To the tenants, credit pressures mean usurious interest rates charged by planters and merchants for advances on food and farming necessities. For the agricultural structure as a whole, credit pressures—themselves partly caused by the dependence on cotton growing—mean a constant stimulus to keep the land in cotton.

4. The Boll Weevil

In this vicious system of economic poverty and exploitation of land and human resources, where every adverse factor is a partial cause of all the others, the boll weevil caused catastrophe. It is often described how it advanced eastward, passing the Mississippi River about 1910.[18] One state after another in the Old South was hit. The destruction was terrible. In many places, particularly in Georgia and South Carolina, farms and planta-

[a] See Part V.
[b] See Chapter 12, Section 11.

tions were permanently abandoned. In Georgia a survey of 59 Lower Piedmont counties showed that the cotton production in 1922 was only one-third of the average for the period 1905-1914, and by 1928 it still did not amount to much more than half of the same average.[19]

But as one state was suffering, those west of it were recovering. Thus, the boll weevil helped the four Southwestern states—Texas, Louisiana, Arkansas, and Oklahoma—to increase their share in the national output from a little more than one-third in 1909 to almost one-half in 1929; and at the latter time they had about three-fifths of the total acreage in cotton.[20] In these Southwestern states cotton cultivation is less dependent on Negro labor and is also more mechanized. For both reasons this geographical dislocation tended, to an extent, to push Negro tenants off the land. The ravages of the boll weevil in the old Cotton Belt had the same effect. The total effects on employment opportunities for Negroes in Southern agriculture have never been calculated, but they must have been considerable.

The boll weevil, in conjunction with the post-war deflation and depression, brought about a temporary decline even in the total national output of cotton around 1921, and it was one of the reasons why the relatively consistent upward production trend—which had been noticeable until the outbreak of the First World War—was broken for a time.[21]

In spite of all misfortunes, cotton was still king when the last agricultural census was taken before the general upheaval of the 'thirties.[22] More than half of the total acreage harvested in the South in 1929 was in farms for which 40 per cent or more of the gross income came from cotton. Also crop-specialty farms (tobacco, potatoes, peanuts, and so on) appeared much more important than in the nation as a whole. Self-sufficing farms, too, were more prevalent in the Southeast than elsewhere, which, however, simply reflects the relatively cashless agricultural economy prevalent among certain groups of poor whites. Dairy farming, on the other hand, has been lagging in the South: in 1929 Southern agriculture did not account for more than one-fifth of the national value production of milk and dairy products.[23]

5. MAIN AGRICULTURAL CLASSES

These are only a few hints about the scene of the rural Negro's struggle for existence. The plantation system and the tenure system, in addition, are institutional factors to be counted heavily when explaining why the agricultural South is even much poorer than can be grasped simply by stating the ratio of population to land and by noting the soil erosion.

The economic chances for small- and middle-sized ownership, in the better part of the South, have been more restricted than in most other American regions. Owner-operated land in 1940 had a lower acreage value in the South ($27.11, including buildings) than in the nation as a whole

($31.37); the fact that Southern land operated by croppers had a per unit value ($33.28) even higher than the latter figure indicates that only in part is this caused by any general inferiority of the Southern soil.[24] In large measure this is due to the fact that so much of the best land in the South originally was taken by the politically, socially, and economically dominant plantation owners. The rest of the Southern farmers had to fight against heavy odds. They had to compete with slave labor at the same time as they had to cultivate soil of lower average quality. The Civil War failed to bring about any fundamental change in this condition. The owners of the plantations soon regained much of their political power. Their land was still superior on the average, in spite of the fact that it was mistreated. And to compete with the plantations was still to compete with sweatshop labor.

In 1930 the total labor force in Southern agriculture—if we except the large but somewhat vaguely defined group of unpaid family workers—was constituted as in Table 1.

Two-thirds of the Negro, as against one-third of the white, "primary" agricultural workers were either croppers or wage laborers. Only one in eight of the Negro, but more than two out of five white workers were owners or part-owners. (Managers constitute an insignificant group.) The white owners outnumbered the Negro owners seven to one. There were more than two white tenants (higher than cropper) for every Negro tenant. The total labor force in the two lowest tenure groups, on the other hand, was almost as large in the Negro as in the white group.

There are great differences in economic status and degree of dependency between the several types of tenants. Highest on the ladder are the renters

TABLE 1

NEGRO AND WHITE AGRICULTURAL WORKERS IN THE SOUTH, BY TENURE: 1930

	Number		Per Cent	
Tenure	Negro	White	Negro	White
Total[a]	1,393,000	2,945,000	100.0	100.0
Owners and managers	183,000	1,250,000	13.1	42.4
Cash tenants	98,000	140,000	7.0	4.8
Other tenants, except croppers	208,000	569,000	15.0	19.3
Croppers	393,000	383,000	28.2	13.0
Wage laborers	511,000	603,000	36.7	20.5

Source: Data on owners, tenants, and croppers are from the *Fifteenth Census of the United States: 1930. Agriculture.* Vol. II, Part 2, County Table I. They include a small number of nonwhites other than Negroes. The data on wage laborers in agriculture are from the *Fifteenth Census of the United States: 1930, Population.* Vol. IV, State Table 11.

[a] Exclusive of unpaid family workers.

and the cash tenants, who rent their farms for a fixed sum of money.[a] Cash tenants usually can be regarded as independent entrepreneurs—or at least they are not in most cases far removed from such a position. All other kinds of arrangements entitle the landlord to a certain share of the main cash crop, for instance, one-fourth, one-third, one-half, sometimes even as much as three-fourths. Those tenants who receive one-half (or less) of the crop are the sharecroppers. The cash tenants usually furnish all the work, stock, feed, fertilizer, and tools themselves. The other groups generally furnish less and less of these things the lower their tenure status. Those lowest down on the scale have little or nothing but their labor to offer.[25] They are really nothing but laborers—or rather their position often tends to be even less independent than that of ordinary wage earners. Before we elaborate on this subject, however, it seems appropriate that we inquire into the reasons why so few of the Negro agricultural workers in the South have been able to reach a position of ownership.

6. The Negro Landowner

The story of the Negro in agriculture would have been a rather different one if the Negro farmer had had greater opportunity to establish himself as an independent owner. In that case he would have become more firmly attached to the soil. He would have known that he worked for his own benefit, that he had a real chance to improve his level of living by his own efforts. "All that is now wanted to make the negro a fixed and conservative element in American society is to give him encouragement to, and facilities for, making himself, by his own exertions, a small landowner," wrote Sir George Campbell in his survey of the South and the Negro problem in the late 'seventies.[26]

There was a time when it really looked as if the rural Negro had some chance of eventually getting established on an ownership basis. True, the development was generally slow, but it seemed to go in the right direction. The number of Negro farm homes in the United States that were owned by their occupants had by 1900 reached a figure of 193,000—constituting about 25 per cent of all Negro farm homes.[27] This percentage marks the peak of the proportion of landowners in the Negro farm population.

The absolute increase continued for some time, but at a slower rate. The absolute number of colored farm owners in the South reached, in 1910, a maximum of about 220,000.[28] After 1920 it gradually declined, and it dropped to 174,000 by 1940.[29] Of all Southern states with any appreciable Negro farm population, only Virginia and Florida showed a majority of owners among the Negro farm operators in 1940. But even in the Virginian stronghold, Negro ownership was weakening, in that the number of

---

[a] Sometimes the farm is rented for a fixed quantity of a certain crop, usually lint cotton ("lint-rental"). We shall include them under the term "cash tenants."

colored farm owners had declined by not less than one-third since 1910. And Florida depends relatively less on tenants and relatively more on wage labor than do other states in the South,[30] so that even there but a minority of the Negro farm population resided on their own places.

There are some general factors to be accounted for in this context. On the one hand, the low land values in the South and the low investment in land improvements, houses, and machines should make landownership easier to attain. On the other hand, the inadequate organization of banking and credit,[31] referred to above, works against both the acquiring and the holding of land. Another general factor making landownership, when it is attained, more precarious than it needs to be, is the old-fashioned system of local real estate taxation, which the South shares with the rest of the nation. This means that a landowner does not get a corresponding decrease in his taxation in a year when his crop has failed or his income drops because of a price fall. The dependence on hazardous cotton growing, of course, makes this institutional deficiency more detrimental to the Southern landowners.[32]

More specifically, in interpreting the reversal in the trend of Negro ownership, Southeastern agriculture after 1910, and particularly during the first years of the 'twenties, was hit by the boll weevil and by the general upheaval caused by the War and the post-war depression. The owner group, of course, should have been less affected than the tenant group, as far as living standards are concerned, but the latter had no ownership to lose. The fact that even the number of white owners in the South declined by more than one-tenth between 1920 and 1930 (from almost 1,400,000 to 1,250,000) suggests that conditions in general were unfavorable for the small farm owner. Between 1930 and 1940 (when the number of white owners was 1,384,000), on the other hand, there was a corresponding large increase in the number of white owners, whereas colored ownership continued to decline. This, however, scarcely means that the prospects for economic success in small ownership had become any brighter. As will be shown in the next chapter, it indicates rather that white owners, or those who were able to get into that class, were the ones who had most opportunity to stay on the land, "if, in view of the paucity of migratory outlets, they preferred to do that."[33]

Data on size of farm, acreage values, and farm values (Figure 5) give a rather good idea of how marginal the existence of the small owner-operators in the South tends to be. They show, further, that this is particularly true about Negro owners. It seems, finally, that their relative position has become even more unfavorable than it was a couple of decades ago. Land operated by croppers, particularly Negro croppers, has the highest average value per acre. This, as we have said, is due to the fact that plantations, by and large, are located on much of the best land of the

FIGURE 5.   AVERAGE SIZE OF FARM, AND AVERAGE VALUE OF LAND AND BUILDINGS PER ACRE AND PER FARM, BY COLOR AND TENURE, IN THE SOUTH: 1920 AND 1940

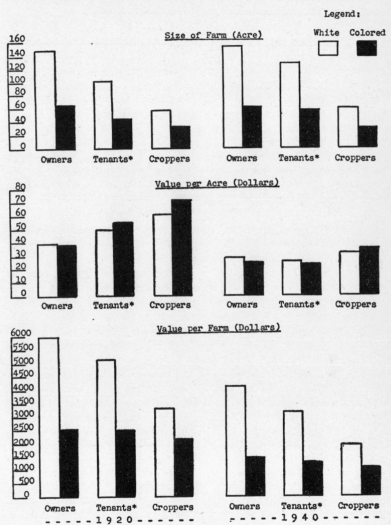

Source: United States Census.
Note: *Tenants include only tenants who are not sharecroppers.

South, leaving less of first choice than of second and third choice land to the middle-sized and small owner-operators. Cash tenants and share renters used to take an intermediate position, but are now pretty close to the owner-operators in this respect. White owners showed a higher average acreage value in 1940 ($27.27) than colored owners ($23.89). The decline in acreage value since 1920 was in every tenure group less pronounced for whites than for Negro operators.

Size of farm increases with tenure status. In every case, however, Negroes have much smaller farms than whites. The consequence is that the average size of Negro owner-operated farms (60.4 acres) is about the same as for white sharecroppers (58.9 acres). The mean value of land and buildings of the farm operated by colored owners ($1,443) is lower even than that of the white sharecropper's plot ($1,908). The value of implements and machinery that the colored owner has ($90) is only a fraction of that which the white owner has at his disposal ($322).[34]

7. HISTORICAL REASONS FOR THE RELATIVE LACK OF NEGRO FARM OWNERS

Even apart from the general economic trends in Southern agriculture, there are several reasons why the Negro has been unable to make a better showing as an independent farm owner.

There is his background in slavery, and the fact that he scarcely ever has been encouraged to show much initiative or been taught that it pays to look after oneself rather than to be dependent. More often he has been given to understand that his racial status provides an excuse for not being able to shift for himself, and that modest acceptance of a low position would rate a reward bigger than that offered for courageous attempts to reach a higher position.[35] In the rural South he has certainly not enjoyed much of that kind of legal security which is a necessary condition for successful entrepreneurship; at any rate, he has had far less of it than the whites with whom he has had to compete.[a] His best security has been to become associated with a white person of some status in the community; and that, in most cases, has presupposed an employer-employee or landlord-tenant relationship.[b] Since his earnings as a farmhand or tenant have always tended to be lower than those of white workers, he has had less chance to save enough money for the purpose of buying land. The belief that he is racially inferior and the social isolation between the two castes have also affected the credit rating even of those individual Negroes who otherwise would have been excellent risks. His educational opportunities in the rural South have been extremely poor.

Although the influence of such general conditions cannot be measured,

[a] See Part VI.
[b] See Chapter 26, Section 2.

there is scarcely any doubt about their being highly significant. In addition, however, a number of specific factors have been operative. Some of them have already been touched upon in the preceding chapters. There is, in the first place, the fact that rural Negroes, to a great extent, are concentrated on plantation areas, where comparatively few small holdings are for sale. There was no general land reform, and the Negro did not participate in the development of the West. But even in Kansas, where one of the few noteworthy attempts to organize new *post-bellum* Negro settlements was made, there were not more than a few hundred Negro owner-operators in 1940; and some of these owners probably were the descendants of persons who had been brought to Kansas as slaves. Undoubtedly the attitudes of the white settlers constituted the main cause for this lack of success. In the largely over-populated, white-dominated districts of the South, these attitudes, if anything, were still more pronounced.

There have, however, always been some small holdings for sale in the areas of Negro concentration, and more have been added to this supply as plantations tended to disintegrate.[36] During the years immediately following the Civil War, land values were low, and that was one of the reasons why a few Negroes, along with many poor whites, managed to get into the landowning class. Some ex-slaves bought land from their former masters, and there are places where such Negro properties still constitute a large proportion of all Negro-owned farms.[37]

The Negro has, however, usually been at a disadvantage when competing with white buyers even in the Black Belt. Apart from economic and other factors already mentioned, he has had to overcome segregational and discriminatory attitudes of the rural white population.

... Negro landownership—even now—can be achieved only by means of a most exacting and highly selective procedure; the would-be owner must be acceptable to the white community, have a white sponsor, be content with the purchase of acreage least desired by the whites, and pay for it in a very few years.

The Negro buys land only when some white man will sell to *him*. Just because a white man has land for sale does not mean that a Negro, even the one most liked and respected by him, can buy it even if he has the money. Whether a particular Negro can buy a particular tract of land depends upon its location, its economic and emotional value to the white owner and other white people, the Negro's cash and credit resources, and, doubtless most important of all, his personal qualities in the light of the local attitudes: He must be acceptable.[38]

Negro ownership emerges in areas where land is rented, rather than where it is worked by croppers or wage hands. Renters do not cultivate the "proud acres" of the plantations. They are common only where the tracts of land are too small, too unproductive, or too distant to warrant supervision; or where the owners, because of other remunerative business, make little effort to secure maximum revenue from their lands. On the out-of-the-way, or neglected tracts, in the nooks and corners between creeks and between white communities, and in areas where white community organization is disintegrating—these are the places where renters are most prevalent, where they move least often, where they are most independent and self-directed, where they accumulate most cash and credit. These are the tracts which are most often for sale to the Negro.[39]

There has always been an active solidarity among white people to prevent Negroes from acquiring land in white neighborhoods. The visitor finds, therefore, that most often he has to get off the main road and into the backwoods if he wants to see a Negro landowner. The intensity of those attitudes on the side of the whites—which closely correspond to the attitudes behind residential segregation in the cities[a]—seems to have been increasing toward the turn of the century. This was the time when the Jim Crow legislation was built up in the South.[b] There actually were even sporadic attempts in the beginning of the century to institute laws in order to block Negro ownership in white rural districts.[40] It is noteworthy that the trend toward increase of Negro landownership was halted at about the same time.[41]

The last decade, finally, has brought a new competitive advantage to the white owner. Government regulations, which have become of great importance, no doubt have helped the Negro owner along with the white owner. The fact, however, that the local administration of the new agricultural policies is entirely, or almost entirely, in the hands of white people cannot fail to make the Negroes a relatively disfavored group. This problem will be touched upon in the next chapter.

8. TENANTS AND WAGE LABORERS

In 1880, 64 per cent of the Southern farms were operated by owners. The corresponding figure for 1900 had fallen to 53 per cent. By 1930 it was down to 44 per cent. A majority of the Southern farm operators were tenants and sharecroppers. There was a similar development in other parts of the country as well. But nowhere else did it go so far.[42] And nowhere else did this trend have quite as serious social implications.

Behind this change are the lagging industrialization, the high rural fertility rates, and the relatively small opportunities for successful ownership in the South. Not only Negroes, but whites also, were affected by these factors. Already by 1900[c] there were more white than Negro tenants in Southern agriculture, and during the following three decades the number of white tenants increased by more than 400,000, or roughly 60 per cent, where as the corresponding figures for nonwhite tenants were 147,000 and 27 per cent, respectively.[43]

There seems to have been a parallel trend in the case of wage laborers,

[a] See Chapter 29, Section 3.
[b] See Chapter 28, Section 4.
[c] There was no breakdown by color in earlier census reports.

although much less pronounced. In 1910 more than half of these workers were Negro—in 1930 less than half of them.[44] It should be kept in mind that their status, by and large, is more insecure even than that of the sharecroppers, who, at least, are assured of year-round employment— although not always of a year-round income. This, however, does not reflect on the wage labor institution as such. If all Southern farm labor had been remunerated on a straight wage basis, the conditions would have been entirely different. A greater proportion of the wage laborers would have had year-round jobs, and these year-round employees would have known in advance for what wages they were working—something which is not true about tenants and croppers. At present most Southern agricultural wage laborers are literally "marginal." It is only at seasonal peaks that most of them can count on full employment. This circumstance, more than anything else, accounts for their inferior position.

The fact that nowadays almost two-thirds of the tenants are white has been emphasized time and again in the discussion. It does not follow, however, that white tenancy is more serious than Negro tenancy. Rather it is the other way around. We have seen that Negroes, more than whites, are concentrated in the lower tenure groups, and that in each tenure group Negroes are economically much weaker than whites. In addition, there are certain other significant differences.

It would be a mistake to believe that the plantation system and the tenant system are synonymous concepts. *The majority of all tenants do not work on plantations, but on small holdings.* In 1910, the last time an enumeration of plantations was made,[45] it was found that 39,000 plantations, located in 325 plantation counties, had about 400,000 tenants;[46] whereas, the total number of tenants in the South was over 1,500,000.[47] The ratio of plantation tenants to all tenants must be still lower now, for the number of tenants has increased much more in non-plantation counties than in plantation counties.[48] During the last decade there has even been a decrease in tenancy on the plantations.[a] It may be, therefore, that three out of four tenants in the South today work on small holdings.

While plantation tenancy belongs to the classical subjects in the rural sociology of the South, much less scientific attention has been given to the Southern nonplantation tenant. It is certain, however, that the great majority of these small-holding tenants are white.[49] A large number of them are related to their landlords.[50] For all we know, their conditions, in many cases, may be similar to those of white tenants in other parts of the country, except that, more likely than not, they have to work and live under poorer circumstances, and their general status, to some extent, may have been influenced by the plantation patterns.

The majority of the plantation tenants, on the other hand, are Negro.[51]

[a] See Chapter 12.

There has been a "white infiltration" even on this mainstay of Negro tenancy, however.[52] It even happens quite frequently that white and Negro tenants work on the same plantations, although usually not in the same capacity. White workers tend to be relatively more concentrated in the outlying districts, or on the least valuable parts of the plantations where the tenants work more independently and have a higher tenure status; whereas, Negroes more often make up the bulk of the labor force on the main part of the plantations, where they can be closely controlled and supervised by the owners or managers.

Thus, some of the main factors which account for the more rapid rise in white over Negro tenancy, until about 1930, are:

1. Negro tenants, more than white tenants, are dependent on the unstable cotton plantation economy.
2. Tenancy has increased more in nonplantation counties than in plantation counties.
3. Cotton culture has been moving toward the Southwest.
4. There has been white "infiltration" into plantation areas. This, however, is not so much an explanation as a description of the change. It still remains a problem why the intensity of rural population pressure increased more for white than for Negro agricultural workers.[a]

Also of relevance in this context is the fact that Negroes are "attached to the soil" much less than whites—that is, they more frequently move from one farm to another.[53] But this does not, in any way, constitute a racial or cultural characteristic. In reality, it is nothing but a consequence of the fact that Negroes, more than whites, are concentrated in the lower tenure groups; the lower the tenure status, the more frequent are the farm-to-farm movements.[54] In every given tenure group, Negroes tend to stay somewhat longer on the same place than do white farmers. In 1935, 38 per cent of the colored, as against 49 per cent of the white, croppers in the South had stayed less than one year on the farms which they were operating. The same proportion for other tenants were 27 and 40 per cent, respectively.

It goes without saying that movements as frequent as those must have an adverse influence on the living conditions of the tenants. No tenant who expects to farm on another place the next year can have much interest in doing any work on his house or in developing a year-round garden; neither can he be interested in maintaining the soil. Negligence in these and other respects naturally tends to become particularly serious in cases of absentee ownership; 15 per cent of the 646 plantations studied by Woofter in 1934 did not have a resident owner or even a special hired overseer.[55]

[a] See Chapter 8.

9. The Plantation Tenant

The plight of the plantation tenant[56] has been described so often and so well[57] that there is no need to give more than a short summary here. But a summary we must present. For, despite all scientific and reformistic publicity, these conditions are still news to a great part of the American people; as we see it, they could not otherwise have prevailed in their present form for such a long time. The subject, in a way, is a fascinating one. It is the problem of an antiquated paternalistic labor institution in the midst of modern American capitalistic society.

If we except cash tenants—who usually, but not always, can be regarded as rather independent entrepreneurs, and who make up only about one-tenth of all Negro tenants—plantation tenants are just ordinary laborers, although they are designated as farmers in the census. Their work is usually supervised, more or less regularly, by the landlord or his representative. In some cases they even work by the clock and in gangs.[58] Their wages, however, are not determined according to supply and demand in a free labor market.

Wages are not fixed per week, per month, or per annum. Nor is the sharecropping agreement modeled after the ordinary piece-wage system. The cropper, rather, gets a share of the product. The quantity of the product depends not only on the efforts of the workers but on the conditions of the soil and on the hazards of wind and weather; and it is not the quantity of the output alone but also its price that determines the final reward for the toils of labor.[a] The wages of the sharecroppers and share tenants, in other words, vary in such a way that there is no reason whatever to assume that they, except accidentally and occasionally, would satisfy the supply-and-demand equations of an ordinary free labor market.[b]

While in other parts of our economic system it has been the accepted ideal that risk of investment should be directly correlated with the size of investment, the sharecropper and the share tenant—although nothing but laborers from economic and social viewpoints—have to carry a considerable share of the entrepreneur's risk. It is possible that it is this practice of

[a] Ordinary piece-rate wages also may vary with the change in general market conditions; but only through the process of price formation in the commodity and labor markets and with a certain time-lag, and seldom, if ever, to the same extent as the price of the product.

[b] As a labor or tenant contract, the share tenant agreement reveals its pre-capitalistic character by the fact that the wage or the land rent is not fixed in a sum of money or product but in a *proportion which remains fixed as a matter of tradition independent of how prices and price relations change.* The products and cost factors in the production other than labor are, however, priced in the market and so is land. Only labor costs (and incomes) are fixed in an arbitrary and traditional proportion. This indicates the dependent status of labor in this economic system. Labor has not even had the protection of being directly related to the objective conditions of price formation in an economic market.

hedging by spreading the risk over the whole tenant working force which has enabled the planters to carry on the cotton crop gamble much more persistently than otherwise would have been possible. It is true that the share tenant shares in the benefit of a good crop and favorable market conditions with the landowner. It is also true that he does not have much capital of his own. If losses run so high that at the end of the year he finds himself indebted to the landlord, he may often be able—at least now-adays—to get rid of this debt simply by moving to another plantation. But many a time he may find himself having invested a full season's work without having received anything near the wages he would have earned had he been a wage laborer with full employment. On such occasions, at least, he has to face long months of semi-starvation for himself and his family. That certainly is a business risk just as much as any. And should he have any livestock or other assets, the landlord is always free to take them to cover possible debts. In nine cotton states "the landlord has the legal right to sell any and all property the tenant may have to secure payment of rent and furnishings."[59]

Indeed, any study of the concrete details of the system will reveal that the sharecropper or share tenant usually has most of the disadvantages of being an independent entrepreneur without having hardly any of the rights that ordinarily go with such a position. Only in relatively few cases are his rights and obligations set down in a written contract.[60] In most cases he does not sell even his own share in the cotton crop himself.[61] According to the crop lien laws in most states, he has no right to dispose of it until he has paid to the landlord all the rent due and the advances he has received during the season. And since he cannot well do that until the crop has been sold and paid for, the landlord is legally entitled to handle all the marketing as he sees fit.[62] Seldom is the tenant even con-sulted about how to sell and when.

Worse than that, however, is the general pattern of making all kinds of account-keeping a unilateral affair. The tenant usually has to take the landlord's word for what price has been obtained for the cotton, for what is the total amount of advances received from the landlord, and for what the interest on these advances is, and so on. An attempt on the part of the Negro tenant to check the accounts against his own itemized annota-tions—if he should have kept any (which is rarely done)—will not accomplish much, in most cases, except possibly to infuriate the landlord.[63] The temptation to cheat the tenants at the final settlement for the year, under such circumstances, must be great. Indeed, Southern plantation owners would be unlike other human beings if they did not sometimes misuse the considerable arbitrary power they have over their tenants.[64]

In several conversations with white planters—as also with employers of Negro labor in cities, particularly of domestics—the writer has noticed the display of a sort of moral double standard. White people of the landowning class who give the impression of being upright and honest in all their other dealings take it for granted and sometimes brag about the fact that they cheat their Negroes. On the other hand, it is equally apparent that there is a strong recognition in the South of the difficulty for a landlord to get and keep good workers if he does not have the reputation of dealing with them on a straight basis. Still, there are too many "settlement jokes" in the Southern folklore[65] and too many statements about the matter in the literature to make a student inclined to dismiss the possibility of outright cheating. There is social significance even in the fact—which every observer will be able to confirm—that "the system leaves the Negro tenant with the *feeling* that he has not been treated justly."[66]

The "advancing" of food, clothing, and other necessities of life is a significant part of the system. Since the tenant is ordinarily without resources—otherwise he would not be a tenant—he cannot usually wait for his wages until the crop has been harvested and sold. He has, therefore, to live on a credit basis at least during a large part of the year. For an average period of seven months, according to Woofter's sample study for 1934, the tenant receives credit from the landlord, often in a special store or commissary, where he can buy household supplies up to a certain amount a month. This amount varies according to the size of the family, the prospects for the crop, the market conditions, and so on. The average in Woofter's sample was $12.80 per month and $88 per year.[67] A study of the Yazoo-Mississippi Delta in 1936 showed an average subsistence advance per year of about $94 for sharecroppers and $138 for share tenants. If operating credit is included, the amounts were $162 and $283, respectively.[68]

The interest rates charged for these advances are extremely high. A flat rate of 10 per cent is usual but, since the duration of the credit is only a few months, the annual rate is several times higher. According to Woofter's sample study in 1934, it was no less than 37 per cent.[69] A plantation study for 1937 on a somewhat smaller sample gave almost the same average. "These rates were two to three times as high as those paid by the operators (landlords) for short-term credit."[70]

In addition, prices in commissaries are often "marked up" to a considerable extent.[71] Some people in the South, however, will tell the visitor that the breaking up of rural isolation and the increased opportunities for tenants to spend week-ends in towns and cities and see the stores has made this latter practice less prevalent than it used to be. When the advances are paid in cash, which sometimes happens, the tenant naturally has greater freedom to buy at ordinary market prices.

According to Woofter's plantation study for the depression period 1930-1934, no less than 13-15 per cent of the tenants ended each crop year in debt to their landlords. This means that, in addition to their having to start the next crop year with a deficit, they have nothing to live on during the winter. The average debt for these tenants varied between $89 and $143.[72] As hinted at before, it is probable that indebted and propertyless tenants are often able nowadays to get rid of their debts simply by moving to another place. This, at least, is likely to be the case when the tenant is an inefficient worker, and the landlord, for this reason, is not interested in keeping him and considers the expense for collecting the debt higher than it is worth. The extremely high number of tenants who have stayed less than one year on their present farms is enough to indicate the relatively unhampered movements of most tenant operators. The practice of forcing an indebted tenant to stay on the plantation in order to work off his debt certainly became less prevalent during the period of relatively abundant agricultural labor which lasted from the beginning of the depression until the present war boom.[73] We do not know whether the present shortage of farm labor has brought about any new increase in such debt-peonage. What we do know is that the whole legal system previously gave the tenants but little protection against such abuses and that, so far, there has been no fundamental change in this legal system. In addition, the planter has at his disposal all the extra-legal caste sanctions. It is certain, anyway, that there is some debt-peonage left.[74]

Apart from the legal and extra-legal pressures, the terms established in the landlord-tenant agreements and settlements will be heavily loaded against the plantation tenants, because of that monopolistic element which was analyzed even in the time of Adam Smith: the purchasers of labor will be bound as neighbors, friends, and gentlemen not to bid against each other for tenants. This monopolistic tendency will be particularly effective in the plantation South where the tenants are usually absolutely unorganized, where, further, there is a racial split and usually extreme prejudice among them, and where—particularly in the case of Negro tenants—the social distance between employers and employees is enormous.

That such a monopolistic tendency is strong has been seen by many observers.[75] To begin with, no planter feels that he can afford to lose a tenant who has started a crop. The claims on solidarity go further, however. To be a "tenant-stealer" is traditionally considered a bad thing.[76] According to the prevailing custom, no landlord is supposed to accept a tenant whom the previous employer does not agree to release.[77]

The basis of this custom is a feeling, on the part of the planters, of a sort of collective ownership of the workers in the community. The resentment against any outsiders coming in for the purpose of hiring labor is even stronger, if possible.[78] The hostility against outside labor agents grew particularly strong during the period of the First World War, when Northern industry made its strongest bid for the Negro agricultural worker. Several states enacted laws against such practices.

The last state law against the enticement of labor was passed in Louisiana early in June, 1935, making it "unlawful for any person to go on the premises or plantation of any citizen between sunset and sunrise and assist in moving any laborers or tenants therefrom without the consent of the owner of said premises or plantation."[79]

This should be the place for "balancing the picture" by looking for positive aspects of the paternalistic labor relations on the Southern plantations. The system doubtless has some positive sides. Even the outsider will occasionally find some evidence of them. There are good landlords, who really try to take care of their tenants to some extent. They are the ones who get and hold the good tenants. They are rightly proud of this fact and tell the interviewer about it. Most studies contain some statement from such a plantation owner who has made the discovery that he can get the best out of his Negro tenant just by treating him decently and by appealing to his ambition to get ahead—in other words, by regarding the Negro like any other human being. Since the general standard is so low, it is not expensive to be an exceptionally good planter and have the best tenants.

Yet the fact that planters, too, are ordinary human beings, and that many of them actually are better than the system which they represent, is not high praise of the plantation system as an economic institution. Every social institution, in this way, presents a whole range of cases—low extremes, normal cases and high extremes. Nevertheless, we can talk about the whole range as being low or high in relation to the corresponding range for alternative institutions. The benevolence of certain landlords certainly is a great help for many individual tenants. But it is, in the final analysis, nothing else than an aspect of the arbitrariness of the whole system.

It is our impression that the predominant feeling among most Negro tenants is that they can get more or less out of the landlord depending upon what kind of landlord he is, and how he is approached. But not often have they been taught to feel that they have definite rights and definite obligations, and that it is up to them to make good. Several local Farm Security officials in the South have informed us of how the inherited paternalistic attitude on the part of the planters and the corresponding attitudes of dependence, carelessness, and lack of ambition on the part of the tenants constitute the toughest problems in their work. The plantation system, in summary, fails flagrantly to meet the standards of social and economic efficiency and justice.[80]

There is no lack of statements in the literature on the plantation system of the South to the effect that its survival through generations is a "proof" that it—compared with other organizations of land, capital, and labor for agricultural production—is superior and best adapted to the circumstances of the region. This is, of course, nothing but the application of the liberalistic (do-nothing) doctrine that "what is, must be"—which from a scientific viewpoint is most doubtful in itself under *any* circumstances[a]—to a tradition-bound, nonliberalistic, economic arrangement. The logical fault is too obvious to need further comment. This particular economic arrangement, as all others, has to be explained in historical terms and to be evaluated in terms of its effects *compared with alternate, possible arrangements.*

In this context the changes actually occurring in the plantation system become important. As we have indicated, the system of slightly modernized Black Codes seems finally to be withering under the assaults of the Supreme Court and other federal agencies as well as of various pro-democratic organizations in both the South and the North. The relative abundance of agricultural labor during the 'thirties has contributed, probably more than anything else, toward the gradual wiping out of the practice of debt-peonage. Attempts to organize plantation tenants have occurred. Efforts of the federal government to rationalize the credit structure and other crucial elements of the plantation system have been started. There are some concerted efforts to begin reforming even the tenure conditions. The cotton acreage has been drastically curtailed. We shall find, however, that new problems have risen—problems which, again, have affected the Negroes much more seriously than the whites.

[a] See Appendix 2.

CHAPTER 12

NEW BLOWS TO SOUTHERN AGRICULTURE DURING
THE THIRTIES: TRENDS AND POLICIES

1. Agricultural Trends During the 'Thirties

Of all the calamities that have struck the rural Negro people in the South in recent decades—soil erosion, the infiltration of white tenants into plantation areas, the ravages of the boll weevil, the southwestern shift in cotton cultivation—none has had such grave consequences, or threatens to have such lasting effect, as the combination of world agricultural trends and federal agricultural policy initiated during the 'thirties. These changes are revolutionizing the whole structure of Southern agricultural economy. They have already rooted out a considerable portion of the Negro farmers and made the future of the remaining group extremely problematic.

For more than a century America has been the leading cotton-producing country in the world. But cotton growing in other countries was slowly increasing, and the increase became substantial in the decade following the First World War. American cotton production, except for annual fluctuations, remained fairly constant during this period. Still during the 'twenties American-grown cotton represented more than half of the total world production. Meanwhile domestic consumption had ceased to increase. The trend of cotton prices was downward during most of the 'twenties.[1] Lange remarks:

> Looking back to this period, it is now rather obvious that cotton production in the United States had already reached its limits of practical expansion. American cotton had to face a keen competition on most markets abroad, as the production in certain foreign countries, primarily China and Egypt, was increasing and new raw material for textiles began to appear at the same time.[2]

But it was during the 'thirties that the over-production problem really became serious. It was then that the demand was declining drastically abroad and at home due to the depression and to the growing competition from other countries and to the increased use of substitutes. The cotton economy suffered much more from the depression and recovered much less afterward than did American agriculture in general.[3]

Southern tobacco also is losing out on the international market, and the slow rise in domestic consumption has failed—at least up to the present war boom—to compensate for the loss.[4] Southern sugar cane is in a similar position.[5] Only in one main commercial crop in the South did a rising demand keep pace with production—namely, the fruit and vegetable production in Florida and the coastal plains. But even for these crops prices have declined, and their cultivation offers workers still worse living conditions than does the cotton plantation.[6]

Under this onslaught on the old cash crops of the South, and also induced by an agricultural policy which we shall comment upon later, dairy farming has made some headway in the South.[7] There does not seem to be much hope, however, that dairy farming ever will become a major Southern industry. In the Lower South there are certain climatic obstacles which so far have been difficult to overcome; and milk and cream require a local market. Beef cattle and hogs, on the other hand, have shown a big increase.[8] Yet the Southeast had, in 1940, still less than one-tenth of all the beef cattle in the country.[9]

These are some of the significant changes which have occurred in Southern agriculture during the decade before the present war boom. The terrific blow to the cotton economy was the most significant, particularly from the viewpoint of the Negro. Some of the other changes indicated a beginning reorientation along new lines. But none of them was large enough to compensate for the shattering disaster in cotton, for cotton is one of the most labor-consuming crops in the South.

> It has been estimated that on the average 30 million acres of land devoted to the production of cotton will furnish about 255 million days of work per year in growing, harvesting, and hauling the crop to the gin. If the same acreage were put in corn it would require only 110 million days of labor, or less than one-half the time required by cotton, and if seeded to oats or hay the total days of labor required to produce and harvest these crops would amount to from 45 to 50 million days, or an equivalent of one-sixth to one-fifth as much labor as if the land were devoted to cotton production.[10]

Thus, even under favorable circumstances it would not have been possible to avoid widespread unemployment of agricultural labor. But circumstances were not favorable. For although extensive and commendable attempts were made to deal with the social aspects of the problem of structural change, the major New Deal efforts, as we shall find, did not fit into constructive long-range program for a reorganization of Southern agriculture.

The present war boom, of course, has brought temporary relief. There has been an increased demand and an increased production of several crops. The growing of peanuts has been stepped up considerably. There is a greater production of tobacco, sugar cane and rice; soybeans, too, have increased, although much more so in the North than in the South. The market for all meats is booming.[11] There is a pronounced scarcity of agricultural labor in the South as well as everywhere else. This new situation may, in a measure, have some positive effects also on the long-range development. The War probably has been a stimulus to greater crop diversification in the South. The encouragement of out-migration from rural areas may make agricultural over-population somewhat less severe even after the War than would have been the case under other circumstances. But there are also great risks in this development. When the results of the destruction in Europe and elsewhere have been overcome, American agriculture will again appear as over-expanded. The long-range employment prospects in Southern agriculture, on the whole, are rather dark.

2. THE DISAPPEARING SHARECROPPER

Up to the time when the data from the 1940 Census were released, the main emphasis in the discussion was placed upon the increase in tenancy—a trend which had been noticeable ever since the Civil War—and upon the decline in number of farm owners—which became apparent during the 'twenties. The 1940 Census, however, showed that the trends had become reversed. Tenancy was on the decline, for there were 192,000 fewer Negro and 150,000 fewer white tenants in 1940 than in 1930. Ownership, on the other hand, was on the increase in Southern agriculture, except for the Negroes (Table 1).

TABLE 1

NUMBER OF FARM OPERATORS IN THE SOUTH, BY TENURE AND COLOR:
1930, 1935, AND 1940
(in thousands)

| | Owners and Managers | | Tenants Other than Croppers | | Croppers | |
Year	Nonwhite	White	Nonwhite	White	Nonwhite	White
1930	183	1,250	306	709	393	383
1935	186	1,404	261	854	368	348
1940	174	1,384	208	700	299	242

Sources: U. S. Bureau of the Census, *Census of Agriculture: 1935*, Vol. III, pp. 106, 107, and 126-133. *Sixteenth Census of the United States: 1940, Agriculture.* United States Summary, First Series, Table VI: Supplemental for the Southern States.

The rise in ownership and decline in tenancy did not balance each other, however. The increase in number of owners occurred altogether between 1930 and 1935 and was restricted to the white group. The decrease in the total number of tenants occurred between 1935 and 1940 and was then divided between the two racial groups. Before 1935, however, white cash and share tenants seem to have become much more numerous, whereas all other tenant groups—Negro cash and share tenants as well as Negro and white croppers—had started to decline. The decrease in number of tenants during the following five years became much more pronounced and affected all four color-tenure groups.

The final results, by 1940, of all these changes were that there was a somewhat larger number of white owners than in 1930; a slightly lower number of Negro owners; a much lower number of Negro cash and share tenants, and of Negro and white croppers. The total number of croppers had declined by almost one-third (somewhat more for whites and somewhat less for Negroes), and the decrease in number of Negro cash and share tenants was at least of the same relative size.

These rather spectacular changes do not mean, observes Sterner,

... that the situation has been ameliorated. By and large it is rather the other way around. While the limitations in the opportunities in Southern agriculture formerly caused an increase in tenancy, they now seem to have been aggravated to such an extent that *the Negro and white sharecropping class as well as the Negro cash and share tenants are in the process of being forced out.*[12]

Yet, many of the ex-tenants and ex-croppers may have stayed in agriculture. They have simply been reduced to wage laborers on the farms. This, of course, means only that their position, in most of the cases, has become still more marginal.[13]

The main reason why the Negro lost out, probably, was the fact that he, much more than the white operator and worker, was dependent on the cotton economy which was hit most severely by the depression and by the falling off of foreign markets. Practically all the increase in number of farm operators as well as the total increase in farm population during the period 1930-1935 occurred outside of the cotton regions;[14] and after that period there were no further increases of that kind. Yet, the depression by itself seems to have had much more immediate effects on income conditions than on employment, for the decline in Negro tenancy before 1935 was relatively limited compared with what was to come after that year. It seems, therefore, that *the agricultural policies, and particularly the Agricultural Adjustment program (A.A.A.), which was instituted in May, 1933, was the factor directly responsible for the drastic curtailment in number of Negro and white sharecroppers and Negro cash and share tenants.*

It is true that behind the A.A.A. was the depression and over-production. If no such thing as the A.A.A. had ever been instituted, the cotton price would have remained low for so long a time that production and employment eventually would have been severely curtailed. And A.A.A. certainly raised the income not only for planters and other owners, but—to an extent —also for those tenants and croppers who were allowed to stay in employment. But hundreds of thousands of them did not get any protection at all. They were pushed off the land, and, if anything, the A.A.A. hastened their elimination.

3. THE ROLE OF THE A.A.A. IN REGARD TO COTTON

In order to understand this, it is necessary to recall what the A.A.A. program is all about and how it works.[a] Its fundamental objective is to raise and stabilize farm income. This objective is sought along four principal lines: (1) limitation of cash crop acreages; (2) removal of price-depressing surpluses from regular markets; (3) payment of direct subsidies to farmers; (4) and encouragement of conservation practices. There is an intimate relationship between all four main aspects of the program. The first two are aimed at restricting the supply brought on the ordinary market. The cash crop limitations make greater emphasis on soil-building crops and practices possible. Subsidies are paid as a remuneration for carrying out acreage restrictions and conservation work; their function is not only to let the farmers have a direct bounty, but also to encourage them to participate in the program, which is not compulsory but voluntary. The voluntary character of the participation, however, seems to be something of a fiction. There is, for instance, a ginning tax on cotton and a marketing tax on tobacco, whereby the nonparticipant is penalized if he markets in excess of what he normally produces on what should be his acreage allotment. The fact that those taxes have to be approved by referendum does not make the participation much more voluntary for the individual operators who would be against it.

The cut in cotton acreage has been drastic.[15] Owing to a tendency to intensify the cultivation and to retain the best land in cotton and, perhaps, to make some improvements in cultivating technique, the production has not decreased to the same extent.[16] Since the acreage cuts were not made large enough to offset the effect of the increased acreage yields, the overproduction problem obviously has not been solved in this way.[17]

The A.A.A. policy of keeping up the level of cotton prices by crop reduction and removal of price-depressing surpluses from the market, of course, helped the United States to lose its foreign market to competing countries. The volume of American cotton export hit a low during the crop year 1938-1939.[18] On the whole, it seems that "of all our crops, cotton has given the

---

[a] The following short description of how the A.A.A. program has affected the Negro is based largely on an unpublished manuscript prepared for this study by Gunnar Lange ("Agricultural Adjustment Programs and the Negro" [January, 1942]). Several significant details and qualifications, as well as certain characteristics of the program during the first years of its operation, are intentionally overlooked in the summary given in the text. Main emphasis is put on those points which facilitate the understanding of how the program has affected the Negro.

New Deal most trouble."[19] In 1939, however, a substantial export bounty on cotton was instituted. This, and perhaps still more the increased consumption during the present war, has brought temporary relief. The carry-over has declined, but it is still significant.

Indeed, the whole program would have failed to bring about any increase in cotton prices had it not been for the removal of surpluses from the ordinary market. Very commendable were the efforts—now discontinued —to increase the cotton consumption of the needy by direct distribution of mattresses and by the Cotton Stamp Plan. Those measures, however, were expensive in relation to their results in reducing the cotton surplus. The fact that the cotton producer receives but 15 cents of the consumer's dollar spent on cotton products[20] makes it much more difficult to make a cotton distribution program effective than it is to take similar measures in regard to most other agricultural products. Therefore, this part of the removal program was only experimental.

Of real importance, on the other hand, have been the commodity loans to individual farmers and associations of farmers for the purpose of encouraging storing (The Ever-Normal Granary Plan). These loans explain the large carry-overs. The existence of such huge and fluctuating surpluses means, however, that the whole system has had complete lack of stability, which was contrary to the official purpose of the Granary Plan to keep the supply in balance. Had it not been for the present War, there could ultimately have been but two alternatives: either further drastic cuts in the cotton acreage, or collapse of the whole program.[a] In either case, the Negro would have been hurt severely.

4. A.A.A. and the Negro

It is something of a problem, however, that most of the reduction in cotton acreage was carried out before 1935, whereas the decrease in number of Negro and white croppers and of Negro cash and share tenants did not start to become really significant until after that year. Of course, there is nothing unnatural in a certain time-lag between acreage curtailment and effects on employment. The intensification of cultivation of the cotton land not eliminated by the A.A.A., the increase in certain other crops, and the uncertainty about the permanence in the change may have contributed to a certain delay in the reorganization of the labor force. The Supreme Court decision of 1936, invalidating the first A.A.A. program, and the actual occurrence of an all-time peak in cotton production in 1937 justifies, to a degree, the hypothesis that the change may have had the appearance to many planters of being only temporary. By letting the employees share

[a] A third alternative would have been to rely consistently on export subsidies; but such a policy, more likely than not, would have been neutralized in the long run through retaliatory measures of foreign competitors.

in the reduction of income which had occurred since 1929, and by letting newly instituted rural relief agencies[a] provide supplementary income for part of the labor force during off-seasons, it was possible for the planters to retain most of the tenants for some time.

Furthermore, it was probably not only by the acreage reduction that the A.A.A. later gave inducement to the reduction in number of tenants.[21] Another factor, perhaps equally important, was the A.A.A. benefit payments. During the first years of the A.A.A. system there was a general complaint that landlords simply grabbed the benefit checks which they were supposed to forward to the tenants.[22] Many of these complaints turned out to be justified—even when investigated by county committees which were almost entirely white, and on which landowners were over-represented.

These practices were, in the main, later abolished. In the last few years, benefits are paid direct to the tenants. Although the credit relations between landlord and tenant, the system of unilateral account-keeping, as well as the legal impotence of the Negro tenants, still may enable the landlord to receive a larger share of the benefits than he is supposed to get, the situation certainly has changed. As early as 1935-1936, the Consumer Purchases Study, for instance, showed that even sharecroppers were receiving some A.A.A. payments.[23] The basis for the division of the payments between landlord and tenant, moreover, has been changed, so that the tenant today is to receive a larger share—about equal to his share in the crop —than according to former stipulations. The average benefit per plantation tenant, according to a sample study for some 3,000 plantation tenant families, had increased from $11 per year in 1934 to $27 in 1937. The latter figure constituted almost 10 per cent of the total net cash income of the average tenant family ($300).[24] In all probability there has been a further increase since 1937.

These changes in favor of the tenants, however, must have had the character of a two-edged sword. They gave the landlord a considerable economic interest in decreasing the number of tenants or lowering their status to wage laborers. And it is particularly during the latter part of the thirties that this temptation became significant. This may well be the main explanation of why most of the decline in number of sharecroppers and tenants occurred after 1935. Landlords have always tended to change the tenure status of their workers whenever that has been compatible with their own economic interests.[25] There is no reason why they should have behaved otherwise when carrying out the A.A.A. regulations.

It is true that the A.A.A. contracts have included stipulations according to which the landlords were obliged to maintain the normal number of tenants and laborers.[26] Yet such a regulation, even under the best conditions, must be difficult to enforce. Landlords cannot well be asked to keep the

[a] See Chapter 15.

same individual tenants and workers as before. When some move away—
and they do move often—it can always be claimed that there just are no
others good enough to take their jobs and farms. There is another stipulation, however, which should be easier to enforce. It is prescribed that a
reduction in the number of tenants and croppers on a farm shall not operate
to increase the payment to the landlord. Yet even this safeguard seems to
have been insufficient. For Negroes, and tenants generally, have practically
no real influence on the local administration of the program. And if a reduction in the number of tenants "is considered justified from the viewpoint
of 'sound management,' the stipulation preventing an increase in the amount
of payments to the landlords shall not apply."[27] Several observers have
noted that landlords actually have substituted wage labor for tenants in
order to secure larger A.A.A. payments for themselves.[28]

In summary: Landlords have been made to reduce drastically the acreage
for their main labor-requiring crops. They have been given a large part of
the power over the local administration of this program. They have a
strong economic incentive to reduce their tenant labor force, a large part
of which consists of politically and legally impotent Negroes. Yet they have
been asked not to make any such reduction. It would certainly not be
compatible with usual human behavior, if this request generally had been
fulfilled. Under the circumstances, there is no reason at all to be surprised
about the wholesale decline in tenancy. Indeed, it would be surprising if
it had not happened.

5. THE LOCAL ADMINISTRATION OF THE A.A.A.

A few remarks on the local administration of the A.A.A. are pertinent
here, as a further explanation of the last point. This administration is in
the hands of the Extension Service—that is, the County Farm Demonstration Agents—and the County Agricultural Conservation Committees
representing local farmers. It is our impression, based upon a large number
of interviews, that the county agents in the plantation South, to a great
extent, have an attitude on economic, social, and racial questions which is
similar to that of the large landowners. Some of them actually are planters
themselves. The committees, at least in plantation counties, are characterized
by an over-representation of big estate owners.[29] Committee members have
often been appointed by the federal administration upon the recommenda-
tion of the county agent, which meant that the Extension Service continued
to control the local committees. The federal administration has continued
attempting to democratize and to decentralize the administration of the
A.A.A. An important development is the recent organization of land-use
planning committees for the purpose of achieving coordination and local
adjustment of the various action programs. The Negro, however, has
scarcely profited by these reforms.[30]

It is true that the Negroes commonly vote in A.A.A. referenda for certain decisions, such as the establishment of marketing quotas.[a] Their votes are needed, since a majority of all farmers, including tenants and croppers, must be in favor of the program for it to be adopted. But Negroes are seldom allowed to vote for committeemen. Even when Negroes do exercise some privileges, it seldom means that they have any real influence on the decisions.

Not only Negro tenants and croppers, but Negro farm owners as well, are jeopardized by their relative lack of influence on the decisions of the local A.A.A. administration. The allotment of cotton acreage and benefit payments is a rather complicated affair. There are certain statistical computations involved, and these computations, in part, are based on records concerning previous farm practices on every individual holding. The accuracy of the records and calculations depends on the good-will, conscientiousness, and competence of those in charge of the local control. If they do not adequately represent all local farm groups, it can scarcely be avoided that the rights and interests of under-represented or entirely unrepresented farmers and tenants are overlooked in many individual cases. This is more likely to be the case since such groups, particularly Negroes, include a large proportion of more or less illiterate people who are unable to understand the intricate regulations well enough even to find out whether or not they have been wronged.[31] Indeed even highly educated persons may have to make a special effort in order to check up on their share.

6. MECHANIZATION

Before we proceed to an evaluation of the A.A.A. program, we must discuss a factor which seems bound to add its influence in displacing Negro labor on Southern plantations: mechanization. We also want to look for tendencies toward concerted defense action on the part of the plantation laborers.

Up to now mechanization has not been important. Cotton cultivation, in the main, is carried on by a technique which has not changed much since slavery. The low degree of mechanization is the reason why cotton growing requires so much labor and keeps this labor down to such low levels of living. At the same time, the cheap labor makes mechanization unprofitable. Otherwise it might be expected that the commercial farming of cotton on the Southern plantations would be more inviting to more efficient production methods than the subsistence production on family farms. But mechanization has actually been slow.[32]

In the last decade, however, there has been a tendency toward a narrowing of the still wide gap between the national and the Southeastern rates of mechanization.[33] That cotton planters in the Southeast would like to

[a] See Chapter 22, Section 3.

buy more machines is evident from a sample inquiry about factors retarding mechanization; half of the informants stressed the difficulty of financing purchases.[34]

It should be noted that the two Southwestern states, Texas and Oklahoma, show a different picture.[35] But what has happened in the Southwest has only a slight direct importance for Negro employment, as Negroes there are so relatively scarce in the rural districts. If mechanization for a long time should fail to become as intensive in the Southeast as in the Southwest, there is no doubt that the Negro, nevertheless, will suffer indirectly.

Great hindrances to mechanization have been both the difficulty of getting credit and the high rate of interest. The recent reforms in the organization of agricultural credit have reduced this obstacle considerably. The A.A.A. benefit payments add to the supply of cash that planters can use for mechanization, though it is true that even with these payments their incomes have not come to the pre-depression level. *The A.A.A. program has, however, another and most important influence toward increasing mechanization because of the premium it offers for reducing the number of tenants.*

Formerly, agricultural machines were not well-adjusted to the rolling terrain in some parts of the South. This is being overcome by newer types of machines constructed to satisfy Southern requirements.[36] As the Southern market for machines increases and, perhaps, other markets contract, the machine manufacturers, no doubt, will direct more of their attention toward the specific needs of the South. The mechanical cotton picker eventually may be perfected to such an extent that it can be used extensively on an economical basis;[37] a mechanical cotton chopper, perhaps, is a nearer possibility.[38] But even without such innovations, there will be more motors running in the agricultural South. The great number of large holdings, in some measure, should facilitate the use of more machine equipment, and Negroes are concentrated in those regions where holdings are large.

The threat against employment opportunities in the rural South is potentially greater, for the very reason that so far there have been but few machines on Southern farms. The displacement of labor which can be brought about by further mechanization is so much greater than anywhere else. Negroes, for several reasons, will feel the effects of this trend more than white workers, in the same way as they have suffered more from the decline in cotton economy. They are more dependent on the cash crop culture. They are more concentrated on plantations. They are objects of prejudice, especially when it comes to handling machinery. To operate an expensive machine is to have a position of responsibility, which, even in the rural South, must draw "white man's pay." Although Negroes have shown that they can acquire the necessary skill for the purpose,[39] there is scarcely any doubt that employers, more often than not, will prefer white labor if farm operations are mechanized. The records show that but a small part of the

machine equipment in the South is on farms where there are colored operators.[40] It will always be easier for employers to find workers who know
how to run machinery in the white group. More and more the Negro will
be reduced to a seasonal worker, and even this opportunity will dwindle if
chopping and picking, too, should become mechanized.[41]

7. LABOR ORGANIZATIONS

In view of the quantitative significance of the labor displacement during
the 'thirties, one would have expected to find widespread evidence of unrest
among the sharecroppers. One would have expected, further, to find a
great number of publicized expressions of a popular concern about what
was happening, as well as a widespread discussion of ameliorative programs.
Finally, one would have expected concrete action to follow these discussions.

There was unrest among the sharecroppers. There was publicity about it.
And the federal government did make highly commendable and rather
sizable attempts to improve the conditions by its various Farm Security
programs.[a] But the organized attempts of the tenants and sharecroppers
to fight for their needs were rather weak and scattered. And the publicity,
largely a result of certain incidents during the organizational work,[42] was
not extensive enough to reach far outside the ranks of such reformers,
administrators, social workers, scientists, journalists, and others who more
or less professionally had to follow the development. The federal government itself called attention to some of the problems involved by publishing
several outstanding reports, including the *Report on Farm Tenancy* by the
President's Committee, Woofter's study on *Landlord and Tenant on the
Cotton Plantation*, and the Holley, Winston, and Woofter volume on
The Plantation South, 1934-1937. But even in these otherwise enlightening
studies there was little, if any, attention given to the wholesale decline
in number of tenants.[b] The general public was rather unaware of the deeper
social significance of such incidents as occasionally made the front page of
the press. What the federal government did for the Southern tenants,
therefore, appeared to the average citizen more or less like a goodhearted
and, perhaps, extravagant benevolence on the part of the New Deal. He
usually had no idea at all that part of the distress was due to government
policy. Popular backing for the protest movement was by no means as strong
as it could have been had the general public been better informed.

[a] See Section 12 of this chapter.
[b] The explanation is largely that the statistics had not yet furnished any conclusive
evidence on the significance of the change. One cannot help feeling, though, that the political
necessity to defend all kinds of farm relief measures against attacks from the nonagrarian
groups caused a certain unwillingness to admit that the A.A.A. program could have contributed to the decline in employment opportunities.

It should not surprise us that organizational efforts among Southern tenants and farmhands were practically absent before the New Deal and remained weak even during the latter part of the 'thirties. Even in countries where the labor movement and collective bargaining have proceeded far in advance of American accomplishments in this field, the organization of agricultural labor has always been a hard task. The spatial dispersion of production and of the labor force and, still more, certain elements of rural culture tend to increase inertia against concerted action. In the South these difficulties are enhanced by the low educational level and the poverty of the agricultural workers; by their complete lack of cooperative habits; by the tradition of paternalism and dependence inherent in the plantation system; by the frequent moving from one locality to another; by the weak legal order which, in this field, has taken the form of ruthlessly beating down all labor organizations; and by the split between Negroes and whites. The last factor is of special importance because in this particular labor market there is intense competition between Negroes and whites. The whites could not possibly attain anything by organizing unions excluding Negroes. Whites and Negroes are exchangeable from the employers' point of view, and there exists a pressing labor surplus, particularly of Negro labor.

This is the general background against which the first labor movement among Southern farm workers should be viewed. The attempt to unionize has been concentrated mainly in the Southwest and in the Western border regions of the Cotton Belt, but the movement is spreading eastward. Arthur Raper, writing in 1940, summarizes the situation thus:

> At present the only three labor unions of farm tenants which are strong enough to be of any consequence have interracial membership. They are: The Farmers' Union, with headquarters at New Orleans and with activities limited largely to Louisiana; the United Cannery, Agricultural, Packing and Allied Workers of America (C.I.O.) with comparatively few members in the cotton area; and the Southern Tenant Farmers' Union, with headquarters in Memphis, Tennessee.[43]

Most of the states in the Southeast are untouched by these activities. Raper explains this limitation in the following way:

> The reasons are varied. In this newest cotton country a considerable proportion of the tenants have a background of small ownership or independent labor at sawmills. They have not been so long schooled in the plantation dependency as have the landless families in the Southeast, where the present plantation roots back into slavery. In the newer plantation region, holdings are larger and absentee ownership prevalent; relationships between management and workers are less personal, and the presence of labor organizers is less noticeable.[44]

Another reason for the regional differential is that the legal order is somewhat stronger in the Southwest. A handbill distributed in 1940 by a group called Missouri Agricultural Workers Council, contained a reference to a previous demonstration, which read:

> We staged the protest in Missouri,—not because cotton labor is treated more unfairly in Missouri than elsewhere. We know that is not true. We staged it in Missouri because we had less fear of bloody violence in Missouri.[45]

It seems that these organizations grow up largely because of the special problems brought about through the A.A.A. and the decline in employment opportunities. The Southern Tenant Farmers' Union, which is still the main organization in the field, started around an organized attempt of sharecroppers, in the neighborhood of Tyronza, Arkansas, to get their share of the A.A.A. payments and to stand up for their rights not to be displaced as a consequence of the A.A.A. program.[46] Indirectly, the results of these activities have been significant, in that the limited publicity around them probably has contributed a great deal to induce the federal government to take certain actions. The direct results, on the other hand, seem not to have been important, except in individual cases. The S.T.F.U. at the beginning of 1942 claimed a membership of 15,000 of which, however, only 2,000 were members who paid dues regularly.[47] Besides the general handicaps of organizing Southern farm workers, mentioned a few pages back, these organizations have been hampered by certain internal differences, particularly between the leadership of the S.T.F.U. and the U.C.A.P.A.W.A. The fact that whites and Negroes have been organized together, has, of course, been a main difficulty, but the pioneers have, on the whole, met it with success. It would seem that the most important single difficulty in the way of these movements is the lack of a legal tradition in the plantation South.[a]

It is difficult to judge about the future chances of trade unionism in the plantation South. On the one hand, the economic pressure is likely to continue and might become aggravated. Reasons for unrest and dissatisfaction are going to mount in the future as they did during the 'thirties. And there are indications of a development toward greater respect for law in the South.[b] In the political sphere there are reasons to expect an increase in participation and power for the working masses.[c] The South is becoming increasingly industrialized, and in its industries unionism is pushing ahead. All these trends favor unionization even in the rural South. On the other hand, the difficulties to be overcome, particularly in the Old Cotton Belt where the Negroes are concentrated, are tremendous.

[a] A more complete story of these attempts, interesting and significant though it might be, would deal more with such problems of law enforcement, or lack of it, that have to be considered elsewhere in our inquiry rather than with questions more immediately related to the social and economic conditions of the Negro in agriculture. See Part VI.

[b] See Part VI.

[c] See Chapters 23 and 33.

It is difficult to see how the federal government would be able to cope more successfully with the displacement problem and with other problems developing as a consequence of economic trends, agricultural policy, and the War, without having the farm workers organized and their interests and opinions articulated. When after the present War the government is faced with the problem of reformulating its agricultural program for the South, we should expect that it will find it necessary at least to protect the Southern tenants in their legal right to organize strong unions.

8. The Dilemma of Agricultural Policy

If the farm workers become organized in the South, whether by their own efforts or by government encouragement, and if their organizations are able to enter into successful collective bargaining with the planters, *any success in raising the earnings and living levels for farm labor on Southern plantations will accentuate, or rather make explicit in form of unemployment, the basic over-population of Southern agriculture.* Any policy which will improve levels of living, thereby increasing costs to plantation owners, will stimulate mechanization and will displace cotton by other crops which do not require so much labor. In the long-range view this might be desirable, in terms both of economic rationality and of human welfare. But the immediate effect, if vigorous countermeasures to remove the surplus population from the cotton land are not taken, would be accentuated unemployment, and the Negroes would be hurt the most. This is the dilemma of agricultural policy in the South.

The dilemma is, of course, much more general. It is at the bottom of all agricultural policy in America and elsewhere. The ultimate objective in attempting to raise the living levels for farmers and to protect their economic security must be to make agricultural production more efficient— be it through the lowering of the credit rates, through the use of more mechanical equipment, through improvement of livestock and plants, through teaching the farmers how to use better techniques and how to plan their operations in a more economical manner. But all this must make the tendency toward over-production even more pronounced. It must lower the number of acres and workers required for satisfying a given demand. Some experts, like the agro-biologist, O. W. Wilcox, even go so far as to believe ". . . that if the most productive methods now known were generally applied, then it would be possible for 1,600,000 farmers on 40,000,000 acres to produce as much of our eight principal crops as are now produced by six or seven million farmers on about 240,000,000."[48]

This may be an exaggeration. But it seems obvious that the increase in production which, within a not-too-distant future, would be technologically possible to achieve, is large compared even with the largest conceivable needs of the American people. According to certain estimates, if all families with a poor diet could be given what the Department of Agriculture characterizes as a "moderate-cost good diet," this would, *with present techniques*, require a crop acreage only about 20 per cent larger than was harvested in 1939.[49] The attempts to increase the demands of low-income families by means of direct distribution of agricultural products, by the Food Stamp Plan and by school lunches, are highly commendable from the viewpoint of national health. But they cannot remove the over-production indefinitely; at best they can merely cushion the effects of it temporarily.

By the same token, the attempts to make farmers go in for a system of almost complete self-sufficiency can scarcely do more than mitigate the effects of the rural over-population.[50] It is true, theoretically, that if a large enough number of farmers went in for self-sufficient agriculture, all over-production would be checked. But this would mean permanently dividing the farming population into two parts, of which only one would be allowed to go in for modern cost-saving specialization and efficient techniques. The other part would have to diversify its efforts and use inefficient techniques to an extent where they would be working hard and getting little in return, including practically nothing in the way of modern conveniences. This plan would never provide the hope of approaching what is understood to be "the American standard of living." Too, it would require the permanent stifling of ambition and an economic dictatorship to separate those retained in commercial agriculture from those forced into self-sufficient agriculture. Such a solution, if it were applied consistently and on a large scale, would not be acceptable to the American people.

This basic dilemma in agricultural policy is now much greater in the South, where over-population is so much more pressing than in the North. The burden of over-population, in the form of both unemployment and extreme poverty among those retained in agricultural employment, falls much more heavily on the Negro population than on the whites.

9. ECONOMIC EVALUATION OF THE A.A.A.

We are now ready to proceed to an evaluation of the A.A.A. program in its relation to cotton cultivation and the Negro farmer.

From the restricted point of view of production efficiency, the reduction of cotton acreage, and the dismissal of tenants consequent to this and to the special inducement contained in the benefit payments, is all to the good. The Southern plantation has altogether too many workers and tenants; cotton cultivation, as it has been carried on in the South, involves an exploitation of labor that is not compatible with American standards and American economic possibilities. From the same point of view, mechanization also is desirable. Any rise in farm labor standards, through collective bargaining or social legislation, would also, for the same reason, be commendable. In fact, economic progress means that we become able to produce our foodstuffs and agricultural raw materials with less of our available labor.

But there is one important consequence of such a policy which must be taken into account if it is to be deemed rational: *Employment must be found for the agricultural labor dismissed as a consequence of trends or of policy*. Theoretically, there is plenty of place for labor in American industry: the masses of people are in need of many more industrial products. Houses need to be rebuilt; people need more and better furniture and other household gadgets; large sectors of the American population do not enjoy health and educational facilities to an optimal degree. An obvious complement to an agricultural policy of the A.A.A. type would be, therefore, *a large-scale effort to move a part of the agricultural population to industry*. It is an equally obvious inference that this effort should be concentrated upon the younger generation, in which should be invested a vocational training making them fit for industrial work. In regard to Negro education in the South, this policy will require a complete reform of the educational system and, particularly, a reformulation of the aims of vocational education.[a]

Unfortunately it happened that this agricultural policy had to be carried out during an unprecedentedly deep and protracted depression. Unfortunately, too, the New Deal was a conspicuous failure in its attempt to turn the depression into economic prosperity.[b] A general defeatism became widespread in regard to the continuation of the trend toward more and more industrialization. Even among experts there was defeatism. This explains both why this rational complement to the policy of agricultural contraction was never undertaken in any wholehearted fashion and why it was not more generally pointed out to the public by informed persons. In the 'thirties, apparently, Americans doubted if there would ever be any place for more workers in American industry. This was, of course, a delusion. The present shortage of labor, and particularly skilled labor, for war production throws light on this mistake in American depression policy; but any improvement of business conditions would have done it, though not so dramatically.

From the point of view of economic rationality a second main shortcoming of the American agricultural policy is closely bound up with the one mentioned. The tremendous scope of the A.A.A. intervention in regard to cotton and other Southern cash crops alone makes it clear from the outset

[a] See Chapter 17, Section 5.

[b] It is the author's considered opinion that this failure was not necessary but was due to specific faults in the economic theory and the coordination of practical policies of the American expansion program. As a discussion of this point would carry us too far and as it is not implied as a premise in our argument, we leave it with this note.

that it was bound to have important effects, not only on acreage in various crops, on labor demand, and on the direction of labor demand, but also on the relative economic advantage of different types of landholdings and of forms of agricultural enterprises. This is a problem of the size of holdings; the relation between ownership, management, and labor; and so on. In the South and to the Negro, it is primarily a problem of whether or not the plantation system shall be protected and conserved. Johnson, Embree, and Alexander rightly emphasized that the "organization of the farm system is basic to reform in other matters."[51] The pretension of "neutrality" in this question is logically untenable when such big measures are taken.

In the planning stage of the program and in the continuous modification, this matter should have been made explicit, a purposeful aim decided upon, and adequate means selected toward this aim. This was not done, except for some efforts to favor agricultural cooperation and except for a tendency—as the defeatism deepened in regard to turning the depression into continued industrialization—to favor self-sufficient farming. These and other efforts were not clearly conceived of in the framework of the entire economic process and of national economic policy as a whole, and they were never attempted on a scale corresponding to the import of the agricultural trends and the scope of the A.A.A. interference in these trends. Arthur Raper, writing in 1936 and not having available the evidence of the 1940 Census, nevertheless saw in his field studies the main facts and formulated this fundamental criticism:

> The New Deal with its cotton restriction program, its relief expenditures, and its loan services, has temporarily revitalized the Black Belt, has rejuvenated the decaying plantation economy. Those who control the plantations are now experiencing relative prosperity. On the other hand *the landless farmers, though able for the most part because of the New Deal to pay their rents and settle their accounts, are not only failing to escape their chronic dependence but are actually losing status.* Many tenants are being pushed off the land while many others are being pushed down the tenure ladder, especially from cropper to wage hand status.[52]

The stipulations against the displacement of labor contained in the law may in some measure have been effective in slowing up the process (at the same time diminishing the gains of economic efficiency to be reached in this way). But they also comforted the policy makers and the general public, and contributed toward keeping off their minds the big unsolved task of moving labor from over-populated cotton-tenancy districts.[53]

10. SOCIAL EVALUATION OF THE A.A.A.

This brings us to a discussion of certain other social aspects of the A.A.A. A primary aim of the program was to bring relief to the rural population which had experienced a serious economic set-back. This aim was first expressed in the price-parity and later in the income-parity formula. From this point of view the A.A.A. was parallel to other relief policies during the depression. Huge amounts have been spent for this purpose. The total appropriations for direct payments to farmers during the period 1934-1941 has been estimated to be over $5,300,000,000, or more than three-fourths of the total costs for all farm policies (including special appropriations for land utilization, soil erosion, rural electrification, farm security, and so on).[54]

In view of these high financial sacrifices, one could have expected much more positive results for those within the agricultural population who were in particularly great need. Yet, for reasons that we have stated, large numbers among those most in need of assistance lost rather than gained because of the A.A.A. More generally, as we shall now point out, the benefits were not distributed in relation to needs.

The total agricultural cash income for nine Southeastern states, according to certain estimates of the Bureau of Agricultural Economics, was twice as high in 1940 as in 1932. Nevertheless, it was still more than 20 per cent below the 1929 level.[55] There is no way of telling how large a share in the income gains the Negroes have received. More Negroes than whites have been made to leave the land, and those who left, of course, got nothing of the increase of farm income or of A.A.A. benefits. In regard to wage workers it can be argued that the higher cotton prices and the A.A.A benefits indirectly allowed higher wages, and that this force on the labor market was stronger than any adverse force due to the increase of labor supply on account of dismissal of tenants. Independent Negro farmers have probably come to share in the benefits rather equally with white farmers of the same economic status, even if the set-up of local administration has not given them much of a voice. Negro tenants have increasingly received their share.

The A.A.A. payments in these nine Southeastern states amounted to about $170,000,000 in 1940, or 13 per cent of the total cash income of agriculture for that year, and more than one-fourth of the cash income gain in agriculture since 1932.[56] The Negroes' share in this agricultural relief was by no means proportionate to their numbers and still less with their greater needs. For every tenant and sharecropper had to let his landlord get part of the benefit payments for the plot of land he was operating, and the wage laborer received no part of it at all. And there are more white landlords and fewer white wage laborers.

But this question of the Negroes' sharing in the A.A.A. benefits is only part of a bigger problem: the distribution of the A.A.A. benefits among various income groups in agriculture. As we mentioned, the distributional objective of the policy was defined in terms of some "parity" *for the agricultural population as a whole*, compared with other population groups and with an eye on conditions prior to the First World War. Specifically, the aim in this respect was "reestablishment, at as rapid a rate as the Secretary of Agriculture determines to be practicable and in the general public interest, of the ratio between the purchasing power of the net income per person on farms and that of the income per person not on farms that prevailed during the five year period August 1909-July 1914."[57]

Such an objective is understandable in view of the fact that the relation between the farm and the nonfarm per capita income in the United States was 39 per cent less satisfactory, from the viewpoint of the agricultural population, in 1932 than during the period 1910-1914.[58] Yet this development, serious though it may be, has never been the only agricultural income problem. Even before the First World War, there certainly were farm families, particularly among the Southern Negroes, who in spite of hard work seldom, if ever, managed to make their living conditions approach a real health standard. Conversely, even in 1932 many farm families had incomes high enough to enjoy more than such a standard would indicate. Nevertheless, in the A.A.A. program no reference is

> . . . made to the fact that there are striking differences as to economic conditions between different groups of the farm population, or that the need for aid is greater for some groups than for others. The A.A.A. programs are concerned with total or average income only. . . . A.A.A. contains important elements of long-time planning already. It is, therefore, difficult to see why so little has been done to secure by legal provisions certain advantages of the policy for the working classes affiliated with commercial agriculture.[59]

One can explain this on several counts. To limit the programs in this way was necessary politically in order to organize a united farm bloc. Public assistance for the needy was to be kept in a separate compartment of federal activities. In the agricultural economics compartment there was to be "social neutrality" as far as the income distribution within agriculture was concerned. In an "economic" policy there was to be nothing that tasted of "relief."

Logically, however, there is a flaw in the argument. As in the case of other relief appropriations, the idea is that the A.A.A. benefits shall be paid by the taxpayers of the nation. To give more out of the public budget to those who have more is not exactly to maintain a position of "social neutrality." A sample study for 246 Southern plantations shows that the planter's average net cash income per plantation was $2,528 in 1934 and $3,590 in 1937. Out of these amounts not less than $979 and $833, respectively, came from A.A.A. payments. The tenants on the same plantations, on the other hand, had a net cash income for these two years of $263 and $300, respectively, out of which but $11 and $27 were A.A.A. payments.[60] Thus, even in proportion to their higher "basic" income, the planters received much more of this assistance than did their plantation tenants.[61] A few large landlords, in the South and elsewhere, may receive as much as $10,000 per year in A.A.A. payments.[62]

It has been observed by many authors that America has to decide whether or not it wants to compete for the cotton world market on a low-wage basis with China, India, Africa and South America. If it does not want to enter any such low-wage competition, it must face the necessity of displacing farm labor on a large scale in the South. Under all conditions America has to face not only the existence of income differentials between the several classes in Southern agriculture, but the effects of its agricultural policy in maintaining or changing these income differentials. Woofter observes:

> There is no clear indication that the choice between various objectives has been made by those in control of policy. The A.A.A. is looked on as a temporary expedient which it is hoped may be gradually relaxed as the underlying economic situation of cotton and tobacco improves.[63]

We know now that the economic policy of the A.A.A. only aggravated the problem of the inability of Southern agriculture to support its population.

The agricultural policy of the period between the two World Wars now belongs to history. The makeshift policy during the present War is of less general interest. When the War is over we shall again, in all countries, face the same problems of agricultural policy as we did prior to this War. Some of the problems will have been aggravated in the meantime. Some may, temporarily at least, look somewhat less pressing. Practically none will have been solved. There is, however, a possibility that they can be taken up more constructively with an international point of view and looking toward an international agreement. We need, in any case, to learn from experience and to analyze unreservedly the shortcomings of agricultural policy. The one-third of the American Negro people in Southern agriculture, who will still at the end of the War be in the bottom layer of the American economic system, has tremendous interests at stake in the new agricultural policy of America. It is necessary for them that agricultural policy be planned with recognition of the serious over-population, of the necessity of large-scale movement of labor, and of the big income differences within the agricultural population.

11. Constructive Measures

Any account of American agricultural policy, even restricted to those aspects of it which relate to cotton and the Negro, would be incomplete if only crop limitations under the A.A.A. program were observed. Besides the A.A.A. there are a number of more or less independent agricultural policies with more constructive long-range aims. Much less has been spent on those policies than on the symptom-treating policy of the A.A.A.

Some of these other policies have begun only recently. Some—the extension work, for instance—are carried on, more intensively than ever, along avenues opened up long before the New Deal. Few, if any, of these efforts are made primarily for the purpose of removing the basic trouble: the excess population on the Southern farm land. But there is an emphasis on new sources of income—both agricultural and nonagricultural. Certain measures, such as the Tennessee Valley Authority and the Rural Electrification program, may facilitate to an extent the growth of nonagricultural rural industries. And even regardless of the over-population, there are, of course, plenty of agricultural problems which need constant attention if any substantial part of the rural people is to have an economically sound future on the Southern farm.

We cannot give an exhaustive description of other agricultural programs now in effect. The array of measures is too wide for even a short summary. No one can fail to become duly impressed by the diversification of efforts when he tries to get some idea of what is going on, either by studying the literature, by running round in the huge buildings of the Department of Agriculture in Washington, by contacting those working in the field in a rural county, or just by looking at the periodical farm supplement of one of the better Southern newspapers. There are soil conservation projects; there is farm demonstration and home demonstration work; there are 4-H Clubs; rural electrification; substantial reforms in the farm credit system; county planning; encouragement of agricultural cooperation; technical research and experimentation; and many similar things. And last but not least, there is adult education, both as a separate program and as an aspect of almost every single part of the entire system of agricultural policies.

Even if the success cannot well be the same all along the line, it is certain that huge gains eventually will be reaped from all these varied activities. An outsider may in the beginning have some doubt about what substantial reforms can be brought about by cooperative planning work in a Southern plantation county, where there is little democracy and social participation, and where issues of any deeper social significance are taboo at public discussions—not to speak of the fact that Negroes are not allowed to participate on an equal footing with whites. Yet exactly in such communities there is a particular need for courageous attempts to democratize agricultural policies, however futile these attempts may seem to be at the start. The very fact that farmers of different social strata get into the habit of coming together for organized discussions cannot fail to bring about some increase in the mutual insight into the problems of the other man; and some real cooperative efforts eventually may come out of it.

The farm and home demonstration work, which has been gradually developed since 1904, is highly significant, and the more so the lower down it reaches on the social ladder. The work with tenants, however, is largely dependent on the good-will of their landlords. The latter have often objected to Negro farm and home demonstration agents approaching families on their holdings—sometimes even to any direct contact between the Extension Service and the tenants. "The Negro tenant farmers and croppers might best receive aid on the agricultural side principally through the white agents working with the landlords and managers," says the Extension Service of the Department of Agriculture,[64] and this admission confirms statements that we have received when interviewing Negro agents in the South about actual conditions in many localities. We have also been told, on the other hand, that nowadays an increasing number of plantation owners do want their tenants to have the benefits of this educational work. The cuts in cotton acreage and the decline in income during the depression made many landlords see the need of more home-use production on the tenants' plots.

Still, it does not seem as if the particularly urgent need for extension work among Negroes has been met to the same extent as has the corresponding need of the white farm population. Even though white agents may give some part of their time to work among the Negro farmers and croppers, they cannot be expected, as a rule, to be as intensively interested in the welfare of the colored people, as are the Negro agents; nor are they as likely to gain the confidence of the Negro farmers. By January 1, 1942, there were altogether 558 Negro extension workers in the South, or about 1.2 per 10,000 Negro persons on the rural farms.[65] The corresponding figure for the total rural farm population in the South by mid-1939 was more than twice as high or 2.7.[66]

Our previous discussion of the practice of "advancing" credit for necessities to croppers and tenants has suggested an unsatisfactory organization of credit. But planters and other landowners, as well as croppers and tenants, have suffered in the same respect. They still have to pay exorbitant interest when borrowing money. But a reform of the credit market is under way. The financial collapse during the depression, which hit both landowners and financial institutions, finally made the federal government intensify its efforts to reform the credit market.[67]

The accomplishments have been particularly noteworthy in the field of mortgage credit. Of the total amount of farm mortgage loans held on January 1, 1939, not less than 39 per cent were Federal Land Bank or Land Bank Commissioner loans; the corresponding proportion for the South was even higher (45 per cent).[68] In the much more difficult sphere of production credit, on the other hand, there has been less success.[69] The average interest rates for all short-term loans, as a consequence of this development, have decreased substantially. Yet it is still very high. The real expense even for government loans, in Woofter's sample study of 1937, was no less than 11.9 per cent. This is not a satisfactory situation.[70] Conditions may have improved since 1937, however, and the gradual development of the government credit system will give some advantages even to the Negroes, at least in an indirect way. The direct gains, on the other hand, have been very slight so far. Sharecroppers and share tenants can seldom use these sources of government credit, for the lien laws, in most cases, make them unable to present any security.[71] The Negro owners and cash renters, however, should have some theoretical chances of getting assistance through the government credit agencies. As usual in cases when government credit activities are based on "ordinary business principles," there are no data by race which would allow us to present any direct evidence. But there is this simple fact, that Negro owners and cash tenants have much smaller and less valuable farms than have their white colleagues and cannot present as much of any kind of security. Therefore, their share in this new government credit must be far smaller than is the proportion of Negroes even among the more independent Southern farmers, who are predominantly white.

Indeed, in all probability it is even smaller than can be explained solely on the ground of the limited resources of the Negro farmers. For the local administration of some of the most significant credit agencies is in the hands of credit cooperatives such as the farm loan associations for Federal Home Loan Bank loans, and the production credit associations for production credit loans. These associations naturally are dominated by white farmers. We have found already[a] so much evidence on how white farmers have misused administrative power given to them under other new economic programs that we cannot believe that this case should constitute an exception. It can almost be taken for granted that the temptation to discriminate against the Negro in many cases has been too strong to resist.

12. FARM SECURITY PROGRAMS

So far we have examined, briefly, only those farm policies which are intended to help agriculture in general. There is, however, a special series of programs for the little man in the farm business—the Farm Security programs. Having observed that the major part of agricultural subsidies and relief has not been administered according to need but has often favored the classes in agriculture which are relatively best off, we must add that this minor part, represented by the Farm Security Administration, has had the function of bringing help to the neediest.

Hundreds of thousands of Southern farm families have received assistance under these programs. As we shall presently show, *Negroes have received a substantial share in the F.S.A. benefits—almost as much, as a matter of fact, as would correspond to their population ratio in Southern*

[a] See also the data on the Negro's share in the benefits under the Farm Security program in Section 12 of this chapter.

farm areas. Even so, it must be said from the beginning that, however well-directed and otherwise commendable these efforts are, they do not quite measure up to the size of the problems involved. We have found that $5,300,000,000 was appropriated for A.A.A. policies during the period 1934-1941.[a] Most of this was A.A.A. benefit payments, a disproportionately large share of which went to the big landlords. The outlays for Farm Security programs during the same period amounted to about one-fifth of this amount ($1,121,000,000), and a considerable part of this sum consisted of loans on which repayment could be expected.[72] And, as for the Negro's share, it must be strongly emphasized that it does not compare with his relative needs. It is, as we shall indicate, much more difficult for a Negro than for a white farmer *in similar circumstances* to receive assistance in this form.

The explanation of this is simple. The disadvantaged groups in Southern agriculture, and particularly the Negroes, are politically impotent.[b] The consequence is not only that the program that has been instituted in their behalf is more limited than is other farm aid, but also there is less assurance about its being continued. At the end of 1941 a congressional committee, headed by Senator Harry F. Byrd of Virginia, one of the leading Southern politicians, while wanting to maintain the A.A.A. payments, in all seriousness proposed that all Farm Security activities be abolished in the interest of wartime economy. There are several reports about the Farm Bureau, under the chairmanship of an Alabama planter, having pushed similar demands.[73] The result was a serious curtailment in the budget of the F.S.A. in 1942; otherwise it has so far been saved. But the incident is an indication of the usually rather noncooperative, and sometimes outright hostile, attitude toward the Farm Security work among those who have command of the power in Southern politics—an attitude which those who attempt to find out about the situation in the South cannot avoid observing time and again. There actually seems to be a notion that since this kind of assistance is given to poor people it is "relief" and, consequently, bad, whereas the fact that A.A.A. payments are distributed to all farmers, so that those in higher income brackets receive a much larger share than others, makes them "business" and not "relief." Farm Security benefits are like manna coming from heaven and there are those in the South who welcome it even outside the beneficiaries themselves. But those who favor the F.S.A. do not have political power.

The differential treatment of the Negro can be explained on similar grounds. The local administration is not entirely in the hand of the officials of the Farm Security Administration. Clients, to be accepted, usually have

[a] The increase in prices brought about by the A.A.A. can be counted as an additional subsidy.
[b] See Chapter 22.

to be passed on by committees of local farmers, over which Negroes have practically no influence.[74] Under such circumstances, it is surprising that Negroes have received a share which almost corresponds to their proportion in the population. The Farm Security Administration has, from the beginning, been fighting courageously and persistently against differential treatment; the agency openly refers to it as "discriminatory" in several of the surveys which it has made.

In a just appraisal of the program all such difficulties must be taken into account. But there are still others. The laws and the system of law enforcement give the tenant little protection against the landlord—in fact, they are largely used for the purpose of making it easier for the landlord to exploit the tenant.[a] This situation must be considered in any evaluation of the Farm Security Administration. It is obvious that it would have been more efficient under a strong and impartial legal system. Further, to rehabilitate tenants or other impoverished farmers, it is not enough merely to give them loans, and then to sit back and expect them to pay it all back while improving their economic status. It is a major educational job, and the great thing is that the F.S.A. has faced it.

It is a question of teaching farmers, who have known about little but specialized cash- and feed-crop production, to diversify their efforts, to grow at home much of what they need for their own consumption. Farmers who have been nothing but dependent tenants have to become independent entrepreneurs. Former croppers, who have been exploited by the planters and have known few other ways of improving their status than to induce their landlords to give them as high advances as possible—and to move away if they fail to get as much as they think they can get some other place—have to learn quite a new kind of game. They have to learn that they, from now on, have definite rights and definite obligations, and that it usually pays to stay at the same place. Detailed farm and household plans are made up for them—if they do not know how to do it themselves; and it is seen to that they stick to those plans as far as possible. They are taught how to keep accounts. Some are illiterate; their children sometimes must be made to help them out. Many clients are without any resources whatever when they start out. Their meager cash income, while they are on the program, may dwindle to almost nothing because of unemployment, occasional crop failure or other circumstances. For such reasons they need not only loans, but also straight subsidies. Clients who retain their status as tenants have to fulfill their obligations to the landlords as well as to the Farm Security Administration; in such cases, there is often a rather complicated three-cornered problem where much depends on the cooperation of all parties concerned. Many clients have difficulties because they are sick; a cooperative health program is organized for them.[75]

[a] See Chapter 11 and Part VI.

Many critics of the program have failed to recognize all of these difficulties. Their criticism should not be directed so much against the Farm Security Administration as against the traditional social and economic patterns in Southern agriculture—against the fact that the small entrepreneur has had so little encouragement, and that the typical tenant has not been accustomed to much independent action and independent planning. This is not to say that no mistakes have been committed. There is no doubt that, particularly during the earlier stages of the development when there had to be much improvisation and experimentation, several projects were unnecessarily expensive. Too, there seems to have been some uncertainty about the objectives. The existence of a considerable rural over-population, the apparent over-production, and the growing belief that industrial stagnation could never be broken, brought about a wide-spread feeling that the only solution would be to let the excess population on the rural farms establish themselves on a basis of almost complete self-sufficiency. The feeling that small owners have difficulties in surviving without an elaborate system of agricultural cooperation was behind the organization of resettlements, where clients were given the chance of becoming owners while engaged in certain cooperative activities. Certain doubts as to whether ownership is really the best form of tenure for the small farmer explain the organization of settlements of rental cooperatives which are particularly favored by the Southern Tenant Farmers' Union.[76] These settlements of various kinds, however, since they are expensive to organize and since many of them have both Negro and white clients working together on the same footing, have caused much resentment in the South. Therefore, this particular part of the program, except for the rental cooperatives, is not being pushed any more.

Already before 1935, during the period of the Federal Emergency Relief Administration (F.E.R.A.), it occurred to some interested persons that it would be far better to help needy rural families, who were competent and willing to work, to grow their own food and earn a little cash income on farms, rather than to give them cash doles. A program to this end was inaugurated in 1934.[77] The activity was soon taken over by the Resettlement Administration and, later, together with certain related programs started by other agencies, by the Farm Security Administration, which was instituted in 1937.

The so-called rehabilitation program, which includes assistance of various kinds on an individual basis, takes up the major part of the work and the appropriations of the F.S.A. The total amount of loans made under this program until the middle of 1941 was $574,000,000; the grants amounted to $132,000,000. The South, although containing more than half of the rural farm population—and an even greater part of those in need of this assistance—has received less than half (43 per cent) of the loans and grants.[78] By December, 1939, there were in the South 154,000 white and 45,000 Negro "standard rehabilitation borrowers." Thus, while more than one-fourth of the Southern rural farm population is Negro, the number of Negroes on the program constituted a somewhat smaller proportion (23 per cent) of the total number of clients. Compared with the total estimated number of white and colored farm families which either were on relief or had an income of less than $500, the participation in the program amounted to 22 per cent of the whites and 11 per cent of the Negroes. This suggests that a low-income white family has had about twice the chance of a Negro family in the same circumstances of being accepted on the program. Too, the average amount of loan advances was somewhat higher for white ($659) than for colored ($606) clients.[79]

It is true that not all of these discrepancies are due to "direct discrimination." The selection of clients and the size of the loans do not depend on need alone. Even in the Farm Security work great attention is given to the credit rating of the individual client, and since Negroes start out with much smaller average resources than do whites, they are more likely to be excluded from the program and less likely to receive large loans.[80] Such an application of "business principles" in relief work, however, can well be called "indirect discrimination," for it must have been obvious from the beginning that it would limit the opportunity to give the Negro a share of the benefits which would correspond to his relative needs. Moreover, there is definite evidence that Negro clients have been selected in a much more cautious manner than have white clients. Although their gross cash income during 1939 was 40 per cent lower than that of white clients in the South, their repayment record was a slightly better one. The absolute amount repaid on the loans actually was almost the same in both cases (about $250). The net income of the Negro clients was rather low—less than $100 in cash and about $240 in home-use production—whereas the corresponding figures for white clients were about $200 and $275, respectively. Both groups of clients bettered their conditions to a considerable extent during the time they were on the program—Negroes relatively more than whites.[81]

The other F.S.A. programs are rather insignificant, as far as Negroes are concerned. By mid-1940 there were less than 2,000 Negro families on various types of F.S.A. settlements and rental cooperatives. They constituted roughly one-fourth of all such families in the South. About 1,900 Negro families were on the so-called tenant-purchase program; there were four times as many white families in the South on the same program.[82] Thus, there was about the same amount of discrimination in these cases as in the rehabilitation work. In the last year (1941-1942), however, the F.S.A. has provided camps for migrant agricultural workers in various parts of the North, and Negroes get a considerable share of these facilities.

Nobody who has had any contact with those doing field work for the Farm Security Administration can escape becoming impressed by these attempts to rehabilitate farm families by making up plans for almost every aspect of the farm-and-household economy and by "helping the clients to help themselves." Attempts are made to introduce written contracts of more than one year's duration for the clients who are tenants—the so-called flexible farm lease. Most tenants on the rehabilitation program have such leases with their landlords.[83] States are urged to adopt legislation for this purpose—so far, however, without any success as far as the South is concerned.[84] The Farm Security work, after this period of rather diversified experimentation, has provided the kind of practical administrative experience which would be needed for a major reform of land and tenure conditions. But it is not likely that there will be enough popular backing for such a system in the South—until the Southern farm population has been hit by at least one more major economic crisis. The coming post-war crisis might furnish this needed impetus.

CHAPTER 13

SEEKING JOBS OUTSIDE AGRICULTURE

1. PERSPECTIVE ON THE URBANIZATION OF THE NEGRO PEOPLE

Only a part of the present farm population in the South has any future on the land. This is particularly true of the Negro farm population, as has been amply demonstrated in the preceding chapter. It is necessary to remind the reader of this important fact. For outside a limited group of experts, few white people realize that, already, almost two-thirds of the Negroes live in nonfarm areas, and that eventually all Negroes, except for a small minority, will have to become integrated into the nonagricultural economy of America. Even the experts, including Negro college teachers in agriculture, seem to have an exaggerated belief in the Negro's possibilities in Southern agriculture. More generally, there is a widespread attitude in the cities that the Negro ought to stay where he belongs—on the Southern farm land. The nonfarm parts of the country simply do not want to accept the responsibility for Negroes who previously have made their living in agriculture. This protectionist attitude is not typical of Americans only. Nor is it confined to the Negro problem alone. In America, as well as in many other countries, there are strong tendencies to build walls around one's own community in order to keep out all sorts of low income people who would press down wage levels, add to the housing shortage and pos-sibly become liabilities in public relief. The recent tendency to make residence requirements for relief more severe is only one of the devices used in this policy of social protectionism.

There is no doubt, however, that this attitude is especially pronounced in regard to rural Negroes from the South. Because of the decadence of agri-culture and the constitutional impossibility of raising barriers against inter-nal migration, this attitude will not be able to stop the gradual urbanization of the Negro people. As we saw in Chapter 8, this has been going on all the time, and since the First World War the Negro farm population has actually been declining because of migration. But the popular attitude that the Negroes had better stay where they are has given, and will probably continue to give, a basis for segregation and discrimination both in housing and in employment. It even tends to perpetuate the ignorance about Negroes by making everyone want to look the other way. The belief that the agricultural South can still accept the main responsibility for the Negroes is a most important ingredient in the "pass-the-buck" mentality which we touched upon in Chapter 2.

In this chapter we shall sketch in broadest outlines the history of the Negro breadwinner outside agriculture and attempt to ascertain where, in more recent times, he has entered industry or has remained unemployed. The sketch is largely based on the facts presented in Appendix 6. The reader who has a special interest in these things will find all the material of this chapter set forth in greater detail in Appendix 6.[a] In Chapter 17 we shall discuss in more general terms the several adverse factors which a Negro encounters when he tries to gain entrance into industry.

2. IN THE SOUTH

Slavery, and the concomitant suppression of free Negroes, gave to Southern Negroes a degree of monopoly on labor for a few years after the Civil War. This was the situation not only on the rural plantations but—excepting areas where Negroes constituted but a minority of the population—in most other types of unskilled work as well. Unskilled work was tainted with inferiority. Negroes were the domestics and the laborers. Negroes were also, to a large extent, the craftsmen and the mechanics. They were carpenters, bricklayers, painters, blacksmiths, harness makers, tailors and shoemakers. For even skilled labor was degraded, and whites had often been denied the opportunity of acquiring training since so many masters had preferred to work with slaves. The high price paid for skilled slaves had encouraged their training in the crafts.[1] Thomas Nelson Page says:

> In 1865, when the Negro was set free, he held without a rival the entire field of industrial labor throughout the South. Ninety-five per cent of all the industrial

[a] Appendix 6 is based mainly on a research memorandum, "Negro Labor and Its Problems," prepared for this study (1940) by Paul H. Norgren. Collaborating with Dr. Norgren were Lloyd H. Bailer, James Healy, Herbert R. Northrup, Gladys L. Palmer, and Arnold M. Rose.

No references will be given when statements in the text are based on Appendix 6.

The literature on the Negro wage earner, although it contains much material that we have not used in this brief summary, is characterized by a certain lack of balance. While great attention has been given to many small industries, particularly when, during recent decades, they have given an increased share of the jobs to Negroes (e.g., the meat-packing and slaughtering industry), other occupations where a much larger number of Negro workers are employed seem to have been largely overlooked. This is true, for instance, about truck, transfer, and cab companies which had 41,000 Negro workers in 1930. It is true also of the menial occupations in wholesale and retail establishments (laborers, porters, and helpers in stores, janitors, chauffeurs, truck drivers, delivery men, elevator tenders, charwomen, and so on) which, in 1930, included over 110,000 Negro workers. (U. S. Bureau of the Census, *Negroes in the United States: 1920-1932*, pp. 354-357.) Perhaps even more significant would be an intensive study of Negro exclusion in those lines of work where few, if any, Negroes are employed.

work of the Southern States was in his hand. And he was fully competent to do it. Every adult was either a skilled laborer or a trained mechanic.[2]

This is a considerable exaggeration. There was, outside agriculture, a fairly large white laboring class, too. And the great majority of Negroes, even in the cities, were domestics and unskilled laborers. But, skilled or unskilled, their protection was that their work was characterized as "Negro jobs" and was usually badly paid.

Right from the beginning the Negroes' position in the Southern non-agricultural labor market has been influenced by two forces or trends of change working in opposite directions. One force is the general expansion of the Southern nonagricultural economy. This tends constantly to increase the employment opportunities for Negroes as well as for whites. The other force is the competition from white job-seekers. This tends to exclude Negroes from employment and to press them downward in the occupational hierarchy. Regarding the second trend, it should be observed that there had been plenty of racial competition before the Civil War. White artisans had often vociferously protested against the use of Negroes for skilled work in the crafts. But as long as the politically most powerful group of whites had a vested interest in Negro mechanics, the protesting was of little avail. Even many of the free Negroes had their white protectors. After Emancipation the Negro artisan was on his own. His former master did not have the same interest in protecting him against white competitors. White men usually had little economic interest in having the young Negro trained for skilled work.

In some cases there were still personal ties between the former slave owners and their ex-slaves. The Black Codes and the dependent status of the Negro still made him amenable to exploitation. But all this could only cushion the effects of Emancipation. It was unthinkable that the white class of ex-masters would protect the Negroes against their white competitors in the same manner as they had done earlier. Many of them were impoverished because of the War. Their places were taken by other whites who had not been brought up in the tradition of "caring for their Negroes." Many of them actually shared the competitive viewpoints of the white working class. This was true for the most part of those contractors, for instance, who rose from the class of white building workers. Generally, the Civil War, the Emancipation, the Reconstruction, and the Restoration were all characterized by a trend toward a consolidation of white interests. And the poorer classes of whites got more of a say, at least as far as the "place" of the Negro was concerned.

The result of this pressure is well known and often discussed by both whites and Negroes in the South. Examples of how Negroes have been driven out from one kind of a job after another are constantly being pointed out. There seems to be a definite pattern in this process. It starts from the top and goes downward. It proceeds more rapidly in the newer cities where there is less regard for tradition. In many of the older Southern cities there are still a considerable number of Negro carpenters, masons, and painters, though usually not so many as earlier, at least not proportionally. In other cities there are only Negro helpers. In still others Negroes are not always allowed to be helpers. In only a few old cities on the Atlantic Coast the observer meets an old Negro barber, catering to a passing generation of Southern gentlemen. Negro waiters are still common, but not so common as even ten years ago. White waitresses are gradually being substituted for them. Whites are entering into hotels even as bell boys and elevator operators. By 1930 whites were in the majority among all workers in hotels, restaurants, and boarding houses in the South. In railroad service there were once a few Negro engineers, and Negroes long held a practical monopoly as firemen. But during the last generation they have been gradually displaced even from those "Negro jobs." A local Negro historian, Charles B. Rousseve, summarizes the trend thus:

> In urban centers like New Orleans, the Negro, who in ante-bellum days, performed all types of labor, skilled and unskilled, found himself gradually almost eliminated from the various trades. In recent years, even from the meanest forms of servile occupations he is being excluded by his fairer-skinned fellow-citizens.[3]

In some Southern cities whites have not disdained to take over the street cleaning and the collecting and carting away of the garbage.

The competition from the white workers, and the gradual loss of protection from the side of the former master class, meant not only that the Negroes' share in the jobs became smaller in many traditional "Negro occupations"; but, perhaps, even more important in the long run was the fact that Negroes, in most cases, failed to get any appreciable share in the jobs whenever new lines of production were opened up. Negro workers, therefore, are likely to be found in stagnating or retrogressing industries and occupations, as the expanding ones are usually the new ones, at least in technique. When there were technical innovations, making work less strenuous, less dirty, and generally more attractive, this often implied a redefinition of the occupations from "Negro jobs" to "white man's work." The decline of handicrafts and the progressive mechanization of industry generally has meant exclusion of Negroes from job opportunities. The rise of commercial laundries, for instance, has brought about a most spectacular decline in the number of Negro home laundresses between 1910 and 1930.

> In the building trades the structure of buildings is changing from lumber to steel. There have been many Negro carpenters but few structural steel workers and few chances for apprenticeship in this new field. . . . Wheelwrights and coopers are gone, probably forever. This work is done in factories by machinery. Moreover, steel drums, pails, sacks, and other containers have replaced the wooden barrel. Machinists

have increased sevenfold, but the machinists' unions bar Negroes. Trucks are replacing drays and also competing with railway transportation; and trucking, increasingly, is becoming a chain proposition instead of an individual venturing.[4]

The increased use of white women in industry meant not only a new source of competition. It also, in a prohibitory way, raised the "social equality" issue. White women and Negroes cannot work together under the Southern code. White workers came more and more to resent working with Negroes, according to what all older Negroes and whites tell the observer. The only way of definitely lifting a certain type of work from the category of "Negro jobs" was to get the Negroes out of it. The Jim Crow legislation, which was enacted just before the turn of the century,[a] drew the color line even sharper, and thus had great importance in the economic sphere.

During this development—which, to an extent, is parallel to the "infiltration" of white tenants in cotton farming and has a similar basic cause in the over-population of Southern agriculture—defensive beliefs were constantly growing among the whites in the South that the Negro was inefficient, unreliable, and incompetent to work with machines. Conditions varied in different localities, and these beliefs were not consistent, as Embree points out:

> To justify their exclusion from the textile mills, it is said that of course Negroes are unable to do skilled tasks. Yet in the next town one hears that they have greater manual dexterity than whites, and therefore hold many of the skilled jobs in the handling of tobacco. Oddly enough, in the textile villages, their lack of competence is given as a proof of their inferiority, while in the tobacco communities the fact that they have manual skill is equally regarded as evidence of low mentality, since it is well known that superior races are not clever with their hands! In the iron and steel mills, since Negroes have been given work about the furnaces, there has grown up a tradition that they are best adapted to work in the presence of great heat. Yet formerly it was held to be foolhardy to try colored laborers in such jobs, because they would not stand up under the trying conditions of blast furnaces.[5]

Thoughtful Southerners, who could not forget that the Negro had earlier been a skilled worker, were compelled to believe that he was deteriorating:

> Meantime, the Negro has retrograded as a workman until he has not only lost the field in which he once had no rival, but is in danger of losing even the ability to compete for its recovery. The superiority of the older farmhands to the younger generation is so universally asserted throughout the South that it must be given some of the validity of general reputation. And whereas, as has been shown a generation ago all the mechanical work of the South was in the hand of the Negroes, only a small proportion of it is done by them to-day.[6]

Another Southerner says:

[a] See Chapter 28, Section 4.

As a laborer, the Negro is not so satisfactory as formerly. The old-time Negro, trained in slavery to work, has about passed away and his successor is far less efficient and faithful to duty. Lately, large numbers of Negro laborers have shown a tendency to leave the farms for work on railroads, in sawmills, and in the cities, large numbers migrating to the cities of the North. They like to work in crowds and this often results in making more work for the police.[7]

In a relative sense there was an element of truth in those statements, at least in so far as fewer and fewer young Negroes could keep up skills when they were not allowed to compete under the better working conditions and the improved techniques, and when they had difficulty in getting training. This was what Booker T. Washington saw when he started out with his endeavor to give Negroes vocational training for crafts and trades.[a]

All these things are, as we said, much in the foreground of public discussion in the South. We must ask: How have the rising numbers of urban Negroes earned their living when they have had all these factors working against them? The explanation is the contrary force or trend, which we mentioned earlier: that there has been a great expansion going on in non-agricultural industries in the South during most of the time since the Civil War. The urbanization of the South has meant, for one thing, that there is a growing number of upper and middle class white families in the cities who can employ domestic servants. This is especially important since it is traditional in the South that every family which can afford it, even down to the lower middle class, should have domestic help. The growing industries, furthermore, created a considerable number of laboring jobs for Negroes, even when they were excluded from the machines. And they did get into some industries.

The employment losses to the Negroes, therefore, have often been more relative than absolute. Even if the Negroes were pressed down in relative status in the occupational hierarchy, and even if they did not get their full share in the number of new jobs so that the proportion of Negroes declined, the absolute number of Negroes for the most part increased, except in stagnating crafts and industries. At least during parts of the period up to the First World War the absolute gains in job opportunities for Negroes in the South, in spite of the relative losses, were considerable. Since then, however, even those absolute gains have declined drastically.

3. A Closer View

From 1890 to 1910, the total number of white male workers in non-agricultural industries in the South more than doubled. The number of Negro male workers in nonagricultural pursuits increased by two-thirds, or by more than 400,000 (Table 1).[b] The latter increase was due mainly

---

[a] See Chapter 41.

[b] There are no occupational census data by race prior to 1890.

to expansion in certain typical "Negro job" industries, such as saw and planing mills, coal mining, and maintenance-of-way work on railroads.[8] From 1910 to 1930, on the other hand, the number of Negro males engaged in nonagricultural pursuits in the South increased by less than one-third and, in absolute numbers, by less than 300,000. This slowing up of the increase of the Negro nonagricultural labor force in the South occurred in spite of the general expansion of industry—which was about as large as during the previous two decades—and in spite of the fact that the

TABLE 1

NUMBER OF ALL MALE WORKERS AND OF NEGRO MALE WORKERS IN NONAGRICULTURAL PURSUITS, BY SECTION: 1890-1930[a]

Section	Number of All Male Workers (in thousands)			Number of Negro Male Workers (in thousands)			Negro Workers as Percentage of All Workers		
	1890	1910	1930	1890	1910	1930	1890	1910	1930
United States	11,053	19,508	28,516	824	1,396	2,170	7.5	7.2	7.6
The North and West	9,028	15,595	22,179	190[b]	350	831	2.1	2.2	3.8
The South	2,025	3,913	6,337	634	1,046	1,339	31.3	26.7	21.1

Sources: *Eleventh Census of the United States: 1890, Population,* Vol. 2, Tables 78, 79, 82 and 116; *Thirteenth Census of the United States: 1910, Population,* Vol. 4, Tables 2, 5, 6 and 7; U.S. Bureau of the Census, *Statistical Abstract of the United States: 1938,* Tables 51, 52 and 53; U.S. Bureau of the Census, *Negroes in the United States: 1920-1932,* pp. 303-309.

[a] Turpentine farm workers have been consistently included among workers in nonagricultural pursuits, in accordance with the procedure adopted in the 1930 Census. In the 1890 Census, however, they were not separated in a special group, but were included in the category "other agricultural pursuits" (Table 79). For Southern states, this group contained mainly turpentine workers, but for the Northern states certain other occupations predominated. Therefore, the workers included under this heading were considered as nonagricultural for the Southern states, and as agricultural for other areas.

[b] This figure includes a few nonwhite workers other than Negro.

previous growth in the Negro farm population had been superseded by a decline. Also during the 'thirties, as we shall show presently, the Negro lost in relative position. This was the more serious because industrial expansion in the South was now much slower, because there were great losses in agricultural employment, and because there were no new openings in the North.

It was of major importance that Negroes were partially excluded as ordinary production workers in the textile industry since it developed into the South's leading industry. The unimportant textile manufacturing which had existed in the South before the Civil War had been based largely on Negro labor, partly slave labor. But the new textile industry broke with this tradition. It arose as a civic welfare movement to create work for poor white people. The Negroes were not needed, as the labor supply of poor whites from the agricultural areas and from the mountains was plentiful.

If those white workers were paid low wages and held in great dependence, they could at least be offered the consolation of being protected from Negro competition. Another factor strengthening the exclusion of Negroes from the textile industry was the employment of white women.

The tobacco industry in Virginia, North Carolina, and Kentucky, up to the Civil War, had had but a small minority of white workers. After the War, however, there were two important innovations which precipitated an increase in the proportion of white labor. One was the taking up of a new line of manufacturing: that of cigarettes. The other change was the introduction of machinery. Both these changes gave an excuse for breaking the traditional Negro labor monopoly. Much of the work became neat and clean, requiring little physical strength, and was adapted to the employment of white women. Negroes were retained, however, as stemmers and in other laboring jobs. The ratio of Negro to white workers around the turn of the century became stabilized at a two-to-one level in these three tobacco-producing states. This ratio seems to have been kept almost constant until about 1930, allowing Negroes to share in the general expansion.[a]

In the skilled building trades, the development had proceeded so far by 1890 that white workers were in the majority although they were not yet represented by any strong unions in the South. The development has continued ever since and the appearance of trade unions in the South helped to give the white building workers even greater power in keeping the Negro out. They have been particularly successful in the new building trades where Negroes had no traditional position. The fact that the proportion of Negroes in these trades already by 1890 had been reduced to 25 per cent or less in the Upper and Lower South made it comparatively easy for the organized white workers to disregard the interests of the Negro workers.

In the trowel trades (bricklayers, masons, plasterers, and cement finishers), on the other hand, the situation is somewhat different. Negroes had managed to retain a large proportion of the jobs when unionization began in the South, and it is probable that it was this circumstance which forced the organizations in these trades to take a more friendly attitude toward Negroes. Discrimination may occur locally, but the national leadership occasionally takes action against such practices. The proportion of Negroes in these trades—roughly one-half in the Upper and Lower South—has remained relatively unchanged during the whole period between 1900 and 1930. The situation is similar in unskilled building work. Negroes and

---

[a] This and the subsequent discussion concerning occupational trends from 1890 to 1930 is based on the following sources: *Eleventh Census of the United States: 1890. Population*, Vol. 2, Table 116; *Thirteenth Census of the United States: 1910, Population*, Vol. 4, Tables 2, 6 and 7; *Fifteenth Census of the United States: 1930, Population*, Vol. III, Part 1, p. 23, and State Table 10, Parts 1 and 2; Vol. IV, State Table 11. See, also, various sources cited in Appendix 6.

whites are usually organized in the same locals even in the South, and race relations in these unions are often comparatively amicable. Nevertheless, there has been a decline in the proportion of Negro workers in Southern states. But Negroes are probably still in the majority in the Upper and Lower South. Taking the building industry in the entire country as a whole, there was a decrease even in the absolute number of Negro workers between 1910 and 1930, in spite of the fact that the total man-power remained unchanged, and although the migration of Negroes to the North broadened the market for their services.[9]

Comparing 1910 and 1930, one finds that, except for a temporary boom during the First World War, the expansion had ceased in some of the most significant "Negro job" industries, such as saw and planing mills, turpentine farms and maintenance-of-way work on railroads. This was one of the main reasons why the general expansion in job opportunities for Southern Negroes was less pronounced during this period than during the previous two decades. In the railroad services the number of Negro engineers, which had never been large, was reduced to virtually nothing. There was, as we mentioned, a decline also in the number of Negro firemen and brakemen. The railroad brotherhoods, most of which exclude Negroes more consistently than almost any other American trade union, eventually became sufficiently powerful to keep the Negroes out of any job which was—or which, through technical development, became—attractive enough to be desirable to the white man.

Again Negroes failed to get into most of the new and expanding industries in the South. Only one per cent of the workers employed at Southern oil and gas wells in 1930 were Negroes. Only as wood cutters and in certain other laboring capacities did Negroes get into the paper and pulp industry. Gas and electric companies have never used Negroes to any appreciable degree. Negroes do not operate streetcars and buses. Telegraph and telephone companies exclude them almost altogether. Furniture factories depend in the main on white labor. The vast expansion in wholesale and retail trade, banking, insurance, and brokerage benefited the Negroes only in so far as they could be used as delivery men, porters, janitors, charwomen and so on. The policy of excluding them from production jobs in the textile factories continued.

There were not many lines of work in which Negroes made any appreciable gains during this period. Coal mines and steel mills continued to expand in the South, and the Negroes had employment gains from their expansion. The same was true of longshore work where Negroes traditionally had such a dominant position in the South that the trade unions never could exclude them to any significant degree, even though there was some local discrimination. Fertilizer factories, which constitute one of the most typical "Negro job" industries, showed a particularly rapid expansion between

1910 and 1930, but this industry is too small and too seasonal to provide much steady employment. There were some cases where Negroes shared in the expansion brought about by motorization: The number of Negro teamsters, truck drivers and chauffeurs increased. So did the number of Negro maintenance and construction workers on streets, highways, sewers and so on. Yet the white labor force in those occupations increased even

TABLE 2

CHANGES IN POPULATION AND IN MALE LABOR FORCE IN
SELECTED NORTHERN AND SOUTHERN CITIES: 1930–1940[a]

Group of Cities	Percentage of Negroes in				Percentage Increase or Decrease (–) 1930–1940			
	Total Population		Male Labor Force 14 years and Over		Negroes		Whites	
	1930	1940	1930	1940	Total Population	Male Labor Force	Total Population	Male Labor Force
11 Northern Cities	7.2	8.6	7.6	7.8	22.8	1.9	1.6	–0.1
15 Southern Cities	25.7	26.9	27.7	25.4	20.7	12.1	13.1	13.3

Source: Sixteenth Census of the United States: 1940, Population, Second Series, State Table 43.
[a] The labor force figures for 1930 refer to the number of gainful workers. The concept of gainful worker in the 1930 Census was approximately the same as that of labor force in the 1940 Census; both include unemployed workers. The cities included in the table are:
In the *North:* New York, Newark, Philadelphia, Pittsburgh, Cleveland, Cincinnati, Indianapolis, Chicago, Detroit, St. Louis and Kansas City (Missouri).
In the *South:* Louisville, Baltimore, Washington, D.C., Richmond, Norfolk, Atlanta, Jacksonville, Miami, Memphis, Chattanooga, Nashville, Birmingham, New Orleans, Houston and Dallas.

more. Soon the white workers were in the majority in these traditional Negro jobs. Rather limited, also, were the employment gains Negroes derived from the appearance of filling and greasing stations, garages, automobile agencies and automobile factories in the South. In 1930 only about one-tenth of all workers at such establishments were Negroes.

4. SOUTHERN TRENDS DURING THE 'THIRTIES

So far we have discussed, mainly, the development in the South up to about 1930. The depression during the 'thirties hit the industrial economy in the South much less severely than in the North, the reason being that the South had fewer heavy industries and that the secular trend of industrialization moves more definitely upward in the South than in the rest of the nation. The number of wage earners employed in manufacturing industries was 1.6 per cent higher in the South in 1939 than in 1929, whereas the nation as a whole showed a decrease of 10.6 per cent.[10] Even so the industrial depression was a serious matter in the South, particularly for Negroes.[a]

Since Negroes, during the 'thirties, were driven out of agriculture at a more rapid rate than were the white farm workers in the South,[b] there is nothing surprising in the fact that the large and middle-sized cities in the South showed a greater increase of the Negro than of the white population (Table 2). Negro farm workers, who had been forced out of employment in rural areas, sooner or later had to go to the cities, which offered varied, even if scarce, employment opportunities. A large labor market always seems to offer a chance; in a plantation area where farm workers are dismissed there is no hope left. Also there were more liberal relief standards in the cities than in rural areas.

The more rapid increase of the Negro than the white urban population in the South during the 'thirties meant that an earlier trend had been broken. During previous decades, when migratory outlets for Negroes in the North had been more ample, there had been a definite decline in the proportion of Negroes in the urban South.[11] In spite of this changing population trend, however, Negroes continued to lose in importance as an element in Southern urban labor. While the white male "labor force"—including unemployed as well as employed workers—increased at about the same rate as the white population, the Negro labor force did not expand even as much as the number of employed white workers. Thus, although the proportion of Negroes in the population showed an increase in the urban South, there was a decline in the percentage of Negro workers in the total male labor force. Undoubtedly the proportion of unemployed among Negro workers in the South increased more than that among white workers during the Great Depression, even if there are no reliable statistics available to prove it.[12]

The general increase in unemployment during the 'thirties made white workers try even more to "drive the Negroes out." That this is one of the main factors behind the continued decline in the proportion of Negro workers in nonagricultural pursuits seems even more probable when we study the data for specific industries in Table 3. To be sure, we have to be cautious in interpreting these figures, for certain technical improvements introduced in the 1940 Census make it difficult to trace the development during the previous decade.[c] Yet we can scarcely be mistaken in the observation that the relative position of the Negro in Southern industry has deteriorated further during the 'thirties.

The textile industry continued to grow tremendously,[13] but only 26,000 out of its 635,000 Southern workers in 1940 were Negroes. Food manu-

[a] See the unemployment rates by race presented in Table 6 of this chapter.
[b] See Chapter 12.
[c] See the footnotes to Table 3.

TABLE 3

NUMBER AND PROPORTION OF NONWHITE WORKERS IN SELECTED INDUSTRIES, 1940;
AND NEGROES AS A PERCENTAGE OF THE GAINFUL WORKERS, 1930—IN THE SOUTH

1	2	3	4
	Nonwhite Employed Workers in 1940		Percentage of Negroes Among GainfulWorkers in 1930[b]
Industry	Number	Percentage of All Races[b]	
1. Coal mining	34,949	15.9	19.4
2. Crude petroleum and natural gas production	1,026	0.9	1.2
3. Construction	108,685	17.8	22.2
4. Food and kindred products	37,390	15.8	19.1
5. Textile-mill products; apparel and other fabricated textile products	26,134	4.1	6.6
6. Chemicals and allied products	33,101	23.5	19.2
7. Logging, sawmills and planing mills; furniture, store fixtures and miscellaneous wooden goods	156,468	36.8	37.6
8. Paper and allied products	9,802	19.1	17.8
9. Printing, publishing and allied industries	5,239	5.0	4.5
10. Iron and steel and their products; machinery; transportation equipment, except automobiles	40,169	14.9	18.5
11. Automobiles and automobile equipment; motor vehicles and accessories, retailing, and filling stations; automobile storage, rental, and repair services	45,855	12.4	11.7
12. Railroads (including railroad repair shops and railway express service)	62,997	21.0	25.0
13. Trucking service	15,856	15.6	(c)
14. Utilities	14,678	12.5	(c)
15. Wholesale trade; food and dairy products stores and milk retailing; other retail trade	146,402	10.6	10.4
16. Finance, insurance and real estate	31,982	11.5	5.2
17. Professional and related services	136,500	16.8	15.0
18. Government	29,884	5.4	(c)
19. Hotels and lodging places; eating and drinking places	129,862	32.1	39.8
20. Laundering, cleaning and dyeing services	43,973	34.6	40.1
21. Domestic service; miscellaneous personal services	837,687	70.9	76.7

Sources: Fifteenth Census of the United States: 1930, Population, Vol. 3, Part 1, p. 23; *Sixteenth Census of the United States: 1940, Population,* Second Series, State Table 18a and 18b.

ᵃ The comparability between the data for 1930 and 1940, in some cases, is affected by changes in the industrial classification. In order to overcome this difficulty, as far as possible, we have added together certain of the original groups. The iron, steel, machinery, and transportation equipment groups in the 1940 Census have been compared with the total for the following 1930 groups: "blast furnaces and steel rolling mills"; "electrical machinery and supply factories," "other iron and steel industries." (This means, however, that workers in car and railroad shops have been included in the 1930 figures for the steel group, whereas in 1940 most of them were counted as railroad workers.) Construction is compared with the total for "building industry" and "construction and maintenance of streets, roads, and sewers" in the 1930 Census. In regard to facturing expanded, but Negroes did not get their full share in the employment gains. The same was true about hotels, lodging places, restaurants, and of laundering, cleaning, and dyeing establishments, where the proportion of Negro workers declined to about one-third. The contraction of railroad employment during the 'thirties made Negroes lose heavily, probably even more than did the white workers. In the iron and steel group they also declined, absolutely as well as in relation to the whites. There is no indication of any gain for the Negroes in coal mining, construction, sawmills or other woodworking industries. It seems that they did share, however, in the expansion in paper, pulp, printing, publishing, and allied industries, but the total number of Negro workers in these groups was not higher than 15,000 in 1940. Domestic service, which is the most important of all "Negro job" industries, seems to have had but a limited expansion during the 'thirties, and it is doubtful whether the Negro gained anything at all, although he still holds a practical monopoly in the South.

5. IN THE NORTH

At the close of the Civil War the Negro wage earner in the North had a quite different position than in the South.[a] The mere fact that there were few Negroes in the North implied that no occupations could take on the character of "Negro jobs." There had not been slavery in the Northern states for some two generations. The Negroes, therefore, had not been protected in their jobs by the vested interests of a white master class. The competition from white workers had always been intense.[14] In most industrial and commercial centers of the North where there were any appreciable number of Negroes, the three decades prior to the Civil War saw recurrent race riots, growing out of this competition for jobs. In the few localities in the North where Negroes actually had come to monopolize certain types of work, their exclusion had thus started much earlier. In 1853 Frederick Douglass complained:

> Every hour sees the black man [in the North] elbowed out of employment by some newly arrived immigrant whose hunger and whose color are thought to give

lumber and lumber products, the total for the groups "logging," "sawmills and planing mills," and "furniture store fixtures, and miscellaneous wooden goods" was compared with the 1930 total for "forestry," "saw and planing mills," and "other woodworking and furniture industries." This procedure was recommended by Dr. Philip M. Hauser, Acting Chief Statistician for Population, Bureau of the Census (letter of May 8, 1942). Certain other minor rearrangements are self-explanatory, since the descriptions in the stub consist of the category titles which comprise the given industry groups in the 1940 Census classification, and from this the comparable 1930 categories may be determined by inspection.

Although the table probably gives a fairly correct general impression—at least if one considers the further qualifications presented in footnote (b)—the comparison is not quite exact in every detail. The increase in the proportion of Negroes in banks, insurance, and real estate companies, for instance, may depend, at least in part, on changes in the classification.

b Gainful workers in 1930 included unemployed workers. Since Negroes are usually unemployed to a greater extent than whites, the proportion of Negro workers may not necessarily have changed if the figure in column 3 is slightly below that in column 4. A difference of several percentage points, however, probably indicates a real change.

a Comparable data not available.

[a] The paucity of statistical or other reliable sources for earlier decades makes it necessary for us to be somewhat vague in several of the following statements.

him a better title to the place; and so we believe it will continue to be until the last prop is leveled beneath us—white men are becoming house servants, cooks, and stewards on vessels; at hotels, they are becoming porters . . . and barbers—a few years ago a white barber would have been a curiosity. Now their poles stand on every street . . .[15]

The constant stream of European immigrants to the North continuously provided new supplies of cheap labor which competed with Negro labor for even the lower jobs such as domestics and common laborers. The trade unions were early stronger in the North than in the South and they were concentrated in the crafts. Most of the time they effectively kept Negroes out of skilled work.[16] They could do it the more successfully as the Northern Negroes did not have the head start which the handicraft training under slavery gave the Southern Negroes.

Having all these things in mind, it is easy to explain why it early became a stereotyped opinion that, as far as the chance to earn a living was concerned, the Negro was actually better off in the South than in the North. This opinion, for natural reasons, became particularly cherished by Southern whites. Henry W. Grady emphasized that the Negro "has ten avenues of employment in this section [the South] where he has one in the North."[17] And Edgar G. Murphy declared:

The race prejudice is . . . as intense at the North as it is anywhere in the world. . . . The negro at the North can be a waiter in hotel and restaurant (in some); he can be a butler or footman in club or household (in some); or the haircutter or bootblack in the barber shop (in some); and I say "in some" because even the more menial offices of industry are being slowly but gradually denied to him.[18]

Booker T. Washington regularly endorsed this view, and it had a strategic importance in his whole philosophy, particularly in his educational program:

. . . whatever other sins the South may be called upon to bear, when it comes to business, pure and simple, it is in the South that the Negro is given a man's chance in the commercial world . . .[19]

Much the same thing is often told the observer in the South today, when it most certainly is an exaggeration. But even for earlier times the proposition sounds questionable. We do not have the comprehensive statistics which would be necessary to ascertain how the two regions actually compared in the opportunities they offered Negroes during various periods. Much scattered information, however, gives an impression quite different from the Southern stereotype. In a general way, the tremendous industrial development in the North and the small number of Negroes compared to the total labor demand were factors which worked to the Negroes' advantage. If we look over the whole period from the Civil War up to 1940, the general picture is that, while the Negroes in the South have been gradually losing out in most lines of work where they had been firmly entrenched at the time of slavery and have been allowed to get a favorable position in but a few of the new industries, Negroes in the North have made some fairly significant gains in some occupations which are new or where few if any Negroes were allowed to work before. Still Negroes are completely, or almost completely, kept out of many manufacturing lines in the North.

The employment gains of Northern Negroes are not a result of a regular trend. It would be much nearer the truth to characterize them as a series of unique happenings. Some of the Northern employers started hiring Negroes on a large scale, as previously explained,[a] mainly because of the temporary scarcity of labor, due to the booms during the First World War and the 'twenties, and to the decline in immigration. The Negro, along with the Southern white worker, actually was the "last immigrant" to the North. At that time there was a much greater need for unskilled labor than is the case nowadays. Then, too, white workers, in so far as they did not come from the South, had little race prejudice. Later many of them developed a deep race prejudice.

Thus, it was a combination of factors which explains the Negroes' gains in the North—but a combination that could not last. The same was true about some of the secondary motives which induced employers to use Negro labor. Many of them wanted to keep their labor force heterogeneous so as to prevent unionization. Some of them even used Negroes as strike-breakers. This had happened several times before the First World War. In many of these cases Negro workers were dismissed when the labor conflict was ended. But, sometimes—particularly between 1910 and 1930— they actually managed to gain a foothold in this way. The motives of these employers, however, could be significant only as long as they believed that there was a possibility of keeping the unions away from their plants. Now they are gradually getting away from this belief and have no reasons to engage Negro labor for this purpose.

6. A Closer View on Northern Trends

Between 1890 and 1910 the increase in number of male Negro workers in the North was only about 160,000 (Table 1). Apart from the service occupations (domestics, laundresses, cooks, waiters, janitors, barbers, and so on) there were in 1910 no particular occupations where Negroes were concentrated. The largest proportion of Negroes in any of the nonservice groups was in the category "general and not specified laborers," many of whom were construction workers; others may have been merely "jacks-of-all-trades." Other groups including a few thousand Negro workers were:

[a] See Chapter 8.

farm laborers; helpers in building and hand trades; road and street laborers; draymen and teamsters; delivery men and helpers in stores; dressmakers and seamstresses. There were some Negro longshoremen in New York and Pennsylvania; coal miners in Pennsylvania, Ohio, and Illinois; iron and steel workers in Pennsylvania. By and large, however, the Negro had scarcely any place at all in ordinary manufacturing industries in the North.[20]

Between 1910 and 1930, on the other hand, the number of male Negro workers in nonagricultural pursuits in the North increased by no less than 480,000 (Table 1). This means that the Negro male labor force in the North more than doubled. Even the absolute increase was much larger than that in the South (about 295,000).

Most of the increase occurred in the nonmanufacturing groups: domestic and nondomestic service workers, helpers and delivery men in stores, draymen, teamsters, truck drivers, and so on. The building industry gave the Negro many additional jobs despite the fact that many craft unions were almost as hostile to the Negro in the North as they were in the South. Indeed, by 1930 almost half of the Negro building workers were in the North. Some gains were made in street and road construction work, as in the maintenance-of-way departments of the railroads. The proportion of Negro longshoremen increased in New York and Philadelphia. Garages, greasing stations, and automobile laundries in the North gave more new jobs to Negroes than did corresponding establishments in the South. The number of Negro coal miners in Pennsylvania quadrupled, even causing some displacement of white workers; still the Negroes did not constitute even 3 per cent of the total labor force in Pennsylvania coal mines by 1930. The bulk of the Negro mine workers remained in the South.[21]

In addition, Negroes managed, almost for the first time, to get a real place in certain purely manufacturing lines in the North. The gains were particularly noteworthy in the iron, steel, machinery and vehicle industries. In 1930, over 100,000, or about 60 per cent of all Negro workers in this group, were in the North. The majority of them were working in blast furnaces, steel rolling mills and automobile factories. Much less significant, but nevertheless noteworthy, were the gains in clothing industries and certain food industries, particularly slaughter and meat-packing houses.

But most other Northern manufacturing industries failed to hire Negro workers in any appreciable numbers. The Negro wage earner in the North has little or no chance in textile factories, sawmills, electrical machinery and supply factories, shoe factories, bakeries, or furniture factories—to mention just a few examples of the numerous Northern manufacturing lines where the Negro has been unable to get in. Only in exceptional cases did Northern railroads use him for other than unskilled jobs. He was not hired by the utility companies. Thus, even in the North, the Negro remained confined to certain jobs—either those where he had earlier acquired something of a traditional position or where he managed to gain a foothold during the extraordinary labor market crisis of the First World War.[a]

This should be emphasized: *large employment gains for Negroes in the North—except for the present war boom—occurred only during the short period from the First World War until the end of the 'twenties.* During the 'thirties (Table 2), the upward trend in number of Negro workers was broken even more definitely than was the case in the urban South—and this in spite of the fact that the Negro population in the large Northern centers of Negro concentration increased by as much as 23 per cent between 1930 and 1940. The white population in the urban North, on the other hand, was almost stationary, as was the white labor force. Thus, while the proportion of Negroes in the total population continued to increase, there was scarcely any change at all in the relative number of Negro male workers. Further, as we shall point out later in this chapter, the unemployment among these Negro workers was much greater in the North than in the South.

All this is explainable on several grounds. The depression hit the North worse than the South. Nevertheless, Negroes continued to go North to such an extent that the relative increase in the Negro urban population was even greater in the North than in the South. As pointed out in Chapter 8, this cannot mean anything but that, once the isolation had been broken and the northward migration had become a pattern, Negroes continued to go North whether or not there were any employment openings for them there. In addition to the general difference in social conditions—less segregation, greater legal security, superior educational and hospital facilities, higher earnings if any jobs are to be had, and so on—the North offers much more public relief to Negroes in economic distress than does the South.[b] This fact has undoubtedly been behind much of the Negro migration to the North during the 'thirties.[c] Also, as in the South, public relief has contributed to the decline in the proportion of Negro youth and Negro aged persons who offer their services on the Northern labor market.[d]

Thus, it was not all due to any greater negligence about the Negro in the North that—as far as employment was concerned—he fared even worse

---

[a] This fact, of course, is one of the main reasons why most of the outstanding Negro leaders are not inclined, during the present War, to postpone the fight for Negro rights until after the War is over. (For a representative expression of their attitude, see "Press Service of the National Association for the Advancement of Colored People." [July 17, 1942].)

[b] See Chapter 15.

[c] See Chapter 8.

[d] See Section 8 of this chapter.

there, during the 'thirties, than he did in the urban South. In part it was just because the North, in other respects, treated him better than the South did that the Northern Negro population tended to outgrow the employment opportunities for Negroes. Still, the record of the North certainly is not a good one either. Many labor unions discriminated against the Negro worker. So did many employers, especially when it came to skilled work.

7. The Employment Hazards of Unskilled Work

We have found that the Negro's participation in the Southern non-agricultural economy has steadily become relatively less significant. In the North there was no further improvement in the Negro's share of the jobs during the 'thirties; the Negro, if anything, lost even more than did the white worker because of the depression.

There is one factor behind this development to which we have not yet given enough emphasis: the fact that the Negro is concentrated in unskilled occupations (Table 4). This circumstance must be considered in any evalua-

TABLE 4

Negro and White Male Workers in Nonagricultural Pursuits by Social-Economic Status, in the North and in the South: 1930
(Cumulative Percentages)

Occupational Status	All Male Workers		Negro Male Workers		White Male Workers	
	The North and the West	The South	The North and the West	The South	The North and the West	The South
All workers	100	100	100	100	100	100
Clerical or lower	83	83	95	95	82	79
Skilled or lower	65	67	91	93	64	60
Semi-skilled or lower	43	48	83	86	41	38
Unskilled	23	32	66	71	21	20

Source: U.S. Bureau of the Census, Alba M. Edwards, Social-Economic Grouping of the Gainful Workers of the United States, 1930 (1938), pp. 36-59.

tion of future prospects. Indeed, the Negro's low occupational status contains a greater danger for future employment than is usually realized. It means generally that his chances not only of getting ahead but of keeping any employment at all are more restricted. The expansion in unskilled occupations has been limited during recent decades compared with that in occupations above the unskilled class.[22] It is necessary to emphasize this point. For, just as many persons believe that Negroes would be able to get along if they only had sense enough to stay in agriculture, there are those who think that Negroes are over-ambitious when they try to get out of their position as common laborers. Negroes *must* become skilled workers, since the demand for unskilled workers is declining.

The proportion of unskilled workers in the nonagricultural labor force is much greater in the South than in the North (Table 4). One of the reasons is that the iron, steel, and machinery industries, with their great need of skilled labor, are less well represented below the Mason-Dixon line than they are in certain other parts of the country. Then, too, there has been comparatively little incentive to mechanization in the low wage regions of the South. But this means, on the other hand, that *there are in the South many more laborers who can be displaced by mechanization.* The Wages and Hours Law tends to spur mechanization by raising wages. It goes without saying that *the Negroes are, and will continue to be, the main sufferers in such a development.* Over 70 per cent of the Negro males in nonagricultural pursuits in the South were in unskilled occupations; the corresponding figure for Southern whites was 20 per cent. The Southern Negroes were, in this respect, somewhat worse off than the Northern Negroes. Southern industry was more "saturated" with unskilled Negro labor than Northern industry. Almost half of all unskilled male workers outside agriculture in the South were Negroes.[23] The occupational status of the Southern whites, on the other hand, was somewhat higher, in certain respects, than was that of the Northern whites. The reason is obvious: white workers in the South had a near monopoly on the higher jobs but were less well represented in the lower occupations.[a]

If the Negro's occupational status was particularly low in the South, it does not mean that it was high in the North. Actually there was little difference: about two-thirds of the male Negro workers in the North were in unskilled occupations. But since these Negro workers constituted only about one-tenth of all laborers in the North,[24] there should be more room for the Negro in the North, even if he remains confined to the bottom of the occupational ladder.

8. THE SIZE OF THE NEGRO LABOR FORCE AND NEGRO EMPLOYMENT

Considering all the limitation that Negroes face in every occupation, even those where they are not completely excluded, it is pertinent to ask: What proportion of Negroes have any jobs at all? Is the Negro merely exchanging his position as a dependent and exploited sharecropper for that of an urban unemployed person and a relief client?

In nonfarm areas of the United States in 1940, 47 per cent of all non-

---

[a] This observation about the occupational status of Southern and Northern whites agrees fairly well with the finding about urban incomes in the South and the North. See Chapter 16. Median incomes for white families, contrary to common belief, are not lower in the urban South than in the urban North, the reason being that the Southern white population —due to the presence of the Negro—has an "incomplete lower class."

white persons, 14 years of age and over, were registered as having employment (exclusive of work relief employment). The corresponding figure
for the white population was slightly lower, or 45 per cent.[25] This, however,
does not mean that employment conditions were any more favorable for
Negroes than for whites. It is only because Negro women to such a great
extent take on gainful work outside their homes that this general employment rate was somewhat higher for nonwhites than for whites. Of all nonwhite women, 36 per cent were employed; for white women the figure was
24 per cent (Table 5).[26] For men it was the other way around: *nonwhite*

TABLE 5

TOTAL PERSONS AND LABOR FORCE IN NONFARM AREAS OF THE UNITED STATES
BY EMPLOYMENT STATUS, SEX, AND RACE: 1940
(Percentages)

Sex and Race	Total Population 14 years of Age and Over, by Employment Status					Labor Force by Employment Status			
			Labor Force					Unemployed	
					Unemployed (emergency workers included)			Total (including emergency workers)	
	Total persons	Non-workers	All Workers	Em-ployed	Total	Em-ployed	Seek-ing Work
Male									
Nonwhite	100.0	21.7	78.3	58.9	19.4	100.0	75.2	24.8	15.2
White	100.0	21.5	78.5	66.1	12.4	100.0	84.2	15.8	10.9
Female									
Nonwhite	100.0	56.8	43.2	35.9	7.3	100.0	83.1	16.9	13.1
White	100.0	72.7	27.3	23.8	3.5	100.0	87.0	13.0	9.7

Source: *Sixteenth Census of the United States: 1940, Population*, Preliminary Release, Series P-4, No. 4

*men had employment less often (59 per cent) than had white men (66
per cent)*. This difference was particularly pronounced in the North. *In
many Northern centers only about one-half of the Negro men had any
employment.*

These race differentials in employment rates are the result of two
opposing factors. One is that the extreme poverty of most Negro families
forces Negro women as well as Negro boys and aged Negro men out on the
labor market to a much greater extent than corresponding categories of
whites.[28] On the other hand, among both men and women who "are in
the labor market," the proportion of those who fail to get any jobs is much
higher for Negroes than for whites. There is often, of course, a causal
relation between these two factors. A Negro woman may take a job because

her husband is without one. On the other hand, if the employment situation is discouraging, some of the workers, particularly if they have secured public assistance, and quite especially if they are getting old, will tend to withdraw permanently from the labor market. Nevertheless, let us consider each of the two factors separately. It is certainly pertinent to our problem to compare the extent to which Negroes and whites offer their services on the labor market. It allows us to comprehend better the data on Negro unemployment[a] which we shall discuss presently. We shall also find that it takes away some of the basis for the popular belief in "Negro laziness."

The total number of both employed and unemployed workers (the so-called "labor force"[b]) has traditionally been much larger, in proportion, among Negroes than among whites. This has been particularly true in the case of women. But such a difference, although smaller, was formerly clearly noticeable in regard to males as well. In part it has been due to the fact that there has been a pronounced time-lag in the elimination of child labor among Negroes. Too, Negroes have retired at a much later age than have white workers. In 1930 over half of the Negro men 75 years of age and over—as against less than one-third of the white men of the same age—were still "in the labor market." While white women used to leave the labor market in great numbers after the age of about 25, there was no very significant drop in the proportion of workers and job-seekers among Negroes until they reached the age of about 65.[29]

Gradually, however, an equalization has taken place in regard to most of these differences. Yet child labor, at least until 1930, dropped more sharply in the white than in the colored group.[30] The proportion of workers among old people, on the other hand, seems to have declined somewhat faster among Negroes than among whites. There has been, for a long time, an upward trend in the proportion of white women gainfully employed; whereas the proportion for Negro women was stationary or declining.[31] This equalization seems to have become particularly pronounced during the decade 1930-1940,[32] which probably was due to the introduction of large-scale public relief, particularly old age assistance, assistance to dependent children, and so on, which, in spite of all discrimination,[c] meant more to the Negro than to the white group. In addition, it is probable that the great unemployment among Negroes during the 'thirties was a contributory factor, in that Negroes who had lost their jobs, more often than whites, were

---

[a] See Section 9 of this chapter.

[b] This designation was used in the 1940 Census; it includes workers on work relief projects (W.P.A., N.Y.A., C.C.C., and so on). The concept "gainful worker" used in earlier census reports was about the same, except in some minor details (see footnote 12 in this chapter).

[c] See Chapter 15.

discouraged from offering their services and, thus, ceased to belong to either the actual or the potential labor force.[33]

This development had gone so far by 1940 that, in urban and other non-farm areas, the proportion of the male population 14 years old and over that belonged to the labor force (those who were either actual workers or job-seekers) was exactly the same in both racial groups (78 per cent; see Table 5). The relative number of female workers and job-seekers, on

TABLE 6

LABOR FORCE AS A PERCENTAGE OF ALL PERSONS, 14 YEARS OF AGE AND OVER, AND
UNEMPLOYED WORKERS AS A PERCENTAGE OF TOTAL LABOR FORCE, IN
SELECTED LARGE CITIES, BY SEX AND RACE: 1940

City	Labor Force as a Percentage of All Persons, 14 Years of Age and Over				Unemployed (exclusive of emergency workers) as a Percentage of Total Labor Force			
	Male		Female		Male		Female	
	Negro	White	Negro	White	Negro	White	Negro	White
New York	80.8	81.1	50.7	32.5	20.1	15.2	18.1	14.8
Philadelphia	78.5	80.8	43.6	31.9	33.1	15.4	23.7	14.6
Cleveland	79.5	81.4	33.0	30.3	16.7	12.4	22.4	11.3
Detroit	84.7	84.7	30.0	28.1	16.1	9.7	19.4	11.3
Chicago	77.9	82.4	35.7	33.3	17.2	11.1	23.2	9.5
St Louis	81.6	82.9	37.4	32.8	19.6	10.5	20.4	9.2
Louisville	79.7	81.8	45.7	29.9	17.6	10.4	18.6	9.8
Baltimore	79.6	80.8	46.8	29.8	13.2	7.3	10.8	7.9
Washington, D.C.	81.0	80.7	51.7	43.0	10.6	5.4	11.3	5.1
Richmond	79.5	81.7	56.1	36.1	15.5	6.6	13.1	6.8
Atlanta	82.0	83.0	54.4	35.5	13.9	6.7	11.6	7.6
Birmingham	82.0	81.9	39.9	26.7	15.9	7.0	14.9	9.1
Memphis	85.4	82.5	44.8	30.9	14.5	6.8	15.5	7.4
New Orleans	80.7	81.1	43.4	28.9	15.3	10.2	15.2	9.6
Houston	84.0	83.8	53.7	28.7	11.9	7.2	9.7	7.0

Source: *Sixteenth Census of the United States: 1940, Population*, Second Series, State Reports, Tables 41 and 43 (for Washington, D.C., Tables 13 and 21).

the other hand, continued in most places to be much higher in the non-white than in the white population, even if the difference was smaller than before. White women still left the labor market at a much faster rate after having reached the age of 25 than did Negro women.[34]

The equalization in the proportion of white and Negro men and women who are workers or job-seekers has proceeded further in the urban North than in the urban South. It has also proceeded further in the cities than in the farm areas of the South. Even in the male agricultural population of the South in 1940 there was still a higher proportion of actual and potential workers in the Negro than in the white group.[35] This may be due, in part, to the fact that unemployment among Negroes is greater in the North than in the South, and much greater in urban than in rural areas. Also, it is an index of the differences in economic standards. Both relief grants and nonrelief earnings are much more adequate in Northern than in Southern cities; both are particularly inadequate in farm areas of the South.[a]

We should not, however, be hasty in jumping to the conclusion that "relief has demoralized the Negro." Of course, something of the sort may have happened in many individual cases, both in the white and in the Negro group. But, by and large, the moral indignation against the Negro that is implied in this stereotype is entirely misplaced. We must keep in mind that so far no appeal has been made to the ambition of the Negro to better himself economically. On the contrary, white people, by means of the severe job restrictions they have imposed upon the Negro—and by denying him sufficient public health facilities—have forced him to accept public relief as one of his "major occupations." Therefore, if the Negro, in a sense, has become "demoralized," it is rather because *white people have given him a smaller share of the steady and worth-while jobs than of the public assistance benefits.*

It should be emphasized, further, that, in spite of the more liberal relief policies of the last decades, there are still, proportionately, a greater number of workers and job-seekers in the Negro than in the white population. The decline has occurred mainly among aged persons who should be allowed to retire,[36] among youth who can use some additional school education, and among women who have their own homes and families to attend to.

In the future, however, this problem may become of increasing significance. There is still, as we shall show,[b] much discrimination against the Negro in the relief system. If these discriminatory practices are removed—and the federal government is working toward that end—but if present job restrictions are maintained, then, of course, *there is a real danger that the Negro will become a burden on the national economy.* This is the basic dilemma in the problem of the Negro's integration into American economic life. It must be faced squarely.

9. NEGRO AND WHITE UNEMPLOYMENT

We have seen that there are more Negroes than whites, in proportion, who offer their services on the labor market. More Negroes need employment than do whites, for the simple reason that the pay for each job that a Negro can get usually is so much lower than are the earnings that a white person can get. Yet the unemployment is much higher for Negroes than for whites. About 25 per cent of the nonwhite male labor force in nonfarm areas was without any employment on the labor market in 1940; and 15

[a] See Chapters 15 and 16.
[b] See Chapter 15.

per cent did not even have any work relief assignments (Table 5). The corresponding figures for white males (16 and 11 per cent, respectively) were significantly lower. There was a similar difference, although on a somewhat lower level, between white and nonwhite females. When the number of jobless female workers is related, not to the "labor force," but to all women, 14 years of age and over, one finds that the unemployment rate was more than twice as high (7 per cent) for Negro as for white women (3 per cent).[37]

Conditions, however, are different in different areas. In the rural farm areas of the South, where only few persons are registered as unemployed, the rates were actually lower for Negroes than for whites. The nonfarm areas of the South show conditions only slightly worse for Negroes than for whites. It is mainly in the cities that unemployment is so much more widespread among Negroes than among whites (Table 6). The difference was usually quite large both in Northern and in Southern cities, but since the North had a higher general level of unemployment, Northern Negroes, of course, were even more adversely affected than were the Negroes in the urban South. In Philadelphia, about one-third of the Negro males, not counting those on work relief projects, were registered as unemployed; in New York and St. Louis the proportion was one-fifth. Negro female workers, as well, showed high unemployment rates in several of the large Northern cities.

Perhaps Negro migration is the cause of this situation. The Negro migrant, as we have seen, prefers the large city. Whenever possible, he wants to go North. It is possible that he could have had a better chance in Southern villages and small cities. But, as explained before,[a] it is natural that the Negro prefers to go where he can escape injustice and restrictions, which are usually particularly great in the small Southern community.

Young workers are suffering from unemployment much more than others. In urban areas roughly one-third of the total labor force in the age group 14 to 19 was without jobs. Nonwhite males (36 per cent) were somewhat above, and white females (29 per cent) were a little below the average; but there was no substantial race differential except in certain individual cities. The situation was better for middle-aged people, but more so for white than for Negro workers. This finding from the 1940 Census is corroborated by other studies.

The Health Survey data for urban male and female workers in 1935-36 . . . and the information from the 1937 Unemployment Census . . . substantiate the conclusion *that the Negro-white difference in unemployment risk is mainly a problem of the Negro's inability to improve his chances on the labor market with increased age and experience to the same extent as the white worker.* If age and

[a] See Chapter 8.

experience help the Negro worker less than the white worker, how about education? Data from the National Health Survey . . . indicate that *the unemployment risk for white urban workers, 16-24 years old, declines progressively with the increased scholastic achievements.* About 56 per cent of the male white workers with less than a sixth-grade education were unemployed in 1935-36, whereas only eighteen per cent of those with a college education were jobless. *Among urban Negro youth, on the other hand, there was no consistent trend of this kind at all* except that persons with college training were somewhat better off than those with less education. Colored urban youth, whose education extended no higher than the sixth grade were somewhat better off than white youth with a similar lack of formal training. The colored and white youth who had completed the seventh grade had the same amount of unemployment (50 per cent for males and 38-39 per cent for females). It was only because such a large proportion of white youth had gone farther than the seventh grade that their general position was better than that of colored youth.[38]

These findings are certainly extremely significant—in fact, so important that one would like to see them confirmed by other similar studies. It seems, however, that they are plausible enough. If white boys and girls do not care for openings that may be available immediately, they can, more often than colored youth, afford to postpone their entry into the labor market. This may explain why those among them who have little education may be even less successful in getting employment than are young colored workers. *Since Negroes are seldom in demand for jobs for which education is necessary, there certainly is nothing surprising in the conclusion that they, unlike whites, usually fail to improve their opportunities by staying in school longer.* Somewhat more astonishing is the finding that those with college education constitute an exception in this regard. But they are not dependent entirely on the white economy, as are most of the less-educated Negroes. The segregated Negro community offers a small but increasing number of jobs to Negro professionals.[a]

[a] See Chapter 14, Section 1. The lower unemployment risk found for youths with college education may be partly fictitious, however, in that many of those who fail to get employment simply continue their studies and, thus, are listed as students rather than as unemployed.

CHAPTER 14

THE NEGRO IN BUSINESS, THE PROFESSIONS, PUBLIC

SERVICE AND OTHER WHITE COLLAR OCCUPATIONS

1. OVERVIEW

The position of the Negro in business, professions, public service, and white collar jobs is far different from that of the Negro wage earner. As a wage earner the Negro is excluded from many trades. Where he works he is commonly held down to the status of laborer and is excluded from skilled work. But there are always possibilities for him to enter these jobs, and he is always struggling to do so. In the occupations traditionally associated with upper or middle class status, the exclusion policy is usually much more complete and "settled." This is because it is fortified by "social" considerations, as well as by economic ones.[a]

The overwhelming majority of all other Negro workers serve the general white-dominated economy, but most Negro businessmen, professionals, and Negro white collar workers are either dependent on the segregated Negro community for their market or they serve in public institutions—like schools and hospitals—set up exclusively for the use of Negroes. (Some civil service employees are the only significant exceptions.)

This has important consequences. The exclusion from the larger white economy means a severe restriction of the opportunities for Negroes to reach an upper or middle class status. It represents one of the main social mechanisms by which the Negro upper and middle classes are kept small. It also makes the occupational distribution in those classes skewed: While the Negro community gives places for a fair number of Negro preachers, teachers, and neighborhood storekeepers, it does not offer much chance for civil engineers and architects. The latter have to work in the white economy which does not want Negroes in such positions. The Negroes' representation among managers of industry, if anything, is still smaller.

The poverty of the Negro people represents a general limitation of opportunity for Negro businessmen and professionals. Since they are excluded from the white market, it becomes important for them to hold

---

[a] The term "social" is here used in the sense of the man in the street, especially the Southerner, and thus has the connotation of "intimate" and "personal." (See Chapter 28.)

the Negro market as a monopoly. The monopoly over the Negro market of teachers, preachers, undertakers, beauticians and others is generally respected. The Negro storekeeper, on the other hand, is in severe competition with the white storekeeper, and only a small fraction of the purchasing power of Negro patrons passes his counter. To a lesser extent this is true also of the Negro doctor. The Negro lawyer has an even worse competitive position. The Negro journalist does not have to compete with whites in the Negro press but, to an extent, the Negro press has to compete with the white press. All Negro businessmen and professionals have to try to make as much use as possible of racial solidarity as a selling point. This means that the entire Negro middle and upper class becomes caught in an ideological dilemma.[a] On the one hand, they find that the caste wall blocks their economic and social opportunities. On the other hand, they have, at the same time, a vested interest in racial segregation since it gives them what opportunity they have.

In the rest of this chapter we shall describe the economic position of upper and middle class Negroes. We shall first present a summary of the situation and then go on to examine each of the occupations separately.

In 1930 there were only 254,000 Negro workers in white collar and higher occupations (Table 1). This means that only one out of fifteen Negro workers in nonagricultural pursuits had a status higher than that of wage earner. In the white nonfarm population as many as two out of every five workers were in business, managerial, professional, and white collar jobs.[1] The number of Negro workers in such occupations had increased by more than three-fourths between 1910 and 1930. But the corresponding increase of white workers had been somewhat greater, so the relative position of the Negro had not improved. In 1910, 1.8 per cent of all these professional, managerial and clerical workers were Negroes. In 1930, 1.7 per cent of them were Negroes. Thus, in spite of the fact that the Negro's share in these jobs was so extremely low, there was no tendency toward equalization. There was not even any great increase in the proportion that professionals, businessmen, and white collar workers constituted of the total Negro labor force in nonagricultural pursuits. In 1910 this proportion was 6 per cent. In 1930 it was 7 per cent.

Conditions differed, however, for different categories. The Negro has had slightly better chances in the professions than in other occupations in this group. Indeed, in 1930 the number of Negro professional workers was larger (116,000) than that of clerical workers (83,000), whereas in the white population there were almost three clerks and kindred workers for every professional person. That the Negroes have as much as a 4 per cent representation among the professional workers is due to two main factors: the segregated Southern school system, and the segregated Negro church

[a] See Chapter 38.

TABLE 1

NEGRO WORKERS IN BUSINESS, PROFESSIONAL, AND WHITE COLLAR
OCCUPATIONS, BY SEX: 1910, 1920, AND 1930

Sex and Occupation	Number of Negro Workers			Negroes as a percentage of all Workers		
	1910	1920	1930	1910	1920	1930
Both Sexes						
Professional persons	64,648	77,118	115,765	4.0	3.8	3.9
Wholesale and retail dealers	20,894	23,593	28,343	1.7	1.7	1.6
Other proprietors, managers, and officials	19,102	17,610	27,648	1.6	1.3	1.5
Clerks and kindred workers	38,698	63,095	82,669	1.0	1.1	1.0
Males						
Professional persons	35,815	39,434	55,610	3.9	3.7	3.7
Wholesale and retail dealers	17,888	20,455	24,493	1.5	1.5	1.5
Other proprietors, managers, and officials	15,487	13,309	21,196	1.4	1.0	1.2
Clerks and kindred workers	31,926	48,046	62,138	1.2	1.4	1.3
Females						
Professional persons	28,833	37,684	60,155	4.0	3.8	4.2
Wholesale and retail dealers	3,006	3,138	3,850	4.4	3.9	3.4
Other proprietors, managers, and officials	3,615	4,301	6,452	6.6	5.5	4.9
Clerks and kindred workers	6,772	15,048	20,531	0.6	0.7	0.7

Source: U. S. Bureau of the Census, Alba M. Edwards, *Social-Economic Grouping of the Gainful Workers of the United States*, 1930 (1938), pp. 7 and 13.

with its numerous small congregations. Teachers and ministers account for almost two-thirds of all Negro professional workers. The small number of Negro clerical workers—only two-thirds of one per cent of all female clerks and kindred workers were Negro—is the result of the fact that few white establishments use any Negro workers in such capacities while most Negro-owned establishments are too small to give employment to others than the entrepreneur and members of his family. Negro storekeepers, other business entrepreneurs, and business officials had an intermediate position between these two groups. They numbered 56,000 and constituted about 1.5 per cent of all American businessmen.

The North is almost as strict as the South in excluding Negroes from middle class jobs in the white-dominated economy. The very lack of segregation in most Northern schools makes it more difficult for a Negro to get a teaching position. Since the educational ladder is made completely available for Negro youths, this subsequent barrier against employment, except as laborers, is more deeply discouraging.[2]

The subsequent detailed account of the various groups of occupations will show that, by and large, the prospects for Negro workers of higher than wage earner status are even more limited than can be learned from the summary data we have just examined.[a]

2. THE NEGRO IN BUSINESS

In 1939 there were not quite 30,000 Negro retail stores, including eating and drinking places, giving employment to an almost equal number of proprietors, and less than 14,000 hired employees, or—apart from 1,000 unpaid family members—a total of 43,000 persons. Thus, Negro retail trade, in terms of employment, is not totally insignificant. Compared with the size of white retail trade, however, it is negligible. The total sales in 1939 were a little more than $71,000,000, which was less than two-tenths of one per cent of the national total. The annual payroll amounted to a little over $400 for each full-time employee.[3] There were no signs of improvement in the relative position of Negro retail trade. The proportion of Negroes among all retail dealers was, if anything, smaller in 1930 than in 1910 (Table 1). The same trend downward is visible during the period of 1929-1939. Total sales declined by 28 per cent in Negro-owned stores and restaurants from 1929 to 1939, whereas the corresponding figure for retail trade in the entire United States was 13 per cent.[4]

The Negro population has much less than one-tenth of the total consumer income in the United States. Certain estimates made of Negro and white family income allow us to guess that the Negro's share in the national income does not exceed 4 per cent, and is probably around 3 per cent.[b] As savings constitute generally a larger part of higher incomes, the Negro's share in total consumption is probably somewhat greater than his share of the national income, though not much. But even when the relatively low level of Negro purchasing power is taken into account, Negro-owned stores and restaurants probably do not have more than 5 or 10 per cent of the total Negro trade. The rest goes to white businesses.

It goes without saying that the small size of the average Negro store increases costs, and thereby causes a competitive disadvantage. Prices tend to be higher than in the white-operated stores, or the margin of profit smaller. It is difficult for the Negro dealer to have a large variety of goods. Reid cites an inquiry made by the Negro Business League in New York's Harlem in 1932, according to which a sample of Negro housewives blamed

---

[a] The facts for the subsequent analysis will be taken, in large part, from an unpublished research memorandum prepared for this study (1940), "The Negro in the American Economic System," by Ira DeA. Reid in conjunction with Norgren's investigations cited in the previous chapter. It deals with the Negro in business, banking, retail trade, professions and white collar occupations.

[b] See Chapter 16.

the insufficient variety of stock and the higher prices as the main reasons for their failure to patronize Negro-owned stores to any large extent. The extreme poverty of most customers puts another difficulty in the way of the Negro dealer: since he must depend on immediate cash turnover, he must avoid giving credit; at the same time he knows that he will lose many of his patrons by not granting them credit.[5] Housing segregation is a factor which generally helps Negro business. When a city, however, contains several small Negro neighborhoods, as often happens in the South, scarcely any one of them can support a prosperous Negro store.[6] Negro sections never contain any primary shopping centers; indeed there are few places, except in the North, where there are even secondary shopping centers in Negro areas. Negroes often reside close to principal business districts where no Negro entrepreneur can ever hope to rent a store.[7]

These things go a long way to explain how narrow the prospects of the Negro retail dealers are. Still, it is not only because Negro consumers buy in white business districts that the Negro dealer gets so little of their patronage. Negro areas, at least in large cities, have a great number of stores and restaurants catering exclusively, or almost exclusively, to Negroes but operated by Jews, Greeks, Italians and other whites. Sometimes this may be a matter of tradition, since it was only a few decades ago that many of the principal Negro neighborhoods in the North had entirely or predominantly white residents. Or it may be that real estate owners—most of whom are white even in Negro areas—do not believe that the Negro dealer is a dependable rent payer. Such an attitude, of course, must jeopardize the Negro's chances of getting a good location. Reid claims, in addition, that the Negro businessman himself has not always seen the advantage of locating his store in a competitive area:

> Besides the fact that the Negro grocery retailer is barred from the main shopping districts by social and economic factors, he believes that his business experiences greater success in a non-competitive area where there are no other stores selling similar merchandise. The general economic truth that competition increases the volume of business does not apply to him, he feels. Such an attitude gives rise to isolation of Negro grocery stores even within the Negro community. The complaint of Negro householders that Negro establishments are inconveniently located is well founded.[8]

The Negro businessman, furthermore, encounters greater difficulties in securing credit. This is partly due to the marginal position of Negro business. It is also partly due to prejudiced opinions among the whites concerning the business ability and personal reliability of Negroes. In either case a vicious circle is in operation keeping Negro business down. Part of this circle is the fact that Negro business generally is not of the size and efficiency necessary to offer many positions which would give good training to Negro youths who want to prepare themselves for a business career.

Whether or not such factors as those mentioned above are sufficient to excuse the Negro's poor showing in business is, of course, a question of judgment. Particularly striking is the fact that only seldom, and then mainly because segregation has provided a monopoly, have Negro business-men succeeded in getting all or most of the Negro trade. In addition to the 10,500 Negro restaurant owners in 1930, there were some 14,000 owners of Negro hotels, boarding and lodging houses (Table 2), constituting 7 per cent of all such entrepreneurs in the country. They probably owned

TABLE 2

NUMBER OF NEGRO ENTREPRENEURS AND WHITE COLLAR WORKERS IN
SELECTED TRADE AND SERVICE INDUSTRIES: 1910[a]

Industry and Occupation	1910	1930
Banking and brokerage: officials, clerks, accountants, etc.	634	994
Insurance: officials, managers, agents, clerks, etc.	2,450	9,325
Real Estate: officials, agents, clerks, etc.	950	4,695
Wholesale and retail trade:		
Retail dealers (except automobiles)	20,644[b]	27,743[b]
Undertakers	953	2,946
Clerks, salesmen, saleswomen, and other white collar workers	10,989	21,017
Hotels, restaurants, boarding houses, etc.		
Hotel, boarding and lodging housekeepers and managers	11,574	14,173
Restaurant, cafe, and lunchroom keepers	6,369	10,543
Clerks, bookkeepers, and other white collar workers	838	1,248
Cleaning, dyeing, and pressing shops:		
Owners and managers	c	1,734
Clerical workers	c	156

Sour e: U.S. Bureau of the Census, Negroes in the U.S.: 1920-1932, pp. 355-358. Thirteenth Census of the U.S.: 1910, Population, Vol. 4, pp. 418-433. It should be noted that these figures differ somewhat from the classification used by Edwards, op. cit., in that, for instance, Edwards includes messengers among white collar workers, which has not been done in this table. It is evident that every classification of this type has to be arbitrary.

[a] Only such trade and service groups as have any appreciable number of Negro entrepreneurs and white collar workers have been included. Regarding barbers and hairdressers, see text in this section.

[b] Figures do not quite agree with those in Table 1 because they are based on different classifications.

[c] Data not available.

most lodging and boarding houses located in Negro sections; few white entrepreneurs would consider competing for this trade. Most of these Negro entrepreneurs were women, usually widowed.[9] The majority of their places probably differed little, if at all, from ordinary private homes with lodgers.

A real "business group," on the other hand, were the 3,000 Negro undertakers, constituting nearly one-tenth of all undertakers in America. In the South they have an almost complete monopoly on Negro funerals, as whites would not want to touch the corpses. In the North their competitive position is almost as strong. They never handle white funerals. Since, in addition, Negroes are likely to spend relatively much on funerals, the funeral homes represent one of the most solid and flourishing Negro businesses. Barbers, beauticians, and hairdressers also have a complete monopoly for similar reasons. In 1930 there were 34,000 Negro entrepreneurs and employees occupied in this line of work, and they constituted almost one-tenth of all such workers in the country.[10] But these are the only Negro businesses in which Negroes are protected from white competition. In all other businesses of any consequence Negro businessmen are able to keep only a small portion of the Negro market. Seldom have Negroes succeeded in keeping a substantial white market.

The Negro's showing in business appears particularly poor when compared with that of certain other "alien" groups. The immigrants offer a case in point. The foreign-born are "under-represented" among industrial entrepreneurs, business managers, officials, and white collar workers, but they constitute a larger proportion of the retail dealers than corresponds to their proportion in the population. In fact, one out of every three wholesale and retail dealers in the United States in 1930 was a foreign-born person.[11] This high proportion may be caused, of course, by their having greater difficulties than native Americans in getting employment in many other occupations. At the same time, it indicates a certain resourcefulness in the struggle against unemployment.

Particularly interesting is the great number of stores and restaurants operated by Chinese and Japanese. In 1929 they owned one-and-a-half times as many stores, restaurants, and eating places per 1,000 population as other residents of the United States. Negroes, on the other hand, operated but one-sixth of the number of such establishments as would correspond to their proportion in the population. Nor is this all. The stores and restaurants operated by the Orientals were larger and gave employment to an average of four persons per store (proprietors and employees), whereas the corresponding ratio for Negro establishments was but 1.6. The net sales of the Oriental-operated stores ($89,000,000) were not much lower than those of the Negro-owned stores ($101,000,000), in spite of the fact that the Negro population was about fifty times larger than the Oriental population of the country.[12]

It is a problem to explain why the Chinese have been able to build up a prosperous restaurant business with white patronage, whereas Negro-owned eating places nowadays have but few white customers, except in a couple of "tourist spots" in the amusement area of Harlem and one or two other publicized Negro sections in other Northern cities; and even those are not always owned by Negroes.[13] It is true that the Chinese restaurant profits from the special appeal that a foreign culture always seems to have to the American. But Southern cooking, in a measure, has a similar reputation outside the South. Since the servants of the Southern aristocracy have usually been Negroes, well-trained Negro cooks and waiters have not been lacking, and one would have expected that the Negro-owned restaurant would have had a particularly good chance, once the Negro had actually made some headway in this business.[14] There are many reports about Negro restaurants having been popular among the white upper class in earlier times.

But already in the 1890's Du Bois described how the Negro caterer was losing out.[15] Part of the explanation is probably the change in the character of the upper class restaurant business. In earlier times, the main requirement was good cooking and service; the caterer may have appeared more as a favored "collective" servant to an upper class circle than as a businessman. But soon requirements were increased. It became necessary to invest large capital in restaurants intended for the wealthy. Or, as Du Bois puts it:

> . . . it is the old development from the small to the large industry, from the house-industry to the concentrated industry, from the private dining room to the palatial hotel. If the Negro caterers of Philadelphia had been white, some of them would have been put in charge of a large hotel, or would have become co-partners in some large restaurant business, for which capitalists furnished funds. . . . As it was, the change in fashion and mode of business changed the methods of the Negro caterers, and their clientele. They began to serve the middle class instead of the rich and exclusive, their prices had to become more reasonable, and their efforts to excel had consequently fewer incentives. Moreover, they now came into sharp competition with a class of small white caterers, who, if they were worse cooks, were better trained in the tricks of trade . . .[16]

Not only has the Negro caterer lost out because he has not had capital, but also because he has often failed to modernize his business and be efficient generally. There have been, of course, social and political pressures, as well as economic ones, against Negro caterers. The few remaining Negro caterers and restaurant owners serve whites mainly, and their business has the character of a novelty rather than of a regularly accepted business.

The famous old Negro barbershops went the same way as the Negro restaurants. Laundry work represents a somewhat similar example. There are more Negro workers in this field than in any other occupation outside of agriculture and domestic service. But it was the whites and the Chinese who started the commercial laundries, which have taken hundreds of thousands of job opportunities away from the Negro home laundresses. There were only a few hundred Negro owners of commercial laundries in 1930, representing about 2 per cent of the total. Not only his experience as a worker but also his self-interest should have provided an inducement for the Negro to go into this kind of business as an independent entrepreneur. Yet he failed to do so.

The building trade offers another example of how the Negro has failed as an entrepreneur, even when he—viewed superficially at least—would seem to have had a comparatively good chance. There are more skilled Negro workers in this industry than in any other line of work. Contractors, at least formerly, were recruited from the ranks of the skilled workers. At the time when, in view of the small size of most construction jobs, most contractors were not much more than master workmen, many Negroes had a certain position in this field in the South, but soon after the Civil War the South started to become industrialized. Many factory buildings and large apartment houses had to be erected, and they required huge amounts of capital. Whites formed an increasing proportion of the skilled workers, and they attempted to monopolize the work on the large projects where the latest technical methods were used. Only in exceptional cases did they accept work under Negro contractors. Under such circumstances it was impossible for Negroes to make any headway. By 1910 there were but 2,900 Negro contractors constituting 1.8 per cent of the total. In 1930 the number was down to 2,400, or 1.6 per cent.

The fact that the Negro has never been able to establish himself as an entrepreneur in ordinary manufacturing industries[a] is less surprising. The public, of course, is not always aware of the racial identity of those who produce. For this reason, the Negro, perhaps, would have been able to sell on the white market had he been allowed to become a manufacturer. But the obstacles have been too great to overcome. In most manufacturing lines he has not even been able to become a skilled worker, much less a foreman, engineer or office worker. The chances of acquiring managerial skills, under such circumstances, were scant. Lack of adequate training made him inferior. His background in slavery enhanced his feeling of inferiority. The general belief that his inferiority was due to his race meant that even those individual Negroes who would have been able to overcome all other difficulties were stopped short. For one thing, it put the would-be Negro entrepreneur at a tremendous disadvantage in respect to the all-important problem of credit. One can almost count on the fingers of one hand the number of types of production where the Negro, as an ordinary working-man, has been allowed to enter when he was not well entrenched already during the time of slavery. If whites put up great restrictions against his activity as a wage earner, how could they be expected to risk their money on his attempts to become an independent producer? In the South it would have been against the doctrine of the inequality of the races. In the North

---

[a] Outside the building industry there were only a little over 1,300 Negro manufacturers in 1930. The main groups were the owners of suit, coat, and overall factories, automobile repair shops, and saw and planing mills. Most of these Negro establishments were probably small and marginal. Some of the largest individual Negro-owned establishments are those producing hair and facial preparations. In most other manufacturing lines there were less than five Negro entrepreneurs. (Edwards, *op. cit.*, pp. 90-113.)

there were few persons of the moneyed class who had any close contact with individual Negroes so that they might judge a Negro on the basis of his personal qualifications.

A comparatively recent development which may have some influence on the Negro's position in business is the "don't buy where you can't work" campaign which started over a decade ago.[a] On its face, this movement is an attempt to get Negro workers into white-owned stores, but it may be considered here because, in part, it is stimulated by Negro businessmen who hope to attract Negro customers away from white-owned business. The right of the Negro to boycott and picket establishments which discriminate against him was long contested from a legal standpoint. It was not until 1938 that this right was finally established through a decision by the Supreme Court.[17] This made it possible for the movement to develop.

The direct purpose of the movement is to increase the number of Negroes employed in white-owned stores, movie theaters and other establishments in Negro districts. Since usually the aim is not to remove white workers already employed but only to make the establishments hire some proportion of Negroes when new workers are taken on, the results cannot immediately be of great quantitative significance for Negro employment. The comparatively small number of white collar workers in most stores with large Negro patronage indicates that even the complete success of the movement must be rather limited. There may be some secondary results, however, in that a number of Negroes receive practical training in efficiently managed businesses—a training which is badly needed but for which there has been little opportunity so far. It may eventually broaden the basis for the recruiting of Negro entrepreneurs. Reid points out that this boycott movement has been used mainly in the urban North where the Negro has greater political and citizenship rights than in the South.[18] Too, it is probably principally in the North that there are a great number of white-owned stores in Negro areas which are large enough to have any employees of white collar status.[19]

Since the boycott movement has had but a few years of full freedom from legal restraint—and in the South, of course, is still met with severe intimidation—one can, perhaps, expect more from it in the future, particularly if the organizations behind it become stronger and more permanent. But we should not forget the limitations of this strategy. Even if all jobs in white stores in Negro sections were given to Negroes, it would be just a drop in the bucket compared with the number of jobs Negroes need to have. The Negro's main concern must be to break down job segregation and job discrimination in the white economy. He might even—as some Negro writers point out[20]—jeopardize this greater objective by asking for

[a] From an ideological and organizational point of view this movement will be treated in Chapters 38 and 39.

all-Negro personnel in Negro neighborhood stores. For this reason he has to content himself with removing practices of complete exclusion of Negroes in such establishments. Not even the ultimate gains can be large under these circumstances.

The very fact, however, that one of the Negro's most spectacular fights for economic improvement has been directed on such rather limited objectives is an indication of how desperate his situation really is. One can well understand his excitement about it. The all-white establishment in the Negro neighborhood has been an offense that he could not possibly be expected to stomach. Even allowing for a possible greater success in the future of the "don't buy where you can't work" campaign, one finds no trend toward any real decisive improvement in the Negro's position in business. He may get a slightly better representation among the white collar workers, and there may be more Negroes who would become competent entrepreneurs. But the days have passed when there was much of a future for the small entrepreneur generally, whether Negro or white.

3. Negro Finance

Since the credit situation certainly has been one of the major obstacles barring the way for the Negro businessman, it is possible that the chances for the Negro in trade might have been somewhat better had he been able to gain a position in the field of finance. But the Negro has been, and still is, almost completely insignificant as a banker. There were not even 1,000 Negro bankers, brokers, cashiers, and other white collar workers in banks in 1930 (Table 2), or less than one for every 600 white workers in such occupations.

The story of the Negro in banking is a story about a handful of fairly successful small institutions—and a somewhat larger number of failures. The Negro has made more progress in the field of insurance. In 1930 there were 9,000 Negro officials and white collar workers in this business, but they constituted scarcely 2 per cent of the national total.[21] It is a well-known fact that one white company has more Negro business than have all Negro-owned establishments together.

Already before the Civil War there were numerous Negro attempts in the field of banking, but the Freedmen's Savings Bank and Trust Company —backed by the Freedmen's Bureau—represented the first noteworthy attempt in the field. It had branches in 36 cities and had an almost phenomenal success; its total deposits at one time reached $57,000,000. Although most of the deposits were covered by United States securities, there was some unwise use of reserve funds, and this contributed to the failure of the bank in the depression of 1874. This event cooled the enthusiasm of the Negroes for ventures of this kind for a long time. Sir George Campbell, traveling in the South during the late 'seventies, had this to report:

I hear much of the Freedman's Savings Bank, which failed with a loss of 4,000,-000, which has never been replaced; and the loss causes much distrust among Negroes inclined to save.[22]

The Capital Savings Bank in Washington started in 1888 and failed in 1904, partly because of unwise and speculative investments and partly because of misappropriation of funds. During the early 1900's a great number of Negro banks were founded, but most of them disappeared after a short time. The bankruptcy rate of small white banks also was high during this period. Conditions became somewhat better, however, after the organization of a state bank inspection system in 1910. In 1940 there were 14 members of the National Negro Bankers Association (organized in 1924).

Today many Negro banks, like almost all white-managed banks, have their deposits insured by the Federal Deposit Insurance Corporation. Although Negro banks certainly are much safer than they used to be, they suffer from several shortcomings. For one thing, they are small, which tends to make operating costs high. This is claimed to be one of the reasons why they invest relatively less in low-yielding government securities than do most other banks. Investments are made in Negro real estate, but they are not easily negotiable, because of the restricted market for Negro property. Financial interests in Negro business are often quite unsafe. A comparatively large part of the borrowers use the loans for consumption rather than for production purposes. Because of the poverty of the Negroes and the relative weakness of most Negro banks, only a small minority of all Negro families residing in localities where Negro banks exist have any savings or checking accounts with them. Some writers believe, however, that Negro banks have brought about certain secondary beneficial effects; white banks are said to treat Negro customers with greater respect whenever there is a competing Negro bank in the locality. It may happen, on the other hand, that the presence of a Negro bank gives the white banks an excuse for advising Negro customers to use their own bank.[23]

The difficulties of the Negroes who wanted to build their own homes and were almost entirely unable to get any assistance from white financial institutions was one of the main driving forces behind the foundation of Negro-managed building and loan associations. The first one started in Virginia in 1883. These associations have shown great progress, but also there have been a great number of failures. By 1930 there were some 70-odd Negro associations with assets totaling $6,600,000, or less than 1 per cent of the total assets of all American building and loan associations. The depression hit the whole group of institutions severely. The Negro institutions were hurt somewhat more than were the white associations, and, by 1938, there were about 50 Negro building and loan associations—22 of which were in Pennsylvania—with combined assets of $3,600,000. It is significant that some of the most successful Negro-managed institutions had a partly white clientele, which means that they had a larger business and a greater diversification of risks than they otherwise could have had, if all the activities were concentrated in one or a few Negro neighborhoods.

Most Negro associations, however, are small, which tends to make costs rather high. The actual average interest rate charged on building loans in 1935-1938 was between 7 and 8 per cent, which was somewhat higher than that charged by white-managed institutions. Obviously, it is practically only upper and upper middle class Negro families who can afford to use them for the purpose of financing their homes. It seems that, at least until 1938, few of the Negro establishments had started to use federal insurance in order to safeguard the depositors and the shareholders, and but a handful of them were affiliated with the Federal Home Loan Bank system. Some of the associations may have done some Federal Housing Administration business, but in all probability it was less than for white-operated institutions. These various federal-sponsored services, by which deposits are made secure, loans inexpensive, operations more rational, and building programs better planned, have more or less revolutionized the whole system of credit, particularly in the housing field. It is a safe bet that Negro-managed institutions will have increased difficulties in competing, unless they are willing and able to qualify for such services, and the various federal credit and housing agencies are prepared to put in some special efforts in order to do something about the Negro's desperate need for better housing.[24]

The fact that Negroes have made much better headway in the life insurance business is due to several factors. For one thing, ever since the 1880's, Negroes have been subject to differential treatment by white insurance companies in that some of them, at that time, started to apply higher premium schedules for Negro than for white customers, whereas others decided not to take on any Negro business at all.[25] The underlying reason, of course, is the fact that mortality rates are much higher for Negroes than for whites.[a] This, however, is a social and economic, rather than a racial, phenomenon, and most Negroes in the upper and middle classes must consider the practice as highly discriminatory. And even when this differential treatment is economically justifiable from the point of view of the life insurance companies, it is only natural that it must be resented by all Negroes, and that they will be inclined to get around it by founding their own insurance institutions.

Discriminatory practices have been followed by other white financial institutions as well. But there is this difference: insurance is used even among the poorest families, Negro as well as white, in America. Sometimes the majority of all families with an income of but $500-$1,000 have some form of insurance, and even among those with less than $500, usually a

[a] See Chapter 7.

quite substantial percentage pays insurance premiums.[26] This type of low-income insurance is, at best, mainly burial insurance. At worst, it gives little, if any, protection, in that persons who are not likely to keep up their payments for more than a few years are induced to take life insurance.[27]

But even when payments are kept up and small life insurance policies reach maturity, they usually fail to give real protection for anybody except the mortician. The burial business in most countries tends to be more or less of a racket, capitalizing on the reluctance of the relatives of a deceased person to economize the last time they can make any sacrifices for him. The American mortician business is no exception. The prices quoted in this country often appear high, at least to an outsider.[28] One cannot avoid the impression that great ingenuity is used to induce even poor patrons to buy unnecessary luxuries. This happens in the Negro communities as well.

We have found that the Negro undertakers numbered around 3,000 in 1930, and that they constituted not far from one-tenth of the total number of such professionals in the country. In other words, one of the few groups of entrepreneurs which has almost the same proportion of Negroes as has the general population happens to be one of those most likely to exploit the consumer. This, incidentally, does not reflect so much on the Negro as on the general pattern of this business. The Negro has had a chance as an undertaker because of the character of his work; corpses usually are segregated even more meticulously than live people. Then, too, there is a close relation between this business and the churches and lodges which are almost completely segregated, both South and North. And Negro insurance men often work hand in hand with the morticians.[29]

Like other Negro financial institutions, the Negro insurance business was originally based in a large measure on Negro church congregations and lodges. This is not to be wondered at, for white-managed insurance has developed similarly. The most direct origin of the insurance company, of course, is the benevolent society, of which there are a great number among the Negroes. New Orleans alone, in the middle of the 'thirties, had several hundred Negro benevolent societies. One of these was founded in the 1780's. It is obvious that most of these societies are extremely small and that they cannot be organized on particularly rational principles or be made to work efficiently. It is not unusual that as much as one-third, or even more, of the expenditures is for administrative purposes, particularly officers' salaries, which means that the sick and burial benefits have to be reduced in proportion.[30]

In 1939 there were 67 Negro insurance companies with 1,677,000 policies and a total income of $13,000,000. They gave employment to about 8,000 workers. Those were the Negro companies which had weathered the depression during the 'thirties. Some of them, nevertheless, have serious shortcomings.[31]

When evaluating the Negro's performance in the world of finance, one should not overlook the fact that similar white institutions have once passed through a period when inefficient and even irregular practices prevailed. In the case of banks and of building and loan associations, that time was not so long ago. The early 'thirties, when thousands of banks failed, revealed some appalling weaknesses in American banking organization. Thus, the difference in performance between Negro- and white-managed institutions may, in part, be a difference in the stage of development. This is not to say, however, that there is much prospect that there will be a second stage in the development when Negro institutions will grow strong enough to be comparable in quality with white financial establishments. The Negro-managed bank and insurance company will not get away from the fact that the Negroes are poor and that the segregated Negro community cannot offer any range of investment opportunities such that investment risk can be minimized.

Indeed, it is difficult to see a real future for a segregated Negro financial system. Basically, it is nothing but a poor substitute for what the Negroes really need: employment of Negroes in white-dominated financial institutions and more consideration for them as insurance or credit seekers.

4. THE NEGRO TEACHER

In 1930 over 5 per cent of all male workers in nonagricultural pursuits and almost 15 per cent of the female nonfarm workers were professionals, that is, teachers, clergymen, physicians, dentists, trained nurses, musicians, artists. The corresponding figures for Negro workers were much lower: 2.6 and 4.5 per cent, respectively.[32] Thus the Negro's chance of getting a job as a professional was only one-third or one-half that of the white worker. Still, compared with the Negro's chances in other "higher" occupations, this is a relatively good record.

For the total American population, the professional occupations had about the same relative importance in the nonagricultural economy in the South as in the North. For Negroes, however, it was different, particularly for women. In the South, more than 5 per cent of the Negro female workers were in professional occupations. The corresponding figure for the North was less than 3 per cent.[33] The main reason, of course, is that the Negro's chances in the teaching profession are much smaller in the North than in the South.

School teaching, of course, is the principal Negro profession. Yet Negroes did not have more than about half the representation in the teaching profession as in the total population. There has been a spectacular increase in the number of Negro teachers, but the white school system, too, has been growing rapidly, so that since 1910 the relative gain for Negroes was limited, except on the college level.[34] By and large, the limitations in the

Negro teaching profession are those of Negro education in general—a subject dealt with elsewhere in this book.[a] Where there are segregated schools the Negro teacher has usually a complete monopoly on the jobs in Negro schools.[b] Where schools are mixed, Negroes have difficulty in getting in.

The Negro teacher in the segregated school has a heavier teaching load than has the white teacher. In Southern elementary schools for Negroes

TABLE 3

PRINCIPAL GROUPS OF NEGRO PROFESSIONAL WORKERS: 1910 AND 1930

Groups	Number of Negro Workers		Negro Workers as a Percentage of all Workers	
	1910	1930	1910	1930
Teachers (school)	29,432	54,439	4.9	5.2
Clergymen	17,495	25,034	14.8	16.8
Musicians and teachers of music	5,666	10,583	4.0	6.4
Trained nurses	2,433	5,587	3.0	1.9
Actors and showmen	2,345	4,130	4.8	5.5
Physicians, surgeons, veterinaries	3,199	3,939	2.0	2.4
College presidents and professors	242	2,146	1.5	3.5
Dentists	478	1,773	1.2	2.5
Lawyers	779	1,175	0.7	0.8

Source: Thirteenth Census of the United States: 1910, Population, Vol. 4, pp. 428-431; and Fifteenth Census of the United States: 1930, Population, Vol. 5, pp. 574-576.

there were 43 pupils for every teacher in 1933-1934, as against a ratio of 34 in schools for white children.[35] This means that 26 per cent more Negro teachers would be needed in Southern elementary and secondary schools if the pupil load in Negro schools were to be brought down to the white level. And the need would be even greater if differences in school attendance were to be eliminated. While Negro teachers had less education than white teachers, on the average, the discrepancy in educational attainment was much smaller than that in salary.[c] The average salary in Southern Negro elementary schools in 1935-1936 was only $510; in Southern white schools it was $833. The corresponding figures for Mississippi alone were

[a] See Chapter 15, Section 3; Chapter 41; and Chapter 43, Section 4.

[b] The only important exceptions are some private colleges.

[c] Almost 25 per cent of the Negro teachers in Southern elementary schools had received no formal education beyond high school, compared to 6 per cent of the white teachers. The difference was less marked, however, in respect to the proportions of those having at least three years of college; they were 22 and 28 per cent, respectively.

$247 and $783, respectively, but in the District of Columbia Negro and white teachers earned an identical high-average salary of $2,376. Apart from the District of Columbia, Delaware, and Missouri, every Southern state paid lower salaries to Negroes than to whites.[36] When the school term is over, the Negro teacher, more often than the white teacher, has to take up some other gainful work—often in domestic service or in agriculture.

Indeed, there are few major cases of racial wage discrimination so clear-cut and so pronounced as that found in the teaching profession in the South. In most other cases there is not so much direct wage discrimination as there is a tendency to let whites monopolize jobs in skilled occupations or in high-paying and expanding industries. Those having the political power in the South have shown a firm determination to maintain these salary differentials in the Negro schools. The writer has heard several rationalizations for it.[a] The only one which has any logical validity is that Negro teachers are not so well trained as whites. But even this argument is not strong. The trouble with it is not only that salary differentials certainly are larger than the differences in competence—and that they exist even when the excuse does not apply—but also that the argument has the character of a vicious circle. By keeping down all appropriations for all kinds of Negro schools,[b] including teachers' colleges, one can, of course, perpetuate the inferiority of training. Frequently Southern school authorities have even gone so far as to hire Negro teachers without teaching certificates only because they could have them at sub-standard salaries.[37]

These facts of discrimination in Negro teachers' salaries have been well known and openly discussed for a long time. Recently, under the general direction of the N.A.A.C.P., the inequality in teachers' salaries has been taken before the courts. Teachers' salary differentials based on race alone were declared unconstitutional in 1940.[38] This court decision and the continued fight in many Southern states have not persuaded Southern school authorities to retreat from their illegal practice. Only the state of Maryland and a few other localities have abided by the decision. Otherwise those states and communities that have shown any readiness to comply have usually contented themselves with plans for a gradual equalization over a period of years. When Negro teachers considered these periods too long, or when the authorities were absolutely unwilling to comply, new court cases were introduced.[39] In spite of this delay, equalization of teachers' salaries is under way in the South. The coming rise in the economic status of the largest Negro professional group will represent a change of no small importance. It is quite likely that it will have certain beneficial secondary effects on Negro education and on Negro leadership.

[a] See Chapter 9, Section 4. See also Horace Mann Bond, *The Education of the Negro in the American Social Order* (1934), pp. 270-271.

[b] See Chapter 15, Section 3.

5. THE NEGRO MINISTER

Clergymen constitute the second largest group among Negro "professional" workers. They also enjoy a complete monopoly behind the caste wall. The ministry is the only profession in which Negroes have more representatives than they have in the general population (Table 3). There are several possible reasons for the large number of Negro ministers: that Negroes are more divided in their religious interest than whites; that restricted opportunities in other desirable fields make a larger number of Negroes become preachers; that more Negroes attend church than do whites.[a]

The educational level of Negro ministers shows great variations; the average is extremely low.[b] The same is true of salaries. A few large Negro churches may pay as much as from $5,000 to $7,500 a year, and salaries of $3,000 or more are not infrequent in the larger city churches. At the other extreme are those ministers, particularly in rural areas, who have to be content with a salary of a few hundred dollars a year or with a fluctuating collection.[40] It goes without saying that a great number of Negro clergymen have to have other employment on the side; it may even be that the ministry is a sideline which gives them their opportunities in other occupations. Some ministers are teachers. Others may be farmers or laborers. Sometimes ministers are offered free shares in business enterprises in return for using their influence in behalf of such economic ventures.[41] Some Negro ministers are associated with morticians. Small gifts from benevolent whites also play a role in many Negro ministers' budgets. Their outside economic connections give some Negro ministers an extra influence over their congregations.[c] The income of many a minister of a small congregation "depends solely upon his ability to demand it from the members for religious purposes."[42] In the Holiness and the Church of God congregations it has been usual that pastors demand a tithe. Even plain misappropriation of money has occurred: once three bishops of the Methodist Church were suspended for this reason.[43]

Although many Negro ministers have been guilty, at one time or another, of these malpractices, it does not follow that they are characteristic of the entire Negro clergy. Part of the explanation is that the position of most

[a] See Chapter 40. While over 16 per cent of all clergymen in 1930 were Negroes, the value of the Negro church edifices in 1926 did not constitute more than about 5 per cent of that of all church buildings in the United States. Even this, however, is a pretty good record compared with the Negro's share in the entire property valuation of the United States which amounted to about 2 per cent (See Carter G. Woodson, *The Negro Professional Man and the Community* [1934], p. 66.)

[b] See Chapter 40.

[c] See Chapter 40.

Negro ministers is marginal and insecure, that their educational level is low, and that they have to sell out to the whites in the South where the latter demand it.

In Chapter 40 we shall deal with the future prospects of the Negro church. It is losing out among the young people, mostly because the Negro preacher has lagged behind the rest of the Negro community and, particularly, behind other professionals, in acquiring a better education. Still the Negro church retains its hold over the Negro community and will continue to give livelihood to a large proportion of Negro professionals.

6. THE NEGRO IN MEDICAL PROFESSIONS

The total number of physicians, surgeons, and veterinaries in the United States was almost stationary between 1910 and 1930. The number of Negro doctors, on the other hand, increased by almost one-fourth (Table 3). The main reason for this is that Negroes have migrated to the North and to cities, where they are more inclined to patronize doctors, and especially Negro doctors. The overwhelming majority of Negro physicians reside in cities, and particularly in large cities.[44] Since the Negro urban population almost doubled during this same period, there was actually a decline in the Negro physician-to-population ratio if we count only communities which are served at all by Negro doctors. In 1930 the Negro's representation in the medical professions, for the whole country, was less than one-fourth that of the whites. There has been no appreciable change since then. In 1940 there were about 4,000 Negro physicians and surgeons,[45] and, if we add the veterinaries, the number was only slightly higher.

There are several reasons for the limitations in the opportunities for the Negro doctor. Most whites would not ordinarily turn to a physician of Negro extraction—partly because of race prejudice, partly because they would not trust his ability. There are some significant exceptions, however, particularly in certain Northern, Eastern, and West Coast centers, where over half the Negro physicians in Woodson's sample said that they had some white patients, mainly among the immigrants. Even in the South it occasionally happens that white patients go to a Negro doctor. But this practice is largely—though not always—of a questionable character, in that some white patients want to conceal venereal diseases and pregnancy from their white friends.[46] In the upland areas of the South—for instance in West Virginia, western Virginia, North Carolina, eastern Tennessee, and so on—where race prejudice is less intense, there are a few Negro doctors who have quite a sizeable white practice. Some of it, of course, consists of cases of abortion and venereal disease, but there are also others, partly because low income whites often have difficulty in getting service from other than inefficient white doctors.[47]

This white clientele has never been large. It is possible that it is shrinking with the assimilation of immigrants and with the gradual institution of public health services for low income families. The Negro doctor, in the main, must depend on Negro patronage. And the overwhelming majority of both the white and the Negro patients of the Negro doctor are poor. Expenditures of private families for medical care increase with income at least proportionately, and sometimes more than proportionately.[48]

Only some of the dollars expended by Negro families on doctor's fees are paid to Negro physicians. Carter G. Woodson, on the basis of certain inquiries he has made, tentatively estimates the proportion of the Negro trade that goes to the Negro doctor to be about 60 per cent. He complains about

> ... the large number of Negro leaders who after preaching race patronage and even boasting of our competent physicians and surgeons as proof of race progress, nevertheless have employed white surgeons in undergoing operations.[49]

He goes on to explain how the trade the Negro doctor gets is not always indicative of any original appreciation of his competence among the Negro people. It has happened that white physicians have had to talk to Negro patients in order to make them believe that doctors of their own race are any good. Often it is only because white physicians want to restrict their practice to white patients that Negroes turn to Negro doctors.[50]

Another reason for the limitation of opportunities for Negro doctors is the fact that most public health services in the South are poorer, in relation to the need, for Negroes than for whites.[a] Even when there are facilities for Negro patients, it does not always mean that they offer any work opportunities for the Negro doctor. White professionals take care of the patients both in the white section and in the "colored wing" of a typical Southern hospital. Dorn observes:

> Until the Flint-Goodridge Hospital was built in New Orleans with the assistance of the Rosenwald Fund and the General Education Board, there was not a single modern hospital in Louisiana where a Negro physician could practice. In Mississippi ... there are no modern hospitals where a Negro physician may take his patients. A corresponding situation prevails in most of the other southern states. North and South Carolina are an exception due mainly to the assistance of the Duke Endowment Fund.[51]

There are only a few hospitals in the United States, such as Harlem Hospital in New York City, where Negro and white doctors work together under a system of absolute equality. Concerning the situation in the South, Reid says:

> Even in cities like Atlanta and Richmond where white medical colleges have control over large public wards of local hospitals, Negro physicians are not permitted

[a] See Chapter 15, Section 4.

to participate in their programs. When the Negro physician receives his degree in medicine and is licensed to practice there is little distinction between his training and that of any other American physician—but the equality ends there, for race proscription then begins. Opportunities for internships and residences are circumscribed, hospital and clinical facilities are denied, membership in county medical and other professional and scientific societies is refused (in the South). Hence the Negro physician becomes the general practitioner par excellence—isolated and serving a low income group.[52]

The prospects of the Negro physician are becoming increasingly uncertain because of the present growth of all kinds of public health facilities. This trend cannot fail to take the low income clientele away from the private practitioner, and this, of course, means that the Negro doctor may lose almost all his patients unless he is given a place in the new public health system. Many Negro doctors, particularly in the South, are quite pessimistic about their chances of getting such a place, and, for this reason, one sometimes finds the most ardent opponents of any program of "socialized medicine" among Negro doctors.[53] They are undoubtedly right in assuming that an extension of the public health services to low income families would constitute a tremendous risk from their point of view. At the same time, however, there are definite possibilities for them in such a development; if they do succeed in getting a fair representation on the public health programs, there will be more employment for them, since these programs must cause a tremendous increase in the use of medical services among low income groups.

The fact that the Negro doctor has such small opportunities for hospital training and specialized work is the reason why there is some justification for the belief that the Negro is less well trained than the white man as a physician or surgeon. The basic training is generally considered adequate. Only a small minority of Negro doctors are trained at white schools. About four-fifths of them get their education at two Negro medical schools: Meharry in Nashville, Tennessee, and Howard in Washington, D.C. The percentage of failures at state board examinations is about the same for graduates of Negro schools as for graduates of white schools.[54] It is obvious, however, that these institutions cannot offer any wide range of opportunities for specialized work.[55]

According to a sample study by Johnson—which contained 510 cases—the median income of the Negro doctors was $2,726.41 in 1936.[56] Nevertheless, some Negro physicians were comparatively wealthy men. Woodson found a few having fortunes of over $50,000. A large proportion of the Negro physicians, however, get a considerable part of their income from sources other than their practice. Several of them work for Negro insurance companies and benevolent societies. Some have made fortunes in real estate. There are those who own drug stores. Others have their own private hospitals, benefiting from a monopoly arising from segregation in public health service.[a] There are observers who characterize some of these business practices as exploitative. In addition, they help to keep down the professional record of the Negro doctor.[57]

Having dealt at such great length with the conditions of the Negro physician, we can content ourselves by touching on the rather similar problems of the Negro in other medical professions. There were only 5,600 Negro nurses in 1930, constituting less than 2 per cent of the total number of nurses in the United States (Table 3). The reason why the proportion of Negroes is even smaller among the nurses than among the physicians is obvious: nurses cannot count on much private practice; usually they have to depend on the public health system, which offers few opportunities for Negro professionals. One would expect, however, that these limitations would be somewhat less rigorous in respect to nurses, since it would seem to be inconsistent with Southern ideas to let white women care for Negro male patients. But a solution to this delicate problem has been found other than that of letting the Negro nurse monopolize the work in the colored hospital wings. White nurses may treat Negro patients, but they are assisted by Negro maids who do most of the dirty work.[58]

The Negro dentist has a position much like that of the Negro physician.[59] He may have some white trade, particularly among foreigners in the North, but also in some Southern communities. On the other hand, large numbers of Negro patients turn to white dentists, in spite of the fact that, in the South at least, they are treated on a segregated basis, with separate instruments, in a separate chair. The fact that Negro dentists, like other Negro professionals, have little representation in rural areas, forces many Negroes to use white dentists even if they want to go to a Negro. The average income of the Negro dentist is somewhat lower than that of the Negro doctor. Like the physician, he is often a businessman on the side. In his practice he may, sometimes, be unethical. It is often alleged that there is a group of Negro dentists—the so-called "glorified blacksmiths"—who satisfy the vanity of patients by decorating sound teeth with gold or by substituting more beautiful artificial teeth for healthy natural teeth. The writer has been told by some observers, however, that this pattern is gradually declining, owing to the rising educational level of the patients.

7. OTHER NEGRO PROFESSIONALS

Potentially, there should be great opportunities for Negro lawyers. So often is the Negro wronged—in the South at least—and so little do most white people understand his plight, that there should be a tremendous need for Negro attorneys to assist Negro clients. Actually, however, the

[a] It has even happened, in Detroit for instance, that municipalities which do not want to accept Negro patients in city hospitals subsidize second-rate Negro-owned institutions.

legal insecurity of the Negro is such that the Negro attorney often has but little chance before a Southern court.[a] Protection by a "respectable" white person usually counts more in the South for a Negro client than would even the best representation on the part of a Negro lawyer.

In 1930 less than 1 per cent of all lawyers were Negroes (Table 3). Almost two-thirds of the 1,200 Negro lawyers resided outside the South. Most Negro lawyers are the products of white law schools in the North. In Mississippi there were but 6 Negro lawyers, as against more than 1,200 white lawyers. The corresponding figures for Alabama were 4 and 1,600, respectively. Of all those in the South only a minority are believed to devote themselves to their law practice, and rarely do they appear in court to defend Negro clients against white parties. Their main legal work concerns internal Negro affairs, such as those connected with churches, fraternal associations, domestic relations and criminal matters.[60]

In 1930 there were less than 1,000 Negroes registered as social workers. The New Deal, however, has brought about a tremendous change in this respect. According to a recent estimate made by Forrester B. Washington, there were over 4,000 Negro social workers in 1940. It is significant that more than half of these were in the North.[61] The South certainly has a smaller representation of Negroes on social work staffs than corresponds to the relative relief needs of the Negro population. This is so for two reasons. One is that, particularly in rural areas of the South, it is usually more difficult for Negroes than for whites in similar economic circumstances to get on the relief rolls.[b] A second reason is that most Negro public assistance clients in the South are handled by white workers. This is quite understandable. The new institution of large-scale public relief for both whites and Negroes in the South has been received with rather mixed feelings by those in power. The appointment of numerous Negro relief officials would have increased the resentment tremendously.[62]

Under such circumstances, it seems like something of an achievement that the Negro, even in a state like Mississippi, is at all represented in the social work profession. There are now Negro case-workers all over the South. Some N.Y.A. officials are Negroes. Negro housing projects usually have Negro management, at least in part. There are Negro officials in the Farm Security Administration and in farm and home extension work.[c] This progress is due, largely, to the influence of the federal government. Then, too, Negroes have had the benefit of two rather good schools of social work, one at Howard University and the other at Atlanta University.

---

[a] See Chapter 26.

[b] See Chapter 15.

[c] Concerning the under-representation of Negroes among farm and home demonstration agents, see Chapter 12, Section 11.

8. NEGRO OFFICIALS AND WHITE COLLAR WORKERS IN PUBLIC SERVICE

In previous sections we have touched upon certain groups of Negro officials and white collar workers, all or some of whom are employed in public service: teachers, physicians and surgeons, nurses, social workers, extension service workers and so on. These categories include the majority of all Negro workers of higher than wage earner status employed by federal, state or county agencies.

The largest of the remaining occupations is postal service, which had 18,000 Negro workers in 1930, of whom 7,000 were clerks, 6,000 were mail carriers and the rest were in various minor categories. This meant a trebling in Negro postal employment since 1910, whereas the number of white workers had increased to a far lesser extent. The gain was due, mainly, to the development outside the South. In Northern states Negroes generally had many more representatives, in proportion, among the postal employees than in the total population, but in the South—and particularly in the Deep South—they were grossly under-represented in the postal service.[63]

In other public services[a] there were scarcely 6,000 Negro officials and white collar workers in 1930, constituting only about 1 per cent of the total. Of these, less than 2,000 were policemen, sheriffs, and detectives; and more than 3,000 were clerks and kindred workers; the remaining 1,000 were in a large variety of other categories.[64] There had been some increase since 1910, but this seems to have been due largely to the development in some Northern state and municipal administrations.[65]

Negroes were driven out of Southern state and local government service after Reconstruction. The decline of Negroes in federal jobs was more gradual. During the Wilson administration, the Negro's position in the federal government became even more critical than previously. The number of Negro postmasters declined from 153 in 1910 to 78 in 1930, and several other Negro officials of the federal government were removed. Segregation was introduced into Washington offices where it had scarcely occurred before. The rule was devised that federal agencies, when employing civil servants, were allowed to choose among the three applicants with the highest rating. Later exclusion of Negroes was made even easier by the requirement that every applicant was to supply his photograph.[66] Moton observed that ". . . an almost perfect system had been devised for eliminating Negroes without violating any specific regulation or officially sanctioning discrimination on account of race."[67] Its effects on the employment of Negroes in federal service was counteracted, to some extent, because of the expansion in the federal administration during the First

[a] The armed forces are discussed in Chapter 19, Section 4.

World War and—at least in the case of postal service—the rapid increase in number of Negro voters in the North.[68]

The New Deal had a more friendly attitude toward employment of Negroes in the federal administration, and this trend has become even more apparent during the present war emergency when the federal government, as well as certain state and municipal governments, have become increasingly concerned about racial discrimination.[a] There are no statistical data available at this time that would enable us to get any idea about how great the improvement has been. We know that the Negroes have made appreciable gains in the number of white collar and higher jobs in public service. But as the general expansion has been extremely rapid ever since the inauguration of the New Deal, it is not even certain that the proportion of Negroes in such positions has increased.

The stipulation about appending photographs to job applications has recently been abolished. This does not mean that discrimination cannot go on. It is almost always possible to ascertain the race of the person certified.[b] Professional workers are almost never employed without having had an interview with the official under whom they are to work. For this reason there are—outside of the special divisions for Negro affairs—only a few Negro federal workers having professional status. When a newly appointed person turns out to be a Negro, it is possible to find his work unsatisfactory and to have him dismissed after a while. Also there is always the possibility of barring Negroes from advancement. In most offices, Negroes—either voluntarily or involuntarily—sit together. Negro stenographers seldom get assignments as private secretaries; most of them work in "pools."[69] In some places there is a more or less rigid segregation in cafeterias, but there are other places where such segregational patterns have been broken up.[70]

The future prospects, of course, are uncertain, but there is more hope for the Negro in public service than in most other work. Government work, for one thing, is steadily expanding; after the War there will, perhaps, be a temporary reduction, particularly of the federal payrolls, but the general trend, more likely than not, will continue upward. Then, too, employment in public service is susceptible to political pressure. It will take a long time, of course, before any efficient pro-Negro pressure can be brought on Southern administrations. On the other hand, it seems that Negroes have not yet exhausted their present possibilities of forcing the federal government and the Northern state governments to employ an increased number of Negro workers. The principle of nondiscrimination is there established and undisputed. The present war emergency, the realization of the low morale among Negroes, and the new consciousness of the American Creed are

[a] See Chapter 19.
[b] See Chapter 19.

forcing the authorities to take action against racial discrimination in civil service.[a]

9. Negro Professionals of the Stage, Screen and Orchestra

The Negro is often praised for his artistic talents—frequently in a rather derogatory way, for the implication is that this is the only domain where he is capable of noteworthy achievements. Many white persons know the names of some outstanding Negro singers and jazz-band leaders, and believe that this is the one professional field where the Negro has been able to make good. He has succeeded in this field to a certain extent, but even here his representation is not as great as in the total population. In the 1930 Census there were about 15,000 Negroes registered as musicians, teachers of music, actors, showmen, and showgirls, and this figure constituted only about 6 per cent of the national total.[71] It is probable that it includes a great number of persons who were not competent, and that many made most of their income in other occupations, including illegal work, such as prostitution.[b] This is true, of course, in respect to many white workers as well.

It is obvious that the competition must be much keener among Negro than among white artists, and this probably for two reasons. The market is smaller, and a number of ambitious Negroes, who, had they been white, would have had a range of good careers to choose from, are likely to try the artistic profession as almost the only one which seems to hold any promise. The relative limitations of the market formerly were even greater than they are now. Before about 1915, Negroes could not make up much of an audience, partly because few of them lived in cities, and it took some time before white people got into the habit of seeing performances of Negro showmen. Even when Negro characters were presented to white audiences, the parts were originally played by whites. This was true of one of the earlier classical caricatures of Negro life, the "Jump Jim Crow," given from 1830 on. After that came a series of so-called minstrels, who were white showmen with blackened faces.[c] Soon, however, Negroes were allowed to help as assistants, and eventually they started out on their own.[72]

The northward migration has helped the Negro artist tremendously. The number of artists doubled between 1910 and 1930, whereas the increase for white artists was far smaller. The majority of Negro workers in this profession are in the North.[73] They are particularly concentrated in New York, which has one permanent Negro stage, the Apollo Theater. In addition, there are intermittent opportunities for Negro actors at down-

[a] See Chapter 19.
[b] However, less than one-third of these 15,000 Negro artists were women.
[c] See Chapter 44, Section 5.

town theaters. Nightclubs, dancing halls, and other places, both in white and in Negro sections, provide additional employment. Most of these places are owned by whites, even though the entertainers are entirely Negro.[74] There are a few hundred Negro artists in Hollywood, but the pattern of using Negroes almost exclusively as extras or in minor parts—which, with a few exceptions, caricature the Negro—makes the economic opportunities for the Negro screen actor extremely limited. In 1935, for example, the total salaries paid to Negro actors by the film industry did not amount to more than $57,000.[75] Negro musicians usually belong to the powerful American Federation of Musicians (A. F. of L.). In the South they are generally organized in separate locals, and the same segregational practice prevails in many Northern cities as well. New York is one of the few centers where Negro musicians are treated as equals by the union. White locals often have jurisdiction over radio stations, theaters, and other large places of employment, and Negro musicians, in such cases, cannot work there without special permission from their white competitors.[76]

10. NOTE ON SHADY OCCUPATIONS

In the cities, particularly in the big cities, there is a Negro "underworld."[77] To it belong not only petty thieves and racketeers, prostitutes and pimps, bootleggers, dope addicts, and so on,[a] but also a number of "big shots" organizing and controlling crime, vice, and racketeering, as well as other more innocent forms of illegal activity such as gambling—particularly the "policy," or the "numbers," game. The underworld has, therefore, an upper class and a middle class as well as a lower class.

The shady upper class is composed mainly of the "policy" kings. They are the most important members of the underworld from the point of view of their numbers, their wealth and their power. The policy game started in the Negro community[78] and has a long history.[79] This game caught on quickly among Negroes because one may bet as little as a penny, and the rewards are high if one wins (as much as 600 to 1). In a community where most of the people are either on relief or in the lowest income brackets such rewards must appear exceptionally alluring. The average amounts bet each year, however, often amount to a staggering sum in relation to the average incomes in the Negro community,[80] and the financial return is, of course, nothing for most people. From the entrepreneur's point of view, the game is a sure thing. During most of its history the policy racket in the Negro community has been monopolized by Negroes.[81] Otherwise respectable businessmen have had a controlling interest in the numbers racket[82] (perhaps because large returns in other enterprises were rare), and many *bona fide* gangsters often own real estate and

---

[a] Crime statistics, as further explained in Chapter 44, Section 2, give a grossly exaggerated idea of how Negro crime and vice compare with white crime.

other Negro businesses, partly as a "front" to give respectability to their gambling enterprise and partly as normal and sound investments for their profits.

While the members of the shady upper class are not accepted by the respectable Negro upper and middle classes, the observer finds that they have a great deal of status in the eyes of lower class Negroes and are not greatly condemned by agencies for Negro concerted action or by the Negro press. There are several reasons for this. Most important is the fact that the policy "kings" are wealthy, and that they are generous in a poor community.[83] Also significant is the fact that when the organized white gangs became interested in the numbers racket, many of the original Negro entrepreneurs, having grown wealthy and not liking violent criminal activities, retired; they thus acquired a sort of second-hand and late respectability. Negroes have not usually been organized into gangs involved in all kinds of criminal activities as have the white gangs; they tend to be individual entrepreneurs usually in the gambling rackets and in machine politics—businesses which are illegal but tacitly accepted by public opinion.

The power of these big racket kings is derived not only from their wealth and their political tie-ups, but from the fact that they provide a large number of jobs in a poor and unemployed community. The numbers racket requires a great number of middlemen who are small fry from the point of view of those at the top but who are not only rich in relation to most members of the community but also lead a free and easy, rather romantic and exciting life.[84] The young Negro fresh from the rural South is even more impressed than is the Northern Negro youth, but even the Northern youth is restricted by caste from the satisfying and economically advantageous jobs and must admire a person who has plenty of money, adventure and status.

The high popularity and prestige of large-scale gamblers and racketeers is a general American pattern and not restricted to the Negro community. This American pattern is exaggerated not only in the Negro ghettos but in all isolated and economically disadvantaged metropolitan groups. Fundamental to its explanation is the odd American tradition of keeping a large number of human activities illegal—for instance, the sale of liquor during prohibition and now gambling—in spite of the fact that they are commonly indulged in by the citizens without serious restrictions by law-enforcement agencies.[a] The American tradition of entangling normal and permitted activities by a great number of impractical, expensive or unenforceable proscriptions has similar effects.

There are several reasons why it is to be expected that the Negro community should be extreme in sheltering a big underworld. One reason is the very great restriction of economic and social opportunities for young

[a] See Chapter 1, Sections 8, 9 and 10.

Negroes in ordinary lines of work, and the consequent experience of frustration. This is particularly strong in the North where educational facilities are flung open to Negroes, and public policy and public discussion are permeated with the equalitarian principles of the American Creed. The low expectation on the part of white people generally and the quite common belief, particularly in the lower classes of whites, that Negroes are "born criminals" must also have demoralizing effects. The Negroes' respect for law and order is constantly undermined by the frequent encroachments upon Negro rights and personal integrity, permitted in the South and sometimes in the North,[a] which are widely publicized throughout the Negro world by the Negro press. This, and the general experience of exclusion and isolation, makes for a fatalistic sense of not belonging. Quite ordinarily the Negro is deprived of the feeling that he is a full-fledged participant in society and that the laws, in this significant sense, are "his" laws.[85] The crowdedness in the Negro ghettos—often bordering white "red light districts"—the poverty and the economic insecurity, the lack of wholesome recreation, are the other factors which all work in the direction of fostering anti-social tendencies. The great unemployment during the 'thirties must have strengthened these tendencies.[b]

In addition, we must remember that much of the vice seen in the Negro community is there, not for Negroes, but for whites; it is carried on in the Negro sections because they are disorganized, without adequate police protection, but with police and politicians looking for graft. This is especially true of vices other than gambling. Elaborate and expensive brothels cater to whites[86] (who have the money to pay for these pleasures) and are largely owned by whites.[87] The ordinary Negro streetwalker is in an unprotected,[88] economically disadvantaged[89] and overcrowded occupation. The peddling of dope, obscene pictures, and other appurtenances of vice, like prostitution, is part of organized vice rings owned by whites.

There are no investigations which allow us to gauge what the Negro underworld means in terms of employment and business opportunities.[90] As to employment, the chances are, as we have pointed out, that, except for the numbers racket, relatively little employment is given, and that what there is is accompanied by a low money return and vicious exploitation. But the numbers racket probably does give a considerable amount of employment at decent pay. As to the extent and size of the business, we cannot even have a reasonably substantiated opinion whether "protected" businesses mean more in the Negro community than in other socially and economically disadvantaged American groups. The observer can testify that he sees much of it in the Negro communities of the bigger cities, both South and North. In the smaller cities and in rural districts, it shades off into petty poolroom and dance hall businesses.

[a] See Part VI.
[b] Negro crime will be dealt with in Chapter 44, Section 2.

CHAPTER 15

THE NEGRO IN THE PUBLIC ECONOMY

1. THE PUBLIC BUDGET

In the preceding four chapters we have been studying the Negro as a factor of production and as an income earner. We have seen how he tries to sell his labor and other productive services in the economic market and what difficulties he meets in competition for jobs with the whites. Further study of the Negro's economic status must now proceed to an analysis of the income he actually earns and the consumption he procures for himself and his family on the basis of his income.

Such a study becomes framed in the general terms of the family budget, which we conceive of as an account over a period of time, usually a year, of the individual household's income and expenditure. But the analysis would be incomplete if we forgot that everyone in our society is a partner in the public budgets, ranging all the way from the budget of the local municipalities to the budget of the federal government. To these public budgets everyone contributes by paying various indirect and direct taxes. And everyone partakes in the consumption of goods and services financed by the public budgets. In modern society the economic status of any individual is to a large and increasing extent determined by how much he puts into the public budgets and how much he gets out of them.

In fact, one of the significant social trends, in America as elsewhere, is the relative growth of the public budgets. The range of "collective consumption" has been steadily increasing. The public budgets are also coming more and more to supplement private budgets, as, for instance, in relief and "social security" payments. Governments have always provided public services in kind, such as police protection; the use of highways, parks, and playgrounds; and free public schools. These public services are continuously improved. Whole items of consumption expenditures are transferred from private budgets to public budgets and at the same time minimum standards are secured, as when to the free schools are added school meals, free school materials and health services for the children. At the same time a gradual centralization and equalization of the public household is going on, so that the higher budgets—the federal budget as compared to the state budgets and the state budget as compared to the municipal budgets—take over more and more items of expenditure from the lower budgets, or provide funds for the lower budgets in order to pay for certain expenditures. Control follows financial responsibility, and minimum standards are raised.

This trend works toward equalization between regions and individuals. It is, indeed, an important part of the general process toward economic democratization in our society. There is a corresponding trend in the structure of taxation. Taxation as a whole is becoming more "progressive," that is, the rate of taxation increases more than proportionately as we go up the income scale. The trend in public services is that they are being made available to all citizens who care to make use of them, or otherwise are being distributed equally according to "needs" as defined in laws and relations. We shall take these two ideals, "ability to pay" for taxation and "equal distribution according to need" for public services, as our value premises for this chapter.

In both respects the principles are still somewhat fluid. The predominance of indirect taxation makes it highly probable that the total burden of taxation, at the outbreak of the Second World War, was "regressive," that is, proportionately higher for the poorer people.[1] In the higher income brackets, however, taxation was steeply progressive. The principle of "need" also is in flux as there is no definite and fixed dividing line between social welfare provisions—as, for instance, unemployment relief—and general benefits for all citizens. Free schools were once for the poor only. Today they are for everybody. Free or subsidized hospitalization can, in this country, usually be used only by low income families. There are other countries where such services are enjoyed by everybody. There is a trend visible in America, as in the rest of the world, not only to increase public benefits for the needy but to make them available to everybody.

Deciding upon the rules to determine the actual distribution of the tax burden among the citizens, and the availability of the public services to them, constitutes a major part of the activity of legislative bodies in a democracy. One principle has been settled for a long time, however, and constitutes a main basis for the legal structure of any democracy: the principle that the individual citizens have equal duties and rights in relation to the public household. In America this principle has constitutional sanction. Our *value premise* in this chapter is this principle: that *the Negro should partake of the burdens and the benefits of the public economy like other citizens in similar circumstances.*[a]

2. Discrimination in Public Service

There is no evidence that there is any direct racial discrimination in regard to taxation, and it has never played much of a role in discussion,

[a] This is only a corollary of the premise of nondiscrimination stated in Chapter 9, Section 3.

although the whites in the South certainly have the power to assess Negro-owned property differently than they assess white-owned property. In regard to public benefits, on the other hand, there is little doubt about the factual situation. Widespread discrimination exists in the entire South. In the North there is little, if any, direct discrimination. In the North the commonly accepted doctrine is that there should be no difference on account of "race, creed or color," and this doctrine is fairly well upheld in all public activity. What inequality there is in the Negro's consumption of public services in the North is due mostly to poverty, lack of education, and other disabilities which he shares with other lower class persons in the region.

In the South, too, all the laws are written upon the principle of full equality. Even the Jim Crow regulations, which in many respects facilitate discrimination in public services and, in fact, have discrimination for their purpose, follow the formula "separate but equal."[a] The actual practice, however, is quite different. It is more difficult for Negroes than for whites in similar economic circumstances to get on the relief rolls, and relief grants are often lower for Negroes than for whites. There is an amazing discrimination against Negroes in the segregated school system of the South. Virtually the whole range of other publicly administered facilities—such as hospitals, libraries, parks, and similar recreational facilities—are much poorer for Negroes than they are for whites. This is true in spite of the fact that the higher sickness rates and the inferior housing conditions in Negro sections make the need for all sorts of health and recreational facilities so much greater in Negro neighborhoods. Every visitor to the South who has given the matter any attention at all knows that streets are not kept up in Negro sections of Southern cities the way they are in white sections. Public utility equipment is often less complete in Negro than in white neighborhoods. Police and judicial protection in the South is not so much organized for Negroes as against them.[b] The Negro's representation on public payrolls is almost everywhere—and particularly in regard to high-paid jobs—much smaller than that of whites. As we have seen, there is discrimination against Negroes in agricultural policy. It can be generally ascertained that, as a result of the relative growth of the federal budget and the increased responsibility for and control of public services by federal agencies, discrimination has been decreasing during the New Deal. The fight between Washington and the Southern state and county administrations goes on continually, yet much discrimination remains.

The popular motivation for discrimination in public service in the South contains, in addition to the elaborated popular theories referred to in Chapter 9, one specific argument which relates to the fiscal sphere. The observer is frequently told by white Southerners that, since Negroes are so

[a] See Chapter 28.
[b] See Part VI.

poor and pay virtually no taxes, they are actually not entitled to get more public services than the whites care to give them. Whatever they get is a charitable gift for which they should be grateful. There can be no sense in talking about discrimination, it is held, as Negroes have no right to anything, but get something out of the whites' benevolence. Negroes are here considered as an "out-group" not on a par with white citizens. Otherwise the same argument would hold true even in regard to poor whites, which is usually not intended.

This popular theory is, of course, contrary to the American Creed and to the Constitution,[2] and also to the democratic individualistic legal structure of the Southern states themselves. The discrimination that exists, therefore, has to be carried out against the laws. Rights, in our Western legal order, are not given to a group or to a race but to individuals. An individual's right to receive public services is not related to the actual amount he has paid in taxes. The poor man should share equally in public consumption with the rich, though his taxes are lower.

Furthermore, there are some Negroes who pay quite high taxes, but they, nevertheless, meet discrimination in getting public service. There are examples of whole Negro communities which actually pay more in taxes than is expended upon the particular public services supported by the taxes.[3] Too, there is plain stealing in giving Negroes public services: when, for example, counties receive state or federal grants on the basis of school population and misappropriate the funds in favor of the white schools.

We shall analyze the basic conflict in the Southern whites' concept of law and order in later parts of this inquiry.[a] It should be observed that the argument of "low taxes, little service," which apparently means so much to the average white Southerner, is no longer publicly expressed by any person who is in a responsible position or who cares for his intellectual reputation. It is openly repudiated by Southern liberals.[4] The factual assertion that Negroes pay practically no taxes because they are so poor is, of course, mistaken or grossly exaggerated. The false belief is explainable only by the fact that most people are inclined to disregard indirect taxes.[5] We have already observed that American taxation, in part, is "regressive" (except for high income groups).[6]

Federal agencies or other groups who want to favor the Negro sometimes have to content themselves by working for the realization of a compromise formula: that Negroes and whites share in the benefits from the public economy in proportion to their numbers.[b] This norm is in conflict with the Constitution, since it refers to the Negro *group* and does not

---

[a] See Part VI.

[b] We have already met this in the activity of the Farm Security Administration; see Chapter 12, Section 12.

guarantee *individuals* their right.[a] It has its utility only as a practical yard-stick in the fight against discrimination. Its very presence in the public debate, and sometimes in public regulations, is an indication of the existing discrimination.[b]

Quite apart from the inappropriateness of distributing public services to any group in relation either to its contributions to the public budgets or to its numbers, it would be highly interesting to be able to analyze in some detail what the Negroes, as a group, do contribute, directly and indirectly, to the public budget and what they do get in return. No such studies have been made. Our analysis in this chapter has to be far from complete. To begin with, we shall have to leave out altogether, for lack of data, the problem of how much Negroes pay in taxes. In regard to benefits, we shall not be able to give anything like a full account.

3. Education

A great proportion of the total budgets of local municipalities and an increasing part of the state and federal budgets are earmarked for public education. From the individual citizen's point of view this form of collective consumption ranks high in importance among public services. The general facts about Negro education are well known, as they have been in the center of public discussion for a long time. In this section we shall restrict our treatment to a presentation of some summary figures on the fiscal costs of education for Negroes as compared to whites, leaving it to other chapters to analyze what these figures mean in terms of what amount and what type of education the Negroes receive.[c]

There are no financial statistics for the North which separate the amount

[a] See footnote 2 of this chapter. The population norm lies somewhere between the con-stitutional norm and the actual discrimination practiced in the South. In several respects, the Negroes as a poor group do not receive a share in public services as large as their pro-portion in the population, though there is no discrimination in the constitutional sense. Since Negroes have fewer automobiles than do whites, for instance, they make less use of public highways. Also Negroes cannot afford to keep their children in school for as long a time as whites can, on the average, but this fact alone does not involve any legal discrimination. Only in one main item of the public budgets do Negroes, in the South as well as in the North, seem to get somewhat more than their share in proportion to their numbers: this is in social welfare. The explanation is that their need for economic assistance is so much greater than is that of the whites that the total sum paid out for relief to Negroes is relatively higher, in spite of discrimination. The causes of their higher needs are, as we have seen: job restric-tions everywhere, lack of ambition, poorer educational facilities, higher sickness and disability rates, greater family disorganization and other direct and indirect effects of dis-crimination.

[b] Theoretically, the population norm could occasionally work to the unusual advantage of the Negroes. For example, to give them a 10 per cent share of desirable jobs would actually wipe out almost the entire problem of economic discrimination. The norm is, of course, never brought up when it refers to such a situation.

[c] See Chapter 41, and Chapter 43, Section 4.

spent on the education of Negroes from the amount spent on the education of whites. In the North, the principle is not questioned that schools should have equal standards, independent of whether a school is all white, all Negro or mixed. It is mainly the Negroes' poverty which keeps them from utilizing existing educational facilities as much as do whites. In fact, were it not for this reason, the Northern Negroes would on the average be better off than the Northern whites, since Negroes are more concentrated in the big cities where school facilities are superior to large parts of the rural North where only white people live. In actual practice, however, schools in needy districts tend to be somewhat older, less well equipped and often more over-crowded. A main cause of this is the migration of Negroes from the South to the slum areas of Northern cities. European immigrants who come to these slum areas also have inferior schools. School facilities have not been adjusted to the rapidly growing need. The city authorities who know about the much more inadequate school facilities for Negroes in the South, and who are usually somewhat reluctant to increase the incentive for Negro migration to their localities, have often not been so active in widening school facilities in Negro districts as they would have been had the districts been white. But the differentials are seldom large and would probably disappear altogether if migration should cease.

In the South, school facilities are generally much poorer. In the year 1935-1936 the average current expenditures per pupil in daily attendance in all public elementary and secondary schools in the country was $74. The range between the different states was extremely wide. In three Northern states, New York, Nevada, and California, the amount was over $115. On the other hand, all the states in the Upper and Lower South, as well as some of the Border states, were far below the national average. At the bottom of the scale were Alabama, Mississippi, and Arkansas, where the average expenditure was less than $30 per pupil.[7]

Obviously, these conditions are related to two factors: the South has the lowest income level and, at the same time, the highest number of children in the whole nation.[8] For these two reasons the South actually sacrifices more for education, in relation to its economic ability, than does the rest of the country, on the average. It has been calculated, for instance, that Mississippi expends about twice as much on schools, compared with its taxable income, as does New York State.[9] Undoubtedly, this goes a long way to explain the lower level of educational facilities in the South. There are two qualifications, however, which we should keep in mind. One is the fact that certain states outside the South, such as Utah, Arizona, and the two Dakotas, where the calculated taxability per child was about as low as in some of the most prosperous Southern states, for example, Virginia and Texas, nevertheless showed much greater expenditures per pupil in 1935-1936.[10] Thus, although public education is burdensome for the Southern economy, there are regions in this country where, relatively, still heavier financial loads for education have been accepted. The other qualification concerns the unequal treatment of Negro and white schools, which makes the claims regarding Southern financial sacrifices for education sound less genuine than they may appear at first sight.

Racial discrimination in the apportionment of school facilities in the South is as spectacular as it is well known.[a] The current expense per pupil in daily attendance per year in elementary and secondary schools in 10 Southern states in 1935-1936 was $17.04 for Negroes and almost three times as much, or $49.30, for white children. In Mississippi and Georgia, only about $9 was spent on every Negro school child, but five times more on the average white pupil. There were two Border states, however (Delaware and Missouri), and one state farther South (Oklahoma) which did not, in this way, discriminate against Negroes.[11] The District of Columbia Negro schools received only slightly smaller appropriations per pupil than did the white schools. They received more than the white schools in any of the Southern states.[12]

The great difference in expenditures per pupil in Negro and white schools in most of the Southern states was due to several factors. The most important one was the great differential in regard to teachers' salaries.[b] Second, there was a difference in number of pupils per teacher.[13] Third, less transportation was provided for Negro children: in 10 Southern states, where Negro children constituted 28 per cent of the total enrollment, only 3 per cent of the public expenditures for school transportation in 1935-1936 was for their benefit.[14] Certain savings on most expenditure items were made

[a] It is not well known to the general public, though. In spite of the fact that few aspects of racial discrimination have been discussed as intensively as this one, the visitor to the South frequently meets white persons even in the educated class who seriously believe that educational facilities for Negroes and whites are quite equal. The very fact that there are Negro schools on different levels is to them enough evidence that Negroes are as well served as are whites. Several times it has happened, for instance, that whites have referred to a nearby Negro college, which they have heard about and passed on the road, to tell me that there Negroes get graduate training to the top. "They graduate lawyers, doctors and all sorts of bigs shots," a white collar girl in Mississippi told me about a poor denominational Negro college in the same city. Such experiences are interesting in several respects: first, they exemplify the growing isolation between the two groups and the ignorance among whites about their Negro neighbors; second, they indicate that the legal fiction which is necessary for constitutional reasons ("separate but equal") actually comes to be believed as true; third, they make it probable that even in this respect ordinary white people in the South would be prepared to give Negroes more justice if they knew the facts.

Another observation is that among ordinary white people in the South it is not well known that Northern philanthropic organizations have much of the credit for the fact that Negro education is not lower than it is, and still less that Negro communities often contribute to building their schools. This distortion in the popular beliefs is, of course, opportunistic.

[b] See Chapter 14, Section 4.

by keeping the average school term in Negro schools about 13 per cent shorter than in white schools.[15]

The same discrimination may be noted in whatever item in the school budget is considered. Every traveler in the South becomes easily aware of the difference in general appearance between Negro and white schools. In rural areas there is still a great number of Negro one-teacher and two-teacher schools,[16] whereas the consolidation movement has proceeded far in respect to white schools. The value of Negro school property per child in 10 Southern states was scarcely one-fifth of the corresponding figure for whites. This was so in spite of the fact that as much as one-third of the total value of Negro school property was in buildings partly financed by the Rosenwald Fund.[17]

Additional savings are made on Negro education because only few Negroes go to high school, and still fewer attend public colleges. In 18 Southern states, where Negroes constituted 23 per cent of the population in 1930, their representation among the high school students in 1933-1934 was but 9 per cent. They had only 6 per cent of the enrollment in publicly controlled institutions of higher learning in 17 Southern states.[18] Savings are also made on Negro education by forcing the Negro community to contribute money or work for its school.[a]

Particularly remarkable is the fact that the differential in school expenditures is often greatest in states which have the highest proportion of Negroes. There is a similar tendency among the counties within each state. A tabulation of the conditions in 7 Southern states in 1929-1930 indicated that the school expenditure per Negro child showed a pronounced tendency to be lower, the higher the proportion of Negro children in the total population of the county. The expenditures for white children, on the other hand, showed a somewhat less marked, but nevertheless unmistakable, tendency to increase with the proportion of Negroes in the counties in spite of the fact that the counties with many Negroes tended to be the poorer counties.[19] In counties with comparatively few (less than 12.5 per cent) Negro children, the expenditure level in white schools was less than twice as high as that in Negro schools; but in counties where the overwhelming

---

[a] "The situation differs, of course, town by town. In a neighboring town the Negroes were given a shell of a building for a school and in one way or another the salaries of the teachers were eked out. The rest of the work was done by Negroes, and an unexpected lot it was. Negro carpenters and masons contributed the work on remodeling the building. Negroes collected the funds to furnish the school with desks, blackboards, and other accessories. No money is provided annually for supplies or fuel by the town; so Negroes contribute for the school supplies and cut and haul their own fuel. This is done in a community where Negro working habits are generally reported to be bad; it is done of course, by zealous individuals with the bright American goal of social advancement before their eyes." (John Dollard, *Caste and Class in a Southern Town* [1937], p. 194.)

majority (at least 75 per cent) of the children were Negro, the standard was more than 13 times higher for white than for Negro pupils.

The explanation of this phenomenon is simple. State appropriations for educational purposes are usually apportioned on a per capita basis. Counties with a high proportion of Negro children, consequently, have a bigger opportunity than have other counties to deprive Negro schools of money intended for them and to use it for white schools.[20] For, in such counties there is more money to "rob" from the Negroes, and the temptation to do it, therefore, must be particularly great. The same principle works even when schools, in the main, depend on local support. If, for instance, there are twice as many Negroes as white children, every dollar per pupil taken from the Negro group means two dollars per pupil added to the appropriation for the white group. This, in conjunction with the low general level of school expenditures in states with a heavy Negro population, explains why it is that expenditures per Negro pupil are so much smaller, the higher the proportion of Negroes among the school children.[21]

It is generally said that school segregation increases the cost of the educational system. This, of course, is quite true. A given average standard can be achieved at a lower expense if the overhead costs can be minimized. This is particularly apparent in respect to higher educational institutions. To maintain two sets of state universities must involve a greatly increased cost. Also, the cost of providing transportation for the children in a consolidated rural school system must be higher when Negro and white children are segregated. And whenever either of the two population groups is small, or distances are large, a segregated system must have a pronounced effect on costs. It seems that only in cities, with a large population of both Negroes and whites, and with a rather clear-cut housing segregation, can it be possible to maintain two separate elementary—and possibly even secondary—school systems without any significant increase in cost.

Yet these conclusions are applicable only when we assume that the problem is to achieve an equal standard at minimum cost. If the objective, however, is not to have equal standards, but rather to use a given appropriation intended for two population groups so as to maximize the benefits for one of them—then, of course, segregation becomes a means of economizing. Whenever the proportion of Negroes in the population is high, and the standard of Negro schools is kept well below that of white schools, the white educational system can derive substantial gains from segregation. Segregation makes discrimination possible; discrimination means lower expenditures for Negro schools, and the white population thus gets a vested interest in separation. If the principle "separate, but equal" were to be realized in practice, and Negro schools were to be just as well provided for as white schools, there would still be a social motive for segregation.[a] White people would,

---

[a] See Chapter 28.

however, lose their economic interest in segregation. In fact they—and the Negroes—would have to pay for it in higher taxes, in so far as a segregated set-up would then be more expensive than a mixed school system. It is open for speculation to what extent this would change popular attitudes in respect to segregation.

The whole system of discrimination in education in the South is not only tremendously harmful to the Negroes but it is flagrantly illegal,[22] and can easily be so proven in the courts. The main organization for guarding civil liberties for Negroes, the N.A.A.C.P., has not waged, up to now, an extensive legal campaign against school discrimination. Recently it has selected a few strategic frontiers for an attack: equalization of teachers' salaries[a] and the admittance of graduate students to Southern universities.[b] In these fields, it is exerting a considerable pressure upon Southern authorities. Not only educators but politicians, even in the Deep South, are heard to say that they must "do something" to raise Negro education so as to avoid too great legal embarrassment. Northern philanthropic institutions have, for a long time, been active in raising Negro education in the South. Many white Southerners are trying to bring about reforms.

There is no doubt that under all these influences a gradual improvement of school facilities for Negroes, as for whites, in the South has been going on and is still in progress. It is less certain, but probable, that Negro schools have lately been improving faster than white schools in the South—that is, in the sense that the *percentage* increase in expenditures may have been greater for Negro than for white schools.[c] But measured in absolute amounts the difference is even larger than it used to be.[23] If we consider the whole Negro group, there is no doubt that the most important factor working to raise the educational level is the continuous migration out of the South to the Northern cities with their good schools.

In the South, the discrimination is still so tremendously great; it is so ingrained; and it is so profitable for the whites, that it is difficult to see how any more rapid reform will be possible unless the federal government enters the field and starts giving financial assistance to the Southern school system. This will mean two things. First, there will be a regional equalization in educational standards over the whole country, from which the South, especially, cannot fail to gain. Such an equalization, as has often been pointed out, is well justified in view of the high birth rate in the South and the migration, which forces the South, as well as other low income, high fertility, "out-migration" areas, to make heavy investments in the education of children who afterwards spend the productive period

[a] See Chapter 14, Section 4.
[b] See Chapter 29, Section 5.
[c] For the nation as a whole there is, undoubtedly, an equalization in educational opportunities, as the proportion of Negroes living in the North is increasing.

of their lives in other states. Second, the federal government is likely to attempt to mitigate discrimination against Negroes. It will acquire an influence over Southern school policies and might eventually stamp out racial discrimination in the school system. This is why, incidentally, many Southern politicians—invoking the doctrine of "states' rights"—are against federal aid in the school system in spite of the fact that their states will gain financially from it.

Federal aid to the educational system would not be an entirely new venture. Indeed, the federal government laid the financial basis for public education in several states by making substantial land grants to them. Considerable discrimination against Negroes has been the rule, however, in these federal educational activities, or, rather, in the way they were carried out by state authorities in the South. In 1935-1936, Negro colleges received only 5.2 per cent of the federal funds given to land-grant colleges in 17 Southern states.[24] Still, land-grant institutions enrolled nearly three-fourths of the students in all public institutions of higher education for Negroes and about one-third of the total in public and private institutions combined.[25] Howard University—in many respects the best Negro university in the country—is supported almost entirely by the federal government.

The New Deal has greatly increased educational benefits to Negroes: The Public Works Administration paid 55 per cent of the costs of building new schools, when the states and the communities paid the rest. But the South saw to it that its whites were provided for much better than its Negroes—despite the much greater needs of the latter. Of some 91 million dollars of federal funds spent for new schools in 16 Southern states, only a little over 7 millions went for Negro schools.[26] Northern communities were much fairer, and—although there are no statistics which distinguish between white and Negro schools in the North—there is reason to believe that Negroes received a share of the P.W.A. funds larger than their proportion in the population, since they lived in older neighborhoods where the schools were more dilapidated. The Works Progress Administration put on its gigantic adult education program employing large numbers of unemployed teachers and educating millions of people;[27] 400,000 Negroes were taught reading and writing.[28] There is also the student aid program of the National Youth Administration and the energetic educational efforts of the Agricultural Extension Service and the Farm Security Administration.

Two national commissions, appointed by administrations of each of the major political parties, have concluded that provisions for adequate educational opportunity for all American children can be made only if the federal government assumes responsibility.[29] When the federal government does give money for education, it usually allows the states to spend it. This grant-in-aid system permits discrimination against Negroes to arise. If the federal authorities take positive action, however, they can reduce discrimination. The trend seems to be in the direction of decreasing discrimination in the distribution of federal aid, and the increasing weight of the Negro vote in the North is strengthening this trend.[30] In spite of all, therefore, we believe that the Negro cannot fail to gain if the federal government should start giving aid on a permanent basis even to the main body of American educational institutions. Some further observations on the problem of federal aid to education will be made in the last section of Chapter 41.

4. PUBLIC HEALTH

Mortality in all age groups is much higher among Negroes than among whites.[a] Negroes suffer more from nearly all sorts of illnesses. We have shown that at least the major part of these differentials is not due to greater susceptibility on the part of Negroes[b] but to the impact of economic, educational, and cultural handicaps, directly or indirectly imposed upon Negroes by discrimination.[c] The fact that Negroes are in greater need of health facilities than are whites, and that discrimination in providing them health facilities hurts the whites themselves, is gradually becoming realized.

The Negroes' need for public health services is higher also because poverty, in conjunction with segregation, prevents them from utilizing private health facilities to the same extent as do whites. Negro families (not on relief) spend only one-third or one-half as much for medical services as do white families (not on relief).[31] Although federal, state, and local governments nowadays carry about half the financial burden for all hospitalization,[32] private hospitals and clinics continue to play a larger role in this country, proportionately, than in most European countries. Even in the North there are many private hospitals which do not accept Negro patients. True, there are several private all-Negro hospitals, both North and South,[33] but they are usually small and qualitatively inferior.

In spite of the greater need for public health services and the interest of the whole society that this need be filled, the pattern of public hospitalization is about the same as that for public instruction. The general level is comparatively high in the North, and there Negroes are seldom discriminated against.[d] The general standard of public hospitalization is much lower in the South.[34] Although no comprehensive data seem to be available on the total number of beds (private as well as public) available to

---

[a] See Chapter 7.

[b] See Chapter 6.

[c] For example, Negro sections of Southern cities have less adequate street cleaning and garbage removal services than white sections. These things are related to disease.

[d] We have already cited one case of discrimination in the North, that of Detroit, where public subsidies have been given to a second-rate Negro hospital so as to exclude Negroes from the ordinary public hospitals.

Negroes in Southern hospitals, there is enough scattered information to establish the fact that discrimination exists.[a]

Since the inauguration of the New Deal, appreciable progress had been made, part of which consisted of the building of hospitals under the P.W.A.[35] The federal government, like most of the philanthropic foundations, usually sees to it that Negroes get their share of the new hospital facilities. Standards have been raised—but, so far, only in a few areas. One Southern city may have a large, completely modern hospital where a great number of indigent people may get treatment free or for low fees. In the next city the main hospital for low income people may be dilapidated and so small that it cannot possibly accommodate more than an insignificant fraction of those in need of hospitalization. Rural hospital facilities are totally inadequate almost everywhere in the South, especially for Negroes.

In this field, as in public education, it seems that no uniformly satisfactory standard can ever be achieved except through a program of permanent federal aid and control. The President's Interdepartmental Committee to Coordinate Health and Welfare Activities published in 1938 a national health program which included a plan for continued federal assistance to public hospitals. On the basis of this program the so-called National Health Bill was introduced in Congress in 1939, and the Hospital Construction Bill in 1940.[36] Although these proposals have not yet been acted upon, they have helped to focus public attention on the problem, and they seem to indicate the general line of future action.

There seems to be less discrimination against Negroes—and in many

[a] Substantiation of this point may be found in Chapter 7, Section 5. Concerning public hospitals alone, the following evidence may be added:

Only 40 of the 450 beds in the State Sanatorium in Mississippi were available to Negroes; almost half of all the beds for the tuberculosis patients were idle because of insufficient funds. (Harold F. Dorn, "The Health of the Negro," unpublished manuscript prepared for this study [first draft, 1940], p. 113. Data based on Council on Medical Education and Hospitals, "Hospitals and Medical Care in Mississippi," *Journal of the American Medical Association* [1939], pp. 2317-2332.)

Sterner visited two of the five state charity hospitals in Mississippi in January, 1940. Both were in bad repair with leaking roofs. Water was dropping down on the floor in one place. In these hospitals half the beds were for Negroes. The doctor in charge of one of the hospitals complained of the inadequate appropriations; about one-sixth of the beds were not in use because of shortage of funds. The reason, he explained, was that money was apportioned by a state board composed of county physicians, who retained as much as possible of state aid for their privately-run county hospitals. He explained, further, that the hospital was unable to receive any normal delivery cases; only emergency cases could be taken care of. Others have to be treated in their homes by midwives. Patients who have any means are asked to make voluntary payments. Others are treated free.

An entirely different impression was given by a new State Charity Hospital in New Orleans, which was visited in January, 1940. As far as the layman could ascertain, it was quite adequate. It had been built as a P.W.A. project. Half the beds were for Negroes. None of the physicians or surgeons was Negro, however, and there were only a few Negro nurses.

cases no discrimination at all—in respect to the so-called "out-patient" services of public health institutions. For this there are several reasons. These services usually cannot be apportioned beforehand between Negroes and whites in the strict manner in which hospital wards are segregated. The federal government has given considerable assistance on a permanent basis to certain important aspects of this medical work. Much of the work concerns venereal diseases, and white people everywhere seem to have become aware of what the high rates of venereal diseases among Negroes mean to themselves.[37]

The building up of a system of general public health clinics, as well as of maternal and child health clinics, is far from completed in America,[38] but there is no doubt that tremendous improvements have been achieved in recent years, and that Negroes have shared in the benefits. One criticism, however, is that too much of the work has been organized on a "categorical" basis. Drives are started against one disease after another,[a] and the objective of rendering assistance to those most in need, regardless of the type of disease they have, has often been almost forgotten. This has sometimes been unfortunate from the point of view of the Negro.[39]

5. Recreational Facilities

America is probably more conscious than any other country of the great importance of recreation. The need for public measures to promote wholesome recreation has been shown to be particularly great for youth in cities and especially in such groups where housing conditions are crowded and unsanitary, where incomes are low and consequently opportunities for enjoying sound commercial entertainment restricted, where many mothers have to leave their homes for gainful work during the day, where the proportion of disorganized families is great, and where juvenile delinquency is high. This all means that, on the average, Negroes have greater need for public recreational facilities than have whites.

In the North there is, occasionally, segregation and discrimination not only in commercial enterprises for entertainment but also in public facilities, as, for instance, in swimming pools.[b] In the South segregation and discrimination are the general rule for all recreational facilities. The visitor finds everywhere in the South that not only beaches and playgrounds, but also public parks, are often entirely closed to Negroes, except for Negro

---

[a] During his field trip in Mississippi (December, 1939-January, 1940), Sterner heard public health officers and nurses talk about the syphilis campaign which had started about a year earlier (before then little, if anything, had been done about it by public health agencies). But he heard nothing about gonorrhea until one public health officer explained that available appropriations were insufficient for treatment of gonorrhea on a large scale in his county.

[b] See Chapter 29. We shall include among public recreational facilities those organized by civic groups and by philanthropists.

nurses watching white children. Public funds are used everywhere in the region for these facilities available to whites only. Often no substitutes at all, or very inferior ones, are offered the Negroes. Like white people, Negroes can use their schools as community centers but they are unsatisfactory for many recreational purposes. More than half of all cities having special Negro community centers listed in the *Negro Year Book* for 1937-1938[40] were in the North and West.[41]

Damaging from both cultural and recreational viewpoints are the restrictions of public library facilities for Negroes. In 1939 it was found that of 774 public libraries in 13 Southern states only 99, or less than one-seventh, served Negroes. Of the 99 libraries, 59 were concentrated in four states.[42]

For a full appraisal of the Negro's share in public recreational facilities, it would be necessary to have access to more material on the quantitative and qualitative adequacy of such facilities for both Negroes and whites. There is no doubt about the fact, however, that provisions for Negroes are much inferior to those for whites. For reasons already suggested, this is a question of no small importance. The visitor finds Negroes everywhere aware of the great damage done Negro youth by the lack of recreational outlets and of the urgency of providing playgrounds for the children. In almost every community visited during the course of this inquiry, these were among the first demands on the program of local Negro organizations.[a]

The Southern whites are unconcerned about how Negroes use their leisure time, as long as they are kept out of the whites' parks and beaches. Recreation involves "social" relationships, and, therefore, Southern whites are strongly opposed to mixed recreation. Nevertheless, considerable improvements have been made even in the South in recent years. Again the federal agencies have been instrumental in giving the Negroes slightly more of their rights. There have been many P.W.A. and W.P.A. projects for new playgrounds, community centers, and other facilities,[43] and Negroes have received some share of them. There are community rooms, playgrounds, nursery schools, and other similar provisions in or around new housing projects for low income families.[44] The National Youth Administration, the Agricultural Extension Service, the Farm Security Administration, and other new agencies, have assisted both Negroes and whites. Yet, there is still a long way to go. So far, only a small part of the distance between "nothing at all" and "full adequacy" has been covered. And, par-

---

[a] When visiting Birmingham, Alabama, in the fall of 1938, we were taken around the town by one of the leaders of the Negro community. "See those tennis courts," said our guide, "they are not much good, as you see. The whites don't care to use them any more. But in spite of that, we had to beg and beg before we got the privilege to play on them. They are the only public courts in town that we are allowed to use. It's just one of those things that make one see red."

ticularly, it has yet to be recognized that quite special provisions are required for the Negroes in order to offset some of the economic, cultural and moral disadvantages from which they suffer.

6. PUBLIC HOUSING POLICIES[a]

Before the depression of the 'thirties, there were few attempts made by public bodies in this country to improve the housing conditions for low income people. Moreover, housing credit was rather unorganized: financial institutions were extremely numerous, there was little integration among them, and the whole system lacked stability and efficiency to such an extent that interest costs on mortgage loans were usually much higher than necessary. High property taxes, then as well as now, also had a damaging effect.[45] These and a number of similar circumstances made decent housing economically unobtainable for millions of families who would have been able to pay the full price if housing had been more efficiently organized.

The Great Depression, however, brought a change. The breakdown of private building construction and the widespread unemployment made the glaring housing needs appear even more irrational than ordinarily. Why let people go unemployed when there is so much work to be done? On top of that, there was the near-collapse in housing credit. These circumstances weakened the resistance against public interference in housing to such an extent that it was possible to launch some rather significant government programs.

Recent housing policies, apart from city planning, building control, and similar activities, have in the main two aspects: making credit available for private housing and providing public housing for low income groups. Quantitatively most important are the credit reforms, carried out by the Home Owners' Loan Corporation (H.O.L.C.), the Federal Home Loan Banks, and the Federal Housing Administration (F.H.A.). The H.O.L.C. was set up primarily for the purpose of rescuing home owners who were threatened with losing their homes during the depression. It is now liquidating. In terms of long-range policies, the F.H.A. is the most important of these housing credit agencies. Its many important contributions are so well known that they scarcely need to be emphasized here.[46] The loans are made by private institutions, but since the insurance eliminates the risk for the lenders, interest rates are kept down to such an extent that F.H.A. houses are well within the reach of middle class and more secure working class families. Particularly significant is the fact that, year by year, it has been possible to reach deeper down into lower economic strata. In spite of that, less than 30 per cent of the main category of new borrowers on one-

[a] For a fuller treatment of the important problems dealt with in this section, see Richard Sterner and Associates, *The Negro's Share*, prepared for this study (1943), Chapters 9, 10 and 18.

family homes in 1940 had incomes under $2,000 and but 5 per cent had less than $1,500.[47]

Under such circumstances, it is apparent that Negroes cannot have had any great benefit from the F.H.A., nor, for that matter, from any other of the federal credit agencies which are organized on the basis of so-called "ordinary business principles."[a] The failure of the F.H.A. to help the Negroes goes even further than can be explained on the basis of their low income. This federal agency has taken over the policy of segregation used by private institutions, like banks, mortgage companies, building and loan associations, real estate companies. When it comes to developing new subdivisions, the F.H.A. is obviously interested in getting such a layout that property values can be maintained. Private operators, in order to secure F.H.A. backing, usually follow the advice of the agency.[48] One of the points which property valuators of the F.H.A. are specifically urged to consider is whether the area or property to be insured is protected from "adverse influences." This, in the official language of the agency, "includes prevention of the infiltration of business and industrial uses, lower class occupancy, and inharmonious racial groups."[49] In the case of undeveloped and sparsely developed areas, the agency lets its valuators consider whether

. . . effective restrictive covenants are recorded against the entire tract, since these provide the surest protection against undesirable encroachment and inharmonious use. To be most effective, deed restrictions should be imposed upon all land in the immediate environment of the subject location.[50]

The restrictions, among other things, should include "prohibition of the occupancy of properties except by the race for which they are intended."[51]

This matter is a serious one for the Negro. It is one thing when private tenants, property owners, and financial institutions maintain and extend patterns of racial segregation in housing. It is quite another matter when a federal agency chooses to side with the segregationists. This fact is particularly harmful since the F.H.A. has become the outstanding leader in the planning of new housing. It seems probable that the F.H.A. has brought about a greatly increased use of all sorts of restrictive covenants and deed restrictions, which are the most reliable legal means of keeping Negroes confined to their ghettos. It may even be that those income groups of the white population which are particularly served by the F.H.A. formerly lived in areas which were much less covered by such restrictions.[b] The damage done to the Negroes is not only that the F.H.A. encourages segregation. There is also the fact *that this segregation is predominantly*

[a] We state this in an *a priori* manner since none of the federal housing credit agencies presents any information on the racial composition of their clientele.

[b] There is little definite knowledge, however, on these matters. A study testing the hypothesis mentioned in the text would be extremely valuable.

negative. It would work much less hardship on the Negro people if it were merely a question of keeping Negroes and whites apart, and not, predominantly, of keeping the Negro out. In other words, if the policy of segregation were coupled with large-scale positive efforts to give the Negro additional new living space, it would be much less harmful. Also such a two-sided policy of segregation, in the end, would have a much greater chance of being successful. The urban Negro population is bound to increase. The present Negro ghettos will not suffice. The Negro will invade new urban territories. Unless these changes are properly planned, they will occur in the same haphazard and friction-causing manner with which we have been only too well acquainted in the past. This, for one thing, will jeopardize the objective of keeping the character of white neighborhoods intact.

The general credit reforms, however, constitute just one part of the present housing policies. The subsidized housing projects for low income families are an entirely different matter. About 7,500, or one-third, of the dwelling units in projects built during 1933-1937 by the Housing Division of the Public Works Administration are for Negro occupancy. The building of subsidized housing projects has since been carried on by local housing authorities with the financial assistance of the United States Housing Authority (U.S.H.A.).[a] By July 31, 1942, there were 122,000 dwelling units built by or under loan contract with the U.S.H.A. and intended for low income families. About 41,000, or 33 per cent, of those were intended for Negro occupancy.[52]

Thus, the Negro has certainly received a large share of the benefits under this program. Indeed, the U.S.H.A. has given him a better deal than has any other major federal public welfare agency. This may be due, in part, to the fact that, so far, subsidized housing projects have been built mainly in urban areas, where, even in the South, there is less reluctance to consider the Negro's needs. The main explanation, however, is just the fact that the U.S.H.A. has had the definite policy of giving the Negro his share. It has a special division for nonwhite races, headed by a Negro who can serve as spokesman for his people. Many of the leading white officials of the agency, as well, are known to have been convinced in principle that discrimination should be actively fought.

So far, however, only about 3 per cent of Negro urban families live in subsidized housing projects. This is a good beginning, but unless these efforts continue, the results are a drop in the bucket compared with the total need.[b]

[a] All housing activities of the federal government were in 1942 brought together into one unit, the National Housing Agency. The F.H.A. and the U.S.H.A. are maintained as departments within this agency. The name of the U.S.H.A. was changed to Federal Public Housing Authority.

[b] For a discussion of actual housing conditions for Negroes, see Chapter 16, Section 6.

It seems that the U.S.H.A. program is well planned in many respects. Yet there are some obvious shortcomings. One is its connection with the slum clearance program. By law, slum dwellings eventually have to be eliminated at the same rate as new units are constructed. It seems that the purpose of this clause is mainly to appease the real estate owners who are afraid of an abundance of housing.[a] It is unfortunate when housing projects are built on old slum sites, and the slum houses have first to be torn down. Such practices work particular hardship on the Negroes since there is usually no place where they can go while the new projects are being built.

Several housing projects, however, among them Negro projects, have been located on vacant land. The experiences, in many cases, have been rather encouraging. Sites for projects have been found where utility services are complete and where streets are well kept up. When there is additional vacant land adjacent to the area, there is the opportunity for the development of some new private housing for Negroes. It seems that such procedures should be followed generally for Negro housing projects. They could and should always be utilized for the purpose of giving the Negro additional "living space" in urban areas—never for binding him with new ties to the over-crowded sections where he is being kept.

Generally, this connection between slum clearance and new construction has made it difficult to make new housing projects fit into constructive and all-inclusive city plans.[b] In too many cases it has been a question of substituting good houses for bad ones without enough consideration of how such piecemeal work can be integrated into a rational city plan. This, of course, is all right for those individual families who happen to get a new dwelling, but it scarcely prepares the ground for an ultimate solution of the housing problem of the entire city. Particularly is this true about Negro housing; Negro sections are almost invariably among the least well-planned areas in a city.

In city planning, which will be necessary for the continuation of the subsidized housing program on a larger scale, the issue of housing segregation will have to be faced squarely. This is the one feature which makes the problem of housing for Negroes different from that of housing for other low income families. The chances are that, in the South at least, segregation will have to be accepted in the surveyable future, for the simple reason that local opposition against subsidized housing projects will otherwise be so strong that no projects can be built. In such cases, the only thing that can be insisted upon is that Negroes get, not only new houses,

---

[a] From a social viewpoint, the only rational thing to do would be to eliminate slum houses whenever there is a sufficient supply of adequate houses—regardless of whether the supply is due to the building of subsidized housing projects or to other causes.

[b] This is a criticism often heard among American planners.

but also additional space, and that both old and new Negro areas become better planned.

In the North, on the other hand, there is some chance that the evils of segregation can be removed by means of the gradual abolition of housing segregation itself. In some Northern places, such as New York City and Albany, there are already projects where white and Negro tenants live scattered within a single project.[53]

Another major problem concerns the financial feasibility of building subsidized housing projects for all families who, for economic reasons, are suffering from bad housing conditions. The American public needs to know whether or not this program will ever solve the entire housing problem for all low income households, or whether it is just going to assist a more or less arbitrarily selected small part of the ill-housed families. This problem has not been adequately faced.[a] Yet a complete financial plan is essential for a rational continuation of the program, as well as for the purpose of convincing the American public that continuation is worth while.

Connected with this matter is the problem of tenant selection. The U.S.H.A. rehouses only families between an upper and a—somewhat unofficial—lower income limit. A great number of relief families are

[a] The average federal net subsidy (gross subsidy minus government profit on loans), according to the U.S.H.A., amounts to $77 per family per year. (Federal Works Agency, *Second Annual Report, 1941*.) In addition, there are municipal subsidies, usually in the form of tax exemptions, averaging $60 (*ibid.*, pp. 145 and 160; United States Housing Authority, "What Does the Housing Program Cost?" [1940], pp. 14-15), which makes a total subsidy of about $137. This means that over 7,000,000 families, or one-fifth of the total in the United States, can be rehoused for an annual cost of $1,000,000,000. It would be necessary, in addition, to make all relief benefits high enough to enable all recipients of public assistance to pay the rents in public housing projects. Such a large program, however, would involve rural families, for which the cost certainly would be considerably smaller. Also, its completion would require several decades. The general income level may be so much higher at the end of this period that the assistance could be restricted to a much smaller number of families. Possible cuts in building and other costs may have the same effect. Even under present conditions, it is doubtful whether the number of households which, for economic reasons, suffer from intolerably bad housing conditions, is really so large; it should be kept in mind that some slum families have incomes which would enable them to purchase adequate housing if they only cared for it. Since the building of the projects ought to be concentrated in periods of unemployment, a substantial part of the cost should be charged to the unemployment relief budget, and not to the housing budget. In other words, as unemployed construction workers must be given jobs on public works programs during depressions, the cost for rehousing slum families is reduced by the utilization of these "free services."

A real cost estimate should include quite a number of such considerations: the future trend in number and size of rural and urban families; the extent to which bad housing conditions are caused by factors other than low income; the intensity of the need of various groups living in substandard houses; the extent to which existing houses can be utilized for subsidized families. Our unpretentious experiment with figures has been made in order to bring home one point: that it is not economically impossible to give the whole people a certain minimum standard of housing.

ineligible because they are unable to pay the rents, which in 1941 averaged $18 per month, including utilities. The average income of the families in the projects was $832.[54] Several projects, particularly those occupied by Negroes, showed much lower rent and income levels. Even so, however, it certainly is true that the U.S.H.A. helps an economic group somewhat above those most in need of assistance. This, of course, is particularly unfortunate in the case of Negroes. To meet this problem a much closer integration between the work of the housing authorities and that of other welfare agencies is needed.

There is one group of economically disadvantaged families to which too little consideration has been given: the large families, partly because they are poorer and cannot pay the rents, and partly because very large dwellings are not provided in public housing projects. The average family size in public housing projects in 1941 was 3.9 which is about the same as for all urban families, exclusive of unattached individuals. This is remarkable in view of the fact that large families suffer much more from bad housing conditions than do small households, at the same time as they are less often economically able to purchase good housing.[55]

It is possible to add other similar criticisms. Still we should not overlook the fact that the problems are extremely complicated, particularly during the initial period of the program. The U.S.H.A. has given two valuable experiences. It has demonstrated that rehousing of slum families can be done in America. And it has shown that a federal agency, with only financial and no administrative power in the local communities, can give the Negro a square deal even in the South.

The lack of integration between the various federal housing programs, however, has been great, especially as the programs have affected Negroes. It is only recently, under the pressure of the war emergency, that the various federal housing offices have been combined into one agency, the National Housing Agency. It remains to be seen to what extent this move will bring about greater consistency.

7. SOCIAL SECURITY AND PUBLIC ASSISTANCE

We have already discussed some of the major social welfare programs, the farm security work, the public health activities and the low cost housing projects. Also, we shall touch upon certain government interferences with the labor market. We want to consider here other principal welfare provisions, such as social security, work relief, youth programs, categorical assistance, home relief, school lunches and other direct distribution of means of subsistence. Under the pressure of shrinking employment opportunities in agriculture and of industrial depression and job restriction in the cities, public relief *has become one of the major Negro occupations; all through the 'thirties it was surpassed only by agriculture and possibly by domestic service.* We must go into some detail in describing how the Negro fares in this substitute form of breadwinning.[a]

Prior to the New Deal period public relief was entirely insignificant in this country. Until the First World War even a state like New York expended less money for relief through public agencies than it did through private charities. In the South such a situation prevailed until the beginning of the 'thirties.[56] Participation on the part of the federal government was restricted to aid to veterans and similar special groups. Most of the states, prior to 1929, enacted programs for aid to dependent children and for workmen's compensation; and some states made special provisions for the blind and for the aged. Otherwise most of the social welfare work was carried on by counties and cities, or by private charity organizations; the poor farm or the almshouse was the main local institution of public welfare.[57] The practice was based on the theory: ". . . making relief deterrent by sending all destitute people to a local almshouse would be a means of preventing pauperism."[58] It was the time of "rugged individualism."

We have previously characterized the institution of large-scale public relief during the 'thirties as the one bright spot in the recent economic history of the Negro. Negroes, for obvious reasons, have gained even more from it than have whites. This is not to say, however, that their needs have everywhere been as much considered as have those of white families in economic distress. On the contrary, in many instances there has been pronounced discrimination against the Negro. Negroes have often found it more difficult to receive any relief at all than have whites in similar

---

[a] We cannot give anything like an exhaustive treatment of the subject. We shall omit, for instance, any discussion of the institutionalized welfare programs—asylums, reform schools, institutions for crippled children, child nurseries. We shall fail to deal with the implications to the Negro of certain major gaps in the social welfare system. Had we discussed all these things, our picture would scarcely be any brighter. Indeed, it would be darker. It is a well-known fact that all institutions for handicapped groups tend to be less adequate for Negroes than they are for whites in the South. The result is that the proportion of feeble-minded and insane persons who are not taken care of in institutions is higher for Negroes than it is for whites—something which, of course, affects the Negro crime rate; a whole Negro community may have to pay for what one subnormal Negro does to a white woman. Negro reform schools in the South usually have a lower standard and are more crowded than are white reform schools. The consequence is that a greater proportion of Negro than of white juvenile delinquents has to be cared for in homes; in the Negro communities there are fewer homes which fit the purpose than there are in white communities. Other juvenile delinquents are simply sent to ordinary penitentiaries when they cannot be taken care of in reform schools. Negroes need more child nurseries than do white people, since their homes are less adequate for the purpose of rearing children, and Negro homemakers more often have to take up gainful work. Yet, at least in the South, they have fewer of them than have whites. There is no public health insurance in America. This is more serious for Negroes than it is for whites, since Negroes have higher rates of sickness. The absence of any adequate form of aid to migrants, likewise, hampers Negroes more than it does whites.

economic circumstances. Moreover, average relief grants per client have often been smaller for Negroes than they have been for whites—and this particularly in communities where Negro relief recipients, to an even greater extent than white recipients, were selected from the poorest people. In such cases Negro clients would have needed even greater assistance than would have been needed by white clients, but relief agencies could not see it that way. The difference, in many cases, may not be more than a few dollars a month, but, still, it counts; for the general level of relief grants in such communities always tends to be low.

The situation, however, is different in various regions. By and large, there are three types of areas that need to be distinguished: urban North, urban South, and rural South.

The urban North has the highest standards in all sorts of social welfare. It shows much more of a consistent pattern than does the South, in respect both to the general level of relief expenditures and to the apportionment of public funds between Negroes and whites. There is no evidence of any direct discrimination against Negroes in respect to any major relief programs. The proportion of Negroes on relief is everywhere higher than is the corresponding proportion of whites, and the difference is so large that it seems that Negroes have about the same chances of receiving public assistance as do whites of equal economic status. Both the Consumer Purchases Study and the National Health Survey indicate that, in the middle of the 'thirties, roughly one-half of the Negro families in the urban North were on relief. This usually was three to four times more than the corresponding proportion of whites. The small residual of nonrelief families with an income of less than $500 was not significantly higher for Negroes than it was for whites.[59]

In the urban South as well, there is usually a higher percentage of relief recipients among Negroes than there is among whites. The difference, in most cases, is quite marked, but it is, nevertheless, much smaller than in the North. Taking a simple average of the relief rates, according to the National Health Survey, for 9 large and middle-sized cities in the South, one finds that in 1935, 25 per cent of the Negro and 11 per cent of the white families were receiving public assistance. The corresponding figures for 9 small cities were 15 and 10 per cent, respectively—indicating a much smaller difference. The Consumer Purchases Study gives about the same impression; it was particularly in the small cities and villages that the difference between the proportions of Negroes and whites on relief was small. This study shows, moreover, that the residual of families who were not on relief but who had incomes of less than $500 was small in the white group in Southern cities and villages, but in the Negro group it was high, often making up as much as one-third or more of all the families. There was even a significant number of Negro families with less than $250 who failed to receive any relief.[60] This, of course, means that, in spite of the higher total relief rates for Negroes, it was usually more difficult for them to get relief than it was for whites with similar needs.

In Southern rural farm areas, the pattern was different. Relief rates were, in the first place, generally lower than they were in the cities and villages. Moreover, in all counties in four Southern states (North Carolina, South Carolina, Georgia, and Mississippi), where both Negro and white farm families were included in the sample investigated by the Study of Consumer Purchases, there were relatively fewer Negroes than whites on the public relief rolls. Thus, not even on a straight population basis did the Negroes get their proportionate share in the relief appropriations. Also, there was a pronounced divergence in the relief rates between various groups of counties. Of the white farmers and croppers, from less than 1 per cent to 15 per cent were on relief; the corresponding rates for Negroes varied between a fraction of one per cent to 11 per cent.[61]

We have chosen to establish these patterns on the basis of the Consumer Purchases Study and the National Health Survey, because they are the only major materials in which data on relief are combined with information on the income distribution of the nonrelief families. Owing to this circumstance, we have been able to prove that discrimination against Negroes may exist even when, as in the urban South, Negro relief rates are two or three times higher than the white rates. Otherwise, however, we can pick almost any material for those years and arrive at substantially the same conclusions concerning the general relations between relief rates for Negroes and whites.[62]

8. SPECIALIZED SOCIAL WELFARE PROGRAMS DURING THE PERIOD AFTER 1935

For the years after 1935 there is little information available on the Negro's share in all benefits from the social welfare programs. Generally there are few data by race in the current reports of federal, state, and local governments—and even less for those states in the Deep South where the Negro population is most dense and discrimination against the Negro is most strongly entrenched.[63]

For most of the specialized programs, however, there are one or several special investigations concerning the representation of Negroes in the clientele and—at least in some cases—their share in the benefits. The main impression from these studies is that there has been no significant change in the Negro's relative position in the public welfare system. He continues to be best off in the North, where the general level of relief expenditures is highest, and where there is little or no direct discrimination against him. In the urban South he usually receives a larger share of the total relief benefits than corresponds to his population ratio, but this difference is much less pronounced than in the North. He is worst off in the rural South, where the most apparent racial discrimination is shown, at the same time as the general relief standards are very low. The South continues to be inconsistent in its treatment of Negroes.

There seems to have been a change for the worse, however, in the position of the Negro women. Those among them who cannot receive old age benefits, old age assistance, or aid for their dependent children seem to have greater difficulties in getting public assistance—other than surplus commodities—than they experienced prior to 1936. On the whole, there is, at least in the South, and particularly in the rural South, little adequate provision for such needy people who happen not to be provided for in any of the specialized programs administered, financed or sponsored by the federal government. There is no public assistance for many unemployed able-bodied workers, for instance, who are not covered by unemployment compensation or when W.P.A. grants do not suffice for more than a part of them. On the other hand, there are certain categories of Negro and white clients who may receive larger grants than were usual under the previous program.

9. THE SOCIAL SECURITY PROGRAM

Conditions are different, however, in different parts of the social welfare system. "Social security" has a position quite apart from the ordinary relief programs. Whether or not there is much direct discrimination against Negroes in the administration of the Social Security Law is difficult to say, since there is comparatively little direct information available on how Negroes are actually treated. Conditions may vary from one part of the system to another. There is little likelihood of any direct discrimination in the old age benefit system which is administered entirely by the federal government.[a] Unemployment compensation is technically administered by the states, but there is a certain federal collaboration, and the basic provisions are comparatively uniform since they were more or less sponsored by the federal government, and all are geared to the federal Social Security Act of 1935. Workmen's compensation for injuries in the course of employment, on the other hand, is entirely a matter of state initiative and state administration.

What we do know, however, is that all these social insurance systems are so constructed that Negroes, along with certain groups of white work-

---

[a] The Old Age and Survivors' Benefit System should be distinguished from Old Age Assistance. The latter is a form of tax-financed relief supported by both federal and state (and often local) governments. The Old Age Benefit System is financed by means of payroll taxes paid by both employers and employees. (See alphabetically listed articles on the various subjects in Russell Sage Foundation, Russell H. Kurtz [Editor], *Social Work Yearbook*, *1941* [1941;] and Richard A. Lester, *Economics of Labor* [1941]. p. 438.)

ers, are in a disadvantaged position.[a] In other words, there is what might be called "indirect discrimination." Particularly, coverage is limited. In the case of the old age pension system there is really no reason at all why it should be related to the labor market, covering only wage earners and salaried workers in specific occupations.

> Here some short circuit in thinking must be at work which involves the position that industrialism is to blame for modern economic problems, so that they have to be remedied by special measures for those connected with industry. . . . It is fallacious, however, to believe that the problem of dependency for maintenance operates only in the sphere of wage earning. . . . Just as old age, death, and illness are not limited to industrial workers, so the risk coverage should not be so limited.[64]

What especially works hardships on the Negro is, of course, the fact that agricultural and domestic workers are excluded. In respect to old age insurance there is some information available which enables us to judge the quantitative significance of these exclusions.[65]

The development of workmen's compensation has depended entirely on state initiative, and there is a great variation in standards.[66] Mississippi does not even have a law requiring compulsory insurance of industrial accident risks.[67] Agriculture and domestic service usually belong to the "uncovered occupations." It has been estimated that only 40 per cent of all gainful workers are within the insurance system.[68] Laws enforcing accident preventive measures are often inadequate in the South.[69]

Thus the Negro's position in the social security programs to some extent differs from that in most other systems of social welfare. By and large, Negroes receive a much smaller share of the social security benefits compared to what they get under most other social welfare programs. They are always "under-represented" among the recipients of benefits, not only from the viewpoint of need, but also in comparison with the proportion of Negroes in the population.

10. ASSISTANCE TO SPECIAL GROUPS[b]

Among the recipients accepted for old age assistance during the period 1937-1940 about 12 per cent were Negroes, whereas of all persons 65 years

---

[a] The following criticisms are directed solely against social insurance systems in the United States, not against workmen's compensation systems. The latter, of course, have other faults.

[b] The Social Security Act of 1935, as amended, entitles the federal government to lend financial assistance to states, on a matching basis (50 per cent of total cost), for public assistance to three distinct categories of needy persons: aged, blind, and children under 16 (sometimes 18) years of age in broken families, provided that state plans adopted for the purpose meet certain specified federal standards. These three programs are called Old Age Assistance (O.A.A), Aid to the Blind (A.B.), and Aid to Dependent Children (A.D.C.). Many states share their parts of the cost with the local communities. The assistance is distributed by local Departments of Welfare.

of age or older, according to the 1940 Census, only 7 per cent were Negroes.[70] Thus, the proportion of Negroes among recipients of old age assistance is much higher than among aged people in general. The difference is particularly pronounced in the North. In the South it is less marked. Mississippi and Oklahoma differed from the other states in the South; in these states Negroes, in spite of their greater poverty, were actually less represented among the old age assistance recipients than among all aged people.[71] It is quite possible that similar flagrant cases of discrimination occurred in the rural areas of some of the other states; but no data exist which would allow us to test this assumption.

The average benefits are much lower in the South than elsewhere.[72] All the Southern states paid lower benefits to Negroes than to whites. The largest race differential appeared in Mississippi, where the average was $7 for Negroes and $11 for whites.

The two other categorical relief programs, aid to the blind and aid to dependent children, are quantitatively much less important than is old age assistance. The need of such relief, however, is particularly urgent among Negroes. It has been estimated, for instance, that the incidence of blindness is twice as high for Negroes as for whites. This means that about one-fifth of all blind persons in the United States are Negroes. It is obvious that Negroes constitute an even higher proportion of those blind persons who are in need of cash assistance. From this viewpoint, Negroes were certainly discriminated against, even though they constituted 20 to 23 per cent of all recipients accepted for aid to the blind during the years 1937-1940. The average benefit in 1939-1940 was $12 for Negroes and $22 for whites. This difference was due, mainly, to the fact that grants tended to be much lower in the South than they were elsewhere. In addition, many of the Southern states paid lower benefits to Negroes than they did to whites.[73]

Aid to dependent children is intended, primarily, for broken families with children. In view of the great number of widows and widowers in the Negro population, and its high divorce, separation, and illegitimacy rates, it is quite apparent that Negroes need this assistance much more than do whites. In 1937-1940 from 14 to 17 per cent of all recipients accepted for such aid were Negroes. In 7 of the Southern states, however, the proportion of Negroes among those accepted for aid to dependent children was smaller even than the proportion of Negroes among all children under 16 years of age. The discrimination was particularly pronounced in Georgia where, in 1940, 38 per cent of all children under 15 were Negroes, where as the proportion of Negroes among those accepted for aid to dependent children during 1937-1940 was but 11 to 12 per cent.[74]

Why is it that, in some Southern states, discrimination can go to such extremes in the case of aid to dependent children? It is quite possible that the special eligibility requirements contained in most state laws concerning the "suitability" of the home may have something to do with it. A few state laws even specify that the parent or guardian be a "proper" person.[75] Such regulations, of course, may easily lend themselves to rather arbitrary interpretations whereby, in particular, many Negro families can be cut off from any chance of receiving this kind of assistance. According to popular belief in the South, few Negro low income families have homes which could be called "suitable" for any purpose; and, of course, it is literally true that the poorer the home the less acceptable it tends to be as a place for rearing children. If standards of conduct have to be considered, unmarried mothers may easily be at a disadvantage; and since often practically all Negroes are believed to be "immoral," almost any discrimination against Negroes can be motivated on such grounds. Even though it is unlikely that professional welfare workers in the South would be taken in by such exaggerated notions, many of them, particularly in rural areas, may have to follow a compromise policy, the actual meaning of which is that Negro children are punished for the real or imaginary faults of their parents.

Average benefits are comparatively high. In 1939-1940 they amounted to $30 to $31 per family, or $13 per child for Negroes and whites alike. Some Northern states even paid higher benefits to Negro than they did to white clients. In the South, of course, it was most often the other way around.[76]

11. Work Relief

Except for unemployment compensation which, as we have seen, is inadequate for Negroes, work relief is the only special form of public assistance to able-bodied unemployed workers in so far as they cannot be placed under any of the youth programs.[a] This situation is unfortunate, for, as we shall find, general relief is virtually nonexistent in many Southern areas, and it is not possible to give work relief to all unemployed persons who fail to get any unemployment compensation benefits. Work projects, for one thing, cannot easily be enlarged and contracted with the fluctuations in total employment and, therefore, they must be kept well below the average level of unemployment. Actually the American work relief system is kept at an even lower level in relation to total unemployment than is necessary.[77] Under such circumstances, an unemployed worker is fortunate if he manages to get on W.P.A.—and the more so since the earnings on work relief are usually much higher than the benefits from the unemployment compensation system or from direct relief.

In April, 1941, there were 237,000 certified Negro workers assigned to work under the Work Projects Administration. They constituted 16 per

See Section 12 of this chapter.

cent of the total labor forces on W.P.A. This means that Negroes had a somewhat larger share in the work relief jobs than corresponded to their representation among the unemployed workers; for, according to the Census of 1940, there were about 13 per cent nonwhites among all persons who were without jobs and who were seeking work, or who were on emergency work.[78]

As usual, however, the situation was different in the North from what it was in the South. Many Northern states had at least twice as high a proportion of Negroes on the W.P.A. rolls as there was among the job seekers, but in most of the Southern states Negroes were less well represented on the work relief rolls than they were among the unemployed workers.[79]

It was particularly in the rural areas of the Southern states that there were relatively few Negroes among the W.P.A. workers. Virginia, exclusive of Richmond and Norfolk, for example, had a lower proportion of Negroes on the work relief rolls than there was in the total population. The same was true about Louisiana, outside of New Orleans. A state like Mississippi, of course, showed even worse conditions in this respect: in counties where there was no city with as much as 10,000 population, only 18 per cent of the W.P.A. workers were Negroes, although they had about as many Negroes as whites in the total population and, no doubt, had a preponderance of Negroes among all persons in need of unemployment relief.[80]

Since wage differentials on W.P.A. are extremely pronounced, the question of what job rating a person gets is important. The lowest wage that is paid the lowest group of unskilled workers in Southern counties with no city or town having as much as 5,000 population was—prior to a recent insignificant raise—$31.20. The highest wage received by professional and technical workers in Northern and Midwestern cities of 100,000 and over was $94.90. Thus, there is social discrimination on the W.P.A., and the consequence is, of course, that average wages for Negroes must be much lower than those paid to white workers. Even the lowest wage rate, however, is higher than that which many Negro workers can receive in private employment.

12. Assistance to Youth

The New Deal has instituted some significant programs for youth. On the one hand, there are the various activities administered by the National Youth Administration. On the other hand, there was the Civilian Conservation Corps, which was abolished in June, 1942.[81]

In the early days of the C.C.C. programs there were but 5 or 6 per cent Negroes among the boys in the camps. From 1936 until 1941 the proportion varied between 9 and 11 per cent. This means that, after 1936, Negroes shared in the benefits of the program in proportion to their numbers in the population, but that no allowance was made for the much greater needs in the Negro population. As usual, however, this general average conceals the differences between the South and the North. In the Fourth Corps Area, comprising 8 Southern states, 21 per cent of the C.C.C. boys, in May, 1939, were Negroes. Since no less than one-third of all males 14 to 24 years of age in these states in 1940 were nonwhite, this means that Negroes were grossly under-represented in the program. In the rest of the country, on the other hand, Negroes had more representatives proportionately in the C.C.C. camps than they had in the general population.[82]

The N.Y.A. programs show similar conditions. In January, 1940, 13 per cent of the workers on the N.Y.A. out-of-school program were Negroes. The corresponding proportion for the school program was 10 per cent. Excepting college and graduate aid, Northern states gave Negroes a much larger share of this assistance than corresponded to their proportion in the population; but in the South they did not receive as much of it as their relative numbers would warrant. In some cases this depended on the difficulties in the South of getting local sponsors for Negro projects. In respect to the school aid, of course, one could explain it simply by the fact that there are much fewer Negroes, in proportion, in secondary and higher schools than there are whites. This explanation has, however, the character of a vicious circle. The purpose of the school aid, of course, is to help low income boys and girls get an education. The fact that so few of them get it is an indication of the need for additional assistance rather than a reason for limiting the aid.[83]

13. GENERAL RELIEF AND ASSISTANCE IN KIND

For categories of people in need of aid, other than those mentioned, there are no chances of receiving any federally subsidized cash relief. In the South this means that their chances of receiving any cash relief at all are extremely small. Ordinary direct relief is insignificant in most of the Southern states. In February, 1941, the proportion of households receiving general relief varied in the South from 2.7 per cent (West Virginia) down to 0.3 per cent (Mississippi). The average benefits per month ranged, in January, 1941, from $25 (District of Columbia) to less than $3 (Mississippi).[84]

There are few data on the subject by race, owing to the fact that general relief is entirely a responsibility of the states and localities. This lack of information, however, does not matter much. The existence or nonexistence of discrimination against Negroes is in this case much less significant than is the fact that both racial groups are inadequately provided for in the South.

Of great quantitative importance, on the other hand, is the direct distribution of federal surplus commodities through local relief agencies. In June, 1940, over 10,000,000 persons, or 8 per cent of the total population, were receiving this kind of assistance, either in combination with other relief or independently. There was great unevenness in the apportionment of this aid among various states. Some states in the South used but little of it. Mississippi, on the other hand, gave this aid to almost one-fifth of its population. There, as well as in certain other Southern states, federal surplus commodities were actually the mainstay of the whole relief system.[85]

This surplus commodity program may fulfill a real function when used for the purpose of supplementing other relief. In the South, however, surplus commodities are often used as the only form of assistance to families in great need. In such cases, of course, they are totally inadequate. The program may even be harmful, then, in that it provides an excuse for not organizing more efficient aid.

The food stamp plan and the school lunch program constitute more rational and better organized attempts to supplement ordinary relief, improve the dietary standards among low income people, and increase the market for agricultural commodities. Just as there is no reporting about how many Negroes and whites are receiving surplus commodities, there is little or no information on how many Negroes there are among the millions of children who eat their school lunches at federal expense every day or on the extent to which food stamps are given and sold to Negroes. Yet these activities include some of the most significant attempts that have ever been made to raise the health standard of the people; and we ought to know whether or not the Negro has received his just share of these benefits, of which he is in such great need.

CHAPTER 16

INCOME, CONSUMPTION AND HOUSING[a]

1. FAMILY INCOME

In a general way we know why the Negro is poor. As a farmer, he has been kept in a dependent position and has been exploited. He was tied to cotton agriculture where the risks were such that at one time it brought sudden riches to white people but now forces surplus workers, particularly Negroes, to leave the Southern land. As a city worker, he has been kept out of jobs, especially the good ones. He has seldom been allowed to prepare himself adequately for jobs requiring high skill or professional training. Because of residential segregation, he is confined to slums to an even greater extent than his low purchasing power makes necessary. He does not share equally with his white fellow citizen in the free services given by the government.

Now, let us ask: What is the result of all this? Just how poor is the Negro? What is his annual income? Does he get a sufficient diet? In what kind of house does he live? How does his level of living, in terms of actual consumption, compare with that of the whites?

The typical Southern Negro farm family has an income of but a few hundred dollars a year. It is considerably lower than that of the average white farm family. This is due, in part, to the fact that Negroes are more concentrated at the bottom of the "agricultural ladder" than are whites. This is not the whole explanation, however, for *the income of the average Negro family at any given tenure status, is always much lower than is the income of the average white family*. Negro farm families of higher than sharecropper status are not any better off, on the average, than are white sharecroppers.[1]

Extremely low, also, are the incomes of most Negro families in the villages of the South. The Consumer Purchases Study indicates that half the "normal"[b] Negro families in 34 Southern villages—located in Georgia, Mississippi, and the Carolinas—had incomes under $330 in 1935-1936.

---

[a] This chapter is based principally on Richard Sterner and Associates, *The Negro's Share* (1943). This book was prepared for our study.

[b] A "normal" family consists of at least husband and wife, living together, with or without children.

The corresponding median income for "normal" white families was $1,220. About 17 per cent of all the "normal" Negro families in villages had incomes under $250, but were, nevertheless, not on relief. Only 4 per cent of the Negro households had incomes of $1,000 or more.[2] It goes without saying that the income level would have appeared still lower if broken families had been included in the estimates.[3]

Small *cities* in the South showed similar conditions, except that the income level for Negro families was somewhat higher.[4] It was still higher in the middle-sized and large cities of the South (Table 1). Nevertheless, half the "normal" Negro families in Atlanta had less than $632, and half the broken Negro families had less than $332. White families had more

TABLE 1

Median Incomes of Negro and Native White Families in Selected Cities: 1935–1936

Race	Normal Families						Broken Families		
	New York N. Y.	Chicago Ill.	Columbus Ohio	Atlanta Ga.	Columbia S. C.	Mobile Ala.	Atlanta Ga.	Columbia S. C.	Mobile Ala.
Negro families	$980 [a]	$726	$831	$632	$576	$481	$332	$254	$301
White families	1930	1687	1622	1876	1876	1419	940	1403	784

Sources: U.S. Department of Labor, Bureau of Labor Statistics, *Study of Consumer Purchases, Urban Series, Family Income in Chicago, 1935–36*, Bulletin No. 642, Vol. I, *Family Income* (1939), p. 162; *Family Income and Expenditure in New York City, 1935–36*, Bulletin No. 643, Vol. I, *Family Income* (1941), p. 19; *Family Income in Nine Cities of the East Central Region, 1935–36*, Bulletin No. 644, Vol. I, *Family Income* (1939), pp. 33 and 443; *Family Income in the Southeastern Region, 1935–36*, Bulletin No. 647, Vol. I, *Family Income* (1939), pp. 46–48.

[a] New York City, so-called "native area" only.

than twice and, in some cities, more than three times as much. Northern cities showed a substantially higher income level for Negroes. In New York City the median income for normal Negro families was $980 and in Chicago it was $726. Moreover, the differential between whites and Negroes was less pronounced than in the South. The reason for this is that—contrary to common belief—*the white urban population in the North does not have any significantly higher median incomes than has the white urban population in the South.*

These conclusions are based not only on the small group of cities sampled in the Study of Consumer Purchases. The National Health Survey for 1935-1936, containing information on income of Negro and white families in 16 Northern and 18 Southern cities, confirms both that race differences in income are much more marked in the urban South than in the urban North, and that median incomes for white urban families are about the same in the South as in the North.[5] The explanation is simple. The urban white population in the South has an "incomplete lower class," due to the presence of the Negro. Domestic service as well as certain other low wage jobs are more or less completely filled by the Negroes. Since, on the other hand, almost all well-paid work is monopolized by the whites, the average income of white workers is fairly high. This more or less balances the consequences of the fact that, in almost any given job, earnings tend to be lower than in the North. In other words, because the Negro is kept down, and because such a large part of the total urban income is retained by the whites, the white population in the urban South is not appreciably worse off than the urban population in the North—in spite of the greater general poverty in the South.

It goes without saying that *the majority of the Negro families are economically unable to live in a way compatible with any modern concepts of a "minimum health standard."* The Works Progress Administration has made up, for 59 cities, as of March, 1935, an "emergency budget" which averaged around $900 per year, estimated on the basis of the needs of a family of four persons.[6] This standard can scarcely be characterized as a real health standard.[7] Yet more than three-fourths of the "normal" Negro families in Columbia, South Carolina; Mobile, Alabama; and Atlanta, Georgia, had incomes below this limit. The conditions were much better in Columbus, Ohio, and in Chicago, Illinois, but even there the majority of the Negro families had sub-standard incomes. In the white urban population of these five cities, on the other hand, almost four out of five "normal" families had incomes high enough to buy at least an "emergency standard." Other income studies confirm that these differences are rather typical.[8]

2. Income and Family Size

The large majority of Negro families have to live on a standard which represents a constant threat to their health. Conditions are difficult for the large families: *Family income did not show any consistent tendency to be higher when the number of children under 16 in the family was greater. Sometimes it was even lower when there were more children in the family.*[9] There is, of course, nothing surprising in this absence of any significant positive correlation between income and number of children. In the main, it can be explained rather easily; and one finds the same phenomenon in other countries.[10] But the phenomenon is a serious one, and it does not seem as though the full implications of it were generally understood.[11] True, large families nowadays are not numerous. But, still, they rear the main part of the coming generation.[12] The condition of these large families, therefore, is much more significant than is suggested by their numbers. This is particularly true about Negroes, who have a greater proportion of large families than has the white population. Then, too, it must be considered that Negro incomes are usually so low to begin with that there is absolutely no leeway in the budget for children. Therefore, it happens more frequently in Negro than in white families that the arrival of children forces the level of living below any minimum health standard—that is, when it was not already below such a standard even before the children arrived.

If family income fails to increase with the number of minors in the family, it does increase somewhat, on the other hand, with the number of adult family members. This is so for two reasons. First, families in which one or more of the children have reached mature age are likely to have a family head who is in his more "productive" age. This factor, however, is much less significant for Negro than for white families. The average earnings of the husbands varied more with age in white than they did in Negro families[13] which is quite understandable in view of the fact that Negroes have slim chances of being promoted, or even of getting "steadier" jobs, as they become more experienced.[a]

The second reason why income tends to increase with the number of adult members in the family is, of course, that, on the average, there are more supplementary earners in the family when it is large. This is particularly true about Negro families. Their greater poverty forces family members out on the labor market much more often than happens in white families.[14]

3. THE FAMILY BUDGET

The Negro is generally believed to be an inefficient consumer. The truth of the matter is that, with few exceptions, we are all more or less bad consumers, regardless of our income and the color of our skin. However, when poor people use their income in a reckless manner, it is, of course, particularly harmful. We have a strong reason, then, to plan educational measures in order to ameliorate the situation, and such educational measures may well become a significant complement to other social welfare efforts. But the need for them should never be used as a moral excuse for not doing anything about poverty itself.

Most Negroes have little education. We cannot expect them to know more about a balanced diet than do the rest of us. Their incomes are not only low but also insecure, which, of course, tends to make budgeting and planning very discouraging. Many of them work in hotels and restaurants where white people do not always display habits of thrift. In the urban areas there are many children of Negro migrants from the rural South who do not believe that their parents can teach them how to organize one's life in a city. In the slums to which they are confined they do not see much prosperity based on thoughtful economic planning, but they may listen to poolroom tales about somebody's making easy money in the numbers

---

[a] See Chapter 13, Section 9, where it is pointed out that unemployment risks of Negro workers show a much less pronounced tendency to decrease with age and experience than do the unemployment risks of white workers.

racket. They, just like white youth in similar circumstances, may too easily be taken in by shallow values. Conspicuous consumption is one of them. The answer to such conditions, of course, is more education, better housing, increased economic security—not moral indignation.

Every observer knows that there is some conspicuous consumption and reckless spending even among poor Negroes. It is not possible to say, however, whether there is more or less of it than there is among whites of equal economic and social status. There are studies made on the subject, of course. By far the best one is the Consumer Purchases Study for 1935-1936. The information on expenditures, however, is limited to nonrelief families, which means that it is less representative for Negroes than for whites.[15] It is limited, furthermore, to such households from which it was possible to obtain information concerning their expenditures for an entire year. In spite of all commendable efforts to contact different sorts of families, and the extensive use of field-workers, we cannot assume that anything near the right proportion of the bad consumers were included in the study; for they generally are much less likely to give reliable information about their expenditures during a whole year than are others. Despite such limitations of the Consumer Purchases Study, it is the best of its kind in the world and can be used to understand all sorts of problems connected with income and consumption.

One result of the study seems especially surprising. Negroes consistently balance their budgets better than do whites in the same income groups. In the low income groups where expenditures usually exceed the income, the average deficits are smaller for Negroes than they are for whites. In the middle income groups (there are too few Negroes in the higher brackets to be considered) the average surpluses are higher for Negroes than they are for whites. It goes without saying, of course, that when all income groups are combined, Negroes have much smaller surpluses—or higher deficits—than have whites, but that is just an effect of the greater Negro poverty. In comparable cases *Negroes almost always seem to be the more careful budgeters.*[16]

These findings are, perhaps, not as unreasonable as they may appear at first sight. There may be several explanations of the phenomenon. Negroes may have greater difficulties in obtaining credit. The lower and lower-middle income groups may include a greater number of whites than of Negroes who have "seen better days" and have not yet become adjusted to their present condition; or who anticipate improved conditions and, for that reason, spend more than they happen to earn at the moment. Negroes, to a greater extent, can be expected to be "adjusted" to their low incomes and, of course, they usually have no economic raises to look forward to. Finally, because of the general limitations in the opportunities for Negroes, it is possible that these income groups include a great number of Negro families whose general economic ability surpasses their actual earnings.[17]

Of course, there is always a possibility of a bias in the sample. Yet it is hard to see how such a bias could so consistently affect the Negro group differently from the white group. At any rate, it seems to have been ascertained that *the general notions about Negro improvidence are greatly exaggerated*. The Negro population includes a substantial number of families who know how to balance their family budgets better than the average white family of corresponding means.

TABLE 2

PER CENT DISTRIBUTION OF TOTAL FAMILY CONSUMPTION ITEMS, FOR NORMAL NONRELIEF FAMILIES IN SELECTED COMMUNITY AND INCOME GROUPS,[a] BY RACE: 1935-1936

Community and Income	Race	Total	Food	Hous- ing	Household Operation and Furnishings	Clothing and Personal Care	Other
New York							
$1,000–1,499	Negro	100.0	35.3	28.2	11.4	10.3	14.8
	White	100.0	39.4	25.7	11.4	8.4	15.1
Atlanta							
$500–999	Negro	100.0	36.7	17.8	14.2	12.1	19.2
	White	100.0	39.9	16.5	17.2	10.5	15.8
$1,000–1,499	Negro	100.0	31.0	16.6	14.6	14.3	23.5
	White	100.0	33.0	16.8	17.0	12.0	21.1
34 Southern Villages							
$500–999	Negro	100.0	41.2	12.4	13.0	14.2	19.2
	White	100.0	38.0	13.3	16.6	13.7	18.3
Georgia and Mississippi farm owners and tenants, except croppers							
Under $500	Negro	100.0	63.0	5.4	10.5	9.8	11.3
	White	100.0	59.7	7.3	10.3	10.5	12.2

Sources: Adapted from U.S. Department of Labor, Bureau of Labor Statistics, *Study of Consumer Purchases, Urban Series, Family Expenditure in New York City, 1935–36*, Bulletin No. 643, Vol. 2, *Family Expenditure* (1939), Tabular Summary, Tables 2, 3, and 4; *Family Income and Expenditure in Selected Southeastern Cities, 1935–36*, Bulletin No. 647, Vol. 2, *Family Expenditure* (1940), Tabular Summary, Tables 2, 3, and 4; and U.S. Department of Agriculture, Bureau of Home Economics, *Study of Consumer Purchases, Part 2, Family Income and Expenditure, Five Regions*, Miscellaneous Publication No. 396, *Family Expenditure* (1940), particularly Table 40; *Farm Series, Family Income and Expenditure, Five Regions*, Miscellaneous Publication No. 465, Part 2, *Family Expenditure* (1941), particularly Table 35.

[a] Where there were too few white families in the sample for income groups most typical for Negro families, it was necessary to select higher income groups. Most other income groups in these communities show about the same race differentials. Data for Columbia, South Carolina, and Mobile, Alabama, indicate about the same race differentials as those for Atlanta, Georgia.

There are many details in the data on family budgets which indicate how Negroes have been taught by their tradition of poverty to economize even more than do white families of similar economic status. To a greater extent than these comparable white families they do their laundry at home rather than send it to a commercial laundry; rarely do they hire any household help; more often do they bake their own bread rather than buy it; less often do they purchase processed foods. They have fewer cars, washing machines, and vacuum cleaners than have white families in similar economic circumstances—partly, perhaps, because it is more difficult for them to obtain installment credit. Most of these things mean that there is more work for Negro women to do in their own homes. Yet they take on gainful work, outside their homes, to a much greater extent than do white women.[18]

It should be mentioned, too, in this context, that expenditures for support of relatives and friends are higher among Negroes than they are among whites even at given income levels.[19] The explanation of this is simple enough. A Negro with an income of, say, $800 is much more likely than a white person with the same earning power to have relatives who are still worse off.

Also it seems that *urban Negroes allocate a somewhat smaller part of their total expenditure to basic necessities, such as food and sometimes housing,*[20] *and a greater part of it for clothing, personal care, and certain miscellaneous items,* such as tobacco, recreation, reading, medical care, than do white families with similar incomes (Table 2). This may possibly be due, to some extent, to poor spending habits.[21] There does not seem to be any significant difference of this kind in rural areas, however. It must be emphasized, further, that the absolute amounts that most Negro families can spend on things other than basic necessities are extremely small.[22] Most Negro families are much too poor to develop into real spendthrifts.

4. BUDGET ITEMS

This becomes even more apparent when the detailed data for various consumption items are inspected. Let us consider clothing. The absolute amount spent by nonrelief Negro families in Atlanta with an income of less than $500 was only $24. Those in the income group $500-$999 spent $72, which was exactly the same amount as that expended by white families of equal economic status. These two income groups, together with the relief families, included more than four-fifths of all "normal" Negro families in Atlanta, whereas almost three-fourths of the white families had incomes above this limit. At successive income levels, Negro outlays for clothing showed a somewhat more rapid increase than did corresponding expenditures in white families.[23] Much more important is the fact that clothing expenditures are so restricted in these income groups in which most Negroes are concentrated.[24]

Expenses for medical care for Atlanta Negro families with incomes under $500 averaged $19. For the group $500-$999 the amount was $42. When we know that white families having incomes of $3,000 and more, although afflicted by sickness to a much lesser extent,[a] spent an average amount of

* See Chapter 7, Section 5, and Chapter 15, Section 4.

$253 for the same purpose, we get some idea about the tremendous health needs in the low-income Negro population. It has been estimated that adequate medical and dental care, when purchased on a group basis, can be had for about $25 per person per year and for about $100 for a family of four.[25] The corresponding minimum cost for Negroes, usually buying such services on an individual basis and suffering from much more illness than the white population is, of course, much higher; it may well run into several hundreds of dollars per family per year. The effect of poverty, in the absence of cooperative organizations and of adequate public health provisions, means that most Negro and white low income families fail to get nearly as much medical care as they need. In addition, some families may have their finances completely upset when hit by severe disease or physical accidents requiring extensive medical care. There were some Negro and white families in Atlanta with incomes under $1,000, who had to spend $100 to $200, or even more, for medical care during the year 1935-1936.[26]

Expenses for recreation and tobacco were quite small for Negro families in the average Negro income brackets.[27] The difference in standard was even greater than the figures indicate, since Negroes had much less access than did whites to free public recreational facilities, like parks, libraries and so on.[a]

One gets the same impression whatever part of the family budget one takes up for closer inspection. The effects of Negro poverty are apparent everywhere. In order to avoid too much detail we must concentrate our attention on the two main items: food and housing. Those are the items for which one would expect the racial differences in standard to be least pronounced. For low income people generally spend a larger part of their budgets on these basic necessities than do more well-to-do families; and for this reason, the percentage of the total Negro income used for buying food and housing is higher than is the corresponding percentage of the white income. Yet we shall find enormous racial differentials in standards even in respect to these items.

5. FOOD CONSUMPTION

Dietary conditions are crucial. The progress of the science of nutrition during the last few decades has made us understand that there is a large difference between barely avoiding starvation and enjoying a real "health diet." We have in this case a more objective basis for formulating the requirements for a minimum standard of living than we can find in regard to any other major item of consumption.

It goes without saying that there are huge differences between the diets of Negro and of white families. In the main, they depend on the obvious fact that Negroes are so much poorer than whites. In addition, however,

[a] See Chapter 15, Section 5.

there seem to be certain interesting differences even when income is kept constant. One may call these latter differences "cultural," but that does not mean that they have nothing to do with economics. In part they may depend on traditions from a time when the Negro's economic conditions were different. In part they may depend on circumstances inherent in the Negro's present economic status. We cannot go into this question and can only state the factual situation.

For one thing, as we have already pointed out, *the average food expenditure per family often tends to be somewhat lower for Negroes than it is for whites even in the same income group*. This condition, of course, helps to make the food consumption of Negroes different from that of whites even at given income levels.[28] The general differences for all income groups combined, of course, are much larger.[29]

If a group has a low average consumption of milk and vegetables, it does

TABLE 3

PERCENTAGE OF NORMAL NONRELIEF FAMILIES WHO DURING A SURVEY PERIOD OF ONE WEEK IN 1936 FAILED TO CONSUME SPECIFIED FOODS

Family Type and Kind of Food	Southern Farm Counties			Southern Villages		Atlanta, Columbia and Mobile	
	Negro Owners, Tenants and Croppers	White Croppers	White Owners and Other Tenants	Negro Families	White Families	Negro Families	White Families
All Normal Families							
Fluid Milk	33.7	25.9	11.2	31.2	11.3	29.0	9.3
Eggs	33.6	17.2	11.4	48.6	10.2	20.2	3.8
Fresh Fruits	66.2	47.2	33.7	51.6	10.6	27.6	5.1
Fresh vegetables	13.6	9.0	8.3	17.7	3.8	5.0	1.7
Potatoes and sweet potatoes	48.0	29.8	26.2	43.6	13.3	29.2	8.9
Large Families [a]							
Fluid milk	37.8	30.0	8.9	34.7	10.7	16.5	(b)
Eggs	37.2	19.4	11.4	54.2	16.8	23.3	(b)
Fresh fruit	68.7	52.4	32.3	56.9	16.8	25.1	(b)
Fresh vegetables	15.0	8.8	5.7	13.9	2.3	4.2	(b)
Potatoes and sweet potatoes	48.1	31.8	27.3	45.8	15.3	25.4	(b)

Source: Adapted from U.S. Department of Labor, Bureau of Labor Statistics, *Study of Consumer Purchases, Urban Technical Series, Family Expenditures in Selected Cities, 1935–36*, Bulletin No. 648, Vol. 2, *Food* (1940), Tabular Summary, Table 4; and U.S. Department of Agriculture, Bureau of Home Economics, *Consumer Purchases Study, Urban and Village Series, Family Food Consumption and Dietary Levels, Five Regions*, Miscellaneous Publication No. 452 (1941), Tables 30, 33, and 34, and *Farm Series, Family Food Consumption and Dietary Levels, Five Regions*, Miscellaneous Publication No. 405 (1941) Tables 48, 51 and 52.
[a] Families of husband and wife and three to four children under 16; and families consisting of husband, wife, one child under 16, as well as four to five others, regardless of age.
[b] Data not available.

not mean that every family in the group consumes the same small quantities of these foodstuffs. Some use more than the average. Others have no regular consumption of them at all. Roughly 30 per cent of the "normal" Negro nonrelief families in the South did not consume any milk during a whole survey week in 1936 (Table 3). There was a similar proportion of Negro families reporting no consumption of eggs. Almost half the Negro farm and village families consumed no potatoes or sweet potatoes. Two-thirds of the farm Negroes, one-half of the village Negroes and over one-fourth of the city Negroes failed to eat any fresh fruit during the week. In rural areas there was a significant number of Negro families who did not get any fresh vegetables. These proportions were in many instances rather high for white families as well, particularly for white croppers. Yet in every single case Negroes were worse off. It should be recalled that all these percentages would be much higher and that the race differential would appear still more pronounced if all the low income groups had been adequately represented in the study.

Such deficiencies in diet, of course, are highly dependent upon income. In Atlanta, Columbia, and Mobile the proportion of nonrelief Negro families who failed to drink any milk during the week was 43 per cent when the income was below $500, but 18 per cent when the income was $2,000-$2,999. The corresponding figures for white families were 26 and 6 per cent, respectively.[30] These differences seem to be rather typical; similar observations can be made for other foodstuffs, and other community groups.[31] They show, however, not only that income means much, but also that it does not mean everything. The fact that even some families in the economic middle class fail to consume milk and other important protective foods is often due just to bad consumption habits or to ignorance. It seems that this particular kind of unwise consumption is especially prevalent among Negroes, since they tend, in every income group, to expend less for food than do whites.

It is startling to find that even among large families, many of whom have three or more children under 16, there are many who do not have any regular consumption of milk, eggs, fresh fruits or potatoes. The proportion of such cases, at least among farm and village Negroes, is often higher among large than among small families. The explanation, of course, is simply that income does not tend to increase with the number of children. This more than offsets the fact that large families always tend to spend a greater proportion of their income on food than do small families.[32] Therefore, the value per meal per food-expenditure-unit (or "average-adult")[a] tends to decline drastically with increased family size (Table 4).

[a] The food-expenditure unit, for which we use the phrase "average-adult," is a measure of the need of an average adult person. The needs of children are expressed in terms of this unit need for purposes of comparison. See footnote (a) to Table 4.

TABLE 4

Average Value (in Cents) per Meal per Food-Expenditure-Unit[a] in
Small and Large Normal Nonrelief Families, by Race

	Southern Farm Areas			Southern Villages	
Family Type[b]	Negro Owners Tenants and Croppers	White Croppers	White Owners and Other Tenants	Negro Families	White Families
Small families	8.6	10.8	12.6	9.7	14.1
Large families	4.9	6.8	8.8	3.8	8.0

Sources: U.S. Department of Agriculture, Bureau of Home Economics, *Consumer Purchases Study, Farm Series, Family Food Consumption and Dietary Levels, Five Regions,* Miscellaneous Publication No. 405 (1941), pp. 176–178, and *Urban and Village Series, Family Food Consumption and Dietary Levels, Five Regions,* Miscellaneous Publication No. 452 (1941), p. 96.

[a] Persons 20 years or older are counted as 1.0 food-expenditure-unit; persons 13 to 19 years as 1.1 food-expenditure-unit; persons 6 to 12 years as 0.9 unit, and children under 6 years as 0.6 unit.

[b] Small families are those consisting of husband and wife without children. Concerning large families, see Table 3, footnote (a).

This is particularly true in the case of Negroes, since they usually have no room whatever in their family budget for the increased needs brought about by a large number of children. Large Negro families in Southern villages expended less than 4 cents per meal per "average-adult." This was not even half of what corresponding white families expended, and it was about 60 per cent less than the figure for Negro two-person families. The plight of the large Negro families is only too evident.

In the economic groups most typical for Southern Negroes,[33] the majority of the families had diets which failed by far to meet modern "optimal" requirements regarding content of proteins, minerals and vitamins.[34] Half the Negroes studied in farm areas and villages, having a food expenditure of $0.69—$1.37 per week per "average-adult," even failed to get the energy value standard of 3,000 calories a day, and between one-fourth and one-fifth of them got less than 2,400 calories—this in spite of the fact that Negroes are concentrated in heavy work for which the requirements are often much higher than is the usual standard. Conditions were decidedly better when food expenditures were from $1.38 to $2.07 per unit per week, but even in this group there were a large number of Negro and white families who failed to get real "health diets."

On the lower levels—that is, in income groups and food-expenditure groups most typical for the Negro population—the majority of the families had diets which failed to meet certain even more restricted requirements and which, for this reason, were characterized as "poor" by the Bureau of Home Economics (Table 5).[35]

It seems, therefore, that we are entitled to draw this rather general but,

TABLE 5

DIETS OF NORMAL NONRELIEF NEGRO AND WHITE FAMILIES IN
THE SOUTHEAST CLASSIFIED BY GRADE: 1936–1937[a]

Food Expenditure Group, Income Class, Community Group, and Race[b]	Number of Families in Sample	Percentage of Diets Graded		
		Good	Fair	Poor
1. Families classified by weekly food value per food-expenditure-unit[c]				
$0.69–$1.37				
Negro city and village families	143	0	4	96
Negro farm owners, tenants, and croppers	109	3	17	80
$1.38–$2.07				
Negro city and village families	124	7	30	63
White city and village families	114	4	30	66
Negro farm owners, tenants, croppers	89	19	39	42
White farm owners and tenants, except croppers	133	26	41	33
2. Families classified by income				
$250–$499				
Negro city and village families	126	14	19	67
$500–$999				
Negro city and village families	145	12	22	66
White city and village families	83	12	37	51
White farm owners and tenants, except croppers	124	45	25	30

Sources: U.S. Department of Agriculture, Bureau of Home Economics, *Consumer Purchases Study, Urban and Village Series, Family Food Consumption and Dietary Levels, Five Regions*, Miscellaneous Publication No. 452 (1941), pp. 55–60 and 71; *Farm Series, Family Food Consumption and Dietary Levels, Five Regions*, Miscellaneous Publication No. 405 (1941), pp. 83–89, 101 and 106.

[a] Diets were classified as *poor* if they failed to meet any one of the following requirements in regard to the food content per nutrition unit per day: protein 50 grams, calcium 0.45 gram, phosphorus 0.88 gram, iron 10 milligrams, vitamin A 3,000 International Units, thiamin 1.0 milligram or 333 International Units, ascorbic acid 30 milligrams or 600 International Units, riboflavin 0.9 milligram. They were classed as *fair* if they met all these requirements by less than a 50 per cent margin with respect to one or more nutrients; as *good* if the diets contained at least 50 per cent more of each nutrient. Not even the last standard is as high, in every respect, as the "dietary yardstick" recommended by the National Research Council (New York *Times* [May 26, 1941]). The Bureau of Home Economics, however, used a somewhat comparable standard (the so-called *excellent* diet) which was 100 per cent higher in respect to vitamins and 50 per cent higher in respect to other nutrients than was the *fair* diet. (U.S. Department of Agriculture, Miscellaneous Publication No. 452, *op. cit.*, pp. 55–56.) There were too few Negro families with such diets to warrant special consideration.

[b] Groups with less than 75 representatives in the sample are excluded. No income grouping has been published for Negro farm families. Income and food-expenditure groups are included only in so far as the sample for them contained at least 75 Negro families.

[c] Food-expenditure-unit is roughly equal to one person. See footnote (a) of Table 4.

nevertheless, significant conclusion: *the majority of the Negro population suffers from severe malnutrition.* This is true at least about the South. Conditions may be somewhat better in the North, for which we do not have any adequate information.

6. HOUSING CONDITIONS

Housing is much more than just shelter. It provides the setting for the whole life of the family. Indeed, whether or not any organized family life will be at all possible depends very much on the character of the house or dwelling unit. Children cannot be reared in a satisfactory manner if there is no place for them at home where they can play without constantly irritating the adults or being irritated by them. Over-crowding may keep them out of their homes more than is good for them—in fact so much that family controls become weak. The result is that some of the children become juvenile delinquents. This danger may become even more pronounced if there are insufficient recreational facilities in the neighborhood, something which is often characteristic of Negro areas.[a] Children in crowded homes usually have great difficulties in doing their home work; their achievements in school may suffer in consequence. The presence of boarders in the homes, or the "doubling up" of families in a single residence unit, which is much more frequent in Negro than in white families, usually means that there cannot be much privacy; often it means a constant threat to family morals. Crowding, in general, has similar effects. In addition to the moral and mental health risks, there are all the obvious physical health hazards.

In fact, the correlation between poor housing, on the one hand, and tuberculosis, venereal diseases, prostitution, juvenile delinquency, and crime, on the other hand, has been demonstrated so often by American experts that we do not have to add anything to the evidence.[36] This point should be kept in mind in any evaluation of Negro family life, of Negro crime and of Negro sickness.

Nothing is so obvious about the Negroes' level of living as the fact that most of them suffer from poor housing conditions. It is a matter of such common knowledge that it does not need much emphasis. We shall, therefore, only sample the great amount of available data.

Let us consider, first, the conditions in rural areas. The South, generally, has the poorest housing conditions in the country.[37] The Negro in every respect is worse off than is the white farmer. Half the white, and four out of five of the Negro farm homes, were made of unpainted wood. The proportion of houses having foundations, floors, roofs, in poor condition, although high for white farmers, was still higher for Negro farm families. One-half of the Negro farm homes in 11 Southern states had foundations in poor condition, and about an equal number had roofs and interior walls and ceilings in poor condition. More than three-fourths of the Negro farm houses were unscreened, and only 3 per cent of all Negro homes—as against 24 per cent of the white homes—had screens which were in good condition. The Consumer Purchases Study, although low income families are under-represented in its sample, shows that 10 per cent of the Negro farm families and over 2 per cent of the white farm families were without any toilet or privy of any kind. It is probable, however, that the situation has improved in this respect, since federal agencies have, during recent years, built a great number of farm privies in the South.[38]

The rural South has the largest number of persons per residential house-

[a] See Chapter 15, Section 5.

hold in the country. Yet the farm houses are smaller on the average than in any other farm region except in the Mountain states where they are just as small.[39] This means, of course, that there is more over-crowding in the farm regions of the South than in any other farm region. Such over-crowding particularly hits the large families of which, in the Negro group, the majority seems to be more or less suffering from cramped housing conditions.[40]

Concerning housing conditions in Southern villages there are comparatively few studies; yet we know that the race differentials are enormous. Just to take an example: more than three-fourths of the Negro village families in the sample for the Consumer Purchases Study were without any indoor water supply; the proportion of such families in the white group was 15 per cent. Two-thirds of the large Negro village families—as against 28 per cent of the white families—were living in homes with more than 1.5 persons per room.[41]

Southern cities, just like Southern rural areas, have, in general, much worse housing conditions than other sections of the country.[42] Negroes are much worse off than are whites both in Northern and in Southern cities. It even happens that *nonrelief* Negro families may suffer from certain specific deficiencies to a greater extent than do white *relief* families. According to the National Health Survey, this was true, for instance, in respect to the frequency of cases where there is no private toilet for each dwelling unit so that two or more residential households have to share one toilet. In one group of Northern cities (Chicago, Cleveland, Detroit, and St. Louis) 27 per cent of the Negro relief households and 21 per cent of the Negro nonrelief families were living under such conditions. The corresponding figures for white relief families and for white nonrelief families with an income of less than $1,000 were 13 and 11 per cent, respectively. There were similar race differentials in other groups of Northern and Southern cities. The proportion of families with private inside flush toilets, likewise, was higher among white relief families than among Negro nonrelief households.[43] The sample for urban nonrelief families in the Consumer Purchases Study indicates similar conditions for different income classes.[44]

These findings are certainly significant. Urban Negro housing is poorer than even the low income status of the Negroes would enable them to buy. This may be due to the fact that, at least in Southern cities and villages, Negroes, even at a given income level, spend less money on housing than do whites. It seems, however, that there is another and even more fundamental cause: the artificial limitation in the choice of housing for Negroes brought about by residential segregation.[a]

[a] A discussion of residential segregation is given in Chapter 29, Section 3. See, also, the section on housing policies (Chapter 15, Section 6).

The racial differential in housing accommodations for all income groups combined is enormous. Let us take just a few examples, picked at random, from recent Real Property Inventories. In Detroit 34 per cent of the Negro-occupied dwelling units were considered to be either unfit for use or in need of major repairs; the same proportion for white-occupied dwelling units was 6 per cent. The corresponding figures for Harrisburg, Pennsylvania, were 73 and 14 per cent, respectively. For Norfolk, Virginia, they were 25 and 5 per cent; for Savannah, Georgia, 55 and 11 per cent. We do not have to add to this list; the differential is quite considerable in almost every place where there is any appreciable Negro population.[45] It even goes so far that the general slum problem in many cities is largely a Negro problem. Wherever there are Negroes in the cities, it will be impossible to eliminate poor housing unless Negro areas are given a significant share of the attention.[a]

Data from the National Health Survey (Table 6) indicate that there is a great race differential also in regard to crowding in urban areas. The situation is particularly serious in the South where the dwelling units are smaller on the average, than elsewhere, at the same time as families tend

TABLE 6

PERCENTAGE OF URBAN FAMILIES SHOWING VARIOUS DEGREES OF CROWDING, BY REGION[a] AND RACE: 1935–1936

	East		Central		South	
Degree of Crowding	Nonwhite	White	Nonwhite	White	Nonwhite	White
Percentage of Families in dwelling units with more than						
1.5 person per room	8.0	3.7	12.9	5.0	21.2	8.3
2.0 or more persons per room	4.7	1.7	9.0	3.3	16.0	5.8

Source: U.S. Public Health Service, *The National Health Survey, 1935–1936*, Bulletin No. 5, Sickness and Medical Care Series (1939), p. 10.

[a] The Eastern sample includes cities in Massachusetts, New York, Pennsylvania, and New Jersey; the Central sample includes Illinois, Ohio, Michigan, Minnesota, and Missouri; the Southern sample includes Virginia, Georgia, Alabama, Louisiana, and Texas.

to be large. Sixteen per cent of the Negro and 6 per cent of the white households in the urban South were living in dwelling units where there were two or more persons per room. These results are confirmed by the Real Property Inventories, many of which have been made in more recent years. They show, furthermore, to what extent crowding is correlated with family size: in many cities the majority of the large Negro families is overcrowded. The fact that large families and children are the main sufferers

[a] This fact has been considered in the federal slum clearance and low cost housing program under the auspices of the United States Housing Authority. See Chapter 15, Section 6.

means that the proportion of the total population that lives under cramped conditions is even higher than is the percentage of crowded dwelling units— a circumstance which is often overlooked.[46]

We have found that Negro families in Southern cities and villages use a somewhat smaller part of their total expenditure for housing than do white families in the same income class. This appears also when rent-paying families are studied separately. The situation seems to be different in New York, however, where Negro families in most income groups pay higher rentals than do whites.[47] When all income groups are combined, urban Negroes are usually found to use a greater proportion of their total expenditures for housing than is usual in the white population. The reason, of course, is the fact that poor families generally have to use a larger part of their income for housing than do the more well-to-do families. The housing item in the budget seems to be particularly cumbersome in New York, where, according to the Consumer Purchases Study, nonrelief Negro families used as much as 27 per cent of their total expenditure for this purpose, whereas the corresponding figure for white families was 22 per cent.[48]

There is a general complaint among Negroes that they have to pay higher rents than do whites for equal housing accommodations. It is difficult to get any unequivocal statistical evidence on this problem, and it seems that this is one of the main aspects of Negro housing on which additional research work is needed.[49] Nevertheless, we feel inclined to believe that rents are higher, on the average, in Negro- than in white-occupied dwelling units even when size and quality are equal. Most housing experts and real estate people who have had experience with Negro housing have made statements to this effect. Not only does there seem to be consensus on the matter among those who have studied the Negro housing problem, but there is also a good logical reason for it: housing segregation.[a] Particularly when the Negro population is increasing in a city, it is hard to see how this factor can fail to make Negro rents increase to an even greater extent than would have been the case if the Negroes had been free to seek accommodations wherever in the city they could afford to pay the rent. The fact that they are not wanted where they have not already been accepted must put them in an extremely disadvantaged position in any question of renting or of buying a house.

[a] Some white real estate dealers attribute the higher rent for Negroes to their carelessness and destructiveness. From our point of view, the important thing is that they observe the fact of higher rents.

CHAPTER 17

THE MECHANICS OF ECONOMIC DISCRIMINATION AS

A PRACTICAL PROBLEM

1. THE PRACTICAL PROBLEM

The picture of the economic situation of the Negro people is dark.[a] The prospects for the future—as far as we have analyzed the trends until now—are discouraging. The main practical problem must be how to open up new possibilities for Negroes to earn a living by their labor.

Southern agriculture offers no such new opportunities. It is, on the contrary, likely that Southern rural Negroes will continue to be pushed off the land and thus increase the number of job-seekers in nonagricultural pursuits. In Northern agriculture the main trend will also be a contraction in the demand for labor. The segregated Negro economy will never provide any great number of jobs. It is on the ordinary nonfarm labor market that Negroes have to look for new opportunities. In the nonagricultural pursuits, Negro job limitations, as we have found, are of four different types:

(1) Negroes are kept out of certain industries, North as well as South.

(2) In industries where Negroes are working, they are often confined to certain establishments, whereas other establishments are kept entirely white.

(3) In practically all industries where Negroes are accepted, they are confined to unskilled occupations and to such semi-skilled and skilled occupations as are unattractive to white workers. The main exceptions to this rule are in the building industry where the Negro had acquired a position during slavery but has been losing ground since then.

(4) Finally, there is a geographical segregation. Negroes in the North are concentrated in a few large cities. In the Western centers there is still only a small number of Negro workers. Negroes are even scarcer in the small Northern and Western cities.

---

[a] Studies on Negro labor deal almost exclusively with such industries and occupations where Negroes have an appreciable share of the jobs. The reader, for this reason, gets an exaggerated impression of the numerical significance of jobs open to Negroes. Therefore, although all such studies present a rather dark picture of actual conditions, the picture is seldom as dark as the facts.

Race prejudice on the part of the whites is the usual explanation given for these various types of job limitations. But to relate discrimination to prejudice means little more than to substitute one word for another.[a] Leaving this problem aside for the moment, we may observe that race prejudice and discrimination, in the economic sphere, operate principally in three different ways:

(1) Many white workers, even if they think that Negroes generally should have a fair share in the job opportunities in this country, tend to be opposed to Negro competition in the particular localities, industries, occupations, and establishments where they themselves work.

(2) Some customers object to being served by Negroes unless the Negro has an apparently menial position.

(3) Many employers believe that Negroes are inferior as workers, except for dirty, heavy, hot or otherwise unattractive work. Perhaps even more important is the fact that they pay much attention to the attitudes of both customers and white workers.

All these conditions, in many different ways, are self-perpetuating. Let us, in this context, just point to one element in this circular process.[b] Suppose that an individual employer would entirely ignore the race of those applying for work at his shop and would consider just the individual capacities of the job-seekers, white or black. The fact that most other employers exclude Negroes means that the individual employer would have a disproportionate number of Negroes applying for his jobs. The rumor about his unusual behavior would draw Negro workers from other localities, and he might soon find a majority of Negroes on his labor force. The consequence might be that his establishment would be shunned by white labor, and it is not impossible that the result would be an almost all-Negro shop. The best he can do if he wants to favor the Negro, without having to face such consequences, is to fix the percentage of Negro workers; but that means giving up the principle of selecting Negro and white workers on an individual basis.

White workers, of course, are up against the same problem, and they have even more reason to be concerned about it than have the employers. Every individual municipality, and even every state, is in a similar situation. Let us imagine that a certain state, by means of strongly enforced legislation, would succeed in abolishing most racial discrimination in the economic sphere. If similar strong measures were not taken simultaneously by other states as well, the result would be a tremendous increase in in-migration of Negroes to that state. *Thus, the very fact that there is economic discrimination constitutes an added motive for every individual white group to maintain such discriminatory practices. Discrimination breeds discrimination.*

[a] See Chapter 3, text footnote in Section 1, and Section 5.

[b] For certain other elements in this vicious circle, see Section 6 of this chapter.

Another major general condition behind the Negro's economic plight, which should be mentioned in this context, is the fact that most white people are ignorant about the total impact of what they have done to the Negro in the economic field. This, of course, is not a "primary cause," either. It only explains how white people have been able to do what they have done without having more of a bad conscience about it. Yet the practical significance of it is tremendous. We frankly do not believe that the Negro's economic status would have been nearly as hopeless as it now appears to be if white people more generally realized how all specific economic discriminations add up, and how effectively they bar the way for the Negro when he attempts to better himself.

In addition, of course, there are any number of secondary factors bolstering discrimination: inadequate vocational and other educational facilities for Negroes particularly in the South; the lack of appeal to the ambition of the Negro worker, who often feels that his fate depends less on his individual efforts than on what white people believe about Negroes in general; the political impotency of the Southern Negro; high sickness rates among Negroes; and so on. In the circular process of cumulative causation many of these handicaps are themselves partly caused by the job limitations which keep the Negro's economic status low.

No interests are served by attempting to brighten this sinister economic situation by undue optimism. The adequate response is instead to turn the problem around and ask the practical question: *How would it be possible by a planned economic policy to increase Negro opportunities for employment?* The possibilities seem to be greatest, of course, on the Northern nonfarm labor market which—whether we study it by geographical regions, industries, or occupations—contains the largest areas where Negroes have yet to gain a position. Still the possibilities in the South, too, must be kept in mind. The South's relative "saturation" with Negro labor is largely artificial. It depends, in the main, on the fact that Negroes are confined to such industries and occupations as are expanding only slightly or are regressing. Production of textiles, the largest manufacturing industry in the South, excludes Negroes entirely, except for certain types of secondary service work. Moreover, the South, up to the present war boom, showed a more rapid increase in industrial employment than did the rest of the country, but the Negro has been unable to get his proportionate share in this expansion. Thus, there are reasons both for defensive and for offensive action in the South as well as in the North.

In this chapter we shall attempt to analyze, in more general terms and from this practical viewpoint,[a] some of the main factors which determine the position of the Negroes in the urban labor market. For reasons already

---

[a] The value premises for the practical analysis in this chapter have been presented in Chapter 9, Section 3.

expressed, we shall give our first attention to the North. Some of the statements we shall make are substantiated, or, at least, illustrated, by the data recorded in Chapter 13 and Appendix 6. But on many points data are lacking, and inferences will have to be conjectural, as they are built, to some extent, on impressionistic observations.

2. THE IGNORANCE AND LACK OF CONCERN OF NORTHERN WHITES

Even in the North the Negro is generally believed to be inferior as a worker. White employees often are strongly against having any Negro co-workers. Yet these attitudes are less general and less well entrenched in the North than they are in the South. Many, perhaps even most, Northerners tend to be rather uncertain and vacillating on such matters. There is nothing in their general ideologies which would support economic discrimination against Negroes. There is no racial etiquette, little emotion about the "social equality" issue, no white solidarity for the purpose of "keeping the Negro in his place."[a] On the contrary, the equalitarian principles of the American Creed dominate people's opinions in the North. Northern states and municipalities, as we saw in Chapter 15, usually uphold nondiscrimination in public relief as well as in politics, justice, and all other relations between public authorities and the citizens.[b] *People in the North are "against" economic discrimination as a general proposition.* If the white Northerners had to vote on the issue, a large majority would probably come out for full equality of opportunities on the labor market: they would be in favor of making employment opportunities "independent of race, creed or color." The actual discrimination is, however, as we have seen, the rule and not the exception.

To understand this apparent contradiction, we shall have to remember, first, that *slight causes, when they cumulate, may have big effects; and second, that the whole issue is enveloped in opportune ignorance and unconcernedness on the part of the whites.*[1] Comparatively few white Northerners are actually engaged in discriminatory behavior which they recognize as such. The practical inference is that *the social engineering required should have its basis in a deliberate and well-planned campaign of popular education.* The education of whites is an important general need in the whole sphere of race relations, but the chances of success are much greater in the economic field than in any other.[c]

There have always been efforts to improve race relations by educational propaganda in American churches, schools, and in the press. But compared to the scope of the problem, these efforts have been quantitatively insignificant. The Negro is usually forgotten. Moreover, the efforts on behalf

---

[a] See Part VII.
[b] See Parts V and VI.
[c] This is related to the theory of the rank order in Chapter 3, Section 4.

of the Negro have largely been ineffective because they have been of a general type and have evaded practical issues. Except for the well-planned and efficiently carried out campaign against lynching in the South,[a] there has been, prior to the present war emergency, no example in recent times of a large-scale endeavor to educate the American white public in the Negro problem and to force it to face the practical consequences of the cherished general principles contained in the American Creed.

The importance of the inculcation of the general principles of democracy in the American people which has been going on for so many generations, should not be under-rated. It is true that practical and specific issues are often avoided in a rather opportunistic way, so as not to disturb the conscience of the white people. The fact that ignorance and unconcernedness are so opportune means, of course, that additional popular education along more concrete lines will meet tremendous emotional resistance. But this resistance is not insurmountable. People are also bent upon rationality. Their allegiance to the ideals of the American Creed is strong and is held consciously. The ideals of Christianity also command their allegiance. One implication of their belief in the principles of democracy and Christianity is that they are susceptible to the more specific and practical consequences of these principles. There are, as we shall find, other important trends that will make ignorance and unconcernedness more difficult to uphold, and that will press for public education in this field. Through unionization and social legislation the labor market is increasingly coming under the control of a formal regulation that will demand equality of opportunity.

There is an observation which we shall find substantiated in every aspect of the Negro problem, that the ordinary white American is the more prejudiced, the more closely individual and personal the matter is. When he becomes formal and, particularly, when he acts as a citizen, he is very much more under the control of the equalitarian national Creed than when he is just an individual worker, neighbor or customer. There is often a similar difference between the leaders and the masses in the North. Leaders are confronted with the wider issues. Therefore, it is more difficult for them to repudiate, openly, the American ideals of equality. The private individual, on the other hand, seeks to pretend that his individual behavior is an exception which is especially motivated and which creates no long-run harm to Negroes. If he fails to hire Negroes in his shop, or to welcome them as fellow workmen, he does not mean that Negroes should not have any jobs, but only that they should not have jobs where his own interests are involved.

Prejudice and discrimination show up devastating social effects only when viewed from a broader perspective. The individual, but not society,

[a] See Chapter 27, Section 4; and Chapter 39, sections on the N.A.A.C.P. and The Interracial Commission.

can raise the question: "Shall I take care of my neighbor?" A citizen of one single community can say, as a manufacturer did recently:

> Negroes here should be in the South. They should never have come to Milwaukee. for by so doing they have created a social problem for the city.[2]

The white Northerner can feel that the Negroes ought to be in the South. The white urban worker can likewise feel that the Negroes should be in the country, and the white farmer that they should not compete for the land. An individual employer or a local trade union may bar Negroes from a particular shop and claim that the Negroes should be somewhere else. But *on a national scale there is no "somewhere else"—unless it be in Africa.* Getting employment for Negroes becomes a concern not only for themselves but for the nation. The alternative is to let them become public charges. A definite policy becomes a necessity.

When, thus, labor market conditions become the concern of the federal and state governments and of a gradually consolidated national labor union movement, the "pass the buck" mentality becomes undermined. Causes and effects will have to be studied, responsibilities will have to be distributed and shouldered. And in this whole process, of which we are just seeing the beginning, a most significant thing is that the ordinary American follows higher ideals and is more of a responsible democrat when he votes as a citizen or elects workers' or employers' representatives to formal assemblies than when he just lives his own life as an anonymous individual.

Also of great importance is the fact that, on the national scene, there is no possibility that Negroes will take over all industrial jobs. The individual employer or the individual group of white workers can always cite the excuse that they have to discriminate since everybody else does; for otherwise, as we have pointed out already, they would have to accept all competent Negro workers excluded by other employers and by other groups of white workers. But there is no such excuse in national employment policies. There are 10 per cent Negroes in the population, and a little more in the total labor force; white workers will never be overwhelmed. By attacking the color bars everywhere, it is possible to minimize the change needed in any individual establishment if the Negro is to be completely integrated into the economic system. The breakdown of discrimination in one part of the labor market facilitates a similar change in all other parts of it. The vicious circle can be reversed.

The trend toward public control of the labor market is the great hope for the Negro at the present time. For the Negro, it is of paramount importance to make the most of it. Public authority is compelled to side with him, in one way or another. The objective of an educational campaign is to minimize prejudice—or, at least, to bring the conflict between prejudice and ideals out into the open and to force the white citizen to take his choice. The practical objective, in the economic sphere, is to break down the barriers against employment of Negroes, to open up new areas for the Negro worker: industrial, occupational and geographical.

3. MIGRATION POLICY

White Northerners do not always have the Negroes with them as do the Southerners. Negroes are almost absent, not only from the large rural areas in the North, but also from most of the smaller cities. Many of the small cities in the North and West have an expanding economy. Together they constitute the most important of all community groups to which Negroes yet have to gain entrance.[a] Their potential importance, in this respect, is the greater, since other barriers to Negro employment will give way only gradually, even in the best case. Because of such barriers the large cities in the North may soon become—or have become already—artificially "saturated" with Negro labor.

But the labor market in these small cities is at present practically closed to the Negro. This does not mean that race prejudice is particularly strong in these communities. But people there have few experiences with Negroes, and Negroes, therefore, appear strange to them.[b] And enough of the ordinary American derogatory stereotypes about the Negroes have spread to them to make the Negroes slightly suspect, both as workers and as citizens. Ordinary conservatism and community solidarity—which are more developed in the smaller cities—prevent employers from attempting to import Negro laborers. The local workers usually keep up a protectionist attitude and are against new competition. All feel vaguely that Negroes would be likely to cause problems—in the jobs, in the community and in other ways. It is always easy to check an influx of Negroes to a small all-white town. There is little of the anonymity that a large city provides. But since usually no employer ever takes the initiative in introducing Negro labor into such a community, and since Negroes themselves practically never try to get in, the white people are not forced to face the issue. They can preserve a clear conscience on the matter and support legislators who follow the American Creed in the state capital and legislate against economic discrimination.

It should not be forgotten, however, that there are many such cities, particularly in New England, which have a few Negroes. Usually the

[a] It is true that intra-regional migration—both white and Negro—is directed, mainly, to large cities; most migrations to small cities probably come from the surrounding country, or from other small cities in the vicinity. Such are the characteristics of the *unplanned* migration which we have experienced in the past. The discussion in the text concerns a migration which is *planned* for the purpose of securing additional job opportunities for Negroes. The degree of "saturation" with Negro labor, under such conditions, is a more important consideration than the maintenance of traditional patterns.

[b] See Chapter 8.

Negroes seem to get along fairly well and are not much discriminated against, at least as far as employment on the working class level is concerned. It is true that these scattered Negro populations have usually been settled there for a long time. Their presence has become part of what is traditional and they have enjoyed for generations the excellent educational facilities which are ordinarily offered in such cities. They are "good Negroes"—in the Northern but not in the Southern sense—educated, conservative, ambitious.

It is open to speculation why Negroes have been so reluctant to move to the smaller Northern cities.[a] In any case, *part of a rational planning to find new employment opportunities for Negroes must be an investigation of the possibilities for some portion of the Negro labor reserve to be settled in the smaller Northern cities where there are now few or no Negroes.* Certain general principles for such a policy—which preferably should be the responsibility of a public employment service qualified for and interested in positive job-finding[b]—seem rather obvious.

For one thing, the attempt should be made at such times and in localities where there is a labor shortage, so that employers would be interested and white workers would be less hurt by the new competition. It should under no circumstances be staged as an "invasion." It should be recognized that Southern Negro migrants are usually less well suited for such a transplantation to small Northern cities than are Northern Negroes.[c] Only individually picked, well-educated, and, preferably, vocationally trained, young Northern Negroes could ordinarily hope to get a permanent foothold in such smaller communities where there is little of the protective anonymity of the big city. The attempt should be prepared and supported by an educational campaign, and local leaders in church, school, business, and labor should be won over to the idea. The most should be made of the American Creed and of the common national responsibility for the economic catastrophe threatening the Negro people.

The task is a most difficult one. Even if fairly successful, such a policy of planned and organized migration to the smaller Northern cities can only have the indirect importance of easing the unemployment situation in the big cities by drawing away part of its existing Negro labor reserve. It will not directly touch the main problem of getting the Negro out of the stagnating rural South.

The small Northern cities, however, cannot accommodate more than a moderate proportion of unemployed and marginally employed Negroes—at least in a short time. Meanwhile, Southern Negroes will continue to go to the larger Northern cities and increase their supply of Negro labor of

[a] Some observations on this problem were made in Chapter 8.

[b] See Chapter 18, Section 2.

[c] See Chapter 28, Section 9.

a comparatively low educational level trained into attitudes and customs which are not favorable for easy adjustment to Northern city life. Even this migration could be steered by rational planning. There may perhaps be some Northern and Western centers which do not have many Negroes but which would be tolerant of a migration of Southern Negroes. Planned migration could be adjusted to employment trends in various localities. Positive measures should be planned for directing this new labor into suitable employment. A program of adult education for the crude Southern Negro laborers coming North should be instituted to familiarize them with the general culture and ways of life of the North and to give them the rudiments of vocational training.[a]

These are practical tasks for a federal employment service working in close collaboration with other private and public institutions for education and social welfare. They are of paramount importance, but until now have been almost entirely neglected. Even under such auspices the Negroes will have to watch the activity carefully through their organizations. The problem is not, let it be stated clearly, whether or not Negroes should migrate. Southern Negroes will continue to migrate under any circumstances, and they are compelled to move out of the South in considerable numbers. But without direction they will migrate to localities which are not best suited to receive them. The problem is rather whether Negro migration should continue to be determined by an irrational tradition, which brings the Negroes haphazardly to a restricted number of places where the Negro population quickly outgrows the existing employment opportunities; or whether it should be expertly planned to cause a minimum of friction and human wastage and a maximum of labor utilization and human efficiency.

4. THE REGULAR INDUSTRIAL LABOR MARKET IN THE NORTH

The situation in the large Northern cities where there are many Negroes is not altogether different from that in the small Northern cities where there are practically no Negroes. Even in those cities in the North where there is a substantial Negro population, Negroes do not work and have never worked in most industrial plants. Taking on a Negro worker sets a precedent and will ordinarily be avoided if possible.

Workers are usually conservative. An attempt by an employer to introduce Negro workers into a hitherto all-white plant will usually be met by more or less active resistance on the part of the workers. This resistance is likely to become more intense if Negroes are to get a share of the skilled jobs. Even a change in the Negroes' position in such plants where they have already been accepted may cause trouble—as, for instance, if Negroes are promoted to higher jobs than they previously have been allowed to

[a] See Chapter 41, Section 5.

have, or if an attempt is made to break up other segregational patterns in workrooms and cafeterias. Yet it is not impossible to overcome such difficulties. Much depends upon the firmness of the decision of the employers and upon the manner of introducing Negro workers. To spring such changes as a surprise on the white workers would not be advisable. But if Negro workers are introduced a few at a time, if they are carefully picked, if the leaders of the white workers are taken into confidence, and if the reasons for the action are explained, then the trouble can be minimized, and the new policy may eventually become successful—provided that the workers do not belong to an especially job-protectionistic and anti-Negro union, and that there is no general scarcity of employment.[3]

Under ordinary circumstances, however, there are few employers who would take so much trouble voluntarily, just for the purpose of contributing to the solution of the race problem. After all, the employer's main interest is to run a business. To continue using white labor only is always the easier way out. When Negroes have managed in the past to get into Northern industries and plants where they had not been allowed to work before, it has been due, almost always, to one of two factors: extreme scarcity of labor or the employers' desire to beat white unions. For the latter purpose employers have often used Negroes as strike-breakers, or they have taken them in just to keep the labor force heterogeneous and divided, thereby preventing unionization. In other words, they have used Negroes in the same way as they were accustomed to use fresh immigrants from Europe.

We shall discuss, subsequently, to what extent the present labor shortage is helping the Negro.[a] We shall find that, until mid-1942, the Negro had gained much less than could have been expected. In respect to the other factor favoring Negro employment—strike-breaking and dividing the workers—it is obvious that its significance has been decreasing rapidly during recent years. Labor unions are, more and more, coming into control of the labor market. The employers' practice of giving jobs to Negroes to keep the workers disunited is, therefore, vanishing. At the same time the American trade union movement is becoming more friendly toward Negroes.[b] Yet exclusionistic unions are still powerful; and even in that part of the labor market which is dominated by unions officially friendly to Negroes, organized labor—at least the local organizations—often resists introduction of Negro workers into all-white plants.

The fact, however, is not always publicized, for often the Negro can be kept out without much trouble. If an establishment is a "white shop," Negroes generally know this. Few of them ever try to get in—and those few who make the attempt can tell the rest of the Negro job-seekers about how futile it has been. In such cases Negroes are excluded with a minimum

[a] See Chapter 19.
[b] See Chapter 18, Section 3.

of effort on the part of both employers and white workers. Most white people never think of the fact that there is a definite policy to keep the Negro out. The "white shop" is part of the tradition and just seems "natural." The issue is not faced. The color bar, although as real as it can be, is almost invisible.

For these reasons it frequently occurs that Negroes are denied entrance to entire industries without anybody feeling much of a bad conscience about it. On the contrary, it may even happen that employers and union leaders exclude the Negro just because they have a conscience. It is an established custom in the South to take Negroes in and let them work under a system of more or less complete segregation; confining them to special jobs and special departments; denying them promotion; giving them separate eating rooms, toilets and water fountains. But such a system of consistent segregation and discrimination is not considered to be right in the North, even though some parts of it may be accepted. In plants where there is a system of fixed rules governing dismissals, rehirings, and promotions based on age, competence, and experience, one would have to face the problem of either excluding the Negro from some of these advantages—thereby breaking the consistency in the system—or of letting some Negroes work themselves up to the position of foremen over white workers. Although several compromises and modifications are possible and are in actual use in most Northern plants, none is satisfactory to the Northern conscience. Even the use of the same toilets or eating places by both races may bring trouble, particularly if there are a few Southerners in the labor force. Again, the employer solves his problem by excluding the Negro altogether.

5. The Problem of Vocational Training

The very fact that an exclusionist policy is established will, furthermore, result in a lack of properly trained Negro workers. This mechanism starts at the bottom of the system of training Negro youths. In the North, where the vocational branches of the public school system are freely open without discrimination, the teachers and the vocational guidance agencies connected with the schools often advise Negro youths not to take courses in those fields where they will later encounter difficulties in getting apprenticeship and employment. This problem is of rapidly increasing significance since formal vocational training is more and more becoming a prerequisite for entering skilled occupations.

The advisors are, like the Negro youths themselves, placed in a difficult dilemma. It must seem unrealistic and even dangerous to the future of young Negroes to encourage them to take vocational training in fields where they will be barred later. On the other hand, to avoid such training means to accept and fortify the exclusionist system, since then no Negroes will ever be equipped to challenge it. If the white persons responsible for vocational guidance are themselves just a little bit prejudiced, this will strengthen their inclination to discourage Negro youths from entering these vocations. At the same time, they can have good consciences and tell themselves and others that they are absolutely unprejudiced and are acting solely in the best interests of Negro youths. It is not their task to reform American society but to give individual guidance. I have seen this particular vicious circle in operation everywhere north of the Mason-Dixon line.[a]

6. THE SELF-PERPETUATING COLOR BAR

The vicious circle of job restrictions, poverty, and all that follows with it tends to fix the tradition that Negroes should be kept out of good jobs and held down in unskilled, dirty, hot or otherwise undesirable work. Residential segregation and segregation at places of work hinder whites from having personal acquaintance with Negroes and recognizing that Negroes are much like themselves. In the eyes of white workers the Negroes easily come to appear "different," as a "low grade people," and it becomes a matter of social prestige not to work under conditions of equality with them. The fact that Negroes actually work almost only in menial tasks makes it more natural to look upon them in this way. The occupations they work in tend to become déclassé.

When once the white workers' desires for social prestige become mobilized against the Negroes in this way, when they have come to look upon Negroes as different from themselves and consequently do not feel a common labor solidarity with them, "economic interests" also will back up discrimination. By excluding Negroes from the competition for jobs, the white workers can decrease the supply of labor in the market, hold up wages and secure employment for themselves. To give white workers a monopoly on all promotions is, of course, to give them a vested interest in job segregation.

Negroes, on their side, have to try to utilize every opening, even if it means working for lower wages or under inferior working conditions. The abundance of Negro labor, kept idle because of exclusionist policies, must always be feared by white workers. If given the chance, Negroes will accept positions as "sweatshop" competitors—something which cannot fail to increase the resentment of the white wage earners. Sometimes they may even work as "scabs" and so white workers get extra justification for the feeling that Negroes represent a danger of "unfair competition." The Negroes react by being suspicious of the white workers and their unions. For this reason, they are sometimes "poor union material" even if white

[a] For information on vocational training under the present war production program, see Chapter 19, Section 3.

workers choose to let them in on a basis of equality. White union members then resent the "ingratitude" of the Negroes.

The racial beliefs are conveniently at hand to rationalize prejudice and discriminatory practices. The whole complex of stereotypes, maintained by limited contacts, is an element in the vicious circle that perpetuates economic discrimination.[a] With some difficulty, white people might be taught that there are all kinds of Negroes as there are all kinds of whites, some good and some bad, and that many—not just a few—individual Negroes are better than many whites. But here the separation between the two groups works strongly against the Negroes. Anyone having to fill a position or a job, having to select a fellow worker at his bench, or a neighbor in the district where he lives, by just drawing a white or a Negro man without knowing anything in particular about him personally, will feel that, in all prudence, he has a better chance to get the more congenial and more capable man if he selects the white. Here the stereotyped concept of the average Negro as it exists in the Northern white man's mind works as an economic bias against the Negro.

7. A Position of "Indifferent Equilibrium"

There is a tremendous initial resistance to overcome when attempting to place even superior Negro labor in a plant where Negroes did not work formerly. Negro labor is often superior to the white man's expectation, partly because the thinking in averages and stereotypes makes him underestimate the individual Negro. Moreover, the fact that Negroes have greater difficulties than do whites in securing any kind of employment renders it probable that there is a greater proportion of capable workers in the Negro than there is in the white unemployed labor reserve. Employers who do employ Negroes, therefore, often get a higher appreciation of them as workers than employers who do not.[b] The same seems to be true of white workers. If they actually come to work together with Negro workers, they come to like them better, or to dislike them less, than they expected to.[4]

Under these circumstances, the extent to which Negroes work in Northern industrial plants is determined not as a stable equilibrium, of the type usually thought of in economic and sociological theory, but as an "indifferent equilibrium," like the one when a cylinder rolls on a horizontal surface and can come to rest in one position as well as in another.[c] *There are tremendous elements of inertia which resist the introduction of Negro labor where there has previously been none. If they get in, however, they*

[a] See Chapters 4 and 9.

[b] In addition, of course, the fact that some employers hire Negroes may indicate by itself that they have had a higher appreciation of them to start with.

[c] For a theoretical discussion of these types of equilibria, see Appendix 3.

will have better chances of staying. It is upon this theory that the Urban League works when trying to sell Negro labor to employers and unions, although with insufficient resources and community support.[a]

Our hypothesis gains plausibility when we look at the history of the Negro in Northern industry. The one period when—mainly due to acute labor shortage—he gained entrance to new fields of employment in the North was during the First World War. During the 'twenties he fortified his position in these new fields. During the Great Depression, of course, he could not make any further gains. But the more remarkable thing is that he kept as well as he did the new positions he had won. Another observation which also supports our hypothesis is the great inconsistency in the pattern of Negro employment in the North. In most industries and most plants Negroes are not hired. But in some they are, mostly for no other particular reason than that they once got entrance because of labor shortage or because the employer wanted to keep out unionism. Charles S. Johnson summarizes a survey of the industrial status of Negroes in Los Angeles, California, in 1926, as follows:

> . . . 456 plants of widely varying character were reached. . . . The most frequently encountered policy was one based upon the belief that "Negro and white workers will not mix." They did "mix," however, in over 50 of the plants studied. In certain plants where Mexicans were regarded as white, Negroes were not allowed to "mix" with them; where Mexicans were classed as colored, Negroes not only worked with them but were given positions over them. In certain plants Mexicans and whites worked together; in some others white workers accepted Negroes and objected to Mexicans; still in others white workers accepted Mexicans and objected to Japanese. White women worked with Mexican and Italian women, but refused to work with Negroes. Mexicans and Negroes worked under a white foreman; Italians and Mexicans under a Negro foreman. . . . Because white elevator men and attendants in a department store disturbed the morale of the organization by constant chattering and flirtations with the salesgirls, Negro men were brought into their places and morale was restored, in spite of the fears that the races would not "mix."[5]

Except for the presence of the Mexicans in Los Angeles, much the same picture of inconsistency can be reproduced from any big Northern city.

Another element of instability—and consequently of changeability—in the situation is the visible *interrelation between the attitudes of the employers and those of the white workers. These attitudes seem to be interdependent in such a manner that either one of the two parties is potentially able to influence the other one for the better or for the worse.* Employers who do not like Negroes almost regularly give as one of their main reasons for their exclusion policy that their white labor would object.[6] There are reasons to believe that they often over-estimate the difficulties of making white employees accept Negroes as fellow workers. As the employers them-

[a] See Chapter 39, Section 10.

selves by this policy are unable to get any practical experience with Negro workers, they often come to believe that Negroes are inferior for all but the most menial tasks. So long as the white labor supply is sufficient they see no reason to check their opinions.

White workers, most of the time, have to adjust themselves to the policy of the employers. There have been few, if any, serious incidents in the Ford factories in Detroit, where for many years the Negroes have had a comparatively good position, whereas most other automobile manufacturers have been reluctant to give Negroes a real break because they expect that the white workers would resent it. The main difference in the two situations seems to be that Henry Ford is known to have the definite policy of letting the Negroes have a fair share of the jobs. The white workers just have to accept this if they want to keep their jobs. Even Southern-born workers, although they usually tend to display much more race prejudice than others, have had to become accustomed to working with Negroes. Northern white workers are often said to start out with a feeling of strangeness and suspicion against Negroes. If they meet a firm policy from the employer, they change, usually quickly.[7]

The large margins of indifference toward the policy of hiring Negro workers, and the instability within these margins, are of tremendous importance for the practical problem we are analyzing in this chapter. In the discussion of the Negro problem there is, as we shall find in many of its various aspects, a constant temptation to over-stress the factors of resistance to change, and the literature is visibly tainted by this bias in the service of the "do nothing" attitude. In the economic field, the depression of the 'thirties has given greater plausibility to this bias. Large-scale unemployment has a tendency to check the trend toward improved race relations in the labor market. One of the main reasons why even in the present war boom Negroes so far have gained little ground[a]—and much less than during the First World War—is that the boom started with much white unemployment. In latter phases of the war boom, the instability discussed in this section might come to be of greatest importance, particularly if it be utilized by a well-planned policy directed toward mitigating economic discrimination. Generally speaking, it is safe to predict that any policy to secure and defend a place for the Negroes in the Northern industrial labor market will depend for its success on the possibility of keeping the general unemployment level low.

8. IN THE SOUTH

These observations have all referred to the North. The situation in the South is not entirely different, but there are certain significant dissimilarities, some advantageous and some disadvantageous. The factor of ignorance

[a] See Chapter 19.

and unconcernedness is important in the South, too. Many white Southerners would undoubtedly give their backing to positive measure to preserve a place for the Negro if they knew more accurately about his plight and about the unfavorable trends. But there is in the South an entrenched and widespread popular theory that the Negro should be held down in his "place." Discrimination in justice, politics, education, and public service creates an atmosphere in which economic discrimination becomes natural or even necessary in order to prevent "social equality."

On the other hand, there are, in the South, many people in the white upper class who feel, as a matter of tradition, that the whites should "look out for" and "take care of" their Negroes. As there are fewer and fewer personal ties between upper class whites and Negroes and the isolation between the two groups is growing,[a] this factor is becoming less and less important as a protection of Negro employment opportunities.

The mere fact that there are many more Negroes in the South makes them less strange to white people. The white Southerner does not react so much, and for such flimsy reasons, as many Northerners do, to having Negroes around. The employers have more experience with Negro labor and are often not so prejudiced against using it. The fact that they are seldom prepared to treat Negro and white workers on a basis of equality often makes it easy for them to employ Negro workers without having any "trouble." The workers are more accustomed in many trades to work with Negroes.

The Negroes have also had a sort of protection in the traditional "Negro jobs." These job monopolies, however, have been largely in stagnating occupations and trades. As we have seen, white workers have always been pressing against these job monopolies. Job exclusion in all desirable and most undesirable jobs has, on the whole, been steadily progressing. The Negro's prospects in Southern industry are not promising. The very fact that there are so many more Negroes working there already means that the possibilities for expansion of Negro employment are slighter than they are in the North. The high natural increase of the white population in the South, and the likelihood that many white farmers will be pushed out of Southern agriculture, means that the white pressure to exclude Negroes from jobs will be strong even if there should be considerable industrial expansion.

Particularly in the South the concentration of Negro workers in the unskilled jobs is dangerous for their future employment, as mechanization means a constantly decreased demand for unskilled labor.[b] Unskilled labor itself is changing character. Modern technical development means that formerly unpleasant jobs are becoming "suitable" for white workers. The

[a] See Chapter 30, Section 2.
[b] See Chapter 13, Section 8.

entrance of women into industry not only means that Negro labor has a new competitor but also intensifies the issue of "social equality." All these trends have been going on for a long time in the South. They are bound to continue. Since there is so much Negro labor in the Southern labor market, and since the resistance against keeping Negro labor in skilled work and "nice" unskilled work is so strong, it is difficult to see much hope for the Negro in Southern industry.

CHAPTER 18

PRE-WAR LABOR MARKET CONTROLS AND THEIR
CONSEQUENCES FOR THE NEGRO

1. THE WAGES AND HOURS LAW AND THE DILEMMA
OF THE MARGINAL WORKER

During the 'thirties the danger of being a marginal worker became increased by social legislation intended to improve conditions on the labor market. The dilemma, as viewed from the Negro angle, is this: on the one hand, Negroes constitute a disproportionately large number of the workers in the nation who work under imperfect safety rules, in unclean and unhealthy shops, for long hours, and for sweatshop wages; on the other hand, it has largely been the availability of such jobs which has given Negroes any employment at all. As exploitative working conditions are gradually being abolished, this, of course, must benefit Negro workers most, as they have been exploited most—but only if they are allowed to keep their employment. But it has mainly been their willingness to accept low labor standards which has been their protection. When government steps in to regulate labor conditions and to enforce minimum standards, it takes away nearly all that is left of the old labor monopoly in the "Negro jobs."

As low wages and sub-standard labor conditions are most prevalent in the South, this danger is mainly restricted to Negro labor in that region. When the jobs are made better, the employer becomes less eager to hire Negroes, and white workers become more eager to take the jobs from the Negroes. There is, in addition, the possibility that the policy of setting minimum standards might cause some jobs to disappear altogether or to become greatly decreased. What has earlier hindered mechanization has often been cheap labor. If labor gets more expensive, it is more likely to be economized and substituted for by machines. Also inefficient industries, which have hitherto existed solely by exploitation of labor, may be put out of business when the government sets minimum standards. These effects will not show up all at once.[a]

The most important of these laws is the Fair Labor Standards Act of

[a] The fact that these effects do not show up all at once is one of the reasons why it is impossible to give statistical evidence of the effects of social legislation upon marginal labor.

1938, usually called the Wages and Hours Law.[1] It provides for a minimum wage, which was 25 cents an hour in 1938, was automatically increased to 30 cents in 1941 and will be 40 cents in 1945.[a] Industrial committees can institute higher wage minima for particular industries. Work over 40 hours a week is overtime and is to be paid at time-and-a-half the usual wage rate. Children under 16 may not be employed.

The law covers only persons employed in interstate commerce or in production of goods for interstate commerce. Since workers in agriculture and domestic service are excluded from the benefits of the law, it is certain that the coverage is much smaller for Negroes than for whites. On the other hand, wherever Negroes are covered, the law must affect their wages more often and more substantially than in the case of white workers. The proportion of workers with wages below the new minima has been much higher among Negroes than among whites.

For the same reason, the law affects the South much more than the rest of the country, since it does not provide for any regional differentials regarding wage minima—not even such differentials as could be motivated by the differences in cost of living between the predominantly urban North and the largely rural South. The law will probably, in some measure, slow up the migration of industries to the South, which certain Southern states, particularly Mississippi, have encouraged by offering manufacturers special tax exemptions, free or low-priced factory lots, or even ready-built plants, as well as other advantages. The main selling point, however, has always been the cheap labor supply—incidentally, with particular emphasis on the fact that white workers are available—and the relative absence of trade union interference. Now, however, it seems that Southern industry will lose one of its main competitive advantages. This effect will increase the competition for jobs in the South and make the Negroes' chances for employment in Southern industry slimmer.

The fact that enforcement seems to have been slower in the South than elsewhere, probably also slower for Negroes than for whites, may have cushioned these effects. Moreover, there is a differential between North and South in respect to supplementary state legislation and enforcement by state agencies. Only three Southern states limit women's work to 48 hours per week, and state legislation restricting child labor is less extensive in the South than elsewhere.[2] Still, it seems safe to conclude that Negroes have been affected already—positively as well as negatively. An estimate quoted by Dabney, to the effect that the wage regulations brought about already under the N.I.R.A. had thrown half a million Negroes on relief by 1934,[3] seems more definite than the complicated character of the problem would permit, and is in all likelihood much exaggerated. It is not possible

---

[a] Similar minimum wages were instituted under the National Industrial Recovery Act of 1933, which was declared unconstitutional in 1935.

to single out what part of Negro unemployment is due to the new wage minima. But there are some data which at least give us a notion of what happened and provide some support to the hypothesis that the change has been considerable.[4]

It would appear as if the danger to the Negro's employment opportunities which is implied in the Wages and Hours Law would become particularly marked by 1945 when the minimum wage rate is to be increased to 40 cents an hour. This danger, however, seems to be passing because the current inflationary trends will probably become intensified to such an extent that it is doubtful whether 40 cents, by 1945, will constitute a higher real minimum than 30 cents now (July, 1942). In fact, it is most probable that it will mean less in terms of actual purchasing power. This would imply that the law, unless amended, soon will become insignificant as "a floor for wages," and also that the negative effects of it will become less serious.

Competing in importance with the Wages and Hours Law is the National Labor Relations Act of 1935 which forbids employers to interfere with unions, to foster company unions, to discriminate against union members, and to refuse to bargain with unions representing the majority of the workers. It superseded similar provisions under the National Industrial Recovery Act of 1933. It was widely ignored by the employers until the Supreme Court upheld its constitutionality in a series of decisions of 1937. This law is the main way in which the government supports trade unionism. The growth of the labor union movement will be discussed in later sections of this chapter. In this context we observe only that, in so far as labor unions succeed in raising wages and labor standards, this law has the same effect on Negro workers as does the Wages and Hours Law.

These various policies to stamp out exploitative labor practices are both in line with economic progress. They all tend to speed up mechanization. Therefore, they are likely to create serious unemployment among Negro labor because it is marginal, unless strong countermeasures are taken to improve employment opportunities for Negroes. Such measures should have been part of a rationally coordinated economic policy.[a]

2. Other Economic Policies

During the period of the New Deal a system of public relief and social security—work relief, direct relief, categorical assistance, old age and survivors' benefits, unemployment compensation, workmen's compensation and similar programs—has been introduced or further developed for the support of citizens in distress. The system is far from complete and by no means does it guarantee that all citizens in great distress will receive public assistance. As shown in Chapter 15, Negroes get fewer benefits, in relation

[a] Concerning federal government policies during the war boom, see Chapter 19, Section 3.

to their needs, than do whites. Nevertheless, since they are so much poorer than whites, their representation on the relief rolls usually exceeds their proportion in the population.

These programs must also have had important effects on supply and demand in the labor market. They must have made it easier for old people and women to stay off the labor market and thus decrease a labor supply which was already much too heavy for the market.[a] Thus they must have tended to make the competition for jobs less desperate in times of unemployment. They also lighten the labor supply because sometimes benefits are higher than ordinary wages. This cannot be helped, for, owing to the extremely wide variation in wage rates and frequent under-employment, the only alternative would be to keep all benefits below adequate standards. It is certain, anyway, that it happens much more frequently to the Negro than to the white clientele.

Public relief and social security have had other purposes, and their effects in keeping away marginal white and Negro labor from the labor market have been more or less incidental, even if not unimportant. On the other hand, those programs must also have had a cumulative effect in strengthening the bargaining power of labor. This, in its turn, must tend to push up wages and improve other labor conditions, which again tend to make the employment prospects for the marginal Negro labor less favorable.

Prior to the present war boom few attempts were made by public agencies to take positive measures in order to secure job opportunities for Negroes. The Public Works Administration and the United States Housing Authority did try to reserve jobs for Negroes in their construction work. Otherwise, no employment policy for Negroes and other similar groups was even discussed much. The Employment Service, which experienced a rapid development under the New Deal, is potentially a powerful instrument for dealing with problems of this kind. But, almost until the time when this country became involved in the War, little, if any, such use was made of it. The usual procedure in this country, as in most other lands, has just been to meet the requirements of the employers. If they want white labor, they get it. If they want Negro labor, they get that. Few employment offices have made any substantial attempts to do more than this one-sided type of employers' agency work—that is, they had not actually tried to "sell" unemployed labor.[5] And it is probable that even less has been done for Negroes than for whites until the present war emergency changed the situation to a limited extent.[b]

Nevertheless, it seems that a long-range development in this direction is to be expected. The Employment Service is the natural starting point

[a] See Chapter 13, Sections 9 and 10.
[b] See Chapter 19.

in any vocational rehabilitation work. It is equally natural that it should go in for educational work among employers who show a tendency to reject certain kinds of potentially useful labor—and if need be, also among white workers who are against letting Negro labor get an adequate share of the jobs. Because of the institution of large-scale public assistance in this country, the government nowadays has even a fiscal interest in the welfare of the Negro. It seems unlikely that the alternative of letting most Negroes become habitual relief recipients will be permanently accepted.

3. LABOR UNIONS AND THE NEGRO

The increasing power of the labor unions, and particularly their rising importance for unskilled and semi-skilled workers, is to the Negroes one of the most significant of all recent changes in the institutional framework of the American economy. Their past experiences with trade unions have been none too good in most cases. The recent development, however, seems to offer some hope. There is now an increased number of strong unions in which Negroes are included on a basis of equality or near-equality. The principal gains, of course, are just that Negroes have more protection in so far as they have been admitted into these industries. In addition, it is of great significance that these more liberal unions usually can be expected to cooperate, or at least to refrain from energetic resistance, when some other party—the employers or the government—wants to break certain occupational barriers against Negroes. Some of them have actually rendered positive assistance in making room for the Negro in plants and occupations where formerly they had not been allowed to work. Such attempts, however, have occurred, for the most part, during the present war boom, when the abundance of employment opportunities made Negro competition less objectionable to the white worker. Even so, they do not seem to have been significant from a quantitative viewpoint, but they may inaugurate an important change in union policy.[a]

There are grave risks, as well, in the increased union power. A greatly strengthened union movement holding the power over employment might, if dominated by monopolistic and prejudiced white workers, finally define the Negro's "place" as outside industrial employment. The post-war unemployment crisis will probably intensify job monopolistic tendencies on the part of white workers. Union leaders who want to protect the Negro's rights may have to face serious rebellions. Weighing the various factors, however, we are inclined to believe that the growth of unionism will in the long run favor the Negro. We have two main reasons for this belief. One is the observation that to exclude one group from full participation in the union movement—and from an equitable share in its positive results —is to put a weapon into the hands of the enemies of trade unionism which

[a] See Chapter 19.

they will know how to use. The American union movement, if it wants to become strong, must be based on a still largely absent, but gradually developing, labor class solidarity, which must be all-inclusive. The declining relative significance of the craft union spirit can be regarded as a first stage of such a development. The other reason is that the labor market and its organization will in all probability be subject to more government control, and the national administration will be forced to attempt to defend a place for the Negro in the labor market against exclusionistic and segregational practices by unions.

When pondering this whole problem, it should be made clear that this is not the first time it has looked as if organized labor definitely were on the move away from discriminatory practices. Time and again, in the history of American trade unions, there have been attempts to build a labor movement on the basis of workers' equality and solidarity, but so far these attempts, except in a few instances, have proved futile.[6]

The fact that the American Federation of Labor as such is officially against racial discrimination does not mean much. The Federation has never done anything to check racial discrimination exercised by its member organizations.[7]

There is no doubt that the rise in industrial unionism has increased the number of unions which do not discriminate against Negroes. The old unions of this group, like the United Mine Workers' Union and the International Ladies' Garment Workers' Union, have grown stronger, and new ones, like the United Steel Workers' Union and the United Automobile, Aircraft, and Agricultural Implement Workers' Union, have been added to the list. When the C.I.O. organized the mass production industries, it followed the principle that Negroes should be organized together with whites, wherever Negroes were working before unionization. Some of the new unions, as previously stated, have recently taken positive measures to give Negroes opportunities to work in occupations where they have not been working before and to defend more equality for them in job advancement.

It is understandable, for several reasons, that these attempts so far have not been significant from a quantitative viewpoint. The rank-and-file members, the majority of whom have only recently become organized, are often biased against Negro fellow workers. Many employers have been rather noncooperative in increasing the range of employment opportunities for Negroes. The Negro workers themselves often have difficulties in overcoming their old suspicions. And the leaders have had to put their main efforts into the work of building up the new unions. The time has been too short to bring about fundamental changes in industrial race relations. The observer finds that the leaders of the new unions are usually much more broad-minded and less prejudiced than the average run of white union workers. Many of the new unions have made a courageous start in workers' education and an important element of this education is to spread the principle of universal labor solidarity and to combat race prejudice.

Still there is much uncertainty in the present situation. The Negro workers have made a gain from the unionization of the mass production industries by becoming included in more unions. They have probably also profited from the very split of the American labor movement into the C.I.O. and the A.F. of L., whereby most of the progressive forces have been concentrated in one group, and both groups have been forced to compete for membership. This split cannot exist forever. Unity, when it comes, may be gained at the expense of the Negro.[8] This may be a pessimistic view, but it is worth considering.

The uncertainty in the situation is further enhanced by the fact that the Negro is really a precarious issue for the American trade unions. He can be used against them in a number of ways. If the unions do take the Negroes in and treat them as equals, employers often find it advantageous to appeal to the race prejudice of the general public and of the white workers themselves. This has happened many times, particularly in the South. Racial equality is one of the standing charges against the Southern Tenant Farmers' Union. On the other hand, if unions exclude Negroes or otherwise discriminate against them, it may be hard to convince the American public, especially in the North, of their consistent democratic ideology. One can gain much support from the general public by fighting persistently for the underdog. But a fight for all underdog groups, save the one most in need of being fought for, can hardly bring the same response. It is not that Americans, even outside the South, are so much concerned about the welfare of the Negro. But they are concerned about the integrity and honesty of those who present themselves as advocates of social and economic equality. As we have pointed out, the Northern whites are "against" economic discrimination as a general proposition, that is, when it does not concern themselves. And even if the general public would fail to react in this way on its own account, it is always open to enemies of unionism to publicize the racial discrimination in trade unions. Such a possibility, of course, is all to the good from the Negro's viewpoint. Still, it adds to the embarrassment of the union movement.

4. A Weak Movement Getting Strong Powers

All these difficulties must be seen against the background of the fact that American trade unionism, in spite of its age and recent progress, is still a comparatively weak movement. Basically, it is this weakness that endangers the Negro's position. At the same time, the weakness depends partly on the presence of the Negro worker.

In 1939, labor unions had only around 8,500,000 members—and this in spite of the fact that they had trebled their membership since 1933.[9] The total labor force of nonagricultural wage earners and salaried workers outside the unions must have amounted to some 36 millions. The membership figures have gone up and down with the business cycle in a manner which reveals an inherent lack of vigor. The main exception was the 'twenties, when the business boom failed to bring about any increase in unionization but was rather accompanied by a regress.

A common explanation of why the American labor movement did not develop more strength is that there has been strong resistance from the employers. American business has undoubtedly kept not only unusual political and social power, but also a militantly individualistic determination not to share its control over labor conditions with anyone. The company town, still to be found in some coal mine and textile areas of the South and in certain other regions as well, is the extreme case of employers' paternalism in the nonagricultural economy. It is characterized by an integration of property rights, municipal administration, and police power that, in some measure, approaches the condition of medieval European feudalism. But even outside the company towns proper, important employers or groups of employers have often had a power over police and court systems which has enabled them to check, in a rather efficient way, any tendencies toward unionization. And many of them have been known to supplement political influence by the use of private, armed police forces and strong-arm squads, often working even outside the premises of their plants. Big corporations, until a few years ago, hired labor spies by the hundreds. Many an attempt at unionization has been stopped by plain murder.[10] Engaging in extreme practices of this kind is not typical of the overwhelming majority of American employers, yet so many of them, particularly in the South, have used some sort of intimidation that there has been a rather effective barrier against the progress of unionism on this account.[11]

The resistance from the side of employers, however, is not only a cause of the weakness in the American trade union movement. To an extent it is an effect of it also. Employers in all countries have initially been hostile to labor unions, and everywhere the police and the courts have to an extent been utilized to strangle a developing union movement at the outset. But as the movement developed strength in the face of all difficulties, both the public authorities and the employers had soon to accept the new order in the labor market. The singularity in the American case is only that the relative laxity of the administration of laws in this country made the police and courts more obedient to the employers' interests and allowed the employers to take the law into their own hands much more than in comparable countries. Further, the labor movement actually had less momentum and for decades did not get strong enough to command respect from the public authorities and the employers. This view becomes strengthened when we witness how the employers' resistance is vanishing as the unions are becoming stronger.

The readiness shown by many American unions to use violence and other extra-legal measures themselves is also a sign of weakness. In discussing labor tactics with American union members, the observer often becomes shocked to find how natural it appears to them to take the law into their own hands when they get into a labor conflict. This characteristic can, of course, be partly explained as a sort of retaliation. The whole atmosphere around labor strife and collective bargaining in America is tainted by a tradition of illegality, and the employers must be blamed for a good part of this. But again, more fundamentally, this trait is an indication of weakness on the part of trade unionism. Strong and well-established unions do not need to fear illegal methods and still less to resort to such methods themselves. The insistence on the part of some American unions on the rule of the "union shop"[a] according to which the worker must become a member in good standing of a union in order to keep his job, is also more understandable as an indication of organizational weakness. A strong union movement does not need to be provided with such pressures.[b]

All those other excellent reasons with which some American unions, particularly among those organized along craft lines, provide the labor-baiters—job monopolism and nepotism, exploitative entrance fees, "closed unions," petty jurisdictional fights, boss rule, even corruption and racketeering—also are nothing more than signs of organizational weakness. They imply that the common worker has been hindered from coming into his

[a] The "union shop," technically defined, is one in which the worker, after he is hired by the employer, must join the union to retain the job. The "union shop" is fairly widespread and is the goal of most American unions. The "closed shop," technically defined, is one in which the worker is selected by the union, and not by the employer, from its own membership. The closed shop has now practically disappeared, and is the goal of only a few reactionary unions. The "closed union" is a union which tries to limit its membership so as to keep a monopoly of the jobs for its members. The closed union usually occurs in conjunction with the closed shop. The closed union is characteristic of a large number of A.F. of L. unions, but it is not the goal of many other unions. The union shop, the closed shop, and the closed union are all signs of the weakness of the American labor movement. For the early stages of organization, however, the union shop has much to commend it.

[b] One important corollary of this, incidentally, is that employers no less than workers have an interest in getting the trade union movement securely established in America. This is true far outside the field of the problems discussed in the text. Neither building contractors nor government agencies will, for instance, ever be able to stamp out the monopolistic wage policies and the practices hampering prefabricated building materials and other labor saving techniques in the building industry. But a hundred per cent strong labor movement, where the majority of workers are suffering economically from the monopolistic practices of building workers, might accomplish it.

own as a worker, as a union member and as a citizen—and maybe has not cared to come into his own. Again it must be emphasized that even the most mature trade union movements once passed through a period when, at least in some degree, there were irregularities of a similar nature. Every trade union movement has, for instance, had to go through the transition from craft unionism to industrial unionism, and the former type always retains some part of the labor market. Jurisdictional fights and job monopolism exist everywhere, although the degree varies. So, when putting the American trade unions beside those of any comparable democratic country, it is possible to state that the glaring shortcomings of the American unions are mainly a matter of degree and stage of development. This thought is often expressed in America and elsewhere, that American trade unionism is suffering from ordinary child diseases.

But there is an important qualification to be made to this statement. The American trade union movement is, as we have said, one of the oldest in the world. The lag in its growth may be thought of as a child disease become chronic. Undesirable union practices have become habitual and established. And, looked at from another point of view, the American trade union movement does not appear at all youthful with the usual faults of youth, but, on the contrary, has shown certain signs of senility. For one thing, the A.F. of L. has lacked, and is still lacking, the militant reformist spirit, the feeling that it is building a new world. It has not been convinced that it was serving economic democracy or, in any case, it has never convinced its membership of it. It has been fighting for petty interests. American business has, in this sense, always had more spirit, more of a feeling that it was carrying the destiny of the nation. The better unions in the A.F. of L. and the C.I.O. have decidedly more spirit and courage, and, therefore, more strictly observed principles.

The basic weakness of many labor unions in America has been their lack of democracy. The rank and file have been allowed too little influence; they have also cared too little about retaining influence. Many of the undesirable practices mentioned are merely symptoms of an underlying lack of democracy in the labor unions. It is significant both that there has been so relatively little workers' education in the American labor movement and that there is more of it in the better unions. The weakness of the American labor movement is only one example of a general trait in America: the weakness, until now, of organized and protracted mass movements—the political passivity of the common people in America. We shall discuss this American cultural trait in Chapter 33 and relate it to the several unique and closely interrelated factors in the social history of the nation: the heterogeneity of the lower classes during the long century of mass immigration, the open frontier up to the turn of the century, the rapid social mobility until the Great Depression, the individualistic middle class ideology, and so on. We shall there also find that important economic changes during the last generation have laid the basis for a fundamental shift to greater participation and solidarity among the masses of people in America. As the trade unions increasingly come to serve workers of all kinds, including those in the mass production industries, the more necessary will it be for the labor movement to embrace a common working class ideology rather than to remain the instrument for job-grabbing and group competition.

But there are other and more specific reasons for our belief that the Negroes will get more consideration from the unions in the future. The labor union movement has recently been growing in strength —due largely to government support. This is, of course, itself a sign of weakness. A strong labor movement is usually just as much against state interference on the labor market as the employers are, and it can afford to take such an attitude because of its independent strength. The American labor movement could not afford to reject government support; it had rather use its political influence to press for it. In the course of time it will become evident that *government support is followed by government influence.*

By its own policy the American labor movement is actually provoking government control. Quite aside from all sorts of irregular practices— which, as long as they exist even as exceptions, are crying for public control over the unions—the labor movement is forced to press for union shops. It is likely that the war emergency will help it to get union shop agreements in an increasing part of the labor market. But such power can be tolerated in a democratic country only if the doors to the unions are kept open and if democratic procedures within the unions are amply protected. As the labor unions are getting stronger, the demand will become ever more vigorous for governmental control protecting democracy in the unions. The important thing, from our point of view, is that the only way by which the unions in the long run would be likely to protect their present independence would be to reform themselves quickly. Either government control or independent democratic control would benefit the Negroes.

As the second alternative is less likely to become realized fast enough, it seems probable that not only the enemies of the labor movement but also its friends and, indeed, many of the organized workers themselves will raise the demand for government control over the unions. It is interesting in this context to refer to a recent article by Norman Thomas, who cannot be accused of being anti-labor or anti-union.[12] Thomas exemplifies the statement that "there are grave evils in the organizational setup and attitude of many American labor unions and their dominant bureaucracies" and sees the fundamental cause in their lack of democracy. He comes out with the following proposal:

Briefly, I propose that every union, to be entitled to recognition as the agency of the workers in collective bargaining (and without that recognition most unions would be doomed), must conform to certain minimum standards of democracy. Its doors must be open to all qualified workers, regardless of race, creed, or color, under reasonable standards of initiation fees and dues. Next, its constitution, by-laws, and practices must provide for orderly elections at reasonable intervals. And finally, a disciplinary procedure must be set up which will protect members of the union from arbitrary punishment more serious than most judges and juries can impose. Possibly some other requirements might be laid down, for instance, with regard to votes on strikes, but those which I have mentioned seem to me essential.[13]

If reform does not come from within the labor movement, it is likely that the government will take a hand, at least with respect to discriminatory practices. At least four states—Pennsylvania, New York, Kansas, and Nebraska—have in recent years been experimenting with legislation against racial discrimination in labor unions.[14] The number of such legislative attempts is increasing during the present war emergency; the federal government, as well, has taken certain action.[a] It is probable that such laws will be much more effective when they become integrated into a government program to preserve democracy and orderly procedures in the labor unions.

This problem should, however, be viewed from a still wider perspective. It is almost certain that the economic problems facing the government after the War will be centered around unemployment. Economic interferences on a huge scale are being planned to meet the post-war crisis. During the War the unions will probably become strengthened. Under these circumstances *it is simply incredible that the government will undertake tremendous financial efforts to create employment and leave to the strengthened trade unions the power of partly sabotaging this policy.* If unemployment becomes concentrated upon Negro laborers and other unpopular groups, which is quite probable, the government, which also carries the financial responsibilities for relief, can hardly abstain from taking efforts to hinder the unions from excluding Negroes from employment.

The Negroes themselves will demand, more strongly than ever, their share in all sorts of jobs, including those in skilled, clerical and professional occupations. And they will demand jobs where the economy is expanding and where there are prospects for the future. Much depends upon what gains they will make—or fail to make—during the present War. This War presents their first big chance since the First World War to gain any new footholds in industries and occupations where they have never worked before. Much will depend, also, on how the post-war liquidation crisis will be handled. These are the main problems that we have yet to consider.

[a] See Chapter 19, Section 3.

CHAPTER 19

THE WAR BOOM—AND THEREAFTER

1. The Negro Wage Earner and the War Boom

The present War is of tremendous importance to the Negro in all respects. He has seen his strategic position strengthened not only because of the desperate scarcity of labor but also because of a revitalization of the democratic Creed.[a] As he finds himself discriminated against in the war effort, he fights with new determination. He cannot allow his grievances to be postponed until after the War, for he knows that the War is his chance. If he fails now to get into new lines of work when labor is scarce, it means that he has missed the best opportunity he is going to have for years. Demobilization and liquidation of the war industries are bound to result in a post-war unemployment crisis. This implies, not only that there will be fewer jobs for everybody, but more likely than not that white workers are going to become even more bent on driving the Negro out of industry. If the Negro does not then have a recognized position, he will certainly not easily gain one as long as there is general unemployment.

We shall not give an exhaustive account of Negro employment during the war boom. Available information on the subject is spotty, or at least not well organized. Moreover, the picture is changing. On the whole, there is a slow improvement. There is a possibility that the situation when this book leaves the press may be more favorable than it was during the first half of 1942, which is as far as our data go.

It can be stated definitely that, until mid-1942, Negroes had not profited from the war boom to the same extent as had white workers. Indeed, until that time the record of the Second World War was, in this respect, much less impressive than was that of the First World War. *There has been no northward migration of Negroes, comparable in size and significance to that which occurred at the beginning of the First World War. Indeed, Negro participation in the migration to war production centers, in both the North and the South, was for a long time extremely restricted.[1] There is no new industry or previously all-white industry where Negroes have made any gains of the same importance as those they made during the First World War in Northern iron and steel plants, shipyards,[2] automobile factories, slaughtering and meat-packing houses.*

[a] See Chapter 45.

Since the war boom has brought about a tremendous scarcity of labor, and since the available labor reserve before the boom was much greater, in proportion, in the Negro than in the white population, one could have expected that unemployment rates would fall more for Negro than for white workers. That, however, has not happened. On the contrary, *the proportion of Negroes among the unemployed workers was considerably higher in the spring of 1942 than it had been two years earlier.*[3]

There are several reasons why the Negro has had much less of a chance during this War than he had during the last War. Let us enumerate the principal ones:[4]

(1) When the present war boom started, there was still widespread unemployment. In the initial stages of war production, therefore, there were large numbers of white workers available.[5]

(2) There is now in the North a much more well-organized resistance to accepting Negroes than was the case during the First World War. This, in part, is due to the fact that there had been much unemployment for about ten years, making white workers more watchful against letting jobs get away from them. Also, the Negro is no longer a new phenomenon in Northern industries; Northern white workers in so far as they are not under the effective influence of certain C.I.O. unions have had a chance to set their minds more definitely against him. Southern-born workers in Northern industries have helped to bring about this change in attitude; the Ku Klux Klan has been active in several Northern places. This is especially true in Detroit, which has an unusually large number of Southern-born workers.[6]

(3) Since employers nowadays to a great extent have accepted trade unions as bargaining agents, their need of the Negro as an ally in the fight against unions is much smaller than it was formerly.

(4) The need for unskilled labor, as previously mentioned, is relatively much smaller than it was during the First World War. This factor is highly significant. For, although the Negro has made several noteworthy "strategic gains" in skilled occupations, those gains, so far, have been rather unimportant from a quantitative point of view. It is not certain that he has improved, or even maintained, his relative position in the skilled labor force.[7] *We know that the Negro has been grossly under-represented in the vocational training program for war workers that has been organized by the government.*[a]

It must be considered, further, that the South, as was the case during the First World War, has received much less than a proportionate share of the war contracts. Although the South has almost one-third of the total population of the country, less than one-fifth of the total value of all war supply and facility contracts and allocations assigned within the United

[a] See Section 3 of this chapter.

States during the period from June, 1940, through May, 1942, were placed in the South.[8] The reason, of course, is that heavy industries are less well represented below the Mason-Dixon line than they are in certain other parts of the country. The result for the Negro is that, even if he were not discriminated against, he could not get his full share in the war jobs, except by moving North.

In spite of all these limitations, it is obvious that the War has brought about a considerable increase in Negro employment, reckoned in absolute figures. Also, it seems that the situation has improved somewhat as the war boom has gone on. Still further improvements can be expected since there will be additional increases in the demand for labor at the same time as more men of working age will leave the labor market for the armed forces. Women and Negroes now constitute almost all of the available labor reserve. This, together with the increased pressure from the government, may cause a certain change in the situation.

The subsequent analysis of certain specific aspects of the war boom will substantiate further the conclusions already drawn.

2. A CLOSER VIEW

The war boom is not a result of armament production alone. In addition, there has been tremendous construction work in camps and war production centers. Then, too, there have been substantial secondary booms in consumption and service industries, transportation and production of raw materials.

It is probable that, so far, the main Negro gains have been in those industries in the last category, where they were already well entrenched before the War. It is not only the expansion by itself which has given them increased employment opportunities in such lines of work; there is also the fact that these industries, generally, are characterized by low wages and other "disutility factors" which cause an outflow of white labor to armament plants. There is an increased demand for Negro labor in Southern agriculture. The Negro domestic has more of a chance when white girls go to factories. There is more work for Negroes in other service occupations (janitors, elevator operators). Many garages, automobile repair shops, and truck owners, in so far as they have not been forced to cut down their business because of gasoline and rubber shortage, have had to substitute Negro workers for white mechanics and drivers. The readiness to hire Negroes as porters and helpers in stores must have increased. There are more jobs for Negroes in production of lumber, coal, and turpentine, in tobacco manufacturing, in longshore work and in railroad transportation. These gains, however, are of little strategic significance. In none of these industries has the Negro been able to gain any substantial foothold in occupations higher than those in which he worked before. In

New York City, and possibly in other places, there are some commercial establishments, even outside of the Negro neighborhoods, which have started to use some Negro clerical assistance; but such cases are quite exceptional.[9]

In the construction industry, as well, there have been substantial gains in Negro employment, particularly in unskilled occupations, in the trowel trades and in carpentry. The Negro skilled worker in building construction was almost on his way out during the Great Depression but now he seems to have gotten a new opportunity. Yet Negroes have not shared equitably with the white workers in this construction boom. Particularly during the early stages of the war expansion, Negroes, as we have found, were grossly under-represented among the in-migrants to defense centers where much of the new construction work has been concentrated. Although some of the skilled crafts have relaxed their exclusionistic practices somewhat—partly due to government pressure, and in many cases only by granting temporary work permits without taking the Negroes into the unions—there are others which still try to keep the Negroes out.[10]

Let us turn now to production of war goods. Certain employment service data suggest that *during the early stages of the war boom the Negro was virtually excluded from most armament industries.* In October, 1940, only 5.4 per cent of all Employment Service placements in 20 selected defense industries (airplanes, automobiles, ships, machinery, iron, steel, chemicals, and so on) were nonwhite, and this proportion had, by April, 1941, *declined* to 2.5 per cent.[11] In September, 1941, it was ascertained that the great bulk of the war plants did not have any Negroes at all among their workers. About one-half of the anticipated further expansion was to occur in plants where the managements said that they would not hire any Negroes in the future either. This is the more astounding in view of the fact that such a declaration meant an open defiance of the President's Order of June 25, 1941, about abolishment of discriminatory practices in all defense work.[12]

The quantitative improvement which has occurred since the autumn of 1941 may concern only the absolute numbers of Negro workers in war production. At least, there is no indication that there has been an increase in the proportion of Negroes in armament plants; there may have been a decline.[13] This must be strongly emphasized, for in the current discussion there has often been a tendency to enumerate Negro employment gains without giving due consideration to the fact that white employment, in many instances, has increased to an even greater extent.

Conditions are different in different lines of war production. Moreover, they change from one region to another and from one plant to another within any given industry. There are cases when even the relative position of the Negro worker has been improved. Shipyards constitute the leading Negro-employing war industry. Many of them are hiring an increased proportion of Negro workers and have widened the occupational range for Negro employees. Some yards use Negroes in all occupations except professional and clerical. Nevertheless, as late as May, 1942, most shipyards still used Negroes almost solely in unskilled jobs. By and large, private yards are more restrictive than are Navy yards and Southern yards are less willing to hire Negro workers at higher occupational levels than are Northern yards, but there were several exceptions to this rule. In Miami, Florida, it has been impossible to use Negroes in skilled and semi-skilled work, since there is a city ordinance forbidding their employment in such occupations outside of the Negro section.[14]

There is an increase in Negro employment in the ordnance industry as well, although it is not proportionate to the general expansion. A few plants are using Negroes in all kinds of skilled occupations, but the general pattern is to keep the Negro down at the bottom of the occupational hierarchy. Again Southern establishments are more bent on keeping the Negroes down than are Northern plants; Army-owned factories tend to be more liberal than private factories.[15]

It is reported that the Negro has recently gained in the automobile industry—or rather in those plants which used to constitute the American automobile industry—although it is not known whether the proportion of Negro workers, as well as the absolute number, has increased. The conversion to war production brought about certain problems. Employment dropped off temporarily when production of passenger cars for civilian consumption was restricted, during the winter of 1941-1942. The Negro skilled workers, most of whom used to work in foundries faced a rather critical situation, since little foundry work is needed in aircraft production. Some can still be used in tank and truck plants, however. The rest have enjoyed much protection from the United Automobile, Aircraft and Agricultural Implement Workers' Union and from the government.[16]

Owing to this protection, the Negro automobile worker has been able to enter skilled occupations where he previously has had little or no representation; it is not certain, however, that this protection in actual practice has been as complete for Negro as it has been for white workers. Newly organized rank-and-file members of the union have shown some opposition to the introduction of Negro workers in plants and occupations where they had not worked earlier. During the winter of 1941-1942 and until the summer of 1942 a few "spontaneous" sit-down strikes occurred in certain plants (Hudson, Packard, Dodge and others). In every case the union leadership immediately went into action, and these "wild-cat strikes" were called off within a day or two—sometimes even within a few hours.[17]

The "original" aircraft plants, on the other hand, present a much less encouraging picture. To be sure, several of them have opened their doors to the Negro worker largely because of the activities of the President's Committee on Fair Employment Practice.[a] Yet shortly before mid-1942 only about 5,000 Negroes, constituting between 1 or 2 per cent of the total, were employed in airplane production.[18] Since this figure includes those employed by automobile factories which had gone into airplane manufacturing, the net gain for the Negro seems to be rather insignificant.

3. GOVERNMENT POLICY IN REGARD TO THE NEGRO IN WAR PRODUCTION

The failure to let the Negro participate fully in war production has not gone unnoticed. Obviously it has embittered the Negroes, and being better organized than ever before, they have known how to protest. Both Negro and white groups have been giving great publicity to the matter. There have been a large number of reports on the subject in the daily press, in both the South and the North, as well as articles in national magazines, and pamphlets.[19] Leading personalities like Wendell Willkie, Pearl Buck, and Eleanor Roosevelt have dealt with the problem repeatedly. This publicity, of course, never reached such proportions that the man in the street came to know about what the barring of Negroes from defense jobs really meant; but the better informed part of the public has some notion about it.

Ever since the defense boom got under way, during the summer of 1940, various attempts to straighten out the problem have been made by the government.[20] Most of these measures, as we have seen, were rather ineffectual. Some of them were just gestures. Under the circumstances, they could not possibly appease the Negro leadership. In January, 1941, A. Philip Randolph, president of the Brotherhood of Sleeping Car Porters, started organizing his famous "March-on-Washington Movement."[b] The President, for reasons of internal and external policy, did not want any such protest march and talked to Randolph in June, 1941, in order to prevent it. Randolph, however, failed to come around until the President agreed to sign an Executive Order "with teeth in it" abolishing discrimination in defense industries as well as in the federal government itself. An agreement to this effect was finally reached, but only a few days before the date of the march. Randolph, thus, got what he wanted, and the march was called off.[21]

The Executive Order 8802 of June 25, 1941, starts with a general statement to the effect that there shall be no discrimination in the employment of workers in defense industries or in government because of "race, creed, color, or national origin." There is a clause to this effect in all

[a] See Section 3 of this chapter.
[b] See Chapter 39, Section 12.

defense contracts. The order contains, further, a confirmation of previous orders about nondiscrimination in defense training programs. Finally, a President's Committee on Fair Employment Practice was to be set up for the purpose of receiving and investigating complaints of discrimination in violation of the order.[22]

The Committee can scarcely institute any punishment for noncompliance. Theoretically, it could recommend the cancellation of war contracts, but, in view of the present emergency, such a measure would hardly ever be considered. Its main weapons are publicity and moral pressure, and those weapons have been used with some success.[23] No employer or trade union likes to appear as the defendant at one of the public hearings, a record of which is published by the Committee together with "findings" and "directives." It is obvious that only a small portion of all offending employers and unions can be reached, since the staff of the Committee, so far, has been small.[24] Yet the Committee has shown that it means business, and that it is not willing to accept a token employment of a few Negroes in custodial and other menial jobs as evidence of nondiscrimination.

There are numerous reports about airplane plants and other previously exclusionistic establishments which have opened their doors to the Negro worker. Some of these gains have a highly strategic value, in that Negro workers have been placed in occupations where they have never worked before. It is hard to say, however, to what extent the gains are due to the activities of the Committee or to the increased scarcity of labor. There is no evidence that the Committee, as yet, has brought about any results which are significant from a quantitative point of view. It is not impossible, however, that the Committee may help to change even the "statistical" picture in the future. In the first place, it was only during the winter 1941-1942 that the Committee established itself in the general consciousness of the employers and the unions. Prestige and publicity have their effectiveness over a period of time, and not all at once.[a] Second, Negroes and women constitute an increasingly important part of the remaining labor reserve, so that any further expansion in war production must mean an increased utilization of Negro and female labor. It is obvious, however, that large-scale results, if they are attained at all, will have to come before the peak in war production has been reached.

The Executive Order and the President's Committee, directly or indirectly, have had a healthy effect on some of the federal government services as well as on private industry.[25] We previously touched upon the fact

[a] While this book is in press, the F.E.P.C. has been moribund, largely because of political pressure from Southern politicians, and partly because the war boom has sharply reduced the number of unemployed Negroes. Whether the F.E.P.C. will ever be revived, it is impossible to say. It officially remains in existence although it has no activity.

that Navy yards and Army ordnance plants tend to be less exclusionistic than are most private establishments in the same lines of work. We also mentioned the abolishment of photographs from job applications in the federal civil service, and the increase in Negro clerical and secretarial employment in certain federal agencies.[a] The improvement, however, is by no means general. Brown and Leighton make the following criticism:

> The committee had not, as late as July 1, 1942, certified to the President any case of job discrimination in the government itself, although, according to one member of the staff, they had found almost as many cases of discrimination in federal departments as in war industries.[26]

Even if, at the end of the war boom, the Negro should find that he had gained only some "strategic" footholds in certain previously all-white occupations, the significance of this progress should not be minimized. "Strategic gains" means that there are so many more practical demonstrations of Negro performance in lines of work where no employer previously tried to give the Negro worker a chance. Further, *the Executive Order and the President's Committee represent the most definite break in the tradition of federal unconcernedness about racial discrimination on the nonfarm labor market that has so far occurred.* They represent something of a promise for the future. Even if the government should temporarily relax its control of the labor market after the War, it is quite possible that there will be some kind of continuation of these efforts.

The President's Committee cooperates with the special branches for Negroes and for other minority groups within the War Manpower Commission. Some of the other federal agencies, as well, have been cooperating to eliminate economic discrimination. In many instances, however, the cooperation has left much to be desired. Two such cases need particular emphasis: the vocational training program and the Employment Service.

In spite of the President's Order there is still widespread discrimination against the Negro in most war production training programs, even though some improvement has been brought about. In December, 1940, only 1,900, or 1.6 per cent, of the trainees were Negroes in the so-called pre-employment and "refresher" courses organized under the auspices of the United States Office of Education and the Employment Service. Taking the whole period July 1, 1941, to April 30, 1942, Negroes still constituted only 4.4 per cent of all trainees enrolled in corresponding educational programs.[27] Thus, the Negro, as yet, is still far from having a 10 per cent representation—in spite of the fact that the need for additional training is much greater among Negroes than it is among whites. This discrimination has been particularly pronounced in the South. In January, 1942, for instance, there were some Southern states, like Florida and

[a] See Chapter 14, Section 8.

Arkansas, where not a single Negro was referred to any public preemployment or refresher defense course, nor to any youth work defense project.[28]

Apart from the President's Committee on Fair Employment Practice, there is no federal agency which has been as frank in its criticism of discriminatory practices in war production as has the United States Employment Service. We have, above, made frequent use of this official criticism. At the same time, the Employment Service itself has undoubtedly been guilty of such practices. This is the more deplorable as it has an extremely strategic position.

It has happened, for instance, as late as February, 1942, that the local Employment Service office in Portsmouth, Virginia, published an advertisement in which available jobs were listed by race; only unskilled and domestic jobs were declared to be open to Negroes, whereas all clerical, skilled, semi-skilled, and even some service jobs (e.g., waitresses) were reserved for whites.[29] The Employment Service offices in the South, of course, are usually segregated. This, obviously, must facilitate discriminatory practices, in that the Negro branches tend to become almost exclusively occupied with "Negro jobs." Under such circumstances Negro officials of the Employment Service may become the more unable to remove discrimination.[30]

One reason for this state of affairs is that the Employment Service did not become completely federalized until January 1, 1942. The consequence is that the bulk of the personnel has been appointed by state governments. In other words, there seems to be a certain difference between, on the one hand, the policy of the headquarters in Washington and certain Northern offices and, on the other hand, that of other state and local offices, especially those in the South.

So far, however, the reorganized United States Employment Service has not made sufficiently energetic attempts to require all the local offices to comply with the government policies. Some of the instructions sent out to state and local offices are such that, to a certain extent, they actually protect Employment Service officials who discriminate against Negroes when making referrals. The main clause in the most recent (July, 1942) instructions has the following formulation:

> . . . it is the policy of the United States Employment Service (1) to make all referrals without regard to race, color, creed or national origin *except when an employer's order includes these specifications which the employer is not willing to eliminate.* [Italics ours.]

And further:

> Employment Service personnel will receive and record all *specifications stated by an employer, including specifications based on race, color, creed, or national origin. If the employer does not include any discriminatory specification in his order, but*

community custom or past hiring practices of the employer indicate that he may refuse to hire individuals of a particular race, color, creed, or national origin, the employment office interviewer shall ascertain whether or not he has any restrictive specifications. . . . [Italics ours.] [31]

In addition, of course, there are certain other, more positive recommendations. [32] They cannot mean much, however. Indeed, it is hard to see how field representatives specializing in race relations, who are sent out by the United States Employment Service, can have much to go on when discriminatory referrals are endorsed in official instructions to this extent.

Certain Northern states have taken special measures against racial discrimination, supplementing those of the federal government; often they go much further than the federal agencies. They deal not only with the position of Negroes and other minority groups in war industries, but also with the policies of the public employment service, with private employment agencies, and with advertisements for workers in newspapers.[a] It is possible that these state policies will lead to substantial results sooner than will the rather uncoordinated work of federal agencies which, to a large extent, is hampered by pressure from Southern congressmen.

There is one important social problem in war production which we have not yet touched upon: housing. The effort to provide shelter for the workers in war production areas had some difficulties to start with, [33] and, for this reason, there is an extreme shortage of housing for Negro as well as for white workers adding to all other community problems brought about by war migration. [34] Nevertheless, much work has been done, even though it is not yet sufficient. The total number of units provided, or to be

[a] New York State can be cited as an example. Various amendments to the Civil Rights Law concerning economic discrimination against Negroes and other minority groups have been adopted. One such amendment, of February 14, 1940, makes union discrimination a misdemeanor subject to fine. The so-called Mahoney Amendment of April 16, 1941, prohibits discrimination in defense industries. The Schwartzwald Amendment of May 6, 1942, gives the State Industrial Commissioner the power to enforce anti-discrimination legislation and to require submission, at regular intervals, of information, records, and reports pertinent to discriminatory practices in industries. The Washburn Amendment makes discrimination in war industries a misdemeanor punishable by fine. A Committee on Discrimination in Employment has been functioning since March, 1941. It has sponsored much of the anti-discrimination legislation, has organized publicity on economic race problems and has put pressure on employers and trade unions. In September, 1941, the New York State Employment Service adopted the rule not to handle any requests from employers containing specifications as to race and creed. A New York City ordinance of May 9, 1942, prohibits, with some exceptions, advertisements by employment agencies which restrict offers of jobs to persons of particular race, color or creed, and forces the agencies to keep their records open for public inspection at all times. (Sources: copies of the various anti-discrimination acts furnished by the Committee on Discrimination in Employment; "History of the Committee on Discrimination in Employment" [mimeographed, August 14, 1942]; the National Association for the Advancement of Colored People, *N.A.A.C.P. Annual Report for 1941*, p. 6; New York *Herald Tribune* [May 10, 1942]; *PM* [May 7, 1942].)

provided, according to allotment records available as of July 31, 1942, was over 400,000, including trailers and accommodations for single persons in dormitories. Some 30,000, or less than 8 per cent of this total, will be used by Negro workers.[35] The share for Negroes may seem high, in view of the limited participation of Negroes in war production.[a] Negro sections were, however, much more crowded to begin with than were the white neighborhoods. Also, private builders seldom pay any attention at all to the Negro's housing needs, which makes the Negro population much more dependent on public efforts.

4. THE NEGRO IN THE ARMED FORCES

The armed forces, today, constitute an important source of employment for Negro as well as for white men. In terms of economic value they offer some of the best opportunities open to many young Negro men. Food and clothing are excellent; the pay is higher than that in many occupations available to Negroes. And these conditions of employment are equal for Negroes and whites. A great number of poor Negroes must have raised their level of living considerably by entering the armed forces. It may be, also, that service in the Army and in the Navy, in many instances, will have a certain educational value[36] that will make many Negroes better prepared for post-war employment.

This is the bright side of the picture. But there is a dark side. There has been a definite reluctance to utilize Negroes in all branches of the armed forces. Like white soldiers, they have been concentrated largely in the South, where they have met hostile community attitudes. This policy, at the same time, has increased the resentment of white Southerners against Negroes. Several unpleasant incidents have occurred, particularly in or around Southern camps. Except for certain officers' training schools, there is complete segregation in the armed forces. There has not even been an attempt made to organize experimental unsegregated outfits, including such whites who would volunteer for unsegregated service. All this has helped to embitter the Negro. He feels that he is not wholeheartedly wanted by white America even when he offers to fight for it.

When given adequate training—and often even without it—the Negro has proven to be a good soldier. He has fought in all the wars in which this country has been engaged.[37] From every war there are numerous records of Negroes who have distinguished themselves for bravery and gallantry. Negroes cherish these memories. An outsider occasionally gets the impression that they sometimes exaggerate their significance; but this is very likely just a natural human reaction in view of all the contempt Negroes have experienced from most whites. White people, generally, know little or

---

[a] It will be recalled, on the other hand, that the Negro's share in the building program for low income families was as high as one-third. See Chapter 15, Section 6.

nothing about the Negro's performance as a soldier. Deliberate attempts have been made to minimize the Negro's military record. For instance, on August 7, 1918, a secret document was issued from General Pershing's headquarters, in which French officers were urged not to treat Negroes with familiarity and indulgence, since this would affront Americans, and "not to commend too highly the black American troops in the presence of white Americans."[38]

After the First World War the Negro became quite an insignificant element in the armed forces. The peacetime strength of Negro troops in the regular Army had been fixed by Congress in 1866 at two infantry and two cavalry regiments, which means that Negroes were much less well represented in the Army than in the general population. Their participation in the National Guard was about equally small. The Navy stopped using Negroes entirely some twenty years ago, except as messmen or in similar menial tasks. There were no Negroes in the Marines. In 1940 there were only two Negro combat officers in the regular Army and none in the Navy. Out of over 100,000 officers in the Army Reserve, only 500 were Negro.[39]

In October, 1940, the War Department announced that the Negro personnel should be increased in such a way that Negroes would constitute the same proportion in the Army as in the general population of the country; and, further, that Negroes would be represented in all major branches of the Army.[40] It seems, however, that at least during the early stages of the expansion, Negro units were not organized as quickly as were white units. There were several complaints about Negro volunteers being turned down with the excuse that there were no vacancies for them.[41] The situation has changed since then, however; it is expected that Negroes will soon have a 10 per cent representation in the Army. The Navy, to a certain extent, has relaxed its policy of excluding Negroes. According to an announcement of April 7, 1942, it has started accepting Negroes for combat and certain other service, but only in the Naval Reserve—which means that, after the War, Negroes will again be allowed to serve only as messmen. Also, Negroes may become promoted to petty officers within segregated Negro reserve outfits, but that is as far as they will be allowed to go.[42] Negro women are completely excluded from the women's branch of the Navy (the "WAVES").

The promise that Negroes would be represented in all major branches of the Army has been fulfilled. But there is no uniform proportional representation. Engineering outfits, quartermaster corps, and other service groups have a larger part of the Negro troops than do other branches of the Army. It seems, however, that the difference is much smaller than was the case during the First World War. What has particularly hurt the feelings of the Negroes has been the unwillingness to give them proportional representation among the Army Air Force pilots. At first they were not accepted at all.[43] In view of the relatively small proportion of Negroes with some college education, and the low number of Negro officers and reserve officers before the War, it is obvious that Negroes cannot get anything near the number of Army officers' positions which would correspond with their proportion in the total population. It is expected, however, that, at least by the end of 1943, the majority of the officers in Negro outfits, except for those in higher ranks, will be Negro. This means that there will be an improvement compared with the conditions during the First World War. There is also an under-representation of Negroes among Army doctors and nurses. Negro women are allowed into the women's branch of the Army (the "WACS") in numbers commensurate with their proportion in the population, but they are segregated.

During his entire military history in this country, the Negro has experienced numerous humiliations of various kinds. He has been abused because of his race by many white officers, by white soldiers and by white civilians. There have been race riots in or around camps. The Negro soldier has usually been punished most severely when he was only one offender among many, and sometimes even when he was the victim.[44]

The present War has already seen a number of such incidents. For example, on August 14, 1941, a group of unarmed Negro soldiers, marching on a highway in Arkansas, under the command of a white officer, were pushed off the road by Arkansas state troopers; the protesting white officer was abused as a "nigger lover" and slapped. In Alexandria, Louisiana, where a small, congested Negro section was the only amusement area for a large number of Negro soldiers, white military police went into this Negro area to arrest a drunken Negro soldier. Negroes resisted, and an hour-long battle followed during which thirty Negroes were wounded. After this, Negro military police were stationed in the Negro area. In the spring of 1941, the body of a Negro soldier was found hanging from a tree in a wood at Fort Benning, Georgia. A white lieutenant of a Coast Artillery Regiment stationed in Pennsylvania (December, 1941) overstepped his authority by issuing an order—soon afterwards withdrawn—in which he threatened with the death penalty "relations between white and colored males and females whether voluntary or not."[45]

To be sure, not all incidents were caused by whites. Some have just been drunken brawls in which the racial element was secondary. In others it may have been the unwillingness of Negro soldiers—particularly Northern soldiers stationed in the South—to comply with Southern segregational patterns which incited the fights. Also, we know more about incidents which have occurred than we do about incidents that have been prevented. In all probability, there are several commanders who know how to minimize racial friction.ᵃ Definite attempts have been made to improve conditions. Negro military police are used more and more to patrol Negro sections. They do not always have the same status as white military police; in many cases they are allowed to carry only clubs while white military police have side arms as well. It may be, nevertheless, that the use of Negro military police has helped to prevent many clashes. As during the First World War, there is a special Negro assistant in the War Department who takes care of the interests of the Negro soldier.ᵇ

There is no point, however, in trying to divide the responsibility equally between both racial groups or to characterize the incidents as exceptional. The white group has the power, and, hence, the responsibility. Minor incidents are certainly frequent; only the most spectacular ones get any publicity in the white press. If Negroes sometimes appear as the ones who start the trouble, this must be seen against the background of their increasing impatience with all humiliations. The constant feeling of not being really wanted must make them sullen and resentful.

There is probably no country where most military leaders have distinguished themselves for any constructive views on delicate social problems —not even when their own services are affected. American white officers cannot be expected to be much better than others; the over-representation of Southerners among officers with peacetime training tends to make those in the higher ranks particularly conservative, on the average, in respect to race relations. Also, they have a huge job on their hands. However wrong they may be in believing a change in race relations to be a matter of secondary or no importance, it is understandable why they believe it. Yet, this attitude is certainly unfortunate. To advertise bad American race relations by maintaining them in armed forces sent overseas is, under present circumstances, highly detrimental to American interests.ᶜ Had the improvements come, not mainly as a result of outside pressure from

---

ᵃ The following story from the First World War is rather illuminating:

"At Camp Upton, New York, General F. Franklin Bell met a similar situation without hesitation:

" 'Now, gentlemen,' said he, 'I am not what you would call "a Negro lover," I have seen service in Texas, and elsewhere in the South. Your men have started the trouble. I don't want any explanations. These colored men did not start it. It doesn't matter how your men feel about these colored men. They are United States soldiers. They must and shall be treated as such. If you can't take care of your men, I can take care of you . . . if there is any more trouble from your men, you will be tried, not by a Texas jury but by General Bell . . .'

"General Bell was talking to white officers of a Southern regiment that came to Camp Upton . . ." (Emmett J. Scott, *The American Negro in the World War* [1919], p. 95).

ᵇ This assistant was William H. Hastie, who was formerly a federal judge in the Virgin Islands. In January, 1943, Mr. Hastie resigned in protest against certain War Department practices. His assistant, Mr. Truman Gibson, remained as an advisor to the War Department.

ᶜ See Chapter 45.

Negroes and others, but because of the action of military leaders who grasped the deeper implications of this War, they would have been much greater and much more significant, not only for the Negro, but for the nation as a whole.

5. . . . AND AFTERWARDS?

What will be the Negro's economic lot in post-war America? There is no definite answer to the question, of course, since it will depend on happenings yet to occur and policies yet to be decided upon. But we can list some of the main factors entering into the problem. When sketching such an analysis of future possibilities and probabilities, it must be kept in mind that now, even less than ordinarily, we have little right to predict from a mere extrapolation of trends. There are no trends independent of fluctuations; the fluctuations create the trend, and the trend is nothing but the cumulative effect of fluctuations.[a]

Thus, the more the Negroes gain during the present war boom, the more will they have advanced themselves permanently; and even if, during a later development, they will have to give up some ground, they are not likely to be driven back as far as they would have been had their previous gains been smaller. Conversely, the more they lose during the next unemployment crisis, the smaller chance will they have of reaching anything near full employment during a subsequent period of labor shortage. Quite especially in regard to the Negro's economic status, we have to emphasize the significance of what happens during the short-term development. The Negro's position in the American economic system depends in a large measure on traditions which have actually become settled because of rather accidental happenings. Whether he does or does not work in a particular occupation depends upon whether a small group among many employers who experienced a labor shortage happened to get the idea of trying him out; or whether his white fellow workers, during a period

---

[a] It is usual, in the analysis of economic changes, to distinguish between cyclical fluctuations and long-time trends. For example, if industrial production increases by 3 per cent per annum, on the average, over a certain long period, but for one particular year the increase is 6 per cent, the difference between these two figures (or some other statistical expression, based on a similar principle) is supposed to measure the cyclical variation for this particular year; the average rate (which can be computed in different ways) is believed to "indicate the long-run trend." Such calculations may be useful for several practical purposes, but they are always arbitrary. There is no "pure" trend and no "pure" cyclical change. Both types of change are closely interwoven. The trend depends largely on the character of the business cycles, and *vice versa*. This fact is often overlooked. The writer, for instance, has heard social scientists express the idea that the employment losses that Negroes have experienced during the 'thirties would not matter "in the long run," since they only constituted "temporary" and "cyclical" fluctuations. In reality, however, there is no guarantee that any of the temporary changes are reversible; if Negroes are driven out of a certain occupation, they may never get in there again.

when job opportunities were scarce, happened to be successful in driving him out. In all probability, there would have been rather few Negroes in the automobile industry if it had not been for Henry Ford. It is even possible that the Negro would not have a foothold at all in Northern manufacturing industries at the present time had it not been for the labor shortage during the First World War.

Assuming for the purpose of our discussion that the War ends with a real peace—not a state of armed truce—and that this peace seems likely to last for a while, this will mean a reduction in the production of arms and ships. There are certain factors in this situation which, to some extent, may tend to minimize the employment losses for the Negro. The very fact that he has not gotten so much of a place in armament production, but rather has made his most significant gains in certain consumption and service industries, may possibly help him then and make the immediate employment losses smaller for him than for the white workers. Also, the over-population in agriculture may for a time make itself less severely felt, since so much labor has been drawn to urban industries during the present emergency. It is probable, as well, that many of the demobilized soldiers from agricultural areas will never return to the farms.

These temporary advantages, however, will be counteracted by other forces. The one armament industry which has the best chances of being maintained, in some measure, after the War is airplane production, where the Negro, so far, has not been allowed to get more than a toehold. The shipyards, which have treated the Negro much better, are more likely to decline.[46] The War has brought about many revolutionary changes in production techniques. These new experiences will probably help to bring about a new mechanization trend as soon as production managers get the time to think of reorganization of production other than that necessitated by the exigencies of the War. Now they are doing everything possible to produce quickly. After the War they will again emphasize economy of production. A speed-up of the mechanization trend will involve new threats to the unskilled worker. Again, the Negro will be one of the principal sufferers.

Of paramount importance will be the general level of employment. The Negroes' hope of becoming integrated into American industry is much greater if the American economy is geared to a full utilization of its productive forces. Should there be widespread unemployment for a protracted period, it will tend to be concentrated on the Negro. Widespread idleness will tend to increase the interest of the white workers in keeping the Negro out. Long-time unemployment always makes for all kinds of socio-psychological tensions. The Negro, as usual, will be a convenient object for those who have been kept brooding long enough to feel the need for some spectacular action. White workers in service industries who have been employed in armament factories during the War will most certainly resent finding Negroes in their old jobs. In the long run, it is rather unfortunate that the present efforts to integrate the Negro into war production have been based, in part, on the motivation that these are unusual times when all kinds of hardships have to be accepted. It is quite probable that this particular kind of motivation will backfire. The same may be true, to an extent, about the argument that Negroes should be given some attention since this country cannot afford to feed the German and the Japanese propaganda machines.

It is not even certain that the leaders of the C.I.O. unions who are friendly to the Negroes will be able to maintain discipline respecting non-discrimination among their rank-and-file membership. During the War the union leaders have alienated themselves from the mass of the members, to a certain extent, by siding with the Administration's anti-strike policy. Although their present difficulties may be due, in part, to the large number of new members, many of whom will perhaps drop out after the War, it is quite possible that they may have to face the alternative of either following the rank-and-filers' anti-Negro attitude or being exchanged for new leaders.

For the period immediately following the War, however, the risk of widespread unemployment may not be great. Those first years will probably be characterized by a large demand for durable consumers' goods, like automobiles, refrigerators, stoves and possibly airplanes. The reconstruction work overseas may constitute another significant source of demand for American products. Sometime, however, a really large post-war unemployment will threaten the entire economic system. It will be largely counteracted, however, by government policies. It is true that unemployment policies during the last depression were not entirely successful; but that was largely because they started too late, and because they constituted the first large-scale attempt of this type in the United States. This time there will be much more rational and experienced planning behind these efforts. The post-war planning work carried on by governmental and other agencies at the present time is extensive.[47] In part it may be somewhat uncoordinated, but certainly many useful things are being done.[a]

[a] It seems, however, that there is reason to warn against over-optimism regarding the success of the policies during the next depression. One often hears the argument that post-war unemployment will not be dangerous at all "since it will be prevented by planning"—just as if this were a perfectly simple thing, or even that the word "planning" would have a magical effect. Yet planning, of course, is never of much use just because it is planning; it is of use only in so far as it is well adapted to the specific problems.

It is quite probable, for instance, that the next depression, to an even greater extent than the last one, will be characterized by structural changes requiring something more than just depression fighting, pump priming, temporary public works. There is always the danger that our planning will fit the last depression more perfectly than the one ahead. Moreover, it is

The Negro will have to be considered in this post-war planning work. As always, he will be unemployed much more often than the white worker. As time goes on, it will become more and more apparent that either the Negro will have to be cared for as a more or less permanent relief client or positive measures must be taken for his integration into the regular economy. The tradition of governmental noninterference on the labor market has been broken during the New Deal, and still more during the War. Trade unions, in so far as they have not themselves abolished monopolistic practices, will increasingly be forced to do so. Employment policies will become less individualistic—more based upon concern about utilization of the total national labor force.

There will be factors, in addition to governmental pressure, which will tend to strengthen the forces friendly to Negroes in the labor movement, at least in the long run. Whenever the unions attempt to leave the Negro out, there may, again, be some risk that employers will tend to use the Negro worker against them. Probably even more important is the fact that some of the most potent anti-Negro forces in the American community are, at the same time, anti-labor. Labor will have to side with the Negro for political reasons. Since labor relations, more and more, are becoming public relations and thus will depend on political action, this will tend to protect the Negro's employment opportunities.

Much more generally, the Negroes' economic fate after the War will depend upon the general development of attitudes toward race in America. There looms a "Negro aspect" over all post-war problems. There may be radical changes ahead—both in the Negro's actual status and in ideologies affecting him. America has lost the protection of the oceans, and there will be many more international implications to national policies. It may well be that the transition, foreboded by the Great Depression and continued by the Second World War and the Peace to come, will change the conditions of life in America to such an extent that the period after the War will stand out as apart from the pre-war time, as does the long period after the Revolutionary War from the colonial era. To this broader perspective we shall return in the last chapter of this book.

---

always somewhat uncertain whether those in political power at the time will select the best plans or whether they will know how to coordinate various plans. It must be considered, finally, that not even the best blueprints are of much use unless there are administrative agencies which are competent to handle them. At present there is a certain tendency to wreck many of the agencies which will be needed for post-war problems. The Civilian Conservation Corps and the Work Projects Administration have already been abolished. The Farm Security Administration has experienced violent attacks, but, so far, it has been saved. If this trend should go further than is warranted by the present decline in relief needs, so that many of the rehabilitation and welfare agencies will not even be allowed to maintain skeleton staffs, it would mean that a great amount of practical experience would be thrown away.

PART V

POLITICS

CHAPTER 20

UNDERLYING FACTORS[a]

1. The Negro *in* American Politics and *as* a Political Issue

Politics and political equality are intrinsically a part of our entire discussion of the many-faceted Negro problem. This chapter, however, is confined to politics in the narrower sense—that is, it will deal with the franchise, political parties and political rewards. We concentrate on the South, not only because this region contains the great majority of the Negro people, but because the South is the only region where Negro suffrage is a problem.

The value premise in this chapter will be *the doctrine of political equality among all citizens of the United States.* Political discrimination, and, more specifically, disfranchisement, is defined in relation to this value premise as the withholding of the vote from citizens merely because they are Negroes. This value premise, as a principle, is prominent in the American Creed and has been given constitutional sanction.

In early colonial times free Negroes apparently often enjoyed the same civic rights and duties as poor white people relieved from indenture servitude.[1] Chief Justice Taney's dictum in the Dred Scott decision of 1857, to the effect that the Negro had nowhere been accorded the status of citizenship in this country, was an overstatement as applied to the contemporary situation and even more so as an historical generalization. With regard to voting in particular, it is well established that there has never, in modern American history, been a period when Negro voters have been totally absent from the polls. At the time of the making of the Constitution, free Negroes had the right of suffrage in all the original states, except South Carolina and Georgia.[2] The greater part of the Negro people was, however, then held in slavery. As a political power the free Negroes were, of course, inconsequential, both in the South and in the North. In the following period up to the Civil War, free Negroes grew in numbers, but all Southern[b] and all the new Western states and territories dis-

---

[a] If we were to adhere strictly to our general plan of presenting the aspects of the Negro problem according to the rank order of interests, hypothesized in Chapter 3, this part on politics should succeed rather than precede the part on justice. We follow the order we do in order to present certain basic facts in a more convenient context.

[b] A partial exception was that free Negroes could vote in North Carolina before 1835. (Harold F. Gosnell, *Negro Politicians* [1935], p. 3, footnote.)

franchised them, as did also some of the older Northern states. At the outbreak of the War, Negroes had votes in only five of the New England States—Maine, Massachusetts, New Hampshire, Rhode Island and Vermont. In addition, New York allowed Negroes suffrage under certain property limitations which did not apply to whites.[3]

As a result of the Civil War and the Reconstruction Amendments, Negro men were enfranchised in the whole Union. In the North this change became permanent. In the South, where most Negroes lived and still live, it was rapidly undone. After Reconstruction, a condition gradually fixed itself upon the nation which has remained fairly unchanged in the twentieth century: that the Negroes in the North enjoy, uninfringed, the right to vote as other American citizens, while, with quantitatively unimportant exceptions, the Negroes in the South are kept disfranchised against the intention and spirit of the amended Constitution. Suffrage for Negroes is one of the patterns in which the two historic regions of America are most dissimilar, and in this respect, the greatest factor of change during the last generation has actually been the migration of one and three-quarter million Negroes from the South to the North. As we shall find in the course of our analysis, the situation is highly unstable, and great changes are impending.

While the Negro people have been kept out of politics in the sense that they have been kept from voting, in another sense, namely, as a political issue, they have been an important factor in the very region where they have been disfranchised, the South. A recent well-qualified student of the Southern political scene has gone so far as to say that "The elementary determinant in Southern politics is an intense Negro phobia which has scarcely abated since Reconstruction."[4] The issue of "white supremacy vs. Negro domination," as it is called in the South, has for more than a hundred years stifled freedom of thought and speech and affected all other civic rights and liberties of both Negroes and whites in the South. It has retarded its economic, social and cultural advance. On this point there is virtual agreement among all competent observers.[5]

In the North, on the contrary, the Negro has nowhere and never been a political issue of primary and lasting importance [a]—except in so far as he

[a] There are secondary reasons for this, other than the main one that the North had never been obsessed with the Negro and the desire to keep him in a low place that characterizes the slavery tradition of the South. Before the great mass migration, the Northern Negro population was numerically small; even after the migration it still remained small in proportion to the total electorates in the cities where they live; Negro voters have usually been tractable and easily managed by the political machines; their voting strength has often been held down by gerrymandering and by the failure to redistrict. Negroes could never by any stretch of the imagination be looked upon as a political danger. They have been a poor, segregated group showing many signs of social pathology, but—except for the classical issues of tariff, money and banking, corporate finance, agriculture, and prohibition—socio-economic problems have, until the New Deal, not played a great role in American politics.

has constituted an issue in national politics. The issue has, then, always been the Negro's status in the South or, earlier, the South's struggle to widen the area over which its concept of the Negro would prevail.

Once, and once only, did the Negro problem become the focus of national attention: in the prolonged conflict with the South over slavery in the Civil War and during Reconstruction. After the national compromise of the 1870's American historians have, by and large, adjusted to the changed political situation and have satisfied the national demand for historical rationalization and justification of the treatment of the Negro. They have stressed that the North did not fight the Civil War to free the Negro slaves. This is apparently correct as far as the immediate political origin of the conflict is concerned. The Emancipation Proclamation was later issued, but only after one hundred days' warning to the rebellious states to lay down their arms, and in it Lincoln declared that the measure was adopted "upon military necessity." But the deeper reality is, nevertheless, that there would have been no Civil War had there been no Negroes in the South, and had not Negro slavery stamped its entire social fabric. The economic, ideological, and political rivalries between the two regions all mainly derived from, or were greatly determined by, the fact of slavery, as were also the peculiar agricultural structure and the social stratification of the *ante-bellum* South.

As the War went on, this deeper cause, the Negro problem, simply had to be brought to the surface in order to uphold Northern morale—in much the same fashion as the notion of democracy and human liberty has had similar functions in the present World War and in the earlier one. The cause of liberating the Negroes and awarding them the status of manhood and citizenship became, during the trials and tribulations of the long and extremely perturbing War, a much-needed strengthening moral justification to the North. It was almost as important as the aim of preserving the Union.

For a decade after the War, the aim of protecting Negro freedom retained its importance in Northern ideology. It gained strength by its capacity to furnish a rationalization for Republican party interests. After the national compromise of the 1870's, the Negro problem dropped out as a national issue. The great majority of Southerners have an interest in keeping it out as long as possible. On the surface, there seem to be no signs that the dominant North will break the compromise and start again trying to reform the South. But it is well to defer judgment on this crucial point until we

---

The presence of European immigrant groups, displaying similar problems, has, in any case, hindered a focusing of such interests upon the Negroes. Negroes have only been one of several problem groups. In regard to the Negroes, the Northerners could always console their social conscience by reminding themselves that Negroes fared still worse in the South. (See Chapter 2, Section 8.)

have considered a number of dynamic factors which are bound to influence the future development both in the South and in the nation at large.

2. THE WAVE OF DEMOCRACY AND THE NEED FOR BUREAUCRACY

In order to understand why the vote, or the lack of it, has such a paramount importance for the daily welfare of the Negro people in America, we have to view the problem in broad perspective. The vote would be of less importance to a group of citizens in this country if America had what it does not have, namely, *the tradition of an independent and law-abiding administration of local and national public affairs.* By this we mean a body of public officials who are independent in two directions: *personally,* as they are holding office under permanent tenure, being appointed and promoted strictly according to merit, and, consequently, vested with economic security and high social prestige; and *officially,* as they are trusted with authority to put the laws into effect without political interference in individual cases. In such an order the political branches of government, legislative as well as executive, would, in the main, be restricted to two functions: (1) to supervise and control the administration as to its efficiency and adherence to the laws and (2) to change the laws and other general instructions when they wished to redirect the course of administration. Such a governmental system is foreign to American traditions. Americans are conditioned by their history to look upon administration as itself a branch of political government: as within "politics." Not only their constitutions—federal and state—but their political philosophies, and what the citizen in various states of sophistication takes for granted, are dominated by this idea.

The struggle of the American colonies against the English Crown and its often corrupt bureaucracy first set this pattern. The rights upheld in this struggle were those of the people and their elected representatives, the colonial legislatures, *against* the administration. Incidentally, the tradition of sending lawyer-advocates as representatives to the legislatures instead of average persons from the midst of the electorate—farmers, workers, preachers, teachers, and businessmen—began in this same period when the legislatures were not sovereign but merely the pleaders against the English Crown, the London Parliament, and the colonial bureaucracy. The lawyer-politicians got such a strong foothold in public affairs in America that they have kept it into the present time.

Out of this struggle emerged not only the fierce American insistence upon the rights and liberties of the individual citizen, but also the American dislike and distrust of state authority. Both were carried forward into the new independent Republic, the latter tendency strengthened by the very disruption of authority during the *interregnum* of the Revolution, during which the old administration and a great portion of the ruling classes (Tories) in America were liquidated.[6] There was thus no inherited bureaucracy to start out with. The results were very different from those in comparable countries—particularly the Scandinavian countries and Great Britain—where the bureaucracy was already in existence when the legislatures developed. In those countries, democracy arose as the legislatures fought to widen their electoral basis and to make the bureaucracy into an effective means of carrying out the popular will. In the United States, on the other hand, bureaucracy developed in a haphazard manner. Protected by the Atlantic Ocean, America was also less exposed to international dangers. Efficient administration of the country was, therefore, not so much of an immediate necessity. The history of American wars for more than a century after the Revolutionary War brings out this point beautifully. The protecting oceans were as important as the frontiers for American domestic development and, particularly, its system of government, a fact not adequately developed by historians.[a]

The attempts of the Hamiltonians to create a stable and independent administration in America were, as is understandable in this historical setting, unfortunately associated with the anti-democratic movement. This, in turn, served to strengthen the anti-bureaucratic tendencies of those men who felt themselves fighting for the liberal ideas of the American Revolution. Thomas Jefferson's election to the Presidency in 1800 was a victory for the latter forces. Even if he was careful to fill the vacancies as they occurred with trusted partisans, he did not, however, start out with a wholesale removal of federal officeholders appointed by the earlier regime. For the next few decades there were, perhaps, rather favorable conditions for the growth of an independent federal administration. But when Andrew Jackson inaugurated the "spoils system," he broke down this hope completely. At the same time he furnished a pattern for the state and local governments, where they were not already ahead of the national government. Underlying this familiar American pattern were, among others, the idea that there should be "rotation in office" and the idea that public service did not require much special training.

Thereafter, through American history until recent decades, there has been a dominant force constantly pressing to increase the *direct* control of the electorate over public affairs. The movement has been self-generating, since in the great American tradition the cure for the inefficiency and cor-

[a] The frontier was actually first given its true significance in American history by Frederick Jackson Turner in his epochal essay, *The Significance of the Frontier in American History* (1893), at a time when the frontier was already disappearing from the national scene. The ocean, on the other hand, has not yet been made the theme of a comprehensive American history. A technical development of communications and warfare, becoming apparent in the present War, has substantially decreased the protection of the oceans. It would not be surprising if there would soon appear, as a consequence, a review of American history in this new light just as revolutionizing as the one stressing the frontier as a main viewpoint.

ruption of the politically closely-controlled administrations has been seen to be "more democracy and not less." In this movement the indirect election of legislative bodies was changed to direct election, appointive public officers were changed to elected ones, and the terms for officials and legislatures were shortened. In some states measures have been instituted enabling the voters, by the use of the petition and special election (the recall), to oust public officials at any time during their term. In some states this applies even to justices, sheriffs and other peace officers. The popular initiative and the referendum, found in many states of the Union, are part of the same pattern.

This movement has always been supported by those in America who defended the rights of the common people and who considered themselves the upholders of the Jeffersonian ideal of democracy. Perhaps in no other respect did the American variant of early nineteenth century political liberalism become so different from the same movement in those European countries mentioned as most comparable. In those countries, liberalism also demanded the ultimate power for the people themselves, and it also wanted to restrict narrowly the sphere of government activity. But, within its proper realm, liberalism in Europe advocated a government in which laws are enforced, while American liberalism since Jefferson and until recent decades has been tinged with philosophical anarchism. By the middle of the nineteenth century, liberals in those other countries largely succeeded in freeing politics from corruption and in perfecting administration as an effective instrument in the hand of governments which were becoming democratized. American liberalism was more suspicious of state authority and suspicious even toward the security and prestige of officeholders. It was more interested in checking bureaucracy than in reforming and utilizing it.

The politically dependent American administrations have, particularly in the states and in the local communities, continuously turned out to be rather inefficient organs for carrying on public affairs and have often been corrupt. This situation has long been recognized in America. The fact that the British rule in colonial times was also inefficient and corrupt has contributed toward the common American belief that politics and administration are always this way and that they must always be so. Gradually "politics" and "politicians" became derogatory words in America. Bureaucracy, even at best, became synonymous with "red tape." The relatively low social prestige of public servants, which is a natural concomitant of their lack of independence and their insecurity of tenure; their subservience to the political game; and the various practices they have to resort to as office-seekers, became accentuated. Public administration thus failed to attract its fair share of the intelligence and ambition of the youth in the nation.

The fact that land speculators, big business, and, generally, the wealthy classes were in a position to utilize the corrupted administration for their interests reinforced the idea, already strong in American liberalism, that only a closer direct control by the electorate would secure a more honest and efficient administration of public affairs. Since this closer control in most cases did not increase, but rather decreased, the independence, security, and prestige of officeholders, the results were, on the whole, negative. When explaining the relatively low professional standards in American administration, there are many other factors to take into account. But an important place should be given to the vicious circle set in motion by the historically rooted American mistrust of bureaucracy and the trust in direct electoral control.[a]

While they are mistrusted and have low standards, public officials have, nevertheless, been invested with much more power for the time they are in office than in comparable countries. Being elected and thus carrying the mandate of the people themselves, they are less dependent on laws and fixed administrative rules. For the same reason, they can even stand more strongly against the representative bodies. They have more discretionary power than the public officials in a more strictly legal system. By long tradition and by their uncertainty of tenure (since their continuation in office depends on the outcome of the next election) they are, on the other hand, conditioned always to try to please their constituents. The individual voters, on their side, are conditioned in America to look to the directly and indirectly elected officials, not only for an honest and firm execution of their duties according to the laws, the established administration procedures, and the officials' best conscience, but, what is dangerous, for special favors.

The relative lack of an independent civil service and of a firm legal pattern in public administration thus means a mutually greater dependence of public officials on the voters and of the voters upon the officials. In this system it has become customary to distribute jobs, protection, and public service in some relation to the voting strength of the various regional, national and religious groups in the community. A disfranchised group like the Southern Negro people will, therefore, be disadvantaged. The effect will be accentuated if, in addition to disfranchisement, the group is segregated. The unpaved streets in the Negro sections of Southern cities, the lack of facilities for sewage disposal, the lack of street lighting, the dilapidated school houses, the scarcity of hospital facilities, and, indeed, all other discrimination in education, health, housing, breadwinning, and justice, give evidence of this important relation in America between the vote and a share in the public services. Since Negroes do not participate in

---

[a] The general problem discussed in this section will be taken up for analysis, from the viewpoints of centralization and decentralization, leadership, and popular participation and responsibility, in Chapter 33.

the election of the representative bodies either, these bodies cannot be expected to give them redress against the officials. No representative will see any immediate reason to please a disfranchised group, and laws and regulations will be drawn up without their interests being represented. If the system becomes corrupted, the odds are placed even more definitely against a poor group without political voice.

Not until very late did forces appear on the American scene trying to reverse the trend. They capitalized on the general mistrust against "politics" in America and on the value attached to keeping things "out of politics," which, paradoxically enough, have been as prevalent as the tendency referred to of increasing the direct electoral controls. The civil service reformers obtained their first success when Congress in 1883 enacted a federal civil service law.[a] States and municipalities have been following the federal government, but the reform is far from consummated. Nevertheless, a professional and fairly independent administration is taking shape in America, and the explanation is primarily the increase in volume and scope of public activity, as public control and social reform proceed. The intricacies and complexities of administration have been increasing, steadily raising the demands on the executors of the public will for professional training and impartiality. The continuation of the old practices is simply impossible, since they threaten a complete breakdown in the management of public affairs.

There have been two other trends which, while apparently opposing each other, actually do not because they both make the administration more independent and less arbitrary. On the one hand, there has been a tendency to write the laws in such a way that the mutual obligations of government and citizen are more specifically defined. For example, the trend of social security legislation has been from the vague promise of government to do something for "paupers" to the legal provision for definite compensation to every specified person when he becomes a certain age or subject to certain disabilities, such as unemployment. It is not left to biased officials to decide what shall be done. On the other hand, as public interest increasingly comes to embrace new fields of social life—for instance, the labor market—the type of detailed laws of the past are giving way to more abstract laws which give the administration greater leeway in making rules to meet new situations but which also force it to lay down such rules rather than to let individual officials use their arbitrary judgments.[b] Both these trends are helping to build up an independent,

[a] This success was partly an accident: support for a civil service system did not become widespread until President Garfield was assassinated by a disappointed office-seeker in 1881.

[b] Some have argued that this has also made it more possible for discrimination to enter. The fact is, however, that it is under the old type of law—detailed and complicated—that discrimination can best flourish. Under the older type of law, there could be few administra-

strong and impartial administration. A fourth trend, having the same effect, is centralization. Public control is gradually moving from municipalities and counties to the states and from the states to the federal government. It is hardly necessary to point out that the New Deal during the 'thirties has speeded up all these trends.

America is thus, finally, well on the way to building up an independent administration. Its rising importance is reflected in higher social prestige of public officials as their tenure and economic security are becoming protected. Public service is beginning to become a professional career which can attract intelligent, well-trained and ambitious youths. A visitor to America who compares attitudes of the late 'twenties with those of the early 'forties notices a great change within this short space of time. It is possible to envisage a very different system of government within a couple of decades: the common people in America are coming to realize that a capable and uncorrupted bureaucracy, independent in its work except for the laws and regulations passed by the legislatures and the continuous control by legislators and executives, is as important for the efficient working of a modern democracy as is the voter's final word on the general direction of this administration.

Although this is the trend in government, America is still far from the goal. This is particularly true in local administration. It is more true in rural than in urban regions, and more true in the South than in the North. Tremendous changes are under way, but they have not yet meant much for the masses of Negroes, since most of them live in regions where the protection of an independent administration and of objectified administrative rules are much less developed than in the country at large. And as we shall find, *Negroes are disfranchised more completely in the very localities where the vote is important because administration is lax.*

3. THE NORTH AND THE SOUTH

In the North Negroes have the vote like other people, and there is nowhere a significant attempt to deprive them of the franchise.[a] To the foreign observer the fact that practically nobody in the North thinks of

---

tive rules since they would illegally modify the law. As a result, the individual official had to use his own personal judgment when the law did not apply to new or odd types of cases. This obviously allows for discrimination. When administrative rules can adjust abstract laws to new situations, there is much less opportunity for individual officials to insert their own biases, and so there is much less discrimination in the individual case. It is not the rules emanating from Washington that are discriminatory in the meaning important to the individual citizen, but rather the arbitrary practices of individual officials who apply the laws to concrete cases.

[a] The only major exceptions—and even these are not restricted to Negroes—are the cases of gerrymandering and the failure to redistrict in some Northern cities. (See Chapter 22, Section 4.)

taking away the Negroes' vote is, in itself, a most important, and even startling, element in the political situation which seems difficult to explain satisfactorily. Negroes are discriminated against in many other respects in the North. Most Northerners seem also to be convinced of the mental and moral inferiority of Negroes, even if their racial beliefs are not so certain, so extreme and so intense as the Southerners'. But the Negroes' right to political participation as voters is actually seldom questioned.

This problem is, indeed, wider, as it can be raised also with respect to many of the immigrant minority groups. They may be despised by the older Americans and discriminated against in various ways. The "Americans" may—often with considerable right—accuse them of being unassimilated and clannish, of not identifying themselves with the community and the nation, and of lacking both the interest in and knowledge of American society prerequisite for a judicious opinion on public matters. It is commonly held—also with much right—that these groups, and the Negroes, form an important part of the basis for the corrupt machine politics which is the disgrace of most big cities and many states. The average Northerner is usually outspoken on these points. But he will generally not draw the conclusion that hence the franchise should be restricted in any measure. The North is apparently sold and settled on the principle of unqualified franchise.

The problem is not even much discussed. A Northern author may incidentally give vent to the remark that "the vote should be a privilege to be earned by evidence of ability and willingness to use it with discretion" and even point to the Southern legislation restricting suffrage as a model also for the North.[7] But such a remark will be made in passing and apparently without hope of public attention. Occasionally the present author has also heard Northerners in various walks of life, when discussing the cultural isolation of Negroes and "foreigners" in the cities, make the observation that "rightly, they shouldn't have the vote." But nobody seems to expect this opinion to be taken as a serious practical proposal.[8]

It is the observation of the author that unrestricted suffrage has become so unquestioned in the North that the ordinary Northerner believes that it has always existed and that, in particular, the free Negroes in the North have always, or at least even prior to the Civil War, enjoyed the privilege of the franchise. The truth is, as we have already pointed out, that the Negroes were disfranchised in almost the whole North and West at the time of the Civil War. During and immediately after the War, attempts were made in some of these states to introduce amendments to the state constitutions for striking out the word "white" in order to enfranchise the Negroes. But, although the Republicans were in absolute control everywhere, these proposals were defeated in one state after another.[9] The Fourteenth and Fifteenth Amendments to the federal Constitution later compelled even these Northern states to change their franchise rules. The amendments were accepted and ratified in the Northern states as part of the Reconstruction program and in order to fortify the Republican party in the South. If the North had not been so bent upon reforming the South, it is doubtful whether and when some of the Northern states would have reformed themselves.[10]

Thus the Negroes' right to vote in the North is not supported by an uninterrupted historical tradition. But when once the great step was taken, it seems almost immediately to have been solidified into the traditionally rooted order of things. The present-day unreserved allegiance to the principle of political nondiscrimination in the North, which has so successfully withstood the increased racial tension due to the huge influx of Southern Negroes in recent decades, is fundamentally, we believe, a direct outflow of the American Creed as it has gradually strengthened its hold upon the American mind. This national *ethos* undoubtedly has a greater force in the North than in the South, as may be observed in other spheres of social life as well. But in most of these other respects, even the Northerner has a split personality. His attitudes toward suffrage and equality in justice[a] seem, in fact, to be the main exceptions where he acts absolutely according to the national Creed.

In explaining these exceptions, we have first to take into account the fact that voting is a rather abstract human relationship between a citizen and the officials representing society. The Northerner tends to adhere to the American Creed in abstract, impersonal things and slips away from it when it involves personal relations. A substantial part of all discrimination is closely connected with snobbishness and petty considerations of status in daily human contacts. When the Northerner gets formal, when he acts in an assembly or reacts as a citizen on grounds of principles, and, particularly, when the question concerns the relations between the state and the individual, he will be more likely to follow the American Creed closely.

Another relevant fact in the explanation is that the Negroes in the North—as well as unpopular immigrant groups—are clustered mostly in the big cities where life is anonymous and where people are conditioned not to be concerned much about one another. These cities have often been dominated by political machines. The machines find the Negroes and the immigrant groups tractable. The politicians themselves have, therefore, no reason to try to eliminate Negro franchise; their difficulty is, rather, the intelligent and independent individual voter. From a conservative point of view, machine politics has favorable effects, at least in so far as it keeps those lower status groups in line and protects them from radicalism. The exploitation of these voters by the machines will, therefore, not be strongly criticized by conservatives. Liberals, for reasons of principle, are not

[a] See Part VI.

inclined to favor any restrictions on suffrage. So there is apparently nobody in the North engaged in the political game who has any particular reasons to object to the Negroes' enjoying their franchise in peace.

Whether or not these explanations are adequate, it seems to be a fact that *Negroes can feel sure that, unless this country undergoes a veritable revolution, their right to vote will remain unquestioned in the North, independent of any increase due to continued migration from the South. Without any doubt, this is one of the strategic protections of the Negro people in American society.* The Negro vote in the North is already of some importance. It could become of much greater importance were it more wisely used. As the educational level of the Negro people is being raised and as the northward migration is continuing, it might become powerful enough within the next couple of decades to demand some real reward not only in local Northern politics but also in national politics. The Northern vote might become the instrument by which the Negroes can increasingly use the machinery of federal legislation and administration to tear down the walls of discrimination.

The white people's attitude in regard to Negro suffrage in the South, and, specifically, in the eleven states which seceded from the Union and formed the Confederacy, is a much more complicated matter. Even a summary interpretation requires sketching the main elements of the historical heritage of the region. Negro disfranchisement is evidently part and parcel of a much more general tendency toward *political conservatism* which stamps the entire life of the region. The Negro is, as we shall find, a main cause of this general conservatism. Southern conservatism is a unique phenomenon in Western civilization in being married to an established pattern of *illegality*.[a] In the South, it is the weak liberal reformers who have had, and have now, to stand up for the majesty of the law. Correspondingly, a person may be ranked as liberal in this region merely by insisting that the law shall be adhered to in practice.

This is a most extraordinary situation. Everywhere else in the world it is the strategy and—from one point of view—the "function" of conservatism in the democratic state to stand for "law and order," while the liberals and, still more, the radicals want to change this order. When the latter succeed in bringing about changes, it is the conservatives' "function" to see to it that due procedure and all legal formalities are observed. Thereby they usually succeed in slowing down the tempo of the induced changes. To function as the guardians of the law, and all it stands for in the way of individual security in an established order, becomes thus a natural strategy for the conservatives who want to check change and preserve the *status quo*.

In the South we have, however, the unmatched political spectacle that

[a] This pattern of illegality will be studied in some detail in Part VI.

the liberals are the party of law and order, while the conservatives are the habitual transgressors. *The party which works for change has the established law on its side, or rather, wants to enforce it, but has not the political power; the party which stands for the* status quo *has the power but not the law.*

To try to understand how this extraordinary situation has come about must be our next task. As a background we shall have to remember the weak development of political legality generally in America, so visible in its relative lack of an independent administration. Even in the North the conservative forces have occasionally faltered in performing their "function" in democracy, to stand for the law. But the difference between the two regions is immense. In the South a veritable reversal of the usual order of democracy has established itself.

4. THE SOUTHERN DEFENSE IDEOLOGY

Part of the explanation is that Southern conservatism is "reactionary" in the literal sense of the word. It has preserved an ideological allegiance not only to *status quo*, but to *status quo ante*. The region is still carrying the heritage of slavery.

In the last part of the eighteenth and the early part of the nineteenth century, the moral righteousness and the socio-economic advantages of slavery came to be doubted very much in the Old Upper South,[11] and even in the Deep South dissenting opinions were heard. But from about the 1830's—under the double influence of the rising profitableness of the slavery and plantation economy and the onslaught from the Northern Abolitionist movement—the apologetic ideology became stabilized and elaborated into a complicated theory of state which every Southerner had to stand for as a matter of regional pride and patriotism.[12]

This ingenious theory was based on the dogma of Negro racial inferiority[a] and also on unique interpretations of the Bible and on general principles for a rational social order. In fact, it is seldom duly recognized that the pro-slavery thought in the South in the decades before the Civil War was the most uncompromising conservative political philosophy which ever developed in Western civilization after the Enlightenment.[13] From a logical point of view, it is the only brand of modern conservatism consistent and courageous enough openly to make human inequality basic to political philosophy, to accept the static state as ideal and to denounce progress. Conservative thinking elsewhere after the Enlightenment was seldom in a position to develop a closed system of principles like liberalism or the various schools of socialism, anarchism and syndicalism. Lack of rigid principles, acceptance of logical compromises, and the view that the growth of society is an arational, organic process was often even pronounced as a

[a] See Chapter 4.

characteristic of conservative thinking.[14] But the pro-slavery philosophy of the Old South, incorporating all ideas dear to conservatism in all countries and in all ages, went the full length and laid down a logical static system just as tight as the competing philosophies to the left.

According to this political philosophy, slavery was not, as earlier Southern writers had been disposed to admit, an inevitable evil. It was instead a positive good, and a good to all parties concerned, including the Negro slaves. Indeed, slavery was only part of a greater social order which established an ideal division of labor and of responsibility in society between the sexes, the age groups, the social classes and the two races. This division should not be left to be worked out by haphazard and ruinous competition. In the South it was intentionally and wisely organized by the state in accordance with the needs, the abilities, and the worth of the individuals in the various groups concerned.

The principle of rational cooperation was, therefore, realized; some authors even talked about "socialism" in a purified and dignified meaning of the term.[15] "By making the labor itself capital, the conflict of interest, so evident in other labor systems, lost its foundation."[16] Radicalism, or rather the reason for radical opposition, was extinguished in this perfect social order. A system of social estates, with the plantation owners as a paternalistic nobility at the top and the toiling Negro slaves at the bottom, was envisaged. "Equality begets universal envy, meanness and uncharitableness—slavery elevates and purifies the sentiments of master and slave."[17] The static nature of this system was accentuated and even exalted by the persistent assertion that the South had actually realized the most happy political, social, and economic conditions ever seen on earth and which were, particularly, much superior to the deplorable conditions in the North. "We are better husbands, better fathers, better friends, and better neighbors than our Northern brethren."[18] The expounders of the pro-slavery doctrine had to go back to Athenian democracy to find a true parallel to the happy South and, indeed, the parallel they used was a highly idealized Athens.

In this static social system all whites, independent of their rank in society, were significantly superior to the slaves. Politically they were all equals, since they were free citizens. Free competition and personal freedom were assured them. The Southern statesmen and writers hammered on this thesis, that slavery, and slavery alone, produced the most perfect equality and the most substantial liberty for the free citizens in society. By relegating—in theory—all menial and domestic labor to the slaves, all the whites became gentlemen. "One of the reconciling features of the existence [of Negro slavery]," argued Jefferson Davis just before the outbreak of the great conflict, "is the fact that it raises white men to the same general level, that it dignifies and exalts every white man by the presence of a lower race."[19] The very basis of white men's equality was the drudgery of the black slaves. In the words of Governor J. H. Hammond of South Carolina:

In all social systems there must be a class to do the menial duties, to perform the drudgery of life. That is, a class requiring but a low order of intellect and but little skill. Its requisites are vigor, docility, fidelity. Such a class you must have or you would not have that other class which leads progress, civilization, and refinement. It constitutes the very mud-sill of society and of political government; and you might as well attempt to build a house in the air, as to build either the one or the other, except on this mud-sill. Fortunately for the South, she found a race adapted to the purpose of her hand. . . . We use them for our purpose and call them slaves.[20]

The slaves were politically the wards of the whites and had no rights against white society. Upon the basis of their labor, civilization could flourish. A high civilization presumed a leisure class and its exploitation of slaves. In the final reckoning, however, even the humble slaves were getting their share of the fruits of that civilization. They were fed, clothed, housed, guarded, and secured in all their needs by their paternalistic owners who, in this wise social order, could have no other interests than to care to the utmost for their welfare. Above this interest solidarity between slaves and slave owners was the solidarity among white men only:

We have among us but one great class, and all who belong to it have a necessary sympathy with one another; we have but one great interest and all who possess it are equally ready to maintain and protect it.[21]

As political ideologies go, this doctrine should not be denied high qualities of structural logic and consistency. It is, of course, an upper class philosophy. It is a rationalization of the interests of the one-fifth of the Southern white population who owned slaves. In its higher spheres the philosophy was hardly understandable to those without a high degree of education. But its basic ideas could be grasped by all. As the conflict with the North drew nearer, it became a regional creed which was pressed upon everybody by all available social controls. It served the South during the Civil War in the same manner as the concept and theory of "democracy" or "the democratic way of life" served all America during the two World Wars. "The parties in this conflict," says the Presbyterian Dr. J. H. Thornwell, who ejected his predecessor, Dr. Cooper, from the presidency of the College of South Carolina for his "infidel" views, "are not merely abolitionists and slaveholders—they are atheists, socialists, communists, red republicans, jacobins on the one side, and the friends of order and regulated freedom on the other. In one word, the world is the battleground—Christianity and atheism the combatants—and the progress of humanity the stake."[22]

Long before the Civil War started, the dissenters from the Southern defense ideology had to keep their opinions to themselves or they risked their social status, their economic advance, their freedom, and, in extreme cases, their bodily security and life, if they did not take refuge in the North. Hinton Rowan Helper's book, *The Impending Crisis of the South* (1857),[23] showed how the South lagged behind the North economically, how the growth of industries was hampered, how the yields were lower in all comparable crops, and how, particularly, the slavery-plantation system was an inefficient and disastrous organization of agricultural production. The author violently accused "the Lords of the Lash" for perpetuating the white majority in unparalleled illiteracy, poverty and dependence. This book became a best seller in the North and exerted a tremendous influence on Northern thinking. It was blacklisted in the South, and the author could not come back to his homeland.

That the book does *not* express the opinions of the lower white strata in the Southern social pyramid, Helper readily admits and regrets. In their poverty, ignorance, and dependence, they knew generally little about the world outside the Southern region which was gradually becoming culturally isolated. And they were offered one great and glittering solace: "white supremacy." They were not at the bottom, they were protected from the status of Negroes by a clear dividing line, and they were told that they could compete freely up to the very top. Few Southerners, even among the nonslaveholding classes, were inclined to dissent from this dogma. Agreeing on the point of "white supremacy," the rest of the elaborated pro-slavery theory offered the most convenient and most efficient rationalization. When they heard that the North wanted to free the Negro slaves, and when they sensed the danger of being thrown into actual competition with the black masses, the great majority of whites even outside the slaveholders felt their solidarity with the latter.

The defeat in the War which followed did not break the general direction of Southern political thinking or the allegiance to it among Southern whites. The harsh measures taken by the victorious North to reform the South quickly favored a consolidation of reactionary forces. This consolidation became particularly effective in disfranchising the Negroes when the North no longer wished to bear the costs and the inconveniences of upholding its military regime indefinitely. Slavery as an institution was, of course, out, as was also the possibility of pretending that the South was God's richest and best social creation. Large sectors of the elaborate philosophy of the *ante-bellum* South therefore had to be consigned to oblivion. But the doctrine of white supremacy became, under these conditions, the more paramount. On this point practically all whites agreed: the impoverished and embittered aristocrats; the *parvenus*, struggling for status; and the masses of poor white people, afraid of competition from the hated and despised black freedmen.

The former Negro slaves, therefore, started their new life as free citizens with a solid mistrust against them, which was crystallized into an elaborate political philosophy, powerful even in its partial disorganization. The very idea of awarding Negroes suffrage was, to the average Southerner, preposterous. The white South *wanted the Negroes to fail as freedmen* and saw in their failure a confirmation of their own wisdom and the Northerners' folly.

5. THE RECONSTRUCTION AMENDMENTS

But the North was in power and Negro suffrage received constitutional sanction. Thus Southern conservatism started out with the law against it. After having lost out as rebels against the Union, the Southern conservatives had now to be rebels in their own land. And as they did not have the power to overthrow the fundamental laws of the Union, they had through generations, and have today, to persist as transgressors of law and order.

The white Southerners' attitudes toward the Reconstruction Amendments deserve some comments. It seems probable, from the literature on the Negro problem after the Civil War, that the abolition of slavery was soon widely accepted as irrevocable. Even if, up to this day, the average Southerner is inclined to paint the institution in somewhat brighter colors than is a Northerner, the opinion early established itself that slavery was incompatible with social and economic progress and, indeed, had been the curse of the Old South. The Fourteenth and Fifteenth Amendments, which granted the Negroes civil rights and suffrage, were not so readily accepted by Southern opinion. They were looked upon as the supreme foolishness of the North, and, worse still, as an expression of ill-will of the Yankees toward the defeated South. The Negro franchise became the symbol of the humiliation of the South.

Later, during the movement to legalize disfranchisement in the decades around the turn of the century, proposals to have the federal Amendments abolished popped up here and there.[24] Such proposals, however, were never part of serious discussion. The obvious impossibility of getting the Northern states to agree was reason enough for that. Corporate business had developed a vested interest in the Fourteenth Amendment. Its proviso guaranteeing all "persons" due process of law turned out to be much more useful in defending corporate business against public interferences and control than in securing political and other civic rights for the Negro.[25] Apart from this particular interest, Northern sentiment could hardly be expected to tolerate such a retreat in principle, even if it was prepared to wink at flagrant circumvention in Southern practice. But it is probable that soon after their passage the two Amendments, and the principle of civic equality they expressed, had acquired a certain amount of idealistic attachment even in the South [26]

In the South of today the writer has observed that many white persons above the least educated strata are inclined to agree in principle that even the Negro has a sort of "right" to vote. With the majority of Southerners, this idea is, of course, only one element in an inconsistent system of thoughts wherein also the very opposite principle is contained and is, indeed, given greater emphasis. This conflict might be important as a symptom of change toward national ideals sanctioned by the American Creed. It shows itself in the fact that the principle as such is seldom denied, except by persons with exceptionally anti-legal leanings.[27]

The statutory requirements of property and poll tax payment, literacy, understanding of the Constitution, good character, and so forth[28]—which at the time of their enactment were openly declared to aim only at circumvention of the constitutional Amendments[29]—are more and more being thought of as within the Constitution. Probably a majority of Southerners, and not only liberal Southerners, are prepared to state that in time to come, when Negroes become educated, the South will have to give them the vote. Attempting to reconcile their electoral practices with constitutional requirements, the Southerners have become accustomed to insist that they are not discriminating against "race, color or previous condition of servitude" but only against ignorance and irresponsibility. Repeating these statements throughout the years, reading them, and hearing them has the effect of conditioning the Southerners to believe them. It is a difficult task for even the most sophisticated person to keep on saying something for a purpose without eventually coming to believe in it—with at least half his soul.

But keeping the Negroes disfranchised in the face of the clear-cut constitutional Amendments allows Southern conservatism nothing more than a pretense of respect for the law. On this most crucial point it is doomed to insincerity.

6. MEMORIES OF RECONSTRUCTION

A review of the various devices by which the Negroes are disfranchised in the South today cannot avoid exposing a rather odious panorama of legal trickery, unfair administration, intimidation and forthright violence.[a] In explanation of this the Southerner will regularly bring forward the horrors of the Reconstruction governments and "black domination." These memories are in a sense cherished. They serve a vital defensive function to the white South. Even the liberal Southerner—and quite particularly when he ventures to criticize these very practices, which he often does with courage and vision—has to express his abhorrence of the Reconstruction atrocities. They are, in fact, symbols of regional allegiance.

The North needs them, also, though to a lesser degree, in order to

[a] See Chapter 22.

rationalize the national compromise of the 1870's and the condoning, since then, of the South's open break with the spirit of the Constitution. Playing up the venality, extravagance, and incompetence of the Reconstruction governments and touching lightly the pride and prejudices of the revolting South is, in addition, a means of reconciling the two regions. It has thus a "patriotic function" in healing the wounds of the Civil War. For all these reasons, it is to be expected that the horrors have been considerably exaggerated. The writing of the history of this epoch has, until recently, responded in a considerable degree to this popular demand of the American whites for rationalization and national comfort.[30]

The dominant history of the period is incompatible with a number of facts that force themselves to our attention. The "carpetbaggers" were not simply Northerners who came down to prey on the devastated South. The great majority of them were either agents sent out by the federal government, to try to help the South to its feet under the principles of the Constitution and its Amendments, or they were New England Abolitionists, often spinsters, who saw their mission in the education of the Negroes.[a] The federal government did not send its agents to the South until 1867, after the South had demonstrated for over two years—by such devices as the Black Codes—that it was determined to retain slavery in fact if not in name. It is true that these carpetbaggers did some stupid things, that their plans were unformulated and inconsistent and that the federal government failed to give them adequate backing. The "scalawags" were mainly poor and ignorant native Southerners who saw a chance—in the South's defeat —to effect something of a revolution against the relatively few wealthy aristocrats. But many of them had honestly and consistently wanted the abolition of slavery, and not a few of them were the Southern inheritors of the great Jeffersonian and, especially, Jacksonian traditions. Some of them had been prominent Whigs before the Civil War.[31] Some of them had consistently favored the Union cause throughout the Civil War when it was extremely unpopular to do so. The masses of Negroes were, of course, uneducated, and a number of them were resentful of their former masters. But they never engaged in organized violence against the whites. They were led by the educated carpetbaggers and by the free Southern and Northern Negroes who had quite often attained a high level of education. Actually, there were only 22 Negro members of Congress[b] from 1870 to 1901; 10 of these had gone to college. The Northern Republicans also came in for their share of vilification. For example, few names in Amer-

[a] Some of the carpetbaggers were businessmen, but these were not always interested in politics.

[b] Twenty of these were in the House of Representatives; the other two were in the Senate (at different times). (Samuel Denny Smith, *The Negro in Congress 1870-1901* [1940], pp. 4-7.)

ican history have come down with such an evil reputation as that of Thaddeus Stevens, the leader of the Republican party in the House of Representatives until his early death in 1868. There are glimmerings of evidence that Stevens had an enlightened plan of social reform far in advance of his time, and that he was not at all violent in inciting Negroes to put their former masters under heel. These few facts, and a consideration of the conditions under which the history of the Reconstruction period has been written, suggest that more efforts ought to be made by American historians to write a complete and dispassionate history of that period, a history which would have to rely on primary rather than on secondary sources.[32]

The school book histories, as well as the more scholarly histories, perpetuate the myths about the Reconstruction period. They still give, for the most part, undue emphasis to the sordid details of the Reconstruction governments but avoid mentioning their accomplishments. They exaggerate the extent of "black domination" and deprecate the Negro politicians even more than they deserve, while they give subtle excuses for the cruelty and fraud employed in the restoration of white supremacy. They usually make all the errors found in the scholarly histories and omit all the complicating qualifications that make the scholarly histories have a semblance of objectivity. Particularly is this true of the history textbooks prepared for Southern schools.[33] The present generation of Southerners, on the whole, is given a more objective picture of the Civil War and Reconstruction than the previous generation received. But their knowledge is still distorted, and their attitudes toward the Negro and the North are correspondingly unfriendly.

It is apparent that, quite independent of what he thinks happened during Reconstruction, the average white Southerner resents the thought of Negroes voting on a par with white men.[34] Yet the Constitution is very clear in specifying that no one is to be kept from voting for reasons of "race, color, or previous condition of servitude." Thus the Southerner is forced to circumvent the Constitution if he is to keep the Negroes from voting. But the Constitution and its principles have a grip on the Southerner's own soul. He therefore needs to believe that when the Negro voted, life was unbearable. The myth of the horrors of Reconstruction thus permits the Southerner to reconcile the two conflicting desires within himself. They are, in our terminology, false beliefs with a purpose.

7. The Tradition of Illegality

While, as we said, the Northerner generally is likely to be less inclined to discriminate against the Negro, the more formal and impersonal a relation is and, specifically, when the relation is between public authority and the individual Negro citizen,[a] the white Southerner is inclined to react

[a] See Section 3 of this chapter.

in nearly the opposite way. Already in the *ante-bellum* elections, political campaigning and voting had acquired a ceremonial significance as marking off a distinct sphere of power and responsibility for the free citizen. From Reconstruction on, voting remained to the white Southerner more than a mere action: it was, and still is, a symbol of superiority. Partly because it is a public activity and does not lend itself to privacy or segregation, it becomes so hard for the white Southerner to admit the Negro to full participation in it.[a] This is one side of the general difference between the two regions so often noticed: that the white Northerners may dislike and ignore the Negro but are prepared to give him his formal rights, while in the South even individual whites who like and care for Negroes cannot afford to give them their rights because this would imply equality.

In order to understand fully Southern conservative illegality, we have also to remember that the actual trickery, cheating and intimidation necessary for the smooth operation of disfranchisement need be indulged in by only a small number of persons. Most people can almost avoid it. Their collaboration is necessary only to the extent of preserving a public sentiment upholding and supporting the system. In most cases, a resolute registrar can himself take care of the matter. And even he does not need to act openly when it has once become generally known among the Negroes in a community that they had better keep away from all politics.

The illegal practices have also the sanction of tradition behind them. The present situation is conceived of as the outcome of the successful revolutionary movement against the Reconstruction governments. The chronicle of the Restoration—symbolized by the Ku Klux Klan and a great number of "protective" leagues and secret terror organizations such as the Pale Faces of Tennessee; the Constitutional Guards and the White Brotherhood of North Carolina; the Knights of the White Camellia in Louisiana and Arkansas; the Council of Safety in South Carolina; the Men of Justice in Alabama; the Society of the White Rose, the Seventy-Six Association, and the Robinson Family in Mississippi; the Knights of the Rising Sun and the Sons of Washington in Texas—offers a most amazing, sometimes ludicrous, but more often pathetic and tragic, reading.

Guy B. Johnson characterizes Reconstruction as, in a sense, "a prolonged race riot":

> The Ku Klux Klan and a dozen similar organizations which sprang up over the South were as inevitable as a chemical reaction. Their purpose was punitive and regulatory, the restoration of absolute white supremacy. They flogged, intimidated, maimed, hanged, murdered, not only for actual attacks and crimes against whites, but for all sorts of trivial and imagined offenses. Every Negro was assumed to be "bad"

---

[a] We do not mean, of course, that the Southerner's purpose in disfranchising the Negro is not to prevent him from having power. We are merely pointing out that the "no social equality" theory applies to politics. (See Chapter 28, Section 6.)

unless he proved by his actions that he was "good.". . . . Every Negro militia drill, every meeting or convention for the political or social advancement of the Negro took on the aspect of a "conspiracy" or an "insurrection." The number of Negroes killed during Reconstruction will never be known. Five thousand would probably be a conservative estimate.[35]

After the overthrow of the Reconstruction government in all Southern states, which was consummated by 1877, a tendency to abstain from violence and threats of violence as a means of keeping the Negroes away from the polls gradually developed. With the state governments safely in their hands, the dominant white Southerners found it easier to buy, steal, or fail to count the Negro vote or to block the Negroes' voting by intricate election laws and manipulation of the election machinery.

Polling places were set up at points remote from colored communities. Ferries between the black districts and voting booths went "out of repair" on election day. Grim-visaged white men carrying arms sauntered through the streets or stood near the polling booths. In districts where the blacks greatly outnumbered the whites, election officials permitted members of the superior race to "stuff the ballot box," and manipulated the count without fear of censure. Fantastic gerrymanders were devised to nullify Negro strength. The payment of poll taxes, striking at the Negro's poverty and carelessness in preserving receipts, was made a requirement for voting. Some states confused the ignorant by enacting multiple ballot box laws which required the voter to place correctly his votes for various candidates in eight or more separate boxes. The bolder members of the colored race met threats of violence, and, in a diminishing number of instances, physical punishment. When the black man succeeded in passing through this maze of restrictions and cast his vote there was no assurance that it would be counted. Highly centralized election codes vested arbitrary powers in the election boards, and these powers were used to complete the elimination of the Negro vote.[36]

The pattern of illegality was thus firmly entrenched in Southern politics and public morals. "A strong man struggling upward under the consciousness of submergence and suffocation strikes right and left with little thought of either principle or policy,"[37] explains an upright Southerner. So, undoubtedly, did the white South feel when justifying the means to the end. But the means became a permanent pattern in the region.

This fatal tradition of illegality has even deeper historical roots. The vigilante conservatives of the 'seventies did not create the patterns anew but simply took over and perfected the methods utilized by the Reconstruction governments themselves in their efforts to remain in power. These governments had often gerrymandered districts in order to gain the full weight of the Negro vote. They had created highly centralized election machinery, which later became so handy to the conservatives, and they had utilized unscrupulously this machinery and the Negro militia for controlling elections. Often these elections were tainted with fraud, intimidation and violence. The post-Reconstruction governments merely went to much greater extremes in illegal practices than already existed.

But even the Reconstruction governments were not entirely original. Already before the Civil War the white South had gradually been conditioned for at least thirty years to sustain increasing suppression of freedom of speech and all other civil liberties in the service of upholding its solidarity.[38]

The methods used and the rationalizations defending them must also be understood against the background of the region's peculiar rural structure. About the South today, Rupert B. Vance points out that:

> . . . it can safely be said that no flavor is stronger than that imparted by the frontier. No traits of the frontier can safely be neglected by the social historian as an antiquarian's item. . . . The South still possesses the largest number of practically self-sufficing farms to be found in any comparable area in the nation. Its rural life is characterized by isolated farmsteads in the open country. If southern conditions of living have often appeared crude to the critics, it is for the reason that they have retained not only the usages but often the conditions of the frontier. More than any other section except the sparsely settled western range it has remained a pioneer belt, and the common man living in the open country faces much the same situation with the cultural heritage left by the frontier. While they were formative the folkways of the South got the stamp of the frontier. From the frontier, part of the area passed to the plantation, but the plantation area retained many of the frontier traits. Institutions and customs are still tinged with the shades of the forest, whether as survivals or as adjustments to ruralism.[39]

If this is true today, it was still more so in the *ante-bellum* South. W. F. Cash, following up this line of thought, comments:

> . . . in this world of ineffective social control, the tradition of vigilante action, which normally lives and dies with the frontier, not only survived but grew so steadily that already long before the Civil War and long before hatred for the black man had begun to play any direct part in the pattern (of more than three hundred persons said to have been hanged or burned by mobs between 1840 and 1860, less than ten per cent were Negroes) the South had become peculiarly the home of lynching.[40]

Thus the opportunistic disrespect for law, order and public morals has a complicated causation and a deep-rooted history in the South. The tradition is today still part of the way of life and as such is often patriotically cherished as distinctively Southern. It is certainly one of the most sinister historical heritages of the region. It spells danger for a democratic society and involves serious maladjustments.

CHAPTER 21

SOUTHERN CONSERVATISM AND LIBERALISM

••

1. THE "SOLID SOUTH"

Except for the Reconstruction period and for the period after Restoration culminating in the Populist movement (1890's), the South has consistently disfranchised the Negroes and has had to cling to the Democratic party to do so. This suppression of normal bi-partisan politics has given the region the appellation "Solid South." The South had a two-party system before 1830, and it was lost in the consolidation of forces against the North just before and during the Civil War. As we noted in the previous chapter, it was lost again at the close of Reconstruction.[1] But already by the end of the 'seventies and increasingly up to the first half of the 'nineties, the Populist movement divided the agrarian middle and lower class from the Democratic party, which was led by the plantation owners, industrialists, merchants and bankers. The rise to political importance of the agrarian radicals resulted in the fulfillment of the prediction that all precautions taken to keep the Negroes disfranchised would crumble if a split occurred in the ranks of the whites. Both factions appealed to the Negro voters. The regular Democrats, who were most familiar with the administrative machinery and who included most of the owners of plantations where Negroes were employed in large numbers, are said to have been most successful. But the agrarians were just as eager to get help where they could find it. In 1896 in North Carolina they joined the Republicans, and as a consequence more Negroes were appointed to offices in that state than ever before.[2] For more than half a decade, the Democratic party was virtually disrupted in most states of the South.

But the reaction soon got under way. A new movement to disfranchise the Negroes by more effective legal means—starting with the Mississippi Constitutional Convention of 1890 and continuing with the adoption of new constitutions in seven other states between 1895 and 1910—drew its main arguments from the danger of a break in white solidarity, demonstrated by the agrarian revolt. When Populism declined, and it did so rapidly after 1896, and the unity between the Populists and the Democrats became restored, the main dish at the love feasts was the disfranchisement of the Negro.[3]

After this crisis, the Democratic one-party rule has persisted practically unbroken until now, with the minor exception of the 1928 presidential campaign. In spite of a formidable armor of constitutional and statutory provisions for disfranchising the Negro and an extra-legal social pressure to complement the statutes, the main regions of the white South still do not dare to have any political division, lest the white factions be tempted to seek Negro support.[a] The irony of the situation is that the disfranchisement of the Negro had been argued as the only means of preventing corruption at the polls and of allowing the whites to divide along natural political lines. The second goal is obviously not reached, as the one-party system is still retained; since it is the only guarantee against Negro franchise, the elimination of the one-party system would be the basis for freedom of the whites to split. And to prevent corruption under a one-party system in a region with the unfortunate traditions of the South—when it is so difficult everywhere in America even when an opposition party is present—is practically impossible. In this vicious circle Southern politics is caught.

The one-party system in the South; its supporting election machine with its restrictions, intricacies, and manipulations; its vast allowances for arbitrary administration; and the low political participation of even the white people favor a *de facto* oligarchic regime, broken here and there, now and then, by demagogues from Tom Watson to Huey Long, who appeal to the lower classes among whites. The oligarchy consists of the big land-owners, the industrialists, the bankers and the merchants.[4] Northern corporate business with big investments in the region has been sharing in the political control by this oligarchy.

There is an amazing avoidance of issues in Southern politics. "The South votes for men—Democratic men—but rarely ever for issues, unless the issue is defined in black and white."[5] We have to remember that in a measure this is a characteristic of all American politics.[b] But in the South, it is driven to its extreme. The chief direct reason for this is, of course, the one-party system which normally keeps politics within a single political machine and restricts the scope of political struggle to personalities and offices. The great Southern orator of the post-Restoration period, Henry W. Grady, gave the best rationalization of this situation as it is even today argued by the majority of the ruling class of the region. The reason is the Negro.

The whites understand that the slightest division on their part will revive those desperate days [of Reconstruction]. . . . So that the whites have agreed everywhere to sink their differences on moral and economic issues, and present solid and

[a] There is a rump Republican party in the South, and in a few isolated areas it is actually dominant. For a discussion of this, see Chapter 22, Section 1.

[b] See Chapter 33.

unbroken ranks to this alien and dangerous element. This once done, the rest is easy. Banded intelligence and responsibility will win everywhere and all the time. Against it numbers cannot prevail.[6]

It is not the Negro himself who is feared but "the baseness of white politicians" who might be tempted to use the Negro vote for "nefarious purposes":

It may be asked, then: "Why do the Southern whites fear the political domination of the blacks?" They do not fear that directly. But the blacks are ignorant, and therefore easily deluded; strong of race instinct, and therefore clannish; without information, and therefore without strong political convictions; passionate, and therefore easily excited; poor, irresponsible, and with no idea of the integrity of the suffrage, and therefore easily bought. The fear is that this vast swarm of ignorant, purchasable and credulous voters will be compacted and controlled by desperate and unscrupulous white men, and made to hold the balance of power wherever the whites are divided. This fear has kept, and will keep, the whites "solid." It would keep the intelligence and responsibility of any community, North or South, solid.[7]

But there is a higher principle invoked to explain why "the whites shall have clear and unmistakable control of public affairs" and why a solid front must be preserved:

They own the property. They have the intelligence. Theirs is the responsibility. For these reasons they are entitled to control. Beyond these reasons is a racial one. They are the superior race, and will not and can not submit to the domination of an inferior race.[8]

Against these arguments the Southern liberals hammer away. They point out that the one-party system fosters mediocrity, demagoguery, political apathy and irrationality. They point out that fear of the Negro shadows every political discussion and prevents the whites from doing anything to improve themselves. The conservative whites counter that the Southern system does allow for political division—in the primaries, though not in the general elections. This, however, is a myth which Southerners have carefully fostered: in 1940 only 36 of the 78 Democratic primaries—less than half—were contested in the eight poll tax states.[9] Thus, even in the primaries there is little opportunity for political division.

But undoubtedly there are sometimes real divisions even in the South on interests and issues: poor people against rich, the hill country against the plantation lands, the coast against the inland. But the fact that the issues have to be fought out under cover of personalities and within a one-party machine must, particularly in a region of inadequate political education, confuse those issues. It has, indeed, been the tradition and the spirit of the "Solid South" to have such confusion, as the party machine is always sensing, and capitalizing upon, the danger of a serious political division. The newspapers usually respect this tradition. They publish the generalities contained in the various candidates' platforms and speeches but usually abstain from giving information on the real issues which might sometimes be involved.

Even admitting, therefore, that the one-party system allows for a certain number of issues and divisions, it must be maintained that, in a considerable degree, the one-party rule of the South obliterates healthy democratic politics, both in national and in local affairs. There is a considerable amount of truth in W. E. Du Bois' bitter characterization:

> The white primary system in the South is simply a system which compels the white man to disenfranchise himself in order to take the vote away from the Negro. . . . The mass of people in the South today have no knowledge as to how they are governed or by whom. Elections have nothing to do with broad policies and social development, but are matters of selection of friends to lucrative offices and punishment of personal enemies. Local administration is a purposely disguised system of intrigue which not even an expert could unravel.[10]

2. SOUTHERN CONSERVATISM

Democratically organized people's movements, giving voice to the needs of the simple citizen and a power basis for his full participation in the control of society, do not thrive in this political atmosphere. To an extent the lack of organized mass participation in government is a general American characteristic.[a] The South shows even less popular political interest than the rest of the country. Except for the Ku Klux Klan, which lacked positive political goals, the Prohibition movement, which was based more on emotion than on reason, and the Populist movement, which, in the South as all over the country, was loose in organization and confused in aims and which achieved little, the South has never experienced organized mass movements of a political character.

There have been few spontaneous movements to improve the well-being of the masses of people, such as trade unions or adult education. Even the farmers' cooperative movement has been lagging in the South,[11] and what has come in has been due mainly to the efforts of the federal government. The Southern masses do not generally organize either for advancing their ideals or for protecting their group interests. The immediate reason most often given by Southern liberals is the resistance from the political oligarchy which wants to keep the masses inarticulate. This has also been the initial situation in most other regions and countries, but in these others eventually the organized and self-disciplined mass movements have come to form the very basis for a revitalized democracy. The deeper reasons are again the low level of political culture in the South, which has become solidified partly in the region's steadfast struggle to keep the Negro from participation.

[a] See Chapter 33.

All modern reform movements which have penetrated the rest of the country and gradually changed American society—woman suffrage and economic equality, collective bargaining, labor legislation, progressive education, child welfare, civil service reform, police and court reform, prison reform—have, until recently, hardly touched the greater part of the South except in so far as the federal government has imposed them from the outside. In particular, there has been no active participation of the masses. Recently they have become the interest of the upper class liberals around the universities and other cultural centers. Southern liberalism—which will be discussed in further detail below—is beautiful and dignified. It preserves much of the philosophical grace of the mythical old aristocratic South. But until the New Deal came, it had no source of power. Even yet it does not have contact with, or support by, the masses. Social reform is now coming rapidly to the South, but it is coming mainly from Washington. For a hundred years this region, which played such an important and distinguished role in the American Revolution and in the early history of the Republic, has not contributed to the nation anything approaching its fair share of fresh political thinking and forward-looking political initiative in national issues. It has, on the whole, served as a reactionary drag against the forces of change and progress.

This political conservatism is directly tied up with the Negro problem in several ways. The devices inaugurated to disfranchise Negroes, the one-party system, the low political participation on the part of the white masses, and other peculiarities of Southern politics, all tend to give a disproportionate power to classes, groups and individuals who feel their interests tied up with conservatism in social issues. But there is also a more direct connection between Southern conservatism and the Negro problem. For constitutional and other reasons, social reform measures will have to include Negroes, and this is resented. The conservative opponents of reform proposals can usually discredit them by pointing out that they will improve the status of the Negroes, and that they prepare for "social equality." This argument has been raised in the South against labor unions, child labor legislation and practically every other proposal for reform.

It has been argued to the white workers that the Wages and Hours Law was an attempt to legislate equality between the races by raising the wage level of Negro workers to that of the whites. The South has never been seriously interested in instituting tenancy legislation to protect the tenants' rights and at the same time to improve agriculture, and the argument has again been that the Negro sharecropper should not be helped against the white man.[a] I have met this same argument everywhere in the South when discussing economic and social reforms: "We don't want our Negroes

[a] See Chapter 10, Section 4.

to ...." The poor white Southerners are apparently still prepared to pay the price of their own distress in order to keep the Negro still lower.

Liberals commonly describe this argument as a "red herring," intentionally used by the reactionaries to distract and deceive the ignorant public and to discredit reforms. But this argument is not merely deceptive. It most certainly has a kernel of truth in it. Of necessity, social reforms involve changes which are general, and social cooperation, to be effective, cannot remain confined exclusively to whites. All social reforms involve an element of economic and social equalization which, by the very logic of things, cannot wholly set the Negroes apart. In addition to technical factors and the constitutional barriers against making social legislation openly discriminatory, there is also the sense of rationality and fairness in the minds of the white Southerners themselves. "Social equality," in a sense, *will* be promoted in a society remade by social reforms; the caste order *was* more easily upheld in a conservative *laissez-faire* society. In spite of much discrimination, this has been the experience of the South during the New Deal. There is, therefore—and this should not be concealed—a measure of logic in the political correlation between the anti-Negro attitude and the traditional conservatism of the South generally. As the South is now gradually accepting social reform, it will also have to give up a considerable part of discrimination against the Negroes both in principle and in practice.

If social reforms have been lacking in the South, certain other changes have been going strong. The Prohibition movement, for example, has had widespread political support. William Archer, when he toured the South in the first decade of the twentieth century, could report that "the most remarkable phenomenon in the recent history of the South is the 'wave of prohibition' which has passed, and is passing, over the country. There are 20,000,000 people in the fourteen Southern States, 17,000,000 of whom are under prohibitory law in some form."[12] Even today, nearly a decade after the abolition of the Eighteenth Amendment, two Southern states—Mississippi and Oklahoma (and one Northern state—Kansas)—have laws prohibiting the sale of hard liquor. Even those states which do not have prohibition laws have strong prohibitionist sentiments. For example: in 1938 the Virginia legislature ordered the burning of a study of the physiological effects of liquor after they had paid to have this study made, simply because it observed that liquor in small quantities was not harmful.[13] These demonstrations against liquor are apparently not meant to affect white people; in most Southern states they are directed solely against the Negro.[a] Archer remarked that: "The presence of the negro in the South is a tower of strength to the prohibitionist."[14]

[a] In Mississippi, which is an absolutely dry state, the author saw more hard drinking

The South is also strongly religious. Not only is the nonchurch member comparatively rare, but the denominations tend to be more fundamentalist and evangelical than in the North. Although it would have to be checked by carefully collected quantitative data, my impression is that the sermons stress the Other World more often than this one and rely for a text more often on the Old Testament than on the New Testament. It would seem that the Southern white man, especially in the lower classes, goes to church more to get an emotional thrill than to get an intellectual framework into which to put his daily problems. These things are true in the North, too, but to a much smaller extent. In spite of his other-worldliness in church, the Southern preacher is often interested in power. Until recently he was often quite important in local politics: during the 1920's clergymen may almost be said to have dominated the South. They were a potent force behind the resuscitation of the Ku Klux Klan. They backed the "Blue Laws." They dominated many universities. The Dayton trial, which was fought over the question of teaching evolution in Tennessee, was only the most spectacular manifestation of the general power of the fundamentalist clergy.[15]

3. Is the South Fascist?

On account of the one-party system and the precarious state of civil liberties, the South is sometimes referred to as fascist. This is, however, wrong and just as wrong of the present as of the earlier South. The South entirely lacks the centralized organization of a fascist state. Southern politics is, on the contrary, decentralized and often even chaotic. The Democratic party is the very opposite of a "state party" in a modern fascist sense. It has no conscious political ideology, no tight regional or state organization and no centralized and efficient bureaucracy. The "regimentation" which keeps the South politically solid is not an organization *for* anything—least of all for a general policy—it is a regimentation *against* the Negro. The South is static and defensive, not dynamic and aggressive.

Fundamentally the white Southerner is—like the Negro, who is molded in the same civilization—even more of an individualist and more of a romantic than the Northerner. This is attested to by recent Southern analysts of "the mind of the South." The point has been particularly well established and explained by W. J. Cash in his recent book of this title.[16] These characteristics are a survival of the frontier civilization of the South. A ruling element of this tradition is "an intense distrust of, and, indeed, downright aversion to, any actual exercise of authority beyond the barest minimum essential to the existence of the social organism."[17] The Southerner wants and expects a personal touch, a measure of arbitrariness, and,

than he has ever before witnessed. Will Rogers is said to have remarked that "Mississippi will hold faithful and steadfast to prohibition as long as the voters can stagger to the polls."

indeed, of adventure in all his relations with public authorities. He wants them to be informal, considerate and personalized.

The South has not yet reached the objectivity and legality of the mature democracy. But still less does it resemble the tight, totalitarian regimentation of the fascist state. It might, perhaps, be said to contain elements of both. But, more fundamentally, the South is a stubbornly lagging American frontier society with a strong paternalistic tinge inherited from the old plantation and slavery system. Paternalism is cherished particularly as the ideal relation between whites and Negroes. The Southerner is proud of his benevolence toward Negro dependents but would resent vigorously their demanding this aid as a right. It must never be forgotten that the caste system has a petty positive angle and not only a gross negative one. Paternalism—as a social pattern which is personal, informal, determined by whimsy and the impulses of the moment, touched by humor and sentimentality, flattering the ego, but, nevertheless, not too expensive—fits ideally into the individualistic and romantic temper of the region.

Registrars and other county officials in the South show surprising indifference to, and sometimes brazen ignorance of, the laws and formal procedures. They are systematically careless, and they are proud of it. Even political discrimination against the Negro is haphazard and accidental in this romantic and individualistic region. Most of the time the Negro is not allowed to register or to vote, and he might risk anything up to his life in attempting to do it. But sometimes he is allowed: because he is a "good nigger," because "he has the right," because his voting "proves" that there is no discrimination, or for no particular reason at all, or just for the fun of doing the opposite of what is expected.

In most districts, most of the time, the Negro has also to be careful about what he indulges in as far as organizational activity and concerted political propaganda is concerned. In many communities leading white citizens make no secret of the fact that they are carefully following—with the assistance of Negro stool-pigeons—all signs of "subversive propaganda" and unrest among the Negroes in the community, and that they interfere to stop even innocent beginnings of Negro group activity. But more often, and again for no visible reason, the Negroes are let alone to organize and plead their causes as they please. The National Association for the Advancement of Colored People is often spoken of by conservative white Southerners as a serious danger, organized from the North to stir up Negroes in the South against the whites and to disrupt the social order there. One is told that anybody from that organization sneaking into the community will have to run fast in order not to be lynched. Incidents are related to show that this is not an empty threat. But the N.A.A.C.P. has local branches in over 100 cities in the South; and Garner, it is said, wanted to have the 1940 N.A.A.C.P. convention in Houston, Texas, and had promised to have the Democratic state committee abolish the white primary rule in return for boosting the Garner candidacy for President among Northern Negroes.

Related to the South's individualism and frontier heritage is its strong democratic temper. Even the old harshly conservative slavery philosophy of the *ante-bellum* South stressed the fundamental equality of all white men.[a] "White supremacy" and, to a lesser degree, the defensive ideology of the alleged superiority of the pure Southern white stock to the mixed Northerners, tended to promote a feeling of fellowship and fundamental equality among Southern white men. In spite of economic class differences, accentuated by the slavery and plantation system, there was also much real democracy in the outer forms of social relations. The planters usually preferred to keep their aristocratic pretensions to themselves and to encourage the high-brow writers in their philosophizing about equality. The literature did not reach the masses anyway. The origin of most of the planter class from the same stock of people as the poor whites was a tie, particularly in the Deep South.[18] Democracy in daily human relations had, thus, much the same origin in the South as in other parts of America. The Civil War and the social convulsions during the succeeding decades certainly did not strengthen the feeling of rigid class differences. Even if in reality the South until this day remains much of a political oligarchy—where, however, the individual oligarchs are often changing—this oligarchy always has to appeal to the common white man as an equal and as the ultimate arbiter of political affairs.

Religion also tends to create a feeling of equality among human beings in the South—not even excluding the Negroes. An even stronger influence has been created by the American Creed. Southerners have been denouncing the North and its leveling theories on every convenient occasion for a hundred years, but they cannot help being gradually drawn into its orbit. In the middle of the 'eighties, Walter Hines Page and George Washington Cable—Page as editor of a weekly magazine, the *State Chronicle* (1883), in North Carolina and Cable with the publication of his book, *The Silent South* (1885)—started Southern self-criticism, and since then the South has had a growing school of nonscalawag liberals, all working in line with the national democratic ideals. They have been violently denounced. Some have abandoned work in the South and moved to the North. Even today they are denounced by perhaps the majority of Southerners. But most of the people who denounce them, nevertheless, take a regional pride in them. Their status in the South is definitely higher than is that of intellectual liberals in the North. And what is more, the Southern liberals have

[a] See Chapter 20, Section 4.

actually influenced considerably the thinking of the South far outside the circle of their direct followers.[a]

Despite all professions to the contrary, the acceptance in principle even by the conservative white Southerners of the American Creed explains why so many exceptions are made to the rule of excluding Negroes from voting. It opens many possibilities for a persistent strategy on the part of the Negro people to increase their political participation. It makes it possible that the barrier against them might, in the future, fall altogether. In fields other than politics, it is equally important to remember that the white conservative Southerner harbors the American Creed. Otherwise it would, for example, be difficult or impossible to explain why the Negroes in the South are getting so much, and are gradually getting even more, education. It would be just as impossible to explain why, in the local application of New Deal measures, Southern discrimination against the Negroes stops where it does. It would generally be inexplicable why the South, with all its traditions of inequality and illegality, is so definitely on the way toward social democracy and law observance, and why it is not headed the other way. The conservative Southerner is not so certain as he

[a] When discussing Southern politics with reactionary intellectuals and semi-intellectuals in the South—among them a high officer of the Ku Klux Klan—the present author had the following type of conversation: after my informant had expounded his social and political theory—a somewhat modified version of the aristocratic, patriarchal, solidarity philosophy discussed above—I tempted him with the following response: I accepted his ideal of political society, but I criticized the methods used to achieve it. We are living in a modern civilization, with vastly improved methods for political domination. In this era the old-fashioned methods of the South—election treachery, intimidation, occasional mob-justice—are outmoded; they are inefficient and socially wasteful. If modern techniques—which I described without going into detail—were to be applied to the Southern situation, a much greater security for the upper strata could be realized with much less cost and effort. It would indeed be beneficial even to poor rural whites and to the Negroes who could rapidly be brought to paint their shacks, screen their windows, keep up gardens, wash their babies, and take better care of their land and their crops. Industry could perhaps afford to pay somewhat higher wages if it were insured against outside interference with its workers, and if the workers were brought to feel a fundamental identity of interest with Capital.

Having thus been shown the ideal fascist state, the Southern reactionary's immediate and emphatic response would invariably be a version of the following: "No, sir! This is a country of liberty and equality of opportunity. Everyone in this American nation, high and low, white and black, rich and poor, values his freedom higher than anything else. Not for any promises of order and material well-being are we Americans willing to give up the fundamental tenets of our democracy."

In these or similar terms I have, time and again, been rewarded for projecting constructively the basic principles sometimes so freely pronounced by conservative white Southerners. The secret, I have been gradually convinced, is that the Southerner, too, and even the reactionary Southerner, harbors the whole American Creed in his bosom. It certainly does not dominate his political behavior: he is inconsistent and ambivalent. But it would be equally wrong to try to analyze the situation in the South without taking his allegiance to the American Creed into account.

sometimes sounds. He is a split personality. Part of his heart belongs to the American Creed. And if one argues that this is mere hypocrisy, he is entirely missing the point. The Southern conservative white man's faith in American democracy, which he is certainly not living up to, and the Constitution, which he is circumventing, are living forces of decisive dynamic significance.

4. The Changing South

The South is changing rapidly. During the 'thirties the changes went into high speed. Those changes cover the whole field of social relations and are being analyzed in other chapters of this inquiry. At this point only a few summary hints are needed to stress their paramount importance for Southern politics.

It is easy to give the false impression that the South is static. The preceding pages of this chapter—taken by themselves—might also have fallen into this error. There are two main causes of this illusion. One is the extremely low starting points, in all respects—general education, political culture, economic standards—of the South at the end of the Civil War. The outside observer, today, who does not himself share in the breath-taking drama of the Southern people, will easily observe that the South is far behind the rest of the nation but might overlook the great changes that have occurred since the Civil War. To guard against this we have tried to be explicit about the humble beginnings.

The second cause is a curious tendency of most Southerners, a tendency related to their conservatism, to stress in conversation and literature that customs are strong and that there is much resistance to change. Reality is actually dynamic in the South, but people's ideas about reality are usually astonishingly static. The average Southerner does not seem to believe in the changes which are going on right before his own eyes. The pessimistic and conservative idea about the "mores" and the "folkways"—which supposedly cannot be changed by the "stateways"—is not only a particularly cherished notion among Southern social scientists, but is something of a regional religion for a large proportion of the literate people. The South is intensely conscious of its history, and there is a high level of historical knowledge among the educated classes. But history is not used, as in the North, to show how society is continuously changing, but rather, on the contrary, to justify the *status quo* and to emphasize society's inertia.

It is true that the presence of this bent of mind itself hampers social change. But the material and spiritual changes under way are so momentous that they cut through these barriers. Southerners are apt to say that "the poll tax will not be abolished in the South, for the courthouse gangs will not allow it," or that "Negroes will never vote in the South, for white people will not stand for it," or that "there are never going to be any labor unions down here, for public opinion is against it." The truth is, of course, that the poll tax *is* abolished in three states (North Carolina, Louisiana, and Florida) already, and that it is likely to be abolished in the others as time passes.[a] The trend is clear and uni-directional: when the poll tax is once abolished in a state it is unlikely that it will be reintroduced there, while in the other states the discussion will continue about its abolition. The courthouse gangs and the local politicians might be against the reform, but there is a general upheaval of social and economic conditions in the South which is changing their basis of power. Likewise, Negroes *are* voting in some places in the South, and white people are tolerating it. In the new annual A.A.A. elections for the crop restriction program they are even voting right in the cotton counties of the Black Belt in perhaps even greater proportion than whites.[b]

Industrialization and urbanization are proceeding at a greater speed in the South than in other parts of the country. Agriculture in the South is facing a more thoroughgoing adjustment to world market conditions than elsewhere, and this structural change means more to the South because its economy is based on agriculture to a greater extent. Because of the coming economic changes and because of the high birth rate, migration may be expected to become more important than it now is, and migration always has far-reaching social effects. Unionization has proceeded in spite of all impediments. The national labor movement in America cannot indefinitely be expected to overlook the fact that the present conservative power constellation in the South is antagonistic to its interests. Indeed, it is something of a riddle that organized labor throughout the country has, for such a long time, acquiesced in the Southern situation.

The economic depression and the following prolonged stagnation during the 'thirties meant distress everywhere and particularly in the poor, backward, harassed South. The liberal New Deal which followed in the wake of the economic pressure was sponsored by the same national party which locally has meant the "Solid South," cultural traditionalism and political reaction. But apart from the fact of party allegiance, the South was actually too poor to scorn systematically the gifts of national charity, even if the price to be paid was the acceptance of social legislation and organized social reform. Not overlooking the considerable discrimination against Negroes in the local administration of New Deal measures in the South,[c] we must see that the New Deal has made a lasting break in Southern racial practices. It has been said that the South was once bought by the Northern capitalists, who did not care much for the Negroes and allowed the Southerners almost complete freedom in the pursuit of any kind of racial discrimination.

[a] While this book is in press, Tennessee has also abolished its poll tax.
[b] See Chapter 12, Section 5, and Chapter 22, Section 3.
[c] See Chapters 12 and 15.

Now Washington is the main "buyer" of the South. And Washington usually seeks to extend its assistance regardless of race.

Washington is not consistent in its racial policy, it is true. The New Deal, whatever its leadership and its aspirations, is bridled by shrewd politicians who must be just as reluctant to break openly with Southern conservatism as with the corrupt city machines in the North. But at the same time these politicians have to look out for the labor vote and for the Negro vote in the North, which again strengthens the forces working for nondiscrimination in the New Deal. There is, in the game, plenty of room for skillful log-rolling; the Southern conservatives in Congress and at home will often succeed in blocking rules and policies drawn up by the New Dealers to protect the Negroes' right to their equal share. The fight goes on under cover. But sometimes it flares into the open, as when Southern reactionary congressmen utilize their strategic committee positions to defeat or restrict some proposal of the New Deal. This blocking of social reform by Southern congressmen and the more general condition—which existed long before the New Deal—for Southern congressmen to exert a disproportionate influence on legislation because of their longer tenure and the consequent importance of their committee assignments and prestige, *is one of the main reasons why the Negro problem is a national one and not merely a sectional one.* Northern politicians are becoming aware of this fact before the Northern public.

If, in the main, the New Deal has to deal tactfully with Southern congressmen, the latter cannot afford to break off entirely from the New Deal either. The Democratic party is their means of reaching out into national politics. And, besides, they have to watch their home front, where the New Deal is getting popular with the masses. The race issue, in these New Deal measures, is never an isolated element which can be cut off; it is always involved in the bigger issue of whether poor people shall be helped or not. The fundamental fact is that the South is poor and in clear need of social assistance and economic reform. To this must be added a personal factor of considerable weight. Roosevelt is not just another Democratic President. He has succeeded in becoming truly popular among the common people in the South, and he has taught them to demand more out of life in terms of security and freedom from want. He has acquired such prestige that the epithet "nigger lover" simply cannot be applied to him. Even the most conservative Southerner will scarcely dare to come out against him personally in the same way as do Republican conservatives in the North.

In this way Southern political conservatism as a whole, and even on the race point, has to retreat and compromise. Meanwhile, the entire South is experiencing the benefits of the various federal policies. A general trend of centralization of governmental functions—from local governments to state governments, and from state governments to federal governments— is helping to give the South a new kind of administration. Even more in the South than in the rest of the country the New Deal takes on the form of a popular movement. Partly under the stimulation of the New Deal, the people of the South are coming to organize themselves for a wide variety of purposes: in county planning and other agricultural groups, in 4-H clubs, in credit associations and cooperatives, in religious reform groups, discussion forums, fact-finding committees, parent-teacher associations, interracial commissions, professional organizations and civic betterment leagues. Some of these organizations are much older than the New Deal, but the whole trend has certainly gained momentum during recent years. The relation to the political New Deal of these variegated civic activities is apparent. The people behind it are the same as those working for the New Deal. Often those organizations are initiated and financed by the N.Y.A., the W.P.A., and the F.S.A. or some of the other government agencies.

Small numbers of Southerners, even in the lower classes, are thus gradually becoming accustomed to meeting together for orderly discussion of their problems. We have already observed the lack, in the South even more than in the North, of self-generating peoples' movements. The activity which we are now considering is certainly not a spontaneous outflow from the intelligent demands of problem-conscious masses. It is spoon-fed from above. But we must be careful not to under-estimate its potentialities. The building up of a social democracy does not, perhaps, follow exactly the same pattern everywhere. It may be that as small groups from the masses are in this way reached by modern political thought, they will, in their turn, act as catalysts bringing political intelligence and organizational solidarity to the vast dormant masses of white and black people in the South.

The New Deal—particularly in the South—does not rate highly when judged by norms of administrative efficiency. There has been lack of careful planning, coordination, and persistency, and there has also been waste of personnel and money. But the New Deal has spirit—particularly in the South. And it has done what many of the more efficient national welfare policies in other countries have rather neglected: it has strongly emphasized the education of the people. Such agencies as, for instance, the Farm Security Administration, have perhaps their most outstanding accomplishment in the education of the masses for a fuller and more efficient life. By actually changing the people, and not only assisting them economically, the New Deal becomes the more potent as a dynamic factor undermining the *status quo* in the South.

The docility of the people on the plantations and in the textile mills— so different from the common stereotype of the independent, upright

American—is, of course, the very thing to be educated away. But in the initial effort at change, this docility gives the public agencies the opportunity to use an element of patriarchal compulsion in the right direction, which speeds up the educational process. The poorest farmer in the Scandinavian countries or in England—or in the Middle West, for that matter —would not take benevolent orders so meekly as Negro and white sharecroppers do in the South. But if use is made of dependence and paternalism, the aim is independence and self-reliance. It has to be remembered that these people have lived in still greater dependence before, and that their close supervision by federal agencies is to be regarded as a weaning process.

If we note further that the long-run trend in the South toward a higher level of general education and cultural participation of both Negroes and whites is steadily proceeding, we have accounted for the main dynamic factors in the Southern political situation. They all accumulate to bring Southern conservatism into a process of gradual disintegration. In this period of accelerated change, the Second World War has come to America. Some of the specific New Deal policies are being discontinued. Undoubtedly this War will have some of the usual effects of all wars in the direction of cultural and political reaction.[19] It is reported that the Ku Klux Klan is preparing for a new and glorious comeback after this War is over. But, more fundamentally, the War will probably work toward a still greater speeding up of most of the changes under way. And the War is fought for democracy, for the "American way of life"—which is certainly not Southern traditionalism.

In these changes, the various areas of the South are proceeding at different levels. The Deep South lags somewhat behind the Upper South, the Southwest, and the Border states, just as these are not as advanced as the Northern and Western regions of the country. These regional differences give us a sort of observational check in our analysis of the changes in time; they are especially useful in foreseeing the future of the Deep South.

No Yankee will be tactless enough to mention it, in so many words, and no Southerner can afford to admit it, but *the main thing happening to the South is that it is gradually becoming Americanized.*

5. Southern Liberalism

Southern liberalism is not liberalism as it is found elsewhere in America or in the world. It is a unique species. It is molded by the forces of the region where it carries out its fight. As an intellectual and ideological phenomenon it is, as we shall find, highly interesting. But in spite of its local, not to say provincial, character, it has always had its chief strategic function as a liaison agent with the North. *It gets its power from outside the South.* For decades Southern liberals have been acting as the trusted advisors and executors of the Northern philanthropists who wanted to do something for the region. During the 'thirties they received a much more potent trusteeship; namely, to bring the New Deal into effect in the South. The power and prestige of this function, and, even more, the entire series of recent changes in the Southern social scene, have given them a high political importance in the South.

As social change gains momentum in the South, the future of Southern liberalism might become great. But it must be recognized that, outside the sphere dominated by Washington, its actual influence today on Southern politics is still minor. It has as yet little organized support among the broad masses of workers, farmers and lower middle class. It is mostly a fraternity of individuals with independent minds, usually living in, and adjusting to, an uncongenial social surrounding. Many of them are tolerated and even respected because of their high standing in their professions, their family background or their general culture. They are the intellectuals of the region and are responsible for a large part of the entire high-grade literary, journalistic and scientific output of the region. They are so relatively few that the student of the South and its problems can hardly avoid coming to know first-hand and personally a representative sample of the group. They are, indeed, the cultural façade of the South.

Here and there they have influenced state and local affairs to a limited extent. During the 'thirties the backing from Washington increased this type of local political influence. But nowhere in the South are they in power. The one exception to prove the rule is former Mayor Maury Maverick of San Antonio, Texas. A few have, however, reached out into national politics. Only two senators in the Upper and Lower South—Claude Pepper of Florida and Lister Hill of Alabama (successor to Justice Hugo Black) —and two or three Southern representatives (notably, Robert Ramspeck of Georgia) could be considered as liberals. It seems to be easier for a Southern liberal to win a seat in Congress than to be really influential at home. One of the most prominent of them, Justice Hugo Black, has entered the Supreme Court after serving as senator. Quite a number of Southern liberals have held important positions in the central New Deal administration and thus, through Washington, moved things quite a bit in their own South. They have been the distinguished "scalawags" of the 'thirties. A representative and prominent man in this group is W. W. Alexander, the former chief of the Farm Security Administration.

But for the rest, Southern liberalism has its main stronghold in a few universities and among newspaper editors, both found most often in the Upper South. President Frank P. Graham of the University of North Carolina is a national figure—which means much in the South—and is thus strong enough even to maintain a thoroughly liberal and, in some respects, unorthodox faculty. North Carolina is, in addition, a fairly liberal state, as Southern states go, and proud of the national reputation of its University. But even in the Deep Southern state of Georgia, the college has a slight liberal influence. When recently Governor Eugené Talmadge, one of the most vicious demagogues of the South, tried to dismiss ten educators in the state's highest institutions, he met the condemnation of the regional educational association, the vociferous protest of the students and even the mild protests of the remaining teachers. Even though the issue was a racial one, the opposition was quite vigorous—much more vigorous than Talmadge had bargained for and much more vigorous than he would have received a generation ago. Mainly as a consequence of his attacks on academic freedom, Talmadge was defeated at the following election.

Some of the liberal editors in the Upper South, such as Jonathan Daniels, Virginius Dabney, and Mark Ethridge, also enjoy a certain amount of protection in their liberal views through the fact that they have achieved positions of national eminence. But many others do not. And all of them have to sell their papers in the local market to make a living.

In this situation it is evident that the result must be a rigorous selection of the liberal professors and editors in the South. For men of humble origin and modest gifts and vision it is actually too dangerous to be liberal in the region. It is an obvious fact—usually never denied in the South even by conservatives—that the liberal professors and editors reach professional standards far superior to the average in the region. This gives to liberalism in the South a flavor of intellectual superiority, which is likely to attract the most ambitious youths. And because it makes such high demands upon a person in the way of talent and courage, mediocre youth avoid it. As some Southern liberals under the New Deal have been awarded important functions in national administration and politics, this adds more appeal but, again, only to the select. To a degree this is the situation everywhere in the world. It is always safest to be a conformer, but there are "glittering prizes for the one who has a brave heart and a cutting blade," as the late British statesman Lord Birkenhead once told an English student assembly.[20] In the South the selective process seems to work with much more sharpness than elsewhere in America.

To the group of outstanding liberals in the South belong also such writers of fiction as Erskine Caldwell, Paul Green, William Faulkner, Ellen Glasgow, Julia Peterkin, Du Bose Heyward, and Thomas S. Stribling. Their direct influence in the South is probably much smaller than could be assumed, as in all likelihood the majority of their readers are Northerners. Book reading is restricted in the South. The North has always been, and still is, the main public for Southern authors.

There are also labor union officials among the Southern liberals. The growing group of social workers and people employed locally in the various federal agencies contain also a significant portion of liberals. In addition, there are solitary idealists living all over the huge region—teachers, some doctors, a few lawyers, occasionally a queer businessman or planter, a number of ministers, and many educated married women of the upper and middle class who enjoy the culture of leisure. Many women's organizations, for instance, the American Association of University Women or the League of Women Voters, are locally strong forces for liberalism. There are other liberal organizations; for example, the interracial commissions[a] or the Fact Finding Committee of Georgia—a Southern state where such a group and such work would be least expected, judging by the office-holders and the policies pursued.

But Southern liberalism has generally not reached even this preliminary stage of organization. The nearest approach to an organized political front was the Southern Conference on Human Welfare, which met in 1938 in Birmingham, Alabama, in 1940 in Chattanooga, Tennessee, and in 1942 in Nashville, Tennessee. The author, who was present at the first occasion, had a feeling that the real importance of this meeting was that here for the first time in the history of the region, since the era of the American Revolution, the lonely Southern liberals met in great numbers—actually more than twelve hundred—coming from all states and joined by their colleagues in Washington; and that they, in this new and unique adventure, experienced a foretaste of the freedom and power which large-scale political organization and concerted action give.

At these conferences Southern Negroes were present and played an important role. It is a fact of more potential than actual political importance that practically all Southern Negro intellectuals and probably a majority of the Negro professionals and business people are, at heart, liberals. It is natural both that their interests are concentrated upon the Negro problem and that their attitudes toward other issues, where they are practically without a voice, are less well considered and articulated.[b]

When attempting to map the political opinions of white Southern liberalism, it must first be recalled that the region is exceptional in Western nonfascist civilization since the Enlightenment in that *it lacks nearly every trace of radical thought.*[c] In the South all progressive thinking going further than mild liberalism has been practically nonexistent for a century.

[a] See Chapter 39, Section 11.

[b] See Part IX.

[c] This *is* unique. Even in a most conservative country like Germany during the nineteenth century, all grades of opinions, from extreme conservatism to extreme radicalism, were represented in the public discussion. The German radicals of that period—various types of intellectual socialists, syndicalists, communists, and anarchists—sometimes met difficulties in getting their stuff into print; sometimes they had to live in exile for a while, as did Karl Marx. But they kept their allegiance and usually they came back and continued their participation in the public debate of their home country.

The full spectrum of opinion is thus never quite completely represented in public discussion in the South.

This is undoubtedly a handicap from the viewpoint of general political culture conceived of as a balanced ensemble of voices, where the richness of the harmony is attained out of the dispute between disparate tones and timbres. The Southern harmony of opinions is based on a narrow range. The explanation of this extraordinary situation is again ultimately the Negro, the slavery institution, the conflict with the North and the strain since then to keep the South solid. The margin of tolerance for political opposition is still narrow. Too, since the region is only a part of the larger America, the few radicals have been able to move freely to the North; and they have stayed there because, not having the difficulties of immigrants, they can easily fit into the new surroundings and find rich outlets for their interests and ideals.

The second main consideration when judging Southern liberalism is that *the liberals are so definitely a political minority*. Liberalism—as well as conservatism—takes on a quite different character depending upon whether it is in opposition or in power. Southern liberalism has not only been in opposition but has also been far from realizing even an expectation to be in political power within the short-range view. This accounts for the rather academic nature of liberal thinking in the South. Until recently Southern liberals planned their programs without thinking in terms of the actual power constellation and without taking account of the detailed demands of practical social engineering. The situation, however, is rapidly changing. The Southern liberals working for the New Deal *have* power and *are* thinking realistically in terms of power and practical plans. In the local issues, not touched by the New Deal, however, liberalism is still largely academic.

For the same reason—lack of expectation to be in power—the Southern liberal, in an extraordinary way, has become inclined to stress the need for patience and to exalt the cautious approach, the slow change, the organic nature of social growth. Southern liberalism is, in these respects, still often expressed in terms which remind one much more of Edmund Burke, the great conservative thinker of a hundred and fifty years ago, than of modern liberalism in the North or in other democratic countries. In their activities Southern liberals have developed the tactics of evading principles; of being very indirect in attacking problems; of cajoling, coaxing and luring the public into giving in on minor issues.

The general public of the South is often spoken of by Southern liberals as hopelessly backward, but at the same time it is flattered in the most extravagant terms of regional mythology. It is made a main point that the Southern public must not be enraged into resistance. It becomes the fine art of politics to get the public to tolerate or accept changes which it does not quite understand, as they are never raised as issues and not talked about straightforwardly. Petty changes are hailed as great victories. Southern liberals are thus conditioned to being opportunistic. They often lack a clear understanding of the common observation from all spheres of politics in all count es and all times: that political actions, which for the moment amount to little more than mere demonstrations and which may actually cause a reaction in the individual case, in the long view may have been tremendously important as powerful stimuli to progressive thinking.

It is apparent that this political approach—which is well understandable in the social context of the present South and against the background of the last hundred years' history of the region—is now much less prevalent than earlier. The New Deal has made liberals accustomed to rather rapid reforms and, what is more important, reforms which have often challenged local prejudices considerably. But as a general attitude, the indirect and cautious Southern approach is still adhered to, especially among liberals of an older generation. In sectors other than those in which they happen to be interested at the moment, many Southern liberals lean over backward to be conservative and so to avoid suspicion. The individual Southern liberal of an older school who is working to defend collective bargaining in his locality, for example, may surprise the interviewer by starting out, without any provocation, to explain why he thinks that birth control is wrong. A stress on church and religion is generally such a front all over the South, by which is meant that these values have a function to the Southern liberal even besides their original one.

The Southern liberal, having to be critical of the South, has to emphasize strongly his *local and regional patriotism*.[21] He has also, if he wants to keep respectability and the possibility of accomplishing something, to tread most cautiously around the Negro problem. Southern liberals time and again explain that they have to respect established rules of racial etiquette in order to be able to do some real good for the South and, incidentally, for the Negro people. It is, for instance, explained by many that it is most important to keep the Negro out of sight in the fight for the abolition of the poll tax, in order not to stir up the anti-Negro complex. The Southern liberal, because he is suspected, has to be more afraid of the deadly blow of being called a "nigger lover" than the conservative, who can more easily shake it off as an absurdity.

Nevertheless—and in spite of the real need for conservatism in some issues, which should not be questioned—the modern Southern liberal will most often actually be liberal not only in the sector where he is active but in other sectors as well. Again we must remember that the recruitment to liberalism in the South is strongly selective in regard to courage. Southern liberals are all fully aware of the function of the Negro issue in the conservatism of the region and how every reform proposal becomes so much more difficult to carry out politically if the Negro angle of it cannot be concealed. But in spite of these formidable drawbacks, Southern liberals have originated and carried out the interracial movement, about which more will be said in a later chapter. Generally the liberals will be found to stand for the most advanced policies in the Negro problem which are possible to advance in the Southern community where they are active. Southern liberals have been standing up for equal justice to the Negroes and have fought the lynching practice. They have often declared themselves against the disfranchisement of the Negroes. They have been active in helping the Negroes get a fairer share of education, housing, employment and relief. They do not, however, go so far as to demand "social" equality for Negroes, and they declare against "intermarriage." They usually direct their main activity on broader problems of economic, social, and educational reforms of the South as a whole, and maintain that, as a result of such a general improvement of the region, the conditions will be eased even for the Negro people.

As the South has the greatest problems of any section of the country, it has been natural for Southern liberals to concentrate their political speculation and action on their own region. Relatively speaking, national and international issues have not loomed so large in the South as in the North. In this sense, the typical Southern liberal has been provincial. On the other hand, he has been more likely than his compeer in the North to think concretely and constructively in terms of the entire Southern region rather than in terms of a state. This is a heritage from the great national split. Against provincialism, however, works the clear understanding among Southern liberals that they derive much of their power from outside their area, and that the future of their cause in the South is vitally interwoven with political developments in the North and in the whole world. This latter tendency has, of course, been strengthened during the New Deal when federal legislation has been the strongest liberalizing force in the South. The editorial pages in liberal newspapers will thus be found to discuss, with increasing courage and insight, national and world issues and events. It should be understood that this is also a practical way of propagating liberalism in the South. In the Southern *milieu*, it is easier to get away with advanced thinking about Germany, India, or New York and even about national legislation if it does not concern concrete Southern problems. The outspoken liberalism in broader issues which can be observed in liberal Southern newspapers is thus often a compensation and an escape for forced conservatism at home.[22] It is also apparent that the "heavier" literature in books and magazine articles, which is written for a less popular and less dangerous public, is more concentrated on Southern problems.

The central concern of the Southern liberal is always the South. The Southern liberals, more than similar groups in other parts of the country, feel themselves as belonging together in a fighting unity. They probably know each other better than liberals elsewhere and have a closer union with one another. Their cause is the improvement of the South. The acute awareness of the pressing problems of the region is likely to make the Southern liberals more definitely practical in their interests even if this has not until recently carried them to think constructively along power lines and in terms of social engineering. Social science in the South has similarly never, as in the North, lost the tradition of reasoning in terms of means and ends; the few leading scientists have not become "purely scientific" to the same extent as in the North.[a] The significance for human happiness of the problems under study is always a present thought in the South, and statesmanship enters more naturally into the writings of its distinguished social scientists.

As suggested previously, Southern liberalism has aristocratic traditions. As a movement it is as yet almost entirely within the upper classes. *Its main weakness lies in its lack of mass support.* If it wants to see its ideals progressively realized, it simply must get its message out from the conference rooms and college lecture halls to the people on the farms and in the shops. Under the pressure of the accumulating structural changes, the "Solid South" might sometime, and perhaps soon, be broken and a two-party system develop. Southern liberalism will then face a political task for which it must be prepared. The leaders for a truly progressive political movement in the South are there; the staff work for the battle is largely done. If Southern liberalism can recruit an army to lead, it will itself, as an ideological force, become one of the major factors of change in the South and in the nation.

[a] See Appendix 2, Section 2.

CHAPTER 22

POLITICAL PRACTICES TODAY

1. THE SOUTHERN POLITICAL SCENE

The future might belong to liberalism, but the South of today is mainly ruled by its conservatives. Though the South, as part of the United States, has, in the main, the same political forms as the North, the activity which goes on within these forms is strikingly different. The difference not only makes internal politics in the South distinctive, but it influences the activities of the federal government. Although there are local and occasional variations which will be considered presently, the South exhibits the following major political divergences from the rest of the nation:[a]

1. For all practical purposes, the South[b] has only one political party. In the 1940 election, for example, 76 per cent of all votes were cast for the Democratic candidate for President. In the extreme cases of Mississippi and South Carolina, 98 per cent of the votes went to the Democratic candidate.[1] This causes the primary to be far more important than the general election. In fact, the general election—most important in the North and West—is usually a formal ritual to satisfy the demand of the federal Constitution. While there is often a real contest in the primaries, on the whole the struggle is one between personalities rather than issues. Although the Democratic party holds unchallenged power over most of the South, this party is not a highly organized political unity. Politics is decentralized.[2]

---

[a] The data on Southern politics presented in this chapter are for the most part taken from Ralph Bunche's seven-volume study, "The Political Status of the Negro," unpublished manuscript prepared for this study (1940). Bunche's investigations, carried out with the help of several field-workers, are particularly rich in material on the South. A significant proportion of the counties in all Southern states was actually visited, and local correspondents from a few areas were used. The present author also made three trips throughout the South and gave special attention to the political scene.

[b] In this chapter we are including in the South only the Upper and Lower South (Alabama, Arkansas, Georgia, Florida, Louisiana, Mississippi, Oklahoma, South Carolina, Texas, North Carolina, Tennessee and Virginia). The Border states (Delaware, Kentucky, Maryland, Missouri, and West Virginia) have two-party systems (Oklahoma does also, but we shall consider it as in the South because it disfranchises Negroes). The people living in the District of Columbia have no vote.

2. A much smaller proportion of the population participates in the elections in the South than in the North. In 1940, only 28 per cent of the adult population voted in 12 Southern states, as compared to 53 per cent in the North and West. In the extreme case of South Carolina, only 10 per cent voted.[3] Most of this voting is carried on with a corruption and disrespect for law that is found in only a few areas of the North and West.[4]

3. For all practical purposes, Negroes are disfranchised in the South. Out of a total Negro adult population of 3,651,256 in the 8 Deep Southern states (excluding Oklahoma) of Alabama, Georgia, Mississippi, Louisiana, Florida, Texas, South Carolina, and Arkansas, Bunche estimates that only 80,000 to 90,000 Negroes voted in the general election of 1940.[a] Practically none voted in the primary.

These three major political facts about the South are really part of one single problem, and—as we shall find—this problem is the Negro problem.[b] Because a Republican administration was at the helm in Washington during the Civil War and Reconstruction, the white South affiliated itself with the Democratic party. It has remained Democratic and has kept the Democratic party in the South a white man's party to prevent Negroes from having any voice in government. A white Republican is generally considered a "nigger lover" but at the same time he is allowed to vote in the Democratic "white primary" in many sections of the South. Every attempt to build up a two-party system is still regarded as a threat of "black domination." As a result, the political issues in the South cannot be fought at the general elections (and not often in the primaries either). No political organization can be built around an issue (except for prohibition). The candidates at a Democratic primary may represent, as we have pointed out,[c] different interests and different points of view, but once the primary has selected the Democratic candidate, usually all opposition to him must cease until he is up for renomination several years later (the "gentleman's agreement"). The necessity of the one-party system as a means of excluding Negroes from suffrage and the danger of "black domination" are kept to the fore of people's attention. In most regions of the South an appeal to white solidar-

---

[a] Except for Louisiana, no record is kept of the color of registered voters. This estimate was made by Ralph Bunche on the basis of extensive interviewing with registrars and Negro and white political leaders throughout the South. Of the 80,000 or 90,000 Negro votes credited to the 8 states, 50,000 are attributed to Texas alone. See Bunche, *op. cit.*, Vol. 4, pp. 771 and 897. For more complete figures, see Section 3 of this chapter. Paul Lewinson (*Race, Class and Party* [1932], pp. 218-220) has some estimates of Negro voting for scattered places in the South around 1930. Lewinson's estimates agree fairly well with Bunche's more recent and more complete estimates.

[b] It is not meant that all these backward conditions are directly traceable to the Negro problem: many are caused by other consequences of the Civil War and by the South's economic structure. But all these things are part of an interconnected whole, of which the Negro problem is certainly a basic element.

[c] See Chapter 20, Section 1.

ity is a great campaign asset for a candidate; in some regions in the Deep South "nigger baiting" still gets votes. All over the South it is dangerous for a candidate to be accused of friendliness to the Negro. As we have observed earlier, political campaigning and election have in the South ceremonial and symbolic significance, and oratorical ability is a first necessity for a Southern politician.

In keeping Negroes from the polls by such devices as the poll tax, white men have been disfranchised. In preventing a two-party system from arising—which might let in the Negro vote—white men have been kept politically apathetic. White Southerners stay away from the polls for the most part.[5] Another large proportion comes to the polls solely because they are given a dollar or two apiece for their vote by the local political machine. As participation in elections is kept low, relatively little money can often control elections in the South. And investigations show that corruption and illegal practices at the polls are the rule—not the exception.[6] The election machinery is in most parts of the region far behind that in the North and in the other democratic countries of the world. For example, the secret, printed, uniform ballot (the so-called "Australian ballot") is not used over large areas of the South, and election officials and hangers-on at the polls know how everyone votes.[7]

At the same time there is a myth in the South that politics is clean, that it became clean when the new state constitutions—inaugurated between 1890 and 1910—completed the process of disfranchising the Negro. Many a story is passed around describing the terrible times before 1890 when Negroes were fed liquor and herded to the polls, first by the Republicans and later by the Democrats and Populists when they split and appealed to the Negro vote.

As a prerequisite for understanding the Negro's role in Southern politics, it is necessary to consider two further aspects of the political scene: the influence of the South in national politics and the position there of the Republican party.

The difference between politics in the South and in the rest of the nation is so great that it visibly affects the personality of Southern members of Congress: they act and think differently in Washington from what they do in their home states. So do Northerners, of course; but the shift undergone by the Southerners is much more drastic. The typical Southern members of Congress are, however, basically so far away from national norms that, in spite of all accommodations, they remain a distinctive force in Washington. This fact becomes all the more important as, for a variety of reasons, they have a disproportionate influence in national politics.

Seats in the House of Representatives are apportioned according to population, and the nine million Negroes in the South give the South a good share of its seats, although so few Negroes are permitted to vote.[a] The large amount of nonvoting among Southern whites similarly makes each vote count more. The small electorate, the one-party system, well-organized local machines, as well as other factors already referred to, create a near permanency of tenure for the average Southern member of Congress which is seldom paralleled in the North. With seniority as a basis for holding important committee posts in Congress, and with acquaintance as an almost necessary means for participating effectively in congressional activities, the Southerner's permanency of tenure gives him a decided advantage in Washington. This is especially true when—as now—the Democratic party is in power: it controls the most important positions in Congress, and it relies heavily on its disproportionate representation from the South.

There are two important limitations, though, to the South's influence on the Democratic party and thereby on the nation. First, it can practically never hope to control the Presidency, since the Democratic candidate for President is almost sure of the South but must be especially attractive to the North.[b] Second, the Democratic party is solicitous of the Northern Negro and has been successfully weaning his vote away from the Republican party.[c]

To the national Republican party, the South has for a long time been a place from which practically no support could be expected, and Southern Republicans were for the most part persons whose votes for nomination had to be bought up at the national conventions.[8] To the Southern Republicans, the national Republican party has been a source of federal patronage. To Negro Republicans it has also been a traditional but failing hope. A major exception to total weakness of the Republican party in the South, of course, was the 1928 presidential election when Texas, Florida, North Carolina, and Virginia bolted the Democratic candidate, Smith, because he was a Catholic and anti-Prohibitionist. Several Republican areas may be found in

[a] In one sense, the South was helped politically by the abolition of slavery and the ratification of the Fourteenth Amendment. Before then, the presence of a Negro gave the South only three-fifths of a vote in terms of representation in Congress. After then, the presence of a Negro—who, in most cases, was still not allowed to vote—gave the South a full vote.

[b] The abolition of the two-thirds rule for nominating candidates for President and Vice-President by the 1936 Democratic Convention removed even the South's veto power on the choice of candidate.

The South's inability to capture the Presidency, coupled with the former weakness of the national Democratic party, has given rise to the myth that the South has little influence in national politics. As the national Democratic party has taken on new importance in recent years, the error in this myth is being seen.

[c] See Section 4 of this chapter.

the Border states of Kentucky, Missouri, Maryland, Delaware, and West Virginia, and also in Tennessee and Oklahoma. The Deep South, too, has its few Republicans: cities always harbor nonconformists, and even a rural area—such as Winston County, Alabama—may be overwhelmingly Republican. In recent years, the small proportion of migrants from the North has occasionally brought its Republican affiliation along and a few native businessmen have considered that their sentiments were with the national Republican party. But these are all exceptions: in most places and at most times in the South, white persons consider it a disgrace to vote Republican. White Republicans have traditionally been labeled "scalawags" and "nigger lovers"—epithets which express the most extreme form of disfavor and which reveal the heart of the political situation in the South.

When the federal government withdrew the army of occupation in the 1870's, and the Klan was left free to terrorize Negro and white Republicans at the polls, the Republican party in the South was broken. With a few Negro and poor white votes—and sometimes in coalition with the Populists—the Republican party retained some representation throughout the South until the new state constitutions of 1890-1910 disfranchised Negroes even more completely. By 1920, in recognition of its lack of significance in the South, the Republican party practically abandoned primaries and often did not even put up candidates in the general election. In 1940, the last remaining strength of Southern Republicans was removed: at future national conventions congressional districts with fewer than 1,000 Republican votes in the previous election will be denied delegates. It is estimated that this will affect 75 congressional districts in the South.[9]

At the same time that the Republican party was declining in the South, the whites within it were splitting off from the Negroes to form what has been commonly called "the lily-white movement." The term seems to date back to 1888 when the Negro Republican leader, N. W. Cuney, applied it to white Republicans who tried to drive Negroes out of the state convention of Texas by fomenting riots.[10] The movement was given impetus by Presidents Taft and Hoover.[11] The aim of the lily-white leaders and of these Republican Presidents was to build up a Republican party in the South by dissociating the party from Negroes, and from the epithets "nigger lover" and "scalawag." They sought to do this by purging the party of Negro influence and a Negro share in the spoils of victory and by attracting the new South's businessmen.

In one sense, the movement has been successful in all but a few Border states: There is now but one "regular" Negro national Republican committeeman—Perry Howard of Mississippi, who resides in Washington, D.C. In recent elections it is probable that a majority of the few Negroes who voted in Southern states voted Democratic, although there is no proof of this.[a] Because there has been no Republican President since Hoover, it cannot be determined whether a national Republican victory would give Southern Negroes a share of the spoils. It should be observed that the lily-white movement is not completely anti-Negro: lily-white leaders want Negro votes but do not want to recognize Negro influence or claims. In some states, as in Louisiana, Negro Republican registrants are needed in order to continue the party's legal recognition and keep its place on the ballot. The rule adopted at the 1940 Convention requiring a congressional district to have 1,000 votes to secure representation may also lead to a courting of Negro Republican votes in the South.

In another sense, the lily-white movement has been a failure: it has led to no mass defection of whites from the Democratic party.[b] The movement is up against the potent myth that, if the whites split, the Negroes will hold the "balance of power" and dominate Southern politics. With the declining proportion of Negroes in the South, and with the recent split in the Negro vote, this myth has even less foundation than formerly. It was a matter of honor for Southern Negroes to be Republican before 1930.[12] Many Negroes in the South feel that the old rump Republican party never did any good for the Negroes but merely gave jobs to a few of their political leaders. They felt hurt by the Republican party's defection when it went lily-white. It cannot, of course, be proven, but it seems likely that there has been a landslide away from the Republican party in the South as well as in the North.[13] Still, many Negroes are shrewd enough to calculate that if the lily-white movement should be successful, there could develop a two-party system in the South, which would give the Negro a chance to become a voter again.

2. SOUTHERN TECHNIQUES FOR DISFRANCHISING THE NEGROES

In discussing techniques for restricting the franchise, the usual procedure has been to list the relevant laws and to describe their administration. While there is nothing incorrect about this procedure, it tends to give a disjointed picture of the situation. Actually, each voting qualification has been made or is enforced according to the basic principles underlying people's conceptions as to who should be allowed to vote. Three principles seem to govern the extension of the franchise to Negroes in the South. In the first place, there is the Constitution of the United States which stipulates:

The right of citizens of the United States to vote shall not be denied or abridged by the United States or by any State on account of race, color, or previous condition of servitude.

[a] It is not only the lily-white movement, of course, which has brought the Negro to the Democratic party. More important were the New Deal reforms and local conditions. (See Section 4 of this chapter.)

[b] Except in the unusual 1928 election.

In perfect opposition to this is the Southern caste principle that no Negro should be allowed to vote. The history of legal voting qualifications in the South since Restoration is the history of the attempt to find some formula which will reconcile these two opposing principles. A third principle may be discerned: this holds that Negroes may be allowed to vote according to the discretion or need of those whites who exercise influence over the conduct of the election. This third principle is the cause of the variation in Negro voting in different parts of the South. Some Negroes may be permitted to vote because they are "good" (a reward for obedience to the caste rules), because an influential white group needs their votes, because so few Negroes vote that it is not worth the effort to hamper them beyond a certain point (lack of "clear and present danger" to the caste principle), or because a few Negro votes are handy to refute the accusation of unconstitutionality.[a]

State laws setting the qualifications for voting have usually been the result of an attempt to get the caste principle around the Constitution. Clearly, the Constitution prohibited any law which explicitly restricted the vote to whites, since this would involve a reference to "race or color." The next best thing was to determine some attribute which was had by whites, but not by Negroes—other than race or color. Perhaps the safest and most ingenious of these discoveries was that of ancestry: the so-called *"grandfather clauses"* restricted registration for voting[14] to those persons who had voted prior to 1861 and to their descendants, or to persons who had served in the federal or Confederate armies or state militias and to their descendants. The United States Supreme Court, however, found these clauses unconstitutional under the Fifteenth Amendment.[15]

Certainly the most efficient device in use today to keep Negroes from voting where the vote would count most in the South is the *"white primary."* The Democratic party prohibited Negroes from participating in its primary[b] by means of state-wide rule (in 1940) in nine Southern states: Mississippi, Alabama, Georgia, Florida, South Carolina, Louisiana, Arkansas, Virginia and Texas. Only in central Texas and some counties of Virginia was the rule relaxed to any significant degree. In North Carolina and Tennessee, the determination of who may vote in the primary is left to the Democratic party committees of the separate counties: Negroes are permitted in the primaries in several counties in these states. Kentucky no longer has even county organizations restricting the primaries.[16]

[a] There are also a few small all-Negro communities in the South—such as Mound Bayou, Mississippi—where Negroes vote unhampered in the local elections. But their votes are not always accepted in county, state and federal elections.

[b] This inability to participate in the primary also involved an exclusion from other party activities, such as conventions, caucuses of voters, mass meetings, party offices and candidacies.

The legal fight with reference to the white primary did not begin in the federal courts until 1927. At that time the law passed by the State Legislature of Texas in 1923 was declared unconstitutional.[17] The Supreme Court held that a state government could not legally declare a white primary. Another decision in 1932[18] simply declared that a state government could not vest the right to restrict the suffrage in the party's State Executive Committee, and so nothing significant was really decided: the restriction was simply declared by the party's State Convention instead of by the Executive Committee. A 1935 decision by the Supreme Court[19] was far more significant—it apparently upheld the white primary by declaring that the primary is an affair of the party alone, and, as a voluntary institution, a political party could restrict its adherents as it pleased. This decision may be limited to the Texas situation where an attempt has been made to divorce the Party from the State. In other states—such as Virginia, Florida, and Louisiana—the expenses of the primary are paid by the state, and the state has formally declared the public character of the primary. In these states, the white primary would seem to be clearly unconstitutional.

The legal issue today hinges around the question as to whether the primary is a public affair: advocates of a white primary claim that the party is a voluntary association and as such it can restrict its participants. Those opposed to the party restrictions against Negroes in the primary claim that the general election is profoundly changed by the existence of the primary, which is the most important election in the South, and that, therefore, voting in the primaries should be subject to the Constitution. One fact which disturbs the legal case of those who would restrict the Negro from voting in the primaries is that in many areas white *Republicans* are permitted to vote in the Democratic primaries, but Negro *Democrats* are not.[a] In a recent decision by the Supreme Court—in a case concerning fraudulent practices and not Negro participation—the position was taken that "the primary in Louisiana is an integral part of the procedure for the popular choice of Congressmen" and that, therefore, no person qualified to vote in the general election can be disqualified in the primary.[20] The legality of the white primary is, therefore, still not settled,[21] and it is under vigorous attack.

Probably the most notorious—although certainly not the most efficient—device to keep the Negro from voting in the South is the *poll tax*. The poll tax is one of the oldest forms of direct taxation, but it was usually compulsory and, therefore, had little effect in restricting the vote. In modern times the compulsory poll tax is being generally abandoned as it is a regressive tax.[22] Eight Southern states have a voluntary poll tax and

---

[a] In the last two decades, few areas in the South have had Republican primaries—partly because the law does not provide for a primary where there are few eligible voters and partly because Southern Republicans are not interested in having a primary.

have it for the express purpose of restricting the vote.[a] They have different kinds of poll taxes, but in general the requirement is the voluntary payment of a small sum (one to three dollars) before registration for voting is permitted; it is thus not actually a "tax" in the strict meaning of the term but a "fee" or "dues" paid for voting.[23]

In many states the poll tax is cumulative, and the payment of more than one year's poll tax is required for the right to vote (in some states back to the time the individual became 21 years of age). Again it may be noted that the states of the Deep South are more restrictive than the states of the Upper South or the Border states.[24] North Carolina, Louisiana and Florida have repealed their poll tax requirements. The latter two states form the only exception to the rule that the more "Southern" the state, the more restrictive its poll tax requirement. While the poll tax is low, except where and when it is applied cumulatively, it means quite a bit to those Negroes and whites who work for a dollar or two a day. It means more for Negroes because they are poorer. But its greatest restrictiveness against Negroes probably results from discrimination in its application: election officials practically always demand to see the poll tax receipts of Negroes and seldom those of whites. Too, it is common in many areas for politicians to pay the poll tax of whites in return for an understanding that those receiving the benefit will vote in accordance with the wishes of the benefactor. But in only a handful of Southern cities is the Negro vote so bought.[25]

Because the poll tax operates to disfranchise the poorer whites as well as Negroes and to bolster political machines, there is a growing movement in the South to abolish it.[26] Some liberals even claim that the primary purpose of the tax was to disfranchise poor whites, since Negroes can be kept from the polls in so many other ways. The case of Louisiana is pointed out: the poll tax was repealed there in 1934, and still only some 2,000 Negroes registered in 1936.[27] The chief popular argument for the poll tax is still, however, that it keeps Negroes from the polls. This argument is buttressed by the case of Miami, where Negroes went to the polls in large numbers in 1939 following the repeal of the poll tax in 1937. Some proponents of the poll tax admit that one of its aims is to disfranchise poor whites, but this—they hold—keeps the primary "manageable" so that the Democratic party does not split and thus open the way for Negroes to vote and get the balance of power.[b] This last argument points to a perhaps

---

[a] While this book is in press, Tennessee has abolished its poll tax. There are now only 7 states with the poll tax.

[b] There have been a few arguments for the poll tax which have no special reference to Negroes. Some of the aristocratic proponents of the tax frankly believe that only those who pay taxes should have the vote. It was also argued that the poll tax is a source of revenue, but it is usually realized that the income from this tax is very small, and that it is not necessary to prohibit voting in order to collect taxes.

fundamental significance of the poll tax: if poor whites are encouraged to vote by the removal of the poll tax, they will not be any friendlier to Negroes, but they may stir up issues and put through legislation that will have the ultimate effect of helping all poor people, including Negroes.

There is no way of measuring to what extent nonvoting in the South is caused by the poll tax. But there is hardly any doubt that it does have such an effect as even a small sum means much to poor people. Many, of course, abstain from paying the poll tax and from voting because of political apathy, which is widespread in the South. But there is a circular causal relationship here of a cumulative and potentially dynamic character. When poor people abstain from voting because of the poll tax or political apathy, this tends to keep issues which interest poor people out of politics. Thereby political apathy and nonpayment of poll tax is enhanced. But if the masses were encouraged to vote by the abolition of the poll tax and other changes, the vicious circle could be set working the other way. The poll tax would then be viewed as one strategic factor in an interrelated causal system, tied up to political apathy and the one-party system.

The poll tax disfranchises and is subject to political manipulation not only because it costs the voter a dollar or two, but because it must be paid by a certain date (which is often long before anyone knows who the candidates will be),[a] because officials often mis-date the receipts to violate the date provision and pay the tax themselves and because employers force their employees to pay the tax.[28] The significance of the poll tax in keeping even whites from voting is suggested by the fact that the states without the tax have a larger proportion of their adult citizens voting than comparable states with the tax.

In 1940, Oklahoma, for example, had 60 per cent of its adult citizenry voting compared to 18 per cent in Arkansas; North Carolina had 43 per cent compared to 22 per cent in Virginia; and Louisiana, which has been without the poll tax only since 1934, had 27 per cent compared to 14 per cent in Mississippi.[29]

Similar to the poll tax, in that they restrict Negroes because they are poor, are *property, educational,* and *"character" requirements* for voting. These, too, are seldom applied to whites but almost always to Negroes, and the requirements are more rigid in the states of the Deep South than in the Border states. Also, like the poll tax, these requirements for voting have been reduced somewhat in recent years, especially in the Upper South. Property requirements for voting are found in Alabama, Georgia, and South Carolina and are applicable only if the prospective voter cannot meet the educational requirements. As such they would seem to serve as a

[a] "Payment of the tax must be made from six to ten months in advance of the election in Georgia, Mississippi, Texas, and Virginia." (Virginius Dabney, *Below the Potomac* [1942] p. 120.)

loophole to white persons who could not read and write. They require the ownership of 40 acres of land or other property worth $300 to $500.

Educational requirements for voting are found in Mississippi, Alabama, Louisiana, Georgia, South Carolina, North Carolina and Virginia. In most states they consist of demonstration of ability to read and write a section of the federal or state constitution to the "satisfaction" of the registrar; in Virginia they consist of writing an application for registration. Relatively seldom is a white man "insulted" by being given the test; yet many cases have been recorded[30] where a Negro "failed" the test when he mispronounced a single word. Even professors at Tuskegee and other Negro universities have been disfranchised by failing to pass these tests. In a few Deep Southern states, not only must a section of the Constitution be read and written, but it must also be interpreted to the "satisfaction" of the registrar. Needless to say, the educational attainments of election registrars are seldom such that they can be fair judges of the meaning of the state and federal constitutions. This "interpretation" requirement is now found only in Mississippi and Louisiana.

The legal "character" requirement for voting registration also has declined in recent years so that it is now found only in Louisiana and Georgia. Actually it is applied illegally to Negroes in many other places in the South: Negroes must be vouched for by whites or they must be known to the registrars in their communities as "good niggers." In some cases, a leading "good nigger" may serve as character witness for other Negroes. In Georgia the character requirement is used not only to disfranchise Negroes but also to permit the registration of whites who cannot meet the property or educational requirements, since it is an alternative to these other requirements.[31]

In addition to these better known legal requirements for voting, there are several others which are, or have been, employed in one or more Southern states to disfranchise Negroes. A tricky registration blank must be filled out: whites will be given assistance, and their errors adjusted or overlooked; Negroes will not be allowed even the most trivial incompleteness or error, and are given no assistance. Certain of the previously discussed requirements (poll tax payment, education, or property) are waived for the war veterans, or for the aged in certain states: in practice whites are informed of such privileges but Negroes who qualify are not expected to ask for them. Some Southern states withhold the vote from anyone convicted of a crime: this is overlooked for most of the whites but applied as rigorously as can be to the Negro.[32]

More important than the legal requirements in disfranchising Negroes in the South are *extra-legal practices*. Laws passed by state or local governments must not conflict with the constitutional provision that there be no discrimination because of race, color or creed. Activities carried on outside the law are seldom subjected to this constitutional test. Laws can disfranchise Negroes only by making a criterion for voting some characteristic which is found more frequently in the Negro population than in the white and by creating opportunities for local administrative discretion. Extralegal activities can disfranchise Negroes to any degree desired.[a]

Violence, terror, and intimidation have been, and still are, effectively used to disfranchise Negroes in the South. Physical coercion is not so often practiced against the Negro, but the mere fact that it can be used with impunity and that it is devastating in its consequences creates a psychic coercion that exists nearly everywhere in the South. A Negro can seldom claim the protection of the police and the courts if a white man knocks him down, or if a mob burns his house or inflicts bodily injuries on him or on members of his family. If he defends himself against a minor violence, he may expect a major violence. If he once "gets in wrong" he may expect the loss of his job or other economic injury, and constant insult and loss of whatever legal rights he may have had.[33] In such circumstances it is no wonder that the great majority of Negroes in the South make no attempt to vote and—if they make attempts which are rebuffed—seldom demand their full rights under the federal Constitution.

Usually a Negro never goes so far as to attempt to cast his vote. In the majority of Southern localities Negroes are prevented from registering, or only a few Negroes are allowed to register. This means that the rebuffs occur in the administration of the legal requirements for registration.[34]

Educational "tests" to disfranchise Negroes are widely used in a bluntly illegal way. One intelligent Negro woman in North Carolina was denied registration when she mispronounced the words "contingency" and "constitutionality" in reading the state constitution.[35] Other rebuffs come as a still more unmistakable extension of the law. A Negro school teacher in the same state was denied registration after the following incident:

> . . . the registrar asked me to read a section of the Constitution, which I did, and then asked me to define terms which I knew was not part of the North Carolina law. I said to him, "That is not a part of the law, to define terms." He said, "You must satisfy me, and don't argue with me."[36]

Many cases are reported where Negroes do not get even this far: "What do you want here, nigger?" has been enough to send them away from the registration or polling place.[37] Other favorite devices are to evade the prospective Negro registrant or voter by ignoring him, by telling him that registration cards have "run out," or that all members of the registration board are not present, that he should go somewhere else, or that he will be notified when he can register, by "losing" his registration card or by "forgetting" to put his name on the list of voters.[38]

[a] For a general discussion of extra-legal devices to coerce Negroes, see Part VI.

The illegal activities of persons not connected with the administration of the election also take many forms. The hangers-on at the polling places insult and stare at Negroes, especially Negro women. Negroes have received threats, such as, "If you vote, you will never return home alive," and "You have always been looked on as a good character. But from now on you shall be looked on as a dangerous character."[39] White newspapers have openly warned Negroes not to vote and intimated violence if they did vote. In the 1939 election in Miami, the Ku Klux Klan rode the streets in full regalia and passed out handbills threatening Negroes if they voted. In the same year, riots and other forms of violence occurred because of Negroes voting in Greenville and Spartanburg, South Carolina.[40] Keeping in mind this review of the techniques for keeping Negroes from voting in the South, we may turn to the question of how many Negroes do vote in spite of this pressure.

3. THE NEGRO VOTE IN THE SOUTH

As has been observed, the general pattern in the South since the "new" constitutions of 1890-1910 has been to deny the vote to Negroes. Still a small proportion of Negroes do vote, and the local variations in the number of their votes are significant.[41] Since no statistics are compiled which separate the Negro votes from the white votes, there is no exact record of these variations. Further, it is practically impossible to compile exact statistics on *registration* of Negroes, as many election officials do not make accurate designations of voters according to color in the registration books. Knowledge of local variations must come, therefore, from a mass of newspaper articles, interviews, registration reports and local studies.[a]

As we have noticed, the most important voting in the South is in the Democratic primaries, and these are restricted to whites. Here and there a community will let one or two "good" Negroes vote in the primary. In some of the cities, especially where political machines can control the Negro vote—such as in San Antonio and Memphis—Negroes vote in the primaries in restricted numbers. With these negligible exceptions, no Negroes are permitted to vote, under a state-wide party rule,[b] in Alabama, Arkansas, Florida, Georgia, Louisiana, Mississippi and South Carolina. Texas and Virginia also have state-wide rules prohibiting Negroes from voting in the primary, but, nevertheless, Negroes are permitted to vote in a few counties. North Carolina and Tennessee leave the primary rule to county party organizations, and several of these do not prohibit

---

[a] Such a collection was made by Ralph J. Bunche and his assistants for this study (*op. cit.*, Vol. 4, Chapter 7; Vol. 5, Chapters 9, 10 and 11; Vol. 8, Appendix 2.) A few of Bunche's most general findings will be summarized here.

[b] See Section 2 of this chapter for a description of the type of rules restricting Negro voting in primaries.

Negroes. Kentucky and the other Border states do not have a white primary at all, but even in such cases it should not be forgotten that Negro voting may be restricted by means other than a formal rule. From the above description of Negro voting in the primary, the greater liberality of the states nearest the North is patent.

While the Democratic primary is the most important election in the South, there are other elections. First, there is the general election, conducted under the Constitution and laws of the United States and administered by the state governments. With the assumed success of the Democratic candidate in most areas, this is not important, except perhaps to keep the Southerner aware that he is politically a member of the United States as well as of the Democratic party. Very rarely, and usually as a matter of "accident," the general election takes on political significance. The defeated Democratic candidate in the primaries may feel that he was defeated only because of corruption, or that he could win the general election with the aid of Republicans and Negroes. He may then break his "gentleman's agreement" and run in the general election as an independent candidate.[42] The general election then takes on the partisan character of a general election in the North. Occasionally, too, death or resignation may create a political vacancy which is fought over in the general election, without a primary.

Besides the primary and the general election, there are two types of so-called "nonpartisan" elections. Both of these are, in large measure, restricted to cities. They are nonpartisan only in the sense that no party label can be put on the ballot, but there may be heated division over the candidates or issues in the election. One type of nonpartisan election occurs in those cities which operate under a city manager or commission form of government. According to Lewinson,[43] there were 115 cities south of the Border states operating under a city manager charter in 1930 in addition to 32 cities of over 30,000 population (1927) operating under the commission plan. Several of these cities retained the primary, but most of them hold only a nonpartisan general election to choose the commissioners.[44] The second type of nonpartisan election is that involving initiative and referendum. Referenda concerning bond issues, tax rates, amendments, city extensions, and so on, are not at all uncommon in Southern cities. For some of these, a certain proportion of registered persons must vote or the referendum does not pass. In such cases, whites who favor the issue may seek to get out the Negro vote.

In general and nonpartisan elections, Negroes vote to a significantly greater extent than in primary elections, since there is no uniform rule barring them. All the other devices outside of the formal no-Negro rule may be applied to keep them from voting, however, and in the 11 states south of the Border states there are probably less than 250,000 Negroes who have voted in the last five or six years.[45] There are the usual variations within the South: there are more Negroes voting in cities than in rural areas. This is not only because there is slightly greater liberality toward Negroes in the cities, but also because the nonpartisan election is a phenomenon almost restricted to cities. There are also more votes permitted to Negroes as we approach the Northern states. The recent increases in Negro voting are registered mainly in the Border states, in the Upper South and in Oklahoma.[a]

There is one other type of election that is important to the Negro in the South. The Agricultural Adjustment Act requires that cotton owner-operators, tenants, and sharecroppers vote to indicate whether they want the application of the crop restriction program. Negroes have participated in unrestricted numbers in these annual elections (since 1938) and have voted in perhaps even greater proportion than whites. They vote at the same polling places as whites and at the same time. There is little physical opposition from the whites because the majority favor crop control, and they know that Negroes will vote in favor of it; they are told that if Negroes are prevented from voting, the election will be illegal. They also know that any irregularity would be observed by federal administra-

---

[a] Bunche's specific estimates are as follows: Mississippi probably has fewest Negroes voting—only a few hundred "good" Negro aristocrats and school teachers. Louisiana had 2,007 "colored persons" registered in 1936, and these were practically all in or around Baton Rouge and New Orleans. Only about half these Negroes actually voted. Next in order came Alabama and South Carolina with about 1,500 Negro votes apiece; South Carolina had so few Negroes voting although there was a spontaneous (that is, not solicited by a white machine) movement to get out the Negro vote in Greenville in 1939. There were 7,000 or 8,000 Negroes voting in recent years in Arkansas, and as many as 10,000 apiece in Georgia (mainly in Atlanta) and Florida (including Miami, where there was an upsurge of Negroes in 1939 against the Klan). Virginia has recently permitted more Negroes to vote so that now there may be as many as 20,000 Negro votes in that state. Texas, North Carolina, Tennessee, and Oklahoma have a Negro vote of about 50,000 apiece. San Antonio is an important center of Negro voting in Texas: Bellinger (formerly the father and now the son) marshals the Negro vote there for the machine. City machines in Raleigh and Durham are mainly responsible for the Negro votes in North Carolina. In Memphis, Tennessee, too, a large number of Negroes are brought out to vote for "Boss" Crump and other members of his machine. Other Negro votes are solicited in Nashville and Chattanooga, partly to challenge the influence of Crump in Tennessee state politics. East Tennessee has some traditionally Republican counties in which a sparse Negro population votes. Kentucky (with 80,000 to 100,000 Negro votes) and Missouri (with about 100,000 to 130,000 Negro votes) have a smaller Negro population than most of the states mentioned thus far; their large Negro vote results from an almost unhampered Negro vote in the cities. Some of the Negro voting in the South comes from towns which are populated and governed almost completely by Negroes. There are probably less than a hundred towns and villages of this sort, and they are small. While Negro voting is unrestricted for local office in these towns, county and state officials usually see to it that they have no voice in county, state or federal elections.

tors and vigorously prosecuted in federal courts.[46] Although the unrestricted voting by Negroes in the A.A.A. referenda does not give them any political power, it, nevertheless, may be of great significance. It accustoms whites to the presence of Negroes at polling places and perhaps makes them think beyond the myth of black domination and consider the real issues involved in Negro voting. It provides the South with an example of elections based on significant issues and with less corruption than usual. It also gives the Negro a chance to vote and perhaps to discover the nature of the political process.

Southerners will often explain that Negroes can vote in the South but that they just do not care to.[47] This is, of course, a rationalization justifying white policy. It is hard to conceive that any Southern politician, well acquainted with the facts, believes it. A few considerations, most of which have already been made, may clarify the situation. A Negro in the South expecting to vote knows that he is up to something extraordinary. In order to register and to appear at the polls, he will have to leave the protective anonymity of being just another Negro. He will become a specific Negro who is "out of his place," trying to attack the caste barriers.[48] He knows further that the primary—which is the main election in the South—is closed to Negroes by formal and express rule in the major part of the South. There is a whole barrage of *formal* devices to keep him from voting in other elections—ranging all the way from the poll tax, which in some states is cumulative from the time the prospective voter is 21 years of age, and a receipt for which must be produced at every election, to the explanation of a statement in the state constitution to the "satisfaction" of the registrar. There is another barrage of *informal* devices to keep Negroes from voting—ranging all the way from the insults and threats presented to the prospective Negro voter as he enters the polling place to the violence administered to his person and property by the Klan. If he should succeed in voting it is likely to be in an election which has been decided long before and, formerly, for a lily-white Republican candidate who openly snubs him.

Another most potent force in keeping the Negro from the polls is his own fear of what *might* happen to him, his job, his family, or his property, in the present or in the future, if he should vote. The Southern Negro often does not know how far he can go, and in such a situation he may take the path of discretion. Some Negroes invoke the law to gain the vote; others stop when it is simply denied them and thereby lose their vote. It is no test of the franchise that some Negroes are permitted to vote in a given community, for what is permitted to a few would never be permitted to the many. The much greater participation of Negroes in the elections in the Northern and Border states and in some cities in the South shows that the Negro votes to the extent that the repressions are relaxed.

In one sense it is true that the Negro is politically apathetic. Like many a white man, he is uneducated and ignorant of the significance of the vote. Because, on the average, the Southern Negro is somewhat less urban, less educated, and poorer than the average Southern white man, and because these traits are universally a cause of low average voting participation, the Negro should be expected to vote less than the white man in the South if there were no special barriers to Negro voting.[49] Even this is not certain, however, if the experience of the A.A.A. referenda be taken as a test, for —if anything—Negroes participate more than whites in these, though perhaps because they are more herded to the polls by the plantation owners. Since Reconstruction days the vote is to many Negroes—as to the whites— a symbol of civic equality.

But it should not be denied that a large proportion of poor Southern Negroes feel that "politics is white folks' business." This attitude is even spread by some "accommodating" Southern Negro leaders. Some of the political apathy is peculiar to the Negroes because the means of disfranchising them have been extraordinary: a tradition of nonvoting is built up that is difficult to break down even in the free elections in the North. Too, there is a psychopathological form of apathy found in some Negroes: they have been so frightened by some experiences when attempting to vote that they swear never to try again.

Another charge levied against the political activity of the Negro is that he is frequently the mere pawn of the political machine. This is true, especially in the South, but it must be seen in the light of other facts. In the first place, it is often a political machine that makes it possible for Negroes to vote at all. If no organized white group backed the Negroes, they would not be allowed to vote in most cases. Too, the machine gives them something for their vote: not only do they often get dollars as individual voters, but they get paved streets and schools as a group. The Negro is accorded better treatment by the city administration, police, and courts in those cities where the machine "votes" him than where he is not permitted to vote at all. In the third place, Southern Negroes can vote only in cities, for all practical purposes, and cities are the places where political machines are most potent. Whites of similar economic status and education are perhaps machine-dominated to the same extent in Southern cities, although there are no statistics to prove this.[50] Finally, it should be remembered that there are places—even Southern cities—where Negroes have voted in significant numbers without machine backing and control: Negroes defied the Klan in 1939 to vote in Miami, and an all-Negro political movement developed in the same year in Greenville, South Carolina.

4. THE NEGRO IN NORTHERN POLITICS

The Negro coming from the South to the North was as politically innocent and ignorant as the immigrant from a country like Italy where democratic politics was not well developed and was very different from politics in the Northern United States. It was quite natural, therefore, for Negro politics in the North to take forms similar to Italo-American politics. Ignorance and poverty caused a disproportionate amount of non-voting among Negroes, although not nearly as much as among Italian immigrants who had to become citizens before they could exercise the franchise. Nonvoting was perhaps accentuated among some Negroes by a timidity caused by violence in the South. Other Negroes, perhaps, felt a stronger urge to vote in the North because they had been disfranchised in the South. Like other immigrants, since young adults migrate to a greater extent than any other age group, Negroes formed a larger proportion of the adult population than of the total population. Therefore they had a potential voting strength greater than their total numbers would indicate.[51] Like other immigrants, they continually got into minor legal difficulties and sought the friendly services of petty politicians. Like other immigrants, they often traded their votes for these material favors, although they were perhaps not as wise or successful as some of the other immigrants in getting a *quid pro quo*. Like other ignorant immigrants, they tended to follow the narrow political leadership of those of their own group who sought political plums for themselves. Still they were not unified, partly because of the rivalry between the recent migrants from the South and those longer established in the North. Du Bois gives an apt summary of the voting behavior of Negroes in one Northern city, Philadelphia, in 1896, and this characterization remained largely valid right up to 1930.

> The experiment of Negro suffrage in Philadelphia has developed three classes of Negro voters: a large majority of voters who vote blindly at the dictates of the party and, while not open to direct bribery, accept the indirect emoluments of office or influence in return for party loyalty; a considerable group, centering in the slum districts, which casts a corrupt purchasable vote for the highest bidder; lastly, a very small group of independent voters who seek to use their vote to better present conditions of municipal life.[52]

There were some peculiarities about the political behavior of Negroes in the North that differentiated it from that of the foreign-born whites as well as from that of the native whites. In the first place, it was strongly attached to the Republican party; gratitude to the symbol of Lincoln, the example of early leaders like Frederick Douglass and Booker T. Washington, and the continuous spectacle of what the name "Democratic party" meant in the South, all tied the bulk of Northern Negro voters to the

Republican party long after it became apparent that a more flexible Negro vote would bring more advantages.[a] In the last decade, however, the Negro vote has shifted radically under the pull of the New Deal and the push of the lily-white movement. Another trait of the Negro vote was that it was, on the whole, passionately aware of the relation of a candidate or issue to the Negro problem. Unlike other native Americans, Negroes, when they thought politically, thought first in terms of their ethnic group and only secondly in terms of the nation as a whole. Foreign-born citizens have this trait also, but it tends to disappear in the second and third generations. With Negroes it is tending to increase as Negroes become more organized and politically conscious. No Negro leader can expect to remain popular if he supports a white man who is reputed to be anti-Negro. A "friend of the Negro people" need not always have the backing of the local Negro leaders to get the Negro vote.

Although individual Negroes are not restricted from voting in the North, there may be one condition which limits the influence of the Negro's vote once it is cast. We refer to the practice of gerrymandering—that is, of so setting the boundaries of election districts that the vote of a minority group is cut up and overwhelmed by the vote of the majority group.[53] Although a comprehensive study of the gerrymandering of the Negro vote in Northern cities is yet to be made, there is evidence that it exists in at least some cities.[54]

Besides gerrymandering, there is another way in which the Negro vote is kept from having its proper weight in the election of candidates. This is by neglecting to redistrict as population grows or declines at different rates in different districts. The practice is especially important with respect to voting for national congressmen and state legislators, and it has some significance for the election of city aldermen. Negroes will flow into a district and still have only the same representation as a declining rural area with perhaps one-tenth the population. This is, of course, a problem far more general than a Negro one: it is the problem of cities to get their fair share of representation in relation to rural areas, and the problem of densely populated city districts to get their fair share in relation to rotten boroughs. While there is probably no special anti-Negro prejudice in the practice, Negroes are hurt far more by it than most other groups since they

[a] Negroes have not been more attached to the Republican party, however, than the Irish, for example, have been to the Democratic party. The Northern Negro vote was not completely inflexible. In New York, it frequently went Democratic. In Chicago, the friendliness of the Democratic candidate for mayor in 1885—Carter Harrison I—secured him about 50 per cent of the Negro vote, and his son, who ran for mayor in 1899, received about 65 per cent of the Negro vote. (See Claudius O. Johnson, *Carter Henry Harrison I* [1928], p. 196, cited in Elmer W. Henderson, "A Study of the Basic Factors Involved in the Change in Party Alignment of Negroes in Chicago, 1932-1938," unpublished M.A. thesis, University of Chicago [1939], pp. 6-7.)

have been moving to Northern cities at a more rapid rate than have others. While the practice is clearly unconstitutional, and the state legislatures are guilty as they are the only ones empowered to make the adjustments, the courts have been loath to interfere. The Constitution, however, gives the United States Congress power to override the state legislatures.[55] The neglect to redistrict also creates a form of "natural" gerrymandering that hurts the Negroes. When migrants come to a city they usually do not happen to distribute themselves according to the boundaries of certain voting districts. As a result their vote becomes split even though they form a single community. In New York, for example, the Harlem Negro vote is split mainly into two congressional districts and Negroes cannot elect a congressman by themselves in either one. If there were redistricting, and if there were no deliberate attempt to perpetuate this gerrymander, Harlem should probably be in one voting district, since it is a natural community area.

No comprehensive study has yet been made on the extent of nonvoting among Negroes in the North. The general impression is that Negroes— like whites with the same average educational and economic status—are somewhat apathetic. The statistical evidence, however, does not present a consistent picture and suggests that Negro apathy is partly a function of local conditions.[56] Litchfield found that Negroes voted one-third less than whites, both native and foreign-born, in Detroit.[57] In Chicago, however, 77 per cent of the adults of a Negro ward registered as compared to 68 per cent for the entire city (1930).[58] Negro apathy in Detroit seems to be due to the city-wide type of election, the nonpartisan character of the election with a concomitant weak party organization and the lack of organization and leadership among Negroes.[59] Negro activity in Chicago seems to be related to the partisan and close character of the election, the solicitation of the Negro vote by white politicians, the support of Negro racketeers and the strength of the Negro organizations.

The fact that Negroes vote to a greater extent than whites in Chicago is startling. All existing studies—made for a few cities in the United States and for many democratic countries in Europe—show a striking relationship between nonvoting and poverty.[60] The correlation may even be stronger for whites in the United States, since there is no labor party to bring out the labor vote, and the political machines bring out only a relatively small selected vote. Since the bulk of the Negroes are very poor, we should expect them to be much more politically apathetic than the whites. The fact that they vote almost as much, or more, in most Northern cities than whites do, indicates that they are relatively more conscious of the vote. The data do not support—so far as voting is concerned—the common stereotype that Negroes are politically apathetic.

Before 1933, Negroes voted the Republican ticket in overwhelming proportion. While there were Negro Democratic organizations in every city, they made little headway except in New York.[61] In Chicago only 23 per cent of the Negro vote went to the Democratic party in the presidential election of 1932, despite Hoover's lily-white tendencies, and perhaps an even smaller proportion went against Republican Mayor Thompson in 1931.[62] Similarly, only 19.5 per cent of Detroit's Negro vote was Democratic in 1930.[63] This attachment to the Republican party both hurt and helped the Negroes politically. It helped them because the Republicans were in power in most of the Northern cities before 1930, and Negroes gave the Republican party a disproportionate number of their votes. In Chicago, for example, Negroes constituted only 6.9 per cent of the total population in 1930, and 8.7 per cent of the population of voting age, but 11.0 per cent of the Republican voters.[64] The strong attachment to the Republican party hurt them because the party felt sure of the Negro vote and hardly made an attempt to solicit it or favor it. When, after 1933, the Negro vote became more fluid, it was more actively solicited by both parties and was rewarded to a greater extent by the Democratic party, which was in office in most Northern cities.[65]

Many Negroes were dissatisfied with the Republican party by 1932. Like other poor people, they were disgusted with the Hoover administration's methods of meeting the depression. They had also become aware of the snubs given them as Negroes by both national and local Republican party organizations. Of course, some Negroes felt a sentimental attachment to the party of Lincoln that could stand almost any amount of snubbing. Some upper class Negroes, too, were quite satisfied with the conservative performance of the Hoover administration or felt that the "best people" voted Republican. In 1932, Roosevelt was relatively unknown outside of New York, and there was some anxiety about the role that Southern Democrats might play in his administration. The whispering campaign, that Roosevelt was in ill health and that his running mate—the Southerner, Garner—would soon take over the Presidency if they were elected, was perhaps influential in keeping the Negro vote Republican in 1932.

But when the New Deal relieved the economic plight of the Negroes during the depression, and—in the North—treated them almost without discrimination,[a] and appointed Negro advisors for many phases of the government's activities, Negroes began to shift to the Democratic party in large numbers. The movement was accelerated when the local Democratic machines proved more grateful for the Negro's vote than had their Republican predecessors.[66] The estimated proportion of Negroes voting for Roosevelt in Chicago was 23 per cent in 1932, 49 per cent in 1936, and

[a] See Chapter 15.

52 per cent in 1940.[67] In Detroit the estimated proportion voting for Roosevelt was 36.7 per cent in 1932, 63.5 per cent in 1936, and 69.3 per cent in 1940.[68]

Table 1 shows the same startling trends toward the Democratic party for these and other cities, using a slightly less adequate technical procedure.

It is not certain whether the Northern Negro vote will remain Democratic, but it is certain that it has become more flexible and will respond more readily to the policies of the two parties toward the Negro.[69] This will probably bring more political advantages to Negroes, since their vote will take on more strategic significance in the close elections often occurring in the North. It is also a sign that politically Negroes are becoming more like other Americans.

There has been a widespread belief that Northern Negroes became radical in large numbers during the depression. All the available data reveal that this is a fallacy. In Detroit about 3.2 per cent of the Negroes voted for a party other than Democratic or Republican in 1930. This was larger than the third-party vote of native whites, but not of foreign-born groups in that city. In 1932, the Negro percentage for third parties fell to 1.5—equal to that of native whites and lower than that of foreign-born groups. It remained low during the depression and by 1940 was only 0.5 per cent.[70] In Chicago, Gosnell estimated that only 500 Negroes joined the Communist party during the depression, although many more participated in parades and other activities.[71] In Cleveland, Davis estimated that the height of the depression saw only 200 Negroes in the Communist party.[72]

Before 1933, when Negroes were attached to the Republican party, there was little, if any, difference between the lower class and middle class Negroes in party affiliation. It is true that Tammany Hall succeeded in attracting more lower class than middle class Negroes in New York, but New York Negroes had already gone quite a way toward the Democratic party before 1930. Since 1933, Negroes have split just as whites have, though probably not so much: Negroes with lower incomes have gone over to the Democratic party in somewhat greater proportion than Negroes with middle incomes. In Detroit, for example, the 1940 election round about 72 per cent of the lower economic group of Negroes for Roosevelt as compared to about 63 per cent of the middle economic group, whereas in 1930 the corresponding percentages were 19 and 22, respectively.[73] Whether this differential between Negroes of different classes will continue or not is problematical. The Negro middle and upper classes are different from white middle and upper classes in that they are more directly dependent on the lower class and in that they are more interested in social reform.

On the whole, *Negroes have come to be rather like whites in their political behavior in the North*. They vote in about the same proportion

TABLE 1

PER CENT OF MAJOR PARTY VOTE FOR ROOSEVELT, 1932, 1936, 1940, IN EACH WARD HAVING MORE THAN HALF ITS POPULATION NEGRO, SELECTED CITIES.[a]

Ward	Baltimore			Chicago		Columbus		Detroit			Kansas City, Kans.	Kansas City, Mo.	New Haven	Pittsburgh	Wilmington
	5	14	17	2	3	6	7	3	5	7	2	4	19	5	6
1932	46.4	49.2	43.0	25.4	20.7	27.9	23.2	46.0	50.2	53.9	41.5	70.8	38.9	53.3	28.3
1936	64.2	54.6	46.9	47.9	50.1	47.7	46.6	71.4	75.0	79.0	61.3	79.4	61.0	76.6	40.1
1940	72.1	60.7	59.6	51.2	54.2	50.7	57.1	75.3	79.2	80.0	59.6	66.5	58.7	77.1	41.5

[a] The cities selected are all those with over 100,000 population, containing wards having 50 per cent or more of their population Negro, where Negroes were allowed to vote unhampered or almost unhampered, and where ward lines were not changed over the period 1932–1940. The only exception is Philadelphia, which refused to supply information. The data in this table were collected for this study by Shirley Star.

as whites; they are no longer tied to the Republican party; they eschew third parties; they have manifested a class differential in their adherence to the Democratic party. On the other hand, *most Negro voters are more keenly aware of a candidate's attitude toward their group than are most other Americans*—perhaps only because they are one of the few ethnic groups against whom politicians ever discriminate. Even though Negroes are seeking only their rights as citizens and a proportionate share of the political spoils, they find they have to be choosy about parties and candidates to get these.

5. WHAT THE NEGRO GETS OUT OF POLITICS

With the great northward migration, Negroes came to vote in large numbers. In spite of the virtual disfranchisement of Negroes in the South, there are about as many Negroes voting today in the United States as there are whites voting in the seven Southern states of Mississippi, Louisiana, Alabama, South Carolina, Arkansas, Georgia, and Florida—that is, in the entire Deep South except Texas and Oklahoma.[74] Yet Southern whites get incomparably more benefits from politics than do Negroes. Negroes are grossly discriminated against in what they get from politics just as they are in their exercise of the right to vote. A striking measure of this fact is that the seven Deep Southern states have 52 members of the House of Representatives and 14 members of the Senate, whereas the Negroes, with the same number of actual votes, have only 1 member of the House of Representatives and no senators. There are many other ways in which Negroes are deprived of the benefits of politics. Unquestionably the most important thing that Negroes get out of politics where they vote is legal justice—justice in the courts; police protection and protection against the persecution of the police; ability to get administrative jobs through civil service; and a fair share in such public facilities as schools, hospitals, public housing, playgrounds, libraries, sewers and street lights. It is hard to demonstrate that a given number of Negro votes will procure a given amount of legal justice for Negroes, because it can be claimed, and correctly so, that these communities which allow Negroes to vote to a given extent will also usually be willing to give them other legal rights to a comparable extent. Yet case after case can be cited to show where white politicians have given community services, justice in the courts, and "civil service" jobs to Negroes just because they have received a certain number of votes from them. These cases may be cited to indicate the nature of the power of the vote and not to measure this power. The Negroes' votes in some parts of the country buy them their rights as citizens to a large extent, while their lack of votes in others cause them to be discriminated against all around.[a]

---

[a] In Chapter 20, Section 2, we have pointed out specific reasons why the vote is of such paramount importance to the individual citizen in America.

Political spoils, favors and "protection" also are given to Negroes for their votes. Any Negro who can control a given number of Negro votes may aspire to an appointive political position for himself or for persons designated by himself. Petty favors to the mass of Negro voters are the stock-in-trade of the local politicians: they can save their supporters from fines and short jail sentences; they can "fix" personal property taxes and traffic violations; they can help poor Negroes to get relief or to get on W.P.A. without the usual red tape. Many a Negro church has been able to avoid closing its doors or to buy a new altar when its minister has made his pulpit available to political candidates, Negro or white. Nearly every Negro newspaper is supported, to some degree, by funds supplied by political parties or candidates. Negro criminals, racketeers, vice "kings," and gamblers get protection from the law and from each other to the extent that they can influence or buy votes. In getting all these illegal and extra-legal returns for their votes, Negroes are quite like whites, except that they probably do not get so much on the average. As Gosnell and Bunche point out, Negroes seldom get the really big graft.[75] While this may be looked on as another form of discrimination, it also allows us to infer that Negroes have not so much to lose if city politics are cleaned up. City reform movements not only tend to be fairer in granting Negroes their civic rights, but in reducing corruption they take away less from the few Negroes than from the few whites who benefit by corruption.[a]

Just as they are practically voteless in the South, Negroes there have a minimum of what we have called "legal justice," as we shall describe in the following part. Where they have a few votes, as in the cities and in the Upper South, they have a roughly corresponding measure of legal justice. While this is the general rule, there are minor exceptions: Lewinson tells the story of the president of a Southern State Normal School for Negroes who was rewarded with new buildings for "minding his business" when it came to politics.[76] But this is—to repeat—an exception. It is not— as the average white Southerner often is heard saying—that Negroes are given a fair share of their legal rights if they do not disturb the smooth course of white men's politics.

Even where Negroes have only a few votes in the South they have at least some opportunity to bargain for police and court protection. The lack of a vote is especially dangerous in many Southern communities where even the police are elected or dependent for their tenure on elected office-holding friends.[77] Even Southerners come to recognize this. After three Negroes were killed in one month by policemen in one Alabama city, a

[a] In some cases, this is not true. The corrupt political machine of Mayor Thompson in Chicago was very friendly to Negroes, and one of the aims of the reformers was to clean out the "Negro influence." Negro racketeers, like other racketeers, also stand to lose if a reform movement is successful.

white newspaper blamed the police and traced the condition to the fact that Negroes had no vote.[78] In Memphis, where Negro votes are an important support of the Crump machine, there are relatively few Negroes killed by the police.[79] In many other ways, too, it is demonstrated that this city, which is cited as the outstanding example of the danger of herding Negroes to the polls, is much fairer to Negroes in granting them elementary civic rights. Similarly it is alleged that Negroes of New Orleans were solidly behind Huey Long because he did not discriminate against Negroes in giving free school books, and because he put Negro nurses in the hospitals, Negro servants in the state capitol and refrained from referring to "niggers" in his campaign speeches.[80] In San Antonio, too, Negroes have received almost a fair share of public facilities and minor political jobs from the Democratic machine. On the other hand, there is a good deal of truth in the assertion that the main return for the Negro vote in the machine-dominated cities is protection for the Negro underworld and minor administrative jobs for the petty Negro politicians who marshal the Negro vote.[81]

In the rural South, a Negro tenant or cropper who seeks to leave his cotton farm will often be apprehended and brought back by the elected sheriffs. Sheriffs seldom, if ever, do this to white croppers and tenants, for the latter may vote just as does the white farm owner, whereas the Negro tenant or cropper cannot vote. In Southern cities, Negro workers are allowed to attend union mass meetings where they can vote.[82] Despite repeated decisions by the federal courts that Negroes must be placed on jury lists, practically no Negroes serve on juries in the South except where they vote in significant numbers.[a] The connection has been directly established in Alabama, for example, where after the Scottsboro decision, Negroes were placed on jury lists only if they had voted—even though no Negroes were ever selected from these lists.

The few hundred Negro votes which were cast in 1939 in Greenville, South Carolina, in the face of Ku Klux Klan violence, has already netted Negroes there two fully equipped playgrounds.[83] Similarly, the first large Negro vote in Miami in 1939—also in the face of Klan violence—has changed the attitude of white politicians greatly; streets in Negro sections have been improved, a low cost housing project has been built and another is under way, and the leader of the Negro movement was a delegate to the Republican National Convention in 1940.[84] In Louisville, Negro votes, shifted to the victorious Democrats in 1933, were rewarded by a Negro fire company in their part of the city and by a score of minor administrative and clerical jobs in the city government.[85]

[a] See Chapter 26. Negroes are found on juries in the South practically only in large cities in the Border states and in Oklahoma and Texas.

In referenda and other nonpartisan elections, Negro votes have often been able to achieve advantages for Negroes in Southern cities. In 1921, Negroes defeated a bond issue for schools in Atlanta until it was agreed that they would receive a share of the funds for new schools; the Booker T. Washington High School and four elementary schools were the outcome. In 1926, a similar deal was made, but the promises made to the Negro leaders were not kept in full.[86] In 1939, Negroes in Dallas received a high school and a grade school for supporting a bond issue.[87] Negro participation in the nonpartisan municipal elections in Austin, Texas, is always rewarded: at present there are four Negro policemen, several garbage collectors, a few janitors in the city buildings, and a well-equipped recreation center for Negroes.[88]

Wherever Negroes vote in the South, white politicians who gain from their votes "repay" them with a few minor administrative or menial jobs, a few streets paved or lighted, and occasionally a school building or community center. If Negro votes are necessary to the success of a referendum and if Negroes are organized enough to make a deal with white leaders, they can get a share of the advantages provided by the success of the referendum. Southern Negro voters are never expected to consider issues broader than the interests of their own group, and they seldom do. On the whole, Southern Negroes have been content to vote *against* discriminatory measures rather than *for* progressive measures.[89] The vote of the average Negro has to be directed toward getting those elementary civic rights which are the unquestioned prerogative of every white citizen. The aims of the Negro political hack can usually be directed no higher than to get the merest left-overs of the political spoils.[a] The rare Negro who has broader political interests has to concentrate on getting out the Negro vote rather than directing a vote that already exists. Partly as a result of this situation, the Negro voter in the South, not unlike the poor white voter, tends to be easily "bought" and not very intelligent on issues. With few exceptions,[b] the only occasions when there is no effort to buy up the Negro vote on the part of white politicians are those when there are so few Negro voters that they can have no influence on the outcome of an election.

In the North, where Negroes are not restricted from voting, they get full police protection and justice in the courts to about the same extent as whites of comparable economic and educational status. They get community services, such as schools, libraries, street paving, and sanitation facilities, in rough proportion to the size of their vote, which is in rough proportion

[a] There are exceptions to this: the Bellingers—father and son—have gotten a great deal for themselves by marshaling the Negro vote of San Antonio.

[b] Such as occurred in the spontaneous Negro political movements in Miami and Greenville in 1939.

to their numbers in the population. Gosnell's summary for Chicago applies, with slight variation, throughout the North.

> Under the existing political system, the Negroes secured about as many concrete benefits from the government as most other minority groups. However, because their needs were greater, these benefits were not sufficient. Inadequate as they were, these services came nearer to meeting the needs than in areas where the Negroes have not developed some political power.[90]

Like whites, Negro racketeers and criminals received protection from politicians to the extent that they could influence votes. Ordinary Negroes received petty favors from politicians almost to the same extent as whites.

Negroes have been elected to office in the North, but not nearly in proportion to their numbers. Even in the Border states of Kentucky, West Virginia, and Missouri, there have been a few Negroes in the state legislatures. Negroes find it hard to attain an elective office: because most whites do not like to be represented by Negroes, because Negroes sometimes do not constitute a large enough proportion in a city to control even small sections like wards, because they have been gerrymandered by Democratic politicians for being Republican, and because they have sometimes not shown political interest or acumen. Except for a few judgeships and memberships on such public bodies as Tax Boards and Boards of Education, no Negro has attained a city-wide elective position. There is only one Negro national congressman[a] and about a dozen Negro state legislators.[b] Most of the large cities in the North containing a significant proportion of Negroes have one or two Negro aldermen or councilmen each. These are all the Negroes who have been elected to public office in the North.[c]

There are more Negroes appointed to public office than elected, relative to the total number of offices available, but even these are nowhere near the proportion of the Negro vote. The main reason cited for not appointing Negroes is that some white citizens have strong objections to dealing with them. It is also noteworthy that when a white politician appoints a Negro to some general office, political motives are always inferred, where as white

[a] William Dawson of Chicago (Democrat). From 1928 to 1934 this seat was held by the Republican De Priest, who became heir to it when Madden, "the white friend of the Negro people," died.

[b] According to Charles S. Johnson, in 1942 there were Negroes in the state legislatures of Michigan, Pennsylvania, New Jersey, New York, Illinois, Kansas, Indiana and Kentucky. ("The Negro," *American Journal of Sociology* [May, 1942], p. 863.) The November, 1942, election brought Negroes into the legislature of Ohio also.

[c] In Chicago, for example, Negroes held the following elective positions in 1939: 1 United States Congressman, 1 State Senator, 4 State Representatives, 1 County Commissioner, 2 City Aldermen. Negroes in Chicago were more favored than Negroes in any other city. (Henderson, *op. cit.*, p. 79.)

men may be appointed without this inference. Both whites and Negroes usually look upon the Negro appointees as representatives only of the Negro population. Negro appointments are usually to minor offices. Since much is made of appointments even to clerical and janitorial positions, while major appointments are regarded as news throughout the country, a white politician is usually well repaid for appointing a Negro to any position he may control. It is astonishingly easy to build up a reputation among Negroes as a "white friend of the Negro people."[91] Mayor La Guardia has appointed Negroes to the Special Sessions Court, Domestic Relations Courts, and Civil Service Commission in New York, and has seen to it that Negroes are allowed to compete freely for positions in the city civil service and relief administration. In Chicago Negroes have been appointed to the posts of Assistant State's Attorney; Assistant Attorney General; Assistant City Prosecutor; Deputy Coroner; Assistant Traction Attorney; Assistant Corporation Counsel; Civil Service Commissioner; member of the Housing Authority, of the Library Board and of the Recreation Board.[92] Mayor Kelly of Chicago has also followed the policy of his Republican predecessor—Thompson—in allowing Negroes a significant number of "civil service" positions—especially in the city school system, the Public Library, the Health Department and the Water Bureau.[93] Other Northern cities have similarly given Negroes minor positions in the local government, although perhaps in a lesser degree than in New York and Chicago where the Negro vote is unusually well organized and flexible.

Because voting Negroes are concentrated in a half dozen Northern cities, they can exert little influence on the federal government.[94] This is more than balanced, however, by the federal government's greater conformity to the principles of the American Creed. The federal courts, especially the United States Supreme Court, have been traditional guardians of the Negro's rights. Congress and the Presidents—even, to a certain extent, the Southern Democrat Wilson and the lily-white Hoover—have usually sought to be fair to Negroes. Negro claims have usually received a sympathetic hearing in Washington: Judge Parker was not confirmed as a Justice of the Supreme Court mainly because of his anti-Negro attitude; the anti-lynching bill has more than once been on the verge of passage—hindered only by a filibuster by Southern senators.

As we had occasion to mention earlier, the only elected Negro representative in Washington is a congressman from Chicago. Few Negroes hold top rank appointive positions, and these few are usually in positions that have "traditionally" been held by Negroes since Reconstruction days (such as Recorder of Deeds for the District of Columbia). These traditional appointments are not so stable as is sometimes thought. There was a steady decline in their number from the Taft administration to the

Franklin D. Roosevelt administration. Once in a while, a new "traditional" Negro position is created: when William Hastie, the Roosevelt-appointed Federal Judge in the Virgin Islands, resigned, another Negro was appointed in his place. There are only about a dozen of these traditional top-rank Negro positions in the federal government.

More important since the beginning of the Roosevelt administration are the positions created in various governmental bureaus to advise or direct the application of federal policies to Negroes. The Negroes selected to fill these positions usually have a superior educational background and only one or two have participated in party politics. The powers of these persons have depended mainly on the liberality of their chiefs, although their own activity has been important. When their function has been to direct the application of their respective bureau's policy toward Negroes—as is the case in the National Youth Administration and the United States Housing Authority—they have been able to exert a good deal of influence and have sometimes succeeded in getting a "fair share" of the government's benefits for Negroes. Where they merely advise their chiefs or are regarded as "trouble shooters" to soothe Negro protests of discrimination—as in the Civilian Conservation Corps—their influence is limited. Some of the New Deal agencies have not had Negro advisors—such as the Federal Housing Administration—and several of these agencies have notoriously discriminated against Negroes.

Between 1933 and 1940 there were 103 Negroes appointed by President Roosevelt to positions in the federal government, including 23 who had resigned by 1940 and 3 who had lost their positions because their functions were abolished. Under the leadership of Mary McLeod Bethune—Director of the Division of Negro Affairs of the N.Y.A. and nationally known educator and leader of Negro women—the most important of these have organized an informal group, the Federal Council, popularly known as "the Black Cabinet." The purpose of this group is to discuss common problems and to encourage coordinated activity, although it never takes public action as a group.[95] The great weaknesses of the holders of these positions are that many of them are in agencies which are not considered to be permanent, and that they are completely subordinated to the white heads of the respective bureaus. Although many Negroes have condemned the appointments to these positions as representing an effort to keep Negroes satisfied, there are important achievements to their credit, and they are the first significant step, in recent years, toward the participation of Negroes in federal government activity.

In addition to the full-time Negro advisors and section chiefs, there are several official part-time advisors who do not live in Washington but only visit there occasionally and upon request. For example, in March, 1942, F. D. Patterson, President of Tuskegee Institute, and Claude A. Barnett,

Director of the Associated Negro Press, were named special assistants to the Secretary of Agriculture to "insure the integration and full participation of Negro farmers in the food-for-freedom campaign." Also there are unofficial Negro advisors—such as Booker T. Washington when he was alive and A. Philip Randolph (President of the Brotherhood of Sleeping Car Porters) today—but their activities are an aspect of Negro leadership more than of federal policy and will be discussed in another context.[a]

According to the Chief of the Statistical Division of the Civil Service Commission, there were about 82,000 Negroes holding federal Civil Service jobs on June 30, 1938, representing about 9.8 per cent of the total federal employment.[96] About 88 per cent of these were stationed outside Washington and were practically all either postal clerks, mail carriers, unskilled laborers or janitors. Most of the 12 per cent stationed in Washington had similar low positions. They were strikingly negligible in the lower salaried white collar jobs which furnish the bulk of employment for white government employees. There was a small proportion of Negroes in the higher paid technical, professional and administrative positions.[b]

During Reconstruction, Negroes succeeded in getting a large share of the lower federal government jobs in the South (mainly in the postal service). After the Southern conservatives regained power, and as the North gradually entered the compromise by which it became blind to actual conditions in the South, Negroes gradually lost these jobs. The fact that the Republican party was in power most of the time after the Civil War, and the fact that Negroes soon came under civil service, prevented them from being thrown out of these jobs completely. By the time of the Hoover administration, Negroes held practically none of the middle or higher federal positions in the South and only a relatively small proportion of the lower ones. The New Deal has reversed the trend slightly, not by opening positions to Negroes in the South, but by being less discriminatory in the lower jobs in Washington.

[a] See Part IX.
[b] For a discussion of discrimination against Negroes in the federal Civil Service, see Chapter 14, Section 8.

CHAPTER 23

TRENDS AND POSSIBILITIES

1. The Negro's Political Bargaining Power

To make political forecasts is hazardous. But forecasts are the aim of factual analysis. Indeed, its sole purpose, aside from scientific curiosity, is to furnish the basis for a practical discussion of future trends and possibilities. In the Negro problem there are certain dominating factors making a forecast considerably simpler than for the American nation at large.

If we focus our attention only on Negro voting in those parts of the country where Negroes have, or will have, the unhampered right to the ballot, it can, with reasonable security, be foretold that *there is not going to be a "Negro party" in American politics.* It is true that there are strong ties of common interests in the Negro group. But Negroes know from bitter experience that there is nothing which can so frustrate their hope of having a voice in public affairs as the arousing of a fear of "Negro domination." Negroes in America are, further, bent on cultural assimilation to the fullest degree allowed by the white majority and are careful to abstain from every move in the political sphere which might be interpreted as group exclusiveness. In addition, Negroes are in a minority in all but a few parts of the country. Where they are a majority, suffrage is a relatively distant hope and will in all probability materialize only gradually. The essential stimulus for party formation—namely, the hope of eventually coming into power—is everywhere entirely lacking. Finally, the peculiar American political system strongly disfavors small parties even when this hope is present.

The Negro voter will, therefore, have to try to exert his influence through one of the two dominant political parties. Since the Negroes broke their traditional allegiance to the Republican party, the Negro vote is fluid. *It is likely to remain fluid.* Neither the Republican party nor the Democratic party will be certain of the Negro vote for any length of time without real exertions. Negro voters will increasingly judge political parties from the viewpoint of their friendliness to the Negro group.

The Democratic and Republican parties will increasingly compete for the Negro vote. The question arises *whether, in this haggling and bargaining, the Negroes will be able to extract the maximum advantage by acting as a political unit, nationally and locally.* One prerequisite for such a tactic is present to a greater degree than in any other large American group of voters. Negroes, as a consequence of the bonds of caste in which they are enclosed, feel a larger degree of interest solidarity in relation to society. It is true that the Negro community is stratified into social classes and that, in general, Negroes are much at variance in political issues, interests and ideals. But the lower classes are, because of the caste situation, a great majority, and the upper classes have strong interests in the economic welfare of the lower classes who constitute the basis of their economic sustenance. As regards Negro issues, therefore, the internal differences have little significance, and those issues are likely to remain primary. There are certain concrete demands—all centering around the insistence that Negroes should be treated like other citizens—about which there is almost universal agreement among Negroes.

In the sphere of national politics, however, the attempt to take up real collective bargaining with the two political parties on behalf of the Negro voters has not been effective.[1] Since the Negro vote became fluid in the 1930's and both parties now recognize this fact, it would be rather natural for a national Negro political leadership to form itself and start negotiations with the two parties in advance of each national election. This has not happened. The "bidding for the Negro vote" has been left almost entirely to the care of the two parties themselves and has principally become directed to the individual Negro voter, through party-appointed Negro leaders, as no bargaining agency for the Negroes has interceded. In local politics collective bargaining has, as we have shown, not been entirely lacking. But taking a broad view, the main observation is again that the situation has not been utilized to any extent approaching the political possibilities. Negro communities everywhere display in the most glaring manner clear-cut problems of housing, employment, education, health, and so on, calling not only for expert planning but for formulation of Negro political programs. It is, indeed, a matter to be explained why Negro pressure in these communities, at least in the North, is so diffuse and inarticulate, and, relatively speaking, so politically ineffective.

Part of the explanation is, undoubtedly, the poverty and the inherited psychology of dependence and apathy among the Negro masses, their low educational and cultural level, and the lack of political tradition and experience both in the masses and in the upper strata of the Negro community. All this is bound to change in time. But there are, in addition, certain intrinsic difficulties inherent in the strategy of not being able to form an independent party with hope of gaining political power but, nevertheless, of wanting to act as a political unit in order to raise the price paid for the Negro votes by the existing parties. The very facts that a Negro is prevented by his caste status from regarding himself as an ordinary American citizen and as a wholehearted supporter of a party, and that—when acting as a representative for his group—he is out to get favors for them, are conducive to a psychology where broad political ideas are put in the background and petty haggling becomes natural. The tendency to cynicism, which the author has observed everywhere in American Negro communities, becomes strengthened by the American party system, which does not correlate closely with broad divisions of real interests and social ideals. If, in addition, the party machines are corrupt, which they are in most places where Negroes live in any numbers, the presence of such moral strength on the part of the Negro leadership as would be prerequisite for efficient bargaining would be a wonder.

But even apart from all this, the Negro leader is in a dilemma. If he pleads allegiance to a political party, he will lose in bargaining power. If, on the other hand, he keeps outside the parties, he loses some of the influence he could exert by being in the inner circle of one of them.[a] Out of the dilemma there is only one possible and rational escape: *a division of labor and responsibility among Negro leaders,* so that the Negro politicians proper and the party workers identify themselves with political parties and work with them and for them, while other Negro representatives, invested with superior prestige among their people, remain independent of close party ties and do the important collective bargaining. The former group represents the Negro people's necessary allegiance to the American party system, the latter group their separate interests as an independent unit. For optimal functioning such a system of minority politics requires a high degree of political sophistication among both leaders and followers and much good-will and cohesion. It is not surprising that it has not materialized in any high degree in this subdued and politically inexperienced group. But it might become more of a reality in the future. The great community of interest in a caste set apart in society, but fighting for fuller assimilation, offers a firm basis for such an organization of the Negro people's political bargaining power.

The political strength of such a dual system of political organization will depend primarily upon the cohesion of the local Negro political blocs in the several communities forming its basis. There are, however, a great number of specific impediments to a further development of the local organization of Negro political power. One is the internal rivalry among leaders in a deeply frustrated group.[b] Power becomes so dear when there is so little of it. Cynicism becomes so widespread among ambitious individuals whose way upward is blocked. There is also the tendency among many Negroes who aspire to prominence, or who have arrived but want to make themselves secure, to take orders from the influential whites and to "sell out"

[a] The problem of Negro leadership will be discussed in Part IX.
[b] See Chapter 36, Section 2, and Chapter 37, Section 8.

their own group. Such persons seem everywhere to be available for utilization in splitting the unity of the Negroes. A third relevant fact is that an even greater group of potential Negro leaders, even if they are not "white men's niggers," nevertheless are so dependent that they cannot afford the integrity required to make them effective bargainers for the Negro group. At bottom is the ease with which the Negro masses can be duped—because they are distressed, poorly educated, politically inexperienced, tractable, and have old traditions of dependence and carelessness.

All this is, however, relative. Even though the Negro voters are weakly organized today, the two parties have to compete for them. The N.A.A.C.P. and all other national and local Negro organizations and the Negro press are constantly doing a service by creating publicity—favorable or unfavorable—in the Negro community for the political parties and the individual officeholders. To some extent the latter become compelled to adjust according to the reactions of Negro voters.

2. THE NEGRO'S PARTY ALLEGIANCE

Our assumption has until now been that the Negro vote will remain fluid but will keep conservatively to the two big parties. One thing seems certain: namely, that the Negroes will not go fascist. All their interests are against right-wing radicalism.[2] More problematic, of course, are Negro attitudes toward Communism. To many white people in America, apparently, it seems natural that they should turn Communist. This is, however, largely only a testimony of their own bad social conscience and of their ignorance of the Negro community. It is true that a majority of the Negro people are in economic distress. It is also true that they are increasingly becoming conscious of being severely maltreated in America and that they sense social exclusion, which must decrease their feeling of full solidarity with the dominant groups in society. All this should make them open to revolutionary propaganda. It is further true that the Communists have seen their chance and have been devoting much zealous work to cultivating the Negroes. They have run a Negro as candidate for Vice-President of the United States. They are the only American group which has in practice offered Negroes full "social equality," and this is highly valued not only among Negro intellectuals but much deeper down in the Negro community, particularly in the North.

Still *the Communists have not succeeded in getting any appreciable following among Negroes in America*[a] and it does not seem likely that they will. No intensive study has been made on this problem. The following observations are presented as impressionistic, even if they are believed to contain the main facts. To begin with, it is a mistake to assume *a priori* that poor, uneducated, and socially disadvantaged groups are particularly

---

[a] See Chapter 22, Section 4.

susceptible to radical propaganda. It is different in a revolutionary situation when those groups might not only come to follow but actually constitute the vanguard of an onslaught on society. But in peaceful, orderly development they are apt to be conservative. Even for liberal reform movements the poorest people have been the most difficult to organize. The trade union movement, for instance, all over the world has had its first and most faithful adherents in the higher strata of the working class. It has had to push downward with difficulty and usually has not succeeded in organizing the lower brackets before they were raised economically and culturally.[3]

The strong impact of church and religion in the Negro community should not be forgotten.[4] This is, however, only one trait of Negro conservatism. Negroes who care so much for society as to have any general political opinions at all are intent upon "respectability" in a middle class sense. Communism is definitely not respectable in America generally or among Negroes specifically. The unpopularity of Communism in America—often reaching the pitch of actual persecution of the Communist party and its adherents—must, furthermore, be uninviting to a group like the American Negroes who know so well that they are unpopular already. As one Negro explained, "It is bad enough being black without being black and red." James Weldon Johnson makes this point:

> In the situation as it now exists, it would be positively foolhardy for us, as a group, to take up the cause of Communistic revolution and thereby bring upon ourselves all of the antagonisms that are directed against it in addition to those we already have to bear. It seems to me that the wholesale allegiance of the Negro to Communistic revolution would be second in futility only to his individual resort to physical force.[5]

and again:

> . . . there is no apparent possibility that a sufficient number of Negro Americans can be won over to give the party the desired strength; and if the entire mass were won over, the increased proscriptions against Negroes would outweigh any advantages that might be gained. Every Negro's dark face would be his party badge, and would leave him an open and often solitary prey to the pack whenever the hunt might be on. And the sign of the times is that the hunt is not yet to be abandoned.[6]

The strong "horse sense" of this argument does not need logical demonstration. It is a foregone conclusion to even the most politically ill-equipped American Negro. Deep in the Negro mind is also a suspicion against the social evangelism of his white Communist friends. "Even after a revolution the country will be full of crackers" is a reflection I have often met when discussing Communism in the Negro community.

> If the United States goes Communistic, where will the Communists come from? They certainly will not be imported from Russia. They will be made from the Americans here on hand. We might well pause and consider what variations Communism in the United States might undergo.[7]

But there is, I have become convinced, a still deeper reason why Negroes are so immune against Communism. Negroes are discriminated against in practically all spheres of life, but in their fight for equal opportunity *they have on their side the law of the land and the religion of the nation*. And they know it, all the way down to the poorest stratum. They know that this is their strategic hold. *No social Utopia can compete with the promises of the American Constitution and with the American Creed which it embodies*. Democracy and lawful government mean so much more to a Negro, just because he enjoys so comparatively little of it in this country. Merely by giving him the solemn promise of equality and liberty, American society has tied the Negroes' faith to itself.

It should be observed, however, that several of the factors mentioned are transitory to a degree. The prospect of stimulating Negro support would also be different if a revolutionary movement once became really important in America and in a position to exert a serious threat of assuming political power. In such a situation a maltreated caste like the Negro people might suddenly become uncertain in its political allegiance. The Negroes' experiences during the present War until the time when this is being written (April, 1942) have undoubtedly had the general effect of loosening their sentimental ties to American society.[a] But such a drift away from national allegiance is the price eventually to be paid by a democratic society which, in the fulfillment of the promises of democracy, makes an exception of one group. It should also be observed that Communism, outside of party membership, has actually had a considerable influence upon the mode of thinking of the small group of Negro intellectuals who are, of course, easiest to move. There has been a growth of general radicalism in this group, and the present investigator has been surprised to find how it has spread also to Negro professionals and, occasionally, even to the Negro press.

If we thus conclude that—for the near future at least—Communism or any similar movement will not be able to muster any numerical support from the Negro voters, we must, on the other hand, be aware that *Negroes as a group will from now on be in strong favor of a political party which stands for social reform and civic equality*. In this respect, the New Deal promises to have permanent effects.[8] It has made this political alignment apparent to the whole Negro people. When once the sentimental allegiance to the Republican party was broken and a modern liberal movement in American politics was inaugurated, this attitude became natural for a group which includes so many who are perennially interested in public assistance in one form or another. Negroes, in both the higher and the lower strata, seem to understand pretty well that a liberal attitude in questions of economic relief and social reform is generally connected with a more equalitarian attitude in racial matters.

[a] See Chapters 19 and 45.

With the vanishing of the frontier, the bar against new immigration, the proceeding Americanization, the growth of labor organizations, and other factors of structural change, the American party system has for a considerable time been headed for a rather fundamental change. During the Roosevelt administration, cleavage seemed to develop within both parties which made for a closer correspondence of party alignment to real interests and ideals. The present War might, of course, inaugurate unforeseen new trends. But extrapolating the trends during the 'thirties and assuming no successful new third party movement, the present author has been inclined to envisage such a reorganization of the two-party system that one of the two parties carrying on the tradition of the New Deal becomes a liberal reform party, while the other remains a conservative party.[a]

If we assume that such a new system will materialize, it seems fairly certain that the great majority of Negroes are going to adhere to the liberal party, provided it be consistently liberal with respect to the Negro problem and manifests its liberalism not only in words but also in deeds. By becoming less fluid politically, the Negro voters would undoubtedly lose some of their bargaining power. But as the cause for their greater party loyalty would be that the party of their choice actually was more liberal, this would not be a real loss. Also, Negro fluidity would not be completely lost, since there will probably never be a return to that type of sentimentality which characterized the Negro's adherence to the Republican party from the Civil War until the New Deal, and since the Conservative party will not ignore the Negro's vote completely, and the Liberal party will realize that it *can* lose the Negro vote. If this realignment of the American party system should emerge, many Negro politicans would be released from the dilemma of double loyalty to the party and to the Negro group. This would remove to a certain extent one of the fundamental causes of political cynicism and corruption among Negro politicians.

Generally speaking, a development of the type here envisaged would, in the present writer's opinion, enhance efficiency and honesty in American politics. The causes of incompetency and corruption are many and varied.[9] But I believe that they have much more to do, than is generally understood, with the system of political parties entirely disconnected from the broad

---

[a] The impediments in the way of such a development are not overlooked. (1) The Democratic party is not likely to develop into a consistently liberal party without endangering its monopoly over the South. We should not deceive ourselves that the South has suddenly become progressive because the Southerners are Democrats, and the Democratic party is progressive under the leadership of Roosevelt. There is no doubt that the fact that the Democratic party is so largely Southern has served as a kind of brake on its progressivism in national politics. The rapid run of change in the South (see Chapter 21, Section 4) might bring a split of the party in the South. (2) Just as there are conservative Democrats, there are progressive Republicans. But even conservative Republicans are not willing to allow their party to play the role of a conservative party.

divisions of interests and ideals in American society. American politics has been comparatively empty of real issues. Often the issue, particularly in local elections, has been simply the demand for efficiency and honesty—the very things which have been generally lacking to such a degree that the ordinary American has come to believe that inefficiency and dishonesty are inexorably connected with politics as such. Honest and efficient politics requires political opinions and, indeed, splits in opinion. It also requires an independent, though democratically controlled, bureaucracy, and a firm tradition of legality. In these latter respects, too, the American government is on the move toward acquiring a structure less conducive to incompetence and graft.[a]

The Negroes as a subordinated group will be among the chief beneficiaries of these changes if they occur. The changes will not come overnight. They are contingent upon the building up of traditions, and that will take time. And there is always the danger that intervening happenings will break the process of orderly growth. Even assuming no such unforeseen causes of deviation, the task before America in reforming its system of government is incomparably grave: it has to cleanse its politics, not—as other nations have done—in an era of noninterference characterized by rigidly restricted state activity, but in an historic stage when state intervention is mounting, when state services are multiplying and when billions of dollars are passing through public budgets.

3. Negro Suffrage in the South as an Issue

The concern of the Southern Negroes is not how they shall use their votes but how to get their constitutional right to vote respected at all. Negro political power in the North is, as we shall see, not inconsequential for this problem in the South. But there are many other forces of change involved in the matter.

That suffrage should be a major interest for Southern Negroes is demonstrated in several chapters of this book. There is, indeed, no single one of the several categories of Southern Negroes' deprivations and sufferings which is unconnected with their disfranchisement. In America, with its tradition of loose and politically dependent administration, there is more than elsewhere a considerable substance of realism in W. E. B. Du Bois' blunt statement:

> I hold this truth to be self-evident, that a disfranchised working class in modern industrial civilization is worse than helpless. It is a menace, not simply to itself, but to every other group in the community . . . it will be ignorant; it will be the plaything of mobs; and it will be insulted by caste restrictions.[10]

[a] See Chapter 20, Section 2.

And Du Bois is also right when, without falling into the fallacy of believing that the voting right would by itself work wonders, he insists on the vote as a key point in all efforts to raise Negro standards. There is, indeed, a strange atmosphere of unreality around much of the discussion of the practical aspects of the Negro problem in America: it is commonly and more or less explicitly assumed that it is possible to raise materially and permanently the condition of living in various respects for the Southern Negro people through Southern white good-will and Northern philanthropy while ". . . Negroes were to have no voice in the selection of local officials, no control of their own taxation, no vote on expenditure. . . ."[11] The Negroes' interests in politics are primarily concerned with the handling of local matters. Negroes need, in order to protect themselves, a voice in deciding who will be the judges of the courts, the public attorneys, the sheriffs and the chiefs of police, the members of the school board and other agencies deciding upon their share of public services. As national politics is increasingly important for all questions of social and economic welfare, they are also interested in who represents their districts in Congress.

On the point of suffrage, as in so many other respects, there has, *in principle*, never really been any great difference of opinion among Negro leaders. It is true that Booker T. Washington found it advisable as a more practical tactic to proceed carefully and to stress that there were many things more important for the Negro's welfare than the vote.[a] But he never gave up the demand for the Negro's right to the vote, nor his expectation that ultimately the South would reach a stage where Negroes were allowed to vote.[12] The Negro leaders have pointed to the moral danger to all society of the resort to extra-legal measures for keeping the Negroes out of politics.[13] The Negro leaders are also at one in not demanding an absolutely unqualified right to suffrage. They only insist that the restrictions of suffrage should be applied impartially to whites and Negroes alike.[14] White liberals in the South are increasingly taking the same position.[15] But the great majority of conservative Southern white people try to appear unconcerned.

While, with a few local and regional exceptions, the Southern Negroes remain disfranchised, we have noted the beginnings of a tendency to increased political participation. In many Southern cities, the present writer has observed how small organizations and civic groups among the Negroes are starting and are attempting to get more Negroes on the registration lists. But first, this is not an entirely new phenomenon and, second, the immediate success is in most cases insignificant. Most Southern Negroes seem to keep their minds turned away from the whole matter. As we have shown, they have, indeed, good reasons for lack of political interest. But

[a] See Chapter 34.

this does not prove that they would not vote if they were allowed to, and if the vote was given due importance.[a]

4. AN UNSTABLE SITUATION

Superficially viewed, the situation looks static and stable. This is, I believe, an illusion. Great changes are working underneath the visible surface, and a dynamic situation full of possibilities is maturing. Let us begin with some of the smaller changes: the declining value of the dollar has, since the inauguration of the disfranchising constitutions and election laws, actually diminished considerably the effectiveness both of the poll tax requirement and of the property clauses. A substantial inflation will probably be the result of the present War. The political pressure from the poorer classes will prevent attempts to raise the money figures in proportion to the rise in price level. The trend actually is in the other direction, to decrease the size of the poll tax and property requirements. A factor similar in its effect to inflation is the trend toward direct taxation and away from indirect taxation. It is possible that when the poll tax becomes only one direct tax among many, it will not appear to be so large. The present War is accentuating this trend.

More important is that the improved education of Negroes is rendering ineffective the literacy and understanding clauses. Every year there is a smaller proportion of the potential Negro electorate—as of the white one—which would be disfranchised by these clauses if they were impartially applied. They are not, as we have seen, applied honestly. This means that *at least the legal foundations for Negro disfranchisement is gradually withering away.* Keeping the Negroes away from the polls will thus increasingly have to be accomplished by intimidation, subterfuge or violence. In a sense, *the entire work around 1900 to legalize political discrimination is being rapidly undone by various social trends.*

For two reasons this work cannot well be made over to meet the changes: first, because the possible means for legal disfranchisement within the loopholes of the federal Constitution have been pretty well exhausted, and, second, because the general political atmosphere of the nation and the attitude of the Supreme Court are not so acquiescent as half a century ago when, in the great reaction after Reconstruction, they condoned the national compromise. Respect for law is being enhanced in the South. It is true that meanwhile a social pattern has been established that politics is white men's business, and that Negroes should not stick their noses into it. This is the main explanation of the calm before the storm. But as far as laws and individual rights mean anything at all in the South—and, as we shall see in the next part, there are reasons to believe that they will

---

[a] See Chapter 22, Sections 3 and 4.

mean increasingly much—this situation is highly unstable and is becoming more so every year.

It comes to this, that the poll tax probably will be abolished in one state after another (the present author would guess within the next decade). The reform elements in the South will become stronger as industrialization is proceeding and as labor is becoming unionized. It is quite possible that abolition of the poll tax might not immediately change the suffrage situation much for the Negroes. The white primary and the extra-legal measures to keep Negroes from the polls might for a time make this reform rather inconsequential as far as the Negroes are concerned.[a] The experiences from the three Southern States which have taken the step make this appear probable. But *by abolishing the poll tax the legal foundation for Negro disfranchisement will be made still weaker;* the South will thus, if it seeks to continue to preserve the *status quo,* have to rely still more exclusively on extra-legal measures. This, and the broadened basis of the white electorate—under the influence of the whole system of social changes which we have reviewed earlier[b]—is bound to rearrange the structure of politics in the South so much that even the white primary might crash. The conservative opponents of any reform in the poll tax, who claim that this will open the road to Negro enfranchisement, are probably right. But the forces that back this reform are getting to be so strong that in all probability they cannot be stopped.

5. THE STAKE OF THE NORTH

This is perhaps the point at which to take up for consideration the stake of the North in the Southern suffrage problem. It is apparent, and rather surprising, that the liberal forces in the North have not until recently given this problem more attention.

There is actually a provision in the Fourteenth Amendment requiring a reduction in representation in Congress as a punishment for disfranchisement.[16] But this provision has never been applied. The conservatives had, of course, no interest in doing it, and it could not be attractive to liberals either, as it would imply a formal sanction of disfranchisement. Further, the Southern conservatives' strategic position became the stronger when it gradually became clear that they were assisted by the Supreme Court decisions which gave a twisted construction to the Reconstruction Amendments and read into them a meaning never intended by their authors. Suits brought by Negroes were dismissed often on formalistic and technical

---

[a] It will also be some time after the legal abolition of the poll tax before the traditions connected with it disappear. Real issues which will stimulate the poorer whites to vote will not appear publicly overnight.

[b] See Chapter 21, Section 4.

grounds.[17] One Southerner—who was not arguing for enfranchising the Negroes but for their deportation—wrote early in the century:

> In the matter of the franchise, the South first desperately intimidated the negro; then systematically cheated him without semblance of law: then cheated him legally; and now defrauds him of his political rights in a duly constitutional fashion with the consent, if not the aid of the United States Supreme Court.[18]

It is generally held that the Supreme Court acted in agreement with and actually expressed what was then the general sentiment even in the North. The North had gotten tired of the Negro problem and, anyhow, saw no immediate alternative other than to let the white Southerners have their own way with their Negroes. But it must not be forgotten that the decisions of the Court had themselves a substantial share in the responsibility for the solidification of the Northern apathy. This was also before the great Negro migration: the Negro vote in the North was still small and safely belonged to the Republican party without any particular political compensation.

The Supreme Court is, however, seemingly changing its attitude and is again looking more to the spirit of the Reconstruction Amendments and not only to their possible loopholes. Since at the same time the legal foundation for Negro discrimination in the South is dissolving, it will be easier to win cases for disfranchised Negroes if they begin again to demand their constitutional right in the state courts. It would be no great surprise if the Supreme Court reversed its earlier stand and, by declaring the primary to be an election, rendered the white primary unconstitutional.

Meanwhile, the forces for social reform in Congress are feeling the opposition from Southern conservative members more and more cumbersome. They are increasingly irritated when they remember that, owing to the peculiar electoral system and the restricted political participation in the Southern states, congressmen from the South are not truly representative of the region. "In the 1940 election about 10% of the voting population of the United States . . . was able to elect . . . one-fourth of the members of Congress,"[19] writes a Southern liberal, and this truth is dawning upon many Northerners too. The stage is being set for attempts to free at least the national elections from poll tax requirements.[a] Both the labor vote and

[a] The current effort to abolish the poll tax by federal legislation is again bringing up the much-debated question of the constitutionality of federal laws to regulate federal elections. The opponents of such laws quote the first part of Article 1, Section 4 of the Constitution: "The times, places, and manner of holding elections for Senators and Representatives shall be prescribed in each State by the Legislature thereof . . ." The advocates of federal action call attention to the continuation of this Section of the Constitution: "but the Congress may at any time by law make or alter such regulations, except as to the places of choosing Senators." In view of the latter statement, it seems to be a myth, carefully fostered by reactionaries, that Congress cannot take a hand in controlling the election of its members. In maintaining this myth, these reactionaries have referred to irrelevant sections of the

the Negro vote in the North will in all probability exert a considerable pressure in this same direction. The labor vote might be primarily interested in freeing the poor whites from the poll tax in the South and, generally, in defeating the conservative hold over Southern politics. But Negro disfranchisement is so thoroughly interwoven with these two other goals that a separation is not possible technically. It is not desirable from a tactical standpoint, either, that labor tolerate discrimination against the Negro, at least as far as legislation and national policy are concerned. This is so because labor must seek support in the industrial South from the Negro, where the Negro constitutes an important element in the industrial population, and it is true also because labor, from the standpoint of national strategy, cannot afford to fall in with the *status quo*.

Northerners far to the right of labor also have cause to feel increasingly uneasy about Southern disfranchisement of Negroes as well as about judicial and economic discrimination. There is a disturbing racial angle to the Second World War, and to the planning for a world order after the War, for which the United States is bound to assume a great responsibility. The issue of democracy is fatefully involved in the War and the coming peace. The Northern press reflects abundantly this growing anxiety around the Negro problem. A recent editorial concludes:

> This is a national, not a sectional problem. . . . It has to be solved if the white-skinned majority is to avoid the sinister hypocrisy of fighting abroad for what it is not willing to accept at home.[20]

Southern conservatives dislike nothing more than the threat of federal interference in their "states' rights." The anti-lynching legislation was fought on this ground. Several conservative Southerners have explained to me that they did not have so much against the measure *per se*, but that they dreaded it as a first step in the regulation of civic rights in the South by federal legislation. Even many liberal white Southerners want to confine the Negro problem, and particularly the Negro suffrage, to a local issue.[21] But the South's strategic position is weakening every day. Southern conservatism is, on this point, defending an indefensible position. There are reasons to anticipate both that the Negro and the labor bloc will exert increasing political power, and that liberalism generally will become stronger both in the South and in the North. The Supreme Court is likely to continue in its new trend. The only means of escaping federal inter-

---

Constitution, such as the Fifteenth Amendment (which says that "the right of citizens of the United States to vote shall not be denied or abridged by the United States or by any State on account of race, color, or previous condition of servitude" but says nothing about poll tax, or similar economic or geographical barriers).

ference might be for the South to start to carry out the reforms on its own initiative.[a]

6. Practical Conclusions

In the South itself, the whole unique political system, particularly the poll tax, is becoming increasingly shaky. And this is realized by Southerners with any insight into politics, even if they do not admit it publicly. More specifically, the disfranchisement of Negroes is losing its entire legal foundation and now depends mainly on illegal measures. From a conservative point of view, this is the more dangerous as respect for law is undoubtedly gaining ground in the South. Not only the legal, but also the political, security of the white primary will crumble, and this is well known to conservative whites. They always stress in discussion that its only basis, and, therefore, the only basis of the one-party system and the "Solid South," is the strict adherence to the "gentleman's agreement" between the defeated and the victorious candidates in the primary. If there are going to be more serious splits on real political issues in the South—and all the changes mentioned earlier tend to build up liberal counterforces in the South—it is not only possible but, as I have often heard Southerners stress, probable that such agreements will not be upheld. As during the period of Populism in the 1890's, the Negroes are then going to be allowed to register and vote. And more Negroes will then have lawful rights to suffrage.

Our conclusion is, thus, that the Southern franchise situation, which on the surface looks so quiet, is highly unstable and that, indeed, *the Southern conservative position on Negro franchise is politically untenable for any length of time.* If this analysis is accepted, and if the value premise is agreed upon, that *changes should, if possible, not be made by sudden upheavals but in gradual steps,* we reach the further practical conclusion that it is an urgent interest and, actually, a truly conservative one, for the South *to start enfranchising its Negro citizens as soon as possible.* This is seen by a small group of Southern liberals.[22]

It is true, as Woofter reminds us in discussing this point, that the situation is complicated. In many areas of the South where the Negro population is most densely concentrated, "this group is less intelligent, less familiar with American institutions, farther down in the economic scale, and most likely to constitute the corrupt mass-voting element."[23] So are also large sectors of the poor white masses in the South. As we have seen, Southern conservative politics is not without guilt in this situation. But for this very reason—the foreseeable changes being what they are—the more urgent is

---

[a] Contrary to a general opinion that the South is conditioned to react only negatively to Northern criticism and pressure, I am convinced that, on the balance, the effect is almost always positive. In all fields—education, civic rights, and suffrage—I have everywhere met this argument in Southern discussion, that a step is necessary in order to forestall this or that move from the North.

it from a conservative point of view *to begin allowing the higher strata of the Negro population to participate in the political process as soon as possible, and to push the movement down to the lowest groups gradually.* The more urgent is it also *to speed up the civic education of these masses who are bound to have votes in the future.* It would, in this late stage of the development, be wise also to go the full way and gradually open the white primary to Negroes. This, actually, would be a means of decreasing the temptation for defeated primary candidates to break the "gentleman's agreement" and, consequently, to preserve the one-party system for a longer time than otherwise would be possible.[a]

In their own history of the past century, the Southern conservatives can see abundantly the negative proofs, and from the history of democratic politics all over the world the positive proofs, for this thesis, that political conservatives, who have been successful for any length of time, have always foreseen impending changes and have put through the needed reforms themselves in time. By following this tactic they have been able to guard fundamental conservative interests even in the framing of the reforms. They have thereby also succeeded in slowing them up; changes have not overwhelmed them as avalanches. They have kept the control and preserved a basis for the retention of their political power. Southern conservatism should further learn from history that, over a period of time, the conservative forces in a society cannot afford to abstain from the tremendous strategic advantage of forming the party of "law and order." This is such an immense interest for conservatism that if—for constitutional and other reasons—the law does not come to the conservatives even when they are in power, the conservatives had better come to the law.

But the great majority of Southern conservative white people do not see the handwriting on the wall. They do not study the impending changes; they live again in the pathetic illusion that the matter is settled. They do not care to have any constructive policies to meet the trends. They think no adjustments are called for. The chances that the future development will be *planned* and *led* intelligently—and that, consequently, it will take the form of cautious, foresighted reforms instead of unexpected, tumultuous,

[a] I am here, looking on the problem from a conservative point of view and assuming that to preserve the one-party system would be desirable. The liberals want, on the contrary, to get away from the white primary and from the one-party system altogether, but they do not anticipate radical changes in the future. They further want to do away with political discrimination and, therefore, come to the same conclusion:

"For the white South, what is needed above all is fairness, a determination to enforce suffrage tests equitably on white and black alike, and resolve to break away from the one-party system and to regain preëminence in the national forums of political action by building a political system around the live national issues and forgetting the more or less dead issue of Negro domination." (T. J. Woofter, Jr., *The Basis of Racial Adjustment* [1925], p. 167.)

haphazard breaks, with mounting discords and anxieties in its wake—are indeed small. But we want to keep this last question open. Man is a free agent, and there are no inevitabilities. All will depend upon the thinking done and the action taken in the region during the next decade or so. History can be made. It is not necessary to receive it as mere destiny.

FOOTNOTES TO VOLUME I

Introduction

[1] (1939), p. 172.

[2] William I. Thomas and Florian Znaniecki, *The Polish Peasant in Europe and America* (1918).

[3] One such exception is E. Franklin Frazier's book, *The Negro Family in the United States* (1939). As Ernest W. Burgess hints at in his Preface, the importance of this work is in no small measure dependent upon Frazier's ability to look at the development of the Negro family in its relation to the trend of changes in the total environmental setting.

[4] *The American Commonwealth* (1911; first edition, 1893), Vol. 1, p. 7.

[5] For a popular but comprehensive attempt at a cultural overview of present-day America, where lights and shadows are distributed in a very different way than in this study concentrated on a problem sector of American civilization, the author can refer to Alva and Gunnar Myrdal, *Kontakt Med Amerika* (1941).

Chapter 1. *American Ideals and the American Conscience*

[1] *Alien Americans* (1936), p. 149.

[2] "Conceptions and Ideologies of the Negro Problem," unpublished manuscript prepared for this study (1940), p. 4.

[3] "Memorial Address on the Life and Character of Abraham Lincoln" (1866), pp. 4 and 6.

[4] Frederick Jackson Turner, *The Frontier in American History* (1921), pp. 281-282.

[5] *Epic of America* (1931), p. 405.

[6] *Main Currents in American Thought*, Vol. 3, "The Beginnings of Critical Realism in America, 1860-1920" (1930), pp. 285 ff.

[7] 1913.

[8] Parrington, *Main Currents in American Thought*, Vol. 3, "The Beginnings of Critical Realism in America, 1860-1920," p. 410.

[9] After a careful survey of American heroes, Dixon Wecter concludes that only Washington could be placed on the side of conservatism, and even he occasionally went over to the liberal side and is popularly identified with liberalism. (Dixon Wecter, *The Hero in America* [1941], pp. 486-487.)

[10] Vernon L. Parrington, *Main Currents in American Thought*, Vol. 1, "The Colonial Mind, 1620-1800" (1927), p. 179.

[11] Charles E. Merriam, "The Meaning of Democracy," *Journal of Negro Education* (July, 1941), p. 309.

[12] It has become customary in the writing of the early history of American ideas

to associate the two fundamental concepts of the Creed and the two conflicting tendencies in American social history: (1) to French eighteenth century humanitarianism and equalitarianism, represented by Rousseau and (2) to English seventeenth century liberalism, represented by Locke.

The difference between the two schools—and the two European influences conditioning the American mind—should, however, not be overemphasized. Both branches of the Enlightenment philosophy believed in "inalienable rights of man," both assumed a harmony between equality of opportunity and liberty. It should not be forgotten that Locke—and *in principle* also the later English liberals—justified only those titles to property which derived from labor as the single "factor of production"; other property titles were "monopolies" and "special privileges." (*In practice* the English school was, however, more conservative than in its principles, particularly in regard to property.) When Jefferson changed "property" to "pursuit of happiness," he followed the more inclusive French idealism, and stuck a radical tone. But as Jefferson and his party did not come out for a state interference in the interest of the poor, and as economic protection of the interests of the rich could not be defended on the grounds of English liberalism, the change was not of great importance for the time being. Both schools had their interests focused on political and civil rights. Both schools thought in terms of *defending* the individual, primarily against the state, not *procuring* for him something by means of the state. The contemporary conservatives were actually more interventionist; they wanted, however, to interfere *against* equality. But they did not have philosophical support from either the French or the English school.

In one single direction Jefferson wanted to extend the scope of government—popular education. And there he could also claim the support of both the English and the French philosophical schools of liberalism; both believed in environment as the chief explanation of human differences and, consequently, the chief means of improving mankind. The French interest was, of course, less platonic. But all *liberalism of the Enlightenment was for intervention in this one field of education.* Belief in education became a part of the American Creed and has since then retained its hold upon the mind of the nation. In this field America early assumed world leadership and has held it up to the present time.

[13] Cited by Ernest S. Bates, *American Faith* (1940), pp. 275 ff.

[14] *Ibid.*, p. 9.

[15] Ralph H. Gabriel, *The Course of American Democratic Thought* (1940), p. 37.

[16] Guion G. Johnson, "History of Racial Ideologies," unpublished manuscript prepared for this study (1940), Vol. 1, p. 67.

[17] James Bryce, *The American Commonwealth* (1911; first edition, 1893), Vol. 2, pp. 289 ff.

[18] "The Price of Free World Victory," mimeographed press release from the Office of the Vice-President.

[19] Lord Bryce, for example, wrote: "The Americans are a good-natured people, kindly, helpful to one another, disposed to take a charitable view even of wrongdoers. Their anger sometimes flames up, but the fire is soon extinct." (*Op. cit.*, Vol. 2, p. 285.)

[20] Gabriel, *op. cit.*, p. 406.

[21] "Popular impatience of restraint is aggravated in the United States by political and legal theories of 'natural law.' As a political doctrine, they lead individuals to put into action a conviction that conformity to the dictates of the individual conscience is a test

of the validity of a law. Accordingly, jurors will disregard statutes in perfect good faith, as in the Sunday-closing prosecutions in Chicago in 1908. In the same spirit a well-known preacher wrote not long since that a prime cause of lawlessness was enactment of legislation at variance with the law of nature. In the same spirit a sincere and, as he believed, a law-abiding labor leader declared in a Labor Day address that he would not obey mandates of the courts which deprived him of his natural 'rights.' In the same spirit the business man may regard evasion of statutes which interfere with his carrying on business as he chooses as something entirely legitimate. In the same spirit public officials in recent addresses have commended administrative violation of the legal rights of certain obnoxious persons, and one of the law officers of the federal government has publicly approved of mob violence toward such persons." (Roscoe Pound, *Criminal Justice in the American City—A Summary* [1922], p. 15.)

[22] When the young Thoreau, for example, wrote his *Civil Disobedience* (1849), he only gave an extreme expression for the common American anti-state attitude: the citizen must not "resign his conscience to the legislator"; "law never made men a whit more just."

[23] "The desire to expunge or cure the visible evils of the world is strong. Nowhere are so many philanthropic and reformatory agencies at work. Zeal outruns discretion, outruns the possibilities of the case, in not a few of the efforts made, as well by legislation as by voluntary action, to suppress vice, to prevent intemperance, to purify popular literature." (Bryce, *op. cit.*, Vol. 2, p. 290.)

[24] One example is the establishment of federal income taxation which touches individual interests directly. It is my opinion that the income tax legislation in America is nearly as effective as, for example, it is in Great Britain, and more effective than it was in France. Many of the New Deal measures belong to the same category of fairly successful legislation. The A.A.A. crop restriction and subsidy program as it has been developed has, on the whole, been carried out successfully (whatever one thinks about its value), in spite of the fact that it would have been a strong local interest everywhere to connive in cheating the government.

[25] Pound, *op. cit.*, p. 18.

[26] Donald R. Young, *American Minority Peoples* (1932), p. 224.

[27] Bryce, *op. cit.*, Vol. 2, p. 371.

[28] Quoted from Guion G. Johnson, *op. cit.*, p. 93.

[29] *Race Questions, Provincialism and other American Problems* (1908), p. 111.

[30] Gabriel, *op. cit.*, p. 418.

[31] *Freedom and Culture* (1939), p. 55. Dewey is here referring to the theory of human freedom that was developed in the writings of the philosophers of the American Revolution, particularly in Jefferson's writings.

[32] *Out of the House of Bondage* (1914), pp. 134-135.

Chapter 2. *Encountering the Negro Problem*

[1] It is interesting to note that the first books having the term "sociology" in their titles were almost exclusively concerned with the Negro problem: (1) George Fitzhugh, *Sociology for the South* (1854); (2) Henry Hughes, *Treatise on Sociology: Theoretical and Practical* (1854).

[2] Possible exceptions are a few natural scientists, such as Ernest E. Just, and a few celebrities, such as Joe Louis. But even they, when they reach national top standards, and probably before that, are forced to become representatives of their "race."

George S. Schuyler, a prominent columnist gives the Negro point of view in his recent criticism of the white press for its "sinister policy of identifying Negro individuals as such":

"This is a subtle form of discrimination designed to segregate these individuals in the mind of the public and thus bolster the national polity of bi-racialism. Thus, Paul Robeson is not a great baritone, he is a great 'Negro' baritone. Dr. Carver is not just a great scientist, he is a great 'Negro' scientist. Anne Brown is not merely a great soprano, she is a great 'Negro' soprano. Langston Hughes is not a poet merely, he is a 'Negro' poet. Augusta Savage is a 'Negro' sculptor, C. C. Spaulding is a 'Negro' insurance executive, R. R. Wright, Sr., is a 'Negro' banker, J. A. Rogers is a 'Negro' historian, Willard Townsend is a 'Negro' labor leader, *etc., etc., ad infinitum.* . . . No other group in this country is so singled out for racial identification, and no one can tell me that there is not a very definite reason for it. No daily newspaper refers to Mr. Morgenthau as 'Jewish' Secretary of the Treasury, or New York's Herbert H. Lehman as the 'Jewish' governor, or Isador Lubin as a 'Jewish' New Dealer. Mayor Rossi is never identified as the 'Italian-American' executive of San Francisco, nor is the millionaire Giannini called an 'Italian' banker. There would be considerable uproar if Senator Robert F. Wagner were termed 'New York's able German-American solon,' or Representative Tenerowicz dubbed 'Detroit's prominent Pole.' When has a Utah legislator in Washington been labeled 'Mormon'?

"One could go on and on, but the point is that 'our' daily newspapers carefully avoid such designations except in the case of so-called Negroes. I cannot recall when I have seen a criminal referred to as a Jew, an Italian, a German or a Catholic, but it is commonplace for colored lawbreakers or suspects to be labeled 'Negro.'

"Personally, I shall not be convinced of the sincerity of these white editors and columnists who shape America's thinking unless and until they begin treating the Negro in the news as they do other Americans. Those who continue this type of journalism are the worst sort of hypocrites when they write about democracy and national unity." (Pittsburgh *Courier,* June 13, 1942.)

Schuyler's point is perfectly clear and his description of the situation correct—except that he does not care to mention that Negro newspapers are, if possible, more unfailing in giving prominent Negroes their "race label."

[3] E. R. Embree, *Brown America* (1931), p. 205.

[4] James Weldon Johnson, *The Autobiography of an Ex-Coloured Man* (1927; first edition, 1912), p. 21.

[5] See Edgar G. Murphy, *Problems of the Present South* (1909; first edition, 1904), especially pp. 188 ff. and Chapter 8; also Jonathan Daniels, *A Southerner Discovers the South* (1938), Chapter 35; and Thomas P. Bailey, *Race Orthodoxy in the South* (1914), especially pp. 341 ff., pp. 368 ff. and p. 380, also William Jenkins, *Pro-Slavery Thought in the Old South* (1935), pp. vii-viii.

[6] *Darker Phases of the South* (1924), pp. 157 ff.

[7] *What the Negro Thinks* (1929), p. 55.

[8] *Following the Color Line* (1908), p. 26.

[9] The important problem of opportune distortion of knowledge has been dealt with

by some outstanding writers in American literature. See, for example, William James' two essays: "The Will to Believe" in *The New World: A Quarterly Review of Religion, Ethics, and Theology* (June, 1896), pp. 327-347, and "On a Certain Blindness in Human Beings" in *On Some of Life's Ideals* (1912), pp. 3-46.

[10] *The Souls of Black Folk* (1924; first edition, 1903), p. 186.

[11] *The Story of the Negro*, Vol. 1 (1909), p. 180.

[12] *The Autobiography of an Ex-Coloured Man*, p. 166. Johnson goes on to draw too optimistic conclusions from this statement when he continues: ". . . and a mental attitude, especially one not based on truth, can be changed more easily than actual conditions. That is to say, the burden of the question is not that the whites are struggling to save ten million despondent and moribund people from sinking into a hopeless slough of ignorance, poverty, and barbarity in their very midst, but that they are unwilling to open certain doors of opportunity and to accord certain treatment to ten million aspiring, education-and-property-acquiring people. In a word, the difficulty of the problem is not so much due to the facts presented as to the hypothesis assumed for its solution." (*idem.*)

He overlooks here that the "actual conditions" of the Negroes actually fortify "a mental attitude" on the part of the whites to form a vicious circle, which will constitute the main viewpoint in this book (see Chapter 3, Section 7).

[13] James Weldon Johnson, *Along This Way* (1934), p. 318.

[14] *Op. Cit.*, p. 65.

[15] *Race Orthodoxy in the South* (1914), pp. 37 and 347.

[16] *What the Negro Thinks* (1929), p. 65.

[17] *Negro Americans, What Now?* (1934), p. 101.

[18] *Along This Way*, p. 142.

[19] *America's Tragedy* (1934), p. 72.

[20] The New York *Times* (May 26, 1942), p. 20.

[21] Murphy, *op. cit.*, p. 23.

[22] *American Minority Peoples* (1932), pp. 205-206. The author, thereafter, describes the subsequent disfranchisement, condones the Southern election laws—without any explicit value premises—criticizes the white primary and generally the unfair administration of the laws, leaving the reader, however, with the impression that measures to enforce the Constitution and the state laws are out of the discussion. There is no other interpretation than that such interferences would mean making the Negro "a ward of the nation."

Chapter 3. *Facets of the Negro Problem*

[1] More recently, Donald R. Young has been most outstanding in arguing this restatement of the Negro problem. We quote from him:

"The view here presented is that the problems and principles of race relations are remarkably similar, regardless of what groups are involved; and that only by an integrated study of all minority peoples in the United States can a real understanding and sociological analysis of the involved social phenomena be achieved." (*American Minority Peoples* [1932], pp. xiii-1.)

In explaining the similarities of the deprivations imposed upon different minority groups, Donald R. Young points out that:

"It is . . . to be expected that dominating majorities in various regions, when faced with the problem of what to think and do about minorities, will fail to be sufficiently inventive to create unique schemes of relationships and action. Variations in intensity of restriction and oppression, special techniques in maintaining superior status and other adaptations to the local scene will always be found, but the choice of fundamental patterns of dominance in majority-minority relations is limited by the nature of man and his circumstances." (*Research Memorandum on Minority Peoples in the Depression*, Social Science Research Council, Bulletin No. 31 [1937], pp. 9-10.)

[2] Even a prominent leader of the Ku Klux Klan, whose conservative attitudes on "racial" questions cannot be doubted, expressed to the writer the considered opinion that, in time, not only the Poles, Italians, Russians, Greeks, and Armenians, but also the Turks, Hindus, Jews, and Mexicans would come to be engulfed in the great American nation and disappear as separate, socially visible population segments. But it would take a very, very long time. I have heard this view affirmed by Americans in all social classes and regions of the country.

[3] Young, *Research Memorandum on Minority Peoples in the Depression*, pp. 18-19.

[4] It is the present writer's impression that anti-Semitism, as he observed it in America during the last years before the Second World War, probably was somewhat stronger than in Germany before the Nazi regime.

[5] See Eugene L. Horowitz, "Race Attitudes" in Otto Klineberg (editor), *Characteristics of the American Negro*, prepared for this study, to be published; manuscript pages 115-123 *et passim*.

[6] Robert R. Moton, *What the Negro Thinks* (1929), p. 219.

[7] This is much to be regretted. Indeed, it is urgently desirable that such impressionistic generalizations be critically examined and replaced by statistically verified and precise knowledge. Meanwhile, because of the lack of such studies, the author has simply been compelled to proceed by building up a system of preliminary hypotheses. The defense is that otherwise intelligent questions cannot be raised in those sectors of the Negro problem where statistics or other kinds of substantiated knowledge are not available.

Some attitude studies and public opinion polls have been made which touch on some of the statements presented in hypothetical form in the text. But they were designed to answer other questions and are practically never comprehensive, and so they cannot be used as conclusive proof of our hypotheses. We shall cite some of the relevant ones in footnotes at certain points. For a summary of all the attitude studies (up to 1940) dealing with the Negro, see the monograph prepared for this study by Eugene L. Horowitz, "Race Attitudes" in Klineberg (editor), *Characteristics of the American Negro*.

[8] There are some studies, however, which provide evidence for the hypothesis of the "rank order of discriminations," even if they are not comprehensive enough to serve as conclusive proof. There are a host of attitude studies showing how whites have different attitudes toward Negroes in different spheres of life. Probably the earliest of these studies was that of Emory S. Bogardus, "Race Friendliness and Social Distance," *Journal of Applied Sociology* (1927), pp. 272-287. As an example of such studies which apply solely to Negro issues, we may cite the study by Euri Relle Bolton, "Measuring Specific Attitudes towards the Social Rights of the Negro," *The Journal of Abnormal*

and Social Psychology (January-March, 1937), pp. 384-397. For a summary of other such studies, see Horowitz, *op. cit.*, pp. 123-148.

⁹ Such studies should not only break the rank order into finer distinctions, but also develop a measure of the distance between the ranks in the order. It would, further, be desirable to ascertain individual differences in the apprehension of this rank order, and to relate these differences to age, sex, social class, educational level and region.

¹⁰ This goes far back. Frederick Douglass nearly endangered his position among Negroes by marrying a white woman. About Douglass, Kelly Miller observed: ". . . he has a hold upon the affection of his race, not on account of his second marriage but in spite of it. He seriously affected his standing with his people by that marriage." (Kelly Miller, *Race Adjustment—Essays on the Negro in America* [1908], p. 50.) And W. E. B. Du Bois tells us in his autobiography: "I resented the assumption that we desired it [racial amalgamation]. I frankly refused the possibility while in Germany and even in America gave up courtship with one 'colored' girl because she looked quite white, and I should resent the inference on the street that I had married outside my race." (*Dusk of Dawn* [1940], p. 101.) See also Chapter 30, Section 2.

¹¹ *Op. cit.*, p. 241.

¹² *Ibid.*, p. 239.

¹³ An exception, which by its uniqueness, and by the angry reception it received from the Negroes, rather proves our thesis, is the remarkable book by William H. Thomas, *The American Negro* (1901). The fact that Negroes privately often enjoy indulging in derogatory statements about Negroes in general is not overlooked. It is, however, a suppression phenomenon of quite another order. See Chapter 36, Section 2.

¹⁴ "The rape which your gentlemen have done against helpless black women in defiance of your own laws is written on the foreheads of two millions of mulattoes, and written in ineffaceable blood." (W. E. B. Du Bois, *The Souls of Black Folk* [1924; first edition, 1903], p. 106.)

¹⁵ *Op. cit.*, pp. 208-209.

¹⁶ *Race Adjustment*, p. 48.

¹⁷ *Out of the House of Bondage* (1914), p. 45.

¹⁸ *Op. cit.*, p. 241.

¹⁹ Editorial, *The Crisis* (January, 1920), p. 106.

²⁰ *Up from Slavery* (1915; first edition, 1900), pp. 221-222.

²¹ "The South, after the war, presented the greatest opportunity for a real national labor movement which the nation ever saw or is likely to see for many decades." (*Black Reconstruction* [1935], p. 353 *passim*.)

Chapter 4. *Racial Beliefs*

¹ See, for example: John H. Russell, *The Free Negro in Virginia, 1619-1865* (1913); J. C. Ballagh, *A History of Slavery in Virginia* (1902); John C. Hurd, *The Law of Freedom and Bondage in the United States* (1858-1862).

² A weak variation of this popular theory—weak because it looked forward only to temporary subordination of backward peoples—was that in making the Negroes slaves, white men were educating and Christianizing them. This variation is known as the "white man's burden" doctrine and played an especially important role in nineteenth

century exploitation. For some statements of this doctrine, see W. O. Brown, "Rationalization of Race Prejudice," *The International Journal of Ethics* (April, 1933), pp. 299-301.

[3] H. A. Washington (editor), *The Writings of Thomas Jefferson* (1859), Vol. 1, p. 49.

[4] Letter to Robert Morris, dated April 12, 1786. Jonas Viles (editor), *Letters and Addresses of George Washington* (1908), p. 285.

[5] "Government and the Negro," *Annals of the Academy of Political and Social Science* (November, 1928), p. 99.

[6] This materialistic explanation is not a new idea. It was already seen clearly by some in the *ante-bellum* South. George Fitzhugh, for example, writes:

"Our Southern patriots, at the time of the Revolution, finding negroes expensive and useless, became warm anti-slavery men. We, their wiser sons, having learned to make cotton and sugar, find slavery very useful and profitable, and think it a most excellent institution. We of the South advocate slavery, no doubt, from just as selfish motives as induce the Yankees and English to deprecate it."

The rationalization comes immediately, however:

"We have, however, almost all human and divine authority on our side of the argument. The Bible nowhere condemns, and throughout recognises slavery." (*Sociology for the South* [1854], p. 269.)

[7] Chancellor William Harper, "Memoir on Slavery," paper read before the Society for the Advancement of Learning of South Carolina, annual meeting at Columbia, South Carolina, 1837 (1838), pp. 6-8.

[8] This stress on moral equality has not been lost through the ages. T. J. Woofter, Jr., a representative of modern Southern liberalism, writes:

"It is desirable frankly to recognize the differences as they actually exist, but there is absolutely no ethical justification for the assumption that an advantaged group has an inherent right to exploit and oppress, and the prejudice based upon the assumptions is the most vicious enemy to human peace and cooperation." (*Basis of Racial Adjustment* [1925], p. 11.)

Vance, another Southern liberal, writes:

"In a field where doubts abound, let us make one sweeping statement. If biological inferiority of the whole Negro group were a proved fact, it would, nevertheless, be to the benefit of both white and black to behave as though it did not exist. Only in this way can the Section be sure of securing, in the economic sphere, the best of which both races are capable." (Rupert B. Vance, *Human Geography of the South* [1932], p. 463.)

[9] "Prejudice of any sort, racial or otherwise, is regarded as derogatory to intellectual integrity, incompatible with good taste, and perhaps morally reprehensible. Hence the prejudiced in order to be secure in their illusions of rationality, impeccable taste, and moral correctness find rationalizations essential. The rationalization inoculates against insights as to the real nature of one's reactions. It secures the individual in his moral universe. It satisfies his impulse to rationality. The mind thus becomes an instrument, a hand-maiden, of the emotions, supplying good reasons for prejudiced reactions in the realm of racial, class, or sectarian contacts." (Brown, *op. cit.*, p. 294.)

[10] In this connection it is interesting to note, as an example of how political reaction **fosters racialism**, that in the *ante-bellum* South racial thinking also turned toward **beliefs** in biological differences between whites. The legend was spread that the white

Southerners were a "master race" of Norman blood while New England was settled by descendants of the ancient British and Saxon serfs. The Northerners and Southerners, it was said, "are the same men who cut each other's throats in England, under the name of Roundheads and Cavaliers." The Southerners were a Nordic race with greater capacity to rule. (See James Truslow Adams, *America's Tragedy* [1934], pp. 95 ff, 121, and 128 ff.) A late example of this ideology will be found in a chapter entitled "The Tropic Nordics," of H. J. Eckenrode, *Jefferson Davis, President of the South* (1923). The present writer has on several occasions in conversation with Southerners met vague reminiscences of this popular theory, usually related to the myth that the South, unlike the North, was settled mainly by English aristocrats. The more common theory of Southern racial superiority nowadays is, however, simply the assertion that the white Southerners belong predominantly to "the pure Anglo-Saxon race," as the South has received so few immigrants in recent decades when these were recruited from other European countries. In addition, one often meets the idea that "the poor whites" and generally the lower classes of whites are racially inferior, as they descend from indentured servants.

[11] Guion G. Johnson, "History of Racial Ideologies," unpublished manuscript written for this study (1940). Vol. 1, pp. 149, *passim;* Vol. 2, pp. 331, *passim.*

[12] The same principle operates also outside the Negro problem. The American Creed, in its demand for equality, has strong support from the very composition of the new nation. As immigrants, or the descendants of immigrants with diverse national origins, Americans have an interest—outside of the Negro problem—in emphasizing the importance of environment and in discounting inheritance. In order to give a human and not only political meaning to the legend *e pluribus unum*, they feel the need to believe in the possibility of shaping a new homogeneous nation out of the disparate elements thrown into the melting pot. This interest plays on a high level of valuations where the individual identifies himself with the destiny of the nation. In daily life, however, the actual and obvious heterogeneity in origin, appearance, and culture of the American people acts as a constant stimulus toward prejudiced racial beliefs.

Thus—even outside the Negro problem—there is in America a considerable ambivalence in people's thoughts on race. On a lower valuational level, there appears to be in America an extreme belief in and preoccupation with all sorts of racial differences, while on a higher level a contrary ideology rules, equally extreme when compared with more homogeneous nations. The former side of the American personality is responsible for much friction and racial snobbishness in social life. The latter side finds its expression not only in empty speeches—what the Americans call "lip-service"—but also in national legislation and in actual social trends.

[13] H. A. Washington (editor), *The Writings of Thomas Jefferson* (1854), Vol. 8, pp. 380-381.

[14] *Ibid.,* pp. 380 ff.

[15] 1915.

[16] Concerning this literature, see G. G. Johnson, *op. cit.,* Vol. 1, pp. 149, *passim;* Vol. 2, pp. 250-258 and 311-338.

[17] Much of the earliest literature of this sort is summarized in W. I. Thomas (editor), *Sourcebook for Social Origins* (1909).

[18] The change toward environmentalism in American psychology has been most

radical in child psychology, psychiatry and educational psychology, applied psychology, "social psychology," and other branches which are in close relation to social practice and social science. Undoubtedly the biologistic approach has still a stronghold in academic psychology proper. But even there a change is under way which can be registered by comparing the present situation with the one prevalent two or three decades ago. An indication is the almost complete abandonment of the "instinct" psychology.

[19] This connection between biology and conservatism will have to be remembered when explaining why, with some outstanding exceptions, the medical profession has, on the whole, in all countries, taken a rather reactionary stand on questions of social and health reforms.

[20] Perhaps the most influential of the popular racialistic writers were: Madison Grant, *The Passing of the Great Race* (1916); Lothrop Stoddard, *The Rising Tide of Color* (1920); Charles W. Gould, *America, A Family Matter* (1920).

[21] The acts restricting immigration not only cut down the total number of immigrants admitted to the country, but also provided that those allowed entrance should be predominantly from Western and Northern Europe. The 1921 act permitted an immigration from each country equal to 3 per cent of the number of foreign-born from that country resident in the United States in 1910. The 1924 act reduced the quota to 2 per cent and set the determining date back to 1890. Immigration from the Orient was completely prohibited, but that from independent countries in the Americas and from Canada was not restricted at all.

[22] As examples we may cite the following: Carl C. Brigham, an outstanding psychologist who has since repudiated his book (*A Study of American Intelligence* [1923]); William McDougall, the father of many trends in psychology (*The Group Mind* [1920], and *Is America Safe for Democracy?* [1921]); Albert Bushnell Hart and H. H. Bancroft, the eminent historians (*The Southern South* [1910], and *Retrospection, Political and Personal* [1912]).

[23] William H. Thomas, a Northern mulatto who went down to the South during Reconstruction and became disillusioned, is an exception. His vitriolic but well-written book, *The American Negro* (1901), has, indeed, its best counterparts in some of the extreme expressions of anti-Semitism which, as is well known, are to be found in occasional writings by Jews.

[24] Kelly Miller, *Out of the House of Bondage* (1914), pp. 221-222.

[25] *Ibid.*, pp. 220-221.

[26] Kelly Miller, *Race Adjustment—Essays on the Negro in America* (1908), pp. 38-39.

[27] *Ibid.*, p. 40.

[28] *Ibid.*, p. 45.

[29] *Ibid.*, p. 40.

[30] *Ibid.*, p. 31.

[31] Frederick Douglass, one of the first Negro leaders, thus argued the case against the race inferiority doctrine:

"It is not necessary, in order to establish the manhood of any one making the claim, to prove that such an one equals Clay in eloquence, or Webster and Calhoun in logical force and directness; for, tried by such standards of mental power as these, it is apprehended that very few could claim the high designation of *man*. Yet something like this folly is seen in the arguments directed against the humanity of the negro. His faculties and powers, uneducated and unimproved, have been contrasted with those of the highest cultivation; and the world has then been called upon to behold the immense and amazing difference between the man admitted, and the man disputed. The fact that these intellects, so powerful and so controlling, are almost, if not quite, as exceptional to the general rule of humanity, in one direction, as the specimen negroes are in the other, is quite overlooked." ("The Claims of the Negro," an Address before the Literary Societies of Western Reserve College at Commencement, July 12, 1854 [1854], pp. 7-8.)

And again:

"We all know, at any rate, that now, what constitutes the very heart of the civilized world—(I allude to England)—has only risen from barbarism to its present lofty eminence, through successive invasions and alliances with her people." (*Ibid.*, p. 33.)

Booker T. Washington pointed out that:

"The Negro is behind the white man because he has not had the same chances, and not from any inherent difference in his nature or desires." (*The Future of the American Negro* [1902], p. 26.)

One of the most brilliant of the early discussions of the biological equality of whites and Negroes is that of a Negro doctor, C. V. Roman (*American Civilization and the Negro* [1916], especially pp. 42-45 and pp. 321-351).

For a similar statement from one of the older leaders, see the answer of T. Thomas Fortune, editor of the New York *Age*, to the speech of W. H. Baldwin, "The Present Problems of Negro Education" (*Proceedings of the American Social Science Association* in *The Journal of Social Science* [1900], pp. 65-66.)

[32] W. E. B. Du Bois, *Black Reconstruction* (1935), Foreword.

[33] For some evidence on this point, see Charles H. Wesley, "The Concept of Negro Inferiority in American Thought," *The Journal of Negro History* (October, 1940), pp. 540-560.

[34] W. E. B. Du Bois, *The Philadelphia Negro*, University of Pennsylvania series in Political Economy and Public Law, No. 14 (1899).

[35] Howard W. Odum, *Social and Mental Traits of the Negro* (1910). For a discussion of Odum's retraction, see Buell G. Gallagher, *American Caste and the Negro College* (1938), pp. 178-179. Brigham repudiated his book (*A Study of American Intelligence* [1923]) in a later article. ("Intelligence Tests of Immigrant Groups," *Psychological Review* [March, 1930], pp. 158-165.) See also Chapter 6, Section 3.

[36] The reader may, for instance, compare the tone in Professor E. B. Reuter's first book, *The Mulatto in the United States* (1918), and particularly its last chapter, with the liberal and nearly warm treatment of the Negro people in his last book, *The American Race Problem* (1938; first edition, 1927).

[37] Reuter, *The Mulatto in the United States*, pp. 99-100.

[38] Edward K. Strong, *The Second-Generation Japanese Problem* (1934), p. 100. The classic statement on the difference between categoric and sympathetic contacts is that of Nathaniel S. Shaler, *The Neighbor* (1904), pp. 207-227.

[39] The tendencies of unsophisticated thinking to be "theoretical" are worthy of much more study than they have been given hitherto. They can be illustrated from all spheres of human life. To give an example outside our problem: The most human concept, *bona fide*, in jurisprudence is a late juristical development in all civilizations; originally legal systems are formalistic and behavioristic (they do not consider people's

intentions); *bona fide* is even today only the trained lawyer's way of thinking and has, as yet, never and nowhere really been understood by the mass of laymen whose thinking on legal matters always seems formalistic to the lawyer. Similarly the simple "economic laws" are thought-forms adhered to by business people when they speculate in this strange field, while the economic theorists, instead, devote their labor to criticising, demolishing, and complicating economic theory. It is the common man, *and not the statistician who* "thinks in averages," or, rather, in pairs of *contrasting types:* good-bad, healthy-sick, man-woman, white-black. And the common man is likely to handle averages and types as if they applied to the individuals. He will confidently tell you something about "all Negroes," in the same breath as he observes an exception.

He is, further, likely to construct his types without a thought as to sampling difficulties. He has a tendency to forget about range and spread. He has, of course, a pragmatic understanding that things and happenings have their causes. Otherwise he would not be able to get on with his several pursuits in a rational way. But particularly when it comes to social questions, causation becomes to the untrained mind divested of complications. Social causation is to him mostly monistic, direct, apparent and simple. The very idea of causal interrelations within a mutually dependent system of a great many factors is usually entirely absent. In his thoughts on social causation he mingles his ideas about what is right and wrong. The unsophisticated mind is not questioning; it answers questions before they are stated.

Generally speaking, it is a fact that "to think in concrete terms" when reaching for generalizations is the endeavor of theoretical training and a mark of the highest intelligence, while "theoretical," abstract and formalistic thinking is the common man's philosophy.

⁴⁰ Stoddard, *op. cit.*, pp. 91-92.

⁴¹ *Ibid.*, pp. 100-102.

⁴² Lewis C. Copeland, "The Negro as a Contrast Conception" in Edgar T. Thompson (editor), *Race Relations and the Race Problem* (1939), pp. 152-179.

⁴³ Like other beliefs of the white man, this one, too, is to some extent taken over by the Negro group, particularly by the mulattoes. (See Chapter 32, Section 6.)

"All the stigmas of the Negro group, as previously mentioned, are associated with physical appearance; and it is the black Negro who is regarded as mean, ignorant, primitive, and animal-like. The light-colored Negro, however, is conceived of as 'smarter,' more intelligent, more 'civilized' (more 'like the whites' in behavior and ability). These beliefs are not restricted to either group but are frequently expressed by both Negroes and whites. Sometimes the comment of Negroes is very extreme, as in the case of two Negroes overheard discussing 'blackness.' One of them said: 'A black nigguh is the meanes' rascal God evah made! I mean it. A black nigguh is jes' natchally mean. He always suspects you of trying to beat him out of something or take something from him.' His companion corroborated his opinion: '. . . My grandmother wuz uh little black woman, an' she wuz one of the evilest black women God evah made! Dat's de truth. He's right about dat. Dey really evil!' Cases were known where light-skinned grandparents trained their children to condemn a black parent, the child saying of her mother: 'Oh, she's black!'" (Allison Davis, Burleigh B. Gardner, and Mary R. Gardner, *Deep South* [1941], pp. 40-41.)

⁴⁴ The following brief autobiography, describing the growth of racial beliefs and their relation to segregation, is taken, in full, from the Preface to a master's thesis by

a white Southerner. The author has unusual insight, even for one who has abandoned his racial beliefs. "It was less than a year ago when I saw for the first time in my life a Negro newspaper. Before that time I had not known that Negroes had papers of their own. They were not to be seen in the places I frequented, though I often went as a boy into the homes of Negro tenants. I do not believe I ever heard one of the Negroes that I then knew say, I read thus and so in the newspaper. If they read at all, it was not of their reading that they talked to white folks.

"I was in college before I read a book written by a Negro. I had been to Negro churches and heard their preachers. Probably the first singing I ever heard was that of Negroes. But I had never associated them with writing, or very much with reading. Those were things, like our Boy Scout troop and school picnics, in which they had no part. I remember the surprise I felt at finding DuBois' *Soul of the Black Folk*, my first contact with Negro writing, not different in outward respects from other books I had read. I don't know what I expected Negro writing to look like; certainly I knew that it would not be white ink on black paper. But I did feel that there would be something physical to show that *this* was done by a Negro. The Negroes that I knew worked in the cotton fields. Around the towns they did all kinds of odd jobs, for small pay. The women washed and cooked and kept house for the white folks. None of them wrote anything that I knew of.

"There must have been more Negroes in the little South Georgia community in which I grew up than whites, for though there were only three or four white boys in the group with which I used to play, there were a half dozen or more Negroes. We did chores together there on the farm, and went ' 'possum huntin' ' and to the swimming hole down on the creek and played ball and did all of those things that boys do in rural Georgia.

"We did them together, and yet the Negroes were always a little apart. If we were swimming, they kept downstream. If we were playing ball, they were in the outfield and we did the batting. If we were gathering plums, the Negroes always left us the best bushes. There was no ill feeling in this. Negroes were different. They knew it, and we knew it. In the fields we all drank from the same jug, but at the pump the Negroes cupped their hands and drank from them and would never have dared to use the cup hanging there. I never knew a Negro to come to the front door of my home, and I am sure that if one had done so, someone would have asked him if he minded stepping around to the back. At the age of ten I understood full well that the Negro had to be kept in his place, and I was resigned to my part in that general responsibility.

"As we grew to adolescence, the relationship with Negro boys became less intimate. We began then to talk of things which the Negro could not understand—of what we were going to do in life, of our little love affairs, of school life, of our hopes for the future. In such things the Negro had no part, and gradually we played together less and less. We were more often with grown Negroes, and I think now that we were always closer to the men than we were to the boys of our own age. They knew where rabbits were, how to tell when a dog had treed, when the wind was too high for squirrels to stir, where it was best to set a trap. I don't know how Southern white boys on the farm would learn anything without Negroes. And they sang a lot too and strummed guitars and were almost always in good humor. They never talked very much about their own affairs, and they never told things on other Negroes. I have never known a Negro to lead a white boy into anything vicious. I knew some of these old Negroes well, after a fashion, and they were in their way good people. They were friends of mine, and still are; and when I go back into my home community, I always look up those whom I knew best. I call them by their first names, as I always have; and they call me 'Mister,' as they always have; and I know that they are glad to see me.

"But they were not like white people. There was a difference that we all recognized. It was to be expected that a Negro would steal a little now and then, not anything of consequence, of course, but petty things: watermelons, sugar cane, fresh meat, and things like that, and now and then a little corn for his shoat. It was a common saying with us that a Negro who wouldn't steal had gold toe-nails. An old Negro cobbler in my home town once said to me: 'That boy workin' for me just ain't no good. I treats him well and gives him a chance to steal a little, and he just don't do nothin' but trifle.' I think all of us must have figured that a little stealing was a part of the wage. Eight dollars a month was considered a fair price for farm help, with a house and some food furnished. Good Negroes were those who knew what not to steal. Stealing food and stealing money may be the same crime in that great chart of the good and the bad, but I have known Negroes who would lift a gallon of syrup without a scruple, and yet they could be trusted implicitly in the house with money and personal effects lying around.

"Their moral codes were different from ours. I don't know that it ever occurred to any of us that a Negro girl was capable of virtue. White men had no hesitation in approaching Negro women. I do not know how often they met with refusal, but I do know that an intimate relationship between white men and Negro women was not uncommon. It is my belief that practically no children and very little disease resulted from this relationship, owing to the general knowledge of preventives that has penetrated even into rural Georgia. The better whites were much opposed to this intimacy, though white boys talked freely with one another of their experiences. Those who did not discontinue the practice when they were older, and they were few, became more reticent. Many Negroes keenly resented this intercourse with whites. An old Negro man once offered this as an explanation of the Negroes leaving the farm in such numbers and going to the city. 'Our women,' he said, 'have no protection against low-down white men in the country and in small towns.'

"I have always understood that a Negro who touches a white woman must die. It is something that we learn in the South without knowing how or when or where. I have heard the statement made by men in the community who were models of right living. Somewhere out of the past this idea came, born of pride in our own culture and possibly of an unrecognized fear that it might not persist. It was intensified by the chivalric ideal of womanhood which has been traditional in the South. In the aftermath of the Civil War the motto of those who rode with the Ku Klux Klan was the protection of Southern womanhood. Whatever might be the law, however courts might rule, whatever amendments might be added to the constitution, the Negro must be kept in his place. It might have been seen even then that most of those Negroes who were lynched were not charged with attempts to assault white women, and that many of those who were so charged were not clearly proved to be guilty. It might have been seen that what claimed to be a defense of white womanhood was more often than not merely a riot of race antagonism, brought into existence by rumors and swept along by a kind of fear. We used to talk a great deal of that race war which was coming, when black and yellows would unite and meet the scorn of whites with violence. It was one of our favorite topics of conversation. It may have been no more than boyish prattling, and now that I can see how foolish is the thought, I wonder that we talked of it at all. But we had it from our elders. They taught us early to keep the Negro in his place, whatever the cost might be.

"I'll never forget one of my first lessons. It was on a very quiet Sunday afternoon, and a group of white boys were lying on the grass beside the road eating peaches. One of the boys was a good deal older than the rest of us, and we looked to him as a leader. I think it was he who made some suggestive remarks to a Negro girl who passed along the road, and certainly it was he who stood up to answer a young Negro man who came to protest when the girl told him what had happened. I think the girl would have been more flattered than annoyed had the remarks been addressed to her privately, for she was a bad sort; but there on the road in the presence of us all, she resented it. The Negro man was mad, and he said more than I have ever heard a Negro say in defense of his women, or for any other cause. We all knew him, and it was not the first time that he had shown a disposition to argue with white folks. Our leader said nothing for a few minutes, and then he walked slowly up to my house, which was not far away, and came back with a shotgun. The Negro went away, and as the white boy lay down beside us and began eating peaches again, he remarked, 'You have to know how to handle Negroes.' I knew then, on that quiet Sunday afternoon almost twenty years ago, and I know now, that he was ready to use that gun, if it were necessary, to keep a Negro in his place. Such incidents were not common, and few white boys would have done a thing like that. But still that was one way.

"I am looking back to the things that I knew. In cities perhaps it was different. It may be a little different in the country now, though I don't think there has been much change. I have known Negroes who were happy, despite poverty and squalid surroundings. I have known whites who were miserable, despite wealth and culture of a kind. Old Negroes have told me, most any kind of Negro gets more out of life any day than a real, high-class white man; and I believe them. We say here in the South that we know the Negro. We believe that we have found for him a place in our culture. Education and the passing of years may change everything, but I know that there are in my community now many white people who will die perpetuating the order as they found it, the scheme of things to which they belong." (Rollin Chambliss, *What Negro Newspapers of Georgia Say about Some Social Problems, 1933*, published thesis submitted in partial fulfillment of requirements for Master's Degree, University of Georgia [1934], pp. 4-8.)

[45] The independent role of the author should not be exaggerated. James Weldon Johnson writes:

"The greater part of white America thinks of us in stereotypes; most of these stereotypes coming to them second-hand by way of the representation of Negro life and character on the stage and in certain books. In the main they are exaggerated, false, and entirely unlike our real selves." (*Negro Americans, What Now?* [1934], p. 52.)

Against this opinion, which is common among intellectual Negroes, it should be pointed out that ordinarily the stereotypes are already in the white society, and that their appearance in the literature is derived rather than *vice versa*. But the latter fix and sometimes magnify the former. This is true in the South. In the North, and particularly in those regions where personal relations to Negroes are scarce or totally absent, Johnson is probably more right: there the literary representations build up the stereotypes. And in the *practical* problem of strategy it is possible to think of fiction as a destroyer of racial stereotypes. The fiction writers are intellectuals, and it is more possible to expose them to modern scientific knowledge than the average reading public. Their resistance is, however, rooted in their interest in keeping their market. People want to meet their stereotyped beliefs in the books they buy.

[46] Sterling A. Brown is the author of a paper "Negro Character as Seen by White Authors," from which we quote:

"The Negro has met with as great injustice in American literature as he has in American life. The majority of books about Negroes merely stereotype Negro character. . . . Those considered important enough for separate classification, although overlappings *do* occur, are seven in number: (1) The Contented Slave, (2) The Wretched Freeman, (3) The Comic Negro, (4) The Brute Negro, (5) The Tragic Mulatto, (6) The Local Color Negro, and (7) The Exotic Primitive.

"A detailed evaluation of each of these is impracticable because of limitations of space. It can be said, however, that all of these stereotypes are marked either by exaggeration or omissions; that they all agree in stressing the Negro's divergence from an Anglo-Saxon norm to the flattery of the latter; they could all be used, as they probably are, as justification of racial proscription; they all illustrate dangerous specious generalizing from a few particulars recorded by a single observer from a restricted point of view—which is itself generally dictated by the desire to perpetuate a stereotype.

"All of these stereotypes are abundantly to be found in American literature, and are generally accepted as contributions to true racial understanding. Thus one critic, setting out imposingly to discuss 'The Negro character' in American literature, can still say, unabashedly, that '*the whole range of the Negro character is revealed thoroughly*' in one twenty-six line sketch by Joel Chandler Harris of Br'er Fox and Br'er Mud Turtle." (*Journal of Negro Education* [April, 1933], p. 180.) Sterling Brown's reference is to John H. Nelson, *The Negro Character in American Literature* (1926), p. 118. This article was expanded by Brown and published in pamphlet form: *The Negro in American Fiction* (1937).

Just to exemplify the type of prejudice transferred by good nonmalicious fiction, a few paragraphs may be quoted from Booth Tarkington's *Penrod*, first published serially in various magazines and later as a book, in several editions from 1913 on (italics ours). The book has been read by a great proportion of all American boys year after year. Its hero is a twelve-year-old middle class white boy living in a middle-sized Midwestern town. The Negro boys in the story, Herman and Verman (the names themselves are significant), live in an alley near Penrod's home. They are having a fight with a white man, Rupe Collins.

"Expressing vocally his indignation and the extremity of his pained surprise, Mr. Collins stepped backward, holding his left hand over his nose, and striking at Herman with his right. Then Verman hit him with the rake.

"Verman struck from behind. He struck as hard as he could. *And he struck with the tines down. For in his simple, direct African way he wished to kill his enemy, and he wished to kill him as soon as possible. That was his single, earnest purpose.*

"On this account, Rupe Collins was peculiarly unfortunate. He was plucky and he enjoyed conflict, but neither his ambitions nor his anticipations had ever included murder. *He had not learned that an habitually aggressive person runs the danger of colliding with beings in one of those lower stages of evolution wherein theories about 'hitting below the belt' have not yet made their appearance. . . .*

"*The struggle increased in primitive simplicity:* Time and again the howling Rupe got to his knees only to go down again as the earnest brothers, in their own way, assisted him to a more reclining position. *Primal forces operated here, and the two blanched, slightly higher products of evolution,* Sam and Penrod, no more thought of interfering than they would have thought of interfering with an earthquake."

[47] *Op. cit.,* pp. 52-53.

[48] W. E. B. Du Bois, *The Souls of Black Folk* (1903), p. 89.

[49] Quoted from Willis D. Weatherford and Charles S. Johnson, *Race Relations* (1934), p. 235. See, also, James Weldon Johnson, *Black Manhattan* (1930), pp. 244-245.

[50] "A careful observation of negro schools, churches and miscellaneous gatherings in all parts of the country convinces the writer that fully three-fourths of the rising generation of the race have some traceable measure of white blood in their veins." (Miller, *Out of the House of Bondage,* p. 58.)

[51] Reuter, *The Mulatto in the United States.*

[52] "One thing is certain: where defense is needed as a result of actions unethical in the light of a personally accepted standard, defensive beliefs will arise." (John Dollard, *Caste and Class in a Southern Town* [1937], p. 388.)

[53] Donald R. Young, *American Minority Peoples* (1932), p. 401.

[54] Ruth Benedict, *Race: Science and Politics* (1940), p. 237.

[55] There have been many studies of the type of racial beliefs held and of the extent to which they are held, but few attempts to show their relation to the functioning of society. An example of a study of the types of racial beliefs is: Bertram Wilbur Doyle, "Racial Traits of the Negro as Negroes Assign Them to Themselves," unpublished master's thesis, University of Chicago (1924). An example of a study of the extent to which racial beliefs are held is: Daniel Katz and Kenneth Braly, "Racial Stereotypes of One Hundred College Students," *Journal of Abnormal and Social Psychology* (1933), pp. 280-290. Much of the attitude measurement research comes under this rubric. An example of functional studies of beliefs—though not racial beliefs and so outside the scope of the present chapter—is Samuel M. Strong, "The Social Type Method: Social Types in the Negro Community of Chicago," unpublished Ph.D. thesis, University of Chicago (1940). W. O. Brown's and Copeland's previously cited studies also belong in this category.

[56] Some recent community studies carried out with a primary psychological interest in people's beliefs have given a vision of the field to be mapped. Dollard's *Caste and Class in a Southern Town* is particularly suggestive of what might be done.

[57] Among the things we want to know are: What do people mean by "race" in reference to the Negro people? To what extent do they allow for influence of environmental factors? How do they relate those factors to the race and to the individual, respectively? What is their idea about the manner in which education, better housing conditions, better nutrition, and so forth, "improve"—or "spoil"—the Negroes. To what extent and how do people allow for individual exceptions from their racial beliefs? Do they believe that all Negroes are worse than all whites, and, if so, in what specific sense? How, more specifically, do they "think in averages"? and in contrast types? What are people's ideas as to the effect of cross-breeding upon the offspring? What specific beliefs are held concerning diverse bodily, intellectual, and moral Negro traits? How are they coordinated in systems of beliefs? How are they coordinated with people's religious faith

and the American Creed? What evidence do people find for their beliefs? How do people feel their own beliefs related to tradition and community consensus? Do people recognize an irrational element in their beliefs, and how do they account for this element? Do people ever sense the opportunistic character of their beliefs? Do people know anything about results of recent research rejecting the racial beliefs or showing that they are without substantiation? What is their reaction to these endeavors of scientific research? What is their reaction to attempts to spread scientific knowledge on racial matters? In all these respects, we want to have the spheres of beliefs recorded for white individuals in different regions of the country, different social and economic classes, on different levels of education, in different age groups, and in the two sexes. We also want to know the beliefs among the Negro people.

Chapter 5. *Race and Ancestry*

[1] James Bryce, *The American Commonwealth*, Vol. 2 (1910; first edition, 1893), p. 555.

[2] Laws defining a Negro vary from state to state and even differ within a single state depending upon the purpose of the law. The most common of these laws are those which define a Negro for the purpose of excluding him from marriage with whites and from going to white schools. Since Northern states east of the Mississippi River do not prohibit intermarriage (except Indiana) and since they have no enforced segregation in public institutions, they have no definition of a Negro in law. Before and during the Civil War such laws existed in some of these Northern states so that the present situation represents a liberal trend in the law. The opposite trend has occurred in the West and South. The West has no Jim Crow laws, but it has enacted vigorous prohibitions against intermarriage. Among all the non-Southern states west of the Mississippi River, only Minnesota, Iowa, Kansas, New Mexico, and Washington now have no such law. Many of the Western states with prohibitions against intermarriage define a Negro as anyone known to have any Negro ancestry whatsoever and have a heavy punishment for violations of the law. Since Southern states have a whole series of legal prohibitions for Negroes, it is common for them to have conflicting definitions of Negroes. (See George S. Schuyler, "Who is 'Negro'? Who is 'White'?" *Common Ground* [Autumn, 1940], pp. 54-55.) It would seem as though the Jim Crow laws were the most drastic since they prohibit persons with the slightest amount of Negro ancestry from using facilities and institutions for whites. The laws against intermarriage are often more liberal, since they permit a person with up to one-eighth Negro blood to be called "white." It is probable, however, that in practice the liberality of these two types of legal restrictions is reversed. Too, there has been a definite trend since Reconstruction to increase the number of situations where Negroes are so defined in law and to broaden the definition of a Negro: states that were formerly content to adopt a rule of one-quarter, one-eighth, or one-sixteenth Negro blood have increasingly tended to diminish the amount of Negro blood that will define a person as a Negro. There is little, if any, differential in law between states of the Deep South and Border, although there may be some differential in practice.

For collections of laws defining Negroes see: (1) Charles S. Mangum, Jr., *The Legal Status of the Negro* (1940), Chapter 1; (2) Louis Wirth and Herbert Goldhamer,

"The Hybrid and the Problem of Miscegenation" in Otto Klineberg, (editor), *Characteristics of the American Negro*, prepared for this study; to be published; manuscript pages 160-162.

[3] A white person, particularly if he has a high status in society, may, in some places and under certain circumstances, be known to have a small amount of Negro blood and yet not lose caste. It must not be made notorious, however; it must not be put on record. And even to this last statement the observer of the American caste system finds curious exceptions, particularly in the old Mother Colony of Virginia and in Louisiana. These and other minor filigree-works on the dominant social pattern are here left out of account.

[4] Sir Harry H. Johnston, *The Negro in the New World* (1910) p. 413.

[5] Madison Grant, *The Passing of the Great Race* (1924; first edition, 1916), pp. 17-18.

[6] Edwin R. Embree, *Brown America* (1933; first edition, 1931), p. 31.

[7] The primary scientific meaning of "race" seems to be ethnological and to refer to a common and distinct ancestry. When population groups live in isolation from each other, the cumulated effects of mutations, combinations, and natural selections in adaptation to the environment produce different genetic constitutions in the groups, expressing themselves in different traits which are more or less common to all the members of each group and which are transmitted by heredity. These traits can then be used for classifying the groups. Such model conditions have rarely existed on earth. If we give up the demand that a racial group should be homogeneous, however, there seems to be a rather common agreement among ethnologists that nearly all mankind can be classified into three major stocks: the Caucasoid, the Mongoloid, and the Negroid peoples. These correspond roughly to the popular division of mankind into White, Yellow, and Brown. The three groups

". . . represent some considerable degree of adaptation to the conditions of the environment. The dark skin, which characterizes most of the peoples living near the tropics, is almost certainly the result of the elimination by natural selection of the fairer types of pigmentation less fitted to afford protection against the actinic rays of the sun. The greater number of sweat glands in the Negro and the reduction of their number among the yellow-skinned peoples, are probably adaptations to hot and to dry conditions respectively. Similarly the striking variations in the breadth of the nose according to latitude may be adaptively perpetuated through natural selection. A white skin is a disadvantage in the Tropics and a wide nostril in the Arctic." (Julian S. Huxley and A. C. Haddon, *We Europeans* [1935], p. 58.)

The major criteria of race mean that two average Caucasoids have more ancestors in common than a Caucasoid and a Negroid, and also that a typical white man is very different from a typical Chinese or a typical Negro. But all variations exist within and between the typical representatives of each group. The isolation has not been complete, and crossing has been widespread through history and pre-history. If it is thus difficult to draw sharp lines of distinction between the major groups, it is still more so within these groups. Migration and hybridization have been going on all the time through the ages and all the national "races" within the three major stocks are the result of extensive hybridization.

[8] If we use Herskovits' sample, and if we further assume that a person who said he was of mixed blood but was more Negro than white is, on the average, 75 per cent Negro, that a person who said he was about half Negro and half white is, on the average,

50 per cent Negro, and that a person who said he was more white than Negro is, on the average, 25 per cent Negro—if we make all these assumptions—the proportion of African Negro ancestors of all ancestors back to any given time is roughly two-thirds. The computations are based on the figures presented on p. 177 of Melville J. Herskovits' *The Anthropometry of the American Negro* (1930).

Of	342 N*	persons,	100 per cent of the ancestors, or in proportion to the total persons	342.00	are assumed to be pure Negro
"	97 NI	"	100	"	97.00	"
"	384 NNW	"	75	"	288.00	"
"	106 NNW(I)	"	75	"	79.50	"
"	260 NW	"	50	"	130.00	"
"	133 NW(I)	"	50	"	66.50	"
"	154 NWW	"	25	"	38.50	"
"	75 NWW(I)	"	25	"	18.75	"
Total 1551					1060.25	

* In the table, N stands for Negro, W for white, I for Indian. Two N's indicate a preponderance of Negro ancestry; two W's indicate a preponderance of white ancestry; an I in parentheses indicates an unknown amount of Indian ancestry.

Since the proportion $\dfrac{1060}{1551}$ neglects the unknown proportion of Caucasoid blood inserted before the Negroes came to the United States, we may reduce the proportion Negro to 2/3. However, in spite of Herskovits' valiant efforts to test the representative-ness of his sample, it undoubtedly contains too many upper class Negroes who have more white ancestry than the average Negro. (See footnote 41 in this chapter.) On the other hand, the persons interviewed by Herskovits may not have known about some of their white ancestry, and, in addition, Indian ancestry is not accounted for in our cal-culation. These counteracting errors must, to some extent, neutralize each other and the proportion of African ancestors is perhaps not too far away from 2/3. As we do not know the magnitude of the errors, the figure should not be taken to be more than our best guess based upon significantly inadequate data.

[9] Most states, including the Southern ones, had laws prohibiting slave importations before 1808, but little attempt was made to enforce them—except in the North where slavery itself was prohibited during and after the Revolutionary War. For the laws, see John Codman Hurd, *The Law of Freedom and Bondage in the United States*, Vol. 2 (1858-1862), p. 2, *passim*.

[10] U. S. Bureau of the Census, *A Century of Population Growth in the United States: 1790-1900*, p. 91.

[11] Melville J. Herskovits, "Social History of the Negro," in C. Murchison (editor), *A Handbook of Social Psychology* (1935), p. 236.

[12] Louis I. Dublin, *Health and Wealth* (1928), p. 256.

[13] The facts in this paragraph on the distribution of the peoples of Africa have been taken from Herskovits, "Social History of the Negro" in *op. cit.*, pp. 207-267.

[14] This sentence should not be taken to imply that the population of Africa is any more homogeneous today.

[15] Evidence as to the geographic homelands of the slaves is summarized in Melville J. Herskovits, "On the Provenience of the New World Negroes," *Social Forces* (Decem-

ber, 1933), pp. 247-262. In addition to this source, we have relied for this paragraph of the text on three memoranda prepared for this study: Melville J. Herskovits, *The Myth of the Negro Past* (1941); Wirth and Goldhamer, *op. cit.*, manuscript pages 6-16; and M. F. Ashley Montagu, "The Origin, Composition, and Physical Characteristics of the American Negro Population," unpublished manuscript (1940), pp. 8-20.

[16] Herskovits (*The Myth of the Negro Past*, pp. 43-53) summarizes the statistical evidence to date on the geographical location in Africa from which the slaves came. His chief sources are two publications by Elizabeth Donnan: "The Slave Trade into South Carolina before the Revolution," *American Historical Review* (1927-1928), pp. 804-828, and "Documents Illustrative of the Slave Trade to America," *Carnegie Institution Publication*, No. 409, Vols. 1-4 (1930-1935). There is a wealth of material in these sources and in others cited by Herskovits, but the statistical proportions cannot be accepted as exact because data are available for only a sample of slaves whose representativeness is not known. The verbal statement in the text, which agrees substantially with Herskovits' conclusion, is, therefore, not more reliable but also not less accurate than the detailed statistical data given.

[17] When the high reproduction rate is taken into account—always increasing the relative importance for genetic composition of a population element in some proportion to its length of domicile in this country—the fact that there was an even greater preponderance of West African slave stock in earlier importation must raise its importance even above its simple aggregate numerical weight.

[18] For discussions of race intermixture in the West Indies see: Matthew G. Lewis, *Journal of a West India Proprietor 1815-17* (1929), pp. 73 and 144; Edward B. Underhill, *The West Indies* (1862), p. 225; W. J. Gardner, *A History of Jamaica* (revised edition, 1909), p. 165; George Pinckard, *Notes on the West Indies* (1816), Vol. 1, pp. 114-118, Vol. 2, pp. 136-137, 328, and 531; Robert T. Hill, *Cuba and Porto Rico with the Other Islands of the West Indies* (1898), pp. 164-169, 226-227, 290 and 311; J. Stewart, *A View of the Past and Present State of the Island of Jamaica* (1823), Chapter 15; E. Goulburn Sinckler, *The Barbados Handbook* (1914), p. 44; Ludwell Lee Montague, *Haiti and the United States 1714-1938* (1940), pp. 4-6; Zora Neale Hurston, *Tell My Horse* (1938), pp. 16-21; *Puerto Rico, American Guide Series* (1940), p. 110; J. Antonio Jarvis, *Brief History of the Virgin Islands* (1938), pp. 44-45, 49, 188-189, and 200-201; George Milton Fowles, *Down in Porto Rico* (1910; first edition, 1906), pp. 60-61 and 96; George Mannington, *The West Indies* (1930; first edition, 1925), pp. 71, 129 and 239-241; James G. Leyburn, *The Haitian People* (1941), pp. 3, 16, 177-179 and 189.

[19] Clyde V. Kiser, "Fertility of Harlem Negroes," *Milbank Memorial Fund Quarterly* (July, 1935), pp. 273-284.

[20] The evidence on the subjects discussed in this paragraph is summarized in Herskovits, *The Myth of the Negro Past*, pp. 293-294. For a discussion of the extent to which slaves sought to escape into free territory, see: Henrietta Buckmaster, *Let My People Go* (1941).

[21] Citations may be made to illustrate these two extreme positions on the extent of mortality during passage. Evidence cited by Willis D. Weatherford and Charles S. Johnson (*Race Relations* [1934], pp. 274-275) supports the position of high mortality: "The physical effects of slavery are often overlooked or understressed because, in certain significant respects, they are more closely related to the commercial than to the

social aspects of the slavery system. Nevertheless, if there is any value in physical selection and survival, there is perhaps no more sensitive example of this in history than the
cold and almost organic selection for which the slave trade was responsible. For every
slave introduced into the routine of the American slave system, from two to five died
or were killed on the way. Thomas F. Buxton estimates that for every slave landed safely
on a plantation five were lost, and he is supported in this estimate by Normal Leys.

"The African slave trade was aided by the intertribal warfare which kept numerous
slaves in the possession of tribes. As the trade became widespread and highly profitable,
there were deliberate slave raids which entailed great loss of life. The march to the coast,
hunger, the harsh measures of the slave drivers, the exposure to contagion in the close
quarters of the slave barracoons, and the horrors of the notorious middle passage, the long
ocean voyage on which the victims were packed close in the foul and unsanitary holds
of the slave ships, resulted in an excessively high toll. It has been estimated that the mortality on the journey from the interior to the coast amounted to five-twelfths of the entire
number captured. Since no careful records were kept, this may be an extreme figure,
but it is known that this mortality was extremely high.

"There are better estimates for the mortality of the middle passage. A journey
required about fifty days. Slaves were cheap in Africa but high in America, and this fact
encouraged overcrowding. The records of the English African Company, for the period
1680 to 1688, show 60,783 Negro slaves shipped, of which number 14,387 were lost in
the middle passage. This is 23.7 per cent of the number. Altogether, this was an experience calculated to eliminate weaklings. Says Le Fevre: 'From the standpoint of the
American slaves, the most significant aspect of the slave-trade was its frightful efficiency
in weeding out feeble bodies and easily depressed minds. Every Negro who survived
proved by the mere fact of being alive, his physical and mental capacity for endurance.' "
Herskovits (*The Myth of the Negro Past*, p. 43) cites evidence of low mortality. He
relies on Père Dieudonné Rinchon. (*Le Trafic Négrier, d'après les livres de commerce
du capitaine Gantois Pierre-Ignace Liévin Van Alstein* [1938], pp. 304 ff.):

"For he [Rinchon] shows that, between 1748 and 1782, 541 slavers bought 146,799
slaves, and disposed of 127,133. The difference, 19,666, or 13 per cent, would indicate
that the losses from all causes during shipment—and it by no means follows that these
were deaths—were much smaller than has been thought."

[22] Frederick Olmsted quotes a slaveholder to this effect: "In the States of Maryland,
Virginia, North Carolina, Kentucky, Tennessee, and Missouri, as much attention is paid
to the breeding and growth of Negroes as to that of horses and mules." (*The Cotton
Kingdom*, Vol. 1 [1862], p. 57.)

[23] Franz Boas, *Changes in Bodily Form of Descendants of Immigrants* (1910) and
various other papers. A critical and appreciative evaluation of Boas' work has been
expressed by F. H. Hankins, *The Racial Basis of Civilization* (1926), pp. 355-356:

"The famous study by Boas already referred to purported to show that the European
immigrant 'changes his type even in the first generation almost entirely'; children born
a few years after the arrival of their parents in this country 'differ essentially from their
foreign-born parents.' Elsewhere Boas contends that 'These observations seem to indicate
a decided plasticity of human types.' In view of the fact that the differences between
parents and offspring as shown in his original data for such a trait as head-form were
not always either positive or negative but frequently conflicting, and in view of the fact
that the general average differences were not always significant when compared with

the probable errors of the measurements, Boas's claims ('entirely,' 'essentially') appear much exaggerated. It is, nevertheless, not necessary to deny that he found some real differences between the ancestral and the American-born generations. Whether the total change, whatever it was, should be attributed to the American climate, food, drink or mores, is open to doubt. It is indeed quite probable that these had nothing whatever to do with the change in head-form assuming such a change to have occurred, whether as a mutation, a recombination of genetic factors, or as a purely somatic modification. One cannot be certain."

Other investigators have followed Boas in studying the physical changes accompanying immigration. For example: Leslie Spier, "Growth of Japanese Children Born in America and Japan," *University of Washington Publications in Anthropology* (July, 1929); H. L. Shapiro, *Migration and Environment* (1939). For a summary of such studies see Maurice H. Krout, "Race and Culture: A Study in Mobility, Segregation, and Selection," *American Journal of Sociology* (September, 1931), pp. 175-189.

[24] There is some inconclusive evidence that the average stature of American Negroes has been increasing since the Civil War. (Stature has been used by anthropologists as a characteristic of race.) The average stature of Civil War Negro troops was 168.99 cm. (reported by Baxter); while that of World War Negro troops, less selected, if anything, was 171.99 cm. (reported by Davenport and Love); and that of Herskovits' more representative sample of 887 male Negroes was 170.49. (See Herskovits, *The Anthropometry of the American Negro*, p. 43.)

[25] L. P. Jackson "Elizabethan Seamen and the African Slave Trade," *The Journal of Negro History* (January, 1924), p. 2.

[26] Most of the evidence on the basis of which this paragraph was written is brought together in Ashley-Montagu, *op. cit.*

[27] "The conversion of new negroes into plantation laborers, a process called 'breaking in,' required always a mingling of delicacy and firmness. Some planters distributed their new purchases among the seasoned households . . ." (Ulrich B. Phillips, *American Negro Slavery* [1918], p. 53.)

James G. Leyburn reports that families were separated to prevent their conspiring and planning revolts. (*The Haitian People* [1941], p. 179.)

[28] See W. E. B. Du Bois, *Black Folk Then and Now* (1939); also, "Africa" *The Encyclopedia Britannica* (eleventh edition), Vol. 1, pp. 325-330.

[29] There have been few attempts by legislation to hinder Negro-Indian intermarriage. Only three states (Louisiana, Oklahoma, and North Carolina) have laws forbidding such intermarriage, and these were never seriously enforced. (See Hurd, *op. cit.*, Vol. 1, p. 295, and Mangum, *op. cit.*, pp. 253-254.)

[30] E. Franklin Frazier, *The Negro Family in the United States* (1939), Chapter 11, "Racial Islands."

[31] K. W. Porter, "Relations between Negroes and Indians Within the Present Limits of the United States," *The Journal of Negro History* (July, 1932), pp. 287-367, and K. W. Porter, "Notes Supplementary to 'Relations between Negroes and Indians,'" *The Journal of Negro History* (July, 1933), pp. 282-321, especially pp. 320-321. These important studies are referred to, and the rest of the evidence on Negro-Indian miscegenation is summarized in Ashley-Montagu, *op. cit.*

[32] Melville J. Herskovits, *The American Negro* (1928), p. 10.

[33] The first census of 1790 showed a white sex ratio of 104 for the United States and 106 for the South. Earlier years would probably show a higher sex ratio, but the data for them are incomplete and otherwise inadequate.

[34] Marcus W. Jernegan, *Laboring and Dependent Classes in Colonial America: 1607-1783* (1931). Also Carter G. Woodson, "The Beginnings of the Miscegenation of the Whites and Blacks," *The Journal of Negro History* (October, 1918), pp. 335-353.

[35] Jernegan, *op. cit.*, p. 55. Also, Woodson, *op. cit.*, pp. 339-340.

[36] Reuter thus states that the miscegenation between Negro slaves and the growing group of poor whites "very greatly decreased as the institution of slavery developed."[a] He summarizes his arguments, which are representative of one vein of scientific opinion on this very controversial question, in the following way:

"As the status of the slave became better defined and a social difference was made, the friendly relation between the Negroes and the white servants gave place to a feeling of hatred between the Negroes and the poor white class. This, together with the more strict discipline over the slaves, generally prevented much intermixture of these classes during the period that slavery existed as a national institution."[b]

And even taking into account the relations between men of the master class and the slave women, he draws the conclusion that "mixture of the races probably went on more slowly during the period that slavery existed as a national institution, than in the period before or the period since."[c]

Reuter's reasoning on this point does not seem quite convincing. It is, first, doubtful to what extent the growing racial antipathies really prevented the type of exploitative sexual intercourse which we are here discussing. Second, only a part of the Negro slaves were employed on great plantations where the type of isolation and regimentation prevailed which would best support Reuter's hypothesis. While the proportion of slaves on the large plantations grew during the period, it never passed 53 per cent.[d] Third, and most important, the slaveholders had no interest at all in directing "the slave system as a working and developed institution" so that it "regulated strictly the conduct of the slaves and thereby restricted, in a measure, irregular relations between them and the general white population."[e] They had rather the opposite interest. The higher sales value of mulatto slaves, especially in the case of women, gave the slaveholders an economic interest in favoring race mixture, and contemporary observers even record

[a] Edward B. Reuter, *The Mulatto in the United States* (1918), p. 158.

[b] *Ibid.*, p. 163.

[c] Reuter is not consistent on this point, since he elsewhere says that there was a decline in mixture after Reconstruction. Compare: E. B. Reuter, *The Mulatto in the United States* (1918), pp. 158-159 *passim*; E. B. Reuter, *Race Mixture* (1931), p. 47 *passim*; E. B. Reuter, *The American Race Problem* (1927), pp. 138-139 *passim*.

[d] The figure of 53 per cent represents the number of slaves owned by persons who held 20 or more slaves each in 1860, in the fifteen slave states. If we reduce the criterion of a "large holding" to 15 slaves, the proportion rises to 62 per cent. If we raise the criterion of a "large holding" to 30 slaves, the proportion falls to 40 per cent. Masters who held 20 or more slaves were 12 per cent of all masters. (Source: U. S. Census Office, *Agriculture of the United States in 1860; Compiled from the Original Returns of the Eighth Census* [1864], p. 247.)

[e] Reuter, *The Mulatto in the United States*, pp. 158-159.

cases where rewards were given to white males who consented to be the fathers of mulattoes.[a]

[37] Wirth and Goldhamer, *op. cit.*, manuscript pages 24-25. Wirth does not here refer to trends, of course.

[38] Concerning the miscegenation between Northern soldiers and Negro women during the period in which the Northern Army occupied the South, Professor E. Franklin Frazier writes (in a communication to the author, July 1, 1942):

"In the genealogies which I have collected, few of the white ancestors were Northern men. It is possible, of course, that the mulatto offspring of Northern soldiers and Southern Negroes do not belong to the upper and middle class in the Negro population as do the offspring of the Southern upper class whites and Negroes. It is possible that the relations between the Northern soldiers and Southern Negroes were more casual than sex relations between Southern whites and Negroes, and the mulatto offspring did not know their white ancestors as well as did the mulatto offspring of Southern whites. Moreover, there is another factor which should be taken into account, namely: Northern soldiers had an aversion to close intimate contacts with the blacks, an attitude which was lacking among the Southern whites."

[39] *Race Mixture*, p. 49.

[40] See, for instance, T. J. Woofter, Jr., *The Basis of Racial Adjustment* (1925), pp. 42-44. Reuter expressed himself more guardedly. (See Reuter, *Race Mixture*, pp. 49-50.) See Wirth and Goldhamer, *op. cit.*, manuscript pages 33-35.

[41] The main evidences are the following:

(a) In his samples of mulattoes drawn from various sections of the country, Herskovits found fewer white parents than white grandparents, who in turn were fewer than white great-grandparents, and so on. For his college group, 2 per cent reported white parentage, while about 10 per cent knew of white grandparents. (*The Anthropometry of the American Negro*, pp. 240-241. Also see *The American Negro*, p. 30.) Herskovits seems to forget that one has more grandparents than parents so that, all other things equal, the probabilities, naturally, increase in geometric fashion—as one goes back through the generations. He also neglects the fact that contraception is more prevalent in recent years—probably especially in sex relations which defy convention—so that the number of offspring cannot be used as an index of the number of sex contacts in time series. Finally, he neglects the possibility of socio-economic differentials—which affect the sample of college students—between white parental and white grandparental groups.

(b) In Mrs. Day's sample of 1,152 persons born before the Civil War, 243 were known to have been partners in interracial unions, while this was true of only 3 out of 1,385 persons born since the Civil War. (Caroline Bond Day, *A Study of Some Negro-White Families in the United States* [1932], p. 108.) Day's sample is not intended to be representative of the general Negro population, and her information is admittedly not complete in this aspect of the study.

(c) Frazier records that of 920 known grandparents of 311 persons listed in *Who's Who in Colored America: 1928-1929*, 137, or 14.9 per cent, were white. (Frazier, *op. cit.*, p. 247.) There is no corresponding sample of recent Negro births for comparison, but this high proportion is undoubtedly not obtained today. The sample is, of course, not representative, and births are no perfect index of sex contacts in time series.

[a] See Wirth and Goldhamer, *op. cit.*, manuscript page 20.

(d) There are a number of observations in the literature to the same effect. Kelly Miller writes in *Out of the House of Bondage*: "As an illustration of the infrequency of the direct mulatto progeny, the student body of Howard University, about fifteen hundred in number, is composed largely of the mixed element. There are probably not a half dozen children of white parents in this entire number. On the other hand, the first pupils in this institution, a generation ago, were very largely the offspring of such parentage." ([1914], p. 55.)

[42] Reuter, who has specialized upon the problem of race mixture, wrote two books on the subject: *The Mulatto in the United States* in 1918 and *Race Mixture* in 1931 and discussed present and future trends without even mentioning contraception and birth control. In his last book, *The American Race Problem* (1927), although Reuter discusses birth control among Negroes in regard to several other problems, he fails to consider the effect of contraception on the number of mixed offspring. More remarkable is, perhaps, that Herskovits in his path-breaking book, *The American Negro*, also is able to discuss the present and future trend of miscegenation and amount of mixed offspring without touching the question of contraception.

[43] John Dollard, *Caste and Class in a Southern Town* (1937), p. 141.

[44] In June, 1932, *The Birth Control Review* devoted its entire issue to a discussion of birth control among Negroes. In this issue, in an article entitled "The Negro Birth Rate," S. J. Holmes states: "There is every reason to believe that the same causes which have led to a decreased birth rate among the whites have occasioned the declining birth rate among the Negroes. As most students of this subject agree, birth control is one of the most potent of these causes" (p. 172).

A social worker gives further evidence: ". . . they [the clients] ask often where they may obtain *bona fide* and scientific information concerning this [contraception]. . . . The Negro client is feeling less and less guilty about asking for and receiving information on birth control and is expressing himself freely as having wanted such guidance for a long time. . . . There are still a great many who have not lost their sense of sinning in seeking such help. . . . Yet there are increasing numbers who seek birth control." (Constance Fisher, "The Negro Social Worker Evaluates Birth Control," *The Birth Control Review*, *op. cit.*, pp. 174-175.)

Confirming evidence is given by Carolyn Bryant: "As far as teachability goes we find that the Negro women seem to learn and accept the method of contraception used in this clinic as easily or more so than the white patients. We have no definite figures to prove this statement." ("The Cincinnati Clinic," *The Birth Control Review*, *op. cit.*, p. 177.)

Norman Himes reports that ". . . at Cleveland, Cincinnati and Detroit the Negro rate of clinic attendance is *approximately three times* the rate in which Negroes exist in the respective city populations." ("Clinical Service for the Negro," *The Birth Control Review*, *op. cit.*, p. 176.)

George S. Schuyler, a Negro journalist, makes the following comments: "There is no great opposition to birth control among the twelve million brown Americans. Certainly none has been expressed in writing. On the contrary one encounters everywhere a profound interest in and desire for information on contraceptive methods among them. . . . Negroes are perhaps more receptive to this information than white folk. Despite their vaunted superiority, the white brethren have a full quota of illusions and, one might say, hypocrisies, especially about anything dealing with sex. Brown Americans are somewhat different because they have been forced to face more frankly the hard facts of life. . . . No wonder one sometimes hears a colored woman say 'it's a sin to bring a black child into the world.'. . . . If anyone should doubt the desire on the part of Negro women and men to limit their families, it is only necessary to note the large scale of 'preventive devices' sold in every drug store in the various Black Belts, and the great number of abortions performed by medical men and quacks." ("Quantity or Quality," *The Birth Control Review, op. cit.,* pp. 165-166.)

Further indirect evidence of the desire for family limitation among Negroes can be presented. "There is reason to believe . . . if one is willing to accept the almost universal testimony of Negro physicians, that . . . birth control of a sort is being attempted on a wide scale among the lower classes of Negroes. . . . Negro women in formidable numbers, without the advantage of contraceptive information, seek relief through abortions performed under highly dangerous conditions. . . ." (Elmer A. Carter, "Eugenics for the Negro," *The Birth Control Review, op. cit.,* p. 169.)

Raymond Pearl's study, however, indicates that Negro women practice contraception less than do white women. (See *The Natural History of Population* [1939], pp. 193-194, and table, p. 231.)

[45] In the only recent study showing quantitative trends in intermarriage, Wirth and Goldhamer state that intermarriage in Boston and New York State (outside of New York City) has been decreasing, but the fact that there are now a larger proportion of Negroes in the North where intermarriage is not illegal may have counterbalanced this trend. (*Op. cit.,* manuscript, pages 37-50.) Recent studies of Southern communities suggest that concubinage hardly exists in the present-day South in the form which it took before the Civil War, or at least if it exists, is more effectively concealed. (See Dollard, *op. cit.,* pp. 141-142; Hortense Powdermaker, *After Freedom* [1939], pp. 195-196.)

[46] ". . . In recent years a new type of contact between the two races has been developing in Northern cities. White collar workers of the two races have been associating more freely and are having, of course, sex relations. Contraceptives are generally used in such contacts." (Communication from E. Franklin Frazier, July 1, 1942.)

[47] Wirth and Goldhamer discuss all these types of passing. (*Op. cit.,* manuscript pages 72-99.)

[48] One of the reasons often overlooked for the ability to pass of persons who still have large proportions of Negro blood is the fact that not all Africans had the black color of the "true Negro." (See Day, *op. cit.,* pp. 10-11.)

[49] Day seems to be the only one who has made an approach to the use of the first method—and that only incidentally in the course of following up other interests. (See Day, *op. cit.,* p. 11.) Her samples of the families were known to have differing amounts of Negro blood in them, but were not intended to be representative of the general Negro population. Out of her 346 families, 35 included one or more individuals who had completely lost their racial identity. Her average family contained about 7.3 persons over 14 years of age, living or dead, so her statement would allow one to estimate that, at the very minimum, 15 out of every 1,000 Negroes passed. This conclusion is worthless, however, in view of the fact that Mrs. Day's sample was not, and was not intended to be, representative since her families were selected as containing some white blood even though individual members in them were full-blooded Negroes.

The second method was employed by Hart—also in following up another interest. (Hornell Hart, *Selective Migration as a Factor in Child Welfare in the United States, with Special Reference to Iowa* [1921], pp. 28-29.) Between 1900 and 1910 he estimated that 25,000 Negroes passed each year into the white community. If the average length of life after the passing be assumed as 20 to 30 years beyond childhood, and if the rate of passing between 1900 and 1910 be assumed to be the average for the years just before 1900 and since 1910, one could estimate that between 4 and 6 per cent of all those with some Negro blood have passed. It is known, however, that census data and vital statistics do not approach the accuracy required to make such refined estimates as are necessary in judging the extent of passing, since the entire error is contained in the relatively small margin used to measure the amount of passing.

The third method of estimating the extent of passing—that of noting discrepancies in sex ratio—was used by Charles S. Johnson ("The Vanishing Mulatto," *Opportunity* [October, 1925], p. 291) and by Everett V. Stonequist (*The Marginal Man* [1937], pp. 190-191.) The application of this technique has not only all the weaknesses of the original census data, but it also could only reveal the extent to which men pass more than women and not the total amount of passing.

[50] The above statement that passing cannot make the population darker refers to the average—since the traits, including skin color, of mixed offspring are usually a blend of the traits of their parents, on the average. The question as to whether passing will create *individual* cases of children with pronounced Negroid traits being born to ostensibly white parents is still a subject of controversy. It seems to be agreed by everyone that the offspring of two passable (or passed) mulattoes may have a darker skin than either of his parents. The controversy is around the question as to whether the offspring of a passed mulatto and a pure-blooded white person can have a darker skin than either parent. Majority opinion among those who have looked into this question seems to be that it cannot happen. Hooton, for example, says:

"There is no reversion to the Negro type in the offspring of mixed parents which would support the traditional notion of seemingly White couples producing fully Negroid infants, but there is no doubt that by a combination of features from both parents an occasional child may intensify the Negroid appearance not particularly obvious in either of his progenitors. In other words, a Negroid child may look more like a Negro than either of his parents, *if both of them carry Negro blood*. This is theoretically impossible if one parent is pure White, and I do not believe that it occurs. Negroid features seem to be attenuated, rather than intensified, by successive generations of inbreeding of mixed types, even when approximately identical proportions of blood are maintained. White features seem to gain upon Negroid features. I am convinced that some sort of Mendelian inheritance, involving many factors, is concerned in this process." (Earnest A. Hooton, "The Anthropometry of Some Small Samples of American Negroes and Negroids" in Day, *op. cit.*, p. 107.)

East makes a similar statement:

"A favourite short-story plot with which melodramatic artists seek to harrow the feelings of their readers is one where the distinguished scion of an aristocratic family marries the beautiful girl with telltale shadows on the half-moons of her nails, and in due time is presented with a coal-black son. It is a good framework, and carries a thrill. One waits shiveringly, even breathlessly, for the first squeal of the dingy infant. There is only this slight imperfection—or is it an advantage?—it could not possibly happen on the stage as set by the author. The most casual examination of the genetic formulae given above demonstrates its absurdity. If there ever was a basis for the plot in real life, the explanation lies in a fracture of the seventh commandment, or in a tinge of negro blood in the aristocrat as dark as that in his wife." (Edward M. East, *Heredity and Human Affairs* [1927], p. 100.)

Wirth has examined the scientific and popular literature exhaustively and has never come across a documented case of a "black baby" being born to a light mulatto and white person:

"One further aspect of Negro-white miscegenation probably requires some comment in view of the persistent error of at least the lay mind on this particular point, namely, the possibility that a white person mating with an individual who passes for white but has some Negro ancestry may produce a child darker than the mixed blood partner. It should be pointed out in this connection that while two parties with Negro blood may very occasionally have an offspring with somewhat more Negroid features than themselves, it is not possible for a white person and a person with some Negro ancestry to have an offspring more Negroid than the partner with Negro blood." (Wirth and Goldhamer, *op. cit.*, manuscript page 113.)

There is at least one biologist, however, who takes the opposite view, and says the "black baby" can happen, and occasionally does happen. (Huxley and Haddon, *op. cit.*, p. 82.)

"In some extreme cases, the offspring of a cross between a white man and a half-breed coloured woman have been fair and almost black respectively."

In a recent (December, 1941) statement to the author, Professor Huxley indicated that he did not wish the above quotation from his book to be taken as final and beyond question.

The Mendelian mechanism of color inheritance, too, is a subject of debate, so that it cannot be relied upon to settle this controversy, since the "white" partner may have had a distant Negro ancestor about whose existence he was completely unaware. The controversy is not very important practically, since if a dark-skinned baby can be born to a light mulatto and a white person, this happens so extremely rarely that one is still justified in branding as a myth the popular belief that it occurs.

Finally, it should be said that it may be that the "black baby" is not given a chance to appear, since belief in the myth might encourage the use of contraceptives in white-mulatto relations.

[51] Southern scholars now discredit the theory that the origin of the Southern planter class was aristocratic, or that it differed much from that of the lower classes. See, for example: Thomas J. Wertenbaker, *The Old South* (1942), p. 21; Virginius Dabney, *Below The Potomac* (1942), p. 2; Frank Owsley, "The Irrepressible Conflict" in *I'll Take My Stand* (1930), p. 69.

[52] Reuter, *Race Mixture*, pp. 160-161. Compare Reuter, *The Mulatto in the United States*, pp. 396-397, *passim*. The cultural and social causes and effects of this selective mating will be discussed further in Chapter 31. The fact itself is referred to by numerous authors, and is, indeed, obvious to any observer. (See Miller, *op. cit.*, p. 57; Herskovits, *The American Negro*, pp. 63-64; and Donald Young, *American Minority Peoples* [1932], p. 356.)

[53] Reuter, *The Mulatto in the United States*. It should also be pointed out that Reuter's estimate of the proportion of mulattoes in the total population—which he uses as a basis for comparison—is much too small in the light of subsequent findings. In his later books, Reuter retains his conclusion, but reverses himself frequently. "No

legitimate inference may be drawn from social prominence to native ability." (*Race Mixture*, p. 110.)

[54] The belief that mulattoes were sterile seems to have been called out when it was desired to discourage miscegenation, and the opposite belief when it was felt necessary to explain the manifest increase in number of mulattoes without admitting the fact of continuing interracial sex relations. In the only careful study of the fecundity of mulattoes, Frazier finds that it is about the same as that of full-blooded Negroes. (E. Franklin Frazier, "Children in Black and Mulatto Families," *The American Journal of Sociology* [July, 1933], pp. 12-29.) This study is not methodologically perfect, but seems to be the best available on the subject. For other literature on the subject, see Wirth and Goldhamer, *op. cit.*, manuscript pages 109-111.

[55] Klineberg has made a painstaking study which tends to show that Negro migrants to Northern cities have not included a disproportionate number of highly intelligent Negroes. (Otto Klineberg, *Negro Intelligence and Selective Migration* [1935].) A similar study done before Klineberg's with data for Washington, D. C. is: Alice S. McAlpin, "Changes in the Intelligence Quotients of Negro Children," *Journal of Negro Education* (April 1, 1932), pp. 44-48.

[56] *The American Negro* and *The Anthropometry of the American Negro*.

[57] *The Anthropometry of the American Negro*, p. 15. Herskovits' full table on p. 177 is reproduced here:

Unmixed Negro	N	342	22.0
Negro, mixed with Indian	N(I)	97	6.3
More Negro than White	NNW	384	24.8
More Negro than White, with Indian	NNW(I)	106	6.9
About the same amount of Negro and White	NW	260	16.7
About the same amount of Negro and White, with Indian	NW(I)	133	8.5
More White than Negro	NWW	154	9.3
More White than Negro, with Indian	NWW(I)	75	5.5
		1551	100.0

These proportions refer to the existing Negro population and do not take into account those hybrids who have passed into the white or Indian populations.

Hrdlička—in searching for full-blooded Negroes on whom he wished to make anthropometric measurements—also reported that over 70 per cent of a group of Negroes in Washington, D. C., had at least one white ancestor.[a] Hrdlička's Washington Negroes were not meant to be considered as representative of the entire population of American Negroes, and undoubtedly contained too many upper class persons who tend to have a relatively large proportion of white blood. The fact that Hrdlička was searching for full-blooded Negroes may, however, have counterbalanced this selective factor. Also Hrdlička says that some of the remaining 30 per cent may have had some white blood.

[58] E. Franklin Frazier writes:

"Many mulattoes in the United States with very little Negro blood consider themselves pure Negroes. I have had mulatto students at Fisk University and Howard University insist that they were pure Negroes. One summer I visited a number of summer

[a] Aleš Hrdlička, "The Full-Blood American Negro," *American Journal of Physical Anthropology* (July-September, 1928), p. 15.

schools in the South in which I had the student teachers fill out blanks indicating their racial identity or racial mixture of their parents, grandparents, and even more remote ancestors. I was forced to give up the attempt to discover the amount of admixture of white blood because the majority of these elementary school teachers regarded themselves, their parents, and more remote ancestors as of pure Negro descent, despite the fact that they were obviously of mixed blood. Some could almost pass for white." (Communication to the author, June 27, 1942.)

[59] Although Herskovits has made valiant efforts to test the representativeness of *his* sample, there has been no attempt to show that the samples of the other groups—measured by other investigators—are representative. Measurements made by different anthropologists, at different times, on different samples of African Negro, American white, and American Indian groups actually show very conflicting results. In many cases the samples are very small, and the errors are correspondingly large—especially in relation to the small differences that actually separate the means and standard deviations of the groups which are compared. There are no comparisons for many important traits—such as skin color and hair form—and even where there are comparable data for the different races, the American Negroes have more traits which show greater variability than lesser variability.

We have analyzed Herskovits' data and can find no striking evidence of lower American Negro variability. This analysis is partly subjective because of the inadequate nature of the original data, but is presented here for what it is worth.

COMPARISON OF VARIABILITIES[a] OF THE AMERICAN NEGRO POPULATION WITH THE AMERICAN WHITE POPULATION AND WITH THE WEST AFRICAN NEGRO POPULATION IN TWENTY-THREE SELECTED TRAITS

	Number of traits in which the American Negro population is more or less homogeneous than:	
	The American White Population	The African Negro Population
Number of traits in which American Negroes are more homogeneous	6	4
Number of traits in which American Negroes are less homogeneous	7	10
Number of traits in which the evidence is conflicting	5	7
Number of traits in which there are no data	5	2
Total	23	23

Source: Melville J. Herskovits, *The Anthropometry of the American Negro* (1930), Chapter 3 and pp. 249–250.
[a] Variability is measured by the standard deviation in all cases.

The reason that Herskovits offers for the supposed greater homogeneity in the American Negro population is that there is no longer much miscegenation with whites and Indians, and that the Negroes themselves are intermarrying. These reasons are invalid even if the data were not: In the first place, the decrease in Negro-white offspring, even if it should be accepted as established, is a rather new phenomenon, while the

African tribes, and possibly even the Old Americans, have had less out-breeding than the American Negroes for a much longer period of time. Secondly, while Negroes with different physical appearance do marry each other, the predominant tendency is for like to marry like. Mulattoes—having a greater concentration in the cities and in the upper income brackets, and having a higher prestige because of their relative physical similarity to whites—tend to marry each other unless they happen to make a particularly good match in the darker, more Negroid group. Finally, Herskovits has not even considered the possibility that, if Negroes were more homogeneous in certain traits, this homogeneity might be due to greater homogeneity of environment rather than of gene composition. Thus, in view of the fact that his data for this purpose are inadequate; that it would seem—*a priori*—that a recently mixed group would show more variability than a more genetically isolated group; and that common observation of the most visible traits (color, hair form, nose breadth, lip thickness) of American Negroes indicate unequivocally that their range—at least—is greater than the range within the American white population —in view of all these things, the burden of proof of greater physical homogeneity of the American Negroes still lies with Herskovits. As far as we know now, the American Negro population may be becoming a homogeneous brown "race"—and it is to Herskovits' credit that he has opened up discussion as to this possibility—but this is a matter of the speculative future and not of the empirical present.

[60] Although there are no adequate data, apparently, to determine trends in class differentials in fertility among Negroes, it is probable that they have been increasing as a Negro upper class has been rising, and as effective contraceptive devices have come into greater use in this upper class.

Chapter 6. *Racial Characteristics*

[1] C. B. Davenport and A. G. Love, *Army Anthropology* (1921).

[2] For an evaluation of this and other studies of the physical anthropology of the Negro, see W. Montague Cobb, "The Physical Constitution of the American Negro," *Journal of Negro Education* (July, 1934), pp. 340-388.

[3] Notable among studies comparing Negro and white traits using small samples has been that of T. Wingate Todd and Anna Lindala, "Dimensions of the Body: Whites and American Negroes of Both Sexes," *American Journal of Physical Anthropology* (July-September, 1928), pp. 35-119. These students had at most 100 cases for each sex-race group. Even less reliable was the study of Aleš Hrdlička, "The Full-Blood American Negro," *American Journal of Physical Anthropology* (July-September, 1928), pp. 15-33. Hrdlička had only 20 males and 6 females. In fairness to these authors, it should be mentioned that they recognize the great limitations of their data, but other authors have used them without making the same reservations.

[4] Aleš Hrdlička, *The Old Americans* (1925).

[5] *Ibid.*, pp. 5-6. Hrdlička did include a series of Southern "Engineers" and Appalachian mountaineers in his sample, but he does not say how many.

[6] This summary is based upon M. F. Ashley-Montagu, "The Origin, Composition and Physical Characteristics of the American Negro Population," unpublished manuscript prepared for this study (1940), and Cobb, *op. cit.*, pp. 340-388. These authors have relied mainly on the following primary sources: Davenport and Love, *op. cit.*;

Todd and Lindala, *op. cit.*; Hrdlička, "The Full-Blood American Negro," *op. cit.*, pp. 15-34; C. B. Davenport and M. Steggerda *et al.*, *Race Crossing in Jamaica* (1929); M. J. Herskovits, *The Anthropometry of the American Negro* (1930); M. J. Herskovits, V. K. Cameron, and H. Smith, "The Physical Form of Mississippi Negroes," *The American Journal of Physical Anthropology* (October-December, 1931), pp. 193-201; C. B. Day, *A Study of Some Negro-White Families in the United States* (1932). Our list is aimed to include only those traits which have been most frequently measured by anthropologists.

After this chapter was written, two other summary sources on the physical anthropology of the Negro became available and we were able to check our statements by them also: (1) Julian Herman Lewis, *The Biology of the Negro* (1942); (2) W. Montague Cobb, "Physical Anthropology of the American Negro: Status and Desiderata," unpublished manuscript (1942).

[7] In addition a number of investigators have reported minor skeletal differences between Negroes and whites. See Lewis, *op. cit.*, pp. 68-73.

[8] Ashley-Montagu, from his experiences in anatomical laboratories, testifies that he "has never had any occasion to remark any appreciable difference of the Negro genitalia as compared with those of whites." (*Op. cit.*, p. 62.) In regard to body odor it should be pointed out that Negroes do have a larger number of sweat glands than do whites. But this does not prove that their body odor is different. Many white authors refer, however, to such a difference as an established fact. (E.g., Donald R. Young, *American Minority Peoples* [1932], p. 406; E. B. Reuter, *The American Race Problem* [1938; first edition, 1927], p. 61; Robert E. Park, "The Bases of Race Prejudice," *The Annals of the American Academy of Political and Social Science* [November, 1928], p. 17.) Some few authors are careful to advance the hypothesis that, if the Negro has a peculiar odor, it might be explained as due to diet and lack of cleanliness (Otto Klineberg, *Race Differences* [1935], p. 131.) William Archer writes (in *Through Afro-America* [1910], p. 144): "Let me take this opportunity of saying that to the best of my belief the 'body odour' of which we hear so much is mainly a superstition. The fact probably is that the negro ought to be at least as scrupulous in his ablutions as the white man—but often is not." Ashley-Montagu (*op. cit.*, pp. 58-59) records "the fact that in his own experience of African and American Negroes he has never observed any particular or general difference in body odor between Negroes and whites." During the course of this study, I have not been able to find that Negro Americans have a different odor than white Americans of similar social and economic status.

Klineberg refers to a suggestive experiment made by Lawrence "who collected in test tubes a little of the perspiration of White and Colored students who had just been exercising violently in the gymnasium. These test tubes were then given to a number of White subjects with instructions to rank them in order of pleasantness. The results showed no consistent preference for the White samples; the test tube considered the most pleasant and the one considered most unpleasant were both taken from Whites." (Klineberg, *Race Differences*, pp. 130-131.) Such experiments should be repeated on larger and more representative groups of whites, and the question should be asked whether the Negro sweat is identifiable, rather than whether it is pleasant.

Even if it were established that Negroes had a different odor, it would not explain why this odor is considered offensive. Likes and dislikes in smells of this sort are a matter of personal taste and cultural conditioning.

[9] Earnest A. Hooton, "The Anthropometry of Some Small Samples of American Negroes and Negroids," in Day, *op. cit.*, pp. 104-106, and Herskovits, *The Anthropometry of the American Negro*, pp. 177-227.

[10] Some anthropologists believe that certain unique Negro traits are exceptions to this rule; some disappear rapidly when even a small admixture of white ancestry is present, and others are tenacious despite large admixtures of white blood.* There is great disagreement even among these few observers, but we may note some of those traits which have been studied: hair form and low hair level are said to have a high degree of "yieldingness," while ear height, interpupillary distance, and hair color are said to be "entrenched." The nature of the inheritance of skin color is still a matter of debate, but the majority opinion seems to be that, on the average, the color of the offspring tends to be a blend of the colors of his parents.

[11] Cobb, "Physical Anthropology of the American Negro: Status and Desiderata," pp. 55-56. Cobb points out that even though Negroes may have continued to hold a certain championship, a white man of today is often better than the Negro champion of twenty years ago. See also Lewis, *op. cit.*, p. 73, and compare Cobb's findings.

[12] See Section 3 of this chapter. A few of the earlier beliefs about Negro susceptibility to disease are cited in Young, *op. cit.*, p. 339; in Harry Bakwin, M.D., "The Negro Infant," *Human Biology* (February, 1932), pp. 1-33; and in Charles S. Johnson and Horace M. Bond, "The Investigation of Racial Differences Prior to 1910," *Journal of Negro Education* (July, 1934), pp. 335-337.

For some of the earlier beliefs about Negro susceptibility to *mental* disease—which generally tried to show that Negroes had little mental disease under the secure condition of slavery—see Lewis, *op. cit.*, pp. 266-267.

[13] Concretely, this experiment should be made by selecting two groups of children— Negro and white—carefully matched in all essentials, keeping them in a controlled laboratory situation for at least a month to test and increase their comparability, and then inoculating them with certain disease germs (just as in ordinary inoculations to develop immunity). Large differentials in reaction ought to suggest, though not measure, differences in racial susceptibility or immunity.

After writing the statement in the text, our attention was called by Lewis' book to the only approach to such an experiment that Lewis notes in his careful survey of the field. Its weaknesses—in terms of inadequate controls and insufficient cases—make its findings completely inconclusive, but its methodology is interesting.

"In order to find the difference between colored and white people in their reactions to tubercle bacilli under controlled conditions, Levine (*American Journal of Diseases of Children* [1936], p. 1052) inoculated 74 white, 38 Negro, and 24 Puerto Rican children with identical amounts of living attenuated bovine tubercle bacilli (BCG). Necrosis of the local lesion on the thigh occurred more rapidly in Negro children than in white. Inguinal abscesses developed in more children and more rapidly among Negroes and Puerto Ricans than among whites. When the effect of such variables as age, previous exposure to tubercle bacilli, economic status, and nutrition were taken into account, there still remained a racial factor that is related to the more severe reaction in Negroes and Puerto Ricans." (Lewis, *op. cit.*, p. 140.)

* T. W. Todd, "Entrenched Negro Physical Features," *Human Biology* (January, 1929), pp. 57-69. Also Hooton, "The Anthropometry of Some Small Samples of American Negroes and Negroids" in Day, *op. cit.*, pp. 104-106, and Herskovits, *The Anthropometry of the American Negro*, pp. 177-227.

[14] Good summaries of research on disease differentials may be found in Bakwin, *op. cit.*, and Harold F. Dorn, "The Health of the Negro," unpublished manuscript prepared for this study (1942).

After this chapter was completed the best summary of disease differentials became available, and we had the opportunity of checking our statements by it: Lewis, *op. cit.*

[15] See Bakwin's summary, *op. cit.*, and Lewis' summary, *op. cit.*

[16] Official death registration statistics underestimate the Negro death rates more than the white rates. Thus the reporting of a slightly higher Negro death rate usually means that the cause of death is more important among Negroes than the statistics show. Studies which are based on a sample instead of the total population, however, are likely to be biased in the other direction—since they miss no cases and may get a poorer selection of Negroes than of whites.

[17] In Charleston, South Carolina, the white rate of tuberculosis in the period 1841-1848 was 268 per 100,000 as compared to 266 for Negroes. Willis D. Weatherford and Charles S. Johnson, *Race Relations* (1934), p. 375, and E. R. Embree, *Brown America* (1933; first edition, 1931), p. 49.

[18] *Race Traits and Tendencies of the American Negro* (1896), p. 69. Also see S. J. Holmes, *The Negro's Struggle for Survival* (1937), p. 39. S. A. Cartwright, a Southern doctor, writing before the Civil War, expressed this opinion:

"To the question, 'Is not Phthisis very common among the slaves of the slave States and unknown among the native Africans at home?' I reply in the negative, that Phthisis, so far from being common among the slaves of the slave States, is very seldom met with. As to the native Africans at home, little or nothing is known of their diseases. . . . Negroes, however, are sometimes, though rarely, afflicted with tubercula pulmonum, or Phthisis, properly so called, which has some peculiarities. . . . Phthisis is, par excellence, a disease of the sanguineous temperament, fair complexion, red or flaxen hair, blue eyes, large blood vessels, and a bony encasement too small to admit the full and free expansion of the lungs, enlarged by the superabundant blood, which is determined to those organs during that first half-score of years immediately succeeding puberty. . . . Hence it is most apt to occur precisely at, and immediately following, that period of life known as matureness. . . . With negroes, the sanguineous never gains the mastery over the lymphatic and nervous systems." ("Slavery in the Light of Ethnology," in E. N. Elliott (editor), *Cotton Is King, and Pro-Slavery Arguments* [1860], pp. 692-693.)

[19] Cited in Charles S. Johnson, "The Negro," *American Journal of Sociology* (May, 1942), p. 863.

[20] Dorn, *op. cit.*, p. 97.

[21] Embree, *op. cit.*, p. 54.

[22] A. G. Love and C. B. Davenport, "A Comparison of White and Colored Troops in Respect to Incidence of Disease," *Proceedings of the National Academy of Sciences* (March, 1919), pp. 58-67.

[23] H. M. Pollock, "Frequency of Dementia Praecox in Relation to Sex, Age, Environment, Nativity, and Race," *Mental Hygiene* (July, 1926), pp. 596-611. Pollock's figures are the numbers of first admissions in 1924 per 100,000 population. A criticism of this study may be found in Solomon P. Rosenthal, "Racial Differences in the Incidence of Mental Disease," *Journal of Negro Education* (July, 1934), p. 490.

[24] Even in 1924, the New York rates were 16.9 and 48.6 for whites and Negroes,

respectively. In 1929-1931, Malzberg found the difference even less: 19.2 for whites and 44.4 for Negroes. See Benjamin Malzberg, "Mental Disease among American Negroes" in Klineberg (editor), *Characteristics of the American Negro,* manuscript page 10.

[25] It is interesting to observe that, almost from the beginning of those studies showing race differences, there has been a minority of scholars who have remained skeptical and have ably contested the findings. In 1897, Charles Horton Cooley beautifully demonstrated the complete invalidity of the findings of Francis Galton, in the famous essay, "Genius, Fame and the Comparison of Races" (*The Annals of the American Academy of Political and Social Science* [May, 1897], pp. 317-358). Other early critics of the use of the doctrine of innate differences included: Franz Boas, "The Mind of Primitive Man," *The Journal of American Folk-lore* (January-March, 1911), pp. 1-11; and *The Mind of Primitive Man* (1911); William I. Thomas, *Sex and Society* (1907), John Dewey, "Interpretation of Savage Mind," *The Psychological Review* (May, 1902), pp. 217-230.

[26] G. O. Ferguson, "The Psychology of the Negro," *Archives of Psychology*, No. 36 (April, 1916). See also, W. H. Pyle, "The Learning Capacity of Negro Children," *Psychological Bulletin* (1916), pp. 82-83.

[27] Ferguson's example, as well as others cited in this section, have been taken from the summary prepared for this project by Klineberg, "Racial Differences as Shown by Tests and Measurements" in Klineberg (editor), *Characteristics of the American Negro.*

[28] Albert L. Crane, "Race Differences in Inhibition," *Archives of Psychology*, No. 63 (March, 1923).

[29] Boas, *The Mind of Primitive Man* (1911), pp. 114-115.

[30] *Ibid.*, pp. 271-272. Boas later changed his position on these points. In the 1938 edition of *The Mind of Primitive Man,* the above statements are not to be found, and there is a new emphasis on "variability of function" accompanying any given structure.

[31] Julian S. Huxley and A. C. Haddon, *We Europeans* (1936), p. 69.

[32] *Ibid.*, pp. 96-97.

[33] A history of these trends in psychological research, with special reference to the Negro is contained in two research memoranda written for this study by Otto Klineberg, "Experimental Studies of Negro Personality" and "Tests of Negro Intelligence," to be published in Klineberg (editor), *Characteristics of the American Negro.*

[34] While some authors report Negro-white differences in memory, others say they cannot find any. For a discussion of this subject, see Klineberg, "Tests of Negro Intelligence," in Klineberg (editor), *Characteristics of the American Negro,* manuscript pages 16 and 118.

[35] No one has sought a representative sample of either white or Negro children to determine what proportions were very superior, but the only investigators who have sought superior Negro children had no special trouble in finding them. Witty and Jenkins studied 26 Negro children with I.Q.'s of 140 and above, who came from grades 3-8 in 7 Chicago public schools. (Paul A. Witty and Martin A. Jenkins, "The Educational Achievement of a Group of Gifted Negro Children," *The Journal of Educational Psychology* (November, 1934), pp. 585-597.) The same authors report on one nine-year old Negro girl with a Stanford-Binet I.Q. of 200. "The Case of 'B'—-

A Gifted Negro Girl," *The Journal of Social Psychology* (February, 1935), pp. 117-124.)

[36] See Klineberg, "Tests of Negro Intelligence" in Klineberg (editor), *Characteristics of the American Negro*, manuscript pages 13-14 and 106-109. Even Ferguson, who has been cited on a previous page as an example of a biased investigator, did not find that Negroes reached their maximum intelligence at an earlier age than did whites. He found, rather, that they continued their mental growth longer than whites, even though they never reached the levels attained by the whites. We need not accept this conclusion either, for the same reasons that his main findings are to be criticized.

[37] See Klineberg, "Experimental Studies of Negro Personality" in Klineberg (editor), *Characteristics of the American Negro*, manuscript page 65.

[38] Subsequent studies have not been able to corroborate Ferguson's finding cited on a previous page—that there is a correlation between Intelligence Quotient and the possession of Negroid traits. See summary by Paul A. Witty and Martin A. Jenkins, "Intra-Race Testing and Negro Intelligence," *The Journal of Psychology* (1935-1936), pp. 179-192. Even if a correlation were found, it would not prove that the high intelligence was caused by white ancestry, since socio-economic differences between mulattoes and full-blooded Negroes would first have to be held constant, and since it would first have to be proved that the inheritance of intelligence does not involve dominant or recessive genes and that the parent population were representative samples of the total Negro and white populations (which they were not) and that passing and differential reproductivity did not bias the sample of mulattoes.

[39] In their study, "Dimensions of the Body: Whites and American Negroes of Both Sexes," p. 48, Todd and Lindala make the point that "it is also irrelevant to suggest that our series are too small. They are quite representative of the series possible to most workers and in numbers they compare favorably with series of other races and stocks which will have to be anthropologically compared."

[40] One of the earliest of the modern physical anthropological studies reported all its findings in frequency polygons. For presentation alone, if not in other respects, few recent studies have approached the excellence of this early study. We refer to Franz Boas, "The Half-Blood Indian," *The Popular Science Monthly* (October, 1894), pp. 761-770.

[41] Franz Boas, *Changes in Bodily Form of Descendants of Immigrants* (1910).

[42] See, Walter H. Eddy and Gessner G. Hawley, *We Need Vitamins* (1931), pp. 36-37.

[43] Social anthropologists have been using the psychologist's devices for some years to quantify culture differences in personality traits. A selection of these studies is summarized in Klineberg, *Characteristics of the American Negro*. There is, for example, the classic experiment of W. H. R. Rivers ("Observations on the Senses of the Todas," *The British Journal of Psychology* [December, 1905], pp. 321-396), which showed the Todas to have a higher pain threshold than his English subjects because they regarded the experiment as a test of their endurance. Another famous example is Margaret Mead's (*Coming of Age in Samoa* [1928]) experiences with the administration of the "ball-and-field" questions in the Binet tests, where she found that Samoan children were much more interested in producing an esthetically satisfying design than in devising a rational means for finding the ball.

[44] An example of the use of intelligence tests to measure cultural differences between

various groups of Negroes may be found in Charles S. Johnson, *Growing Up in the Black Belt* (1941), pp. 334-335.

[45] A recent evaluative summary of such research has been made by Robert S. Woodworth, *Heredity and Environment* (1941).

[46] Klineberg, *Negro Intelligence and Selective Migration*.

[47] H. G. Canady, "The Effect of 'Rapport' on the I.Q.: A New Approach to the Problem of Racial Psychology," *Journal of Negro Education* (April, 1936), p. 217.

[48] The present War may provide some data to do some of these dynamic studies. In the first place, measurements are being made of the psychic traits of a large number of individuals with diverse backgrounds. In the second place, these individuals are being subjected to experiences which are drastically different from any they have known before. To get the fullest use out of the data being brought up by the War, it would be necessary to test the members of the armed forces after the War is over, and to compare the later measurements with the earlier ones.

[49] Paul Horst and Associates, *The Prediction of Personal Adjustment* (1941), p. 14.

[50] Another revolutionary development in psychological measurement is the trend away from the concept of "general intelligence." Mainly under the leadership of Thurstone, contemporary psychologists are trying to get at the "factors" in intelligence, and to arrive at an "intelligence profile" of an individual rather than a general I.Q. An allied development is that toward "item analysis"—the analysis of responses to specific questions and tasks in a personality inventory or battery. To go into these developments is beyond the scope of this book, but when they are applied to measurements of Negro-white differences, they may become important to our problem.

Chapter 7. *Population*

[1] Under the 1924 law, the President is permitted to reduce the quota. President Hoover did so on March 26, 1931. See Niles Carpenter, "The New American Immigration Law and the Labor Market," *Quarterly Journal of Economics* (August, 1931), pp. 720-723.

[2] American population statisticians have long known how inaccurate the *birth* registration statistics are, but not until recently have we come across any specific information regarding the inadequacy of *death* registration data. Harold F. Dorn cites a study by Isabella C. Wilson which indicates that about 50 per cent of the deaths of Negroes in Chicot County, Arkansas, were unreported. (Harold F. Dorn, "The Health of the Negro," unpublished manuscript prepared for this study [1940; revised, 1942], Appendix; Isabella C. Wilson, "Sickness and Medical Care among the Negro Population in a Delta Area of Arkansas," University of Arkansas Agricultural Experiment Station Bulletin 372 [1939]). Other discussions of under-registration of deaths are cited by Dorn and by Lyonel C. Florant, "Critique of the Census of the United States," unpublished manscript prepared for this study (1939).

[3] Despite these inadequacies, as well as the difficulty of having special registrations for voting, social insurance, unemployment, army draft, consumption goods' rationing, observation of aliens and other purposes, America has avoided the far more efficient and less expensive system of a continuous registration of population. Such a system would

not only substitute one registration for all these and make available more accurate statistics, but it would reduce the possibility of error and fraud in voting, facilitate the substitution of direct taxation for indirect, aid in the detection of criminals, reduce the use of the oath (the notary public is an inconvenient and inefficient institution). The main reason why Americans do not seem to like continuous registration is that they are afraid it will lead to regimentation. But large sectors of the American public are already under continuous government registration (all who come under the Social Security Act, all who have postal savings accounts, and so forth) and the democratic nations of Northern Europe have it for their entire populations. There are other reasons why Americans do not have this system: most Americans do not realize its advantages, those experts who do realize its advantages have a strong tendency to avoid the political battle necessary to institute it, and many politicians do not want to lose the petty patronage involved in census-taking. If continuous registration were to be instituted in the United States, probably the post office would be the best organization to administer it; since practically every community has a post office; since its employees usually are reasonably well-educated and have a respected status, and since it has the necessary office facilities.

[4] *Sixteenth Census of the United States: 1940, Population.* Preliminary Release: Series P-5, No. 13. Nonwhites include Chinese, Japanese, and a few other colored peoples as well as Negroes, but non-Negroes are eclipsed by Negroes in the computation of nonwhite rates. Estimates made by Kirk on the basis of registered births and deaths show a similar picture: the net reproduction rate for Negroes in 1933-1937 was 104, while that for whites in 1933-1935 was 98. (Dudley Kirk, "The Fertility of the Negroes," unpublished manuscript prepared for this study [1940], p. 14.)

[5] *Sixteenth Census of the United States: 1940, Population.* Preliminary Release: Series P-5, No. 13. Kirk's computations show both whites and Negroes to have a net reproduction rate of 108 in 1930 (*op. cit.*, p. 14).

[6] Thompson and Whelpton's various estimates of future trends in population place the Negro proportion in the American population in 1980 between 10.8 per cent and 12.0 per cent as compared to 9.7 per cent in 1930. (Warren S. Thompson and P. K. Whelpton, "Estimates of the Future Population of the United States—1940 to 1980," *Population Statistics.* 1. National Data. National Resources Committee [1937].) The lowest proportion of 10.8 was calculated assuming a medium fertility, high mortality, and net annual immigration of 100,000. The highest proportion of 12.0 was calculated assuming a high fertility, medium mortality, and no net migration. The terms "high," "medium," and "low" are used with reference to the period 1930-1934: "high fertility" is the actual birth rate of that period; "high mortality" is a declining death rate after that period at a greatly decreasing rate. Different assumptions are made for native whites, foreign-born whites, and colored peoples. For a detailed description of the assumptions used see: P. K. Whelpton, "An Empirical Method of Calculating Future Population," *Journal of the American Statistical Association* (September, 1936), pp. 457-473. See also: National Resources Board, *The Problems of a Changing Population* (1938), p. 128.

[7] These figures were calculated by A. J. Jaffe, "Population Growth and Fertility Trends in the United States," *Journal of Heredity* (December, 1941), p. 444. The rates here are standardized for rural-urban residence only and not for region. Since practically all Negroes living in the North and West are urban, and since there is

practically no difference in the urban rates for the whites and nonwhites, this is practically equivalent to standardizing for regions as well as for rural-urban residence.

It is not yet possible to standardize for both region and rural-urban residence at the same time, since the necessary breakdowns have not yet been made available by the Census Bureau and since Negro net reproduction rates were not calculated for rural areas in the North or for rural or urban areas in the West. It is possible, however, to standardize for region alone just as Jaffe standardized for urban-rural alone. The white rate then becomes 95 and the Negro rate 96. The Negro rate is below the white rate, of course, since—as we have just said—region and urban-rural residence are comparable.

[8] The net reproduction rate we have used is more reliable than the birth and death rates which compose it because it is calculated from the decennial census statistics rather than from the annual registration statistics, and the former are generally more reliable than the latter. Even when annual registration statistics are used, however, the net reproduction rate is usually more reliable since the under-registration of births and the under-registration of deaths tend to cancel each other out, even when their exact magnitude is unknown.

[9] Kirk, *op. cit.*, p. 7 and Figure 1. Since birth registration statistics have become available for a significant number of states only since 1915, Kirk was forced to use the number of children under 5 years per 1,000 women aged 15-44 as an index of the birth rate. In 1880 this was about 760 for Negroes, and in 1930 about 390.

[10] *Ibid.*, p. 14.

The changes in the uncorrected crude birth rates were as follows:

	1930	1940
White	18.7	17.5
Negro	21.7	21.7

These figures are, of course, subject to many errors, but they can be relied on for the following two conclusions: (1) The white birth rate is lower than the Negro birth rate. (2) The fall in the white birth rate between 1930 and 1940 was probably greater than the fall in the Negro birth rate. The figures fail to show what is likely—that the Negro birth rate fell between 1930 and 1940. (Texas—with a high birth rate—was not included in the 1930 figures, but was included in the 1940 ones.) These figures were calculated from: U.S. Bureau of the Census, *Vital Statistics—Special Reports*, Vol. 14, No. 2, p. 9. The population bases were taken from the *Sixteenth Census of the United States: 1940, Population*. Preliminary Release: Series P-10, No. 1.

[11] U.S. Bureau of the Census, *Vital Statistics—Special Reports: 1940*, Vol. 14, No. 2, p. 9.

[12] Dorn, *op. cit.* (1942, first draft, 1940), Figures 17 and 18.

[13] The number of still-births per 1,000 live births, according to the inadequate official figures, was 2.76 for the whites and 5.81 for the Negroes during 1930. (U.S. Bureau of the Census, *Vital Statistics—Special Reports: 1940*, Vol. 14, No. 2, p. 9.)

[14] Dorn, *op. cit.* (1942; first draft, 1940), p. 3. By 1939 the expectation of life at birth had increased to 55.4 for *nonwhite* females and to 52.4 for *nonwhite* males. The corresponding expectations for white infants were 66.8 and 62.6, or 11.4 and 10.2 years greater, respectively. (*Idem*)

[15] U.S. Bureau of the Census, *Vital Statistics—Special Reports: 1940*, Vol. 14, No. 2, p. 9.

¹⁶ Kirk reports the following corrected gross reproduction rates:

	Negro		White
1928-32	136	1930	122
1933-37	130	1931-35	109

See *op. cit.*, p. 14, and footnote on p. 161 of this chapter. Other evidence of the greater fall in the white birth rate may be had from the net reproduction rates reported in Table 1 and from the crude birth rates in footnote 10 of this chapter.

¹⁷ Dorn reports the trends in the following manner: "Although it is impossible to state definitely the amount of change in the average length of life of the Negro population, the available data indicate that, except for the first few years of life, there has been very little improvement since the beginning of the century. The only series of data covering the entire period are for Negroes living in the original registration states of 1900, the New England States, New York, New Jersey, Michigan, Indiana and the District of Columbia. In 1900, the Negro population of these states comprised 3.9 per cent of the total; by 1930, it had increased to 9.5 per cent of the total. Although the trend in mortality among Negroes in these states is probably representative of the trend among Negroes living in the North there is no way of determining the closeness with which it represents the trend of mortality among Negroes living in the South.

"As shown in Figure 21, the expectation of life among Negroes living in the North actually decreased during the first three decades of this century except for persons 20 years of age and younger. The increase in expectation of life at birth was greater both absolutely and relatively among Negroes than among whites, but at other ages it was much less. (Figure 22.)

"Better representation of the entire Negro population can be obtained by considering the trend of mortality in the death registration states of 1920. This group of states included about 65 per cent of the Negro population in 1920 and nearly 70 per cent in 1930. The trend of mortality among Negroes in these states presents an even more unfavorable picture than the trend in the original registration states. (Figure 23.) The expectation of life for Negro males decreased at every age including birth; the decrease among Negro females occurred at ages 20 and over. The only increase in expectation of life during the decade was for females under 20 years of age.

"The trend in the expectation of life among Negroes in the general population agrees in general with that among the colored policy-holders of the Industrial Department of the Metropolitan Life Insurance Company (Louis I. Dublin and Alfred J. Lotka, *Twenty-five Years of Health Progress* [1937]). From 1921 to 1931 the expectation of life for both males and females from 10 to 60 years of age either decreased or failed to increase. However, from 1911 to 1921 the expectation of life definitely increased at the same ages. Since 1931 the downward trend in the expectation of life has been stopped and slight increases have occurred at most ages. But even so, in 1938 the expectation of life for colored males was less than in 1921 at 40 years of age and over and among colored females it was less at 50 years of age and over." (Metropolitan Life Insurance Company, *Statistical Bulletin* [June, 1939]. Dorn, *op. cit.* [1942; first draft, 1940], pp. 36-37a). (Figures referred to are in Dorn's manuscript.)

¹⁸ *Ibid.*, p. 4c.

¹⁹ For the death registration states at each of the years, the white death rate was 10.8 per 1,000 population in 1930, and 10.4 in 1940. The corresponding drop in the

Negro death rate was from 16.5 to 13.9. These figures are subject to several types of error, but the comparative drops in the two rates are fairly reliable. Calculated from data in: U. S. Bureau of the Census, *Vital Statistics—Special Reports: 1940*, Vol. 14, No. 2, p. 9. Population bases for 1940 taken from: *Sixteenth Census of the United States: 1940, Population.* Preliminary release: Series P-10, No. 1.

See also the quotation from Dorn in the preceding footnote.

[20] *Sixteenth Census of the United States: 1940, Population.* Preliminary Release: Series P-5, No. 3.

[21] A. J. Jaffe, "Urbanization and Fertility," *American Journal of Sociology* (July, 1942).

[22] If we use the net reproduction rate as an index of birth rate, and recognize the general deficiencies of the data, it is something of a measure of the truth of this statement that the relevant net reproduction rates were as follows in 1940.

	Rural Farm	Urban
Nonwhite	154	76
White	132	76

Sixteenth Census of the United States: 1940, Population. Preliminary Release: Series P-5, No. 4.

[23] "In 19 counties most of which immediately adjoin the lower Mississippi River in Arkansas, Mississippi, and Louisiana, the fertility of the Negro rural-farm population drops to comparatively low levels. In the year 1930, the ratio of children under 5 per 1,000 women 20-44 among rural-farm Negroes was 885 in the entire United States, 725 in Mississippi, 768 in Louisiana, and 718 in Arkansas, but only 518 in this group of counties. In some counties the ratio of children to women, even after correction for under-enumeration, was approximately at replacement levels (491) or even below." (Conrad and Irene B. Taeuber, "Negro Rural Fertility Ratios in the Mississippi Delta," *The Southwestern Social Science Quarterly* [December, 1940], p. 210.) This study was made from unpublished tables of the Metropolitan Life Insurance Company.

[24] If we use net reproduction rates to give us an index of birth rates, Series P-5a of the preliminary 1940 census releases (Nos. 14, 15, 16) permits a rough comparison of the Negro-white net reproduction rates in the urban South and of eastern and western urban areas within the South:

NET REPRODUCTION RATES IN SOUTHERN REGIONS: 1940

Census Division	Urban		Rural Nonfarm		Rural Farm	
	White	Nonwhite	White	Nonwhite	White	Nonwhite
South Atlantic	71	73	119	118	144	159
East South Central	79	70	128	101	150	163
West South Central	81	68	115	109	142	158

[25] See, for example, E. R. Groves and W. F. Ogburn, *American Marriage and Family Relations* (1928), pp. 447-448.

[26] Registration statistics indicate a higher death rate for Negroes in the North than

in the South, but there is notorious under-registration of deaths in the South and expert opinion seems to hold to a lower specific death rate in the North. While there are influences which tend to raise the death rate for Negroes in the North—such as novel climate, novel diet, and perhaps greater exposure to venereal disease—the influences which work to make the Negro death rate lower in the North than in the South seem— *a priori*—to be more important. In the North there is much easier access to modern medical facilities; the standard of living is higher; and Negroes are better educated. The death rate of infants and children is unequivocally lower in the North, even if that for adults is not.

[27] *Sixteenth Census of the United States: 1940, Population.* Preliminary Release: Series P-5, No. 4. Because of deficiencies in census enumeration, these figures are not perfect. Also the nonwhite rate covers colored persons other than Negroes. A large difference in the declines, however, is certain.

[28] Studies showing the relation between income and vital rates among Negroes are: Philip M. Hauser, "Differential Fertility, Mortality, and Net Reproduction in Chicago, 1930," unpublished Ph.D. thesis. The University of Chicago (1938). Frank W. Notestein, "Differential Fertility in the East North Central States," *The Milbank Memorial Fund Quarterly* (April, 1938). Clyde V. Kiser, "Birth Rates and Socio-Economic Attributes in 1935," *The Milbank Memorial Fund Quarterly* (April, 1939).

[29] *Sixteenth Census of the United States: 1940, Population.* Second Series, State Table 4.

[30] U. S. Bureau of the Census, *A Century of Population Growth in the United States: 1790-1900*, p. 86, and U. S. Bureau of the Census, *Negroes in the United States: 1920-1932*, p. 21.

[31] Clyde V. Kiser, "Fertility of Harlem Negroes," *The Milbank Memorial Fund Quarterly* (July, 1935), p. 275.

[32] For a short review of this discussion, see Samuel A. Stouffer and Lyonel C. Florant, "Negro Population and Negro Population Movements, 1860 to 1940, in Relation to Social and Economic Factors," unpublished manuscript prepared for this study (1940); (revised by Lyonel C. Florant under title, "Negro Migration—1860-1940" [1942]) Chapter III, pp. 15-25.

[33] There are several other factors to take into account when explaining the general inarticulateness of practical thinking on population in America; see Gunnar Myrdal, *Population: A Problem for Democracy* (1940), pp. 24-30 and 66-72, and Alva Myrdal, *Nation and Family* (1941), pp. 9-10. General statements on American population policy may be found in Frank Lorimer, Ellen Winston, and Louise K. Kiser, *Foundations of American Population Policy* (1940); and Frederick Osborn, *Preface to Eugenics* (1940).

It is a public secret that the National Resources Committee before publishing its report, *The Problems of a Changing Population* (1938), found itself obliged to take out the discussion of birth control contained in the original draft.

[34] Compare Alva Myrdal, *op. cit.*, Chapters VII and VIII.

[35] W. Montague Cobb, "The Negro as a Biological Element in the American Population," *Journal of Negro Education* (July, 1939), p. 347.

[36] W. E. B. Du Bois, "Black Folk and Birth Control," *Birth Control Review* (June, 1932), p. 167. George S. Schuyler takes a position similar to that of Du Bois in the following statement:

"The question for Negroes is this: Shall they go in for quantity or quality in children?

Shall they bring children into the world to enrich the undertakers, the physicians and furnish work for social workers and jailers, or shall they produce children who are going to be an asset to the group and to American society. Most Negroes, especially the women, would go in for quality production if they only knew how." ("Quantity or Quality," *Birth Control Review* [June, 1932], p. 166.)

Another indication that Negroes favor quality even at the expense of quantity is the fact that 34 of the most eminent Negro leaders have endorsed the work of the Planned Parenthood Federation of America and have lent their names to the letterhead of its Division of Negro Service.

[37] This point has been made in detail by Osborn, *op. cit.*

[38] Council on Medical Education and Hospitals, "Hospitals and Medical Care in Mississippi," *Journal of the American Medical Association* (June 3, 1939), p. 2319.

[39] The Duke Endowment, *Fourteenth Annual Report of the Hospital Section* (1939), p. 6.

[40] H. M. Green, "Hospitals and Public Health Facilities for Negroes," *Proceedings of the National Conference of Social Work* (1928), pp. 178-180. In 1942, Edwin R. Embree reports that, for the United States as a whole, there are now "110 Negro hospitals in the United States, of which some 25 have been accredited, 13 of them approved for the full training of internes by the Council on Medical Education and Hospitals of the American Hospital Association. . . . While there are today 10,000 hospital beds for Negroes in the country, in some areas where the population is heavily Negro there are as few as 75 beds set aside for over one million of this group." (Julius Rosenwald Fund, *Review for the Two-Year Period 1940-1942* [1942], pp. 13-14).

[41] Dorn, *op. cit.* (1940), p. 97.

[42] Compared to a proportion of 21.3 per cent of all Negroes, 55.0 per cent of the Negro dentists, 42.6 per cent of the Negro physicians and surgeons and 36.3 per cent of the Negro nurses were outside the South in 1930. (U. S. Bureau of the Census, *Negroes in the United States: 1920-1932*, p. 293.)

[43] For a description of how Negro folk practices are dangerous to health, see Newbell N. Puckett, *Folk Beliefs of the Southern Negro* (1926).

[44] U. S. Bureau of the Census, *Vital Statistics—Special Reports: 1940*, Vol. 14, No. 2, p. 9. The infant mortality rate was 43.2 for 1,000 live births for whites and 72.9 for Negroes.

[45] *Idem.* The maternal mortality rate per 1,000 live births was 3.2 for whites and 7.8 for Negroes.

[46] Vance has calculated that for the Southeastern states in 1930, 27 per cent of Negro women have no births as compared to 19 per cent of white women, while 29 per cent of Negroes have one birth as compared to 18 per cent of white women. (Rupert B. Vance, "The Regional Approach to the Study of High Fertility," *The Milbank Memorial Fund Quarterly* [October, 1941], pp. 356-374.)

In 1930, the following proportions of families had no children under 10 years of age.

	Negro	Native White
North: Urban	68.1	62.6
South: Urban	67.1	58.1
Rural farm	46.7	44.2
Rural nonfarm	59.0	47.9

Calculated from census data by Richard Sterner and Associates, *The Negro's Share*, prepared for this study (1943), Appendix Table 17. Also see Notestein, *op. cit.*, and Kirk, *op. cit.*, pp. 51-65.

[47] Raymond Pearl, "Fertility and Contraception in Urban Whites and Negroes," *Science* (May, 1936), pp. 503-506. Also see by the same author, *The Natural History of Population* (1939), p. 113, *passim*.

[48] U.S. Bureau of the Census, *Vital Statistics—Special Reports: 1940*, Vol. 14, No. 2, p. 9.

[49] Dorn, *op. cit.*, (1942; first draft, 1940), pp. 35-44.

[50] "Sterilization laws have been passed by 29 states, and over 1,000 operations have been performed in each of 7 states, namely, California, Kansas, Michigan, Minnesota, Oregon, Virginia, and Wisconsin. The total number of sterilizations performed in the United States up to January 1, 1940, was approximately 33,000 of which 17,212 were on insane cases and 15,231 on feeble-minded; 592 were sterilized for other reasons." (Publications of the Human Betterment Foundation, Pasadena, California [1940]. Cited by Osborn, *op. cit.*, p. 31.)

[51] Practically every modern discussion of birth control in every scientific book and every propaganda pamphlet contains a list of such reasons.

[52] Official mortality statistics of the death registration states of 1930 which are defective, not only in revealing total numbers of deaths, but also in classifying these deaths by causes, show a syphilis rate of 42.5 for Negroes and 5.2 for whites (per 100,000 population, 1929-1931). Death rates may not accurately reflect the relative incidence of syphilis, but Dorn summarizes sample studies which also show the Negro rate to be between 3 and 9 times as great as the white rate in various communities. (Dorn, *op. cit.* [1940], p. 71.)

Recently some excellent data have become available on syphilis. Examination of the first million draft registrants—who are a selected sample of the population but a significant sample—showed that the syphilis rate was 18.5 per thousand for whites and 241.2 for Negroes. That is, Negroes had 13 times as much syphilis as whites. (See: New York *Herald Tribune* [October 16, 1941], p. 5; and *PM* [February 10, 1942], p. 20.)

Since much less is known about gonorrhea, and since it does not seem to be much more prevalent among Negroes than among whites, it will not be discussed here.

[53] H. Poindexter, "Special Health Problems of Negroes in Rural Areas," *Journal of Negro Education* (July, 1937), p. 407.

[54] On January 1, 1940, there were 2,527 such clinics. Dorn, *op. cit.* (1940), p. 155.

[55] The LaFollette-Bulwinkle Act (1938) authorized federal grants-in-aid to the various states for venereal disease control.

[56] Dorn, *op. cit.*, (1940), p. 114-b-3.

[57] "For the most part, the only time that a doctor may legally interrupt pregnancy in the United States is when its continuance threatens the life of a mother. Six states— Florida, Louisiana, Massachusetts, New Hampshire, Pennsylvania, and New Jersey— overlook even this contingency, having no specific provision for therapeutic abortion. Seven states—Arkansas, Georgia, Kansas, Missouri, Ohio, Texas, and Wisconsin expressly require medical advice prior to the act, while thirty-one states, including New York, sanction abortion to save the life of the mother, with no provision for medical counsel. Only three states—Colorado, Maryland, and New Mexico—and the District

of Columbia countenance the interruption of pregnancy not only to save the life of the mother but also to preserve her health. The Mississippi law forbids abortions but adds the cryptic provision, 'unless the same shall have been advised by a physician to be necessary for such purpose.'" (B. B. Tolnai, "Abortions and the Law," *Nation* [April 15, 1939], p. 425.)

[58] U.S. Bureau of the Census, *Births, Stillbirths and Infant Mortality Statistics: 1936*, p. 9.

[59] Alva Myrdal, *op. cit.*

[60] For the dramatic history of the movement see: Margaret Sanger, *My Fight for Birth Control* (1931) or *Autobiography* (1938).

[61] The legal fight began in 1873 when the anti-birth control forces led by Anthony Comstock secured a federal law prohibiting the use of the mails for the dissemination of birth control information and prohibiting the importation of contraceptives. Many of the state governments before or after this year took steps to stop the sale of contraceptives and the encouragement of their use. The scope of the federal law was somewhat narrowed by a series of court decisions, but a major setback to this law did not come until 1936, when the United States Court of Appeals for the Second Circuit declared that birth control devices and information could be imported and sent through the mails by *doctors* "for the purpose of saving life or promoting the well-being of their patients." In the meantime some states have repealed or nullified their laws.

In July, 1942, 19 states make no mention of the prevention of conception in their statutes; 13 states have statutes which restrict the distribution and dissemination of information regarding the prevention of conception, but expressly exempt medical practice; 14 states have statutes aimed at the advertising and distribution of information regarding the prevention of conception, but exempt medical practice by implication or construction; only two states—Massachusetts and Connecticut—have laws which penalize even physicians for giving information. (See: "The Legal Status of Contraception," mimeographed leaflet distributed by the Planned Parenthood Federation of America, July, 1942.) Three states actually sponsor birth control clinics. But the fight is far from won: the federal law remains on the books for all nonmedical persons and even for medical persons in the Territories and the District of Columbia; in 1937 a private clinic was closed in Massachusetts and the personnel subjected to criminal prosecution (there was a similar occurrence in Connecticut); 45 states do not give the birth control movement the active support it needs to be really effective.

[62] E. Mae McCarroll, "A Report on the Two-Year Negro Demonstration Health Program of the Planned Parenthood Federation of America, Inc." A talk delivered at the annual convention of the National Medical Association, Cleveland, August 17, 1942. Of the 803 birth control centers, 225 were located in hospitals, 265 in health department quarters, and 313 in settlement houses, churches and similar institutions.

[63] The only three states with birth control officially incorporated into the general public health program—North Carolina, South Carolina, and Alabama—are in the South. Several other Southern states are expected to join this group shortly, but no Northern ones. By July, 1942, there were, in the United States, 345 contraceptive centers deriving all or part of their support from taxes. North Carolina, South Carolina, and Alabama had 47 per cent of these. Over 24 per cent more were found in 13 other Southern states (among Southern states only Louisiana and Mississippi had none). Twenty-one Northern and Western states had the remaining 29 per cent (almost half

of these were in California). Clearly the South leads in the public acceptance of birth control. ("Distribution of Birth Control Centers and Services," mimeographed sheet, Planned Parenthood Federation of America, Inc. [July, 1942].)

[64] The facts for this paragraph have been generously provided by Miss Florence Rose of the Planned Parenthood Federation of America (interview, August 21, 1942). Also see:

1. Claude C. Pierce, "State Programs for Planned Parenthood," address read at the Conference of State and Provincial Health Authorities of North America, Washington, D.C., March 23-24, 1942.

2. G. M. Cooper, F. R. Pratt, and M. J. Hagood, "Four Years of Contraception as a Public Health Service in North Carolina," *American Journal of Public Health* (December 1941), p. 2.

3. George M. Cooper, "Birth Control in the North Carolina Health Department," *North Carolina Medical Journal* (September, 1940), p. 463.

4. Robert Seibels, "The Integration of Pregnancy Spacing into a State Maternal Welfare Program," *Southern Medicine and Surgery* (May, 1940), pp. 230-233.

5. J. N. Baker, Director, Alabama State Department of Health, "Alabama's Program for Planned Parenthood," address delivered at the Third Southern Conference on Tomorrow's Children, Nashville, Tennessee, October 31, 1941.

[65] Address by Dorothy Boulding Ferebee at the Annual Meeting of the Birth Control Federation of America, January 29, 1942.

[66] Information made available by Miss Florence Rose of the Planned Parenthood Federation of America (interview, August 21, 1942).

[67] For a discussion of these prejudices among Negroes, see an address given by Dr. Dorothy Boulding Ferebee, "Planned Parenthood as a Public Health Measure for the Negro Race," delivered at the annual meeting of the Birth Control Federation of America, January 29, 1942. Dr. Ferebee lists the popular objections as:

1. the concept that when birth control is proposed to them, it is motivated by a clever bit of machination to persuade them to commit race suicide;

2. the so-called "husband-objection" which Dr. Robert E. Seibels of the South Carolina rural project observes "is often blamed on physical reactions to the material, but apparently is related more to superstitious fear of impairment of function through interference with a vital process."

3. the fact that birth control is confused with abortion, and,

4. the belief that it is inherently immoral.

[68] *Ibid.*, for a study showing the greater inefficiency of Negro women in using contraceptives, see Pearl, *The Natural History of Population*, pp. 113-114, 193. On the other hand, the Planned Parenthood Federation's experiment in Berkeley County, South Carolina, led to the conclusion that "80 per cent of the contacted population of Negroes of low income and low intelligence level will use pregnancy spacing methods when this is properly presented to them." (Robert E. Seibels, "A Rural Project in Negro Maternal Health," *Human Fertility* [April, 1941], p. 44.) After two years of the Federation's project at Nashville, 58 per cent of the 610 patients instructed used the method prescribed "consistently" and successfully (McCarroll, *op. cit.*, p. 8.)

[69] The following discussion is largely based on a similar one regarding Sweden, by Alva Myrdal, *op. cit.*, p. 200 ff.

[70] There are several controversial issues involved in the above suggestion that an

educational campaign be instigated to reach the masses with specific birth control advice. The first is a legal question: The Comstock Law still stands on the federal statutes books for all nonmedical people and would probably be involved if general advice—not directed to specific cases investigated by a doctor—were distributed through the mails. Twenty-nine states also still have laws which prohibit nonmedical people from giving birth control advice. But the birth control organizations are no longer fighting the Comstock Law or the state laws (outside of those in Massachusetts and Connecticut, which apply to doctors). They are content to let them stand since they no longer apply to doctors. The second problem is one of quackery: if nonmedical people were allowed to give advice, there would be all sorts of dangerous or useless contraceptives put on the market and advertised. But this is already happening, except that the mails are not used, even in those states where it is illegal. People know that physicians can give contraceptive information; to overcome quackery it is necessary to disseminate correct information on a mass scale without waiting for people to consult physicians. Too, it is possible to have laws which practically eliminate quackery. A third issue is the question of what the popular reaction might be: birth control organizations are afraid of losing the support of doctors and others of the "best people" and of being called "immoral." This is probably the decisive issue which prevents the birth control organizations from giving concrete information to the masses of the people. But the question remains as to whether there would be such a popular reaction, whether this reaction would nullify all the small but positive gains that have been made, and whether an extensive publicity campaign would not counterbalance any reaction.

[71] Because of the tendency to work through physicians, even greater emphasis than is necessitated by facts has been laid on the contraceptive techniques which require a doctor's advice; the pessary and the foam-and-sponge techniques. The simple methods of the condom and *coitus interruptus* are deplored. Yet the leading medical authorities, Dickinson and Morris, in a manual issued by the Birth Control Federation itself, have the following to say about the condom:

"Properly tested, the condom provides protection as efficient as any method, and, skillfully used, *furnishes security*. . . . It ought to enjoy a much more favorable attitude on the part of the clinician." (Robert L. Dickinson and Woodbridge E. Morris, *Techniques of Conception Control* [1941], p. 34.)

It may be that when all people know about birth control, and when the task is to get its methods perfected and individualized, it will be wise to shift emphasis back again from the condom to the pessary, since the latter is supposed to be the most efficient and least annoying method. Since it happens that the condom and *coitus interruptus* methods are for men, the pessary and other methods available to women should be spread so that women, too, should have opportunity to control conception.

[72] The public clinics now in existence disseminate information about birth control solely by mentioning it to women who have come into the public health office for other purposes, especially to women who have just had a child. Only indigent women use the public clinic; others are referred to a private physician.

The demonstration projects sponsored by the Planned Parenthood Federation have a similarly slow method of reaching the public. During two years of the project at Nashville, only 638 patients were advised, and during 21 months of the project in Berkeley County, South Carolina, only 1,008 patients were advised. (McCarroll, *op. cit.*, pp. 7, 11.) It should be recognized, however, that completeness and not extensive coverage was the aim of these projects. Still, the achievements were small in view of the large amount of money spent. Not even the governments could afford to maintain permanent birth control clinics all over if they were as expensive as these two, and yet far from all persons needing contraceptive information in the two areas were reached. Despite the excellent work of the projects with those women contacted, the small number of women contacted shows how limited such clinics are.

Chapter 8. *Migration*

[1] The primary census data are somewhat unreliable, particularly for the South, and especially for Negroes. They are, furthermore, unreliable in a different degree from one census to another. Apart from this, such data as exist can only account for the composite *result* of migration together with all other factors of population change during a preceding decade, or the extent to which all persons living at the time of a census resided elsewhere than in their states of birth. We cannot, therefore, expect to gain any intensive and accurate knowledge of the movement of the population. All short-distance mobility is out of the picture. So also are stages and steps in migration, and all moves in one direction which are compensated for by the same persons' (or other persons') migration in the opposite direction (within the decade between two censuses). All yearly fluctuations are canceled out in the aggregate figures. Only a suggestion of stages of migration may be had by comparing different states as to the character of their populations born outside the state. Only to a limited extent are there studies available for small parts of the population, allowing us to make valid inferences in these several respects. Perhaps the most useful of these is the information that may be had from the question asked of all farmers for the 1935 Census of Agriculture, "Where were you living five years ago?"

The 1940 Census attempts to correct many of the earlier deficiencies by supplying information from all persons in the United States on the same question: "Where were you living five years ago?" This does not meet all requirements for knowledge about migration, but it will offer a body of information vastly superior to anything that now exists. Unfortunately the information is not yet available at the time of writing (summer, 1942).

[2] U.S. Census Office, *Statistics of the United States in 1860*, pp. 337-338.

[3] There are no data available to determine the exact size of the net migration of Negroes from South to North between 1910 and 1940. The figure of one and three-quarters million presented in the text is simply the difference between the Northern Negro population for 1940 and that for 1910. To use this figure as an index of net migration involves making two assumptions: (1) The net reproduction rate of Negroes in the North during this period was 1.00, on the average. Actually it probably averaged less than 1.00. (2) The age distribution of the Northern Negro population was, on the average, that of a life table population. Actually there was probably a greater proportion of persons in the child-bearing ages. The errors in our two assumptions affect our estimate of net migration in opposite ways. We have, therefore, only one assumption—that these two errors cancel each other.

Du Bois estimated that two million Negroes migrated North by 1930. But his estimate is of total migration and does not exclude those who returned South. (W. E. B. Du Bois, "A Negro Nation within the Nation," *Current History* [June, 1935], p. 265.)

⁴ Stouffer and Florant, *op. cit.*, p. 36. According to W. D. Weatherford and Charles S. Johnson (*Race Relations* [1934], p. 257) most of the Negroes who went to Liberia at first were ex-slaves who were freed on the condition that they emigrate.

⁵ The Negro population of Kansas increased from 627 to 43,107 between 1860 and 1880 according to the census. Part of this was natural increase, of course, and only some of the increase occurred during the period when there was agitation for Negro migration to Kansas. But there was also some return migration to the South.

⁶ James Weldon Johnson, *Along This Way* (1934), pp. 206-207 and 208.

⁷ This reclassification was prepared by the Bureau of the Census with the aid of O. E. Baker of the United States Department of Agriculture. The computation of the Negro population of these areas back to 1860 was done by Stouffer and Wyant.

⁸ Stouffer and Florant, *op cit.* (1940), pp. 1-58 and technical appendix prepared by Rowena Wyant.

⁹ Stouffer and Florant, *op. cit.* (1940), p. 5.

¹⁰ As the National Resources Committee points out, part of the migration northward was by stages and part of it was direct from the Deep South.

"Much of the Negro migration has been a State-to-State displacement. By 1930, for example, 72,000 Negroes had moved into North Carolina from South Carolina, but 47,000 had moved out of North Carolina to Virginia and Maryland. More than 50 per cent of the Negroes leaving South Carolina, Georgia, Alabama, Mississippi, and Louisiana have settled in other Southern states, while about 90 per cent of those leaving Kentucky and 65 per cent of those leaving Virginia and Tennessee have settled in the North. At the same time there has been considerable migration directly from the deep South to the North." (National Resources Committee, *The Problems of a Changing Population* [1938], p. 99.)

¹¹ Stouffer and Florant, *op. cit.* (1942), pp. 54-58.

¹² These calculations are taken from Stouffer and Florant, *op. cit.* (1940), Chapter I, pp. 17-18. These authors include Missouri in the Border states, and their definition of the North, as noted in the text, is confined to the Northern states east of the Mississippi River.

¹³ U. S. Bureau of Census, *Negroes in the United States: 1920-1932*, p. 22.

¹⁴ *Fifteenth Census of the United States: 1930, Population*, Vol. 2, pp. 158-162.

¹⁵ *Ibid.*, pp. 163-167.

¹⁶ The literature on Negro migration is too large to be surveyed, even too large to be sampled for purposes of this section. In 1934, F. A. Ross and L. V. Kennedy prepared a whole book entitled *A Bibliography of Negro Migration*, and since then many other titles would have to be added to their list. In the monograph prepared for this study by Stouffer and Florant, a large and selected sample of this tremendous literature was integrated. For this section we have relied largely on this monograph and on a few of the better-known books on the subject, such as those by C. G. Woodson (*A Century of Negro Migration* [1918]), The Chicago Commission on Race Relations (*The Negro in Chicago* [1922]), L. V. Kennedy (*The Negro Peasant Turns City-ward* [1930]), C. V. Kiser (*Sea Island to City* [1932]). The general literature on the Negro also has much on migration. Because of the size of this literature we have felt that it would be best to make this section rather abstract. The conditions which are

referred to here in passing are usually taken up in greater detail in other parts of this book.

17 Woodson, *op. cit.*, Chapter 8. Also see Ray Stannard Baker, *Following the Color Line* (1908), p. 110.

18 Some experts on the problem hold a single-cause theory of Negro migration. They believe that migration is a result only of new economic opportunities in cities. Negroes went North because the cities were in the North, and if the cities had been in the South, Negroes should never have left the South in spite of its traditional prejudice and discrimination against them. (See, for example, Donald R. Young, *American Minority Peoples* [1932], pp. 46 ff; and T. J. Woofter, Jr., *Races and Ethnic Groups in American Life* [1933], p. 113.)

The incorrectness of this theory can be judged by speculating what would happen if the situation were to be reversed. If suddenly there should be a new development of industry in the South which would open many new jobs of the unskilled and service type to Negroes, at the same time as there was economic stagnation and unemployment in the North, it is not likely that Northern Negroes would migrate South in such numbers as Southern Negroes migrated North under comparable circumstances after 1915.

19 In other words, the real "causes" of migration were as numerous as the Negroes who migrated and as complex as the entire life-experiences of these Negroes. These real causes were not simply a series of "conditions" or "factors" impinging on the individual, but they were complexes of factors actively interpreted, weighed, and integrated in the conscious and unconscious minds of individuals. What the analyst must do, however, is to resolve into elements the complex structure of the motivations of individuals, group these elements, and determine which are the important ones—the ones without which the migration would have involved significantly fewer numbers than it did. Such important classes of elements in the motivation of the migrants are usually termed "causes" of the migration, but they must be recognized to be causes in only a special sense—neither inevitable in their influence nor all-inclusive as explanations for the migration of all those who migrated. Unfortunately, due to the complexity of migration and the fact that it is always an event in the past and to the poorness of the data, the relative importance of the factors cannot be measured. The significance assigned to them is a function of the observer's judgment, based upon his knowledge of the history of the migration.

20 The returning migrants probably mounted up to the thousands in the early days of the depression of the 1930's when jobs were no longer available and the relief machinery was not yet set up. Some local Urban Leagues and certain city governments sponsored plans to send Negroes back to the South.

21 Richard Sterner and Associates, *The Negro's Share*. Prepared for this study (1943), p. 40.

22 Unpublished estimates by Stouffer and Florant indicate that the net migration of Negroes from the South was 317,000 between 1930 and 1940 as compared to 716,000 between 1920 and 1930. As the authors recognize, there is a considerable margin of error in both figures. (*Op. cit.*, [1940], p. 124.)

23 Two recent incidents are illustrative of this point.

   1. A California law prohibiting the entry of indigents from other states was declared unconstitutional by the Supreme Court of the United States (No. 17, October

term 1941; Fred F. Edwards, Appellant *vs.* The People of the State of California; November 24, 1941).

2. In attempting to build a labor camp for Southern Negroes near Burlington, New Jersey, in May, 1942, the Farm Security Administration met the opposition of the nearby township government. Nevertheless the F.S.A. went right ahead with its plans and there was no opposition from Congress (including the local congressman). The F.S.A. was supported by the local farmers who needed the labor which the camp would provide.

[24] Between 1930 and 1940, the Negro population of California increased 53 per cent.

[25] There are some new agricultural job opportunities on the West Coast—such as in cotton planting and commercial fruit growing in California—but these are likely to go to whites now migrating from the West Plains and from the South, and to Mexicans.

[26] Tannenbaum, for instance, says:

"The South, in a search for solutions, must turn to the gradual migration of the negro and his replacement by foreign labor. These two factors are the only available means at hand for the breaking up of emotional concentration upon the negro, the gradual achievement of objectivity in attitude towards him, the slow softening of the burden of fear and hate that has seared and seared the South to this very day." (Frank Tannenbaum, *Darker Phases of the South* [1924], p. 182.)

[27] See Woofter, *op. cit.*, p. 198; John Temple Graves, "The Southern Negro and the War Crisis," *Virginia Quarterly Review* (Autumn, 1942), pp. 512-513.

[28] Woodson, *op. cit.*, pp. 183-186; W. E. B. Du Bois, "The Hosts of Black Labor," *Nation* (May 9, 1923), pp. 539-541; and James Weldon Johnson, *Black Manhattan* (1930), p. 152.

Chapter 9. *Economic Inequality*

[1] Charles S. Johnson, Edwin R. Embree, and W. W. Alexander, *The Collapse of Cotton Tenancy* (1935), pp. 14-15 and 21-22.

[2] National Resources Planning Board, *National Resources Development, Report for 1942* (1942), p. 3. Points 6-8 are omitted here as irrelevant to our present discussion.

[3] This is a world-wide trend; for a discussion of the basic principles involved, see Alva Myrdal, *Nation and Family* (1941).

[4] See *The Public Opinion Quarterly* (October, 1939), pp. 586-587 and (Fall, 1941), p. 475.

[5] See *The Public Opinion Quarterly* (October, 1939), p. 592; (March, 1940), p. 91; (September, 1940), p. 547; and (Fall, 1941), p. 477.

[6] *Bulletin of the Bureau of School Service, University of Kentucky*, "A Salary Study for the Lexington Public Schools" (March, 1935), p. 26.

[7] For an excellent example of how a wide variety of these arguments are marshaled one after the other, we may quote in full a letter to the editor of the Richmond *News Leader* concerning differential salaries for school teachers:

"ARGUES NEGRO TEACHERS SHOULD RECEIVE LESS

"Editor of the News Leader:

"Sir,—There is a sort of soft-soap piety floating around in our part of the world that is like the will-o-the-wisp that rises from miasmic swampland. It floats majestically over the 'Negro question,' but when analyzed there is nothing to it. The special point about which it is bobbing now is 'equalization of teachers' salaries.' Let's cast the light of reality (or, should I say, the sunlight of truth?) over the shadowed point and present it as many of us vitally interested really see it.

"Should Negro teachers receive the same salary that white teachers receive? Emphatically, No! Why not?

"(1) Less than 10 per cent. of our taxes is paid by Negroes. Of course, destitute white children attend the same schools that wealthy ones attend, but they are of the same race, an identical social unit, with co-ordinating future obligations.

"(2) Negroes do not teach the same type of future citizens that white teachers instruct. God made the two races different and exacts of them their own best contributions. White people have and will continue to have responsibility 'the brothers in black' cannot assume.

"(3) Negroes do not teach the same things in reality and in the same way that white instructors do. The average Negro has an honorable service to render outside the academic field.

"(4) White people owe Negroes no especial debt, save to 'love one another' in a Christian way. The Negro race has gained far more from the civic contact with the white than can be here portrayed—and Negro people generally know this and appreciate it, the 'soft-soap piety' generally bubbling from the caucasian mouth . . . Why do these people bubble and babble? Perhaps because it is a psychological truth that everyone wants to make a 'splash' in life's 'mud-puddle!'

"(5) If Negro people are paid the same salaries the white teachers receive, salaries will not be equalized, but Negro teachers will have more, as their living expenses are less. This economic fact should have weight. Compare rent lists in good sections for white and Negro, for instance.

"Let's not 'fly in the face of God' and His great plan. While He made all men of one blood, He gave them gifts differing. Let not the white girl's salary for service in the schoolroom be lessened, as it has already been markedly in a few cases, for her financial responsibilities, as well as her pedagogical efforts, must be greater than her Negro sister's. And above all, don't confuse piety with bubbles!

Montrose."[a]

8 "A Salary Study for the Lexington Public Schools," *op. cit.*, p. 25. See Chapter 14, Section 4.

Chapter 10. *The Tradition of Slavery*

[1] Rupert B. Vance, *Human Geography of the South* (1932), p. 467.

[2] *Ibid.*, p. 474.

[3] *Ibid.*, p. 467.

[4] John Dollard, *Caste and Class in a Southern Town* (1937), p. 55.

[5] W. E. B. Du Bois, *Black Reconstruction* (1935), p. 13.

[a] "The News Leader Forum," Richmond *News Leader* (December 6, 1941).

[6] Sir George Campbell, traveling in the South in the 'seventies, listened to many old slave breeders who told him about the same story:

". . . the slaves were not worked out like omnibus horses; in fact, the capital sunk in slaves was so heavy, and produce had become so cheap, that the principal source of profit was what was called the 'increase' of the slaves—the breeding them for the market or for new plantations opened in the more Western States. As in breeding-farms for other kinds of stock, the human stock was carefully, and, on the whole, kindly treated; and although the selling off the young stock as it became fit for the market was a barbarous process, still, the family relations being so weak, as I have described, those who remained did not feel it so much as we should; and I think it may be said that the relations between the masters and the slaves were generally not unkindly. One old gentlemen in Carolina dwelt much on the kindness and success with which he had treated his slaves, adding as the proof and the moral that they had doubled in twenty years." (*White and Black in the United States* [1879], pp. 140-141.)

[7] Large numbers of ex-slaves lapsed into temporary vagrancy at the end of the Civil War. They, naturally, wanted to test their new freedom. Not without reason, they also feared re-enslavement. The general upheaval and the curtailment of production during and after the War were also responsible for the vagrancy. The hope which was never fulfilled, that the federal government would provide them with land of their own, also contributed to the unrest. "This belief is seriously interfering with the willingness of the freedmen to make contracts for the coming year," reported General Grant to the President in 1865.[a] Many of them regarded steady employment with a white plantation owner as slavery. Heavy work and slavery then appeared to them as pretty synonymous concepts:

> Mammy don't you cook no mo',
> You's free! You's free!
> Rooster don't you crow no mo',
> You's free! You's free!
> Ol' hen, don't you lay no mo' eggs,
> You's free! You's free!
> Ol' pig, don't you grunt no mo',
> You's free! You's free!
> Ol' cow, don't you give no mo' milk,
> You's free! You's free!
> Ain't got to slave no mo',
> We's free! We's free![b]

Such a reaction was by no means general. The accounts of it probably have been exaggerated considerably,[c] because of the need to rationalize the system which was then being built up to keep the Negro worker in his place. In comparison with Southern whites, especially upper class whites and white women of all classes, Negroes were probably never characterized by unusual laziness. It was only by comparison with the continuous labor under slavery, and aided by forced unemployment, that Negroes suddenly appeared lazy. If Negroes ever manifested an unusual unwillingness to work,

[a] Cited by Hilary A. Herbert, *Why the Solid South?* (1890), p. 17.
[b] Cited by Federal Writers' Project, *The Negro in Virginia* (1940), p. 210.
[c] *Ibid.*, pp. 223-224.

it was only in the first year or two after the end of the War. In so far as it did appear during this period of general disorganization, it was just plain human. The institution of slavery to a great extent had debased ordinary work in the appreciation of black and white alike. It was psychologically inescapable that slavery should backfire in this way, particularly during the initial period of freedom.

[8] Rupert B. Vance gives this concentrated account of how the system of share tenancy came into being and how it became fixed upon the region:

"A stricken upper class possessing nothing but lands met a servile population possessed of nought except the labor of their hands. In what must have been an era of primitive barter, a system was arrived at whereby labor was secured without money wages and land without money rent. Up and down the Cotton Belt southern states after 1865 vied with one another in passing crop lien laws. Accepted as the temporary salvation of a wrecked economic structure, the system has increasingly set the mode for southern agriculture. Under the crop lien system the unpropertied farmer mortgages his ungrown crop for the supplies necessary to grow it. He also pledges a portion, third, fourth, or half of his crop, for use of the land. The most outstanding commentary one can make on the South is to point out the fact that from that day to this the percentage of those who must secure their year's livelihood by crop liens has steadily increased. Many of the enfeebled aristocracy saw their once proud acres go on the block for ridiculously low prices; but the hopes for the rise of a vigorous yeomanry to take their places never materialized. The crop lien system was developed to readjust the Negro to cotton production on terms more fitting a modern economy than slavery. Its success was so great as to be disastrous. Congregated on its original fringes the unpropertied poor white farmers poured into the new scheme and helped to make temporary expediency a permanent arrangement." [a]

And so the stage was set for human tragedy. From the Negro angle Du Bois explains:

"Now it happens that both master and men have just enough argument on their respective sides to make it difficult for them to understand each other. The Negro dimly personifies in the white man all his ills and misfortunes; if he is poor, it is because the white man seizes the fruit of his toil; if he is ignorant, it is because the white man gives him neither time nor facilities to learn; and, indeed, if any misfortune happens to him, it is because of some hidden machinations of 'white folks.' On the other hand, the masters and the masters' sons have never been able to see why the Negro, instead of settling down to be day-laborers for bread and clothes, are infected with a silly desire to rise in the world, and why they are sulky, dissatisfied, and careless, where their fathers were happy and dumb and faithful. 'Why, you niggers have an easier time than I do,' said a puzzled Albany merchant to his black customer. 'Yes,' he replied, 'and so does yo' hogs.' " [b]

[9] Du Bois, *Black Reconstruction*, p. 368. Others who saw the need for basic economic reform were Carl Schurz, congressman from Wisconsin (*The Condition of the South, Report to the President* [1865] and "For the Great Empire of Liberty, Forward." Speech delivered at Concert Hall, Philadelphia [September 16, 1864]), and Hinton Helper (*The Impending Crisis of the South* [1860], especially Chapters 1 and 2 and pp. 180-186.)

[10] Paul S. Peirce, *The Freedmen's Bureau* (1904), pp. 44, 74 and 110.

[11] Du Bois, *Black Reconstruction*, p. 602.

[a] Vance, *op. cit.*, p. 187.
[b] W. E. B. Du Bois, *The Souls of Black Folk* (1903), pp. 155-156.

[12] See Federal Writers' Project, *op. cit.*, pp. 215-225.

[13] Josephus Daniels, *Tar Heel Editor* (1939), pp. 171-172.

[14] Woofter only expresses the common sense and the actual experience of social tenant legislation when he points out:

"It is to the advantage both of the tenant and the landlord that the tenant treat the land as if it were his own; that he build the necessary fences and terraces, improve the farm buildings, and drain the swampy places." [a]

Without legal claims on improvements he may make, the tenant is robbed of interest in conserving or improving the land or the buildings:

"On the contrary, just as it is to his advantage to rob the soil of its fertility, so he is tempted to burn the fire wood rails from any nearby fence or planks from the porch floor or from an out-house—if the place happens to be distinguished by having any movable materials that have not already succumbed to the ravages of time and tenants. The tenant is not likely to trouble to make any repairs that are not absolutely necessary, and these few will be so made as not to outlast his stay on the place." [b]

[15] Stipulations to this effect were, however, included in some of the Black Codes, which also set up some requirements for the protection of the freedmen; see Gilbert T. Stephenson, *Race Distinctions in American Law* (1910), pp. 62-63.

[16] Charles S. Mangum, Jr., *The Legal Status of the Negro* (1940), p. 27.

[17] Prior to Reconstruction some of the Northern free states had similar laws; see, for instance, Frank U. Quillin, *The Color Line in Ohio* (1913), pp. 21-34 and 88-92.

[18] In some states the lien applies not only to the crop but also to livestock, or even to all the tenant's property; in a number of states the cropper—in spite of sharing in the risk—has no legal title to the crop at all but is legally classified as a laborer.

[19] This may be exemplified by the following recent Georgia statute:

"PROCURING MONEY ON CONTRACT FOR SERVICES FRAUDULENTLY

"Any person who shall contract with another to perform for him services of any kind with intent to procure money or other things of value thereby, and not perform the service contracted for, to the loss and damage of the hirer, or after having so contracted, shall procure from the hirer money, or other things of value, with intent not to perform such service, to the loss and damage of the hirer, shall be deemed a common cheat and a swindler, and upon conviction shall be punished as for a misdemeanor." [c]

[20] Mangum, *op. cit.*, pp. 164-170. The Georgia law was a formulation which the Southern legislators had hoped would pass the test. Yet it failed. By a United States Supreme Court decision of January 12, 1942, it was declared unconstitutional. The case involved a Negro whose employer claimed to have paid the cost for the Negro's release from a previous debt charge. The Negro in return had promised to work the debt off ($19.50) but failed to do so (New York *Times*, [January 13, 1942]).

[21] Baker gives the following picture of a typical situation one generation ago:

"If he attempts to leave he is arrested and taken before a friendly justice of the peace, and fined or threatened with imprisonment. If he is not in debt, it sometimes happens

[a] T. J. Woofter, Jr., *The Basis of Racial Adjustment* (1925), p. 89.

[b] Charles S. Johnson, Edwin R. Embree, and W. W. Alexander, *The Collapse of Cotton Tenancy* (1935), p. 20.

[c] Georgia Code of 1933, 26-7048. Quoted by Arthur Raper, "Race and Class Pressures," unpublished manuscript prepared for this study (1940), p. 184.

that the landlord will have him arrested on the charge of stealing a bridle or a few potatoes (for it is easy to find something against almost any Negro), and he is brought into court. In several cases I know of the escaping Negro has even been chased down with bloodhounds. On appearing in court the Negro is naturally badly frightened. The white man is there and offers as a special favour to take him back and let him work out the fine —which sometimes requires six months—often a whole year. In this way Negroes are kept in debt—so called debt-slavery or peonage—year after year, they and their whole family. One of the things that I couldn't at first understand in some of the courts I visited was the presence of so many white men to stand sponsor for Negroes who had committed various offences. Often this grows out of the feudal protective instinct which the landlord feels for the tenant or servant of whom he is fond; but often it is merely the desire of the white man to get another Negro worker."[a]

For a discussion of these practices today, see Raper, *op. cit.*, pp. 187-188, and Chapter 26, Section 2. For a recent report of a case of peonage see the New York *Sun* (November 5, 1942), p. 9.

Chapter 11. *The Southern Plantation Economy and the Negro Farmer*

[1] Hinton R. Helper, *The Impending Crisis* (1857), pp. 57-58.

[2] *Sixteenth Census of the United States: 1940, Population*. Preliminary Release: Series P-5a, Nos. 14-16; and *Sixteenth Census of the United States: 1940, Agriculture*, United States Summary, First Series, Table VI.

[3] T. J. Woofter, Jr., "The Negro and Agricultural Policy," unpublished manuscript prepared for this study (1940), p. 30.

[4] T. J. Woofter, Jr., and Associates, *Landlord and Tenant on the Cotton Plantation* (1936), p. 11.

[5] Herman Clarence Nixon, *Forty Acres and Steel Mules* (1938), p. 13.

[6] Carter Goodrich and Others, *Migration and Economic Opportunity* (1936), pp. 125-126. A similar reconnaissance survey for 1934 indicated that conditions were even worse in Virginia, Georgia, Alabama, Mississippi, Tennessee, Texas, Oklahoma, and Kentucky where more than half of the land was believed to be eroded, at least "moderately."[b] In a third source, 53 per cent of the land in the East South Central Division (Kentucky, Tennessee, Alabama, and Mississippi) is reckoned as "moderately eroded," 23 per cent is "severely eroded," and 7 per cent is "essentially destroyed for tillage."[c] This has contributed to make the Southeast contain the largest contiguous area in the country characterized by a low per capita value of farm land.[d] For the whole South, in 1940, the average value of land and buildings amounted to $596 per capita of the rural farm population. The corresponding national figure was $1,116.[e]

[a] Ray Stannard Baker, *Following the Color Line* (1908), p. 98.

[b] Letter with manuscript table, July 12, 1939, from Dr. E. A. Norton, Head, Physical Surveys Division, Soil Conservation Service, Department of Agriculture, to Dr. T. C. McCormick.

[c] Department of Agriculture, *Yearbook of Agriculture* (1938), p. 90.

[d] See map published by the National Resources Committee in *The Problems of a Changing Population* (1938), p. 57.

[e] *Sixteenth Census of the United States: 1940, Agriculture. United States Summary*, First Series, Table VI.

[7] Gunnar Lange, "Trends in Southern Agriculture," unpublished manuscript prepared for this study (1940), pp. 23 ff.

[8] Woofter, "The Negro and Agricultural Policy," p. 31.

[9] Lange, *op. cit.*, p. 27.

[10] *Fifteenth Census of the United States: 1930, Agriculture*, Vol. III, Part 2, p. 62.

[11] U. S. Bureau of the Census, *Negroes in the United States: 1930-1932*, pp. 587-588, and *Fifteenth Census of the United States: 1930, Agriculture*, Vol. III, p. 12.

[12] *Fifteenth Census of the United States: 1930, Agriculture*, Vol. IV, p. 510.

[13] *Ibid.*, p. 891.

[14] Frank Tannenbaum, *Darker Phases of the South* (1924), pp. 117-118.

[15] U. S. Department of Agriculture, *Agricultural Statistics, 1940*, pp. 108-109.

[16] Planters and other cotton farmers, it is sometimes claimed, have shown that they know how to diversify their crops whenever the cotton price is low.[a] Indeed, it has been statistically ascertained that the cotton acreage—before the A.A.A.—varied with the price to a much greater extent than is true about most other crops.[b] But this means, on the other hand, that Southern farmers, in spite of their poverty and their need for a stabilized economy, have been unable to resist the temptation of making large temporary profits whenever the price exceeds a certain point.

[17] See, for instance, Rupert B. Vance, *Human Geography of the South* (1932), pp. 198-199; and Woofter and Associates, *Landlord and Tenant*, pp. 49-64.

[18] See, for instance, Goodrich and Others, *op. cit.*, pp. 134-138.

[19] Woofter and Associates, *Landlord and Tenant*, pp. 23 and 39.

[20] *Fifteenth Census of the United States: 1930, Agriculture*, Vol. II, Part 2, Table 46; *Thirteenth Census of the United States: 1910, Agriculture*, Vol. V, p. 681.

[21] U. S. Department of Agriculture, *Agricultural Statistics, 1940*, pp. 108-109.

"The average annual loss from insect ravages during the period 1910 to 1928 has been estimated to be about 15 percent, whereof the boll weevil is held responsible for 12 percent." (Lange, *op. cit.*, p. 30.)

[22] In 1929, on the basis of crop value, cotton had the first place in eight Southern states and held second place in North Carolina, where it was next to tobacco, and in Tennessee, where corn was more important. In seven of the states (South Carolina, Georgia, Alabama, Mississippi, Louisiana, Texas, and Arkansas) it accounted for half or more (in Mississippi, three-fourths) of the total crop value. Of the Southern states outside the Border only Virginia (corn, tobacco, potatoes) and Florida (citrus fruits) failed to have cotton among their principal crops. Corn, in most of the states, had second place. Rice came third in Louisiana, just before sugar cane, and fourth in Arkansas.[c]

[23] *Ibid.*, pp. 657, 892-893.

[24] *Sixteenth Census of the United States: 1940, Agriculture*, United States Summary, First Series, Table VI.

[25] Woofter and Associates, *Landlord and Tenant*, p. 10. See also Davis, Gardner, and Gardner, *op. cit.*, pp. 280-288.

[26] *White and Black in the United States* (1879), p. 160.

[a] Allison Davis, Burleigh B. Gardner, Mary R. Gardner, *Deep South* (1941), pp. 272-273.

[b] Rupert B. Vance, *Human Factors in Cotton Culture* (1929), pp. 118-119.

[c] *Fifteenth Census of the United States: 1930, Agriculture*, Vol. IV, pp. 715-716.

[27] U.S. Bureau of the Census, *Negro Population in the United States: 1790-1915*, p. 461. The number of owned farm homes is approximately the same as the number of owned farms. It is possible, however, that the *proportion* of owned homes was somewhat lower than the statistics indicate, for 1890, 1900, and 1910; the total number of farm homes for these years was scarcely higher than the number of farm operators (owners and tenants), whereas there was a large difference in 1930—indicating a substantial number of farm homes occupied by wage laborers.

[28] The number of owner-occupied Negro farm homes in the whole United States was almost exactly the same (221,000).

[29] U.S. Bureau of the Census, *Negroes in the United States: 1920-1932*, pp. 257 and 577; and *Sixteenth Census of the United States: 1940, Agriculture*, United States Summary, First Series, Table VI.

[30] See J. C. Folsom and O. E. Baker, *A Graphic Summary of Farm Labor and Population*, United States Department of Agriculture Miscellaneous Publication No. 265 (1937), p. 10.

[31] The degree of extension of credit itself, as well as the organization of the credit market, is a factor relevant to Negro landownership. But this factor works in a complicated way, and a discussion of it is beyond the scope of this book.

[32] Folsom and Baker, *op. cit.*, p. 14.

[33] Richard Sterner and Associates, *The Negro's Share*, prepared for this study (1943), p. 19.

[34] *Sixteenth Census of the United States: 1940, Agriculture*, United States Summary, First Series, Table VI.

[35] Similar interpretations are given by Rupert B. Vance, "Racial Competition for the Land," in *Race Relations and the Race Problem*, edited by Edgar C. Thompson (1939), pp. 102-103.

[36] There are no complete statistics on the extent to which large holdings have or have not maintained their relative position in Southern agriculture. Plantations do not even exist in ordinary census statistics; a farm is defined in such a way that even a sharecropper's plot is regarded as an independent unit. This procedure has often been criticized. See, for example, Karl Brandt, "Fallacious Census Terminology and Its Consequences in Agriculture" *Social Research* (March, 1938). However, there was a special enumeration of plantations in 325 counties in the Census of 1910 (*Thirteenth Census of the United States: 1910, Agriculture*, Vol. V, Chapter 12, "Plantations in the South," pp. 877-889). A similar enumeration was planned for the Census of 1940, but the results have, at this writing, not yet been published. Tax digest data for certain plantation areas in the Southeast indicate, however, that there has been a decline in the number of large holdings (over 500 acres) and a large increase in the number of small- and middle-sized holdings. These comparisons cover in one case (20 Georgia counties) the whole period 1873-1934, and in other cases the period 1911-1934 or 1922-1934 (Woofter and Associates, *Landlord and Tenant*, pp. 18, 197). This trend does not seem to be quite general, however; another study indicates an opposite trend in 20 Louisiana parishes (T. Lynn Smith, *The Sociology of Rural Life* (1940), pp. 305-307).

[37] Davis, Gardner, and Gardner, *op. cit.*, pp. 296-297.

[38] Arthur F. Raper, *Preface to Peasantry* (1936), pp. 121-122.

[39] *Ibid.*, p. 129. Dr. Raper cites the following example of how an attempt by acceptable Negroes to buy land in a more desirable neighborhood of Greene County, Georgia,

was turned down. An old plantation was for sale by public auction in lots of sixty to ninety acres. Two Negroes wanted to buy two of the lots for a price nearly double the market value, but were discouraged by both the owner and the auction company.

"The Negroes then went to a local white friend and asked him if he would bid in the two lots for them at the auction, whereupon he advised; 'Now, I am going to help you get some land, for you fellows ought to have some; but I don't believe I could try to buy any of those lots—you know there aren't any Negro owners right in there, and besides that land is right on the main road. Now understand, I want to help you—you just keep in touch with me and I will help you to locate some land in the neighborhood where you will like it better.' "[a]

[40] Vance, "Racial Competition for the Land," p. 107.

[41] White landlords in the South have even been accused of "selling" land to Negroes without letting them have the proper title to it. An outsider cannot have any opinion about the prevalence of such practices, but all available information about the legal status of the rural Negro in the South makes it seem probable that such cases occur and that Negroes, more often than whites, are the victims in such transactions. See for example, Davis, Gardner, and Gardner, *op. cit.*, p. 294; Campbell, *op. cit.*, p. 335.

[42] *Farm Tenancy*. Report of the President's Committee, prepared under the auspices of the National Resources Committee (1937), p. 39.

[43] *Twelfth Census of the United States: 1900, Agriculture*, Vol.V, Part I, pp. xcviii, civ; and *Fifteenth Census of the United States: 1930, Agriculture*, Vol. II, Part 2, p. 35.

[44] *Thirteenth Census of the United States: 1910, Population*, Vol. IV, pp. 96-152; U.S. Bureau of the Census, *Negro Population in the United States: 1790-1915*, pp. 506-508 and Table 1. It is somewhat difficult to follow this trend, for few of the Southern wage earners in agriculture have steady employment, and this makes it difficult to enumerate them. Too, there have been certain changes in the census classifications. The conditions of the Negro wage laborers in the Southern states, on the whole, have been studied far less extensively than have those of the Negro tenants. Therefore it will not be possible for us to pay as much attention to them as their numerical significance would warrant.

[45] A similar enumeration was planned for the 1940 Census, but the results, at this writing, are not yet available.

[46] *Thirteenth Census of the United States: 1910, Agriculture*, Vol. V, Chapter 12, "The Plantations in the South." A plantation was defined as a continuous holding with five or more tenants. It is probable that there were some plantation tenants also in "non-plantation counties," but even so the majority of the tenants certainly resided on small holdings.

[47] *Farm Tenancy*, Report of the President's Committee, pp. 91-95.

[48] Sterner and Associates, *op. cit.*, p. 15.

[49] *Ibid.*, p. 15. In nonplantation counties in 1930 only one-fourth of the tenants were Negroes.

[50] The proportion of all tenants who rented from their own or their wives' parents, grandparents, brothers, or sisters was, in 1930, not quite 30 per cent in the North, 17

[a] *Ibid.*, p. 128.

per cent in the West, and 15 per cent in the South.[a] The figure for the South, however, includes Negroes; for white tenants alone, it must be considerably higher.

[51] In counties designated as plantation counties in 1910, almost 60 per cent of the tenants were colored in 1930.[b] Woofter's sample study of plantations in 1934 indicates that 53 per cent of the plantations had Negro tenants only; 42 per cent had both Negro and white tenants, and 5 per cent had white tenants only.[c]

[52] Of 289 Southern counties which were designated as plantation counties in the Census of 1910, more than half, or 165, showed increase in number of both white and colored tenants between 1900 and 1930. In most of the cases these increases were proportionally greater for white than for colored tenants. In 50 counties there was a decline in number of tenants in both racial groups. When changes went in opposite directions, it was most often the white tenants who gained at the expense of the colored tenants (65 counties). The reverse was true in but a few cases (9 counties). This information was based on a special adaptation of the census material [d] made by Richard Sterner, "Standard of Living of the Negro and Social Welfare Policies," unpublished manuscript prepared for this study (1940).

[53] U. S. Bureau of the Census, *Census of Agriculture: 1935*, Vol. III, pp. 204-205; and Sterner and Associates, *op. cit.*, p. 13.

[54] As early as 1879 Sir George Campbell observed about the constant movement from one plantation to another:

"It is a form of strike as a counter-move against ill-treatment; and under the circumstances the move may be a bold and effective measure."[e] Compare in modern literature, for instance, Lawrence W. Neff, *Race Relations at Close Range* (1911), p. 22; and John Dollard, *Class and Caste in a Southern Town* (1937), pp. 445-497.

[55] Woofter and Associates, *Landlord and Tenant*, p. 200.

[56] It will be recalled that there is but scant information on the conditions of the non-plantation tenants, who are quite numerous even in the Negro group (although Negroes, much more than whites, are concentrated on large holdings).

[57] Some of the best works on the subject are: T. J. Woofter, Jr., and Associates, *Landlord and Tenant on the Cotton Plantation* (1937); William C. Holley, Ellen Winston, T. J. Woofter, Jr., *The Plantation South, 1934-1937*, Works Projects Administration Research Bulletin No. 22 (1940); *Farm Tenancy*, Report of the President's Committee (1937); Arthur Raper, *Preface to Peasantry* (1936), particularly pp. 157-180; Allison Davis, Burleigh B. Gardner, and Mary R. Gardner, *Deep South* (1941), pp. 255-421; E. L. Langsford and B. H. Thibodeaux, *Plantation Organization and Operation in the Yazoo-Mississippi Delta Area*, United States Department of Agriculture Technical Bulletin No. 682 (1939); Edgar T. Thompson, "Population Expansion and the Plantation System," *American Journal of Sociology* (November, 1935), pp. 314-326.

[58] Davis, Gardner, and Gardner, *op. cit.*, pp. 329-332.

[a] *Farm Tenancy*, Report of the President's Committee, p. 47.

[b] Sterner and Associates, *op. cit.*, p. 15.

[c] Woofter and Associates, *Landlord and Tenant*, p. 196.

[d] *Fifteenth Census of the United States: 1930, Agriculture*, Vol. II, Part 2, County table 1, Supplemental for Southern States, and *Twelfth Census of the United States: 1900, Agriculture*, Vol. V, Part 1, pp. 58-141.

[e] *Op. cit.*, pp. ix-x.

[59] Arthur Raper, "Race and Class Pressures," unpublished manuscript prepared for this study (1940), p. 181.

[60] Woofter and Associates, *Landlord and Tenant*, p. 11.

[61] *Ibid.*, p. 29.

[62] Raper, "Race and Class Pressures," p. 180.

[63] Rupert B. Vance observes:

"For the tenant to seek to keep his own accounts within the credit system is often regarded as a personal insult to the landlord or credit merchant."[a]

[64] Davis, Gardner, and Gardner, for instance, have this to say on the problem:

"One large planter in Rural County attributed the existence of a large number of landlords who stole from their tenants to the difficulty of raising cotton profitably otherwise, under the present economy.

" 'The only way a man can make money from farming is by stealing it from the Negroes, or by living close. Some people get ahead by living close and saving every cent, and then there are lots that steal from the Negroes. Some of them will take everything a Negro has, down to his last chicken and hog.'

"A businessman, in one of the counties, whose business furnished him with a close knowledge of the credit dealings of most landlords and tenants in the county, stated that 'practically all landlords' cheated their tenants 'in one way or another.' "[b]

[65] Raper, "Race and Class Pressures," p. 183.

[66] Charles S. Johnson, *Growing up in the Black Belt* (1941), p. 309. Italics ours.

[67] Woofter and Associates, *Landlord and Tenant*, p. 59.

[68] Langsford and Thibodeaux, *op. cit.*, p. 48.

[69] Woofter and Associates, *Landlord and Tenant*, p. 63.

[70] Holley, Winston, and Woofter, *op. cit.*, pp. 27-28.

[71] Davis, Gardner, and Gardner, *op. cit.*, p. 350.

[72] Woofter and Associates, *Landlord and Tenant*, p. 60.

[73] Information from officials of the Southern Tenant Farmers' Union, at conference in Memphis, January 31, 1939.

[74] There is probably not so much debt-peonage left, however, as is suggested by the following statement, taken from the resolution of the Georgia Baptist Convention's Social Service Commission meeting in Augusta, November, 1939:

"Peonage or debt slavery has by no means disappeared from our land. There are more white people affected by this diabolical practice than there were slave owners. There are more Negroes held by these debt slavers than were actually owned as slaves. . . . The method is the only thing which has changed."[c]

Davis, Gardner, and Gardner quoted the following statement made by a Negro landlord in the middle of the 'thirties:

" 'You don't get any more by being a good tenant! Grosvenor still takes it all and charges them besides! . . . They all do it. I do it myself—some of these things. . . . How can the tenant get his share? Most of them can't read or write. They can't sell

[a] "Cotton and Tenancy" in *Problems of the Cotton Economy*, Proceedings of the Southern Social Science Research Conference, New Orleans, Louisiana (March, 1935), p. 19. See also Raper, "Race and Class Pressures," p. 181, and Federal Writers' Project, *These Are Our Lives* (1939), pp. 21-22.

[b] *Op. cit.*, p. 351.

[c] Cited by Raper, "Race and Class Pressures," p. 198.

their own cotton. . . . They can't dispute the landlord's word, if he is white, and they can't move if they owe him. Even if they don't owe him, another landlord won't take them unless the one they're renting from is willing for him to go.' "[a]

[75] For example, see Raper, "Race and Class Pressures," pp. 178-180.

[76] Ray Stannard Baker, *Following the Color Line* (1908), p. 79.

[77] See Davis, Gardner, and Gardner, *op. cit.*, p. 356.

Mangum informs us:

There is a common-law rule that one can recover damages from anyone who entices away one's servant. Moreover, an Arkansas enticement statute, applying to the luring of renters as well as laborers, has been held not to be in conflict with the Thirteenth Amendment or the peonage statutes."[b]

[78] Raper tells a story about a case in Warren County, Georgia, where almost two-thirds of the population are Negro. Adjoining Glasscock County, where the population includes a relatively large proportion of small white farmers, had an unusually good cotton crop in 1937 and sent to Warren County for pickers, bidding a higher price than planters in that county wanted to give. The result was a series of rather violent demonstrations and intimidations by organized vigilantes. The trucks from Glasscock County had to turn back without any pickers, and the enraged Warren farmers forced all Negroes they could get hold of to work for them, entering their homes in order to find them, scarcely even leaving the domestics employed by other white families in peace.[c]

[79] *Ibid.*, p. 179.

[80] "Where the system flourishes, ignorance, prejudice, and cruelty are the rule, not the exception. The arrangement has behind it the weight of tradition and public opinion, tainted by fear and hate. The white owners know no other order. The Negro tenant is poor, illiterate, and intimidated. There are few better landlords to whom he could transfer his allegiance if he tried."[d]

Chapter 12. *New Blows to Southern Agriculture During the Thirties: Trends and Policies*

[1] U. S. Department of Agriculture, *Agricultural Statistics: 1940*, pp. 108-111; Gunnar Lange, "Trends in Southern Agriculture," unpublished manuscript prepared for this study (1940), pp. 17 ff. and Table A5.

[2] Lange, "Trends in Southern Agriculture," p. 18.

[3] The situation was aggravated by the depression after 1929. Domestic and foreign demand for textiles dropped sharply with increased unemployment and reduced industrial income. As a result the demand for cotton lint fell off rapidly, and prices dropped to half the pre-war level. The textile industries in the main cotton manufacturing countries abroad began to place more of their purchasing contracts with producers elsewhere than in the United States. England and France took larger shares of their cotton import from their dominions and from Egypt and Brazil. In Brazil cotton production

[a] *Op. cit.*, p. 356.

[b] Charles S. Mangum, Jr., *The Legal Status of the Negro* (1940), p. 170.

[c] "Race and Class Pressures," pp. 202-203.

[d] Edwin R. Embree, *Brown America* (1933; first edition, 1931), p. 143.

rose from an average of 492 million bales annually in 1925-1929 to 1,856 million bales in 1933-1937. At the same time a tremendous increase in the production of synthetic fibres occurred. World production of rayon and rayon staple fibres, which in 1920 had been only 33 million pounds, increased from 458 million in 1930 to 1,948 million pounds in 1938. It has been estimated that the production of these fibres was equivalent to 78,000 bales of cotton in 1920 and 4,583,000 bales in 1938.[a]

"These two factors, the upward trend of cotton production abroad and the shift in demand to rayon, are the most responsible for the sharp reduction of the demand for American cotton. It seems to be certain that these factors will continue to influence the situation in the future and the American cotton producers cannot be expected to retain their present markets—much less to regain what they lost, unless some way of expanding domestic consumption can be found. Other innovations—for instance, nylon, recently introduced on a commercial basis—have come into the picture lately and do not brighten the market outlook for cotton."[b]

That the cotton economy has suffered much more during the depression and recovered much less after the depression than American agriculture in general is evident from the following figures:[c]

INDEX NUMBERS FOR GROSS CASH INCOME FROM MARKETINGS

Year	All Products	Cotton and Cotton Seed
1925–1929	100	100
1932	43	31
1939	71	41

Yet, even so, cotton was still in 1939 the leading money-income crop of the whole country, giving the American farmers $609,000,000 in cash as compared to $397,-000,000 from wheat, $367,000,000 from truck crops (all vegetables, except dry edible beans, potatoes, and certain garden plot crops), $326,000,000 from corn, and $264,000,000 from tobacco. None of the crops, however, could compete with milk ($1,355,000,000), cattle and calves ($1,274,000,000) or hogs ($821,000,000).[d]

[4] Lange, "Trends in Southern Agriculture," p. 43.

[5] Ibid., pp. 23 ff.

[6] Ibid., pp. 11 and 24 ff.

[7] The number of cows and heifers kept mainly for milk production increased by 23 per cent between 1930 and 1940. The national increase (17 per cent) was not much

[a] See: I. W. Duggan, "Cotton Land and People," Journal of Farm Economics (February, 1940), p. 197.

[b] Lange, "Trends in Southern Agriculture," pp. 16-17.

[c] Adapted by Lange ("Trends in Southern Agriculture,"   ) from U. S. Department of Agriculture, Agricultural Statistics: 1940, pp. 544 and 552, and Bureau of Agricultural Economics, Income Parity for Agriculture, Part I, Section 1. Calendar Years 1910-1937 (Preliminary, 1938). The figure 41, used as the index for cotton and cotton seed for 1939, is only approximate.

[d] U. S. Department of Agriculture, Agricultural Statistics: 1940, pp. 544-545.

smaller, however, and the South's share in all milk produced (21 per cent) or sold (12 per cent) was still very small in 1940.[a]

[8] If we exclude the West South Central states, where the raising of beef cattle always has been large but never has provided much employment for Negroes, we find that the rest of the South had an increase between 1930 and 1940 of no less than 69 per cent in number of cows and heifers kept mainly for beef production. The production of hay increased by 53 per cent in the South, whereas the rest of the country showed a small decline. The number of hogs and pigs increased by 41 per cent in the South, as against 4 per cent for the country as a whole. (The last figures are somewhat too low, owing to a change in the enumeration method.)[b]

[9] *Idem.*

[10] M. R. Cooper and Associates, "Defects in Farming System and Tenancy," U. S. Department of Agriculture, *Yearbook of Agriculture, 1938,* p. 144.

[11] Concerning these present trends, see U. S. Department of Agriculture, *The Agricultural Situation* (particularly the issues for March, April, and August, 1942) and *Crops and Markets* (for instance, the issue for July, 1942).

[12] Richard Sterner and Associates, *The Negro's Share,* prepared for this study (1943), p. 19. Italics ours.

[13] We shall have to say more about this change later. At this writing it is not yet known how large the increase in number of wage laborers is compared with the decrease in number of tenants. Indeed, it is not even certain whether there was any significant increase at all in number of wage workers between 1930 and 1940.[c] It is certain, however, that the increase in number of Negro day laborers—if it did occur—was much smaller than the decline in number of Negro tenants. For the total Negro rural-farm population in the South declined by 4.5 per cent between 1930 and 1940. This decline was relatively smaller than during the decade 1920-1930 (8.6 per cent), but it is remarkable that it could go on at all in spite of the lack of industrial employment opportunities during the 'thirties. The Southern white rural-farm population, on the other hand, which had been slowly decreasing during the 'twenties (— 3.0 per cent) showed a small gain during the 'thirties (2.1 per cent). The fact that white people have greater opportunities in farm ownership than have Negroes apparently meant more than their greater employment chances in nonfarm areas. The records for this decade show clearly, as we have found, that farm ownership and high tenure status tend to keep the people on the land.[d]

One of the reasons why Negro tenants were losing out seems to be that *the increased population pressure had brought about an intensified racial competition for the land.*

[a] *Sixteenth Census of the United States: 1940, Agriculture,* United States Summary, First Series, pp. 30-31.

[b] *Sixteenth Census of the United States: 1940, Agriculture,* United States Summary, First Series, pp. 30-31 and 52.

[c] The number of Negro and white agricultural wage workers in the South, in 1930, was 511,000 and 603,000 respectively (see Table 1 of Chapter 11). These figures include unemployed workers. The number of *employed* wage laborers in 1940 was 471,000 (includes a few nonwhites other than Negroes) and 495,000, respectively (*Sixteenth Census of the United States: 1940, Population,* Second Series, State table 18a-b). It is obvious, however, that these two sets of figures are incomparable, so in spite of the two last ones being lower, a certain increase may, nevertheless, have occurred.

[d] See Sterner and Associates, *op. cit.,* pp. 11-18.

Among 288 counties in six selected Southern states, no less than 199 showed at the same time (between 1930 and 1935) an increase in number of white and a decrease in number of Negro cash and share tenants; the reverse of this happened in only one of the counties studied.[a]

Woofter's plantation study indicates that the proportion of white families on the plantation increased during these years.[b]

[14] W. C. Holley, Ellen Winston, and T. J. Woofter, Jr., *The Plantation South, 1934-1937* (1940), p. 49.

[15] The harvested area, because of the depression, had already declined from 43,000,-000 acres in 1929 to 36,000,000 in 1932. In 1933, because of the A.A.A., it was down to 29,000,000. There was a further decline to 22,000,000 in 1941.[c]

[16] From a peak of 17,000,000 bales in 1931, it fell to less than 10,000,000 in 1934; but then it started to climb again and reached an all-time peak of 19,000,000 bales in 1937, when the acreage had been allowed, temporarily, to increase to a little more than three-fourths of the 1929 level.[d] In 1940, however, it was down to 12,500,000 bales.[e]

[17] The carry-over, which was almost 10,000,000 bales in 1932, had decreased to less than half of that figure by 1937 but reached a new, even higher peak of 13,000,000 bales in 1939.[f]

Behind this was the huge crop of 1937.

[a] Richard Sterner, "The Standard of Living of the Negro and Social Welfare Policies," unpublished manuscript prepared for this study (1940). These data are based on a special adaptation of census materials for all counties in Virginia, North Carolina, South Carolina, Georgia, Alabama, and Arkansas, which had at least 100 colored and 100 white tenants (other than croppers). Corresponding tabulations were made for farm owners (241 counties) and croppers (269 counties). The following table gives a complete summary of the main results:

COUNTIES IN SELECTED SOUTHERN STATES BY INCREASE OR DECREASE IN NUMBER OF COLORED [AND WHITE OWNERS, TENANTS (other than croppers), AND CROPPERS: 1930-1935

Counties by Decrease or Increase of *White* Operators	Counties by Decrease or Increase of Colored Operators					
	Owners		Tenants other than Croppers		Croppers	
	Decrease	Increase	Decrease	Increase	Decrease	Increase
Decrease	31	8	15	1	165	25
Increase	57	145	199	73	40	39

Source: U.S. Bureau of the Census, *Census of Agriculture; 1935*, Vol. I, County Table 1, Supplemental for Southern States. *Fifteenth Census of the United States: 1930, Agriculture*, Vol. II, Part 2, County Table 1, Supplemental for Southern States.

[b] T. J. Woofter and Associates, *Landlord and Tenant on the Cotton Plantation* (1936), p. 157.

[c] Bureau of Agricultural Economics, "The Agricultural Situation" (August, 1942), p. 9.

[d] U. S. Department of Agriculture, *Agricultural Statistics: 1940*, p. 109.

[e] U. S. Department of Agriculture, *Agricultural Statistics: 1941*, p. 120. The preliminary figure for 1941 was 11,000,000 bales (The National Industrial Conference Board, *The Economic Almanac for 1942-1943* [1942], p. 266.)

[f] U. S. Department of Agriculture, *Agricultural Statistics: 1940*, p. 119

[18] Carl T. Schmidt, *American Farmers in the World Crisis* (1941), p. 156.

[19] *Ibid.*, p. 155.

[20] U.S. Department of Agriculture, *Yearbook of Agriculture: 1940*, p. 654.

[21] According to certain estimates (Holley, Winston, and Woofter, *op. cit.*, p. 116), the labor requirements for cotton do not at all vary with the acreage, but only with the number of bales produced. It is understandable that this would be true about chopping and picking—but less so about operations which have to do with the soil rather than the plants. It does not seem, therefore, that these estimates would disprove that the acreage cuts have brought about a decrease in the need for year-round labor.

[22] Henry I. Richards, *Cotton and the A.A.A.* (1936), p. 146.

[23] Sterner and Associates, *op. cit.*, pp. 75-76.

[24] Holley, Winston, and Woofter, *op. cit.*, p. 44.

[25] Edwin G. Nourse, Joseph S. Davis, and John D. Black, *Three Years of the Agricultural Adjustment Administration* (1937), p. 344. See also Allison Davis, B. B. Gardner, and M. R. Gardner, *Deep South* (1941), pp. 283-284.

[26] Nourse, Davis, and Black, *op. cit.*, p. 344. See also Carl T. Schmidt, *op. cit.*, p. 265: "The Act . . . obligates landlords not to reduce the number of their tenants below the average number on their farms during the last three years. The loophole is that the limitation applies only if the county committee finds that the change or reduction is not justified and disapproves such a change or reduction."

[27] Lange, "Agricultural Adjustment Programs and the Negro," p. 37.

[28] Thomas J. Woofter, Jr., "The Negro and Agricultural Policy," unpublished manuscript prepared for this study (1940), pp. 104 ff. Particularly illuminating is the following statement by a Missouri planter, quoted by Schmidt, *op. cit.*, p. 265: "What happens after a landlord decides upon a change [from tenants to wage labor]? He goes to the committee, and thereupon the three harassed men who are trying to run a complicated cotton program find themselves in an impossible position. They know very well that, since 1933, other owners have shifted to day labor and are getting all the payments. Why, therefore, should they discriminate against this late-comer? . . . They get very little credit if they stand firm and try to run a good program."

[29] Concrete examples of how the local administration in the Deep South is dominated by large landlords are given by Davis, Gardner, and Gardner. See, for instance *op. cit.*, pp. 283-284.

[30] Lange observes: "The decentralization of A.A.A. might give the programs a more democratic character. *That so much of the responsibility of promoting the programs has been placed upon the local committees is, however, in many respects to the disadvantage of the Negroes.* The local administration of the A.A.A. in the South has been fitted into the traditional pattern of racial segregation. This segregation prevents the Negro from participating actively in the county associations. . . It is possible that A.A.A. to some extent has contributed to a breakdown of the racial barriers, for the Negroes are allowed to attend A.A.A. meetings together with white farm operators in a few Southern states, as, for example, in North Carolina. But, with rare exceptions, they would not be permitted at those meetings in Alabama or Mississippi . . . although the Negro farm operators actually are in the majority in many counties. The influence of the Negro farm agents over the administration of A.A.A. is, of course, only through the white agents. This brings us to the conclusion that the Negro farmers have very

little influence over the local operation and enforcement of the A.A.A. legislation. This means that complaints from Negroes about acreage allotment and illegal diversion of payment practically always are judged by a committee of white farmers.[a]

[31] About the importance of the literacy factor in this context, see, for instance, Davis, Gardner, and Gardner, *op. cit.*, p. 419.

[32] *Changes in Technology and Labor Requirements in Crop Production, Cotton.* Work Projects Administration, National Research Project (1938). Cited by Lange, "Trends in Southern Agriculture," p. 33.

NUMBER OF MOTOR TRUCKS AND TRACTORS ON FARMS: 1930 AND 1940

Item and Year	United States	The North and West	The South	Texas and Oklahoma	All other Southern States
Motor trucks					
1930	900,000	663,000	237,000	76,000	161,000
1940	1,047,000	737,000	310,000	85,000	225,000
Per Cent Increase	16%	11%	31%	12%	40%
Tractors					
1930	920,000	774,000	146,000	63,000	83,000
1940	1,567,000	1,296,000	271,000	144,000	127,000
Per Cent Increase	70%	67%	86%	129%	64%

Sources: Fifteenth Census of the United States: 1930, Agriculture, Vol. IV, pp. 536, 537. *Sixteenth Census of the United States: 1940, Agriculture,* United States Summary, Second Series, pp. 27-31.

[34] Holley, Winston, and Woofter, *op. cit.*, p. 20.

[35] By 1940, Texas and Oklahoma had more than half of all farm tractors in the South. They also showed a more rapid increase during the 'thirties than did the rest of the South or the nation. This, in conjunction with the drought which hit Oklahoma particularly, brought about a more spectacular decline in the rural farm population than in any other Southern state. The white farm population between 1930 and 1940 decreased by 6 per cent in Oklahoma and by 7 per cent in Texas. The corresponding figures for the much smaller Negro farm population, as usual, were higher: 27 and 13 per cent, respectively.[b] Speaking of mechanization trends as affected by the A.A.A. in these parts of the South, Carl T. Schmidt says:

"To be sure, technological changes in cotton cultivation have been accelerated by the A.A.A., not only in the extent that it has given cotton planters cash with which to buy machinery, but also because the substitution of machines for tenants and croppers enables the landlords to double their share of the Government subsidy."[c]

The continuance of the differential in mechanization rates between the two parts of the South must give the Southwest a considerable competitive advantage, re-emphasizing the old shift in cotton culture to the Southwest. And under the pressure of this competition, the Southeast will probably intensify its own efforts to make the change. It seems to be only a question of time until an extensive mechanization of the cotton

[a] Lange, "Agricultural Adjustment Programs and the Negro," pp. 24-25. Italics ours.
[b] *Sixteenth Census of the United States:* 1940, Preliminary Release, Series P-5a, No. 16.
[c] "Power Farming and Labor Displacement," *Monthly Labor Review* (March, 1938). Quoted by Schmidt, *op. cit.*, pp. 263-264.

culture in the Delta will occur. An appraisal of what that would mean has been given by Horace C. Hamilton.[a]

"Langsford and Thibodeaux[b] have shown how the mechanization of plantations in the Mississippi Delta area would reduce the plantation labor force per plantation (having 750 acres of crops) from 40 families under the horse-drawn one-row system, to 24 families under a four-row tractor system. This amounts to a decrease of 40 per cent. In this estimate they are quite conservative, because they are assuming that some of the 24 families would be kept there primarily for the purpose of hoeing and picking cotton. If the Delta should come to depend upon transient labor as the Plains and Blacklands of Texas do, then less than 24 families might be kept on the plantation. Already we know of many instances where transient cotton pickers have been transported in trucks from Texas to Mississippi."

It should be added that such transient workers are often Mexicans, who have actually started to compete on a small scale with Negroes even in this stronghold of Negro agricultural labor.[c]

[36] Schmidt, *op. cit.*, p. 65.

[37] ". . . the general history of such machines suggests that the cotton-picker will eventually be perfected, for use in relatively flat country at least—and the greater part of the richer cotton lands of the South are located in just such country . . . it is an ominous machine . . . since it overcomes the last and principal barrier to the mechanization of Southern cotton farming . . . huge mechanized land units are plainly indicated as the easiest way to recovering, so far as it is possible, the foreign market, lost precisely because of the high production costs of the present methods of growing cotton."[d]

[38] Schmidt, *op. cit.*, p. 69.

[39] "Many planters throughout the South agree that the cropper's necessity of keeping his second-hand Ford on the road, coupled with his inability to part with any cash for repairs, had made of him a good mechanic. Thus when the plantation comes to mechanize it will find its Negro labor machine conscious and able to make the transition."[e]

[40] *Fifteenth Census of the United States: 1930, Agriculture*, Vol. IV, pp. 530 and 536-537. There were 38,000 tractors on tenant-operated farms in the South, but only 2,000 on farms operated by colored tenants in the whole country. Most tractors used by tenants may have been registered as belonging to the owner-operated parts of the plantations.

[41] "If . . . the mechanical cotton pickers should be applied to half of the 10 million acres of cotton in the Delta Lands, the Gulf Coast Prairie and the Texas Black Waxy Prairie, we might expect a saving . . . of half a million pickers during the cotton picking season. . . . Mechanization of other phases of cotton production should undoubt-

[a] "The Social Effects of Recent Trends in the Mechanization of Agriculture," *Rural Sociology* (March, 1939), p. 11.

[b] E. L. Langsford and B. H. Thibodeaux, *Plantation Organization and Operation in the Yazoo-Mississippi Delta Area*, U.S. Department of Agriculture Technical Bulletin 682 (1939), p. 80.

[c] Information received by Sterner during interview, Department of Welfare, Clarksdale, Mississippi, January, 1940.

[d] W. F. Cash, *The Mind of the South* (1941), p. 411. Compare Rupert B. Vance, *Human Geography of the South* (1936), p. 497.

[e] Vance, *op. cit.*, p. 497.

edly accompany widespread use of the mechanical picker thereby decreasing the labor required prior to harvest."[a]

[42] Oren Stephens, "Revolt on the Delta," *Harper's Magazine* (November, 1941), p. 664.

[43] Arthur Raper, "Race and Class Pressures," unpublished manuscript prepared for this study (1940), p. 206.

[44] *Idem.*

[45] Quoted by Raper, "Race and Class Pressures," p. 213. Often even the attempts to organize the tenants in the Southwest met with violence. One woman sympathizer was whipped while studying the activities of the Southern Tenant Farmers' Union in Arkansas. (See Oren Stephens, *op. cit.*, p. 661.) A Negro member, who had received a leaflet from the Union containing an admonition that members take part in the election of the county conservation committee, showed this leaflet in the office of the county agent, while inquiring about the date of the election. He failed to receive the information, but later he was handcuffed, beaten and "run out of the county."[b]

A white attorney in Arkansas, although not particularly progressive,[c] was aroused by the illegal practices in the dealings with tenants and, therefore, used to assist them at court. Because he had helped some members of the Southern Tenant Farmers' Union, his house was once attacked by a group of vigilantes, who, however, left when they found him armed.[d] The police generally take orders from the planters. Lower courts tend to decide against the tenants, but when cases are brought to higher courts, as by this attorney, they are frequently reversed.[e]

[46] Southern Tenant Farmers' Union, "History of S.T.F.U., S.T.F.U. Study Course," mimeographed, pp. 102. See also Raper, "Race and Class Pressures," p. 208.

One of the most spectacular incidents occurred in January, 1939, when a group of displaced sharecroppers and other discontented rural workers of both races, led by persons connected with both the Southern Tenant Farmers' Union (S.T.F.U.) and the United Cannery, Agricultural, Packing, and Allied Workers of America (U. C. A. P. A. W. A.), camped near a Missouri highway, thereby demonstrating their plight. After the state health authorities had delivered the somewhat peculiar declaration that their presence at this place constituted "a menace to the public health," they were moved to a less conspicuous location, where they were left stranded for some time, until the Farm Security Administration managed to take care of some of them. The organizers referred to this demonstration as an "organized peaceable protest against unfairness of cotton control to cotton workers" and against the "defeat of labor policy in cotton control."[f]

[a] Roman L. Horne and Eugene G. McKibben, "Changes in Farm Power and Equipment, Mechanical Cotton Picker" (1937), Works Progress Administration, National Research Project, Report A-2, p. 18.

[b] Information received by Sterner from the directors of the Southern Tenant Farmers' Union at conference in Memphis, December 31, 1939. A number of similar cases are reported in issues of *The Tenant Farmer*, monthly magazine of the S.T.F.U.

[c] Stephens, *op. cit.*, p. 659.

[d] Interview by Sterner, October, 1938. Story confirmed by Raper, "Race and Class Pressures," pp. 216-217.

[e] *Ibid.*, pp. 210-211 and 217.

[f] Raper, "Race and Class Pressures," pp. 211-213. See also New York *Times* (January 11, 1939) and New York *Post* (January 20, and November 9, 1939).

[47] H. L. Mitchell, "The Southern Tenant Farmers Union in 1941," Report of the Secretary (1942), p. 2.

[48] Cited by Schmidt, *op. cit.*, p. 71.

[49] *Ibid.*, p. 286; and *Sixteenth Census of the United States: 1940, Agriculture*, United States Summary, First Series, p. 10.

[50] Bertram Schrieke, who, with a background in Dutch colonial policy, surveyed the American Negro problem in the early 'thirties, painted the future for a new American peasantry quite rosy:

"America, and particularly the South, offers a unique opportunity for the development of the new peasant. He will do as the old peasant did, produce his own food and the feed for his stock. With his fruit, maple syrup, cream and butter, home-cured hams, cereals, and vegetables, he will provide himself a healthier and more abundant diet than he has ever known. At the same time, in this age of radios, automobiles, movies, and telephones, he will not be isolated as was the pioneer. The word 'peasant' brings unfavourable associations to the American mind. It suggests feudalism. The agriculturist wishes to be called a 'farmer,' but farming implies the production of commercial crops. However, the peasant is not a serf; he is a hard-working stubborn character, proud of his freedom and independence on his self-owned land."[a]

It should be recalled, however, that this new American peasant, in order to have a decent living standard—and particularly if he were to be provided with those gadgets of modern civilization which Schrieke would give him—would need a substantial cash income. This is not, under present trends in agricultural technique and in world production of agricultural goods, compatible with anything like the present ratio of labor to land in the South.

The so-called "agrarians"—a small group of Southern university professors, journalists, and so on—also have advocated a return to the land. Their reasons are sentimental rather than economic and they seem to have had no influence. See: Twelve Southerners, *I'll Take My Stand* (1930).

[51] *The Collapse of Cotton Tenancy* (1935), pp. 68-69.

[52] *Preface to Peasantry* (1936), pp. 6-7. Italics ours.

[53] A tendency in Administration circles to abstain from publicly criticizing government policies has not been without responsibility for allowing the general public to be less well-informed on technical points of such public questions than corresponds to its intelligence and general education. The attitudes toward labor unions, social insurance, and agricultural policy are as a result too often in black and white: one is either for a policy as a whole, or against it. The tendency to extreme loyalty on the part of government experts has to be understood against the background (1) that the technical plans for policy are often originally drawn up without much public discussion; (2) that the Administration seems always to fear that the opposition will make undue use of any admission of unfavorable effects of a policy; (3) that the public expects all members of the Administration to agree, and if they do not agree they are said to be "bickering" or "showing jealousy." This spreads an air of one-mindedness and secretiveness around policy making, and makes the policy adopted partly a matter of accident. One administrator, when discussing certain features of the A.A.A. for which he was not responsible, privately remarked: "You cannot expect me to criticize the policy of the govern-

[a] *Alien Americans* (1936), p. 193.

ment." The whole set-up is much like the often-criticized Russian scheme of having discussion until a policy is voted upon and then a complete stifling of discussion.

[54] Schmidt, *op. cit.*, p. 280. These estimates do not include future losses on commodity loans. Because of the War, such losses perhaps will not be so large.

[55] The full series of estimates for the latter part of this period is given below:

	1929	1932	1933	1934	1935	1936	1937	1938	1939	1940
Millions of dollars	1651	648	807	1190	1245	1360	1473	1342	1354	1292
Index Nos.	100	39	49	72	75	82	89	81	82	78

Figures are from *Farm Income* (February 19, 1941) and from figures made available through the Division of History and Statistics, Bureau of Agricultural Economics, United States Department of Agriculture, in Lange, "The Agricultural Administration Program and the Negro," p. 39. The nine Southeastern states included in the analysis were: North Carolina, South Carolina, Georgia, Florida, Alabama, Louisiana, Mississippi, Kentucky and Tennessee. A.A.A. payments are included for the years 1933-1940.

[56] Computed from Lange, "Agricultural Adjustment Programs and the Negro," p. 39. Lange gets his figures from *Farm Income* (February 19, 1941) and from figures made available through the Division of History and Statistics, Bureau of Agricultural Economics, United States Department of Agriculture.

[57] U.S. Department of Agriculture, *Annotated Compilation of Soil Conservation and Domestic Allotment Act, as amended* (1938), Section 7a (5). Quoted by Lange, "Agricultural Adjustment Programs and the Negro," p. 9.

[58] Lange, "Agricultural Adjustment Programs and the Negro," p. 7.

[59] *Ibid.*, pp. 10-11.

[60] Holley, Winston, and Woofter, *op. cit.*, pp. 40, 41 and 44.

[61] True, not all planters receive incomes such as these averages indicate. Some even have to suffer losses. This was true of about 7 per cent of the 646 plantations in Woofter's larger plantation sample of 1934. But over one-third of the planters had a net cash income of at least $2,000, and the average for this group was $5,393.[a] On the whole, it seems that the statement, often heard in the South, that not only tenants but planters as well are poor, is greatly exaggerated. Those who want to argue that planters generally are badly off, often taken their recourse to certain computations of percentage returns on plantations; such computations cannot always be accepted without important qualifications.

Woofter estimates that the operator's average "capital investment" (total value of land, buildings, livestock and machinery) for a sample of 632 plantations was $28,694 in 1934. If the operator's salary for his own work is considered to be only $1,000 a year, the residual net return on this capital would be 5.5 per cent.[b] Such a capital return may seem low, but it is questionable whether it is low also for agricultural conditions. The author, who is somewhat familiar with Swedish agricultural economics, can testify that similar calculations for Swedish farms indicate the prevalence of much lower returns. This argument, however, cannot be stressed much, for computations of

[a] Woofter, *Landlord and Tenant*, p. 86.
[b] *Ibid.*, p. 218.

this kind are always rather arbitrary and more or less incomparable. The main objection is, rather, that such calculations seldom give any exact and meaningful indices on the economic success of the operations. For the capital value is not an independent unit; it is a reflection of the anticipated net income (as well as of the anticipated returns on competing investment opportunities and of anticipated risks). The A.A.A. payments, for instance, undoubtedly have contributed to an increase in plantation values, and, although they constitute part of an increase in income, it is not certain that they have helped to bring about any rise in the percentage return. If they should have brought about such an increase, this is only because the investor considers them temporary and, consequently, bases his calculation on the assumption that his net income eventually will decline. Indeed, the greater the assurance that a certain increase in income will last, the less likely is it to cause any rise in the percentage return.

[62] Schmidt, *op. cit.*, p. 152.

[63] Woofter, "The Negro and Agricultural Policy," p. 110.

[64] United States Department of Agriculture, "Extension Work with Negroes," mimeographed, p. 5.

[65] Figures made available through the courtesy of Dr. M. L. Wilson, Director of Extension Work, U.S. Department of Agriculture.

[66] U.S. Department of Agriculture, *Agricultural Statistics: 1940*, p. 719. In Mississippi, for instance, where in 1942 the majority of the rural farm people are colored, less than one-fourth of the extension workers were Negro. Tennessee had but 20 colored workers in 1942, whereas the total number of extension workers, even in 1939, was fifteen times greater. Among all Southern counties with 500 or more Negro farm families almost two out of five were without any colored extension workers in 1941.[a]

It has already been mentioned that the Extension Service has frequently failed to stand up for the rights of tenants when landlords have appropriated A.A.A. payments intended for them or in other ways have misused the aid given under the A.A.A. program. A somewhat less serious charge is that some county agents, who frequently are the secretaries of local chapters of the Farm Bureau, have helped to force tenants, including Negroes, to become dues-paying members of this organization, which rarely, if ever, represents the interests of the Southern tenant class.[b] The county agents may rarely express an explicit command to the tenants to join the Farm Bureau; but a mere suggestion, often made when benefit checks are distributed, is enough to make a Negro believe that he has not much choice. About similar pressure from the side of landlords, see *PM* (February 23, 1942.)

[67] This system of federally organized credit agencies was begun by the institution of the Federal Land Banks (for mortgage loans) in 1916 and the Federal Intermediate Credit Banks (for certain types of production credit) in 1923. The Farm Credit Act of 1933 provided for the organization of the Farm Credit Administration (F.C.A.) which now includes half a dozen federally sponsored credit agencies working for various purposes, among those the older institutions which were just mentioned, as well as the Production Credit Corporations and Associations (for short-term credit), the Banks for Cooperatives, and the Emergency Crop and Feed Loan Offices (short-term credit for farmers unable to get assistance from other institutions). In addition, certain indepen-

[a] U. S. Department of Agriculture, "Extension Work among Negroes," Table II.
[b] Information from the Southern Tenant Farmers' Union, December 31, 1939.

dent new federal agencies give more specialized types of agricultural credit, such as the Farm Security Administration, which will be discussed subsequently, the Commodity Credit Corporation, which is part of the previously mentioned "Ever-Normal Granary Plan" system, and the Rural Electrification Administration.

Even this incomplete list is impressive enough. Possibly it may reflect a certain overlapping between various offices, but in the main it indicates a real effort to solve the problem of agricultural credit in its various phases.

[68] U.S. Department of Agriculture, *Agricultural Statistics: 1940*, p. 599.

[69] The total amount of such credit held by the various F.C.A. agencies and by the Commodity Credit Corporation on January 1, 1940, was not much more than half of that held by one single group of private institutions, the insured commercial banks; it was about the same in the South.[a] Woofter's study of 646 plantations in 1934 shows that a little more than one-fourth of the short-term credit came from government institutions.[b] The follow-up study of 246 plantations showed that less than half of them used any short-term credit at all in 1937; among those who did, over two-thirds used private sources of credit, usually banks, but in a few cases used supply merchants and fertilizer companies. The government institutions, however, had become more important at the expense of the private organizations. They were used somewhat less infrequently than in 1934, and they granted higher average amounts of credit.[c]

[70] *Ibid.*, p. 25.

[71] Woofter, *Landlord and Tenant*, p. 55.

[72] Schmidt, *op. cit.*, p. 280.

[73] See, for instance, *The Tenant Farmer* (February 15, 1942).

[74] Sterner and Associates, *op. cit.*, p. 305.

[75] Information from field offices in Mississippi, January, 1940. See also Sterner and Associates, *op. cit.*, p. 297.

[76] Schmidt, *op. cit.*, p. 238.

[77] *Monthly Report of the Federal Emergency Relief Administration, May 1, through May 31, 1934*, p. 6.

[78] *Report of the Administrator of the Farm Security Administration, 1941*, pp. 28-29.

[79] Sterner and Associates, *op. cit.*, pp. 300-301.

[80] *Ibid.*, pp. 300 and 305.

[81] *Ibid.*, pp. 301, 302, 304, and 308-309.

[82] *Ibid*, Table 125, p. 306.

[83] *Report of the Administrator of the Farm Security Administration, 1941*, p. 10.

[84] Schmidt, *op. cit.*, p. 233.

Chapter 13. *Seeking Jobs Outside Agriculture*

[1] "Whether upon the plantation or in towns, whether in the cruder trades or the artistic crafts, the Negroes played an important role. We find them on the rice or the tobacco plantations, serving their masters as carpenters, coopers, blacksmiths, sawyers,

[a] U. S. Department of Agriculture, *Agricultural Statistics: 1940*, pp. 619, 620, 632, and 633.

[b] Woofter, *Landlord and Tenant*, p. 212.

[c] Holley, Winston, and Woofter, *op. cit.*, p. 25.

wheelwrights, shoemakers, painters, etc. We may assume that they were, as a rule, not the most skilled or exact craftsmen, but they were capable of doing satisfactory work in shoeing horses and mules, making hogsheads, repairing barns and slave quarters, making wagons, cutting timber. The slave who had been trained to a craft always commanded a higher price than the ordinary field hand . . .

"In the larger towns in all parts of the South, slaves were trained to various crafts and used in the shops of the larger shipwrights, cabinetmakers, shoemakers, wigmakers, etc. . . .

"The custom of hiring out Negro artisans was common in many parts of the South. When a master craftsman died, his widow often found that she could depend on a fair revenue from the work of her slave helpers.

"This use of Negro craftsmen tended to run white men out of the trades, since it not only lowered wages, but cast a stigma on skilled labor. Slave labor in the rice and tobacco fields had already struck a deadly blow at the yeomanry, now it began to undermine the small but important artisan class. . . . In the old South, after the passing of wigs and elaborate hair dressing for men, the barber business fell largely into the hands of blacks. An old Southern gentleman once told me that on his first visit to the North he experienced a kind of shame for the white man who cut his hair and the white girls who waited on him at table. Thousands in the South were shocked when the first Negro postman delivered mail to their front doors. Thus, when the master craftsmen of the old South began to employ Negroes in large number, it tended to make carpentry, or bricklaying, or wheelmaking, or cooperage, or tanning the profession of slaves. Slave workers not only degraded labor, but cheapened it." (Thomas J. Wertenbaker, *The Old South* [1942], pp. 229-232.)

[2] *The Negro: The Southerner's Problem* (1904), p. 127.

[3] *The Negro in Louisiana* (1937), pp. 135-136.

[4] Willis D. Weatherford and Charles S. Johnson, *Race Relations* (1934), p. 315.

[5] Edwin R. Embree, *Brown America* (1933; first edition, 1931), p. 151.

[6] Page, *op. cit.*, p. 77.

[7] Winfield H. Collins, *The Truth about Lynching and the Negro in the South* (1918), p. 138.

[8] *Eleventh Census of the United States: 1890, Population*, Vol. II, Table 116; *Thirteenth Census of the United States: 1910, Population*, Vol. IV, Table 7.

[9] *Thirteenth Census of the United States: 1910, Population*, Vol. IV, pp. 313-314; *Fifteenth Census of the United States: 1930, Population*, Vol. V, pp. 408-411.

[10] Although the South had 32 per cent of the nation's population in 1940, only about 20 per cent of all wage earners in manufacturing industries in 1939 were in the South. (U.S. Bureau of the Census, *Statistical Abstract of the United States: 1938*, Tables 6 and 793; U.S. Bureau of the Census, *Statistical Abstract of the United States: 1941*, Table 868; and *Sixteenth Census of the United States: 1940, Population*. Preliminary Release, Series P-10, No. 1.)

[11] U.S. Bureau of the Census, *Negroes in the United States: 1920-1932*, p. 53.

[12] It should be noted that the concept of "labor force" in the 1940 Census, like the concept of "gainful worker" in earlier census enumerations, includes unemployed workers. This circumstance, owing to the increase in unemployment, affects the comparison between 1930 and 1940 to a greater extent than corresponding comparisons between previous census years. There are no reliable data for 1930 which could be compared

with the 1940 figures on employed workers. To be sure, a census of unemployment was taken in 1930 which indicated a much lower unemployment than in 1940, particularly for Negroes (*Fifteenth Census of the United States: 1930, Unemployment*, Vol. II, pp. 232 ff.), but this study probably involves an under-enumeration, especially for Negroes. (There was little indication of unemployment rates being significantly higher for Negroes than for whites.) It is not likely, however, that a comparison based on accurate data for employed workers would have shown any smaller decrease in the proportion of Negroes in the urban labor force than do the figures in Table 2, since this would have presupposed that the race differential in unemployment had become smaller. Rather it was the other way around; in spite of the lack of reliable statistical data, it seems most probable that, between 1930 and 1940, unemployment increased more for Negroes than for whites.

This development is not restricted to the South. The discrepancy between the increase in urban Negro population and the increase in the Negro labor force was even greater in the North than in the South during this period. We shall discuss the causes later.

In both regions the development is to some extent explained by the institution of old age benefits and large-scale relief and by the increase in the numbers of Negro youths who attended schools: these factors caused a certain tendency for Negroes to withdraw from the labor market. (See Chapter 13, Section 9.) However, these withdrawals from the labor market were certainly due, in part, also to the lack of employment opportunities for Negroes which have tended to cause elderly people, particularly, to abstain from seeking jobs and from considering themselves as workers.

[13] See source reference to Table 3. Data available at this writing do not enable us to indicate the exact size of the change in total employment, since the 1940 figures refer to employed workers 14 years of age and over, and those for 1930 to both employed and unemployed workers 10 years of age and over. These circumstances have been considered in the text comment, which refers only to some of the most apparent changes.

[14] The Negroes in New York not only had to bear the pressure of general sentiment against free Negroes, but were called on to stand up under an economic pressure stronger than that endured by any other of the free groups. For generations the New York Negroes had had an almost uncontested field in many of the gainful occupations. They were domestic servants, laborers, boot-blacks, chimney-sweeps, whitewashers, barbers, hotel waiters, cooks, sailors, stevedores, seamstresses, ladies' hairdressers, janitors, caterers, coachmen. (At that time a black coachman was almost as sure a guarantee of aristocracy for a Northern white family as a black mammy for a family of the South.) In a limited way they were engaged in the skilled trades. The United States Census of 1850 lists New York Negroes in fourteen trades. In two occupations—as janitors of business buildings and as caterers—a number of individuals actually grew wealthy. (James Weldon Johnson, *Black Manhattan* [1930], pp. 43-44.)

[15] Frederick Douglass, cited by B. Schrieke, *Alien Americans* (1936), p. 122.

[16] There were many exceptions though. Ray Stannard Baker relates from the North:

"And yet, although I expected to find the Negro wholly ostracised by union labour, I discovered that where the Negro becomes numerous or skillful enough, he, like the Italian or the Russian Jew, begins to force his way into the unions. The very first

Negro carpenter I chanced to meet in the North (from whom I had expected a complaint of discrimination) said to me:

" 'I'm all right. I'm a member of the union and get union wages.'

"And I found after inquiry that there are a few Negroes in most of the unions of skilled workers, carpenters, masons, iron-workers, even in the exclusive typographical union and in the railroad organizations a few here and there, mostly mulattoes. They have got in just as the Italians get in, not because they are wanted, or because they are liked, but because by being prepared, skilled, energetic, the unions have had to take them in as a matter of self-protection. In the South the Negro is more readily accepted as a carpenter, blacksmith, or brick-layer than in the North not because he is more highly regarded but because (unlike the North) the South has almost no other labour supply." (*Following the Color Line* [1908], p. 135.)

[17] *The New South* (1890), pp. 249-250.

[18] *Problems of the Present South* (1909; first edition, 1904), pp. 186-187. The thesis that the South provided industrial opportunities for Negroes had a vital role in its defense for abridging their rights as citizens:

"The South has sometimes abridged the Negro's right to vote, but the South has not yet abridged his right, in any direction of human interest or of honest effort, to earn his bread. To the Negro, just now, the opportunity, by honest labor, to earn his bread is very much more important than the opportunity to cast his vote. The one opportunity is secondary, the other is primary; the one is incidental,—the greater number of enlightened peoples have lived happily for centuries without it,—the other is elemental, structural, indispensable; it lies at the very basis of life and integrity—whether individual or social." (*Ibid.*, pp. 187-188.)

[19] *Up From Slavery* (1901; first edition, 1900), pp. 219-220.

[20] *Thirteenth Census of the United States: 1910, Population*, Vol. IV, Table 7.

[21] *Thirteenth Census of the United States: 1910, Population*, Vol. IV, Table 7; and *Fifteenth Census of the United States: 1930, Population*, Vol. IV, State Table 11.

[22] The data for the nation as a whole indicate that, between 1910 and 1930, there was a 46 per cent increase of male workers (all races) in nonagricultural pursuits. For unskilled workers the rate of expansion was only 20 per cent. (U.S. Bureau of the Census, Alba M. Edwards, *Social-Economic Grouping of the Gainful Workers of the United States in 1930* [1938], p. 7.) Yet it was due, mainly, to this limited expansion in laboring jobs that the Negro was able to make any inroads into industry. Sterner points out:

"There were 1,171,000 more male unskilled workers in 1930 than in 1910; 40 per cent of these [additional] workers were Negroes. Of the 2,121,000 additional semi-skilled workers, 8 per cent were Negroes. The total increase in number of skilled, clerical, managerial, and professional male workers amounted to 5,739,000 persons, of whom only 2 per cent were Negroes." (Richard Sterner and Associates, *The Negro's Share*, prepared for this study [1943], p. 27.)

Nevertheless, there had been some improvement in the Negroes' occupational status; the proportion of all Negro workers who were in semi-skilled occupations had increased, at the same time as the proportion of those in unskilled occupations had declined somewhat. Yet in relation to the white workers, the position of the Negro had become worse. (*Idem.*)

[23] Edwards, *op. cit.*, pp. 47 and 59.

[24] *Ibid.*, pp. 46-59.

[25] *Sixteenth Census of the United States: 1940, Population,* Preliminary Release, Series P-4, No. 4.

[26] The employment rates for white females were comparatively uniform all over the country. In most large cities, North as well as South, from one-fifth to one-third of the white women were reported as employed. The rates for Negro women in large Southern cities usually ranged from one-third to one-half. In the North they were less consistent, and frequently much lower. In some cities, like Chicago, Cleveland, Detroit, and Pittsburgh, they were even lower than those for white women. (*Sixteenth Census of the United States: 1940, Population,* Second Series, State Reports, Table 41.)

[27] In the nine Northern cities having the heaviest Negro population (New York, Chicago, Philadelphia, Detroit, Cleveland, Los Angeles, Pittsburgh, Cincinnati, Indianapolis), the proportion of actually employed persons among Negro men 14 years and over ranged around one-half (from 45 to 56 per cent), whereas the corresponding figure for white males varied between two-thirds and three-fourths (from 63 to 73 per cent). Southern cities showed a somewhat smaller difference, but even there Negroes were worse off than whites. The large cities in the Upper and Lower South showed a rather uniform pattern; in most of them about two-thirds of the Negro men and three-fourths of the white men were registered as being employed. (*Idem.*)

[28] *Sixteenth Census of the United States: 1940, Population,* Preliminary Release, Series P-4, No. 8.

[29] *Sixteenth Census of the United States: 1940, Population.* Preliminary Release, Series P-4, No. 8. See also Sterner and Associates, *op. cit.,* p. 31.

[30] Sterner and Associates, *op. cit.,* p. 31. At the Census of 1930 no less than 20 per cent of the Negro boys and 12 per cent of the girls, 10 to 15 years of age, were registered as gainful workers. The corresponding figures for white boys and girls were 5 and 2 per cent, respectively. Corresponding data from the 1940 Census are not available at this writing. It is known, however, that the rate for colored boys and girls, 14 years of age, dropped from 23 per cent in 1930 to 11 per cent in 1940; whereas, the corresponding figures for white boys and girls were 5 per cent in 1930 and 3 per cent in 1940. (*Sixteenth Census of the United States: 1940, Population,* Preliminary Release, Series P-4, No. 8).

[31] The general rate for Negro women was about stationary for the period 1900-1930, but this was probably due to the migration from rural areas, where but a small proportion of females are registered as gainful workers. Urban areas seem to have shown a slight decline during the period. (Sterner and Associates, *op. cit.,* pp. 29-30.)

[32] *Ibid.,* p. 33.

[33] It should be noted, however, that data for 1930 and 1940 are not quite comparable since the basic census definitions have been changed. Seasonal workers, who were neither working nor seeking work during the time of the census, were not included as members of the "labor force" in 1940; but in 1930 they were reckoned as "gainful workers." Since they may have been particularly numerous among the Negroes, it is possible that this, to some extent, may have made the equalization between Negroes and whites, in regard to proportion of persons in the labor force, appear as somewhat more pronounced than it actually was. This error in the comparison may have been counteracted, to some extent, by another difference in definition: young workers, who had never had any unemployment, are included as members of the "labor force" in 1940;

but they were not considered as gainful workers in 1930. This group, however, is small. (Regarding these problems of definition, see the previously quoted census publications.)

[34] *Sixteenth Census of the United States: 1940, Population*, Preliminary Release, Series P-4, No. 8. There were several cities, however, particularly in the North, where the proportion of all workers (employed and unemployed) had become smaller among Negro than among white males (Table 6). Also, there were in the North some large cities where the relative number of female workers and job-seekers was only slightly higher in the Negro than in the white group. In such cases Negro rates usually tended to be even lower than white rates for girls under 25, at the same time as they were higher for other age groups. (*Ibid.*, Series P-4, No. 6.) One sometimes hears that many Negro mothers would rather work than let their daughters lose status in the eyes of possible suitors by accepting positions as domestics. We can take it for granted, at any rate, that the extremely limited range of job opportunities for Negro women is behind this phenomenon; after all, of all Negro women workers in nonagricultural pursuits in 1930, less than one-half were able to find work other than as servants or cooks in private families. (U.S. Bureau of the Census, *Negroes in the United States: 1920-1932*, pp. 303 and 358.) There has not been any substantial improvement since then.

[35] *Sixteenth Census of the United States: 1940, Population*, Second Series, State Reports, Table 17.

[36] The proportion of old Negro men (75 years of age and over) who were still "in the labor market" declined from 53 per cent in 1930 to 23 per cent in 1940 (the corresponding figures for whites were 31 and 18 per cent, respectively). (*Sixteenth Census of the United States: 1940, Population*, Preliminary Release, Series P-4, No. 8.)

[37] The discussion in this section is based, mainly, on the 1940 Census. There are no major studies which would enable us to get an idea about the trends in employment and unemployment rates by race. In addition to the 1940 Census, there are only two general studies reliable enough to be used, viz. the Unemployment Check Census studies of November, 1937 (Calvert L. Dedrick and Morris H. Hansen, *Final Report on Total and Partial Unemployment, 1937* [1938], Vol. 4) and the National Health Survey of 1935-1936 (Bernard D. Karpinos, *The Socio-Economic and Employment Status of the Urban Youth of the United States, 1935-1936* [1941].) Both of these studies give about the same picture of the character of the race differences in regard to the size of the "labor force," employment and unemployment as does the 1940 Census. (Sterner and Associates, *op. cit.*, pp. 39-45.) Yet the three sets of data are not comparable to such an extent that any conclusions regarding the trends could be drawn on the basis of them.

[38] *Ibid.*, pp. 44-45. Italics ours.

Chapter 14. *The Negro in Business, the Professions, Public Service and Other White Collar Occupations*

[1] U.S. Bureau of the Census, Alba M. Edwards, *Social-Economic Grouping of the Gainful Workers of the United States: 1930* (1938), p. 86, Table 31.

[2] Sutherland reports:

"The field studies indicated that there was no better place to study frustration of this type than in the small northern community. Here the tradition of liberalism in race relations has given Negro youth an expectation of freedom in community life. In their childhood experiences they are accepted in the churches, in the schools, and on the playgrounds. Some are favored by white teachers who, recognizing their traditional handicap, give them special encouragement. Service clubs allocate part of their educational funds to Negro youth. Honors in athletics, in class offices, and in scholastic attainment also come their way. Responding to these incentives, the boy or girl feels no isolation and expects his good fortune to continue. He has already experienced some of the blessings of the American dream.

"Sad, therefore, is the awakening which comes to many of these youth when, upon graduation from high school, they find that the communities did not mean to be really liberal; that, although a service club would help a Negro boy to complete his high school course, its members would not give him a job after his schooling was over. Even before graduation day the lines of participation had been drawn and his social contacts were limited largely to other Negroes in the community, and in many small towns there are too few of them to provide any satisfactory kind of society. Unless he could manage to continue his education in college and settle in a larger community, his prospect of success was exceedingly slight." (Robert L. Sutherland, *Color, Class, and Personality* [1942], pp. 31-32.)

[3] *Sixteenth Census of the United States: 1940*, Preliminary Release, "Retail Trade. Retail Negro Proprietorship—The United States—1939" (August 29, 1941). The description in this section is based both on the Census of Business and on occupational information from the Census of Population. They are not comparable in that the population census is much more complete in regard to very small establishments, but the discrepancy does not affect the main conclusions.

[4] *Idem.*

[5] Ira DeA. Reid, "The Negro in the American Economic System," unpublished manuscript prepared for this study (1940), Vol. 1, pp. 102-103.

[6] Charleston, South Carolina, where Negroes live widely scattered, has little Negro business; Savannah, Georgia, where Negroes are concentrated in one area, has much more Negro business.

[7] This is true, for instance, in Richmond, Virginia, where the principal Negro neighborhood borders Broad Street.

[8] Reid, *op. cit.*, Vol. 1, p. 105.

[9] U.S. Bureau of the Census, *Negroes in the United States: 1920-1932*, pp. 332-333.

[10] U.S. Bureau of the Census, *Negroes in the United States: 1920-1932*, p. 358; and U.S. Bureau of the Census, *Statistical Abstract of the United States, 1938*, p. 66.

[11] Edwards, *op. cit.*, p. 10.

[12] U.S. Bureau of the Census, *Negroes in the United States: 1920-1932*, p. 497.

[13] For a statement of how few of the "Negro entertainment" places in Harlem are owned by Negroes, see Claude McKay, *Harlem: Negro Metropolis* (1940), pp. 117-120.

[14] See James Weldon Johnson, *Black Manhattan* (1930), pp. 43-44.

[15] W. E. Burghardt Du Bois, *The Philadelphia Negro* (1899), pp. 119-121.

[16] *Ibid.*, p. 120.

[17] *New Negro Alliance* v. *Sanitary Grocery Co.*, 303 U.S. 552 (1938).

[18] *Op. cit.*, p. 143.

[19] One or two of the more noteworthy campaigns may be mentioned. Certain Harlem organizations, in the middle of the 'thirties, forced some stores to take on a few Negro clerks. The merchants, however, secured an injunction against them for "restraint of trade" and the new colored workers were dismissed. The great discontent caused by this incident was the major force behind the Harlem race riot of 1935. The fight was continued by an organization called Greater New York Coordinating Committee for Employment which, in 1938, succeeded in getting a written agreement with the Uptown Chamber of Commerce to the effect that all stores in Harlem under the jurisdiction of the Chamber should increase the proportion of Negroes among their white collar workers to at least one-third, as soon as white employees resigned or were dismissed for cause. Negro workers should have the same chance of being promoted as other workers. Another campaign in New York which, according to Reid, has turned out to be "singularly effective," concerns public utilities. In this case there are several possible tactics: to force white telephone operators to make the connections instead of using the mechanical dialing system, to demand out-of-turn inspection of electricity and gas connections, to avoid using electricity, and so on. The St. Louis Urban League has organized "block units," some with 100 per cent membership. These and the Colored Clerk's Circle, as well as other organizations, have succeeded in getting jobs for several hundreds of colored clerks. There are some campaigns, however, which have miscarried, as for instance, one in Atlanta in the middle of the 'thirties. (Reid, *op. cit.*, Vol. 1, pp. 149-161.)

[20] *Ibid.*, Vol. 1, p. 163.

[21] Edwards, *op. cit.*, pp. 118-119.

[22] Sir George Campbell, *White and Black in the United States* (1879), p. 286. Du Bois comments as follows:

"Morally and practically, the Freedmen's Bank was part of the Freedmen's Bureau, although it had no legal connection with it. With the prestige of the government back of it, and a directing board of unusual respectability and national reputation, this banking institution had made a remarkable start in the development of that thrift among black folk which slavery had kept them from knowing. Then in one sad day came the crash,—all the hard-earned dollars of the freedmen disappeared; but that was the least of the loss,—all the faith in saving went too, and much of the faith in men; and that was a loss that a Nation which to-day sneers at Negro shiftlessness has never yet made good. Not even ten additional years of slavery could have done so much to throttle the thrift of the freedmen as the mismanagement and bankruptcy of the series of savings banks chartered by the Nation for their especial aid." (W. E. B. Du Bois, *The Souls of Black Folk* [1903], pp. 36-37.)

[23] Most data in this and the preceding paragraphs are based on Reid, *op. cit.*, Vol. 1, pp. 70-83. Some of the main sources used by Reid are: Abram L. Harris, *The Negro as Capitalist* (1936); Jesse B. Blayton, "The Negro in Banking," *The Bankers Magazine* (December, 1936), pp. 511-514; and J. B. Blayton, "Are Negro Banks Safe?" *Opportunity* (May, 1937), pp. 139-141.

[24] All data on Negro insurance, except when otherwise stated, have been drawn from Reid, *op. cit.*, Vol. 1, pp. 84-92. The main basic source used by Reid was Samuel A. Rosenberg, *Negro Managed Building and Loan Associations in the United States* (1939). Concerning the general problem of Negro housing credit, see Chapter 15, Section 6.

[25] Some Northern states have made attempts to stop discrimination in insurance; the New York act even forbids the refusal of a Negro's application because of his race alone. (See Charles S. Mangum, Jr., *The Legal Status of the Negro* [1940], p. 70.) Most data on Negro life insurance, except when otherwise stated, are based on Reid, *op. cit.*, Vol. 1, pp. 37-69.

[26] See, for instance, U.S. Department of Labor, Bureau of Labor Statistics, *Study of Consumer Purchases, Family Expenditures in Selected Cities: 1935-36*, Bulletin No. 648, Vol. 8, "Changes in Assets and Liabilities" (1941), pp. 70-179. U.S. Department of Agriculture, Bureau of Home Economics, *Consumer Purchases Study, Changes in Assets and Liabilities of Families*, Miscellaneous Publication No. 464 (1941), pp. 50 and 79. Concerning average amounts of premiums, see also, Richard Sterner and Associates, *The Negro's Share*, prepared for this study (1943), p. 152 and Appendix Table 35.

[27] According to the Consumer Purchases Study it is quite usual that every year as much as 5 or 10 per cent—sometimes up to 15 per cent—of the low income families surrender their insurance policies; the proportion of policies which fail to reach maturity must under such circumstances be extremely high. (U. S. Department of Labor, Bureau of Labor Statistics, *Study of Consumer Purchases, Family Expenditures in Selected Cities: 1935-36*, pp. 70-179.)

[28] A survey of funeral expenses connected with 7,871 "adult deaths" of industrial policyholders in 1927 revealed that the average cost of burial was $363. The average insurance carried was somewhat lower ($309). Another group studied was composed of 3,121 veterans, for whom the average burial cost ranged from $241 in towns with less than 10,000 population to $336 in cities of over 250,000. Funeral expenditures of 319 dependent widows applying for pensions to the New York Board of Child Welfare averaged $247 in the Jewish group, $421 in the Italian group, and $452 in the Irish group. It happened frequently that low income families spent large sums on an extravagant funeral and a few weeks later applied for relief. The high fees apparently had caused an over-expansion in this business; it was ascertained that 92 per cent of the undertakers in New York City made a living on an average of but 25 funerals a year. (John C. Gebhard, *Funeral Costs*, Miscellaneous Contributions on the Costs of Medical Care, Number 3, The Committee on the Costs of Medical Care [1930], pp. 3-7.) Although conditions may have changed since the time of this study, it is a well-known fact that funeral costs are still high.

[29] We have asked Negro insurance officials whether it would not be in the public interest for the insurance companies to develop policies which would set limits to the extraordinary expenses that poor Negro families incur when one of the family dies, and whether they would not start an educational campaign to teach people the importance of keeping insurance for the survivors instead of spending it on funerals. The answers have, in general, been the following: (1) one should not interfere with the desires of people to use their money as they please; (2) the intense desire among even the poorest Negroes to guarantee a decent funeral after death is one of the strongest incentives for keeping up insurance, and the insurance companies should not be expected to demolish the basis for their own business; (3) even granted that the morticians artificially stimulate in an unsocial way conspicuous consumption in luxurious funerals, and that, particularly, they exploit the poor people, one business should not be expected to take a stand against another business; (4) the morticians are so powerful in the Negro community,

and are so entrenched in the churches, that not even the big insurance company dares to take up a fight against them.

[30] A detailed account of these societies is given in Harry J. Walker, "Negro Benevolent Societies in New Orleans," unpublished manuscript, Department of Social Science, Fisk University (1936).

[31] Modern Negro insurance history centers around four institutions: the North Carolina Mutual Life Insurance Company of Durham, the Standard Life Insurance Company of Atlanta, the National Benefit Life Insurance Company of Washington, D. C., and the Supreme Liberty Life Insurance Company of Chicago. The history of the North Carolina Mutual goes back to 1898. C. C. Spaulding, still the leading Negro finance official, soon became its most prominent officer. The Standard Life Insurance Company of Atlanta, which was organized in 1913, has had a more turbulent history. Its activities rose rapidly but soon they became too involved, in that investments were made in quite a number of business and real estate projects, many of which were far outside the sphere of ordinary life insurance investment. The company was finally dissolved in the middle of the 'twenties. The National Benefit Life Insurance Company in Washington also was one of those concerns which went too far in its investment policies. It failed in 1931. There are several other Negro life insurance ventures which have been characterized by similar shortcomings, such as unwise spending, high administrative costs, lack of prudent management, excessive investment in real estate, too great a readiness to help Negro business establishments, marginal trading in stock. Irregularities have not been infrequent. The personnel is often underpaid. Premiums, it is claimed, are computed from tables which do not reflect the true mortality of the Negro population. The turnover among those insured is described as high.

Unsuccessful Negro insurance companies have been made the subject of a special study by the Department of Commerce, Bureau of Foreign and Domestic Commerce, entitled *Causes of Negro Insurance Company Failures*, Bulletin No. 15 (1937).

[32] Edwards, *op. cit.*, pp. 7 and 13.

[33] *Ibid.*, pp. 46-49 and 58-61.

[34] It should be noted, in passing, that these data seem to suggest a certain equalization in the educational facilities for Negroes and whites. At the same time as the Negro school system expanded somewhat more than the white school system, there was a great increase in the number of Negro pupils in unsegregated Northern schools.

[35] Doxey A. Wilkerson, *Special Problems of Negro Education* (1939), p. 21. Among sources used by Wilkerson are Ambrose Caliver, *Education of Negro Teachers*, U. S. Office of Education, Bulletin No. 10 (1933); David T. Blose and Ambrose Caliver, *Statistics of the Education of Negroes, 1933-34 and 1935-36*, U. S. Office of Education, Bulletin No. 13 (1938).

[36] Wilkerson, *op. cit.*, pp. 23-25.

[37] Bond, *op. cit.*, pp. 264-265.

[38] Decision of the United States Circuit Court of Appeals of June 18, 1940, in the case of *Melvin Alston* v. *the School Board of Norfolk, Virginia*.

[39] An account of these developments is given in recent issues of the magazines, *The Crisis* and *Opportunity*. A summary of the development until mid-1941 is given in the National Association for the Advancement of Colored People, *Teachers' Salaries in Black and White. A Pamphlet for Teachers and Their Friends* (September, 1941).

[40] Reid, *op. cit.*, Vol. 2, p. 248; Woodson, *op. cit.*, pp. 68-69; Charles S. Johnson, *The Negro College Graduate* (1938), p. 137.

[41] It seems that the majority of the churches give at least moral support to Negro business establishments in one form or another. (Woodson, *op. cit.*, p. 76.)

[42] Reid, *op. cit.*, Vol. 2, p. 242.

[43] Woodson, *op. cit.*, pp. 69-70. See also Chapter 40 of this book.

[44] Woodson, *op. cit.*, p. 89.

[45] Reid, *op. cit.*, Vol. 2, p. 182.

[46] Woodson, *op. cit.*, pp. 98-102. Although Woodson does not say so, it is quite likely that some of this white trade consists of abortion cases.

[47] *Idem.*

[48] The average amount per year for different community groups ranges between $10 and $20 for families with an income of less than $500; they usually run into several hundreds of dollars for families with more than $3,000. Negroes, since they are poorer, often use a somewhat smaller percentage of their income for this purpose than do whites, and the actual amounts they spend are only one-third or one-half of those spent by the average white family.[a]

[49] Woodson, *op. cit.*, p. 96.

[50] *Ibid.*, p. 97.

[51] Harold F. Dorn, "Health of the Negro," unpublished manuscript prepared for this study (1940), p. 113 a.

[52] Reid, *op. cit.*, Vol. 2, pp. 186-187.

[53] Sterner once interviewed one of the leaders of the National Medical Association (the Negro professional organization for physicians and surgeons) who resides in the Deep South. He complained about how a patient brought to a hospital was always a patient lost to him. He described how he had tried to make Negroes understand that the treatment at the public clinic was not in any real sense free, as the patients had to pay "with their good name." One of the reasons why the Negro private practitioner was losing out, he explained, was that employers send their workers to the public clinic; they are not even allowed to retain jobs at a shirt factory unless they are free from syphilis. The informant seemed to be against any further increase in public health facilities for Negroes, but apparently mainly for the reason that he feared that Negro doctors would never get any chance to work at public clinics and hospitals. His repeated requests to the state government that the Negro doctor be given a real place in the public health service of the state had been in vain. (Interview, January 8, 1940.)

[54] Howard University with 276 candidates had only 33 failures, or 12 per cent. This ranks favorably with other medical schools; Harvard University, at the top, had 1.1 per cent of its 276 candidates failing; Loyola University, at the bottom, had 20.9 per cent of its 254 candidates failing. (Albert E. Casey, "Research Activity and the Quality of Teaching in Medical Schools," *Science* [July 31, 1942], pp. 110-111.)

[55] Reid, *op. cit.*, Vol. 2, pp. 185-187. During the 'thirties, there was a decline in the number of students at Negro medical schools, but this was probably a depression phenomenon. The number of internships available to Negroes has increased from 68 in 1931 to 168 in 1939.

[56] Charles S. Johnson, *op. cit.*, p. 137.

[a] Sterner and Associates, *op. cit.*, pp. 149-153. Data based on *Study of Consumer Purchases: 1935-36.* Data refer to nonrelief families only.

[57] Woodson, *op. cit.*, pp. 104-113.

[58] Reid, *op. cit.*, Vol. 2, p. 215.

[59] Woodson, *op. cit.*, pp. 165-183.

[60] Reid, *op. cit.*, Vol. 2, pp. 283-290.

[61] Cited in *ibid.*, Vol. 2, p. 296.

[62] Sterner once met a white Farm Security supervisor in the Deep South who complained about the restricted possibilities of having Negro assistants and cooperating freely with them. He asserted that Negro workers, in general, gained the confidence of Negro clients much more easily than did white workers. He once had a male Negro assistant who had been forced to leave because of the resentment in the community. According to another informant in the community, a young educated Negro who said that he was the friend of this Negro assistant, the departure had been brought about by a group of whites who had entered the office of the assistant and told him to get out of town before a certain time. There was still a female Negro co-worker, but she had to work outside the town and the daily communications with her had to be made over the telephone—an arrangement which the white Farm Security official described as extremely inconvenient.

[63] *Thirteenth Census of the United States: 1910, Population,* Vol. IV, pp. 416-419; *Fifteenth Census of the United States: 1930, Population,* Vol. III, Part 1, p. 23; Vol. 5, p. 548.

[64] *Fifteenth Census of the United States: 1930, Population,* Vol. V, p. 83.

[65] *Thirteenth Census of the United States: 1910, Population,* Vol. IV, pp. 426-431; *Fifteenth Census of the United States: 1930, Population,* Vol. V, pp. 572-574.

[66] Laurence J. W. Hayes, *The Negro Federal Government Worker* (1941), pp. 37-56.

[67] Robert R. Moton, *What the Negro Thinks* (1929), p. 169.

[68] The total number of Negro federal employees (including custodial workers and laborers), according to the estimates cited by Hayes (*op. cit.*, p. 153), increased regularly —even during the Wilson administration:

	Number	Per cent
1892	2,000	1.4
1900	1,000	0.4
1912	20,000	5.0
1918	45,000	4.9
1933	53,000	9.8
1938	82,000	9.9

Only a minority of these workers, however, were officials and clerical employees.

[69] A very light Negro stenographer told Sterner that she had at first worked in the stenographic pool of one large Washington agency. After some time she was sent to work in another building of the same agency where those in charge of assignment did not know her race. Immediately she was put to work as a private secretary to one of the white officials. The white girls associated with her. This situation embarrassed her, for she had not intended to "pass" but feared the expression of resentment from her boss and the white girls if she told them that she was a Negro.

[70] This has happened, for instance, in the Bureau of the Census owing to the activity of the Federal Workers' Union, to which, however, only a minority of the employees

in the Bureau belong. Some time afterwards, a mimeographed sheet denouncing Negro employees was secretly distributed among the employees.

Another incident, as related by the Washington Bureau of the National Association for the Advancement of Colored People:

"A suit in criminal court against . . . a guard at the War Department building in Arlington, Va., is expected to be filed by the Bureau within the next few days.

"Trouble came May 18, when James Harold, a War Department draftsman, was struck over the head . . . when Harold and other colored workers in the department attempted to enter the cafeteria in the building.

"Quick action by the Bureau resulted in the removal of the ban against Negroes at the cafeteria." (N.A.A.C.P., *Bulletin*, [June, 1942].)

[71] *Fifteenth Census of the United States: 1930, Population*, Vol. V, pp. 574-576.

[72] Woodson, *op. cit.*, pp. 250-251.

[73] *Thirteenth Census of the United States: 1910, Population*, Vol. IV, Table VII; U. S. Bureau of the Census, *Negroes in the United States: 1920-1932*, Table 23; U. S. Bureau of the Census, *Statistical Abstract of the United States, 1938*, Table 51.

[74] For an enumeration of the white-owned and Negro-owned places of amusement featuring Negro entertainers in New York, see McKay, *op. cit.*, pp. 117-120.

[75] Reid, *op. cit.*, Vol. 2, p. 358. Based on unpublished manuscript by William T. Smith (editor), *Silhouette*, Los Angeles, California.

[76] *PM* (June 23, 1942), p. 22.

[77] Frazier describes a district of Louisville in the following words:

"Within the boundaries of this zone the tempo of Negro life in Louisville is most rapid and all forms of illegal and anti-social practices flourish. Throughout the area 'hustlers,' thieves, 'con' men, pimps, policy writers, and race horse bookies ply their trades. Under the guise of legitimate business, traffic is carried on in dope or 'reefers,' liquor, and prostitution. Though the number of legitimate liquor stores is increasing monthly, bootleg liquor known as 'mammy,' 'splo,' and 'derail' is sold in the dens of vice to which men go for all types of sexual pleasures. There are homosexual 'joints' masquerading under the names of clubs and inns. And, as in all cities, there are the 'exclusive' dens of vice where Negro women cater to the perverted as well as normal sexual desires of white men." (E. Franklin Frazier, *Negro Youth at the Crossways* [1940], p. 16.)

Fortune magazine describes the underworld of Harlem:

"There are reefer pads (marihuana dens), gambling houses, and countless houses of prostitution. Most 'hotels' are brothels, and it is a usual sight to see a dozen street-walkers on every corner in lower Harlem . . .

"Almost every grocery, cigar store, beauty parlor, barbershop, and tavern in Harlem is a numbers 'drop' where the collectors pick up the play for the day . . . Harlem . . . has . . . the city's highest record of . . . dope peddling." (This quotation and others in this section are reprinted through the courtesy of *Fortune* magazine, "Harlem," July, 1939, p. 170.)

[78] See Claude McKay, *op. cit.*, pp. 101-116.

[79] Du Bois mentions this type of gambling as early as 1897. (See *The Philadelphia Negro*, p. 265.)

[80] See J. Saunders Redding, "Playing the Numbers," *The North American Review* (December, 1934), pp. 533-542.

[81] During the prohibition era and afterwards when bootlegging became less profitable, the organized white criminal gangs "muscled in" and not only took control of the numbers racket in the Negro community but introduced it into the white community where it now flourishes all over the United States. The New York investigation into the activities of "Dutch" Schultz, head of the numbers racket, revealed a close tie between his activities and those of the Tammany political machine. (See *Newsweek* [August 1, 1938], pp. 7-8.)

At the present time, although the heads of the national numbers syndicates are whites, Negroes run the number rackets in Negro communities. *Fortune* points out:

". . . the hottest game in Harlem is the numbers game, the policy racket, which is going stronger than ever since the publicity of the Jimmy Hines [Tammany leader] trial. The racket, run by Negroes who have a working agreement with the white bankers of Manhattan and Hoboken, grosses about $20,000,000 a year." (*Fortune, op. cit.*, p. 170.)

For a description of the "numbers" racket in Chicago, see J. G. St. Clair Drake, "The Negro Church and Associations in Chicago," unpublished manuscript prepared for this study (1941), pp. 274-277; and J. G. St. Clair Drake, *Churches and Voluntary Associations in the Chicago Negro Community*, Work Projects Administration Report (1940), pp. 179-182.

[82] See Redding, *op. cit.*, pp. 537 and 540.

[83] Gosnell tells about Daniel M. Jackson, before his death in 1927 the most powerful vice and gambling king in Chicago, that he was noted for his generosity to poor people. He quotes the following statement, made during an interview, by a Negro journalist:

"I don't like to admit it, but an open town is far better for the Negroes than a closed town. . . . Of course, these bosses make a lot of money, but while Jackson was in control he donated thousands to charities, the N.A.A.C.P., working girls' homes and the like. While Jackson was in power the colored people always had a friend to go to. . . . " (Harold F. Gosnell, *Negro Politicans* [1935], pp. 131-132.)

Regarding the reasons for the power of the Negro underworld leaders, Gosnell states:

"In commenting on this situation one prominent Negro said: '. . . Now, if I were to run for a political office, I would have to raise campaign expenses. If I went to every professional man in the town, I would not be able to raise two hundred dollars. But if I went to the vice lords and policy kings, I would get two or three thousand from a couple of them.' . . . In relation to other enterprises run or partly controlled by Negroes the total amount of money involved in the undercover activities is large. The drug stores, the taxi cab companies, the beauty parlors, the bonding houses, the small shops, the criminal lawyers, the real estate companies, and even the bankers in the communities where the 'racketeers' are numerous and well supplied with cash may depend in part for their own prosperity upon the patronage of those engaged in illegal activities." (*Ibid.*, pp. 134-135.)

[84] In addition to the jobs connected directly with the numbers game, there are a whole parallel series of "shady" businesses that exist partly for the purpose of turning up the lucky number; these are the occult enterprises, the astrologers, charm sellers, crystal-ball readers, fortune tellers:

"A subsidiary of the [numbers] game is the dream-book and incense business.

Dream books containing lucky numbers are sold for two bits or half a dollar. The incense sells for a dime and, when it has burned down, three numbers (the right ones, of course) can be seen in the ashes." (*Fortune, op. cit.*, p. 170. See also, Redding, *op. cit.*, pp. 539 ff; and John B. Kennedy, "So This is Harlem," *Collier's* [October 28, 1933], pp. 22 and 50-52.)

Many of these enterprises are owned and operated by the policy kings on a syndicated basis, and the employees belong to the shady middle or lower class; they have relatively little power or wealth. Some few of the astrologers, many of them women, however, build up a reputation and clientele and exert considerable influence in the shady upper classes. See McKay, *op. cit.*, pp. 73-81.)

[85] Frazier has some pertinent observations on the mechanism of the tendencies to asociality among Negroes:

"The . . . pathological feature of the Negro community is of a more general character and grows out of the fact that the Negro is kept behind the walls of segregation and is not permitted to compete in the larger community. This produces an artificial situation in which inferior standards of excellence and efficiency are set up. Since the Negro is not required to compete in the larger world and to assume its responsibilities and suffer its penalties, he does not have an opportunity to mature. Moreover, living within a small world with its peculiar valuations and distinctions, he may easily develop on the basis of some superficial distinction a conception of his role and status which may militate against the stability of his own little world. This is manifested not only in the activities of racketeers who are known as such, but also in the behavior of those who because of color, of 'good looks' or education maintain a professional or upper-class 'front' while engaging in antisocial practices." (*Op. cit.*, p. 290.)

[86] Frazier, *op. cit.*, p. 16 *passim*.

[87] One observer reports:

"I have seen colored prostitutes galore, catering to a white clientele who are satisfied to pay fancy prices for novelties offered. It is said that about ninety per cent of these dives are owned and managed by whites . . .; five per cent are owned and managed by whites and negroes jointly, and the balance are managed by colored people. (Hendrik de Leeuw, *Sinful Cities of the Western World* [1934], p. 266.)

Fortune states:

"In recent years white prostitutes have also been imported from downtown." (*Op. cit.*, p. 170.)

[88] Gosnell observes:

"Since it is easier to observe immoral conditions among a poor and unprotected people, colored prostitutes are much more liable to arrest than white prostitutes. White women may use the big hotels or private apartments for their illicit trade, but the colored women are more commonly forced to walk the streets."

And he goes on to explain how officers often tend to arrest Negro girls solely because they find them in company with white men, whereas white women can approach white men without being conspicuous. (*Op. cit.*, pp. 120-121.)

[89] The *Nation* reports that prices for Negro prostitutes range from 25 cents to $2 while those for whites are $1 to $5. ("Prostitution in New York City," editorial, *Nation* [March 25, 1936], p. 369.)

[90] Merely as an illustration we quote the following estimates about the Chicago Negro community:

"Protected business is important in the economic life of the community. Some $10,000,000 is spent annually on policy playing alone. The game gives employment to more than 4,000 people and maintains a weekly payroll of $40,000 in salaries and commissions. No other business in the Negro community is so large or so influential." (W. Lloyd Warner, Buford H. Junker, and Walter A. Adams, *Color and Human Nature* [1941], p. 19.)

Chapter 15. *The Negro In The Public Economy*

[1] Clearly regressive indirect taxation, such as property, tobacco, liquor, and sales taxes, and custom duties, made up more than half the total national tax receipts in 1937. (See the Twentieth Century Fund, *Facing the Tax Problem* [1937], pp. 9-25. For a similar estimate for 1936, see Clarence Heer, *Federal Aid and the Tax Problem*, The Advisory Committee on Education, Staff Study No. 4 [1939], p. 34.) Some estimates are presented in this study illustrating the point in the text that taxes were regressive for the lower and middle income groups; see *ibid.*, p. 232.

[2] The Constitution of the United States does not, of course, say anything directly about the distribution of public services, or about the principle of "need." The relevant phrasing is in Section 1 of the Fourteenth Amendment:

"No State shall make or enforce any law which shall abridge the privileges or immunities of citizens of the United States; nor shall any State deprive any person of life, liberty, or property, without due process of law; nor deny to any person within its jurisdiction the equal protection of the laws."

It is to be noted that this requires not only equality but also equality applied to *individuals* and not to groups. Under the Fourteenth Amendment, the Supreme Court has consistently required the states to provide equal facilities to individual Negroes, and this in effect turns out to be the principle of need. If, for example, a state has an unemployment insurance law, it must apply equally to individual Negroes and individual whites, even though Negroes as a group are more benefited because more of them are unemployed. Similarly, individual Negroes do not have to pay higher gasoline taxes than individual whites, even though the entire group of Negroes pays less gasoline taxes because it buys less gasoline. For this reason we shall refer to the principle of need as the "constitutional" norm, and we shall regard as unconstitutional any attempt to relate the distribution of general public services either to a group or to the amount of taxes paid by an individual or group.

[3] An example of this is presented in T. J. Woofter, Jr., and Associates, *Black Yeomanry* (1930). The total tax levy for an almost all-Negro community during the period 1921-1927 was $16,437, while the total value of services was estimated at $6,837, or 42 per cent of the former amount. (See *ibid.*, pp. 158-185 and 275.)

[4] T. J. Woofter, Jr., for instance, has this to say:

"The democratic theory of public expenditure demands more than common justice. It demands that the money raised from public taxation be spent where it is most needed, regardless of the sums which the needy group have paid in. If the policy of expending money for education in proportion to the amount paid in were adopted, then the rich districts and wards would have magnificent palaces for public schools and the poorer districts and wards would have schools little better than those provided for the Negroes now. . . .

"Some communities are . . . so far behind the realization of this democratic ideal that it is necessary to hold up before them the amount of money which the Negroes actually contribute in order to emphasize the fact that common justice demands the more liberal support of colored institutions.

"Many communities in the South have never expended a cent of public money for a colored public school building, but have relied on the use of a church or a school building erected by private agencies. In some of these communities bonds have been issued recently to build expensive schools for whites. This means that colored property holders are taxed to build school buildings for white people. . . ." (*The Basis of Racial Adjustment* [1925], pp. 154-155.)

[5] "The universality of the property tax burden is often ignored in current tax discussion. Many members of the community, it is sometimes said, are 'exempt' from taxes, since they are so poor that they pay no income taxes, health duties, or gift taxes, and own no taxable property. They are, however, exempt only in the sense that they have no direct contact with the tax collector." (The Twentieth Century Fund, *op. cit.*, p. 296.)

[6] It is indicative of the opportunism of popular beliefs that, while the observer finds most white people in the South inclined to stress that Negroes pay practically no taxes, Negroes, on the other hand, show themselves quite sophisticated in the theory of the incidence of indirect taxation. In 1873 a Negro Reconstruction politician, the Mississippi State Superintendent of Education, Cardozo, expressed what is the Negro theory in the matter:

"Again it is objected that a general tax compels white men of the State to educate the children of the Negro. But as the Negro forms a majority of the entire population of the State, and in an eminent degree a majority of the producing classes, as such classes of every population—the laborer, tenant, and consumer—indirectly bear the burdens of taxation, it follows that an assessment upon the property of the State would be principally paid by the Negro. . . ." (Quoted in Horace Mann Bond, *The Education of the Negro in the American Social Order* [1934], p. 71.)

[7] The Advisory Committee on Education, *Report of the Committee* (1938), pp. 20-22.

[8] The mean family income in 1935-1936, according to the estimates of the National Resources Committee, was $1,622 for the country as a whole and $1,326 for the South. The Mountain and Plains regions, however, which include several states with rather high expenditures per pupil, showed an average family income ($1,363) which was not much higher than that for the South. (National Resources Committee, *Consumer Incomes in the United States, Their Distribution in 1935-36* [1938], pp. 21-22.) In the South there were in 1930 about 6 children, 5 to 17 years of age, to every 10 adults, 20 to 64 years of age; in the rest of the country there were about 4 children to every 10 adults. (*Report on Economic Conditions of the South*, prepared for the President by the National Emergency Council [1938], p. 25; The Advisory Committee on Education, *Report of the Committee*, p. 25). Additional information on income and on number of children is presented in Chapter 16 of this book.

[9] A calculation made by the Advisory Committee on Education (*The Federal Government and Education* [1938], pp. 8 and 12-13), of the yield of a uniform state tax,

indicates that the state-to-state variations in these yields are much greater than are the differences in actual expenditures for education. In Mississippi the yield per child would be only one-tenth of that in New York State, whereas the actual expenditure per child was one-fifth of the amount expended in New York State.

[10] In Arizona and in the two Dakotas, the expenditure level was even higher than the national average, and in Utah it was not far below this national figure. (Advisory Committee on Education, *The Federal Government and Education*, pp. 8 and 12-13.)

[11] Missouri and Oklahoma even showed somewhat higher per pupil expenditures for Negro schools than they showed for white schools. This is due to the fact that Negroes in these two states, to a greater extent than whites, are concentrated in cities, where school expenses always tend to be higher than they are in the country.

[12] David T. Blose and Ambrose Caliver, *Statistics of the Education of Negroes, 1933-34 and 1935-36* (1939), pp. 14-16.

[13] Doxey Wilkerson, *Special Problems of Negro Education* (1938), p. 21.

[14] *Ibid.*, p. 19.

[15] *Ibid.*, p. 9. Also see Chapter 43, Section 4, of this book.

[16] Sixty-five per cent of all the Negro public schools in Louisiana are one-teacher schools, and another 27 per cent are two- or three-teacher schools. (See Charles S. Johnson, "The Negro Public Schools," *Louisiana Educational Survey* [1942], p. 43.)

[17] Wilkerson, *op. cit.*, p. 33.

[18] *Ibid.*, pp. 40, 45, and 60.

[19] The main figures in the tabulation are as follows:

Race	Number of Counties	Median Expenditure for Teachers' Salaries in Counties With Specified Proportion of Negroes in the School Population, Aged 5-19: 1930-1931							
		0 – 12.4%	12.5– 24.9%	25.0– 37.4%	37.5– 49.9%	50.0– 62.4%	62.5– 74.9%	75.0– 87.4%	87.5– 99.9%
Negro Schools	521	$8.62	$5.28	$5.56	$4.46	$3.05	$2.85	$2.12	(only 1
White Schools	526	14.31	16.87	21.25	21.25	22.58	26.25	28.50	county)

Source: Horace Mann Bond, *The Education of the Negro in the American Social Order* (1934), pp. 240-241.

[20] Bond, *op. cit.*, pp. 232-245.

[21] "Experience with a number of Federal funds has demonstrated that when the division of Federal grants between separate white and Negro schools or institutions is left entirely to administrative discretion, it is exceedingly difficult to secure an equitable distribution. Experience with some State distributive funds has also indicated that when such funds are allocated to local jurisdictions for Negro schools, frequently either the funds for Negro schools are diverted in part to white schools or the local support of Negro schools is reduced and the effect of State aid is cancelled in whole or in part." (The Advisory Committee on Education, *Report of the Committee*, p. 51.)

[22] See Charles S. Mangum, Jr., *The Legal Status of the Negro* (1940), pp. 88, *passim*. Mangum summarizes his discussion as follows:

"The central theme running through the above discussion of the statutes and decisions on this important subject is the guarantee of equal educational opportunity for the children of all races. The fact that such a guarantee of equal facilities exists does not mean that it is carried out in the southern states. In fact it is the exception and not the rule for the Negro schools in that part of the nation to be anywhere near as efficient as those for the whites. The inequalities are manifest to anyone who has even a cursory knowledge of the present status of education in the South." (*Ibid.*, pp. 129-130; Compare p. 137.)

[23] Charles H. Thompson, "The Status of Education *Of* and *For* the Negro in the American Social Order," *Journal of Negro Education* (July, 1939), pp. 494-495. See also, Bond, *op. cit.*, p. 171.

[24] Wilkerson, *op. cit.*, p. 79. Where the federal government has left it up to the state legislatures to allocate the funds for agricultural, industrial, or home economics training, Negroes have received little of the benefits. According to Wilkerson, such federal acts include: Hatch Act (1887), Adams Act (1906), Smith-Lever Act (1914), Clarke-McNary Act (1924), Purnell Act (1925), Capper-Ketcham Act (1928), and Bankhead-Jones Act, Sections 1-8 and 21 (1935). But where the federal law stipulates that Negro schools are to receive an equitable share of the funds, Negroes have received benefits. Such laws include: Nelson Amendment (1907) to the Morrill Act (1890) and Bankhead-Jones Act, Section 22 (1935). Negroes have received about half their proportionate share of the Smith-Hughes Act (1917) funds. (*Idem.*)

[25] *Ibid.*, p. 72.

[26] Robert M. Lester, "Corporation Grants for Education of the Negro," A Report of the Carnegie Corporation of New York (1941), p. 26.

[27] Advisory Committee on Education, *The Federal Government and Education*, pp. 17-18.

[28] Ira DeA. Reid, *In a Minor Key* (1940), p. 39.

[29] Advisory Committee on Education, *Federal Relations to Education*, two vols. (1931); Advisory Committee on Education, *Report of the Committee* (1938), p. 243. More recently the American Youth Commission, headed by Owen D. Young and composed of eight laymen and eight educators, came to a similar conclusion after extensive investigation. (Educational Policies Commission, *Education and Economic Well-Being in American Democracy* [1940].) The conclusion of the former of the two commissions was summarized as follows:

"The facts presented previously in this report indicate that no sound plan of local or state taxation can be devised and instituted that will support in every local community a school system which meets minimum acceptable standards. Unless the Federal Government participates in the financial support of the schools and related services, several millions of the children in the United States will continue to be largely denied the educational opportunities that should be regarded as their birthright." (Advisory Committee on Education, *Report of the Committee*, p. 47; compare Clarence Heer, *op. cit.*, particularly pp. 86-87.)

[30] The subject is touchy, and the Advisory Committee on Education is anything but clear in its pronouncements on this point. On the one hand, it recommends, in its main report, that:

". . . all Federal action should reserve explicitly to State and local auspices the general administration of schools, control over the processes of education, and the determination of the best uses of the allotments of Federal funds within the types of expenditure for which Federal funds may be made available." (*Report of the Committee*, p. 42.)

On the other hand, it advises that:

"All Federal grants for educational purposes to States maintaining separate schools and institutions for Negroes should be conditioned upon an equitable distribution of the Federal funds between facilities for the two races." (*Ibid.*, p. 43.)

In the last statement it does not seem to be implied that federal authorities should make it a condition for federal aid that *state and local* appropriations be equitably distributed between Negro and white schools. It is only said that the proportion of state and local funds spent for Negro schools should "not be reduced" when the federal government gives money. (*Ibid.*, p. 51.)

[31] Sterner and Associates, *The Negro's Share*, prepared for this study (1943), pp. 152 ff.

[32] According to Elliot H. Pennell, Joseph W. Mountin, Kay Pearson, *Business Census of Hospitals, 1935*, Supplement No. 154 to the Public Health Reports (1939), 47 per cent of the total income came from government funds, 43 per cent from patients and 10 per cent from private endowments and gifts. (Russell Sage Foundation, Russell H. Kurtz (editor), *Social Work Yearbook, 1941* [1941], p. 329.)

[33] Monroe N. Work (editor), *Negro Year Book, 1937-1938* (1937), pp. 290-292.

[34] According to a survey for 1935, none of the states in the Upper and Lower South had as many as 345 beds per 100,000 population in all registered general and special hospitals, and all but three of them (Virginia, Florida, and Louisiana) had less than 264. On the other hand, Maryland, District of Columbia, as well as several Northern and Western states, had rates higher than 445. (Joseph W. Mountin, Elliot H. Pennell, and Evelyn Flook, *Hospital Facilities in the United States*, U.S. Public Health Service Bulletin No. 243 [1938], quoted by Harold F. Dorn, "The Health of the Negro," unpublished manuscript prepared for this study [1940], Figure 44.) Conditions have certainly improved since then, however, in part due to increased efforts on the part of the federal government which has rendered assistance, through its program of public works, for the erection of several new hospitals.

[35] According to Charles S. Johnson, the P.W.A. provided, either by direct aid or by loans, 8,000 hospitals beds for Negroes in 17 Southern states. (See "The Negro," *American Journal of Sociology* [May, 1942], p. 857.) Also see: Federal Works Agency, *Second Annual Report* (1941), pp. 116, 191, 315, 460.

[36] *Social Work Yearbook, 1941*, pp. 332-336 and 427-430.

[37] Sterner, when visiting the public health clinic in a Mississippi county in December, 1939, was told how planters brought truckloads of their tenants to the clinic for treatment of syphilis. A prominent Negro doctor in another Mississippi town told him how white manufacturers did not even let Negroes do factory work unless they received treatment for veneral diseases at the public clinic. The public health officer in this city said that about 90 per cent of the clients at the clinic were Negroes.

[38] At the end of 1939, almost two-thirds of the rural counties were still without any complete health departments directed by full-time medical officers, but the increase in number of units where satisfactory public health services are rendered has been extremely rapid during the last decade. In 1940 more than two-thirds of the counties had at least public health nurses. The federal government, under special provisions in the Social Security Act of 1935 and the Venereal Disease Control Act of 1938, has rendered financial assistance on a matching basis to several programs, including general health

clinics as well as maternal and child health services, venereal disease clinics, and so on. (*Social Work Yearbook, 1941*, pp. 324-325 and 432-433.) Considerable extension of this federal assistance was proposed in the National Health Bill.

³⁹ Michael M. Davis observes:

"Programs have been planned by categories of disease. Tuberculosis, diphtheria, infant and maternal mortality, venereal disease, hookworm, malaria, mental disease, and some others, have each been the objective of specific programs. General sanitation, the disposal of excreta, and the control of epidemics represent other, historically older objectives which are really categorical. The diseases of people have been studied and a series of technical procedures have been discovered for control or prevention. The people have rarely been studied, to determine the health needs they had, the needs they felt, and the relative urgency of those recognized needs—so as to plan a health campaign, which would meet a social situation as well as a series of biological ones.

"In order to be both wise and efficient, public health policy needs to take into account both the social and categorical points of view. The issue is one of balance. If the balance had not been so heavily weighted on the categorical side, the Mexicans in a few states, the whites of the Appalachian highlands in several states, and the Negroes in many states, would have had much more attention from public health departments and voluntary agencies." ("Preface" to Harold F. Dorn, "Health for the Negro," unpublished manuscript prepared for this study [1940], p. 10.)

⁴⁰ *Negro Year Book, 1937-38*, pp. 559-560.

⁴¹ As there are no comprehensive statistics on recreational facilities and their distribution between whites and Negroes, we are restricted to citing examples. Concerning the conditions in small Southern cities, E. Franklin Frazier makes the following statement:

"The dominant white group in these areas simply pay little or no attention to the recreational needs of Negroes. For example, for the white residents of Greenville, South Carolina, there is within thirty miles a state park available but there is no public reservation for Negroes. In the city of Greenville there are two small areas without any equipment in which Negroes are allowed to play. Negroes are denied the use of a tract of land, eighteen acres in area, between two densely populated Negro areas, chiefly because it is used as a playing field for the white baseball team. Even the areas adjacent to the Negro high and elementary schools are too small to provide adequate recreation for the school children." ᵃ

Yet Greenville is one of the few small cities in the South having a Negro community center. It has been organized by a private agency. Frazier characterizes it by quoting the following statement by the National Recreation Association (April, 1939):

"It is not adequately supported and does not have a budget consistent with its service. The outdoor area is too small to be considered in contemplating even the Negro child school population of nearly 4,000. It does have a side yard with a tennis court and a tot lot." ᵇ

The large cities in the South, where the need for recreational facilities is greater, also have inadequate provisions. Frazier gives a complete description of the recreational

ᵃ "Recreation and Amusement among American Negroes," unpublished manuscript prepared for this study (1940), p. 36.

ᵇ Report of the Field Director, Bureau of Colored Work, National Recreation Association (August, 1939); cited in *ibid.*, p. 37.

facilities in North Carolina, where conditions, however, are superior to those in the Deep South. In 1940, Raleigh had three playgrounds, one park with a swimming pool, and one community center for Negroes. Greensboro had one park with a community building, a swimming pool, a golf course, and a playground; it also had three independent supervised playgrounds, one handicraft center and a skating rink. There were similar provisions in Durham and Charlotte. On the other hand, Winston-Salem, which has the largest Negro population in the state (36,000 in 1940), did not have any special recreational facilities for Negroes, except a swimming pool; for the rest, school houses were used as recreational centers, with special recreational leaders.[a]

In respect to the situation in Virginia's urban areas—likewise above the average for the entire South—we may quote the following statement:

". . . Negro children of smaller cities have for their only playgrounds their school yard, vacant lots of outlying regions, or the alleys. The Community Center of Richmond, sponsored by the Colored Recreation Association, a Richmond Community Fund agency, offers courses in vocational arts and crafts and in home-making, music and folk-dancing. The gymnasium and playground affords such recreations as boxing, ten pins, volley ball, basketball, ping pong, baseball, and tennis for young and old. In July, 1938, the Richmond city council approved the purchase of a large plot of ground in North Richmond, upon which is to be erected a playground and recreation center with space and equipment for games, a swimming pool, and modern gymnasium and field house. By means of a P.W.A. grant the outdoor swimming pool was completed for use during the summer of 1939.

"Likewise Lynchburg, Norfolk and Newport News have inadequate recreational facilities for Negroes. Happyland, a private park of Lynchburg, has a lake for swimming and boating, picnic grounds, recreational fields, and what has been described as the 'most beautiful dance floor in Virginia.' The Recreation Center of Newport News was completed in January, 1938, out of funds contributed principally by the Newport News Shipbuilding and Dry Dock Company." [b]

Birmingham, Alabama, a city in the lower South, has no Negro parks. In Houston, Texas, there is a ten-acre park for Negroes donated to the city by ex-slaves; the white parks comprise 2,600 acres.[c]

[42] The four states were Virginia, Kentucky, Texas and North Carolina. The remaining nine states were Alabama, Arkansas, Florida, Georgia, Louisiana, Mississippi, Oklahoma, South Carolina and Tennessee. It was estimated that only 21 per cent of the Negroes in these 13 states had access to public library services.[d]

In some large cities with public branch libraries, like Atlanta and Birmingham, Negroes can use only books stored in the special Negro branches. In Richmond and Houston, on the other hand, books can be secured through the Negro branches from the main library.[e]

The Virginia State Library in Richmond can be used by Negroes, although they have to sit at segregated tables in the main reading room. On the whole, there may be some-

---

[a] See op. cit., p. 39.
[b] The Federal Writers' Project, The Negro in Virginia (1940), p. 344.
[c] See Frazier, op. cit., pp. 45-46.
[d] Survey made by Eliza Atkins Gleason, The Southern Negro and the Public Library (1941), p. 90.
[e] See Frazier, op. cit., pp. 49-50.

what greater freedom in the case of 'higher" library services than there is in respect to the "popular" public libraries.

The Rosenwald Fund has tried to improve the situation by supplying money on a matching basis for the extension of library service. But only 11 counties cooperated between 1930 and 1935 and even they were quite discriminating in the distribution of these funds between Negroes and whites.[a]

[43] Federal Works Agency, *Second Annual Report* (1941), pp. 116, 191, 315 and 460.

[44] *Ibid.*, pp. 121-125.

[45] Not only do real property taxes increase housing expenses for the consumer in a way which must be particularly burdensome for low income families; even more important, perhaps, is the fact that they must make investments in housing more risky than they otherwise would be. For what they really mean is that states, counties, and municipalities have a first mortgage on all real estate, leaving less room and less security for other mortgages, and making the owner's equity much more likely to fluctuate in value than would have been the case if taxes were on income only.

[46] Suffice it to say that, in 1940, when most of the building construction was of single family homes, 171,440 new small homes, or 40 per cent of all new dwellings in this category, in nonfarm areas were covered by F.H.A. insurance. (U.S. Federal Housing Administration, *Seventh Annual Report* [1941], pp. 6 and 15.) In 1941, 218,035 new small homes, or 41 per cent of new single family homes, were covered by F.H.A. insurance. (U.S. Federal Housing Administration, *Eighth Annual Report* [1942], p. 3.)

[47] U.S. Federal Housing Administration, *Seventh Annual Report* (1941), pp. 15 and 77. See also Sterner and Associates, *op. cit.*, p. 314.

[48] Sterner and Associates, *op. cit.*, p. 313. See also U.S. Federal Housing Administration, *Successful Subdivisions*, Planning Bulletin No. 1 (1940); and National Association of Housing Officials, *Housing Yearbook* (1940), pp. 161-162.

[49] U.S. Federal Housing Administration, *Underwriting Manual* (1938), par. 935.

[50] *Ibid.*, par. 980.

[51] *Idem.*

[52] Corienne K. Robinson, Federal Public Housing Authority, letter (August 28, 1942). It should be noted, in addition, that a considerable number of projects originally intended for low income families were turned over to defense workers for the duration of the War. Concerning the Negro's share in the war housing program, see Chapter 19.

[53] One New York project, for instance, the South Jamaica Houses, has 1,050 Negro and 459 white residents thus intermingled. The John Jay Homes in Springfield, Illinois, also have about 100 Negro and 400 white families living without any segregation. The experiences, so far, have been good; there have been extremely few expressions of bad interracial feeling. (New York *Herald Tribune*, [June 10, 1942]; William M. Ashby, "No Jim Crow in Springfield Federal Housing," *Opportunity* [June, 1942], pp. 170-171; and Sterner and Associates, *op. cit.*, p. 320.) This may be due, in part, to the fact that the white inhabitants in such projects are often Italians, Poles, and

[a] Louis R. Wilson and Edward A. Wight, *County Library Service in the South* (1935), pp. 67-96; cited by Doxey A. Wilkerson, *Special Problems of Negro Education* (1939), pp. 148-149.

other immigrants, not yet imbued with American race prejudice. Then, too, there is no guarantee that conflicts would be avoided, were this practice to be followed on a larger scale than hitherto. Still it should be tried. Even a partial success would be extremely valuable.

[54] Federal Works Agency, *Second Annual Report*, p. 382.

[55] *Ibid.*, p. 8.

[56] Anne E. Geddes, *Trends in Relief Expenditures, 1910-1935* (1937), pp. 21 and 92-94.

[57] In 1890 somewhat more than 1 per cent of the total population and somewhat less than 1 per cent of the Negro population was cared for in public almshouses. The difference was due to the fact that almshouse care was less extensive, in proportion, in the South than it was elsewhere. In the South, Negroes and whites had about the same proportions cared for in almshouses; in the North the proportion of Negroes cared for was twice as high as the proportion of whites. Thus, public relief agencies in the North and in the South showed about the same difference in their attitude toward Negroes as has characterized them during recent years. See the following table:

"PAUPERS" IN ALMSHOUSES IN 1890

Race	United States	The North and the West	The South
Numbers			
All Races	73,045	59,896	13,149
Negro	6,467	2,013	4,454
Percentage of total population			
All Races	1.2	1.4	.6
Negro	.9	2.8	.7

Sources: *Eleventh Census of the United States: 1890. Report on Crime,* "Pauperism and Benevolence in the United States," Part 2, p. 651. U.S. Bureau of the Census, *Negroes in the United States: 1920-1932,* p. 5.

[58] Grace Abbott, *From Relief to Social Security* (1941), p. 9.

[59] Sterner and Associates, *op. cit.*, Part 2, particularly pp. 219-230.

[60] *Idem.*

[61] *Idem.*

[62] The period 1933-1935 stands somewhat apart in the history of public assistance. We may call this the F.E.R.A. period, since the main welfare agency during these years was the Federal Emergency Relief Administration. State and local agencies were being organized, but the federal government carried the main financial responsibility over the whole field and particularly in the South. Eventually a certain specialization among various aspects of the relief work was brought about, and this trend was precipitated around 1935-1936 when the social security program and various special programs were inaugurated; at the same time a strict demarcation line was drawn between, on the one hand, the responsibilities of the federal government and, on the other, those of state and local governments.

In October, 1933, Negro relief rates in urban areas of Northern states with 100,000 or more Negroes varied between 25 and 40 per cent, and they were usually between three and four times higher than the white rates. The corresponding state figures for urban Negroes in the South varied between 10 and 33 per cent and were usually two or three times higher than those for whites. In the rural South, on the other hand, which, of course, comprises both villages and open country, Negro relief rates were sometimes lower—as, for instance, in Mississippi, Arkansas, and Louisiana—and sometimes higher than the white rates. Both Negro and white rates were quite heterogeneous in the rural South, the lowest one being 2 per cent and the highest 27 per cent.[a]

A special survey of urban workers on relief in May, 1934, indicated a higher general level but about the same differential. Half the Negro families in a sample of cities in the North and in the Border states were receiving public assistance; the corresponding proportion of white families was 10 to 13 per cent. Cities in the Upper and Lower South showed a proportion of Negro relief of one-third, whereas the white figure was about the same as it was in the North.[b] The Census of Workers on Relief in March, 1935, showed a similar pattern for urban areas in the North and the South. There was one state (Mississippi), however, where even the urban rate was slightly higher (17 per cent) for whites than for Negroes (16 per cent). The rural areas in the South, of course, showed an even greater lack of uniformity. The relief incidence was sometimes higher and sometimes lower for Negroes than it was for whites.[c]

The lack of uniformity in the South becomes even more evident when data for individual cities and counties are considered. There were some Southern cities which definitely showed a Northern pattern. Even more pronounced, however, were the divergencies in rural areas. Georgia had two counties, both with an appreciable proportion of Negroes in the population, where there were no Negroes at all on the relief rolls in March, 1935, whereas as much as 12 and 19 per cent, respectively, of the white families were receiving public assistance. Most of the other Georgia counties had lower relief rates for Negroes than they had for whites, but there were a few where the relations were reversed. In Eastern Texas, there were some counties where relief rates for Negroes were less than half those for whites; on the other hand, there were other counties where the Negro relief incidence was four times higher than the white relief incidence.[d]

Since Negroes are always poorer than whites, on the average, this heterogeneity cannot be explained on the basis of "local conditions." In the main, it is just a matter of lack of uniformity in the administration of relief. One can well understand how this came about. On the one hand, there were the federal relief officials demanding equal treatment of Negroes and whites. On the other hand, there were the traditional local attitudes. The dominant group in the South was against racial equality. Public relief was a new thing. The politically and economically most potent among them tended to be against it, except when their attitudes were conditioned by obvious needs during the worst depression years when even they welcomed the assistance in carrying their laborers through the off-seasons. It is frequently said that, in many places, planters even

[a] Sterner and Associates, *op. cit.*, p. 22. Data based on Federal Emergency Relief Administration, *Unemployment Relief Census, October, 1933*, Report No. 2 (1934), pp. 14 and 15.

[b] Sterner and Associates, *op. cit.*, p. 228. Data based on Katherine D. Wood, *Urban Workers on Relief*, Part 2 (1936), pp. 72-73.

[c] See Sterner and Associates, *op. cit.*, p. 223. Data based on Philip M. Hauser, *Workers on Relief in the United States in March, 1935, A Census of Usual Occupations* (1938), Vol. 1, pp. 102-103.

[d] See Sterner and Associates, *op. cit.*, p. 223.

took command of public welfare agencies, making them accept their workers on the relief rolls when they were not in need of their services, and making them turn them back to work as soon as there was any work to do.

It seems that in every country where large-scale public relief has been introduced, employers have been against it because of their interest in having an abundant labor supply competing for low wages. It goes without saying that such an attitude has been prevalent in the South, where planters have shown in so many other ways (social sanctions for "tenant stealing," laws against "enticement of labor," remnants of peonage, and so on) how far they can go in order to secure absolute command over the services of "their Negroes." We have run across this several times during our field work in the South.

"The conventional attitude of the landlord was that the tenant, and particularly the share-cropper, was dependent on him for direction and aid. More than nine out of every ten landlords interviewed stated that it was one of the functions of the landlord to maintain his tenants, if possible, in times of distress. At first sight it would seem difficult to reconcile this statement with the fact that approximately 80 per cent of the landlords actually wanted their tenants to get on relief. The contradiction is partially explained, however, by the fact that 50 per cent of the landlords reported financial inability to care for their tenants . . . a considerable number of unscrupulous landlords used government relief as a means of furnishing their tenants with goods which could and should have been furnished by themselves. On the other hand, nearly 40 per cent of the landlords who had tenants on relief were opposed to governmental aid for their tenants on the grounds of its demoralizing effects upon them. . . . Among the landlords who had no tenants on relief, more than 70 per cent stated that they objected to relief because of its demoralizing influence on the tenant."[a]

Caught in the middle were the local social workers. In the beginning, comparatively few of them had much of a professional background, but the proportion of trained workers has gradually increased, and practical experience must have given many others an outlook rather different from the prevalent one. Under such circumstances, almost anything could happen. The treatment of the Negro is a matter of chance. A good social worker, for instance, can treat Negroes and whites on a basis of equality. In the cities, where professional standards are higher than in rural areas, the chances of giving Negroes something approaching their just share is, of course, much greater. Even there, however, it may well happen that welfare workers are hampered by politicians.

In the beginning of November, 1938, Sterner visited the Department of Welfare in Birmingham, Alabama. Negroes and whites were received in segregated parts of the offices. The statistical data revealed the higher relief needs of Negroes, but, nevertheless, a large proportion of the clientele was white. Just after this, there was reported in a local newspaper an interview with a member of the state legislature who claimed that he had found evidence of discrimination against whites; Negroes, he said, could go into the department and get what they asked for, but a white applicant had a hard time getting a fair hearing.

Relief grants, during this period, were much lower in the South than they were elsewhere. In July, 1935, for instance, the national average benefit per case per month

[a] Harold Hoffsommer, *Landlord-Tenant Relations and Relief in Alabama*, Federal Emergency Relief Administration, Division of Research, Statistics and Finance, Research Bulletin, Series II, No. 9 (1935), pp. 1 and 4.

was about $30, but all the states in the Upper and Lower South showed lower figures; most of them paid between $10 and $18. Negroes usually received less than did whites, at least in rural areas. In the Eastern cotton area, for instance, the average grant to whites in June, 1935, was $16, whereas Negroes received $13.[a]

[63] This tendency to disregard the Negro in most of the current reporting on relief may often be due, of course, to a desire not to publicize racial discrimination. Some social workers have given Sterner another explanation which, in many cases, may be almost equally feasible: when there are relatively more Negroes on the relief rolls than in the general population, such statistics could bring about pressure from white tax-payers wanting to limit relief appropriations to Negroes. Quite unrealistic, on the other hand, is the following rather usual explanation: "Since we don't discriminate against Negroes, we have no reason to count them separately in the statistics."

[64] Alva Myrdal, *Nation and Family* (1941), p. 134.

[65] In 1937 over 32,000,000 workers were covered by old age insurance. Of those over 2,240,000, or 6.9 per cent, were Negroes. Together with other nonwhites they constituted still not more than 7.8 per cent of the total coverage. According to the 1940 Census, on the other hand, 10.7 per cent of the total labor force (including unemployed persons and relief workers) was nonwhite.[b]

Those covered by insurance in 1937 constituted over 70 per cent of all workers actually employed in 1940. Three-fourths of the white workers but only one-half of nonwhite workers were covered. There was a great difference, however, between the South and the rest of the country. In the North the overwhelming majority not only of the white but also of the nonwhite workers were within the old age system. In the South, on the other hand, about three-fifths of the Negro workers and almost half the white workers were in uncovered occupations. The old age pension system was particularly inefficient in regard to female nonwhite workers, North as well as South; only about one-fourth of them were covered.[c]

The real race differential is even greater, however, than these figures suggest. Even in covered occupations, low-wage workers are often denied any benefits from the system. Since Negro covered workers had only 3 per cent of the total taxable wage income,[d] it is obvious that such additional restrictions must hit them worse than the whites. In general, in order to qualify for old age benefits, a worker "must have had at least 1 quarter of coverage for each 2 calendar quarters elapsing during his working lifetime."[e] Quarters during which he has had a wage income of less than $50 are not counted as having been "covered." Not less than 42 per cent of the covered Negro

[a] Sterner and Associates, *op. cit.*, p. 227.

[b] Social Security Board, *Old Age and Survivors Insurance Statistics, Employment and Wages of Covered Workers, 1938* (1940), pp. 16-18. *Sixteenth Census of the United States: 1940, Population*, Preliminary Release, Series P-4, No. 4.

[c] *Idem*, and *Sixteenth Census of the United States: 1940, Population*, Preliminary Release, Series P-4a, Nos. 14 to 16. It is obvious that these percentages cannot be exact. Not only is there a time differential; there is also the fact that covered workers include unemployed as well as employed persons. The comparison gives some idea, however, about the relative efficiency of the system for various groups.

[d] *Idem.*

[e] Wayne F. Caskey, "Workers with Annual Taxable Wages of less than $200 in 1937-39," *Social Security Bulletin* (October, 1941), pp. 17-24.

workers, as against 22 per cent of the white workers in 1935, had wage incomes of less than $200 per year; more than half the female Negro workers had wages below the limit.[a] This means, of course, that a substantial proportion even of the covered Negro workers are not going to get any old age benefits at all, if present regulations are to be maintained.

The benefits range between $10 and $85, depending upon the number of dependents, the years of coverage and the average previous wage income. The last two stipulations mean that Negro average benefits must be lower than are those for whites. (A large number of covered workers moves between covered and uncovered occupations. Since the field of uncovered occupations is larger for Negroes than it is for whites, they are more likely to have spent considerable time outside the system of old age insurance.) Even persons with fairly low previous wage incomes, however, receive benefits which, at least in the South, must appear high compared to average relief benefits under many other social welfare programs. For instance, a worker who has had an average monthly wage of $50 and a coverage of five years will receive for himself and his wife, when both have reached the age of 65, a monthly benefit of $31.50.[b] There are additional benefits for children under 16 (sometimes 18) years of age. There are benefits, as well, for surviving wives and children.

Unemployment compensation has limitations in coverage similar to those of the Old Age and Survivors' Insurance. In the rural South, of course, Negroes have little help from the unemployment insurance. Although the system is fairly uniform, benefits may vary to some extent.[c] In the South, most clients receive between $5 and $10 per month; in most other states the majority of recipients get benefits in excess of $10.[d]

[66] *Social Work Yearbook, 1941*, op. cit., p. 611.

[67] *Ibid.*, p. 609, and Virginius Dabney, *Below the Potomac* (1942), p. 114.

[68] *Social Work Yearbook, 1941, op. cit.*, p. 612.

[69] Even in Virginia, where conditions are probably better than in many other Southern states, there remains much to be done. The state labor commissioner officially refers to the "inadequacy of the State safety laws" and refers, among other things, to the fact that, for factories and buildings for public use, there are no legal "standards and controls over the width, pitch and general repair of stairways or the condition of floors . . . aisles, passageways, ladders, platforms, and scaffolding." (Department of Labor and Industry, State of Virginia, *Forty-third Annual Report, Industrial Statistics, Calendar Year, 1939* [1941], p. 21.)

[70] *Sixteenth Census of the United States: 1940, Population,* Preliminary Release, Series P-10, No. 6.

[71] Sterner and Associates, *op. cit.*, pp. 272-274.

[72] California paid $34 per month in 1939-1940; several Northern states, as well as the District of Columbia, paid between $20 and $30. In the South, on the other hand, there were eight states which paid less than $10.

[73] Sterner and Associates, *op. cit.*, p. 280.

[74] *Ibid.*, pp. 282-283. The last percentage was between one-and-a-half and two

[a] *Idem.*

[b] *Social Work Yearbook, 1941, op. cit.*, p. 384.

[c] *Ibid.*, p. 570.

[d] Social Security Board, "Operation of the Employment Security Board," *Social Security Bulletin* (October, 1941), p. 63.

times higher in New York, New Jersey, and Pennsylvania, although in these Northern states Negroes constitute only a small minority of the total population.

[75] *Ibid.*, p. 281.

[76] *Ibid.*, p. 284.

[77] In April, 1940, for instance, there were in this country 8,000,000 unemployed persons, of whom 2,900,000 were taken care of by the W.P.A., C.C.C., or N.Y.A. (those on the Student Work Program are not included in either of the figures). (See *Sixteenth Census of the United States: 1940, Population*, Preliminary Release, Series P-4, No. 5.)

[78] Sterner and Associates, *op. cit.*, pp. 239-241.

[79] This discrepancy was particularly pronounced in Tennessee, where 23 per cent of all unemployed workers, those on emergency work included, in 1940 were Negroes, whereas the proportion of Negroes among relief workers was but 11 per cent. (*Idem.* and *Sixteenth Census of the United States: 1940, Population*, Second Series, Tennessee, State Table 16.)

[80] Sterner and Associates, *op. cit.*, pp. 241-242. One of the reasons why Negroes are discriminated against to such an extent in rural areas of the South is, of course, that agricultural employers are against seeing Negroes get wages on relief work high enough to compete with those paid on the farms. For similar reasons, in part, there is a pronounced special discrimination against Negro women on W.P.A., as evidenced by the following figures for February, 1939:

Negroes as a Percentage of All W.P.A. Workers in:	*Male*	*Female*
13 Southern states and the District of Columbia	26.2	15.9
All other states	10.2	15.7

(*Ibid.*, p. 244.) Thus, the Southern states gave Negro women a share of the work relief employment which was no greater than that given to them by states in the North and West; and it was only about half as great as the proportion of Negroes among all unemployed women in the South in 1940. (*Sixteenth Census of the United States: 1940, Population*, Preliminary Release, Series P-4a, Nos. 14 to 16.)

This phenomenon is due not only to the popular belief in the South that Negro women always can and should earn their living as domestics. Even more significant, perhaps, are the Southern segregational practices and the rules about local sponsorship of W.P.A. projects. Negro men probably would be even worse off than they are under present conditions had it not been for the fact that most W.P.A. projects for men are outdoor projects. This means that, even according to Southern rules, both Negroes and whites can work on the same project, although in separate gangs. Projects for women, on the other hand, are indoor affairs. Seldom, if ever, is it possible in the South to have a sewing room for Negro women in the same building where there is such a room for white women. The consequence is that separate projects have to be organized for Negro women if they are to have any share in the jobs. Since there are few local agencies which would even think of sponsoring projects especially for Negroes, Negro women, in most places, have to be without them. (Sterner and Associates, *op. cit.*, pp. 245-246.)

It goes without saying that the situation is similar in regard to projects for professional and clerical workers. On the whole, there is a general complaint among Negroes to the effect that their chances of being assigned to other than the lowest and least well-paid jobs on W.P.A. are much smaller than corresponds to the actual skills of Negro unemployed workers. Certain evidence presented by Sterner, although not quite conclusive, makes it seem probable that such complaints are justified, at least as far as the South is concerned. (*Ibid.*, pp. 249 and 251.)

[81] The C.C.C. organized work projects at rural camps principally for boys aged 17 to 23 who were unemployed and eligible for relief or otherwise came from low income groups. The work consisted of soil conservation, development of forests and parks for recreational use, flood control and so forth. The objectives of the National Youth Administration have been stated as follows:

"(a) to provide funds for the part-time employment of needy school, college, and graduate students between sixteen and twenty-five years of age so that they can continue their education; (b) to provide funds for the part-time employment on work projects of young persons, chiefly from families certified as in need of relief, between eighteen and twenty-five years of age, the projects being designed not only to provide valuable work experience but to benefit youth generally and the communities in which they live; (c) to encourage the establishment of job training and counseling service . . . ; and (d) to encourage the development and extension of constructive leisure-times activities." M. M. Chambers, "Youth Programs" in *Social Work Yearbook, 1941, op. cit.*, p. 614.

[82] Sterner and Associates, *op. cit.*, p. 258.

[83] *Ibid.*, pp. 263-265.

[84] *Ibid.*, p. 287.

[85] *Ibid.*, p. 291.

Chapter 16. *Income, Consumption and Housing*

[1] A great number of studies on income of farm families have been made, but there are probably none that give an exact picture of the income distribution of all Southern farm families. Owing to the importance of income "in kind" in agricultural areas, it is always difficult to get reliable statistics on farm income. Besides, many samples are biased in either a high or a low direction. By surveying different studies having different characteristics, however, it is possible to arrive at fairly safe general conclusions. Such a survey has been made by Sterner and Associates, *The Negro's Share*, prepared for this study (1943), pp. 62-70. In this context, we may content ourselves by citing the main results of the two most important studies.

The plantation study made by T. J. Woofter, Jr., in 1934, indicates the average annual income for families of Negro tenants and wage laborers on plantations was but $278, whereas the corresponding figure for whites was $452. Negro wage laborers earned as little as $175 per year. Even the Negro cash renters and share tenants were not far above the $300 mark, being worse off than white sharecroppers, who earned $417.[a]

[a] Unpublished figures made available by Woofter, cited in Sterner and Associates, *op. cit.*, pp. 67-68.

These figures, however, are probably slightly too low. While the value of home-use production was included, certain other items, such as housing, fuel, relief, and wages earned off the plantation, were not. The sample of farm families of the Consumer Purchases Study for 1935-1936 (see table in this footnote) indicates higher incomes for Negroes and whites alike, but these data are biased upward.[a] The reason is that large groups among the poorest families, such as unemployed workers, wage laborers, broken families, and farmers who had moved within the year, were completely excluded from the sample. Almost half the families approached during the survey turned out to be ineligible for the sample because they were of these types.[b] Since the groups studied must have had much higher average incomes than the excluded groups, the fact that they included such extremely high proportions of destitute families is remarkable. Since wage laborers were excluded, it was, of course, the Negro sharecroppers who were lowest on the scale. A significant number of them had less than $250. White share-

MEDIAN INCOMES[a] FOR NEGRO AND WHITE FARM FAMILIES IN THREE SOUTHEASTERN SAMPLE AREAS: 1935-1936

State	Owners and Tenants Except Croppers		Croppers	
	Negro	White	Negro	White
South Carolina	$599	$1,035	$424	$541
Georgia	491	708	409	544
Mississippi	576	1,091	416	574

Source: U. S. Department of Agriculture, Bureau of Home Economics, Consumer Purchases Study, Farm Series, Family Income and Expenditures, Southeast Region, Miscellaneous Publication No. 462, Part 1, Family Income (1941), pp. 5 and 77-80.

[a] These as well as all following median income figures are calculated under the assumption that relief families, for which no complete income data were gathered, had incomes below the median. This assumption is certainly correct, except for some rare cases.

[a] The sample for the eastern part of North Carolina (not used in the table) gave income figures which cannot, by any stretch of the imagination, be characterized as typical for the Southeast. The median income varied between $797 for Negro sharecroppers and $1,587 for white operators (other tenants and owners). Negro operators and white croppers, as usual, had about the same position; they earned $1,046 and $1,023, respectively. Another sample for North Carolina which included only white operators in the western part of the state indicated an opposite extreme. The median income was but $611, which is lower than that for any other group of white operators sampled in the Southeast. (U. S. Department of Agriculture, Bureau of Home Economics, Consumer Purchases Study, Farm Series, Family Income and Expenditures, Southeast Region, Miscellaneous Publication No. 462, Part 1, Family Income [1941], p. 5.) The figure cited for white operators in eastern North Carolina ($1,587) is higher than that for any of the states sampled in farm regions of the Northeast and of the Middle West; the latter varied between $936 (Iowa) and $1,503 (Illinois). (See U. S. Department of Agriculture, Bureau of Home Economics, Consumer Purchases Study, Farm Series, Family Income and Expenditures, Middle Atlantic, North Central and New England Regions, Miscellaneous Publication No. 383, Part 1, Family Income [1940], p. 19.)

[b] U. S. Department of Agriculture, Miscellaneous Publication No. 462, op. cit., p. 185.

croppers were somewhat better off. They had about the same position as the combined group of Negro owners, cash tenants and share tenants. Highest on the scale was the corresponding group of white operators.

2 Sterner and Associates, *op. cit.*, p. 71. Data based on U.S. Department of Agriculture, Bureau of Home Economics, *Consumer Purchases Study, Urban and Village Series, Family Income and Expenditure, Southeast Region*, Miscellaneous Publication No. 375, Part 1, *Family Income* (1941), p. 92.

3 In this case the only low income group excluded from the sample was broken families. This is probably the main reason why Negro incomes in villages appear so low compared with the income data for farm families contained in the same study. In addition, it is probable that the great number of displaced Negro farm families in Southern villages helps to drag the income level down. White village families in these 34 villages earned between three and four times as much as did Negro families. Their median income was $1,220. For nonrelief families alone, it was $1,410. These figures compare very well with those for the 8 groups of villages studied in other parts of the country, which—if relief families are included—showed a range in median incomes of from $737 (Illinois and Iowa) to $1,355 (California). In fact, only 3 of these 8 non-Southern village groups had income levels higher than those for white families in Southern villages.[a]

4 Sterner and Associates, *op. cit.*, p. 71.

5 *Idem.* Data based on U.S. Public Health Service, *National Health Survey: 1935-1936*, Preliminary Reports, Population Series, Bulletins A and C (1938). An additional confirmation, based on data for 14 Southern cities but only 3 Northern cities is presented in Department of Commerce, *Consumer Use of Selected Goods and Services, by Income Classes*, Market Research Series, No. 5 (1935-1937).

The mean income, on the other hand, seems to be significantly higher in Northern than in Southern cities, since the frequency of very high incomes is greater in the North. See, for instance, the estimates in National Resources Committee, *Consumer Incomes in the United States, 1935-1936* (1938), p. 28.

6 Margaret Loomis Stecker, *Intercity Differences in Costs of Living in March, 1935, 59 Cities* (1937), p. xix.

7 While the allowances for food may be sufficient, at least for a limited time, they are not as large as the minimum amount for what the Bureau of Home Economics calls a "good" diet, determined by what families in actual practice had been found able to purchase. Only a few adequate dwelling units which can be rented for the amount intended for housing in this budget are available in American cities.[b]

8 Sterner and Associates, *op. cit.*, pp. 84-88.

9 For example, the median income for *nonrelief* Negro families in Atlanta, consisting of husband, wife and 0, 1, 2, and 3 to 4 children under 16, was $710, $685, $675 and $655, respectively. This was so in spite of the fact that the proportion of low income families receiving public assistance—who were not included in these figures—

[a] U. S. Department of Agriculture, Bureau of Home Economics, *Consumer Purchases Study, Urban and Village Series, Family Income and Expenditure, Southeast Region*, Miscellaneous Publication No. 375, Part 1, *Family Income* (1941), p. 14.

[b] Sterner and Associates, *op. cit.*, pp. 86 and 316.

was positively correlated with the number of children in the family, which means that the sample of larger families had fewer poor cases. (*Ibid.*, p. 82.)

[10] Alva Myrdal, *Nation and Family* (1941), pp. 61-76.

[11] Large families do not benefit from subsidized housing in proportion to their greater sufferings from bad housing conditions. (See Chapter 15, Section 6.) The whole program is designated primarily for low income families; family size, at best, is given secondary consideration only. The new social welfare system includes a special program for broken families (Aid to Dependent Children); but there are no corresponding special provisions for large families. While urban relief authorities generally give assistance to a greater proportion of the large than of the small families, it has sometimes happened that welfare agencies in the farm areas of the South have failed to consider the special plight of the large families, particularly in the case of Negroes. (See data from the Consumer Purchases Study cited in Sterner and Associates, *op. cit.*, p. 81.)

[12] In 1930, 59 per cent of all Negro children under 21 years of age in private families belonged to households which had at least four children, whereas the corresponding proportion for native white families was 44 per cent. (See Sterner and Associates, *op. cit.*, p. 49.) The figures would be still higher if one added families having four or more children, of which some were over 21 or had already left home.

[13] The Consumer Purchases Study shows that, for instance, in Atlanta, white husbands, 50 to 59 years of age, in "normal" nonrelief families, earned over one-half more than did husbands 20 to 29 years of age. The corresponding difference for Negro families was only about one-third. The absolute amount of difference was over $700 for white families and $190 for Negro families. (*Ibid.*, p. 83. U.S. Department of Labor, Bureau of Labor Statistics, *Study of Consumer Purchases, Urban Series, Family Income in the Southeastern Region 1935-36*, Bulletin No. 647, Vol. 1, *Family Income* [1939], Tabular Summary, Section B, Tables 8 and 18.)

[14] In Atlanta, Mobile, and Columbia, for instance, there were about twice as many supplementary earners in "normal" nonrelief Negro households as there were in corresponding white families. But each one of them did not earn more than one-fourth or one-third as much as did the supplementary earners in white families, and their total earnings per family, therefore, were only one-half or two-thirds of those of the fewer white supplementary earners. Even so, their contributions made up a larger percentage of the total family income than was the case in white families. (Sterner and Associates, *op. cit.*, pp. 57 and 77-79.)

[15] In the urban North, where 40 to 50 per cent of the Negro families were on relief at that time, and in addition, a great number were broken families, the study represented less than half the Negro population. Groups covered by the study were, on the average, better off than those excluded. The exclusions were somewhat less important in the urban South; still they were considerable. In the rural farm South, the exclusion of relief families meant comparatively little; but in view of the exclusion of wage laborers, and of farmers and tenants who had stayed less than one year on the farm, and of broken families, this rural sample was, at least, just as much too "high" as was that for the urban North.

[16] Sterner and Associates, *op. cit.*, p. 93. Basic data available in U.S. Department of

Labor, Bureau of Labor Statistics, *Study of Consumer Purchases, Urban Series, Family Expenditure in Chicago, 1935-36,* Bulletin No. 642, Vol. 2, *Family Expenditure* (1939); *Family Income and Expenditure in New York City, 1935-36,* Bulletin No. 643, Vol. 2, *Family Expenditure* (1939); *Family Expenditure in Nine Cities of the East Central Region,* Bulletin No. 644, Vol. 2, *Family Expenditure* (1941); *Family Expenditure in Three Southeastern Cities, 1935-36,* Bulletin No. 647, Vol. 2, *Family Expenditure* (1940); and *Urban Technical Series, Family Expenditure in Selected Cities, 1935-36,* Bulletin No. 648, Vol. 8, *Changes in Assets and Liabilities* (1941), Tabular Summary, Tables 2 and 3; U.S. Department of Agriculture, Bureau of Home Economics, *Consumer Purchases Study, Urban and Village Series, Family Income and Expenditure, Five Regions,* Miscellaneous Publication No. 396, Part 2, *Family Expenditure* (1940), pp. 182-189; *Farm Series, Family Income and Expenditure, Five Regions,* Miscellaneous Publication No. 465, Part 2, *Family Expenditure* (1941), p. 113.

[17] Sterner and Associates, *op. cit.,* p. 93.

[18] *Ibid.,* pp. 31 and 94-165.

[19] *Ibid.,* pp. 163 and 165.

[20] The general data on value of housing are not quite reliable since they have to be estimated for families residing in their own homes or in houses owned by their employers. In the case of rent-paying families in Atlanta, Georgia; Mobile, Alabama; Columbia, South Carolina; Albany, Georgia; and Columbus, Ohio, however, it can be ascertained unequivocally that Negro tenants usually pay lower rents than do white families with the same income; but in New York it is the other way around. (U.S. Department of Labor, Bureau of Labor Statistics, *Study of Consumer Purchases, Urban Technical Series, Family Expenditures in Selected Cities, 1935-36,* Bulletin No. 648, Vol. 1, *Housing* [1941], pp. 20 and 26; and Bulletin No. 647, Vol. 1, *op. cit.,* p. 104, and *Family Income in Nine Cities of the East Central Region, 1935-36,* Bulletin No. 644, Vol. 1, *Family Income* [1939], p. 88.)

[21] It should be remembered that it is particularly difficult to get complete reports on Negro food consumption, since Negro domestic servants, as well as hotel and restaurant workers, often eat the food of their employers. The fact that the expenditures for housing are sometimes lower, in relation to income, in Negro than they are in white families may be due to the greater insecurity in Negro income. The phenomenon is also characteristic of groups of lower social status generally. Wage earners often pay lower rents than do business, professional and clerical workers in the same income classes. (U.S. Department of Labor, Bulletin, No. 644, Vol. 1, *op. cit.,* p. 90.)

[22] Atlanta Negro families, in the average Negro income group $500-$999, had an average of $241 to spend for clothing, personal care, medical care, recreation, and all other items, after food, housing, household operation and furnishings had been paid for. Negro sharecroppers with an income of less than $500 spend, on the average, $73 on the same "extra" items (clothing, medical care and so on). (Sterner and Associates, *op. cit.,* pp. 96 and 97.)

[23] In the "average white" income class $1,500-$1,999, for instance, clothing expenditures in Negro and white families were $206 and $180, respectively. Yet such a difference is of little practical significance, as the number of Negro families in this economic group is exceedingly small.

[24] In Negro families with less than $500 in income, $9 worth of clothing was bought for the husband, an equal amount was spent on the wife, and $6 was left over for children and other family members; when there were more than four persons in the family, husband and wife could each spend but $5 on themselves. In the income group $500-$999, the husband's share in the clothing budget was $24, the wife's share was $27 and that of children and other family members was $21. (Sterner and Associates, *op. cit.*, p. 140.) The following description gives some idea about what such sums meant in concrete terms:

"The figures for the husbands in low-income families were far below the annual clothing requirements suggested in the WPA budget for an emergency standard of living. [Margaret Loomis Stecker, *Quantity Budgets for Basic Maintenance and Emergency Standards of Living*, Research Bulletin, Series 1, No. 21 (1936), p. 15.] For example, while an annual replacement of one cotton work shirt and one other shirt with attached collar and purchase of a wool work shirt every other year is suggested, it appears that one-third of the Negro men at the lowest income level and almost one-fifth of the white and Negro men at the next level bought no shirts at all during the year. Likewise, in contrast to the annual purchase of two pairs of work shoes and one pair of oxfords suggested in the emergency budget, work shoes were purchased barely every other year, on the average; two-thirds of the Negro men in families with incomes below $500 bought no street shoes, and approximately one-third of the white and Negro men at the next income level failed to purchase any during the year of the study." (Sterner and Associates, *op. cit.*, pp. 140-141.)

[25] Interdepartmental Committee to Coordinate Health and Welfare Activities, *Proceedings of the National Health Conference, July, 1938*, "Report of the Technical Committee on Medical Care" (1938), p. 57. Quoted in Sterner and Associates, *op. cit.*, p. 153.

[26] Sterner and Associates, *op. cit.*, Appendix Table 32.

[27] Negro sharecroppers with incomes under $500 spent, for the entire family, an annual average of $1 for reading matter, less than 50¢ for movies and other admissions, $1 for games and sports equipment, $1 for other recreation, and $12 for tobacco. Atlanta Negroes in the income group $500-999 spent for these same items $9, $5, $1, $7 and $17. The corresponding figures for white Atlanta families in the income bracket $1,500-$2,249 were $17, $22, $5, $22 and $44. (*Ibid.*, pp. 154-159 and Appendix Table 36.)

[28] In cities, villages, and farm areas of the South, Negroes consumed larger quantities of fish and other seafoods, but smaller quantities of milk, eggs, potatoes, other vegetables, and fruits, than did white families of similar means. In order to cut down on their expenditures they bought less baked goods, but more flour and cereals than was usual in white households. Largely for the same reason, they consumed less processed foods than did white families of the same economic classes. These are among the most usual differences, but there were others which appeared more or less consistently; some of them were mainly "cultural."[a]

[a] U.S. Department of Labor, Bureau of Labor Statistics, *Study of Consumer Purchases, Urban Technical Series, Family Expenditures in Selected Cities*, Bulletin No. 648, Vol. 2, *Food* (1940), Tabular Summary, Table 5; U. S. Department of Agriculture, Bureau of

29 Exactly how great this difference is we cannot say, since the low income groups were greatly under-represented in the expenditure sample of the Consumer Purchases Study (which, of course, must affect the data for Negroes much more than it does those for whites). Yet the records, despite this fact, show a considerable discrepancy in regard to several important items. Negro *farmers and tenants* consumed even less than did white sharecroppers of pork, poultry, eggs, fats, potatoes, vegetables, fruits, sugar, and particularly milk. Of fish and other seafoods they consumed somewhat larger quantities, of beef and grain products about the same amount as white sharecroppers. Compared with owners and more independent tenants among the whites, their inferior position was even more pronounced. In Southern *villages* whites consumed four times as much milk, three times as many eggs and fruits, twice as many potatoes and other vegetables as did Negroes. Although Negroes, in villages as in other community groups, were greater consumers of fish and seafood, the combined consumption of meats, pork and fish was one-and-a-half times as high in white as it was in Negro households. Even of fats and sugar, whites bought larger quantities than did Negroes.[a] Concerning the situation in Southern *cities* we may quote the analysis of Sterner and Epstein:

"Whites reported the consumption of nearly six times as much whole fresh milk and twice as much canned milk as Negroes. On the average, white families used more than twice as many eggs, over three times as many tomatoes, five times as many oranges, and over twice as many pounds of white potatoes as Negro families. Negroes used somewhat less butter and other table fats but more lard products. Beef was used in considerably larger quantities by whites than by Negroes. . . . While [Negroes used] more fresh pork and salt-side, they consumed less bacon, ham, and poultry than white families. On the other hand, Negroes used twice as much fresh fish as whites."[b]

30 U.S. Department of Labor, Bureau of Labor Statistics, *Study of Consumer Purchases, Urban Technical Series, Family Expenditures in Selected Cities*, Bulletin No. 648, Vol. 2, *Food* (1940), Tabular Summary, Table 4.

31 Sterner and Associates, *op. cit.*, Appendix Table 27.

32 *Ibid.*, pp. 99-100.

33 Almost half the Negro families sampled in small cities, villages, and farm areas of the Southeast had a food-value per week and per food-expenditure-unit of less than $1.38. The same was true of over one-fourth of the Negro families sampled in Atlanta, Columbia and Mobile. White families, on the other hand, usually had relatively few representatives in this economic group (U.S. Department of Agriculture, Bureau of Home Economics, *Consumer Purchases Study, Urban and Village Series, Family Food Consumption and Dietary Levels, Five Regions*, Miscellaneous Publication No. 452 [1941], p. 188; and *Farm Series, Family Food Consumption and Dietary Levels, Five Regions*, Miscellaneous Publication No. 405 [1941], p. 328.)

Home Economics, *Consumer Purchases Study, Urban and Village Series, Family Food Consumption and Dietary Levels, Five Regions*, Miscellaneous Publication No. 452 (1941), Tables 30 to 34; and *Farm Series, Family Food Consumption and Dietary Levels, Five Regions*, Miscellaneous Publication No. 405 (1941), Tables 48 to 52.

[a] U. S. Department of Agriculture, Miscellaneous Publication No. 405, *op. cit.*, Tables 48-52; and No. 452, *op. cit.*, Tables 30-34.

[b] Sterner and Associates, *op. cit.*, p. 112.

PERCENTAGE OF NEGRO AND WHITE FAMILIES IN THE SOUTHEAST WITH DIETS FURNISHING LESS THAN OPTIMUM REQUIREMENTS OF SPECIFIED NUTRIENTS: 1936-1937[a]

Families by Weekly Food Value per Food-expenditure-unit	No. of Families in Sample	Energy Value	Protein	Phos-phorus	Cal-cium	Iron	Vita-min	Thia-min	Ascor-bic Acid	Ribo-flavin
	No.	Pct.	Pct.	Pct.	Pct.	Pct.	Pct.	Pct.	Pct.	Pct.
$0.69 - $1.37										
Village families, Negro	84	48	70	66	93	58	67	68	96	94
Farm families, Negro[b]	109	50	57	24	60	22	52	47	96	79
$1.38 - $2.07										
City families, Negro[c]	54	16	41	45	33	21	24	44	67	91
Village families, Negro	53	17	26	25	15	24	63	43	73	79
Village families, White	69	22	49	30	73	39	68	61	69	74
Farm Families, Negro[b]	89	7	14	9	34	9	23	30	81	48
Farm families, White[d]	133	16	4	2	23	4	44	17	79	38

Sources: U. S. Department of Agriculture, Bureau of Home Economics, *Consumer Purchases Study, Farm Series, Family Food Consumption and Dietary Levels, Five Regions,* Miscellaneous Publication No. 405 (1941), pp. 52-61 and 103; and *Urban and Village Series, Family Food Consumption and Dietary Levels, Five Regions,* Miscellaneous Publication No. 452 (1941), pp. 209-229.

[a] The following requirements were used for this tabulation: energy value 3,000 calories, protein 67 grams, phosphorus 1.32 grams, calcium 0.68 gram, iron 12 milligrams, vitamin A 6,000 International Units, thiamin 1.5 milligrams, ascorbic acid 75 milligrams, and riboflavin 1.8 milligrams. These requirements refer to the daily needs of a moderately active full-grown man. Needs of women and younger persons may be different from these—often lower but sometimes higher. This complication is taken care of by computing the consumption per nutrition unit, whereby the needs of a full-grown man are used as a unit. The number of food expenditure units are computed in a similar way (U.S. Department of Agriculture, Miscellaneous Publication No. 452, *op. cit.*, pp. 251-252).
Groups having less than 50 representatives in the sample are excluded from the table.
[b] Owners, tenants and croppers.
[c] Atlanta, Georgia; Mobile, Alabama; Columbia, South Carolina.
[d] Owners and tenants, except croppers.

[35] To be sure, these observations are based on rather small samples. For this reason, we cannot draw many detailed conclusions. It is extremely unlikely, however, that the data would give us an exaggerated general impression regarding the frequency of dietary deficiencies in the Negro population. Rather, it is not unlikely that they minimize the occurrence of such deficiencies. For we must keep in mind that large groups at the very bottom of the income ladder, such as relief families, broken families, agricultural wage laborers, farmers and tenants who have moved within the year, are completely excluded from the sample.

[36] To be sure, statistical correlation does not prove anything about causation. Sick people may live in slums because their sickness has kept them so poor that they cannot afford adequate housing. Prostitutes may not get housing accommodation in decent neighborhoods, and so are forced to live in slums. Poor slum families may get tuberculosis because their diet is bad. Nevertheless, any common sense evaluation will tell us that the causation, in part, goes *from* poor housing *to* bad moral, mental and physical health.

[37] The material in more than one-half of the Southern farm houses in 1934 was unpainted wood. This was true about less than one-tenth of the farm houses in Northern states east of the Mississippi River. About one-third of the Southern farm houses had foundations in poor condition. The corresponding proportions for other areas varied between 7 and 28 per cent. There were about the same differences in

regard to the condition of other parts of the house, such as exterior walls, roofs, floors and so on. In regard to almost every equipment item, for which data are available, conditions were worse in the South than they were in other regions. This was true even in regard to such conveniences and necessities as are particularly needed in the Southern climate. Only a minority of the farm families in the country have bathrooms in their homes, but in the South bathrooms were scarcer than they were anywhere else. From one-third to one-half of the Southern farm houses were without screens in 1934, whereas the corresponding proportions for other regions varied between 4 and 14 per cent. One-fourth of the farm houses in the country were equipped with ice boxes or other refrigeration; in New England two-thirds of the farm houses had refrigeration of some kind. But in the South the proportion was below the national average. (Sterner and Associates, *op. cit.*, p. 168.)

[38] *Ibid.*, pp. 172-173.

[39] The average number of occupants per farm house ranged in the South from 4.6 in the West South Central division to 5.2 in the South Atlantic division. In Northern states east of the Mississippi it was about 4.4. The number of rooms per house ranged in the South from 4.2 in the West South Central area to 5.2 in the South Atlantic area, whereas the average for the four Northeastern divisions ranged from 6.0 to 8.9. (*Ibid.*, p. 177.)

[40] The Consumer Purchases Study, based on a sample which omits the poorest families, gives proportions of crowded large families, in farm areas of the South, as shown in the following table:

LARGE FAMILIES LIVING IN HOMES WITH MORE THAN 1.5 PERSONS PER ROOM AS A PERCENTAGE OF ALL LARGE FARM FAMILIES, BY COLOR AND TENURE: IN 1935-1936

Area	Owners and Tenants Except Croppers		Croppers	
	Negro	White	Negro	White
North Carolina and South Carolina	59.4	27.1	63.6	46.4
Georgia and Mississippi	68.3	35.0	60.4	45.7

Source: Richard Sterner and Associates, *The Negro's Share* (1943), p. 180. Data based on U.S. Department of Agriculture, Bureau of Home Economics, *Consumer Purchases Study, Urban, Village, and Farm Series, Family Housing and Facilities, Five Regions,* Miscellaneous Publication No. 399 (1940), Table 36. Concerning the definition of large family, see footnote (a) of Table 3 in this chapter.

[41] Sterner and Associates, *op. cit.*, pp. 181 and 179.

[42] One-third of the dwelling units in the urban Southeast (including the South Atlantic states, the East South Central states and Louisiana) and one-fourth of those in the Southwest were without any private indoor flush toilets in 1934-1936, whereas the corresponding proportion for the country as a whole was 15 per cent. There were similar differences in regard to other equipment items. Almost one-fourth of the dwelling units in the Southeast and close to one-fifth of those in the Southwest were characterized as either in need of major repairs or unfit for use. The national figure—excluding New York City—was 16 per cent. The median dwelling unit was one of four rooms in the South; in other regions it was one of five rooms. The proportion of "doubled-up" families and of crowded households was higher in the South than any-

where else. (Sterner and Associates, *op. cit.*, p. 186. Data based on Peyton Stapp, *Urban Housing; A Summary of Real Property Inventories Conducted as Work Projects, 1934-36*, Works Progress Administration [1938], *passim.*)

[43] Sterner and Associates, *op. cit.*, pp. 182-183. Data based on U.S. Public Health Service, *The National Health Survey, 1935-36*, Sickness and Medical Care Series, Bulletin No. 5 (1939), *passim.*

[44] The proportion of families having living quarters equipped with running hot and cold water, inside flush toilet, and electric lights, for Atlanta Negro families in the income group $1,000-$1,249 was only 23 per cent. For white families in the same income class it was 58 per cent. The corresponding figure for white families having an income of $750-$999 was 51 per cent; not until one comes to the lowest income group listed for the white population ($500-$749) does one find a figure (24 per cent) on about the same level as that quoted for Negro families in the income group $1,000-$1,249. By the same token, one has to go as high up on the Negro income scale as to the class $1,750-$1,999 in order to find a percentage (57 per cent) about as high as that for white families in the income group $1,000-$1,249. (U.S. Department of Labor, Bulletin No. 648, Vol. 1, *op. cit.*, p. 75.)

[45] Sterner and Associates, *op. cit.*, Table 79.

[46] In Augusta, Georgia, 8 per cent of the Negro and 3 per cent of the white households were living in dwelling units where there were *more* than two persons per room. These crowded households included 15 and 6 per cent, respectively, of the population. In all probability they included an even larger proportion of all minor children. (*Ibid.*, p. 194.)

The statement that children are more crowded than are adults is based on the fact that they, to a greater extent, belong to large families. It is corroborated by Swedish experiences. (Myrdal, *op. cit.*, p. 246.) The Real Property Inventories, however, do not contain any data on the number of children in crowded households. The important point about children as the main sufferers of poor housing conditions seems to have been overlooked in American housing statistics.

[47] U.S. Department of Labor, Bulletin No. 648, Vol. 1, *op. cit.*, p. 26; U.S. Department of Agriculture, Bureau of Home Economics, *Consumer Purchases Study, Urban and Village Series, Family Expenditures for Housing and Household Operation, Five Regions*, Miscellaneous Publication No. 432 (1941), p. 86.

[48] Sterner and Associates, *op. cit.*, p. 99.

[49] *Ibid.*, p. 197.

Chapter 17. *The Mechanics of Economic Discrimination as a Practical Problem*

[1] The following experiences of the author may serve as illustrations:

A Negro lad in Minneapolis, Minnesota, had successfully prepared himself in the excellent vocational school of this Midwestern city to become an electrician. As he had been told before he started to take these courses, he encountered difficulties in getting apprenticeship training and employment, in spite of the best personal recommendations and in spite of assistance from the local Urban League. Most of the contractors declared that they themselves had nothing against engaging him. They were not prejudiced, they explained, but they had to abstain on account of occasional customers who were prejudiced.

I made some inquiries and found that most housewives I questioned did not mind. A few stated that they felt that they rather wanted to have white workers around in the house when something was to be repaired. They did not realize how their slight and unmotivated bias had the cumulated effect of closing employment opportunities to great numbers of Negro youths. They were actually shocked when informed of what they were doing. One young lady announced that she was immediately going to take up the matter in the church club.

The incident from Minneapolis could be duplicated in any similar Northern city. In Minneapolis at the time of my visit (Christmas, 1939) the majority of Negro workers was unemployed. The total Negro population was estimated to be only four or five thousand in a total population of half a million. The local Urban League worked hard to find employment outlets but with scant success. The white people I met were all well informed about the criminality and viciousness in the Negro slum quarters but, on the whole, totally ignorant about Negro unemployment. They had given practically no thought to the possible causal relations between economic distress and morals.

The following example, drawn from a different line of work, also illustrates the ignorance of white people. A Negro clerk told Sterner that he had been unable to convince a white friend about the fact that a Negro (before the recent change in policy) was unable to enlist for ordinary combat service in the Navy. He had to take his white friend to a naval recruiting office and try to enlist in order to make the friend believe that his statement was correct.

[2] Cited by Earl Brown, "American Negroes and the War," *Harper's Magazine* (April, 1942) p. 551.

[3] The technique of introducing Negro labor has often been discussed during this war emergency. See, for instance, "The Negro's War," *Fortune* (June, 1942), p. 157; and "Found: A Million Manpower," *Modern Industry* (May 14, 1942), p. 31.

[4] Comparatively little good research work seems to have been made on employers' and workers' opinions regarding Negro labor. Some of the most noteworthy studies of employers' attitudes have been summarized by Charles S. Johnson (*The Negro in American Civilization* [1930], pp. 68-86). Usually it was found that the bulk of the employers considered Negroes to be about as good workers as whites. There was a significant proportion of them, however, who believed Negroes to be inferior to whites, but also a large number who held that they were superior to their white competitors. Indeed, according to some of the most significant studies, the number of those believing Negroes to be better than were whites was actually larger than the number of those who held the opposite view. These judgments referred to general efficiency at the place of work. In regard to regularity, punctuality, and so forth, the results were somewhat less encouraging; the opinion that Negroes in this respect were less dependable than were whites, according to certain studies, was more frequently voiced by employers than was the opposite contention that whites were less dependable.

A recent inquiry made by the National Industrial Conference Board (William Barnes O'Connor, "The Use of Colored Persons in Skilled Occupations," *The Conference Board Management Record* [December, 1941], pp. 156-158. Quoted by permission of the National Industrial Conference Board) gives, in part, similar results. The overwhelming majority, among over 100 employers and company officials questioned, thought that Negroes were about as good as whites on comparable skilled and semi-skilled work; but there was a large minority who thought they were poorer than whites, and only a few who believed them to be superior to their white competitors. The judgments were particularly favorable to the Negro in regard to actual performance in production; 85 employers thought they were equal to whites, 12 that they were poorer, and 5 that they were better than whites. A minority of over 30 employers thought that Negroes were poorer than whites in regard to ability, skill and regularity in attendance. Least favorable were the judgments on general intelligence; 49 informants believed Negroes to be inferior to whites, and about the same number believed them to be equal to whites. It is interesting to find, however, that many employers characterized the problem as "distinctly individual rather than group."

Such studies, of course, indicate merely employers' opinions—not the actual performance record of the Negro worker, and still less his potentialities. It can be taken for granted that many informants voice preconceived ideas rather than findings based on actual measurements of the workers' performance; for some of the "experiences" quoted (Johnson, *op. cit.*, p. 78, and O'Connor, *op. cit.*, p. 158) are just familiar stereotypes about Negroes being particularly good at hot, greasy, dirty or other disagreeable work. It is a well-known fact that most managers and foremen are likely to make mistakes about their workers' actual ability unless they use some kind of numerical measurement as a basis for their judgment. Such measurements are often made, of course, but it is questionable how often they are used for the purpose of finding out how the range of Negro performance records compares with that for white workers. The fact that Negroes are often segregated in special occupations increases the difficulty of making sound comparisons of this type.

It seems that additional research work, where these complications were given due consideration, would be extremely valuable. It would be of great interest, for instance, to find out how the opinions of those employers who have organized systematic tests of the abilities of Negro and white workers may differ from those of other employers. The results could be highly significant, even though they, of course, would not measure the real potentialities of the Negro worker.

It would be profitable, as well, to make some intensive studies of the attitudes of white workers. The opinion poll technique should make such inquiries fairly easy to organize. The emphasis should be put on how the attitudes may differ among various groups of white workers. Classifications according to region, sex, employment condition (whether unemployed or not), occupational status (unskilled, skilled, clerical worker, and so on), union and nonunion, craft or industrial union, and so forth would often give strategically significant results. It might be corroborated, for instance, that white women are more biased than are white men, as has already been suggested by certain experiences and findings (O'Connor, *op. cit.*, p. 157). It could be ascertained to what extent the rank-and-file membership in the new industrial unions agrees with its leaders on the policy of treating Negro workers as equals. Still more important would be to find out about the difference in attitude among workers with various kinds of experiences of collaboration with Negroes (those in all-white plants; those in establishments where Negroes are segregated; those who compete with Negroes on equal terms). It would be necessary, of course, to ask not only whether the informant *in general* is prepared to let Negroes compete with white workers on equal terms; but also whether he would accept such competition *in his own occupation and in his own workplace.*

[5] Johnson, *op cit.*, pp. 78-79.

[6] See O'Connor, *op. cit.*, pp. 156-158.

[7] Actually, there have been only few examples—and those mainly during the period 1915 to 1930—when employers have made serious attempts to make white workers accept Negroes as fellow workers. The instances when white-dominated labor unions have attempted to educate the employers to hire Negro workers have been even less significant.

Chapter 18. *Pre-War Labor Market Controls and Their Consequences for the Negro*

[1] Most data on legal provisions in this section are based on Richard A. Lester, *Economics of Labor* (1940). (Mimeographed; now printed.)

[2] Virginius Dabney, *Below the Potomac* (1942), p. 114.

[3] *Ibid.*, p. 87.

[4] In 1930, a few years before the introduction of these minimum wage regulations, the average hourly wage for Negro male workers in Virginia manufacturing industries was 28 cents, as against 39 cents for white workers. The corresponding figures for Negro and white manufacturing workers in the female group were 16 and 21 cents, respectively. None of the specific industry groups which had more than a handful of Negro women paid as much as 25 cents an hour to Negro females. (Department of Labor and Industry, State of Virginia, *Forty-Third Annual Report*, Calendar Year 1939, Industrial Statistics [1941]; *Thirty-fourth Annual Report*, Calendar Year 1931, Industrial Statistics, [1932], pp. 24-26). Yet Negroes certainly had higher earnings in Virginia than in most other Southern states. This confirms the impression that Negroes, albeit the law's coverage is particularly limited as far as they are concerned, ought to be much more affected by it than the whites.

We quoted these Virginia figures because they seem to be the only data with breakdown by race covering a whole state. (By and large, there is a greater paucity of information by race in the Deep South than in the Upper South in official state reports on labor conditions, public welfare and so on. Actually, the more federal or private investigations indicate the occurrence of discrimination against the Negroes, and the greater the proportion of Negroes in the population, the more are the Negroes forgotten in official state reports. There are exceptions to this rule, but the general trend is unmistakable.) A complete series of such wage data, by race, would be extremely valuable for the purpose of checking up on the enforcement of the Wages and Hours Law. Unfortunately, the breakdown by race in the Virginia wage statistics has been discontinued during recent years. Certain over-all wage data suggest, however, that by 1939 the total averages for both races combined in virtually all specific industries were at least up to, or in the neighborhood of, the 30-cent limit. This seems to be true even about certain industries where Negro women predominate and where the wage level previously had been extremely low (such as where there prevailed an average rate of only 12 cents per hour for Negro female workers in 1930).

One of these industries was peanut shelling and cleaning. Despite the substantial increase in wages, there was no tendency to displace the Negro women in this line of work. The candy industry, on the other hand, which started from an equally low wage-level, had but a small minority of white workers in 1930, but in 1939 about half the workers were white, most of them women.

The total number of Negro workers in all manufacturing industries did not decrease but showed a rather substantial increase, at least in the male group. Yet this has to be seen against the background of the tremendous expansion in Virginia manufacturing industries, which occurred between 1930 and 1939. The rates of increase for all four color-sex groups of wage earners and the proportions of workers who were colored were:

PERCENTAGE INCREASE IN NUMBER OF WAGE EARNERS IN VIRGINIA MANUFACTURING INDUS-TRIES: 1930-1939, AND PERCENTAGE OF NONWHITE WAGE EARNERS: 1930-1939.

	Nonwhite	White	1930	1939
Male	23%	39%	28.3%	26.0%
Female	4	32	34.5	28.6

Sources: Department of Labor and Industry, State of Virginia, *Forty-third Annual Report*, Calendar Year 1939, Industrial Statistics (1941); *Thirty-fourth Annual Report*, Calendar Year 1930, Industrial Statistics (1932), pp. 24-26.

The facts that whites profited much more from the expansion than did Negroes, and that the proportion of Negro workers declined, particularly among women, was probably not all due to the improved working conditions and the increased competition brought about by the unemployment among whites. But, unless we are much mistaken, those circumstances must have been operating as important contributing factors.

[5] Such a program has been developed in Cincinnati. One of the main "selling points" was that employers should hire local labor rather than allow unemployed workers with legal residence in the community to become public charges. (Information from Dr. Lorin A. Thompson, who formerly was connected with this program.)

[6] The National Labor Union of the 1860's represented the first noteworthy endeavor to unite all organized labor on a national basis. The leadership showed a liberal attitude toward Negroes, but, in order not to alienate monopolistically inclined groups of white workers, it tolerated separate unions for Negroes and whites, probably even outright exclusion of Negroes. Negroes sometimes met in separate state and national conventions. The union's interest in organizing a political labor party interested Negroes even less than whites; this interest eventually contributed to the union's downfall after a few years. The Industrial Congress of 1873, on the other hand, foreshadowed the principle of "trade unionism pure and simple" of the American Federation of Labor, but it was soon destroyed by the big depression which started the same year. Negroes were hardly at all represented in these efforts.

The Knights of Labor originally started as a secret order in 1869, but did not grow into importance until the 1880's. It again manifested a liberal attitude toward Negroes, and soon met enthusiastic response from them. It was the goal of the Knights to organize and develop a general working class solidarity of all workers. Those who did not belong to trade unions were organized in local assemblies. Several of these local assemblies were segregated, however, and the Knights had little power to combat the tendency of ordinary trade unions, composed mainly of skilled workers, to organize Negroes into separate unions.[a]

[a] The historical notes are based mainly on Sterling D. Spero and Abram L. Harris, *The Black Worker* (1931), particularly pp. 23-47.

The craft unions, mainly composed of the labor aristocracy of skilled workers, became increasingly dissatisfied with the all-inclusive objectives of the Knights. Already in 1881, before the Knights had reached their peak, the craft unions had organized a special federation of their own, which in 1886 withdrew from the Knights and adopted the name "American Federation of Labor" (A.F. of L.). After this, the Knights of Labor disintegrated. The development toward craft unionism naturally hit the Negroes more than the whites, not only on account of their race, but also because they were mainly unskilled workers. The A.F. of L. was not left completely unchallenged during the whole period before the institution of the C.I.O. There were some attempts to organize workers on the basis of a common, nonracial and nondiscriminatory, working class solidarity. The most noteworthy example is the syndicalist group, International Workers of the World (I.W.W.), which was started in 1905 and lasted until the early 'twenties. It meant something for Negroes in lumber and longshore work in certain areas of the South. With such exceptions, however, it was the American Federation of Labor and the independent Railroad Brotherhoods which governed organized labor during the long period from the early 1890's until the middle of the 1930's.

The A.F. of L. was never an association of craft unions only. Some unions were organized on an industrial basis, at least in name, but in some cases also in fact. In the latter group we find those few unions—for instance, the United Mine Workers' Union and the International Ladies' Garment Workers' Union—which during the entire period of their existence have recognized the necessity of including the Negro on the basis of equality, and also, in spite of certain unavoidable racial frictions and with some limitations, have succeeded in giving the Negro a square deal. It must also be recognized that part of the failure of the Federation to organize a more substantial proportion of all wage earners was due to the energetic anti-union work of the employers. During the decade before the First World War there was a series of vicious intimidations. It was during this time that one of the presidents of the National Association of Manufacturers expressed the belief that "the American Federation of Labor is engaged in an open warfare against Jesus Christ and His cause."[a] The 'twenties brought a new attack from the employers in the form of labor espionage, blacklisting, strike-breaking, violence. This was also the heyday of the company unions, which by 1928 had about 1,500,000 members.[b]

These circumstances, however, should not be allowed to overshadow the fact that the Federation, by and large, has been governed by the craft spirit, and that its main purpose has been to regulate the monopolistic competitive interests of the crafts. Its principal business was not to fight for labor in general. It was to draw the jurisdictional borderlines among its various member groups by means of the "charter." This explains why mass production industries, like steel and automobiles, were practically unorganized until the C.I.O. was instituted in 1935. The policy of the Federation was that the mass production workers were to be divided among the crafts. But this could be done only if they were first organized on an industrial basis, and then there was the danger that they would like to stay organized that way. This was exactly what finally happened, and the Committee for Industrial Organization (C.I.O.)[c] grew out of the resistance

[a] Richard A. Lester, op. cit., p. 310.

[b] Ibid., p. 313.

[c] In 1938, the name of the Committee for Industrial Organization was changed to Congress of Industrial Organizations.

of the newly organized industrial workers against the attempts of the crafts to take them over.[a]

[7] On this matter we may quote Paul H. Norgren:

"From its very beginning, the Federation has professed adherence to the principle of racial equality. Time and again it has 'resolved,' and its leaders have reaffirmed that it knows no color bar, and that 'the workers must unite and organize' irrespective of race or creed.

"For a few years immediately after its formation, the leaders of the Federation apparently made an attempt to enforce this principle. Thus the Executive Council, in an early publication, states that 'a union that [draws the color line] cannot be admitted into affiliation with this body.' (Quoted by Spero and Harris, *op. cit.*, p. 88.) However, the dictates of expediency and the desire for increased membership soon gained the upper hand, with the result that in 1895 the International Association of Machinists, a strictly Negro-excluding body, was admitted as a full-fledged affiliate.

". . . there is no way of knowing whether the Federation will in the future attempt . . . to bring an end to racial discrimination by its constituent unions. The present writer, for one, is extremely skeptical as to the possibilities. There was some hope in this direction in earlier years, when several large industrial unions, including the United Mine Workers, and the Amalgamated Clothing Workers, were still affiliated with the Federation. But after the expulsion of these unions in 1937, the craft union leaders came into virtually complete control of the Federation. . . .

"It is, in fact, abundantly clear even to the casual student of the labor movement in this country, that one of the principal functions of the American Federation of Labor, as it exists today, is to provide a centralized source of pious propaganda through which the craft unions which control it can issue frequent public reassurances of their firm adherence to the principles of democracy, equality, and unity among the laboring masses, while at the same time they continue with impunity to practice exclusionism and restriction of job opportunities in their own particular fields. . . . The 'control make-up' of the Federation is well adapted to this Jekyll-Hyde role. The Executive Council—which makes all the important decisions concerning policy—is made up principally of the heads of the craft unions which, in one way or another, practice racial discrimination." (Paul H. Norgren and Associates, "Negro Labor and Its Problems," unpublished manuscript, prepared for this study [1940], pp. 303-308, *passim.*)

Making a survey of the Negro-excluding unions within and without the Federation, Norgren says:

"No less than twenty American trade unions explicitly exclude Negroes from membership, either by constitutional provision or in their rituals. Only eleven of these, however, are of any appreciable importance from the standpoint of barring Negroes from jobs. . . . The eleven larger unions include the Boilermakers, the Machinists, the Commercial Telegraphers, the Railroad Telegraphers, the Railway Mail Clerks, the Railway Clerks and Freight Handlers, the Switchmen, the Firemen and Enginemen, the Trainmen, the Conductors, and the Locomotive Engineers. . . . In addition, five unions—the Electricians, the Plumbers and Steamfitters, the Bridge and Structural Iron Workers, the Granite Cutters, and the Flint Glass Workers—exclude Negroes by tacit agreement." (*Ibid.*, pp. 300-301.)

[a] See, for instance, J. Raymond Walsh, *C.I.O. Industrial Unionism in Action* (1937), pp. 28-47.

It should be noted that almost all the Negro-excluding unions are either A.F. of L. affiliates or independent railroad brotherhoods. (See Florence Murray [editor], *The Negro Handbook* [1942], pp. 134-135.)

These are the cases of complete exclusion. But most other craft unions show more or less partial discrimination:

"Most of the other national craft unions, while they do not bar Negroes from their ranks, either curtail their rights and privileges within the union, or allow their local components to do so. Thus the national rules of the Motion Picture Operators, the Blacksmiths and Drop Forgers, the Sheet Metal Workers, and the Maintenance-of-Way Employees (an unskilled craft union) permit the organization of colored workers in 'auxiliary' locals, but prohibit them from having any voice in union affairs. And if they are subjected to unfair or arbitrary treatment by the employers, their only means of obtaining redress is to request the officials of the 'regular' (white) local to present their grievances for them. . . .

"The Carpenters and the Painters do not have any constitutional provisions or other explicitly stated rules in their national set-up providing for the exclusion or segregation of colored workers. Nevertheless, there is a great deal of discrimination against Negroes among the locals of both these unions which, while not openly sanctioned, is always tacitly condoned by the central organizations. The national leadership of the Bricklayers' Union, on the other hand, has on a number of occasions attempted to enforce racial equality in the constituent bodies. As far as the writer has been able to learn, however, these attempts have been sporadic, and not very vigorous; and there are still a number of local bricklayers' organizations which openly practice discrimination." (Norgren and Associates, *op. cit.*, p. 302.)

More recently (September, 1942) Northrup has classified the unions according to degree of discrimination and nondiscrimination as follows:

"Unions excluding Negroes by ritual—(1.) International Association of Machinists (A.F.L.)

"Unions excluding Negroes by constitution,—(1) Masters, Mates, and Pilots; (2) Commercial Telegraphers; (3) Railroad Telegraphers; (4) Railway Mail Association; (5) Switchmen's Union; (6) Airline Pilots; (7) Sleeping Car Conductors; (8) Wire Weavers; (all A.F.L.); (9) American Federation of Railroad Workers; (10) Locomotive Engineers; (11) Locomotive Firemen and Enginemen; (12) Railroad Trainmen; (13) Railway Conductors; (14) Train Dispatchers; (15) Railroad Yardmasters of America; (16) Railroad Yardmasters of North America; (all independents).

"Unions which generally refuse admittance to Negroes by tacit consent:—(1) Brotherhood of Electrical Workers; (2) Journeymen Plumbers and Steamfitters; (3) Asbestos Workers, Heat and Frost Insulators; (4) Granite Cutters; (5) Flint Glass Workers; (all A.F.L.).

"Unions which provide Negroes with Jim Crow auxiliary status which gives them the privilege of paying dues but no say in the organization—(1) Boilermakers, Iron Ship Builders, Welders and Helpers; (2) Blacksmiths, Drop Forgers, and Helpers; (3) Railway Carmen; (4) Railway and Steamship Clerks, Freight Handlers, Express and Station Employees; (5) Maintenance of Way Employees; (6) Federation of Rural Letter Carriers; (all A.F.L.) (7) Rural Letter Carriers' Association (Independent)."

(Herbert R. Northrup, unpublished memorandum made available by the courtesy of the author [September, 1942]; this memorandum is to be incorporated in a forthcoming article.)

[8] The C.I.O. has, however, demanded that the A.F. of L. take positive steps to eliminate racial discrimination before any alliance between the two organizations can be reached.

[9] Richard A. Lester, *op. cit.*, p. 309.

[10] See the reports by the La Follette Committee: *Violations of Free Speech and Assembly and Interference with Rights of Labor*. Hearings before a Subcommittee of the Committee on Education and Labor. United States Senate, Second Session on S. Res. 266, Washington, 1936, *passim*; *Oppressive Labor Practices Act*. Hearings before a Subcommittee of the Committee on Education and Labor, United States Senate, Seventy-sixth Congress, first session on S. 1970, Washington, 1939, *passim*.

[11] Concerning the widespread use of violence as a weapon in labor strikes in the South, Virginius Dabney writes:

"It is interesting to note, on the basis of material gathered by Dr. Arthur Raper of Atlanta, that far more strikers and labor organizers were killed in the South in the period immediately preceding the birth of the C.I.O. than subsequently. In 1929 and 1930, when Gastonia and Marion were in the headlines and the first great textile strike was on, seven strikers and one police chief were slain. In 1934 and 1935, no fewer than forty-two Southern laborers and organizers were killed in strikes. In 1936 and 1937, with the coming of the C.I.O., only five workers and organizers were killed in Southern labor disorders; the total for 1938 and 1939 was 14, while the figure for 1940 and 1941 is six. But while slayings have become less numerous, beatings have increased, and organizers are all too frequently set upon by company deputies, sometimes accompanied by irate citizens, or by non-union workers who have been persuaded, whether rightly or wrongly, that unionization will bankrupt their employers." (Dabney, *op. cit.*, p. 131.)

[12] "How Democratic are Labor Unions?" *Harper's Magazine* (May, 1942), pp. 655-662.

[13] *Ibid.*, p. 662.

[14] Herbert R. Northrup, "Negro Labor and Union Policy," unpublished Ph.D. thesis, Harvard University (1942), pp. 408-409.

Norgren describes two of the state laws against race discrimination:

"The Pennsylvania Labor Relations Act of 1937 contains a clause stipulating that unions which exclude workers from membership because of their color shall be denied the protection of the State Labor Relations Board. (Correspondence with Reginald A. Johnson of the Urban League of Pittsburgh, July, 1940.) In January, 1940, the New York state legislature passed a law expressly forbidding unions to 'deny a person or persons membership . . . by reason of race, color or creed.' A union which violates this statute is subject to court action, and the aggrieved person may recover up to $500 for the injury. In addition, union officers or members found guilty of violating the law are subject to fine or imprisonment. . . . According to the above-mentioned correspondent, the Pennsylvania anti-discrimination clause has up to now been almost completely ineffective, owing largely to the difficulty of finding 'a dispute under a clear cut circumstance where the racial clause of the Act can be put into effect.' The New York Act is still too new to permit of appraising its effectiveness or otherwise." (Norgren and Associates, *op. cit.*, p. 307.)

Chapter 19. *The War Boom—and Thereafter*

[1] A study made by the Work Projects Administration indicates unequivocally that, at least until the latter half of 1941, Negroes were grossly under-represented among the in-migrants to certain large cities including many primary war production areas. (See table in this footnote.) This was true in the North as well as in the South. In most cases there were not even half as many Negroes among those moving to the cities as among those already in the cities. This means that the war boom had reversed an earlier migration trend. While the Negro population until 1940 had been increasing faster than the white population in urban areas, both in the North and in the South, during this early stage of the defense boom, it was the white population that showed the most rapid growth. This pattern was, of course, wholly different from that during the First World War.

Conditions may have changed somewhat since the fall of 1941. The Bureau of Employment Security reports in September, 1942, that:

"These developments [the federal government's stand on discrimination and cooperation by some industries] have resulted in some slight increases in Negro employment from 3.5 percent in May to 4.7 percent in July of employment in the major war manufacturing establishments. . . . It is reported [however] that many employers in war production industries plan to continue their discriminatory policy until other available sources of labor are exhausted. This appears to be true especially of the aircraft, ordnance, rubber

PERCENTAGE OF NONWHITES IN THE TOTAL POPULATION, 1940, AND AMONG RECENT IN-MIGRANTS ACCORDING TO SURVEYS MADE DURING THE LATTER HALF OF 1941, IN SELECTED CITIES[a]

City	Percentage of Nonwhite Persons		City	Percentage of Nonwhite Persons	
	In Total Population	Among recent In-migrants		In Total Population	Among recent In-migrants
North and West			*North and West* (cont.)		
Bridgeport	3	1	San Diego	3	1
Philadelphia	13	6	Los Angeles	6	3
Pittsburgh	9	8	Oakland	5	3
Dayton	10	5			
Indianapolis	13	4	*South*		
South Bend	4	2	Baltimore	19	11
Detroit	9	4	Washington, D.C.	29	7
Des Moines	4	(b)	Norfolk	32	14
Wichita	5	2	Atlanta	35	16
Seattle	4	(b)	Nashville	28	8
San Francisco	5	(b)	Oklahoma City	10	1
Long Beach	0	1	Houston	22	7
			St. Louis	13	3

Source: Migration figures furnished by courtesy of Work Projects Adminstration, Division of Research; Population figures from *Sixteenth Census of the United States: 1940, Population,* Preliminary Release, Series P-5, No. 10.
[a] The data on in-migrants are based on rather small samples. The figures for individual cities, therefore, should not be stressed as much as the fact that virtually all data give about the same general impression of Negroes being under-represented among the in-migrants.
[b] Less than 0.5 per cent.

products, electrical machinery, machinery, and textile-mill products industries." (Federal Security Agency, Social Security Board, Bureau of Employment Security, *The Labor Market* [September, 1942], p. 13.)

[2] At the close of the First World War about 39,000 Negroes were employed in plants under the jurisdiction of the United States Shipping Board. (George E. Haynes, *The Negro at Work During the World War and During Reconstruction* [1921] p. 58. Quoted by Robert C. Weaver in "Racial Employment Trends in National Defense," Part I, *Phylon* [Fourth Quarter, 1941], p. 342.)

[3] The Federal Security Agency, as late as June, 1942, made the following significant statements:

"In April, 1940, Negroes constituted 9.8 per cent of the population, 10.7 per cent of the Nation's labor force, and 12.5 per cent of the unemployed. Since 1940 Negroes have constituted an increasing proportion of the unemployed—during the past year from 15 to 20 per cent—because industry has recruited its war workers almost exclusively from among the white labor force." (*The Labor Market* [June, 1942], p. 10.) And:

"Over 500,000 Negroes who should be utilized for war production are now idle because of the discriminatory hiring practices of war industries. In addition, several million other Negroes engaged in unskilled occupations are prevented from making a greater contribution to the war effort because employers, with few exceptions, are unwilling to train and promote them to jobs of higher skills. Persistent discrimination is accentuating the shortage of labor in areas where acute problems already exist. Discriminatory hiring practices in these areas result in the recruitment of white in-migrants while Negroes remain unemployed. With the influx of outside workers into these cities housing, transportation, health, educational and sanitation facilities in many localities have become inadequate and local problems have increased." (*Ibid.*, p. 9.)

[4] Lester B. Granger of the National Urban League (interview, August 10, 1942) emphasized particularly the reasons given under (1), (2) and (4). Paul H. Norgren of the War Production Board, Labor Division, stressed especially the declining need for unskilled labor (interview, August 3, 1942).

[5] "During the depression of the 1930's employers could set almost any combination of job specifications and still be assured an ample supply of applicants. As a result, 'native, Protestant, white,' came to be a fairly widespread personal qualification for employment. Maintenance of such qualifications not only contradicts democratic principles but in the present situation also greatly intensifies disruptive recruiting practices and encourages unnecessary migration of unskilled as well as skilled workers. Discrimination by one company has resulted in over 40 per cent of its 34,000 workers coming from outside the State while there yet remains a large number of unemployed Negroes in the local community who could have been trained and hired." (*The Labor Market* [May, 1942], p. 6.)

[6] For a report of alleged Ku Klux Klan activity in the U.A.W. in Detroit, see *PM* (February 13, 1942), p. 14.

[7] Again we may quote the Federal Security Agency:

"Moreover, the bulk of placements of Negroes was concentrated in service and unskilled occupational groups. In the first quarter of 1941 only 51 per cent of all white placements, as against 90 per cent of all Negro placements were made in service and unskilled occupations. In the first quarter of 1942 the corresponding proportions were

53 per cent and 93 per cent. . . . In the first quarter of 1941 16 per cent of all white placements compared to 1.9 per cent of all nonwhite placements were made in either skilled or professional occupations. In the first quarter of 1942 the corresponding proportions were 14.6 per cent of all white placements, and only 1.2 per cent of all nonwhite placements." (*The Labor Market* [June, 1942], p. 11.)

These figures, however, are not quite representative. It appears that the Employment Service handles a larger part of the turnover in unskilled than in skilled occupations. A comparison with Edwards' classification indicates that there is a much higher proportion of skilled, clerical, and professional workers in the total labor force than in the Employment Service placements. (U. S. Bureau of the Census, Alba M. Edwards, *Social-Economic Grouping of the Gainful Workers in the United States, 1930* [1938], p. 7.) The Employment Service data, furthermore, cannot cover promotions of workers within an establishment.

8 War Production Board, Statistics Division, "State Distribution of War Supply and Facility Contracts, June 1940 through May 1942" (mimeographed, June 30, 1942).

9 Robert C. Weaver, "Racial Employment Trends in National Defense," Part II, *Phylon* (First Quarter, 1942), p. 28; Federal Security Agency, Social Security Board, Bureau of Employment Security, *Negro Workers and the National Defense Program* (September 16, 1941), p. 5; Robert C. Weaver, "With the Negro's Help," *Atlantic Monthly* (June, 1942), pp. 699-700; interviews with Lester B. Granger, Executive Secretary, National Urban League (August 10, 1942), and Paul H. Norgren, War Production Board, Labor Division (August 3, 1942).

10 "Throughout the country there was a heavy demand for unskilled labor needed for the construction of airports, military cantonments, barracks. . . . Negro unskilled labor shared substantially in these employment opportunities and benefited by the wage rates paid on these projects, which were generally higher than wages usually earned in unskilled work.

"The extraordinary demand for skilled construction workers, particularly carpenters . . . resulted in many job opportunities particularly for union members. There is evidence, however, that in some localities, in spite of the acute shortage of carpenters, Negroes were not employed. In skilled building trades occupations other than carpenters and cement finishers, and to some extent, bricklayers and masons, there is no evidence that discriminatory practices were being noticeably relaxed." (*Negro Workers and the National Defense Program*, p. 5.)

Weaver ("Racial Employment Trends in National Defense," Part I, pp. 352-356) cites a number of instances where Negro carpenters have been employed on defense projects—and others where they have not been able to get in. As a result of increased employment there was a growth in the number and strength of Negro carpenters' locals.

Some other building crafts, however, have maintained a more consistent exclusionistic policy. The President's Committee on Fair Employment Practice found in 1942 that the Chicago Journeymen Plumbers' Union excluded Negroes from membership; that the Union for several years had had a written agreement with the Plumbing Contractors' Association of Chicago, according to which the contractors were to accept as workers on certain defense projects (Great Lakes Naval Training Station and the Cabrini Housing Project) only plumbers who were members of the union; and that Negroes, for this reason, had been unable to work as plumbers on those projects. The Committee directed that these practices be abolished. ("Summary of Hearings on Complaints of

Negro Plumbers against the Chicago Journeymen Plumbers' Union Local 130 held in Chicago, Illinois, April 4, 1942, before the President's Committee on Fair Employment Practice, with Findings and Directions" [mimeographed, 1942].) It goes without saying that this is just one example of barriers instituted by some of the unions in the building trades.

[11] In the female group only six-tenths of 1 per cent of all placements in defense industries made by the Employment Service, during the period October, 1940, through March, 1941, were nonwhite. On the other hand, for all male and female defense and nondefense placements taken together, the Negro's share amounted to about 20 per cent. It should be considered, however, that only a part of the newly hired workers were recruited through the Employment Service. (*Negro Workers and the National Defense Program*, p. 10.)

[12] Only 19 per cent of all the hiring that was planned for the period September, 1941, to February, 1942, was to occur in plants where Negroes were represented in the labor force. Even in the South more than two-thirds of the anticipated expansion referred to establishments which barred the Negro entirely. To be sure, several employers indicated their willingness to start hiring Negroes, but it is evident that a great number of them were just paying lip-service to government regulations. What makes their statements particularly suspect is the fact that the expressed readiness to change policies was particularly pronounced in the case of professional, managerial and skilled workers. (Federal Security Agency, Social Security Board, Bureau of Employment Security, "Survey of Employment Prospects for Negroes," undated mimeographed release.)

[13] White placements through the Employment Service in 18 selected war industries tripled from the last quarter of 1940 to the beginning of 1942, whereas Negro placements in the same industries increased by only 80 per cent. (*The Labor Market* [June, 1942], p. 11.) These data give strong support to the theory that the proportion of Negro workers in the war industries has actually declined. However, since it is uncertain what relation there is between Employment Service placements and total placements, the evidence is not quite conclusive. It is possible, for instance, that there has been a greater increase in the utilization of the Employment Service for white workers than there has been for Negro workers.

[14] "Not always, however, are the employment practices of shipyards the obstacle to maximum utilization of local labor supplies. A city ordinance in Miami, Florida, for example, prohibits Negroes from working in skilled and semiskilled occupations in sections of the city other than Negro and has consequently affected shipbuilding expansion in the area. Negro boatbuilder and joiner trainees, needed in the local yards, cannot be hired because of this ordinance." (*The Labor Market* [June, 1942], p. 14. See also: *ibid.*, p. 10; Weaver, "With the Negro's Help," pp. 700-791; and the National Urban League, "The Integration of Negroes into Defense Training and Employment. The Barriers faced, the Progress made," typescript [February 17, 1942]. This source indicates, for instance, that the number of Negro workers at the Charleston Navy Yard increased during 1941 from 453, or 9.5 per cent of the total, to 1,302, or 17.7 per cent. The number of Negro workers at the Norfolk Navy Yard in Portsmouth, Virginia, had, by November, 1941, increased to about 6,000, or 23 per cent. Supplementary information from Mr. Lester B. Granger of the National Urban League, interview [August 10, 1942].)

15 The Bureau of Employment Security observes, with respect to the ordnance industry:

"Hiring of Negroes is not commensurate with rapidly expanding job opportunities, and it is doubtful that there will be a general acceptance of Negro workers in the near future. Jobs filled by Negroes at present are chiefly in the custodial services and in the unskilled categories, with few instances of upgrading reported. Virtually every important employer has indicated that hiring of nonwhites will begin 'when necessary,' that is when the supply of white workers is exhausted. Employment prospects for Negroes in southern war plants, even as unskilled workers, are limited, due to the availability of a large pool of whites. Almost without exception, job opportunities for Negroes are negligible in the large ordnance plants of the Great Lakes and Middle Atlantic States." (*The Labor Market* [June, 1942], p. 15. See also other sources cited in the preceding footnote.)

16 There are certain instructions issued, after conferences with unions and employers, by the Office of Production Management (September 17, 1941) and jointly by the War Manpower Commission and the War Production Board (June 18, 1942), regulating the seniority rights of workers moved from one production line to another, or from one establishment to another within the industry.

17 Interview with Lloyd H. Bailer of the War Production Board, Labor Division (August 2-3, 1942). See also Lester B. Granger, "Negroes in War Production," *Survey Graphic* (November, 1942), p. 544.

18 *The Labor Market* (June, 1942), p. 10; and Weaver, "With the Negro's Help," p. 701.

19 The Richmond *Times-Dispatch*, for instance, carried a series of articles on the subject during the winter of 1940-1941. Among the most noteworthy pamphlets are: Council for Democracy, *The Negro and Defense* (1941); Frank R. Crosswaith and Alfred Baker Lewis, "Discrimination, Incorporated," *Social Action* (January 15, 1942); Earl Brown and George R. Leighton, *The Negro and the War*, Public Affairs Pamphlet No. 71 (1942); The National Urban League, "Report of Progress in the War Employment of Negro Labor" (mimeographed, July, 1942). Prominent magazine articles are: "The Negro's War," *Fortune* (June, 1942), pp. 77-80, 157-164; "Found: A Million Manpower," *Modern Industry* (May 15, 1942), pp. 28-31; Earl Brown, "American Negroes and the War," *Harper's Magazine* (April, 1942), pp. 545-572; Stanley High, "How the Negro Fights for Freedom," *Readers Digest* (July, 1942), pp. 113-118. Walter White, "It's Our Country, Too," *The Saturday Evening Post* (December 14, 1940), pp. 27 and 61-68. See, also, other sources cited in this and the preceding Section.

20 The National Defense Advisory Commission instituted a special Department of Negro Affairs in its Labor Division in July, 1942. In August, the N.D.A.C. made a statement to the effect that defense workers should not be discriminated against because of age, sex or race. This declaration was backed up by the President in September and by Congress in October, 1940. A few days later the N.D.A.C. reached an agreement with the Congress of Industrial Organizations and the American Federation of Labor to the effect that all trade union barriers against the Negro should be removed. In November, 1940, the U. S. Commissioner of Education urged those in charge of public defense training programs to consider the nondiscrimination clause in existing defense training legislation. In April, 1941, a Negro Employment and Training Branch was

instituted in the Office of Production Management, later the War Production Board. During 1942 it was moved to the War Manpower Commission. (President's Committee on Fair Employment Practice, Negro Employment and Training Branch, Labor Division, O.P.M., Minority Groups Branch, Labor Division, O.P.M., "Minorities in Defense" [1941], pp. 10-12.)

[21] Brown, "American Negroes and the War," pp. 548-550.

[22] The President's Committee on Fair Employment Practice was originally set up as a division within the Office of Production Management. Later it became independent. In 1942, it was moved over to the War Manpower Commission.

[23] Lester Granger points out that allowing the Committee to fine employers who discriminate would give them an effective method of control. ("Negroes in War Production, p. 470.)

[24] Brown and Leighton, op. cit., pp. 26-27.

[25] On September 6, 1941, the President issued a second, and much stronger, condemnation of discrimination, but this one applied to federal government agencies only.

Mr. Roosevelt's new letter "to heads of all departments and independent establishments" read:

"It has come to my attention that there is in the Federal establishment a lack of uniformity and possibly some lack of sympathetic attitude toward the problems of minority groups, particularly those relating to the employment and assignment of Negroes in the Federal civil service.

"With a view to improving the situation, it is my desire that all departments and independent establishments in the Federal Government make a thorough examination of their personnel policies and practices to the end that they may be able to assure me that in the Federal service the doors of employment are open to all loyal and qualified workers regardless of creed, race or national origin.

"It is imperative that we deal with this problem speedily and effectively. I shall look for immediate steps to be taken by all departments and independent establishments of the government to facilitate and put into effect this policy of non-discrimination in Federal employment."

[26] Brown and Leighton, op. cit., p. 27. During the winter of 1941 it happened that about 200 Negro stenographers and typists hired by the War Department had to spend their time in enforced idleness since most office heads refused to use their services. (Ibid., p. 19.)

It seems that many hiring officials in federal offices have recourse to various tricks when they find out that they have employed a Negro. There are numerous stories told by Negroes about how, when they report for work, they are told that "some mistake must have been made," and a technical excuse is found for dismissing them. Hiring officials have even been accused of asking the Negro for the letter of employment—and then keeping it, leaving the employee without proof of his employment. According to one white informant who has collected material on practices in various federal offices, one of the most usual tricks is based on the fact that job descriptions are often oral. They can simply be changed when the hired persons turns out to be a Negro. (For instance, a secretary who is good at typing, but less well trained in taking dictation, is told that dictation is the main part of the job.) The use of detailed, written job descriptions is the only answer in such cases. The same informant believed that it would not be impossible even to overcome the discriminations in dismissals made possible by the stipulation of a probationary period. "When you fire a veteran, you have to show cause. When you fire a Negro, you don't have to." (Interview, August 3, 1942.) See also, Granger, "Negroes in War Production," pp. 471 and 543.

[27] In addition there were the so-called supplementary courses, where Negroes, during the same period, constituted but 1.7 per cent of the total. (*Negro Workers and the National Defense Program*, pp. 17-18; *The Labor Market* [June, 1942], p. 11.) It is a well-known fact that Negroes are under-represented on most in-plant training programs organized by employers. The Work Projects Administration and the National Youth Administration, on the other hand, have, to a comparatively large extent, included them in their war work training programs. (High, *op. cit.*, p. 115.)

[28] For the whole South the percentages of nonwhites among those referred to such courses and projects was only 7.5 per cent, although 26.2 per cent of the total Southern labor force in 1940 was nonwhite. The corresponding figures for the rest of the nation were 2.9 and 4.8 per cent, respectively, indicating a much smaller discrepancy. (Federal Security Agency, Social Security Board, Bureau of Employment Security, "Vocational Training Activities of Public Employment Offices, January, 1942," mimeographed; *Sixteenth Census of the United States: 1940, Population*, Preliminary Releases, Series P-4, No. 4, and P-4a, Nos. 14 to 16.)

Workers are referred to these training courses by the Employment Service. The latest instructions issued by the Bureau of Employment Security to local offices have the following rather unfortunate formulation:

". . . it is the policy of the United States Employment Service . . . to fill requisitions for trainees without regard to race, color, creed or national origin, except in those States where separate educational facilities for whites and Negroes are required by law, namely . . ." [Eighteen Southern and Border states enumerated.] (Federal Security Agency, Social Security Board, Bureau of Employment Security, "U.S.E.S. Operations Bulletin No. C-45" [July 1, 1942], p. 2.)

The intention, of course, is just to acknowledge the segregation in the Southern educational system. The formulation, however, leaves the door open for almost any kind of discrimination.

[29] *Journal and Guide*, Norfolk, Virginia (February 28, 1942).

[30] Information from Lester B. Granger, National Urban League (August 10, 1942). According to Mr. Granger all Southern states, except Georgia, have Negro Employment Service offices.

[31] "U.S.E.S. Operations Bulletin, No. C-45," pp. 2-3.

[32] The recommendations and requirements sent out by the U.S.E.S. to its local offices included the following injunctions:

". . . it is the policy of the United States Employment Service: . . .

(2) To make definite effort to persuade employers to eliminate specifications which prevent the consideration of local qualified workers because of their race, color, creed, or national origin . . .

"(3) To omit discretionary specifications from advertising sponsored or approved by the United States Employment Service:

"(4) To report to the Director of the United States Employment Service for appropriate disposition each instance in which an employer refuses to relax discriminatory specifications;

"(5) To refuse to make referrals on employer orders which include discriminatory specifications in those states where such specifications are contrary to State law; . . ." (*Ibid.*, p. 2.)

[33] The war housing work, for a long time, was extremely uncoordinated, particularly from a local viewpoint. This was due, largely, to the fact that the local Housing Authorities were kept from leadership since they worked under the auspices of the United States Housing Authority which happened to be rather unpopular in Congress. Most of these organizational difficulties, however, have been overcome since the integration of all public housing programs under the National Housing Agency in 1942.

[34] The following description of the conditions in the Negro section of Norfolk, Virginia, in the spring of 1942 is pertinent in this context:

"Three recent field trips to the area have convinced the writer that there is an immediate demand for dormitory accommodations. All rooming houses are overcrowded. Such community agencies as the Young Men's and Young Women's Christian Associations have canvassed the city for spare rooms that residents would be willing to rent out to new-comers. All available sleeping space has been utilized: porches have been closed in, two and three double beds have been placed in rooms, couches have been placed in halls, and as many as 35 men a night can be found sleeping in chairs or on the floor of the recreation room of the Y.M.C.A. It is difficult to find single accommodations. A man has to share his bed with a second occupant. The 'hot bed' practice of sleeping men in shifts without a change of linen has been reported . . ." (Lyonel C. Florant, Population Study, Virginia State Planning Board, "Memorandum re: Negro Housing in Norfolk, Virginia," typescript [June 3, 1942], p. 3.)

[35] Information from Miss Corienne K. Robinson, National Housing Agency, Federal Public Housing Administration (letter, [August 28, 1942]).

[36] See, for instance, Emmett J. Scott, *The American Negro in the World War* (1919), pp. 77-78.

[37] Monroe N. Work (editor), *Negro Year Book, 1931-32* (1931), pp. 327-334. Negro soldiers were used on both sides in the Revolutionary War—often in unsegregated outfits. There were almost 180,000 Negro troops on the Union side in the Civil War; some fought on the Confederate side. During the First World War there were 380,000 Negroes in the Army. About 200,000 Negro soldiers were sent to France. Most of these were in labor battalions and service units; only 42,000 were combat troops, and Negroes had to fight for the right to be represented at all among the line soldiers. About 1,400 Negroes were commissioned as officers in the Army of the First World War, although it took some time before the Army leadership could be induced to make provisions for giving officer's training to any Negro soldiers.

[38] Scott, *op. cit.*, particularly, pp. 82-91, 315-327 and 442-443.

[39] Brown and Leighton, *op. cit.*, p. 7; "The Negro's War," p. 164; "The Negro in the Army Today," typewritten statement issued by Judge William Hastie, Special Assistant, War Department; White, *op. cit.*, p. 63.

[40] "The Negro in the Army Today."

[41] See, for example, White, *op. cit.*, p. 61.

[42] High, *op. cit.*, p. 114; Brown and Leighton, *op. cit.*, p. 7.

[43] The Negro pilot school at Tuskegee at present (August, 1942) accepts only some 20-odd Negro pupils every five weeks. At the present time (September, 1942), however, there are plans for a considerable expansion in the Negro aviation cadet training program.

[44] During the First World War, for instance, there was a serious riot in Houston, Texas, in 1917, which ended in the execution of thirteen Negro soldiers. Another large riot in Spartanburg, South Carolina, was barely avoided. A Negro soldier had been beaten up while buying a newspaper in a hotel; the next night a group of soldiers started marching from their camp to the city in order to "shoot it up," but were stopped by a white officer. There were numerous other clashes. Special investigations revealed widespread discrimination against Negroes in certain camps, such as Camp Lee, Virginia, where the military police was accused of treating Negroes unfairly. Passes were said to be issued more freely to white than to Negro soldiers. Officers sometimes inflicted bodily punishment on Negroes. When selecting Negro soldiers for promotion to the rank of noncommissioned officers, they often showed a tendency to prefer illiterate "funny fellows" to men of greater ability. The chief of the only Negro combat division stationed in the North caused a general resentment among Negroes when he issued a bulletin urging Negro officers and men to refrain from their legal right to visit theaters and other places "where their presence will be resented," giving as a reason the argument that "white men made the Division, and they can break it just as easily if it becomes a trouble maker." (Scott, *op. cit.*, pp. 80-110.)

[45] *N.A.A.C.P. Annual Report for 1941*, pp. 7-9; Brown and Leighton, *op. cit.*, p. 7. It goes without saying that these are only a sample of the incidents which have occurred.

[46] To be sure, the merchant marine may, in large part, have to be rebuilt after the War, and this may, for a time, minimize the decline in shipbuilding. It is possible, as well, that the government, for the purpose of meeting another future emergency, will subsidize ship production in order to maintain some part of the present shipbuilding capacity. Even so, there must be a substantial decline. At present, facilities are being geared to the purpose of replacing ships that have been sunk; to the transportation of military supplies and troops; to provide for the increase in need due to the tremendous slowing up of transportation.

[47] See, for instance, George B. Galloway, *Postwar Planning in the United States* (1942).

Chapter 20. *Underlying Factors*

[1] W. E. B. Du Bois, *The Philadelphia Negro* (1899), pp. 368-370.

[2] Gilbert T. Stephenson, *Race Distinctions in American Law* (1910), p. 284.

[3] Stephenson, *op. cit.*, pp. 282-284, and Charles S. Mangum, Jr., *The Legal Status of the Negro* (1940), pp. 371-374. The five New England states mentioned had, in 1860, a total Negro population of 16,084, constituting 4.5 per cent of the total free Negro population outside the 11 secession states; New York had, in addition, 49,005 Negroes of which, however, probably the great majority were disfranchised under the limitation.

"The Constitution of Tennessee of 1834 provided that no person should be disqualified from voting in any election who was then by the laws of the State a competent witness in a court of justice against a white person."[a] It is impossible to tell, however, how many Negroes were thus qualified to vote.

The Wisconsin Constitution (1848) limited voting to whites, but the Supreme

[a] Stephenson, *op. cit.*, p. 284.

Court of the State held in 1866 that suffrage had been extended to Negroes by a referendum at the general election on November 6, 1849; since the result of the election was in dispute from 1849 until 1866, it is probable that no Negroes voted during that period.[a]

[4] Marian D. Irish, "The Southern One-Party System and National Politics," *The Journal of Politics* (February, 1942), p. 80.

[5] To quote two representative liberal Southern authors; Willis D. Weatherford:

"Who among us has not seen how the presence of the Negro has moulded our political history since emancipation? We have been slow to pass laws for compulsory school attendance, lest we tie ourselves to the task of classical education of the Negro. We are slow enough about extending the suffrage, lest the colored man should become too influential. No major political issue has faced the South in the last hundred years that has not been decided largely in the light of the presence of the Negro."[b]

T. J. Woofter, Jr.:

"It is . . . apparent that in excluding the Negro the South is, in a way, politically dominated by the Negro question. Before all others it looms as the bulwark of the one-party system. It was a determining factor in the prohibition vote. It affected the South's stand on woman suffrage and it ramifies into hundreds of questions of public policy, it influences the South's position on child labor, it is a stumbling block in the administration of compulsory school laws, standing as an ever-present shadow across the door of political councils."[c]

The conservative Southerner is not so likely to write books on the Negro problem as is his liberal compatriot. The present writer recalls, however, from his talks with many Southerners of conservative leanings that they too usually complained about how the Negro problem has entered into all public questions of the region and hindered their consideration upon their own merits. But they consider this situation without remedy or, rather, hold that even a gradual enfranchisement of the Negro could only accentuate this "plight of the South."

[6] Charles A. Beard and Mary R. Beard, *The Rise of American Civilization* (1927), pp. 298-306.

[7] Donald Young, *American Minority Peoples* (1932), p. 212; compare *ibid.*, pp. 201 ff. especially p. 207.

[8] Some Northern states—Massachusetts, Connecticut, New York, Maine, Delaware, Wyoming, California—actually have literacy requirements for registration in their constitutions or election laws.[d] In addition, in some Northern states, paupers are disfranchised; some criminals are prohibited from voting. In Utah, anyone who advocates polygamy, or belongs to an organization that advocates it, may not vote.[e]

When these requirements are enforced, they are done so regardless of race or national origin; Northern states that have literacy requirements also provide adult education schools to teach illiterates how to read and write.

[9] Frank U. Quillin, *The Color Line in Ohio* (1913), p. 9.

[a] *Idem.*

[b] Willis D. Weatherford and Charles S. Johnson, *Race Relations* (1934), p. 298.

[c] *The Basis of Racial Adjustment* (1925), p. 166.

[d] Stephenson, *op. cit.*, pp. 301-302; and Osmond K. Fraenkel, "Restrictions on Voting in the United States," in *The National Lawyers' Guild Quarterly* (March, 1938), pp. 135-143.

[e] Fraenkel, *op. cit.*, p. 138.

[10] Stephenson, *op. cit.*, pp. 284-287, and W. E. B. Du Bois, *Black Reconstruction* (1935), p. 341.

[11] As late as 1831 the Virginia legislature considered a plan for the gradual emancipation of the slaves; the plan, inspired by Thomas Jefferson, and introduced into the legislature by his grandson, Thomas Jefferson Randolph, was debated for months and finally defeated by a single vote.[a]

[12] William Sumner Jenkins, *Pro-Slavery Thought in the Old South* (1935).

[13] From the judgment in the text, we do not make exceptions of modern fascism and nazism. Those ideologies, however, fall outside our classification: they are no more like conservatism than radicalism but could, perhaps, best be characterized as a peculiar blend of reactionism and radicalism.

[14] The reluctance of modern conservatism to build up closed systems of compendent logical propositions varies, of course, considerably. Catholic conservatism, for instance, tends more toward a closed system of principles. Hegelianism was also, in some respects, a conservative philosophy and was developed into a system, though not a static one.

[15] George Fitzhugh, *Sociology for the South* (1854), Chapter 2.

[16] Jenkins, *op. cit.*, p. 295. See also Chapter 10 of this book.

[17] Fitzhugh, *op. cit.*, p. 289.

[18] *Ibid.*, p. 248.

[19] Speech in the Senate, March 2, 1859, quoted in Jenkins, *op. cit.*, p. 192.

[20] *Congressional Globe*, 35th Congress, 1st Session, App. p. 71 (March 4, 1858); quoted from Jenkins, *op. cit.*, p. 286.

[21] Judge Upshur, quoted by Jenkins, *op. cit.*, p. 288.

[22] Quoted from: W. F. Cash, *The Mind of the South* (1941), p. 80.

[23] A few quotations on the last point from this remarkable book should be given:

"Notwithstanding the fact that the white non-slaveholders of the South are in the majority, as five to one, they have never yet had any part or lot in framing the laws under which they live. There is no legislation except for the benefit of slavery, and slaveholders. As a general rule, poor white persons are regarded with less esteem and attention than negroes, and though the condition of the latter is wretched beyond description, vast numbers of the former are infinitely worse off. A cunningly devised mockery of freedom is guaranteed to them, and that is all. To all intents and purposes they are disfranchised, and outlawed, and the only privilege extended to them is a shallow and circumscribed participation in the political movements that usher slaveholders into office."[b]

"The lords of the lash are not only absolute masters of the blacks, who are bought and sold, and driven about like so many cattle, but they are also the oracles and arbiters of all non-slaveholding whites, whose freedom is merely nominal, and whose unparalleled illiteracy and degradation is purposely and fiendishly perpetuated. How little the 'poor white trash,' the great majority of the Southern people, know of the real condition of the country is, indeed, sadly astonishing. The truth is, they know nothing of public measures, and little of private affairs, except what their imperious masters, the slave-drivers, condescend to tell, and that is but precious little, and even the little, always garbled and one-sided, is never told except in public harangues; for the haughty

[a] See William E. Dodd, *Statesmen of the Old South* (1911), p. 80.
[b] Hinton R. Helper, *The Impending Crisis of the South* (1857), p. 42.

cavaliers of shackles and handcuffs will not degrade themselves by holding private converse with those who have neither dimes nor hereditary rights in human flesh."[a]

"It is expected that the stupid and sequacious masses, the white victims of slavery, will believe, and as a general thing, they do believe, whatever the slaveholders tell them; and thus it is that they are cajoled into the notion that they are the freest, happiest and most intelligent people in the world, and are taught to look with prejudice and disapprobation upon every new principle or progressive movement. Thus it is that the South, woefully inert and inventionless, has lagged behind the North, and is now weltering in the cesspool of ignorance and degradation."[b]

[24] "The most tangible reform that he [Tillman] could suggest was that the Fifteenth —and sometimes the Fourteenth—Amendment be repealed . . . [but] . . . he did not arouse [Northern] public opinion to effect the repeal of the Fifteenth Amendment."[c]

[25] "Less than 5 per cent of all cases involving the Fourteenth Amendment have dealt with Negro rights and most of those have been lost."[d]

"Since 1868 some 575 cases involving the 14th amendment have come before the supreme court for adjudication. Only 27, or less than 5% of these have dealt with the negro. By far the greater portion of the litigation under this act has been concerned with the federal regulation of industrial combinations. Organized capital rather than the negro race has invoked the protection of the 14th amendment against state interference. Of the 27 cases concerned with the negro, 20 were decided adversely to the race for whose benefit the act was framed. The six decisions favouring federal intervention in modified forms are concerned for the most part with the refusal to admit negroes to jury service in the state courts."[e]

[26] For example, two leading Southern Restoration statesmen, L. Q. C. Lamar and Wade Hampton, in a symposium in 1879, stood by the post-war Amendments. In presenting his opinion, Lamar first states the two propositions for the symposium:

"1. That the disfranchisement of the negro is a political impossibility under any circumstances short of revolution.

"2. That the ballot in the hands of the negro, however its exercise may have been embarrassed and diminished by what he considers, erroneously, a general southern policy, has been to that race a means of defense and an element of progress.

"I agree to both propositions. In all my experience of southern opinion I know no southern man of influence or consideration who believes that the disfranchisement of the negro on account of race, color, or former condition of servitude is a political possibility. I am not now discussing the propriety or wisdom of universal suffrage, or whether, in the interests of wise, safe, and orderly government, all suffrage ought not to be qualified. What I mean to say is that universal suffrage being given as the condition of our political life, the negro once made a citizen can not be placed under any other condition. And in this connection it may surprise some of the readers of this discussion

[a] *Ibid.*, pp. 43-44.

[b] *Ibid.*, pp. 44-45.

[c] Butler Simkins, "Ben Tillman's View of the Negro," in *The Journal of Southern History* (May, 1937), pp. 170-173. See also Paul Lewinson, *Race, Class and Party* (1932), p. 84. footnote.

[d] Charles S. Johnson, *The Negro in American Civilization* (1930), p. 337.

[e] John Moffat Mecklin, *Democracy and Race Friction* (1914), pp. 231-232.

to learn that in 1869 the white people of Mississippi unanimously voted at the polls in favor of ratifying the enfranchising amendment. . . ."[a]

"Whatever may have been the policy of conferring the right of voting upon the negro, ignorant and incompetent as he was to comprehend the high responsibility thrust upon him, and whatever may have been the reasons which dictated this dangerous experiment, the deed has been done and is irrevocable. It is now the part of true statesmanship to give it as far as possible that direction which will be most beneficial or least hurtful to the body politic."[b]

[27] The editor of *The News and Courier* of Charleston, South Carolina, is such an exception:

"Again let it be said and clearly understood that were The News and Courier a democratic newspaper, if it believed in democracy as President Roosevelt believes in it, as he described it in his North Carolina speech last week, it would demand that every white man and woman and every black man and woman in the South be protected in the right to vote. It would demand the abolition of all 'Jim Crow' cars, of all drawing of the color line by law. That is democracy. But The News and Courier is not a democrat. It fears and hates democratic government. The News and Courier believes in Democratic government—Democratic with a big 'D' and that is another word for a measure of aristocratic government that ought to be more aristocratic than it is."[c]

"In South Carolina, the Democratic party, has been, so far as the negro vote is concerned, a Fascist party, and that is why The News and Courier 'cooperates' with it. In the North the Democratic party has become so democratic that it turns Southern stomachs."[d]

A prominent white lawyer in a letter observed:

"We have a newspaper in Charleston, S.C., which fills its editorial column with daily blasts against the Negro. It is, so far as I know, the last surviving representative of a school of journalism which was at one time quite common in the state. Its own influence is rapidly dwindling."[e]

[28] The "grandfather clause" no longer belongs to this list since it was declared unconstitutional by the United States Supreme Court in 1915.

[29] The author of the disfranchisement amendments of the Virginia Constitution (1902), Carter Glass, later U. S. senator, replied to a question whether the elimination of the Negro vote would not be accomplished by "fraud and discrimination":

"By fraud, no; by discrimination, yes. But it will be discrimination within the letter of the law. . . . Discrimination! Why, that is precisely what we propose. That, exactly, is what this convention was elected for—to discriminate to the very extremity of per-

[a] L. Q. C. Lamar, "Ought the Negro to be Disfranchised?—Ought He to Have Been Enfranchised?" in *The North American Review* (March, 1879), p. 231.

[b] Wade Hampton, "Ought the Negro to be Disfranchised?—Ought He to Have Been Enfranchised?" in *The North American Review* (March, 1879), p. 240.

For similar expressions of opinion from other leading Southerners, see the "Symposium: Ought the Negro to be Disfranchised?—Ought He to Have Been Enfranchised?" in *The North American Review* (March, 1879), pp. 225-281, from which the above statements are taken.

[c] August 26, 1937. Quoted from Rayford W. Logan (editor), *The Attitude of the Southern White Press toward Negro Suffrage, 1932-1940* (1940), p. 69.

[d] July 20, 1938. *Ibid.*, p. 70.

[e] July 2, 1940.

missible action under the limitations of the Federal Constitution, with a view to the elimination of every Negro voter who can be gotten rid of, legally, without materially impairing the numerical strength of the white electorate. . . . It is a fine discrimination, indeed, that we have practiced in the fabrication of this plan."[a]

Moffat states:

"There can be no reasonable doubt that the *intent* of the delegates to these various conventions [Mississippi, South Carolina, Louisiana, North Carolina, Maryland, Alabama, and Virginia] was to frame their constitutions in such wise as to stand the test of the Fifteenth Amendment to the Constitution and at the same time withhold the ballot from the great mass of negro voters in their respective states."[b]

Moffat backs his statement with many pages of quotes from the legislators who participated in the conventions.[c]

James Weldon Johnson makes the following statements:

"Not long ago, in a widely circulated weekly magazine, Senator George, formerly a member of the Supreme Court of Georgia, was quoted as saying in the course of an interview:

" 'Why apologize or evade? We have been very careful to obey the letter of the Federal Constitution—but we have been very diligent and astute in violating the spirit of such amendments and such statutes as would lead the Negro to believe himself the equal of a white man. And we shall continue to conduct ourselves in that way.'

"Senator Glass was quoted by the same interviewer as saying:

" 'The people of the original thirteen Southern States curse and spit upon the Fifteenth Amendment—and have no intention of letting the Negro vote. We obey the letter of the amendments and the Federal Statutes, but we frankly evade the spirit thereof—and purpose to continue doing so. White supremacy is too precious a thing to surrender for the sake of a theoretical justice that would let a brutish African deem himself the equal of white men and women in Dixie.' "[d]

[30] Bertram Schrieke reflects likewise:

"National history strongly believes in the *fait accompli*. If a revolution is successful, its promoters are heroes, their opponents tyrants; if a revolution is unsuccessful, the promoters are dishonest agitators or at least impractical but dangerous idealists. Since the revolution that undid reconstruction, no new revolution in the South has occurred; therefore no need has been felt for a new evaluation. The slogans of the struggle of the southern Democrats—'Negro domination,' 'carpet-bagger governments,' 'corruption, frauds, and maladministration because of Negro participation in politics,' and so on— have now become 'historical verities.' As a matter of fact, there had never been a Negro majority in the reconstruction governments, whereas Southerners of standing had prominently participated in them. As for political corruption and 'spending,' these had not been much worse than in the North, especially in New York, during the same

[a] *Virginia Debates: 1901-02.* Vol. 2. Quoted from Lewinson, *op. cit.*, p. 86.

[b] R. Burnham Moffat, "The Disfranchisement of the Negro from a Lawyer's Standpoint," *The Journal of the American Social Science Association* (September, 1904), p. 33.

[c] *Ibid.*, pp. 34-62. See also James A. Hamilton, *Negro Suffrage and Congressional Representation* (1910).

[d] "A Negro Looks at Politics," *The American Mercury* (September, 1929), p. 92. See also, *The Journal of the American Social Science Association* (December, 1899), p. 67, a statement by Mr. Woods of Marion, South Carolina in a discussion of a paper by W. H. Baldwin; and Edward M. Sait, *American Parties and Elections* (1939; first edition, 1927), pp. 53-54.

period. However, not facts but opinions about facts determine national history. . . . The whole attitude of the North towards the South was changed, softened. The desire to forget the regrettable misunderstanding between the states for the sake of the unity of the nation made it necessary to adopt the southern version of the history, at least in part. The *fait accompli* of the undoing of reconstruction stamped reconstruction as a failure and established the southern evaluation of reconstruction governments as historical truth."[a]

[31] Josephus Daniels, *Tar-Heel Editor* (1939), pp. 281-282. Some of them had consistently favored the Union cause throughout the Civil War when it was extremely unpopular to do so.

[32] A few white historians—Louis Hacker, for example—have given a history of the Reconstruction that corresponds with the facts. But these are far from dominant among writers of history. Two great historians, J. W. Burgess and W. A. Dunning, set the pattern for the dominant historical interpretation of the Reconstruction period.[b]

Negro writers have had a contrary need for rationalization which is equally understandable. W. E. B. Du Bois' *Black Reconstruction* (1935) is expressly written to counterbalance the common bias in favor of the unreconstructed white Southerners. Carter Woodson and other Negro historians have the same purpose in their books.[c] The Negro authors concede that the Reconstruction governments were guilty of extravagance, theft, and incompetence in many cases, but insist that the charges have been grossly exaggerated. They point to the very difficult conditions in the war-ridden, poverty-stricken Southern regions, where the former ruling aristocracy and a large portion of the entire white population were openly hostile and obstructive and wished Negroes to fail. They also emphasize that political corruption was widespread and common in the whole country in this period and point particularly to the Tweed machine in New York. They observe that the historians they criticize have not given the Reconstruction governments their due credit for their remarkable initiative in establishing a public school system in the South and beginning social legislation. They stress finally that there was nowhere "black domination," but that the Negroes were usually in a minority among the electors, and that whites always held the great majority of the higher, policy-making offices. There are also quixotic attempts made from the side of some Negro writers on the period to picture the Negro legislators as great reformers and statesmen who introduced the democratic institutions to the South.

The English observer of the South during Reconstruction, Sir George Campbell, gives first-hand evidence that the Negroes' position is justified, that the South was no worse off nor more corrupt during Reconstruction than was the rest of the country.[d]

Ralph J. Bunche is one Negro author who has probably struck a balanced picture of the Reconstruction period.[e] He points out that there was no "black domination" but

[a] *Alien Americans* (1936), pp. 112-113.

[b] For a discussion of historians of the Reconstruction by a Negro, see A. A. Taylor, "Historians of the Reconstruction," *The Journal of Negro History* (January, 1938), pp. 18-24.

[c] See, for example, Kelly Miller, *Out of the House of Bondage* (1914), pp. 116-117; Robert R. Moton, *What the Negro Thinks* (1929), pp. 128-130.

[d] *White and Black in the United States* (1879), pp.176-180.

[e] "The Political Status of the Negro," unpublished manuscript prepared for this study (1940), Vol. 1, pp. 220-240.

rather that there were Negro carpetbagger and scalawag governments operating, in the presence of federal troops, under the dominance of Congress. The North had a variety of conflicting interests, some selfish, some altruistic, with respect to the South and considered that its victory gave it the right to satisfy these interests. The bulk of the Negroes, he concludes, were ignorant peasants who played only a feeble role in the political drama of the period.

In surveying the literature on Reconstruction, the present author has gained the impression that in explanation of the imperfections of the Reconstruction regime—besides the factors of physical war, destruction, and general poverty in the South; the wave of political corruption in the whole nation which reached a culmination in this period; and the psychology of defeat among the Southern people—the lack of political education generally in the South has been given too little weight. Successful democracy has never been established anywhere in the world except by considerable exertions of the masses themselves, masses who have been fairly well educated and who are public spirited from the start, and who, in addition, during the struggle for representation and power, have acquired political experience and built up organized civic movements of their own. What happened in Reconstruction was, on the contrary, that, without their asking for it, almost a million Negro men, most of whom had not only been kept in total ignorance, but who in the protected slave existence had lacked any opportunity to live a self-directed life, were suddenly enfranchised. "Rights which the agricultural laborers of England did not obtain until 1885 were . . . thrust upon these children of nature . . ." reflected James Bryce.[a] At the same time, one hundred thousand men of the not much larger white population were disfranchised and, in addition, another hundred thousand white men were not only disfranchised but were disqualified for office because they had taken up arms against the Union. The disfranchised and disqualified group contained a great over-representation of the educated and politically alert and experienced classes of the South. Under the guard and direction of the Union army and federal agencies, the political power in the Southern states was thus conferred on the masses of totally uneducated Negroes and the nearly as ignorant white masses, both abruptly freed from the controls of the politically experienced upper strata under which they had been held in the *ante-bellum* South.

Even the staunchest believer in democracy must feel anxious and skeptical when contemplating this situation. One must be surprised that the actual outcome was not worse. The agents for the federal government, the "carpetbaggers"—operating without much of a rational plan and often lacking support from Washington—must have been, on the average, considerably better than their reputation, as transmitted through the historical mythology. One also feels that the freedmen—led by the carpetbaggers and the scalawags and also by some educated free Negroes from the North—if not a success as responsible citizens, were less of a complete failure than could have been reasonably expected.

A basic flaw of the Reconstruction regime was thus, according to the present author's view, the almost total lack of general education of the black and white masses in the South. It is true that "the ballot is a school-master." It is true also that the Reconstruction governments took immediate and courageous measures to establish a public school system in the South, and that the Negroes especially went in enthusiastically for educa-

---

[a] *The American Commonwealth* (1900; first edition, 1893), Vol. 2, p. 495.

tion. But education, not least political education, takes time. And the Negroes were not given time.

[33] See William J. Robertson, *The Changing South* (1927), p. 144; Bessie L. Pierce, *Public Opinion and the Teaching of History in the United States* (1926), pp. 136-169; Marie E. Carpenter, *The Treatment of the Negro in American History School Textbooks* (1941), especially pp. 43-48; and Lawrence D. Reddick, "Racial Attitudes in American History Textbooks of the South," in *The Journal of Negro History* (July, 1934), pp. 225-265.

[34] Thomas P. Bailey testified:

"I found that the younger white voters were bent on causing trouble at the polls during a municipal election. I inquired whether they feared that the negroes might carry the election. The reply was in the negative. The 'audacity' and 'impertinence' of the negroes in 'daring' or 'presuming' to vote was the trouble."[a] The same attitude is frequently displayed today.

[35] "Patterns of Race Conflict," in *Race Relations and the Race Problem*, Edgar T. Thompson (editor) (1939), p. 138.

[36] Paul H. Buck, *The Road to Reunion—1865-1900* (1937), pp. 284-285.

[37] Edgar G. Murphy, *The Basis of Ascendancy* (1910), p. 39.

[38] "The South accustomed itself to denying this essential condition of democratic government [freedom of speech] during the days of slavery."[b]

[39] *Human Geography of the South* (1932), pp. 75-76.

[40] *Op. cit.*, p. 43.

Chapter 21. *Southern Conservatism and Liberalism*

[1] Because there were several occasions on which the South split politically, as we note in the text, Lewinson claims that the South is not generally "solid."[c] On another ground, Ray Stannard Baker prefers not to consider the South as "solid," although he does use the term:

"In the South to-day there are, as inevitably as human nature, two parties and two political points of view. The one is aristocratic and the other is democratic."[d]
Nevertheless, one party is completely dominant in the South today, despite freak elections such as in 1928 and despite splits within the party. There is a "Solid South" and it has a one-party system.

[2] John D. Hicks, *The Populist Revolt* (1931), p. 391. For a brief history of the Populist party in the Southern states see Lewinson, *op. cit.*, pp. 69, 75 and 164.

[3] The principal idea of this movement to disfranchise the Negro by "constitutional" means was to invent statutory formulations which discriminated against "Negro characteristics" rather than against the Negro race. Poll tax requirements and property, literacy, "understanding" and "good character" clauses were the main devices used. (See Chapter 22.) Some of these techniques for disfranchising the Negroes were

[a] *Race Orthodoxy in the South* (1914), p. 38.
[b] William E. Dodd in a communication to the editor of *Nation* (April 25, 1907), p. 383. See also William E. Dodd, *The Cotton Kingdom* (1919), pp. 23, 69-70, and 146.
[c] Paul Lewinson, *Race, Class and Party* (1932), p. 101.
[d] *Following the Color Line* (1908), p. 242.

already on the law books of some Southern states. The task was now to build them into a unified and efficient system.

The educated upper classes in the South faced a dilemma. On the one hand, it must have seemed to be both advisable on general grounds and constitutionally more correct to allow these clauses to disfranchise also the poor white people in the South. It is obvious that, in addition, such a course also favored the political interests of those classes to keep the political power firmly in their own hands. On the other hand, the white supremacy doctrine asserted a principle of democracy among all white people and established a gulf between them and all Negroes. More important was the fact that the lower classes had tasted political power and were most suspicious of anything that might disfranchise them; their suspicion had only been accentuated during the agrarian revolt.

The question of disfranchising the Negroes was, for this reason and in spite of the great unanimity in the main purpose, the cause of heated campaigns. The debates in the constitutional assemblies were long and extremely controversial. Indeed, the controversy has lasted until this day; it now concerns principally the poll tax. In principle the upper classes had to give up; the compromises reached were everywhere openly announced as aiming at disfranchising the largest possible number of Negroes without depriving any white man of his vote. Devices such as permanent registration, the "grandfather clause," or the exception of war veterans were intentionally framed in order to enable all the white voters to evade the force of the clauses aimed at disfranchising the Negroes; in addition, a sufficient discretionary power was reserved for the registrars to give effect to the promise of a "right-minded" administration of the election statutes. The upper classes felt a certain satisfaction in the reflection that some of the corrective devices were bound to have decreasing importance as time passed. In practice, particularly the poll tax requirement has turned out to be a barrier to great masses of lower class white people.

The dilemma of the "best people" in the upper strata and their interpretation of the result is interestingly revealed by Edgar G. Murphy, who himself had taken an active part in the struggle about the new constitution (1901) in his home state, Alabama, and who is distinguished as one of the most sincere friends of the Negro among the conservative-minded old Southerners and the author of two books on the Negro problem. In *Problems of the Present South* (1909; first edition, 1904) he writes:

"Had the negro masses presented the only illiterate elements, that method (namely to require literacy for voting) might have been pursued. But there were two defective classes—the unqualified negroes of voting age and the unqualified white men. Both could not be dropped at once. A working constitution is not an *a priori* theoretic creation; it must pass the people. The unqualified white men of voting age might be first included in the partnership of reorganization. Such a decision was a political necessity. . . . Moreover . . . no amended Constitution, *no suffrage reform*, no legal status for a saner and purer political administration, *was possible without their votes*. . . .

"Terms were given them. Under skillfully drawn provisions the mass of illiterate negro voters were deprived of suffrage and the *then voting* white population—with certain variously defined exceptions—was permitted to retain the ballot. Care was taken, however, that *all the rising generation and all future generations of white workers* should be constrained to accept the suffrage test, a test applicable, therefore, after a brief fixed period, to white and black alike. Such is the law."[a]

[a] Pp. 192-193; italics ours.

The ultimate goal to be reached as new generations of white Southerners rose to voting age was what he called "the supremacy of intelligence and property."[a] Murphy did not want to disfranchise the Negroes entirely:

"Take out of his life all incentive to the franchise and you will partly destroy his interest in the acquisition of knowledge and of property, because no people will, in the long run, accept as a working principle of life the theory of taxation without representation."[b]

He understood that the reaching of his goal presumed honest administration of the provisions decided upon:

"If these boards of registrars—the essential and distinctive provision in the suffrage system of the South—be administered arbitrarily and unfairly, if they perpetuate the moral confusion and the debasing traditions which they were intended to supplant, then the South will stand condemned both to the world and to herself. She will have defeated the purpose of her own deepest political and moral forces."[c]

In *The Basis of Ascendancy*, published in 1909, Murphy already thought that his policy had proven successful:

"The clouds of conflict have rolled away. Within less than ten years thousands of the worthier black men, under our amended constitutions, have been admitted to the ballot; and in Alabama alone, in the first presidential election after the readjustment of the suffrage, more than half of our adult *white* men did not qualify and vote. Despite all the frank assertions of discrimination on the part of the South, despite all the imputations of discrimination from the side of the North, the thing which the Southern majority declared should happen and which the Northern majority denounced as having happened has not happened at all. Many negroes have been admitted. Many white men have been excluded."[d]

As to the disfranchisement of white men, Murphy was correct as we shall see in Chapter 22. But otherwise this last quotation and the next to the last one indicate wishful thinking.

[4] Lewinson, *op. cit.*, pp. 189-199. See also, Marian D. Irish, "The Southern One-Party System and National Politics," *The Journal of Politics* (February, 1942), pp. 80-94, and George E. Stoney, "Suffrage in the South. Part II: The One Party System," *Survey Graphic* (March, 1940), pp. 163-167 and 204-205.

[5] Ralph Bunche, "The Political Status of the Negro," unpublished manuscript prepared for this study (1940), Vol. 1, p. 36.

[6] Henry W. Grady, *The New South* (1890), pp. 242-243.

[7] *Ibid.*, pp. 240-241.

[8] *Ibid.*, p. 239.

[9] Virginius Dabney, *Below the Potomac* (1942), pp. 112-113.

[10] "The Negro Citizen" in Charles S. Johnson, *The Negro in American Civilization* (1930), pp. 467-468.

[11] Sixteenth Census of the United States: 1940, Agriculture, United States Summary, Second Series, Table 26.

[12] William Archer, *Through Afro-America* (1910), p. 146.

[a] *Ibid.*, p. 199.
[b] *Ibid.*, p. 195.
[c] *Ibid.*, pp. 197-198.
[d] P. 4.

[13] Dabney, *op. cit.*, pp. 241-244.

[14] Archer, *op. cit.*, p. 154.

[15] For a general description of intolerance in the South, see Dabney, *op. cit.*, pp. 237-256.

[16] *The Mind of the South* (1941).

[17] *Ibid.*, p. 33.

[18] W. J. Cash, who stressed these factors, concludes that:

"If the yoke of law and government weighed but lightly, so also did that of class. Prior to the last ten or fifteen years before Secession, the Old South may be said, in truth, to have been nearly innocent of the notion of class in any rigid and complete sense."[a]

On the other hand, there was the myth among the Southern aristocrats that they were descended from Cavalier Norman stock, whereas the lower classes in the South were of Roundhead Saxon stock. As we said, they kept these ideas to themselves.

[19] For a discussion of the effect of the last War on the South, see Frank Tannenbaum, *Darker Phases of the South* (1924), pp. 13-20.

[20] Quoted from memory.

[21] One Southern liberal has given us the following lyrical picture of the South:

"In particular here was a large segment of "America's Tragedy" with its harvest of later conflict and confusion, born of undesigned and unbalanced programs of reconstruction. So came an American epoch that was the South. Old golden pages of history, shining parchment records of culture, then yellow and faded, scorched and seared with years of embattled conflict, and epic struggle. . . . Gallant figures on black horses and white . . . and crude, simple folk, sore with the footfall of time, passing across an epoch which was to be destroyed by physical and cultural conflagration and to rise up again in another American epoch strangely different and vivid and powerful. Cultures in the making, social processes at work, portraiture descriptive of how civilizations grow. All the South's yesterdays, with their brilliant episodes and with their sordid pictures receding, giving way to the South's tomorrows, through a sweeping American development reminiscent of universal culture. Thus, there are many Souths yet *the* South. It is pre-eminently national in backgrounds, yet provincial in its processes. There are remnants of European culture framed in intolerant Americanism. There are romance, beauty, glamor, gaiety, comedy, gentleness, and there are sordidness, ugliness, dullness, sorrow, tragedy, cruelty. There are wealth, culture, education, generosity, chivalry, manners, courage, nobility, and there are poverty, crudeness, ignorance, narrowness, brutality, cowardice, depravity. The South is American and un-American, Christian and barbaric. It is strong and weak, white and black, rich and poor. There are great white mansions on hilltops among the trees, and there are unpainted houses perched on pillars along hillside gullies or lowland marshes. Yet, here is reflected a composite region-in-the-making, descriptive of American reality, rich in power, range, and contrast, shaped and proportioned by strong backgrounds whose unfolding episodes were vivid with the quiver of life. Here are epic and romantic materials of history and literature alongside measurable elements for the scientific study of human society. Here are illuminating materials for the better understanding of American life through the study of regional situations and folk society. Their consistency is often in their contradictions, their unity in their diversity, like some masterpiece of orchestral harmony. Or, like some unfold-

[a] *Ibid.*, p. 34.

ing evolution of social culture or some masterpiece of narrative, charm and power are revealed only through dramatic unfolding, episode upon episode, year upon year. Here is a civilization slowly gathering together its processes and patterns until the magnitude of the whole has been fashioned, nevertheless, whose power and brilliance are cumulative, residing unescapably in separate units, yet also, and more, in the high potentiality of the final unity."[a]

A milder example may be taken from a more recent book of an outstanding Southern liberal:

"Not content with such flagrant misrepresentations as the foregoing, certain professional Northerners delight in reading lectures to all Southerners for their 'narrow-mindedness,' their 'provincialism,' and their general lack of decency and intelligence. Such criticisms of the South are heard most often with respect to its handling of the race problem. Fantastic statements in Northern magazines and newspapers, by self-constituted authorities who know little or nothing about the subject, naturally contribute only slightly to intersectional goodwill. For example, the following pontification appeared not long ago in the editorial columns of the Lowell, Massachusetts, *Sun*: 'Any Negro in the South who dares go near a polling booth on election day invites a bullet through his brain. That is fact, not fiction.' A Virginia editor promptly pointed out that many thousands of Negroes vote every election day in the South, without any such retribution as the Lowell paper declared to be universal, and three Northern-born residents of Virginia protested the *Sun's* extravagant assertion. The Massachusetts daily promptly modified its charge with respect to Negro voting, but was equally absurd in its comment upon one of the above mentioned letters. The author of the letter, a native New Englander, had declared, on the basis of residence in both Florida and Virginia, that 'the lot of the Southern Negro is no worse than that of the average Northern laborer.' This declaration, it is true, was distinctly vulnerable, but the *Sun's* editor went to the extreme length of saying, in rebuttal, that 'no Northern laborer would for one moment tolerate conditions under which the Southern Negro lives.' He should have read the series of newspaper articles by Harry Ashmore, a young South Carolina newspaperman, lovingly describing the unspeakably foul slums of various Northern cities—a series which was published with gusto in 1938 by more than a score of Southern dailies grown weary of excursions by Northern journalists into the cabins and back alleys of the cotton belt."[b]

[22] The present author was traveling in the South in the fall of 1938 when the outburst of anti-Semitism in Germany disheartened and infuriated liberals all over the world. The Southern liberal newspapers—and many of the conservative ones—were outraged and denounced in no uncertain terms the barbarous actions taken by the German Nazis against the Jews: the cheating and beating, the arbitrary justice, the discriminations against the Jews by attempts at residential segregation and Jim-Crowing in streetcars, and beaches, in the labor market, in business. But the intellectual association to the conditions of Negroes in America was skillfully and completely avoided. One liberal editor with whom I discussed this point told me that such an association, if expressed, would "altogether spoil the educational effect." It had to be left to "the deeper forces in the Southern soul" to make this comparison.

[a] Howard W. Odum, *An American Epoch* (1930), pp. 329-330, adapted in Howard W. Odum and Harry E. Moore, *American Regionalism* (1938), pp. 521 and 523.

[b] Dabney, *op. cit.*, pp. 21-22.

Chapter 22. *Political Practices Today*

[1] *The World Almanac: 1942*, p. 813. These percentages should not be taken as an exact measure of the South's adherence to the Democratic party, since, if the Republican party were to get enough votes to challenge it, the Democratic party in time would get more persons to vote.

[2] "The one-party system of the South expresses itself through the local political machines. These are the courthouse gangs, the county cliques, which are the main props of the southern political structure as it exists today. The real venality of southern politics is revealed in the operation of the courthouse gangs. Though they are technically subject to the controls of the county and state Democratic party committees, in their own domain they are supreme. Here offices are bought and sold, and there is found an almost complete anarchy of political thought and law. By and large, they tend to make their own rules, and are rarely ever well-informed upon the laws of the state that they are sworn to uphold. In the courthouse gangs will be found the probate judges, the ordinaries, the county clerks, the registrars or the members of the county registration committees or boards, the sheriffs, the beat committeemen, the members of the election committees and the county Democratic party officers.

"The political power of these local machines is so great that it is virtually impossible to make any generalizations concerning the pattern of any particular aspects of southern politics. For example, if we are to consider the qualifications for registration required of Negroes in Georgia and Alabama, it is not enough to study the state laws on the subject. The local registrars take the law into their own hands and there are almost as many variations of the laws as there are counties. Even within the white population, the laws are not administered uniformly. The county officials are often known to grant favors with respect to the application of the laws, to friends or political partisans." (Ralph J. Bunche, "The Political Status of the Negro," unpublished manuscript prepared for this study [1940], Vol. 1, pp. 35-36.)

[3] *The World Almanac: 1942*, p. 813, and *Sixteenth Census of the United States: 1940, Population*, Preliminary Release, Series P-10, No. 6, Table 3.

[4] For detailed evidence of the general corruption in Southern elections see: (1) Bunche, "The Political Status of the Negro," especially Vols. 1 and 2; (2) George C. Stoney, "Suffrage in the South. Part II: The One Party System," *Survey Graphic* (March, 1940), pp. 163-167 and 204-205. For other excellent surveys of the Southern political scene, see (3) Paul Lewinson, *Race, Class and Party* (1932); and (4) Marian D. Irish, "The Southern One-Party System and National Politics," *The Journal of Politics* (February, 1942), pp. 80-94.

[5] It is by no means certain that it is the poor whites who stay away from the polls in greatest proportion, even though it is certain that they get least out of politics. Rosenstein found that, for a single Mississippi county, the poorest white farm operators were registered in greater proportion than white farm operators of middle income. (Joseph Rosenstein, "Government and Social Structure in a Deep South Community," unpublished M.A. thesis, University of Chicago [1941], pp. 17-18.)

[6] A detailed county-for-county description of election practices in the South is available in Bunche, "The Political Status of the Negro," Vols. 1 and 2.

[7] "The *Citizen-Georgian* of Macon County, Georgia, in an editorial of November

5, 1936, attacks the absence of a secret ballot in Georgia and the need for an Australian Ballot, stating, in part: '. . . the present method can hardly be called a secret ballot because friends, relatives, supporters, and sometimes even the candidates themselves, literally stand over the voting booths, making it impossible for a person to mark his ticket without several persons knowing for whom the vote has been cast.' " (*Ibid.*, Vol. 1, p. 194.)

"The numbers on the ballot are used to check up on how people vote in almost every precinct. Almost every election after the official burning of the ballots, lists of names of those who voted and how they voted on major offices are 'for sale.' " (Interview with a member of the Alabama Legislature, February, 1940, cited in *ibid.*, p. 125.)

[8] V. O. Key, Jr., *Political Parties and Pressure Groups* (1942), pp. 402-407.

[9] Bunche, "The Political Status of the Negro," Vol. 5, p. 1180.

[10] Lewinson, *op. cit.*, pp. 110 and 170.

[11] For a history of the movement, see *ibid.*, pp. 166 ff.

[12] This is a tradition from Reconstruction. Many Southerners find a partial motivation for the disfranchisement of the Negroes in the fact that Negroes voted *against* the whites. Many stories are told to illustrate this tendency. The best one is Booker T. Washington's about an old Negro in Reconstruction time who relates:

"We watches de white man, and we keeps watching de white man till we finds out which way de white man's gwine to vote; an' when we finds out which way de white man's gwine to vote, den we votes 'xactly de other way. Den we knows we's right." (Booker T. Washington, *Up from Slavery* [1915; first edition, 1900], p. 111.)

[13] See Section 4 of this chapter. Wendell Willkie, the defeated Republican candidate for President in 1940, has recently made a number of speeches condemning race prejudice and discrimination against Negroes. He even delivered the keynote speech at the 1942 convention of the N.A.A.C.P. If he should again become the Republican candidate for President, which does not seem likely at the present time, it is probable that he would get many Negroes to vote for him who had voted for Roosevelt in 1936 and 1940. The same would happen if any other Republican candidate should demonstrate friendliness toward the Negro, or if the Democratic candidate should be a Southerner.

[14] Theoretically, anyone not qualified by the grandfather clause (i.e., Negroes) could still register if he paid taxes and met a battery of other restrictions. Another theoretical weakness of the grandfather clause arose from the fact that many Negroes had white fathers and grandfathers who had voted before 1861 or who had served in a military capacity; such white ancestors could not be formally claimed by Negroes, however.

[15] *Guinn* v. *United States*, 238 U. S. 347 (1915).

[16] Bunche, *op. cit.*, Vol. 4, p. 982.

[17] *Nixon* v. *Herndon*, 273 U. S. 536 (March, 1927). In this brief résumé of the legal status of the white primary, we shall not present the decisions reached by state courts or lower federal courts, but only those of the United States Supreme Court.

[18] *Nixon* v. *Condon*, 286 U. S. 73 (1932).

[19] *Grovey* v. *Townsend*, 295 U. S. 45 (1935).

[20] *United States* v. *Patrick B. Classic et al.*, No. 618 (October Term, 1940). See Ralph J. Bunche, "The Negro in the Political Life of the United States," *Journal of Negro Education* (July, 1941), p. 574.

[21] Charles S. Mangum, Jr., *The Legal Status of the Negro* (1940), p. 371.

[22] A few Northern states still have a compulsory poll tax for everyone. In such a form it has no effect on voting. The compulsory poll tax is so different from the voluntary poll tax that modern experts give it a new name, "capitation tax." The compulsory poll tax, or capitation tax, is compulsory in that if one does not pay it, he is subject to criminal prosecution, just as for nonpayment of other taxes. The voluntary poll tax, which is found only in the South, does not carry any penalty for nonpayment other than inability to vote.

[23] In a few Southern states the payment of poll taxes by landowners is compulsory.

[24] Mississippi is perhaps the most restrictive state: the payment of *all* state taxes is made a prerequisite to voting in the general election, but only the poll tax of two dollars per year for two years is necessary for voting in the primary. Alabama and Georgia, while they charge only $1.50 and $1.00 per year respectively, make this hard on older persons by requiring all back taxes (back to the time the individual became twenty-one years of age) before registration. South Carolina requires payment of a poll tax of $1.00 for voting in the general election, but no poll tax need be paid to vote in the primary. Virginia has a three-year cumulative tax. Tennessee, Texas, and Arkansas are relatively lenient with a small tax ($1.00 in Tennessee and Arkansas, $1.50 in Texas with an additional $0.25 optional to the county), without the cumulative features and without any distinction between primary and general election. (Bunche, "The Political Status of the Negro," Vol. 3.)

[25] *Ibid.*, Vol. 3, p. 630.

[26] There also has been an attempt recently to abolish the poll tax by federal law. In 1938, a bill to this effect was introduced in Congress by Representative Lee E. Geyer, California Democrat. The Southern-dominated House Judiciary Committee stifled the bill for four years (as did a Senate Committee for the bill introduced by Senator Pepper of Florida), but in 1942 the bill was forced to the floor of the House by sentiment created by the disfranchisement of soldiers. As this is being written (October, 1942), the House has passed the bill, and it is now up before the Senate. Liberals throughout the South are fighting the poll tax, but many would much prefer that the individual states abolish it, rather than see it killed by the United States Congress or by the federal courts. (See Virginius Dabney, *Below the Potomac* [1942], Chapter 4.)

[27] While Louisiana no longer requires the payment of the poll tax, it does require the possession of a "poll tax certificate," which is available without cost. This is confusing to many voters.

[28] Bunche, "The Political Status of the Negro," Vol. 3, and Lewinson, *op. cit.*, p. 80.

[29] *The World Almanac: 1942*, p. 813; and *Sixteenth Census of the United States: 1940, Population*, Preliminary Release, Series P-10, No. 6, Table 3.

[30] For cases of this and other kinds of discrimination in the application of requirements for voting, see Bunche, "The Political Status of the Negro," Vol. 3, esp. p. 774, and Vols. 4 and 5.

[31] *Ibid.*, Vol. 4, p. 839, and Vol. 7, pp. 1563-1565.

[32] *Ibid.*, Vol. 2, pp. 316, 330 and 436-506 *passim*. The South generally has more rigid residence requirements for voting than the North, but whether there is any special discrimination against Negroes in this respect in the South is not known. (See: Leo Alilunas, "Legal Restrictions on the Negro in Politics," *The Journal of Negro History* [April, 1940], p. 158.)

[33] For documented cases of each of these types of violence and intimidation, see the unpublished monographs prepared for this study (1940): Bunche, "The Political Status of the Negro," especially Vols. 2 and 4, and Arthur Raper, "Race and Class Pressures." See also Lewinson, *op. cit.*, Chapter 6.

[34] I have talked to a great number of registration officers in various Southern states, and they have usually been very outspoken on this point. They have also been astonishingly frank in describing the methods they used. A tax collector in Georgia, for example, referred to the Supreme Court jurisdiction clause of the State Constitution and said:

"I can keep the President of the United States from registering, if I want to. God, Himself, couldn't understand that sentence. I, myself, am the judge. It must be written to my satisfaction." (Interview by Myrdal, November 3, 1939.)

[35] Interview by Wilhelmina Jackson, December, 1939, in Bunche, "The Political Status of the Negro," Vol. 4, p. 941.

[36] Interview by Wilhelmina Jackson, December, 1939, in *Ibid.*, Vol. 4, p. 940.

[37] Sometimes a vague excuse may accompany a refusal to permit a Negro to register or vote, such as that "there is no provision in the law for registering Negroes," or that the "quota" of Negro voters had been filled. (See Lewinson, *op. cit.*, p. 118.)

[38] *Idem.*

[39] *Ibid.*, p. 119.

[40] Raper, *op. cit.*, pp. 288-291.

[41] The causes of local variations are discussed in Lewinson, *op. cit.*, pp. 120-124, 132-138.

[42] A candidate who does this is sometimes a "reform" candidate. For a description of several "reform" campaigns leading up to general elections, see Lewinson, *op. cit.* pp. 148 ff. When the 1928 campaign split the South, there were contests in the general elections for a few years afterwards where pro-Hoover Democrats joined the Republicans to battle the regular Democratic candidates. (See *ibid.*, pp. 159 ff.)

[43] *Ibid.*, p. 147.

[44] In one case at least the commission form of government is known to have hurt Negroes politically: In Chattanooga before 1920 the city had an aldermanic government, and there were Negro aldermen from Negro sections of the city. In 1920 a nonpartisan commission form of government was instituted and—since elections became city-wide—Negroes were outvoted. From that time on, according to a local labor leader, Negroes received less consideration in politics. (Interview by George Stoney, January, 1940, in Bunche, "The Political Status of the Negro," Vol. 4, p. 973.)

[45] Here again we rely on Bunche's estimates.

[46] See Chapter 12, Section 5. Corruption is absent only in the sense that Negroes are not intimidated at the polls. There have been reports of white plantation owners bringing their Negro croppers to the polling place and "voting" them. Too, the voting is not secret, so that white plantation owners know their tenants' vote. On the other hand, some Southern whites feel that the A.A.A. elections are bad because they are giving Negroes the idea that they can vote. Other whites satisfy themselves by believing that the Negroes do not know what they are voting for anyway or by telling Negroes how to vote. While Negroes vote in the main A.A.A. referenda, they are often not permitted to vote for the committeemen who administer the program locally. In some cases they are permitted to vote, but only for white nominees. In all Alabama, for example, there was only one county which had Negro committeemen in the A.A.A. program. (Hale

County, which had three Negro committeemen in 1940, representing three separate communities.) See Bunche, "The Political Status of the Negro," Vol. 5, p. 1066.

[47] Lewinson, *op. cit.*, pp. 107 ff; Bunche, "The Political Status of the Negro," Vol. 4. Bunche quotes a number of these statements from his interviews, including some by Southern senators. They represent one of the traditional stereotypes. Stone says:

"The Negro masses in fact do not have to be excluded. They will disfranchise themselves if left to their own devices." (A. H. Stone, *Studies in the American Race Problem* [1908], p. 374.)

Occasionally a Negro author will agree to the white rationalization. Bertram W. Doyle writes:

". . . the Negro masses are, in general, not interested. The situation serves as an illustration to draw the distinction between the controls established by laws and formal regulation and those fixed in custom and habit. The Negro masses look on the white man as chosen to rule and on the ballot as a means to that end. They feel out of place participating in such. They accept their status as nonvoters and expect to be guided thereby. They would much prefer that "quality" white people govern them; but, even in other instances, they exhibit a lack of interest. From this standpoint the battle for and against Negro suffrage, on principle, or on a platform of the enforcement of the fourteenth and fifteenth amendments of the Constitution, is hampered by the underlying sentiments and habits of the Negroes themselves. Voting and participation in governmental affairs seem not to be in the mores of the Negro group." (*The Etiquette of Race Relations in the South* [1937], pp. 139-140.)

[48] Allison Davis, Burleigh B. Gardner, and Mary R. Gardner, *Deep South* (1941), p. 487.

[49] For general traits of nonvoters, see Charles E. Merriam and Harold F. Gossnell, *Non-Voting* (1924), and Herbert Tingsten, *Political Behavior* (1937).

[50] The political boss of a large city in the Deep South, who openly conceded to the author that he bought votes, gave a sort of democratic motivation for vote-buying which might be recorded because of the light it throws on the psychology of corrupt politics. "Why," he said, "shouldn't the poor devil, who doesn't own more than his shirt, have the right to expect a couple of dollars for his vote, when the big shots get so much more out of politics. . . . If you were a local business man," he continued, "wouldn't you expect favors from me, if you helped me into office? Well, what about the common citizen? Should he be entirely forgotten in this big game?"

[51] In Detroit in 1940, for example, Negroes constituted 9.2 per cent of the total population but 11.0 per cent of the population 21 years of age and over.

[52] W. E. B. Du Bois, *The Philadelphia Negro* (1899), p. 373.

[53] There are many forms of gerrymandering: in addition to cutting up a minority group, it may also take the form of concentrating a group in one election district when that group could control several districts if otherwise distributed. Since the modification of the boundaries of an election district always affects the influence of the vote in that district, the only test for the presence of gerrymandering is to equate the total votes of all groups over several election districts with the total influence of these groups in electing candidates.

Gerrymandering is possible because Negroes are segregated in certain areas of the city and because the multi-district system is used instead of proportional representation or other systems without districts. If Negroes were distributed throughout a city or if a district's boundaries meant nothing (as under a proportional representation system), there would be no gerrymandering. But there would also be much less chance of electing Negroes to office (except under a proportional representation system). When Negroes are scattered throughout a city, they cannot exert much influence in any district. Segregation usually gives them control of at least one district, and also makes apparent to politicians how they vote in city-wide elections. Voting on a city-wide basis takes away the advantage of being a majority in a single district. In Detroit and Chattanooga, the Negroes have little political influence, partly because of the city-wide election system for local office. But if the city-wide system is combined with proportional representation it gives greater weight to the votes of those Negroes living in non-Negro areas. Between 1930 and 1938 the New York City Council, operating under the single-member-district plan, had a Negro alderman. When proportional representation was put into effect in 1938, the Negro alderman was lost. But in 1941, Negroes managed to concentrate their votes, and with the help of some white votes, sent a representative to the Council again.

[54] In 1933 the victorious Democrats of St. Louis redistricted the city for the election of state legislators. A large number of the Negroes formerly concentrated in the Twelfth District were shifted into the huge Eleventh District and their vote in both districts was completely overwhelmed. Previous to 1933, one or two Negro legislators were always elected from St. Louis; after that year no Negro has ever been elected. Negro leaders have been working to stop this gerrymander. (Memorandum by David M. Grant in Bunche, "The Political Status of the Negro," Vol. 6, p. 1316.) The re-apportionment of 1931 in Detroit also served to prevent Negroes from electing a congressman. The Negro majority in the First District was wiped out by putting some of its Negro constituents in the predominantly white Thirteenth and Fifteenth Districts. Both of these cases of gerrymandering were perpetuated by the Democratic party, apparently not because it was making a racial discrimination against Negroes but because Negroes were tied to the Republican party before 1933. A more exhaustive study needs to be made to determine whether Negro areas have ever been gerrymandered in the North on account of race prejudice.

[55] Recently a congressman was successful in forcing the New York Legislature to promise to make the long overdue adjustments.

[56] Since there are no registration or voting statistics in the North which differentiate Negroes from whites, all quantitative studies of Negro voting and nonvoting are based on differences between areas inhabited mainly by Negroes and areas inhabited mainly by whites.

[57] Edward H. Litchfield, "A Case Study of Negro Political Behavior in Detroit," *Public Opinion Quarterly* (June, 1941), pp. 267-274. Litchfield found that this greater political apathy among Negroes existed even when economic status is held constant. In the absence of figures on income, measures of economic status used to compare Negroes and whites may be called into question. Rents, for example, are not comparable when Negroes are segregated and crowded. Such weaknesses of economic indices do not apply, however, to differences *within* the Negro group.

[58] Harold F. Gosnell, *Negro Politicians* (1935), p. 17. In Cleveland, too, it has been claimed that Negroes vote more than whites, although statistics have not been compiled to prove this. See memorandum prepared for this study by Harry E. Davis, cited in Bunche, "The Political Status of the Negro," Vol. 6, p. 1279.

[59] One student reports that, while Negroes *vote* much less than whites in Detroit, they *register* for voting almost to the same extent. This is because some Negro men hope to get jobs in the Ford factories by registering and forming Republican clubs. (My interviews.) See also: T. R. Solomon, "Participation of Negroes in Detroit Elections," unpublished Ph.D. thesis, University of Michigan (1939), pp. 101-102. Quoted in Bunche, "The Political Status of the Negro," Vol. 6, p. 1308.

[60] Tingsten, *op. cit.*, Chapter 3, has a complete summary of all these studies. Although Gosnell, Arneson, and others have made such studies for two or three such communities in America, it is difficult to do this, since voting statistics are not broken down by race, and it is difficult to find suitable economic indices. (See: Harold F. Gosnell, *Getting Out the Vote* (1927); Harold F. Gosnell and Norman N. Gill, "An Analysis of the 1932 Presidential Vote in Chicago," *The American Political Science Review* (December, 1935), pp. 967-984; Ben A. Arneson, "Non-Voting in a Typical Ohio Community," *The American Political Science Review* (November, 1925), pp. 816-822; W. Donaldson, "Compulsory Voting," *National Municipal Review* (July, 1915), pp. 460-465. There is, however, a simple substitute for voting statistics in America and that is the already collected public opinion polls made by Gallup, *Fortune* magazine and others. Many of these polls give information as to whether the informant voted or not in the previous election, and they have a rough estimate of the informant's economic status. A retabulation of several such polls ought to provide a reasonable estimate of the extent of nonvoting in different income groups.

[61] Tammany sought the Negro vote in New York City as early as 1886 when they got John A. Nail, a saloon-keeper and leading Negro citizen, to set up a Negro Democratic club. After 1900 Ferdinand Q. Morton took over leadership of Negro Democrats. He was skillfully supported after 1920 by Mrs. Bessye Bearden. The Garvey movement helped the Democratic party in New York to a large extent. (Bunche, "The Political Status of the Negro," Vol. 6, pp. 1335-1356.) For a detailed description of Negroes in recent New York politics, see Claude McKay, *Harlem* (1940), pp. 124-131.

[62] Henderson, *op. cit.*, p. 19.

[63] Litchfield, *op. cit.*, pp. 271, 273.

[64] Gosnell, *Negro Politicians*, p. 36.

[65] In St. Louis, for example, Negroes were given only three upper-bracket political jobs by the Republicans. The incoming Democrats, despite a general curtailment due to the depression, opened up eleven more jobs to Negroes and built one hospital and three community centers for them. (Democratic Campaign Booklet, prepared by Negro Division of the Democratic Campaign Headquarters of St. Louis. Quoted by Bunche, "The Political Status of the Negro," Vol. 6, pp. 1315-1316, 1320.)

[66] New York was something of an exception, since the nominal Republican, La Guardia, was the mayor during the depression after beating Tammany candidates. La Guardia supported Roosevelt nationally, however. Chicago too, was something of an exception since the pre-depression Republican mayor, Thompson, was very pro-Negro. After Thompson's defeat in 1931, however, he was rapidly forgotten, and the Negro vote shifted to the Democratic party after a few years.

[67] The figures for 1932 and 1936 are from Henderson, *op. cit.*, pp. 19-21. The figure for 1940 is from H. F. Gosnell, "The Negro Vote in Northern Cities," *National Municipal Review* (May, 1941), p. 267. Since Gosnell used a slightly different basis for calculation than Henderson, the 1936 and 1940 figures may not be exactly com-

parable. Henderson showed a Negro vote of 59.5 per cent for the Democratic candidate for Mayor in 1939.

[68] Litchfield, *op. cit.*, p. 271. The percentage Democratic among Detroit Negroes in 1930 was 19.5.

[69] In addition to the factors mentioned as causing the shift in the Negro vote toward the Democratic party, Gosnell observes that there was one other factor that influenced the local elections if not the national ones. As Northern city administrations fell into the hands of Democrats after 1930, the Negro underworld was forced to back them.

"This year one syndicate had 1,500 policy writers on the streets canvassing for the Democratic ticket. One of the leaders of this syndicate recently made a settlement with the federal government of $500,000 for his back income taxes in 1938. A rival syndicate that sponsored a Willkie meeting was raided and practically closed down. The police have this element of the Negro community well under control." (Gosnell, "The Negro Vote in Northern Cities," *National Municipal Review*, p. 267.)

[70] Litchfield, *op. cit.*, p. 273.

[71] Gosnell, *Negro Politicians*, p. 352.

[72] Davis, in Bunche, "The Political Status of the Negro," Vol. 6, pp. 1289-1290.

[73] Litchfield, *op. cit.*, p. 272. Negroes, by economic class, had about the same proportions Democratic as the city as a whole. This comparison, however, has methodological weaknesses. Henderson found a similar class differential in voting among Chicago Negroes. Henderson, *op. cit.*, pp. 30-31.

[74] The estimate that there are as many Negroes voting today in the United States as there are Southern whites voting in seven Deep Southern states was made in the following manner: to get the approximate number of Negro voters in all Northern and Western states and in the Border states of Delaware, West Virginia, and Maryland, the proportion of all voters for President in 1940 to the total population in 1940, for each state, was applied to the Negro population of the respective state. That is, it was assumed that Negroes voted in the same proportion in these states as did whites. The only empirical evidence we have on this point is Gosnell's finding that in Chicago Negroes voted more than did whites and Litchfield's finding that in Detroit Negroes voted less than did whites. (See Section 4 of this chapter.) If Negroes voted less than did eligible whites in the entire North, we feel that this is compensated for by the fact that many of the foreign-born whites are not citizens and so cannot vote. A similar procedure was used to estimate the number of Negroes voting in the Border states of Missouri and Kentucky except that the percentage was arbitrarily reduced by 10 per cent before being applied to the Negro population, in order to compensate for the minor restrictions on Negro voting in some areas of those states. Our estimates showed that over 1,263,000 Negroes voted for President in 1940 in the North and West, and that over 348,000 Negroes voted in the five Border states. For the 12 states of the Upper and Lower South we used Bunche's estimate of 250,000 Negro votes. The total number of Negro votes in the United States was thus about 1,861,000.

To determine how many Southern states had this many whites voting, we subtracted the estimated Negro vote from the total vote for each state, and added these white votes together (beginning with the states that disfranchised the Negroes most) until our total was close to 1,861,000. The total white vote for the six Deep Southern states of Mississippi, Louisiana, Alabama, South Carolina, Arkansas and Georgia was 1,430,000.

By adding Florida, the total was brought up to 1,905,000, which is close to the total number of Negro votes.

[75] Gosnell, *Negro Politicians*, pp. 364-367; Bunche, "The Political Status of the Negro," Vol. 6, p. 1272 *passim*.

[76] Lewinson, *op. cit.*, p. 130.

[77] See Raper, *op. cit.*, pp. 27 ff.

[78] Editorial in the Montgomery *Advertiser* (April 23, 1940). Cited in Raper, *op. cit.*, p. 45.

[79] *Ibid.*, p. 50.

[80] According to a Negro political leader in an interview in November, 1939. See Bunche, "The Political Status of the Negro," Vol. 4, p. 923.

[81] *Ibid.*, p. 994.

[82] Raper, *op. cit.*, p. 13.

[83] Bunche, "The Political Status of the Negro," Vol. 4, pp. 866-867.

[84] *Ibid.*, p. 911.

[85] *Ibid.*, p. 985.

[86] *Ibid.*, Vol. 6, p. 1490, and Lewinson, *op. cit.*, pp. 150-151.

[87] Bunche, "The Political Status of the Negro," Vol. 4, p. 906.

[88] *Idem.*

[89] *Ibid.*, Vol. 4, p. 782.

[90] Gosnell, *Negro Politicians*, p. 373.

[91] Gosnell describes the political loyalty of the Negroes in the following terms:

"The greatest contribution which the rank and file of the Negro group had to offer to the white political leaders was personal loyalty. The politician who won their confidence could count on their support even in the most adverse of circumstance. It was common belief among certain white politicians that the Negro vote was influenced primarily by large expenditures of money. It is true that colored party workers demand compensation for their services on behalf of given candidates. Other things being equal, the colored voters, like the white voters in many parts of the United States, support the candidates who spend the most money. However, these candidates had to measure up to given standards of acceptability if the money spent was to yield the best returns. In other words, money, jobs, and other rewards might not influence the Negro voters to support a candidate who was regarded as hostile to the interests of the race in preference to one who had a reputation of fair dealing in race matters. This is not to say that the favored candidate, if he wanted a large vote, could neglect to spend the money that was commonly put into districts of the same economic status. Another evidence of the loyalty of the colored voters was their behavior when the political fortunes of their favorite candidates were sinking. The Negroes, like other minority groups, do not enjoy supporting losing causes, but when their friends are going down they stick with them to the last." (*Negro Politicians*, pp. 365-366.)

[92] Henderson, *op. cit.*, pp. 78-79.

[93] Gosnell, *Negro Politicians*, p. 367.

[94] Negro political leaders have sometimes claimed that Negroes control the "balance of power" in as many as 17 states. This estimate is based on the dubious assumptions that all Negroes of voting age do vote, that the Negro vote is perfectly organized and flexible, that white voters are always divided as closely as they were in 1940, and that white voters would be uninfluenced if an organized Negro movement were afoot.

[95] The tradition of a "Black Cabinet" dates further back. (See James Weldon Johnson, *Along This Way* [1934], p. 239.)

[96] Archie C. Edwards, quoted by Laurence J. W. Hayes, *The Negro Federal Government Worker*, Howard University Studies in the Social Sciences (1941), pp. 73, 153. According to Kiplinger, at the end of 1941 there were more than 150,000 Negroes in the federal civil service, and they were increasing as the war boom continued. (W. M. Kiplinger, *Washington Is Like That* [1942], p. 148.)

Chapter 23. *Trends and Possibilities*

[1] We are not overlooking the watchdog service on behalf of the Negro interests carried on primarily by the national office of the N.A.A.C.P. (see Chapter 39). W. E. B. Du Bois, a former leader of the organization, gives in his autobiography an inside view of how political strategy appeared to Negro leadership up until recently:

"We had calculated that increased independence in the Negro vote would bring a bid for the Negro vote from opposing parties; but it did not until many years later. Indeed, it was not until the re-election of the second Roosevelt in 1936 that the Negro vote in the North came to be eagerly contended for by the two major parties. In 1914 we tried to make congressional candidates declare themselves as to our demands, but were only partially successful. The Sixty-fourth Congress saw eleven bills introduced advocating color caste and the state legislatures continued to be bombarded by similar legislation. Thus, in 1916, we found ourselves politically helpless. We had no choice. We could vote for Wilson who had segregated us or for Hughes who, despite all our requests, remained doggedly dumb on our problems."[a]

[2] I have observed in the big cities a certain amount of anti-Semitism among Negroes, which is rather natural as Jews in the role of businessmen and real estate owners are frequently the ones among the whites who are in closest contact with the Negro and are thus likely to be identified as the exploiters of the Negro people. Rarely, however, does an anti-Semitic tone creep into the Negro press. This is not only due to the fact that Jewish merchants usually contribute so large a part of the tiny local advertising for every Negro paper, but more fundamentally to a clear knowledge by almost everybody writing or talking in the Negro group that as a people they cannot afford any negative racialism but have to stick to racial equalitarianism.

[3] Robert E. Park points to one important aspect of this general "law" at the end of the following statement:

"The freedman was not able at once to enter into the spirit and tradition of a free competition and industrial society. He had no conception, for example, of the secret terror that haunts the free laborer; the fear, namely, of losing his job and of being out of work. On the contrary, his first conception of freedom was that of a condition in which he would be permanently out of work. So far, therefore, from being possessed by that mania for owning things which is the characteristic, as the communists tell us, of a capitalistic society, his first impulse and aim were to get as deeply in debt as possible. If, therefore, the agents of the 'Third International' find that such Negroes

[a] *Dusk of Dawn* (1940), p. 237.

are as yet not ripe for communism, it is undoubtedly because they have not had as yet the opportunity to realize the evils of a free and competitive society."[a]

[4] The Communists have tried to circumvent this difficulty. The church is often the only meeting place.[b] But the great majority of Negro preachers will not only keep them out of their churches, but use all their influence to stamp out Communism as a "Godless," anti-religious creed.

[5] *Negro Americans, What Now?* (1934), p. 11.

[6] *Ibid.*, p. 68. Compare James Weldon Johnson, *Along this Way* (1934), p. 411.

[7] James Weldon Johnson, *Negro Americans, What Now?*, p. 9.

[8] The following figures taken from a survey made by *Fortune* magazine show to what a great extent Negroes support the New Deal:

	Per cent in Favor
"Do you approve:	
"in general of F.D.R.?	84.7
"of his economic objectives?	87.3
"of Wages and Hours Legislation?	91.3
"of F.D.R.'s attitude toward Business?	85.2
"of F.D.R.'s Advisors and Associates?	73.6"

These figures are quoted by courtesy of *Fortune* magazine. "The Fortune Quarterly Survey: XIII," *Fortune* (July, 1938), pp. 36-37 and 74-80.

[9] The most comprehensive and penetrating study of the subject is still, after half a century, James Bryce, *The American Commonwealth* (1893).

[10] W. E. B. Du Bois, "The Negro Citizen" in Charles S. Johnson, *The Negro in American Civilization* (1930), p. 466.

[11] Du Bois, "The Negro Citizen," *op. cit.*, pp. 465-466.

"I do not for a moment argue that political power will immediately abolish color caste, make ignorant men intelligent or bad men good. We have caste and discrimination in the North with the vote, and social progress in some parts of the South without it. But there is this vast difference: in states like New York, where we are beginning to learn the meaning and use of the ballot, we are building a firm and unshakeable basis of permanent freedom, while every advance in the South, unprotected by political power, is based on chance and changing personalities. I maintain that political power is the beginning of all permanent reform and the only hope for maintaining gains.

"There are today a surprisingly large number of intelligent and sincere people, both white and black, who really believe that the Negro problem in the United States can ultimately be solved without our being compelled to face and settle the question of the Negro vote.

"Nearly all of our social studies apparently come to this conclusion, either openly or by assumption, and do not say, as they ought to say, that granted impulse by philanthropy, help by enlightened public opinion and the aid of time, no permanent improvement in the economic and social condition of Negroes is going to be made, so long as they are deprived of political power to support and defend it.

"Nowhere else in the world is there any suggestion that a modern laboring class can

---

[a] Introduction to Charles S. Johnson's *Shadow of the Plantation* (1934), p. xxii.

[b] See J. G. St. Clair Drake, "The Negro Church and Associations in Chicago," unpublished manuscript prepared for this study (1940), p. 409.

permanently better itself without political power. It may be a question, it certainly is a question, as to just how labor is going to use this power ultimately so as to raise its economic and social status. But there is no question but that such power must be had."[a]

[12] See, for instance, Booker T. Washington, *The Future of the American Negro* (1899), pp. 141, 156 and 212.

[13] "The more I consider the subject, the more strongly I am convinced that the most harmful effect of the practice to which the people in certain sections of the South have felt themselves compelled to resort, in order to get rid of the force of the Negroes' ballot, is not wholly in the wrong done to the Negro, but in the permanent injury to the morals of the white man. The wrong to the Negro is temporary, but to the morals of the white man the injury is permanent. I have noted time and time again that when an individual perjures himself in order to break the force of the black man's ballot, he soon learns to practise dishonesty in other relations of life, not only where the Negro is concerned, but equally so where a white man is concerned. The white man who begins by cheating a Negro usually ends up cheating a white man. The white man who begins to break the law by lynching a Negro soon yields to the temptation to lynch a white man. All this, it seems to me, makes it important that the whole Nation lend a hand in trying to lift the burden of ignorance from the South."[b]

"These disfranchisement measures, harsh and severe as they are in many features, meet with little or no opposition from the nation at large. Although the clear and unmistakable intent of the Federal Constitution is set at naught, yet the nation suffereth it to be so. There is no moral force in the nation at present that will lead to their undoing, and no political exigency seems to demand it. That they violate the spirit, if not the letter, of the Federal Constitution is notorious. Every fourteen year old child in America is fully aware of this fact, and yet the nation winks at the violation of its own fundamental law. Men of the highest patriotic and personal probity ignore their oath to execute the law, and condone its annulment. If there is a growing disrespect for law in the attitude of the American mind, the cause is not far to seek nor hard to find. If one portion of the organic law may be violated with impunity, why not another if it seems to conflict with our interests or with our prejudices?"[c]

[14] "I am not saying a word against all legitimate efforts to purge the ballot of ignorance, pauperism, and crime. But few have pretended that the present movement for disfranchisement in the South is for such a purpose; it has been plainly and frankly declared in nearly every case that the object of the disfranchising laws is the elimination of the black man from politics."[d]

"More and more I am convinced that the final solution of the political end of our race problem will be for each state that finds it necessary to change the law bearing upon the franchise to make the law apply with absolute honesty, and without opportunity for double dealing or evasion, to both races alike. Any other course my daily observation in the South convinces me, will be unjust to the Negro, unjust to the white man, and unfair to the rest of the states in the Union, and will be, like slavery, a sin that at some time we shall have to pay for."[e]

[a] *Ibid.*, pp. 464-465.
[b] Booker T. Washington, *Up from Slavery* (1901; first edition, 1900), pp. 165-166.
[c] Kelly Miller, *Out of the House of Bondage* (1914), p. 130.
[d] W. E. B. Du Bois, *The Souls of Black Folk* (1903), p. 175.
[e] Washington, *Up from Slavery*, pp. 86-87.

[15] "There is a growing school of thought in the South which holds that any man, no matter what his race, who is qualified to vote ought to be permitted to vote, and that it is wholly unjust for election officials to disqualify thousands of Negroes arbitrarily while permitting other thousands of white illiterates to troop to the polls. It is the view of the element that an educated and respectable Negro is a greater asset to the community and more deserving of the franchise than an unlettered white swineherd from the pine barrens. It cannot be said that this view is held by anything remotely approaching a majority of the Southern whites, but it undoubtedly is gaining in favor. As reconstruction and its atrocities recede further and further into the background, more and more white Southerners are coming to feel that the cry of 'white supremacy,' raised so often in the past, is in the twentieth century a mere rawhead and bloodybones without substance or meaning."[a]

[16] The relevant section of the Fourteenth Amendment reads: ". . . when the right to vote at any election for the choice of Electors for President of the United States, Representatives in Congress, the executive and judicial officers of a State, or the members of the Legislature thereof, is denied to any of the male inhabitants of such State, being twenty-one years of age, and citizens of the United States, or in any way abridged, except for participation in rebellion, or other crime, the basis of representation therein shall be reduced in the proportion which the number of such male citizens shall bear to the whole number of male citizens twenty-one years of age in such State."

There was some discussion about applying the penalty to the South demanded by this section of the Constitution after the disfranchising laws were adopted by the South. In 1904, the so-called Crumpacker Resolution was before Congress demanding that the representation of the disfranchising states be reduced after a careful investigation. In 1904 the Republican Party platform carried the same demand. By the end of the first decade of the twentieth century discussion on this point was dead.

There was some question as to the constitutionality of such a resolution. Some held that the Fifteenth Amendment superseded the Fourteenth, and that a disfranchising state's representation should not be reduced but the disfranchising stopped. James G. Blaine, the great statesman of the last decades of the nineteenth century, for example said:

"Before the adoption of the Fifteenth Amendment, if a State should exclude the negro from suffrage the next step would be for Congress to exclude the negro from the basis of apportionment. After the adoption of the Fifteenth Amendment, if a State should exclude the negro from suffrage, the next step would be for the Supreme Court to declare the act unconstitutional and therefore null and void."[b]

The relevant section of the Fifteenth Amendment reads: "The right of citizens of the United States to vote shall not be denied or abridged by the United States or by any State on account of race, color, or previous condition of servitude."

[17] Compare Charles S. Mangum, Jr., *The Legal Status of the Negro* (1940), pp. 388 ff. J. W. Johnson comments from the Negro side: "More than once he took his case to the Supreme Court of the United States, but the Court pointed out that he had failed to show that the *state* had abridged or denied his right to vote or that persons who prevented him from voting had done so because of his *race, color or previous condition of servitude*. So, unable to prove that the committee which had met him at

[a] Virginius Dabney, *Liberalism in the South* (1932), pp. 253-254.
[b] *Twenty Years of Congress* (1886), Vol. 2, pp. 418-419.

the polls with shotguns was actuated by any such base and unconstitutional motives, he found his case thrown out. In the last analysis, he lost his vote because of the attitude of the Supreme Court."[a]

[18] Thomas P. Bailey, *Race Orthodoxy in the South* (1914), pp. 60-61.

[19] Marian D. Irish, "The Southern One-Party System and National Politics," *The Journal of Politics* (February, 1942), p. 82.

[20] "A Minority of Our Own," New York *Times* (April 3, 1942).

[21] "For the nation, therefore, the fair position would seem to be that the South is entitled to work out this extremely important and extremely delicate question in the way in which they have begun, without further disastrous interference such as occurred during the reconstruction period."[b]

[22] "For the dominant political party in a third of the United States to rule that in 1942 only qualified 'white voters' shall be allowed to participate in the selection of the officials of our democratic government would be an anachronism too dangerous to democratic principles and Christian ideals to be preserved for the sake of old days and old ways."[c]

[23] Woofter, *op. cit.*, p. 151.

INDEX TO BOTH VOLUMES

549n.; Negro police in, 543n.; poll tax in, 1324; terror organization in, 449; transportation, Jim Crow in, 635; voting in, 488n.; white primary in, 486

Alabama Women's Democratic Club, 812n.

Alabama Women's League for White Supremacy, 812n.

Alcohol, use of, by Negroes, 980-981

Alexander, W. W., 467, 843, 844, 847, 849

Allen, James S., cited, 750

Allen, William G., 737

All-Negro communities, 480n., 488n., 621

All-Negro political movements, 490, 500n., 817-819, 851-852

Amalgamated Association of Iron, Steel and Tin Workers, 1118

Amalgamated Clothing Workers, 1110

Amalgamated Meat Cutters and Butcher Workmen, 1123

Amalgamation (see also Miscegenation), 105-106, 113, 728, 808, 927; beliefs fostered to discourage, 108; denial of, to Negroes, see Anti-amalgamation doctrine; fear of, 586-587, 589, 590-591; feeling against, in the North, 57-58, 603; of foreign-born, 50, 51-53; Negro attitudes toward, 56-57, 1187

Ambivalence of attitude: emotional and intellectual, 39-40; of Negro leaders, 772-773, 774, 775; of Negro upper class, 794-797; of whites, 957, 959, 1189

American Association of University Women, 469

American Civil Liberties Union, 812n., 855n.

American Colonization Society, 805-806

American Creed, lxviii-lxix, 209, 581, 717n.; acceptance of, in South, 461-462, 690, 888, 893, 895, 896; as basis for Negro struggle for equality, 799; belief of Negroes in, 4, 510, 808-809, 880, 900, 946; changing, 574; conflict of, with caste system, 812, 899; and democracy, 783; departure of South from, 87; development of new consciousness of, 568; economic phase of, 212, 214; and education, 709, 879, 882, 893, 1182; and equality, 213, 429, 671-672, 1189; formative stage of, 23-24; and freedom of mobility, 198; gradual realization of, 1021-1024; influence of, 80, 88-89, 110, 383, 460, 585, 591, 662, 792, 1010, 1020; and living conditions, 169; as national conscience, 23; and national unity, 7-8, 13; not lived up to, 13-14, 21, 52, 326; an obstacle to elimination of Negro population, 170; restraining influence of, 800; revitalization of, 409, 439; rooted

in Christianity, 9-12, 757; rooted in English law, 12; rooted in philosophy of Enlightenment, 8-9, 1181-1182; substantiation of, by science and education, 92-93, 96-97, 110; as system of ideals, 3-5; as value premises for this book, 23-25, 526, 573, 852-853, 927

American Federation of Labor, 402, 403, 405n., 406, 855, 1096, 1102; discrimination in, 1298-1299, 1300; founding of, 1297; principle of nondiscrimination in, 792

American Federation of Musicians, 330

American Institute of Public Opinion, 893n.

American League for Peace and Democracy, 812n.

American Medical Association, 179

American Red Cross, segregation policy of, 631, 1367

American Revolution, 710, 997; Negro soldiers in, 1308

American society and the Negro problem, relationship between, lxxiv-lxxvii

American Youth Commission, 649, 699n., 893n., 1272

Americanization: and class etiquette, 614; of immigrants, 927-928; and race prejudice, 603; of the South, 1011

Ames, Jessie Daniel, 846; cited, 1335; on Interracial Commission, 844, 845

Anarchism: philosophical, 434; tendency toward, 16

Ancestry: African, 117-120, 698, 1200, 1201; Indian, 113n.; pride of, 747, 901; qualification for voting, 480

Anderson, Marian, 734, 735, 988, 991n.

"Anglo-Saxon race"; see "Nordic race"

Anthony, Susan B., 1075

Anti-amalgamation doctrine 52n., 53-58, 586-587, 589-591, 928, 1354; bolstered by inferiority theory, 102; Negro attitude toward, 62-65; psychological nature of, 59-60

Anti-democratic movement, 433

Anti-lynching legislation, 502, 517, 565, 829, 1350

Anti-Semitism, 53, 852, 1186, 1190, 1321, 1331, 1424

Anti-Slavery Convention, 1076n.

Anti-social tendencies, factors fostering, 331-332

Anti-strike policy, 425

Apathy: on Negro problem in the North, 516; political, 476, 483, 490, 493

Apollo Theater, 329

Appointive offices, Negroes in, 501-502, 503-504, 535

Archer, William, 676, 697; cited, 562, 676; on anomalous position of Negro,

~79-280, 302; Negro residences in, 1125-1128; Northern, segregation in, 626; political machines in, 439; racial etiquette in, 615; small, Negroes in, 386-387, 601; unemployment in, 302

City planning, 351-352, 626-627

Citizens' Fact Finding Movement, 812n.

Citizenship, education for, 778, 949

Civil liberties, fight for, 790, 794

Civil Liberties Union; see American Civil Liberties Union

Civil rights laws, 418n., 528, 533, 579, 580, 601n., 1367

Civil service: discrimination in, 327-329, 416, 839; Negroes in, 497, 502, 504, 778, 1331; police systems and, 539, 544; reform of, 436

Civil War, 431, 997; class differences not strengthened by, 460; economic interpretation of, 222; increased violence in period following, 533; lingering resentment in South over, 45; Negro troops in, 738, 1308; Northern attitude toward, 45, 47; slavery issue in, 431, 443

Civilian Conservation Corps, 361-362, 426n., 503, 1283

Class: in American society, 6, 50-51; and caste, 58, 675, 693-695, 727, 1129-1132, 1381; in church, 868; concept of, 667-669, 1130, 1377-1378; in early New England, 1362-1363; as escape from caste, 792; factors accentuating, 213, 671; factors hindering rigid system of, 670-671; Marxian theory of, 68, 73; "meaning" of, 670-674; the result of restricted competition, 673-674; as social continuum, 675-676, 700; solidarity of, see Labor solidarity

Class attitudes in South, on social inequality, 592-599

Class Consciousness, 674

Class discrimination in Europe, 670

"Class problem," 75

Class stratification, Negro, 580, 593, 662, 700-705, 764-765, 1386-1388; in caste system, 689-693; and education, 875, 879; importance of relationship to white society in, 695; and leadership, 727-733, 1390; in under world, 704-705

"Class struggle," 673

"Classical" versus "vocational" education, 888-889, 896-900, 906

Clay, C. C., on economic life in the South, 230

Clay, Emily H., on Interracial Commission, 844, 846, 1408-1409, 1410

Clergymen; see Ministers, Negro

Cleveland, Negro vote in, 1327

Closed shop, 405n.

Closed union, 405n.

Clothing, Negro, 962-963; expenditures for, 370, 1287-1288

Club activity, 952-953

Cobb, W. Montague: cited, 1214; on racial strength, 169

Collective bargaining, political, of Negroes, 498-500, 505-508; need for agency for, 835, 855

Collective consumption, 333

Colleges: discrimination in, 633; Negro, 632, 732-733, 765, 881, 888, 889, 890, 891, 892, 901, 904-905, 945, 951, 1415, 1429; poll of, on mix~d education, 1421; segregation in, 1420

Collins, Henry Hill, on Cranbury Terror Case, 528

Collins, Winfield H.: on "vocational" education, 898-899; on Negro laborers, 284

Colonization schemes, 185-186, 698, 746-749, 805-807

Color, 1382-1384; and caste, 695-700; consciousness of, in children, 1429; and leadership, 1390; question of, in World War II, 915, 1004, 1006, 1016

Color bar; see Discrimination and Segregation

Color caste; see Caste system

Color line; see Caste line

Colored Clerks' Circle, 816, 1261

Colored Merchants' Association, 815

Commercial establishments, discrimination and segregation in, 636-638

Commissary system, 247, 1090, 1095

Commission form of government, 487, 1325

Commission on Interracial Cooperation; see Interracial Commission

Committee on Africa, the War, and Peace Aims, 807

Committee on Discrimination in Employment, 418n.

Committee on Economic and Racial Justice, 812n.

Committee for Improving the Industrial Conditions of Negroes in New York City, 837

Committee on Urban Conditions Among Negroes, 837

Common-law marriage; see Marriage, common-law

Common welfare, 1046-1047

Communism: experiments in, 712; influence of, on Negro intellectuals, 510; Marx's idea of, 1051n.; Negro attitudes toward, 508-510, 754, 807, 1332

Communist party, 812n.; appeal of, to Negroes, 750; in National Negro Congress,

Funeral expenditures, 1262

Gabriel, Ralph H., on democracy and moral law, 10, 15, 23
Gaines Case, 830, 833
Gallagher, Buell G., 1377; cited, 563; caste and class diagrams by, 1381
Gambling, 330-331, 940, 983-984, 985, 1266, 1267, 1269; laws against, 17
Garner, John N., 459-460, 494, 754
Garnet, Henry Highland, 737
Garrison, William Lloyd, 806, 1075
Garvey, Marcus, 746-749, 836n., 1390
Garvey movement 698, 746-749, 806, 1328
Gaudiness, Negro love of, 962-963
Gebhard, John C., cited, 1262
Geddes, Anne E., cited, 354
General Education Board, 891, 893
General Motors Corporation, 1119
Genetic composition of Negro people, 121-122, 124, 131-132, 590, 1199-1200; present and future trends, 132-136
Geographic conditions, effect of, on man, 116
Geographical distribution of Negroes, 183-185, 189, 190-191, 205-206; effect of, on reproduction rate, 161; of Negro policemen, 543n.
Georgia: incomes from fines in, 549n.; liberal influence in, 468, 469; Negro police in, 543n.; riot in, 567; voting in, 488n.; voting requirements in, 484, 1324; white primary in, 486
Gerrymandering, 430n., 437n., 450, 492, 633, 901, 1326-1327; "natural," 493
Gibson, Truman, 422n.
Gillard, John Thomas, cited, 864n.-865n., 870n., 871n.
Gist, Noel P., cited, 1373
Glasgow, Ellen, 468
Glass, Carter, on discrimination, 1313-1314
"Glass plate," 680, 724-727
Gleason, Eliza Atkins, cited, 1275
God, Negro youth's conception of, 1411
Goldberg, Isaac, on white enjoyment of Negro songs, 1437
Goldhamer, Herbert, cited, 952
Good Shepherd Church, 863n.
Goodell, William, cited, 531-532
Goodrich, Carter, cited, 232
Gosnell, Harold F.: cited, 493, 494, 495, 498, 502, 941; on Negro benefits from government, 501; on Negro political loyalty, 1330; on Negro prostitution, 1268; on Negro underworld and election, 1329; on Negro underworld leaders, 1267
Gould, Howard D., 1123n.
Government: Jeffersonian distrust of, 16;

increasing power of labor in, 788; Negroes employed by, 327-328, 416, 788, 1265-1266; non-criticism of, 1251-1252; reform of, 511-512
Government jobs, discrimination in, 1306-1307
Gradualism, 787-788, 845, 1119
Grady, Henry W., 230; on *ante-bellum* South, 1375-1376; on employment opportunities for Negroes, 292; on racial separation, 581, 1353; on slaves, 1357; on white solidarity, 453-454; on white supremacy, 1354
Graft; *see* Corruption
Graham, Frank P., 467
Granger, Lester B., 837, 987; cited, 417, 1302, 1306, 1307; on Urban League, 1408
Grandfather clauses, 480, 829, 833, 1313, 1318, 1323
Grant, Madison, on racial definition, 114
Grant, Ulysses S., on hope of freedmen for land, 1234
Grants-in-aid system, 343, 892-893, 1225
Graves, John Temple, 1013
Great Depression, 348, 394, 1243-1244; effect of, on migration, 196; effect of, on Negroes, 206-207, 295, 296, 315, 393, 754-755; in the North 295; in the South, 197, 289, 463
Great Migration (*see also* Migration), 46, 183, 189, 191-196, 295, 329-330, 527, 568, 599, 602, 652, 999, 1229-1232
Great Revival of 1800, 938
Greeley, Horace, 1075
Green, H. M., cited, 172
Green, Paul, 468
Green, William, 718
Greene, Harry W., on education of Negro leaders, 1402
Greene, Lorenzo J., and Woodson, Carter G., on opposition of unions to Negroes, 1102n.
Grimke, Angelina and Sarah, 1075
Gross reproduction rate, 161-162, 1221
Guardian, Boston, 913-914, 1392
Guggenheim Memorial Foundation, 892n.

Hacker, Louis, 1315
Hailey, Malcolm, cited, 807
Hairdressers, Negro, 1088
Haiti, immigration to, 186
Hamilton, Horace C., on mechanization in the South, 1249
Hammon, Jupiter, 992
Hammond, J. H., on slavery, 443
Hampton, Wade, on Reconstruction Amendments, 1313

Human inclinations, etiquette in cases involving, 616-617

Humanitarianism, 6-7; of American Creed, 598; in Reconstruction period, 739, 741

Humor, Negro, 959-961, 1431; function of, in race question, 38-39; simulated, 960

Hurd, John C., cited, 531-532

Hurston, Zora Neale, cited, 965

Huxley, Julian S.; on adaptation to environment, 1199; on miscegenation, 1209

Huxley, J. S., and Haddon, A. C., on genetic racial differences, 146

Idealism, American, lxviii, lxx, 712, 810; and behavior, disparity between, 21-23; 745, 755-756, 1008; history of, 6-8; inscribed in laws, 14

Ideals: conflict of, 209; lip-service to, 21-23; unity of, 3-5

Ideology: business, 800-803; defense, 30-32, 56-57, 62, 88, 104-105, 283-284, 441-445, 460, 962n., 1432; equalitarianism, see Equalitarianism; national, see American Creed; Negro, see Popular theories, Negro; Northern, 603, 1375-1376; "pure woman," 1356; Southern (see also Liberalism, Southern), 441-445, 670; working class, 407; of World War II, 517, 745, 755, 790n., 915, 1004, 1006, 1007, 1012, 1016

Ignorance, mutual, of Negroes and whites, 762, 956, 957

Ignorance, Negro, 961, 970; simulated, 961; of whites, 659

Ignorance about social affairs, 1034

Ignorance, white, about Negroes (see also Misinformation about Negroes), 40-42, 279, 339n., 382, 600, 647, 1010, 1143n., 1293, 1370-1371, 1373-1374; convenience of, 40-42, 48; as a factor in social inequality, 656-659; in the North, 383-386, 606, 644; in the South, 394-395

Illegality: pattern of, 558-560, 1346; tradition of (see also Law, lack of respect for, in America), 405, 435, 440, 441, 448-451, 525, 526, 536

Illegitimacy, 177-178, 932, 933, 935

Illinois: death penalty in, 554n.; lynching in, 561; riots in, 567; school segregation in, 633

Immigrants: competition of, with Negroes, 603; exploitation of, 50, 292; inferior schools for, 338; newspapers for, 911, 912; physical changes in, 122, 1202-1203; voting among, 491; voting rights of, 438

Immigration, 17, 50-52, 157-159, 166, 196, 713, 714, 927; decline of, 715; legislation on, 92, 196, 198; of Mexicans and Canadians, 159; Negro, 120, 135, 165, 166; restricted, 998, 1190

Imperialism, American, 1020

Improvement organizations, 744, 800, 812-852, 877

Income: farm, 255, 1283-1285; Southern white, 45n., 297n.

Income, Negro (see also Salaries and Wages), 307, 364-366, 1270, 1283-1285, 1288; of artists 329 330; differential in, 164-165; of doctors, 324-325; and family size, 366-367; of teachers and ministers, 319-320, 321

Inconsistency: between American ideals and practices 21-23; 745, 755-756, 1008; of attitudes in America, lxvii, lxx, 1140-1141; of beliefs, 111, 283-284, 446; intellectual and moral, 39-40; of Negro clergymen, 940; in social orientation, 52-53; of valuations, see Valuations, conflicts of

Independent Labor League of America, 812n.

India, potential revolt in, 1006

Indians, American, assimilability of, 53

Indiana: lynching in, 561; school segregation in, 633

"Indifferent equilibrium": in the North, 392-394; in the South, 394-396

Individual enterprise, decreased sanctity of, 213

Individualism, 709, 710; of immigrants, 714; Negro, 961; Southern, 458-459

Inequality; see Discrimination and "No social equality," doctrine of

Industrial Congress of 1873, 1296

"Industrial" education; see "Vocational" education

Industrial Revolution, effect of, on Negroes and women, 1077

Industrialization: future, of "backward" countries, 1017-1018; impact of, on Negroes, 645; in the South, 44, 199, 263, 398, 463, 515

Industry: Negroes in, 198, 199, 279-303, 380, 424, 1079-1124, 1256-1259, 1295-1296, 1386; exclusion of Negroes from, 389-390; history of Negroes in, 393-394

Infant mortality, 162, 171, 174, 1223, 1224

Inferiority doctrine, 54-55, 97-101, 577-578, 583, 642, 751; applied to women, 1077; deliberate fostering of, 101-106; disproving of, 76; Negro attitude toward, 62-65, 208, 758-759, 760; un-

ational facilities in, 1275; riots in, 568n.; terror organizations in, 449; voting in, 483, 488n.

North Carolina Mutual Life Insurance Company, 1263

North Dakota, expenditures for education in, 1271

North Star, 913

Northrup, Herbert R.: cited, 408, 1097, 1099, 1101, 1102, 1103-1104, 1106, 1108-1110, 1113, 1118, 1119n.; on discrimination in unions, 1299-1300

Nourse, E. G., Davis, J. S., and Black, J. D., cited, 257

Number of Negroes in America; *see* Quantitative goal for Negro population policy

Numbers game, 330-331, 940, 985, 1267, 1269

Nurses, Negro, 172, 325, 638, 796, 1224

Oberlin College, 1076n., 1415

Occupational mobility, 213

Occupational status of Southern whites, 297

O'Connor, W. B., cited, 393

Odum, Howard W., 96, 844; on criticism of Interracial Commission, 847; description of South by, 1320-1321

Office of Civilian Defense, discrimination in, 1367

Officeholders: Negro, 497, 501-504, 535, 542-543, 723-724, 755; power of, 435, 716, 717n.; publicity afforded, 718

Offord, Carl, cited, 1085

Ogburn, William, 1389; on institutional changes, 1051; on materials of social planning, 1052

Ohio: lynching in, 561; school segregation in, 633

Oklahoma: expenditures for education in, 1271; prohibition in, 457; transportation segregation in, 635; voting in, 483, 488

Old age benefit system, 357, 358, 359, 400, 1280-1281; occupations not covered by, 358, 1280-1281

Old Age and Survivors' Benefit System, 357n.

"Old Americans," 47, 114n., 138

Oliver, King, 988

Olmsted, Frederick, on slave-breeding, 1202

One-party system in the South, 452-455, 474, 475, 519, 1322

Oneida Community, 712

Operative Plasterers' and Cement Finishers' International Association, 1102

Opinion correlation, system of, 72-73

Opinion research; *see* Public opinion polls

Opinions, "personal" and "political," 1139-1141

Opportunism, 208, 471, 600, 774, 796, 830, 834n., 840, 843, 848, 854, 893, 1010, 1139, 1270, 1410

Opportunistic beliefs; *see* Stereotypes about Negroes

Opportunity, equality of, 573, 671-672, 884, 893

Opportunity, 837, 839, 909

Optimism-pessimism, scale of, 1038-1039

Order of Railway Conductors, 1105

Ordnance industry, Negroes in, 413

Organization (*see also* Trade Unions and Unionization): of Negroes to resist attack, 681n.; of plantation tenants, 250, 262, 263, 1250

Organizations: anti-Negro, 812n.; duplication of, 825, 854; left-wing, 812n.; Negro, 812-852, 952-955

Organizers, labor: importance of, 713, 714; terrorization of, 1300

Orientals; *see* Chinese *and* Japanese

Out-patient services, 346

Over-crowding in Negro homes, 376, 377, 378-379, 977, 978, 1127, 1291, 1308, 1426

Over-population in rural South, 205, 231-232, 253, 264, 265, 424

Over-production of cotton, 251

Overtime, payment for, 398

Ovington, Mary White, 819

Owen, Chandler, 749

Owenites, 712

Owens, Jesse, 734

Owens, John R., cited, 1099

Packing House Workers' Industrial Union, 1123

Page, Thomas Nelson, 732; characterization of Negro masses by, 1386-1387; on fight for race purity, 586, 1354-1355; on interracial friendship, 741n.; on interracial work, 843; on Negro education, 888, 896, 1419; on Northern teachers for Southern Negroes, 1415-1416; on retrogression of Negro workmen, 283; on Southern industrial labor, 280-281

Page, Walter Hines, 460

Paige, "Hot Lips," 645n.

Pale Faces, 449

Palmer, Edward Nelson, cited, 871n., 955; 1086

Panunzio, Constantine, cited, 1360

"Parallel civilizations," 578-582, 595, 741, 754, 1358

Parent-Teacher Associations, 948-949, 954n.

Park, Robert E., 1049-1050; on accommodation, 1050; on advertisements in Negro press, 922; on bi-racial organization,

Politics: clergy in, 458; growth of bureaucracy in, 432-437; honest, 511-512; labor and farmer, 714; leadership in, 716-719; machine, 331, 439, 453, 476, 486, 488n., 490, 499, 733, 810, 1322; Negro bargaining power in, 498-500, 505-508, 835, 855; Negro church in, 940-941; Negro power in, 777, 778; and Negro problem, 475-476; Negroes in, 429-432, 475-476, 478, 491-497, 725-726, 733, 852, 987, 1000, 1328, 1330; police systems subject to, 539

Poll tax, 446, 450, 476, 481-483, 489, 514; abolition of, 463, 482, 1000; arguments for, 482; compulsory 1324; fight to abolish, 471, 515, 516-517, 791, 833, 1318, 1324; in the North, 1324

Pollock, H. M., cited, 143

Poor whites, 597-598, 689, 1189, 1388; effect of Negro discrimination and segregation on, 644; legal rights of, 525; social inferiority of, 582

Popular beliefs; see Stereotypes about Negroes

Popular movements; see Mass movements

Popular theories, Negro, 781-809, 1030-1031; on colonization schemes, 805-807; derived from white aristocrats, 786-788; instability of, 781-783; on labor solidarity, 788-794; on Negro business, 800-805; on the Negro problem, 27-30, 31-32, 38, 786; provincialism in, 783-785; on segregation, 797-800; upper class, 794-797

Population, Negro: age structure of, 162-163; in Chicago, 1126-1127; growth of, 157-161, 165-166; in New York City, 1125-1126; policy of, 167-171; registration of, 1218-1219; rural, decline of, 279; in Southern cities, 1127-1128; trends in, 1219

Population, white, decreased expansion rate of, 1017

Populist movement, 452, 455

Porter, K. W., cited, 1203

Postal service: Negro trust in, 1343; Negroes employed in, 327, 545

Post-war plans, 425, 425n.-426n., 806-807, 1018-1021, 1023

Post-war world, 408; housing in, 627; Negroes in, 423-426; unemployment in, 401, 408, 409, 424, 425, 1010-1011

Pound, Roscoe: on law-making, 20; on natural law, 1182-1183

Poverty, Negro, 205-207, 304; of consumer, 804; and crime, 976, 977; and drinking, 980-981; and education, 946,

948; and health, 344; and housing conditions, 375-379, 619; and judicial discrimination, 534, 548, 550; and nonvoting, correlation between, 493

Poverty, white, a background factor in lynching, 563

Powdermaker, Hortense: cited, 607, 689, 700, 1207; on age differentials within class, 1131; on disparity of information between races, 1372; on emotionalism in Negro church, 1426; on Negro attitude to law, 1336; on Negro middle class, 704n.; on Negro upper class and poor whites, 1388; on social equality and amalgamation, 1355; on Southern custom of carrying arms, 1346; on superstition, 965; on upper class Negro marriage, 1425

Powell, A. Clayton, 863n., 987

Power: of American President, 717n.; of officeholder, 716; overlapping, 718

Power relations, lxxiii, lxxiv, 724-726, 858, 859

Pragmatism, 882

Preachers, Negro; see Ministers, Negro

Prejudice: of Negroes against Negroes, lxix; race, see Race prejudice

Premises; see Value premises

President's Interdepartmental Committee to Coordinate Health and Welfare Activities, 345

Press, Negro; see Negro press

Press, white: anti-lynching position of, 565; and disfranchisement policy, 486; growing anxiety of, around Negro problem, 517; influence of, toward reform, 556; liberal, in the South, 472, 646, 661, 726, 915; "minority," 911, 912; Southern, support of one-party system by, 454-455; treatment of Negro news by, 37, 48, 104, 422, 600, 656, 661, 916, 924, 957, 1184, 1372-1373

Pressure groups, 811, 851-852

Primary elections, Southern (see also White primary), 454, 474, 475

Princeton University, Negro students not enrolled in, 633, 1367

Prisons, 554-555; profit from, 548; reform of, 555-557; segregation in, 555, 634; self-segregation in, 648; in the South, 554-555, 977n.

Production credit associations, 273

Production techniques, changes in (see also Mechanization), 424

Professional monopolies, 685, 686, 690, 693

Professional organizations, Negro; see Business and professional organizations, Negro

Professionals, Negro, 172, 305, 306, 318-

(tags)

ABOUT THE AUTHOR

Gunnar Myrdal is one of the world's leading social scientists. In a career of over fifty years he has been a lawyer, a member of the Swedish cabinet, executive secretary of the United Nations Economic Commission for Europe, a member of various government commissions, and professor of International Economics at the University of Stockholm, where he is now professor emeritus. Founder and director of the Institute for International Economic Studies in Stockholm, Gunnar Myrdal is now chairman of the board of two new research institutions: the Stockholm International Peace Research Institute (SIPRI) and the Latin American Institute.

His recent works include *Asian Drama: An Inquiry into the Poverty of Nations*, *Objectivity in Social Research*, *The Challenge of World Poverty*, and, in 1973, *Against the Stream: Critical Essays on Economics*, all published by Pantheon. *An American Dilemma* was the result of a study which he headed for the Carnegie Corporation from 1938 to 1942.

In 1974, Gunnar Myrdal was awarded jointly with Friedrich August von Hayek the Nobel Memorial Prize in Economic Science.